# The Logic of American Politics

## Ninth Edition

*To Dianne, Marty, Kate, and Jeff*

The following dedication to James Madison is from the oldest American government textbook we have found: William Alexander Duer's *Outlines of the Constitutional Jurisprudence of the United States,* published in 1833.

*To you, Sir, as the surviving member of the august assembly that framed the Constitution, and of the illustrious triumvirate who, in vindicating it from the objections of its first assailants, succeeded in recommending it to the adoption of their country; to you, who, in discharging the highest duties of its administration, proved the stability and excellence of the Constitution, in war as well as in peace, and determined the experiment in favor of republican institutions and the right of self-government; to you, who in your retirement, raised a warning voice against those heresies in the construction of that Constitution which for a moment threatened to impair it; to you, Sir, as alone amongst the earliest and the latest of its defenders,—this brief exposition of the organization and principles of the National Government, intended especially for the instruction of our American youth, is most respectfully, and, in reference to your public services, most properly inscribed.*

*Columbia College, N.Y.*
*August 1st, 1833.*

# The Logic of American Politics

## Ninth Edition

**Samuel Kernell**
*University of California, San Diego*

**Gary C. Jacobson**
*University of California, San Diego*

**Thad Kousser**
*University of California, San Diego*

**Lynn Vavreck**
*University of California, Los Angeles*

FOR INFORMATION:

CQ Press
An Imprint of SAGE Publications, Inc.
2455 Teller Road
Thousand Oaks, California 91320
E-mail: order@sagepub.com

SAGE Publications Ltd.
1 Oliver's Yard
55 City Road
London EC1Y 1SP
United Kingdom

SAGE Publications India Pvt. Ltd.
B 1/I 1 Mohan Cooperative Industrial Area
Mathura Road, New Delhi 110 044
India

SAGE Publications Asia-Pacific Pte. Ltd.
18 Cross Street #10-10/11/12
China Square Central
Singapore 048423

Printed in Canada

*Library of Congress Cataloging-in-Publication Data*

Names: Kernell, Samuel, 1945- author.

Title: The logic of American politics / Samuel Kernell, Gary C. Jacobson, Thad Kousser, Lynn Vavreck.

Description: 9th edition. | Thousand Oaks, California : CQ Press/SAGE, 2020. | Includes bibliographical references and index.

Identifiers: LCCN 2018055112 | ISBN 9781544322995 (pbk. : alk. paper)

Subjects: LCSH: United States—Politics and government—Textbooks.

Classification: LCC JK276 .K47 2020 | DDC 320.47301—dc23
LC record available at https://lccn.loc.gov/2018055112

This book is printed on acid-free paper.

Executive Publisher:   Monica Eckman
Acquisitions Editor:   Lauren Schultz
Content Development Editor:   Anna Villarruel
Editorial Assistant:   Sam Rosenberg
Production Editor:   Tracy Buyan
Copy Editor:   Mark Bast
Typesetter:   C&M Digitals (P) Ltd.
Proofreader:   Sue Schon
Indexer:   Maria Sosnowski
Cover Designer:   Anthony Paular
Marketing Manager:   Erica DeLuca

19 20 21 22 23 10 9 8 7 6 5 4 3 2 1

# Brief Contents

## Part IV. Conclusion

# Detailed Contents

AP Photo/Evan Vucci

Alex Wong/Getty Images

## Chapter 3 • Federalism    93

AP Photo/Jeff Chiu

## Chapter 4 • Civil Rights                                                 135

John Moore/Getty Images

## Chapter 5 • Civil Liberties 185

Reuters/Jonathan Bachman

## Part II: The Institutions of Government

## Chapter 6 • Congress 231

Mark Wilson/Getty Images

Reuters/Kevin Lamarque

## Chapter 8 • The Bureaucracy 345

REUTERS/Esam Al-Fetori

Bill Clark/CQ Roll Call

## Chapter 11 • Voting, Campaigns, and Elections — 475

## Chapter 12 • Political Parties
513

Win McNamee/Getty Images

## Chapter 13 • Interest Groups
563

Jeff J Mitchell/Getty Images

## Chapter 14 • Media        607

as no agenda.
an't be manufactured.
oesn't take sides.
sn't red or blue.
hard to accept.
ulls no punches.
powerful.
under attack.
worth defending.
equires taking a stand.

New York Times

# Part IV: Conclusion

## Chapter 15 • Is There a Logic to American Policy?  645

J. Scott Applewhite - Pool/Getty Images

# Preface

Donald Trump's election and his first two years in office seem only to point out the *illogic* of American politics. Since writing this book's last edition, shortly after the 2016 election, America's politics has been in continuous tumult. The question we confront as we take the Trump presidency into account asks, does Donald Trump's election and first two years in office break the mold, requiring us to rethink *Logic*'s approach to the systematic forces and processes that govern the play of politics in Washington and across the nation? Perhaps not. The tumultuous events might represent the proverbial "exception that proves the rule." If the latter, Trump's election and presidency would allow us to glean new insights into American politics in other political actors' responses to Trump's unconventional behavior. Answering this question lies at the heart of this revision.

Obviously, assessment of the extraordinary 2016 election and the 2018 midterms are major topics of **Chapter 11**'s coverage of voting and elections, and sizing up Trump's first two years in office occupies much of the attention of **Chapter 7** on the presidency. In both we seek to square the Trump years with the stable systematic forces at work in both arenas. But this question pervades every other chapter as well. We close **Chapter 2** ("The Constitution") by considering the proliferation of contentious separation of powers issues that in some instances preceded the Trump presidency but that his policies have made more salient and problematic. **Chapter 3**'s coverage of federalism introduces the Democratic and Republican cadres of state attorneys general signed on to lawsuits challenging or supporting administration policies according to their partisan alignment with the president. **Chapter 4** reports on the ongoing tribulations over the still unresolved Deferred Action for Childhood Arrivals (DACA) policy affecting several hundred thousand children brought into the country illegally. With Republicans controlling both chambers of the 115th Congress and Trump in the White House, the Republicans were poised to fulfill their dream of repealing Obamacare; **Chapter 6** explains why they could not.

We learn in **Chapter 8** just how extensive presidents' administrative authority is, in chronicling President Trump's directions to administration officials to roll back the Obama administration's extensive formal and informal regulations of businesses and state administration of federal programs. **Chapter 9** finds the federal judiciary giving new meaning to activism in which an increasing number of district judges in the states weigh in on national policy by issuing national injunctions, again lining up consistently with the preferences of the party of the president who appointed them. **Chapter 10** takes a close look at public opinion, paying particular attention to issues on which it has changed over the last several decades but also to issues on which opinion has been remarkably stable. **Chapter 12** notes how intense opposition to Trump and his Republican partners energized Democratic partisans in 2018, especially women, producing a dramatic upsurge in activism, unprecedented levels of campaign spending, the highest midterm turnout in more than a century, and a Democratic House majority.

**Chapter 13** shows how students from Parkland, Florida, adopted and refreshed the techniques of interest group influence to put pressure on President Trump and Congress to make progress to reduce gun violence. **Chapter 14** addresses the ever-changing role of the media in American politics. In this edition, we separate media into legacy media, digital-only media, and social media and discuss how the news is produced and consumed for each type. We also examine the role of fake news—all while addressing the threat to democracy that comes when the president refers to legacy news outlets as "fake news" and labels media "the enemy of the people." And in **Chapter 15**, we use the logic of collective action to explain why President Trump's tax reform of 2017 succeeded in passing, whereas prior efforts by President Obama and by Republican leaders in Congress had failed.

One of the themes of *The Logic of American Politics* is that, alongside the outsized personalities that inhabit Washington, D.C., and the idiosyncratic events that appear to drive it, systematic forces remain at work. The book's goal is to help students understand these forces and to see how they shape the choices of political leaders today. We want to help readers discern the rationale embedded in the extraordinary and complex array of American political institutions and practices. To accomplish this goal, we analyze political institutions and practices as (imperfect) solutions to problems facing people who need to act collectively. We highlight recurring obstacles to collective action in various contexts to illuminate the diverse institutional means that American politicians have created to overcome them. These obstacles include the conflict over values and interests, the difficulty of aggregating individual preferences into collective decisions, the need for coordination, and the threat of reneging implicit in every collective undertaking. Stable political communities strengthen their capacity to act collectively and reduce the costs of doing so by fashioning appropriate institutions. These institutions feature majority and plurality rules and procedures that convert votes into representation, delegate authority to agents, and permit some institutional actors to propose courses of action while allocating to others the right to veto proposals. Throughout the book we emphasize the strategic dimension of political action, from the Framers' tradeoffs in crafting the Constitution to the efforts of contemporary officeholders to shape policy, so students can understand current institutions as the products of political conflicts, as well as the venues for resolving them.

New challenges pose fresh problems for collective action for which current institutions may seem inadequate. The institutions created to deal with the challenges of collective action at one historical moment can continue to shape politics long after those challenges have receded. Therefore, we pay a good deal of attention to the historical development of political institutions, a narrative that reveals politicians and citizens grappling intellectually, as well as politically, with their collective action problems and discovering the institutional means to resolve them.

This book is the product of our nearly forty years of teaching American politics in a way that seeks to go beyond the basics. In addition to introducing students to descriptive facts and fundamental principles, we have sought to help them cultivate an ability to analyze and understand American politics for themselves. Each of us is variously associated with the rational choice school, yet over time our research and teaching have benefited from many of its insights, especially those familiarly referred to as "the new institutionalism." We have found these insights helpful in making sense of American politics in terms that students can grasp intuitively. Having absorbed these ideas into our own scholarly thinking, we employ them here to help students understand what the American political system looks like and why it has assumed its present shape.

## Approach

Our emphasis on the primacy of institutions extends well beyond collecting and processing the preferences of citizens and politicians. In that institutions may structure the choices available to voters and their leaders, we view them as indispensable in explaining public opinion and the strategic behavior of the political organizations that seek to influence and mobilize these preferences. We therefore have adopted a somewhat unorthodox structure for the book. We cover the rules of the game and the formal institutions of government before discussing the "input" side of the political process—public opinion, elections, parties, and interest groups—because we emphasize the way rules and institutions structure the actions and choices of citizens and politicians alike.

The introduction offers ideas and concepts employed throughout the text. They can be classified under two broad categories: *collective action problems* and *institutional design concepts*. Both sets of ideas have deeply informed each chapter's argument. Because this is an introduction to American politics, rather than to political theory, we have intentionally sublimated the analytic ideas in favor of enlisting them to explicate real politics. Along with traditional concepts that remain indispensable to understanding American politics—such as representation, majority rule, and separation of powers—we introduce students to a number of ideas from economics that political scientists have found increasingly useful for exploring American politics. These include the focal points of coordination, prisoner's dilemma, free riding, tragedy of the commons, transaction costs, principal–agent relations, and public goods.

## Organization of the Book

The substantive chapters are arranged in four parts.

**Part I** covers the foundational elements of American politics: the Constitution, federalism, civil rights, and civil liberties. The chapters that cover these topics give students an understanding of the political origins and development of the basic structure and rules of the national polity.

**Part II** examines the major formal institutions of national government: Congress, the presidency, the bureaucracy, and the federal judiciary. These chapters reveal how the politics and logic of their development have shaped their current organizational features, practices, and relations with one another.

**Part III** analyzes the institutions that link citizens with government officials, again in terms of their historical development, political logic, and present-day operations. Chapters in this section are devoted to public opinion; voting, campaigns, and elections; political parties; interest groups; and the news media.

**Part IV** features a concluding chapter that evaluates American policymaking through the lens of our collective action framework. Through five vignettes that span policies from health care reform to global climate change, this chapter uses the concepts covered throughout the book to yield insights into the sources of policy problems, point to possible solutions, and explain why agreement on those solutions is often difficult to achieve. Equipped with this understanding of the logic of policymaking, students can apply the same logic underlying these examples to other policy challenges, from immigration reform to pork barrel spending and U.S. disputes with other nations. Students come away from the chapter and the book as a whole with the tools needed to think in new ways about how American government works.

## Instructional Features

*The Logic of American Politics* includes special features designed to engage students' attention and to help them think analytically about the subject.

- Learning objectives and key thematic questions at the beginning of each chapter preview important themes and set the tone for critical thinking.

- Each chapter opens with a story from the real world of politics that introduces one or more of the central issues to be explored in that chapter.

- To help the student reader spot the collective action and institutional design concepts when they occasionally break to the surface, we have highlighted these passages in bright blue text.

- In addition, important terms and concepts throughout the text appear in boldface the first time they are defined. These key terms are listed at the end of each chapter, with page references to their explanations, and are defined in a glossary at the back of the book.

- The **Logic of Politics** boxes explain the logical rationale or implications of some institutional feature presented in the text.

- Another set of boxes, **Strategy and Choice**, explores how politicians use institutions and respond to the incentives that institutions provide in pursuing their personal or constituencies' interests.

- In addition to examining the logic of the policymaking process in our concluding chapter, we continue to cover public policy where it is most relevant to the discussion, incorporating policy issues throughout the book. **Politics to Policy** boxes explain how policies reflect the underlying political rationale of the institutions that produce them.

- To encourage students to continue their studies of American politics beyond the pages of this volume, we have included annotated reading lists at the end of each chapter.

## Digital Resources

We know how important good resources can be in the teaching of American government. Our goal has been to create resources that not only support but also enhance the text's themes and features. **SAGE edge** offers a robust online environment featuring an impressive array of tools and resources for review, study, and further exploration, keeping both instructors and students on the cutting edge of teaching and learning. SAGE edge content is open access and available on demand. Learning and teaching have never been easier!

**SAGE coursepacks for instructors** make it easy to import our quality content into your school's learning management system (LMS).* Intuitive and simple to use, the coursepacks allow you to

**Say NO to . . .**

- required access codes
- learning a new system

**Say YES to . . .**

- using only the content you want and need
- high-quality assessment and multimedia exercises

*For use in Blackboard, Canvas, Brightspace by Desire2Learn (D2L), and Moodle.

**Don't use an LMS platform?** No problem, you can still access many of the online resources for your text via SAGE edge.

**With SAGE coursepacks, you get the following:**

- Quality textbook content delivered **directly into your LMS**
- An **intuitive, simple format** that makes it easy to integrate the material into your course with minimal effort
- **Assessment tools** that foster review, practice, and critical thinking, including the following:
  - diagnostic chapter **pretests and posttests** that identify opportunities for improvement, track student progress, and ensure mastery of key learning objectives
  - **test banks** built on Bloom's taxonomy that provide a diverse range of test items with ExamView test generation
  - a **test bank grading rubric** to support the grading of essay and short-answer questions
  - **activity and quiz options** that allow you to choose only the assignments and tests you want

- instructions on how to use and integrate the comprehensive assessments and resources provided

- **Assignable data exercises** in each chapter help students build essential data literacy skills using interactive data visualization tools from **SAGE Stats** and **U.S. Political Stats**. Drawing on key data series ranging from demographic patterns to state budgets to voting behavior, these exercises offer students a dynamic way to analyze real-world data and think critically about the numbers.

- **Assignable SAGE Premium Video** (available via the interactive eBook version, linked through SAGE coursepacks) tied to learning objectives and curated exclusively for this text to bring concepts to life, featuring the following:

  - **corresponding multimedia assessment options** that automatically feed to your gradebook

  - a comprehensive, downloadable, easy-to-use **media guide in the coursepack for every video resource**, listing the chapter to which the video content is tied, matching learning objective(s), a helpful description of the video content, and assessment questions

  - **"Topics in American Government" videos** that recap the fundamentals of American politics in every chapter—from the Bill of Rights to voter turnout to the powers of the presidency

  - **Newsclips from the Associated Press** that bring extra coverage of current events into the book, connecting multiple, brief two- to four-minute newsclips to core American government chapter content

- Editable, chapter-specific **PowerPoint® slides** that offer flexibility when creating multimedia lectures so you don't have to start from scratch

- **Sample course syllabi** with suggested models for structuring your course that give you options to customize your course to your exact needs

- An **instructor manual** for each chapter, including a chapter summary, learning objectives, discussion questions and ideas, and in-class activities, to support your teaching

- **Integrated links to the interactive eBook** that make it easy for students to maximize their study time with this anywhere, anytime mobile-friendly version of the text. It also offers access to more digital tools and resources, including SAGE Premium Video.

- All **tables and figures** from the textbook

**SAGE edge for students** enhances learning, is easy to use, and offers the following:

- An **open-access site** that makes it easy for students to maximize their study time, anywhere, anytime

- **eFlashcards** that strengthen understanding of key terms and concepts

- **Quizzes** that allow students to practice and assess how much they've learned and where they need to focus their attention

- Meaningful **video and web links** that facilitate student use of Internet resources, further exploration of topics, and responses to critical thinking questions

## Acknowledgments

Without the help and encouragement of department colleagues, friends, students, and the editorial staff at CQ Press, this book never would have been completed. The book also has benefited from the insightful and astute comments of colleagues at other institutions who took time from their busy schedules to review chapters. We are deeply obliged to everyone who has helped us along the way. In particular, we wish to thank Lawrence Baum, Lee Epstein, Rosalind Gold, Richard Hart, and Vickie Stangl for their assistance in procuring data for tables and figures and clarifying historical events.

Our colleagues and students at the University of California, San Diego and the University of California, Los Angeles have contributed to every aspect of the book, often in ways they might not realize, for the way we think about politics is permeated by the intellectual atmosphere they have created and continue to sustain. Lee Dionne assisted us in revising those sections covering the judiciary and case law; Derek Bonnett collected information for updating the presidency chapter. We are indebted to Charisse Kiino, who regularly summoned her nonpareil skills as a diplomat, critic, dispatcher, coach, and booster, and Monica Eckman for her steady oversight of the whole. Anna Villarruel diligently managed the book's many gangling features, including not only the manuscript and digital resources but, with the able help of Sam Rosenberg, also photographs and cartoons, tables and figures, and citations. Mark Bast cheerfully entered the ring with the authors to wrestle the prose into submission, and Tracy Buyan coordinated the editing and production processes. We also wish to thank Eric Garner, who managed production; Amanda Simpson, who managed the manufacturing; Anthony Paular, who designed the cover; and Erica DeLuca and Jennifer Jones for brochures, advertisements, and displays for the professional meetings.

The following are colleagues across the country who have read and commented on the past four editions and given us an abundance of good advice, much of which we took in writing this revision. Equally essential, they kept us from making many embarrassing mistakes.

Roberta Adams, Salisbury University

Danny M. Adkison, Oklahoma State University

E. Scott Adler, University of Colorado

Scott H. Ainsworth, University of Georgia

Richard A. Almeida, Francis Marion University

Ellen Andersen, University of Vermont

Phillip J. Ardoin, Appalachian State University

Ross K. Baker, Rutgers University

Lawrence A. Baum, Ohio State University

Michelle Belco, University of Houston

William T. Bianco, Indiana University

Sarah Binder, Brookings Institution and George Washington University

Rachel Bitecofer, University of Georgia

Ray Block, University of Wisconsin–La Crosse

Christopher Bonneau, University of Pittsburgh

Shenita Brazelton, Old Dominion University

Jeremy Buchman, Long Island University

Michael Burton, Ohio University

Suzanne Chod, North Central College

Rosalee Clawson, Purdue University

Christopher Austin Clemens, Texas A&M University

Ann H. Cohen, Hunter College of the City University of New York

Marty Cohen, James Madison University

Richard S. Conley, University of Florida

Michael Crespin, University of Georgia

Laura Mayate-DeAndreis, Modesto Junior College

Michelle D. Deardorff, Jackson State University

Katharine Destler, George Mason University

John Domino, Sam Houston State University

Keith Dougherty, University of Georgia

Justin Dyer, University of Missouri

Michael J. Faber, Texas State University

Jason Fichtner, Georgetown University

Richard S. Fleisher, Fordham University

John Freemuth, Boise State University

Yvonne Gastelum, San Diego State University

John B. Gilmour, College of William & Mary

Lawrence L. Giventer, California State University–Stanislaus

Brad Gomez, Florida State University

Craig Goodman, University of Houston–Victoria

Sanford Gordon, New York University

Andrew Green, Central College

Paul Gronke, Reed College

Edward B. Hasecke, Wittenberg University

Danny Hayes, George Washington University

Valerie Heitshusen, Georgetown University

Richard Herrera, Arizona State University

Marc Hetherington, Vanderbilt University

Leif Hoffman, Lewis-Clark State College

Brian D. Humes, Georgetown University

Jeffery Jenkins, University of Virginia

Joel W. Johnson, Colorado State University–Pueblo

Paul E. Johnson, University of Kansas

Timothy Johnson, University of Minnesota

Nicole Kalaf-Hughes, Bowling Green State University

Chris Koski, James Madison University

Doug Kuberski, Florida State College at Jacksonville

Timothy M. LaPira, James Madison University

Dan Lee, Michigan State University

Joel Lefkowitz, State University of New York–New Paltz

Brad Lockerbie, East Carolina University

Amy Lauren Lovecraft, University of Alaska–Fairbanks

Roger Lukoff, American University

Anthony Madonna, University of Georgia

Forrest A. Maltzman, George Washington University

Wendy Martinek, Binghamton University

John McAdams, Marquette University

Madhavi McCall, San Diego State University

Ian McDonald, Lewis & Clark College

Scott R. Meinke, Bucknell University

Rob Mellen Jr., Mississippi State University

John Mercurio, San Diego State University

Eric Miller, Blinn College, Bryan Campus

Will Miller, Ohio University

William J. Miller, Southeast Missouri State University

Richard Millsap, University of Texas at Arlington

Ashley Moraguez, University of North Carolina–Asheville

Tracy F. Munsil, Arizona Christian University

Timothy Nokken, Texas Tech University

Shannon O'Brien, University of Texas at Austin

Bruce I. Oppenheimer, Vanderbilt University

L. Marvin Overby, University of Missouri–Columbia

Carl Palmer, Illinois State University

Hong Min Park, University of Wisconsin–Milwaukee

Bryan Parsons, University of Tennessee at Martin

Justin Phillips, Columbia University

Andrew J. Polsky, Hunter College

Alexandra Reckendorf, Virginia Commonwealth University

Suzanne M. Robbins, George Mason University

Jason Roberts, University of Minnesota

Beth Rosenson, University of Florida

Mikhail Rybalko, Texas Tech University

Eric Schicker, University of California–Berkeley

Ronnee Schreiber, San Diego State University

Mark Shanahan, University of Reading

Charles Shipan, University of Michigan

David Shock, Kennesaw State University

James D. Slack, University of Alabama at Birmingham

Charles Anthony Smith, University of California–Irvine

Carl Snook, Southern Polytechnic State University

Tara Stricko-Neubauer, Kennesaw State University

Joseph Ura, Texas A&M University

Brian Vargus, Indiana University–Purdue University Indianapolis

Charles E. Walcott, Virginia Polytechnic Institute and State University

Hanes Walton Jr., University of Michigan

Wendy Watson, University of North Texas

Christopher Weible, University of Colorado–Denver

Patrick C. Wohlfarth, University of Maryland–College Park

Frederick Wood, Coastal Carolina University

Garry Young, George Washington University

Finally, our families. Dianne Kernell; Marty BlakeJacobson; Jeff Lewis; and Kate, Will, and Kat Kousser also deserve our gratitude for putting up with what occasionally seemed an interminable drain on our time and attention. We are sure they are as delighted as we are to have this revision finished.

# A Note to Students

## Plan of the Book

Our analysis of the logic of American politics begins in Chapter 1 with an introduction to the analytical concepts we draw on throughout the text. Although these concepts are straightforward and intuitive, we do not expect you to understand them fully until they have been applied in later chapters. The rest of the text is arranged in four main parts.

**Part I** looks at the foundational elements of the political system that are especially relevant to understanding modern American politics. It begins with the constitutional system (Chapter 2, "The Constitution") and then moves on to the relations between the national government and the states (Chapter 3, "Federalism"); the evolution of civil rights and the definition of citizenship (Chapter 4, "Civil Rights"); and the establishment of civil liberties, such as freedom of speech and religion (Chapter 5, "Civil Liberties"). A recurring theme of Part I is *nationalization*, the gradual shift of authority from state and local governments to the national government.

**Part II** examines the four basic institutions of America's national government: Congress (Chapter 6), the presidency (Chapter 7), the bureaucracy (Chapter 8), and the federal judiciary (Chapter 9). The development of effective, resourceful institutions at the national level has made it possible for modern-day politicians to tackle problems that in an earlier time they would have been helpless to solve. We explain how all four institutions have evolved along the paths initiated and confined by the Constitution in response to the forces of nationalization and other social and economic changes.

**Part III** surveys the institutions that keep citizens informed about what their representatives are doing and enable them to influence their elected officials through voting and other forms of participation. Chapter 10, "Public Opinion," explores the nature of modern political communication by focusing on the ins and outs of mass public opinion. Chapter 11, "Voting, Campaigns, and Elections," examines the ways in which candidates' strategies and voters' preferences interact at the polls to produce national leaders and, on occasion, create mandates for policies. The Constitution mentions neither political parties nor interest groups, and the Framers were deeply suspicious of both. But they are vital to helping citizens make sense of politics and pursue political goals effectively. In Chapter 12, "Political Parties," and Chapter 13, "Interest Groups," we explain how and why parties and interest groups have flourished as intermediaries between citizens and government officials. President Woodrow Wilson once aptly observed that "news is the atmosphere of politics." Chapter 14 looks at the news media both as channels of communication from elected leaders to their constituents and as independent sources of information about the leaders' performance. The chapter also considers the implications of the rise of the Internet in coordinating the collective efforts of unorganized publics.

Part IV, which consists of Chapter 15, concludes our inquiry by evaluating American public policymaking through the lens of our collective action framework to discern the logic of the policymaking process.

## Special Features

This book contains several special features designed to help you grasp the logic of American politics. Because these features, including the substantive captions, play an integral role in the presentation and discussion, *you should read them with as much care as you do the text.*

- At the outset of each chapter are key questions that preview important themes and, we hope, will pique your curiosity.

- To help you more easily spot discussions of collective action problems and institutional design concepts, important passages and analytic points are highlighted in bright blue text.

- Within each chapter, thematic boxes labeled **Logic of Politics** consider more fully the logical rationale and implications of certain features of government design introduced in the core text.

- Another set of boxes, **Strategy and Choice**, focuses on the sometimes imaginative ways politicians enlist institutions to advance their agendas and their constituents' goals.

- A third set of thematic boxes, **Politics to Policy**, treats some of the public policy issues that have sprung forth from the political process.

- Additional boxes, tables, figures, photographs, and other visuals clarify and enliven the text.

- To encourage you to pursue more information on topics you find particularly interesting, we have included annotated lists of suggested readings at the end of each chapter.

## How to Read the Graphs

A picture is worth a thousand words. You may think this book is too long as it is, but it would be a lot longer if we couldn't use figures and graphs to show you important relationships. Figures tell stories, and if we have a figure in a chapter it is because the story it tells is important to your understanding or thinking about the concepts in the chapter. Don't skip the figures! They are an important element in really understanding what we're talking about.

Because figures are so important to learning, imagination, and discovery, it is important you are comfortable interpreting them and feel at home looking at data presented visually.

Before we get started with substantive material, we wanted to make sure you know how to evaluate the figures we use.

There are several types of figures. We use a few repeatedly:

- **Bar graphs** show numbers that are ***independent*** of each other. Examples might include things like the number of people who preferred each of the presidential candidates in the last election.

- **Line graphs** show you how numbers have ***changed over time***. They are used when you have data that are connected, and to show trends, for example, average support for the president in each month of the year.

- **Cartesian graphs** or **scatter plots** have numbers on both axes, which therefore allow you to see ***how changes in one thing affect another***. For example, we may want to show how changes in consumer sentiment are related to changes in presidential approval.

The first step in reading any figure or graph is understanding what you are looking at.

- The place to start is with the axes. Graphs generally have two axes, the lines that run across the bottom of the figure and typically up the left side.

- The line along the bottom is called the horizontal or x-axis, and the line up the side is called the vertical or y-axis. (An easy way to remember which one is which is to think of the letter *Y* and it's stem extending down the vertical axis line.)

- Both axes can contain either numbers or categories of things. They generally start with the lowest value at the origin of the axes (the place where both lines meet, the bottom left corner of the figure). The numbers or categories typically increase (if they are cardinal in nature) as you move to the right on the horizontal axis and up on the vertical axis.

- A good figure has labels on both axes to help the reader interpret the data. A good figure also starts and ends at reasonable numbers. Checking the axes is an important first step in reading a figure. They answer the questions, what is the purpose of this figure, and how will it show me the data?

- The data in figures are often presented as lines, markers (like dots), or bars. In scatter plots, which show the relationship between what is on the horizontal and vertical axes, figures often contain a line across the diagonal at forty-five degrees. This line is called the forty-five-degree line. It is helpful especially if the axes of the figure take on the same values. In this case, the forty-five-degree line represents the cases (the dots) where the values on the horizontal axis match the values on the vertical axis *exactly*. Dots on the line are exact matches. Dots off the line are not—specifically, those above the line are cases in which values are higher on the y-axis than on the x-axis, and dots below the line are the opposite.

- In addition to these important elements on the graph, the information around the figure is also important. Good figures have a title that tells you exactly what the story in the figure is. Figures should also give you a time frame for the data they present and a note that tells you the source of the data shown and when it was collected.

Practice interpreting a few graphs so you will be ready to think about the figures in the chapters to come!

## One More Thing

Politics, like every significant human endeavor, becomes more intriguing the more deeply it is explored and understood. Our book aims to give you not only a strong basic foundation for understanding political life in the present-day United States but also a glimpse of how intellectually enjoyable it can be to grapple with its puzzles and paradoxes.

Sara Miller McCune founded SAGE Publishing in 1965 to support the dissemination of usable knowledge and educate a global community. SAGE publishes more than 1000 journals and over 800 new books each year, spanning a wide range of subject areas. Our growing selection of library products includes archives, data, case studies and video. SAGE remains majority owned by our founder and after her lifetime will become owned by a charitable trust that secures the company's continued independence.

Los Angeles | London | New Delhi | Singapore | Washington DC | Melbourne

AP Photo/Evan Vucci

Drew Angerer/Getty Images

President Barack Obama signs the Every Student Succeeds Act (ESSA) in 2015, after both houses of Congress worked together—for different reasons—to replace the unpopular and flawed No Child Left Behind law. It serves as an example of the compromises often required in government, where no side can get exactly what it wants and through collective effort must strive to find a mutually acceptable policy. With the confirmation of President Trump's appointment of Betsy DeVos as secretary of the Department of Education—an appointment opposed by every Democratic senator (and a couple of Republicans)—the prospect of cutting future education reform deals will be more difficult.

# The Logic of American Politics

# 1

"This is a Christmas miracle," a beaming President Obama proclaimed on signing the Every Student Succeeds Act (ESSA) in December 2015. Flanked at the signing ceremony by congressional leaders from both political parties, the president added, "We should do this more often." Indeed, in Washington's present-day polarized politics, bipartisan agreement on major policy is a rare sight. But ESSA—affecting 50 million students and their teachers across 100,000 schools—passed with huge majorities in both houses of Congress. What occurred differently that allowed Congress and the president to break their normal gridlock and pass this major law? Answering this question may or may not provide Washington with a roadmap past gridlock. What it certainly offers students of American politics, however, is insight into the process that leads politicians who are ideologically and politically distant from one another to settle on a policy that they (and their like-minded colleagues) prefer to current policy.

The Every Student Succeeds Act represents a sweeping revision of the fourteen-year-old No Child Left Behind (NCLB) law.* That law, championed by Republican president George W. Bush, sought to strengthen K–12 education by holding laggard schools up to strict performance standards. To qualify for indispensable federal grants under NCLB, schools needed to track students' performance with standardized tests. Schools in the bottom 5 percent of test scores that failed to significantly improve student performance would be overhauled and possibly closed.

The goal of strengthening education was laudable, but Democrats and Republicans in Congress had different reasons for supporting President Bush's initiative. Republicans were helping their president fulfill a campaign promise to improve K–12 education across the nation. In addition, NCLB gave them a way of preventing school districts from taking and freely spending federal money without accountability—schools had to demonstrate that they were using it to improve their programs. Democrats were perhaps even more enthusiastic about the Republican president's initiative. They had long promoted federal aid in education, and impoverished, minority students appeared to stand to gain the most

## CHAPTER OBJECTIVES

**1.1** Summarize the importance of institutional design in governance.

**1.2** Discuss the role of a constitution in establishing the rules and procedures that government institutions must follow for collective agreement.

**1.3** Identify different types of collective action problems.

**1.4** Explain the costs of collective action.

**1.5** Relate the different ways that representative government works.

**1.6** Discuss the similarities and differences between private, public, and collective goods.

**1.7** Explain what motivated the Founders to try to solve collective action problems.

---

*Welcome to the world of acronyms, where staff on Capitol Hill can be heard saying such things as, "OMB sent over a SAP threatening SSA." Translation: The Office of Management and Budget (OMB) issued a Statement of Administration Policy (SAP) in which President Obama threatened to veto Republicans' 2013 legislation, the Student Success Act (SSA).

from close scrutiny of failing schools. To satisfy the objectives of accountability and reform, both parties agreed to the creation of a standardized national test of students' verbal and math skills.* Each side quickly found something it liked in NCLB and passed it promptly, at least when compared with the normal lengthy vetting that accompanies most legislation that creates new policy.

Not long into the administration of NCLB, however, problems started cropping up. The success envisioned in the law's timelines for student improvement in reading and math test scores failed to materialize, as was bound to happen. NCLB mandated an ambitious 100 percent student proficiency on these tests within 12 years (2014). Moreover, many center city and rural schools that faced special challenges in educating their students continued to fail—some miserably—in improving their students' tests scores. According to critics, as pressures to meet Department of Education performance deadlines approached, schools began concentrating on student performance on standardized tests to the neglect of a broader, quality education. A few teachers responded to the pressures with direct action—coaching students on answers during tests and, afterward, even correcting students' answers. School districts and state agencies began requesting deadline exemptions and extensions of deadlines to accommodate their inability to meet NCLB's stiff standards.† By 2015, forty-three of the fifty states had received waivers.

Clearly, NCLB failed to live up to its aspirations. Democrats and Republicans initially responded differently to this failure. Republicans focused on the duress Washington's "one size fits all" performance standards presented to their states' educational systems. Even though NCLB had been their president's initiative, many Republicans in Congress chafed at the way it had dramatically shifted educational policy from local control to Washington. In 2013 the Republican-majority House of Representatives passed a bill that eliminated most of NCLB's federal oversight provisions, as well as the unreachable 2014 target date for 100 percent proficiency. States would be able to set achievement standards and develop their own testing methods for measuring success and identifying underachieving schools. President Obama, prodded by civil rights groups who worried that the legislation would allow states to abandon efforts to upgrade failing schools, threatened a veto of the bill, and it died in the Senate.

At the same time, numerous states were seeking waivers to NCLB's unrealistic test score goals. The Obama administration agreed to the requested waivers, but only after a state agreed to institute teacher evaluation procedures that took standardized test scores into account in teacher retention and promotion. Teachers' organizations—traditional supporters of Democratic members of Congress—objected strenuously to this sudden, externally imposed policy that upset many long-standing contracts with local school districts. By 2015 Democrats and Republicans in Congress each had their own compelling reasons to rewrite No Child Left Behind.

NCLB had become so unpopular that it forced Democrats and Republicans to search for and settle on a new law that neither side embraced as ideal but accepted as better than the status quo. Over the fall of 2015, bipartisan teams in both chambers and, later, in conference committee negotiations hammered out a compromise bill—the Every Student Succeeds Act.

---

*This became the Common Core, one of the most controversial features of NCLB.

†Federal mandates attached to financial aid are a standard practice whereby Congress asserts a national policy without directly taking over administration. We explore the "carrot/stick" properties of federal grants in Chapter 3.

Republicans won major concessions that allowed states to develop their own student and teacher performance goals and tests. Moreover, the Department of Education would no longer mandate changes in teacher evaluation or dictate changes in failing schools. Democrats won a major concession requiring states to continue some form of student testing and results reporting to the Department of Education. With these instruments, failing schools could still be identified and efforts to improve them assessed.

As this example shows, social choices inevitably breed conflict, especially when they involve issues that affect the political parties' core constituencies. Through politics, people try to manage such conflicts. Neither side may be thrilled by the results, but when politics succeeds, both sides discover a course of action that satisfies them more than the status quo. However, politics does not always end in success. Resources are too scarce to satisfy the competing claimants, and values prove irreconcilable. Even when the configuration of preferences might allow reconciliation, the political process itself may impede lawmakers' efforts to agree on a new policy. (You will soon discover that this text is concerned with understanding how America's political institutions expedite or interfere with citizens' and their representatives' ability to discover and pursue a collectively agreed-to policy.) Finally, successful politics does not always lead to happy endings. In the example of the ESSA, no one in either political party expressed enthusiasm for the education package beyond "the best deal we could get."

In more formal terms, **politics** is *the process through which individuals and groups seek agreement on a course of common, or collective,\* action—even as they disagree on the intended goals of that action.* Politics matters because each party's success in finding a solution requires the cooperation of others who are looking to solve a different problem. When their goals conflict, cooperation may be costly and difficult to achieve.

Success at politics almost invariably requires bargaining and compromise. Where the issues are simple and the participants know and trust one another, **bargaining** may be all that is needed for the group to reach a collective decision. Generally, success requires bargaining and ends in a **compromise**, or a settlement in which each side concedes some preferences to secure others.

Those who create government institutions (and the political scientists who study them) tend to regard **preferences** as "givens"—individuals and groups know what they want—that must be reconciled if they are to agree to some common course of action. Preferences may reflect the individual's economic situation, religious values, ethnic identity, or some other valued interest. We commonly associate preferences with some perception of self-interest, but they need not be so restrictive. Millions of Americans oppose capital punishment, but few of those who do so expect to benefit personally from its ban.

Reconciling disagreement over government action represents a fundamental problem of politics. James Madison played a dominant role in drafting the Constitution, and we repeatedly

---

\*This text concentrates on politics in the American national government, but it also draws freely on examples from other settings because the logic embedded in political processes is not confined to matters related to government. Consequently, throughout the text we frequently refer to some generic *collectivity*, whose members engage each other in reaching a *collective decision* either to undertake some *collective action* or to produce some *collective good*. We enlist these general terms whenever we offer a definition, an observation, or a conclusion that has a general application.

Library of Congress

During the Great Depression, when millions of Americans were suddenly impoverished, many critics blamed unfettered capitalism. The National Association of Manufacturers, still a politically active industry association, posted billboards like this one around the country to bolster support for "private enterprise" by associating it with other fundamental preferences.

turn to him for guidance throughout this book. In one of the most memorable and instructive statements justifying the new Constitution to delegates at the state conventions who were deciding whether to ratify it, he explained that the new government must be devised to represent and reconcile society's many diverse preferences that are "sown into the nature of man":

> A zeal for different opinions concerning religion, concerning government, and many other points . . . have, in turn, divided mankind into parties, inflamed them with mutual animosity, and rendered them much more disposed to vex and oppress each other than to co-operate for their common good. So strong is this propensity of mankind to fall into mutual animosities, that where no substantial occasion presents itself, the most frivolous and fanciful distinctions have been sufficient to kindle their unfriendly passions and excite their most violent conflicts.*

Certainly, Madison's observation appears no less true today than when he wrote it in 1787.

---

*This passage is from Madison's *Federalist* No. 10, published initially in 1787 as a newspaper editorial supporting the Constitution's ratification. We examine this truly exceptional essay in Chapter 2. We encourage you to read and study it; it is reprinted in its entirety in the appendix.

## The Importance of Institutional Design

As participants and preferences in politics multiply and as issues become more complex and divisive, unstructured negotiation rarely yields success. It may simply require too much time and effort. It may require some participants to surrender too much of what they value in order to win concessions from the other side. In other words, a compromise solution simply may not be present. And finally, and this is crucial, because here the careful study of institutional design can make a difference, negotiation may expose each side to too great a risk that the other will not live up to its agreements.

Fear of reneging may foster mutual suspicions and lead each side to conclude that "politics" will not work. When this occurs, war may become the preferred alternative. The conflict in the 1990s among Serbs, Croats, and Muslims in Bosnia followed such a dynamic. The earlier collapse of Yugoslavia's communist government resurrected ancient enmities among people who had lived peacefully as neighbors for decades. In the absence of effective political institutions they could count on to manage potential conflicts, ethnic and religious rivals became trapped in a spiral of mutual suspicion, fear, and hostility. Without a set of rules prescribing a political process for reaching and enforcing collective agreements, they were joining militias and killing one another with shocking brutality within a year. Today the former Yugoslav states are separate national governments striving to build institutions that replace violence with politics.

Whether at war or simply at odds over the mundane matter of scheduling employee coffee breaks, parties to a conflict benefit from prior agreement on rules and procedures for negotiations. Indeed, this theme reappears throughout this book: a stable community, whether a club or a nation-state, endures by establishing rules and procedures for promoting successful collective action. In January 1999, when the Senate turned to the impeachment trial of President Bill Clinton, the stage was set for an escalation of the partisan rancor that had marred the same proceedings in the House of Representatives. Yet the Senate managed to perform its constitutional responsibility speedily and with a surprising degree of decorum thanks to an early, closed-door meeting in which all one hundred senators endorsed a resolution that laid out the trial's ground rules. More important, they agreed to give the chamber's Democratic and Republican leaders the right to reject any changes to these rules. Thus members on both sides of the partisan divide could proceed toward a decision without fear that the other side would resort to trickery to get the results it favored. That the Senate would find a way to manage its disagreements is not surprising. Its leaders take pride in finding collegial ways of containing the potential conflicts that daily threaten to disrupt its business.

Reliance on rules and procedures designed to reconcile society's competing preferences is nothing new. In an era of arbitrary kings and aristocrats, republican political theorists understood their value. In a 1656 treatise exploring how institutions might be constructed to allow conflicting interests to find solutions in a more egalitarian way, English political theorist James Harrington described two young girls who were arguing about how to share a single slice of cake. Suddenly one of the girls proposed a rule: "'Divide,' said one to the other, 'and I will choose; or let me divide, and you shall choose.'" At this moment, Harrington stepped away from his story and seemingly shouted to the reader, "My God! These 'silly girls' have discovered the secret of republican institutions."* With that ingenious rule, both girls were able to pursue their self-interest (the largest possible slice of cake) and yet have the collective decision result in a division both could happily live with.[1] This became, for Harrington, a parable about the virtues of **bicameralism**—a legislature comprised of two chambers with each holding a veto over the other.

More than one hundred years after Harrington's treatise, the Framers of the Constitution spent the entire summer of 1787 in Philadelphia debating what new rules and offices to create for their fledgling government. They were guided by their best guesses about how the alternatives they were contemplating would affect the interests of their states and the preferences of their constituencies (see Chapter 2). The result of their efforts, the Constitution, is a collection of rules fundamentally akin to the one discovered by the girls in Harrington's story. (Think about it: both the House of Representatives and the Senate must agree to a bill before it can be sent to the president to be signed into law.) The events in Philadelphia remind us that however lofty the goal that gives rise to reform, **institutional design** is a product of politics. As a result, institutions may confer advantages on some interests over others. Indeed, sometimes one side, enjoying a temporary advantage, will try to permanently implant its preferences in difficult-to-change rules and procedures. The present-day Department of Education, for example, arose from the former Department of Health, Education, and Welfare in 1977 after newly elected president Jimmy Carter proposed this split as a reward for early support from teacher organizations that had long regarded a separate department as key to their ability to win increased federal funding for schools and teacher training. The history of this department bears out the wisdom of their strategy. Republican Ronald Reagan followed Carter into the White House with the full intention of returning the education bureaucracy to its former status. But before long the cabinet secretary he appointed to dismantle the department began championing it, as did many Republicans in Congress whose committees oversaw the department's activities and budgets. Nearly four decades later, the Department of Education is entrenched in Washington, and as we found in the introduction, national education policy has become a central issue for politicians from both political parties.

## Constitutions and Governments

All organizations are governed by rules and procedures for making and implementing decisions. Within colleges and universities, the student government, the faculty senate, staff associations, academic departments, and, of course, the university itself follow rules and procedures when transacting regular business. Although rules and procedures go by different names (for example, *constitution*, *bylaw*, *charter*), their purpose is the same: to guide an organization's members in making essentially political decisions—that is, decisions in which the participants initially disagree about what they would like the organization to do.

And what happens when the organization is a nation? Consider the problems: the number of participants is great, the many unsettled issues are complex, and each participant's

---

*Actually, Harrington exclaimed, "Mon Dieu!" Note that the lowercase "republican" refers to a form of government and not the (uppercase) Republican Party. The same case distinction applies to "democratic" and the Democratic Party. Both of these forms of government are examined later in the chapter.

performance in living up to agreements cannot be easily monitored. Yet even with their conflicts, entire populations engage in politics every day. Their degree of success depends largely on whether they have developed constitutions and governments that work.

The **constitution** of a nation establishes its governing **institutions** and *the set of rules and procedures these institutions must (and must not) follow to reach and enforce collective agreements.* A constitution may be a highly formal legal document, such as that of the United States, or it may resemble Britain's unwritten constitution, an informal "understanding" based on centuries of precedents and laws. A **government**, then, consists of these institutions and the legally prescribed process for making and enforcing collective agreements. Governments may assume various forms, including a monarchy, a representative democracy, a theocracy (a government of religious leaders), or a dictatorship.

## Authority versus Power

The simple observation that governments are composed of institutions actually says a great deal and implies even more. Government institutions consist of **offices** that confer on their occupants specific authority and responsibilities. Rules and procedures prescribe how an institution transacts business and what authority relations will link offices together. **Authority** is the acknowledged right to make a particular decision. Only the president possesses the authority to nominate federal judges. However, a majority of the Senate's membership retains sole authority to confirm these appointments and allow the nominees to take office.

Authority is distinguishable from **power**, a related but broader concept that we employ throughout the book. Power refers to a politician's actual influence over others whose cooperation she needs in order to achieve her political goals. An office's authority is an important ingredient, conferring influence—that is, power—to those who enlist it skillfully. For instance, President Trump has the authority to instruct the Department of Homeland Security (DHS) to test alternative prototypes for a new and extended wall at the U.S.-Mexican border. As of the fall of 2018, however, he did not have the authority to spend the billions necessary to build the wall. This authority rests with Congress. Whether Trump succeeds in achieving this major campaign promise will rest on his ability to persuade Congress to give him the necessary funds to build the wall. His success or failure in persuading Congress to appropriate the money will be a measure of his power.

Another instructive example of the distinction between authority and power comes from the same time in the Trump presidency. For months, the president tweeted almost nightly his displeasure with Attorney General Jeff Sessions. At one point, he even proclaimed, "I don't have an Attorney General, Very Sad." So why did Trump continue to rant for months, even calling Sessions a "wimp" and "ignorant" and a "Mr. Magoo" (a cartoon bumpkin), instead of just firing him? Unquestionably, the Constitution gives him the authority to do so. He might well have hesitated because Republicans in Washington cautioned that firing Sessions might lead the public and politicians to conclude that he was trying to cover up misdeeds and that he deserved to be impeached. So, here the president has the authority, but to use it might be so risky that one could say he lacked the power to fire his subordinate.

GUILLERMO ARIAS/AFP/Getty Images

Prototypes of President Donald Trump's southern border wall built near San Diego, California.

## Institutional Durability

Institutions are by no means unchangeable, but they tend to be stable and resist change for several reasons. First, with authority assigned to the office, not to the individual holding the office, established institutions persist well beyond the tenure of the individuals who occupy them. A university remains the same institution even though all of its students, professors, and administrators are eventually replaced. Institutions, therefore, contribute a fundamental continuity and orderliness to collective action. Second, the people affected by institutions make plans on the expectation that current arrangements will remain. Imagine how senior college students would react if, during their last semester, their college or university increased the required course units for a degree. Or consider the anxiety the millions of workers approaching retirement must feel whenever politicians in Washington talk about changing Social Security.*

Sometimes institutions are altered to make them perform more efficiently or to accomplish new collective goals. In 1970 an executive reorganization plan consolidated components of five executive departments and agencies into a single independent agency, the Environmental Protection Agency, with a strong mandate and commensurate regulatory authority to protect the environment. By coordinating their actions and centralizing authority, these formerly dispersed agencies could more effectively monitor and regulate polluting industries.

---

*In his 2005 State of the Union address President George W. Bush sought to reassure the most anxious segment of the public approaching retirement—specifically, those over age fifty-five—that his sweeping reform proposal would not apply to them.

### The Political System's Logic

The quality of democracy in modern America reflects the quality of its governing institutions. Embedded in these institutions are certain core values, such as the belief that those entrusted with important government authority must periodically stand before the citizenry in elections. Balanced against this ideal of popular rule is the equally fundamental belief that government must protect certain individual liberties even when a majority of the public insists otherwise. Throughout this text we find politicians and citizens disagreeing on the precise meaning of these basic beliefs and values as they are applied or redefined to fit modern society.

Also embedded in these institutions—initially by the Framers of the Constitution and later by amendment and two centuries of precedents based on past political practices—is a logic based on principles about how members of a community should engage one another politically to identify and pursue their common goals. Although the Framers did not use the vocabulary of modern political science, they intuitively discerned this logic and realized that they must apply it correctly if the "American Experiment" were to succeed.* For us, too, this logic is essential for understanding the behavior of America's political institutions, the politicians who occupy them, and the citizens who monitor politicians' actions. To that end, the concepts presented in the remainder of this chapter are the keys to "open up" America's political institutions and to reveal their underlying logic. We begin with the problems (or one can think of them as puzzles) that confront all attempts at collective action. Many institutional arrangements have been devised over time to solve these problems. Those we examine here are especially important to America's political system, and the concepts reappear as key issues throughout the book.

## Collective Action Problems

By virtue of their size and complexity, nations encounter special difficulties in conducting political business. In those nations where citizens participate in decisions through voting and other civic activities, still more complex issues arise. Successful **collective action** challenges a group's members to figure out what they want to do and how to do it. The former involves comparing preferences and finding a course of action that sufficient numbers of participants agree is preferable to proposed alternatives or to doing nothing. The latter concerns implementation—not just the nuts and bolts of performing some task, but reassuring participants that everyone will share the costs (such as taxes) and otherwise live up to agreements.

Even when members basically agree to solve a problem or achieve some other collective goal, there is no guarantee that they will find a solution and implement it. Two fundamental

---

*They were, after all, contemporaries of Isaac Newton and found in his theory of mechanics inspiration to search for similar natural laws to create a well-functioning polity. With Britain's monarchy the only real-world model to guide them—and one they tended to judge more as a model of what to avoid than to emulate—the Framers depended heavily on carefully reasoned ideas, which took them to Newtonian physics. Consequently, the terms *force*, *counterweight*, and *balance* were familiarly used during debates at the Constitutional Convention and by both sides in the Constitution's subsequent ratification campaign.

barriers—coordination problems and prisoner's dilemmas—may block effective collective action. Coordination can be problematic at both stages of collective action—as members decide to undertake a task and subsequently work together to achieve it. **Coordination** in making a joint decision mostly involves members sharing information about their preferences; coordination in undertaking a collective effort involves effectively organizing everyone's contribution. On this second matter, coordination may become problematic when individual members realize that the success of the collective enterprise will depend on their contribution, which may be costly. For instance, individual members may be asked to make a severe contribution such as going to war, and despite their costly effort, the collective effort might fail.

This fundamental problem introduces a class of issues commonly referred to as the **prisoner's dilemma**. It refers to a variety of settings in which individuals find themselves personally better off by pursuing their private interests and undermining the collective effort even when they want it to succeed. Prisoner's dilemmas pervade all of politics, from neighbors petitioning city hall for a stop sign to legislators collaborating to strike budget deals in Congress. These dilemmas especially interest us because the "solution"—that is, having everyone contribute to the collective undertaking—depends heavily on providing the kinds of incentives to individuals that governments are well suited to provide.

## Coordination

Whether in deciding what to do or how to do it, coordination is more difficult for large than for small groups. Several friends can easily share their preferences in great detail on how to spend the weekend together. Now consider Republican voters in the spring of 2016 trying to decide who their presidential nominee should be. An NBC/*Wall Street Journal* survey in early March found 30 percent favoring Donald Trump, with Ted Cruz, John Kasich, and Marco Rubio following with 27, 22, and 20 percent support, respectively. But this only scratched the surface of their preferences on what they wanted their party to do. The survey followed up by pitting Trump against each of the other candidates in a two-man race. In Figure 1.1 we find that Trump loses each contest. A lot of Republican respondents to the survey wanted anyone but Trump. Each candidate's "true" supporters teamed with the "anyone but Trump" respondents formed a clear majority. But as primaries and caucuses continued through early June, the coordination problem persisted. In the end, the "anyone but Trump" Republicans never managed to coordinate on an alternative candidate.

Now consider how size affects the capacity of a group to coordinate in achieving an agreed-to goal. Here, a classical music performance offers an education in the costs of coordinating collective action. During a concert the members of a string quartet coordinate their individual performances by spending nearly as much time looking at one another as they do following their music. Volume, tempo, and ornamentation must all be executed precisely and in tandem. By the end of a successful concert, the effort required is evident on the triumphant musicians' perspiring faces. A symphony orchestra, by contrast, achieves comparable coordination, despite its greater numbers, by retaining one of its members to put aside the musical instrument and take up the conductor's baton. By focusing on the conductor, orchestra members are able to coordinate their playing and produce beautiful music. And at the end of the concert, the conductor is the first one to mop a perspiring brow.

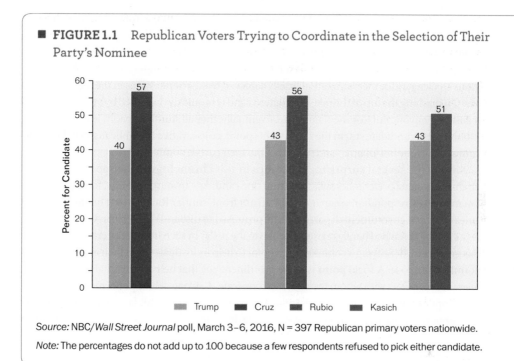

**■ FIGURE 1.1**    Republican Voters Trying to Coordinate in the Selection of Their Party's Nominee

*Source:* NBC/*Wall Street Journal* poll, March 3–6, 2016, N = 397 Republican primary voters nationwide.

*Note:* The percentages do not add up to 100 because a few respondents refused to pick either candidate.

Large groups trying to reach a shared goal might emulate the symphony in designating and following a leader. Members of the House of Representatives and the Senate configure procedures to enable Congress to decide policy for the hundreds of issues presented each session. But to achieve the same objective, the 435-member House and the 100-member Senate proceed differently, following a logic reflecting the size of their organizations. The House delegates to a Rules Committee the responsibility for scheduling the flow of legislation onto the floor and setting limits on deliberations and amendments. This important committee becomes the "leader" in setting the body's agenda. The entire House cedes this authority to a committee because coordination is vital if the chamber is to identify and pass the most preferred legislation. By contrast, the smaller Senate has found that it can achieve comparable levels of coordination without having to surrender authority to a specialized committee. In the Senate, informal discussions among members and party leaders suffice.

When the number of participants desiring to coordinate is very large—say, a state's voters—coordination may generally be unachievable. This explains why a society's collective decisions are generally delegated to a small group of professionals, namely **politicians**, who intensively engage one another in structured settings, namely government, to discover mutually attractive collective decisions.

The challenges to successful coordination increase with size. For some problems simple, self-enforcing rules—such as traffic staying to the right side of the street—might be all that is required. For other kinds of collective choices, institutions severely limit options, allowing like-minded individuals to coordinate easily. Political party nominations offer voters an obvious common choice.

Successful mass coordination occasionally arises even in the absence of institutions channeling individuals' choices. The 2012 presidential primaries saw conservative Republican voters race en masse from one candidate to another in search of an alternative—apparently any alternative—to the moderate and eventual winner Mitt Romney. As displayed in Figure 1.2, four of Romney's serious challengers for the nomination briefly achieved front-runner status in the public opinion polls. On reaching the top of the pile, each faltered and was quickly discarded by voters in favor of yet another "anyone but Romney" nominee. Eventually, they all stumbled badly, leaving Romney the only viable candidate still in the race. At this point, conservative Republicans switched their mantra to "anyone but Obama" and rallied behind their party's nominee.

Among the several surprising outcomes in this chronology is the speed with which Republican voters' preferences switched from one candidate to another. How, for example, did so many survey respondents manage to shift from front-runner Rick Perry (after he forgot the names of several government departments he promised to disband) to Herman Cain, who until Perry's debate fiasco had barely registered a blip in the polls? In such instances a critical ingredient of success lies in identifying a common focal point to help individuals target their energies toward a common purpose. A **focal point** is some prominent cue that helps individuals recognize the preferences of others with whom they want to cooperate. A strong debate performance might win some supporters, but equally important, it might identify to all the candidates who will attract the most support. Similarly, a narrow victory in a state delegate caucus could signal which candidate

**◼ FIGURE 1.2**    Republicans Pick a Presidential Nominee, 2012

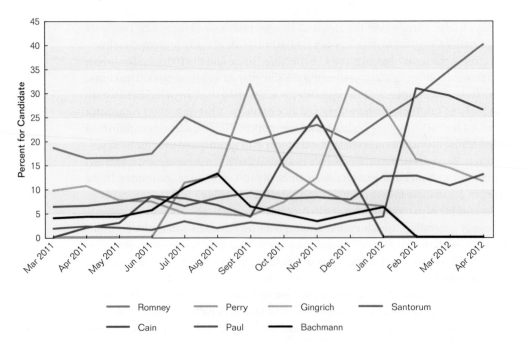

*Source:* Data from RealClearPolitics.com, 2012 Republican Presidential Nomination, accessed at www.realclearpolitics.com/epolls/2012/president/us/republican_presidential_nomination-1452.html#polls.

all like-minded voters should gather behind. Or endorsement by some accepted authority—like the conservative Tea Party movement—could concentrate support. Each of these kinds of focal point cues guided conservative Republicans as they settled on an "anyone but Romney" alternative who, shortly thereafter, displayed some fatal flaw that sent them searching for another candidate.

Internet-based social networks offer levels of focal point coordination unimaginable in earlier decades. A remarkable example of nearly spontaneously coordinated protest activity occurred in 2006, when a Los Angeles union and church organized a protest march against anti-immigrant legislation under consideration by the House of Representatives. The organizers hoped to arouse twenty thousand participants, but after they persuaded several Spanish-radio DJs to publicize the rally, over half a million protesters showed up. The size of the turnout amazed everyone, including the organizers, and the crowd quickly overwhelmed the police force. Clearly, there was a pent-up demand needing only a cue as to when and where everyone would show up.

Coordination problems essentially arise from uncertainty and insufficient information and may prevent collective undertakings even when a great majority agrees on a course of action, such as Republicans' desire to win back the presidency in 2012. We now turn to potentially more problematic challenges to collective action—the problems of the prisoner's dilemma. Unlike a lack of coordination, where mutual ignorance prevents participants from identifying and working together for a common goal, prisoner's dilemma problems find participants privately calculating that they would be better off by not contributing to the collective action even when they wholeheartedly agree with its purpose. Where coordination problems frequently require no more than direction and information, prisoner's dilemmas generally necessitate monitoring and the threat of coercion.

## The Prisoner's Dilemma

Since it was first formally introduced in the late 1950s, the prisoner's dilemma has become one of the most widely used concepts in the social sciences. A casual Google search generated over half a million hits on this phrase, bringing up websites on subjects far afield from political science and economics (where systematic consideration of the concept originated), including psychiatry, evolutionary biology, and drama theory. The prisoner's dilemma depicts a specific tension in social relations, one long intuitively understood by political thinkers. Solving this dilemma fundamentally distinguishes political success and failure and is a cornerstone of our inquiry. What precisely is the prisoner's dilemma, and why is it so important for the study of American politics?

The prisoner's dilemma arises whenever individuals who ultimately would benefit from cooperating with each other also have a powerful and irresistible incentive to break the agreement and exploit the other side. Only when each party is confident that the other will live up to an agreement can they successfully break out of the dilemma and work to their mutual advantage. A simple example of how this works is the original exercise that gives the prisoner's dilemma its name. In the movie stills from the 1941 drama *I Wake Up Screaming* (see photos), homicide detectives are subjecting screen legends Victor Mature and Betty Grable to the prisoner's dilemma. Specifically, each murder suspect is being advised to confess and testify against the other, in return for a lighter prison sentence. The diagram on the next page maps out the likely prison term each faces. Deep down Mature and Grable know that the police do not have enough evidence to convict them of murder. All they have to do is stick to their story (i.e., cooperate), and, at worst, they may have to spend six months in jail on a gun possession charge. If both were to confess, each would get a five-year sentence. Each of them is offered a deal: in exchange for a full confession, the "squealer" will get off scot-free, whereas the "fall guy" or "sucker" will be convicted and likely receive a ten-year prison term. In the movie both suspects are isolated in their cells for a few days, with the detectives hinting that their partner is "singing like a canary." As the days pass, each begins to recognize the other's character flaws and panics. If Mature squeals, Grable realizes, she must also in order to avoid a ten-year stretch. If, however, she has underestimated his virtues and he holds out, well, that would be unfortunate, but she gains some solace in knowing that her lone confession will be her "get-out-of-jail" card. Of course, Mature, stewing in his cell, reaches the same conclusion. Why this movie presents a genuine dilemma is that *in this setting* confessing offers the best outcome for each suspect, regardless of what the other individual does. So, in the end, they both confess and spend the next five years in the slammer.*

|  |  | VICTOR MATURE | |
|  |  | STAYS SILENT | CONFESSES |
| Betty Grable | Stays silent | 6 months, 6 months | 10 years, no jail |
|  | Confesses | No jail, 10 years | 5 years, 5 years |

(Grable's sentence is listed first.)

Subjected to the classic prisoner's dilemma interrogation, Victor Mature and Betty Grable turn out to have nothing to confess in the 1941 whodunit *I Wake Up Screaming*. Since its introduction in the 1950s, thousands of articles have enlisted this metaphor to explore the fundamental conflict between what is rational behavior for each member of a group and what is in the best interest of the group as a whole.

*For this reason police have traditionally objected to giving suspects early access to lawyers, who might help the otherwise isolated prisoners coordinate their plan. But this is a different story we return to in Chapter 5. By the way, the movie offers a happy ending.

So what does this dilemma have to do with American politics? Everything. Every successful political exchange must tacitly solve the prisoner's dilemma. Exchanges occur because each side recognizes that it will be better off with a collective outcome rather than with trying to act alone. Had Mature and Grable somehow managed to stay silent, their cooperation would have shaved all but six months from their five-year terms. And both knew this. Yet neither could be sure the other confederate would stay silent. To get something worthwhile, both sides must typically give up something of value in return. The moral: unless participants in a collective decision can trust each other to abide by their commitments, they will not achieve a mutually profitable exchange.

How do the Matures and Grables shift the outcome from that quadrant, where neither cooperates, to the one where they both do? One solution involves making reneging and defection very expensive. In some settings this can be achieved informally. For example, politicians who repeatedly make campaign promises that they subsequently fail to act on lose credibility with voters and become vulnerable to defeat in the next election. Once in office, reneging on an agreement will quickly damage a politician's reputation, and others will refuse to deal with her in the future. Where failure to live up to one's agreements imposes costs down the road, politicians will think twice before doing so.

Another common solution is to create institutions that help parties discover opportunities to profit through cooperation and, most important, guarantee that agreements are honored. Here government's coercive authority is useful. An anthropologist once reported that two tribes in a remote region of New Guinea lived in a state of continual warfare, to the point that many more men from both tribes had died in battle than from natural causes. The anthropologist summed up their dilemma: "In the absence of any central authority, they are condemned to fight forever . . . since for any group to cease defending itself would be suicidal." He added that these tribes might "welcome pacification." One day the distant government in Papua sent a ranger armed with a handgun to establish territorial boundaries between the tribes and rules governing their chance encounters. Suddenly, the decades-long warfare ended. Each side believed the ranger with his single sidearm presented sufficient force to punish any breaches (defection) of the peace agreements, and the now-peaceful neighbors began to use politics—not war—to solve their conflicts.[2] Members of a society must be able to engage one another politically. Without confidence that agreements will be enforced, the political process quickly unravels. Participants will balk at undertaking mutual obligations they suspect their bargaining partners will not honor.

In his 1651 treatise on the origin and purposes of government, *Leviathan*, political philosopher Thomas Hobbes examined the straits to which society is reduced when its government is unable to enforce collective obligations and agreements. (See the Logic of Politics box "Hobbes on Monarchs.") In a famous passage he warned that life would return to "a state of nature . . . solitary, poor, nasty, brutish and short."[3] The mortality rate of New Guinea tribesmen confirmed Hobbes's insight. They were not naturally combative; rather, these tribes simply could not trust each other. Thus enforcement succeeded in encouraging cooperation, but not through flaunting overwhelming force or imposing a solution on the contending parties. The ranger's presence simply rendered any party's defection costlier than its compliance.

Hopefully, the relevance of the prisoner's dilemma to American politics is becoming clearer. Virtually every policy the government adopts represents a successful resolution of

## LOGIC OF POLITICS
# Hobbes on Monarchs

In 1651 Thomas Hobbes argued in *Leviathan*, one of the most important books in political theory, that the English monarch was a necessary guarantor of collective agreements.[a] He proposed that because the king and his offspring derived their wealth directly from the population in taxes and labor, they would pursue the nation's welfare because it would enrich them as well. Even if the monarch were wicked and expropriated too much of the nation's wealth for himself, the citizenry was still better off with him wielding power arbitrarily than if no one had enforcement authority. Restated in the vocabulary of this text, Hobbes argued that monarchs offered a cost-effective means to collective action.

North Wind Picture Archives

a. Thomas Hobbes, *Leviathan, or The matter, forme, & power of a commonwealth ecclesiasticall and civill* (1651; reprint, Oxford: Clarendon Press, 1958).

this dilemma. Constituencies and their representatives cooperate to achieve their separate goals—recall our definition of politics earlier—because institutions have developed to help diverse constituencies discover opportunities for mutual gain through cooperation and, just as important, to deter them from reneging on their agreements. Like the ranger with a handgun from Papua, America's political institutions foster collective action by solving the prisoner's dilemma.

There are failures, to be sure. Antitrust laws are designed to prevent competitors in the marketplace from colluding to fix prices or restrain trade in other ways, but they can have unintended consequences. For instance, in 2014 new oil production technologies combined with a slumping world economy to suddenly create a worldwide oversupply of oil. Crude oil prices plummeted to less than half their value of a couple of years earlier, leaving the American oil industry in a predicament. Many drillers that had recently taken on debt to expand production now found themselves contributing to an oil glut. One obvious solution would be for everyone to cut back production. And yet, unable to coordinate, they individually drilled harder to service their debt in the face of depressed prices while hoping that their competitors would cut back.[4]

Other issues simply do not offer mutual gains through cooperation. One party's gain is the other's loss, and politics may break down and give way to force. National policy on rights to abortion frequently becomes just such an issue where irreconcilable preferences seek to control policy. Chapter 4 recounts the most intractable issue of all in American political history—the failure, despite repeated compromise attempts, to come up with a policy on slavery's extension into the territories during the 1850s. This issue was resolved only by the deadliest war of its time.

Even when each side can envision opportunities for mutual gains, American politics is far from failure proof. Everyone agrees that in several decades the Social Security program will be unable to keep up current levels of benefits long before the millennial generation approaches retirement. Both Republicans and Democrats in Washington want to fix it, and from time to time one side will gingerly make an overture to the other. But all of the solutions are costly or otherwise unpopular, either requiring hefty new taxes or curtailing benefits. Both political parties worry that as soon as they offer a tough solution, the other side will exploit it to score points in the next election. Until politicians figure out a way to cooperate and share the blame, Social Security reform will remain the proverbial "third rail" of politics: "Touch it and you are dead."*

### Free-Rider Problem

A form of the prisoner's dilemma that afflicts large groups is the **free-rider problem**. Whenever an individual's contribution to the success of the collective effort is so small as to seem inconsequential, one will be tempted to free ride—that is, to fail to contribute to the group's undertaking while enjoying the benefits of its success. Even those who enthusiastically support the group's goal realize that they can escape fulfilling their obligations. When the motivation to free ride is a serious possibility, several outcomes are possible.

First, it may stymie collective action altogether. Just knowing that the other participants might free ride might at times even dissuade those ready to pony up their share of money or effort from doing so. If many people react this way—and many do—and suspect their neighbors of doing so as well, too few contribute to collective effort, and, thus, it fails. During Barack Obama's 2008 presidential campaign, "get out the vote" operatives discovered that organizing volunteers into groups of more than ten volunteers reduced the group's success in contacting prospective voters. Instead of crusaders making a difference, they felt like "numbers on a spreadsheet." A lot of them dropped out of the campaign. Having learned this lesson, in 2012 the Obama campaign organized volunteers into smaller teams where they could more easily see that their contribution made a difference. As a result, the campaign's voter contact efforts proved more successful.[5]

A second possible outcome arises when the collective undertaking will benefit some participants more than others. When those who have a small stake in the outcome discern that one or several other participants will derive so much value that they would be prepared to absorb the full cost of the undertaking, the setting is ripe for free riding. But in this case, the collective enterprise is still successful. This is the dilemma the United States has grappled with unsuccessfully over the years in trying to persuade our NATO partners to contribute their agreed-to resources—a contribution equal to 2 percent of the country's GDP—for their common defense. In Figure 1.3 we find that only five countries have matched or exceeded

---

*The third rail metaphor refers to the third rail of subway tracks, the one that carries the electricity.

their allocated share. Some, such as Canada, have cut their contributions sharply over the past several decades. Every president has complained about this at NATO gatherings, but President Trump is the first to threaten to pull the United States out of NATO and by doing so, prompted our allies to acknowledge the current imbalance. (Whether they go the next step and contribute greater support remains to be seen.)*

From the first two scenarios we see that individuals' contributions to a collective enterprise is carefully calculated, even when everyone agrees that the collective good is well worth pursuing. Successful collective action in most settings requires an organization that can

■ **FIGURE 1.3**   Defense Expenditures of NATO Countries, 2017

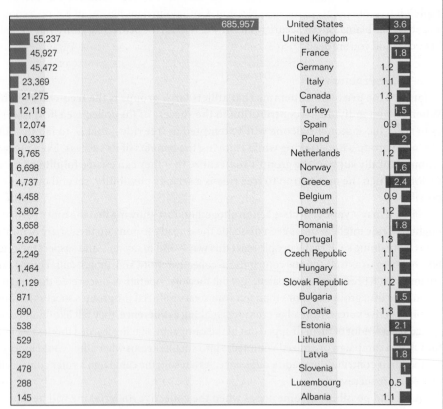

| Military spending | Country | Estimated share of GDP |
|---|---|---|
| 685,957 | United States | 3.6 |
| 55,237 | United Kingdom | 2.1 |
| 45,927 | France | 1.8 |
| 45,472 | Germany | 1.2 |
| 23,369 | Italy | 1.1 |
| 21,275 | Canada | 1.3 |
| 12,118 | Turkey | 1.5 |
| 12,074 | Spain | 0.9 |
| 10,337 | Poland | 2 |
| 9,765 | Netherlands | 1.2 |
| 6,698 | Norway | 1.6 |
| 4,737 | Greece | 2.4 |
| 4,458 | Belgium | 0.9 |
| 3,802 | Denmark | 1.2 |
| 3,658 | Romania | 1.8 |
| 2,824 | Portugal | 1.3 |
| 2,249 | Czech Republic | 1.1 |
| 1,464 | Hungary | 1.1 |
| 1,129 | Slovak Republic | 1.2 |
| 871 | Bulgaria | 1.5 |
| 690 | Croatia | 1.3 |
| 538 | Estonia | 2.1 |
| 529 | Lithuania | 1.7 |
| 529 | Latvia | 1.8 |
| 478 | Slovenia | 1 |
| 288 | Luxembourg | 0.5 |
| 145 | Albania | 1.1 |

■ Military spending (millions of U.S. dollars)

■ Estimated share of GDP (percent)

*Source:* Adapted from NATO, "Defence Expenditure of NATO Countries (2010-2017)," March 15, 2018. https://www.nato.int/nato_static_fl2014/assets/pdf/pdf_2018_03/20180315_180315-pr2018-16-en.pdf.

*Note:* Gross domestic product is one of the most commonly used benchmarks of nations' wealth.

---

*Mancur Olson, who introduced free riding to generations of scholars beyond economics, referred to this setting as the "tyranny of the great by the small."

monitor and where necessary intervene to induce individuals' contributions. These organizations may be either private or the government. One advantage the latter enjoys is the use of force. Immediately after the United States declared war on Japan after the attack on Pearl Harbor, thousands of patriotic young men rushed to army and navy recruiters. In case they did not, however, Congress passed a draft law. One of the most controversial features of the national health care law enacted in 2010 was the requirement that everyone sign up for health care insurance. Failing to do so would result in an extra tax added to the individual's income tax to contribute to these premiums. Clearly the intuition behind the mandate was that in a setting where no one could be denied insurance coverage, many people would wait until they got sick to sign up. In a sense they would free ride—that is, not contribute to the overall financing of the program—but avail themselves of the collective good whenever they liked.*

For many voluntary associations, this strategy is unavailable. With about 10 percent of its regular viewers donating to their local PBS affiliates, the Public Broadcasting System requires an annual government subsidy to stay in business. Given the logic of nonparticipation, why does anyone ever contribute to a collective enterprise? Clearly some people find certain activities intrinsically rewarding, however minor their contributions. That said, most of the people, most of the time, are inclined to free ride. If a collective effort is to succeed, it must provide potential participants with a private inducement.

Labor unions represent a class of voluntary organization that has been particularly susceptible to free riding. Whether in following the organization's call to strike or simply in paying monthly union dues, unions grapple with workers who want the benefits of the unions collective effort without having to pay the fees or endure the pain of a strike. Traditionally, the Republican Party in Washington and across state capitals has sympathized with workers inclined to free ride by passing "right-to-work" laws forbidding enforced union membership. In 2018 the Supreme Court ruled that required union dues for public employee workers—the largest groups are teachers and service employees—violated workers' First Amendment free speech right (we return to the modern understanding of this civil liberty in Chapter 5). The ruling directly affects the nation's largest union, the National Education Association (NEA), which announced that it expected to lose more than 200,000 of its 3 million teacher members during the first year alone.[6]

## The Tragedy of the Commons

Another distinctive and important form of the prisoner's dilemma is the **tragedy of the commons**. It resembles free riding in that the provision of a collective good is divorced from its consumption. Where free riding emphasizes efforts of individuals to shirk their contribution, tragedy of the commons problems concentrate on individuals' costless consumption of a public good (the "commons") that results in its ruination. Having a large number of participants encourages each to renege on contributions to the public good. The chief difference is that the good already exists and will be destroyed if its exploitation is not brought under control.

---

*In 2017 Congress rescinded this unpopular mandate, putting the Affordable Care Act on a less secure financial footing.

This dilemma takes its name from another instructive allegory. A number of herdsmen graze their cattle in a common pasture. Gradually, they increase the sizes of their herds, destroying the pasture and with it their livelihood. With each herdsman reasoning that adding one more cow to the herd will increase his income while having negligible impact on the pasture, they all add cattle, and do so repeatedly. The end result is a disaster—eventually, overgrazing strips the pasture of fodder, the cows starve, and the herdsmen go broke.

A real-world analogy is the collapse of the cod fishing industry off New England. Entire communities based their economies on fishing cod in nearby waters, but so many fishermen exploited this resource, without allowing nature to replenish it adequately, that they managed to wipe out the fishery on which their jobs depended.[7] Kansas wheat growers confront the same dilemma when they overirrigate their fields even while recognizing that they are rapidly depleting the underground aquifer and, consequently, their long-term livelihood.

Where virtually all examples of tragedy of the commons dilemmas emphasize the inability of individual actors to work together to protect a shared resource, here is a recent example of the government relaxing environmental regulations and opening up this commons (i.e., clean air) to individuals' use. In the fall of 2018 the Environmental Protection Agency (EPA) proposed a new regulation that would return to the states authority to oversee energy production of coal. The coal industry would love this change because every state administrator would be tempted to free ride by issuing lax use permits out of suspicion that the other state regulators are. Because one state, acting alone, can achieve little by way of protecting the environment, it might as well reap the same benefits for its coal producers.

AP Photo/Daily Sitka Sentinel, James Poulson

A classic tragedy of the commons scene: too many boats chasing too few fish, not because the skippers are greedy, but because in the absence of an agreement, none can afford to stop fishing and surrender the harvest to others. Here, ships collide at an opening of the Sitka Sound herring fishery as they compete to catch the remaining tons of herring left in the year's quota.

The trick to avoiding the tragedy of the commons lies in proper institutional design. As with free riding, the solution links the individual's personal interest to provision (in this instance, preservation) of the collective good. A decision to squander or conserve resources must somehow be made to affect each participant's personal welfare. One solution is **regulation**—setting up rules limiting access to the common resource and monitoring and penalizing those who violate them. But enforcement can be costly because individuals will be tempted to exploit the collective good if they see their neighbors and colleagues flouting the rules.

In many settings, a less costly and more effective alternative

Proposed redesigned coal pollution regulatory regime.

solution to conserving the commons is to **privatize** it—that is, converting it from a collective good to a private good. After a second straight disastrous harvest in 1622, the residents of Plymouth Plantation found themselves as close to starvation as at any time since their arrival on the *Mayflower*. In desperation, the community's leader, William Bradford, announced an end to communal farming. He divided the acreage into family plots and left each family to provide for itself. This ended the famine. As one historian noted, "The change in attitude was stunning. Families were now willing to work much harder than they had ever worked before."[8] After instituting the reform Bradford observed, "The women now went willingly into the field and took their little ones with them to set corn." Similarly, confronted with decreasing stock, modern fishery management has increasingly switched from regulations (i.e., catch quotas) to privatization by granting fishermen exclusive access to parts of the ocean in the hope that this will motivate them to harvest prudently. Whether regulation or privatization, the solution involves aligning personal gain with promotion of the collective good.

## The Costs of Collective Action

Collective action offers a group benefits that its members cannot achieve on their own. But participating in a collective enterprise also entails various costs. The key to successful collective action lies in designing a system that achieves the benefits of a collective effort while minimizing its costs. For example, the Senate, with its 100 members, efficiently accomplishes its business with fewer and less restrictive rules than those required for the much larger 435-member House of Representatives.

Don't waste your time: stop circling the block, find a spot in a button tap
Broadcast your parking request to our community: you could park on other people's vacant driveways!

**Broadcast a request**
Our nearby community will be notified

**Check the closest driveway**
Instant access, $10 flat rate

**Get directions and park**
Contact the driveway-owner for any further information

Privatizing the Commons. Citing the headaches that hundreds of city drivers face each day, an enterprising entrepreneur has developed an app-based service, MonkeyParking, that identifies vacant parking spots on city streets. He took service one step further in Los Angeles and proposed that, for a fee, the service would send someone out to reserve the slot for the subscriber. This would have effectively privatized this commons—that is, street parking. City Hall, however, decided that the commons is not his to privatize and banned the practice.

Some of the costs associated with collective enterprises are not hard to spot. An obvious one is each person's monetary contribution to an enterprise—for example, tax payments funding road construction or staffing of a police department. Less obvious are the "overhead" costs of enforcing agreements, such as the ranger's salary in New Guinea or the costs associated with the judicial system and the lawyers needed to ensure that those who enter into business agreements live up to their contracts. Overhead costs also include the government's effort to combat free riding. If people were not inclined to free ride, the federal government could disband the large bureaucracy that goes after tax cheats.

Two kinds of costs that are especially relevant for designing and evaluating institutions are transaction costs and conformity costs. Though they represent separate aspects of how a community tackles collective enterprises, they often involve a trade-off with each other. In creating institutions to achieve desirable collective goods, a society should collectively weigh the balance between members' private autonomy and the requirements for achieving the collective good.

## Transaction Costs

**Transaction costs** are the time, effort, and resources required to make collective decisions. Consider a student activities committee that selects which band to bring to campus. First, do students want rock, hip-hop, or some other kind of music? Then, what bands are available, how good are they, and what do they charge? Of course, unsatisfactory answers to the second set of questions might return the committee to the first. Once a decision has been made, the bands must be contacted, dates and prices negotiated, and a venue found. The time and effort

Deputies in Ukraine's parliament struggled with high transaction costs during a debate before a vote on the country's 2014 budget.

spent researching available bands, debating preferences, and implementing decisions are all transaction costs of the collective good of campus entertainment.

Transaction costs can pose a formidable barrier to political agreements. These costs rise sharply as the number of participants whose preferences must be taken into account increases. In the absence of institutions for negotiating and implementing collective agreements, these costs might overwhelm the ability of participants to identify with and commit themselves to collective enterprises. With well-designed institutions, however, agreements become easier to make. In the previous example, the student body greatly reduced its transaction costs by authorizing a committee to make a collective choice for it.

Sometimes, though, high transaction costs are intentionally put in place to make some collective activities more, not less, difficult. Having fashioned a delicately balanced plan of government, the Framers were understandably uninterested in making it easy for some group down the road to rewrite the Constitution. Indeed, the prospect that their labors might soon be undone could have prevented them from reaching agreement in the first place. The Framers ratcheted up the transaction costs of future constitutional change. A proposed amendment to the Constitution must be endorsed by two-thirds of the membership of both houses of Congress and ratified by three-fourths of the states.*

---

*Alternatively, two-thirds of the state legislatures can ask Congress to call a national convention to propose amendments, but this has never been done.

## Conformity Costs

In negotiating a common course of action, parties advocating competing interests rarely discover that they want precisely the same thing. Politics invariably means compromise. Most of the time there are losers—parties whose preferences receive little accommodation but who must still contribute to a collective undertaking. To the extent that collective decisions obligate participants to do something they prefer not to—and all resolutions of the prisoner's dilemma involve this—we refer to this necessity as a **conformity cost**. Conformity costs range from an ordinary task such as paying property taxes to extraordinary sacrifices such as serving overseas in the military, away from home and family. Rules that require fishermen to stay at the dock during a portion of the fishing season, rules that make a citizen spend part of her income to fund government programs she opposes, and rules that limit the time allotted to a member of Congress for a floor speech all impose conformity costs on individuals to achieve a collective goal. Not surprisingly, members of a community prefer minimum conformity costs. But because collective goals never come effortlessly, elected representatives must continually weigh what kinds of and how much costs its citizens are prepared to bear for a particular good. Failure to do so, as Democrats discovered in the 2010 congressional elections shortly after passage of comprehensive health care policy, could find them ushered out of office.

In that transaction and conformity costs generally entail a trade-off: those institutions that minimize transaction costs, making it easy to act, may do so by imposing excessive conformity costs. An extreme case would be a dictator who arbitrarily decides national policies (minimal transaction costs) by insisting that everyone do what he, not they, prefers (maximum conformity costs). At the opposite end of the continuum would be government by consensus. The group does nothing unless everyone agrees to it. Of course, governments based on consensus often have a difficult time undertaking any collective enterprise, although they expend great effort (exorbitant transaction costs) discovering this.

Perhaps the best way to appreciate the trade-off of these costs is to play the following mind game: you've accumulated $40,000 and are ready to fulfill your lifelong dream to climb Mount Everest. One of the first (and probably most consequential) choices you have to make is selecting an expedition to sign up with.

*Frank Cotham/The New Yorker Collection/The Cartoon Bank*

"*It's either this or a country run by lawyers.*"

Not just another lawyer joke. . . . Clearly the guards prefer the high conformity costs imposed by this hapless leviathan to the transaction costs of more democratic institutions.

With about 800 soul mates trekking toward the summit each year, you have some choices. Do you sign up with an expedition whose leader has the reputation as a real taskmaster? This seasoned, grizzled veteran rarely, if ever, pays customers' opinions any regard and brooks no dissent. A real dictator. Or do you opt for an equally experienced but more solicitous leader— someone who shares decisions with the group and values their input? (Consider how these expeditions have opted for different mixes of conformity and transaction costs.) Back to the decision: which group do you sign up with? Recent research on this subject suggests that your answer should depend on your priority. If above all else you want to reach the summit, go with the dictator. Statistics show that over the years, the more hierarchically organized expeditions have greater success in reaching the top. If, however, survival is a higher priority, go with the more democratically organized expedition. Fewer members of these teams die along the way.[9]

These extreme mixes of transaction and conformity costs might seem far-fetched when referring to national governments, but for many of the Constitution's Framers this was precisely the issue that brought them to Philadelphia. Chapter 2 examines America's unhappy, precarious experience with government by consensus in the decade following independence. The Articles of Confederation, the nation's first constitution, allowed any state to block national action on important policies such as taxes. Moreover, the absence of enforcement authority fostered rampant free riding even when the states could agree on a course of action. Consequently, even in a country with only thirteen participating states—each with one vote in the Confederation Congress—the transaction costs of consensus government proved

Christian Kober/AWL Images

Climbers make their way toward the peak on Mount Everest. Those who want to summit Everest must calculate both transaction and conformity costs in selecting the guide to get them there, from the dollar expense to leadership style. Data show that more hierarchically organized expeditions have a greater success rate in reaching the top.

impossibly difficult and prompted all but one state, Rhode Island, to send delegates to a constitutional convention to create a more viable arrangement.

More commonly, governmental reform occurs within a narrow range of trade-offs between transaction and conformity costs. Rules, procedures, and resources are frequently changed to reduce transaction costs and make government more efficient and decisive. But sometimes the opposite scheme is adopted to prevent abuses. After the civil rights movement and the Vietnam War era, scandals uncovered widespread abuses by the Federal Bureau of Investigation and Central Intelligence Agency in spying on civil rights activists (including Martin Luther King Jr.) and antiwar leaders. Congress enacted procedures requiring judicial approval before these investigative agencies could undertake wiretaps and other forms of intrusive surveillance of citizens. Such reforms to prevent abuses were adopted with little opposition in Washington and represent a classic instance of increasing transaction costs as a way to hamstring action—in this instance, action taken against those who opposed current government policies. Over the objections of law enforcement officials, the government decided to preserve individuals' freedom of dissent (reduce conformity costs) by jacking up transaction costs on law enforcement officials. After September 11, 2001, the balance shifted back to reducing the transaction costs involved in going after potential terrorists (via the USA PATRIOT Act), and conformity costs increased.

## Representative Government

Modern democracies blend delegation with majority rule into what is known as **representative government**. Citizens limit their decisions to the selection of government officials who, acting as their agents, deliberate and commit the citizenry to collective enterprises. This form of democracy eliminates the massive confusion that would ensue if large communities tried to craft policies directly, and it frees most citizens from having to attend constantly to civic business. For a large group or society, representative government, through delegation, makes large-scale democracy possible. **Direct democracy**, in which citizens participate directly in collective decision-making, is reserved primarily for small communities and organizations.*

At the time of the adoption of the U.S. Constitution, the idea of majority rule was controversial. The ancient city-state of Athens, one of the few experiments with democracy known at the time, had ended ignominiously in mob rule and ultimately dictatorship. The eighteenth-century political theorists who influenced the Constitution's Framers endorsed a form of government called a **republic**, designed to allow some degree of popular control and also avoid **tyranny**.[10] The Framers designed the new Constitution to pose formidable transaction costs on collective action. The Framers especially favored some form of veto or "check" of one institution over another. In a republic, voters elect their representatives, but these representatives are constrained

---

*Another approach to direct democracy that is adapted to a large electorate is the **referendum**. Nearly half the states allow the legislature to propose a change to the state's laws or constitution, which all the voters subsequently vote on. An alternative and even purer form of direct democracy is the **initiative**, which places a proposal on the ballot when the requisite number of registered voters have signed petitions to place the issue on an election ballot.

in following the majority's dictates by constitutional guarantees for minorities and by institutions and rules requiring exceptionally large majorities for certain decisions.

The notion of an independent, unelected judiciary challenges the paramount democratic principle of majority rule, but it presents no problem for the republican creed. By ratifying the Constitution and retaining the power to amend it, the people may choose to set up an institution independent of the others and unconcerned with short-term swings in public opinion to referee the political process and preserve the values on which the government is founded. In short, republican theorists, who had the allegiance of virtually everyone attending the Constitutional Convention in 1787, *really* believed in the role of institutions in reaching and preserving agreements. And by making some collective decisions more difficult than others, the Framers consciously built in higher transaction costs, even if they did not use those terms.

Since the American Experiment was launched over two hundred years ago, experience with majority rule throughout the world has proved that it is a viable approach to self-governance. Although constitutions written in the twentieth century—such as those in France and Germany—may still divide authority in ways that allow their countries to be referred to as republics, they do not include the elaborate rules and institutions designed to constrain majority rule by ratcheting up transaction costs in the American system. Instead of separating the executive from the legislature, most of the world's modern democracies have fused them in **parliamentary government**. Many varieties of parliamentary government exist, but they all lodge decisive authority in a popularly elected legislature, whose actions are not subject to the same severe checks by executive and judicial vetoes. The legislature in turn elects a team of executives called a **cabinet**, one of whose members serves as the premier or prime minister (see Figure 1.4). This system promotes majority rule in the sense that the

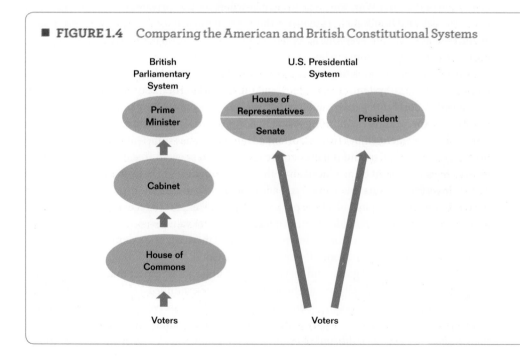

■ **FIGURE 1.4**   Comparing the American and British Constitutional Systems

political party or **coalition** of parties that controls the legislature controls the executive. In effect, parliamentary systems are able to forgo the higher transaction costs embedded in the U.S. Constitution's **separation of powers**. At the same time, as the majority gains the capacity to act on its preferences, those who disagree are obliged to accept the majority's preferences.

## The Work of Government

Given the variety of costs and risks associated with collective action, Americans weigh such undertakings carefully. Among other things, they calculate whether the prospective gains from a collective public effort are sufficiently greater than what they could achieve privately. The vast majority of these calculations favor private action, perhaps explaining why much of what Americans do and consume as individuals has little or nothing to do with government. Their homes, cars, clothes, food, and sources of entertainment fall into a realm called **private goods**—that is, things people buy and consume themselves in a marketplace that supplies these goods according to the demand for them.

What we discuss in this book is the provision of **public goods**, which everyone participates in supplying—say, through tax dollars—and which anyone can freely consume, as much as he or she desires. Stated another way, the two distinguishing features of all public goods are that their costs are borne collectively and that no one can be excluded from their benefits. An example of a public good is a freeway, which, as its name implies, may be used by anyone. A toll road is a private good because its costs are met by the motorists who pay a fee (toll) for its use. A quintessential public good is national defense. However, in the early 1950s, at the beginning of the Cold War, some fearful homeowners took a "private goods approach" and installed backyard bomb shelters to use in the event of nuclear attack. They were eventually abandoned as just about everyone accepted the logic of relying on national defense—a public good—to protect them from nuclear assault.

Citizens frequently look to government to provide positive public goods: national defense, public order, a legal system, civil liberties, and public parks. They also count on government to prevent or correct negative public goods such as laws controlling pollution; protecting endangered species; and establishing residential, commercial, and industrial zones. For these tasks, the government enjoys two important advantages: it has sufficient resources to undertake expensive projects, and it has coercive authority to prevent free riding. Many public goods simply could not be produced any other way. Some are too risky financially to attract private investment. What business could afford to build a multibillion-dollar supercollider to research nuclear fusion and, at the project's inception, expect to recover its costs within a period reasonable to shareholders? Other goods offer better value when converted from a private to a public good. The history of fire protection in America is one example (see Politics to Policy box "Fire Protection: From a Private to a Public Good").

Another large class of goods and services has a "public good" aspect that justifies the collective provision of essentially private benefits. Earlier we examined a class of mixed policies where government privatizes the "commons" in order to conserve it. Federal and state tax codes are complicated because many of their provisions are intended not to raise revenue, but to motivate the public to contribute to some collective policy goal. Tax deductions or credits

## POLITICS TO POLICY
# Fire Protection

### From a Private to a Public Good

The history of fire protection in America offers a classic example of the evolution of private goods to a government responsibility. During the nation's colonial era, fire protection assumed the form of an insurance policy. Homeowners subscribed to a local protection service, mounted its identifying shield on the front of the house, and hoped that if they had a fire it would show up.

In many small communities voluntary fire departments formed to turn fire protection into a public good. The coordination problems were resolved, and the service's responsiveness limited the spread of fires across structures. This arrangement worked reasonably well in towns and villages where everyone knew everyone else. Any "volunteer" who chronically slept through the fire bell might well have found his neighbors doing the same when the bell sounded for his house.

As communities grew and social controls on free riding weakened, voluntary fire protection gave way to government-run, professional fire protection. Typically, governments created a special fire district with taxing authority and hired professional firefighters to supply this public good.

*Missouri History Museum, St. Louis*

for charitable contributions, for contributions to personal retirement accounts, for installing solar heating, for restoring historic homes, and for investing in new equipment are just a few of a long list of federal incentives promoting some collective good.

In reality, most of the goods and services that governments provide cannot be easily sorted into either the private or the public bin. Public education is a classic example. A well-educated citizenry undeniably strengthens the civic and economic life of a society, but public education also bestows substantial *private* benefits on students and educators. The immediate beneficiary of a flu vaccination is the person who received it. But so too is everyone with whom

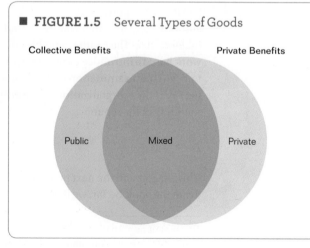

**■ FIGURE 1.5**  Several Types of Goods

Collective Benefits                          Private Benefits

Public          Mixed          Private

he or she comes into contact, even if only by pushing the same elevator button. Because the work of modern governments typically belongs in this class of *mixed* goods, public policy is frequently referred to as dealing in **collective goods**. Throughout our discussion, we will use this less restrictive term that includes both true *public goods* and mixed policies that also confer private benefits (see Figure 1.5).

## Collective Action and America's Constitution

The Constitution's Framers, who assembled in Philadelphia during the summer of 1787, did not use the modern vocabulary of collective action problems, such as *prisoner's dilemma* or *tragedy of the commons*. Nor did they formally label and classify their institutional design mechanisms. Yet they were intimately preoccupied with the collective action issues that afflicted society and overwhelmed the capacity of the nation under the Articles of Confederation to solve them. Although they sometimes disagreed on the design of the new government, delegates to the Philadelphia Convention all understood that the nation's previous failures stemmed from weak institutions. Citizens and state governments engaged in rampant free riding, and politicians failed to honor commitments because the institutions made reneging easy and cooperation risky. Americans were trapped in the same fundamental prisoner's dilemma that ensnared Victor Mature and Betty Grable. The Framers undertook the enormous task of refashioning the nation's governmental system, knowing that the survival of the republic was at stake.*

To solve the nation's pervasive collective action problems, the Framers designed a new government that, by modern standards, minimized conformity costs. Some delegates worried that the states were being reduced to minor administrative districts. Others, including James Madison, were far more concerned that self-interested majorities might tyrannize minorities and exploit the public good. The solution to both extremes lay in escalating transaction costs so the new government could better address the nation's collective problems. At the same time, the government would possess too little authority to allow self-interested politicians or a majority coalition to turn its power against the citizenry. Separation of powers, staggered legislative terms, an unelected judiciary, limited national authority, and the other features explored in the chapters that follow all effectively constrain majority rule. The result is a highly complex constitutional system in which politicians must work hard to introduce even minor changes in national policy. The most appropriate place to begin our examination of *modern* American politics and apply the concepts presented here is at the reorganization of the entire government, and so in Chapter 2, we turn to the founding of the republic.

## Nota Bene

This chapter and the next present concepts that our discussion uses throughout the remainder of the book. So far, we have examined the various kinds of collective action problems that

---

*Rival nations abroad also knew that U.S. survival was at stake and tried to pry the nation apart by pitting states against one another in bidding for trade agreements that would weaken and eventually destroy the national union.

invariably arise within society and government whenever differently minded individuals attempt to work together. In the next chapter we identify some simple institutional design principles that guided the Framers in drafting the Constitution and can be used to dissect the underlying logic of all forms of governmental organization. For those chapters examining the several branches of government and federalism, problems of collective action and institutional design are naturally more prominent than in the political behavior chapters. Yet these issues arise in every chapter, and when they do, we will highlight the text (including the important topics located in the boxes!) to alert you that the concepts introduced here and in the next chapter are being put to work.

**$SAGE edge™**
**for CQ Press**

**Want a better grade?**

Get the tools you need to sharpen your study skills. Access practice quizzes, eFlashcards, video, and multimedia at **edge.sagepub.com/kernell9e.**

## KEY TERMS

authority   9
bargaining   5
bicameralism   8
cabinet   29
coalition   30
collective action   11
collective goods   32
compromise   5
conformity costs   26
constitution   9
coordination   12
direct democracy   28

focal point   14
free-rider problem   19
government   9
initiative   28
institution   9
institutional design   8
office   9
parliamentary government   29
politicians   13
politics   5
power   9
preferences   5

prisoner's dilemma   12
private goods   30
privatize   23
public goods   30
referendum   28
regulation   23
representative government   28
republic   28
separation of powers   30
tragedy of the commons   21
transaction costs   24
tyranny   28

## SUGGESTED READINGS

Safire, William. *Safire's New Political Dictionary.* New York: Ballantine Books, 1993. Arguably, Safire understood the American version of English better than any other modern popular writer. Fortunately, the former presidential speechwriter also had an especially keen eye for politics.

Stanley, Harold W., and Richard G. Niemi. *Vital Statistics on American Politics, 2009–2010.* Washington,

DC: CQ Press, 2009. If the text does not satisfy your appetite for tables and figures, this book, filled with well-organized data about American politics, will.

Tocqueville, Alexis de. *Democracy in America.* Many good paperback translations of Tocqueville are available, but beware of abridged versions in which, invariably, the lively asides and incidental observations are lost.

## REVIEW QUESTIONS

1. Why can't we solve our disputes through simple bargaining all the time? What factors undermine bargaining in different settings? What can people or governments do to help solve disputes despite these factors?

2. What sorts of institutions are commonly used to manage conflicts in societies? What are some examples of where these institutions have failed?

3. In what ways are challenges to today's government a consequence of collective action problems?

4. In what ways is the parliamentary system of representative government designed to work with fewer transaction costs than the U.S. presidential system?

5. What are some examples of public and private goods that you have consumed today? How did you acquire them?

Khizr Khan, his wife, Ghazala, beside him, holds up a copy of the U.S. Constitution as he speaks at the Democratic National Convention in July 2016. Khan, whose son, army captain Humayun S. M. Khan, was killed in the line of duty in Iraq, challenged Republican candidate Donald Trump by asking if he had ever read the Constitution. Politicians often turn to the nation's founding documents to provide support for their positions, and Khan admits to frequently referencing it in his work as a lawyer and as an immigrant and American citizen.

# The Constitution

**2**

## KEY QUESTIONS

- The Constitution has not changed much over the past two hundred years. Were the Framers really geniuses, or are Americans simply very lucky?

- Why is the U.S. Constitution so complicated, where even the word *majority* has several meanings?

- How can the United States call itself a democracy when so many features of its national political system are designed to frustrate majority rule?

## CHAPTER OBJECTIVES

**2.1** Describe how the colonies' experience in self-government contributed to their willingness to revolt.

**2.2** Explain how the challenges of collective action under the Articles of Confederation undermined early American independence.

**2.3** Identify the issues the Founders considered when drafting the Constitution.

**2.4** Discuss the debates over ratification of the Constitution.

**2.5** Summarize the influences of *Federalist* Nos. 10 and 51 on the underlying theory of the Constitution.

**2.6** Define the five design principles that contribute to the framework and functions of our government.

**2.7** Discuss how the Constitution put mechanisms in place that allowed subsequent U.S. political development to lead to the nationalization of American politics.

The year 1780 was a disastrous one for the American Revolution. Three years into the war the Continental Army, the revolutionary fighting force, teetered on total collapse. In May an entire garrison of five thousand men surrendered to the British at Charleston, South Carolina. In late summer, across the state in Camden, nearly nine hundred Continental soldiers were killed, and one thousand were taken prisoner in a single engagement. When the army regrouped, only seven hundred of the original four thousand men showed up. The fall brought no respite from the army's woes. Indeed, the young nation learned that one of its few illustrious military commanders, General Benedict Arnold, had switched sides; his name became a byword for treason.

By the end of 1780, General George Washington's American forces had shrunk from 26,000 to 15,000. New Year's Day 1781 saw even further deterioration in the campaign—1,300 mutinous Pennsylvania troops, camped in Princeton, New Jersey, demanded Congress give them a year's back pay and an immediate discharge. A congressional committee met the soldiers outside Philadelphia and agreed to some of their demands.

Although all of these difficulties appeared to stem from unfit commanders or unwilling troops, the real problem was the fledgling national government, the Continental Congress. It simply was unable to act decisively or rapidly because all matters of consequence (such as taxes) required the approval of all the state governments. And it had virtually no administrative apparatus to implement policy, even those that enjoyed unanimous support. As a result, members of congressional committees sometimes found themselves deadlocked over how many uniforms the army needed. Long into the war the army remained underfed, ill clothed, poorly armed, unpaid (at least in currency of value), and despised by civilians uncompensated for requisitioned supplies. The troops struggled just to survive as a unit. Ultimately, of course, this depleted army had to confront the well-equipped British on the battlefield. During the winter of 1780, General Washington desperately exhorted Congress, "Where are the Men? Where are the provisions? Where are the Cloaths?"

The bitter irony was that many of the desperately needed provisions existed in ample supply. The war caused shortages, but they were not severe enough to account for the deprivations hampering the army. Nor was the problem the strictly logistical exercise of keeping a traveling army supplied. Despite the difficulty of that task, British troops and their German mercenaries were reasonably well provisioned. Undermining the Revolution's cause was an epidemic of free riding by Americans—from political leaders to ordinary soldiers. States agreed to contribute money and supplies but failed to do so in a timely fashion, if at all. Contractors, paid with a currency that was losing about 10 percent of its value every month, sold the American army spoiled food, shoddy clothing, and poorly manufactured arms, and then shortchanged the Continental Army even on those inferior provisions when the suppliers thought they could get away with it. Many recruits enlisted, received their requisitions, and then deserted with their new booty.

Although all of the politicians, merchants, and soldiers involved in the war effort may have been patriots, they were unprepared to shoulder the costs of serving the public good while their neighbors and colleagues conspicuously shirked the same duties. If, as we argued in Chapter 1, the enforcement of contracts and other collective agreements is the fundamental responsibility of government, then we must blame ineffective government for the free riding and other shirking that sap a community's will to achieve its collective goals. General Washington understood the problem and warned darkly that if the Continental Congress did not soon take charge, "our Independence fails, [our government] will be annihilated, and we must once more return to the Government of Great Britain, and be made to kiss the rod preparing for our correction."[1] Over the next year Washington continued to endure the government's ineptitude, narrowly avoiding a catastrophic military defeat. Then, with time, the Revolution gained credibility abroad. France, England's archrival, agreed to loan Congress money to continue the war effort and, finally, to commit French naval and land forces to the battlefield. On October 17, 1781, the collaboration paid off with a decisive victory at Yorktown, Virginia, which ended the war.

The year 1783 brought a formal end to the hostilities and independence for the American colonies. But the young nation, still saddled with a government that could not act, was confronted with many of the same problems it had labored under during the Revolution. Indeed, many observers feared that independence, won in war, would soon be lost in peace as the nation threatened to unravel into thirteen disputatious nation-states.

In the summer of 1787 fifty-five delegates from all the states except Rhode Island assembled in Philadelphia to consider revising the nation's constitution, known as the Articles of Confederation. (Content with the Articles, the citizens and politicians of Rhode Island feared correctly that their small state would lose influence under any reforms.) General Washington, presiding over this convention, and the twenty other delegates who had served under him in the field, knew firsthand the failings of the current government. The rest of the delegates similarly drew on their varied governing experiences, some stretching back into the colonial era, as they worked together first to revise the Articles and then to formulate an entirely new constitution. How did these delegates use their experience and their familiarity with the new nation's struggle to solve the problems inherent in collective action? A closer look at the events leading up to the Constitutional Convention and the creative process it spawned reveals the thinking that gave birth to America's constitutional system (see Table 2.1).

**TABLE 2.1**  Countdown to the Constitution

| DATE | EVENT | COLONIAL ACTION |
| --- | --- | --- |
| 1750s | French and Indian War (1754–1763) drains the British treasury | Albany Congress calls for colonial unity (1754) |
| 1760s | Stamp Act enacted by British Parliament (1765) | Stamp Act Congress attended by delegates from nine of the thirteen colonies (1765) |
| 1770s | Tea Act (1773) | Boston Tea Party (1773) |
|  | British adopt Coercive Acts to punish colonies (1774) | First Continental Congress rejects plan of union but adopts Declaration of American Rights denying Parliament's authority over internal colonial affairs (1774) |
|  | Battles of Lexington and Concord (1775) | Second Continental Congress assumes role of revolutionary government (1775); adopts Declaration of Independence (1776) |
|  | Thomas Paine's *Common Sense* (1776) published | Congress adopts Articles of Confederation as constitution for new government (1777) |
| 1780s | British defeat Americans at Camden and Charleston (1780) | |
|  | Hartford Convention (1781) | Articles of Confederation ratified (1781) |
|  | British surrender at Yorktown (1781) | |
|  | Shays's Rebellion (1786) | Constitutional Convention drafts blueprint for new government (1787) |
|  | *The Federalist* (1787–1788) published | Constitution ratified (1789) |

*Source:* Created by authors from data.

## The Road to Independence

Geographically, America was well situated to be the first nation to break with monarchy and embrace republicanism; distance limited Britain's capacity to govern the colonies—a problem that gained painful significance during the Revolutionary War. Beginning early in the colonial era, Britain had ceded to Americans responsibility for managing their domestic affairs, including taxation. The colonists enjoyed this **home rule**, and the British also found it agreeable. After all, Britain's first concern was to control America's foreign commerce, thereby guaranteeing itself a market for British manufactured goods and a steady supply of cheap raw materials. Thus, for more than a century before independence the colonists had routinely elected their own leaders and held them accountable for local policies and taxes. Breaking with Great Britain may have been emotionally wrenching for many Americans, but unfamiliarity with self-governance was not a factor in their hesitancy to seek independence.

### A Legacy of Self-Governance

The first colonial representative assembly convened in Virginia in August 1619. By about 1650 all of the colonies had established elective assemblies, which eventually gained the authority to initiate laws and levy taxes. The British appointed governors, colonial councils, and judges in most colonies, and some of these officials vigorously resisted the expansion of local prerogatives. But because the elective assemblies paid their salaries and funded their offices, these officers of the Crown found that they, too, had to accommodate popular opinion. The colonial experience thus taught Americans that a popularly elected legislature in control of the purse strings could dominate other governmental institutions. The next generation of leaders recalled this important and enduring lesson as they convened in Philadelphia to revamp the new nation's constitutional system.

In addition to experience in self-governance, the state assemblies supplied the nation with another vital resource: elected politicians experienced in negotiating collective agreements. As the vanguard of the independence movement, these politicians provided the nation with an era of exceptional leadership.

Americans also entered independence well versed in constitution writing. A royal charter or contract between the Crown and a British company or business entrepreneur

Library of Congress

In what is recognized as America's first political cartoon, Benjamin Franklin's drawing depicts the colonies as caught in a classic collective action dilemma. If united, the colonies represent a formidable force for England to reckon with. But if any colony attempts to free ride, the collective effort will survive no better than a dismembered snake.

had provided the foundation for most colonies. Later, the colonists themselves wrote constitutions, which they periodically revised. When in 1776 and again in 1787 the nation's leaders confronted the task of designing new government institutions, a written constitution was, not surprisingly, the instrument of choice.

Home rule may have had its benefits for the American colonies, but as training for self-governance it shortchanged the nation. As with the rest of its far-flung empire, Britain regulated all of its colonies' commerce and provided them with military security by means of its navy, the world's largest. Under this arrangement the colonies prospered and managed their own local affairs, but this ingrained free riding and gave them little experience in managing collective action. Britain preferred to deal with the thirteen colonies

On March 5, 1770, British troops fired into a crowd of men and boys in Boston, killing five and wounding others. The massacre, depicted in this classic engraving by Paul Revere, gave the word *tyranny* new meaning. These and other events were instrumental in rousing colonial resistance to British rule on the eve of the American Revolution.

individually rather than through some national assembly that might discover and pursue their common interests. Later, after the nation had declared its independence, politicians who had stridently resisted the Crown's incursions into their local authority found themselves incapable of addressing their collective problems as a nation. With nationhood, the free ride on Britain would end.

Home rule experienced its first strains during Britain's war with France in the 1750s. Known in America as the French and Indian War and in Europe as the Seven Years' War, this lengthy, multicontinent conflict drained both Britain's treasury and its military resources. Searching for assistance, Britain in 1754 summoned delegates from each of the colonies to a conference in Albany, New York, to invite their collective assistance in defending the western frontier against the French military and its Indian allies. Because six of the thirteen colonies failed to send delegates, this would-be first national assembly failed even before it convened.

Yet the Albany Congress produced the first serious proposal for a national government. One of Pennsylvania's delegates, Benjamin Franklin, already renowned throughout the country as the man who had tamed lightning, proposed a "Plan of the Union" that would have created a national government. The plan called for an American army to provide for the colonies' defense, a popularly elected national legislature with the power to levy taxes, and an executive appointed by the British king. (On learning of Franklin's plan, King George II declared, "I am the colonies' legislature.") But none of the colonial assemblies could muster much enthusiasm for Franklin's ideas. Why should they share their tax base with some dubiously mandated new governmental entity? And why should they undertake Britain's burden of providing for the colonies' security and overseeing trade? For them, free riding made eminent sense as long as they could get away with it. And they did get away with it; another decade would pass before Britain tried to force Americans to contribute to their defense. Only then did Franklin's proposal attract interest.

## Dismantling Home Rule

France's 1763 defeat in the French and Indian War ended its aspirations for extensive colonization of America. The British, relishing their victory, had little idea, however, that the war would trigger events that would severely compromise Britain's claims in America over the next decade.

By the end of the war Britain was broke. With its citizenry already among the most heavily taxed in the world, the British government looked to the colonies to share in the empire's upkeep. At the time, the only British taxes on the colonies were duties on imports from outside the British Empire, designed less to raise revenue than to regulate commerce. To raise needed revenues, Britain decided to impose taxes. Moreover, to consolidate its power Britain began to violate home rule. Every revenue law the British government enacted during the decade after the French and Indian War contained provisions tightening its control over the internal affairs of the colonies.

The most aggressive challenge to home rule came in 1765 with passage of the Stamp Act.* This law imposed a tax on all printed materials, including legal documents, licenses, insurance papers, and land titles, as well as a variety of consumer goods, including newspapers and playing cards. (Proof of payment of the tax was the stamp affixed to the taxed document.) The tax had long been familiar to the British public, but it inflamed American public opinion, not so much because of the money extracted but because of the instruments used to extract it. Americans had paid taxes before, but they had been self-imposed, levied by the colonial assemblies to provide local services. Thus the American response, "No taxation without representation," was not simply the rallying cry of a tax revolt. In fact, Americans were not genuinely interested in representation in the British Parliament. Rather, the colonists were asserting home rule. A more accurate rallying cry would have been "No taxation by a government in which we want no part!"

The colonial assemblies passed resolutions demanding the tax be repealed, and most sent delegates to a national conference, the Stamp Act Congress, to craft a unified response. For the first time they united against Britain by agreeing unanimously on a resolution condemning the tax. They could not agree, however, on a course of action.

---

*Earlier, the Sugar Act of 1764 had levied new duties on certain foreign imports and introduced new efforts to interdict Yankee smuggling to circumvent import duties. At the same time Parliament passed another inflammatory law, the Currency Act, which forbade the colonies from printing their own currency, thus requiring merchants to raise scarce hard cash to do business.

The organized resistance of ordinary citizens was more successful.* Throughout the colonies local groups confronted tax collectors and prevented them from performing their duties. Over the next decade these scenes were repeated as Britain imposed a half-dozen new tax and administrative laws designed to weaken the colonial assemblies. Americans countered by boycotting British products and forming protest organizations, such as the Sons of Liberty, the Daughters of Liberty, and the more militant Committees of Correspondence. Vigilantism and public demonstrations overshadowed assembly resolutions.

The most famous of these demonstrations was the Boston Tea Party. No colony had chafed under Britain's new rules and import taxes more than Massachusetts, whose economy depended heavily on international trade and shipping. On a winter night in 1773 a group of patriots donned Indian dress and dumped 342 chests of tea owned by the East India Company into Boston Harbor to protest a new tax on Americans' favorite non-alcoholic beverage. Britain responded with the Restraining Acts and Coercive Acts, which closed the port of Boston to all commerce, dissolved the Massachusetts assembly, decreed that British troops in Boston must be quartered in American homes, and ordered that Americans charged with protest crimes and British soldiers charged with crimes against the colonists be sent to England for trial. Colonists viewed these last provisions as ensuring serious punishment for the first group and lax punishment for the second.

In this eighteenth-century satirical drawing by a British artist, Bostonians gleefully pour tea down the throat of a customs official, who has just been tarred and feathered. In the distance colonists dump tea into Boston Harbor, just as they did in 1773 at the Boston Tea Party. And, lest one British misdeed go unnoticed, a symbol of the hated Stamp Act, passed in 1765, appears on the tree.

## The Continental Congresses

When colonists elsewhere witnessed Britain's heavy-handed policies in Massachusetts, they recognized their own vulnerability. Without hesitation, they answered the call of Boston resistance leader Samuel Adams to assemble at Philadelphia in the fall of 1774 for what became the First Continental Congress. Each colony sent its leading professionals, merchants, and planters. These men had mostly known one another only by reputation, but at this meeting they would form a nucleus of national leadership for the next decade. Among them were the future nation's first presidents: George Washington, John Adams, and Thomas Jefferson.

---

*"Nothing else is talked of," wrote Sally Franklin to her father, Benjamin, in London. "The Dutch [Germans] talk of the stompt act the Negroes of the tamp, in short every body has something to say." Mary Beth Norton et al., *A People and a Nation: A History of the United States* (Boston: Houghton Mifflin, 1990), 117.

The Continental Congress promptly passed resolutions condemning British taxes and administrative decrees. When the idea of creating a national government was raised, Franklin's plan of union, the only existing proposal for unification, was introduced and briefly but inconclusively debated. The most significant actions of the First Continental Congress were adoption of a Declaration of American Rights, which essentially reasserted home rule, and endorsement of an agreement to ban all trade with Britain until it rescinded the despised taxes and regulations. To enforce the boycott against the prospect of massive free riding, Congress called for the formation of local elective "committees of observation" in every county, town, and hamlet in the country. Soon many of these newly formed organizations began imposing patriotic morality with investigations of "treasonable" conversations and public rebukes of more ordinary vices. Earlier import boycotts had been modestly successful—enough to alter British policy—but with the capacity to identify and sanction potential free riders, the new boycott won almost total compliance.

The eight thousand or so members of these local committees provided a base for the statewide conventions that sprang up throughout the colonies when the British prevented the colonial assemblies from meeting. Unhampered by local British authorities, these conventions quickly became de facto governments. (When some colonies' assemblies were enjoined from meeting, they would adjourn to a local tavern and resume doing business as an unofficial provincial convention.) They collected taxes, raised militias, passed "laws" forbidding the judiciary from enforcing British decrees, and selected delegates to the Second Continental Congress, which met in Philadelphia in May 1775.

By the time the Second Continental Congress gathered, war had broken out. Spontaneous bloody uprisings in the spring of 1775 at Lexington and Concord in Massachusetts had provoked the state conventions to mobilize local volunteer militias and disarm suspected British loyalists. Events demanded concerted action, and the Second Continental Congress responded by acting like a national government. Congress had no legal authority to conduct a war effort, but throughout the colonies patriots desperately required coordination, and it was the only national institution available.

Congress first instructed the conventions to reconstitute themselves as state governments based on republican principles. Using their former colonial governments as a model, most states adopted **bicameral** (two-chamber) **legislatures**, and all created governorships. Accustomed to difficult relations with the royal governors, the states severely limited the terms and authority of these newly minted American executives. This antiexecutive bias would persist and influence deliberations at the Constitutional Convention a decade later.

Then, acting even more like a government, the Second Continental Congress issued the nation's first bonds and established a national currency. It also authorized delegate George Washington to expand the shrinking Massachusetts militia into a full-fledged national army. (As if his colleagues had needed a hint, Washington attended the convention in full military dress of his own design.)

## The Declaration of Independence

During its first year's work of creating states and raising and financing an army, Congress did not consider the fundamental issue of separation from England. But it was discussed on street corners and in taverns throughout the nation. In January 1776 the pamphleteer Thomas Paine published *Common Sense*, which moved the independence issue to center stage. Within three months

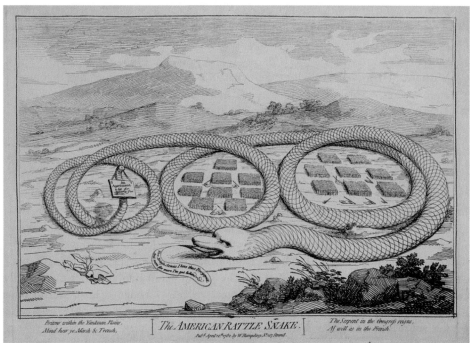

Library of Congress

In this 1782 British cartoon at the close of the Revolutionary War, Benjamin Franklin's diminutive, garden-variety snake, struggling to stay whole (see page 36), has become through unity a voracious "American rattlesnake," eager to consume British armies. "Two British Armies I have thus Burgoyn'd, And room for more I've got behind," it boasts. A sign posted on its rattle advertises ominously to British readers, "An Apartment to Lett for Military Gentlemen."

120,000 copies had been sold, and Americans were talking about Paine's plainly stated, irresistible argument that only in the creation of an independent republic would the people find contentment.

The restless citizenry's anticipation that Congress would consider a resolution of separation was realized in June when Virginia delegate Richard Henry Lee called for creation of a new nation separate from Britain. Congress referred his proposal to a committee of delegates from every region with instructions to draft the proper resolution. One member of this committee was a thirty-three-year-old lawyer from Virginia, Thomas Jefferson. Asked to draft a statement because of "his peculiar felicity of expression," Jefferson modestly demurred. This prompted the always-direct John Adams of Massachusetts to protest, "You can write ten times better than I can."[2] Jefferson's qualifications to articulate the rationale for independence extended well beyond his writing skills. Possessing aristocratic tastes but democratic values, he never wavered from an abiding confidence in the innate goodness and wisdom of common people. "State a moral case to a ploughman and a professor," he once challenged a friend. "The former will decide it as well, and often better than the latter, because he has not been led astray by artificial rules."* In the end, Jefferson agreed to draft the resolution of separation.

---

*Whether drafting Virginia's first law guaranteeing religious freedom as a member of its House of Burgesses, revising Virginia's constitution, or founding the University of Virginia, Jefferson consistently engaged in activities liberating the inherent capacities of his fellow citizens. Joseph R. Conlin, *The Morrow Book of Quotations in American History* (New York: Morrow, 1984).

Jefferson concurred with the other delegates in many of the specific grievances itemized in the resolution he drafted, but for him the real rationale for throwing off British rule rested on the fundamental right of self-government. Such conviction produced this famous passage:

> We hold these truths to be self-evident, that all men are created equal, that they are endowed by their creator with certain unalienable Rights, that among these are Life, Liberty and the pursuit of Happiness. That to secure these rights, Governments are instituted among Men, deriving their just powers from the consent of the governed. That whenever any form of government becomes destructive of these ends, it is the Right of the People to alter or abolish it, and to institute new Government.

Jefferson's colleagues made only slight changes in this centerpiece of the **Declaration of Independence**, but they did amend his list of grievances. Foreshadowing the future conflict over race, Jefferson's indictment of Britain for introducing slavery into the colonies offended the sensibilities of slave-owning southern delegates. At their insistence this grievance was stricken from the final resolution.* (The full text of the Declaration of Independence appears in the appendix.)

In a solemn ceremony on July 4, 1776, the Second Continental Congress officially accepted the document. Rebelling against a colonial power with a huge occupation army was a dangerous enterprise. The conclusion of the Declaration—"we mutually pledge to each other our lives, our Fortunes, and our sacred Honor"—was no mere rhetoric.

## America's First Constitution: The Articles of Confederation

With the Declaration of Independence in hand, the delegates to the Second Continental Congress proceeded to "institute a new Government," as called for in the Declaration. Over the next several weeks they drafted and sent to the new states for ratification the nation's first constitution, the **Articles of Confederation**. Although not ratified until 1781, the Articles served as the nation's de facto constitution during the intervening war years.

As its name implies, the first American constitution created a **confederation**, a highly decentralized system in which the national government derives limited authority from the states rather than directly from citizens. Not only do the states select officials of the national government, but they also retain the authority to override that government's decisions.

The Articles transferred the form and functions of the Continental Congress to the new, permanent Congress, in which each state received one vote. Major laws required the endorsement of nine of the thirteen state delegations, whereas more fundamental changes, such as direct taxation, necessitated unanimous agreement to amend the Constitution. National authority was so restricted that the delegates saw little purpose for an executive branch or a

---

*Among the items deleted: "He [King George III] has waged cruel war against human nature itself, violating its most sacred rights of life and liberty in the persons of a distant people who never offended him, captivating them and carrying them into slavery in another hemisphere, or to incur miserable death in their transportation thither." In *Thomas Jefferson*, ed. Merrill D. Peterson (New York: Library of America, 1984), 21–22.

judiciary. From time to time administrators might be required, but they could be hired as needed and directly supervised by the new Congress.

In adopting a confederation, the delegates sought to replicate the home rule they had lost in the 1760s. Clearly, after years of free riding under British rule, they were not yet willing to absorb the collective action costs associated with nationhood. Yet they also recognized that in declaring their independence they thrust upon themselves responsibility for supplying essential public goods—most important, defense and commercial markets—that Britain had provided under home rule. The same delegates who had pressed hardest for independence, knowing that it was likely to lead to war, were among those who most vigorously favored a confederation over a more centralized and powerful national government. Undoubtedly, the new nation's leaders still had a great deal to learn about the logic of collective action. But they would learn in time—the hard way. Their suspicion of national authority very nearly cost the fledgling nation its independence.

## The Confederation at War

Faced with a war raging for over a year, the states, unwilling to give the national government sufficient authority to conduct the war, became chiefly responsible for recruiting troops and outfitting them for battle. The national military command, which answered to Congress, assumed responsibility for organizing the various state regiments into a single fighting force. In principle, Congress was assigned the role of coordinator. It would identify military requirements, assess the states, and channel their (voluntary) contributions to the army. Congress also was empowered to borrow money through bonds, but its lack of taxation authority made bonds a risky and expensive venture for the government, which had to offer high interest rates to attract investors.

The public's deep suspicion of government also prevented national officeholders from creating the administrative structures suitable for the new government's wartime responsibilities. John Adams even wanted to prevent Washington from appointing his own staff officers for fear that "there be too much Connection between them." Instead, he argued, Congress should select all officers so that these "officers are checks upon the General." Adams's appeal to the "proper Rule and Principle" stimulated serious debate, but he did not prevail in this instance. Adams was, however, more successful in other attempts to dilute executive powers.

The administrative vacuum sucked congressional committees into the daily affairs of requisitioning an army. These legislators struggled mightily, even heroically, to do their duty, but most were unskilled in administration and frequently unable to make timely decisions. In fact, the members of one committee expressed such a variety of views on the number of uniforms to be ordered that they were unable to come to a decision. The desperate plight of General Washington's army as the war continued attests to the naiveté and ineffectiveness of the confederation's structure. Thus the collective action problems described in Chapter 1 were evident in America's war effort: contagious levels of free riding and the reluctance of some states to contribute their fair share for fear that the other states would hold back (a classic prisoner's dilemma). Moreover, the undeveloped national administration provided fertile soil for equally debilitating free riding in the form of corruption.

Without the authority to play a more central role in administering the war, Congress responded to the quickly deteriorating military situation by decentralizing authority even further. Among other things, it passed resolutions instructing the states to supply their troops directly. Perhaps, some members reasoned, the states would be more forthcoming with support for their own sons in uniform. This scheme had the merit of converting a public good—military supplies that all state regiments could consume regardless of their state's contribution—into a more or less private good that linked the welfare of each state's troops to its legislature's effort. But the actual practice of thirteen states locating and supplying intermingled regiments scattered up and down the Atlantic seaboard presented a logistical nightmare. On hearing of it, General Washington caustically remarked that members of Congress "think it is but to say 'Presto begone,' and everything is done." At the same time pressure mounted on various fronts, including within Congress itself, for Congress to assume greater authority to conduct the war.* Understandably, the military commanders were the most outspoken in lobbying Congress and state governors for a "new plan of civil constitution."[3] General Washington advised Congress that an "entire new plan" providing it with the authority "adequate to all of the purposes of the war" must be instituted immediately. Washington's aide Alexander Hamilton, later one of the architects of the Constitution, showered members of Congress with correspondence urging them to grasp the emergency authority he claimed was inherent in the Articles. Without the "complete sovereignty" that could come only with an independent source of revenue, he argued, Congress would have neither the resources nor the credibility necessary to conduct the war. And, as the states' dismal performance had proved, if Congress did not take control, no one else could.[†]

The addition of the second major group—state officials—to the chorus for reform reveals the pervasiveness of frustration with the confederation. Although the confederation had sought to empower these officials above all others, many found themselves trapped in a classic prisoner's dilemma. They were prepared to sacrifice for the war, but only if they could be confident that the other states would also do their part. Moreover, many of their colleagues who had been outspoken champions of volunteerism were defeated in the 1780 elections by challengers calling for a strengthened national authority that could enforce agreements.

By the summer of 1780 some states were taking direct action. In August representatives of several New England states met and passed a resolution calling for investing Congress with "powers competent for the government." Several months later five northern states met at what is now known as the Hartford Convention to urge Congress to grant itself the power to tax. In a remarkable resolution the convention called for Congress to delegate to General Washington the authority "to induce . . . punctual compliance" from states that ignored their obligations to supply the army. The delegates realized that states would only cooperate (and end their prisoner's dilemma) under the threat of coercion.

Congress responded as best it could, but it labored under a constitution designed to frustrate national action. In 1781 Rhode Island, with less than 2 percent of the nation's population,

---

*Ten years later these advocates of congressional authority would form the core group of nationalists, led by James Madison and Alexander Hamilton, pressing the nation for a new constitution.

†Hamilton also argued that Congress must delegate administration to "great officers of State—A secretary for foreign affairs—A President of War—A President of Marine—A Financier." In effect, he was calling for an autonomous national government with a legislature at its center and a separate executive branch.

vetoed a bill giving Congress the authority to levy taxes. Various administrative reforms were enacted but had to be watered down to win unanimous endorsement. Congress could not agree on how much independent authority to delegate to the executive offices it created. As a result, the offices had no authority, and their occupants served at the beck and call of the legislature's committees.

The tide turned after France, England's long-standing adversary, agreed to lend the Americans hard currency. By 1782 General Washington could write for the first time since the beginning of the war that his army was well fed, clothed, and armed. A reinvigorated American army and France's continued participation in the war presented Britain with the prospect of a far longer conflict. (France formally recognized American independence and agreed to support the United States unilaterally in 1778.) In October 1781 British troops, under General Charles Cornwallis, suffered defeat at Yorktown, Virginia, and Britain sued for peace. Thus the United States had somehow survived a war with an occupying army. In the jubilation of victory, however, momentum for political reform was lost.

## The Confederation's Troubled Peace

Shortly after signing the peace treaty with Britain, the nation lunged toward new perils—indeed, to the point that many Americans and even more Europeans wondered whether the hard-won independence might still be lost in national disintegration. By 1787 American leaders were openly speculating about the prospect of Britain reasserting its authority over the barely united and internally divided states. "America is a nation without a national government," one critic observed, "and it is not a pretty sight."

### The War-Torn Economy

After six years of war, the nation's debt was staggering. Congress owed Americans about $25 million and foreign governments another $10 million. The most urgent concern was the back pay owed the army. In the spring of 1783 General Washington learned of a conspiracy forming among disgruntled officers to march on Congress. Greatly alarmed, he wrote his former aide Alexander Hamilton, now a member of Congress, that the army should be paid and "disbanded without delay." The army is "a dangerous instrument to play with," he warned ominously. Prudently, Congress followed Washington's advice.

Creditors who had supplied the troops formed another long line. But Congress was more successful in ignoring these unarmed claimants, some of whom eventually received partial payment from the states. Abroad, debts to Britain negotiated in the peace settlement and loans from European governments and private interests all had to be repaid before normal commercial relations with these countries could resume. In the face of so much debt, the national currency plummeted to approximately one-tenth of its prewar value.

The complexities of governing by confederation compounded the problem. Congress held the debt, but the states controlled the purse strings. As it had during the war, Congress prescribed annual state contributions to reduce the debt over twenty-five years. But no one expressed confidence that the states, having proved so unreliable in war, would step forward in peace to accept fiscal responsibility for the nation. With no enforcement mechanism in place, the states again individually confronted a classic prisoner's dilemma: no state would contribute its share of the revenue so long as it suspected one or more of the other states might not meet its obligations. Congress faced two tough choices. It could try to penalize those states that reneged, or it could try to finance the debt on its own. The latter proved more feasible. Thus in the same bill that mapped long-term debt reduction Congress proposed a constitutional amendment giving the national government a source of direct revenue in the form of import duties. As in the past, however, the Articles' unanimous consent rule for amendments frustrated action. Unwilling to share the revenue from its already active port city of New York, the New York legislature killed this proposal.

### Trade Barriers at Home and Abroad

The nation's shaky finances were not helped by its trade problems, which also stemmed from the confederation's explicit reservation of all matters of commerce to the states. For example, Congress lacked the authority to negotiate credible trade agreements with other nations. European governments found this arrangement, in which trade agreements required the endorsement of each state's legislature, unwieldy. The national government also proved incapable of responding to discriminatory trade sanctions and other actions abroad. When the British and later the French closed their West Indies possessions to U.S. exports, the action threatened the fragile, war-torn economy that depended heavily on exports.

Economic relations among the states were nearly as unsatisfactory. States with international ports charged exporters from other states stiff user fees. New York victimized New Jersey; Virginia and South Carolina both extracted a toll from North Carolina. And each state minted its own currency. Some states, responding to political pressures from indebted farmers, inflated their currencies. Exchange rates fluctuated widely across states, rendering interstate commerce a speculative financial exercise.

To no one's surprise, many sectors of the economy clamored loudly for reform. The nation's creditors wanted a government able to pay its debts. Importers and the mercantile class desperately needed a sound currency and an end to capricious state policies toward other states' goods. The profits of southern tobacco and indigo growers depended wholly on open export markets, which only a national government could negotiate effectively. The need for a central authority that could create and manage a common market at home and implement a unified commercial policy abroad spurred diverse economic interests to call for a revision of the Articles of Confederation.

In the summer of 1786 Virginia made the first move, inviting delegates of other states to convene that fall in Annapolis, Maryland, to consider ways of strengthening the national government's role in commerce. Eight states named delegates, but when those from only five states showed up, the Annapolis convention adjourned after passing a resolution calling for another convention in Philadelphia nine months later. Thus the Annapolis convention earned a place in history by setting the stage for the Constitutional Convention in May 1787. Although the delegates had no reason to believe the next meeting would generate any better turnout, events during the intervening months, including **Shays's Rebellion**, galvanized interest and mobilized the states behind constitutional reform.

### Popular Discontent

In the economic depression that followed the Revolution, many small farmers lost their land and other assets. Markets were disrupted, credit became scarce, and personal debt mounted.

The financial straits of small farmers spawned occasional demonstrations, but none so threatening as the one that erupted in the fall of 1786 in western Massachusetts, where taxes were especially onerous and the local courts unforgiving. Many farmers lost their land and possessions at the auction block, and some were even being hauled off to debtors' prison. The protest movement began with town meetings and petitions to the state legislature to suspend taxes and foreclosures. When their appeals failed to win much sympathy, these disaffected citizens found more aggressive ways to remonstrate their grievances. Under the leadership of Daniel Shays, a former captain in the Continental Army and a bankrupt farmer, an armed group composed mostly of farmers marched on the Massachusetts Supreme Court session in Springfield to demand that state judges stop prosecuting debtors. Shays's band was met by the state militia, but the confrontation ended peacefully after the magistrates adjourned the court.

In late January 1787, Massachusetts erupted once more, this time with enough violence to convince the states to convene in Philadelphia. Having learned that Shays planned an assault on a government arsenal in Springfield, delegates from Massachusetts appealed to the national government to send funds and troops. Once again unable to muster compliance among the states, Congress could offer neither troops nor money. A similar appeal to neighboring states proved no more productive. Finally, the state organized a militia (in part with private donations) that intercepted and repulsed Shays's "army" of about a thousand farmers outside the arsenal. Over the next several weeks some of Shays's men were captured, others dispersed, and the rebellion ended.

Had it been an isolated incident, even this event might not have persuaded state leaders of the need for a stronger national government. But Shays's Rebellion coincided with a wave of popular uprisings sweeping across the country. The same winter, two hundred armed farmers in Pennsylvania had tried to reclaim neighbors' possessions that had been seized by tax collectors. On the same day as Shays's defeat, these farmers rescued a neighbor's cattle from a tax sale. Virginia protesters, following the example of the insurgents in Massachusetts, burned down public buildings. Their favorite targets were jails and courthouses where tax and debt records were kept.

State legislatures, either intimidated by threats of force or genuinely sympathetic with farmers' demands, started to cave in under the slightest pressure from these constituencies. At times, these bodies' knee-jerk responses caused them to behave in ways more in keeping with revolutionary tribunals than with deliberative republican legislatures respectful of property rights. Throughout the country they summarily overturned unpopular court decisions, altered property assessments, and issued quickly devalued paper money, which they then forced creditors to accept as full payment of farmers' debts. One scholar offered this assessment: "The economic and social instability engendered by the Revolution was finding political expression in the state legislatures at the very time they were larger, more representative, and more powerful than ever before in American history."[4] Observing all this, the troubled James Madison of Virginia wrote his friend Thomas Jefferson in Paris, where Jefferson was serving as the states' ambassador: "In our Governments the real power lies in the majority, and the invasion of private rights . . . chiefly [arises] . . . not from acts of Government contrary to the sense of its constituents, but from acts in which the Government is the mere instrument of the major number of the constituents."[5] Madison's discomfort with arbitrary majority action guided his efforts and those of like-minded delegates throughout the Constitutional Convention.

Despite their defeat, the protesting farmers led by Daniel Shays won a number of reforms from the Massachusetts state legislature, which lowered court costs and exempted household necessities and workmen's tools from the debt collection process. The unintended impact of Shays's Rebellion on national reform was far more dramatic. It demonstrated that the confederation could not perform the most basic function of government—keeping peace.

SHAYS'S FORCES IN MASSACHUSETTS.

To many observers, Shays's Rebellion represented a wildfire threatening to sweep the country into anarchy.[6] No matter how persuasive Hamilton, the beloved Washington, or any of the other **nationalists** were in promoting the cause of constitutional reform, it was Daniel Shays who offered the most compelling reason for states to send delegates to the Philadelphia Convention. Ultimately, the states took the first steps toward true unification not in response to their collective dilemma, but rather out of a more fundamental concern with self-preservation. When they assembled in Philadelphia the next spring, delegates from all states except Rhode Island showed up.

## Drafting a New Constitution

 In their deliberations the fifty-five youngish, well-educated white men who gathered in Philadelphia in 1787 drew on their shared experience of war and its aftermath, but they did not do so reflexively or out of narrowly construed self-interest. They also were highly conversant in the ideas and theories swirling "in the air" during the Enlightenment, as the dominant intellectual current of the eighteenth century was known. Influenced by recent advances in science, scholars—and even America's politicians—sought through careful reasoning to discern the "natural laws" that governed economics, politics, and morality. The impact of these ideas was a matter not merely of their novelty and intellectual appeal, but also of how they illuminated Americans' experiences.

 Thus the Constitution that eventually arose out of the Convention was grounded in theories of politics, economics, and even science that were attracting attention at the time throughout Europe. The delegates cited dozens of contemporary and ancient philosophers during floor deliberations, often quoting them in their original language of Latin or French. Of these thinkers, several deserve to be singled out because their ideas are clearly discernible in the Constitution.

## Philosophical Influences

Heading any list of influential Enlightenment thinkers is the English philosopher John Locke (1632–1704), whose brilliant writings on political theory and design of government read in some places as if the Framers were his sole audience. In 1690 Locke vigorously defended the still-novel idea of **popular sovereignty**—that is, citizens' delegation of authority to their agents in government, with the ability to rescind that authority.[7] This argument clearly influenced Jefferson's words in the Declaration of Independence. Moreover, Locke stressed individual rights and the limited scope of government authority. If Locke's ideas strike the modern student as unexceptional, it is because they are so thoroughly embedded in the U.S. Constitution and governmental system that they are taken for granted.

During the same era another Englishman, Sir Isaac Newton (1642–1727), established the foundations of modern mechanics and physics. His discovery of the laws of physical relations (such as gravity) inspired the Framers to search for comparable laws governing social relations. Evidence of Newton's influence can be seen in the Framers' descriptions of their design proposals to one another and later to the nation. Concepts such as "force," "balance," and "fulcrum" and phrases such as "laws of politics" and "check power with power" that seemed borrowed from a physics textbook were bandied about with great familiarity.

Perhaps more than anyone else, the French philosopher Charles, Baron de Montesquieu (1689–1755), supplied the Framers with the nuts and bolts of a design of government, particularly his classification of governmental functions and forms as legislative, executive, and judicial. Like Locke, Montesquieu championed limited government—limited not only in the nature of its authority but also in the size of the political community it encompassed. Thus during and after the Convention opponents of reform invoked Montesquieu's case for the superiority of small republics as a powerful counterargument to those who advocated empowering the national government.

Finally, the Scottish philosopher David Hume (1711–1776) treated politics as a competition among contending interests, in much the same way that his fellow countryman Adam Smith described competition in the marketplace of an emerging capitalist economy. An ocean away, James Madison adapted Hume's arguments to his own purposes, much as Jefferson did Locke's.

America's founding leaders, though politicians, often behaved as if they were philosophers, carefully studying and even writing treatises on government. The most important is James Madison's three-thousand-word essay "Vices of the Political System of the U. States," which he drafted in the spring of 1787 after extensive research on ancient and modern confederations. (Madison had Jefferson scour Paris bookstores for source materials.) Madison circulated copies of his manuscript among fellow Virginians who would be attending the Philadelphia Convention to prepare them for the reform proposal he was writing. Madison's sophisticated understanding of politics is apparent in a passage attributing the confederation's failure not to a moral breakdown of the citizenry but to the classic prisoner's dilemma embedded in faulty institutions: "A distrust of the voluntary compliance of each other may prevent the compliance of any, although . . . [cooperation is] the latent disposition of all."

## Getting Down to Business

Most of the delegates representing their states in Philadelphia probably were unaware of the grand scope of the enterprise on which they were about to embark. Some undoubtedly assumed that the Convention would simply return to the Annapolis agenda that sought to resolve commercial disputes at home and coordinate the states' commercial policies abroad. Others anticipated minor reforms of the Articles and were prepared to take the positions dictated by their state legislatures. But at least a few, most notably James Madison, were planning—indeed, plotting with others of like mind—to scrap the Articles of Confederation altogether and start over.

Sensing his fellow Virginian's hidden agenda, war hero Patrick Henry announced he "smelt a rat" and refused to join the delegation to Philadelphia. The Delaware legislature was similarly suspicious and instructed its delegates to oppose any scheme that undermined the equality of the states. Another small state, the ever-independent Rhode Island, boycotted Philadelphia altogether.

The Convention opened on a rainy Friday, May 25, 1787. By near universal acclamation, the delegates elected General Washington to preside over the deliberations, and the Convention began on a harmonious note. Madison sat at the front, where he could easily participate in floor debates and record the arguments of his colleagues.* The Convention agreed to keep the proceedings secret to allow a frank exchange of views and to facilitate compromise. This decision also meant keeping the window shutters closed during one of the hottest summers in Philadelphia's history.

## The Virginia and New Jersey Plans

On the first day of substantive business Madison and his nationalist colleagues sprang their surprise. Edmund Randolph, also from Virginia, introduced Madison's blueprint for a new constitution. In this revised constitution Madison favored those institutional design features more closely resembling parliamentary systems than those of the future American republic. In the Virginia Plan, as it came to be known, Madison appears to have been more concerned with fashioning an active national government, even if it imposed high conformity costs on the states. The **Virginia Plan** dominated floor debate well into July. Although few of its provisions survived intact in the final draft of the Constitution, the Virginia Plan succeeded in shifting the deliberations from patching up the confederation to considering anew the requirements of a national union.

The centerpiece of the Virginia Plan was a bicameral national legislature. Members of the lower chamber would be apportioned among the states by population and directly elected by the citizenry. The lower chamber would, in turn, elect the members of the upper chamber from lists of nominees supplied by the state legislatures. It also would elect the officers of the proposed executive and judicial branches (see Figure 2.1). Madison's intent was clear: only representatives, whose direct election by the people gave them special legitimacy in formulating national policy, would control the selection of the other officers of government.

---

*Unable to fathom the purpose of certain provisions of the ancient constitutions he had examined in his preparation for the convention, Madison was determined not to leave future generations in the dark about the rationale of this new constitution. Thus he carefully recorded the business of the convention. *Notes on the Federal Convention* was discovered among Madison's papers after his death in 1837. The federal government paid his widow, Dolley, $30,000 for the papers and published them three years later. This discussion closely follows Madison's *Notes*.

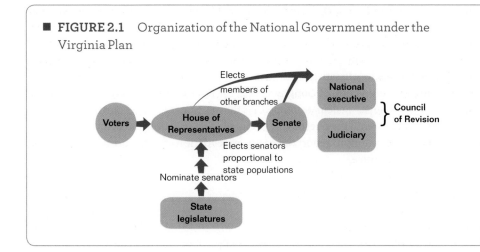

■ **FIGURE 2.1**    Organization of the National Government under the Virginia Plan

To solve the nation's collective action problems, the Virginia Plan also gave the national government enforcement authority. It could make whatever laws it deemed appropriate and veto any state laws it regarded as unfit. If a state failed to fulfill its legal obligations, the national government could summon military force against it. This provision proved to be a tactical mistake because it inflamed opposition. In the meantime, the nationalists realized belatedly that military force would never be needed because the national government could directly implement its own policies and would no longer depend on the cooperation of the states.

With the states reduced to the status of junior partners, the national legislature would assume a standing comparable with that of the British Parliament. Madison did provide one check on this legislative dynamo: a Council of Revision, composed of the executive and certain judges, which could veto legislation. Its members, however, would be elected by the legislature. Thus skeptical delegates reasonably questioned how effective such a check could be. In any event, Madison proposed allowing Congress to override a council veto.

After Madison achieved early success in some preliminary floor votes, opposition, mainly from two sources, to his radical reforms solidified. Delegates representing the less populous states were understandably upset. They could easily calculate that they (and their citizens) would have far less representation under the Virginia Plan than they presently enjoyed with equal state representation and the one-state veto rule. Another bloc (mostly from small states as well) wanted stronger safeguards of state sovereignty. For these **states' rights** delegates, continued state participation in the selection of national officeholders was as important an issue as how legislative seats were to be apportioned.

Both groups coalesced around an alternative proposed by New Jersey delegate William Paterson, known as the **New Jersey Plan**. This late, hastily drafted response to the Virginia Plan was not as thoroughly thought through as Madison's proposal. It satisfied the requirements of its states' rights supporters, however, by perpetuating the composition and selection of Congress as it functioned under the Articles of Confederation and continuing to give each state one vote. But the New Jersey Plan broke with the Articles by giving Congress the authority to force the states to comply with its tax requisitions. This plan also allowed a simple majority vote to enact national policy rather than the supermajority required in the Articles. The New Jersey Plan thus eliminated the most objectionable features of the confederation. But its retention of a seriously malapportioned Congress representing the states rather than the citizenry did not come close to satisfying the demands of the nationalists.

Debate on the composition of Congress raged for weeks, with each side steadfastly and heatedly refusing to budge.* Stalemate loomed. As the meetings neared a Fourth of July recess, the delegates agreed to send the question of Congress—its selection and composition—to a committee with instructions to report out a recommendation after the break. Madison was not named to the committee.

## The Great Compromise

The committee's solution was a Solomon-like compromise that split control of the legislature's two chambers between the large (House of Representatives) and small (Senate) states. The upper chamber, or Senate, would retain many of the features of Congress under the Articles of Confederation: each state legislature would send two senators to serve six-year terms. Madison's population-based, elective legislature became the House of Representatives. To sweeten the deal for the nationalists, who had rejected a similar compromise earlier in floor deliberations, the committee reserved to the House alone the authority to originate revenue legislation (see Figure 2.2).

■ **FIGURE 2.2**    Virginia Plan, New Jersey Plan, and Great Compromise

| Virginia Plan | New Jersey Plan | Great Compromise |
|---|---|---|
| ★ Two-chamber legislature; representation based on state population | ★ Single-house chamber; equal representation for each state regardless of population | ★ Two-chamber legislature, with lower chamber (House of Representatives) representation based on population and upper chamber (Senate) representation equal for every state |
| ★ Lower chamber of legislature elected by the citizenry; upper chamber, executive, and courts elected by the lower house | ★ Legislature has same power as under Articles, with added authority to levy taxes and regulate commerce; can exercise supremacy clause over state legislation | |
| ★ Legislature can make any law and veto any state legislation | ★ Plural executive can be removed by legislature (on petition of a majority of states); courts appointed by executive | ★ Authority to levy taxes reserved to the lower chamber |
| ★ Council of Revision (composed of executive and court) can veto legislation, but legislature can override by majority vote | ★ Supreme Court hears appeals in limited number of cases | |

*Madison's allies did make one significant concession, accepting an amendment that gave the states sole authority to select the members of the upper house. Thus the Senate began to assume its ultimate form. But the delegates from small states pressed for more: equal state representation in both chambers.

The unanimous agreement rule that had hobbled the Confederation Congress was gone, replaced by a rule that wholly ignored states as voting entities and instead empowered a majority of each chamber's membership to pass legislation. Moreover, the delegates agreed to a broad list of enumerated or expressed powers, contained in Article I, Section 8, of the Constitution, that extended the authority of the national legislature far beyond that available to Congress under the confederation. These powers included the authority to declare war, maintain an army and a navy, and borrow money. Another item on the list of new powers stood out: the authority "to regulate Commerce with foreign Nations, and among the several States." This **commerce clause** greatly expanded the new Congress's—and, in turn, the national government's—sphere of action. And another clause in Section 8 further compounded its impact. The Framers closed the long list of explicit powers with the following general provision: Congress shall enjoy the authority "to make all Laws which shall be necessary and proper for carrying into Execution the foregoing Powers, and all other Powers vested by this Constitution in the Government of the United States." This critical provision, called the **necessary and proper clause**, left the door open for a major expansion of Congress's legislative power and the nationalization of public policy during the twentieth century.*

Both defenders and critics of an activist federal government agree that all national policies affect interstate commerce in some way. Together these clauses have provided a rationale for enacting far-reaching national legislation, including federal laws against interstate kidnapping and bank robbery; regulations on agricultural production (covering even the growth of feed that never leaves the farm where it was grown); bans on racial and other discrimination in restaurants, hotels, and public transportation; laws against possession of guns near public schools; and thousands of other wide-ranging national policies.

The committee's proposal was adopted by a vote of 5–4, with the other states abstaining or absent. Opposition came uniformly from the nationalists, who viewed the compromise as one sided. Through the Senate a majority of the states could still prevail over national policy. But the nationalists also recognized that this was the best deal they could get. Because the preferences of the states' rights delegates were more closely aligned with those of the status quo, they could more credibly present the nationalist side with a take-it-or-leave-it proposition.

Now, more than two centuries later, the political logic of dividing representation in Congress between the citizens and the states no longer matches reality. The supremacy of the national government over the states was decided by the Civil War. Senators have been elected directly by the voters since adoption of the Seventeenth Amendment in 1913. Despite the new reality, the Senate—the institution that embodies the initial logic of states' rights—persists. Indeed, as noted in Chapter 1, once in place an institution tends to survive long after the circumstances that fashioned it in a particular form have changed beyond all recognition.

---

*Chapter 3, "Federalism," traces the nationalization of public policy via the necessary and proper clause. In addition to listing what Congress can do, the Constitution lists what it—and the states— cannot do. Article I, Section 9, restricts Congress from granting titles of nobility, spending unappropriated funds, suspending the writ of habeas corpus, passing ex post facto laws, levying income taxes (the Sixteenth Amendment ratified in 1913 rescinded this provision), and taxing state exports. Section 10 imposes restrictions on states, prohibiting them from conducting foreign policy (through entering into treaties or alliances or conducting war), printing money, passing laws undermining contracts, and imposing tariffs or duties on trade.

Although it is difficult today to justify a system in which, for example, citizens of Wyoming count for sixty-five times as much as citizens of California in one chamber of the national legislature, Americans are stuck with it. Yet, although still badly malapportioned, the modern Senate has become as attuned as the House of Representatives to changes in popular sentiments (see Chapter 6, "Congress").

Because the compromise plan substantially strengthened the national government's capacity for action, most nationalists except Madison reconciled themselves to it—at least initially. The man who during his lifetime was called "the father of the Constitution" maintained that ultimately the nationalists would prevail by letting the country stew a while longer under the Articles. Eventually he was talked out of that idea, but he remained profoundly disillusioned. Then, perhaps literally overnight, Madison scrapped the rest of the Virginia Plan and made what amounted to a 180-degree turn in his views on the proper relations among government institutions. A new, more strategic politician had emerged. Suddenly Madison expressed enthusiasm for a genuine separation of powers between the branches, with each side exercising **checks and balances** over the others. The reasoning behind his hurried reassessment might have gone something like this: if the state legislatures could corrupt the new Congress through their hold on the Senate, they also could corrupt the entire national government through Congress's power to select the officers of the other branches of government. The solution: insulate the executive and judicial branches and enlist them in containing any efforts by the states through the Senate to subvert national policy. Thus in early July, with the summer half over and the proceedings gathering momentum, Madison turned his attention to fashioning an independent executive and judiciary.

## Designing the Executive Branch

Of all the delegates, Alexander Hamilton had shown the greatest enthusiasm for a strengthened, independent executive. His fixation on an executive elected for life, however, left him so far on the fringe that he enjoyed little influence on the rest of the delegates as they turned their attention to this institution. His eloquent speeches were "praised by everybody . . . [but] supported by none," reported one candid delegate.

The delegates' lack of enthusiasm for an active, authoritative presidency is understandable. They had just finished dividing legislative authority into two coequal chambers with representatives and senators to be elected for different terms and from different constituencies. With each chamber able to block intemperate policies arising from the other, the Framers could more safely invest in them broad authority to make policy. Once the delegates dismissed the idea of a plural executive as impractical, the presidency no longer contained the internal checks that would have it control its excessive impulses.

This posed a serious dilemma for the Convention. Even a casual survey of world history would turn up a panoply of absolute monarchs and other tyrants. Such a list supplied ample examples of the techniques arbitrary executives used to exploit the citizenry and preserve their power. Indeed, all of the delegates had lived under an arbitrary executive's thumb. They despised King George III and his agents, the vilified colonial governors, who chronically were at odds with the colonial legislature over who had what authority. After the Revolution the new states had overreacted by creating weak governors. Based on his brief experience as Virginia's wartime governor, Jefferson dismissed the office as a "cipher," a nonentity.

**LOGIC OF POLITICS**

# Checks and Balances in the Constitution

The Framers feared that a concentration of power in any one group or branch of government would lead to tyranny—that is, one group would gain enough power to dominate the government and strip other groups of their basic rights. Thus they devised in the Constitution something of a political game in which each of the three branches of government has some capacity to limit, or trump, the power of the other two.

This system of checks and balances largely originated with the French philosopher Charles,

Baron de Montesquieu (1689–1755), who argued that the concentration of government power could be effectively limited by locating the several functions of government—legislative, executive, and judicial—in separate and independent institutions. Notice in the diagram that rather than defining "separation of powers" according to these functions, the Constitution described separate institutions *sharing* power. All three branches possess legislative, executive, and judicial authority.

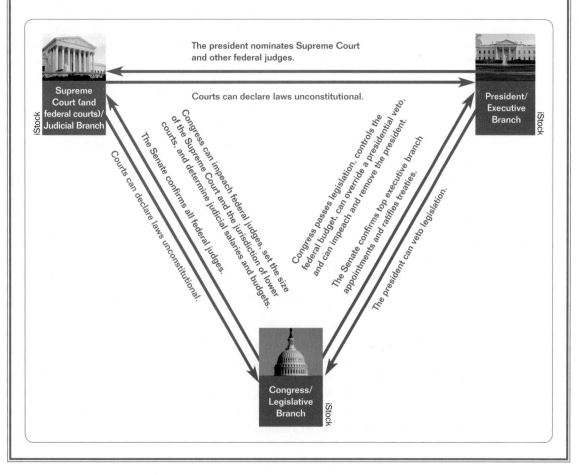

In the end the only acceptable model of the new American president was, in the words of one historian, "sitting there in front of them . . . dignified, silent, universally admired and respected . . . impartial, honored for his selfless devotion to the common good, not intervening in, but presiding over, their councils—a presider, a *president*. The executive was to be— George Washington."[8] The presence of a real-life example of an ideal executive presiding over the Convention kept in view the kind of leadership the delegates sought to institutionalize, yet it does not appear to have made their task any easier. In the end, the delegates largely succeeded in fashioning an independent executive branch that might be incapable of abusing authority and might actually moderate excesses by an overreaching legislature. To achieve this, they designed several features. First, they limited the scope of presidential responsibilities and particularly the office's command authority. (The presidency of the twenty-first century might appear to belie their success. In Chapter 7 we survey the evolution of the presidency and reconcile the modern with the early office.) Article II states, almost as an afterthought, that the president "shall take Care that the Laws be faithfully executed." Modern presidents sometimes assert that the **"take care" clause** allows them to undertake whatever actions the nation's well-being requires and are not expressly forbidden by the Constitution or public law. Yet, unlike Congress's expansive necessary and proper clause that bolsters their discretion in performing a long list of responsibilities, this mandate is not attached to any specific duty. Specifically, this new executive will appoint officers to fill vacancies in the executive department, receive and appoint ambassadors, negotiate treaties, serve as commander in chief of the army and navy, and periodically report to Congress on the state of the nation. The second design feature attached a legislative check, or veto, to each presidential duty. The Senate would confirm appointments and ratify any treaties (in this instance with a two-thirds vote) before they could take effect. Only Congress could declare war.

The third significant design feature was the veto, a negative action that would allow the executive to perform a "checking" function on the legislature. Unlike some constitutional executives, presidents cannot make policy or appropriate funds for programs, except as allowed in public laws. By requiring a **supermajority** vote of two-thirds of the members of each house to override a presidential veto, the Framers carved out an important role for the modern president in domestic legislation.

Over the next two centuries, the presidency became a much more consequential office, both in its duties and in its authority. But at least with respect to domestic policy, it has done so within a constitutional framework that has not changed. Most of the expansion has occurred through statutory provisions delegating policy responsibilities to the White House. If the Framers observed the president's role in domestic policy today, they might be shocked with what they found, but they would quickly recognize it as an extension of the office they envisioned.

One cannot be so confident that the Framers would come to the same assessment regarding the president's dominant role in foreign policy and national defense. Beginning with World War II the United States became a leader in international affairs. Whatever advantages its status conferred, it also entailed numerous—well over a hundred— military actions. None began with Congress declaring "war," although all of the large-scale conflicts—Korea, Vietnam, and both Iraq wars, among others—found Congress passing resolutions backing the president's actions that initiated the conflict. Some analysts argue

Library of Congress

Mark Wilson/Getty Images

The Framers, as do students of modern American government, considered how much military authority to grant the president and how Congress could constrain potential abuses of this authority. With Britain, Spain, and France controlling territories on America's borders, providing for the nation's security preoccupied the Framers. So, too, did an executive who might usurp power and turn the military against the other branches of government. Yet giving Congress the "power of the purse and the sword" clearly violated the accepted guiding principle of checks and balances.

that contemporary international affairs and modern military technology have eclipsed the Constitution's capacity to prescribe appropriate authority and responsibilities available to the executive and legislature in modern wartime. In part the Constitution's limited and general language regarding foreign affairs has contributed to this uncertainty. During the George W. Bush presidency, administration and congressional views on the constitutional prerogatives for these branches during wartime diverged sharply. In Chapter 7 we consider occasions during which White House officials have asserted that Congress has no role. Invariably the federal courts have had to resolve these constitutional disputes and have groped for answers along with the president and Congress. We take up these issues in detail later. The important point here is that the Constitution contains gaps—at times chasms—that have Americans more than two hundred years after the document was ratified asking fundamental questions about the appropriate role of Congress and the presidency. Much of the uncertainty occurs with subjects that Article II's creation of the presidency failed to resolve.

At the Constitutional Convention, the delegates found that the only workable formula for agreement between the nationalists and states' rights advocates was to give both sides pretty much what they wanted, an approach that yielded the **Great Compromise**, and multiple routes for amending the Constitution. When the drafters turned to devising a procedure for electing the president, they returned to arduous committee deliberations and floor wrangling to find a compromise. This time Constitutional Convention politics produced arguably the most convoluted rules to be found in the Constitution: the workings of the **Electoral College**.

As a device, the Electoral College tries to mix state, congressional, and popular participation in the election process and in doing so has managed to confuse citizens for more than two hundred years. In two of the past five elections the candidate who won the Electoral College majority failed to win even a plurality of the popular vote. George W. Bush in 2000 and Donald Trump in 2016 did so by having their popular votes fortuitously distributed across the states in such a fashion as to maximize their electoral votes. Each state is awarded as many electors as it has members of the House and Senate. The Constitution left it to the states to decide how electors are selected, but the Framers generally and correctly expected that the states would rely on statewide elections. If any candidate fails to receive an absolute majority (270) of the 538 votes in the Electoral College, the election is thrown into the House of Representatives, which chooses from among the three candidates who received the largest number of electoral votes. In making its selection, the House votes by state delegation; each state gets one vote, and a majority is required to elect a president (see Chapter 11 for more on the Electoral College). Until the Twelfth Amendment corrected the most egregious flaws of the Electoral College, votes for the president and the vice president were tallied side by side, resulting in a vice presidential candidate almost winning the presidency in the election of 1800.

## Designing the Judicial Branch

The Convention spent comparatively little time designing the new federal judiciary, a somewhat surprising development given that the Constitution gives the Supreme Court final jurisdiction in resolving differences between the state and national levels of government. Armed with that jurisdiction and with the **supremacy clause** (Article VI), which declares that national laws take precedence over state laws when both properly discharge their governments' respective responsibilities, the Supreme Court emerged from the Convention as a major, probably underappreciated, lever for expanding the scope of national policymaking.

States' rights advocates and nationalists did, however, spar over two lesser questions: Who would appoint Supreme Court justices—the president or the Senate? And should a network of lower federal courts be created, or should state courts handle all cases until they reached the Supreme Court, the only federal court? The Convention split the difference over appointments by giving the president appointment powers and the Senate confirmation powers, and they left it to some future Congress to decide whether the national government needed its own lower-level judiciary. The First Congress exercised this option almost immediately, creating a lower federal court system with the Judiciary Act of 1789.

An important issue never quite resolved by the Constitutional Convention was the extent of the Court's authority to overturn federal laws and executive actions as unconstitutional—a concept known as **judicial review**. Although the supremacy clause appears to establish the Court's authority to review state laws, there is no formal language extending this authority to veto federal laws. Yet many of the Framers, including Hamilton, claimed that the Constitution implicitly provides for judicial review. Later in life Madison protested that he never would have agreed to a provision that allowed an unelected branch of government to have the final say in lawmaking. But in one of the great ironies of American history, Madison was a litigant in an early Supreme Court decision, *Marbury v. Madison* (1803), in which the Court laid claim to the authority to strike down any legislation it deemed unconstitutional.[9] In Chapter 9 we return to this historic case and its profound effects on the development of the judiciary's role in policymaking.

## Substantive Issues

In remapping federal-state responsibilities the Framers largely intended to eliminate the collective action dilemmas that had plagued states' efforts to cooperate under the Articles of Confederation. The states had to surrender some autonomy to the national government to eliminate the threat of free riding and reneging on collective agreements.

### Foreign Policy

Trade and foreign policy were at the top of the list of federal-state issues the Framers wanted the Constitution to solve. Shortly after the Revolutionary War, the states had found themselves engaged in cutthroat competition for foreign commerce. The Framers solved this dilemma by placing foreign policy under the administration of the president and giving Congress the explicit legislative authority to regulate commerce. As for common defense and security, the Framers placed those responsibilities squarely on the shoulders of the national government. The Constitution (Article I, Section 10) forbids any state from entering into a foreign alliance or treaty, maintaining a military during peacetime, or engaging in war unless invaded.

### Interstate Commerce

Relations among the states, a longtime source of friction, also figured prominently in the Framers' deliberations. As a result, Article I, Section 10, prohibits states from discriminating against each other in various ways. They may not enter into agreements without the consent of Congress, tax imports or exports entering local ports, print money not backed by gold or silver, or make laws prejudicial to citizens of other states.

The Framers balanced these concessions with important benefits for the states. The new national government would assume outstanding debts the states had incurred during the war, protect the states from invasion and insurrection, and guarantee that all states would be governed by republican institutions.

All these provisions of the Constitution are less well known than those creating and conferring powers on the several branches of government or the amendments known as the **Bill of Rights**. But the fact that Americans take them for granted reflects their success, not their irrelevance. With these provisions the Framers solved the most serious collective action dilemmas confronting the young nation, including trade. Taken together, the provisions to prevent states from interfering with commerce that crossed their borders established the essentials of a common market among the former colonies. As a result, the Constitution contributed vitally to the nation's economic development during the next century, not only through its directives on interstate commerce but also through the other trade- and business-related provisions in Article I. One such provision prevents the government from passing laws impairing the obligations of private contracts; others mandate that the national government create bankruptcy and patent laws.

### Slavery

Throughout America's history the issue of race has never been far removed from politics. It certainly was present in Philadelphia, despite some delegates' best efforts to prevent a regional

## POLITICS TO POLICY
# Why Women Were Left Out of the Constitution

Why is it that nowhere in the original Constitution or in the floor debates at Philadelphia are women mentioned? One reason is that the delegates to the Constitutional Convention, faced with the glaring deficiencies of the national government under the Articles of Confederation, were less concerned with individual rights than with making government more effective and establishing proper relations among the institutions they were creating. Early on, delegates agreed to allow the individual states to continue to decide which citizens should have the right to vote. Thus no one actually gained the right to vote in the Constitution.

Second, although it tacitly accepts franchise restrictions imposed by the states, the Constitution reads as though it were drafted to be as free of gender bias as eighteenth-century usage allowed. Throughout, the words *persons* and *citizens*, not *men*, appear. Eligibility to serve as a member of Congress, for example, begins with the statement "No Person shall be a Representative." Elsewhere: "The Citizens of each State shall be entitled to all Privileges and Immunities of Citizens in the several States." A few passages of the Constitution use the pronoun *he* (in each instance, however, the masculine pronoun refers back to a gender-free noun), but until the twentieth century, this referent was commonly used and legally interpreted to include women. In this respect, then, women were not left out of the Constitution.

The third reason is that women's political rights simply had not yet become an issue. Absence of the issue, however, did not mean that women remained apolitical during the Revolution and the subsequent crisis in governance or that they

Abigail Adams

failed to protest other aspects of their inferior legal standing. The ample evidence in private correspondence indicates that many women followed politics carefully. A few even published monographs that received wide circulation. One of the most famous correspondents of either sex during this era was Abigail Adams, the wife of John Adams and the mother of John Quincy Adams. Her numerous letters to her husband and leaders, such as Thomas Jefferson, exhibit a candor and insight that make them compelling to modern readers as well. To her husband, who was away attending the Continental Congress, she wrote, "In the new code of laws which I suppose it will be necessary for you to make, I desire you would remember the ladies, and be more generous to them than your ancestors. Do not put such unlimited power in the hands of husbands. Remember, all men would be tyrants if they could." This passage often has been celebrated as one of the first expressions of women's political rights in America. But, in fact, Adams was addressing various civil laws that allowed husbands to confiscate their wives' property and made divorce all but impossible. Lack of a woman's rights in marriage—not suffrage—was the grievance of these early feminists.

Not until publication of Sarah Grimké's *Letters on the Equality of the Sexes, and the Condition of Woman* in 1838 and the Seneca Falls Convention declaration—"All men and women are created equal"—a decade later would women's suffrage be placed on the national political agenda. In 1869 Wyoming became the first state to add

women to the voter rolls. Later in the nineteenth century, Susan B. Anthony of Massachusetts led a suffragist movement that claimed the right to vote under the Fourteenth Amendment and sought a constitutional suffrage amendment. In 1887 Congress defeated the proposal for the amendment, but the suffrage movement continued. President Woodrow Wilson (1913–1921) initially opposed the amendment, arguing that state action was more appropriate. But when protests grew into hunger strikes in 1918, he announced his support. The Nineteenth Amendment to the Constitution, guaranteeing women the right to vote, was ratified in 1920.

*Source:* Adapted from James Q. Wilson and John J. DiIulio Jr., *American Government: Institutions and Policies*, 7th ed. (Boston: Houghton Mifflin, 1998), 43.

disagreement on slavery from thwarting the purpose of the Convention. But how could delegates construct a government based on popular sovereignty and inalienable rights without addressing the fact that one-sixth of Americans were in bondage? They could not. Slavery figured importantly in many delegates' private calculations, especially those from the South. At several junctures, it broke to the surface.

The first effort to grapple with slavery was the most acrimonious and threatening. How should slaves be counted in allocating congressional representatives to the states? Madison had persuaded delegates to postpone this issue until they had finalized the design of the new Congress, but the issue soon loomed again. Trying to maximize their representation in the population-based House of Representatives, southern delegates insisted that slaves were undeniably people and should be included fully in any population count to determine representation. Northerners resisted this attempted power grab by arguing that because slaves did not enjoy the freedom to act as autonomous citizens, they should not be counted at all. In the end each side accepted a formula initially used to levy taxes under the Articles of Confederation, a plan that assigned states their financial obligations to the national government proportionate to population. Accordingly, the Constitution apportioned each state seats in the House of Representatives based on population totals in which each slave would count as three-fifths of a citizen.*

---

*The three-fifths rule had been devised under the Articles to resolve a sectional dispute over apportioning states' tax contributions according to population. At that time the northerners had a stake in recognizing the humanity of slaves—if slaves were people, their numbers should be fully counted in apportioning tax obligations. Southerners had countered that, because they marketed slaves as property, slaves should be counted no more than any other property. After extended haggling, the groups agreed to add three-fifths of the number of slaves to a state's free population.

Later in the Convention some southern delegates insisted on two guarantees for their "peculiar institution" as conditions for remaining at the Convention and endorsing the Constitution in the ratification debates. One was the unrestricted right to continue importing slaves. The delegates from northern states, most of which had outlawed slavery, preferred to leave the issue to some future government. But in the end they conceded by writing into the Constitution a ban on regulation of the slave trade until 1808.* (A total ban on slave imports went into effect on January 1, 1808.) Late in the Convention southerners introduced the Constitution's second slavery protection clause. It required northern states to return runaway slaves to their masters. After some delegates first resisted and then softened the language of the clause, the proposal passed.

Why did the delegations from the more numerous northern states cave in to the southerners? The handling of the slavery issue was likely another instance of intense private interests prevailing over more diffuse notions of the public good. Reporting to Jefferson in Paris, Madison wrote that "South Carolina and Georgia were inflexible on the point of slaves," implying that without the slave trade and fugitive provisions they would not have endorsed the Constitution. And because the southerners' preferences were secure under the Articles of Confederation, their threat to defect during the subsequent ratification campaign was credible. After launching anguished, caustic criticisms of southerners' demands during floor debates, the northerners cooled down and reassessed their situation. In the end, they conceded many of their antislavery provisions and adopted a more strategic posture that would allow them to gain something in exchange.

With neither side able to persuade the other to adopt its preferred position and yet with each effectively able to veto ratification, both sides began searching for a mutually acceptable alternative. Their first such attempt had produced the Great Compromise. This time the solution took the form of a **logroll**—a standard bargaining strategy in which two sides swap support for dissimilar policies. In the end, New England accommodated the South by agreeing to two provisions: Article I, Section 9, protecting the importation of slaves until at least 1808; and Article IV, Section 2, requiring that northern states return fugitive slaves. In return, southern delegates dropped their opposition on an altogether different issue that was dear to the commercial interests of the northern states. Article I, Section 8, allows Congress to regulate commerce and tax imports with a simple majority vote (see Strategy and Choice box "Logrolling a Constitution," page 67).

## Amending the Constitution

In their efforts to provide a suitable means for amending the Constitution, the Framers broke new ground. (Amending the Articles of Confederation required the unanimous consent of the states, and the constitution creating the French republic in 1789 contained no amendment procedure whatsoever.) Perhaps the futility of trying to win unanimous consent

---

*The committee that drafted this language proposed that the ban on regulation end in 1800, but a coalition of New Englanders and southerners added eight years to the ban. Only Madison spoke out against extending the deadline. The delegates from Virginia, all of whom had owned slaves at one time or another, voted against extension.

## STRATEGY AND CHOICE
# Logrolling a Constitution

Many of the New England delegates who came to Philadelphia were frustrated by the nation's inability to conduct a coordinated commercial policy at home or abroad. Southerners, however, liked things pretty much the way they were, fearing that additional government controls might lead to taxes and regulations on their extensive agricultural exports to Europe. If the national government insisted, as in time it did, that a substantial share of exports must travel on U.S. ships, the Northeast (with its ports and shipping companies) would gain financially at the expense of southern producers. Consequently, the South had opposed giving the national government such commercial authority without the assent of two-thirds of both houses of Congress. This large supermajority would have given the South, in effect, a veto over any objectionable policy, and as a result no commercial provision would have been adopted. Southerners also were committed to warding off an antislavery measure that most northerners and their state legislatures were on record as supporting.

Consider the range of policy options before the delegates. We can rank the policy preferences of any individual delegate or group of like-minded delegates. Although northern delegates preferred an antislavery policy, they desired a strong commercial policy even more. We can illustrate their preferences for various policy combinations by assigning letters to the alternatives: a strong commercial policy, C; no commercial policy, c; proslavery, S; and antislavery, s. Northern delegates most preferred a strong commercial policy coupled with antislavery, followed by a strong commercial provision and an allowance for slavery, and so on. Using letter combinations and the mathematical symbol for "is greater

A Slave-Coffle passing the Capitol.

than," we can rank the northern delegates' preferences for possible policy combinations:

Northerners: $Cs > CS > cs > cS$

The South, on the other hand, preferred to maintain a proslavery policy and to defeat a commercial one. In floor debates at the Convention, southern delegates said they felt more strongly about maintaining slavery than about avoiding marginally more costly shipping. Using the same set of symbols, we can rank southern delegates' preferred policy combinations:

Southerners: $cS > CS > cs > Cs$

Note that the North's most preferred combination of constitutional provisions—strong commercial institutions and a ban on the slave trade—was the least preferred

*(Continued)*

(Continued)

combination in the South. And, conversely, the South's most preferred position was the least desired in the North. With their sincere preferences so opposed, frustrations mounted, as did the temperature of the rhetoric. Finally, each side realized that it could not win its most preferred combination of policies, and a search for a compromise began. Look carefully and locate the compromise package that each side found comparatively more attractive, bearing in mind that failure to reach agreement on these issues might well have endangered the success of the Convention and left thorny issues unresolved during the ratification process. The compromise solution, CS, was a policy that combined strong commercial language and a provision permitting slavery. It took a while for the delegates to find it, but they did.

This solution took the form of a classic logroll. Instead of finding separate compromise policies on each issue, the delegates engaged in vote trading. To win its most important preference, each side conceded to the other its least important choice.

Finding a solution and implementing it are separate exercises that may be equally susceptible to failure. After all, each side must give up something important to win a concession in return. It is a situation rife with the possibility of reneging, an instance of the classic prisoner's dilemma that always threatens cooperation. (We found such a situation in Chapter 1, where we discussed the classic prisoner's dilemma interrogation in the film *I Wake Up Screaming*.) And because delegates from each side appreciated the difficulty of having to

return home and explain their agreement to an unpopular policy, the fear of reneging was real. New England delegates would have to justify writing slavery into the Constitution, whereas southerners would have to defend opening the door to dreaded commercial regulations.

To succeed, the logroll had to be consummated delicately and discreetly. In his record of the Convention's proceeding, James Madison noted the careful language Charles Pinckney of South Carolina had used to signal to the other side that he and his southern colleagues were in agreement. "The true interest of the S[outhern] States is to have no regulation of commerce," said Pinckney, who then cited "the loss brought on the commerce of the Eastern States by the revolution" and the "liberal conduct [of those states] toward the views of South Carolina." Here, Madison inserted a footnote translating Pinckney's circumlocutions for future readers: by "liberal conduct," Pinckney "meant the permission to import slaves. An understanding on the two subjects of navigation and *slavery* had taken place between those parts of the Union."[1]

Logrolling is ubiquitous in all legislatures, whether they are constitutional conventions or student government committees. This form of strategic behavior is, in fact, essential for a society composed of many different and competing interests to transact its politics successfully. We encounter numerous instances of it throughout this text.

---

1. Quoted in William Lee Miller, *The Business of May Next: James Madison and the Founding* (Charlottesville: University Press of Virginia, 1992), 135.

for changing the Articles persuaded the Framers to find a more reasonable method for amending the Constitution, one that did not require a full convention like the Philadelphia Convention. Yet they did not want to place the amendment option within easy reach of a popular majority. After all, some future majority frustrated by executive and judicial vetoes might try to change the Constitution rather than accommodate its opponents. So, again, the Framers solved the dilemma by imposing heavy transaction costs on changing the Constitution.

The concept of providing for future amendment of the Constitution proved less controversial than the amendment procedure itself. Intent on preserving their hard-won gains in the face of future amendment proposals, both the nationalists and states' rights advocates approached this matter warily. Delegates from small states insisted on endorsement of amendments by a large number of states, whereas the nationalists argued that the Constitution derived its legitimacy directly from the citizenry and that the citizens alone should approve any change. Unable to muster a majority for either position, the delegates again used the formula of accepting parts of both proposals. As a result, the Constitution allows an amendment to be proposed either by a two-thirds vote of both houses of Congress or by an "application" from two-thirds of the states. Enactment occurs when three-fourths of the states, acting either through their state legislatures or in special conventions, accept the amendment (see Figure 2.3).

Since its ratification, the Constitution has been amended twenty-seven times. In every instance, Congress initiated the process, and in all but one case, the state legislatures did the ratifying. (The Constitution and its amendments appear in the appendix.) Six additional amendments—including the Equal Rights Amendment (see Chapter 4, "Civil Rights")—were sent to the states but failed to win endorsement from a sufficient number. The paucity of near misses is deceiving, however. Each year, dozens of amendments are proposed in Congress, but they fail to go any further either because they fail to attract the requisite two-thirds support in both chambers or because supporters foresee little chance of success in the states. During the 108th Congress (2003–2004), for example, members proposed amendments restricting marriage to a man and a woman; ensuring "God" is included in the Pledge of Allegiance; and providing a mechanism for Congress to replenish its membership should more than a quarter of its members be killed, as in a terrorist attack.

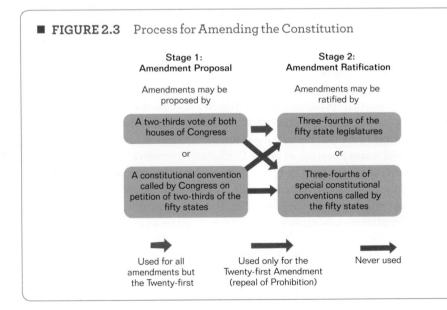

■ **FIGURE 2.3**    Process for Amending the Constitution

# The Fight for Ratification

The seventh and final article of the Constitution spells out an important procedure endorsed by delegates in the final days of the Convention: "The Ratification of the Conventions of nine States, shall be sufficient for the Establishment of this Constitution between the States so ratifying the Same." Everyone knew that this deceptively straightforward provision was critical for the success of the enterprise. The delegates improvised by adapting the nine-state rule used by the Articles for passing normal legislation, even though the Articles did not provide for amendment. And the ratification provision withdrew ratification authority from the state legislatures, which might have misgivings about surrendering autonomy, and gave it instead to elective special conventions. In sum, the delegates succeeded in a bit of legalistic legerdemain—appearing to conform to the requirements of the existing Constitution while breaking radically from it.

## The Federalist and Antifederalist Debate

At the close of the Convention, only three delegates refused to sign the Constitution. This consensus, however, is misleading; others who probably would have objected left early, and many prominent political leaders such as Virginians Patrick Henry and Richard Henry Lee had refused even to participate.

Over the next year every state but Rhode Island (it held out until 1790) elected delegates to state conventions that proceeded to dissect the Constitution and ponder its individual provisions. This was truly a time of national debate over the future of the country. As one observer noted, "Almost every American pen . . . [and] peasants and their wives in every part of the land" began "to dispute on politics and positively to determine upon our liberties."[10] On a lighter note, the *Boston Daily Advertiser*, responding to General Washington's call for public debate, admonished its readers: "Come on brother scribblers, 'tis idle to lag! The Convention has let the cat out of the bag."[11] Delegates to the state conventions concentrated, predictably, on the concerns of their states and communities. Southern states carefully inspected each article for a northern avenue of attack on their "peculiar institution" of slavery. Finding none, all except North Carolina lined up behind the Constitution.

Constituencies and their delegates similarly aligned themselves for or against the Constitution according to its perceived impact on their pocketbooks. Small farmers, struck hard by declining markets and high property taxes after the war, had succeeded in gaining sympathetic majorities in many of the state legislatures and so looked suspiciously on the proposed national government's new role in public finance and commerce. Under pressure from small farmers, many state legislatures had printed cheap paper money (making it easier for the farmers to pay off their debts), overturned court decisions unfavorable to debt-laden farmers, and provided some with direct subsidies and relief. Thus these constituencies were reluctant to see their state legislatures subordinated to some future national policy over currency and bankruptcy.

In the public campaign for ratification these issues tended to be reduced to the rhetoric of nationalism, voiced by the **Federalists**, versus the rhetoric of states' rights, voiced by the **Antifederalists**. The divisiveness characterizing the Philadelphia Convention thus continued. But the labels given the two sides were confusing. Although they consistently distinguished the Constitution's supporters and opponents, the labels confused the positions of these camps on the issue of federalism. *Federalism*, a topic so central to understanding America's political system that we devote all of the next chapter to it, refers to the distribution of authority between the national and state governments. Many of those who opposed ratification were more protective of state prerogatives, as the term *federalist* implies, than were many of the prominent "Federalists." Appreciating the depth of state loyalties, Madison and his colleagues early on tactically maneuvered to neutralize this issue by claiming that the Constitution provided a true federal system, making those seeking ratification Federalists. Their success in expropriating this label put their opponents at a disadvantage in the public relations campaign. One disgruntled Antifederalist proposed that the labels be changed so that Madison and his crowd would be called the "Rats" (for proratification) and his side the "Antirats."

With the New York ratification narrowly divided, proratification forces staged a massive rally. The parade was graced by a "ship of state," an already well-developed metaphor. At the time, New Yorker Alexander Hamilton was widely regarded as one of the Constitution's most effective sponsors.

North Wind Picture Archives

Although in the end the Federalists prevailed and are today revered as the nation's "Founders," the Antifederalists included a comparable number and quality of proven patriots. Foremost among them was Patrick Henry, who led his side's counterattack. With him were fellow Virginians Richard Henry Lee, George Mason, and a young James Monroe, who would become the nation's fifth president under the Constitution he had opposed. Other famous outspoken opponents included Boston's Revolutionary War hero Samuel Adams and New York governor George Clinton.

In their opposition to the Constitution, the Antifederalists raised serious theoretical objections—ones that can still be heard more than two hundred years later. They argued that only local democracy, the kind found in small homogeneous communities, could approach true democracy. The United States, they asserted, already was too large and too diverse to be well ruled by a single set of laws. Turning their sights to the Constitution itself, the Antifederalists argued that a stronger national government must be accompanied by explicit safeguards against tyranny. Specifically, the Constitution needed a bill of rights—a familiar feature of most state constitutions. Some delegates to the Convention proposed a bill of rights, but Madison and others had argued that it was unnecessary because the Constitution did not give the national government any powers that could be construed as invading the citizenry's rights. This argument, however, worked better at the Convention than it did in the public campaign. The Antifederalists quickly realized they had identified a chink in the Constitution's armor and began pounding the issue hard. Even Madison's ally Jefferson wrote him from France insisting that individual rights were too important to be "left to inference." Suddenly on the defensive, Madison made a strategic capitulation and announced that at the convening of the First Congress under the new Constitution, he would introduce constitutional amendments providing a bill of rights. His strategy worked; the issue receded. In a sense, though, the Antifederalist strategy had worked as well. Madison kept his promise, and by 1791, the Constitution contained the Bill of Rights (see Table 2.2).

In June 1788 New Hampshire became the ninth and technically decisive state to ratify the Constitution. But Virginia and New York had still not voted, and until these two large, centrally located states became a part of the Union, no one gave the new government much chance of getting off the ground. But by the end of July both states had narrowly ratified the Constitution, and the new Union was a reality.

Despite their efforts, Madison and fellow nationalists won only a partial victory with the launching of the Constitution. The nation still added up to little more than a collection of states, but the mechanisms were put in place to allow the eventual emergence of the national

**TABLE 2.2**  The First Ten Amendments to the Constitution: The Bill of Rights

| AMENDMENT | PURPOSE |
|---|---|
| I | Guarantees freedom of religion, speech, assembly, and press, and the right of people to petition the government for redress of grievances |
| II | Protects the right of states to maintain militias |
| III | Restricts quartering of troops in private homes |
| IV | Protects against "unreasonable searches and seizures" |
| V | Ensures the right not to be deprived of "life, liberty, or property, without due process of law," including protections against double jeopardy, self-incrimination, and government seizure of property without just compensation |
| VI | Guarantees the right to a speedy and public trial by an impartial jury |
| VII | Ensures the right to a jury trial in cases involving the common law (judge-made law originating in England) |
| VIII | Protects against excessive bail or cruel and unusual punishment |
| IX | Provides that people's rights are not restricted to those specified in Amendments I–VIII |
| X | Reiterates the Constitution's principle of federalism by providing that powers not granted to the national government are reserved to the states or to the people |

government. For example, by basing the Constitution's adoption on the consent of the governed rather than endorsement by the states, the nationalists successfully denied state governments any claim that they could ignore national policy. Over the next several decades, although state politicians would from time to time threaten to secede or to "nullify" objectionable federal laws, none of the attempts at **nullification** reached a full-fledged constitutional crisis until the Civil War in 1861. With the Union victory, this threat to the national government ended conclusively. Yet, as we shall see in the next chapter, "Federalism," until the twentieth century national authority remained limited by modern standards. Nowhere is this more evident than in the domains of civil rights and civil liberties, the subjects of Chapters 4 and 5.

## The Influence of *The Federalist*

Aside from eventually yielding a new constitution, the ratification debates fostered another national resource: eighty-five essays collected under the title *The Federalist*. Published under the shared pseudonym Publius in 1787 and 1788, the essays were written by Alexander Hamilton (who wrote the majority), John Jay (who wrote five), and James Madison (who arguably wrote the best). In one of history's interesting twists of fate, Hamilton initially recruited fellow New Yorker William Duer to join the Publius team.*

Because their immediate purpose was to influence the delegates to the New York convention, where ratification was in trouble, the *Federalist* essays first appeared in New York City newspapers. At one point Hamilton and Madison were cranking out four essays a week, prompting the Antifederalists to complain that by the time they had rebutted one argument in print, several others had appeared. Reprinted widely, the essays provided rhetorical ammunition to those supporting ratification.†

Whatever their role in the Constitution's ratification, *The Federalist Papers*, as they are also called, have profoundly affected the way Americans then and now have understood their government. A few years after their publication, Thomas Jefferson, describing the curriculum of the University of Virginia to its board of overseers, declared *The Federalist* to be indispensable reading for all undergraduates. It is "agreed by all," he explained, that these essays convey "the genuine meaning" of the Constitution.

---

*Duer's submissions were judged inadequate, however, and Hamilton turned to Madison. Duer, a professor at Columbia University, later found his appropriate medium in a highly successful American government textbook in which he introduced students to the already famous *Federalist* essays, to which he almost contributed. Writing perhaps the first textbook on American government in 1833, William Alexander Duer penned a heartfelt dedication to James Madison, which is reproduced as the front piece, just after *Logic*'s title page.

†Although they became famous, the *Federalist* essays, according to most historians, had a negligible impact on the outcome of the ratification process. Perhaps too many hard economic interests were in play for abstract arguments about the general welfare to do more than justify and dress up positions grounded firmly in self-interests. The New York convention shifted toward ratification only after New York City threatened to secede from the state if the vote went against ratification.

## The Theory Underlying the Constitution

Two of Madison's essays, *Federalist* No. 10 and *Federalist* No. 51, offer special insights into the theory underlying the Constitution. (The full text of these essays is available in the appendix.) In different ways, each essay tackles the fundamental problem of self-governance, which Madison poses in a famous passage from *Federalist* No. 51:

> If men were angels, no government would be necessary. If angels were to govern men, neither external nor internal controls on government would be necessary. In framing a government which is to be administered by men over men, the great difficulty lies in this: you must first enable the government to control the governed; and in the next place oblige it to control itself.

The last goal is tricky. *Federalist* No. 10 tackles the problem by both exploring the likelihood that tyranny by the majority would arise within a democracy and identifying a solution. It is a powerful, cogent argument grounded in logic. *Federalist* No. 51 deals with the problem of keeping government officeholders honest and under control. The solution lies in pitting ambitious politicians against one another through the Constitution's separation of powers and checks and balances. This way, politicians can counteract one another's temptation to engage in mischief. Whatever their differences, these two essays can be read as following parallel paths—one at the societal level, the other at the governmental level—toward the same destination of a self-regulating polity free from tyranny.

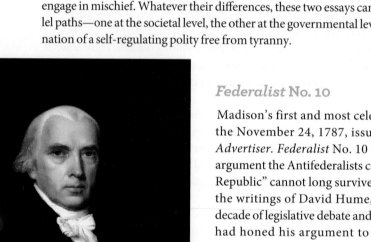

The White House Historical Association

When James Madison was introduced with the accolade "Father of the Constitution," he frequently demurred, probably less from modesty than from disagreement with many of its provisions.

### *Federalist* No. 10

Madison's first and most celebrated essay appeared in the November 24, 1787, issue of the New York *Daily Advertiser*. *Federalist* No. 10 responds to the strongest argument the Antifederalists could muster—that a "large Republic" cannot long survive. This essay borrows from the writings of David Hume, but over the course of a decade of legislative debate and correspondence, Madison had honed his argument to fit the American case.[12] Indeed, Madison had made the argument before—at the Constitutional Convention when defending the Virginia Plan in a floor debate.

The major task Madison sets out for himself in *Federalist* No. 10 is to devise a republic in which a majority of citizens will be unable to tyrannize the minority. Madison wastes no time identifying the rotten apple. It is **factions**, which he describes as "mortal diseases under which popular governments have everywhere perished." He defines a faction as "a number of citizens, whether amounting to a majority or minority of the whole, who are united and actuated by some common impulse of passion, or of *interest*, adverse to the rights of other citizens, or to the permanent and aggregate interests of the community" (emphasis added). Madison's factions appear to have many of the attributes of modern-day interest groups and even political parties.

Madison then identifies two ways to eliminate factions—authoritarianism and conformism—neither of which he finds acceptable. Authoritarianism, a form of government that actively suppresses factions, is a remedy worse than the disease. In a famous passage of *Federalist* No. 10, Madison offers an analogy: "Liberty is to faction what air is to fire, an aliment without which it instantly expires."

Conformism, the second solution, is, as Madison notes, "as impracticable as the first would be unwise." People cannot somehow be made to have the same goals, for "the latent causes of faction are . . . sown in the nature of man." Thus two individuals who are precisely alike in wealth, education, and other characteristics will nonetheless have different views on many issues. Even the "most frivolous and fanciful distinction" can "kindle their unfriendly passions," Madison observes, but most of the important political cleavages that divide a citizenry are predictably rooted in their life circumstances. In another famous passage, the author anticipates by nearly a century Karl Marx's class-based analysis of politics under capitalism:

> But the most common and durable source of faction has been the various and unequal distribution of property. Those who hold and those who are without property have ever formed distinct interests in society. . . . A landed interest, a manufacturing interest, a mercantile interest, a moneyed interest, with many lesser interests, grow up of necessity in civilized nations, and divide them into different classes, actuated by different sentiments and views.*

If the causes of faction cannot be removed without snuffing out liberty, then one must control their effects. Madison identifies two kinds of factions—those composed of a minority of the citizenry and those composed of a majority—that have to be controlled in different ways. During the late eighteenth century, the ubiquitous problem of factional tyranny occurred at the hands of the monarchy and aristocracy, a "minority" faction, for which democracy provides the remedy. A minority faction "may clog the administration, it may convulse the society; but it will be unable to execute and mask its violence under the forms of the Constitution." Democracy, however, introduces its own special brand of factional tyranny—that emanating from a self-interested majority. In Madison's era many people—especially those opposed to reform—ranted that majority rule equaled mob rule. Thus supporters of the new constitutional plan had to explain how a society could give government authority to a majority without fear that it would trample on minority rights. Madison explained: "To secure the public good and private rights against the danger of . . . a [majority] faction, and

---

*In an earlier version of this passage, delivered at the Convention in defense of the Virginia Plan, Madison had added that those who owned slaves and those who did not had distinct and antithetical interests. He may well have omitted this reference to slavery here because it had proved controversial with southern delegates. After all, this is a public argument intended to persuade readers to support adoption of the Constitution.

at the same time to preserve the spirit and the form of popular government, is then the great object to which our inquiries are directed."

Parting ways with some of the leading political philosophers of his era, Madison dismisses direct democracy as the solution:

> There is nothing to check the inducements to sacrifice the weaker party or an obnoxious individual. Hence it is that such democracies have ever been spectacles of turbulence and contention; have ever been found incompatible with personal security or the rights of property; and have in general been as short in their lives as they have been violent in their deaths.

So much for town meetings.

Madison contends that the republican form of government, in which elected representatives are delegated responsibility for making governmental decisions, addresses the tyranny of the majority problem in two ways. First, representation dilutes the factious spirit. Madison does not trust politicians to be more virtuous than their constituents, but he recognizes that, to get elected, they will tend to moderate their views to appeal to a diverse constituency. Here Madison subtly introduces his *size principle*, on which the rest of the argument hinges: up to a point, the larger and more diverse the constituency, the more diluted is the influence of any particular faction on the preferences of the representative.

A legislature composed of representatives elected from districts, each containing diverse interests, is unlikely to allow a faction or a small coalition of them to so dominate the institution that it can deny rights to factions in the minority. This line of reasoning allows Madison to introduce a second distinct virtue of a republic. Unlike a direct democracy, it can advantageously encompass a large population and a large territory. As Madison argues,

> Extend the sphere, and you take in a greater variety of parties and interests; you make it less probable that a majority of the whole will have a common motive to invade the rights of other citizens; or if such a common motive exists, it will be more difficult for all who feel it to discover their own strength and to act in unison with each other.

In other words, their differences will pose a benign collective action problem. Any attempted collusion would confront such steep transaction costs that any efforts to engage in mischief would inevitably be frustrated.

What has Madison accomplished here? He has turned the Antifederalists' "small is beautiful" mantra on its head by pointing out that an encompassing national government would be less susceptible to the influence of factions than would state governments: "A rage for paper money, for an abolition of debts, for an equal division of property, or for any other improper or wicked project, would be less apt to pervade the whole body of the Union than a particular member of it." A geographically large republic would encompass dispersed, diverse populations, thereby imposing serious transaction costs on their representatives in maintaining a majority coalition and minimizing the prospect of majority tyranny. Madison concludes: "In the extent and proper structure of the Union, therefore, we behold a republican remedy for the disease most incident to republican government."

Until the twentieth century, *Federalist* No. 10 attracted less attention than did some of its companion essays. Yet as the nation has grown in size and diversity, the essay won new prominence for the prescience with which Madison explained how such growth strengthens the republic. This Madisonian view of democracy often is referred to as **pluralism**. It welcomes society's numerous diverse interests and generally endorses the idea that those competing interests most affected by a public policy will have the greatest say in what the policy will be.

## *Federalist* No. 51

By giving free expression to all of society's diversity, *Federalist* No. 10 offers an essentially organic solution to the danger of majority tyranny. *Federalist* No. 51, by contrast, takes a more mechanistic approach of separating government officers into different branches and giving them the authority to interfere with each other's actions. The authority of each branch must "be made commensurate to the danger of attack," Madison asserts. As for incentive: "Ambition must be made to counteract ambition. The interest of the man must be connected with the constitutional rights of the place." In other words, the Framers' efforts will have failed if future generations of politicians do not jealously defend the integrity of their offices.

Because popular election is the supreme basis for legitimacy and independence in a democracy, no constitutional contrivances can place appointive offices on an equal footing with elective offices. Madison explains:

> In republican government, the legislative authority necessarily predominates. The remedy for this inconvenience is to divide the legislature into different branches; and to render them, by different modes of election and different principles of action, as little connected with each other as the nature of their common functions and their common dependence on the society will admit.

Bicameralism is intended to weaken the legislature's capacity to act too quickly and impulsively, but even so it may not prevent the legislature from encroaching on the other branches. Madison offers the president's veto as a strong countervailing force and speculates that, by refusing to override the president's veto, the Senate might team up with the executive to keep the popularly elected House of Representatives in check. Madison even finds virtue in the considerable prerogatives reserved to the states: "In a compound republic of America, the power surrendered by the people is first divided between two distinct governments. . . . Hence a double security arises to the rights of the people. The different governments will control each other, at the same time that each will be controlled by itself."

Could this be the same James Madison who wanted to abandon the Convention rather than agree to a Senate elected by the state legislatures, the same man who had wanted Congress to have an absolute veto over state actions? Madison's Virginia Plan had vested ultimate authority in a popularly elected national legislature, and this model of a legislature became the House of Representatives. So why is he commending a Constitution that severely constrains this institution's influence over policy?

Madison probably was playing to his audience.[13] *Federalist* No. 51 seeks to reassure those fence-sitters listening to Antifederalist propaganda that the Constitution would take a giant step down the short path to tyranny. After all, the Antifederalists were presenting the specter of a powerful and remote national government and, within it, the possible emergence of a junta composed of unelected senators and an indirectly elected president bent on usurping the authority of the states, undermining the one popularly elected branch of government (the House of Representatives), and ultimately subjugating the citizenry. Madison is countering with a portrait of a weak, fragmented system that appears virtually incapable of purposive action, much less of hatching plots. He must have grimaced as he (anonymously) drafted the passage extolling the Constitution's checks on his House of Representatives.

In summary, *Federalist* No. 10 conveys the theory of pluralism that guided the Constitution's chief architect; *Federalist* No. 51 explores how and why the governmental system that emerged from the political process in Philadelphia might actually work. Since these essays were written, Madison's insight into the operation of the Constitution has been largely borne out.

Both the pluralism of competing interests and separated institutions have been judged less favorably by many modern students of American politics. With authority so fragmented, they argue, government cannot function effectively. And by adding a layer of institutional fragmentation on top of pluralism, the Framers simply overdid it. The result is an inherently conservative political process in which legitimate majorities are frequently frustrated by some minority faction that happens to control a critical lever of government. Furthermore, if the logic of *Federalist* No. 10 is correct, Americans do not need all of this constitutional architecture of checks and balances to get the job done. Critics also point to the many other stable democracies throughout the world that function well with institutions designed to allow majorities to govern effectively. Would Madison have privately agreed with this critique? Probably so—after all, his Virginia Plan incorporated those checks and balances necessary to foster the healthy competition of factions and no more.

## Designing Institutions for Collective Action: The Framers' Tool Kit

The careful attention that Madison gave to the design of Congress and the presidency in order to channel politics into a productive course preoccupied everyone at the Constitutional Convention. What constitutional arrangements will allow future generations to stand the best chance of solving their collective problems with the least conformity costs or risk of falling into tyranny? Clearly the majority of delegates recognized the need for institutions that could act more decisively but they feared equally of establishing one that might someday intrude too far into their private lives. This latter concern explains why so many delegates who subsequently attended their states' ratification conventions favored adding a Bill of Rights to limit the ability of national majorities to demand religious and political conformity.

In devising the several branches of the national government and its relations with the states, the Framers relied on design principles that instituted varying trade-offs between the transaction and conformity costs introduced in the last chapter to fit the purposes of the institutions they were creating. And they sought balance—keeping the branches in "their proper orbits"—so that none would gradually gain a permanent advantage over the others.

By intent, the Constitution provides only a general framework for government. As its institutions have evolved over the past two centuries, the same design principles have shaped their subsequent development. Consequently, the principles summarized in Table 2.3 are just

**TABLE 2.3**   The Framers' Tool Kit

| DESIGN PRINCIPLE | DEFINING FEATURE | EXAMPLE |
| --- | --- | --- |
| Command | Authority to dictate others' actions | President's commander-in-chief authority |
| Veto | Authority to block a proposal or stop an action | President's veto; Senate confirmation of the president's appointments; judicial review |
| Agenda control | Authority to place proposals before others for their decision, as well as preventing proposals from being considered | Congress presenting enrolled bill to president; congressional committees' recommendations to the full chamber |
| Voting rules | Rules prescribing who votes and the minimum number of votes required to accept a proposal or elect a candidate | Supreme Court decisions; Electoral College; selection of the Speaker of the House of Representatives |
| Delegation | Authority to assign an agent responsibility to act on your behalf | Representation, bureaucracy |

as useful for dissecting the internal organization of the modern House of Representatives as they are for studying the Framers' plan. The Framers' tool kit informs our analyses throughout the text—especially those chapters that delve into the logic of the governmental system.*

## Command

This refers to the authority of one actor to prescribe the actions of another. Unlike the other design concepts presented here, **command** is unilateral. It cuts through both coordination and prisoner's dilemma problems by allowing one of the actors to impose a solution or policy. Command certainly achieves efficiencies in reducing transaction costs, but it does so by imposing potentially huge conformity costs on those who prefer some other policy or course of action. For decades, Cuba's Fidel Castro banned whole genres of music from the radio. For

*We do not present this list of design principles as exhaustive. One can think of other principles—such as the principles in the Bill of Rights prohibiting certain classes of government actions—but we do find that the tool kit's principles are indispensable for understanding how America's political institutions work the way they do.

Hobbes (see box "Hobbes on Monarchs," page 18), the command authority conferred (by God, or so they liked to argue!) prevented society from deteriorating into anarchy.*

The Framers, and republican theorists before them, sought other institutional arrangements that would enable efficiency yet minimize the conformity costs imposed by command. Consequently, "command" was rarely used in designing the Constitution. The only provision (Article II, Section 2) that comes close makes the president "the *commander* in chief of the army and navy." The military, then and now, is the one component of government designed to place a premium on action over deliberation. Hence, the authority to issue commands flows down the military branches' "command structure." Any squad member under enemy fire can appreciate the value of not having others in the unit calculating whether to cover for their buddies or to engage in free riding.

During this era of divided party control of government in Washington, presidents have increasingly relied on *executive orders* to change or implement a policy. Historically, executive orders were authorized by Congress. In the late nineteenth century presidents were given the authority to unilaterally expand the types of federal jobs (e.g., letter carriers) that would fall under the newly created civil services system. The president issued an executive order according to the law's provisions; it would stay in place unless it was rescinded by an act of Congress. In recent times presidents have invoked an implicit, and consequently somewhat vague, authority that comes with their constitutional status as the nation's chief executive. Although executive orders give presidents the opportunity to act unilaterally, they do not fully qualify as "commands" because the judiciary can (and is willing to) rescind the order when it decides that a president's action exceeded the office's implicit executive authority. This is precisely what happened with President Obama's order temporarily blocking deportation of undocumented parents of children who are American citizens and additionally giving them work permits. We return to this case and numerous others when considering the modern presidency in Chapter 5. The president may be the supreme commander, but the Framers made sure any pretense of command authority ends there.

BORN TO COMMAND.

OF VETO MEMORY.

HAD I BEEN CONSULTED.

KING ANDREW THE FIRST.

Library of Congress

Widely published in opposition Whig newspapers, this cartoon depicts President Andrew Jackson trampling on the Constitution and public works legislation. However imperiously Jackson dealt with the opposition-controlled Congress and the Supreme Court, whose decisions he selectively ignored, the veto in his left hand hardly sufficed to allow him "to rule" the country.

---

*Moreover, Hobbes argued that in monarchies, the inherited right to rule was not just necessary but also salutary; monarchs had a long-term stake in their subjects' prosperity in order to maximize their own power and prosperity.

Vivid evidence of their success appears in outgoing president Harry Truman's prediction about his successor, army general Dwight Eisenhower: "He'll sit here, and he'll say, 'Do this! Do that!' And nothing will happen. Poor Ike—it won't be a bit like the Army. He'll find it very frustrating."*

## Veto

The **veto** embodies the right of an official or institution to say no to a proposal from another official or institution. Like command, the veto is unilateral, allowing its possessors to impose their views regardless of the preferences of others. Yet it is far less potent than command because of one critical difference: it is a "negative" or blocking action that preserves the status quo.[†] The veto confers little direct advantage in shifting government policy, but in Chapter 7 we find that a president's threat to use it may induce Congress to address the president's objections as it prepares legislation. Moreover, the blocking effects of the veto can be limited by providing those subject to a veto the means of circumventing it. After weighing the pros and cons of giving the president an absolute veto, the Framers backed off and added an override provision. With a two-thirds vote in each chamber, the House of Representatives and Senate can enact a vetoed bill without the president's endorsement. A policy that withstands the huge transaction costs entailed in mustering supermajorities in both chambers has demonstrated its merits and deserves enactment despite the president.[‡]

The president's veto is the only explicit use of this instrument in the Constitution, but the Constitution implicitly creates other important veto relationships. Both the House of Representatives and the Senate must agree to identical legislation before it can proceed to the president's desk for his signature (or veto). In effect, then, each legislative chamber holds a veto over the legislation emanating from the other chamber. Yet another unnamed veto resides with the Supreme Court. Shortly after the new government was launched, the Supreme Court claimed the power of *judicial review*, asserting its authority to overturn public laws and executive actions it deemed unconstitutional. (We discuss fully this important "discovered" authority in Chapter 9.) The greater the number of veto holders, the higher the transaction costs in making new policy. Consequently, with its numerous veto holders, the American political system deserves its reputation as being inherently conservative.

## Agenda Control

This refers to the right of an actor to set choices for others. The choices might concern legislation, proposed regulations, or any other decision presented to a collectivity. Political parties nominate candidates who define the choices available to voters on Election Day. Those who exercise **agenda control** gain both positive and negative influence over collective decisions.

---

*According to most contemporary observers, Eisenhower's experiences in office bore out Truman's prediction. According to one description of Ike's sixth year in office, "The President still feels that when he has decided something, that *ought* to be the end of it . . . and when it bounces back undone or done wrong, he tends to react with shocked surprise." Richard E. Neustadt, *Presidential Power and the Modern Presidents* (New York: Wiley, 1960), 10.

[†]In fact, many of the Constitution's Framers referred to the veto as a "negative."

[‡]All state governors possess some form of veto over legislation; many of these vetoes differ significantly from the president's in allowing the governor to veto parts of bills and flexibility in appropriating expenditures less than those prescribed in the legislation.

On the positive side, an agenda setter can introduce a choice to the collectivity—a senator proposing an amendment to a bill under consideration, for example—which then decides to accept or reject it. Where everyone enjoys this right—when, say, any fellow senator can offer an amendment to any colleague's proposal—access to the agenda will be of little consequence in explaining collective decisions. Agenda control becomes consequential in settings where some members of the group exercise proposal power and others do not. Congress presents the president with a bill that he must sign or veto. This is an example of strong agenda control. For an example of weaker agenda control, many state governors can reduce but not increase spending in an appropriation bill sent to them by the state legislature.

Consider the advantage this right confers. The agenda setter can propose a course of action, leaving other participants the more limited authority to accept or reject. The agenda controller thus *limits* the choices available to the collectivity. Unlike the Senate, where proposal rights are universal, the House has long been governed by rules that empower leaders to set the choices members will vote on. Leaders determine what, if any, amendments will be allowed, and limit the time available for debating alternatives. This procedural authority can have huge consequences. In fact, it probably led to that chamber's impeachment of President Bill Clinton in 1998. In late fall 1998 the Republican-controlled Judiciary Committee sent to the floor articles of impeachment against President Clinton. Republican floor leaders faced a potential problem. They favored impeaching the president as well, but they were fairly certain that a majority of members did not favor this drastic course. Republicans held only a nine-vote majority overall. Moreover, with Democrats appearing unified in opposing impeachment, four to six Republicans informed their leaders that they preferred a softer punishment—specifically, a resolution censuring President Clinton—to impeachment. Yet the Republican leadership's agenda control held a trump card that guaranteed their ultimate success. With the authority to decide which proposals would be available for the members to vote on, the leadership disallowed censure motions and forced Republican fence-sitters to decide between impeachment and no action. In the end the fence-sitters joined their colleagues, and on a nearly perfect party-line vote, the House of Representatives impeached the president, even though a majority of the membership preferred censure.[14] House members confer so much power on their leaders and knowingly bear heavy conformity costs because in the absence of agenda control the transaction costs would be unmanageable. Without leaders orchestrating the chamber's decisions, the institution would be at the mercy of its 435 members—each, like their colleagues in the smaller Senate, jealously protecting and exercising his or her right to offer any bill or amendment at any time.

To appreciate how the solution to some issues appears to require agenda control authority, Congress has from time to time passed laws giving presidents **fast-track authority** to negotiate trade agreements to bring to Congress for its approval. To give the president credibility when negotiating with other governments (and with various industries), Congress ties its hands by limiting itself to either approval or disapproval. And if it does neither by a certain deadline, the president's proposal becomes law. Some have proposed that a good way to break gridlock in Washington would be to give presidents this kind of authority across the board.[15]

## Voting Rules

Any government that aspires to democracy must allow diverse interests to be expressed in government policy. When members of a collectivity share decision-making authority, the outcomes are determined by some previously agreed-to **voting rule**. The most prominent option in classical democratic theory is **majority rule**. Normally this term refers to a **simple majority**, or one-half plus one.

Majority rule embodies the hallowed democratic principle of political equality. Equality requires that each citizen's vote carries the same weight and offers all citizens the same opportunity to participate in the nation's civic life. When all votes count the same, majority rule becomes an obvious principle: when disagreements arise, the more widely shared preference should prevail.

Yet majority rule offers no magic balance between transaction and conformity costs. It is just one possible constitutional rule midway between dictatorship and consensus. Governments controlled by popular majorities are less likely to engage in *tyranny*—that is, impose very high conformity costs—than are dictatorships, but this knowledge did not fully reassure the Constitution's Framers. Worried about tyranny by the majority, they carefully constructed institutions that would temper transient passions of majorities in the new government. Separation of powers with checks and balances, two concepts we examine in detail in the next chapter; different term lengths for members of the House and Senate, the president, and federal judges; and explicit provision for states' rights all make it difficult for majorities to take charge of the new government.

Although majority rule figures prominently in the Constitution, it is explicitly required in only a few instances. Almost all popular vote elections require the winner to receive not a majority, but simply a **plurality** of the votes cast—that is, more votes than received by any of the other candidates. A majority of the Electoral College is required to elect the president, and a quorum, a majority of the membership of the House of Representatives, must be present before the House can conduct business. Much of what the government does requires action by Congress, which, the Framers seemed to assume, would conduct its business by majority vote.

Voting Rules of the U.S. Senate*

| MOTION | VOTING RULE |
|---|---|
| Passage of ordinary bills and amendments | Simple majority of members present and voting |
| Rule 22 (cloture to set time limit on debate) | Three-fifths of the full Senate (normally sixty votes) |
| Veto override | Two-thirds of members present and voting |
| Unanimous consent to take up legislation out of turn | Unanimous agreement of members present |

*These rules are fully explained in Chapter 6.

Yet the Constitution permits or tacitly authorizes other voting rules. The Constitution leaves it to the states to specify rules electing members of Congress, and states almost always have preferred the plurality rule (the candidate receiving the most votes, regardless of whether the plurality reaches a majority) in deciding winners. Elsewhere in the Constitution supermajorities of various amounts are required. If the president vetoes a bill passed by both houses of Congress, two-thirds of the House and of the Senate must vote to override the veto, or the bill is defeated. And in another example of steep transaction costs, three-quarters of the states must agree to any amendments to the Constitution.

## Delegation

When individuals or groups authorize others to make and implement decisions for them, **delegation** occurs. Every time Americans go to the polls, they *delegate* to representatives the responsibility for making collective decisions for them. Similarly, members of the House of Representatives elect leaders empowered to orchestrate their chamber's business, thereby reducing coordination and other costs of collective action. The House also delegates the task of drafting legislation to standing committees, which are more manageable subsets of members. As in this instance, decisions are frequently delegated in order to control their transaction costs.

Social scientists who analyze delegation note that **principals**, those who possess decision-making authority, may delegate their authority to **agents**, who then exercise it on behalf of the principals. Every spring, millions of Americans hire agents—say, H&R Block—to fill out their tax forms for them and, they hope, save them some money. Similarly, the president (principal) appoints hundreds of staff members (agents) to monitor and promote the administration's interests within the bureaucracy and on Capitol Hill. We use these terms to identify and illuminate a variety of important political relationships that involve some form of delegation.

Delegation is so pervasive because it addresses common collective action problems. It is indispensable whenever special expertise is required to make and carry out sound decisions. The vast and complex federal bureaucracy requires a full chapter (Chapter 8) to describe and explain—because Congress has pursued so many diverse public policies and delegated their implementation to agencies. A legislature could not possibly administer its policies directly without tying itself in knots. The Continental Congress's failed attempts to directly supply Washington's army during the Revolutionary War, resulting in the chronically inadequate provision of essential supplies to the troops, provided a lesson not lost on the delegates to the Constitutional Convention in Philadelphia two decades later.

Beyond the need for technical expertise, majorities may sometimes find it desirable politically to delegate decisions. For example, the government allocates space on the frequency band to prevent radio or television stations from interfering with each other's signals. In 1934 Congress stopped allocating frequencies itself, leaving decisions instead to the five members of the Federal Communications Commission. Congress had learned early that assigning frequencies was difficult and politically unrewarding, for its decisions were regularly greeted with charges of favoritism or worse. Congress therefore delegated such decisions to a body of experts while retaining the authority to pass new laws that could override the commission's decisions. Thus Congress retains the ultimate authority to set the nation's technical broadcasting policies when it chooses to exercise it.

Finally, almost all enforcement authority—the key to solving prisoner's dilemmas of all types—involves delegation to a policing agent. It might be the Internal Revenue Service (IRS), the Securities and Exchange Commission, the Equal Employment Opportunity Commission, or any of the hundreds of other federal, state, and local agencies that make sure that individuals abide by their collective agreements.

Delegation solves some problems for a collectivity, but it introduces others. A principal runs the risk that its agents will use their authority to serve their own rather than the principal's interest. The discrepancy between what a principal would ideally like its agents to do and what they actually do is called **agency loss**. Agency losses might arise "accidentally" by incompetence or the principal's failure to communicate goals clearly. Or losses might reflect the inherent differences between the goals of a principal and its agents. A principal wants its agents to be exceedingly diligent in protecting its interests while asking for very little in return. Agents, on the other hand, prefer to be generously compensated for minimal effort. The balance in most principal–agent relationships lies on a continuum between these extremes. Mild examples of agency loss include various forms of shirking, or "slacking off." Our agents in the legislature might attend to their own business rather than to the public's, nod off in committee meetings, or accept Super Bowl tickets or golf vacations from someone who wants a special favor. Citizens warily appreciate the opportunities available to their agents in Washington to "feather their own nest." So voters are quick to respond to information, typically from opponents who covet the job, suggesting that the incumbent is not serving constituents well. Members of Congress who miss more than a few roll-call votes usually do so at their peril.

So how can a principal determine whether its agents are being faithful when it cannot observe or understand their actions? Car owners face a similar problem when an auto mechanic says the strange engine noise will require replacement of an obscure part costing a month's pay. How do owners know whether to trust the mechanic, especially because they know the mechanic's financial interest clashes with theirs? They could get a second opinion, investigate the mechanic's reputation, or learn more about cars and check for themselves, but all these solutions take time and energy. Governments use all of these techniques and others to minimize agency loss. **Whistle-blower laws** generously reward members of the bureaucracy who report instances of malfeasance. Governments can create an agent who monitors the performance of other agents. Congress has created about eighty inspectors general offices within the federal bureaucracy to check and report to the president and Congress on agency failures to perform assigned duties faithfully and honestly. Delegation always entails a trade-off between the benefits of having the agent take care of decisions on the principal's behalf and the costs associated with the risks that agents will pursue their own interests.

A virulent form of agency loss occurs when the agent turns its delegated authority against the principal. This possible scenario arises when principals provide agents with the coercive authority to ward off external threats or to discourage free riding. What prevents these agents—the police, the army, the IRS, the FBI, and many others—from exploiting their advantage not only to enrich but also to entrench themselves by preventing challenges to their authority? Certainly many have. World history—indeed, current affairs—is rife with news of military takeovers, secret police, rigged elections, imprisoned opponents, ethnic cleansing, and national treasuries drained into Swiss bank accounts. Institutions created to minimize transaction costs may, as the trade-off indicates, impose unacceptably high conformity costs.

## Assessing the Constitution's Performance in Today's American Politics

America's polarized politics poses several challenges for America's Constitutional system. One is **gridlock**, the inability of the House of Representatives, the Senate, and the president to agree on new policies. Even when all agree that a government program is broken, all too often there appears to be little prospect that it will soon be fixed. In large part, of course, gridlock in addressing universally recognized problems simply reflects the fact that Americans and their representatives disagree on a solution. Everyone appears to dislike the nation's current immigration policy, but with solutions ranging from "build a wall" to dismantling the Immigration and Customs Enforcement (ICE), there is little prospect of agreement on any new policy.

But gridlock also results from a more fundamental difficulty in reaching collective decisions. Our constitutional system intentionally disperses government authority. Separation of powers and federalism necessitate broad agreement among officeholders across the different branches in order for new policies to be successfully enacted and subsequently implemented. And by adding a layer of institutional fragmentation on top of pluralism, the Framers simply overdid it. The result is an inherently conservative political process. The president, the House of Representatives, and the Senate all hold a veto over new laws, and if they agree, the federal judiciary typically is invited by the disgruntled loser to weigh in and declare the policy unconstitutional. Those opposed to the policy need only prevail in one of those institutions to veto a new policy.

The Framers intentionally left unstated important aspects about how government should work on a daily basis. As a result we are still working through whether separation of powers and checks and balances allow government officials the discretion to pursue a course of action they claim they have the authority to do. Was Obama's executive order protecting "Dreamers" from deportation constitutional? (As of the end of 2018, the courts were still pondering the answer.) Can a president to whom the Constitution assigns broad pardon power pardon himself or even be indicted for a crime? (President Trump emphatically says he can pardon himself, and his Justice Department claims that separation of powers prevents such an indictment while the president remains in office.)

Today, trying to figure out what the Constitution permits and prohibits its government officials from doing occupies much of the waking hours of numerous politicians, judges, and lawyers. Divided party control of government in Washington finds presidents acting unilaterally, testing the boundaries of their authority. Not only will the opposition party in Congress challenge their actions, so too will the thoroughly "red" (aka Republican) and thoroughly "blue" (aka Democratic) states challenge objectionable polices in federal courts. The recent separation-of-powers controversies listed in Table 2.4 illustrate the scope of this disagreement. This list could have easily been twice as long.

The familiar issues summarized in the table share a couple of features that one finds generally. All seek to rein in presidents in some way. Typically, this involves challenging a policy or

**TABLE 2.4**   Recent Separation-of-Powers Issues

| | DESCRIPTION |
|---|---|
| **DACA (Obama)** | After several failed attempts to pass immigration reform stalled in Congress, President Obama issued an executive memorandum in 2012 establishing the Deferred Action for Childhood Arrivals (DACA) program. DACA exempts eligible recipients—most of whom arrived in the United States as children under the age of 10—from deportation for renewable two-year terms. Republicans argued that the president was usurping authority over the nation's immigration policy. In 2014, the Republican governors of twenty-six states sued in federal court and won an injunction to stop efforts to expand DACA to cover more people and to create a comparable deferred action program for the parents of DACA recipients. In a 4–4 decision, the Supreme Court left the injunction in place. |
| **DACA (Trump)** | The Trump administration rescinded DACA in September 2017, subjecting program recipients to the risk of deportation after their permits expired. The Regents of the University of California successfully sued in district court to block Trump's rescission. The Supreme Court refused to hear an extraordinary appeal from that ruling, leaving the program in place as the federal courts considered the appeal from the Department of Justice. A federal district court in New York similarly ruled that DACA recipients could renew their exemptions. Meanwhile, a district court judge in Texas refused to grant the State of Texas a national injunction against DACA—although the judge noted that Texas had demonstrated the legal merits of its case. The future of DACA thus remains uncertain as the case approaches eventual Supreme Court resolution. |

*(Continued)*

(Continued)

| | DESCRIPTION |
|---|---|
| **CFPB** | In 2010 Congress created the Consumer Financial Protection Bureau (CFPB) to protect consumers from financial institutions' abusive or fraudulent practices. Wary of the industry's strenuous opposition to the agency's mission, proponents designed CFPB to insulate it from future attacks. It set up CFPB as an independent agency (we examine this type of agency in Chapter 8) headed by a single director appointed for a fixed term and removable only for cause. Moreover, the agency is funded by another independent agency, the Federal Reserve, and consequently does not depend on congressional appropriations. Critics allege that the CFPB is unconstitutionally unaccountable. The DC Circuit Court of Appeals disagreed in January 2018, holding that the structure of the CFPB satisfied constitutional requirements. However, a district court in New York contradicts the DC Circuit Court. This decision could foreshadow conflicting appellate court rulings and an eventual Supreme Court decision. |
| **Muslim Ban** | In January 2017, the Trump administration suspended all travel from seven countries, all but one of which hosted majority Muslim populations. After a district court ruled the order discriminatory, the administration replaced it with a new order modifying the targeted countries and emphasizing the national security implications. After losing again in several federal court rulings, the Supreme Court rescued the ban by holding that the president's order fell within his constitutional authority. |
| **Sanctuary Cities** | Many cities in California and other states with large undocumented populations have instituted rules and procedures to shield undocumented people from deportation. Among other things, they require local law enforcement to not cooperate with federal immigration authorities. Trump's Justice Department responded by blocking federal law enforcement grants to sanctuary cities. Chicago, Los Angeles, San Francisco, and other cities immediately went to federal court to challenge the administration's policy as unconstitutional. Thus far (as of January 2019), they have won each district and appellate court decision, but the administration has appealed these rulings to the Supreme Court. |
| **Firing Federal Employees** | Donald Trump issued an executive order in May 2018 tightening work and performance rules for federal employees. The administration called for sharp reductions in the time given to poor performers to improve before facing termination, as well as making it more difficult for them to appeal performance evaluations. Employee unions challenged the order in court with a federal district judge who agreed with them and instructed federal agencies to ignore the president's order. |

### for CQ Press

**Want a better grade?**

Get the tools you need to sharpen your study skills. Access practice quizzes, eFlashcards, video, and multimedia at **edge.sagepub.com/kernell9e.**

action in court. In the case of the law creating the CFPB, legislators sought to insulate the agency from some future president's control. It too ended up in federal courts. We return to these and similar cases throughout the book. The point here is simply that these and numerous other uncertainties about the boundaries of each branch's authority have been present since the founding of the United States. They are surfacing now because of partisan polarization in Washington and across the country.

# KEY TERMS

agency loss   85
agenda control   81
agent   84
Antifederalists   70
Articles of Confederation   46
bicameral legislature   44
Bill of Rights   63
checks and balances   58
command   79
commerce clause   57
confederation   46
Declaration of Independence   46
delegation   84
Electoral College   62

faction   74
fast-track authority   82
Federalists   70
Great Compromise   61
gridlock   86
home rule   40
judicial review   62
logroll   66
majority rule   83
nationalists   52
necessary and proper clause   57
New Jersey Plan   55
nullification   73
pluralism   77

plurality   83
popular sovereignty   53
principal   84
Shays's Rebellion   50
simple majority   83
states' rights   55
supermajority   60
supremacy clause   62
"take care" clause   60
veto   81
Virginia Plan   54
voting rule   83
whistle-blower laws   85

# SUGGESTED READINGS

Draper, Theodore. *A Struggle for Power: The American Revolution.* New York: Times Books, 1996. According to Draper, the Revolution represented the politics of self-interest rather than ideology. His account also examines the greater political context of the Revolution, in particular the long-standing conflict between the French and the British.

Howell, William G. and Terry M. Moe. *Relic: How Our Constitution Undermines Effective Government.* New York: Basic Books, 2006. The authors propose a constitutional solution to Washington's chronic gridlock by shifting agenda control from Congress to the president. Specifically, the president would propose laws that Congress could vote up or down. If it failed to do either within a fixed time period, the president's proposal would become law.

Ketcham, Ralph. *James Madison: A Biography.* Charlottesville: University Press of Virginia, 1990. An authoritative and highly readable biography of America's first political scientist.

Miller, William Lee. *The Business of May Next: James Madison and the Founding.* Charlottesville: University Press of Virginia, 1992. An absorbing account of the politics leading up to and at the Constitutional Convention. This history served as the chief source of the account reported in this chapter.

Norton, Mary Beth. *Liberty's Daughters.* Boston: Little, Brown, 1980. A systematic and persuasive assessment of the considerable behind-the-scenes contribution of women during the Revolution and the impact of the war on the transformation of family relationships.

Riker, William. *The Strategy of Rhetoric.* New Haven, CT: Yale University Press, 1996. A lively yet keenly analytical and systematic account of the Constitution's ratification as a political campaign.

Wills, Garry. *Explaining America.* New York: Doubleday, 1981. An analysis of the logic and ideas of *The Federalist.* Few authors can match Wills's talent for rendering abstract concepts and ideas intelligible to the general audience.

Wood, Gordon S. *The Creation of the American Republic, 1776–1787.* New York: Norton, 1969. An indispensable intellectual history of the transformation of America from the Revolution through the adoption of the Constitution.

## REVIEW QUESTIONS

1. What steps were taken to construct a national government before the Articles of Confederation? What resulted from these steps?

2. How were decisions made under the Articles? What sorts of decisions were not made by the confederation? How did this system affect the war effort? How did it affect the conduct of the national and state governments once the war was over?

3. Why is the Electoral College so complicated?

4. How did the Framers balance the powers and independence of the executive and legislative branches?

5. Discuss how the coordination and transaction costs for states changed when the national government moved from the Articles of Confederation to the Constitution.

6. What are principals and agents? When in your life have you been one or the other?

7. What mechanisms for constitutional amendment were included in the Constitution? Why were multiple methods included?

Pro-immigrant protesters in California made an explicit appeal to states' rights in 2018 when they called on Attorney General Jeff Sessions to stay out of California's sanctuary state law. An irony of this defense of the law, which restricts state and local law enforcement officials from cooperating with federal immigration officials, is that states' rights arguments were also advanced throughout much of America's history to stop the federal government from enforcing civil rights laws, environmental protections, and even the abolition of slavery.

# Federalism

# 3

On March 7, 2018, the federal government of the United States of America declared war against the sovereign state of California. At least that's how Golden State governor Jerry Brown, a Democrat, characterized the speech that Attorney General Jeff Sessions gave to a gathering of law enforcement officials in Sacramento. Accusing the federal government of initiating a "reign of terror," Governor Brown announced that "this is basically going to war against the state of California." The rhetoric employed by Attorney General Sessions was no less overheated. Sessions accused state leaders of advancing the agendas of "radical extremists" and of passing "irrational, unfair, and unconstitutional policies."[1]

What issue so dramatically inflamed tensions between the nation's top law enforcement officer and the governor of its most populous state? The policy in question was the so-called "sanctuary state" bill that Governor Brown had signed in 2017, a law that prevented state and local law enforcement officials from carrying out the work of federal immigration authorities. The bill, authored by state senate leader Kevin de Leon, forbid police officers and sheriffs in the state from asking about a person's immigration status and put restrictions on how these officials could communicate with agents of the federal Immigration and Customs Enforcement (ICE) agency. In a compromise hammered out between the more moderate Brown and the liberal de Leon, when California police and sheriffs arrested an undocumented immigrant who had committed one of 800 serious or violent felonies, they could communicate and cooperate with ICE agents and transfer the arrested person. But if the immigrant was arrested for a lesser crime and due to be released, California officers could not hold the accused for transfer to ICE.

As if illegal immigration and crime were not hot-button issues enough, what truly elevated the tensions between California's leaders and the Trump administration was that the sanctuary state bill raised the question of where federal authority ends and where a state's power begins. Could Sacramento lawmakers even do this, in the face of opposition from Washington, D.C.? At stake in the controversy over the bill was the issue of *states' rights*, the perennial push and pull between America's state and federal governments that has been fought out on legal, political, and literal battlefields throughout our history. What policies should be entirely under the control of each state, and what issues should be governed by a single federal policy crafted in Washington, D.C.? This is the fundamental question of federalism. It has been debated since America's founding and at crucial points in our nation's development, with the sanctuary state bill and the sanctuary city laws that preceded it again providing an example of the legitimate arguments on both sides.

From the perspective of Attorney General Sessions and President Donald Trump, the ability to enforce a uniform set of laws was crucial to implementing a national immigration policy. After all, a strict approach to preventing illegal immigration was a central plank of Trump's campaign and helped win him the presidency. Being able to enforce a national plan all across the country was critical to controlling the nation's borders, they argued. If a city, county, or especially the nation's largest state provided sanctuary to those who did not immigrate legally, this would prevent the federal government from delivering the public good of strong borders. In the terms outlined in Chapter 1 of this book, this posed a collective action problem for Sessions and leaders in other states who wanted to prevent California from defecting from a national approach to illegal immigration. Of course, the attorney general framed his dilemma in more stark terms. "This state of lawlessness allows gangs to smuggle guns, drugs, and even humans across borders and around cities and communities," declared Sessions. "That makes a sanctuary city a trafficker, smuggler or gang member's best friend."[2]

California's leaders countered with a public safety argument of their own and with a claim that police and sheriffs employed by state and local governments should not be compelled to carry out federal policies. They pointed out that violent felons were not protected by the sanctuary laws and that victims or witnesses of crimes would be discouraged from reporting them if they feared that this would lead to deportation. State leaders also made the implicit argument that the federal government's solution to its collective action problem imposed conformity costs on California: being forced to spend state resources to enforce federal policies staunchly opposed by many of the state's voters essentially nationalized state and local law enforcement, against the will of the taxpayers who paid their salaries. The sanctuary state bill's author, Kevin de Leon, argued that the law "will prevent state and local law enforcement officers and resources from being commandeered by President Trump to enforce federal laws. Our undocumented neighbors will be able to interact with local law enforcement to report crimes and help in prosecutions without fear of deportation—and that will make our communities safer."[3]

The struggle between a national standard of immigration enforcement and states' rights to pass sanctuary laws was fought not just in political rhetoric but in a series of bills, executive orders, and high-profile court cases in the first years of the Trump administration. In the first week after he was inaugurated, President Trump issued an executive order withholding federal funding to any cities and counties that refused to cooperate fully with federal immigration agents. "These grants are not an entitlement," said Sessions, attempting to use federal grants as a carrot to compel state and local governments to adhere to federal policy (a strategy outlined later in this chapter). Rather than complying, Chicago and a group of other cities sued, arguing for states' rights. Soon after California passed its sanctuary state law, Sessions and the federal government sued, arguing for federal supremacy. And when Texas went in the opposite direction from California, passing a state law that prevented its cities from declaring themselves to be sanctuaries, cities sued Texas, arguing for their local right to diverge from national policy.

Fighting out a critical policy issue through a battle over states' right puts the sanctuary state policy controversy squarely in line with American political tradition. There are both immediate policy questions and long-standing governing principles underlying these debates. Consistent backers of states' rights have a philosophical commitment to the decentralization of authority, believing that it leads to greater governmental innovation and to a set of state policies that better represent the desires of each state's residents than a single, one-size-fits-all national policy. The proponents of federal power counter that the patchwork of policies created when states are free to do as they please makes it difficult to govern a nation where problems can spill over state lines as easily as Americans can drive across them. They point out that majority votes in states can often threaten the civil rights of minorities. The debate over exactly which powers should belong to the federal government and which are reserved to the states goes back to the very founding of the nation, as Chapter 2 illustrates. This conflict has been fought out at constitutional conventions, in courtrooms, and on the battlefields of the Civil War.

The idea of states' rights has been invoked by proponents of policies at both ends of the ideological spectrum. It is used as often to defend state gun control laws as it is to challenge the current federal preemption of many state abortion restrictions. Historically, states' rights arguments were wielded by the alcohol prohibition movement and, most shamefully, by defenders of slavery and the decades of state-sponsored racial segregation that soon followed slavery's abolition (see Chapter 4). Today, many liberals argue that states should have the right to allow medical or recreational marijuana. Arguments about the legitimacy of states' rights

Attorney General Jeff Sessions harshly criticized cities across the country that had declared themselves as sanctuaries for undocumented immigrants, preventing their local police officers from asking residents about their immigration status or from collaborating with Immigration and Customs Enforcement (ICE) agents. "That makes a sanctuary city a trafficker, smuggler, or gang member's best friend," Sessions warned.

Alex Wong/Getty Images

come down to the debate over whether state or national majorities should govern, and how far courts should go to protect the rights of minorities.

Even though the nation has grappled with these key questions of federalism for its entire history, the debate has never been completely resolved. The recent judicial battle over the constitutionality of President Obama's Patient Protection and Affordable Care Act (ACA), covered in greater depth in Chapter 7, was a fight over states' rights in which the national government won only a very limited victory. The Supreme Court's ruling in the landmark 2005 case *Gonzales v. Raich* upheld the supremacy of federal restrictions on medical marijuana over state laws, but states have continued to pass bills and propositions to relax access to pot ever since the decision was issued.

The ultimate arbiter in controversies of American federalism is the U.S. Supreme Court. Yet just because the federal judiciary decides whether national or state policy will prevail does not mean that Washington, D.C., always wins out. Chicago won in its initial case against the federal government, and in August 2018, judges in the U.S. Ninth Circuit Court of Appeals ruled in favor of cities and against the Trump administration's policy of threatening to withhold federal funds from sanctuary cities. The month before, California won an initial decision defending its sanctuary law. But Attorney General Sessions looked likely to appeal both cases, setting in place a longer legal battle over another high-stakes question of federalism. After losing one early decision that defended a sanctuary city law, President Trump tweeted "See you in the Supreme Court!"

## American-Style Federalism

In a federal system, the constitution divides authority between two or more distinct levels of government. For example, the system in the United States divides the national (federal) government and the states.* **Federalism** is a hybrid arrangement that mixes elements of a *confederation*, in which lower-level governments possess primary authority, and **unitary government**, in which the national government monopolizes constitutional authority, as shown in Figure 3.1.

Before adopting a federal system in the Constitution, the nation experienced first a unitary government and then a confederation. The decision by the distant British government to impose a central, unitary authority to tax and administer the subordinate colonies precipitated the American War of Independence. After the war, the citizens of the newly independent states reacted to the colonial experience by rejecting unitary authority in favor of a confederation in which smaller state governments held ultimate power. But because the Articles of Confederation failed to give the national government any enforcement authority, the individual states could, and did, ignore legislation from Congress that they did not like. Consequently, the national government accomplished little.

---

*In this text and elsewhere, the terms *federal* and *national* are used interchangeably. This practice also characterized discussions leading to the formation of the Union. Any difference in usage was largely a matter of stress—that is, *federal* reflected the user's cognizance of the state elements also present in the national government. Hans Sperber and Travis Trittschuh, *American Political Terms* (Detroit, MI: Wayne State University Press, 1962), 148–149.

■ **FIGURE 3.1**   Comparing Three Systems of Government

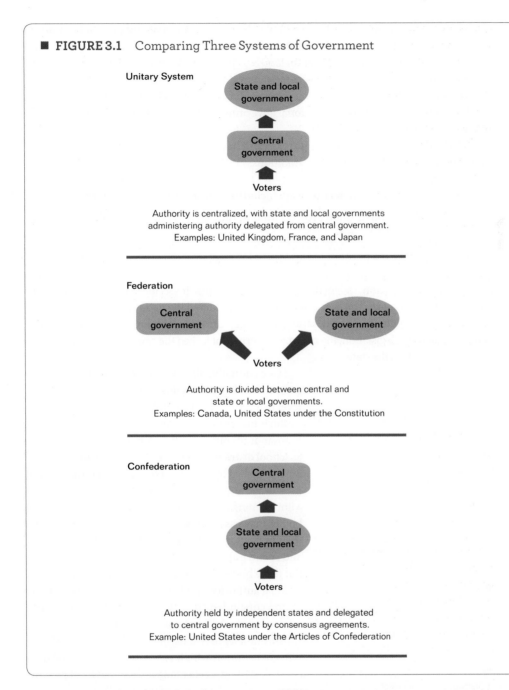

Unitary System

Authority is centralized, with state and local governments
administering authority delegated from central government.
Examples: United Kingdom, France, and Japan

Federation

Authority is divided between central and
state or local governments.
Examples: Canada, United States under the Constitution

Confederation

Authority held by independent states and delegated
to central government by consensus agreements.
Example: United States under the Articles of Confederation

Across the world, unitary governments are far more common than federations and confederations combined. Under unitary systems, the lower-level governmental entities—such as counties and metropolitan districts in Britain and departments in France—are created by and ultimately depend on the national government for authority and resources. Typically, the central government establishes national policies, raises money, and distributes funds to the local units to carry these policies out. However deliberative and authoritative these subnational units may appear, they function largely as part of the administrative apparatus of the national government. A unitary government may decentralize its power by delegating some decisions and administration to a lower government entity, but even so the constitutional system remains unitary because the national government retains ultimate authority to alter or rescind this delegation.

In a federal system, however, a government has constitutional relations across levels, interactions that satisfy three general conditions:

- The same people and territory are included in both levels of government.
- The nation's constitution protects units at each level of government from encroachment by the other units.
- Each unit is in a position to exert some leverage over the other(s).[4]

The second condition, independence, is critical because it sets the stage for the third condition, mutual influence. The lack of independence rendered the national government impotent under the Articles of Confederation. With the states commanding a veto over the most important national legislation, the national government lacked the resources and authority to act independently of the states.

**TABLE 3.1**  Numerous Governments Constitute America's Federalism

| | |
|---|---|
| National | 1 |
| State | 50 |
| County | 3,031 |
| Municipal | 19,519 |
| Township or town | 16,360 |
| School district | 12,880 |
| Other special districts | 38,266 |
| Total | 90,056 |

Source: U.S. Census Bureau, 2012 Census of Governments, "Local Governments by Type and State: 2012," accessed at https://www.census.gov/programs-surveys/cog.html, September 2018.

Occasionally, observers of American federalism refer to local governments as if they were a separate level in a three-tiered federal system. This characterization is inaccurate. Local governments, which include thousands of counties, cities, and *special districts*—such as school districts, water boards, and port authorities—are established by the states (see Table 3.1). They are not mentioned anywhere in the Constitution. In providing a limited range of government services, local governing bodies may pass laws, worry each year about balancing their budgets, generate revenue through taxes and fees, and spend public money through their own agencies, but these bodies do not exercise independent, constitutional authority. In a famous decision, Judge John F. Dillon concluded "that the great weight of authority denies *in toto* the existence, in the absence of special constitutional provisions, of any inherent right of local self-government which is beyond [state] legislative control." Dillon's rule made it clear that local governments are mere "creatures of the state."[5]

State officials can and often do exercise their power to intervene in local affairs. They may determine matters as fundamental as the governing structures of cities, counties, and special districts; their taxation powers; and even their geographic boundaries. They can wield authority over local issues that are important to voters state-wide, as New York's state legislature did in early 2008 when its members halted New York City mayor Michael Bloomberg's plan to charge an $8 toll to drivers entering Manhattan during rush hours. State officials, such as the Alabama legislature in its 1880 session, can also intervene in areas as trivial as "prohibiting the sale, giving away, or otherwise disposing of, spirituous, vinous, or malt liquors within two and one-half miles of the Forest Home (Methodist) church, in Butler county."

Former New York City mayor Michael Bloomberg's plan to charge a steep toll on all commuters entering Manhattan needed approval from the state legislature, just as many local government policies do. As this cartoon shows, his commuter tax was not well received by state legislators meeting in Albany.

Even when metropolitan areas are ceded great discretion to decide local policies through state home-rule provisions, they remain the legal creations of states, which retain the authority to rescind or preempt local ordinances. Whereas the relations between the state and national governments are premised on separate constitutional authority and qualify as "federal," those between state and local governments are not and therefore can best be classified as "unitary."[6]

## Evolving Definitions of Federalism

The three defining features of federalism listed earlier leave room for different kinds of relations between state and national governments. Two distinct forms of American federalism have been identified: dual and shared. **Dual federalism** is perhaps the simplest possible arrangement, leaving the states and the national government to preside over mutually exclusive "spheres of sovereignty." James Madison described this arrangement (and the intent of the Framers of the Constitution) in *Federalist* No. 45: "The powers delegated by the proposed Constitution to the Federal Government are few and defined. Those which are to remain to the State Governments are numerous and indefinite." For example, foreign policy and national defense are purely national concerns; matters that "in the ordinary course of affairs, concern the lives" of the citizens are the responsibility of the individual states.

A second conception, called **shared** (or "cooperative") **federalism**, recognizes that the national and state governments jointly supply services to the citizenry. Although each level of government has exclusive authority over some policy realms, state and federal powers intersect over many of the most important functions. Figure 3.2 gives examples of these areas of exclusive and shared authority.

■ **FIGURE 3.2**  The Constitutional Basis for Dual and Shared Federalism

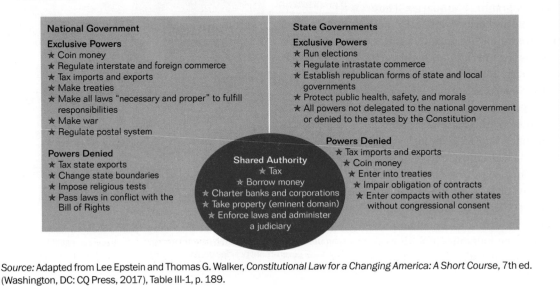

*Source:* Adapted from Lee Epstein and Thomas G. Walker, *Constitutional Law for a Changing America: A Short Course*, 7th ed. (Washington, DC: CQ Press, 2017), Table III-1, p. 189.

Throughout American history, the nation's practices better resemble the overlapping arrangements of shared federalism than the neat divisions of dual federalism. In the early years of the nationhood, states exercised national authority on important matters. In the Civil War the Union forces assembled to put down the Confederacy were recruited and initially provisioned by the states. Only after the men joined the ranks of other states' enlistees did the federal government assume control.

Soon after that war, however, **nationalization** shifted the "indefinite" authority Madison had assigned to state governments to the national side. Today, in fact, the national government has a hand in almost all policies that "concern the lives" of the citizenry. The most important expansions of national power are described later in this chapter. These include the New Deal policies of the 1930s and the Great Society programs of the 1960s, through which the federal government redesigned more limited state and local pension, welfare, and health care programs by providing most of the funding for them, designing a basic framework for each state to work through and opening up eligibility to all qualifying Americans. In the past decade, the testing and funding provisions of the No Child Left Behind Act (NCLB) have sharply increased federal authority over the way local schools operate. The trend toward nationalization has not been entirely a one-way street. Both the Nixon and Reagan administrations pushed for a "new federalism" by giving states more control over the implementation of some federal programs and grants, and Bill Clinton worked with Congress to increase state control over other federal policies through the "devolution revolution" of the 1990s. Before he became Speaker, House budget chair Paul Ryan and other congressional Republicans proposed giving states much more control over how to spend the federal grants they receive to provide health care to their aged, disabled, and poor residents (though the plan would also dramatically cut the size of these grants). Yet these exceptions to the rule of ever-increasing federal power have occurred only with the willing agreement of federal leaders.

Overall, then, the United States has moved from Madison's dual federalism to a shared federalism in which federal officials generally decide how authority over intersecting state and federal policy areas should be divided. Indeed, the modern ascendancy of the national government surely would have amazed all (and horrified most) of the delegates to the Constitutional Convention. After all, protecting the states from encroachment by a stronger national government was, in the words of one nationalist delegate, "the favorite object of the Convention." All but a handful of the states' rights delegates were satisfied with the final product, and most of them later publicly advocated the Constitution's ratification. So why have their efforts to partition federal and state responsibilities into separate, self-contained spheres been so thoroughly eclipsed?

Part of the answer is that modern policy challenges and a political consensus that "the government" should provide more services and solve more problems than the Founders anticipated have made a joint, cooperative strategy across states and levels of government necessary. Pollution does not honor state boundaries; neither do unemployment, inflation, crime, greenhouse gases, methamphetamines, or irresponsible mortgage lenders. Then there is the Internet, which knows no boundaries whatsoever. National disasters such as Hurricane Katrina and the 2010 BP oil spill in the Gulf of Mexico affect areas far beyond the reach of floodwaters or oil slicks and require responses on a scale that no single state can provide. The increasing complexity of policy dilemmas and the growing interrelationship between American states have driven the move toward nationalization.

But political logic in tandem with the rules that govern the boundaries of American federalism are just as important in explaining the increasing involvement of the federal government in matters that "in the ordinary course of affairs, concern the lives" of Americans. Federal officials have many incentives to increase federal power. Presidents are often rewarded when they bring state or regional policies into line with what their national constituency desires. Members of Congress can claim political credit when they work through the federal government to help their districts, and often draw on the immense national tax base to do so. When either logic leads to an expansion of federal authority that the states resist, the critical question becomes, who gets to decide whether this expansion is legitimate? As the next section shows, the Constitution opened the door to nationalization by granting the federal government ultimate power to determine (within certain bounds) the extent of its authority over the states.

## Federalism and the Constitution

In countering Antifederalist alarms about an overly powerful national government, Madison cited two kinds of protections in the Constitution: first, the "structure of the Federal Government," referring mostly to the Senate; and second, explicit rules reserving important prerogatives to the states. Neither has proved an effective barrier to national action.

### Transformation of the Senate

In the nineteenth century the equal representation of states regardless of population, combined with the selection of senators by state legislatures, gave the Senate the motive and the means to defend state prerogatives against national encroachment. The history of slavery reveals just how effective the institution was in this task. At first, some state legislatures were so possessive of the Senate and its members that they would pass resolutions instructing their senators how to vote on particular issues. Senators who failed to comply were asked to resign, and some did.[7] Even after this practice died out in the 1840s, most senators continued to regard themselves as agents of the state party organizations that controlled the state legislatures and elected them.

The real coup de grâce for the Senate as the bulwark of federalism came with ratification in 1913 of the Seventeenth Amendment, which mandated direct, popular election of senators. Amid persistent, widespread, and sometimes well-founded charges that senators bribed legislators to buy seats (and instances when divided state legislatures failed to agree on a nominee, leaving the state without representation for an extended period), a public consensus formed against indirect election of senators. Public pressure mounted to such an extent that more than three-quarters of state legislatures surrendered control and turned Senate selection over to popular election. The amendment, however, while targeting dysfunctional political practices, also knocked out an important prop of federalism because it removed senators' ties to the state legislatures. Today, the Senate is a central pillar of the national government. Senators may, incidentally, protect states' interests as they serve those of their constituents, but there are no guarantees. In fact, major extensions of federal authority have originated on the floor of the Senate, where more than a few of that chamber's members have cultivated a national constituency with an eye toward future presidential campaigns. Hillary Clinton, Ted Cruz, Bernie Sanders, and Marco Rubio all burnished their national credentials and launched their bids for the White House from the Senate, and members of the upper house made many of the key policy deals to pass the landmark pieces of legislation that characterized the early years of Obama's presidency.[8]

## Constitutional Provisions Governing Federalism

The Constitution gives the national government at least as much responsibility for overseeing the integrity of the states as it does the states for overseeing the integrity of the national government. All but the original thirteen states entered the Union by an act of Congress; the national government defined the boundaries of territories, oversaw their administration, and eventually ushered them into the Union. Moreover, Article IV of the Constitution obliges the federal government to ensure that all states adhere to republican principles. Although Congress may create new states, it cannot destroy an established state—say, by dividing it in half—without its consent. For their part, two-thirds of the states may petition Congress to convene a special constitutional convention to propose amendments. In these seldom-invoked provisions, the Constitution enlists each level of government to keep the other in check.

Language distinguishing the authority and responsibilities of the states from those of the national government runs throughout the Constitution. In partitioning responsibilities, the Framers worked within a structure of dual federalism. Thus in three major sections of the Constitution they attempted to specify boundaries between the two levels of government. By understanding what these provisions sought but largely failed to do, we can better appreciate how the U.S. governmental system has yielded to nationalizing forces.

### The Supremacy Clause

The provision of the Constitution with the most profound implication for modern American federalism is the so-called supremacy clause in Article VI: "This Constitution, and the Laws of the United States which shall be made in Pursuance thereof [that is, in keeping with the principles of the Constitution] . . . shall be the supreme Law of the Land." Although this clause appears to give the national government license to do whatever it wants, the text actually contains an important qualifier: the national government enjoys supremacy, but only insofar as its policies conform to a Constitution that prohibits certain kinds of federal activities.[9] This qualifier restricted national authority throughout most of the nineteenth century. The original intent was simply to have the national government prevail over states when both governments were acting in a constitutionally correct manner. Thus the supremacy clause was framed to avoid impasses over jurisdiction rather than to cede authority to the national government. Over the next two hundred years, however, the sphere of legitimate national action expanded, allowing national policy to enter domains once occupied only by the states. Wherever the national government carved out new authority, it automatically became supreme.

### The Powers of Congress

Article I, Section 8, lists the powers reserved to Congress. But these provisions have as much to do with federalism—that is, creating jurisdictional boundaries between the states and the national government—as they do with parceling out authority among Congress, the president, and the Supreme Court. After protracted deliberations in which many possibilities were considered, the Framers finally agreed to list in the Constitution a dozen or so **enumerated powers** that should be in the domain of the national government—specific authority that would enable the government to address problems the states had not grappled with effectively under the Articles of Confederation. One example: even Antifederalists conceded that a national postal system made better sense than trying to stitch together thirteen individual state systems.

Recognizing that contingencies requiring a national response might arise in the future, the Framers added to Section 8 what is now known as the **elastic clause**. It allows Congress to "make all Laws which shall be necessary and proper for carrying into Execution the foregoing Powers."[10] This open-ended provision, whose interpretation later would undermine the restrictive purpose of the carefully worded list of enumerated powers, apparently escaped the attention of many of the delegates because the convention accepted it with little debate. Later, the Antifederalists detected in it an opening for broad national authority, as did the generations of national officeholders who followed them. As the variety of economic

Although the Constitution may guarantee that it is the "supreme Law of the Land," constitutional battles today still address fundamental issues such as which governments—federal or state—reign supreme. Soon after Donald Trump was elected president, California's legislative leaders, anticipating a spate of legal battles with the Trump administration over whether state or federal law should govern critical issues such as the environment, immigration, health care, and consumer protections, lawyered up. They hired Eric Holder, who served as attorney general under Barack Obama, and by July 2018 the state had filed 38 legal actions against the federal government.

transactions that directly involve interstate commerce has grown sharply over the past two centuries, so too has the sphere of policy over which the national government can claim some jurisdiction. Moreover, laws governing a broad variety of social relations that are only incidentally economic—such as racial discrimination in access to public accommodations and possession of handguns near public schools—have invoked the commerce clause to justify federal involvement in these longtime state responsibilities.

### The Tenth Amendment

In the ratification debates Madison answered Antifederalist charges of impending tyranny by promising that once the new government was in place, he would immediately introduce a bill of rights (see Chapter 2). In view of the controversy surrounding federal power in the ratification debates, it is not surprising that many members of the First Congress insisted that the first ten constitutional amendments include protections for the states as well as for individual citizens.

The **Tenth Amendment** offers the most explicit endorsement of federalism to be found in the Constitution: "The powers not delegated to the United States by the Constitution, nor prohibited by it to the States, are reserved to the States respectively, or to the people." Yet, despite its plain language, the Tenth Amendment has failed to fend off federal authority. The powerful combination of the supremacy and elastic clauses reduces the Tenth Amendment to little more than a truism: those powers not taken by the national government *do* belong to the states. About all that it offers critics of nationalization is lip service to the principle of states' rights.

## Interpreting the Constitution's Provisions

The sweeping language with which the Constitution variously endorses national power and states' rights has given politicians easy openings to interpret the Constitution according to their own political objectives. Thus the Framers envisioned a Supreme Court that would referee jurisdictional disputes among the states and between states and the national government. Among the thousands of judicial decisions that have grappled with the appropriate roles of the national and state governments, one early Supreme Court ruling stands out for protecting the national government from incursions by the states. In 1816 Congress created a national bank that proved unpopular with many state-level politicians who preferred the state-chartered banks over which they exercised control. To nip this federal meddling into what it viewed as a state matter, Maryland levied a heavy tax on all non-state-chartered banks. James McCulloch, an agent for the national bank in Baltimore, refused to pay the tax, and the two sides went to court. The historic decision *McCulloch v. Maryland* (1819) brought together the supremacy and elastic clauses and moved them to the forefront of constitutional interpretation.[11] Writing for the Court, Chief Justice John Marshall declared that because the national bank assisted Congress in performing several of its responsibilities enumerated in Article I, Section 8—namely borrowing money, levying taxes, and issuing a national currency—the elastic clause gave the national government the implicit authority to create the bank. In one of the most famous passages in Supreme Court opinion, Marshall enunciated this definitive constitutional doctrine:

> Let the end be legitimate, let it be within the scope of the Constitution, and all means which are appropriate, which are plainly adapted to that end, which are not prohibited, but consistent with the letter and spirit of the Constitution, are constitutional.

# The Constitution's Provisions for Federalism

### Article I, Section 8, Commerce Clause

The Congress shall have Power … to regulate Commerce with foreign Nations, and among the several States, and with the Indian Tribes; …

### Article I, Section 8, Elastic Clause

The Congress shall have Power … to make all Laws which shall be necessary and proper for carrying into Execution the foregoing Powers, and all other Powers vested by this Constitution in the Government of the United States, or in any Department or Officer thereof.

### Article IV, Section 3, Admission of New States

New States may be admitted by the Congress into this Union; but no new State shall be formed or erected within the Jurisdiction of any other State; nor any State be formed by the Junction of two or more States, or Parts of States, without the Consent of the Legislatures of the States concerned as well as of the Congress.

### Article IV, Section 4, Enforcement of Republican Form of Government

The United States shall guarantee to every State in this Union a Republican Form of Government, and shall protect each of them against Invasion; and on Application of the Legislature, or of the Executive (when the Legislature cannot be convened) against domestic Violence.

### Article VI, Supremacy Clause

This Constitution, and the Laws of the United States which shall be made in Pursuance thereof; and all Treaties made, or which shall be made, under the Authority of the United States, shall be the supreme Law of the Land; and the Judges in every State shall be bound thereby, any Thing in the Constitution or Laws of any State to the Contrary notwithstanding.

### Tenth Amendment

The powers not delegated to the United States by the Constitution, nor prohibited by it to the States, are reserved to the States respectively, or to the people.

Marshall iced the cake by removing the young national government from the purview of the states. Because "the power to tax involves the power to destroy," the supremacy clause implicitly exempts the federal government from state taxes.

Five years later, in 1824, the Marshall Court handed down another decision that must have appeared far less significant to contemporaries than it came to be regarded in the twentieth century. In settling a dispute between New Jersey and New York over each state's efforts to give a favored steam company a monopoly over shipping on the Hudson River, the Court held in *Gibbons v. Ogden* that neither state could control such a concession.[12] Only Congress possessed the authority to regulate interstate commerce.

In combination, these two cases created powerful precedents that would allow future national policy to develop free of the constraints of state prerogatives. Once the Court in

**STRATEGY AND CHOICE**

# Chris Christie and an Ambitious Governor's Dilemma

America's federal system gives governors great flexibility to practice politics in a way that fits their state. Unlike the members of Congress or senators who have to go back to Washington, D.C., and cast party-line votes on divisive issues, governors can craft their own policy agendas and find a middle ground between the two parties. The freedom of federalism means that state governments can seek compromise when D.C. is gridlocked, with governors often taking pragmatic, moderate positions.

Yet with this freedom comes great responsibility for owning these positions throughout a political career. When ambitious governors want to move up the political ladder to the White House, their past pragmatism can create future political obstacles. Winning the presidency first requires candidates to please their party's voters in the primary. Those voters often demand more ideological purity than governors provide. A major obstacle in Mitt Romney's run for the 2012 Republican nomination was the fact that he had championed Massachusetts's "Romneycare" universal health care law when he served as governor of that heavily Democratic state. This made it hard for him to convince GOP primary voters that he would aggressively oppose the

Obamacare law (which was modeled after Romneycare) and complicated his attacks on it in the general election. The position that he had taken was popular in heavily Democratic Massachusetts, but not in the nation's red states.

Less substantive but symbolically powerful was New Jersey governor Chris Christie's literal embrace of President Obama in the aftermath of the devastating "Superstorm Sandy" in October 2012. Especially in this blue-leaning state, it seemed uncontroversial to welcome the president—and the prospect of federal emergency relief funds—right after the storm. Yet four years later, when Christie entered the presidential race, his record as a moderate who would hazard a cordial relationship with Obama hurt him. Christie's picture with Obama came back to haunt him, and his centrist record did him no favors in a race in which voters wanted an antiestablishment conservative. Governor Christie eventually dropped out of the race and endorsed Donald Trump while becoming an Internet meme. His experience highlighted the dilemma faced by all ambitious state chief executives: meeting your own state's voters in the political center can pay off while you are governor but hurt your presidential prospects.

AP Photo/Charles Dharapak

AP Photo/LM Otero

As governor of New Jersey when its shore was battered by Superstorm Sandy, Chris Christie gave President Obama a friendly welcome when he arrived in October 2012. Yet his aisle-crossing image hurt him with Republican primary voters in 2016, with perhaps the most notable event of his candidacy coming when he dropped out of the race and endorsed Donald Trump.

*Gibbons* had sanctioned federal authority to regulate commerce, the supremacy clause gave the national government the authority to preempt the states in virtually all policies involving interstate commerce. Many traditional tasks of states, such as providing for public safety, enforcing fair advertising laws, and overseeing waste disposal, would slip easily into federal control via the commerce clause.

As national politicians sought over the years to expand their authority and responsibilities, they discovered that the wall between the federal government and the states was not as impregnable as most of the Framers had apparently supposed. The Constitution's provisions and language leave ample room for a variety of federal-state relations. Thus nationalization of public policy reshaped federalism largely unfettered by constitutional constraints and without triggering a constitutional crisis. Nationalization did not just happen, however. As many problems outgrew state borders, pressure usually built for a greater national role. But whether the federal government actually assumed responsibility remained—and still is—a political decision, reflecting as much the competition of interests as any objective rationale for national action. The buildup of antislavery sentiment in the northern states, which led to Abraham Lincoln's election in 1860, the South's secession, and the Civil War, remains the nation's most bitter and tragic conflict involving federalism. Yet whereas the war was nominally triggered by a dispute over the bounds of federal authority to abolish slavery, it should be seen as a larger political and moral clash that broke down into military conflict rather than a battle over the principles of federalism.

## The Paths to Nationalization

Throughout the first half of the nineteenth century, the United States remained a nation of segmented communities whose commercial intercourse required minimal coordination across states. But as American workers began to produce more and more goods to be traded on distant markets, lawmakers began to shift their attention from strictly state and local matters to national problems and solutions. With growth, industrialization, urbanization, and the development of national transportation and communication systems, the nation's appetite grew for public goods that outstripped the scope and resources of local communities and states.[13] In the early 1870s, for example, the farm states tried in vain to prohibit the railroads from engaging in rate discrimination and exorbitant charges. They finally turned to Washington for regulation, and in 1887 Congress obliged by passing the Interstate Commerce Act. A similar process spurred the federal government to enforce national food safety standards, enact antimonopoly laws, and undertake numerous other services.

The nationalization of public policy, which altered federal-state relations, was propelled by a rationale, or logic, that grew out of the requirements of collective action. Played out historically, the logic of collective action has assumed several forms. First, Americans have at times decided collectively to adopt policies of such magnitude and scope that they outstripped the resources of states. The result has been a historic movement of large blocks of domestic policy from the state capitals to Washington. We soon examine two important historical instances of this movement: Franklin Roosevelt's New Deal and Lyndon Johnson's Great Society.

Second, states have solicited federal intervention when they could not solve their problems by working together individually. Considering that the U.S. mainland is carved into forty-eight separate state jurisdictions, one can easily imagine a great variety of issues arising that require states' cooperation. And yet the Constitution prohibits formal interstate agreements

(Article I, Section 10) in the absence of the national government's consent. Voluntary cooperation, by definition, holds the potential for reneging, particularly when serious, costly commitments are required. For that reason, following the 1906 San Francisco earthquake, which overwhelmed the capacity of California's state government to respond to $500 million in property damage and assist over 250,000 homeless residents, the states welcomed a national insurance policy against such disasters even though it meant surrendering control of disaster relief to federal agencies.

Photos 12/Alamy

One major step toward nationalization that literally connected states was the building of the Interstate Highway System, now 46,837 miles long, beginning in the late 1950s. Promoted by President Dwight D. Eisenhower, this massive public works project allowed people and products to move much more quickly within and across states, accelerating the nation's postwar economic boom. Yet it also imposed sharp costs—economic and cultural—on the small towns bypassed by the new highways. Many of the "mom and pop" diners, gas stations, and souvenir shops located on the main streets of towns along old roads such as Route 66 disappeared. (Their passing was mourned in the animated film *Cars*, which tells the sad tale of what happened when Interstate 40 bypassed the fictional town of Radiator Springs.) Because decisions about the new highway system were made at the federal level, small-town residents who might have been able to influence their local or state governments had little say in the national policy.

Finally, national majorities have increasingly insisted on federal involvement in what were formerly state and local matters. Sometimes mere expediency is at work as a national majority finds it easier to succeed in Washington than in each of the states. Similarly, companies with business around the country sometimes lobby for national regulations simply so that they do not have to deal with fifty different states' policies. On other occasions, the cause has been just and noble, as the history of civil rights policy in the United States shows. In asserting its authority to protect the rights of African Americans—from the Civil War in the 1860s to the civil rights laws a century later—the national government breached the separation of national from state spheres of control. Although the impact of civil rights on federalism has been profound, it is a subject with broad implications for all Americans and warrants separate consideration (see Chapter 4).

## Historic Transfers of Policy to Washington

President Roosevelt's New Deal, enacted in the 1930s, and President Johnson's Great Society program, realized in the mid-1960s, represented two equally historic shifts toward nationalization. In addition to broadening the scope of federal responsibilities, these watershed programs followed the election of large national majorities to Congress from the president's party, with an apparent mandate to create a broad new array of collective goods.

Roosevelt's New Deal was a comprehensive set of economic regulations and relief programs intended to fight the Great Depression

(1929–1940). The innovation of the New Deal stemmed less from the form of its policies than from their size and scope. During Roosevelt's first two terms (1933–1941), he and the huge Democratic majorities in Congress established economic management as one of the national government's primary responsibilities. Federal policy took two basic forms: regulating and financing (and with it prescribing) state action. Despite the continuing debate between present-day Republicans and Democrats over the proper division of federal and state responsibilities, no one has seriously proposed dismantling the framework of economic management constructed by the New Deal.

At the outset of the Depression, 40 percent unemployment rates were not uncommon in many communities. The states, responsible for welfare programs, had to reduce services to fend off insolvency. In the process, they also had to abandon people in need of help. When the Roosevelt administration's offer to fund 90 percent of the costs for relief and new make-work programs finally came, the principle of federalism did not prevent state leaders from

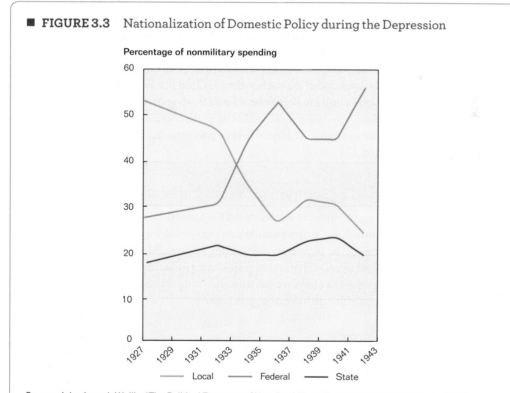

■ **FIGURE 3.3**   Nationalization of Domestic Policy during the Depression

Percentage of nonmilitary spending

——— Local     ——— Federal     ——— State

*Source:* John Joseph Wallis, "The Political Economy of New Deal Fiscal Federalism," *Economic Inquiry* 29 (July 1991): 511.

*Note:* About half of the increase in federal spending in this figure took the form of direct financial support to indigent citizens.

cheerfully accepting the help.* All forty-eight states quickly signed up for the Works Progress Administration, Old Age Assistance, Civilian Conservation Corps, Social Security, and other federally sponsored public assistance programs. During these Depression years the dramatic growth in federal spending, coupled with corresponding reductions in funds at the state and local levels, provided evidence of the sharp shift from state to federal responsibility for social programs (see Figure 3.3).

Another great wave of nationalization of domestic policy occurred in the mid-1960s. Elected in 1964 in an even larger landslide than FDR's 1932 victory, Lyndon Johnson and the overwhelmingly Democratic Congress launched the War on Poverty as part of their Great Society agenda. In 1964–1965 Congress passed more than a hundred new programs that would be carried out by states but funded (and controlled) through federal grants, spending over $5 billion. The largest of these was Medicaid, which provides health insurance to low-income families, senior citizens in nursing homes, and disabled Americans. Other traditional state and local responsibilities such as school funding, teacher training, urban renewal, and public housing became important federal responsibilities. As with the New Deal, these grants subsidized state programs that implemented national goals.

But all these grants came with strings attached. To qualify for funding, state and local authorities had to follow detailed programmatic guidelines prescribing how funds were to be spent. These strings greatly expanded the federal government's power, even over services such as schools that are still funded mostly by state and local governments. Because states now rely on the federal education grants that were created during the Great Society era, they have been forced to accept federal policy dictates such as the No Child Left Behind testing requirements and the **Common Core** in order to keep federal funds flowing. Without paying all of the costs of education, the federal government can still exert much control over it. Even though grant programs transfer money from the national to state governments, they often transfer authority back to Washington, D.C.

## Nationalization—The Solution to States' Collective Dilemmas

When modern state governments encountered the same collective action dilemmas that prompted their eighteenth-century counterparts to send delegates to Philadelphia, they solved these dilemmas in the same way—by shifting responsibility from the state to federal authorities. Every kind of collective action problem introduced in Chapter 1, from simple coordination to the prisoner's dilemma, has frustrated state action at one time or another and repeatedly required states to turn to Washington for help.

### Coordination Problems

A nation composed of fifty states inevitably faces coordination problems—some dramatic, some mundane. Even when the states agree to cooperate, thereby allowing each to deal more

---

*Unlike the federal government, most state governments are forbidden by their constitutions from enacting annual budgets that incur deficits. But although they may have to balance their budgets, most states can and do frequently borrow billions of dollars to build schools, roads, parks, dams, hospitals, canals, railroads, and other vital parts of their infrastructures.

effectively with a common responsibility, they may have difficulty figuring out precisely how to work together. For example, until 1986, the principle that each state administers its own driver's license laws appeared unassailable. But after heavy lobbying by state officials, Congress passed the Commercial Motor Vehicle Safety Act, which standardized state driver's licenses for interstate truckers and created a bureau within the Department of Transportation to centralize traffic violation records. What prompted federal intervention was the practice common among truckers of obtaining licenses in several states to maintain a valid license regardless of the number of traffic tickets accumulated. Centralized record keeping offered a far simpler solution to state coordination than requiring each state to update its records with those from every other state. Disgruntled truckers pointed to the new law as another example of interference by "heavy-handed Washington bureaucrats," but in fact it precisely fulfilled the states' request.

Even when the need for coordination is evident, there is no guarantee that the states will agree to shift this responsibility to Washington. In addition to the transaction costs of conforming to national standards, state politicians may worry that surrendering authority for one accepted purpose might lead the federal government to undertake less desirable policies. Such considerations are holding up agreement in Congress to strengthen national regulation of electrical transmission across the country. Every state exercises some regulatory control over its

Franklin Roosevelt's New Deal included the federal Works Progress Administration, which among other employment opportunities promoted "Jobs for Girls and Women."

electricity industry. In an earlier era, when most utilities were local monopolies with in-state generation and transmission, state-level policy made sense. Today, however, power flows through an extensive continental grid; residents of one state consume electricity from dozens of sources throughout the region. As demonstrated by a massive blackout that began with a minor power outage in Ohio but cascaded across the East Coast on August 13, 2003, state regulation no longer works. The question still being deliberated in Congress and the states is, can regulatory coordination be delegated to the Federal Energy Regulatory Commission without surrendering state control over rates? (Nearly ten years after the blackouts of the Midwest and East Coast, members of Congress from the South and Northwest still have not agreed to new federal authority for fear that their cheap local electricity would chase market prices and drive up their local costs.)

### Reneging and Shirking

In the nation's early years, states agreed to a course of common action but then failed to honor their commitments. The Constitution and national laws solve many of these dilemmas by

## POLITICS TO POLICY
# Free Federal Dollars?

### No Thanks, I'll Take Political Currency Instead

A critical component of President Obama's Affordable Care Act—popularly known as "Obamacare"—was the expansion of state Medicaid programs. Federal lawmakers (or, to be more specific, the Democratic federal lawmakers who passed the ACA by the slimmest of majorities) wanted to provide health coverage for Americans who held low-paying jobs at businesses that did not offer health insurance benefits. Because Medicaid programs—which are run by the states but funded mostly by the federal government—already cover many low-income individuals, it made policy sense to give states the money to cover the working poor. By requiring states to cover families making up to $31,000 a year under Medicaid, and paying for all this expansion for many years with federal dollars, the ACA was expected to bring health coverage to 17 million people spread across the nation. Then the courts, and political logic, intervened.

The Supreme Court's 2012 *National Federation of Independent Business v. Sebelius* decision, which upheld the constitutionality of nearly all parts of Obamacare, contained one narrow ruling that proved to be enormously consequential. The court ruled that Congress could not force the states to expand Medicaid by threatening their existing Medicaid funding, but it did not take away the vast financial incentive to expand these state programs with billions of federal dollars. Essentially, the Supreme Court took away the federal government's stick, but not the carrots it could offer states. State leaders were granted new policy discretion. They could, at no cost to their state budgets, provide health care to many of their residents, making doctors and hospitals happy for the new business at the same time. Or they could leave federal dollars on the table,

angering the powerful medical lobby and leaving many of their most needy residents uninsured.

To the shock and dismay of many observers, six years after this decision, thirty-two states expanded their Medicaid programs, but eighteen have so far refused the free federal dollars. This has left many millions of low-income Americans without health insurance, stymieing a major component of the ACA. Why did so many states turn down an apparent free lunch? Because accepting Obamacare dollars and looking complicit in an unpopular policy sent down from Washington, D.C., ran counter to the policy preferences and political incentives of many Republican governors and state legislators. Many had been elected with campaigns that railed against Obamacare's individual insurance mandate, coming to power in red states that voted overwhelmingly for Mitt Romney in 2012 and Donald Trump in 2016. Yet with the Supreme Court upholding the mandate and attempts to repeal the ACA failing in the first year of the Trump presidency, the only way to oppose Obamacare was to fight Medicaid expansion. And in the eyes of conservative governors, taking federal money is not "free": these are, after all, taxpayer dollars. To register their opposition to Obamacare, and to follow the fiscally conservative path that brought them to office, state leaders—especially those associated with the Tea Party—have made this a central political issue in their states. All but one of the states that refused Medicaid expansion have been led by Republican governors. The most recent state to expand its Medicaid program, Virginia, did so in May 2018 after a five-year fight between Republican state legislators and Democratic governors. In a concrete sense, these are proxy battles over a defining national issue of the day—mandatory national health insurance—being played out in the states while Washington, D.C., remains in a political deadlock.

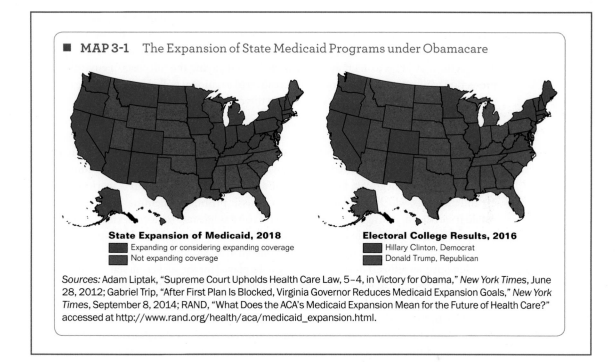

■ **MAP 3-1**    The Expansion of State Medicaid Programs under Obamacare

**State Expansion of Medicaid, 2018**
- Expanding or considering expanding coverage
- Not expanding coverage

**Electoral College Results, 2016**
- Hillary Clinton, Democrat
- Donald Trump, Republican

*Sources:* Adam Liptak, "Supreme Court Upholds Health Care Law, 5–4, in Victory for Obama," *New York Times*, June 28, 2012; Gabriel Trip, "After First Plan Is Blocked, Virginia Governor Reduces Medicaid Expansion Goals," *New York Times*, September 8, 2014; RAND, "What Does the ACA's Medicaid Expansion Mean for the Future of Health Care?" accessed at http://www.rand.org/health/aca/medicaid_expansion.html.

authorizing the federal government to take direct action in raising resources and administering policy. However, in certain situations national responsibility and jurisdiction either are undecided or allow the states a prominent role. Movements to reduce pollution and conserve natural resources, among the most pervasive and thorny challenges to effective collective action in recent years, have inspired innovative approaches enlisting federalism as a solution. Both problems qualify as tragedies of the commons, introduced in Chapter 1. No one wants to breathe polluted air, but without some mechanism to arrange and enforce agreements, everyone continues to pollute under the assumption that doing otherwise will not by itself clean up the atmosphere (that is, promote the public good or lead to the betterment of the "commons"). Coordinated national policies are necessary to solve this collective action problem, but they can sometimes emerge through state pressure. The clearest example of this comes from recent responses to the most pressing environmental concern of our era: climate change. Climate change presents a policy challenge that crosses state borders. Exhaust from the tailpipe of a California car can cause smog in the Los Angeles basin, but the carbon emissions can also trap heat in Earth's atmosphere and affect the global climate. Because many people are affected by the car's emissions, not just its driver, the environmental damage done represents an *externality*, an effect felt by more people than just the one who chose to cause it. When the federal government made little effort to combat greenhouse gas emissions, a group of states pushed the United States toward national action. California passed a landmark climate change bill under Governor Arnold Schwarzenegger's leadership and was soon followed by fourteen states from Arizona to Maine. The federal government initially opposed the state laws, arguing that they could create a policy patchwork, but after Obama's election, the EPA embraced California's tough fuel economy standards, making them the national standard by 2016. Though the first states to act may have worried about paying the full costs of environmental protection while other states shirked, the creation of a national policy to address the negative externality of greenhouse gas emissions solved this collective action problem.

### Cutthroat Competition

Under the Articles of Confederation each state was free to conduct its own international trade policy. This arrangement allowed foreign governments and merchants to exploit competition among the states to negotiate profitable trade agreements. The losers were American producers and the states, which found themselves in a classic prisoner's dilemma. Their best strategy would have been first to agree among themselves on a single rate (to form a kind of cartel) and then to negotiate with Britain from a united front. But this approach would have required that none of the states break rank when the British offered to reward the first "defector" with an especially lucrative, sweetheart deal. Not wanting to be played for the sucker, all states underbid one another, or engaged in **cutthroat competition**. Searching for a solution, both nationalists and advocates of states' rights readily agreed at the Constitutional Convention that the states were best served by the national government assuming control in foreign affairs, including trade.

At various times cutthroat competition has prompted state officials to lobby Washington to prevent bidding wars. When the national government defended a 1937 federal minimum wage law before the Supreme Court, it reminded the justices that rather than usurping state prerogatives, Washington was actually serving the states: "State legislators . . . over a period of time have realized that no state, acting alone, could require labor standards substantially higher than those obtained in other states whose producers and manufacturers competed in the interstate market."[14]

Environmental regulation is another area in which the national government has taken action. To lure new business, states sometimes are tempted to relax their environmental standards to give them a competitive edge over their neighbors. Thus one state's strong environmental policies may expose it to other states' gamesmanship. As much as state officials like to complain about the policies of the EPA, the presence of national standards insulates environmental protection from cutthroat competition.

Competition among states can take other forms as well. Companies considering relocating facilities will strategically select two or three "finalist" sites in different states and then sit back and let them bid against one another by offering tax breaks or special services. Although the states generally would be better off if they could avoid this competition, none can afford to do so. Each state will raise its bid until the costs of subsidizing a new company through property improvements and reduced taxes exceed the expected economic benefits. States also face incentives to engage in a **race to the bottom** in social services by cutting back on things like the size of the monthly check a state pays to welfare recipients so that it will not become a "welfare magnet" that attracts the low-income residents of its neighbors. There remains much debate over whether states do indeed race toward the bottom,[15] but the incentives that a decentralized welfare policy creates to do so might harm society's most vulnerable.

Whether pitting the states against one another in a bidding war is a good thing depends wholly on whose interests are being served. By one recent estimate cities and states are paying

A participant in the "Original Redneck Fishing Tournament" swings at carp flying out of the Illinois River. This aggressive, voracious species of fish was imported by southern states in the 1970s to help keep wastewater treatment facilities clean, but Mississippi River flooding freed the carp to ravage the Missouri and Illinois Rivers (and their kayakers) throughout the 1990s. Five states situated on the Great Lakes have asked the U.S. Army Corps of Engineers to shut down the locks connecting Chicago's rivers to the lake to help fight the carp's spread. Illinois business leaders, though, fought the request, because in protecting the other states it would badly threaten Chicago's economy and flood control system. A federal court ruled in December 2010 that the locks could stay open, but the five Great Lakes states appealed the decision.

about $40 billion annually in direct compensation, special services, and tax exemptions to lure and retain large employers.[16] In these fights, states even spend money on billboards, television, and radio advertisements to steal one another's businesses. Corporate executives seeking attractive concessions would understandably view any agreement among the states to avoid competition as unwelcome collusion. Alternatively, one could argue that these bidding wars represent a market mechanism establishing the true price of a project and hence promote efficiency.

Moreover, competition among states and performance comparisons may allow politicians across the country to discover which innovative solutions to common policy challenges actually work. The idea—that one state can experiment and, if successful, that other states and the national government may replicate it—presents a compelling justification for competitive federalism. Many state policy innovations have spread across the country. Less certain is that the innovations copied are always the most successful ones. In response to negative public opinion after Texas rated poorly in many national rankings of primary and secondary school test scores, politicians, including then-governor George W. Bush, made the state's low education scores a political issue. During the next several years, educational expenditures increased significantly across Texas, as did, eventually, its test scores and national ranking. After he was elected president, Bush applied some parts of the Texas plan on a national scale through the No Child Left Behind legislation. Opponents of this approach to education and critics of competitive federalism in general might ask how we know which parts of Texas's plan improved

*AP Photo/Detroit Free Press, Eric Sharp*

test scores and whether we can be sure that the nation copied a state's successful innovations rather than its failures.

## The Political Logic of Nationalization

As countless political controversies teach us, promoters of a policy will sometimes try to shift it from the states to the national government because either they expect more sympathetic treatment in Washington or they find it easier than lobbying fifty state governments. National campaigns for legislation banning automatic weapons and handguns, regulating hazardous waste disposal, and mandating special education programs in public schools are instances in which "state" issues have been strategically shifted to Washington.

If a cause enjoys widespread national support, lobbying Congress is far more efficient than lobbying fifty state legislatures. After all, a single federal law can change a policy in all fifty states. In 1980 a mother whose teenage daughter was killed by a drunk driver formed Mothers Against Drunk Driving (MADD), which quickly mushroomed into a national organization with thousands of members. Initially, MADD pressed state legislatures for stiffer laws and higher drinking ages. And although all proclaimed their enthusiasm for removing drunks from the highways, those states with lower drinking ages had a financial interest in maintaining the status quo. Such states profited from underage customers who visited from neighboring states with higher legal drinking ages. As a result, variations in the states' drinking ages perversely encouraged some young people to take to the highways in search of alcohol.

In 1984 MADD took its case to Congress.* Few politicians proved willing to defend federalism against the movement to reduce drunk driving. In 1985 Congress passed legislation that instituted a simple, effective way to regulate drinking age laws. If a state failed to raise its drinking age to twenty-one in 1986, it would lose 5 percent of its federal highway funds. Failure to do so in 1987 would trigger a 10 percent deduction. All the states got the message and promptly raised the drinking age by 1988. They also brought suit in the Supreme Court, claiming extortion and federal intrusion into strictly state jurisdictions. The Court sided with the national government.[17]

Even those who do not desire national action sometimes invite it to avoid burdensome and varied regulations from each of the states. In recent years many state attorneys general have charged airlines with practicing illegal "bait and switch" advertising when they run local newspaper promotions for steeply discounted fares that few customers find available. The airlines, however, have successfully evaded state prosecution by persuading the Department of Transportation to assert its preemptive federal authority to regulate airline rates and advertising. Thus even businesses wanting to remain free of any government regulation may prefer to deal with one federal agency rather than having to fend off regulation attempts from fifty states.†

---

*MADD did meet some resistance in the low-drinking-age states that benefited economically from the commerce in alcohol.

†Similarly, major software companies, including Microsoft and AOL, assembled in 2004 to respond to Utah's recently enacted law requiring any company loading cookies and other software onto a personal computer via the Internet to first obtain permission from the computer owner. With several other states poised to pass similar legislation, the software firms feared patchwork regulations would hamstring their capacity to innovate in this area. John Schwartz and Saul Hansell, "The Latest High-Tech Legal Issue: Rooting Out the Spy in Your Computer," *New York Times*, April 26, 2004.

STRATEGY AND CHOICE

## STRATEGY AND CHOICE
# Maryland Declares
# Its Political Independence

### Partisan Passage of the "Maryland Defense Act"

When red state voters deliver a sweeping Republican victory at the federal level, what can the political leaders of a blue state do? After President Trump's surprise victory in 2016 left the GOP in control over every branch of the national government, Democratic lawmakers across the states looked for ways to fight back. Never considering an all-out rebellion or challenging the legitimacy of the election—an important adherence to the nation's norms since the end of the Civil War—they looked for legal avenues to protect the policies they had passed in their states. They didn't mind scoring political points, too, in states where voters were aligned with them against President Trump.

In deep blue states like New York, California, Washington, Hawaii, Delaware, Oregon, and New Jersey, where Democrats hold all the levers of political power, launching and funding state lawsuits against the federal government has been a straightforward task. Because it is in everyone's political and policy interests to join the resistance, fully Democratic states have led the legal charge against Trump administration policies. The political and legal strategy has been much more complicated, though, in a state where control of the legislature and governor's office is divided between red and blue parties.

That is exactly the dilemma faced by Democrats in the Maryland state legislature in 2017. Though Democrats ruled both houses of the legislature by overwhelming margins in a state where Donald Trump received less than 34% of the vote, moderate Republican Larry Hogan has served as

C-SPAN, "Trump Administration and Federal Deregulation, Panel Discussion," June 5, 2018

Just three weeks after Donald Trump was inaugurated as president, Democratic legislators in Maryland were willing to give their attorney general the unchecked power to sue the federal government, without the governor's or legislature's approval. The Maryland Defense Act stopped the state's Republican governor from halting lawsuits launched by its Democratic attorney general, Brian Frosh (pictured here), a sign of how the policy and political fights between state and federal leaders have become intense enough to reshape the structure of some state governments.

governor since his election in 2014. Democratic lawmakers worried that Republican governor Hogan would not aggressively pursue lawsuits against the Trump administration. Their fears were confirmed when Hogan did not respond to the legislature's request that he challenge President Trump's ban on travel by visitors from predominantly Muslim nations. So, just three weeks after President Trump's inauguration, they changed the balance of power within Maryland government to bolster the fight against the federal administration.

With the party-line passage of the "Maryland Defense Act," Democrats in Maryland's legislature gave the state's attorney general the unchecked power to sue the president on a range of issues. Before passage of the act, the governor's

*(Continued)*

(Continued)

approval was needed to launch a lawsuit. Yet the act empowered the attorney general, independently elected Democrat Brian Frosh, to sue on his own without first obtaining approval by the governor. Attorney General Frosh, and all his successors, were also empowered to file lawsuits without seeking the legislature's approval. This amounted to "an unprecedented expansion of power for the office," in the words of the *Baltimore Sun*, reshaping the formal lines of authority within state government to fight a political battle. The act outlined nine areas in which the attorney general could unilaterally move to sue, ranging from "protecting the health of the residents of the State and ensuring the availability of affordable health care" to "protecting civil liberties" and "protecting the natural resources and environment of the State."

In the first year of the act, Frosh filed suits against the travel ban, to protect the state's greenhouse gas emissions and energy efficiency standards, to safeguard Obamacare, to maintain net neutrality, and to protect Deferred Action for Childhood Arrivals (DACA) participants. All were attempts to frustrate Trump administration policies as they were being implemented in Maryland and other states. They were thus declarations of political and policy independence for Maryland from the decisions being made just across its border, in the District of Columbia. Empowering the attorney general to do so required giving him the right to work around the authority of both the Republican governor and the Democratic legislature, a significant change in the governance structure of Maryland that could only be justified by the intensity of the partisan and policy battles that followed Donald Trump's victory.

*Sources:* Erin Cox, "Maryland Attorney General Frosh Awarded Expanded Power to Sue the Trump Administration," *Baltimore Sun*, February 15, 2017, and Maryland Office of the Attorney General, "Maryland Defense Act: 2017 Report," Annapolis, Maryland, December 2017.

Perhaps the most compelling strategic reason for a group to prefer national over state policy is that the national arena may be the only place in which it can hope to prevail, especially when a policy is opposed in the community where it would need to be enforced. This situation characterized civil rights in the South during the 1960s, but virtually any domain of public policy in which the state and national governments share responsibility is subject to this political maneuver. After increasing their majority in both the House and the Senate in the 2004 elections, Republicans opened the 109th Congress by promptly passing a law that moved most class-action lawsuits from state to federal court jurisdictions. Some state courts had earned reputations for favoring plaintiffs, which aggrieved Republican-supporting business groups and endeared them to Democratic-supporting trial lawyers' associations.

Perhaps no area of national policy has so thoroughly been reshaped by this dynamic than the extension of environmental protections at the expense of state and local constituencies. Protection of environmental resources can be costly—directly or indirectly—in lost jobs and business. Either way, local residents typically pay the bulk of the costs. Idaho ranchers worry that the reintroduction of wolves in the nearby national parks will endanger their sheep. The Navajos' coal-burning, electricity-generating plant in Arizona may blanket the Grand Canyon in dense fog, but they prefer the profits gained from selling electricity to a national market. The lumber industry in northern California and Oregon believes jobs will be imperiled if it must curtail the harvest of old-growth forest to protect the endangered spotted owl.

The rest of the country, by comparison, bears little of these costs. It can "afford" the appropriate environmental measures far better than can those whose livelihoods are adversely affected by them. Restoring the original ecology of Yellowstone National Park, maintaining a smoke-free Grand Canyon, and protecting an endangered owl are all desirable and essentially free public goods. Thus conflicts arising over the environment frequently pit local resource users (such as ranchers and developers) who bear the costs of environmental regulation against nationally organized environmental constituencies that do not.

As James Madison emphasized in *Federalist* No. 10, states and the national government combine the citizenry's preferences into different groupings, with the result that the two levels of government may adopt different, even opposite, policies to address the same problem. Although Madison was prepared to take his chances with national majorities, whose decisions, he believed, would be moderated by the collective preferences of a broad, diverse nation, he also knew what we learned in our discussion of sanctuary cities and of federal environmental policy: that national majorities will at times impose costs on local constituencies. Thus federalism presents opportunities for two kinds of majorities—state and national—to pursue

On Patriots' Day in April 2010, armed activists marched to demonstrate their right to bear arms in northern Virginia across the Potomac River from Washington, D.C. Even though the Supreme Court's *District of Columbia v. Heller* decision struck down the district's handgun ban in 2008, gun control laws are still much stricter in the district than in Virginia. As a consequence, the activists did not march on the National Mall itself—the location of their protest was dictated by the nation's patchwork of gun control laws, itself a product of federalism.

their interests in competition with each other. For better or worse, national majorities have the institutional resources to nationalize many policy questions that once were the exclusive domain of state majorities.

## Modern Federalism

Early in the twenty-first century, the national government's primacy in setting domestic policy is secure, even in domains that once belonged exclusively to the states. Whether through outright takeover of a function or by selective financial inducements, Washington can pretty much dictate state policy when its policymakers are so inclined. Some observers find recent Supreme Court decisions beginning to fence in the federal government's ability to dictate policy. Even so, the shift has been modest and easily circumvented by an alternative strategy of financial inducements.

### The National Government's Advantage in the Courts

Indicative of how far nationalization has shifted the balance of power, today's constitutional litigation over federalism typically concerns direct efforts by the federal government to regulate the activities of state and local governments and their employees. In *Garcia v. San Antonio Metropolitan Transit Authority* (1985) the Supreme Court approved the application of federal wage-and-hour laws to state and local employees. Writing for the majority, Justice Harry Blackmun dismissed the Tenth Amendment as too ambiguous to guide federal-state relations. But this was no great matter, he added, because the proper relations between the states and the national government were protected in other ways. The states' "sovereign interests," he wrote, "are more properly protected by procedural safeguards inherent in the structure of the federal system than by judicially created limitation on federal power." Because members of Congress come from the states, the majority opinion concluded, "the political process ensures that laws that unduly burden the States will not be promulgated."[18] Such an argument may have befitted federalism during the days when senators really were agents of their state legislatures, but, at the time of *Garcia v. San Antonio*, the Court had little basis for expecting the states' interests to win a sympathetic audience in Washington. Indeed, this decision illustrates just how much over the years the Supreme Court favored the national government in refereeing federal-state relations.

In recent years the Supreme Court has begun to take a more circumspect view of federal authority and has sought to preserve some semblance of state independence in federal-state relations. For example, in *United States v. Lopez* (1995) the Court narrowly decided in favor of a student who had been caught carrying a handgun onto campus in violation of the federal Gun-Free School Zones Act of 1990.* For the first time in many years the Court held that some "empirical connection" needed to be established between a law's provisions and its actual effect on interstate *commerce* before the national government could make policy that would supersede state policy in the traditional domains of state jurisdiction.[19] The Court first

---

*The Gun-Free School Zones Act established a zone around public schools in which anyone caught with a gun was charged with a federal felony. *United States v. Lopez*, 514 U.S. 549 (1995).

applied the *Lopez* rationale in 2000, when it overturned the 1994 Violence Against Women Act allowing female victims of gender-motivated violence to sue their attackers in federal court. Writing for a narrow majority, then–chief justice William H. Rehnquist argued that Congress had exceeded its commerce clause authority by intruding into state control of law enforcement. Unpersuaded by Congress's concerted effort to show that violence affected interstate commerce, Rehnquist responded, "Simply because Congress may conclude that a particular activity substantially affects interstate commerce does not necessarily make it so."* After applying this precedent in several decisions, however, the Court in 2005 rejected the *Lopez*-based argument that California's and nine other states' laws protecting the noncommercial cultivation of marijuana for personal, medical use prevent the federal government from enforcing national antidrug laws. However heartening recent small victories may be for defenders of states' rights, the medical marijuana decision reminds us that they have not seriously undermined the extensive authority nationalization has thrust on the federal government.

## Preemption Legislation

Today the clearest and most unequivocal expression of nationalization's impact on public policy appears in the growth of **preemption legislation**—federal laws that assert the national government's prerogative to control public policy in a particular field. Preemption owes its existence to the supremacy clause and its frequent use to the nationalizing forces described earlier. Over the 150 years prior to the New Deal, Congress enacted 83 laws that in some way substituted federal policy for that of the states. From 1933 to 1969, 123 such statutes were adopted, and since 1969 twice that number.[20] If preemption were all that had changed federal-state relations, modern American federalism might still be described as dual. The national government's "sphere of sovereignty" would merely have grown at the expense of the states. But preemption accounts for only a small part of the impact of nationalization on federal-state relations. Generally, the jurisdictions of the states have not been curtailed so much as the national government has joined with the states in formulating policy. The result is the shared federalism described earlier in this chapter.

A cursory examination of trends in government growth during the twentieth century might raise the question of whether the impact of nationalization on reshaping modern federalism has been overstated here. Today states and localities employ more workers than ever before, their largest increases occurring since the nationalizing thrust of the New Deal (see Figure 3.4). Paradoxically, state governments have grown because of, rather than despite, nationalization. Just as the New Deal grafted national policy onto state administrations, much federal domestic policy continues to be implemented through the states instead of directly through the federal bureaucracy.

---

*Elizabeth A. Palmer, "High Court Further Circumscribes Congress' Power in Ruling on Violence Against Women Act," *CQ Weekly*, May 20, 2000, 1188. The Court again invoked *Lopez* in 2001, ruling by a 5–4 vote that state employees could not use the federal Americans with Disabilities Act (see Chapter 4) to sue their employers.

■ **FIGURE 3.4**   The Postwar Growth of Government Occurred at the Local Level

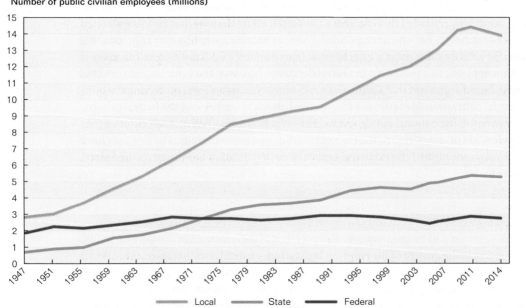

Number of public civilian employees (millions)

*Sources:* For 1949, 1952, 1954, 1959, 1964, 1969–1988, and 2012: data from U.S. Advisory Commission on Intergovernmental Relations, *Significant Features of Fiscal Federalism, 1990,* vol. 2 (Washington, DC: Author, 1990), 177; for 1989–1992, 1994, 151; for other years: data from U.S. Census Bureau, *Historical Statistics of the United States,* Series Y189–198 (Washington, DC: U.S. Government Printing Office, 1975), 1100; U.S. Census Bureau, *Statistical Abstract of the United States, 2000* (Washington, DC: U.S. Government Printing Office, 2000), Tables 524 and 525; U.S. Census Bureau, *Statistical Abstract of the United States, 2004* (Washington, DC: U.S. Government Printing Office, 2004), Table 453; U.S. Census Bureau, *Statistical Abstract of the United States, 2008* (Washington, DC: U.S. Government Printing Office, 2008), Table 448; U.S. Census Bureau, *Statistical Abstract of the United States, 2010* (Washington, DC: U.S. Government Printing Office, 2012), Table 450; U.S. Census Bureau, *Statistical Abstract of the United States, 2012* (Washington, DC: U.S. Government Printing Office, 2012), Table 461; U.S. Census Bureau, American Fact Finder, "Government Employment & Payroll," accessed at http://www.census.gov/govs/apes/, March 2016.

The national government has developed two ways—the carrot and the stick—to induce cooperation from the constitutionally independent states. The carrot consists of financial inducements, usually in the form of grants to states. The stick is regulation and mandates. Since the 1980s, chronic federal budget deficits have led national politicians to rely more heavily on the stick to achieve their policy objectives, and thus pass the costs on to the states.

### The Carrot: Federal Grants to the States

Although federal aid dates back to the Articles of Confederation, when the national government doled out public lands to the states, only during the past half-century have federal **grants-in-aid** become an important feature of intergovernmental relations. By one count, a mere handful of these programs that provide money to a state for a specific purpose existed before the New Deal; today they number in the hundreds. Typically these grants amount to more than just inducements for states to provide services that they otherwise might not be disposed to offer or could not afford. Rather, they give the national government opportunities to define these "state" programs with great specificity. The federal Race to the Top grants have generated enormous controversy by pushing states to adopt a national set of Common Core standards in education. (See the Politics to Policy box, "States' Rights Meet Reading, Writing, and 'Rithmetic," on page 124.)

The exact structure of a grant can have an enormous impact on how much control the federal government exercises over the scope of state programs and even over the ideological direction in which policy is likely to move. Though it may seem like a bureaucratic detail, the difference between a **block grant** and a **matching grant** is crucial. When the federal government makes a block grant, it gives each state or local government an exact amount of money to spend for some purpose. If the state wants to do more in the policy area, it can, but the state's government must pay all the costs of this program expansion by itself. If state officials do not place a high priority on the policy area, they are free to spend less than the block grant, but all of the savings will stay in the federal treasury. States thus have little incentive to control their costs below the level of the block grant, and a huge disincentive to spend above it. They generally spend exactly as much as the block grant gives them, which effectively lets the federal government set state spending levels.

The logic and consequences of a matching grant work differently. With a matching grant, the federal government promises to provide matching funds, usually between one and four dollars, for every dollar that a state spends in some area. These blank checks, not surprisingly, often lead to major program expansions. A matching grant creates a "moral hazard," a situation in which people or groups behave differently, and often take more risks, when they do not have to pay all the costs of their actions.

Consider the logic of Medicaid, the state health insurance program funded through federal matching grants. States are required to cover some of their poorest residents and provide a minimum number of health care services through Medicaid but can choose to insure more people or pay for more services if they want. When a state's budget is flush and its leaders decide to expand Medicaid, a state that receives a $2-to-$1 federal match can cover an extra $300 million of services and spend only $100 million, because the federal government will pay the other $200 million. Its residents receive a lot of benefit, and its taxpayers assume little financial risk. This makes Medicaid expansion a relatively easy decision for state lawmakers. But when the state faces a budget crunch, the matching rate makes Medicaid cuts a bad deal. To save $100 million in state spending, state officials would have to trim Medicaid services by $300 million, leaving $200 million of federal grants on the table. This ensures a lot of pain for little gain and explains why state and federal Medicaid spending has grown steeply over the past few decades. When states are not forced to pay the full costs of a new program, they take advantage of their blank checks to spend more and more federal money.

Why would the federal government ever give states matching grants? National lawmakers have long realized the implications of this moral hazard for the growth of government. One explicit rationale behind matching grants is that they can help capture the positive externality created when states care for the welfare and health care of their residents. Because Americans often move across state lines, these benefits—by ensuring that even those below the poverty

**POLITICS TO POLICY**

# States' Rights Meet Reading, Writing, and 'Rithmetic

## The Battle over the Common Core

The language used by governors leading the fight against the imposition of a national set of educational testing standards known as the Common Core evokes every states' rights battle fought over the past two centuries. Texas governor Rick Perry declared that "Texas is on the right path toward improved education, and we would be foolish and irresponsible to place our children's future in the hands of unelected bureaucrats and special interest groups thousands of miles away in Washington." Indiana's Mike Pence, pledging that his state would adopt its own demanding standards, vowed that "they will be written by Hoosiers, for Hoosiers, and will be among the best in the nation." When Louisiana governor Bobby Jindal filed a lawsuit against the Obama administration in August 2014, he charged that "the federal government has hijacked and destroyed the Common Core initiative. Common Core is the latest effort by big government disciples to strip away state rights and put Washington, D.C. in control of everything."

Where did this federal power grab come from, and how did it generate so much political heat? The Common Core, the target of so much incendiary rhetoric by governors in the lead-up to the 2014 elections, was initiated by governors themselves five years earlier. The National Governors Association, working with a council of school superintendents, funded the development of a set of rigorous national standards in education to give clear guidance to teachers across the nation in what colleges and employers expected from high school graduates. In a 2009

press release announcing the state collaboration creating these standards, Virginia governor Tim Kaine made the case that national standards were in each state's best interests. "Today, we live in a world without borders," Governor Kaine observed. "It not only matters how Virginia students compare to those in surrounding states—it matters how we compete with countries across the world."

Then the federal government got involved. Barack Obama's Department of Education used the federal government's ability to compel the states to action by dangling the carrot of a grant. The Obama administration offered $4.35 billion in "Race to the Top" education grants to states, giving bonus points to state applications that adopted common learning goals. State officials understood what they needed to do to get a shot at the federal largesse, and by 2012, forty-six states and the District of Columbia had adopted the Common Core.

Yet as the standards, which emphasized critical thinking, explaining answers, nonfiction reading, and computerized testing, began to roll out in schools across the country, rebellion against them brewed on both sides of the political spectrum. Those on the left saw them as too focused on testing and not enough on teaching, with New York's governor, Andrew Cuomo, calling for a delay in their implementation. Objections on the right were far more vociferous, especially among lawmakers associated with the Tea Party who saw this, in the words of Governor Jindal's lawsuit, as a policy shift that "effectively forces states down a path toward a national curriculum" in violation of the state sovereignty clause in the Constitution. In 2014 legislators across the country introduced more than one hundred bills seeking to stop or to delay the Common Core in their states. Backers

of the Common Core have responded that the fight is all about election-year politics. Former U.S. education secretary Arne Duncan noted that Jindal—a candidate for president in 2016—initially supported the Common Core, and attacked Jindal for switching positions: "It's all about politics, it's not about education." Yet this fight, which is likely to play out over many years as states implement the new standards or adopt their own, is but another example of the age-old push and pull between national policy and states' rights.

*Sources:* Allie Bidwell, "The Politics of Common Core," *U.S. News and World Report*, March 6, 2014; National Governors Association, "Forty-Nine States and Territories Join Common Core Standards Initiative," press release, June 1, 2009; Stephanie Banchero, "School-Standards Pushback," *Wall Street Journal*, May 8, 2012; "Gov. Bobby Jindal to Sue Feds over Common Core," Associated Press, August 27, 2014.

line receive medical services and basic necessities—spill across the nation, and the grants help state lawmakers internalize the benefits they create for their neighbors. According to Wallace Oates, a prominent theorist of fiscal federalism, matching grants should "be employed where the provision of local services generates benefits for residents of other jurisdictions."[21] Matching grants, because they can treat each state differently, ironically allow the federal government to equalize living conditions across states with radically unequal economies. Richer states receive smaller federal matches, and poorer states get larger matching grants, as Table 3.2 illustrates. The differences in these rates translate into billions more in federal dollars going to less affluent states.

Because matching rates incentivize higher state spending and redistribute money across the nation, they have become an issue of partisan contention. The Democratically controlled Congresses that created and expanded Medicaid and welfare programs funded them through matching grants because they knew this financial arrangement would spur

**TABLE 3.2** How Many Federal Dollars Match One Dollar of State Spending?

| STATE | FEDERAL MATCH FOR MEDICAID SPENDING |
|---|---|
| Arkansas | $2.39 |
| California | $1.00 |
| Kansas | $1.33 |
| Mississippi | $3.24 |
| Montana | $1.90 |
| New York | $1.00 |
| New Mexico | $2.60 |
| Texas | $1.39 |

*Sources:* These matching rates are from the 2019 fiscal year, reported in reports by the Kaiser Family Foundation ("Federal Medical Assistance Percentage [FMAP] for Medicaid and Multiplier")

New York Governor Andrew Cuomo announced in January 2018 that his state would join with Connecticut and New Jersey—all blue states that had voted strongly for Hillary Clinton in 2016—in suing the Trump Administration over its 2017 tax law. The law hit hard at the pocketbooks of homeowners and those with big salaries in states like Cuomo's that charged high rates on property and income. The lawsuit opened up yet another legal front in the episodic battle between various states and federal government.

even the most conservative and cash-strapped states to spend freely on social services. When Republicans took control of Congress in 1994, they wanted to remove this moral hazard to restrain state and federal spending. After trying and failing to shift Medicaid to a block grant program in 1995, the Newt Gingrich–led Congress succeeded in block granting the Temporary Assistance for Needy Families program as part of a 1996 welfare reform deal with Bill Clinton. The ideological stakes of these battles over funding formulas were clear; both sides knew that government would grow more quickly under matching grants than under block grants. The combatants also likely realized that shifting responsibility for funding a program from the national to the state governments dramatically changes who pays for it, as the Politics to Policy box, "Who Pays for Government?," on page 131 shows. These episodes illustrate once again that in fights over federalism, each combatant is usually more concerned with a policy goal than with shaping the proper relationship between national and state governments.

## The Stick: Unfunded Mandates

Until the 1960s the only federal regulations applied to the states were those governing the routine reporting and accounting for grants.* Since then, Washington has relied increasingly on rules to pursue policy objectives. Not only are states required to administer policies they might object to, but, adding insult to injury, the federal government may not even compensate the states for the costs of administration. One of the most controversial examples is the Education for All Handicapped Children Act of 1975, which requires states and school districts to offer prescribed, and in many cases costly, levels of special education for children with disabilities without providing more than a fraction of the funds needed to finance these mandated programs. Many school districts, as a consequence, find themselves strapped for resources and must curtail existing instructional programs to satisfy this federal mandate.

*Crosscutting requirements* are statutes that apply certain rules and guidelines to a broad array of federally subsidized state programs. Since the 1960s this device has been used widely

---

*The one exception was the Hatch Act (1940), which sought to clean up corruption by preventing federal and state employees from engaging in a variety of partisan political activities.

to enforce civil rights laws. For example, the failure of any state to follow federal guidelines that prohibit discriminatory employment practices can result in prosecution of state officials as well as loss of grants. Another prominent area of crosscutting requirements is the environment. All state programs that include major construction and changes in land use must file environmental impact statements with the federal government.

*Crossover sanctions* are stipulations that a state, to remain eligible for full federal funding for one program, must adhere to the guidelines of an unrelated program. One example, mentioned earlier, is Congress's stipulation tying federal highway funds to state adoption of a minimum drinking age of twenty-one. Similarly, the Education for All Handicapped Children Act requires that a school district develop special education programs meeting federal guidelines to remain eligible for a broad variety of previously created grants-in-aid programs, including school construction and teacher-training subsidies.

National politicians frequently use crossover sanctions to influence state policies beyond their jurisdiction. In 1994 Senator Patrick Leahy, D-Vt., proposed legislation banning the sale of soft drinks on public school campuses, and Senator Dianne Feinstein, D-Calif., introduced a bill requiring that all students caught entering school with a handgun be suspended for a minimum of one year. Both bills provided for a cutoff in school aid funds if the districts failed to comply.

*Direct orders* are requirements that can be enforced by legal and civil penalties. The Clean Water Act, for example, bans ocean dumping of sewage sludge. In 1996, when the city of San Diego resisted a multibillion-dollar investment in a sophisticated sewage treatment facility that would alleviate the problem, the EPA brought suit in federal court to impose punitive financial penalties on the city.

Certain federal laws allow the states to administer joint federal-state programs as long as they conform to federal guidelines—a practice known as *partial preemption*. If a state agency fails to follow the instructions of federal agencies, the state might lose control of the program altogether; alternatively, federal grants might be suspended via crossover regulations. Good examples of partial preemption

In a dizzying twist on the fiscal tools of federalism, the federal government has actually unfunded itself in order to protect states that have legalized medical marijuana. An amendment passed by Congress in 2014 by Dana Rohrabacher (a conservative Republican) and Sam Farr (a liberal Democrat), and renewed each year since then, prevents the U.S. Department of Justice from spending money to obstruct states "from implementing their own state laws that authorize the use, distribution, possession, or cultivation of medical marijuana." When two California pot growers were caught with 300 marijuana plants, $225,000 in cash, and bars of gold and silver, the amendment saved them. Even though they pleaded guilty to federal drug charges, charges against the growers were thrown out when a federal district judge ruled that federal laws could not be used to crack down on medical marijuana in a state, like California, that had legalized it.

regulations are state air pollution policies. Public law and the EPA set minimally acceptable standards, but enforcement of these standards rests mostly with state agencies.

Hardly any area of state policy is unaffected by federal regulations of one kind or another. A close look at the major federal laws listed in Table 3.3 reveals several interesting trends and characteristics. First, although federal grants were plentiful before the 1970s, few regulatory policies were in place. Second, since the 1970s the more coercive forms of regulation—direct orders and partial preemption—have been favored. Finally, the content of the policies reveals the political processes that produced them. Federal regulation of the states is concentrated on civil rights and the environment—the two sectors in which national majorities are likely to be at odds with state majorities. The same policy disagreements also may explain why coercion is such a favored policy instrument today. Regulatory statutes compel states to administer policies they would spurn if federal regulations did not legally require their compliance.

**TABLE 3.3**  Examples of Major Unfunded Mandates

| PUBLIC LAW | KIND OF MANDATE |
|---|---|
| **Civil Rights Act of 1964 (Title VI)**<br>Prevents discrimination on the basis of race, color, or national origin in federally assisted programs | Crosscutting |
| **Age Discrimination in Employment Act (1967)**<br>Prevents discrimination on the basis of age in federally assisted programs | Crosscutting |
| **Clean Air Act (1970)**<br>Established national air quality and emissions standards | Crosscutting, crossover sanctions, partial preemption |
| **Occupational Safety and Health Act (1970)**<br>Sets standards for safe and healthful working conditions | Partial preemption |
| **Endangered Species Act (1973)**<br>Protects and conserves endangered and threatened animal and plant species | Crosscutting, partial preemption |
| **Fair Labor Standards Act Amendments (1974)**<br>Extend federal minimum wage and overtime pay protections to state and local government employees | Direct order |
| **Education for All Handicapped Children Act (1975)**<br>Provides free, appropriate public education to all handicapped children | Crossover sanctions |
| **Hazardous and Solid Waste Amendments (1984)**<br>Reauthorize and strengthen the scope and enforcement of the Resource Conservation and Recovery Act of 1976; establish a program to regulate underground storage tanks for petroleum and hazardous substances; require annual EPA inspections of state and locally operated hazardous waste sites | Partial preemption |

| PUBLIC LAW | KIND OF MANDATE |
|---|---|
| **Asbestos Hazard Emergency Response Act (1986)** Directs school districts to inspect for asbestos hazards and take the necessary actions to protect health and the environment; requires state review and approval of local management response plans | Direct order |
| **Americans with Disabilities Act (1990)** Established comprehensive national standards to prohibit discrimination in public services and accommodations and to promote handicapped access to public buildings and transportation | Crosscutting, direct order |
| **Clean Air Act Amendments (1990)** Impose strict new deadlines and requirements dealing with urban smog, municipal incinerators, and toxic emissions; enacted a program for controlling acid rain | Partial preemption |
| **National Voter Registration Act (1993)** Requires states to provide all eligible citizens the chance to register to vote when they apply for renewal of their driver's license | Direct order |
| **Ban on Internet sales tax (rider on 1998 appropriations law)** Placed a three-year moratorium on state sales taxes on Internet commerce and created a commission of state and industry representatives to recommend permanent policy | Direct order |
| **No Child Left Behind Act (2001)** Established standards for performance of schools with frequent standardized testing required and prescribed levels of credentialed instructors | Crossover sanction |
| **Help America Vote Act (2003)** Established standards and partially financed changes in voting procedures | Direct order |
| **Fair Minimum Wage Act (2007)** Increased the federal minimum wage from $5.15 to $7.25 per hour by 2009 | Direct order |
| **Internet Tax Freedom Act Amendments (2007)** Extended the moratorium on states charging sales tax on Internet purchases until 2014 | Direct order |

*Sources:* Data from Advisory Commission on Intergovernmental Relations and various issues of *Congressional Quarterly Weekly Report* and *CQ Weekly.*

When members of Congress pass a law that obligates the states to provide particular services, they are yielding to a temptation all politicians share: the desire to respond to some citizens' demands without being held responsible for the costs. In forcing the states to pay for a program, members are imposing costs for which they will not be held accountable. Like the grants process, mandates deprive state political representatives of their rightful decision-making authority. Of greater concern to fiscal conservatives, unfunded mandates increase government spending. In 1995 President Clinton and the Republican Congress agreed to rein in future temptations to "spend" the states' revenues. The result was the Unfunded Mandates Reform Act, which required that new federal laws pay for the programs and regulations they imposed on the states. A 1998 study, however, found that the law was exerting minimal constraint on mandates.[22] Perhaps the temptation to respond to demands for services while avoiding costs overwhelms the ideologies of even conservative politicians. In any event, Congress has continued to enact preemptive and mandate legislation.

## Evolving Federalism: A By-Product of National Policy

No feature of American government was more dramatically transformed during the twentieth century than federal-state relations. Some of the most important contributions to this development came through sudden bursts of national policymaking in which the federal government assumed jurisdiction over and responsibility for large sectors of public policy once reserved to the states. President Roosevelt's New Deal response to the Depression and President Johnson's Great Society initiatives against poverty in the United States are two notable examples. It is instructive that both occurred when the Democratic Party controlled the White House and enjoyed the largest majorities in Congress ever seen in the twentieth century. In other instances, changes in federal-state relations have occurred more gradually and inconspicuously as interest groups and constituencies have pressed for national action after failing to win in the states. On still other occasions, the states themselves have invited federal participation to tap federal funding or to institute federal oversight and sanctioning authority to solve their own collective action problems.

The nationalization of public policy that proceeded from these causes did not arise from some grand design. Rather, it occurred as politicians sought solutions to problems and responded to the demands of their constituencies. No one had a stake in trying to rationalize intergovernmental relations or wrest authority away from the states. In this sense, then, the condition of modern federalism has had little to do with responses to collective action dilemmas and much to do with the interplay of political interests. And if the behavior of recent presidents and Congresses is any indication, federal-state relations will continue to evolve in this way.

In Chapter 4 we turn to a series of national decisions that even more dramatically refashioned federalism in the United States. The issue is civil rights for African Americans. The Civil War, Reconstruction, and the civil rights movement of the 1960s all required vigorous national action against entrenched state policies instituting slavery and, later, segregation. Southerners, recognizing that their positions on slavery and segregation were untenable, nevertheless sought to rationalize and defend their policies from the higher ground of federalism. The Confederacy's only president, Jefferson Davis, went to his grave steadfastly maintaining that the South's secession was not about slavery but about states' rights. Nearly a century later, Alabama governor George Wallace used the same rhetoric when confronted

**POLITICS TO POLICY**
# Who Pays for Government?

## Comparing State and Federal Tax Burdens

One central fact of federalism that is seldom discussed but deserves serious contemplation is that shifting the responsibility for funding programs to the states also shifts the burden of paying for them to less affluent Americans, for better or worse. Most federal tax dollars are raised from income and payroll taxes, with higher earners paying a higher rate. This creates a progressive tax system, with the following figure showing that the richest 1 percent of Americans pay a federal tax rate that is more than three times as high as the rate paid by those whose incomes put them in the lowest 20 percent.

Yet states typically raise less money from income taxes—with Florida and Texas charging no income taxes at all. Instead, many rely on large sales and property taxes, which hit the poor harder because they spend so much of their money on housing and consumer purchases. This makes state taxes regressive, with poorer residents paying more cents on every dollar they earn to state governments than do the affluent. The graph shows that in Texas, the poorest residents pay the largest share of their income in state and local taxes. Some states are more regressive than others, but in all states those in the bottom 20 percent pay a higher tax rate than the top 1 percent. As a consequence, any shift in responsibility for health care or welfare services from the federal government changes who will pay the bill. To many, this is fair, because poor residents receive the bulk of these services and because the rich are already paying such a high federal tax rate. To others, including the protesters who took to the streets during the 2011 Occupy movement, state tax structures represent an unfair advantage for the richest 1 percent.

*Sources:* Tax data are drawn from the Institute on Taxation and Economic Policy, *Who Pays Taxes in America in 2018?*, April 2018, and the Institute on Taxation and Economic Policy, *Who Pays? A Distributional Analysis of the Tax Systems of All 50 States*, 5th ed., January 2015.

## Texas State and Local Taxes

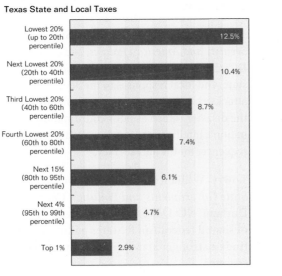

**Texas State and Local Taxes**

| Income Group | Tax Rate |
| --- | --- |
| Lowest 20% (up to 20th percentile) | 12.5% |
| Next Lowest 20% (20th to 40th percentile) | 10.4% |
| Third Lowest 20% (40th to 60th percentile) | 8.7% |
| Fourth Lowest 20% (60th to 80th percentile) | 7.4% |
| Next 15% (80th to 95th percentile) | 6.1% |
| Next 4% (95th to 99th percentile) | 4.7% |
| Top 1% | 2.9% |

## Federal Government Taxes

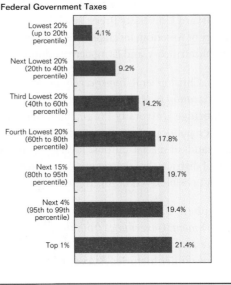

**Federal Government Taxes**

| Income Group | Tax Rate |
| --- | --- |
| Lowest 20% (up to 20th percentile) | 4.1% |
| Next Lowest 20% (20th to 40th percentile) | 9.2% |
| Third Lowest 20% (40th to 60th percentile) | 14.2% |
| Fourth Lowest 20% (60th to 80th percentile) | 17.8% |
| Next 15% (80th to 95th percentile) | 19.7% |
| Next 4% (95th to 99th percentile) | 19.4% |
| Top 1% | 21.4% |

**Want a better grade?**

Get the tools you need to sharpen your study skills. Access practice quizzes, eFlashcards, video, and multimedia at **edge.sagepub.com/kernell9e.**

by federal officers seeking to enforce national laws and court orders. Because of the South's experience with civil rights, federalism came to be viewed as a hollow ruse that could be brushed aside without serious consideration whenever national action appeared necessary. Whether hollow or not, the concept of federalism will always be debated in American politics because the stakes of this fight are so high for policies critical to American life. "From the start," one scholar of the history of American federalism notes, "political opponents have fought about federalism because it affects who wins and who loses a particular fight."[23]

## KEY TERMS

block grant   123
Common Core   110
cutthroat competition   114
dual federalism   99
elastic clause   103
enumerated powers   103

externality   113
federalism   96
grants-in-aid   122
matching grant   123
nationalization   100
preemption legislation   121

race to the bottom   114
shared federalism   99
Tenth Amendment   104
unitary government   96

## SUGGESTED READINGS

Beer, Samuel H. *To Make a Nation: The Rediscovery of American Federalism.* Cambridge, MA: Belknap Press of Harvard University Press, 1993. Beer reviews the history of American federalism, its roots in traditional republican theory, and its modern evolution.

Berry, Christopher R. *Imperfect Union: Representation and Taxation in Multilevel Governments.* New York: Cambridge University Press, 2009. Berry looks at politics, public participation, and policy in the tens of thousands of special-purpose local governments and school districts that deliver critical services yet form nearly invisible layers of government within America.

Campbell, Ballard C. *The Growth of American Government: Governance from the Cleveland Era to the Present.* Bloomington: Indiana University Press, 1995. Another historical survey of nationalization that focuses almost exclusively on the national government.

Kettl, Donald H. *System under Stress: Homeland Security and American Politics,* 2nd ed. Washington, DC: CQ Press, 2007. This balanced look at federal, state, and local responses to the September 11, 2001, attacks examines the system-wide failures that led to the disaster—such as poor coordination among the nation's intelligence agencies—and assesses the consequences for the bureaucracy.

Lowry, William R. *The Dimensions of Federalism: State Governments and Pollution Control Policies.* Durham, NC: Duke University Press, 1992. A study of shared federalism in water pollution policy that finds a stronger state presence than is commonly assumed.

Peterson, Paul E., Barry G. Rabe, and Kenneth K. Wong. *When Federalism Works.* Washington, DC: Brookings, 1986. A thorough and authoritative study of modern federalism in the United States.

Skowronek, Stephen. *Building a New American State: The Expansion of National Administrative Capacities, 1877–1920.* New York: Cambridge University Press, 1982. A modern classic on the institutional conflicts involved in shifting the center of public policy from the states to Washington.

Wiebe, Robert H. *The Search for Order, 1877–1920.* New York: Hill & Wang, 1967. An authoritative, well-written historical survey of the nationalization of American life.

## REVIEW QUESTIONS

1. What are the main differences between unitary governments, confederations, and federal governments? Which type of government is most common?

2. Most of the Framers felt that the Constitution adequately protected the states against encroachment by the national government. How, then, did proponents of nationalization succeed in expanding the power of the national government?

3. When states encounter problems that cross state borders, why don't they just make formal agreements with each other to solve the problems? What happens in the absence of such arrangements?

4. Why would national majorities sometimes find it easier to work through the national government than through state governments? What are some examples of policy areas in which this strategy has been used?

5. What are the three main types of collective action problems faced by state governments? Give an example of each.

Honduran immigrants, some of more than 1,500 people in a migrant caravan, travel north on October 16, 2018, near Quezaltepeque, Guatemala. The caravan, the second of its size in 2018, began the previous week in San Pedro Sula, Honduras, with plans to march north through Guatemala and Mexico en route to the United States.

# Civil Rights

## KEY QUESTIONS

- How could a nation that embraced the Declaration of Independence's creed that "all men are created equal" condone slavery?

- Why would a majority in society ever seek to extend and protect the rights of its minorities in the face of huge costs—even those imposed by a tragic civil war?

- Does America's constitutional system impede or promote the cause of civil rights?

- Are "civil rights" generic, or do we define them differently across groups according to issues for which they seek protection?

## CHAPTER OBJECTIVES

**4.1** Define civil rights.

**4.2** Identify two obstacles in the way of civil rights for African Americans historically.

**4.3** Discuss the political efforts to seek civil rights for African Americans from the nineteenth century to the present.

**4.4** Explain the legacy of the civil rights movement for groups such as women, Hispanics, and members of the LGBT community.

**4.5** Assess the role of collective action efforts in the civil rights movement.

All nineteen hijackers who coordinated, commandeered, and launched the September 11, 2001, airline attacks on the World Trade Center and Pentagon were Middle Eastern men. In the subsequent investigations, authorities found that other terrorist cell members implicated in the assaults were also Middle Eastern.

For the next five months, as federal agencies issued reports and advisories about terrorist threats, their communiqués frequently included mug shots of Arab suspects who allegedly were in the United States. Unavoidably, perhaps, government officials and ordinary citizens alike began to regard male Arab strangers with suspicion. This wariness took on more specificity as the Justice Department systematically interviewed twelve hundred male Middle Eastern visa holders in the United States; Attorney General John Ashcroft unveiled new procedures to expedite expulsion hearings for people who had overstayed or violated their visas; some pilots and flight crews refused to fly with "suspicious-looking" passengers (including, in one case, Rep. Darrell Issa, R-Calif., and, in another, a member of President George W. Bush's secret service). Critics of these measures charged discrimination and **racial profiling** (enlisting race or ethnicity as the primary criterion for identifying a suspect), starting a national debate over how government and airline officials should prevent the next terrorist attack, which nearly everyone thought was imminent.

One national survey taken soon after September 11 found that 58 percent of the public endorsed more intensive security checks for Arabs, and two-thirds supported "random stops" of people of Middle Eastern descent.[1] Arab American support groups and some local American Civil Liberties Union (ACLU) chapters opened hotlines for registering discrimination complaints. Civil liberties watchdogs argued that because only a tiny fraction of individuals posed a threat, treating with suspicion everyone who fit the Middle Eastern profile constituted discrimination. The reaction to September 11 recalled the internment of Japanese Americans nearly sixty years earlier. In 1941 after Japan bombed Pearl Harbor in Hawaii, the same fear of imminent attack—fueled by government alerts, air-raid drills, and other civil defense activities—gripped the nation. Within months government officials in Washington spawned the plan—in hindsight, clearly unwarranted—to intern thousands of West Coast Japanese Americans in camps as far away as Arkansas for the duration of World War II.

The Transportation Department recalled this misguided relocation as it dealt with the September 11 crisis. To counteract charges of racial profiling in airport screening, which began in the aftermath of the terrorist attack, the department issued rules for airport and other security personnel that sought to balance protecting the public's right to security with preventing civil rights violations. The department prohibited screeners from giving travelers special attention based solely on their "race, color, national origin, religion, sex, or ancestry." "Arab-looking" men who spoke no English were to be screened no differently than other passengers, including, for example, elderly grandmothers who had their knitting needles confiscated by security guards.[2] Critics of the policy countered that because dozens of known terrorists fit the same distinctive gender and ethnic profile, public officials were justified in using this information to identify hard-to-find suspects. One nationally prominent civil libertarian condoned racial profiling as "entirely appropriate," repeating former Supreme Court justice Robert Jackson's declaration that "the Constitution is not a suicide pact." In any event, observed one leading civil rights lawyer, it was expecting too much of screeners who must "make on the spot decisions about whom to detain and whom to question [to] disregard ethnicity."[3] The racial profiling debate will not be resolved anytime soon. Indeed, in 2010 it flared up again in a new arena of law enforcement—spotting and deporting illegal immigrants. The construction of a border fence from San Diego, California, into Arizona during the previous five years channeled increasing numbers of illegal border crossings along Arizona's unfenced border with Mexico. In April 2010 the public's frustration culminated in the passage of a local and highly popular but nationally controversial Arizona law requiring local law enforcement officers to check individuals' immigration status if, during the course of a legal stop for violation of a traffic or other law, the officer reasonably suspects that the person is in the United States illegally.

The Arizona law raises issues of what civil rights, if any, *illegal* immigrants are entitled to. It also poses the question of how law enforcement officers could implement the law while *avoiding* racially profiling citizens of Hispanic descent. If, for example, a subject's dress, language skills, and general demeanor give an officer reasonable suspicion that the person is in the United States illegally, the law prescribes that the officer determine the individual's immigration status. If the person is unable to produce valid Arizona identification (such as a driver's license or nonoperating identification license) or a federally issued identification or immigrant registration document, the officer then should ask to see the individual's visa. If these papers are also unavailable, are out of date, or contain some other problem, the law enforcement officer must turn the individual over to the federal immigration service. Immediately, lawsuits were filed in federal court to block implementation of the law, and the U.S. Supreme Court ruled on the case in June 2012. Although the Court struck down other parts of the Arizona law as "preempted" by federal law, it let stand the key provision requiring local and state law enforcement officers to verify immigration status of individuals stopped for traffic violations and other minor offenses.*

With Hispanics constituting nearly a third of the state's citizenry, the new law virtually ensured repeated instances of ordinary citizens who lost or left their driver's licenses at home being detained because they "look" illegal to officers.

Well before the Arizona law and September 11 attacks, racial profiling had already become a controversial practice. It remains one today. In 2003 the Bush Justice Department issued guidelines for all federal officials to limit racial profiling but made exceptions for protecting the borders against illegal entry and searching for suspected terrorists. Late in 2014 the Obama administration revised the guidelines to prohibit profiling based on other criteria, but it still exempted many of the standard screening procedures at border and transportation centers. In fall 2016 the Justice Department filed criminal charges against Arizona's Maricopa County sheriff, Joe Arpaio, for his department's continuing practice of pulling over and arresting hundreds of Latinos while searching for undocumented aliens.

Most individuals encounter law enforcement at the local level. Across the states profiling policies vary dramatically. About half have laws

Shortly after the attack on Pearl Harbor, President Franklin Roosevelt began issuing executive orders that placed restrictions on Japanese Americans living on the West Coast. Eventually, more than 110,000 Japanese Americans—including native-born U.S. citizens—were removed to internment camps throughout the nation. The internees were given little time to dispose of their homes, businesses, or other property, causing financial ruin for many.

---

*A half-dozen other states used the Arizona law as a model for their own legislation to take direct action to enforce federal immigration laws. Since the Supreme Court issued its decision on the Arizona law, lower federal courts have upheld the "show-me-your-papers" provisions of laws in Alabama, Georgia, and South Carolina. Robbie Brown, "South Carolina: Federal Court Delivers Mixed Verdict on Immigration Measure," *New York Times*, November 15, 2012.

AP Photo/Marcio Jose

People rally in opposition to a proposed stop-and-frisk policy in San Francisco. Similar policies in major cities such as New York have resulted in a backlash and concerns about racial profiling among African American and Hispanic communities in particular.

limiting profiling, but only seventeen by one count have put reporting requirements in place for enforcing racial profiling bans. Although after 9/11 national attention focused mostly on racial profiling of individuals from the Mideast and non-English-speaking Hispanics in the border regions, various research suggests that black men remain the class of Americans law enforcement is most likely to profile.*

The controversies over airport screening and local enforcement of federal immigration laws remind us that civil rights established for one group apply to everyone. For many years, the term *civil rights* referred almost exclusively to the rights and privileges of African Americans. Certainly, the nation's history of civil rights concerned the emancipation of African Americans—first from slavery and then, in the twentieth century, from segregation. The legacy concerns the rights of everyone. The new federal laws, administrative practices, and agencies to secure the rights of African Americans became available to enforce the rights of "new" claimants. Voting rights laws authorizing Justice Department intervention against discriminatory practices in the 1960s were summoned by Hispanic voters fearing arbitrary rules, such as challenges of citizenship, that would disenfranchise them in the 2004 presidential election. The civil rights struggle of African Americans ends with all Americans changing their view of their own rights and privileges. In this respect, the debate over how closely airport screeners should consider the ethnicity and gender of passengers reflects prior debates over the civil rights of African Americans.

## What Are Civil Rights?

Throughout the nation's history, Americans have applied the terms **civil rights** and **civil liberties** to a variety of rights and privileges. Although they have sometimes been used interchangeably, *rights* and *liberties* do offer useful distinctions for organizing our discussion in this and the next chapter. We classify as civil liberties the Constitution's protections *from*

---

*Racial profiling has proved difficult to verify. Without any racial profiling, local police would detain young black men far more often than their white counterparts just by virtue of patrolling high-crime neighborhoods. For a review of this research, see Emily Badger, "Why It's So Hard to Study Racial Profiling by Police," at the *Washington Post*'s Wonkblog site: www.washingtonpost.com/blogs/wonkblog/wp/2014/04/30/it-is-exceptionally-hard-to-get-good-data-on-racial-bias-in-policing/.

government power, meaning the government *may not* take these freedoms—including the freedoms of speech, liberty, and the right to privacy—away. Typically, violations of these liberties occur when some government agency, at any level, oversteps its authority. Civil rights, on the other hand, represent those protections *by* government or that government secures on behalf of its citizens. The crucial difference is that civil rights require governments to act, whereas civil liberties are well served when government does nothing.[4] In colonial times civil rights equaled "civic" rights—protections against arbitrary action by the distant British Crown. Although the term *civil rights* was not commonly used until the late 1760s, when colonial Americans rallied to the slogan "No taxation without representation," the colonists were clearly seeking these rights, including the right to vote and have their views represented in the British Parliament. Thomas Jefferson's eloquent statement in the Declaration of Independence that all governments must defer to humanity's "unalienable Rights" of "Life, Liberty and the pursuit of Happiness" gave the Revolutionary War its moral certitude.

Once they had gained their independence and established republican institutions, Americans turned from seeking protection from an arbitrary and distant government to looking for it from one another. In *Federalist* No. 10 James Madison explored whether a majority of citizens could use government authority to strip adversaries of their rights and thereby gain a permanent advantage. This prospect bothered leaders on both sides of the Constitution's ratification issue. For Madison and the other nationalists, the pluralism of a large republic provided the best insurance against such factionally inspired tyranny; as the number and diversity of groups increased, the likelihood that any one group could impose its will on another decreased. But Patrick Henry and others opposing ratification insisted on a bill of rights to further deter the new national government from usurping power. Along with voting (an issue the Constitution resolved by allowing the states to set voting requirements), virtually everyone's list of freedoms included freedom of speech, free assembly, and a free press.

Modern-day "civil rights" encompass much more than these "civic" rights of political expression and participation. They also include safeguards against any effort by government and dominant groups in a community to subjugate another group and take unfair, mostly economic, advantage of it. Before the American Civil War, southern governments teamed up with white slave owners to configure state laws and institutions to legalize and preserve slavery. (In most southern states, for example, it was illegal for slave masters to free their slaves.) Many decades later, segregation in the South, also regulated by the states, dominated virtually all interpersonal contact between the races. Civil rights, then, also include the rights of individuals in their relations with one another: to live free from bondage and intimidation, to enter into contracts and own property, to have access to businesses that serve the public, and to enjoy equal educational opportunities.

## The Civil Rights of African Americans

In December 1997 Bill Lann Lee, a second-generation Chinese American, opened his acceptance statement as President Bill Clinton's acting assistant attorney general for civil rights by describing his post as "haunted by the ghosts of slavery, the Civil War, Jim Crow." He then proceeded to cite modern instances of racial, ethnic, and religious discrimination.[5] Indeed, as Lee knew and the history books describe, African Americans have been engaged in a two-hundred-year struggle for civil rights, spanning slavery to full citizenship. As we will see in this chapter and the next, the results have redefined the rights and liberties of *all* Americans.

The history of black civil rights provided a laboratory to test James Madison's ideas on democracy in America, laid out in his *Federalist* essays. Dominant white majorities throughout the South instituted slavery—and later segregation—to gain a permanent advantage over the black minority. And what is the solution to such tyranny? As Madison argued in *Federalist* No. 10, a diverse national community would be less inclined than state-level majorities to engage in tyranny and more likely to halt it.

The history of black civil rights follows Madison's script in another respect. The effort to secure civil rights rested less on making formal rules—which Madison noted had little impact on intemperate majorities—and more on configuring politics to allow society's competing interests to check one another. This chapter, as did Madison, recognizes civil rights in America as products of the political process. But the abuses of slavery and segregation endured for almost two centuries before the national majority struck out against local tyranny. The effect of institutions on democracy explains this disturbing situation. For one thing, the Framers rejected a national veto over all state laws, as Madison had repeatedly proposed. Public policy, such as public safety and regulation of elections, was left to state control, allowing slavery to flourish within the South.

African Americans faced two major obstacles in securing rights. First, the Constitution reserves important authority for the states, such as the power to determine voting eligibility. It also separates powers among the three branches of government, making it difficult for national majorities to control the federal government to the extent required to strike against tyranny in the states.

Madison's observation that government is controlled by "men" and not "angels" sums up the second obstacle to obtaining civil rights for African Americans. People do not engage in costly behavior without some expected return. Madison, recognizing that citizens and politicians alike act most forcefully when they have a personal stake in the outcome, believed that tyranny could best be avoided by empowering every faction to look out for its own interests. But what of a faction without the capacity to defend itself? This predicament is central to the nation's long ordeal over civil rights for African Americans. Indeed, politics based on self-interest in a fragmented constitutional system largely explains why it took so long to eradicate slavery, segregation, and other discrimination. Instead, the real question is why the civil rights of African Americans were ever addressed at all.

## The Politics of Black Civil Rights

The efforts to seek civil rights for African Americans took different forms at different times. Notably, in 1787 Benjamin Franklin convened an abolition society meeting in his home and invited delegates to the Constitutional Convention to attend. Throughout the antebellum era and during the Civil War, a small but persistent abolitionist movement forced the nation to face the discrepancy between the ideal of "Life, Liberty and the pursuit of Happiness" and the enslavement of 10 percent of its population. Emancipation shifted the issue from fundamental "life and liberty" rights to those of full citizenship.* Several years later the Fifteenth Amendment granted former slaves the right to vote,† but another century would pass before most could safely exercise this right. With civic rights secured, the dominant issue again shifted, this time to equal opportunity in the marketplace—particularly in education, employment, and housing.

By and large, national majorities have over the decades consistently favored civil rights for African Americans, but only twice did they strike out forcefully against discrimination. The first time was Reconstruction after the Civil War; the second was the national attack on segregation in the 1960s. Why were rights advanced at these particular moments in American history and not at others? A look at the successes and failures will answer this question and illuminate the conditions under which national majorities are able to dictate national policy.

## The Height of Slavery: 1808–1865

Late in 1807, with the Constitution's prohibition against the federal government's regulation of the slave trade about to expire, Congress passed a law ending the importation of slaves. Southern representatives in Congress, not yet aware that the rise of "King Cotton" would soon give rise to a slave-centered, plantation economy, did not vigorously contest the new law. In fact, some probably anticipated that the restricted supply of new slaves might drive up the market value of their human property. Thus the nation took this first step toward eradicating slavery with deceptive ease. It would never be easy again.

Over the next decade slavery remained a side issue only because the northern and southern states carefully maintained regional balance in the Senate, thereby preserving the South's veto over national policy. This balance required matching states' entry—one slave state with one free state—into the Union. As we learned earlier, institutions created to achieve one goal can over time come to serve other purposes. Where equal apportionment of the Senate reassured small states that their interests would not be ignored in the new national government, by the 1820s this same rule guaranteed the South a veto over policy curtailing slavery. Many northern politicians found the practice objectionable but did not press for its eradication against intransigent southerners for fear of fracturing fragile regional party alliances. Indeed, the North hoped that slavery would eventually wither away.

---

*As late as 1858 Abraham Lincoln, in his famous Senate race debates in Illinois with Stephen Douglas, distinguished between citizenship rights based on equality and fundamental rights. He protected his flank by stating there was "no purpose to introduce political and social equality between the white and black races." But then, in one of the most progressive statements made by any elected officeholder of the time, he asserted, "There is no reason in the world why the negro is not entitled to all the natural rights enumerated in the Declaration of Independence. . . . I hold that he is as much entitled to these as the white man." Donald G. Nieman, *Promises to Keep: African-Americans and the Constitutional Order, 1776 to the Present* (New York: Oxford University Press, 1991), 43.

†This achievement stemmed in part from the Senate's insistence that the former Confederate states ratify the amendment as a condition of their reentry into the Union.

### The Missouri Compromise

Then in 1819 the citizens of Missouri, most of whom had emigrated from the slave states of Kentucky and Tennessee, petitioned Congress for admission as a slave state. Instead of shriveling up, slavery threatened to expand beyond its southern borders, upset the balance, and ignite the nation. "Like a fire bell in the night," wrote a retired Thomas Jefferson, the political conflagration he foresaw "awakened and filled me with terror."[6] After months of debate in Washington and throughout the country, Congress enacted the Missouri Compromise in 1820. The plan matched Missouri's entry as a slave state with Maine's as a free state, thereby maintaining the balance in the Senate between free and slave states. Moreover, the South agreed to accept Missouri's southern border as the northern boundary beyond which slavery could not extend in the future (see Map 4.1). The boundary at latitude 36°30' stretched to the end of

### ■ MAP 4.1    The Missouri Compromise and the State of the Union, 1820

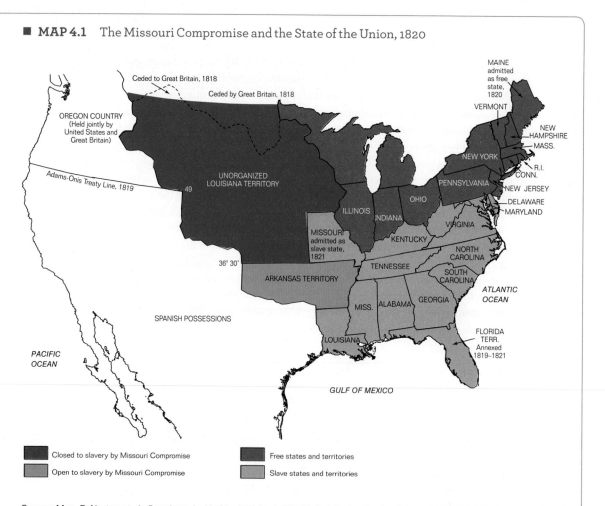

*Source:* Mary B. Norton et al., *People and a Nation: A History of the United States*, 2 vols., 5th ed. © 1998 Wadsworth, a part of Cengage Learning, Inc. Reproduced by permission. www.cengage.com/permissions.

the Louisiana Territory, where Spain's possessions began. Once again, slavery appeared to be fenced in. The compromise itself was a classic "political" solution—one that was not entirely satisfactory to either side but that allowed agreement on a national policy applicable to the foreseeable future.

For the next decade or so this compromise worked. It began to unravel, however, as territories applying for statehood were not conveniently paired off as slave and free states. Gradually southern senators realized that, under the current formula, their ability to block national policy was doomed as more free than slave states joined the Union with continued westward expansion. Thus they began searching for an effective alternative to their Senate veto that would ensure continuation of the institution of slavery.

Meanwhile, the containment strategy also was losing favor in the North, where a small but highly vocal group of abolitionists had never accepted the compromise. More broadly, the abolitionist movement, under the banner of the Liberty Party, reminded the nation of its hypocrisy in condoning slavery. Voters were angry about slavery's territorial expansion, although few endorsed its outright eradication.*

## The Wilmot Proviso and the Compromise of 1850

In 1846 David Wilmot, a Democratic representative from Pennsylvania, introduced a bill that would have gutted the compromise by banning

Do not look at the Negro.

His earthly problems are ended.

Instead, look at the seven WHITE children who gaze at this gruesome spectacle.

Is it horror or gloating on the face of the neatly dressed seven-year-old girl on the right?

Is the tiny four-year-old on the left old enough, one wonders, to comprehend the barbarism her elders have perpetrated?

Rubin Stacy, the Negro, who was lynched at Fort Lauderdale, Florida, on July 19, 1935, for "threatening and frightening a white woman," suffered PHYSICAL torture for a few short hours. But what psychological havoc is being wrought in the minds of the white children? Into what kinds of citizens

Between 1882 and 1950, 4,729 lynchings were reported in the United States. African Americans were the victims in about three-quarters of the cases. This 1930s NAACP poster graphically featured this tyrannical practice designed to intimidate the entire black population.

slavery in the recently acquired territories. Wilmot denied any "squeamish sensitivities" or "morbid sympathy for the slave." Rather, he professed devotion to "the rights of white freemen . . . [and] white free labor."[7] Simply put, slave labor depressed wages for free, white workers. The Wilmot proviso was introduced twice and passed the House of Representatives both times, but it made no headway in the evenly divided Senate. Still, the failure of Wilmot's proposal eventually led significant numbers of northern whites to recognize they had a stake in containing slavery.

---

*After its recent war with Mexico, the United States had annexed territory in the Southwest, almost all of it falling into the slavery zone. Moreover, California was petitioning for statehood, and southerners were proposing that the 36°30' line be projected to the Pacific Ocean and California be split into one slave and one free state.

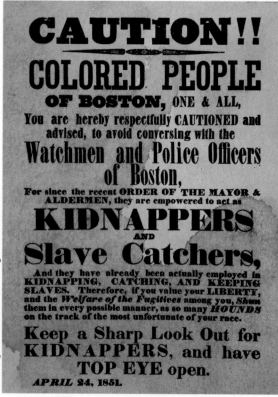

The Fugitive Slave Law of 1850 forced law enforcement authorities in both the North and the South to act as slaveholders' agents in seizing and returning their "property." As this broadside warned, even free African Americans were in danger of being seized and sent into slavery as unscrupulous law enforcement officials colluded with slaveholders in making bogus claims that these free citizens were actually runaway slaves.

By 1848 Wilmot's allies joined the abolitionists in the new antislavery Free Soil Party. Its election slate that year was headed by presidential candidate Martin Van Buren, who already had served one term as president, as a Democrat, in 1836. His 1848 campaign revolved around a single issue: opposition to the extension of slavery on behalf of "free labor." The Free Soil Party managed to scare the two major political parties, the Democrats and the Whigs, by winning 10 percent of the national popular vote and finishing second in several states. Six years later the Free Soil Party joined a broader coalition against slavery's extension that called itself the Republican Party.

In 1850 the Missouri Compromise buckled under the weight of southern and northern grievances. Southerners had complained that runaway slaves who reached the North via the "Underground Railroad"—a network of abolitionists who hid slaves and provided them with transportation northward—were not being returned to their owners. At the same time, northerners were repulsed by slave auctions in Washington, D.C., "within the shadow of the Capitol." But the compromise finally collapsed when California applied in 1849 for admission to the Union as a free state. If the South agreed to admit California, it would lose its ability to block legislation in the Senate. Ultimately the South did agree, but only in return for passage of the **Fugitive Slave Law** compelling northerners to honor southerners' property claims to slaves. Moreover, the new Compromise of 1850, introduced by aging Whig senator Henry Clay of Kentucky, allowed the residents of the territories to decide for themselves whether to apply for statehood as a slave or free state.

### Dred Scott Galvanizes the North

The South may have lost its Senate veto, but a few years later it would unexpectedly acquire a new one. In 1857 the Supreme Court delivered one of its most unfortunate decisions in *Dred Scott v. Sandford*.[8] With every justice writing a separate opinion, a 7–2 majority of the Court concurred that the federal government could not prevent slavery in the territories. The Herculean effort to legislate mutually acceptable policy over the previous half-century was undone in a single decision by the nine unelected justices. The mostly southern majority argued that the Constitution's Framers had never intended African Americans to be citizens. Consequently, African Americans enjoyed "no rights which a white man was bound to respect," and any federal law that interfered with the right of an individual to his property, including slaves, was unconstitutional. Sympathetic lower-court judges appeared ready to extend the logic of this argument and rule that state laws banning slavery also were unconstitutional. The specter of the whole nation being opened to slaveholding by judicial fiat galvanized the North. Campaigning vigorously on the slogan "Free Soil, Free Labor, Free Men," Republican candidate Abraham Lincoln won the 1860 presidential election. So too did so many fellow Republican congressional candidates that this young party took majority control of the House of Representatives and, in alliance with splinter parties, formed a narrow antislavery majority in the Senate. For the first time in American history, the president and a majority of both houses of Congress were aligned against slavery's extension.

Recognizing that the seemingly insurmountable transaction costs to effective majority action had finally and suddenly been swept away, the South did not wait to contest new antislavery policy in Congress. Once president-elect Lincoln announced that the national government would no longer tolerate "the minority [the South] over the majority," the southern states seceded, with South Carolina the first to proclaim its independence on December 20, 1860. By June 1861 ten more states had left the Union and established a new, confederation-style government. On April 12, 1861, the "Confederates" fired on Fort Sumter, a federal garrison in Charleston harbor. The American Civil War had begun, a war that would claim the lives of more than six hundred thousand American soldiers with many thousands more maimed for life.

Thus the first half-century of racial politics in the United States closely followed Madison's prediction of tyranny in the states unconstrained by national majorities. In the South white majorities enlisted state authority to preserve slavery. They were aided and abetted by their agents in the Senate who, as Madison had warned, succeeded in frustrating national action. Only the decisive 1860 Republican electoral victory and the secession of the slave states from the Union gave the national majority sufficient control over government to enforce its preferences. Along the way, strategic politicians, including Wilmot and Lincoln, transformed a losing issue into a winning one by focusing narrowly on the territories and the interests of northern whites more concerned about their own welfare than the welfare of slaves. In the end, this appeal enabled these politicians to win control of the government and eventually eradicate slavery (see the Strategy and Choice box, "The Emancipation Proclamation").

## Reconstruction: 1865–1877

In the five-year period from 1865 to 1870, slaves were formally emancipated (Thirteenth Amendment), granted citizenship (Fourteenth Amendment), and guaranteed the right to vote (Fifteenth Amendment). At the close of the Civil War, however, only a handful of Union states gave black citizens equal access to the ballot box. Some subjected African Americans to special criteria—such as proof of property ownership and literacy—that effectively disenfranchised most of them. Other northern states simply barred African Americans from voting.*

---

*Of the eleven referendum votes held from 1865 through 1869 in eight northern states on constitutional changes to provide African Americans with the ballot, only those in Iowa and Minnesota in 1868 succeeded. The white voters of Illinois, Indiana, Pennsylvania, and New Jersey never voted on the issue, which may have indicated a higher intensity of racial prejudice in those states than in Connecticut, New York, and Ohio, where equal suffrage was defeated. LaWanda and John H. Cox, "Negro Suffrage and Republican Politics: The Problem of Motivation in Reconstruction Historiography," *Journal of Southern History* 33 (August 1967): 318–319.

### STRATEGY AND CHOICE
# The Emancipation Proclamation

Emancipation of the slaves was born of war rather than politics, but its planning and implementation were nonetheless highly strategic. When read carefully, President Abraham Lincoln's Emancipation Proclamation, issued in the fall of 1862, appears to have been composed more with an eye to encouraging southern defections from the Confederacy than to emancipating slaves. Lincoln announced that slaves would be freed in those states that persisted with the rebellion. Slavery was to remain intact in the border states that had stayed in the Union, and even in those sections of the Confederacy that had fallen under Union control.

This policy exposed the president to the criticism that he had failed to free the slaves where he could and freed them where he could not. But by mapping emancipation this way, he prevented it from becoming politically divisive among the Union states (a few still allowed slave ownership), while simultaneously trying to drive a wedge into the Confederacy. Moreover, the rebel states might have to deal with slaves asserting their freedom.

Library of Congress

In 1863 David Gilmour Blythe depicted a homespun Lincoln (his rail-splitter's maul is in the foreground) at work in his study writing the Emancipation Proclamation. Pushed to one side, unheeded, are the states' rights theories of John C. Calhoun and John Randolph. Instead, Lincoln rests his hand on the Holy Bible and heeds Andrew Jackson's call: "The Union Must & Shall Be Preserved."

Not until the 1864 presidential campaign did Lincoln openly endorse the universal abolition of slavery.

For most states, then, freeing slaves and granting them full-fledged citizenship were two different things, and the latter was regarded as radical even by abolitionists. Militant abolitionist newspaper publisher William Lloyd Garrison concluded that "according to the laws of development and progress," voting "is not practical."[†] So how did the Fifteenth Amendment manage to clear, with remarkable alacrity, the formidable hurdles of the amendment process?

The ability to count is invaluable to a politician. Shortly after the war ended in 1865, House Republican leader Thaddeus Stevens of Pennsylvania calculated the probable partisan makeup of Congress after the South returned to the Union. Taking into account that African Americans now counted as full rather than three-fifths citizens for apportioning

---

[†]Another enemy of slavery who conceded that freedmen could not be transformed instantly into full citizens was Republican senator Charles Sumner of Massachusetts, who before the war had earned his abolitionist credentials the hard way by being severely caned by an enraged southern member of the House after a floor speech denouncing slavery.

congressional seats across the states, Stevens estimated that the South would gain thirteen seats over its prewar level. Moreover, with southern legislatures busily enacting laws, called **black codes**, that effectively prevented former slaves from voting (and thus from supporting the party of Lincoln), Stevens rightly suspected that all thirteen seats would be added to the Democratic column. Southerners, he noted, "with their kindred Copperheads [Democrats] of the North, would always elect the President [as well as] control Congress."[9] The outlook was bleak for the Republican Party. Even as Andrew Johnson of Tennessee, Lincoln's Democratic successor in the White House, planned for the South's rapid readmission to the Union, congressional Republicans were staring at possible defeat in the next national election. The Republican response was Reconstruction, whereby under the watchful eye of federal troops, the South would be transformed from a slave society into a free one in which African Americans would fully enjoy the privileges of citizenship. At least that was the plan.

### The Fourteenth and Fifteenth Amendments

The Republicans' foray into political and social reconstruction began with the Fourteenth Amendment. It is difficult to overstate its significance for Americans a century and a half later. It opens with a straightforward definition of citizenship that encompasses former slaves: "All persons born or naturalized in the United States, and subject to the jurisdiction thereof, are citizens of the United States and of the State wherein they reside." Birthright citizenship, as it is sometimes called, has become a flashpoint issue for President Trump. In the fall of 2018 he issued an executive order trying to end it, claiming dubiously that illegal migrants were not in states' "jurisdictions," which requires tortured reasoning to reach this conclusion.* The qualifier does exclude some groups, such as the families of diplomats, foreign soldiers who are in the country temporarily, and others who do clearly fall under their home country's jurisdiction. Then the amendment declares that no state shall "deprive any person of life, liberty, or property, without the *due process of law*; nor deny to any person within its jurisdiction the *equal protection of the laws*" (emphasis added). Note that this statement blankets all "persons," not just citizens with due process and equal protection. This provision is the cornerstone—as important arguably as the Bill of Rights—of our present-day rights and liberties. We devote all of the next chapter to examining the impact of the due process and equal protection clauses on the liberties of all Americans.

Section 2 of the Fourteenth Amendment turns to the immediate business of Reconstruction. It reaffirms the constitutional prescription of apportioning seats in the House of Representatives according to a state's population but then makes an exception: if a state fails to allow black men to vote in federal and state elections, the number of seats allocated to it will be reduced proportionately. A purely political calculation dictated the provision of additional seats only where the Republican Party stood a fighting chance of winning. The amendment was intended to protect two constituencies: African Americans in the South and the Republican majority in Washington, D.C. After the war, as before, civil rights rode on the shoulders of partisan, self-interested politics.

---

*As of early 2019, the president's executive order seeking to end birthright citizenship is tied up in the courts.

But how did this skillfully crafted amendment gain the necessary support when new legislatures in the South were rejecting it by nearly unanimous majorities? The Republicans in Congress, enjoying veto-proof majorities and a recent landslide victory in the 1866 midterm elections, devised an ingenious plan to foil southern opposition. The First Reconstruction Act of 1867 disbanded the governments of the southern states (with the exception of Tennessee, which already had been readmitted to the Union), thereby voiding their votes against the amendment. It then replaced the state governments with five military districts, headed by generals and administered by more than twenty thousand northern troops. To ensure ratification once the state governments were reinstituted, the law bluntly extended the vote to all freedmen and withheld it from the white, rebel ex-soldiers. In Louisiana, where the racial composition of the adult male population was roughly evenly split, black voter registration soon doubled the registration of whites.* Then, putting one last nail in the Confederacy's coffin, Congress made readmission to the Union contingent on a state's ratification of the Fourteenth Amendment.

The narrow partisan purpose of Reconstruction is evident in what the Republican policy omitted. Abolitionists and black leaders pressed Congress for land reform and a degree of economic independence for slaves from their former masters. Instead, all that the freed slaves got from Congress was the ballot. Republican cabinet secretary Gideon Welles concluded cynically, "It is evident that intense partisanship rather than philanthropy is the root of the movement."[10] Two years later congressional Republicans sought to make the black franchise inviolable by passing and sending to the states the Fifteenth Amendment. Quickly ratified, it simply states, "The right of citizens of the United States to vote shall not be denied or abridged by the United States or by any State on account of race, color, or previous condition of servitude."

### Rights Lost: The Failure of Reconstruction

Despite these efforts, Reconstruction's advancement of black civil rights proved temporary. Relying heavily on black support, Republicans dominated southern state legislatures for a few years, but white Democrats seized control of Tennessee and Virginia as early as 1869, and by 1877 all of the former Confederate states had reverted to white Democratic control. Once this happened, Reconstruction was doomed, and African Americans saw their newly acquired status as freed men and women slide back to near servitude.

Power slipped away from African Americans during these years for several reasons. Vigilante violence as a political resource erupted in the late 1860s. Murderous white rioters in New Orleans, Memphis, and other southern cities targeted politically active African Americans and their white allies. In the countryside, the Ku Klux Klan, a secret society of white supremacist men, perfected intimidation through selective brutality.

Meanwhile, northern politicians' commitment to Reconstruction was waning. After many Republicans went down to defeat in the 1874 midterm congressional elections, apparently because of an economic recession, the new Democratic majority in the House of Representatives refused to appropriate funds to support the military forces that remained

---

*Similarly, in Alabama there were approximately twenty thousand more white than black men but forty thousand more black voters. C. Vann Woodward, *The Burden of Southern History* (Baton Rouge: Louisiana State University Press, 1968), 98–99.

Photofest

Originally titled *The Clansman*, *The Birth of a Nation* is recognized as both one of the most important films in the development of American cinema and one of the most racist. D. W. Griffith's 1915 film was the first to use natural settings, night photography, original music, panning shots, moving cameras, and dozens of other innovations. It remains shocking today in part because it looks like a documentary. The blatant racism that depicted freed slaves as villains and the Ku Klux Klan as the salvation of humanity reveals the state of the nation's attitude toward African Americans at the time. It became a blockbuster hit, but not without severe criticism. President Woodrow Wilson described it as "like writing history with lightning. And my only regret is that it is all terribly true." Stung by the criticism, Griffith followed it with *Intolerance*, on the effects of bigotry and inhumanity. Though less famous, many critics consider it his greatest achievement.

in the South. Northern constituents wanted their sons returned home. Congress passed additional laws to protect the freed slaves, but without serious enforcement provisions, they offered African Americans in the distant South little real support. With the rise of the Ku Klux Klan, accompanied by the rapid demobilization of the occupying Union Army, the trajectory of southern politics became clear.

Killed by the same short-term partisan considerations that gave birth to it, Reconstruction officially ended with the 1876 presidential election. The Democratic candidate, Samuel Tilden, came within one vote of an Electoral College majority, but in the disputed states of Florida and Louisiana both parties produced their own favorable vote counts. As a result, the election was thrown into the House of Representatives, where a Republican pledge to end Reconstruction induced southerners to break ranks and support the Republican candidate, Rutherford B.

This jarring photo of segregation was taken outside a Mobile, Alabama, department store in 1956 by Gordon Parks, the first black photographer at *Life* magazine.

Hayes. In 1877 federal troops pulled out of the South, leaving African Americans at the mercy of their former masters.[11] During the early post–Civil War years, therefore, the Constitution presented fewer barriers to majority rule than in any other period in American history. The Republican majority in Congress and the White House opted for a middle course of political reform. Rather than undertaking a massive social and economic reconstruction of the South, they limited Reconstruction to making the South Republican, thereby realizing the party's goal of remaining the nation's majority party and satisfying the interests of their constituents. Even so, local interests in northern congressional districts soon rose against this limited reconstruction. Twenty thousand war-weary northern soldiers remained in the South, and the government continued to assess high wartime taxes nationwide to achieve in the South what few white citizens anywhere would have tolerated in their own communities—the creation of a sizable black electorate. In the North voters no longer wanted to sacrifice to solve distant problems, and the Republican majority soon lost the will to act. Full citizenship for African Americans would wait one hundred years for the emergence of northern politicians whose constituencies favored intervention in race relations in the South.

## The Jim Crow Era and Segregation: 1877–1933

In the 1890s **Jim Crow laws** (named after a popular minstrel show character of the era) were adopted throughout the South to disenfranchise black citizens and physically separate African Americans and whites. These laws institutionalized **segregation** of African Americans and whites in their access to schools, hospitals, prisons, public parks, restrooms, housing, and public conveyances. Indeed, hardly any government service or social interaction between the races was unaffected.

But to secure segregation the southern states had to prevent black citizens from voting, and so they did. By the end of the century all southern states constructed a maze of electoral laws that systematically excluded African Americans from civic life. One common device, the **white primary**, excluded African Americans from voting in primary elections. Because winning the Democratic primary in the solidly Democratic South was tantamount to winning the general election, this law effectively disenfranchised southern black voters. Another effective barrier was the **poll tax** levied on all registered voters, which typically had to be paid months before the election.

Perhaps the most notorious and effective legal barrier was the **literacy test**. Local white registrars would require prospective black voters to read and interpret arcane passages of the state's constitution. Few could satisfy the registrars' rigorous demands, and by 1910 fewer than 10 percent of black men were voting in the South. These restrictive laws also caught many poor and illiterate whites. Most states, however, provided **grandfather clauses**, which exempted from these registration requirements those whose grandfathers had voted before the Civil War.

Without the backing of the Supreme Court, the southern state legislatures would have found it harder to strip away black civil rights. The Court generally upheld segregation and disenfranchisement laws against challenges. Conversely, when federal laws extending rights to African Americans were challenged, the Court summarily overturned them. The Court based these decisions on a tortuously narrow reading of the Fourteenth and Fifteenth Amendments. Consider this passage from the Fourteenth Amendment: "No State shall make or enforce any law which shall abridge the privileges or immunities of citizens of the United States." The Supreme Court interpreted this clause to mean only that states could not abridge privileges conferred explicitly by the Constitution to the national government, such as unrestricted interstate travel and open navigation of rivers. The justices excluded state laws from the guarantees of the Bill of Rights. Decades later, the Supreme Court would reject this interpretation of the Fourteenth Amendment and rediscover the broad national guarantees this clause provides.*

The coup de grâce came in 1896 when the Supreme Court, ruling in *Plessy v. Ferguson*, declared the South's Jim Crow laws and systematic segregation constitutional.[12] The case arose when shoemaker Homer Plessy, who was seven-eighths white (but still black, according to law), appealed his conviction for having violated Louisiana's segregation law by sitting in

---

*Similarly, interpreting the Fifteenth Amendment, the Supreme Court held that state laws denying voting rights to African Americans were permissible unless they could be shown to be motivated by race. By applying the poll tax or literacy test to everyone, or even claiming to, the southern legislatures could satisfy the Court.

a "whites only" railroad car. The Court argued that the Fourteenth Amendment's guarantee of equal protection of the law referred only to "political" equality. If African Americans were socially inferior to whites, the Court reasoned, laws such as Louisiana's could reflect that inferiority so long as political equality was not compromised. The Court then ruled that government-enforced segregation of the races was constitutional as long as the facilities for African Americans and whites were equal. And apparently they were, the Court reasoned; after all, whites were prohibited from sitting in the black passenger car. With that ruling, the Court established nationally the **separate but equal doctrine**, which officially sanctioned segregation throughout the South for the next half-century. Dissenting justice John Marshall Harlan vigorously attacked the majority's reasoning in language that would provide a foundation for overturning the "separate but equal" doctrine a half-century later. Appearances of equality were a sham, he argued. "Everyone knows that the statute in question had its origin in the purpose, not so much to exclude white persons from railroad cars occupied by blacks, as to exclude colored people from coaches occupied by or assigned to white persons."*

## Democratic Party Sponsorship of Civil Rights: 1933–1940s

From 1929 until 1933 the Republican Party presided over the worst depression in American history. Among the many victims of the economic hard times was the party itself. The Great Depression ended Republican dominance in national politics for the next fifty years. Ironically, while the rest of the nation was abandoning the Republican incumbent, Herbert Hoover, in favor of Democrat Franklin Roosevelt, most black voters were sticking with their party's ticket in the presidential election of 1932, despite being hit harder by the Great Depression than any other group of Americans. (By 1936, however, three-quarters of African Americans supported Roosevelt's reelection.) Today, the appeal of mostly liberal Democratic politicians to black voters appears quite natural, requiring no special explanation. This partnership took nearly three decades to establish.

Both future partners first had to break enduring ties that pulled in opposing directions. The loyalty of black voters to the Republican Party grew out of emancipation and Reconstruction, and Democratic politicians had done nothing in the intervening years to prompt African Americans to question their partisanship. But their loyalty was rooted more in habit than reward and thus was susceptible to a Democratic appeal. For Democratic politicians, taking up the cause of African Americans was fraught with risk. Ever since its return to the Union, the South had provided the Democratic Party with the electoral base it needed to compete nationally. Northern Democratic members of Congress had long depended on the automatic victories of their southern colleagues to win majority control of Congress. Democratic presidential candidates could count on the South's large bloc of electoral votes; all they had to do was ignore segregation, just as their counterparts before the war had disregarded slavery.

---

*Why did a mostly Republican-appointed Supreme Court interpret the Fourteenth and Fifteenth Amendments in ways that negated Reconstruction? C. Vann Woodward reasonably conjectures that as Republican politicians reoriented their party toward rapidly emerging business constituencies, black civil rights became a low priority. See Woodward, *Reunion and Reaction: The Compromise of 1877 and the End of Reconstruction* (Boston: Little, Brown, 1966), 22–50.

## The New Deal

Neither Franklin Roosevelt's winning electoral campaign in 1932 nor his "New Deal" to pull the nation out of the Depression overtly championed the cause of African Americans. Both did, however, alter political circumstances in a way that prompted black Americans and Democratic politicians to contemplate their mutual interests. When pressed, Roosevelt refused to battle southern Democratic senators for passage of popular antilynching legislation, privately citing his need for friendly relations with southern Democrats to enact his emergency economic policies.* Yet the New Deal's evenhanded treatment of the black community appealed to black voters. Many of its programs offered African Americans government assistance for the first time since Reconstruction. (Other programs, however, such as Social Security, excluded many low-income occupations that were disproportionately black.) Federal authorities investigated racial discrimination in relief aid distribution, especially prevalent in the South, and largely rooted it out. Roosevelt also appointed more than one hundred black administrators, some to prominent posts. Finally, the Justice Department rejuvenated its long-dormant civil liberties division.

Following the White House initiative, congressional Democrats added nondiscrimination language to a score of public laws creating federal programs. In 1941 Roosevelt issued an executive order banning employment discrimination in federal agencies, and he established the Committee on Fair Employment Practices to enforce nondiscrimination in defense-related industries. These measures, requiring that African Americans be treated as ordinary citizens, represented a major breakthrough for America's civil rights policy.

## African Americans and the New Deal Coalition

During the Roosevelt years, Democratic politicians continued to woo black voters, but from a sufficient distance to allow the Democratic Party to maintain its southern alliance. Nonetheless, hindsight reveals that subtle changes were under way in the political landscape, leading up to political realignment and the Democratic Party's embrace of black voters. In Washington twenty years of nearly uninterrupted Democratic control of both the presidency and Congress replenished the Supreme Court and lower federal judiciary with judges more sympathetic to civil rights claims. This laid the groundwork for an era of active judicial intervention against state laws enforcing segregation, particularly in public education.

More important, African Americans gradually shifted their party loyalties from the "party of Lincoln" to the "party of Roosevelt." The political transformation could not have been timed more propitiously for the Democratic Party, for hundreds of thousands of these potential new Democrats were migrating from the South, where they could not vote, to northern and midwestern cities, where Democratic political organizations eagerly registered and ushered them to the polls. The resulting demographic transformation of U.S. cities, recorded in

---

*Whereas President Roosevelt had been reluctant to back federal antilynching and anti–poll tax legislation, many congressional Democrats introduced and championed hundreds of bills targeted at these and other civil rights issues. (The legislation repeatedly passed in the House of Representatives but, just as in the antebellum era, failed in the Senate, where the South held a greater share of the membership.)

Table 4.1, reflects the cumulative effects of several distinct forces.* For a century black share-croppers and tenant farmers had been one of the least mobile population groups in the nation. But World War II (1939–1945) sent many young black men from the segregated Deep South into the armed services, where they were stationed in less racist, or at least less intimidating, communities. Other southern African Americans were lured north by relatively high-paying jobs in wartime industry. Still others followed after the war as farm mechanization rendered labor-intensive farming obsolete. Migration transformed these black citizens from political nonentities into pivotal voters.

**TABLE 4.1**   The Road to Political Power: African Americans Migrate North

|                        | 1930 | 1940 | 1950 | 1960 | 1970 |
|------------------------|------|------|------|------|------|
| **All 12 SMSAs**       | 7.6  | 9.0  | 13.7 | 21.4 | 30.8 |
| New York               | 4.9  | 6.9  | 9.8  | 14.7 | 23.4 |
| Los Angeles–Long Beach | 5.0  | 6.0  | 9.8  | 15.3 | 21.2 |
| Chicago                | 7.1  | 8.3  | 14.1 | 23.6 | 34.4 |
| Philadelphia           | 11.4 | 13.1 | 18.3 | 26.7 | 34.4 |
| Detroit                | 7.8  | 9.3  | 16.4 | 29.2 | 44.0 |
| San Francisco–Oakland  | 4.9  | 4.9  | 11.8 | 21.1 | 32.7 |
| Boston                 | 2.9  | 3.3  | 12.3 | 9.8  | 18.2 |
| Pittsburgh             | 8.3  | 9.3  | 18.0 | 16.8 | 27.0 |
| St. Louis              | 11.5 | 13.4 | 5.3  | 28.8 | 41.3 |
| Washington, D.C.       | 27.3 | 28.5 | 35.4 | 54.8 | 72.3 |
| Cleveland              | 8.1  | 9.7  | 16.3 | 28.9 | 39.0 |
| Baltimore              | 17.7 | 19.4 | 23.8 | 35.0 | 47.0 |

*Source:* Adapted from Leo F. Schnore, Carolyn D. Andre, and Harry Sharp, "Black Suburbanization, 1930–1970," *The Changing Face of the Suburbs*, ed. Barry Schwartz (Chicago: University of Chicago Press, 1976), 80. The figures were transposed to yield data on black percentages.

*Note:* The table shows the percentage of African Americans in central cities of the twelve largest standard metropolitan statistical areas (SMSAs).

---

*In Detroit, for example, the black population doubled from 8 percent in 1930 to 16 percent in 1950, and increased to 44 percent by 1970. Although Detroit had the most dramatic growth in black population, every major urban center throughout the nation experienced a similar trend. Edward G. Carmines and James A. Stimson, *Issue Evolution: Race and the Transformation of American Politics* (Princeton, NJ: Princeton University Press, 1989), Table 4-1.

Despite the increasing numbers of Democratic politicians committing to civil rights reforms, segregation remained entrenched for as long as these politicians needed southern Democrats to keep control of Congress and the presidency. This coalition began to crack in 1948, however, when Democratic president Harry Truman openly courted the black vote for reelection, even at the risk of alienating the South. A faltering, strike-plagued economy appeared to doom the unpopular president to electoral defeat. Desperately searching for a winning campaign plan, Truman's advisers proposed a novel strategy for the Democratic Party: "Unless there are real and new efforts . . . to help the Negro," stated one strategy memo, "the Negro bloc, which, certainly in Illinois and probably in New York and Ohio, *does* hold the balance of power, will go Republican." This strategy prompted President Truman to issue an executive order integrating the armed services and introduce legislation making Roosevelt's Committee on Fair Employment Practices a permanent agency. He also sponsored a comprehensive civil rights bill, the first since the end of Reconstruction, that finally made racial lynching a federal

■ **MAP 4.2**  Truman Wins the Presidency in 1948 Despite Dixiecrat Defection

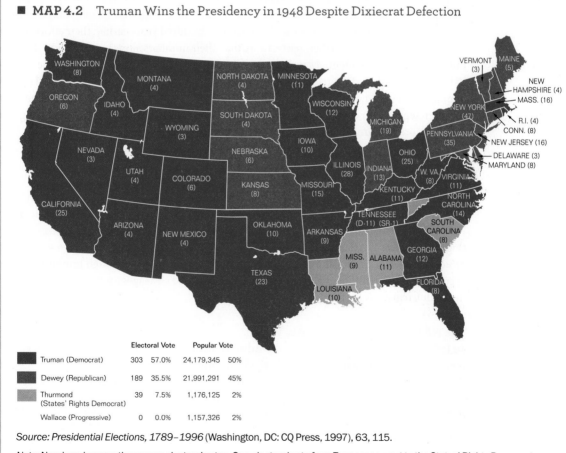

| | | Electoral Vote | | Popular Vote | |
|---|---|---|---|---|---|
| | Truman (Democrat) | 303 | 57.0% | 24,179,345 | 50% |
| | Dewey (Republican) | 189 | 35.5% | 21,991,291 | 45% |
| | Thurmond (States' Rights Democrat) | 39 | 7.5% | 1,176,125 | 2% |
| | Wallace (Progressive) | 0 | 0.0% | 1,157,326 | 2% |

*Source: Presidential Elections, 1789–1996* (Washington, DC: CQ Press, 1997), 63, 115.

*Note:* Numbers in parentheses are electoral votes. One electoral vote from Tennessee went to the States' Rights Democrat.

crime, provided federal guarantees for voting rights, and prohibited employment and housing discrimination.* With no chance of passing the legislation in the face of a certain southern filibuster in the Senate, knowledgeable observers knew that the president's gesture was symbolic. Nonetheless, it placed civil rights on the Democrats' "to do" agenda, along with national health care.

At the Democratic Party's national convention in the summer of 1948, liberal northern Democrats pressed fellow delegates to adopt a strong civil rights platform. Southern delegates were outraged and bolted from the meeting. In the fall these "Dixiecrats," as they were called, ran their own candidate, Strom Thurmond, under the States' Rights Party banner and pulled several southern states' electoral votes away from the Democratic ticket (see Map 4.2). The defection reminded national Democrats that the South could be taken for granted only so long as the party left segregation alone. Despite losing this traditional stronghold, Truman won reelection.

The Truman administration's unsuccessful 1948 attempts to enact a civil rights law, like the defeat of the Wilmot proviso a century earlier, presaged a later victory by identifying a political rationale for northern politicians to attack southern tyranny. With the New Deal, the Democratic Party attracted activist liberals and union leaders who were ideologically committed to civil rights. Like Republican abolitionists one hundred years earlier, their efforts made these activists important to their party, more than their numbers alone would attest.[13] But not until Democratic presidential candidates realized that the black vote might offset the potential southern losses did the party's politicians have a collective stake in advancing civil rights. Similarly, not until northern congressional Democrats discovered that speaking out against southern segregation won them the votes of the recent southern black migrants did a congressional majority committed to breaking up segregation coalesce.

## Emergence of a Civil Rights Coalition: 1940s–1950s

The 1950s saw only modest advances in civil rights, but a new coalition—requiring renewed support for civil rights from the Republican Party and profound shifts within the Democratic Party, whose leaders historically had been hostile to the cause of African Americans—set the stage for success. Two landmark events of the 1950s stand out: the historic *Brown v. Board of Education of Topeka* decision and the Civil Rights Act of 1957.[14] Although important, both events proved more influential in identifying the issues and cleavages for the next decade than in yielding real gains in civil rights.

### The NAACP's Litigation Strategy

In 1909 the National Association for the Advancement of Colored People (NAACP) began to represent black defendants throughout the South and to use the federal judiciary to challenge the legal structure of segregation. Although southern opposition in the Senate blocked legislative solutions, a decade of Roosevelt judicial appointments had recast the Supreme Court and many federal district and appeals courts with judges more sympathetic to the southern blacks'

---

*The legislation, predictably, died in the Senate, where, armed with the filibuster, southern members prevented it from coming to a vote.

cause. One of its most important landmark victories during these early years came in 1944, when the NAACP persuaded the Supreme Court in *Smith v. Allwright* to throw out white primary laws.[15] The Court ruled that because race was the explicit criterion for discrimination, such laws violated the Fifteenth Amendment.

Nowhere in the South, however, was the electoral potential of the black vote close to being realized. Long-standing Supreme Court doctrine requiring that plaintiffs prove a law's discriminatory *intent* rather than simply demonstrate a bias in its *effect* frustrated the NAACP's efforts to dismantle other racial barriers. For example, in trying to eradicate the poll tax, which also disenfranchised poor whites, the NAACP could not satisfy the Court's tough requirements.

In the 1940s the NAACP launched a second line of attack against Jim Crow laws, this time targeting segregated public education. Since *Plessy v. Ferguson* in 1896, the federal judiciary had upheld segregation in the South, but the "separate but equal" doctrine proved to be an easy target. The soft underbelly of segregation was the word *equal*. Nowhere in the South did the separate facilities for African Americans equal those for whites.

The NAACP targeted the most blatant disparities. Because many states did not provide black graduate and professional schools and black residents were shut out of both public and private white facilities, the NAACP had a relatively easy time convincing the Court of the inequality of separating the races in education. In *Sweatt v. Painter* (1950) the Court unanimously agreed that the University of Texas could not stave off desegregation at its law school by instantly creating a black-only facility.[16] Then the NAACP successfully attacked segregated schools where separate facilities existed but were patently unequal in the education offered students. Less conspicuous forms of inequality were taken on next. In a 1950 decision the Court accepted the argument that intangible factors such as faculty reputation and alumni prestige contributed to educational inequality.

### *Brown* Trumps *Plessy*

Having established that "separate but equal" could be unconstitutional, the NAACP directly attacked *Plessy*. The opportunity came in 1950 when Oliver Brown, an assistant pastor from Topeka, Kansas, violated local segregation laws when he tried to enroll his daughter, Linda, in a white neighborhood public school. Representing the NAACP, future Supreme Court justice Thurgood Marshall took up Brown's case, which four years later brought the pivotal Supreme Court ruling in *Brown v. Board of Education of Topeka*. Writing for a unanimous Court, Chief Justice Earl Warren argued that education is the foundation of good citizenship and thus constitutes "a right which must be made available to all on equal terms." Stipulating that racial segregation "generates a feeling of inferiority as to [black children's] status in the community that may affect their hearts and minds in a way unlikely ever to be undone," Warren concluded, "separate educational facilities are inherently unequal." With this 1954 ruling, *Plessy*, the principal legal prop of Jim Crow, crumbled.

The *Brown* decision, argued as a class-action suit on behalf of all citizens similarly denied access to white public schools, had broad legal ramifications. The next year the Court empowered lower federal courts to hear segregation cases and oversee the desegregation of public schools with "all deliberate speed."[17] Hundreds of school desegregation cases were filed in the federal courts in the decade after *Brown*.

Yet even this flurry of litigation did not end segregation. Efforts to implement *Brown* encountered all of the problems associated with enforcing judicial rulings. The decision was met by massive resistance across the South. Acting as if the nation were still governed by the Articles of Confederation, some state legislatures boldly asserted that public education lay beyond the national government's jurisdiction and that they would ignore the Court's "illegal" decision. When this bluff failed, state politicians devised more imaginative blocking tactics. In Virginia public schools were closed and "private" ones, created with state financing, opened in the vain hope that the new schools would be exempt from the *Brown* ruling. When these and other legal tricks were exhausted, state officials simply defied black parents and federal marshals sent to implement a desegregation ruling. The Supreme Court itself intervened in 1957, ordering the city of Little Rock, Arkansas, to enroll black students in all-white Central High School. When Arkansas governor Orval Faubus and school officials failed to comply, President Dwight Eisenhower sent in U.S. Army troops to escort black students to their new school.

The last bulwark of segregation's defense was tokenism—perhaps the most successful dilatory tactic of all. A school district would admit a handful of black students and then rush to federal court claiming compliance. The result would be another round of litigation during which further desegregation would be suspended. Civil rights lawyers may have won many cases during this era, but their clients had little success in gaining access to "whites-only" schools. In 1962, eight years after *Brown*, fewer than one-half of 1 percent of black students in the South were actually attending desegregated schools.

At least symbolically, Labor Day 1957 was a watershed event in school integration. Elizabeth Eckford, textbooks in arm, and eight other black students were escorted through a hostile crowd into Little Rock's Central High School. The jeering student behind Eckford, Hazel Bryan, would later rue this moment when she became "the poster child for the hate generation, trapped in the image captured in the photograph." Later Bryan contacted Eckford to apologize, and subsequently they jointly participated in local racial tolerance workshops. The second photo was taken at the same site and by the same photographer on the fortieth anniversary of this historic moment.

## The 1957 Civil Rights Act: Rehearsal for the 1960s

The year 1957 was rife with political opportunity for the Democrats. With Republican two-term president Dwight Eisenhower ineligible for reelection in 1960, the Senate was full of ambitious Democrats grooming themselves for a presidential bid. John Kennedy of Massachusetts, Stuart Symington of Missouri, and Hubert Humphrey of Minnesota would later declare their candidacies and campaign actively in the 1960 presidential primaries. Other, less daring Senate colleagues could barely contain their aspirations for the top spot. Among them was Democratic majority leader Lyndon Johnson from Texas.

Daring or not, all would-be Democratic candidates had to appeal to a national constituency that now included substantial numbers of black voters in the large, vote-rich industrial states. For Johnson, a southerner, this requirement posed a serious problem. How could this Texan establish his credentials with African Americans and therefore be taken seriously by the northern Democratic Party leaders who controlled the nomination?

Johnson's vehicle into the national arena was the 1957 Civil Rights Act, which he introduced. This modest law allowed African Americans who felt their right to vote had been denied because of race to sue their state in federal court. But the prospect of expensive litigation and the provision that defendants—say, a local voter registrar—would be entitled to jury trials proved such formidable barriers that the NAACP and similar civil rights organizations filed suits designed only to establish widespread voting discrimination. To no one's surprise, few, if indeed any, black citizens gained the vote by virtue of this limited law.

The significance of Johnson's strategic sponsorship of the 1957 Civil Rights Act, then, lay more in what it represented politically than in any real gains it produced for African Americans. Southern senators, who wanted to boost Johnson's presidential bid over those of northern liberals Humphrey and Kennedy, strategically refrained from vigorous opposition and, in a few cases, abstained in the final floor vote. This message was reinforced by the passage of another, slightly less anemic, voting rights bill in the spring of 1960, only weeks before many of these senators headed for the Democratic presidential **nominating convention**. Although Johnson lost the Democratic presidential nomination to Kennedy, he won the consolation prize—the vice presidential nomination. And ever mindful of the black vote, Johnson and his colleagues oversaw enactment of yet another minority voting rights law during the summer before the 1960 presidential election.

With passage of the Civil Rights Act of 1957, the first civil rights law since Reconstruction, Democratic congressional leaders committed themselves to passing civil rights legislation. This and other early civil rights laws represented a transition, not so much for African Americans seeking full citizenship as for the Democratic Party.

Kennedy's narrow victory in 1960 reminded Democrats once again that winning the presidency without the South was virtually impossible. Even majority control of Congress would be jeopardized if more southern politicians decided—as a few in fact had—to disassociate themselves from northern Democrats and change parties. But even if the party accepted these risks and championed civil rights, it still lacked sufficient votes to enact the kinds of policies necessary to dismantle segregation. To jettison the party's southern wing by embracing civil rights and then fail to deliver on its commitment to the cause would constitute political suicide.

Yet during the 1960s Democratic presidents Kennedy and Johnson and their congressional colleagues broke with the South and committed the nation to an activist civil rights policy before it was politically expedient to do so. Why? Because doing nothing suddenly became the riskier strategy. A civil rights movement based on demonstrations and protest was generating a groundswell of support throughout the nation that the Democratic Party, which controlled Congress and the presidency, could not ignore. Failure to deal with this issue would have jeopardized the political relations of many Democratic politicians with their core supporters. Then, in the 1964 election, an event rarer than Halley's Comet occurred: the emergence of a *dominant* governing coalition in Washington. Not only did Democrats retain the presidency, but they also greatly enlarged their majorities in both chambers of Congress. Like a comet, this coalition did not last long, but while present it burned brightly. The result was half a decade of legislation followed by vigorous enforcement of laws dismantling segregation and voting discrimination. Finally, the national government had decided to finish the project of Reconstruction and assume responsibility for every citizen's civil rights.

## The Civil Rights Movement: 1960s

Before the early 1960s, the civil rights movement, led by the NAACP, followed a strategy designed to influence judges more than politicians. This strategy had garnered some impressive court victories, but judicial successes had not translated into real gains in civil rights. Entering the 1960s, the civil rights movement took a new course—public protests directed against segregation and the authorities who administered it. Ultimately, the protests sought to influence public opinion and, in turn, Congress and the president.

This new course began in December 1955, when a black seamstress, Rosa Parks, boarded a city bus in Montgomery, Alabama. When Parks refused to surrender her seat to a white patron and move to the back of the vehicle, as the law required, she launched the historic Montgomery bus boycott, which became the model for later boycotts. In 1960 the first "sit-in" was held when several black college students in Greensboro, North Carolina, occupied seats reserved for whites in a local restaurant and refused to move until they were served or arrested.

Shifting strategy from litigation to mass demonstrations introduced collective action problems that had to be solved for the civil rights movement to succeed. Who would lead the movement in this new direction? Could the NAACP, an organization of lawyers—many of them white, nonsouthern volunteers—be expected to engage in, much less organize, massive civil disobedience? Disenfranchised black southerners did not have politicians—professionals in the art of solving collective action problems—to inspire and organize efforts to bring down Jim Crow through confrontation.

Ironically, segregation itself supplied the leaders who would press for its dissolution. Segregation in the South separated the races in all aspects of social organization: schools, churches, entertainment, hospitals, and professions; even cemeteries were segregated. Two largely parallel social groups coexisted in every community. Some black professionals—such as public school teachers—worked under the supervision of white-controlled institutions and would suffer serious repercussions if they challenged segregation. Other black professionals, however, served an exclusively black clientele and were fairly well insulated from white retribution: shop owners, morticians, and especially preachers—the latter were already well versed in organizing congregations and enjoyed credibility among those they would ask to make sacrifices. With control of scarce resources—skill at organizing and the trust of their congregations—and largely exempt from the potentially severe white reprisals, it is not surprising that black southern preachers participated in planning and coordinating demonstrations. Hundreds of them mobilized their congregations and coordinated with colleagues from other communities to generate large, effective demonstrations. The most important of these leaders, Reverend Martin Luther King Jr., was a Methodist minister. His organization, which during the next decade spearheaded demonstrations throughout the South, was appropriately named the Southern Christian Leadership Conference (SCLC).

King's strategy of nonviolent demonstrations and other forms of resistance may have been inspired by the Indian leader Mahatma Gandhi (1869–1948), but his political pragmatism was a page out of James Madison's playbook. Ultimately, King reasoned, rights would be won not in the courts through cogent argument but in legislatures through direct engagement with opponents whose interests were at stake.

AP Photo/Gene Herrick

Rosa Parks, whose refusal to move to the back of a city bus in December 1955 touched off the historic Montgomery, Alabama, bus boycott, is fingerprinted by Montgomery deputy sheriff D. H. Lackey. Her courageous act and subsequent arrest triggered massive demonstrations in the city and a boycott of local public transportation and white businesses. These events led eventually to the dismantling of local segregation policies and stimulated other acts of civil disobedience elsewhere.

"Needless fighting in lower courts," King argued, is "exactly what the white man wants the Negro to do. Then he can draw out the fight."[18] If African Americans were to realize their rights, he knew they would have to claim them.

The first serious hurdle for the protest strategy was finding leaders who could bear the heavy transaction costs and personal risks, and who possessed the communication and organizational skills to mobilize a population inexperienced in expressing its grievances. The second problem, just as formidable, concerned the movement's followers. Specifically, would ordinary African Americans agree to demonstrate in the streets, boycott public transportation and white businesses, and confront local registrars bent on denying them their right to vote? Many of these activities violated state and local segregation laws; participants would face a legal system administered by unsympathetic officials. More important, the vast majority of black southerners worked for white employers who would actively discourage participation. With these disincentives, many (perhaps too many) of those sympathetic with this new strategy might instead free ride.[19] A successful demonstration requires lots of people

*Jackson Daily News/Clarion-Ledger*

The scene is Jackson, Mississippi, where the local lunch crowd is drenching lunch counter demonstrators with mustard and ketchup. Such demonstrations occurred throughout the South in the 1960s. Most of the demonstrators were local black and northern white college students.

to voluntarily expose themselves to danger and other sanctions. Yet every individual knew that his or her participation would not make or break the demonstration. What would become of the civil rights movement if insufficient numbers answered the call to action?

History showed otherwise. Demonstrations began in earnest in 1960, and over the next six years almost 2,500 were held, with many receiving national news coverage.[20] In retrospect, the success of the movement is easy to understand. In addition to the nationally prominent clergy in SCLC headquarters, ministers with the professional and rhetorical skills to mobilize direct action ran most of the eighty-five local chapters throughout the South. Moreover, these local leaders enjoyed exceptional credibility with those whom they needed to motivate. When King and other SCLC leaders endorsed a boycott or some other action, the local chapters served as a focal point to coordinate a joint action. Without the organizational efforts of these local leaders, the movement would not have enjoyed such broad-based support.

The pivotal protest of spring 1963 in Birmingham, Alabama, forced the Democratic Party to commit to an aggressive civil rights policy and led directly to passage of the landmark Civil Rights Act of 1964.

### The Birmingham Demonstration

In early 1963 President Kennedy pleaded for patience from King and other leaders, arguing that Congress should enact his less controversial social programs before tackling segregation. Civil rights leaders suspected that Kennedy's real motivation was to keep the South in the Democratic column in the upcoming 1964 election. King and the other leaders had their own strategic reasons for impatience; demonstrations were turning violent, and events were only partially under their control. To keep the movement directed toward civil disobedience and peaceful protest, SCLC leaders needed to start producing results.

The selection of Birmingham as a protest venue reflected the broad strategic purpose of the demonstrations. Birmingham's segregation was no worse than in many other cities throughout the Deep South. But Birmingham had a notoriously intolerant local police chief, Eugene "Bull" Connor, known for rough treatment of civil rights demonstrators. He would provide a graphic display of the institutional violence that enforced segregation. As the nation watched on network television, Connor arrested and jailed two thousand marchers for not having a parade permit. The local law enforcement officers then resorted to police dogs and fire hoses to disperse peaceful demonstrators, including children barely old enough to go to school.

The Birmingham demonstrations succeeded when the city's business community agreed to negotiate with the protesters. But more important, the protesters created a national crisis that President Kennedy could not ignore. From April to July 1963, the percentage of Gallup poll respondents mentioning civil rights as the most important problem facing the country shot up from 10 percent to nearly 50 percent.

Suddenly, continued accommodation of southern Democrats imposed significant political costs for Kennedy. Failure to act might irreparably damage his reputation among black voters who might well provide a margin of victory in a reelection bid. These events, orchestrated by the civil rights movement, turned the president into a reluctant champion of its cause. Shortly after a televised address to the nation unveiling the new civil rights legislation, Kennedy invited movement leaders to the White House to plan a legislative strategy. The president explained to the group the bind he and the Democratic Party were in:

AP Photo/Bill Hudson

Protesters parading down the streets of Birmingham, Alabama, in 1963 were bent on focusing national attention on their cause. The local police proved quite accommodating in demonstrating to the horror of television viewers throughout the nation the brutality with which segregation was enforced.

> This is a very serious fight. The Vice-President [Lyndon Johnson] and I know what it will mean if we fail. I have just seen a new poll—national approval of the administration has fallen from 60 to 47 percent. We're in this up to the neck. The worst trouble of all would be to lose the fight in the Congress. We'll have enough trouble if we win; but, if we win, we can deal with those. A good many programs I care about may go down the drain as a result of this—we may go down the drain as a result of this—so we are putting a lot on the line.[21]

Democrats were about to commit to a strong civil rights program without having the means to succeed.[22]

## POLITICS TO POLICY
# The 1964 Civil Rights Act and Integration of Public Schools

One of the most effective provisions of the 1964 Civil Rights Act authorized the Department of Health, Education, and Welfare to withhold federal grants from school districts that failed to integrate their schools. No longer could southern school boards hide behind token desegregation and endless visits to the federal courts. The effects were quick and dramatic: within a year more black children were admitted to formerly all-white schools than in the entire decade after the 1954 *Brown v. Board of Education of Topeka* decision. Within ten years over 90 percent of black children in the South were attending desegregated schools.

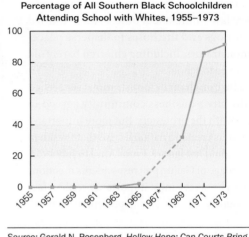

Percentage of All Southern Black Schoolchildren Attending School with Whites, 1955–1973

Source: Gerald N. Rosenberg, *Hollow Hope: Can Courts Bring about Social Change?* (Chicago: University of Chicago Press, 1991), 50–51.

*Dashed line indicates missing data for 1967.

### The Democratic Party's Commitment to Civil Rights

On June 11, 1963, President Kennedy addressed the nation, proclaiming his full support for the aspirations of African Americans and announcing a major revision of the civil rights bill then before Congress. The courts would no longer determine violations; for the first time federal agencies could independently identify discrimination and impose remedies. Although this new proposal was far weaker than the sweeping civil rights reforms King and his colleagues had requested, they accepted it as a solid step in the right direction.

Five months later Kennedy was assassinated, and Vice President Johnson succeeded to the presidency. At the time, a strengthened version of the legislation, which had passed the House of Representatives on a bipartisan vote, was predictably stalled in the Senate. Southern senators did not have enough votes to defeat the legislation outright, but they were prepared to filibuster it indefinitely.*

---

*The filibuster, allowing a minority of the Senate membership to delay floor consideration of legislation, is discussed more fully in Chapter 6.

Within a few days of assuming the presidency, Johnson addressed a joint session of Congress and a nationwide television audience to announce that a strong civil rights law would be the nation's memorial to the fallen president. This proclamation set the stage for a struggle in Washington. The outcome would make 1964 a year of historic successes for both civil rights and the Democratic Party.

### The 1964 Civil Rights Act

Once Johnson persuaded Senate Republicans to join northern Democrats in breaking the southern filibuster, the Senate promptly passed the Civil Rights Act of 1964. This law, which was substantially stronger than the legislation President Kennedy

Lyndon B. Johnson Library Collection

For years Georgia senator Richard Russell (right) and other southerners had blocked civil rights legislation with the threat of a filibuster. New president Lyndon Johnson (left), however, was not deterred in his push for civil rights legislation. Here, two weeks after President John Kennedy's assassination, Johnson warns his Senate mentor to stand aside or be run down.

had introduced, authorized the national government to end segregation in public education and public accommodations (see the Politics to Policy box, "The 1964 Civil Rights Act and Integration of Public Schools").

The Democratic administration's high-profile sponsorship of the civil rights law put forth civil rights as a decisive campaign issue in the 1964 presidential election. The Republican Party in Congress traditionally had been more supportive of civil rights than the Democrats, but in 1964 it began to veer sharply away from its long-standing support. At their national convention Republicans chose Barry Goldwater of Arizona as their presidential candidate, one of the few senators outside the South to oppose the 1964 civil rights bill. When the Democrats convened to nominate the incumbent president Johnson, they underlined the party differences on this issue by seating delegates who challenged segregationist Democrats and by selecting as Johnson's running mate Senator Hubert Humphrey, a longtime vocal proponent of civil rights.

The outcome of the election was the largest presidential landslide in history up to that time. The Democrats also racked up huge majorities in the congressional elections. Goldwater won only five states in the Deep South and his home state of Arizona. With over 95 percent of black voters preferring Johnson, the Democratic and Republican Parties swapped constituencies in the South.[23] When the new Congress convened in 1965, northern Democrats dominated both chambers. Even some border states elected Democrats who were moderate supporters of civil rights and who were prepared to support national policies that would dismantle segregation. Finally, the sheer magnitude of the Democratic victory swamped the Constitution's separation-of-powers barrier to collective action. With the severe transaction costs of policymaking swept away, the Washington cognoscenti and ordinary voters alike sensed that the Johnson landslide would bring about an onslaught of civil rights legislation (see Map 4.3).

### The Voting Rights Act of 1965

Every civil rights law enacted since 1957 addressed voting rights, but throughout much of the South black registration remained at low levels. Only 7 percent of eligible black citizens

**■ MAP 4.3**   The Key to Unlocking Black Voting Rights: Vigilant Administration of Civil Rights Laws

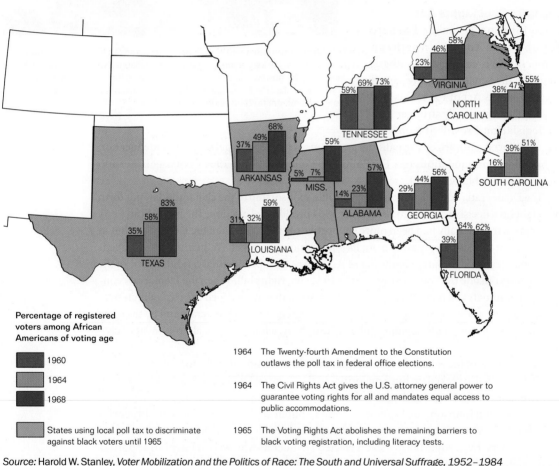

Percentage of registered voters among African Americans of voting age

- 1960
- 1964
- 1968

States using local poll tax to discriminate against black voters until 1965

1964   The Twenty-fourth Amendment to the Constitution outlaws the poll tax in federal office elections.

1964   The Civil Rights Act gives the U.S. attorney general power to guarantee voting rights for all and mandates equal access to public accommodations.

1965   The Voting Rights Act abolishes the remaining barriers to black voting registration, including literacy tests.

*Source:* Harold W. Stanley, *Voter Mobilization and the Politics of Race: The South and Universal Suffrage, 1952–1984* (Westport, CT: Praeger, 1987), 97. Copyright © 1987 by Harold W. Stanley. Reproduced with permission of ABC-CLIO, LLC.

in Mississippi were registered in 1964; in Alabama the figure was 23 percent. Each of these civil rights laws had the same fatal flaw: they required individuals to prove discrimination in court. Black leaders thus pressed the White House to authorize federal agencies to guarantee the right to vote by taking over voter registration or directly supervising local officials, just as the 1964 Civil Rights Act authorized government action against segregation in education and public accommodations.

Responding to their pleas, President Johnson asked King and other leaders to "give the nation a chance to catch its breath" on civil rights. After all, African Americans would be well served, Johnson argued, by his Great Society programs in employment, education, and health care. But for movement leaders, Johnson's request asked too much. King and his colleagues knew that not since Reconstruction had such large, sympathetic majorities controlled both houses of Congress, yet from recent experience, they also knew precisely what was needed to spur legislative action.

The spring 1965 demonstrations in Selma, Alabama, closely paralleled the 1963 Birmingham actions. Brutal local law enforcement—attack dogs, club-wielding police on horseback, and liberal use of powerful fire hoses—yielded vivid television images of the official violence that enforced segregation. Civil rights leaders again succeeded when President Johnson went on prime-time television to introduce new civil rights legislation.

Ignoring the outcry of southern senators, Congress passed and the president promptly signed the Voting Rights Act of 1965. The law was aggressive—its drafters knew that virtually everyone added to the registration rolls would soon be voting Democratic. Its main provision authorized the Department of Justice to suspend restrictive electoral tests in southern states that had a history of low black turnout. In these states the Justice Department could (and did) send federal officers into uncooperative communities to register voters directly. The states also had to obtain clearance from the Justice Department before changing their election laws. Though the Antifederalist Patrick Henry might have turned over in his grave at the thought of the Voting Rights Act and federal registrars entering his home state of Virginia, the policy was perfectly consistent with Madison's proposed national veto over objectionable state laws.

Few laws have ever achieved their goals more dramatically or quickly. Registration soared, yielding dramatic effects. For the first time southern politicians paid attention to their newly registered black constituents. In 1970, when several southern senators polled their colleagues about opposing an extension of the voting rights law, they found little enthusiasm. Democratic conservative Herman Talmadge of Georgia begged off: "Look, fellows, I was the principal speaker at the NAACP conference in my state last year." And South Carolina Democrat Ernest Hollings was direct: "I'm not going home to my state and explain a filibuster to black voters."[24] Moreover, from 1970 to 2011, the number of black elected officials at all levels of government grew from 1,469 to 10,500.[25] Many of these men and women won office by appealing in part to white voters. In a real sense these many local officeholders paved the way for Barack Obama's success.

# Major Events in the Civil Rights Movement, 1955–1968

| | |
|---|---|
| December 1955 | African Americans in Montgomery, Alabama, begin boycott of city buses in protest of segregated seating. |
| September 1, 1957 | Central High School in Little Rock, Arkansas, engulfed in turmoil as the governor calls out Arkansas National Guard to prevent enrollment of nine black students. President Dwight Eisenhower forced to send in federal troops to restore order. |
| February 1, 1960 | Wave of "sit-ins" touched off across the South by four students in Greensboro, North Carolina, who are refused service at a segregated lunch counter. |
| May 4, 1961 | "Freedom rides" begin as African Americans try to occupy "whites only" sections of interstate buses. U.S. marshals ultimately are called in to settle violent reaction to black efforts. |
| September 30, 1962 | Federal troops are used to quell a fifteen-hour uprising by University of Mississippi students protesting the enrollment of a single black student, James Meredith. Two students are killed. (Televised live across the nation.) |
| April 1963 | Demonstrations begin in Birmingham, Alabama. Local authorities use fire hoses and police dogs to disperse demonstrators. |
| August 28, 1963 | March on Washington by more than two hundred thousand African Americans and whites. Reverend Martin Luther King Jr. delivers his "I Have a Dream" speech, and "We Shall Overcome" becomes the anthem of the civil rights movement. |
| September 1963 | Demonstrations begin in St. Augustine, Florida, to protest the arrest and detention of seven students. African Americans boycott several northern schools in protest of de facto segregation. Four black children are killed in bombing of Birmingham, Alabama, church. |
| June 1964 | Three civil rights workers, two white and one black, working to register black voters are killed in Mississippi. Murderers include sheriff's deputies. |
| July 1964 | First in a wave of ghetto riots breaks out in New York City's Harlem. |
| January 1965 | King organizes protest marches in Selma, Alabama. Marches end in violent attacks by police. |
| August 11, 1965 | Ghetto riots erupt in Watts section of Los Angeles. Four thousand rioters are arrested; thirty-four are killed. |
| June 6, 1966 | James Meredith suffers gunshot wound in march across Mississippi. |
| Summers 1966 and 1967 | Riots and violent demonstrations occur in cities across the nation. |
| April 4, 1968 | Martin Luther King Jr. assassinated in Memphis, Tennessee. |

## Current Civil Rights Policy

With one exception, the civil rights laws enacted in the 1960s remain in force today, and many of them have been strengthened through new legislation, regulations, and judicial decisions. The federal bureaucracy has assumed a prominent role in implementing policies enacted during the civil rights movement. Revised public accommodations and fair housing laws specifically redelegated principal enforcement authority from the courts to federal agencies. Rather than having to investigate and prove a specific discriminatory act in a judicial proceeding, the government could focus instead on the "outcome" of local practices. An early target of administrative agencies' implementation of the recent civil rights laws was public primary and secondary schools. When the enforcement agencies searched for evidence of discrimination in the proportions of black versus white enrollments, they netted many schools outside the South where **de facto segregation** was generating the same patterns as those mandated by state law (**de jure segregation**) in the South. Outside the South, residential segregation was the culprit. It too was a by-product of former discriminatory housing laws that kept neighborhoods and their schools segregated.* When the courts and federal agencies decided jointly to force school districts to bus students to sometimes distant schools for the sake of integration, the measure produced waves of public protests. Indeed, busing proved to be one of the most contentious civil rights policies of the modern era. In many communities, it spurred "white flight" to districts that lay beyond busing, with the unintended consequence of increasing racial segregation. In recent years as busing has declined as the judicially preferred remedy, it has also waned as a political issue.

### Beyond the Voting Rights Act

The 1965 Voting Rights Act was, then, a culminating achievement of the civil rights movement of the 1960s. For the next four decades the nine southern states falling under the law routinely submitted changes in state election laws and redistricting decisions to the Department of Justice for preclearance. Congress reauthorized the law each time it was set to expire. In 2013, however, the Supreme Court ruled that nearly half a century after preclearance had been put in place, it was no longer needed to prevent discrimination, and, as such, it posed an undue burden on states, thus violating the Constitution's delegation to the states responsibility for conducting elections.[26] This decision left much of the law in place, but it shifted the burden to voters to challenge a state's or community's changes in voting rules in court.

At about the same time recently elected Republican state legislatures throughout the country began tightening voter qualification laws and election procedures that immediately ignited controversy. Most of these laws have been challenged in the courts as intentionally discriminatory against minorities, who happened to be predominantly Democrats. Laws requiring photo identification—such as a driver's license or a state identification card—pose a difficulty for thousands of mostly minority citizens who do not drive to get to their DMV to obtain photo identification. The Supreme Court had previously upheld the right of states

---

*Until the Supreme Court ruled them illegal in 1968, *restrictive covenants* were commonly embedded in property deeds, preventing owners from selling the property to Jews and African Americans. *Jones v. Alfred H. Mayer Co.*, 392 U.S. 409 (1968).

# Key Provisions of Federal Civil Rights Legislation

## Civil Rights Act, 1957

Established U.S. Commission on Civil Rights to investigate the status of civil rights in the country. Made it a federal crime to attempt to prevent a person from voting.

## Civil Rights Act, 1960

Increased sanctions against abridging or denying the right to vote. Permitted federal government to appoint "referees," under the jurisdiction of the courts, to register voters denied the right to vote by a pattern or practice of discrimination.

## Civil Rights Act, 1964

*Voting:* By equating a sixth-grade education with literacy, the act made it more difficult to disenfranchise African Americans through literacy tests.

*Public accommodations:* Barred discrimination on basis of race, color, religion, or nationality in restaurants, service stations, theaters, transportation, and hotels with five rooms or more. Empowered attorney general to initiate suits.

*Schools:* Authorized attorney general to bring suit against segregated schools. Also permitted federal government to withhold funds from segregated schools.

*Employment:* Barred discrimination on the basis of race, color, religion, nationality, or sex in a range of employment practices. Established Equal Employment Opportunity Commission to enforce this provision.

## Voting Rights Act, 1965

Permitted appointment, under Civil Service Commission, of voting examiners in place of local registrars in all areas where less than 50 percent of those eligible to vote actually voted in the 1964 presidential election. Use of literacy tests and similar mechanisms suspended.

## Age Discrimination in Employment Act, 1967

Prevented employment discrimination based on age for workers forty to sixty-five years old. Later amended to prevent mandatory retirement.

## Fair Housing Act, 1968

Outlawed refusal to rent or sell housing on grounds of race or religion, but exempted citizens who rented or sold their homes without using a real estate agent.

## Rehabilitation Act, 1973

Instituted affirmative action programs for employers to hire "qualified handicapped individuals" and barred discrimination solely on the basis of a disability.

## Restoration of Civil Rights Act, 1988

Applied anti–sex discrimination standards to all institutions' programs if the institution received federal funding.

## Civil Rights Act, 1991

Gave victims of intentional discrimination based on sex, religion, or disability the right to sue for monetary damages. (Victims of racial discrimination had had this right since a Reconstruction-era law.)

■ **MAP 4.4**   States with Voter ID Requirements, 2018

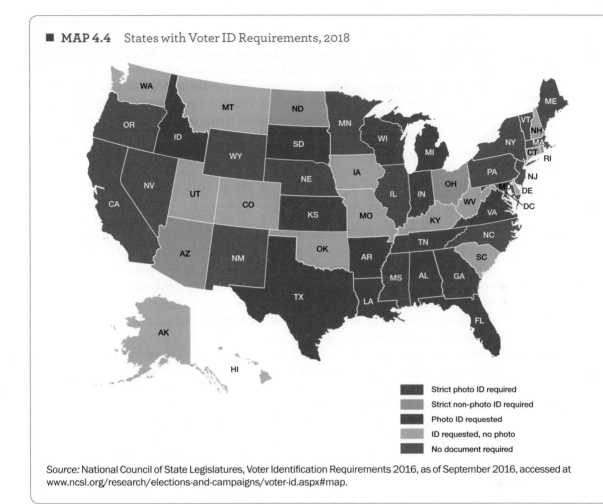

| | |
|---|---|
| ■ | Strict photo ID required |
| ■ | Strict non-photo ID required |
| ■ | Photo ID requested |
| ■ | ID requested, no photo |
| ■ | No document required |

*Source:* National Council of State Legislatures, Voter Identification Requirements 2016, as of September 2016, accessed at www.ncsl.org/research/elections-and-campaigns/voter-id.aspx#map.

to require photo identification—generally speaking—as a justifiable protection against voter fraud, but not for purposes of discrimination.[27] (In many of these states, employer and school photo identification cards did not suffice.) Other state laws reduced the time available for early voting in ways that dampened minority turnout; still others make voter registration more difficult by eliminating same-day registration and/or limiting voter mobilization drives.[28] Entering the 2016 campaign federal courts were reviewing and in many instance overturning recent changes in these laws. Map 4.4 displays the voting laws and procedures across the states that were in place during the 2016 election.

## Affirmative Action in Higher Education

In the 1980s and 1990s civil rights enforcement moved beyond the South to include a broad range of government and private actions that appeared racially discriminatory. Note that the government found straightforward solutions for redressing discrimination in voting rights and schools: it enrolled previously disenfranchised black voters and redirected students from segregated to racially integrated schools. Beginning in the 1970s and continuing today, national policy has sought not just to eradicate discrimination, but also to redress the lingering effects of past discrimination on opportunities currently available to minorities. If entry into the construction trade depended on acquiring specific skills and training to which African Americans had for generations been barred, then mandating that a contractor not discriminate in hiring skilled workers and subcontractors would have no practical effect. Ending discrimination would not in itself necessarily introduce equal opportunity, much less lead eventually to an integrated society.

Enter affirmative action. In the early 1970s **affirmative action** represented a policy that requires those employers and schools that had practiced past discrimination to compensate minorities (and, subsequently, women) by giving them special consideration in hiring and school admissions. The simplest way to implement this policy involved **quotas** requiring recruitment of an equal or some proportionate number of minorities. This early form of affirmative action has been thoroughly rejected by both the federal courts and the American public. In the first and still definitive case, *Regents of the University of California v. Bakke* (1978), the Supreme Court decided that, though creating an admission quota for minority students might serve the laudable goals of addressing past wrongs and attaining a diverse student body, the university medical school's approach violated the equal protection rights of white applicants.[29]

During the intervening decades the Supreme Court has decided numerous affirmative action cases without resolving the issue of preferential treatment beyond outlawing quotas. Virtually all of the tough cases that have reached the Court have been decided by a single vote, with the balance teetering in favor of or opposition to affirmative action. Where in 1987 the Court ruled that gender could be considered along with other criteria in promotion decisions, and apparently even without evidence of past discrimination, by 1995 it was sanctioning only "narrowly tailored" standards designed to achieve a "compelling government interest."[30]

During the past two decades the main arena for affirmative action in education has shifted to higher education. The most recent decisions find the Court still grappling to identify acceptable avenues for favoring some applicants over others without using quotas. In 2003 it decided a pair of long-anticipated University of Michigan cases that had received apparently contradictory rulings at the appeals level. The Court's decisions reflected its own ambivalence over affirmative action; both were 5–4 and reached opposite results.[31] In the undergraduate case, the Court ruled that although diversity in higher education could be a "compelling interest," the university's assignment of one-fifth of the total points for admission on the basis of race was unconstitutional. The law school program, however, passed muster because race was merely *one* of the factors that the law school considered. But even that ruling provoked a vigorous dissent, and since then changes in membership have shifted the Court in a more conservative direction.*

---

*Sandra Day O'Connor, the pivotal vote and author of the majority's opinion in the law school case, retired to be replaced by the distinctly more conservative justice Samuel Alito.

Nine years later, the Supreme Court returned to the issue in a case brought by a white student who was denied admission to the University of Texas. The plaintiff argued that because the University of Texas's policy of admitting any high school student who ranked in the top 10 percent of his or her class had resulted in the admission of substantial numbers of African American and Hispanic students, it did not need to reserve a share of admissions in which the applicant's race would be a criteria for admission. After a series of intermediate decisions in which the case bounced around federal courts, the Supreme Court ruled in 2016 that the university could overenroll black students in order to attain diversity. Although it allowed the university discretion in this case, the majority advised that other kinds of affirmative action policies used by universities might not pass muster.[32]

One can find parallels in public opinion with the judiciary's collective ambivalence with affirmative action policy. National surveys convey a public that mostly favors the principle of affirmative action while disapproving of almost every specific approach for achieving it. One 2012 survey taken during the Court's deliberation of the Michigan cases found most respondents strongly opposing preferential treatment. When asked, "As you may know, the U.S. Supreme Court will be deciding whether public universities can use race as one of the factors in admissions to increase diversity in the student body. Do you favor or oppose this practice?" sixty-five percent registered opposition, and 26 percent registered support. Yet the same survey found a majority (49 to 43 percent) endorsing affirmative action in order to overcome past discrimination as long as it did not involve "rigid" quotas. Moreover, whenever voters have been presented with this issue in a referendum, a clear majority voted to outlaw racial and other preferences in university admissions.

## The Legacy of the Civil Rights Movement

Although race remained a prominent civil rights issue in the 1970s, the civil rights movement branched out to include women, the elderly, the disabled, the LGBT community, and virtually every ethnic minority. The new directions of civil rights over the past several decades owe their progress, however, to African Americans' two-hundred-year struggle for civil rights. It paved the way politically for these new efforts, both in honing the techniques of demonstrations and protests and in creating a receptive audience in the news media and American public opinion. But most important, the black civil rights movement built a foundation of federal laws, judicial precedents, and administrative regulations that could be easily extended to other groups.

### Equal Rights for Women: The Right to Vote

Long before abolitionists took up the cause of slavery, early feminists, later calling themselves **suffragists**, were campaigning for the vote. (Many early suffragists also were active in movements for prison reform, public education, temperance, and, above all, abolition of slavery.) These women viewed their cause as inextricably linked to full citizenship for African Americans in the "rising tide of prodemocratic sentiment."*

Despite the efforts of the suffragists, voting rights for African Americans tracked very different courses from the late 1840s to the late 1860s. Ironically, slaves were liberated and black males given the vote, whereas women, despite needing to traverse a much shorter distance, had progressed little toward gaining the franchise. (On two other issues—allowing inheritance and access to public education—the movement successfully revised many state laws.)

Suffrage leaders Elizabeth Cady Stanton and Susan B. Anthony actively lobbied to include women in the Fourteenth Amendment and probably expected to succeed.[33] As Stanton famously declared, black suffrage opened the "constitutional door," and the suffragists intended to avail [themselves] of the strong arm and the blue uniform of the black soldier to walk in by his side."† Their expectations were dashed when Republican leaders explicitly limited the amendment to male citizens. Claiming that including women would have endangered ratification, Republican politicians clearly viewed women's suffrage to be a costly issue.‡

Unlike the black vote, which contemporaries agreed would go directly to the Republicans, the women's vote appeared to confer little advantage to either party. Without a compelling political advantage to be gained, few politicians were prepared to absorb the heavy political costs of extending the vote to women. This is consistent with the history of suffrage. Enthusiasm for women's suffrage appears to have been concentrated among the urban, upper-middle class. Various other women's groups either opposed or ignored the issue. Unlike the black vote—desperately needed by Republicans if they hoped to retain control of Congress and the presidency after the rebel states were readmitted into the Union—the women's vote, especially given the narrow support base for this reform, conferred little political advantage to Republicans.§ "Sex" was excluded from the Fifteenth Amendment. Except for local school board elections and liquor referenda in twenty states, women did not obtain the franchise until 1869, when the territory of Wyoming passed the first women's suffrage law.[34]

---

*During the colonial era, single property-owning women in New Jersey could vote. See Alexander Keyssar, *The Right to Vote* (New York: Basic Books, 2000); and Judith Apter Klinghoffer and Lois Elkis, "The Petticoat Electors: Women's Suffrage in New Jersey, 1776–1807," *Journal of the Early Republic* 12 (1992): 159–193.

†See Ellen Carol Dubois, "Outgrowing the Compact of the Fathers: Equal Rights, Women's Suffrage, and the United States Constitution, 1820–1878," *Journal of American History* 74, no. 3 (December 1987): 836–862, at 845.

‡In one particularly heated exchange, Frederick Douglass—a former slave who had been present at the first national suffrage conference at Seneca Falls in 1848—argued that only when white women were "dragged from their houses and hung upon lamp-posts" would they have "an urgency to obtain the ballot equal to our own." Susan B. Anthony gave the withering response: "If you will not give the whole loaf of suffrage to the entire people, give it to the most intelligent first." Mari Jo Buhle and Paul Buhle, *The Concise History of Woman Suffrage* (University of Illinois Press, 1978), 258.

§Ironically, the difference in the partisan advantage between black and female vote extensions might well explain the historical differences in the success of these groups in exercising their newly won franchise. The reemergent Democratic Party throughout the South later systematically stripped the vote from ex-slaves with literacy tests, white primary laws, and poll taxes. Threatening no one, other than saloon proprietors, women exercised their franchise largely unhindered. Indeed, both political parties took credit for their newly won right and appealed for their support.

Having lost out in the Reconstruction amendments, the women's movement set out to build national support. Yet with only women remaining on the outside of the polling booth (at least formally), the movement no longer could cast its appeal in terms of universal suffrage. Now, women's suffrage became a women's issue and gave rise to two widely circulated and seemingly incompatible lines of arguments. Some proponents struck a conservative note. The more conservative line queried the inconsistency of denying women the vote when so many ill-informed and illiterate immigrant men were voting. The southern variant of this argument had the white women's vote diluting any chance of African Americans winning elections. At the other end of the ideological continuum, recasting the women's vote as a women's issue connected with a broader feminist platform. Denial of the franchise was simply emblematic of women's subjugation, a condition entrenched in the traditional family structure. Prominent women's issues today found their origins in the arguments of many late-nineteenth-century suffragists. These strongly held, incompatible views invariably competed for leadership of the movement. Whether these organizational weaknesses reflected or contributed to the failure of women's suffrage to win public support is difficult to say. As long as these fissures persisted the women's movement continued to attract supporters for various causes all along the ideological spectrum—including vocal pacifism during World War I—and it took nearly four decades to achieve the Nineteenth Amendment. Gradually, public support for women's suffrage increased, first in Wyoming in 1869 and over the next several decades in other, mostly western states. By 1919, fifteen states had given women the right to vote in at least some elections. Congress renewed consideration repeatedly from the mid-1880s until 1919, when, with President Woodrow Wilson's strong endorsement, two-thirds of both the House and the Senate sent the Nineteenth Amendment to the states for ratification. The next year, the states ratified it.

Women, unlike African Americans, experienced little delay in implementing the right to vote. Although registration rates varied across states, women's rates approached three-quarters of men's within a decade after ratification. Over the next decade or so women were voting regularly at a rate only slightly below that of men.

## The Modern History of Women's Rights

The modern extension of subsequent civil rights guarantees to women clearly followed the civil rights movement. In fact, through a political miscalculation, sex discrimination was outlawed in the 1964 Civil Rights Act. Initially the legislation included language that covered discrimination based only on religion, national origin, and race. Southern opponents proposed and voted to add sex to this list, certain that it would decrease overall support for and ultimately defeat the civil rights bill. This strategy of weighing the legislation down with controversial provisions backfired, however, when Congress accepted their amendment and proceeded to pass the legislation.

The surprising legislative victory did not lead to immediate enforcement, however, even though the 1964 law created an enforcement mechanism—the new Equal Employment Opportunity Commission (EEOC)—authorized to investigate and file suits against racial discrimination in the workplace. With one early EEOC commissioner calling the sex discrimination policy "a fluke," the commission initially balked at enforcing the employment

Victoria Claflin Woodhull was one of the most outspoken feminists of the late nineteenth century. The first woman to declare herself a candidate for the presidency, she also ran a brokerage firm and published a Marxist-tinged newspaper. In her 1871 keynote address to the National Woman Suffrage Association, Woodhull admitted her ultimate goal was the overthrow of the government, by treason if necessary. Her subsequent announcement that she practiced as well as preached free love lent credibility to opponents' claims that female suffrage would be the first step toward some brave new world.

discrimination protections for women. But the agency revised its orientation after a successful political campaign focused national attention on employment discrimination against women.

The National Organization for Women (NOW) was formed in 1966 in direct reaction to the EEOC's refusal to enforce this provision. Organized along the same lines as the NAACP, NOW initially pursued a litigation strategy with mixed success. To establish a stronger legal foundation, NOW and other women's rights organizations dusted off the Equal Rights Amendment (ERA), which had been introduced in Congress in 1923 and every year thereafter with little fanfare and poor prospects. The amendment gave Congress the authority to implement the following statement: "Equality of rights under the law shall not be denied or abridged by the United States or by any State on account of sex."

Using many of the same tactics honed by the civil rights movement—demonstrations, televised appeals, Washington rallies, and intense lobbying—NOW and other feminist organizations won over a sympathetic public. The mostly male members of Congress were not far behind. After languishing for years, the ERA was sent to the states in 1972, and within the first year twenty-two of the required thirty-eight states voted for ratification. But then the amendment hit a brick wall with the abortion issue (discussed more fully in Chapter 5).[35] Thus instead of pitting men against women, as the Nineteenth Amendment had done earlier in the century, the ERA divided feminist and antiabortion women's groups. What began as an uncontroversial endorsement of women's rights—after all, the amendment's wording simply asserts that women enjoy the same rights as men—ended in strident, contentious rhetoric between opposing camps.* On June 30, 1982, the timetable for ratification expired, and the ERA became history.

Feminists may have lost the battle over the ERA, but they appear to have won the war. During the decades since the failed ERA campaign, national civil rights policy in areas of special concern to women has advanced steadily. In 1972 Congress enacted **Title IX** of the Higher Education Act, which prohibits funding for schools and universities that discriminate against women, including the size of their intercollegiate sports programs. When the Supreme Court in 1984 limited the law's coverage of private groups, ruling that it prohibited discrimination

---

*Public support waned. By 1981 less than half of all voters still endorsed the amendment in those states where it had not yet been ratified. Gallup poll cited in Jane Mansbridge, *Why We Lost the ERA* (Chicago: University of Chicago Press, 1986), 214.

only in those programs of a private organization that directly benefited from federal funding, Congress responded by passing, over President Ronald Reagan's veto, a law that overturned the Court's decision.[36] And to send a message to the conservative Court, the Democratic majorities deliberately titled the new law the Restoration of Civil Rights Act of 1988.

Most significant developments in civil rights policy on employment practices have occurred during the past two decades, reflecting women's increasing presence in the workforce. However measured—whether by percentage of women in the workplace, or numbers of working mothers, or the share of women who are their family's primary breadwinner—the numbers indicate dramatic growth in women's workforce participation.

As employment issues increased, working women and their legal advocates discovered that the Civil Rights Act of 1964—just as some critics of the ERA had argued—offered ample legal protections for their discrimination claims. Though drafted principally to eradicate racial discrimination, the language of Title VII of that law is unequivocal in its provisions against sex discrimination in the workplace: "[It is] an unlawful employment practice for an employer. . . to discriminate against any individual with respect to his compensation, term, conditions, or privileges of employment, because of such individual's race, color, religion, sex, or national origin." During the past twenty years, as the Supreme Court has considered the merits of women's lawsuits charging sexual harassment by male supervisors, the Court has relied heavily on the 1964 provision to find that sexual harassment violates the federal civil rights law.

Congress further strengthened employment discrimination claims on various fronts. The Pregnancy Discrimination Act (1978) and the Family and Medical Leave Act (1993) prevent firing and demotion during absences for childbirth and family medical emergencies. The Civil Rights Act of 1991 required employers to show that unequal hiring and compensation practices did not reflect gender discrimination and gave victims the right to sue for damages. In recent years gender has replaced race at the top of the civil rights agenda. The courts, Congress, federal agencies, and state legislatures devote a significant amount of time to policies governing gender relations in the workplace. Today, claims of sexual discrimination in hiring, pregnancy discrimination in retention and advancement, and harassment in the workplace constitute more than one-third of all complaints presented to the EEOC.[37]

## Rights for Hispanics

According to the U.S. Census Bureau, in 2009 the Hispanic population totaled forty-eight million, about 16 percent of the U.S. population.* The 2010 census figures indicate that slightly less than four in ten Hispanics are foreign born, with most arriving from Mexico and Central America. Over the years Hispanics have experienced many of the same civil rights injustices endured by African Americans. As "national origin" became a protected rights category and as the Hispanic population has grown rapidly, so have the number of discrimination complaints. In many respects, Hispanics have successfully enlisted the legal, administrative, and judicial structures constructed to protect African Americans.

---

*African Americans and Asian Americans by comparison constitute 13.6 percent and 5 percent of the population, respectively. "U.S. Hispanic Population Surpasses 45 Million, Now 15 Percent of Total," U.S. Census Bureau Population Division, May 2008.

Yet their civil rights concerns are also distinctive. Many lack the language skills to exercise their civic responsibilities in English. Recognizing this problem early on, Congress passed the 1970 extension of the Voting Rights Act of 1965, requiring that ballots also be available in Spanish in those constituencies where at least 5 percent of the population is Hispanic.

Other recent government actions concerning language have been less accommodating, however. Whether from discrimination or the expressed difficulty of administering multilingual applications, a few states have adopted English-only laws mandating that most state business be conducted in English. When an applicant for an Alabama driver's license challenged the state's English-only law as a civil rights violation, a narrowly divided Supreme Court in *Alexander v. Sandoval* (2001) ruled that an individual could not challenge Alabama's regulation that all driver's license tests and applications be written in English. The 1964 Civil Rights Act allowed individual suits only in cases of "intentional discrimination." The law, according to the majority opinion, left to federal enforcement agencies the determination of whether English-only rules had an inherently discriminatory outcome. The decision, in effect, turned this class of civil rights complaints away from the courts and to political and administrative institutions.

Undocumented, or illegal, immigrants, the largest share of whom are Hispanic, enjoy fewer civil rights protections than do legal immigrants. But legal immigrants, in turn, enjoy fewer Bill of Rights protections than do those immigrants who have become citizens. For one, they cannot vote. But their status is more complex and fraught with risk. If a legal immigrant commits a crime—say, drug possession or driving without a license—he or she is subject to deportation. Yet how long can the government wait before taking the person into custody? According to Homeland Security, they can do so anytime. A current case before the Supreme Court (to be decided in 2019) has the Homeland Security Administration squaring off against the ACLU over whether the government can seize and deport these individuals years (in some instances, decades) after the case is resolved. The ACLU and the Ninth Circuit Court of Appeals, which had ruled in favor of the immigrant, argued that such late seizure and deportation violated the defendant's due process rights. (We will post the outcome of this case on this book's website.)

This is a nontrivial argument. Recall that the Fourteenth Amendment's due process clause explicitly extends basic rights to noncitizens: "No state shall . . . deprive any person of life, liberty or property, without due process of law; nor deny to any person within its jurisdiction the equal protection of the laws." In the next chapter we find the due process clause having its greatest impact in applying basic privacy and criminal rights protections to citizens and noncitizens alike.

When it comes to the panoply of government services, eligibility for the benefits available to all citizens varies from state to state and changes from one year to the next. This creates great confusion and underuse of benefits even among noncitizens eligible for them. Take, for example, the food stamp program (today called the Supplemental Nutrition Assistance Program, or SNAP). In 1996 the law was changed to restrict eligibility with few exceptions to citizens. Then over time, the law was amended, opening eligibility to the following groups of legal immigrants: Cuban/Haitian entrants, Afghan and Iraqi immigrants, survivors of human trafficking, lawful residents who had logged ten years of work, Hmong and Laotian tribe members, immigrant seniors born before 1931, and the list goes on. Complicating matters further, five states extended food credits to everyone regardless of legal status. The same hodgepodge of eligibility rules can be found for rent and health subsidy programs. Undocumented immigrants do have automatic access to some federal programs such as Emergency Medicaid, Head Start, and school meal programs. Moreover, states are required to enroll undocumented children in their K–12 programs. Finally, unlike legal residents, undocumented immigrants are ineligible to receive Social Security benefits even if they otherwise qualify by paying their contribution for a sufficient number of quarters.

Adding to the confusion, these policies can change from one administration to the next. Eligibility for permanent legal status has always emphasized applicants' self-reliance. Generally, this precluded participation in those federal programs providing cash subsidies, compared to services, such as the children's health program. In 2019 the Trump administration tightened eligibility by ruling that use of any government service would demonstrate dependence on the government, rendering them ineligible for legal status. Nowhere is there greater uncertainty than for the 700,000 children who entered the United States illegally with their parents. Failing to win immigration reform from a Republican-controlled Congress, Democratic president Obama in 2012 created by executive action the DACA program (Deferred Action for Childhood Arrivals). This would move these children to the lowest deportation priority. It allowed them to register and apply for a green card, permitting them to be legally employable. Two years later, the president again unilaterally sought to expand eligibility to over 300,000 more individuals—specifically, the parents of DACA participants. This time states took the administration to a federal district court in Texas, which ruled that the president's order exceeded his legal authority.* Since then federal district courts appear poised to declare the original program illegal. Compounding the uncertainty, President Trump announced the end of DACA, but a federal court in the summer of 2018 ruled that it could not be ended abruptly. So, eligible immigrant children can still apply for DACA status, work permits, driver's licenses, and the like, but for how long?

The extent to which Hispanics succeed in having their complaints addressed by political and bureaucratic institutions may depend on their ability to maximize a fundamental political resource reserved for citizens—the right to vote. One of every four foreign-born Hispanics is a naturalized citizen.† Added to the 60 percent who are native born, about seven in ten Hispanics in the United States are citizens. In the absence of immigration reforms that open the pathway to citizenship, population numbers will continue to overstate the Hispanic community's potential political power.

Despite the obstacles facing immigrants with illegal status and other Hispanics, the long-term prognosis for this group's civic gains is bright. The population is growing rapidly (see Map 4.5), as are naturalization rates. Moreover, the population as a whole is quite young, with about 40 percent of Hispanics below voting age. As these young people, most of whom are native-born citizens, become eligible to vote, this group's electoral power is bound to surge. Finally, the Hispanic population is distributed geographically in a manner that promises it political influence. The population's residential concentration ensures that a sizable number

---

*The Supreme Court upheld the district court decision in a 4–4 vote in *United States v. Texas,* 579 U.S. ___ (2016).

†To be eligible for naturalization, immigrants must have permanent resident visas for five years or, if married to a U.S. citizen, have lived in the country for three years.

of Hispanics will compete in Hispanic plurality districts. This bodes well for aspiring Hispanic politicians. Indeed, from 1996 to 2014 the number of elected Hispanic officials increased from 3,743 to 6,084. The fact that over 90 percent of these officials who occupy partisan offices are registered as Democrats harbingers tough times ahead for the Republican Party in those constituencies where Hispanics constitute a sizable share of the electorate. Moreover, Hispanic voters reside in some major swing states such as Florida and Colorado, and soon it appears they will become pivotal in Arizona and Texas. (We revisit Hispanics' growing political clout in Chapter 12 on political parties.)

■ **MAP 4.5**    High Concentration of U.S. Hispanics: A Guarantee of Political Influence

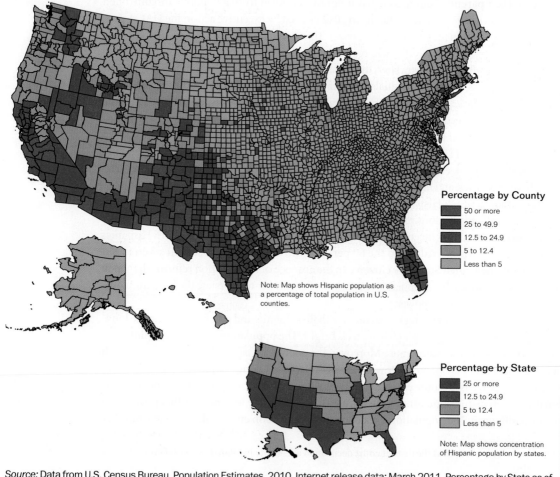

Percentage by County

- 50 or more
- 25 to 49.9
- 12.5 to 24.9
- 5 to 12.4
- Less than 5

Note: Map shows Hispanic population as a percentage of total population in U.S. counties.

Percentage by State

- 25 or more
- 12.5 to 24.9
- 5 to 12.4
- Less than 5

Note: Map shows concentration of Hispanic population by states.

*Source:* Data from U.S. Census Bureau, Population Estimates, 2010. Internet release data: March 2011. Percentage by State as of 2009, U.S. Census Bureau QuickFacts.

## Gay Rights

The favorable "rights" climate generally has encouraged other groups to come forward—most prominently, the gay community.* But civil rights protections for gays remain a murky area of national policy largely because the public's views and, consequently, elected officials' commitments are still forming. Moreover, many claims of the gay community have not always fit neatly into the statutory provisions or judicial precedents created during the civil rights era that have over time become the basis for civil rights protection of other groups.

A decade or so ago some observers foresaw the Supreme Court establishing a beachhead for an expanding gay rights movement, when it struck down a voter-approved amendment to Colorado's constitution that *prohibited* state and local governments from protecting gays and lesbians against discrimination based on sexual orientation. The Supreme Court ruled that the amendment unconstitutionally denied gays equal protection, yet the Court did not actually confer any specific rights to gays. Nonetheless, by applying the critical Fourteenth Amendment to gay rights claims, *Romer v. Evans* made this group eligible for positive protections if state and local jurisdictions deemed them appropriate.[38]

But in 1995 Congress voted down legislation that would have incorporated sexual orientation into existing employment rights laws. The next year it passed the Defense of Marriage Act (popularly known as "DOMA"), which not only rejects same-sex marriage but allows states to ignore these unions sanctioned in other states. More than symbolism was at stake in this law. By one count, over a thousand federal rights and benefits are available to married couples, including Social Security survivor's benefits, Medicaid eligibility, and estate tax exemptions or reductions.[39]

Despite these setbacks, the gay rights movement has celebrated some major successes. In 2009, Congress expanded federal hate crimes protections to gays. (The **hate crime** designation refers to those provisions of the criminal code that make illegal—or stiffen penalties for—violence directed against individuals, property, or organizations because of the victims' race, gender, national origin, or sexual orientation.) The next year it ended the military's "don't ask, don't tell" policy that permitted service by gays only as long as they did not disclose their sexual preference.

In the spring of 2013, the Supreme Court issued a landmark ruling that DOMA violated the constitutional rights of same-sex couples, but the majority opinion read as though it left room for the states to set their own marriage rules.[40] At that time, thirty states permitted either marriage or "unions" in lieu of marriage. Two years later the Court revisited the issue, and it decided 5–4 that marriage choice is a fundamental right provided for by the Fourteenth Amendment, yet another legacy of black Americans' two-hundred-year pursuit of their civil rights.[41]

# Challenging Tyranny

This historical survey of civil rights in America reveals courageous men and women advocating for their fellow citizens who were suffering injustice. But this history also reveals that these

---

*Throughout our discussion we refer to the rights of "gays" in the broad use of this word, which includes lesbian, transgender, and bisexual individuals in addition to gay men.

efforts did not always suffice. True to James Madison's observation in *Federalist* No. 10, the cause of civil rights is advanced only when a large national majority fully takes control of the federal government and challenges tyranny in the states. The politicians who assembled these broad national coalitions were keen political strategists. Abraham Lincoln and the Republican Party rode into office advocating "Free Soil, Free Labor, Free Men," not eradication of slavery. Nonetheless, their political success allowed them to conduct a costly and bloody war to preserve the Union and abolish slavery.

From the 1880s through the 1950s neither party could muster a majority even within itself, much less the government, on behalf of civil rights for African Americans. Consequently, the cause languished, and generations of African Americans were doomed to lives marred by segregation's shameful regimen. Then, in the 1960s, the Democratic Party rode the crest of public opinion generated by the civil rights movement. The 1964 election gave Democrats the presidency and huge majorities in both chambers of Congress. They enacted strong new civil rights policies and enforced them. Advances in civil rights since those years rest on a firm foundation of laws and institutions created in response to these historic events.

What does the difficult history of the civil rights movement say about the operation of America's political system? The struggle for civil rights has seriously tested the politics of self-interest. Yet all of the politicians who worked to advance black civil rights offer a more confident depiction of political ambition than the one James Madison presented in *Federalist* No. 51. Whereas Madison viewed the Constitution as neutralizing the ambition of politicians and factions, the history of civil rights portrays these same vote-seeking politicians and political parties as transforming moral justice into public policy.

**for CQ Press**

**Want a better grade?**

Get the tools you need to sharpen your study skills. Access practice quizzes, eFlashcards, video, and multimedia at **edge.sagepub.com/kernell9e.**

## KEY TERMS

affirmative action    172
black codes    147
civil liberties    138
civil rights    138
de facto segregation    169
de jure segregation    169
Fugitive Slave Law    144
grandfather clauses    151

hate crime    181
Jim Crow laws    151
literacy test    151
nominating convention    159
poll tax    151
quotas    172
racial profiling    135
segregation    151

separate but equal doctrine    152
suffragists    173
Title IX    176
white primary    151

# SUGGESTED READINGS

Anderson, Kristi. *After Suffrage*. Chicago: University of Chicago Press, 1996. Anderson assembles all of the available voting and registration data in providing a detailed and varied history of the entry of women into American politics.

Branch, Taylor. *Parting the Waters: America in the King Years, 1954–63*. New York: Simon & Schuster, 1988; and *Pillar of Fire: America in the King Years, 1963–65*. New York: Simon & Schuster, 1998. These two installments of Branch's detailed political history of civil rights offer a wealth of instruction to students of politics and history alike.

Carmines, Edward G., and James A. Stimson. *Issue Evolution: Race and the Transformation of American Politics*. Princeton, NJ: Princeton University Press, 1989. Although these scholars use sophisticated statistical techniques, they offer an accessible and convincing account of the evolution of the Democratic Party among politicians and citizens as the party of civil rights.

Garrow, David J. *Bearing the Cross: Martin Luther King Jr. and the Southern Christian Leadership Conference*. New York: Morrow, 1986. An absorbing account of the rise of King from the Montgomery bus boycott to his assassination in 1968.

Keyssar, Alexander. *The Right to Vote*. New York: Basic Books, 2000. This highly readable history of the extension of voting rights in the United States has emerged as the authoritative source on the subject.

Oates, Stephen B. *With Malice toward None: The Life of Abraham Lincoln*. New York: New American Library–Dutton, 1978. Our favorite Lincoln biography has two great virtues: Lincoln is shown to be a masterful politician, and the gradual emergence of emancipation as a wartime issue is described clearly.

# REVIEW QUESTIONS

1. What features of government did the southern states use to prevent the eradication of slavery? What steps were necessary to remove the obstacles to emancipation?

2. What benefits did Reconstruction produce for former slaves? For northern whites? What benefits and which groups did Reconstruction "leave out," and why?

3. What party did most African Americans support prior to the 1930s, and why? Why did this change after the 1930s, and what was responsible for the change?

4. How did the civil rights demonstrations of the 1960s change the political calculations of Democratic politicians? How were the demonstrations planned strategically to increase pressure on politicians?

5. What challenges and opportunities do Hispanics face in their current civil rights efforts? How do these challenges differ from those blacks faced in their civil rights campaigns?

Following the shooting deaths of Philando Castile and Alton Sterling by the police in summer 2016, thousands of protesters took to the streets. Here, Iesha Evans is detained by law enforcement in Baton Rouge, Louisiana. Evans was one of more than one hundred protesters arrested in Baton Rouge that day, with civil unrest taking place across the nation in response to police shootings of African Americans.

# Civil Liberties

# 5

In 2016, after a series of citizens' video recordings of unjustified police shootings of African Americans around the country were initially posted and later broadcast on national news, the issue of police brutality gained national awareness. The American public was galvanized by the images, and most were outraged by what they saw. During the summer, the Pew Research Center, which tracks national opinions about racial relations in the United States, found a surge of public opinion holding that police discriminated in their treatment of African Americans. By late spring 2016, four in five black respondents held that they were treated less fairly by the police. Perhaps even more indicative of the effects of social media, half of white respondents also expressed this opinion.[1]

Chicago has probably experienced as many chronic problems between the police and the city's racial and ethnic minorities as any other large metropolitan area within the United States. In 2016, after a number of police shootings of black suspects failed to lead to indictments, disciplinary actions, or even public reports, Chicago's African American leaders began clamoring for action. Their appeal attracted national attention. That same year Chicago city officials released a number of videos of various police encounters with black Chicagoans. One that received prominent national coverage recorded a 2012 police confrontation with an unarmed but muscular man, Ismael Jamison. Conflict escalated, and Jamison was shot.* The video recording of this encounter raises the question of what constitutes an acceptable level of force. Along with other digital footage, it also reminds us that emerging technology continually recasts constitutional questions about our civil liberties.

Police had been alerted that a passenger was physically abusing people on a nearby bus. (Both the driver and a passenger required treatment in a hospital.) Video shows Jamison approaching a policeman, who then shoots him. Other police, quick to arrive on the scene, subsequently used a stun gun on Jamison several times to subdue him before he was put into an ambulance. (Jamison recovered from his injuries.) Was the shooting justified? Did it constitute an acceptable level of force? These are the questions the police review commission and the Chicago district attorney had to ask in deciding whether to take action against the police officer. As graphic as the video is, it omits what might be critical information to answer that question. There is no audio, so we do not know what transpired between the two men at the outset of the confrontation.

From the information contained in the video, judicial doctrine would appear to side with the police officers. The Fourth Amendment's ban on "illegal searches and seizures," examined more fully shortly, is the constitutional issue that police shootings invoke. In 1985 the Supreme Court took up a case in which a Memphis police officer shot a fleeing burglary suspect in the back, killing him. The Court ruled that such shootings are justified only if "the officer has probable cause to believe that the suspect poses a significant threat of death or serious injury to the officer or others."[2] Subsequent decisions have favored the use of force in close calls. In the most recent case in 2015, the Court ruled that an officer who shot and killed a suspect who was racing away from police in a stolen car was justified because of the likelihood that the high-speed chase would result in serious injuries to others.[3] But the issue remains unresolved. Police departments are being pressed by federal authorities and in many communities by local officials and the citizenry to revamp procedures to deescalate difficult but nonthreatening situations without drawing their firearms.

## Nationalization of Civil Liberties

Civil liberties claims—of all kinds—dominate today's newspaper headlines and frequently lead television evening news programs, and for good reason. Occasionally, an authority, whether the local police or Congress, acts in such a way that some argue abridges an established freedom. In other instances, new laws or judicial interpretations expand personal liberties or extend established civil liberties into new domains. The rapid emergence of advanced information and communication technologies has introduced a panoply of new applications of civil liberties claims and policy. The expansion of civil liberties is often controversial. As the previous cases illustrate, civil liberties claims frequently run up against the ardent preferences of a majority of the citizenry, the nation's legitimate security needs, or even the rights claims of others.

---

*The video of this confrontation is posted on numerous sites. Here is one that accompanies news coverage of the incident: https://www.dnainfo.com/chicago/20160603/chicago-lawn/ismael-jamison-2012-chicago-police-shooting-video-released.

Civil liberties have not always been so prominent in the nation's news and policy deliberations. At the end of the nineteenth century readers might have had to scour newspapers for more than a month to discover claims invoking such constitutionally established privileges as freedom of the press, speech, and religion. Many modern-day civil liberties assertions would have struck the nineteenth-century public as bizarre. If and when same-sex marriages, physician-assisted suicides, and abortions occurred in nineteenth-century America, they were clandestine, and ultimately criminal, enterprises.

Over the past century, determination of national civil liberties policy has shifted from nearly the exclusive jurisdiction of states and communities to Washington. Previously, defendants' rights amounted to little more than what the local police and sheriff permitted. In many states local judges, prosecutors, and legal associations agreed that exclusively white (and mostly older) male jurors satisfied their standards of impartiality and that an attorney for indigent defendants represented an unneeded luxury. Local ministers tendered prayers to school principals, who handed them to teachers and students for morning recitations. Eventually, though, the national government assumed jurisdiction over defendants' rights and school prayer. With a new, expansive interpretation of the Constitution, the courts applied the Bill of Rights to state and local policies as well as national policy.

The histories of civil rights and civil liberties have much in common. Indeed, the constitutional amendments conferring full citizenship to recently freed slaves would later provide the Supreme Court with a rationale for the national government to enter the civil liberties arena. In both histories the judiciary played a pivotal role in accepting the claims of individuals' and groups' rights over the objections of a local or national majority. But in other important respects, the history of civil liberties proceeds down a different path. As discussed in Chapter 4, the greatest advances in civil rights occurred when a national majority took up a minority's cause; so long as the national government remained silent, slavery and segregation were secure. Although the federal judiciary struck the first blows against segregation, the rights of African Americans did not substantially improve until congressional majorities and presidents staked their party's electoral fortunes on intervening directly against segregation and black disenfranchisement. In the end, civil rights required the sustained efforts of a national majority exerting the full force of the federal government. By contrast, advances in civil liberties have frequently involved the intervention of the federal judiciary to protect flag-burning demonstrators from incarceration, to bar public prayers at school graduations, and to prevent juries from hearing confessions from defendants before they were read their rights. These are just a few examples we encounter in this chapter of the Supreme Court's acting to frustrate the preferences of local and even national majorities.

## The Bill of Rights Checks Majority Rule

Where the history of civil rights emphasizes the capacity of majorities to control policy, the history of civil liberties reminds us that the United States is a republic whose institutions are designed to temper the passions of majorities. The First Amendment of the Bill of Rights begins with the emphatic and revealing language "Congress shall make no law" and covers six areas of personal and political liberty. This opening phrase invited the Supreme Court to eventually define civil liberties. Appropriately to this task, the Framers insulated the judicial branch from popular pressures by making judges unelected and tenured for life. The courts "will consider themselves in a peculiar manner the guardians of [civil liberties]," the ever-prescient James Madison predicted. He then added, "They will be an impenetrable bulwark against every assumption of power in the legislative or executive; they will be naturally led to resist every encroachment upon rights."[4]

The Bill of Rights (see box "The Bill of Rights") was designed to limit the capacity of the government to impose conformity costs on those individuals and minorities whose views differ from those of the majority. By insisting that these first ten amendments be placed in the Constitution, the Antifederalist critics of ratification sought assurance that these rights could not be easily removed or abridged. Only if the majority was overwhelming and enduring could it absorb the high transaction costs required to modify these rights via a constitutional amendment. Thus the Supreme Court's authority to veto Congress and state governments on these policies places civil liberties under the protective purview of an institution insulated by design from the pressures of democracy.

The seemingly unequivocal language of the Bill of Rights provides government officials with little latitude to relax its proscriptions. Yet no amendment has ever been judged absolute, and some are downright ambiguous. What precisely does the First Amendment clause "Congress shall make no law respecting an establishment of religion" really mean? Certainly Congress cannot "establish" a particular faith as the "official" religion of the country. Beyond that, the clause offers little guidance and has even fostered opposing interpretations of the relationship between church and state. Does it prevent a moment of silent prayer in public schools? Does it deny government transportation and textbook subsidies for children attending private, church-sponsored schools? Would it permit the immigration service from screening out Muslims for visas to enter the country? Similarly, what does the Eighth Amendment's prohibition of "cruel and unusual" punishment mean, and, of greater practical significance, who decides? Are the justices of the Supreme Court endowed with special insight on appropriate punishment? If not, should states' citizens decide the matter in their criminal statutes, as is largely the case today? If so, what did the Framers have in mind when they used this language in the national Constitution?

Sometimes ambiguity arises from two or more clearly worded constitutional provisions that directly oppose each other. Does unfettered press reportage (a First Amendment right) that introduces highly incriminating or biased information and opinions before the trial undermine a criminal defendant's Sixth Amendment right to an impartial jury?

Other constitutional responsibilities, especially those concerning the country's collective security, may bring official actions into conflict with individual rights. The preamble to the Constitution charges the national government to "provide for the common defence," and Article II designates the president as "Commander in Chief." Does this presidential responsibility allow the government to restrict freedom of the press during times of war, as President Abraham Lincoln claimed, or allow the National Security Agency to collect the phone records of Americans without a court warrant? Whether liberties are competing with one another or with other parts of the Constitution, the Bill of Rights represents a Pandora's box of unanswered policy questions.

The absolute language of the Bill of Rights notwithstanding, civil liberties policy is essentially a line-drawing or boundary-setting activity separating what government actions are

# The Bill of Rights

## Amendment I

Congress shall make no law respecting an establishment of religion, or prohibiting the free exercise thereof; or abridging the freedom of speech, or of the press; or the right of the people peacefully to assemble, and to petition the Government for a redress of grievances.

## Amendment II

A well regulated Militia, being necessary to the security of a free State, the right of the people to keep and bear Arms, shall not be infringed.

## Amendment III

No Soldier shall, in time of peace be quartered in any house, without the consent of the Owner, nor in time of war, but in a manner to be prescribed by law.

## Amendment IV

The right of the people to be secure in their persons, houses, papers, and effects, against unreasonable searches and seizures, shall not be violated, and no Warrants shall issue, but upon probable cause, supported by Oath or affirmation, and particularly describing the place to be searched, and the persons or things to be seized.

## Amendment V

No person shall be held to answer for a capital, or otherwise infamous crime, unless on a presentment or indictment of a Grand Jury, except in cases arising in the land or naval forces, or in the Militia, when in actual service in time of War or public danger; nor shall any person be subject for the same offence to be twice put in jeopardy of life or limb; nor shall be compelled in any criminal case to be a witness against himself, nor be deprived of life, liberty, or property, without due process of law; nor shall private property be taken for public use, without just compensation.

## Amendment VI

In all criminal prosecutions, the accused shall enjoy the right to a speedy and public trial, by an impartial jury of the State and district wherein the crime shall have been committed, which district shall have been previously ascertained by law, and to be informed of the nature and cause of the accusation; to be confronted with the witnesses against him; to have compulsory process for obtaining witnesses in his favor, and to have the Assistance of Counsel for his defence.

## Amendment VII

In Suits at common law, where the value in controversy shall exceed twenty dollars, the right of trial by jury shall be preserved, and no fact tried by a jury, shall be otherwise re-examined in any Court of the United States, than according to the rules of the common law.

## Amendment VIII

Excessive bail shall not be required, nor excessive fines imposed, nor cruel and unusual punishments inflicted.

## Amendment IX

The enumeration in the Constitution, of certain rights, shall not be construed to deny or disparage others retained by the people.

## Amendment X

The powers not delegated to the United States by the Constitution, nor prohibited by it to the States, are reserved to the States respectively, or to the people.

and are not permissible. At times all three branches of the national government grapple with an issue and come to disagree over the meaning of the Bill of Rights. In a series of rulings beginning in 1990, the Supreme Court started a protracted disagreement over a new standard for whether state and local laws impinged on protected religious practices. Initially the Court ruled that otherwise valid, neutral laws of general applicability that incidentally impinge on a particular religious practice do not violate the First Amendment's free exercise clause.[5] Seeking to blunt the impact of the decision, religious organizations of every persuasion that had been exempt from a wide variety of laws, ranging from antidrug statutes to zoning restrictions, then lobbied Congress to enact a blanket law that would effectively exempt them from local regulations. Congress responded in 1993 with the Religious Freedom Restoration Act, which voided any law or regulation that "substantially burdened" religious practices if it could not be shown to serve a "compelling government interest . . . by the least restrictive means." At the bill-signing ceremony, President Bill Clinton noted that it effectively reversed the Court's 1990 decision and in his judgment was "far more consistent with the intent of the Founders than [was] the Supreme Court." Four years later the Court ruled that Congress had overstepped its constitutional authority in applying the new law to the states (as opposed to the federal government) and struck down the act to that extent. The Court majority reminded Congress and the president that "the power to interpret a case or controversy remains in the Judiciary."[6] Congress promptly reopened hearings and in 2000 enacted legislation making it harder for local governments to enforce zoning decisions against religious organizations.

AP Photo/Patrick Semansky

The Obama administration in 2013 defended the National Security Agency's collection of Americans' phone records—without a warrant—as an important tool in protecting the nation from terrorist threats. Several federal courts heard challenges to the program's constitutionality in 2014, and in June 2015 Congress passed the USA Freedom Act, which prohibited the bulk collection of Americans' phone records.

Arguably the Supreme Court still has the last word. Yet it has declined to hear several cases related to the Religious Freedom Restoration Act and let stand lower courts' decisions overturning government regulation based on the act.* So, even in *not* deciding a case, the Supreme Court has been able to implement its policy preferences, despite attempts by Congress and the president to emphasize and restore the prerogatives of religious organizations. This rare demonstration of these institutions squaring off against each other contrasted with their usual practice of jointly defining current liberties and rights. The conflict also illustrates how the Constitution's language

*In 2006 the Court did unanimously uphold application of the Religious Freedom Restoration Act against the *federal* government. *Gonzales v. O Centro Espirita Beneficente Uniao Do Vegetal*, 546 U.S. 418 (2006). And in 2014 *Burwell v. Hobby Lobby Stores* cited the law in overturning part of the Affordable Care Act.

permitted the Supreme Court to carve out a broad swath of veto authority called *judicial review,* which we take up in Chapter 9. Judicial review, the authority to rule on the constitutionality of laws, has allowed this branch to move to the forefront of civil liberties policy and created a revolution in rights and liberties, an important theme of this chapter.

## Writing Rights and Liberties into the Constitution

The Constitution, as it emerged from the 1787 Philadelphia Convention, did not seriously address civil liberties. Late in the Convention George Mason of Virginia had proposed prefacing the document with a bill of rights (many state constitutions already had one), but most delegates were skeptical about the need for such an addition.[7] (Mason subsequently cited this omission as the reason he turned against the Constitution's ratification.) The delegates reasoned that the solution to tyranny lay in correctly designed institutions that balanced interests through competition. Some delegates also feared that a list of rights in the Constitution might imply that the federal government had the authority to restrict the freedoms not expressly protected. Alexander Hamilton posed the question famously in *Federalist* No. 84: "Why declare that things shall not be done which there is no power to do? Why, for instance, should it be said that the liberty of the press shall not be restrained, when no power is given by which restrictions may be imposed?"

Mason was not the only advocate of a federal bill of rights. Throughout the ratifying process Antifederalists rallied opposition by arguing vigorously that the new constitutional plan flirted with tyranny by omitting explicit protections for the citizenry. Recognizing a chink in their armor, Madison and fellow supporters of the Constitution conceded the point and agreed that after its ratification they would introduce at the first session of the new Congress the amendments required for a bill of rights.

The Constitution actually acquired civil liberties protections in several steps over a long period of time. The first step was inclusion of the Bill of Rights, which insulated citizens from interference by the federal government in a variety of areas. The second, taken more than seventy-five years later, after the Civil War, was ratification of the Fourteenth Amendment, which gave the national government the authority to protect the rights of former slaves. And in a third step, which occurred over the twentieth century and continues into the twenty-first, the Supreme Court interpreted the Fourteenth Amendment to apply the Bill of Rights to the actions of state and local governments. Judicial scholars commonly refer to this process as **incorporation**—that is, using the Fourteenth Amendment to make the Bill of Rights binding on *state* governments, not just the federal government. Thus, the nationalization of civil liberties has not only altered the balance of power between Washington and the states, but also dramatically expanded the range of protections offered by the Bill of Rights.

### The First Ten Amendments

In June 1789 James Madison, elected to the First Congress as a representative from Virginia, followed through on his commitment during the ratification debate to a bill of rights by introducing seventeen constitutional amendments. His letters indicate that he may even have been persuaded of the merit of having these government proscriptions stated explicitly. Writing to his friend Thomas Jefferson, Madison conjectured that constitutionally guaranteed rights "acquire by degrees the character of fundamental maxims of free Governments, and as they become incorporated with the national sentiment, counteract the impulses of interest and passion."[8]

Madison may have been won over to the Bill of Rights, but he steadfastly believed that the states and not the national government provided the most fertile soil for tyranny. Acting on that belief, one of the amendments he submitted to the First Congress limited state authority. It read: "No state shall infringe the right of trial by jury in criminal cases, nor the right of conscience, nor the freedom of speech or of the press." States' rights advocates, however, were suspicious. Madison's effort to restrain the states smacked of another "nationalist" ruse, and they struck it from the list of amendments sent to the states for ratification. Two years then passed before the required three-quarters of the states ratified the Bill of Rights. Although the Antifederalists lost the ratification fight, they salvaged a major political concession in the Bill of Rights, their chief legacy to future generations of Americans.

In 1833 states' righters secured a victory in a landmark Supreme Court decision that governed the Court's posture and removed civil liberties from the national agenda for nearly a century. *Barron v. Baltimore* concerned road repairs made by the city of Baltimore that caused a buildup of gravel and sand in the area of John Barron's wharf, impeding access of deep-bottomed vessels.[9] Barron sued the city of Baltimore for violating his constitutionally guaranteed property rights. Pointing out that the Fifth Amendment forbade the public "taking" of private property without "just compensation," Barron argued that this provision applied to the states as well as the federal government and, therefore, Baltimore owed him money.

The Supreme Court ruled unanimously against Barron, holding that the Bill of Rights restrained only the actions of the national government. The whole thrust of the Bill of Rights, the justices reasoned, was directed exclusively at federal power. In short, the federal courts could not alleviate the excesses of state and local governments. Handed down in an era of limited federal responsibilities, the ruling rendered the Bill of Rights virtually meaningless, for most citizens' quarrels were with their state governments. If a state's residents wanted the rights that Barron claimed, they should amend their state constitution, suggested the Court. The other option—to amend the U.S. Constitution to apply the Bill of Rights to the states— was left unsaid. Yet achievements on the civil liberties front continued, and instead of serving as the last word on the subject, *Barron* today is a historical relic.* For us, it provides a baseline for measuring the extent to which civil liberties have become nationalized.

## Incorporation via the Fourteenth Amendment

Among the several constitutional amendments proposed during Reconstruction was the Fourteenth—a text crammed with now-familiar phrases (see box "Fourteenth Amendment: Section 1"). Although the amendment, passed in 1868, was intended initially to protect former slaves by explicitly declaring that rights of citizenship were not subject to

---

*Reflecting the low salience of civil liberties in the nation's civic discourse, Andrew W. Young's 1843 introductory American government textbook *Introduction to the Science of Government* devoted fewer than 5 of its 332 pages to the Bill of Rights. This would change in the next century with the doctrine of incorporation.

## Fourteenth Amendment: Section 1

All persons born or naturalized in the United States and subject to the jurisdiction thereof, are citizens of the United States and of the State wherein they reside. No State shall make or enforce any law which shall abridge the *privileges* *or immunities* of citizens of the United States; nor shall any State deprive any person of life, liberty, or property, without *due process of law;* nor deny to any person within its jurisdiction the *equal protection of the laws* [emphasis added].

state controls, over time its sweeping language led other groups to seek its umbrella protections. Yet nearly a half-century of jurisprudence passed before the Supreme Court began to interpret the Fourteenth Amendment language as requiring the states to adhere to the national government's Bill of Rights protections.[10] One of the great ironies of American history is that although this amendment failed to achieve its immediate objective, a century later it extended the rights and liberties of all citizens in directions unimaginable to its authors.

The first sentence of the amendment provides for a unified national citizenship and thereby directly contradicts the Court's assertion in *Barron* that state citizenship and national citizenship are separate affiliations. The second sentence, in articulating both the **due process clause** and the **equal protection clause**, states flatly that *all* persons enjoy the same civil liberties and rights, which the states cannot deny "without due process of law" (that is, without following reasonable, legally established procedures) and which the states must apply equally to everyone. To the modern reader this language seems plainly to say that states cannot violate the Bill of Rights, but in 1868 this broad interpretation of the Fourteenth Amendment continued to elude most readers—at least those on the Supreme Court.

In 1873 the Court rejected its first opportunity to incorporate the Bill of Rights into the Fourteenth Amendment. In the *Slaughterhouse Cases* a group of disgruntled butchers sued to invalidate a New Orleans ordinance that gave a single company a monopoly over all slaughterhouse business.[11] They based their appeal on the Fourteenth Amendment, arguing that the monopoly denied them the "privileges and immunities" (that is, the constitutionally protected rights) of citizens. The Court did not agree. By a 5–4 decision it ruled that the monopoly did not violate the Fourteenth Amendment because the amendment was intended to protect black citizens. Moreover, broad application of the amendment to state policy would "fetter and degrade the State governments by subjecting them to the control of Congress." With that decision, the Court effectively short-circuited any future development of the **privileges and immunities clause**.

Subsequently, lawyers targeted the due process provision in trying to persuade the Court that the Fourteenth Amendment applied to the states. Although plaintiffs in these cases consistently lost their arguments as well, most justices agreed that the due process clause might be construed to protect certain unspecified "fundamental rights."[12]

**TABLE 5.1** The Supreme Court's Civil Liberties Cases: A Major Share of Decisions

| CIVIL LIBERTIES CASES PER TERM | | |
|---|---|---|
| **YEAR** | **NO.** | **%** |
| 1946 | 31 | 22 |
| 1950 | 20 | 21 |
| 1955 | 18 | 19 |
| 1960 | 53 | 41 |
| 1965 | 32 | 32 |
| 1970 | 53 | 43 |
| 1975 | 61 | 40 |
| 1980 | 42 | 33 |
| 1985 | 69 | 45 |
| 1990 | 40 | 35 |
| 1995 | 29 | 38 |
| 2000 | 35 | 44 |
| 2005 | 34 | 46 |
| 2010 | 33 | 43 |

*Source:* Adapted from Lee Epstein et al., *The Supreme Court Compendium: Data, Decisions, and Developments,* 6th ed. (Washington, DC: CQ Press, 2016), Tables 2-11 and 3-8. Updates provided by Lee Epstein.

*Notes:* In the table the term *civil liberties* encompasses the following issue areas: criminal procedure, First Amendment, due process, privacy, and attorneys. For 1995 to 2006, the totals on which the percentages are based do not include interstate relations cases. From 1946 to 1994, the Court heard fifty-five such cases, or an average of about one per term.

Some twenty-five years into the twentieth century, the Court gingerly began to incorporate into the Fourteenth Amendment those provisions of the Bill of Rights dealing with personal freedoms.* Only gradually did the Supreme Court assume guardianship of civil liberties by applying piecemeal the various provisions of the Bill of Rights to state laws and practices. Table 5.1 shows the growth in the number of civil liberties cases the Court considered. Through this process, called **selective incorporation**, civil liberties have been gradually "nationalized." The Supreme Court first incorporated a provision of the Bill of Rights into the Fourteenth Amendment's due process clause in 1897, when it selected for incorporation the Fifth Amendment's ban on taking private property without compensation.

From the 1920s through the 1940s, the Court took up the First Amendment freedoms (speech, press, and religion), which remain the rights most carefully protected. At first, the justices viewed criminal rights as a special class for which incorporation did not apply.† But then, in the 1960s, the Court also covered most of the provisions of the Fourth, Fifth, and Sixth Amendments through the due process and equal protection clauses. Today, a third wave of advances in civil liberties may be forming as judges and politicians explore the right to privacy.

The Supreme Court's post-1925 incorporation decisions have served as precedents in guiding lower federal and state courts and, by offering new opportunities for litigation, have generated the dramatic growth in the civil liberties docket of the Court. Yet incorporation has occurred incrementally, case by case (see Table 5.2). Indeed, some provisions of the Bill of Rights are still not applied to the states: the Third Amendment prohibition against quartering soldiers, the Fifth Amendment provisions concerning grand jury hearings, the Seventh Amendment right to a jury trial in civil cases, and the Eighth Amendment right against excessive bail and fines. The states retain broad discretion in regulating these areas. Nonetheless, the accumulated precedents mean that Madison's vision of the national government as the ultimate guarantor of individual rights has largely been realized.

---

*Throughout the nineteenth century litigants mostly contested property rights, not personal liberties. As a result, little case law on the subject accumulated.

†*Palko v. Connecticut*, 302 U.S. 319 (1937). At the same time, the Court also refused to assume federal jurisdiction over a double jeopardy case, finding that protection against double jeopardy was not as fundamental to "liberty" and "justice" as were the First Amendment guarantees.

**TABLE 5.2** Cases Incorporating Provisions of the Bill of Rights into the Due Process Clause of the Fourteenth Amendment

| CONSTITUTIONAL PROVISION | CASE | YEAR |
|---|---|---|
| **First Amendment** | | |
| Freedom of speech and press | *Gitlow v. New York* | 1925 |
| Freedom of assembly | *DeJonge v. Oregon* | 1937 |
| Freedom of petition | *Hague v. CIO* | 1939 |
| Free exercise of religion | *Cantwell v. Connecticut* | 1940 |
| Establishment of religion | *Everson v. Board of Education* | 1947 |
| **Second Amendment** | | |
| Right to bear arms | *McDonald v. Chicago* | 2010 |
| **Fourth Amendment** | | |
| Unreasonable search and seizure | *Wolf v. Colorado* | 1949 |
| Exclusionary rule | *Mapp v. Ohio* | 1961 |
| **Fifth Amendment** | | |
| Payment of compensation for the taking of private property | *Chicago, Burlington & Quincy R. Co. v. Chicago* | 1897 |
| Self-incrimination | *Malloy v. Hogan* | 1964 |
| Double jeopardy | *Benton v. Maryland* | 1969 |
| When jeopardy attaches | *Crist v. Bretz* | 1978 |
| **Sixth Amendment** | | |
| Public trial | *In re Oliver* | 1948 |
| Due notice | *Cole v. Arkansas* | 1948 |
| Right to counsel (felonies) | *Gideon v. Wainwright* | 1963 |
| Confrontation and cross-examination of adverse witnesses | *Pointer v. Texas* | 1965 |
| Speedy trial | *Klopfer v. North Carolina* | 1967 |
| Compulsory process to obtain witnesses | *Washington v. Texas* | 1967 |
| Jury trial | *Duncan v. Louisiana* | 1968 |
| Right to counsel (misdemeanor when jail is possible) | *Argersinger v. Hamlin* | 1972 |
| **Eighth Amendment** | | |
| Cruel and unusual punishment | *Louisiana ex rel. Francis v. Resweber* | 1947 |
| **Ninth Amendment** | | |
| *Privacy*[a] | *Griswold v. Connecticut* | 1965 |

*Source:* Adapted from Lee Epstein and Thomas G. Walker, *Constitutional Law for a Changing America: Rights, Liberties, and Justice,* 9th ed. (Washington, DC: CQ Press, 2016), Table 3-1.

[a]The word *privacy* does not appear in the Ninth Amendment or anywhere in the text of the Constitution. In *Griswold* several members of the Court viewed the Ninth Amendment as guaranteeing (and incorporating) that right.

## Judicial Interpretation

The incorporation of Bill of Rights provisions into the Fourteenth Amendment was a historic development in civil liberties, comparable with the adoption of the Bill of Rights itself. As we have seen, incorporation occurred not through legislative mandate or the amendment process but through judicial interpretation. Once this was done, the Supreme Court could turn to the more substantive issue of whether particular state policies violated constitutional protections and, if so, what the remedies should be.

Supreme Court justices agree that as jurists they are obligated to interpret the Constitution as objectively as possible. Yet on any particular ruling they frequently disagree—sometimes sharply—over what an "objective" interpretation prescribes. A literalist, finding no language in the Constitution that protects burning of the U.S. flag, might conclude that the Bill of Rights does not defend this act. Another justice might view flag burning as a kind of political expression sufficiently close to speech and deserving of First Amendment protection.

All self-respecting judges believe that when they occupy the bench they must shed all of their personal preferences, ideologies, and partisanship. But evidence reveals that the personal and political ideologies of the nine justices on the Supreme Court are evident in almost every decision. Consequently, as justices come and go from the Court, judicial doctrine may change. Nativity scenes deemed objectionable and removed one Christmas may pass constitutional scrutiny and be reinstalled the next. Students of jurisprudence have long accepted that justices, like members of Congress and presidents, can be accurately classified as liberals and conservatives. As a result, trends in civil liberties tend to reflect the shifting ideological composition of the Court (see Figure 5.1).

■ **FIGURE 5.1**   The Supreme Court's Shifting Ideology on Civil Liberties Cases

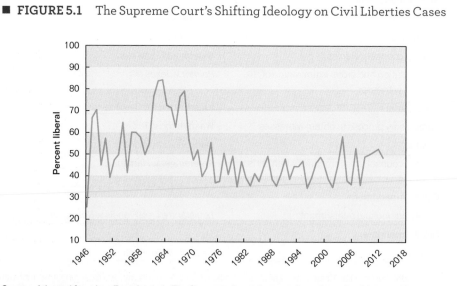

*Source:* Adapted from Lee Epstein et al., *The Supreme Court Compendium: Data, Decisions, and Developments*, 6th ed. (Washington, DC: CQ Press, 2016), Table 3-9.

## Major versus Peripheral Rights

This chapter focuses on the major rights in the Bill of Rights—that is, those that have been litigated heavily and developed in detail by the Supreme Court over the past two centuries. However, the rights given detailed treatment in this chapter are not the *only* rights in the Bill of Rights. There are other, more peripheral rights—meaning that their parameters have not been fully developed by the Supreme Court. These more peripheral rights include, for example, the right of assembly under the First Amendment and the Fifth Amendment's protection against having private property taken by the government without just compensation (known as the "takings clause").

# Freedom of Speech

> Amendment I: *Congress shall make no law . . . abridging the freedom of speech.*

Freedom of speech is essential to representative government and the exercise of individual autonomy. But what exactly constitutes legitimate expression? And how does one balance free speech against other rights and claims?

Generally speaking, the Supreme Court has given a high level of protection to speech that is expressly political. However, there are limits to even this kind of speech. One of the most useful ways to make sense of the Court's free speech jurisprudence is to consider major categories of speech that are *excluded* from First Amendment protection. The sections that follow focus on two of the most controversial categories: speech that advocates illegal action and obscenity.

## Political Protest

In a historic decision in 1925 the Court applied the First Amendment's free speech clause to actions of *state* governments.[13] The case was brought to the Court by Benjamin Gitlow, the leader of a radical faction of the Socialist Party who was arrested in New York City at the height of the Red Scare. Charged with advocating "criminal anarchy" through organized labor strikes, Gitlow was found guilty in a New York State court. In its review of his case, the Supreme Court ruled that states could not interfere with the "fundamental personal rights and 'liberties'" contained in the First Amendment. The Court thus established the Fourteenth Amendment's jurisdiction over the states, at least when it came to free speech. But, moving cautiously, the Court continued, "the State cannot reasonably be required to measure the danger from every such utterance in the nice balance of a jeweler's scale. A single revolutionary spark may kindle a fire that, smoldering for a time, may burst into a sweeping and destructive conflagration." So, despite the application of the First Amendment free speech clause to the states, Gitlow went to prison.

Even during World War II and the conflicts that followed, the Court persisted in giving the government the benefit of the doubt during times of crisis. During the Korean War (1950–1953) the Court upheld the Alien Registration Act of 1940 by affirming the conviction of eleven top members of the American Communist Party for having advocated the violent overthrow of the government. After all, the government could not idly watch traitors hatch a rebellion, the Court argued. Indeed, Chief Justice Fred Vinson, in *Dennis v. United States,* adopted the interpretation of the **clear and present danger test** put forward by famed lower-court judge Learned Hand; this interpretation is also known as the **clear and probable danger test**: "In each case [the courts] must ask whether the gravity of the 'evil,' discounted by its probability, justifies such invasion of free speech as is necessary to avoid the danger."[14] Although this test introduced the idea of probability or likelihood into the analysis (which in theory was more likely to protect the speaker), Dennis and his comrades suffered the same fate as Gitlow.

A quarter century later the Court narrowed this rule in *Brandenburg v. Ohio. Brandenburg* involved not a Socialist or a Communist, but a member of the Ku Klux Klan. He was charged with violating the Ohio criminal syndicalism law, which among other things made it illegal to advocate crime and violence as a means of accomplishing political reform.[15] Brandenburg spoke at a televised rally in which he used racial slurs and warned that if the U.S. government continued to suppress the Caucasian race, "it's possible that there might have to be some revengeance [*sic*] taken." In a unanimous decision, the Court eschewed the clear and present danger test and announced a new **incitement** test: the government cannot forbid "advocacy of the use of force or of law violation" unless the advocacy is "directed to inciting or producing imminent lawless action and is likely to incite or produce such action." Although this formulation acknowledged the time element of the clear and present danger test by using the word *imminent,* it added two important conditions: first, the speaker must have the *intent* to incite others (the "directed to" language); and second, the illegal action must be *likely* to occur. These additions offer more protections to the speaker, by making the government's case harder to prove.

Although it took the Court several decades to settle on the appropriate test for government regulation of speech that advocates illegal activity, the **Brandenburg test** created a high bar that has endured in broadening the scope of protected speech. The Politics to Policy box, "The Legacy of Brandenburg" (see page 199) illustrates its scope with three important subsequent cases that showed the full implications of this precedent. Justice William Brennan summed up the Court's views in these cases when he wrote in the flag burning decision, "If there is a bedrock principle underlying the First Amendment, it is that the Government may not prohibit the expression of an idea simply because society finds the idea itself offensive or disagreeable."

## Disturbing Speech

Yet this permissive judicial principle has limits. Various lower courts have ruled that speech can go beyond expressions of preference and actually present a direct threat of violence. Publishing a book on how to become a hired assassin, posting the names and addresses of abortion providers while arguing that they should be dealt with for crimes against humanity, and distributing instructions on how to fabricate undetectable plastic automatic weapons with a 3-D printer are several such instances.[16]

## Sexually Explicit Expression

Everyone seems to agree that the First Amendment does not protect **obscenity**. Where local, state, and national politicians and judges disagree concerns what kinds of sexual expression,

## POLITICS TO POLICY
# The Legacy of Brandenburg

Surrounded by fellow Nazis, Frank Collins (left), the American Nazi Party leader whose father is Jewish, appealed a court order blocking the march. Although the Supreme Court sided with them, the march on Skokie was eventually abandoned.

Members of the Westboro Baptist Church in Topeka, Kansas, protested at the funeral of a soldier killed in Iraq by carrying inflammatory signs such as "Thank God for Dead Soldiers."

In recent years, disagreement over hate speech has largely taken up residence on college and university campuses. As student bodies have become more diverse, universities have sought to become more welcoming and supportive of "first generation" students. By one recent count, over 300 schools have modified their student codes of conduct to proscribe language that some students would likely find injurious. Lafayette College issued the following guideline for its entering class in 2018 that is typical of these rules intended to promote civility and mutual respect.

> Students and student organizations are expected to so conduct themselves that they cause no physical, emotional, or mental harm to others; that they neither break laws nor contribute to the delinquency of others; and

that they do not destroy property. Participation in any activity that harms or demeans others may lead to dismissal of individuals and dissolution of groups.[17]

The problem here is that free speech doctrine has evolved in a direction that stresses an individual's freedom of expression. In the dozens of lawsuits involving student plaintiffs who ran afoul of university "harmful" speech rules, the courts have mostly sided with the students and against the university or college. The central problem of these guidelines is that when set against the modern judicial reading of the First Amendment, they are too broadly and vaguely worded to state what speech is protected and what speech will land a student in front of a disciplinary board. In 2010 the Third Circuit Court rejected a campus's guidelines

*(Continued)*

(Continued)

as inappropriately responsive to a listener's distressed reaction to a speech.

This poses a special challenge to universities that over the course of the twentieth century came to embrace an expansive view of free speech as academic creed. Consider that elsewhere in its student handbook Lafayette confirms its commitment to open inquiry: "As citizens [students] enjoy the same rights—for example, freedom of speech, peaceful assembly, and right of petition—and obligations that other citizens enjoy" and that "freedom of inquiry and freedom of expression are indispensable to the attainment of the goals of Lafayette College." Both espousing free inquiry and upholding community civility are laudable, but frequently on present-day campuses they conflict with one another.

Students are not impervious to these issues, and student opinion surveys reflect the same tension as that expressed in student handbooks.[18] A 2018 survey of 3,000 college students unsurprisingly found majorities endorsing both students' free speech rights and the university's role in promoting an inclusive society. When students were asked to select which of the principles was more important, inclusiveness won out 53 to 46 percent. In Figure 5.2 student answers to this question were broken down by respondents' personal characteristics and their party identification. Men significantly favored "free speech," whereas women favored rules promoting "diversity and inclusiveness" by an even larger majority. And one finds partisan separation here, as with almost every other public issue examined in this text. Two-thirds of Democratic students opted for inclusiveness whereas an even larger share of Republican students embraced free speech.

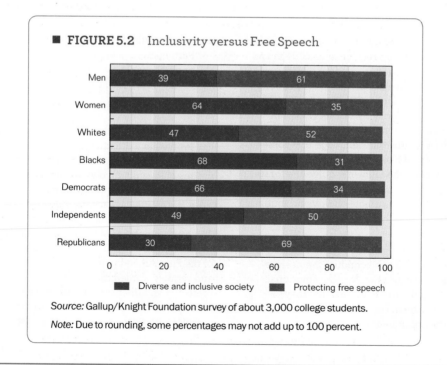

■ **FIGURE 5.2**   Inclusivity versus Free Speech

*Source:* Gallup/Knight Foundation survey of about 3,000 college students.

*Note:* Due to rounding, some percentages may not add up to 100 percent.

or pornography, cross the line over to obscenity. The Supreme Court, Congress, and local law enforcement, however, have run up against two serious obstacles in banning obscenity. The first is definitional: where does obscenity begin? Struggling to formulate an objective, enforceable definition, an exasperated Justice Potter Stewart declared, "I know it when I see it."[19] The second is the Internet. How does local law enforcement or even the Federal Bureau of Investigation (FBI) effectively ban obscene videos posted on the Internet somewhere in the Balkans?

The war on obscenity began in 1873 with the passage of what came to be known as the Comstock Act. It left to others to define obscenity by declaring simply that the sale and possession of obscene materials is a federal crime.[20] Obscenity became pretty much what local officials—from librarians, to movie censors, to beat cops—said it was. In one famous case in the 1930s, a diligent postal official spotted and presumably read and then seized copies of James Joyce's novel *Ulysses,* claiming it contained "obscene" passages. Some postmasters judged even anatomy textbooks destined for medical schools as crossing the line. In deciding whether these and other Comstock enforcement actions were legal, state and federal courts tended to follow guidelines laid down in British law defining obscenity as any text or images designed "to deprave and corrupt those whose minds are open to such immoral influences." Despite this highly restrictive legal setting, pornography flourished.

The Supreme Court revised obscenity policy in 1957 and issued a new doctrine in *Roth v. United States.*[21] A work was obscene if it was "utterly without redeeming social importance" and "to the average person, applying contemporary **community standards**, the dominant theme of the material, taken as a whole, appeals to prurient interests." With this language the Court tried to thread its way between conservative forces calling for tight local regulation and libertarians who sought to banish the notion of obscenity from jurisprudence. But every key word in the passage is ambiguous and subject to lenient or stringent interpretation. Who decides the tastes of the "average person"? Which "community's" standards come into play? How much obscenity needs to be in the material before it "dominates" the work's themes? And while they were at it, lawyers attacking *Roth* added, just what does *prurient* mean? Only as the Court tried to answer these questions did the full extent of the libertarian victory become clear. Nude pole dancing in bars could be (and was) construed as a form of artistic expression and hence fell within the First Amendment's "freedom of speech" protection.

During the early 1970s an increasingly conservative Supreme Court began retrenching the "anything goes" doctrine of the 1960s. In *Miller v. California* the Court shifted primary authority for obscenity policy back to the state—and, implicitly, to a local—government.[22] Local authorities could ban and otherwise regulate materials "which, taken as a whole, appeal to the prurient interest in sex, which portray sexual conduct in a patently offensive way, and which, taken as a whole, do not have serious literary, artistic, political or scientific value." This new standard greatly strengthened local authorities' hands in regulating a variety of sex purveyors such as massage parlors, topless bars, and pornographic book and video stores. And this delegation of enforcement authority to the states helped the Court clear its docket. Since adoption of *Miller,* the Court has decided fewer than a quarter of its obscenity cases in favor of First Amendment claims.[23]

Over the next two decades the regime of local control was turned on its head by the Internet. How could a city council regulate pornography that was flowing to library patrons from Bulgaria?

## POLITICS TO POLICY
# Corporate Free Speech

Prior to the Supreme Court's decision in *Citizens United v. Federal Election Commission,* federal law prohibited corporations and unions from using their general treasury funds to make direct contributions to candidates. It also prohibited them from using general treasury funds to make independent expenditures for speech that expressly advocated either the election or the defeat of a candidate (or speech defined as an "electioneering communication"). However, corporations and unions were allowed to establish political action committees, or PACs, which could receive contributions from individuals within a union or business and use the funds to support candidates and political causes (see Chapter 11).

In a 1990 case, *Austin v. Michigan Chamber of Commerce,* the Court upheld the prohibition on political expenditures by corporations and unions, citing the government's compelling interest in preventing "the corrosive and distorting effects of immense aggregations of wealth that are accumulated with the help of the corporate form and that have little or no correlation to the public's support for the corporation's political ideas."[a]

In 2010, in a 5–4 vote, the Court reversed this policy. In *Citizens United,* the majority held that Congress cannot restrict political speech based on the speaker's corporate identity. In other words, Congress cannot single out corporations (and unions) and thereby discriminate on the basis of their identity (i.e., their identity as legal entities instead of individual human beings). The majority viewed the 2002 McCain-Feingold campaign finance law's attempts to regulate the speech of corporations as essentially viewpoint discrimination, based on not liking the particular speaker (and, therefore, that particular speaker's message). As a result, the majority held that the federal law at issue violated corporations' and unions' First Amendment rights.

*SIPRESS*

*"If you prick a corporation, does it not bleed? If you tickle it, does it not laugh? If you poison it, does it not die?"*

David Sipress/The New Yorker Collection/The Cartoon Bank

Justice Stevens's impassioned dissent (joined by Justices Breyer, Ginsburg, and Sotomayor) questioned the wisdom of the majority's equating the First Amendment rights of corporations with the First Amendment rights of individuals—a practice that, according to Justice Stevens, ignores the guarded skepticism with which the Framers viewed corporations and the fact that they conceptualized the First Amendment as protecting the free speech of individuals. As Justice Stevens derisively put it, "Under the majority's view, I suppose it may be a First Amendment problem that corporations are not permitted to vote, given that voting is, among other things, a form of speech."[b]

More recently, the same majority extended corporate rights to include religious freedom. In *Burwell v. Hobby Lobby Stores* it ruled that businesses owned by few members could exercise their personal freedoms in its policy. In this case, the owners cited their religious views for refusing to pay for contraceptives for employees as required by the Affordable Care Act.

---

[a]494 U.S. 652, 660 (1990).

[b]558 U.S. ___ (2010); dissent at 33–34.

# Freedom of the Press

> Amendment I: *Congress shall make no law . . . abridging the freedom . . . of the press.*

An independent press is indispensable in maintaining a representative democracy. Without reliable information about the performance of officeholders, citizens would be hard-pressed to monitor their elected agents. Without the news media, politicians would find it difficult to communicate with their constituents and to keep an eye on one another. The role of the news media is so critical, in fact, we devote a full chapter to this "fourth branch" of government (see Chapter 14). The laws and judicial policy regulating the modern news media reflect the sweeping language of the First Amendment. We take up the privacy of news sources, government censorship, and publication of classified information in Chapter 14. Here we consider conflicts between press freedom and individuals' privacy and defendant rights.

The Sixth Amendment guarantees that "the accused shall enjoy the right to . . . an impartial jury of the State." The importance of an impartial jury is obvious. As for a public trial, the history of the concept has less to do with prosecuting criminals than with preventing law enforcement officials from meting out arbitrary justice. By exposing the judicial process to public scrutiny and, by implication, the press, the Framers intended to keep police, judges, and prosecutors in check.

In one famous trial, however, public scrutiny led to public chaos that threatened the defendant's right to a fair hearing. In 1954 Ohio osteopath Samuel Sheppard (whose case inspired the long-running television series and movie *The Fugitive*) was convicted of murdering his wife. His trial attracted almost as much news coverage as the O. J. Simpson trial some forty years later. Yet the Simpson trial, however tumultuous, was a model of judicial and press decorum compared with the Sheppard proceedings. The testimony of witnesses could not be heard at times because of the din in a courtroom packed with reporters. Moreover, the jurors, who were not sequestered, were exposed to the media circus throughout the trial. Order was eventually restored, but only years after Sheppard's imprisonment: in 1966 the Supreme Court found that the "carnival atmosphere" surrounding the trial had undermined Sheppard's right to a fair day in court, and it reversed his conviction.[24]

Does the *Sheppard* case require a uniform ban on the press in trials involving sensitive issues or famous defendants? Apparently not. In 1982 the Supreme Court overturned a Massachusetts law that excluded the public from trials of sex crimes involving victims under the age of eighteen.[25] Although it conceded the value of protecting an underage victim, the majority argued that the victim's welfare did not justify the mandatory exclusion of the public. Rather, the question of public access should be decided on a case-by-case basis.*

# Freedom of Religion

> Amendment I: *Congress shall make no law respecting an establishment of religion, or prohibiting the free exercise thereof.*

Although the First Amendment is best known for its free speech guarantees, it actually begins with freedom of religion. Many of the early colonies designated official churches, which

---

*A similar strain of judicial reasoning crops up in libel doctrine examined in Chapter 14.

believers and nonbelievers alike were forced to attend and support with their taxes (a practice that continued in some states even after independence). And yet, by the Revolution, America already was home to a great variety of religious denominations. In *Federalist* No. 10 Madison identified religious conflict as one of the issues bound to generate factional struggle.* In fact, Virginia's religious fights gave Madison the insight that factional conflict could provide a solid foundation for democracy. One of Madison's favorite observations on this score came from Voltaire: "If one religion only were allowed in England, the government would possibly be arbitrary; if there were but two, the people would cut each other's throats; but, as there are such a multitude, they all live happy and in peace."[26]

The religious freedom provision of the First Amendment prohibits Congress from passing any legislation "respecting an *establishment* of religion, or prohibiting the *free exercise* thereof" (emphasis added). But like the rest of the amendment, the **establishment of religion clause** and the **free exercise clause** at first applied only to actions of the federal government. In fact, some states retained laws discriminating against particular religions for years after the Bill of Rights was added to the Constitution.

Madison and Jefferson both subscribed to the frequently stated view that the First Amendment erects "a wall of separation" between church and state.† But theirs was merely one interpretation. Separation is not mentioned in the Constitution itself, and it has not been followed consistently by Congress or the Court. Nor can it be in many instances. Indeed, the Court has argued that tensions between the free exercise and establishment clauses may allow government to support religious institutions in various ways.

## Establishment

Because the national government rarely had occasion to subsidize religious institutions or their ancillary activities during the nineteenth century, the first real establishment of religion decision did not come until 1899, when the Supreme Court allowed the federal government to subsidize a Catholic hospital that was open to all patients.[27] In 1947 the Supreme Court applied the due process clause to the establishment provision and thereby placed the states under the same restraints as those limiting the federal government.[28] As the Court entered this field of state policy, it found some states subsidizing parochial schools and others offering religious training in public schools. A 1960 survey of school districts revealed that 77 percent of schools in the South and 68 percent in the East were conducting Bible readings.[29] And throughout the nation most students accompanied the Pledge of Allegiance to the American flag with a prayer.

### The *Lemon* Test

Over the years, most of the controversial policies triggering establishment arguments have concerned the various ways states have subsidized private schools. Tuition grants, textbooks,

---

*In private correspondence with Jefferson, Madison stated precisely the same argument in favor of religious diversity that he later would offer for factions. By letting a thousand denominations bloom, he reasoned, none would attract sufficient popular support to dominate the others.

†Jefferson referred to a "wall of separation" between church and state in an 1802 letter written to the Danbury Baptist Association.

and school buses have all had their day in court. The most far-reaching of these cases was *Lemon v. Kurtzman* (1971), in which the Court specified three conditions every state law must satisfy to avoid running afoul of the establishment prohibition[30]:

1. The statute in question "must have a secular legislative purpose," such as remedial education.

2. The statute's "primary effect must be one that neither advances nor inhibits religion."

3. The statute must not foster "an excessive government entanglement with religion."

If any of these conditions are violated, the policy fails the ***Lemon* test**. The Court was trying mightily to construct clear doctrine, but with highly subjective criteria such as "primary" and "excessive" it succeeded better perhaps in describing how justices thought these issues through than in identifying to the states those policies that would satisfy the Court's interpretation of the "establishment" clause.

The problems inherent in applying *Lemon* soon became evident in the highly inconsistent decisions that followed its adoption. For example, sometimes the federal courts applied the test to dismantle nativity scenes on public property; at other times judges enlisted the same guidelines to approve official displays of nativity scenes as a celebration of the historic origins of Christmas.[31]

The Supreme Court viewed prayer at school football games and convocation exercises as clear violations of the Constitution but had no problem with the devotions that begin each day's business in Congress. In the judgment of one constitutional scholar, the vague, three-pronged *Lemon* test inspired judges to engage in reasoning "that would glaze the minds of medieval scholastics."[32]

## Testing a Policy's "Neutrality"

By the 1990s the *Lemon* test was fading from establishment decisions as the justices increasingly tested a policy's "neutrality." They used the **neutrality test** not so much to prevent favoritism among religious groups as to root out policies that preferred religious groups generally over nonreligious groups engaged in a similar activity. Tax credits for religious school tuition were permissible if they also were available for secular, private instruction. Religious organizations could meet on public school property as long as they observed the same access rules governing any other school club.

In 1994 the Supreme Court applied the emerging neutrality doctrine in *Board of Education of Kiryas Joel Village School District v. Grumet*.[33] A sect of Orthodox Jews in upstate New York persuaded the state legislature to carve out a new, publicly financed school district that would include only their community. Because students from that district who had no special needs already attended a private religious school, the new district would offer only special education classes for the community's disabled children. The Court ruled, however, that creation of this school district breached the rule of neutrality and was thus unconstitutional: "The district's creation ran uniquely counter to state practice, following the lines of a religious community where the customary and neutral principles would not have dictated the same result." Since then the Court has followed its neutrality rule in permitting public funding

Reuters/Mario Anzuoni

Can a baker refuse on religious grounds to bake a wedding cake for a gay marriage? The state of Colorado said no, but the U.S. Supreme Court ruled that the state had behaved arbitrarily. Yet it did not actually rule whether in the end the baker would or would not have to bake that cake.

of mandated special education courses in parochial schools; in allowing state subsidies for some instructional materials in private schools, such as school computers and library resources; and in upholding as constitutional a school voucher program that allowed thousands of Cleveland, Ohio, students to attend religious schools.[34] This last decision in 2002 rekindled a hot political issue championed by President George W. Bush in the 2000 election but left out of his No Child Left Behind legislation in order to garner support for his education reforms. Now that the Court has removed this legal issue, vouchers may find renewed interest in Washington and many state capitals as a way of exposing public education to the discipline of market forces—that is, giving students and their parents the freedom to choose schools.

Just as the neutrality standard appeared to allow a host of subsidies for religious education, a 2004 Supreme Court decision made a critical distinction between funding religious institutions for their secular activities and funding religious training. The issue involved a college student in Washington State who received a state scholarship to help finance his undergraduate education. After he declared his intention to major in religious studies designed to train him to become a minister, however, the state withdrew the scholarship. This was standard practice in thirty-seven states at the time, and in a 7–2 opinion the Court found the state's decision appropriate.[35]

Although the Court continues to sustain the neutrality standard as the governing establishment doctrine, some question whether it has achieved the intended result. Critics charge that the Court has dismantled the chief barrier to expanded public subsidies for church-sponsored education, which some states have been eager to provide. With President Trump's appointment of two socially conservative justices in 2018, groups are preparing cases to probe the extent to which the Supreme Court will maintain its traditional "wall" of preventing outright tax support for religion-based elementary and secondary education.

## School Prayer and Bible Reading

None of the establishment issues has aroused more enduring enmity among religious conservatives than the Supreme Court doctrine banning prayer and Bible readings in public schools. This issue is, arguably, the only real wall separating church and state not yet breached by the Supreme Court. In *Engel v. Vitale* (1962) the Court ruled the following New York State–composed prayer unconstitutional: "Almighty God, we acknowledge our dependence on Thee, and we beg thy blessings upon us, our parents, our teachers, and our country."[36] The next year it invalidated Bible readings in public schools.[37] Over the years these decisions and the later ones that bolstered them have angered many Americans. Indeed, neither a majority of the public nor those politicians who periodically ask for people's votes have ever been won over to the Supreme Court's point of view. Congress has periodically considered a constitutional amendment allowing school prayer, most recently in 1998. Each time, however, proponents have attracted majority support in Congress but have failed to win the two-thirds support necessary to send an amendment to the states.[38] In the absence of a national policy alternative, states have continued to pass laws trying to circumvent or accommodate the federal courts, but with no success. In 1985, for example, the Court ruled unconstitutional an Alabama state law that mandated a moment of silence at the beginning of the school day.[39] Seven years later it found invocation and benediction prayers at gradua- tion equally objectionable.[40] Moreover, in a throwback to the days of school desegregation in the 1950s and early 1960s, many local school districts throughout the South have simply ignored the federal courts' instructions on school prayer. Three years after the 1963 unequiv- ocal banning of Bible reading, one study revealed that only one Tennessee school official of the 121 interviewed even bothered to claim compliance with the Court decision.[41] In 1997 a federal district judge found school prayers to pervade school life in Alabama despite the federal courts' efforts to forbid these practices. When the judge appointed a "monitor" to fer- ret out classroom violations of his order to end prayers, the Alabama governor denounced his action as tantamount to employing "secret police." Nearly 500 of the 636 students in the affected district, as well as students in other states, protested the judge's ban by walking out of class.[42] This is just one example of the judiciary's inability to enforce its own decisions, which is discussed more fully in Chapter 9.

Until recently school prayer seemed to be an exception to the rule that the Court's pol- icy decisions do not stray far beyond the bounds of citizen opinion. In 2001, however, a fed- eral appeals court turned away a challenge to a Virginia law permitting a moment of silence at the start of each class day in the state's high schools. And later in the year, the Supreme Court refused to review the decision, thereby letting it stand as state policy. So although it is safe to assume that these issues will remain contentious and that the judiciary will revisit them fre- quently, the courts might have found a way to accommodate the states and public opinion without seriously undermining the establishment clause.

## Free Exercise

The case law delineating the free exercise doctrine is relatively clear and simple when com- pared with the tortured history of religious establishment cases. The doctrine's incorpora- tion into the Fourteenth Amendment began on a spring day in 1938, when the Cantwells, a family of Jehovah's Witnesses, drove into New Haven, Connecticut, to proselytize their faith and solicit donations. Jehovah's Witnesses believe that each member of the church, as one of its ministers, is obligated to spread the gospel of salvation. Some local residents, however, objected to the Witnesses' intrusion on their privacy and called the police, who arrested the Cantwells for soliciting money door to door without a permit.

Ruling on this case in 1940, the Supreme Court decided for the first time that First Amendment protections of free exercise of religion were incorporated in the "fundamental concept of liberty embodied" in the Fourteenth Amendment. Connecticut's regulation of financial solicitation by religious groups, the Court ruled, represented an unconstitutional "censoring" of religion.

What makes many free exercise cases difficult is that rarely is a particular religious practice specifically targeted by a law. Instead, many generally applicable laws—laws passed to solve some general societal problem and applied to everyone—interfere with some group's religious practice (such as rules requiring compulsory education up to a certain age). For years, when the Court was confronted with these situations, it generally asked whether the government had a compelling interest and then attempted to balance that interest against the degree of infringement on the individual's free exercise of religion.*

This all changed with the Court's decision in *Employment Division v. Smith* (1990), involving two Native American church members who were dismissed from their drug counseling jobs for ingesting peyote (a hallucinogenic derived from cactus) as part of a religious ceremony.[43] When the state of Oregon denied their request for unemployment benefits, the church members sued the state for infringing on their free exercise of religion. In a surprising 5–4 decision, the Court ruled that otherwise valid, neutral laws of general applicability that incidentally impinge on a particular religious practice do not violate the First Amendment's free exercise clause. As discussed earlier in the chapter, Congress responded by passing the Religious Freedom Restoration Act, part of which has been upheld by the Court and part of which has been found unconstitutional.

Still, as the Court reiterated in 1993, if a law is *not* neutral (in other words, if the law targets a specific religious practice), "it is invalid unless it is justified by a compelling interest and is narrowly tailored to advance that interest."[44] As a result, the Court struck down a Hialeah, Florida, city ordinance after determining that the real purpose of the law was to stop the animal sacrifice performed by a Santeria church as part of a religious rite.

Both the free exercise and establishment issues spark competing rights claims that require careful balancing from courts. The problems are rooted in the language of the First Amendment. Does "free exercise" extend to behavior that imposes costs on the larger community—whether it be drug use, proselytizing, or disregard of local zoning ordinances? Does the prohibition against establishing a state religion cover moments of silence, church-sponsored school clubs, or overtly religious Christmas displays? As the Supreme Court's wavering decisions reveal so clearly, there is no single "correct" answer to the questions raised by the First Amendment's guarantee of religious freedom. The courts, politicians, and public, then, have ample room to decide for themselves and thus disagree.

## Gun Rights

Amendment II: *A well regulated Militia, being necessary to the security of a free State, the right of the people to keep and bear Arms, shall not be infringed.*

Until recently, the Second Amendment could have been placed in the category of peripheral rights—not because the right to own a gun is less important to many Americans than

---

*Cantwell v. Connecticut*, 310 U.S. 296 (1940). The Court concluded that "in spite of the probability of excesses and abuses, [religious] liberties are, in the long view, essential to enlightened opinion and right conduct on the part of citizens of a democracy." See Richard C. Cortner, *The Supreme Court and the Second Bill of Rights* (Madison: University of Wisconsin Press, 1981), 99–108, for a thoughtful review of this case.

A man checks out a display of rifles at the SHOT Show in Las Vegas, the world's largest gun and outdoor trade show.

rights such as free speech, but because for over two hundred years, the Supreme Court interpreted the cited clause as a collective good rather than a personal freedom. Easily the Second Amendment presents the most ambiguous language in the Bill of Rights. When Congress debated this amendment, the Revolution against the autocratic British regime was still a fresh memory. Indeed, the representatives expanded on this theme in the historically inconsequential Third Amendment banning the government from commandeering private homes to garrison troops. Most historians and judicial scholars have read the congressional deliberations and the wording of the amendment itself as guaranteeing the right of local militias to bear arms—a kind of collective good. What "good" it was intended to provide is somewhat vague. A modern reading and one preferred by pro-gun advocates has it represent the people's ultimate check against government tyranny. Yet a careful reading of the history suggests that the "State" refers actually to states' right to maintain militias (a forerunner of the national guard) to counter insurrections such as the Whiskey Rebellion.

Although the judiciary for decades consistently read the amendment as guaranteeing this limited collective right, this opinion had never wholly become a national consensus. And in fact, over the decades the collective good interpretation had rarely been litigated—perhaps as few as six cases in the first two centuries of the Republic.

Over the years a number of resourceful interest groups and elected officeholders have taken exception to this collective good interpretation. The National Rifle Association and others vigorously advanced the interpretation that the amendment guarantees an *individual right* to own a gun. Until 2008, the last word from the Court dated to 1939, when the justices upheld required registration of a sawed-off shotgun, using a rationale that seemed to deny an individual right. This line of interpretation would change in 2008, however, when the Supreme Court issued its most important Second Amendment ruling to date: *District of Columbia v. Heller.* In a bitterly divided 5–4 opinion split predictably along conservative-liberal lines, the majority explicitly adopted the *individual* right interpretation of the Second Amendment. To do so it rejected the long-standing interpretation that the phrase "to keep and bear Arms" was limited to weapons used in military service.[45] Specifically, the Court held that Washington, D.C.'s, absolute prohibition of handguns used for self-defense in the home was unconstitutional under the Second Amendment.

Two years later the Court issued another watershed Second Amendment ruling, holding that the Fourteenth Amendment incorporates the Second Amendment right announced in *Heller* to keep and bear arms for the purpose of self-defense.[46] As a result, the Court struck down a Chicago law that effectively banned handgun possession by almost all private citizens who reside in the city. These two major decisions (with a bare five-member majority, consisting of the Court's conservative justices) have changed the political game when it comes to Second Amendment rights and have shifted the final word on gun rights from Congress, state legislatures, and municipalities to the Supreme Court.

In the short term, what this really means is that the *lower* federal courts are left to define the parameters of Second Amendment rights, without much guidance from the two Supreme Court decisions on the subject. As one appeals court judge mused, "There may or may not be a Second Amendment right in some places beyond the home, but we have no idea what those places are, what the criteria for selecting them should be, what [level] of scrutiny might apply to them, or any one of a number of other questions."[47] By one count over 1,090 Second Amendment cases have been filed since *Heller,* with the courts upholding state and local gun laws in 94 percent of the cases. Throughout this period, the Supreme Court has refused to accept cases challenging restrictions on firearms in public, challenges to restrictions of possession of machine guns and other military weapons, and challenges to local requirements that guns be registered and associated fees.

In 1994 Congress passed a ban on the sale of newly manufactured assault weapons. But the law expired ten years later, and all efforts to extend it have failed in Congress. Even though the Supreme Court may have barely opened the door to gun rights, the political impasse in Washington created a policy vacuum that has allowed some states to rush in to ensure the right of gun ownership. The result has been a flurry of state legislation over the past decade or so covering such issues as gun registration, background checks, open and concealed carry of handguns and long guns, and assault weapons restrictions. Some states, such as California, have passed restrictive laws, whereas others, such as Texas, have passed minimal conditions on the possession and open carrying of guns.

The series of mass killings at schools such as Columbine High School, Virginia Tech, and Sandy Hook Elementary School and in San Bernardino, Orlando, and Las Vegas has fueled a demand for action. And yet these same events have caused many Americans to favor gun ownership for protection. The first mass shooting, which occurred at Columbine High in 2000, triggered an outpouring of support for tighter gun laws, but we can see in Figure 5.3 that subsequent, similarly horrendous shootings have barely moved the needle in public opinion. What did make a difference was the Supreme Court's *Heller* decision. In Figure 5.3 we see support for gun rights rising to about half of survey respondents and staying there.

■ **FIGURE 5.3**    The Public's Changing Attitude toward Gun Control

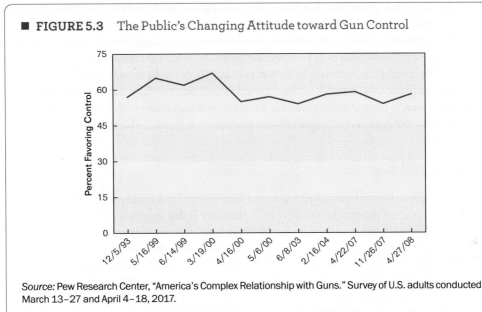

Source: Pew Research Center, "America's Complex Relationship with Guns." Survey of U.S. adults conducted March 13–27 and April 4–18, 2017.

(http://www.pewsocialtrends.org/2017/06/22/americas-complex-relationship-with-guns/).

■ **FIGURE 5.4**    The Public's View of Gun Rights by Party Identification

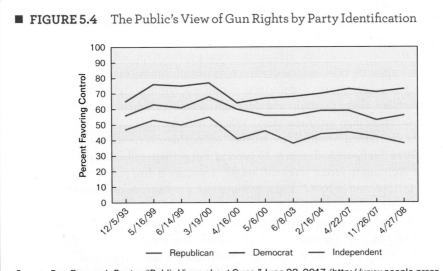

Source: Pew Research Center, "Public Views about Guns," June 22, 2017. (http://www.people-press
.org/2017/06/22/public-views-about-guns/#total).

Public opinion has not been altogether static since 2008, however. Republicans have embraced the individual right interpretation to the Second Amendment, whereas Democrats have not. Figure 5.4 documents the steady rise of gun control as a highly partisan issue—in reality, a litmus test that politicians from both political parties must answer correctly to secure their party identifiers' support. Several reasons for this partisan divide can be found in the composition of party supporters. As women have drifted toward Democrats, they have shifted that party's stance more squarely in favor of gun control. Similarly, the growing urban-rural divide in party identification contributes the widening gulf between partisans in both the electorate and in Washington.

## Criminal Rights

"The history of liberty," remarked Supreme Court Justice Felix Frankfurter, "has largely been the observance of procedural safeguards."[48] Nowhere is this insight more applicable than to criminal rights. In fact, an article on world affairs in today's newspaper is highly likely to confirm Frankfurter's comment. Leaders in nondemocratic societies often throw their adversaries in prison on trumped-up criminal charges as an easy way of quelling the opposition.

But procedural safeguards remove the criminal process from politics and protect the individual citizen from the raw power of the state. The Framers had firsthand experience in this area: Britain had used criminal statutes and prosecutions in its attempts to tighten its political control over the colonies. The wary drafters of the Bill of Rights carefully and systematically constructed barriers to arbitrary law enforcement.

Public safety and law enforcement are quintessentially state and local responsibilities. This fact probably explains why the Bill of Rights provisions in Figure 5.5 were among the last to be incorporated into the Fourteenth Amendment and applied to all levels of government. Until the 1960s the Supreme Court applied the Fourteenth Amendment's due process clause to defendants only in egregious instances of state misconduct, such as a 1936 case in which a suspect was tortured to near death before he confessed.[49] Clearly, for a long time a majority of the Court wanted to avoid overseeing the state criminal justice system. Even when it did accept the argument that a particular constitutional provision applied to the states, the Court hesitated to impose the rules and standards used in federal criminal cases.

The public has disapproved of the incorporation of criminal rights into the Fourteenth Amendment; law-abiding citizens and their representatives tend to sympathize more with the victims of crime than with the accused. When a national survey asked Americans in 1972 whether the courts treat criminals "too harshly" or "not harshly enough," two-thirds said the latter. By 1994 this figure had risen to 85 percent, but perhaps reflecting the effects of more restrictive decisions in recent years and longer sentences, it dropped to 78 percent in 1996 and again to 64 percent in 2008.[50] Today criminal rights remain one of the most controversial aspects of modern civil liberties policy.

Elected officeholders have responded to these opinions and controversies by paying closer attention to the legal opinions of the men and women they are appointing and confirming to the federal judiciary. Although criminal rights have not been "unincorporated" or sharply curtailed, vigilant recruitment appears to have brought criminal rights court rulings into closer alignment with the preferences of the American public. As a consequence, Supreme Court decisions have on average become less supportive of criminal rights than they were during the 1960s, when major policy changes occurred in this field (see Figure 5.6). After the September 11

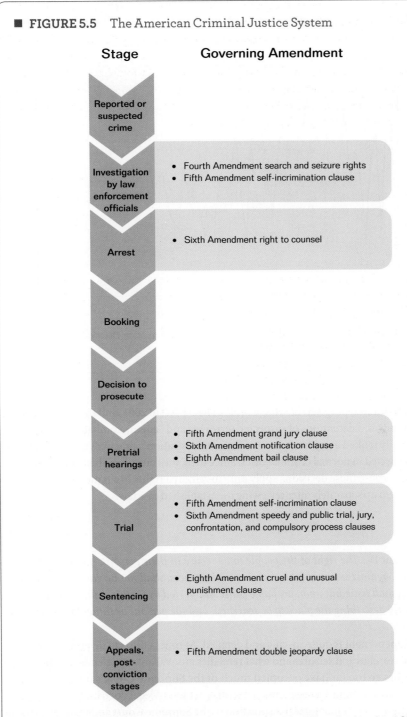

**■ FIGURE 5.5**    The American Criminal Justice System

*Source:* Lee Epstein and Thomas G. Walker, *Constitutional Law for a Changing America: A Short Course,* 4th ed. (Washington, DC: CQ Press, 2009), Table VI-1, 558.

**■ FIGURE 5.6** The Supreme Court's Criminal Rights Decisions in Favor of the Accused

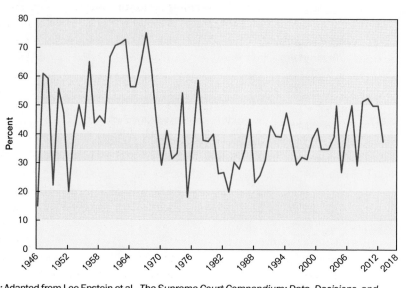

*Source:* Adapted from Lee Epstein et al., *The Supreme Court Compendium: Data, Decisions, and Developments*, 6th ed. (Washington, DC: CQ Press, 2016), Table 3-9.

attacks led first to a sweeping new law, the USA PATRIOT Act of 2001, and shortly thereafter to numerous arrests and detentions of suspected terrorists and "enemy combatants," the federal judiciary initially looked away from most of the administration's practices to which it would clearly have objected in normal criminal cases. Since then, the courts have become increasingly circumspect. Because these decisions apply only to criminal rights in a national security context, we take them up separately after reviewing the established case law.

## Fourth Amendment: Illegal Searches and Seizures

Amendment IV: *The right of the people to be secure in their persons, houses, papers, and effects, against unreasonable searches and seizures, shall not be violated, and no Warrants shall issue, but upon probable cause, supported by Oath or affirmation, and particularly describing the place to be searched, and the persons or things to be seized.*

The Fourth Amendment is quite specific and detailed. At times efforts to determine what constitutes illegal searches and seizures and what remedies are available to defendants when police and prosecutors go too far have occupied much of the Supreme Court's time. Attempts to answer these two questions have generated two distinct sets of legal doctrine that continue to evolve with the changing ideological disposition of the Supreme Court and the ever-growing capacity of technology to monitor both our behavior and police enforcement actions.

For centuries the principle was commonly asserted and eventually accepted that unless the police convinced a judge to give them a search warrant, the home was indeed a "castle" from which ordinary citizens could escape government intrusion. Indeed, colonists' vivid memories of British official intrusions at the advent of the Revolution probably guaranteed the Fourth Amendment's place in the Bill of Rights. Until recently the Supreme Court followed this principle—almost literally. The Court deemed out of bounds only police investigations that violated an individual's private *physical space.* Accordingly, the Court ruled that phone wiretaps performed without search warrants were legal and that any evidence obtained in this way could be introduced in a trial. The first real limitations on search and seizure "beyond the domicile" came not from the judiciary but from Congress, which, in setting up rules and administrative structures for regulating broadcast and telephone communications (the federal Communications Act of 1934), added language proscribing most police use of wiretaps.

Not until 1967 did the Supreme Court start expanding the domain of privacy and limiting police use of technology to conduct warrantless searches. Following accepted procedures, FBI agents placed a listening device outside the phone booth used by a suspected bookie, Charles Katz. They were rewarded with incriminating evidence that helped convict Katz. The case did not end there, however, because his lawyers challenged the wiretap, arguing that a telephone booth is a "constitutionally protected area." In *Katz v. United States* the Court agreed, breaking new legal ground in two respects.[51] First, the Court did not limit protections to discovery of physical evidence, and second, it indicated that even searches not involving "physical penetration" of an individual's space might be illegal. This decision opened a vast realm of possibilities, as reflected in the thousands of legal challenges and dozens of Supreme Court decisions that *Katz* spawned. In 2001 the Court ruled that police cannot use a thermal imaging device to perform a blanket sweep of neighborhoods to look for basement marijuana fields.[52] In 2014 it required law enforcement to obtain a search warrant before opening a suspect's cell phone messages.[53] This and other recent decisions have helped clarify the Court's approach to search and seizure cases. The Court generally allows police searches and seizure of evidence without a warrant under the following circumstances:

- during a valid arrest (after all, the police must be sure those they arrest do not remain armed);
- when searching to ensure that evidence is not lost;
- when searching with the consent of the suspect;
- when the search occurs in "hot pursuit" of a suspect in the act of committing a crime;
- when seizing evidence that is in plain view; and
- when searching places other than residences that the Court has decided merit low protection (such as automobiles).[54]

One of the most difficult questions the Court has faced is what should be done with illegally obtained incriminating evidence. The Court grappled with this question as early as 1914, when it decided that such material must be excluded from consideration by the trial judge and jury. But as late as 1949 the Court resisted incorporating this **exclusionary rule**, reasoning that if police act improperly, the accused person could complain to police superiors or file a private lawsuit (the main recourse provided by British law). Not until the early 1960s did an increasingly liberal Supreme Court, under the leadership of Chief Justice Earl Warren, turn to incorporation of criminal rights. In *Mapp v. Ohio* (1961) the Court finally extended the exclusionary policy to the states.[55] Unlike its decisions on obscenity or religious establishment, the Court's ruling on the exclusionary rule was clear and simple: improperly obtained evidence could not be admitted at any trial.

The Court majority must have believed it created an absolute standard. Over the next few years it and lower federal courts unflinchingly threw out improperly acquired evidence, no matter how incriminating. The public grew outraged. But as membership on the Court became more conservative, the seemingly absolute standard set down in *Mapp* became more ambiguous and flexible. In two 1984 cases the Court ruled that if law enforcement officers made a "good faith" effort to abide by established procedures, the evidence retrieved could still be introduced,[56] and in 2006, the Court ruled in a 5–4 decision that the exclusionary rule does not apply to evidence obtained after police failed to follow properly the "knock and announce" rule required by the Fourth Amendment.[57] The Court has also ruled that improperly acquired evidence is admissible if one could reasonably assume it would have been discovered anyway. (In the case on which this ruling was based, the evidence was the body of the murder victim, lying exposed in a field.*)

Although the exclusionary rule has been around for decades, modern technology is introducing new Fourth Amendment issues. In 2012 the Supreme Court launched a series of decisions that increasingly scrutinize police use of cell phone and GPS technology for monitoring citizens' behavior. It ruled unanimously that the police could not place a GPS tracking device on a suspect's vehicle without a warrant.[58] For four of the justices, the case seemed to turn on the fact that the vehicle was on private property at the time of placement. But others, such as Justice Alito, seemed to be concerned more broadly about expectations of privacy in the digital age, claiming that individuals did not expect that law enforcement would "secretly monitor and catalogue" their movements.[59] One thing is clear: this will not be the last case the Court decides involving modern technology and the gathering of electronic information about individuals. As we discuss later in the chapter, concerns about informational privacy are not limited to "search and seizure" issues.

## Fifth Amendment: Self-Incrimination

Amendment V: *No person . . . shall be compelled . . . to be a witness against himself.*

This protection applies not only to testimony in a trial but also to any statement made by a defendant awaiting trial. The principle against self-incrimination has been a bedrock of

---

*Nix v. Williams*, 467 U.S. 431 (1984). In its first case of exclusionary evidence in five years, the Court in 2016 weakened the rule further in finding that evidence gathered during a legal arrest is admissible, even though the initial contact with the suspect was inadvertent and probably unconstitutional. *Utah v. Strieff*, 14–1373 (2016).

American jurisprudence. Only if granted immunity from prosecution, based on requested testimony, can an individual be legally compelled to testify. But what happens when defendants claim they were coerced or tricked into confessing?

---

PD 47 METROPOLITAN POLICE DEPARTMENT

Rev. 8/73 **WARNING AS TO YOUR RIGHTS**

You are under arrest. Before we ask you any questions, you must understand what your rights are.

You have the right to remain silent. You are not required to say anything to us at any time or to answer any questions. Anything you say can be used against you in court.

You have the right to talk to a lawyer for advice before we question you and to have him with you during questioning.

If you cannot afford a lawyer and want one, a lawyer will be provided for you.

If you want to answer questions now without a lawyer present you will still have the right to stop answering at any time. You also have the right to stop answering at any time until you talk to a lawyer.

**WAIVER**

1. Have you read or had read to you the warning as to your rights? _____

2. Do you understand these rights?

   _____

3. Do you wish to answer any questions?

   _____

4. Are you willing to answer questions without having an attorney present? _____

5. Signature of defendant on line below.

   _____

6. Time _____ Date _____

7. Signature of Officer _____

8. Signature of Witness _____

---

Reading this statement, or one very much like it, is standard operating procedure for police and sheriffs all across the country when making arrests.

Law enforcement officials have always preferred obtaining confessions to preparing for trials. The alternative, gathering evidence and building a case, can be time consuming and risky. As late as the 1960s, many police departments throughout the nation routinely induced confessions by beatings, threats, and severe deprivations. Moreover, "tricks of the trade," including placing codefendants in a prisoner's dilemma situation, induced some of the accused—even some who were innocent—to confess.

In 1964 the Supreme Court took the first step toward eradicating these abuses by applying the Fifth Amendment to the states.[60] It followed that decision with a controversial ruling two years later in *Miranda v. Arizona*, aimed at protecting suspects from self-incrimination during the critical time between arrest and arraignment.[61] In the *Miranda* case the Warren Court held that police custody is inherently threatening and that confessions obtained during that period can be admitted as evidence only if suspects have been advised of their constitutional right to remain silent. Moreover, defendants must be warned that what they say can be used against them in a trial, informed that they have a right to have a lawyer present for any statements (and that the state will provide an attorney if they cannot afford one), and told of the right to end the interrogation at any time.

In 1968, as part of a more encompassing crime law, Congress enacted legislation that sought to overturn *Miranda* by permitting all demonstrably voluntary confessions. Lawmakers intended the provision to return the judiciary's focus *to* the nature of the confession and *away* from strict adherence to the **Miranda rule**. For the next three decades, attorneys general and local prosecutors did not enforce this provision of the law, perhaps believing it to be unconstitutional. Then in 2000 a case involving the provision finally reached the Supreme Court. Arguing that the *Miranda* rule was a fundamental "constitutional principle," the Court held that Congress did not have the authority to change the *Miranda* decision.[62] This does not mean, however, that the Court lacks the authority to change its own rule. In 2010, the Court issued three different decisions concerning *Miranda* rights, all of which lessen to some degree the protections under *Miranda*. Most significantly, the Court ruled that a suspect being interrogated must *unambiguously* invoke his or her right to remain silent under *Miranda*.

## Sixth Amendment: Right to Counsel and Impartial Jury of Peers

> Amendment VI: *In all criminal prosecutions, the accused shall . . . have the Assistance of Counsel for his defence.*

Defendants in any American courtroom can take comfort in the Sixth Amendment assurances that they are entitled to "a speedy and public trial, by an impartial jury of the State and district wherein the crime shall have been committed," a "compulsory process for obtaining witnesses in [their] favor," and "the Assistance of Counsel." The protections offered in this amendment have been subject to little controversy.

In 1932 the Supreme Court partially applied the Sixth Amendment to the states when it required them to provide all indigent defendants in capital cases (that is, those potentially involving the death penalty) with a lawyer. Full incorporation, however, had to wait until 1963, when Clarence Earl Gideon won one of the most famous decisions in Court history.[63] Gideon, a drifter, was accused of breaking into a pool hall. Unable to afford a lawyer, he asked the Florida trial judge for representation but was turned down, convicted, and promptly sent to prison. There he became an inspiration for "prison lawyers" everywhere.

With classic David-versus-Goliath determination, Gideon researched the law and sent to the Supreme Court a handwritten petition claiming that his five-year prison sentence was unconstitutional because he had been too poor to hire an attorney and, as a result, had been required to defend himself.

Upon taking his case, the Court assigned Gideon a first-class attorney (and future Supreme Court justice), Abe Fortas, who successfully argued that Gideon's constitutional right to counsel had been denied. Indeed, the decision in *Gideon v. Wainwright* decreed that anyone charged with a felony must be offered legal representation. Later the Court expanded eligibility to include any defendant whose conviction might result in incarceration.[64] With over 94 percent of all federal and state prosecutions resulting in guilty pleas, the Supreme Court recently extended the Sixth Amendment throughout the process.[65]

In many conviction appeals the Sixth Amendment claim has turned from the availability of counsel to the adequacy of the defense that court-appointed attorneys provide. The appeals courts are reluctant to become closely involved with this part of the process, lest they find themselves asked to second-guess the defense whenever a guilty verdict occurs. Nonetheless, beginning with a 1984 case, the Court has prescribed that "counsel has a duty to make reasonable investigations or to make a reasonable decision that makes particular investigations unnecessary."[66] Evidence that the defense failed to perform at a minimal competence level offered the defendant grounds to request retrial. Generally, cases involving the death penalty have received the most careful appellate review.[67]

As for the Sixth Amendment's reference to juries and their procedures, the federal courts have largely allowed the states to determine jury size and whether unanimous agreement is required for conviction. However, the courts have concentrated on whether juries are adequately composed of the defendant's peers. Unrepresentative juries can arise in two ways: the pool of potential jurors is itself unrepresentative, or the selection process is biased. Until the 1960s African Americans in the South were effectively excluded from juries because jury pools were drawn from voter registration lists (see Chapter 4). When federal registrars signed up black voters, however, this discrimination was automatically dismantled.

Potential jurors may be rejected from service either for "cause" (arising from suspected prejudice) or as the target of a peremptory challenge. The latter, a pervasive practice in state and local courts, allows attorneys on both sides to reject a certain number of individuals without having to establish cause. Lawyers, seeking the most sympathetic jury possible, routinely exempt certain types of people depending on the nature of the case and the personal characteristics of the defendant. They may not, however, use their challenges to eliminate jurors on the basis of race or sex.

## Eighth Amendment: "Cruel and Unusual" Punishment

> Amendment VIII: *Excessive bail shall not be required, nor excessive fines imposed, nor cruel and unusual punishments inflicted.*

Both "excesses" targeted by the Eighth Amendment have recently come under reassessment. Reflecting Britain's arbitrary practices, those promoting this amendment with Madison sought to limit the discretion of government to jail and punish those charged with crimes. Yet the amendment leaves ample room for discretion by judges—and hence, room for discrimination—in setting bail and sentences. Advocates of reform have railed against America's bail system for decades, until recently without success. Incarcerating poor people, including those who will eventually be found not guilty, can add up to months in jail simply because they could not post bail. During this time, they may lose their jobs, cars, homes, and in some instances, their families. This all because they did not have the funds or credit rating to secure a bail bond. In 2018 the California governor and state legislature agreed with critics and enacted a reform ending bail in state courts. In its place judges have the discretion to release or hold defendants based on pretrial assessment of their flight risk, danger to others, and similar criteria. Other states are considering similar reforms and will surely pay close attention to the California reform's success or failure over the next couple of years.

The Eighth Amendment's second excess deals with the highly subjective phrase "**cruel and unusual punishments.**" Its vague language assured that the courts would become involved in deciding where to draw the line. Moreover, as society's norms and mores about punishment change, the provision was bound to be periodically revisited. Judges generally prefer to have elected representatives set the specific fines and penalties and reserve their oversight to appraising whether police, judges, and juries applied the rules correctly ("due process") and fairly ("equal protection"). An example of this has been the judiciary's reticence to strike down California's and other states' "three strikes" law, which sharply stiffens sentences for third-time offenders.*

Instead, the Supreme Court has largely limited application of this amendment to death penalty cases. After decades of refusing to address whether capital punishment in itself constituted cruel and unusual punishment, the Supreme Court entered the fray through a back door in a stunning 1972 decision, *Furman v. Georgia*. It did not overturn the death penalty per se, but citing quantitative research indicating racial bias, ruled that as meted out in most states, it violated the Fourteenth Amendment's "equal protection." African Americans convicted of murdering whites were far more likely to receive the death penalty than were whites convicted of the same crime. A close inspection of the 243-page decision, the longest in Court history, reveals that only three justices maintained that the death penalty inherently violates the Bill of Rights. The others who joined the majority took a narrow approach, citing discriminatory practice as the basis for their ruling.

Immediately the federal government and thirty-five states redrafted laws to deal with the Court's objection to Georgia's sentencing procedures. Some states tried to eliminate discrimination by mandating that certain heinous crimes carry an automatic death penalty. But these laws were also later rejected as inherently arbitrary and because they did not allow consideration of mitigating circumstances in sentencing. The solution was found in a new Georgia statute that separated the conviction from the sentencing stage of the trial, allowing juries to weigh the particular crime and defendant and any mitigating and aggravating circumstances. In 1976 the 7–2 majority in *Gregg v. Georgia* proclaimed the new Georgia statute to be a "model" law, and the death penalty ceased to constitute cruel and unusual punishment.[68] Indeed, the Georgia solution appears to have become an acceptable option for the state governments that rewrote sentencing procedures shortly after the *Gregg* decision and for the prosecutors, judges, and juries that implement them.†

In other cases over the past ten years, the Court has found the following to be cruel and unusual punishment under the Eighth Amendment: the execution of defendants with "mental retardation"; the execution of juveniles; and the execution of a defendant who raped, but did not murder, a child.[69] In addition, in 2009 the Roberts Court (with both Justice Roberts and Justice Kennedy in the majority) ruled that it violated the Eighth Amendment to sentence a juvenile to life in prison without the possibility of parole if the crime did not involve a murder.

---

*Ten years after the legislation was enacted, the state had over seven thousand people incarcerated under the three-strikes law for twenty-five years or more. This number includes three hundred whose last conviction was for "petty theft." Linda Greenhouse, "Justices Uphold Long Prison Terms in Repeat Crimes," *New York Times*, March 6, 2004.

†In 2016 it vacated a death sentence for a black defendant in a trial in which the prosecutor appeared to have used race as the criterion for striking all potential jurors from hearing the case. It also ruled against a Florida law that allowed trial judges to levy the death penalty instead of strictly following a jury's decision. *Foster v. Chatman*, 14-8349 (2016).

Despite these rulings from the Supreme Court finding violations of the Eighth Amendment in death penalty cases, more than 1,224 death sentences have been carried out since reinstatement of the death penalty in 1976. As of October 2009, over three thousand inmates were sitting on death row.* Both the escalation of executions in the mid-1990s and more recently the equally sharp decline (see Figure 5.7) have tracked trends in public opinion favoring capital punishment. Although public opinion has gradually grown less supportive of the death penalty over the past quarter century, a clear majority of the public still favors it for murder cases.

Time has shown that the rights of the accused are not always easy to appreciate or enforce. Criminal rights almost always trigger precarious balancing between the defendant's due process and equal protection rights and the community's interest in punishing the guilty and maintaining social order. When a court frees a guilty person because of some technical glitch in the criminal justice system—such as from an improperly filled-out search warrant or an untimely prosecution—controversy erupts. Perhaps the morass of legal technicalities, as much as the other thorny issues described in this section, account for the delayed incorporation of criminal rights (see Table 5.3). By the late 1940s the Supreme Court had applied to the states the entire First Amendment—as well as the Fourth Amendment (without mandating the

■ **FIGURE 5.7**   As More Americans Oppose the Death Penalty, the Number of Executions Has Declined

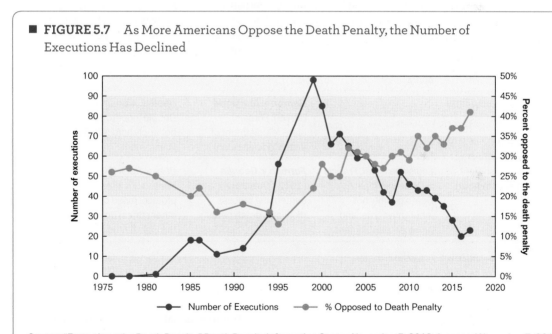

*Source:* "Facts about the Death Penalty." Death Penalty Information Center. November 5, 2018. Accessed November 7, 2018. https://deathpenaltyinfo.org/documents/FactSheet.pdf.

*Note:* The percentage opposed reflects responses to the Gallup poll question: "Are you in favor of the death penalty for a person convicted of murder?"

---

*About 38 percent of all executions since 1976 have taken place in Texas alone; its total of 460 executions far surpasses that of any other state.

**TABLE 5.3**    The Meandering Path of Criminal Rights

| | EARLY | 1960S AND 1970S | RECENT DEVELOPMENTS |
|---|---|---|---|
| Search and seizure (Fourth Amendment) | *Wolf v. Colorado* (1949): Fourth Amendment applies to states but exclusionary rule not mandated. | **Mapp v. Ohio** (1961): Improperly obtained evidence cannot be introduced at trial. | *United States v. Leon* (1984): Exclusionary rule not constitutionally protected but a means to deter police illegality. Allows good faith and inevitable discovery exceptions. |
| Non-self-incrimination (Fifth Amendment) | *Brown v. Mississippi* (1936): Outlaws confessions extracted by torture. | **Miranda v. Arizona** (1966): Officers must inform suspects of their rights before interrogation. | *Illinois v. Perkins* (1990): For confessions heard by undercover police, the Court rules: "*Miranda* forbids coercion, not strategic deception." |
| Right to lawyer (Sixth Amendment) | *Betts v. Brady* (1942): Denies right to lawyer in state prosecutions where special circumstances do not apply. | **Gideon v. Wainwright** (1963): Reverses *Betts,* guaranteeing all defendants charged with a felony a lawyer at trial. | *Ross v. Moffitt* (1974): Right to counsel is not required for discretionary appeals after conviction. |
| Double jeopardy (Fifth Amendment) | | **Benton v. Maryland** (1969): Forbids state reindictment of acquitted defendant. | *Heath v. Alabama* (1985): Double jeopardy does not apply across levels of government. |
| Capital punishment (Eighth Amendment) | *Louisiana ex rel. Francis v. Resweber* (1947): Death penalty not inherently "cruel and unusual" punishment. | **Furman v. Georgia** (1972): "Arbitrary" sentencing process disallows death penalty. | *Baze v. Rees* (2008): Kentucky's lethal injection protocol (used by almost thirty other states) does not violate the Eighth Amendment. |

*Note:* Cases in ***boldface*** are discussed in the text.

exclusionary rule)—but it hesitated until the 1960s to nationalize the remainder of the Bill of Rights.

## Privacy

A right to privacy, unlike other civil liberties, is not explicitly stated in the Bill of Rights or elsewhere in the Constitution. Indeed, although an implicit "right of privacy" had been postulated by legal jurists as early as the 1890s, the Supreme Court did not explicitly recognize its existence until 1965.

But how could the Court "recognize" as constitutional a right that is nowhere mentioned in the Constitution? In 1965 the Court reasoned in *Griswold v. Connecticut* that Americans' guaranteed rights are not limited to those specifically identified in the Constitution.[70] Indeed, the Ninth Amendment says as much: "The enumeration in the Constitution, of certain rights, shall not be construed to deny or disparage others retained by the people." This amendment opened the door to unstated rights. Moreover, a reasonable reading of other amendments invites privacy into the Constitution's protected liberties. After all, what does the Constitution's guarantee of "liberty" mean if not privacy from state surveillance? Other explicit rights such as freedom of speech and assembly and the prohibitions against self-incrimination and unreasonable search and seizure require some measure of privacy if they are to be secure. These explicitly guaranteed rights form **penumbras**, or implicit zones of protected privacy rights on which the existence of explicit rights depends. For example, freedom of speech and a free press must include not only an individual's right to engage in these activities but also the right to distribute, receive, and read others' views. Without these other rights, the specific rights would be insecure.

Once identified, the right to privacy became subject to all the complexities of interpretation and enforcement associated with other civil liberties. But the overriding question was, in the absence of constitutional standards, what actions and practices are so personal or private that they should be shielded from interference by the government?

## Childbearing Choices

The Supreme Court's attentiveness to privacy claims has largely been confined to an important but narrow domain of public policy: reproductive rights. In extending privacy in childbearing choices, the courts began not with abortion but with access to contraceptives. In 1961 Estelle Griswold, executive director of the Planned Parenthood League of Connecticut, opened a Planned Parenthood clinic, which dispensed contraceptives. Three days after the clinic opened, Griswold was arrested for violating an 1879 Connecticut law prohibiting the use of contraceptives. After losing her case in the state courts, the defendant appealed her test case in federal court. Not only did she win, but the Supreme Court decision, *Griswold v. Connecticut,* laid precedents that emboldened feminist and reproductive freedom groups to pursue abortion rights.

In 1972 Justice William Brennan's argument in *Eisenstadt v. Baird* bolstered the efforts of such groups: "If the right of privacy means anything, it is the right of the individual, married or single, to be free from unwanted governmental intrusion into matters so fundamentally affecting a person as the decision to bear or beget a child."[71] One year later, in the landmark abortion rights decision *Roe v. Wade,* a Court majority ruled, "The right of privacy, whether it be founded in the Fourteenth Amendment's concept of liberty ... or ... in the Ninth Amendment's reservation of rights to the people, is broad enough to encompass a woman's decision whether or not to terminate her pregnancy."*

---

*But as Justice Byron White wrote in his dissent from the *Roe* decision, "The upshot is that the people and the legislatures of the fifty states are constitutionally disentitled to weigh the relative importance of the continued existence and development of the fetus, on the one hand, against a spectrum of possible impacts on the mother, on the other hand." *Roe v. Wade*, 410 U.S. 113 (1973).

Abortion rights in the United States did not begin with this historic and controversial decision; many states permitted abortion until the late nineteenth century. Moreover, in the ten years leading up to the *Roe* decision, eighteen states either relaxed or repealed their statutes prohibiting abortion. Thus the Court's nationalization in 1973 of a woman's right to terminate her pregnancy ended abortion's varying legality across the states.

This said, *Roe v. Wade* did not remove the states from abortion rights policy. This decision established that a woman's decision to end her pregnancy belongs within the protected sphere of privacy, but it did not wholly exempt abortion from government regulation. Rather, the Court ruled that in the interest of the mother's health and the "potential" life of the fetus, state governments could regulate abortions from the end of the first trimester of pregnancy to fetus viability (months four through six). Within the final trimester the states could forbid all abortions except those required "for the preservation of the life or health of the mother." In 1992 the Court backed away from the trimester standard, choosing instead the demarcating line of "viability" (which the Court did not define with precision) and substituted a more ambiguous "undue burden" criterion: prior to viability, states cannot ban abortions, but they can impose certain regulations on both the women who seek abortions and the doctors who perform them, as long as those regulations do not pose an "undue burden" on the woman's right to an abortion.[72] Waiting periods, counseling sessions, and parental consent were deemed constitutional as long as they did not place an undue burden on the abortion right.

Indeed, abortion politics remains the subject of an intense political debate that takes many forms—confrontational demonstrations by the antiabortion movement, platform fights at

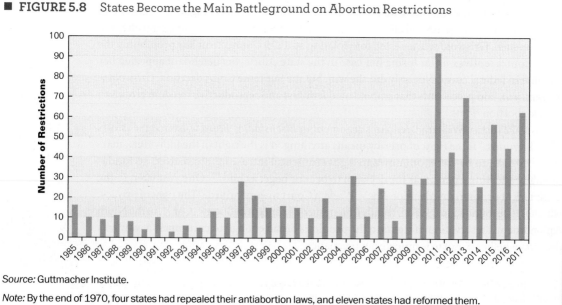

**■ FIGURE 5.8**   States Become the Main Battleground on Abortion Restrictions

*Source:* Guttmacher Institute.

*Note:* By the end of 1970, four states had repealed their antiabortion laws, and eleven states had reformed them.

presidential nominating conventions, and legislation both extending and voiding the *Roe* decision. Dozens of new state laws adjusting the boundaries of this privacy right have been enacted and amended over the past decade (see Figure 5.8). For example, at least ten state legislatures have passed laws requiring a woman seeking an abortion to have an ultrasound examination before the procedure is performed. Thirty-five years after *Roe*, abortion remains controversial. As a candidate, Donald Trump promised to put pro-life justices on the Court, and as president he made good on that promise by appointing Judge Neil Gorsuch, a past critic of *Roe v. Wade*. If *Roe* is retrenched or overturned, states will play an even greater role in defining a woman's right to an abortion.

## Privacy on the Internet

Although this chapter focuses on the protection of citizens from intrusions on liberty by the government, increasingly, circumstances arise that blur the line between gathering of information by government and that by third parties. The proliferation of e-mail, text messages, GPS technology, cloud computing, and smartphones and an explosion in the number of consumers who are conducting business online have led to concerns about (1) third parties that create and maintain massive online databases and (2) the extent to which the government easily can access that information. For example, employers, credit agencies, health providers, insurance companies, credit card companies, banks, and e-mail providers like Google all gather information on users, in ways that may be highly intrusive of individuals' privacy.

So why are the courts not flooded with suits charging the people and organizations that control these databases with invasion of privacy? Perhaps the long-standing judicial doctrine that information loses its privacy privilege once conveyed to third parties has discouraged claims. Or perhaps this area of civil liberties has simply failed to attract the kinds of group sponsorship typically needed to make strong cases and sustain them through the judicial system. But the biggest problem with regard to protecting informational privacy is that federal and state laws have trouble keeping up with changing technology. For example, the Electronic Communications Privacy Act was passed in 1986, well before most Americans knew what e-mail was. That law allows the government to obtain electronic communications that are over 180 days old without a warrant; only a subpoena is required. Finally, there is inherent tension between the idea of informational privacy and the reality that so many Americans voluntarily share personal, private details about their lives every day on the Internet. But as Justice Sotomayor stated in her concurrence in the GPS case, "It may be necessary to reconsider the premise that an individual has no reasonable expectation of privacy in information voluntarily

A Trojan Dino: To set this child's toy to access the Internet for entertainment, Dino has unencrypted access to the home's wireless system, exposing the home to hacking.

disclosed to third parties." In the end, individuals, legislators, and judges will need to reevaluate their ideas of privacy to match the realities of the digital age.

## Civil Liberties as Public Policy

At first, the nationalization of civil liberties in the Bill of Rights was not a popular idea. Madison's proposal to amend the Constitution to apply them directly to the states was handily defeated in Congress as those members sympathetic with the Antifederalists, who had insisted that civic freedoms be written into the Constitution, explicitly rejected the idea of extending them to the states.

Only during the twentieth century, and gradually by incorporation, has the Bill of Rights come to be accepted as *national* policy that applies to every level of government. Yet states still formulate the rules that implement many of the rights guaranteed. For example, the Supreme Court allows states to determine the size of juries and level of agreement required to convict in state courts. Similarly, the states are free to decide the legality of physician-assisted suicide and have plenty of room to regulate the availability of abortions.

The members of Congress who drafted and deliberated these liberties and the state legislators who ratified them probably had in mind essentially "civic" rights: the right to dissent; to organize opposition; and, in extreme instances, to resist—essential bulwarks against the impulses of any intemperate majorities and tyrannical government officials. As we have seen, these rights have been broadened, in some instances dramatically, to create personal spheres of expression and privacy. This evolution is evident in modern case law on search and seizure, unconventional religious practices, nude dancing, the right to die, abortion, guns and property, gay marriage, and many other issues reviewed in this and the previous chapter.

Americans, however, do not see eye to eye on these matters. In fact, modern civil liberties number among the most divisive and unsettled issues facing the nation. The modern Supreme Court's dominant role in deciding these policies contributes to their controversy. Once, these issues resided exclusively in the political arena—that is, with state and local governments and with Congress. But as the Supreme Court carved out a larger role in these policies, its insulation from public opinion exposed its decisions to criticism and second-guessing. And, of course, its insulation has allowed it at times to issue highly unpopular decisions, such as its stance on flag burning and, during the 1960s, its restrictions on established law enforcement practices.

How does the image of a small number of unelected, life-tenured justices deciding public policy comport with the principles of democracy? Those who insist that majority rule must prevail in a democracy cannot justify the Court's having any role at all other than duties delegated to it by the democratic (that is, elected) branches of government. Others, however, may accept the authority of a national community to impose limits on itself and future majorities in making certain decisions. The elaborate rules to amend the Constitution are a prime example. Other limits can be found in the Bill of Rights. It removes various personal prerogatives and private behavior from casual government intrusion. The First Amendment opens with "Congress shall make no law . . . ," and the list of proscriptions continues throughout the ten amendments. Madison recognized at the outset that the Supreme Court was well designed to enforce these antimajoritarian rules. The Court's unelected, life-tenured members are well insulated from the "popular passions" that can run roughshod over personal freedoms. Moreover, the explicit prohibitions to congressional action create space for the Court to enter as the Constitution's guardian. If a national majority wants to ban flag burning, it can wait for new justices to be appointed and hope they are sympathetic with its position, or it can try to pass a constitutional amendment. Both avenues promise a lengthy delay and high transaction costs for the majority with little guarantee of success.

Finally, still others may point out that the majority is not as frustrated in exerting its preferences as it might appear. Supreme Court justices are subject to many of the same social and civic influences as are ordinary citizens, and as these circumstances change, so might justices' opinions—in tandem with those of the citizenry. Two weeks after the September 11 attacks, Justice O'Connor observed without alarm, "We are likely to experience more restrictions on our personal freedom than has ever been the case in our country."[73] That these heightened restrictions may occur and be sanctioned in future judicial policy reflects not so much the compromise of principle in the face of reality as the fact that judicial doctrine includes provisions for balancing these elements. The phrase "compelling government interest," for example, allows evidence to inform doctrine and hence opens the way for doctrine to change with conditions.

Given the absolute language of the Bill of Rights, someone who is unfamiliar with the modern history of civil liberties policy might assume that it is settled policy. As we have seen here, however, civil liberties seem to be constantly changing. When judges come and go, they permit Court ideology to be brought into closer alignment with partisan control of the rest of the government. To the extent that citizens disagree on many of these civil liberties issues, so too will their elected officeholders and, in turn, the judges these politicians appoint. Other, more direct influences on the Court can be found in the efforts of organized interests as they sponsor clients and submit "friend of the court" briefs. And finally, ever-changing technology throws into question (and sometimes into confusion) civil liberties policies based on old realities. All of these forces guarantee that civil liberties policy, far from settled, as the Framers might have envisioned, will be continuously revisited and frequently revised.

$\circledS$SAGE edge™

for CQ Press

**Want a better grade?**

Get the tools you need to sharpen your study skills. Access practice quizzes, eFlashcards, video, and multimedia at **edge.sagepub.com/kernell9e.**

## KEY TERMS

*Brandenburg* test   198

clear and present danger test   198

clear and probable danger test   198

community standards   201

cruel and unusual punishments   219

due process clause   193

equal protection clause   193

establishment of religion clause   204

exclusionary rule   216

free exercise clause   204

incitement   198

## SUGGESTED READINGS

Carter, Stephen L. *The Culture of Disbelief: How American Law and Politics Trivialize Religious Devotion.* New York: Basic Books, 1993. A thoughtful argument against prevailing Supreme Court doctrine on the separation of church and state.

Hentoff, Nat. *Free Speech for Me . . . but Not for Thee: How the American Left and Right Relentlessly Censor Each Other.* New York: HarperPerennial, 1992. A highly original account of how political groups gain a political advantage through censorship.

Lewis, Anthony. *Freedom for the Thought That We Hate: A Biography of the First Amendment.* New York: Basic Books, 2007. Although on balance Lewis is more comfortable with established free speech doctrine that embraces the marketplace metaphor, he does not consider it sacrosanct. Might hate speech and libel doctrines, among others, impose real costs on society? Once again, Lewis poses serious questions in a style and language appropriate for a general audience.

Wheeler, Leigh Ann. *How Sex Became a Civil Liberty.* New York: Oxford University Press, 2012. This fascinating history of the emergence of sexual expression as a form of free speech emphasizes the critical role played by the American Civil Liberties Union.

Winkler, Adam. *Gunfight: The Battle over the Right to Bear Arms in America.* New York: Norton, 2011. Excellent history of the evolution of the National Rifle Association and its role in promoting gun ownership as a personal freedom.

## REVIEW QUESTIONS

1. Through what individual steps did the Constitution acquire civil liberties protections?

2. How has individual liberty been elevated from a private local matter into a prominent national policy issue?

3. How has the role of national government differed in the development of civil rights policy versus that of civil liberties?

4. How did the Bill of Rights come to apply to states?

5. Do the states still have a role in defining civil liberties?

Democrat Nancy Pelosi, surrounded by her grandchildren and children of other members, is sworn in once more as Speaker of the House, an office she first won after the 2006 election, lost with the Republican victory in 2010, and retook when the Democrats captured a 235–200 majority in the 2018 midterm election.

# Congress

# 6

←

## KEY QUESTIONS

- Why do members of the House and Senate follow complex, arcane rules and precedents in processing legislation even when such devices keep majorities from getting their way?

- Congressional incumbents rarely lose elections. Why, then, are they obsessed with the electoral implications of nearly everything they do?

- Why have the House and Senate become so much more polarized along partisan and ideological lines over the past several decades?

- Why have congressional party leaders grown more powerful and committees less powerful over the same period?

## CHAPTER OBJECTIVES

**6.1** Describe the requirements and powers of Congress and how the congressional electoral system works.

**6.2** Identify the factors that create advantages and disadvantages in congressional electoral politics.

**6.3** Discuss the racial and ethnic makeup of Congress.

**6.4** Explain six basic problems of legislative organization.

**6.5** Relate the institutional structures in the House and Senate that help members overcome barriers to collective action.

**6.6** Describe what influences public opinion about Congress and its performance.

In March 2010, Democratic majorities in Congress passed the landmark Patient Protection and Affordable Care Act (ACA) without the support of a single Republican vote in either the House of Representatives or the Senate. Nicknamed "Obamacare" after its prime sponsor, the ACA was a sweeping revision of the rules governing the dauntingly complicated American health care system, which accounts for one-sixth of the national economy. The legislation's carefully integrated package of provisions, running to 2,300 pages, was intended to reduce costs while extending health care coverage to many of the approximately 50 million Americans then lacking insurance.

Major changes included making it illegal for insurance companies to discriminate against people with preexisting health problems or to drop coverage of people who get sick, requiring coverage of "essential health benefits," expanding the Medicaid program for poorer citizens, taxing the wealthy to cover some of the costs, and requiring individuals to purchase coverage if not available through their workplace or otherwise. The law was popular in these details—except for the individual purchase mandate—but not overall, with initial polls reporting that, among people with an opinion, an average of 45 percent liked the ACA whereas 55 percent did not, a balance of opinion that changed little during the remaining years of the Obama administration.[1]

AP Photo/Andrew Harnik

House Speaker Paul Ryan and Senate majority leader Mitch McConnell's efforts to repeal and replace Obamacare during the 115th Congress were doomed by internal party divisions; evidently weary of leading the fractious House Republicans, Ryan gave up his seat and retired from Congress in 2018.

Although the ACA was based on ideas developed by conservative think tanks, Republican leaders decided to portray it as a ruinous big-government takeover of the health care sector and, recognizing its shaky public support, included a vow to "repeal and replace" it in every subsequent election campaign. After winning control of the House in 2010 and the Senate in 2014, the Republican majorities voted more than sixty times to repeal or gut the ACA. With Barack Obama wielding the veto, these votes were merely symbolic, but when Donald Trump's victory in 2016 gave Republicans control of the White House as well as Congress, Obamacare's legislative demise seemed imminent. As House Speaker Paul Ryan said in his postelection press conference, "This Congress, this House majority, this Senate majority has already demonstrated and proven that we're able to pass that legislation and put it on the president's desk. The problem is that President Obama vetoed it. Now we have President Trump."[2]

Despite Republican control of the Congress and the presidency, the ACA survived the 115th Congress (2017–2018), although not without absorbing some damage. Simply repealing the law without replacing it, although urged by some conservative Republicans, was a political nonstarter in an assembly of lawmakers who owe their jobs to voters; only about 20 percent of the public favored this option, which according to the Congressional Budget Office (CBO) would have cost an estimated thirty-two million Americans their health insurance coverage. A substitute was thus imperative, but congressional Republicans, though united in opposing the ACA, had never mapped out an alternative because they never agreed on what its replacement should look like. The hard-line conservatives happy to kill it outright were opposed by a larger set of Republicans who wanted to find a way to preserve the popular elements of the law and some of the benefits now enjoyed by their constituents.

After initial failure—a proposal rejected on one side by conservatives for leaving too much of the ACA intact and on the other by vulnerable members in competitive districts hearing from angry constituents fearful of losing coverage—the House Republicans succeeded in passing by a narrow margin a compromise repeal package. The bill was not acceptable to Senate Republicans, however, who were also badly divided over how to revise the law. To reconcile internal party conflicts without the glare of publicity and pressure from the vast array of interest groups with a stake in the health care system, Senate majority leader Mitch McConnell took the negotiations behind closed doors. A thirteen-member all-male Republican working group spent two months drafting a proposal called the Better Care Reconciliation Act (BCRA) in secret, with no hearings, no expert testimony, and no input from either the health care sector or the public. Among other things, the bill would have reduced Medicaid spending, repealed the tax that paid for the ACA's benefits, and let states waive consumer protections. The CBO estimated that it would add twenty-two million people to the uninsured. Procedurally, the bill was handled through the budget reconciliation process to prevent a Democratic filibuster that would have required an unattainable super-majority of sixty votes to overcome; the original ACA had itself been enacted through this same special process, explained later in this chapter, for the same reason.

On July 25, 2017, by a 51–50 vote, with the tie broken by vice president Mike Pence, the Senate voted to begin debate on repealing and replacing Obamacare. None of the alternatives, including BCRA with or without amendments and a repeal-only bill, could win majority support. Senate leaders then called for a vote on a scaled-down version of the bill, dubbed "skinny repeal," that eliminated the individual and employer mandates and made some other minor changes but left much of the ACA intact, although with sixteen million people still projected to lose their coverage.

The bill was seriously defective from almost everyone's perspective, and no one actually wanted it to become law. McConnell's argument to his Republicans was that the skeletal bill would move the process forward, giving the conference committee that would be appointed to reconcile the House and Senate bills a chance to come up with a full, comprehensive proposal. Four Republican senators said they would vote for it only if Ryan promised not to bring it to the House floor unchanged—that is, they would vote for it only if they were assured it would never actually become law. Ryan refused. One of them, John McCain of Arizona, finally joined two moderate Republican women, Lisa Murkowski of Alaska and Susan Collins of Maine, to vote against skinny repeal. McCain's vote shocked Republican leaders and ended the repeal-and-replace effort, at least for the time being. McCain, afflicted with brain cancer that ended his life a year later, objected as much to the procedure—the secrecy, absence of hearings, a flawed proposal concocted behind closed doors and sprung on members at the last minute—as to the substance of the legislation. McCain also lamented the absence of bipartisanship in the process: not a single Democrat in either chamber supported any of the proposed bills.

The effort to unite Republicans behind a replacement for the ACA got warm encouragement but little practical help from the White House. The Obama administration had been deeply involved in both designing the ACA and moving it through Congress. Trump was as eager to undo Obama's handiwork as Obama had been to produce it, but, unfamiliar with the issues involved, he left it to Ryan, McConnell, and other Republicans in Congress to devise its replacement.* During his 2016 campaign, Trump had promised to replace the ACA with a health care program that would deliver "insurance for everyone," with no cuts in Medicare or Medicaid, no loss of coverage to anyone, and leaving no one worse off financially.[3] How this outcome might be achieved was never explained. Lacking a blueprint from the administration, the various pieces of legislation Republican leaders brought to the floor kept none of these

---

*Addressing an audience of the nation's governors in February 2017, the president said, "I have to tell you, it's an unbelievably complex subject. Nobody knew that health care could be so complicated." His audience, deeply engaged in administering their states' health care systems, certainly knew (https://www.nytimes.com/2017/02/27/us/politics/trump-concedes-health-law-overhaul-is-unbelievably-complex.html).

promises. Trump nonetheless held a celebration in the White House's Rose Garden to mark the House bill's passage, prematurely announcing the demise of Obamacare, but later told Republican senators that the House bill was "mean" and they should produce something "more generous," adding to the uncertainty about what sort of legislation the administration wanted.[4]

Regardless of the details, the president seemed eager to sign any bill revamping the ACA that reached his desk. After the Senate failure, he continued to urge Republican leaders to act despite abundant signs that their proposals for revising the ACA were highly unpopular; on average in polls, only about a quarter of the public supported any of the Republican alternatives, and about half opposed them (the rest were uncertain). Efforts to repeal and replace the ACA had the ironic effect of swinging majority support to the legislation's side for the first time since it was enacted.[5] In September 2017, Republicans did manage to eliminate the individual mandate, the least popular part of the ACA, and the Trump administration took numerous small steps intended to weaken it further. It remains largely in place, however, with the share of uninsured ticking up but remaining much lower than before the ACA took effect.

What do these events begin to tell us about the contemporary Congress?

- The House and Senate occupy the center stage in national policymaking, although their power over legislation is not unalloyed, for the Constitution gives an important share of legislative authority to the president via the veto.

- The congressional parties have become highly polarized, making it exceedingly difficult to act in a bipartisan fashion on any issue touching on basic party ideology or commitments. Neither the original ACA nor its proposed replacements receive any cross-party support. Intense partisanship also encourages the pursuit of victory on the floor as an end in itself.

- Electoral politics influences almost everything members of Congress do, collectively and individually. Republicans' commitment to repeal and replace the ACA had been a central theme of every campaign since 2010, leaving many of them torn between keeping a promise to their primary supporters and campaign contributors and responding to their broader constituencies who had come to appreciate the ACA's benefits and might punish them at the polls if these benefits were taken away (and some of them were indeed punished with loss of office in 2018).

- The majority party, through its leaders, directs and sometimes dominates the action in the House and Senate. The degree to which leaders exercise control depends, however, on how unified the parties are internally. Disunity on health care presented a difficult challenge to Ryan and McConnell, and despite using every resource at his disposal to forge a consensus, McConnell was unsuccessful. Ryan did shepherd a bill through his chamber but not without great difficulty; in April 2018, he announced he would not run for reelection.

- "Regular order"—the traditional procedures for drafting and moving legislation through subcommittees and committees, with public hearings, open debate, and broad participation by members, is readily set aside when leaders believe irregular, ad hoc procedures are needed for their party to unify and prevail on significant legislative matters. But resorting to such means carries its own costs in effectiveness, legitimacy, partisan rancor, and discontent among colleagues left out of the process.

- Presidents can sometimes help their congressional parties solve the collective action problems inherent in crafting and enacting laws but do not always try to do so; the absence of the central coordination provided by presidential leadership can make it harder for the president's party to resolve conflicts over difficult and controversial legislation within and between the two chambers.

- It is always far easier to stop things from happening in Congress than to make things happen in Congress. The legislative process contains multiple points where action can be blocked (bicameralism creates only one of many). Even a status quo that is broadly disliked can prevail if there is no agreement on what constitutes improvement. It is also harder to take away benefits than to block their extension in the first place, because the prospect of concrete losses motivates stronger political reactions than the promise of eventual gains.

This chapter explores these themes while explaining how and why the House and Senate operate as they do. It also looks at how these institutions have evolved in response to the changing motives and opportunities, personal and political, of the politicians elected to them. Any such discussion must be prefaced, however, by a review of the constitutional design of Congress and the extensive powers granted it by the Framers.

## Congress in the Constitution

The basic structure of Congress is the product of the Great Compromise at the Constitutional Convention, described in Chapter 2. Balancing the demands of the large states for national representation against those of the small states for protection of states' rights, the Framers established in the Constitution a House of Representatives, with seats allocated by population and members elected by the citizenry, and a Senate composed of two members from each state chosen by the state legislature. Bicameralism (two houses) also resolved another dispute. Delegates to the convention disagreed about the appropriate degree of popular influence on government. Using the bicameral structure, they were able to devise a mixed solution. Representatives would be "popularly" chosen in biennial elections held in even-numbered years. Broad suffrage—the qualification for voting was to be the same as for the "most numerous Branch of the State Legislature" (Article I, Section 2)—and short tenure were intended to keep the House as close as possible to the people.

The Senate, by contrast, would be much more insulated from transient shifts in the public mood. Senators would be chosen by state legislatures, not directly by the voters. The term of office was set at six years, and continuity was ensured by requiring that one-third of the Senate's membership stand for election every two years. The Senate could thus act as a stable, dispassionate counterweight to the more popular and radical House, protecting the new government from the dangerous volatility thought to be characteristic of democracies. As

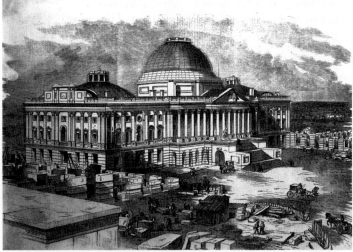

Library of Congress

Washington's city planner, the young Frenchman Pierre L'Enfant, consulted the Constitution before placing the Capitol on the highest hill in the city. From 1825 to 1856 the Capitol lacked a large dome—the original low wooden dome is depicted here—causing L'Enfant to describe it as "a pedestal waiting for a monument."

James Madison put it in *Federalist* No. 62, "The necessity of the Senate is . . . indicated by the propensity of all single and numerous assemblies to yield to the impulse of sudden and violent passions, and to be seduced by factious leaders into intemperate and pernicious resolutions." The Senate also incorporated remnants of state sovereignty into the new national government.

Qualifications for office also reflected the Framers' concept of the Senate as the more "mature" of the two chambers (*senate* is derived from the Latin *senex,* old man). The minimum age for representatives was set at twenty-five years; for senators, thirty years. Representatives had to be citizens for at least seven years; senators, for nine years. Both were required to reside in the state they represented. Representatives do not have to live in the districts they serve, but in practice they almost always do. These are the only qualifications for office specified in the Constitution. The property-holding and religious qualifications included in many state constitutions were explicitly rejected, as was a proposal to forbid a member's reelection to office after serving a term. The Articles of Confederation had included a reelection restriction, but the Framers thought it had weakened Congress by depriving it of some of its ablest members.

## Powers of Congress

As we saw in Chapter 2, the Constitution established a truly national government by giving Congress broad power over crucial economic matters. Article I, Section 8, authorizes Congress to impose taxes, coin and borrow money, regulate interstate and foreign commerce, and spend money for the "common Defence" and "general Welfare." Tacked on at the end of this list of specific powers is a residual clause authorizing Congress "to make all Laws which shall be necessary and proper for carrying into Execution the foregoing Powers, and all other Powers vested by this Constitution in the Government of the United States, or in any Department or Officer thereof." Accepted by many delegates as an afterthought, this *necessary and proper clause*—often known as the elastic clause because it "stretches" the powers of Congress—has proved to be the single most extensive grant of power in the Constitution, giving lawmakers authority over many spheres of public policy (see Chapter 3).

Congress was given significant authority in foreign affairs as well. Although the president is designated commander in chief of the armed forces, only Congress may declare war, raise and finance an army and a navy, and call out the state militias "to execute the Laws of the Union, suppress Insurrections and repel Invasions" (Article I, Section 8). The Senate was granted some special powers over foreign relations. In its "advice and consent" capacity, the Senate ratifies treaties and confirms presidential appointments of ambassadors.

The Senate also confirms the president's nominees to all federal courts and top executive branch positions. These powers reveal that, in part, the Framers viewed the Senate as an advisory council to the executive, modeled on the upper chambers of some state legislatures. But they also reflect the Framers' belief that the more "aristocratic" and insulated of the two houses would keep a steadier eye on the nation's long-term interests.

In distributing power between the House and the Senate, the delegates sought a proper balance of authority. One bone of contention was the power to raise and spend money. Some delegates wanted to give the House, as the chamber closer to the people, the exclusive authority to enact legislation to raise or spend money; the Senate would be allowed to vote on House bills but not amend them. The final compromise required merely that bills raising revenue originate in the House, with the Senate having an unrestricted right to amend them. The House was given no special mandate to initiate spending bills, but it has assumed that right by custom as an extension of its special authority over revenue bills.

Despite its many legislative powers, Congress does not have exclusive authority over legislation. The president may recommend new laws and, in emergencies, call Congress into special session. Most important, the president has the power to veto laws passed by Congress, killing them unless two-thirds of each chamber votes to override the veto.

## The Electoral System

Two choices made by the Framers regarding the electoral system have profoundly affected the development of Congress. First, members of Congress and presidents are elected separately. In parliamentary systems like those found in most European countries, government authority rests with the legislature, which chooses the chief executive (called the prime minister or premier). Thus voters' choices for legislators depend mainly on voter preferences for leader of the executive branch. In the United States, voters are presented separate choices for senator, representative, and president.

Second, members of Congress are elected from states and congressional districts by plurality vote—that is, whoever gets the most votes wins.* Some parliamentary systems employ **proportional representation**, which gives a party a share of seats in the legislature matching the share of the votes it wins on Election Day. For example, if a party's share of votes entitles it to eighty-five seats, the first eighty-five candidates on the party's slate go to parliament. The voters, then, choose among parties, not individual candidates, and candidates need not have local connections. Party leaders under this system are very powerful because they control parliamentary careers by deciding who goes on the list and in what order.

---

*In the past, some states elected some or all of their U.S. representatives in statewide "at-large" districts. A 1964 Supreme Court decision, *Wesberry v. Sanders*, ended the practice by requiring that districts have equal populations. One state, Georgia, requires an absolute majority of votes to win general elections to Congress. If no candidate wins such a majority, a runoff election is held between the top two finishers.

American legislators are elected from territorial units, not party lists. Parties do matter in congressional elections, and with rare exceptions, only major-party nominees have any chance of winning (see Chapter 12). But the parties do not control nominations. Almost all congressional nominees are now chosen by voters in primary elections—preliminary contests in which voters select the parties' nominees. Candidates thus get their party's nomination directly from voters, not from party activists or leaders.

## Congressional Districts

After the first census in 1790, each state was allotted one House seat for every 33,000 inhabitants, for a total of 105 seats. Until the twentieth century the House grew as population increased and new states joined the Union. Total membership was finally fixed at its current ceiling of 435 in 1911, when House leaders concluded that further growth would impede the House's work. Since 1911, states have both lost and gained seats to reflect population shifts between the decennial (ten-year) censuses. Changes in the sizes of state delegations to the House since World War II illustrate vividly the major population movements in the United States (see Map 6.1). States in the West and South have gained at the expense of the large industrial states in the Northeast and Midwest.

Federal law may apportion House seats among states after each census, but each state draws the lines that divide its territory into the allotted number of districts. In 1964 the Supreme Court ruled in *Wesberry v. Sanders* that districts must have equal populations.[6] In *Thornburg v. Gingles* (1986) the Court ruled that district lines may not dilute minority representation but neither may they be drawn with race as the predominant consideration.[7] Within these limits states can draw districts pretty much as they please. If one party controls both the legislature and the governorship, it may attempt to draw district lines that favor its own candidates. The idea is to concentrate the opposition party's voters in a small number of districts that the party wins by large margins, thus "wasting" many of its votes, while creating as many districts as possible where one's own party has a secure, though not overwhelming, majority. Called **gerrymandering**, these tactics sometimes produce bizarrely shaped districts (see box "The Original Gerrymander").

The constitutionality of partisan gerrymanders has been challenged in court, but so far with limited success. In *Davis v. Bandemer* (1986) the Supreme Court held that a gerrymander would be unconstitutional if it were too strongly biased against a party's candidates but has yet to declare any districting scheme to be in violation of this vague standard.[8] None of the challenges to the Republican gerrymanders executed after the 2010 reapportionment (see box Strategy and Choice: "The Republican Gerrymander in 2012") has prevailed, but in 2018 the Court refused to stay a decision of the Pennsylvania Supreme Court overturning a pro-Republican gerrymander as violating the state's constitution. Ongoing litigation in lower federal courts will oblige the Supreme Court to revisit the issue in the near future.

### Racial Gerrymandering

The Court's 1986 *Thornburg* decision, requiring that legislative district lines not discriminate, even unintentionally, against racial minorities, was widely interpreted as directing mapmakers to design districts in which racial and ethnic minorities constituted a majority

■ **MAP 6.1**   Apportionment's Winners and Losers

Since 1950, the South and West have been gaining House seats at the expense of the Northeast and Midwest

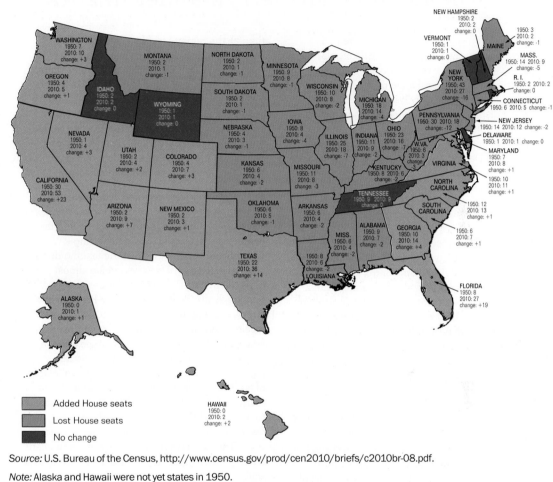

Added House seats

Lost House seats

No change

HAWAII
1950: 0
2010: 2
change: +2

*Source:* U.S. Bureau of the Census, http://www.census.gov/prod/cen2010/briefs/c2010br-08.pdf.

*Note:* Alaska and Hawaii were not yet states in 1950.

of voters wherever residence patterns made this feasible.[9] Attempts to conform to this decision after the 1990 census inspired some artistry that would have made Massachusetts governor Elbridge Gerry, from whom the gerrymander got its name, proud (see box "The Original Gerrymander"). For example, North Carolina legislators carved out two majority black districts (First and Twelfth) that eventually came before the Court (see Map 6.2). The Court decided in 1993 that such irregular districts went too far,[10] and in 1995 that districts could not be drawn solely to benefit one race.[11] Thus, the North Carolina districts had to be redrawn.

# The Republican Gerrymander in 2012

The Republican Party has long enjoyed an advantage in the House because its regular voters are distributed more efficiently across House districts than are regular Democratic voters. The advantage exists mainly because Democrats win a disproportionate share of minority, single, young, LBGTQ, and highly educated voters who are concentrated in urban districts that deliver lopsided Democratic majorities. Loyal Republican voters are spread more evenly across suburbs, smaller cities, and rural areas, so that fewer Republican votes are "wasted" in highly skewed districts.

The Republicans' sweeping national victory in 2010 enabled them to strengthen this structural advantage by giving them control of the redistricting process in eighteen states with a total of 202 House seats. Democrats controlled the process in only six states with a total of forty-seven seats. (In twelve of the remaining states, the parties shared control; seven were redistricted by commissions, and seven were single-district states.) Republican-controlled states made the most of this gerrymandering opportunity. To see this, we can use the *Cook Political Report*'s Partisan Voting Index (PVI), which is computed as the difference between the average district-level presidential vote in 2004 and 2008 and the national presidential vote averages for these elections.[a] For example, the national average of the Democratic presidential vote in these two elections was 51.2 percent, so a district with a two-election average of 54.2 percent would have a PVI of +3, whereas a district with an average of 48.2 percent would have a PVI of –3.

Republicans already held a considerable advantage by this measure before the 2012 redistricting, with 210 Republican-leaning districts (defined here as having a partisan voting index less than –2) compared with 175 Democratic-leaning districts (index greater than 2); the remaining fifty districts were balanced, with indexes between –2 and +2 (see the table in this box). After redistricting, there were eleven more Republican-leaning districts, five fewer Democratic-leaning districts, and six fewer balanced districts. This result was clearly intended; where Republicans controlled redistricting, the party gained sixteen favorable districts while the Democrats lost one and balanced districts were reduced by eleven.

Once the votes were counted, House election results matched district leanings with remarkable consistency. Only ten Democrats won Republican-leaning districts in 2012, and not a single Republican won in a Democratic-leaning district. The balanced districts were divided almost perfectly in half. These distributions changed only modestly in 2014 despite the Republicans' strong showing nationally. In 2016, with the PVI recalculated using the 2008 and 2012 presidential votes, both the Republican advantage and the extremely close match of results to district partisanship remained. In the "blue wave" election of 2018, however, the Democrats' national vote margin of 8.6 percentage points was large enough to overcome their structural disadvantage, delivering their largest net gain since 1974, forty seats. They won twenty-four seats in Republican-leaning districts (mostly in upscale suburbs) as well as all but two of the balanced districts to reach their 235–200 majority. But they might have done even better if Republican gerrymanders had not proven so effective in several states. In Ohio, the Democrats' share of House votes cast rose from 40 percent to 48 percent from 2014 to 2018, but they still won only the same four of the state's sixteen seats; in North Carolina, their vote share rose from 44 percent to 49 percent, but their seat share remained unchanged at three of thirteen; in Wisconsin, the Democratic vote rose from 47 percent to 54 percent without changing the Republicans' 5–3 seat advantage. In

Pennsylvania, by contrast, after the state supreme court determined that Republicans violated the state constitution and compelled new districts to be drawn (hence the totals in each column for 2018 do not match 2016), the Democrats ended up winning nine of the state's eighteen seats, up from four in 2014, as their vote share rose from 44 percent to 55 percent. Gerrymandering did not preserve the Republicans' House majority in 2018, then, but it did reduce their losses.

| CONTROL OF REDISTRICTING AND CHANGES IN DISTRICT PARTISANSHIP, 2010–2018 ||||
|---|---|---|---|---|
| CONTROL OF REDISTRICTING | | DEMOCRAT > 2 | BALANCED | REPUBLICAN > 2 |
| All districts | 2010 | 175 | 50 | 210 |
| | 2012 | 170 | 44 | 221 |
| | Change | −5 | −6 | +11 |
| Republican control | 2010 | 51 | 24 | 123 |
| | 2012 | 50 | 13 | 139 |
| | Change | −1 | −11 | +16 |
| Other control | 2010 | 124 | 26 | 87 |
| | 2012 | 120 | 31 | 82 |
| | Change | −4 | +5 | −5 |
| *Election Results, 2012* | | | | |
| Democrat won | | 170 | 21 | 10 |
| Republican won | | 0 | 23 | 211 |
| *Election Results, 2014* | | | | |
| Democrat won | | 166 | 16 | 6 |
| Republican won | | 4 | 28 | 215 |
| *Election Results, 2016* | | | | |
| Democrat won | | 178 | 13 | 3 |
| Republican won | | 2 | 29 | 220 |
| *Election Results, 2018* | | | | |
| Democrat won | | 174 | 37 | 24 |
| Republican won | | 4 | 2 | 194 |

*Note:* District partisan advantage is based on the *Cook* PVI; see text for a description.

[a]David Wasserman and Ally Flinn, "Introducing the 2017 Cook Political Report Partisan Index," *The Cook Political Report*, April 7, 2017, at https://www.cookpolitical.com/introducing-2017-cook-political-report-partisan-voter-index.

# The Original Gerrymander

Library of Congress

The practice of "gerrymandering"—the extensive manipulation of the shape of a legislative district to benefit a certain incumbent or party—is probably as old as the Republic, but the name originated in 1812. That year, the Massachusetts legislature carved out of Essex County a district that historian John Fiske said had a "dragonlike contour." When the painter Gilbert Stuart saw the misshapen district, he penciled in a head, wings, and claws and exclaimed, "That will do for a salamander!" Editor Benjamin Russell replied, "Better say a Gerrymander"—after Elbridge Gerry, then governor of Massachusetts.

Modified twice before receiving final Court approval, the districts had some of their rough edges smoothed off but retained all the earmarks of a painstaking gerrymander. The post-2010 North Carolina districts were again successfully challenged in court on racial grounds, and the lines in place under court order for the 2016 election modified the First and radically altered the Twelfth. The North Carolina legislature responded by drawing new lines, this time as an explicitly partisan gerrymander intended to assure Republicans would win ten of the state's thirteen House seats even with less than half the statewide vote. A U.S. district court ruled this map unconstitutional but not in time for new lines to be drawn before the 2018 election, in which Democratic candidates won 49 percent of the House vote statewide but still only their current three seats.

## Unequal Representation in the Senate

The fifty Senate constituencies—entire states—may not change boundaries with each census, but they vary greatly in size of population. Senator Dianne Feinstein, D-Calif., represents nearly forty million people, whereas Senator Mike Enzi, R-Wyo., has fewer constituents (574,000) than does the average U.S. representative (750,000). The nine largest states are home to 51 percent of the total U.S. population, whereas the smallest twenty-six states, with 52 percent of Senate seats, hold only 18 percent of the population. Unequal Senate representation currently favors Republicans, who tend to do better in the smaller states.*

---

*In the 116th Congress, Republicans held 60 percent of the Senate seats in the twenty-nine states with seven or fewer House districts, whereas Democrats held 57 percent of the seats in the twenty-one states with more than seven districts.

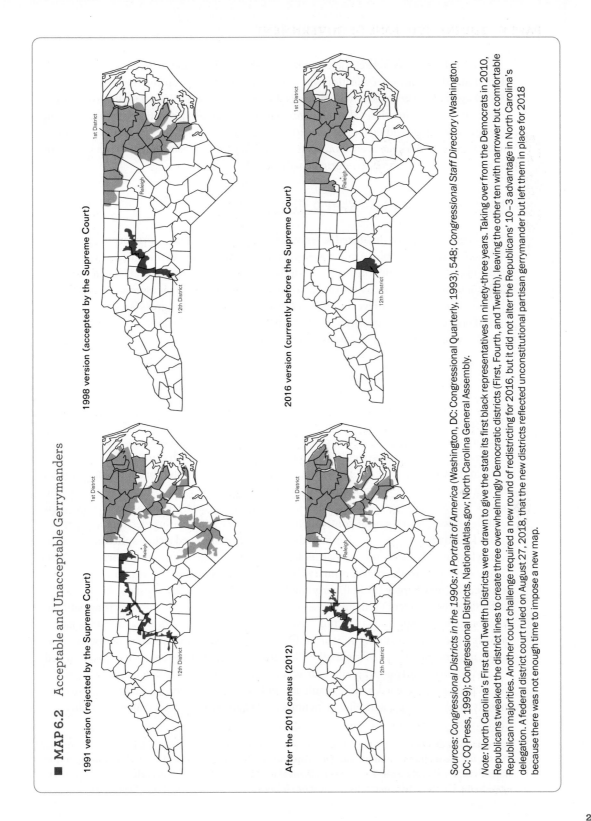

■ **MAP 6.2** Acceptable and Unacceptable Gerrymanders

1991 version (rejected by the Supreme Court)

1998 version (accepted by the Supreme Court)

After the 2010 census (2012)

2016 version (currently before the Supreme Court)

*Sources: Congressional Districts in the 1990s: A Portrait of America* (Washington, DC: Congressional Quarterly, 1993), 548; *Congressional Staff Directory* (Washington, DC: CQ Press, 1999); Congressional Districts, NationalAtlas.gov; North Carolina General Assembly.

*Note:* North Carolina's First and Twelfth Districts were drawn to give the state its first black representatives in ninety-three years. Taking over from the Democrats in 2010, Republicans tweaked the district lines to create three overwhelmingly Democratic districts (First, Fourth, and Twelfth), leaving the other ten with narrower but comfortable Republican majorities. Another court challenge required a new round of redistricting for 2016, but it did not alter the Republicans' 10–3 advantage in North Carolina's delegation. A federal district court ruled on August 27, 2018, that the new districts reflected unconstitutional partisan gerrymander but left them in place for 2018 because there was not enough time to impose a new map.

Until 1913 senators were chosen by state legislatures. Most Americans had long since concluded that this method of selection was undemocratic and corrupting (between 1890 and 1905 charges of bribery shadowed Senate elections in seven states).[12] But it took the reforming spirit of Progressivism at its peak to convince senators to agree to a constitutional amendment (the Seventeenth) providing for popular election.[13] As it turned out, they had little to fear from the change; senators have been about as successful in winning reelection as they had been in persuading state legislatures to return them to office.*

## Congress and Electoral Politics

The modern Congress is organized to serve the goals of its members. A primary goal for most of them is to keep their jobs. And because voters have the final say in their hiring and firing, a career in Congress depends on members winning the voters' endorsement at regular intervals. Reelection is not their only objective, but winning regular reelection is essential to everything else members want to achieve in office. A rewarding career in Congress is also much more likely if one serves in the majority party, so a party victory is also a major goal. Electoral imperatives thus shape all important aspects of congressional life.

### Candidate-Centered versus Party-Centered Electoral Politics

The electoral environment that members of Congress must negotiate to win and hold their seats has undergone notable changes over time, varying between more party-centered and more candidate-centered systems. During much of the nineteenth century, the system was predominantly party centered. Party-line voting was prevalent; voters based their choices on the top of the ticket—the presidential candidates in presidential election years—and on the parties' platforms. Congressional candidates' fates were decided by national trends they could do little personally to shape or control. Changes in the laws regulating elections and parties around the turn of the century weakened parties and encouraged **ticket-splitting**—that is, voting for candidates of different parties for different offices.[14] The most important of these changes was the introduction of primary elections for choosing the parties' nominees and the secret ballot (see Chapter 12). Still, party conflicts over national policy, most notably the political battles over President Franklin Roosevelt's New Deal, continued to inject a strong national component into congressional elections until the 1950s. As the New Deal controversies faded, however, the party coalitions built around them fractured under the stress of divisive new issues, most prominently civil rights, the Vietnam War, and social issues such as abortion and the environment. Party lines became blurred, and party loyalty among voters declined.

As party ties weakened, a more candidate-centered electoral process emerged. The decline in party loyalty among voters offered incumbents a chance to win votes that once would have

---

*A remaining democratic anomaly is the absence of representation of any kind, in the Senate or the House, for the six hundred thousand Americans who live in Washington, D.C. Citizens living in the nation's capital do get to vote for three presidential electors, however. They also elect a nonvoting delegate to the House of Representatives (Eleanor Holmes Norton during the 116th Congress).

gone routinely to the other party's candidate. Members sought to expand their electoral base by emphasizing individual character, legislative performance, and constituency services, encouraging voters to use such criteria in deciding how to vote.[15] Realizing that the growth of candidate-centered electoral politics worked to the advantage of incumbents willing to build a personal following, members of Congress voted themselves greater resources for servicing their states and districts—that is, higher allowances for staff, travel, local offices, and communication. These allowances are now worth more than $1.2 million annually per legislator in the House and up to three times as much per senator, depending on the population of the state represented.[16] Electoral data demonstrate the success of these efforts. The House incumbency advantage, measured in the extra share of votes a candidate typically received by running as an incumbent (see Figure 6.1)[17], rose from 1 to 2 percentage points prior to the mid-1960s to an average of 8 percentage points in elections from 1966 through 2002. Since then, however, it has declined sharply and in the four most recent elections was back to the low levels typical of the 1950s.[18]

In the earlier period, incumbents were successful largely because they represented districts that voted consistently for one party's candidates. From the mid-1960s through the 1980s, they became much more successful in winning in districts where their party did not have a natural majority. Since then, incumbents have continued to win at high rates but to an increasing extent because they represent districts with electorates that favor their parties' candidates, incumbent or not.

■ **FIGURE 6.1**    The Incumbency Advantage in U.S. House Elections, 1952–2018 (Average of Three Measures)

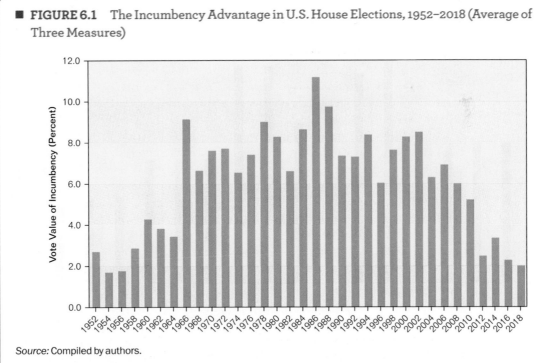

*Source:* Compiled by authors.

*Note:* See endnote 17 for a description of this index.

The changing ability of congressional candidates to win against the partisan grain, measured by their ability to win a state or district their party's presidential candidate lost, is illustrated in Figure 6.2. Both House and Senate candidates were unusually successful in winning seats in the other party's presidential territory in the 1970s and 1980s, but such victories have since become rarer. They were particularly scarce in 2012, when only twenty-six of the 435 House districts delivered a split verdict, and again in 2016 when, for the first time in history, every Senate contest was won by the party that won the state's electoral votes. This trend reflects the growth in party-line voting discussed in Chapter 12 and the decline in the ability of incumbents (and other candidates) to separate themselves from their party's collective fate. In particular, electoral fortunes of congressional candidates are increasingly tied to those of their presidential candidates; the correlations between the vote shares won by presidential candidates and congressional candidates at the state and district levels have become much stronger in recent years (see Figure 6.3).* Congressional elections are increasingly treated by voters as national events, with presidents and presidential candidates as a major focus. The 2018 midterm election was the most nationalized, president-centered midterm election yet observed, with the correlation between the House and presidential vote two years earlier at a record 0.97 and with the smallest incumbency advantage since the 1950s (see Figure 6.1).[19]

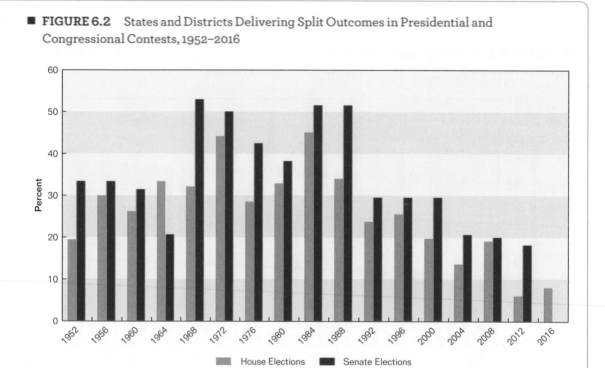

■ **FIGURE 6.2**   States and Districts Delivering Split Outcomes in Presidential and Congressional Contests, 1952–2016

*Source:* Compiled by author.

---

*Correlations take values from 0.0 (no relationship at all) to 1.0 (a perfect relationship).

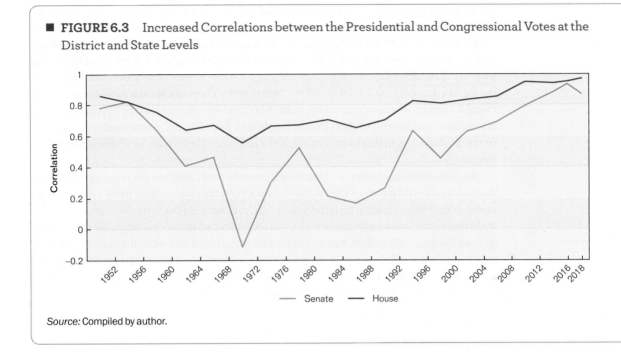

■ **FIGURE 6.3** Increased Correlations between the Presidential and Congressional Votes at the District and State Levels

*Source:* Compiled by author.

The emergence of a more nationalized, party-centered electoral process has contributed directly to the increase in the partisan and ideological polarization in the House and Senate, discussed later in this chapter, for it has given the congressional parties much more distinctly partisan electoral constituencies. For example, back in 1976, the average vote for Democratic presidential candidate Jimmy Carter in House districts won by Democrats was 56 percent, whereas the average vote for Carter in districts won by Republicans was 45 percent, a difference of 11 percentage points. This gap has grown steadily since then; in 2016, Trump's average vote in districts won by Republicans was 62 percent, whereas his average in districts won by Democrats was 33 percent, a difference of 29 percentage points. The comparable gap between states won by Republican and Democratic senators was 6 points in 1976 and 19 points in 2016. With their constituencies so far apart politically, the congressional parties have found it increasingly difficult to find common ground where mutually agreeable compromises are feasible.

## National Politics in Congressional Elections

The resurgence of party- and president-centered voting over the past two decades has strengthened the national component of congressional election politics, but even during the heyday of locally focused, candidate-centered elections, national forces continued to have a palpable effect on electoral fates and thus the partisan composition of Congress. In midterm elections the president's party almost always loses congressional seats, but the size of its losses depends in part on the performances of the national economy and the president. Losses tend to be fewer when the economy is booming and the president is popular and greater when the economy or the administration's popularity sags. Thus, George W. Bush's leadership in the war on terrorism produced high approval ratings in 2002 that helped his party achieve small gains in the House and Senate, a rarity for the president's party in midterm elections. With Bush's ratings 25 points lower in 2006, Democrats picked up enough seats to take control of both chambers. In 2010 high unemployment, public dissatisfaction with the direction of the economy, and Barack Obama's mediocre approval ratings cost the Democrats sixty-four House and six Senate seats. Despite a robust national economy, Donald Trump's low approval ratings in 2018 (around 40 percent) cost the Republicans forty House seats and control of that chamber, although Republicans maintained control of the Senate by defeating incumbents in four of the ten states Democrats were defending where Trump had won in 2016.

As these elections showed so dramatically, members of Congress can no longer dissociate themselves from their party's fate, so they retain a personal stake in their party's public image as well as the public standing of the president. Nor can they separate themselves from Congress itself, though incumbents frequently try to do so. Individual members remain far more popular than Congress collectively, but they still suffer at the ballot box when the public's normally mild hostility toward Congress becomes intense, at least if one party controls both chambers and thus absorbs all the blame. Individual members cannot do much about such sentiments by themselves, so they often focus on personal efforts that can make a difference.

### Serving Constituents

Recognizing that they hold their jobs at the sufferance of sometimes-fickle electorates, members of Congress are highly responsive to their constituencies. Decisions on legislative issues are shaped by the potential need to explain and defend them in future campaigns.[20] This includes future primary campaigns; for many members now representing districts safe for their parties, the biggest threat to reelection comes from primary challengers. Most members also spend a great deal of time back home, keeping in touch and staying visible. They solicit and process **casework**, requests from constituents for information and help in dealing with government agencies. A lost Social Security check? A bureaucratic mix-up over veterans' benefits? A representative or senator (or more precisely, their staff) is ready to help.

### Vulnerable Senators

Although senators have engaged in many of the same constituency-building activities as representatives, they have never been as successful in keeping their jobs, and now they, too, find it more difficult to win states where the other party is ascendant. Since 1946 their overall rate of reelection, 80 percent, has left them three times more likely to lose their seats than House incumbents. But because senators face reelection only one-third as often, tenure in office tends to even out between the chambers. Even when Senate incumbents do win, their margins of victory tend to be narrower than those of representatives. Senate incumbents win less consistently and typically by narrower margins for several reasons. States (other than the seven with only one representative) are more populous and diverse than congressional districts and are thus more likely than congressional districts to have balanced party competition. Senate races attract a larger proportion of experienced, politically talented, well-financed challengers. They also usually fit media markets—formed by cities and their suburbs reached by local TV and radio stations and newspapers—better than House districts, making it easier for challengers to get out their messages. And finally, senators are more readily associated with controversial and divisive issues, and they do not have the pressure of a two-year election cycle to keep them attuned to the folks back home.

## Representation versus Responsibility

Different electoral processes produce different forms of representation. In a party-centered electoral process, for example, legislators represent citizens by carrying out the policies promised by the party

The 2018 midterm elections were the most nationalized in modern American history and were centered on the highly polarizing figure of President Donald Trump. Democrats' ads sought to link the Republican to Trump and his policies in areas where both were unpopular—illustrated by this ad run in Republican Barbara Comstock's suburban Virginia House district—while Republican candidates trumpeted their support for Trump where he was popular. Comstock lost her reelection bid.

winning a majority of seats. Legislators know they will be held responsible by voters for their party's performance in governing, so ensuring the success of their party and the government takes top priority.

The candidate-centered electoral process that flourished during the long period of Democratic control prior to 1994 gave members of Congress far more incentive to be individually responsive than collectively responsible. Trends since then have reduced but by no means eliminated this imbalance, which is a primary source of Congress's collective action problems. For example, electoral logic induces members to promote narrowly targeted programs, projects, or tax breaks for constituents or campaign contributors without worrying about the impacts of such measures on spending or revenues. Recipients notice and appreciate such specific and identifiable benefits and show their gratitude at election time. Because the benefits come at the expense of general revenues (money supplied by the taxes that everyone pays), no one's share of the cost of any specific project or tax break is large enough to notice. Thus it makes political sense for members of Congress to pursue local or group benefits that are paid for nationally even if the costs clearly outweigh the benefits. Conversely, no obvious payoff arises from opposing any particular local or group benefit because the savings are spread so thinly among taxpayers that no one notices.

The pursuit of reelection therefore makes logrolling—a legislative practice in which members of Congress offer reciprocal support to each other's vote-gaining projects or tax breaks—an attractive strategy (see Chapter 2). But this situation creates a classic prisoner's dilemma. When everyone follows such an individually productive strategy, all may end up in worse shape politically when shackled with collective blame for the overall consequences. Spending rises, revenues fall, the deficit grows, government programs proliferate, and the opposition attacks the logrolling coalition—in practice, the majority party—for wastefulness and incompetence. Individual responsiveness leads to collective irresponsibility.

Democratic candidates suffered across the board in 2010 as voters turned against the aggregate consequences of collective irresponsibility: a government they perceived as too big, too expensive, and too inept. To demonstrate that they were different, the triumphant Republicans promised to shrink government, cut taxes, and change how the government operates. In particular, many pledged to abstain from **earmarks**—items individual members routinely insert into spending bills or revenue bills providing special benefits to their states, districts, and campaign contributors. Although earmarks account for less than one-half of 1 percent of federal spending, they are easy targets of public criticism—**"pork barrel" legislation** always turns up projects of dubious worth*—and was especially scorned by the Republican Party's very conservative Tea Party wing, so forgoing earmarks was thought to have considerable symbolic importance. House Republicans adopted rules inhibiting earmarks, but a true end to earmarking and pork-barreling would be a remarkable transformation. Most members are convinced that delivering such local benefits pays important electoral dividends. A comment by Michele Bachmann, R-Minn., a leading voice of the Tea Party faction at the time, suggests that symbolism does not necessarily trump more practical considerations: "Advocating for transportation projects for one's district does not in my mind equate to an earmark."[21] The budget bill passed early in 2018 was replete with provisions looking suspiciously like earmarks, and one estimate put their price at $14.7 billion, more than five times as much as in 2014.[22]

## Who Serves in Congress?

The people who win seats in the Senate and House are by no means "representative" of the American people in any demographic sense. Almost all members have graduated from college; law (41 percent) and business (39 percent) were the most common prior occupations in the 115th Congress, followed by education (19 percent). A large majority are professionals of one kind or another; only a handful have blue-collar backgrounds. Most have served in lower elected offices. The true vocation of the average member is, in fact, politics.

Women and racial minorities continue to be underrepresented in Congress, though their numbers have been increasing (see Figures 6.4 and 6.5). In 1961 only three African Americans and twenty women held House or Senate seats; by 1981 the number of black members had grown to seventeen, and only one more woman had been added. Growth continued to be slow until 1992, when the number of African Americans and Hispanics in the House increased sharply after the 1982 Voting Rights Act was interpreted to require states to maximize the number of "majority-minority" districts when drawing new district lines. The 1992 election also saw women candidates and campaign donors mobilized in unprecedented numbers in response to an event widely publicized in 1991: the insensitive handling by an all-male Senate committee of sexual harassment charges made by college professor Anita Hill against Supreme Court nominee Clarence Thomas. In 2018, Donald Trump's rhetoric and actions on health care, immigration, reproductive rights, sexual harassment, and the environment provoked a remarkable upsurge in women's electoral involvement on the Democratic side. Of the 254 nonincumbent Democrats winning House nominations, 128 (50 percent) were women; counting incumbent Democrats, 181 of the party's 427 nominees (42 percent) were

---

*According to the C-SPAN Congressional Glossary, *pork barrel* came into use as a political term in the post–Civil War era. It comes from the plantation practice of distributing rations of salt pork to slaves from wooden barrels. When used to describe a bill, it implies the legislation is loaded with special projects for members of Congress to distribute to their constituents back home as an act of largesse, courtesy of the federal taxpayer.

■ **FIGURE 6.4** Women in Congress: Higher Numbers but Still Underrepresented

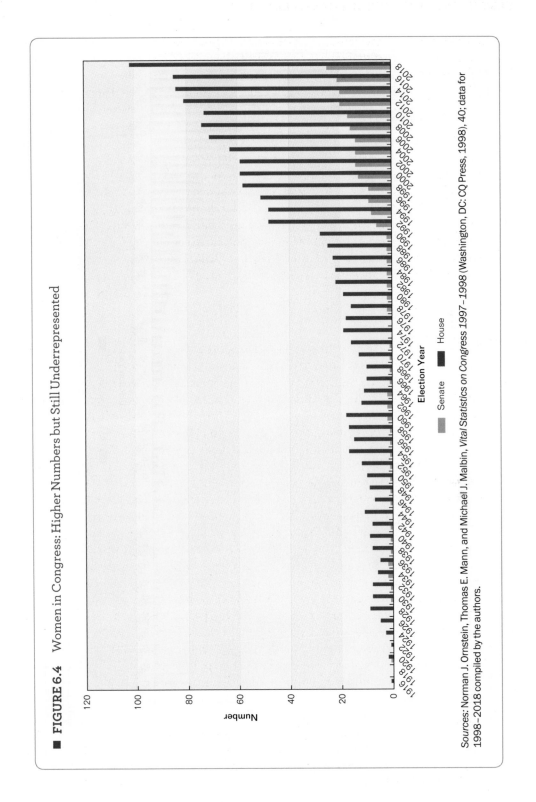

*Sources:* Norman J. Ornstein, Thomas E. Mann, and Michael J. Malbin, *Vital Statistics on Congress 1997–1998* (Washington, DC: CQ Press, 1998), 40; data for 1998–2018 compiled by the authors.

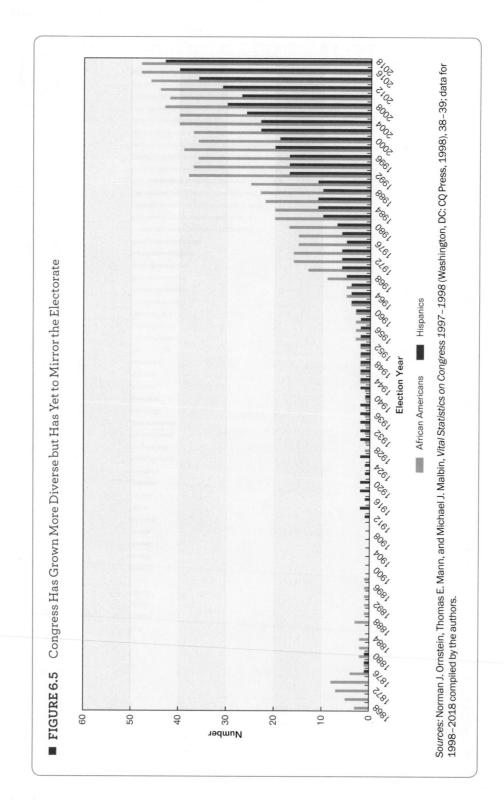

■ **FIGURE 6.5** Congress Has Grown More Diverse but Has Yet to Mirror the Electorate

*Sources:* Norman J. Ornstein, Thomas E. Mann, and Michael J. Malbin, *Vital Statistics on Congress 1997–1998* (Washington, DC: CQ Press, 1998), 38–39; data for 1998–2018 compiled by the authors.

women. About half of them won, and thirty-five of the sixty newly elected Democrats are women. All of these are record numbers.

After the 2018 elections, the Senate included twenty-five women, four Hispanics, three African Americans, and two Asian Americans; the House included 102 women, fifty-five African Americans, thirty-nine Hispanics, and eleven Asian Americans. The congressional parties differ sharply in diversity. In the 116th Congress (2019–2020), women and ethnic minorities made up a majority (61 percent) of the House Democratic membership; in contrast, white men constitute 90 percent of the Republican House

Emblematic of the changes in the House arriving with the new class of Democrats in the 116th Congress, Alexandria Ocasio-Cortez, a self-described Democratic Socialist of Puerto Rican descent, defeated ten-term incumbent Joseph Crowley in the primary and then went on to win the general election to become, at twenty-nine, the youngest woman ever elected to Congress.

membership. Seventeen of the twenty-five women Senators are Democrats, as are six of the nine ethnic minority Senators. All ten openly gay or bisexual members of Congress are Democrats; all but two Republicans are Christians, but more than 20 percent of Democrats are not. Altogether, 79 percent of congressional Republicans, but only 34 percent of congressional Democrats, are straight white Christian men. The congressional parties thus echo, to a greatly exaggerated degree, demographic differences in their electoral coalitions (see Chapter 12).

Congress remained overwhelmingly white and male for so long because white males predominated in the lower-level public offices and private careers that are the most common stepping-stones to Congress. As women and minorities have continued, albeit slowly, to assume a larger share of state and local offices and professional careers in law and business, their representation in Congress has continued to rise as well.

The gender and racial makeup of Congress makes a difference. For example, black members led the fight for sanctions punishing South Africa for its apartheid system in the 1980s. And the influx of women has made Congress far more attentive to issues of sex discrimination and sexual harassment.[23] The stark differences in diversity between the Republicans and Democrats elected to the 116th Congress may also contribute a demographic dimension to the growing ideological polarization of the congressional parties.

## Basic Problems of Legislative Organization

The Constitution established a basic framework for a national legislature, but today's Congress is the product of more than two centuries of institutional development. Although the House and Senate have evolved into highly complex institutions with remarkably elaborate and arcane rules, procedures, and customs, a logic underlies this sometimes bewildering complexity. To understand how Congress reflects the diverse and conflicting needs and intentions of its members, one must understand what representatives and senators want to accomplish and what obstacles they have to overcome to achieve their goals.

The delegates in Philadelphia created and empowered a national legislature—on paper at least; it was up to members of Congress to make the words into an institutional reality. To exercise the powers conferred on them by the Constitution, the House and Senate had to solve some basic problems: how to acquire information, how to coordinate action, how to resolve conflicts, and how to get members to work for common as well as personal goals. As these problems have become more acute over the years, members of Congress have scrambled to adapt the institution to cope with them more effectively while recognizing that every solution raises problems of its own. The challenges that spurred members to develop the modern Congress fall into two classes: problems besetting the House and Senate as organizations and problems arising from the competing individual and collective needs of members.

## Need for Information

Legislation is only as effective as the quality of knowledge underlying its inception. For example, a legislator cannot regulate the stock market sensibly without knowing how the market works or attack environmental pollution effectively without knowing how pollution is produced. As the United States has become more and more complex—socially, economically, and technologically—and the activities of the federal government have expanded, the informational demands on Congress have grown enormously.

Congress has responded with a solution common to the problem of performing complex social tasks efficiently: division of labor and specialization. The division of labor has given rise to the committee and subcommittee systems, large personal and committee staffs, and specialized research agencies that characterize the modern Congress. Specialists are able to develop a deeper understanding of their domains. By becoming specialists themselves or by drawing on the knowledge of other specialists, members of Congress can make better-informed decisions, and Congress, in turn, becomes a more effective institution. To provide the chamber with expertise, members must invest a lot of time and effort in mastering an area of specialization (as we learned earlier, public goods are more attractive in their consumption than in their production). Congress compensates members who master an area of specialization and supply specialized information with enhanced influence in their area of expertise. For example, unparalleled mastery of health care issues made Representative Henry A. Waxman, D-Calif., for many years the most influential House Democrat in this important policy area. One problem, however, is that specialists may dominate policymaking in their domains, shutting out the broader viewpoints of other members. Thus, the efficiencies gained by a division of labor are paid for by diminished participation in policymaking outside one's specialty.

## Coordination Problems

As noted in Chapter 1, any group of people trying to act in concert faces coordination problems. Coordination becomes more difficult—and necessary—the greater the group's workload and the more elaborate its division of labor. As the volume and complexity of Congress's work have grown, so has its need for traffic management: dividing up the work, directing the flow of bills through the legislative process, and scheduling debates and votes on the floor.

Coordination problems of this kind usually are solved by a group giving one or several of its members the authority to coordinate—that is, take on the role of "traffic cop." In Congress party leaders serve this function, but procedures also shape policy. Control over the agenda— deciding what gets voted on when—is a powerful legislative tool. For example, a majority of House members probably would have preferred to censure rather than impeach Bill Clinton in 1998, but the Republican House leaders refused to allow a vote on censure, leaving a vote for impeachment as the only alternative to letting the president off completely. (Had they allowed a vote on censure, Clinton probably would have avoided impeachment and trial in the Senate.) Members thus sacrifice a measure of their autonomy in return for the gains in efficiency accrued by delegating agenda control to party leaders.

## Resolving Conflicts

Legislation is not passed until the majorities in both houses agree to its passage. The rich pluralism of American society guarantees that resolving conflicts is a fundamental task of any institution that reflects America's diversity. Agreement requires successful politicking: getting people who are pursuing divergent, even conflicting, ends to take a common course of action. Even when there is a consensus on ends, Congress often must resolve disagreements about means. During the 108th Congress (2003–2004), for example, almost all members agreed that a major overhaul of intelligence gathering was needed to combat terrorist threats, but leaders had to reconcile competing ideas about what should replace the current system in order to reform intelligence. Disagreements that divide the parties fundamentally can be extremely difficult to resolve, as the struggles over health care policy attest.

Many of Congress's rules, customs, and procedures are aimed at resolving or deflecting conflicts so it can get on with the business of legislating. For example, when representatives speak on the floor of the House, all remarks are officially addressed to the Speaker, making it less likely that debates will degenerate into personal confrontations. More substantively, members delegate the task of building legislative coalitions to party leaders, who hold such positions by virtue of their demonstrated skills at negotiating legislative deals. The political parties in Congress themselves serve as ready-made coalitions. Party members agree on matters often enough to adopt a common label and to cooperate routinely on many—but by no means all—of the matters that come before the House and Senate. The presence of ready-made coalitions resolves many conflicts in advance, reducing the transaction costs of negotiating agreements on legislation. The price, however, is loss of autonomy to the party and of authority to leaders: individual members incur greater conformity costs because they cannot always do what is politically best for themselves rather than their party.

## Collective Action

Everyone who wins a seat in the House or Senate wants to belong to a well-informed, effective legislature capable of fulfilling its constitutional mandate. Moreover, senators and representatives run under party labels and so have a stake in their party's reputation. But all of them have personal interests as well: winning reelection or advancing to higher office by pleasing constituents and campaign contributors, enacting pet policies, and attaining influence and respect in Washington. The problem is that what members do to pursue individual goals— tax breaks for local firms, special projects for their constituents, maintaining their ideological purity by rejecting compromise—may undermine the reputation of their party or of Congress as a whole. The tension between individual and collective political welfare—the standard prisoner's dilemma—pervades congressional life. Congress has responded to the problem by developing devices such as the committee system that give members individual incentives to work for collectively beneficial ends. As noted, members who contribute to Congress's performance by becoming well informed about issues in their subcommittee's jurisdiction are rewarded with preeminent influence over policy in that area.[24] But as lawmaking has increasingly become centralized in the congressional parties in recent years, the incentives for specialization have weakened—and not to Congress's collective benefit.

## Transaction Costs

In trying to meet its many challenges, Congress must cope with another pressing problem: high transaction costs. These costs, as noted in Chapter 1, are literally the price of doing politics—the time, effort, and bargaining resources (favors to be exchanged) that go into negotiating agreements on action in the absence of agreement on the purposes of the action. Because many of the transaction costs involved in building legislative coalitions are unavoidable—such as the conflicts to be ironed out, compromises to be arranged, and favors to be traded—Congress has organized itself to reduce other transaction costs. One way is the use of fixed **rules** to automate decisions. For example, the **seniority rule**, by routinely allocating first choice in committee chairs, offices, and committee assignments to majority-party members who have served longest, reduces the time and energy members would otherwise put into competing for these valued positions. Another way is to follow precedent; battles over legislative turf, for example, are minimized by strict adherence to precedent in assigning bills to House committees. The pressing need to reduce transaction costs explains, then, why Congress does its work within an elaborate structure of rules and precedents. Like any attempt to reduce transaction costs, following precedent or seniority can have its own downside, for it inevitably increases the power of some members at the expense of others. Rules are never politically neutral.

## Time Pressures

The pressure to avoid unnecessary transaction costs is intensified by the ticking clock—both within the one-year session of Congress and over the two-year tenure of each Congress. The chief source of Congress's authority is its power of the purse over government revenue raising and spending. But if it fails to enact a federal budget in some form each year (or session), large portions of the federal government have to shut down, something that has actually happened twenty-one times in the past fifty years, on nine occasions for more than a week.[25] As budgets have grown larger, broader in scope, and, in recent years, more hotly contested, Congress often has found it difficult to enact them on schedule. Other legislation has to pass through all the hurdles (outlined later in this chapter) within the two-year life of a Congress. Bills in the pipeline but not enacted by the end of the second session of one Congress must be reintroduced in the next Congress.

The organization and rules of the House and Senate have evolved over two centuries through the accumulation of solutions deliberately chosen to overcome the pressing challenges just described (as well as, of course, to serve the immediate political needs of the majority then in power).[26] The much larger House experiences organizational problems more acutely than the Senate. Senators can get away with looser organization and retain more individual autonomy and equality simply because there are fewer of them. Their counterparts in the House, to solve their coordination problems, have to follow stricter rules of procedure and tolerate greater control by leaders.

## Organizing Congress

To preserve the House and Senate as the powerful legislative bodies envisioned in the Constitution, members of Congress have had to devise means to overcome the formidable barriers to effective collective action discussed in the previous section. The crucial institutional structures they have created to exercise, and therefore preserve, Congress's power in the federal system are the party and committee systems.

### The Parties

Decisions in the House and Senate are made (with a few important exceptions) by majority vote. Majorities not only enact bills but also set rules, establish procedures, choose leaders, and decide how to organize their respective houses. This reality creates powerful incentives for members of Congress to join and maintain durable coalitions—that is, political parties (for a broader analysis of the logic of party formation, see Chapter 12). What individual members give up in freedom to go their own way is more than made up for by what they can gain by cooperating with one another.

Parties do not arise through spontaneous, voluntary cooperation, however. Like other coalitions, political parties are formed when people recognize it is in their best interests to cooperate despite their disagreements. Party coalitions are assembled and maintained by party leaders. But leaders cannot lead without effective means to resolve conflicts, coordinate action, and induce members to cooperate when they are tempted to do otherwise. Members, in turn, must sacrifice independence by conceding some authority to party leaders. Yet as we noted in Chapter 1, when a group delegates authority to a leader to achieve coordination and reduce transaction costs, it risks incurring conformity costs and agency losses.

Members of Congress, aware of the risks, relinquish autonomy only so far as necessary, which accounts for the notable differences in the evolution of party leadership between the House and Senate as well as the changes over time in the power of House and Senate leaders.[27]

### Development of Congressional Parties

Parties began to form in the first session of the First Congress. A majority of members in the House favored the program for national economic development proposed by Alexander Hamilton, President George Washington's secretary of the Treasury, and worked together under his leadership to enact it. James Madison, a member of the House, and Thomas Jefferson, the secretary of state, led the opposition to what they saw as an unwarranted expansion of federal activity. These "factions" soon had names—Hamilton's Federalists and Jefferson's Republicans (later called Democratic-Republicans and then Democrats)—and party competition was under way. (See Chapter 12 for a fuller account of these developments.)

When the House and Senate divided into parties, congressional and party leadership merged. Formal leadership was established more quickly and more powerfully in the House because, because it was the larger and busier body, its collective action problems were more acute. Elected by the reigning majority, the **Speaker of the House** became the majority's leader and agent. Speakers were given the authority to appoint committees, make rules, and manage the legislative process on the majority party's behalf.

### Speaker of the House

Centralized authority reached its peak under Thomas Brackett "Czar" Reed, a Republican from Maine, who served as Speaker in the Fifty-First (1889–1890), Fifty-Fourth (1895–1896), and Fifty-Fifth (1897–1898) Congresses. Reed appointed all committees and committee chairs, exercised unlimited power of recognition (that is, decided who would speak on the floor of the House), and imposed new rules that made it much more difficult for a minority to prevent action through endless procedural delays. He also chaired the Rules Committee, which controlled the flow of legislation from the other committees to the floor of the House.

Although denounced by his opponents as a tyrant, Reed could not have amassed so much power without the full support of the Republican House majority. They were willing to delegate so much authority for two reasons. First, disagreements within the Republican Party were, at the time, muted; no important faction thought its interests could be threatened by a powerful leader allied with a competing faction. Second, service in the House had not yet become a career; the average member served only two terms. Without long-term career prospects and accustomed to party discipline, most members had little reason to object to strong leadership.

But once these conditions no longer held, the House revolted. Republican Speaker Joseph Cannon of Illinois (served 1903–1911) made the mistake of offending the progressive faction of the Republican Party that had emerged since Reed's day. In response, the Republican insurgents formed an alliance with Democrats who voted in 1910 to strip the Speaker of his power to appoint committees and chairs, forced him off the Rules Committee, and limited his power of recognition. The increasingly career-oriented membership

Joseph Cannon was the last of a generation of powerful Speakers of the House of Representatives. During his tenure as Speaker of the House, "Uncle Joe" swatted many an opponent. Too many of his victims were fellow Republicans, however, and in 1910 thirty-six of them joined with Democrats in the historic revolt that dismantled the strong Speaker system and decentralized House administration.

filled the power vacuum with a more decentralized and impersonal leadership structure, making seniority the criterion for selecting committee chairs. By weakening the Speaker, House members in effect chose to tolerate higher transaction costs to reduce their conformity costs.

The degree of consensus within a party continues to affect how much authority party members are willing to delegate to party leaders. In the 1970s, for example, the Democrats strengthened the hand of the Speaker and curbed the independence of committee chairs by making them subject to election by secret ballot in the Democratic Caucus (the organization of all House Democrats). The party had grown more cohesive as its conservative southern wing shrank (for reasons explained in Chapter 12), and so its members saw smaller potential conformity costs in centralizing. By the 1990s congressional Democrats were more unified than they had been in decades.[28]

Republicans granted even more authority to their leaders when in 1995 they took control of the House for the first time in forty-two years. Unified by the party's Contract with America, House Republicans made Newt Gingrich the most powerful Speaker since Cannon. At his behest, the Republican Conference (the Republican counterpart of the Democratic Caucus) ignored seniority in appointing committee chairs, ratifying without dissent the slate proposed by Gingrich. The Speaker also had a strong say in all committee assignments, which he used to reward loyal junior members. The new majority party also adopted a rule limiting committee chairs to three two-year terms, preventing anyone from building an independent committee domain. House Republicans gave their leader an unusually strong hand to overcome their coordination and other collective action problems because they believed that keeping their promise to act on every item in the Contract with America within one hundred days of taking office was crucial to their and their party's future electoral fates.

By 1997, however, House Republicans' unity had frayed badly, and one faction mounted a quickly aborted attempt to depose the Speaker. Gingrich hung on until Republican members, angry at the party's losses in the 1998 midterm election, forced him to resign—a pointed reminder that party leaders, as the majority's agents, are subject to dismissal if they do not satisfy their principals. Gingrich's eventual replacement, Dennis Hastert of Illinois, was able to maintain a high level of party unity, notably keeping his narrow but overwhelmingly conservative House majority together in support of the George W. Bush administration's legislative proposals. Leading the Democrats in opposition to the Bush administration after they won control of the 110th Congress (2007–2008) and in alliance with the Obama administration during the 111th Congress, Speaker Nancy Pelosi presided over the most unified Democratic majority in at least fifty years. Her leadership was crucial to Obama's major legislative victories on economic stimulus, health care reform, and economic regulation legislation.

The Republican majority after 2010 under Pelosi's successor, John Boehner, also sought to present a highly unified front on the House floor, although Boehner often found it hard to resolve intraparty disputes between the party's conventional conservatives and its more radically antigovernment faction associated with the Tea Party and, later, the Freedom Caucus. On several occasions during the 112th and 113th Congresses this faction's intransigence left Boehner no choice but to rely on a majority of Democratic votes to pass important legislation, breaking an unwritten rule that any legislation not supported by a majority of the House majority party will not be brought up for a vote. Under steady fire from his right, Boehner resigned in 2015, handing the chore of managing the fractious Republican majority to Paul

Ryan, who found it no easier than Boehner and retired from Congress in 2018. Pelosi is back leading the energized but far from unified Democratic majority in the 116th Congress, but she had to promise to limit the terms she and other senior party leaders would serve to quell internal opposition to her speakership. In sum, Congress is subject to what political scientists have labeled *conditional party government*, meaning that the degree of authority delegated to and exercised by congressional party leaders varies with—is conditioned by—the extent of election-driven ideological consensus among members.[29]

## Increased Partisanship

The decline and resurgence of congressional partisanship since the 1950s is evident in Figure 6.6. The proportion of "party unity" votes—those on which the party majorities took opposite positions—has increased since the 1970s (although more steeply and uniformly in the Senate than in the House). More importantly, as the party coalitions have become more homogeneous, the proportion of representatives and senators of both parties who vote with their party's majority on these party unity votes has risen steadily and was about 15 percentage points higher during the three most recent administrations than it was during the Nixon-Ford administration.

As the congressional parties became more unified, they also became more polarized along ideological lines. The ideological gap between the two parties in both houses of Congress has widened appreciably since the 1970s (see Figure 6.7) and reached its widest point since Reconstruction in the 115th Congress (2017–2018). Republicans have grown, on average, steadily more conservative, accounting for most of the polarization. But Democrats have also become more liberal as their party's conservative southern members were gradually replaced in Congress by Republicans, leaving the remaining southern Democrats ideologically more similar to other congressional Democrats. Ideological polarization thus helped to unite the parties internally, separate them from each other, and strengthen party leaders.

### Party Organization

The majority party in the House is led by the Speaker of the House, whose chief assistants are the **majority leader** and the **majority whip** (see Table 6.1 for a list of major-party offices and organizations in the House and Senate). The structure of the minority party, the Republicans in the 116th Congress (2019–2020), is similar to that of the majority party but without the Speaker; the minority leader is its head. The party whips head up the whip organization—the members who form the communication network connecting leaders with other members— whose purpose is to help solve the party's coordination problems. (The term *whip* comes from Great Britain, where the "whipper-in" keeps the hounds together in a pack during a foxhunt.) In addition to these official party committees, the Rules Committee is, in effect, an instrument of the majority party.

Party members give House party leaders resources for inducing members to cooperate when they are tempted to go their own way as free riders (for example, by breaking ranks on roll-call votes to enhance their own electoral fortunes). These resources mainly take the form of favors the leaders may grant or withhold. For example, party leaders have a strong voice in all committee assignments (officially the province of the Steering Committees); Speaker Boehner used this influence prior to the 113th Congress (2013–2014) to strip four

## ■ FIGURE 6.6　Rising Party Unity in Congress

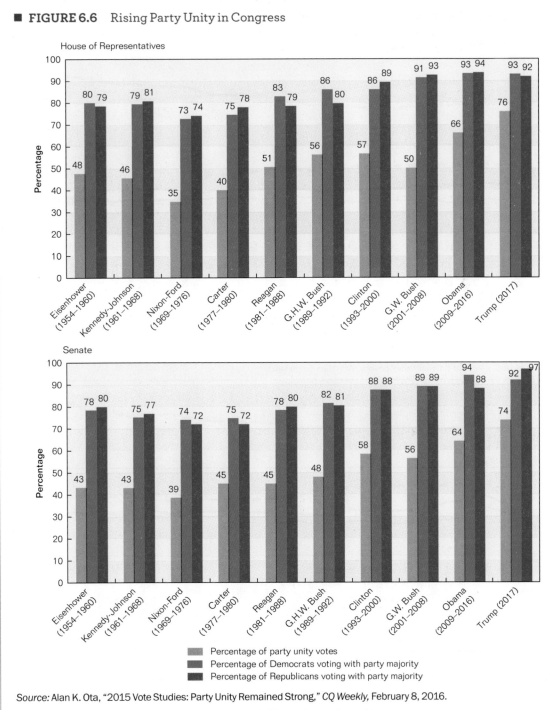

*Source:* Alan K. Ota, "2015 Vote Studies: Party Unity Remained Strong," *CQ Weekly,* February 8, 2016.

*Note:* Party unity votes are those votes on which party majorities took opposite positions.

■ **FIGURE 6.7**    The Widening Ideological Gap between the Parties

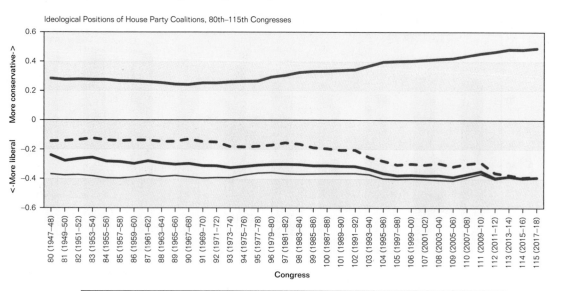

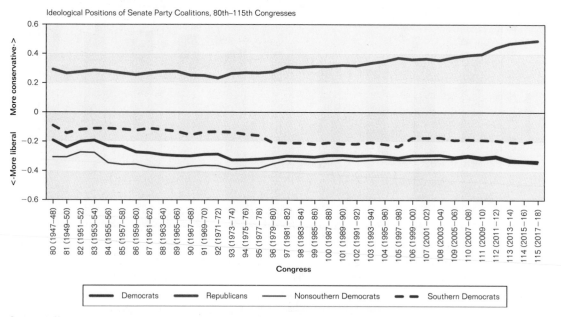

*Source:* Jeff Lewis, "Polarization in Congress," at https://www.voteview.com/articles/party_polarization.

Republicans of their plum committee assignments for bucking his leadership too flagrantly and as a warning to other potentially disloyal members.[30] Leaders also control the legislative agenda. Because a place on the agenda is a scarce resource, scheduling decisions determine the fates of many bills. Leaders also choose how much of their own time, energy, and organizational resources to devote to each legislative proposal. In the past, they have also controlled access to pork, routinely using earmarked projects to win support of wavering members; Boehner's 2011 pledge to ban earmarks thus deprived him of an important customary bargaining resource.[31] Party leaders can also help with reelection campaigns, especially the fund-raising component. Party leaders are therefore in a position to make it easier (or more difficult) for members to attain positions of influence, shape policy, and win reelection.

House party leaders are members' agents, however—not their bosses. They do not hire and fire party members; voters do, and so voters come first. Members, then, choose the style of leadership they believe will best serve their goals. Party leaders are elected or reelected to their positions at the beginning of every Congress, so the principals can regularly review their agents' performance. In the pre-Gingrich decades when Democrats held a majority of seats, they chose leaders, such as Thomas "Tip" O'Neill of Massachusetts (majority leader, 1973–1977; Speaker 1977–1987), who were experts on procedure rather than policy and who cared more about building successful coalitions than about achieving specific legislative goals. But when the Republicans took over the majority in 1995, Speaker Gingrich pursued a legislative agenda much more policy and ideologically focused than those undertaken by the Democratic Speakers before him. This has since become the norm for Speakers of both parties.

For the minority party in the House, legislative leadership is less crucial because the party's legislative role has usually been modest. When the party balance is very close, minority leaders can sometimes influence legislation by forming alliances with more moderate members of the majority party, although this has happened rarely in recent Congresses. When

**TABLE 6.1**   Party Committees and Leaders in Congress

| HOUSE OF REPRESENTATIVES | |
| --- | --- |
| **DEMOCRATS** | **REPUBLICANS** |
| Speaker | |
| Majority leader | Minority leader |
| Majority whip | Minority whip |
| Caucus (all Democrats) | Conference (all Republicans) |
| Steering Committee | Steering Committee |
| Policy Committee | Policy Committee |
| Democratic Congressional Campaign Committee | National Republican Congressional Committee |
| **SENATE** | |
| **REPUBLICANS** | **DEMOCRATS** |
| President pro tempore | |
| Majority leader | Minority leader |
| Assistant majority leader (whip) | Assistant minority leader (whip) |
| Conference (all Republicans) | Conference (all Democrats) |
| Policy Committee | Policy Committee |
| National Republican Senatorial Committee | Steering and Outreach Committee |
| | Democratic Senatorial Campaign Committee |

*Source:* Compiled by authors.

*Note:* Table covers the 116th Congress (2019–2020).

the majority enjoys a wider margin, minority leaders can do little more than oppose and attack the majority to position their party for future electoral battles. This leaves them in a bind when a president of their party sits in the White House, because the president has to cut deals with the majority to accomplish anything at all. When the other party holds the White House, they are freer to engage in unalloyed opposition, a strategy for winning a majority and moving up to the Speakership pursued successfully by Gingrich, Pelosi, and Boehner, and again by Pelosi.

## Parties and Party Leaders in the Senate

Over the years the Senate has been slower than the House to develop formal leadership positions, and senators have never delegated as much authority to their leaders as have representatives. Senators initially saw themselves as ambassadors from sovereign states and as such could accept no less than equal rights with one another. In the years since, they have retained wide freedom of individual action because, with its smaller size, the Senate is able to get by without elaborate procedural shackles.*

Under the Constitution, the vice president is the presiding officer of the Senate. The designated **president pro tempore** presides when the vice president is absent. But neither office has a real leadership role—after all, the vice president, who seldom presides, is not chosen by the Senate, and the president pro tempore, as the Latin term suggests, is formally a temporary position. In fact, in the first few Congresses a new president pro tempore was elected every time the vice president was away. In practice, no one led the Senate during the pre–Civil War period. Parties formed in the Senate almost from the start, but party members were little inclined to delegate authority. The party caucuses did not take full control of committee appointments until 1846, after which they avoided intraparty conflicts over committee control by resorting to a strict seniority rule. Not until the end of the nineteenth century did senators concede the means to enforce party discipline—on procedural matters only—to party leaders. The positions of majority leader and minority leader were not formalized until 1913.

The power and influence exerted by Senate leaders have depended largely on their personal political skills and the extent of intraparty divisions. Lyndon Johnson, who led the Senate Democrats from 1953 until resigning to become vice president in 1961, exercised extraordinary influence over the Senate through skillful persuasion and manipulation. The resources at his disposal were no greater than those of other Senate leaders, but he used them to greater effect. No majority leader has since matched Johnson's fire or authority, and more

---

*The Senate began with twenty-six members and did not reach one hundred until 1959; the House already had exceeded one hundred members by 1793.

recent leaders have had a much more divided and contentious Senate to manage. Still, party leadership in the Senate remains more collegial and less formal than in the House. The minority party has greater influence in the Senate because so much of that body's business is conducted under **unanimous consent agreements** negotiated by party leaders. These agreements, which can be killed by a single objection, might govern, for example, the order in which bills are considered and the length of debate allotted to them. However, the majority party in the Senate is still at a considerable advantage because its leader strongly shapes, if not fully controls, the Senate's agenda. Hence the switch in party control to the Republicans in January 2015 por-

President pro tempore is now, by tradition, the majority member with the greatest Senate seniority. In the 106th Congress (1999–2000), ninety-six-year-old Strom Thurmond, a South Carolina Republican first elected to the Senate in 1954, filled the position. For the 116th Congress (2019–2020), the comparatively youthful Charles Grassley (R-Iowa), eighty-six, assumed the office. Grassley, pictured here, is third in line of presidential succession after Vice President Mike Pence and House Speaker Nancy Pelosi.

tended much more than a simple reshuffling of offices. Unanimous consent agreements serve as only the most extreme examples of the general rule: the capacity of House and Senate party leaders to lead depends largely on the willingness of party members to follow.

### Other Groups in Congress

Although parties are by far the most important of Congress's coalitions, members have formed dozens of other groups. Some are explicitly ideological (Republican Study Committee, Progressive Caucus, New Democrat Coalition, Blue Dog Coalition, Tea Party Caucus, Freedom Caucus). Others are based on demographics (Black Caucus, Hispanic Caucus, Asian Pacific American Caucus, Caucus for Women's Issues). Bipartisan groups form around shared regional interests (Mississippi River Caucus, Western Caucus, Ohio River Basin Caucus) and economic concerns (Steel Caucus, Automotive Caucus, Entertainment Industries Caucus, Biotechnology Caucus). Other groups focus on specific issues (Second Amendment Caucus, Victims' Rights Caucus, Human Rights Caucus). More than thirty foreign countries enjoyed the attention of a congressional caucus in the 115th Congress.

Such groups give members better access to information and allies on issues of special concern to them (or their constituents) that do not fit neatly into regular party or committee categories. The groups reflect the value of ready-made alliances in a system where success depends on building majority coalitions.

### The Committee Systems

The committee systems of the House and Senate are the second organizational pillar upholding the institutional power of Congress in the federal system. Although committee power has

Bill Pugliano/Getty Images

Although intense partisan rivals, Chuck Schumer, D-NY, and Mitch McConnell, R-Ky., confer regularly on procedural matters. The Senate's rules make it easy for a disgruntled minority to block action, so like it or not, McConnell has to accommodate Schumer, just as former majority leader Harry Reid, D-Nev., had to accommodate McConnell before Republicans won the Senate in the 2014 midterm election. Here, Schumer treats the Kentucky senator with a bottle of bourbon—from Brooklyn.

at times been used to frustrate party majorities and leaders, committees are ultimately subject to the majority party, and the committee and party systems are closely integrated and mutually dependent. House committees, like House party leaders, are more powerful than their counterparts in the Senate, again reflecting the need for tighter organization in the larger body.

### Evolution of Congressional Committees

The first Congresses delegated authority to committees sparingly. Instead, the House would turn itself into a Committee of the Whole (sitting as a committee, the House operates under a more flexible set of rules), frame a piece of legislation, elect a temporary committee to draft the bill, then debate and amend the bill line by line. After reassuming its guise as the House, it would vote on final passage.

From the start, this process was intolerably cumbersome. One early member, Fisher Ames of Massachusetts, likened it to trying to make a delicate etching with an elephant's foot.[32] Thus, the House began to delegate more and more work to permanent committees. Ten were in place by 1809, twenty-eight by 1825. Transaction costs were further reduced by having committee members appointed by the Speaker rather than elected. As the Speaker emerged as leader of the majority party, appointments became partisan affairs, and choice committee assignments became rewards for party loyalty and bargaining chips in campaigns for the Speakership.

The Senate was slower to set up permanent committees. Despite their smaller numbers and lighter workload, senators also found they were spending too much time on electing a new committee to draft each bill, and the Senate began to accumulate **standing committees**—those that exist from one Congress to the next unless they are explicitly disbanded. The initial twelve were established in 1816; by 1841 there were twenty-two. The Senate also was slower to delegate legislative action to committees and has never gone as far in this direction as the House. After the Senate's parties assumed the right to make committee assignments, seniority became the criterion for selecting committee chairs: the office was awarded to the majority-party member with the longest term of service on the committee. Reducing transaction and conformity costs, the seniority rule avoided two unwelcome alternatives: election, which would have led to divisive, time-consuming intraparty squabbles, and appointment by party leaders, which would have given the leaders more power than senators thought desirable or necessary.

## Types of Committees

The standing committees of the House and Senate embody Congress's division of legislative labor. Standing committees have fixed jurisdictions (that is, they always deal with the same legislative topics) and stable memberships, both of which facilitate specialization. Once appointed, a member in good standing (that is, one who has not flagrantly annoyed party leaders) can expect to keep the seat unless his or her party suffers large electoral losses. Party ratios on committees generally match party ratios in the House and Senate. A House party with a narrow overall majority usually gives itself somewhat larger committee majorities, and it always accords itself extra seats on the most important committees. The job security associated with standing committees gives committee members both the motive and the opportunity to become knowledgeable about policy issues under their committee's jurisdiction. Expertise brings influence—other members defer to the judgment of committee experts they trust—and therefore a chance to make a real difference in at least one area of national policy.

Although committee membership is generally stable, changes occur when legislators seize the opportunity to move up to the committees deemed more important and desirable than the others. At the top of the heap in both chambers are the money committees—the Ways and Means and the Appropriations Committees in the House, the Finance and the Appropriations Committees in the Senate—because their activities are so central to Congress's main source of power in the federal system, its control over the budget. The House and Senate Budget Committees share some of this prestige. Seats on the Senate Foreign Relations and Judiciary Committees also are in demand because of the Senate's special authority over treaties and diplomatic and judicial appointments. In the House the powerful Rules Committee, which controls the flow of legislation from committees to the floor, is especially attractive. Among the least desirable committees are those dealing with the internal administration of Congress, particularly its members' ethics; many members feel uncomfortable sitting in judgment on their colleagues.

## Committee Assignments

Assignments to committees are made by party committees under the firm control of senior party leaders and are ratified by the party membership. Members pursue committee assignments that allow them to serve special constituent interests as well as their own policy and power goals. For example, the Agriculture Committees attract members from farm states, and the Armed Services Committees attract members from regions with large military installations.

Because party leaders want to keep their followers in office, they are responsive to arguments that a particular assignment will help a member win reelection. Moreover, when members are assigned to the committees that best serve their personal and political interests, they will take committee work more seriously, making a larger contribution to their party's overall performance. The danger is that committees may become stacked with members whose views do not represent those of their party's majority. By and large, party leaders have managed to avoid this problem by judicious distribution of assignments, especially to the committees whose jurisdictions are most important to the party. A party's committee members are, like party leaders, the party's agents, and party majorities use their ultimate control over committee assignments to keep their agents responsive to the party's desires.[33]

Most committees are divided into subcommittees, many of which also have fixed juris-dictions and stable memberships. Like full committees, subcommittees encourage specializa-tion and, at the same time, reward members who develop expertise with special influence over their own small pieces of legislative turf. Both committees and, in the Senate, subcommittees come with staffs of experts to help members do their work. Most committee staffers report to committee and subcommittee chairs; the ranking minority committee members control a much smaller set of staff assistants.

In addition to the standing committees, Congress also forms special, select, joint, ad hoc, and conference committees. In theory, most **special committees** and **select committees** (the terms are interchangeable) are appointed to deal with specific problems and then disappear. A good example was the House's Select Committee on U.S. National Security and Military/Commercial Concerns with the People's Republic of China, appointed in 1998 to inves-tigate technology transfers to China and disbanded a year later after issuing a 1,016-page report detailing the loss of military secrets to that country and recommending steps to stop it. However, some special and select committees sometimes last through many Congresses—for example, the Senate's Special Committee on Aging has been around since 1961.

## Joint Committees

These are permanent committees composed of members from both chambers; the commit-tee leaderships rotate between the chambers at the beginning of each newly elected Congress. **Joint committees** gather information and oversee executive agencies but do not report leg-islation. One joint committee (Library) oversees the Library of Congress, the U.S. Botanic Garden, and public statuary; another (Printing) oversees the U.S. Government Printing Office and the arrangement and style of the *Congressional Record,* which publishes all of the speeches and debates on the floors of the House and Senate. **Conference committees** are appointed to resolve differences between the House and Senate versions of bills (see section "Making Laws" in this chapter). The committees of the 116th Congress are listed in Table 6.2.

## Committee Power

A century ago House committees were dominated by the Speaker, who appointed committee members and chairs. The revolt against Speaker Cannon in 1910 effectively transferred con-trol over committees to committee chairs, who, under the altered rules, owed their positions to seniority, not loyalty to their party or its leaders. By the 1950s both chambers were run by a handful of powerful committee chairs who could safely ignore the wishes of party majorities. Conservative southern Democrats, continually reelected from one-party strongholds, chaired the most powerful committees and cooperated with Republicans to thwart policies supported by a majority of Democrats, especially in the area of civil rights. The rules allowed chairs to run committees like dictators, and some of them did.

In 1959 frustrated younger liberals formed the Democratic Study Group (DSG) to take on the conservative Democrats, hoping that they could make up in numbers what they lacked in institutional clout. Over the next decade the DSG grew large enough to take over and revitalize the Democratic Caucus. The most important changes occurred after the 1974 election, when the public reaction to the Watergate scandal brought seventy-four new Democrats, eager for action and disdainful of seniority, into the House. At their instigation, the Democratic Caucus

**TABLE 6.2** Committees of the 116th Congress

| | PARTY RATIO | NUMBER OF SUBCOMMITTEES | | PARTY RATIO | NUMBER OF SUBCOMMITTEES |
|---|---|---|---|---|---|
| **House of Representatives** | | | **Senate 116th** | | |
| *Standing Committees* | | | *Standing Committees* | | |
| Agriculture | 26D:21R | 6 | Agriculture, Nutrition, and Forestry | 11R:10D | 5 |
| Appropriations | 30D:23R | 12 | Appropriations | 16R:15D | 12 |
| Armed Services | 31D:26R | 7 | Armed Services | 14R:13D | 7 |
| Budget | 19D:14R | — | Banking, Housing, and Urban Affairs | 13R:12D | 5 |
| Education and Labor | 28D:22R | 4 | | | |
| Energy and Commerce | 31D:24R | 6 | Budget | 11R:10D | — |
| Ethics | 5D:5R | — | Commerce, Science, and Transportation | 14R:12D | 6 |
| Financial Services | 34D:26R | 5 | | | |
| Foreign Affairs | 26D:21R | 6 | Energy and Natural Resources | 11R:9D | 4 |
| Homeland Security | 18D:13R | 6 | Environment and Public Works | 11R:10D | 6 |
| House Administration | 6D:3R | — | | | |
| Judiciary | 24D:17R | 5 | Finance | 15R:13D | 6 |
| Natural Resources | 23D:19R | 5 | Foreign Relations | 12R:10D | 7 |
| Oversight and Reform | 24D:18R | 6 | Health, Education, Labor and Pensions | 12R:11D | 3 |
| Rules | 9D:4R | 2 | Homeland Security and Governmental Affairs | 8R:6D | 3 |
| Science, Space, and Technology | 22D:15R | 5 | | | |
| Small Business | 13D:10R | 5 | Indian Affairs | 7R:6D | — |
| Transportation and Infrastructure | 37D:30R | 6 | Judiciary | 12R:10D | 6 |
| | | | Rules and Administration | 10R:9D | — |
| Veteran's Affairs | 16D:12R | 4 | Small Business and Entrepreneurship | 10R:9D | — |
| Ways and Means | 25D:17R | 6 | Veterans' Affairs | 7R:8D | — |
| *Select Committees* | | | *Select Committees* | | |
| Permanent Select Committee on Intelligence | 13D:9R | 4 | Select Committee on Ethics | 3R:3D | — |
| | | | Select Committee on Intelligence | 10R:9D | — |
| | | | Special Committee on Aging | 8R:7D | — |
| | | | Joint Economic Committee | 6R:4D | — |

*Source:* Compiled by authors.

*Note:* The two independents in the Senate organize with the Democrats and are included in the Democratic totals.

adopted a rule that forbade any individual from chairing more than one committee or sub-committee; this way, many more members could enjoy this privilege. Committee members and the caucus, rather than chairs, assumed control over committee rules, budgets, and sub-committee organization. Committee nominations were transferred from Democrats on the Ways and Means Committee, who had held this authority since the revolt against Cannon, to the caucus's own new Steering and Policy Committee.* The caucus itself elected commit-tee chairs by secret ballot (secrecy removed the threat of retaliation). In 1975 the caucus actu-ally deposed three committee chairs, all elderly southern conservatives, underlining the new reality that the party's majority, not strict seniority, would now have the final say in who runs committees.

These changes produced a more fragmented and decentralized committee system in which fully half of the Democrats in the House chaired a committee or subcommittee. Although members benefited individually, they found it more difficult to act collectively. The simultaneous strengthening of the Speaker's authority, described earlier, logically comple-mented these changes. The party leaders may have found the task of coordination more dif-ficult, but they also were given more tools (for example, control of nominations to the Rules Committee) to carry it out. The net effect was a strengthened party capacity for collective action and a decline in the power of conservative southern Democrats.

The new Republican majority that took over the House in 1995 revised committee rules to ensure that the legislative agenda outlined in its Contract with America would move swiftly to enactment. The new rules gave committee chairs greater control over subcommittees by authorizing them to appoint all subcommittee chairs and control the work of the majority's committee staff. But committee chairs themselves now had to report to the Speaker and were limited to three consecutive terms (six years) as chair. All these changes gave the Republican majority more control over its committees than any House majority had exercised since the early years of the twentieth century. Since then, Republicans have maintained **term limits** but otherwise usually respected seniority in appointing chairs; the Democrats follow seniority in choosing committee chairs and do not limit their terms.

### Jurisdiction

In the House, does international trade policy fall within the jurisdiction of the Energy and Commerce Committee or the Foreign Affairs Committee? Should education programs for veterans be handled in the Senate by Veterans Affairs or by Health, Education, Labor, and Pensions? Where does something like homeland security, which affects virtually every aspect of American life—transportation, energy, infrastructure, international trade, admin-istration of justice, national defense—fit? Moreover, such technical issues are overlaid with political agendas. Committees and subcommittees compete for jurisdiction over important policy areas, but the supply of legislative turf is always insufficient to meet the demand. Thus, it is not surprising that the House and Senate have altered the number and jurisdictions of their committees from time to time; nor is it surprising that such changes have been highly contentious.

---

*The Steering and Policy Committee was subsequently split into a Steering Committee, which retained the authority to make committee assignments, and a separate Policy Committee.

Over the past century, the House and Senate have trimmed their committee systems several times, notably in the Legislative Reorganization Act of 1946, which sharply reduced the number of standing committees in both chambers (from thirty-three to fifteen in the Senate; from forty-eight to nineteen in the House). The act also rearranged committee jurisdictions to reduce the overlap and confusion and to make the House and Senate systems more similar. Reductions were achieved by consolidation, however, so many former committees simply became subcommittees. The most recent committee changes occurred in 1995, when the victorious House Republicans abolished three standing committees and made other modest alterations in committee jurisdictions.

The political problem with trying to distribute committee jurisdictions more sensibly is that changes redistribute power and upset long-established relationships among committee members, administrative agencies, and interest groups. Nevertheless, Congress must rationalize jurisdictions occasionally, or the emergence of new issues will lead to turf battles, overlapping jurisdictions, uneven workloads, and confusion. For example, homeland security policy is so multifaceted that by one count made in 2003, eighty-eight congressional committees and subcommittees, which included as members every senator and all but twenty representatives, held jurisdiction over one or more of its components.[34] Outsiders (and a few insiders) advocated the creation of new committees in both houses to handle the new Department of Homeland Security's nominations, budget, and legislation and to oversee its operation. As one former deputy defense secretary put it, "If they don't create a separate oversight committee in the House and Senate, there's never going to be a functioning department. You can't create a new department if all the elements of the new department keep going back to their old bosses."[35] But members of Congress relinquish jurisdiction over important matters with great reluctance, and homeland security was no exception. Congress established the new department in 2002, but the House and Senate did not form new standing committees on homeland security until 2005. Powerful leaders of existing committees resisted giving up jurisdiction—and not only out of pure self-interest, for they could plausibly argue that the deep fund of experience and expertise, both of members and of staff, regarding the department's diverse component agencies (see Chapter 8) held by their old committee overseers might be lost if a new committee took full jurisdiction over them. The result could be enfeebled congressional oversight.[36]

Party leaders regularly cope with the problem of multiple jurisdictions by using **multiple referrals**—that is, sending bills, in whole or piece by piece, to several committees at the same time or in sequence. In the 108th Congress (2003–2004), for example, a bill to reorganize government intelligence operations was sent to thirteen House committees. In recent Congresses, about 20 percent of all bills and 40 percent of major bills have been subject to multiple referrals in the House.[37]

### The Money Committees

The "power of the purse" has inspired the most contentious jurisdictional fights. In the earliest years of government, revenue and spending bills were handled by Ways and Means in the House and Finance in the Senate. Then, during the 1860s, the spending power was transferred to a separate Appropriations Committee in each house to help deal with the extraordinary financial demands of the Civil War. Other committees in both houses later broke the

Appropriations Committees' monopoly on spending, and by 1900 authority over national finances was spread among nearly twenty House and Senate committees. In the House this devolution of authority was not such a great impediment to action when powerful Speakers dominated the chamber, but a few years after the revolt against Cannon the Republican House majority underlined its commitment to parsimony by restoring the Appropriations Committee's monopoly. The Senate followed suit in 1922.

Since then, legislative spending has been a two-step process in each chamber. In the first step the committee with jurisdiction over a program *authorizes* expenditures for it, and in the second the Appropriations Committee *appropriates* the money—that is, writes a bill designating that specific sums be spent on authorized programs. The sums appropriated need not and often do not match the amounts authorized because more spending may be authorized than the appropriators, concerned with the total size of the budget, are willing to appropriate. For some important programs expenditures take the form of **entitlements**, which designate specific classes of people who are entitled to a legally defined benefit. Social Security and Medicare payments and military pensions are examples. Congress must spend whatever it takes to cover those who are eligible for entitlements—unless it changes the eligibility standards or the amounts to which the eligible are entitled.

After 1921 the money committees took on the institutional task of protecting congressional majorities from the collective damage that the pursuit of individual electoral goals threatened to impose. In the House the powerful Appropriations Committee used its authority to keep members' desires for locally popular projects (such as dams, highways, and harbor improvements) and programs (such as housing, urban renewal, and police equipment) from pushing up taxes or deficits to politically intolerable levels. Tax legislation emerging from Ways and Means was routinely deemed ineligible for amendment to prevent a scramble for revenue-draining tax breaks for local firms or well-connected interests.

### Budget Reform

By the early 1970s the ability of the money committees to enforce collective self-control had been seriously eroded. The committee reforms weakened committee leaders, and a move toward congressional "openness"—doing more business in public—made it harder for individual members to resist the temptation to promote locally popular projects of doubtful value. At about the same time, President Richard Nixon used his authority to impound—refuse to spend—some of the funds authorized and appropriated by Congress to subvert the spending priorities of its Democratic majorities. Nixon even impounded appropriations passed over his veto. His actions posed fundamental challenges to the House and Senate as institutions as well as to their Democratic majorities.

Congress responded with the Budget and Impoundment Control Act of 1974. The act subjected presidential impoundment authority to strict congressional control. More important, it revamped Congress's budgetary process with the goal of making impoundment unnecessary. Among other things, the act established a Budget Committee in each chamber to oversee the coordination of taxing and spending policies. It also instituted procedures and timetables for setting budget targets, supervising the committees' decisions on revenues and spending, and reconciling the tax and spending bills enacted by Congress with the targets. The system was designed to compel members to vote on explicit levels of taxation, expenditures,

*Sesame Street*'s Elmo and others appear before the House Appropriations Committee on Labor, Health and Human Services, and Education to ask for federal funding to help ensure every child has access to quality music instruction. The Muppet's appearance provided a livelier spectacle—and got more media attention—than the more typical parade of bureaucrats requesting funding for programs.

and deficits, thereby taking direct responsibility for the fiscal consequences of the many separate decisions made during a session.

Despite Congress's good intentions, the reformed budget process proved entirely incapable of preventing the huge deficits produced by budget politics during the Reagan and Bush administrations of the 1980s and early 1990s. Orderly budgeting fell victim to the sharp partisan conflict between the Republican presidents and congressional Democrats over budget priorities. Presidents Ronald Reagan and George H. W. Bush sought to keep taxes low, congressional Democrats to protect popular domestic spending programs. Because both low taxes and spending for popular programs proved politically irresistible, the budget was left unbalanced. No amount of reform, then, could have prevented the massive budget deficits of the 1980s and early 1990s because nothing can force Congress to follow the rules it makes for itself. Procedures are chosen to produce desired outcomes; when the rules stand in the way of desired outcomes, members can always find ways around them.[38]

Attempts to reduce the deficit by procedural devices failed repeatedly. Congress and the president chipped away at the deficit with unpopular combinations of tax increases and spending cuts in 1990 (in a deal between Republican president George H. W. Bush and a Democratic Congress) and 1993 (enacted by a unified Democratic government led by Bill Clinton). Still the budget did not come into balance, requiring yet another round of budget confrontations and negotiations, stretching from 1995 to 1997—and this time between a Republican Congress and a Democratic president.

The agreement became possible when the booming economy produced a bonanza of tax revenues, making it much easier to accommodate the desires of both sides. By 1998 the economy had produced so much in new tax revenues that the budget was in surplus, and budget politics turned, temporarily, to the happier task of choosing among tax cuts, additional spending for government programs, or paying down the national debt. But a slowing economy put the squeeze on resources in 2001, and revenues were further reduced by major tax cuts enacted at the behest of the George W. Bush administration. As spending rose with the cost of homeland security and the wars in Afghanistan and Iraq, deficits returned. The severe recession that began in late 2007 and lasted for the next eighteen months, combined with the Obama administration's package of tax cuts and spending programs intended to revive economic growth, produced huge budget shortfalls and made deep spending cuts the primary objective of congressional Republicans when they took control of the House in 2011. Democrats, meanwhile, wanted new tax revenues to balance the cuts, leading to another major showdown in 2012 in which the formal budget process was again largely ignored. Assuming full control of the federal government in 2017, Republicans forgot their aversion to red ink and enacted large corporate and individual tax cuts that reduced revenues and sent the deficit steeply upward. Offsetting spending cuts were left for the future.

Inevitably, partisan politics dominates the budgeting process, and the formal budget rules guide the action only insofar as they do not prevent congressional majorities from doing what they want. The rules are also used strategically. For example, the reconciliation bill that finalizes congressional budget action cannot be filibustered, needing only a simple majority to pass the Senate. Senate leaders thus use reconciliation legislation to push through bills strongly opposed by the minority, as with the enactment of health care reform in 2010 and the tax cuts adopted in 2017. The rules forbid "extraneous" provisions, so this stratagem works only when legislation can be made to fit budgetary categories.

## Congressional Staff and Support Groups

In addition to relying heavily on its committee system, Congress has sought to cope with its expanding workload by adding staff (see Figure 6.8) and specialized research agencies. Staff doubled between the mid-1950s and the late 1970s (with most of the growth in personal staff); the numbers then remained stable until 1995, when House Republicans reduced House committee staffs by 30 percent. Personal staff assistants manage members' offices in Washington and back in the state or district. They also draft bills, suggest policy, prepare position papers, write press releases, handle casework for constituents, deal with lobbyists, and negotiate with other staff on their boss's behalf. Almost any political or legislative chore short of casting formal votes in committee or on the floor can be delegated to staff assistants. Committee staffs are deeply involved in all legislative activities. They organize hearings and investigations; research policy options; attend to legislative details; and negotiate with legislators, lobbyists, and executive branch officials on behalf of the party faction or the committee that employs them. The sharp decline in House committee staff visible in Figure 6.8 has by some informed accounts made the institution less competent and weaker relative to the executive branch and lobbying industry.[39]

Members receive additional help in gathering and processing information from several specialized congressional agencies. The Government Accountability Office (GAO) audits and

■ **FIGURE 6.8**    Expanding Congressional Staff

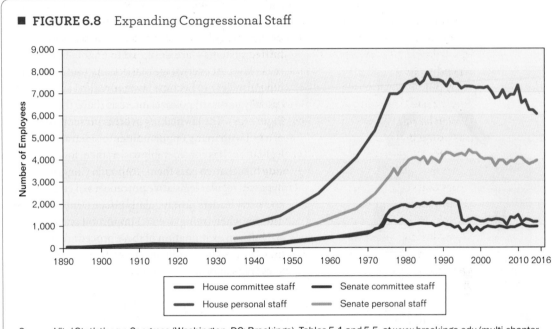

Source: *Vital Statistics on Congress* (Washington, DC: Brookings), Tables 5-1 and 5-5, at www.brookings.edu/multi-chapter-report/vital-statistics-on-congress.

investigates federal programs and expenditures, probing for waste, fraud, and inefficiency. The Congressional Research Service (CRS) gives Congress access to a highly skilled team of researchers. The Congressional Budget Office (CBO), created as part of the 1974 budget reforms, provides Congress with the economic expertise it needs to make informed fiscal decisions and to hold its own in conflicts with the president's Office of Management and Budget (see Chapter 7). Among its tasks are economic forecasting and policy analysis; its estimates of the number of people who would lose their health insurance were, for example, central to the debates about options for repealing and replacing the ACA. Although the CBO was mainly designed to serve the collective institutional needs of Congress, it also serves members individually; it will, on request, provide analyses to let members know how various budget alternatives would affect their home states and districts.

By using the expert advisers within committee staff and congressional support agencies, members of Congress do not have to take the word of experts from the executive branch or interest groups, who cannot always be trusted to impart unbiased information. Although officially bipartisan, the support agencies are the most valuable to the majority party in Congress when the other party controls the executive branch. Indeed, it was no accident that a Democratic Congress created the CBO and initiated a major expansion of the CRS during the Nixon administration or that Republicans replaced the CBO director when they took full control of Congress in 2015.

■ **FIGURE 6.9**    How a Bill Becomes a Law

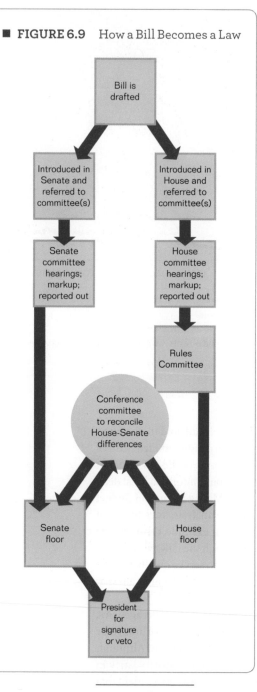

## Making Laws

Congress's rules and structures—the parties and committee systems—are designed to enable majorities to make laws. At every stage of the many routine hurdles a bill must clear to become law, individual and collective (usually partisan) political interests shape the action (see Figure 6.9). The lawmaking process presents opponents of a bill with many opportunities to sidetrack or kill the legislation. It is considerably easier, then, for members to stop bills than to pass them. Although Congress quickly bypasses regular legislative procedures in emergencies,* and party leaders now regularly circumvent normal procedures when trying to enact important and controversial bills, an examination of these procedures completes the picture of how ordinary legislative politics—referred to as "regular order"—is supposed to work.[40]

### Introducing Legislation

Only members may submit legislation to the House or Senate. Many proposals originate outside Congress—from the executive branch, interest groups, and constituents—but they must have a congressional sponsor to enter the legislative process. The process itself is largely routine and routinely political. Some bills carry (informally) their authors' names; for example, the America Invents Act, a patent reform bill enacted in 2011, is better known as the Leahy-Smith Act after its principal sponsors Senator Patrick Leahy, D-Vt., and Representative Lamar Smith, R-Texas. Even whole programs may be named after their authors. For example, the government helps college students finance their educations through Pell Grants, named after Democrat Claiborne Pell of Rhode Island, who championed the program when he was in the Senate. Personal credit for what is, after all, a collective act of Congress (one vote is never sufficient and rarely necessary to accomplish anything) is a valuable commodity. Proponents of bills try to line up cosponsors both to build support (by sharing

---

*For example, within three days of the attacks of September 11, 2001, Congress passed a joint resolution (PL 107-40) authorizing the president "to use all necessary and appropriate force against the nations, organizations, or people that he determines planned, authorized, committed, or aided the terrorist attacks." Congress also passed a major antiterrorism bill (PL 107-56) on October 25, a little more than a month after President Bush had requested it.

credit) and to display it (increasing the chances for legislative action). Most important bills are introduced in the House and Senate at the same time so the chambers can work on them simultaneously.

The parties and the president (with the cooperation of congressional friends) also use legislative proposals to stake out political positions and to make political statements. Presidents freely submit proposals they know are "dead on arrival" to establish a record that their party could run on in the future. Members of Congress regularly do the same.

## Assignment to Committee

After a bill is introduced, it is assigned a number (preceded by *H.R.* in the House and *S.* in the Senate) and referred to a committee. Even the number assigned can make a political point. In 2019, Speaker Nancy Pelosi assigned H.R. 1 to a package of reforms aimed at reducing the influence of money in politics and strengthening ethics rules and voting laws to underline her new Democratic majority's commitment to government reform. Most bills are routinely assigned to the appropriate committee; complex bills are often referred to several committees, and especially difficult bills have sometimes been handled by temporary ad hoc committees appointed for that single purpose. The Speaker makes the nonroutine decisions in the House, manipulating the committee process to ensure more friendly or expeditious treatment of legislation important to the majority party. In the Senate, party leaders negotiate agreements to settle disputed referrals.

Once a bill has been referred to a committee, the most common thing that happens next is *nothing*. Most bills die of neglect—and are meant to—in committee. Many more bills are introduced than members have time to deal with—more than ten thousand in a typical two-year Congress. Some bills are introduced "by request," meaning the introducer was doing someone—a constituent or campaign contributor—a favor by offering the bill but has no further interest in its fate. Bills introduced by the minority party to score political points or embarrass the majority are deliberately buried. Like party leaders, committee chairs and their allies strive to avoid situations in which their party colleagues might have to cast potentially embarrassing votes. If the committee decides on further action, the bill may be taken up directly by the full committee, but more commonly it is referred to the appropriate subcommittee.

## Hearings

Once the subcommittee decides to act, it (or the full committee) may hold hearings, inviting interested people—from executive agencies, interest groups, academia, or almost anywhere—to testify in person or in writing about the issue at stake and proposals to deal with it. In a typical recent two-year Congress, the Senate held about 1,200 hearings; the House, about 2,300.

Hearings may be orchestrated to make a record for (or against) a particular proposal, to evaluate how a program is working, or simply to generate publicity—for committee members as well as issues. Committees can investigate almost anything, including the White House or Congress itself. The White House is especially likely to be targeted when controlled by a congressional majority's rival party, as is the case in the 116th Congress (see the Logic of Politics box, "Congressional Investigations"). The rival party's prospective presidential nominee may get special attention as well. For instance, in March 2015 Hillary Clinton was grilled for eleven hours by the House Select Committee on Benghazi about her response to a 2012 terrorist attack on the American diplomatic mission in that Libyan city. Senate committees also hold hearings to evaluate judicial, diplomatic, and senior administrative appointments; these can be very contentious, as in the hearings on Brett Kavanaugh's appointment to the Supreme Court in 2018 during which he was accused of and adamantly denied youthful sexual misdeeds.

Hearings also provide a formal occasion for Congress to monitor the administration of the laws and programs it enacts. The heaviest duty falls on the Appropriations subcommittees in the House, for government agencies have to justify their budget requests to these panels every year. Congress often is criticized for shirking its duty to oversee the administration of laws. After all, if carried out, comprehensive oversight would be a tedious, time-consuming, politically unrewarding chore. Instead, members of Congress set up administrative procedures that give affected interests an opportunity to protest damaging bureaucratic policies and decisions. In this way, members can confine their oversight to those areas of administration where the political stakes are demonstrably high. Members operate more like firefighters than police, waiting for fire alarms to go off before taking action rather than patrolling the streets looking for crime.[41] By relying on people affected by administrative decisions to alert it to problems, Congress, in effect, puts a big bumper sticker on bureaucrats that says, "How am I driving? Call 1–800-Congress" (see Chapter 8).

### Reporting a Bill

If the subcommittee decides to act on a bill (and often it does not), it marks it up—that is, edits it line by line—and reports it to the full committee. The full committee then accepts, rejects, or amends the bill. With the exception of important and controversial bills, committees usually defer to subcommittees; otherwise, they lose the benefits of a division of labor.

Much of the coalition building that produces successful legislation takes place as subcommittees and committees work out the details of bills. No one wants to waste time on a bill that has no chance of passing—unless political points could be scored, as with the numerous votes congressional Republicans took on bills aimed at undoing Obama's health care reforms knowing full well that Obama would veto any that passed. If a bill cannot attract solid support from at least the majority-party committee members (and perhaps minority-party members as well), its chances on the House or Senate floor are slim indeed. But if amendments, compromises, and deals can build a strong committee coalition for a bill, its chances on the floor are much better. The committee system, then, also divides the labor of coalition building.

The written report that accompanies every bill reported out of committee is the most important source of information on legislation for members of Congress not on the committee and for other people in government, including the agencies and courts that have to implement and interpret the law once it is passed. These reports summarize the bill's purposes,

# Congressional Investigations

Under divided government, the party controlling Congress has to share lawmaking power with the party controlling the White House, and the party's more ambitious legislative goals are likely to be frustrated. But divided government does not impair Congress's powers of oversight—the authority to hold hearings and investigations, issue subpoenas compelling testimony from individuals in and out of the executive branch, and generally pry into any matter that catches a member's eye. Indeed, under divided government the use of this authority becomes more attractive for both partisan and institutional reasons: to embarrass the rival party by exposing its supposed misgovernment and to assert Congress's authority as a branch of government coequal to the executive branch that the rival party controls.

During the 2006 campaign, Democrats had criticized the Republican Congress for lax oversight of the Bush administration. With the Republican members' electoral fates linked by shared party label to the public's evaluation of the president and his policies, the Republican leaders' reluctance to draw attention to the administration's shortcomings is understandable. As one Republican House member candidly observed, "Our party controls the levers of government. We're not about to go out and look beneath a bunch of rocks to try to cause heartburn."[a] But protecting the administration led to Democratic accusations that the Republican Congress had given up its constitutional status as a coequal branch of government.

After the 2006 elections, recognizing that the president would limit what they could accomplish legislatively, the victorious Democrats immediately initiated a series of investigations targeting the administration and its officials,

Chip Somodevilla/Getty Images

The new Democratic House majority planned wide-ranging oversight of the Trump administration in the 116th Congress, targeting among other things Trump's tax returns, Russian meddling in the U.S. election, the Department of Homeland Security's separation of immigrant families, and financial transactions between foreign governments and Trump's businesses. Representative Adam Schiff, D-Calif., as chair of the House Intelligence Committee, seen here with a poster of President Trump and Russian Foreign Minister Sergey Lavrov, will take a prominent part in these efforts.

holding at least one hundred hearings in the first one hundred days. Few of these hearings and investigations led to legislation, but Democrats hoped they would expose the administration's alleged misgovernment and become grist for election campaigns in 2008. The administration fought back through assertions of executive privilege (see Chapter 7) and stalling in response to committees' demands for documents.

Four years later, it was the Republicans' turn to pepper the now-Democratic White House with subpoenas. Darrell Issa, R-Calif., incoming chair of the House Oversight and Government Reform Committee, who had once declared Obama "one of the most corrupt presidents in modern times" (he later apologized, saying the president was not personally corrupt), drew up a long list of targets

*(Continued)*

(Continued)

for inquiries, as did other Republican committee chairs.[b] Like the Democrats before them, Republicans aimed to expose and perhaps rectify real problems and mistakes but also to score political points and embarrass the administration with an eye to the 2012 and later 2016 elections. And like the Bush administration before it, the Obama administration was quick to invoke executive privilege whenever possible to avoid revealing sensitive or embarrassing information.

Predictably, congressional Republicans were much less keen on investigating the Trump

administration, leaving a variety of inviting targets for the incoming Democrats in 2019, including the Trump campaign's possible collusion with Russia during the 2016 election, the financial activities of the president and his family, and various questionable actions by Trump's appointees.

[a]Zachary Roth, "Investi-gate," *Washington Monthly,* June 2006.

[b]Philip Rucker, "Incoming GOP Chairmen Have a Long List of Issues to Investigate," *Washington Post,* January 4, 2011.

[c]"10 Key lawmakers to watch in the new Congress," KPBS, November 9, 2018, at www.pbs.org/newshour/politics/10-key-lawmakers-to-watch-in-the-new-congress.

major provisions, and changes from existing law. They also summarize the arguments for and against the bill.

### Scheduling Debate

When a committee agrees to report a bill to the floor, the bill is put on the House or Senate calendar—a list of bills scheduled for action. Each chamber has different calendars for different types of bills. In the House, noncontroversial bills are put on the Consent Calendar (public bills) or Private Calendar (bills concerning individuals) to be passed without debate. Such bills also may be dealt with expeditiously under a suspension of the rules, which waives almost all of the formalities to allow swift action. Most legislation passed by the House follows one of these routes.

Controversial or important bills are placed on the Union Calendar (money bills) or House Calendar (other public bills). The committee reporting such bills must ask the Rules Committee for a rule, a resolution that specifies when and how long a bill will be debated and under what procedures. The rule may permit amendments—changes in wording—from the floor (**open rule**), only certain amendments (**restricted rule**), or no amendments (**closed rule**). A rule may also specify the order in which amendments are considered, thereby stacking the deck to favor particular outcomes. Majority-party leaders use restricted or closed rules to keep unwanted amendments off the agenda, both to protect their party's members from casting embarrassing votes and to keep legislative packages from unraveling. Closed rules help to solve the majority's prisoner's dilemmas; many proposals that would not be enacted piece by piece because different members would defect on different sections can pass if they are voted on as packages. As partisan competition became more intense during the 1980s, Democratic House leaders used restricted or closed rules to maintain control of the floor agenda. Republicans objected strenuously but, after taking over in 1995, regularly resorted to restrictive rules themselves (see Table 6.3). Tight

**TABLE 6.3** Growth of Restricted Rules in the U.S. House

| CONGRESS | TOTAL RULES GRANTED | OPEN RULES | | RESTRICTIVE/CLOSED RULES | |
| --- | --- | --- | --- | --- | --- |
| | | NUMBER | PERCENTAGE | NUMBER | PERCENTAGE |
| 95th, 1977–1978 | 211 | 179 | 85 | 32 | 15 |
| 96th, 1979–1980 | 214 | 161 | 75 | 53 | 25 |
| 97th, 1981–1982 | 120 | 90 | 75 | 30 | 25 |
| 98th, 1983–1984 | 155 | 105 | 68 | 50 | 32 |
| 99th, 1985–1986 | 115 | 65 | 57 | 50 | 43 |
| 100th, 1987–1988 | 123 | 66 | 54 | 57 | 46 |
| 101st, 1989–1990 | 104 | 47 | 45 | 57 | 55 |
| 102nd, 1991–1992 | 109 | 37 | 34 | 72 | 66 |
| 103rd, 1993–1994 | 104 | 31 | 30 | 73 | 70 |
| 104th, 1995–1996 | 151 | 86 | 57 | 65 | 43 |
| 105th, 1997–1998 | 142 | 72 | 51 | 70 | 49 |
| 106th, 1999–2000 | 184 | 93 | 51 | 91 | 49 |
| 107th, 2001–2002 | 112 | 41 | 37 | 71 | 63 |
| 108th, 2003–2004 | 128 | 33 | 26 | 95 | 74 |
| 109th, 2005–2006 | 138 | 24 | 17 | 114 | 83 |
| 110th, 2007–2008 | 159 | 23 | 15 | 136 | 85 |
| 111th, 2009–2010 | 95 | 0 | 0 | 95 | 100 |
| 112th, 2011–2012 | 144 | 14 | 10 | 130 | 90 |
| 113th, 2013–2014 | 162 | 13 | 8 | 149 | 92 |
| 114th, 2015–2016 | 172 | 8 | 5 | 164 | 95 |
| 115th, 2017–2018 | 103 | 0 | 0 | 103 | 100 |

*Sources:* Roger H. Davidson and Walter J. Oleszek, *Congress and Its Members,* 13th ed. (Washington, DC: CQ Press, 2012); *Survey of Activities of the House Committee on Rules for the 112th Congress* (Washington, DC: U.S. Government Printing Office, 2013); and *Survey of Activities of the House Committee on Rules for the 113th Congress* (Washington, DC: U.S. Government Printing Office, 2015). The 114th and 115th Congresses compiled by authors from data at https://rules.house .gov/legislation.

*Note:* Democrats claim that Republicans misclassified rules in the 104th–106th Congresses, thereby overstating the frequency of open rules.

majority-party control of the legislative process has since become the norm, and open rules have been rare in recent Congresses; not a single open rule was allowed in the House during the 115th Congress.

If the Rules Committee holds hearings on a rule, interested members may express their views on the legislation. After hearings, a bill may be granted a rule, or it may be denied a rule entirely, at least until its sponsors have revised it to the Rules Committee's satisfaction. Once the Rules Committee grants a rule, it must be adopted by a majority vote on the floor. When floor action on a bill is constrained by its rule, a House majority has, in fact, consciously chosen to constrain itself. Sometimes the House kills a bill by voting against the rule rather than against the bill itself. In 1994, for example, the House rejected a rule for a bill to elevate the Environmental Protection Agency (EPA) to cabinet status because the bill did not require the new department to consider the economic costs and benefits of new environmental regulations. The House's action killed the legislation.

In 2001, Republican House leaders tried to kill a campaign finance reform bill they strongly opposed by proposing a rule so unacceptable to the bill's proponents that they joined in voting the rule down. When the Republican leaders refused to act further on the bill, its supporters eventually got it out of Rules through a **discharge petition**, which brings a bill directly to the floor without committee approval when signed by a majority of House members (218). This discharge petition was a rare success; since 1967, only thirteen such petitions have received the required 218 signatures.*

The Senate has no equivalent of the House Rules Committee or, indeed, any rules limiting debate or amendments. The majority leader can exercise some agenda control by using a device called "filling the amendment tree," preempting all opportunities for offering amendments to avoid votes party members would prefer not to cast. Doing so, however, annoys the minority party, which has many other tools for obstructing the majority. Thus, the leaders of both parties routinely negotiate unanimous consent agreements to arrange for the orderly consideration of legislation. Unanimous consent agreements are similar to rules from the House Rules Committee in that they limit time for debate, determine which amendments are allowable, and provide for waivers of standard Senate procedures. The difference is that the minority party always has a say in them.

Without a unanimous consent agreement, there is no limit on how long senators can talk or on how many amendments they can offer. Individuals or small groups can even **filibuster**—hold the floor making endless speeches so that no action can be taken on the bill or anything else—to try to kill bills that the majority would otherwise enact. And breaking a filibuster is difficult. Under Senate rules an extraordinary three-fifths majority of the Senate membership (sixty votes) is required to invoke **cloture**, which allows a maximum of thirty additional hours of debate on a bill before a vote must be taken.

Conservative southern senators used filibusters most notoriously in their rear-guard action against civil rights laws a generation ago, but senators of all ideological stripes now use

---

*Ultimate success is even rarer for discharged bills. Since 1910, when the procedure was first instituted, only four bills brought to the House floor via discharge have become law: in 1931; 1960; 2002, when Congress passed the Shays-Meehan campaign finance reforms; and 2015, when Congress passed a bill reauthorizing the Import-Export Bank.

the tactic. In fact, filibustering has become much more common in recent years and was especially rife after Republicans lost control of the Senate in 2007. During the 111th Congress (2009–2010), Democratic majority leader Harry Reid, facing a Republican minority bent on obstructing Barack Obama's legislative agenda, filed a record 139 cloture motions, of which ninety-one came to a vote and sixty-three received at least sixty votes, thus ending debate and opening the way to a final vote. All of these numbers were much higher for the 113th Congress, but they include a large number of cloture on presidential nominations to the federal courts and the executive branch invoked by simple majorities under new rules pushed through at Reid's behest in late 2013 (see Strategy and Choice box, "The Origin and Evolution of the Senate Filibuster"). The old rules remain in place for legislation, where even the threat of a filibuster can stop action because Senate leaders dislike wasting time on bills not likely to pass. With filibustering now so routine—more than half of the major legislation considered by the Senate in recent Congresses has been subject to filibusters and other delaying tactics[42]—the reality is that the support of sixty senators is needed to pass any controversial piece of legislation except the budget resolution, which is protected from filibusters by a special rule. Whether the filibuster can survive the current era of unrestrained partisan warfare is an open question, for the ploy used by Reid to amend the cloture rules is available to any sufficiently frustrated Senate majority.

Strom Thurmond Collection, Clemson University

The longest speech in the history of the Senate was made by Strom Thurmond of South Carolina. Thurmond, a Democrat who later became a Republican, spoke for twenty-four hours and eighteen minutes during a filibuster against passage of the Civil Rights Act of 1957. This display of stamina was no fluke; in 2002 at the age of ninety-nine Strom Thurmond finally decided to retire from the Senate.

In addition to permitting filibusters on legislation, the rules allow individual members to tie the Senate up in knots by refusing to concur with unanimous consent agreements aimed at facilitating the chamber's work. Senators, then, must depend on mutual restraint and bipartisan cooperation to get their work done. When cooperation breaks down, the Senate is immobilized. Senators thus buy lower conformity costs at the price of higher transaction costs.

### Debate and Amendment

In the House, the time for debate is divided equally between the proponents and opponents of a bill. Each side's time is controlled by a floor manager, typically the committee or subcommittee chair and the opposing ranking member. If amendments to a bill are allowed under the rule, they must be germane (pertinent) to the purpose of the bill; extraneous proposals, known as **riders**,

**STRATEGY AND CHOICE**

# The Origin and Evolution of the Senate Filibuster

Nothing is more emblematic of the Senate's special character than the filibuster—the ability of a minority of senators to block action on legislation or presidential appointments by extending debate, holding the floor until the majority gives up or grows to a supermajority that wields the sixty votes now necessary to adopt a cloture motion, which terminates debate and allows the Senate to proceed to a vote on the matter. Ironically, this hallowed practice originated more by accident than by design. Between 1789 and 1806, the Senate's rules included a motion "to move the previous question," which if adopted by a simple majority ended debate and compelled a final vote on the matter at hand. When the rules were revised that year, the previous question motion was dropped because it was rarely used and did not seem necessary for the Senate to do its business. Three decades then passed before a Senate minority bent on obstruction found it could exploit the absence of any formal procedure for ending debate by conducting a filibuster.

From 1806 until 1917, a single senator could block action by refusing to end debate. That year, under strong pressure from President Woodrow Wilson and a public appalled that twelve antiwar senators had successfully filibustered a bill to arm U.S. merchant ships threatened by German submarines, the Senate adopted Rule 22, which allowed a two-thirds majority to invoke cloture. Cloture was made a bit easier in 1975 when the required majority was reduced to three-fifths of the Senate's membership (sixty).

Before the 1970s, filibusters were rare, but their use has since increased dramatically, producing a "sixty-vote Senate" for bills other than budget resolutions, which may not be filibustered. Why this increase? One reason is that majorities no longer forced filibusterers to exhaust themselves speaking round the clock in order to hold the floor. Growing demands on senators' time—for travel back home and raising campaign money as well as for managing their formidable legislative workloads—made them reluctant to adopt such a time-consuming strategy of attrition. Instead, senators in opposition to the filibusters now fight them with cloture motions, which minimize the filibusters' expense because they no longer shut down other Senate business. This low cost makes the filibuster an attractive option for individual senators bent on extracting legislative concessions as well as killing legislation. The filibuster has also become a standard weapon of partisan warfare in an increasingly polarized Senate, epitomized by its use in the 111th Congress (2009–2010) as a key component of the minority Republicans' strategy of root-and-branch obstruction of Barack Obama's legislative agenda.

By the 113th Congress (2013–2014), Senate Democrats had become so frustrated with Republicans' blocking of votes on Obama's nominations to executive and judicial offices that they changed the rules (using a parliamentary maneuver that allowed the rules to be amended by a simple majority vote of fifty-one) so that cloture on presidential nominees (except for the Supreme Court) could be accomplished by a simple majority vote. Republicans expressed outrage; Minority Leader Mitch McConnell suggested that were his party to hold a majority in the next Congress, it just might subject all Senate action to a simple majority vote. It has yet to go that far, but in 2017 the Republican majority eliminated the filibuster for Supreme Court nominees as well as other nominees, paving the way for the ascension of conservative justices Neil Gorsuch and Brett Kavanaugh along with the broader stacking of the federal courts with conservative Republicans. At various times, both Republican and Democratic Senate majorities have contemplated eliminating the filibuster entirely, a move dubbed the "nuclear option" because it would escalate partisan conflict to total war. But the filibuster has survived this long for reasons other than pure custom. First, the next election could turn a majority into a minority, and while in the majority, senators have been willing to tolerate obstruction in order to retain the right to obstruct. Second, minorities have usually avoided pushing obstruction to the point where the majority becomes sufficiently angry and frustrated to risk the fallout from

using the nuclear option. Third, that fallout would be heavy; an infuriated Senate minority has a variety of options beyond the filibuster for frustrating and harassing the majority. Still, extreme partisan polarization in Washington currently leaves the filibuster in considerable jeopardy.

*Sources:* Gregory Koger, *Filibustering: A Political History of Obstruction in the House and Senate* (Chicago: University of Chicago Press, 2011); Sarah A. Binder and Steven S. Smith, *Politics or Principal? Filibustering in the United States Senate* (Washington, DC: Brookings, 1997); Brian Friel and Niels Lesniewski, "Senate Limits 'Holds,' Keeps Filibuster," *CQ Weekly*, January 31, 2011, 260; "McConnell in 2013: No Reason for GOP Senate to Reverse 'Nuclear Option,'" *Roll Call*, December 19, 2014, at www.rollcall.com/multimedia/-238492-1.html.

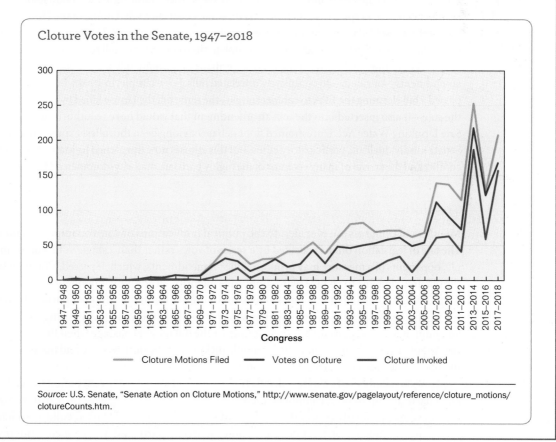

Cloture Votes in the Senate, 1947–2018

Cloture Motions Filed    Votes on Cloture    Cloture Invoked

*Source:* U.S. Senate, "Senate Action on Cloture Motions," http://www.senate.gov/pagelayout/reference/cloture_motions/clotureCounts.htm.

are not allowed. Debate on amendments usually is restricted to five minutes for each side. The House often debates bills as a Committee of the Whole because, acting in the guise of a committee, the House is less encumbered by formal procedures. For example, for the Committee of the Whole, a **quorum**—the number of members who must be present for the House to act officially—is 100 rather than the usual majority of 218, and a member chosen by the Speaker wields the gavel. The House must revert back to itself, however, to vote on legislation.

Floor debates change few minds because, jaded by experience, politicians are rarely swayed by one another's eloquence. Debates are for public consumption: to make arguments members will use to justify their votes to constituents and others; to shape public perceptions through the media; to guide administrators and courts when they apply and interpret the legislation; to stake out partisan positions; to show off. More important, formal floor debates serve to legitimize policy. Whatever deals and compromises went into building a legislative coalition, whatever the real purposes of its supporters, they have to make a case that the proposed action will serve the public interest. The opposition has equal time to argue, on the same grounds, against the action.

Floor action does more to shape legislation in the Senate than in the House. Because unanimous consent is required to limit Senate debate (except when cloture is used to end a filibuster), members are free to spend as much time as they like debating a bill. Unlike in the House, few conflicts are resolved in Senate committees or subcommittees; senators do much more legislating on the floor, offering amendments or complete alternatives to the bill reported by the committee. Senate amendments need not even be germane; important bills are sometimes passed as amendments—or riders—to completely unrelated bills. For example, in 1994 when the Senate passed a bill elevating the EPA to cabinet status—the same bill the House killed by voting down the rule—it also inserted into the text an amendment that would have reauthorized the 1974 Safe Drinking Water Act. Unrestrained floor debate has long been the fullest expression of the Senate's individualistic, participatory ethos. But this ethos is now threatened by intensified party conflict and the arrival of many veterans of the highly partisan, majority-dominated House.[43]

## The Vote

Members of Congress are ever alert to the political implications of votes on important bills. The fate of legislation often is decided by a series of votes rather than a single vote. For example, opponents of a measure may propose "killer" amendments, which, if passed, would make the bill unacceptable to an otherwise supportive majority. In addition, opponents may move to recommit the bill—that is, to send it back to committee for modification or burial—before the final vote. And on occasion, members may try to straddle an issue by voting for killer amendments or to recommit but then voting for the bill on final passage when these moves fail. Sophisticated observers have little trouble picking out the decisive vote and discerning a member's true position, but inattentive constituents may be fooled.

How do members of Congress decide how to vote? Prior to the current period of heightened partisanship in both chambers, members reported that, along with their own views, the opinions of constituents and the advice of knowledgeable and trusted colleagues had the strongest influence on their decisions; other sources—party leaders, presidents, interest groups, the press—were said to be much less influential. Constituents and colleagues are still important, but the pressure for party conformity has made party leaders considerably more influential than they were a generation ago. Often members are aware of what their constituents want without anyone having to tell them. At other times they rely on letters, phone calls, faxes, e-mails, text messages, editorials, and polls to get a sense of what people think. Even on issues on which constituency opinion is unformed, members try to anticipate how constituents would react if they were to think about the issue. The idea is to cast an *explainable vote,* one that can be defended publicly if brought up by a challenger in some future campaign. This is not always easy, for a vote that is explainable to the strong partisans who vote in primary elections may not be explainable to the broader, more moderate voters needed to win the general election, and vice versa. The votes in 2017 to undo the ACA presented such a dilemma to some Republicans. Not every vote has to please the people who hire and fire members of Congress, but too many "bad" votes can expose a member to the charge of being out of touch with the folks back home.[44]

Most constituents know and care little about most of the issues on which members vote. The minority of the public that does pay attention varies from issue to issue. The relevant constituency opinions are those held by people who care, pay attention, and are not securely in the other party's camp, for their support will be affected by how the member handles the issue. In other words, the politically relevant interests on most issues are special interests. For that reason, in Congress intense minorities often prevail over apathetic majorities. One example: opponents of gun control, led by the National Rifle Association, have blocked gun control legislation many times over the years despite widespread public support for tighter regulation of firearms. Even the recent rash of deadly school shootings has not changed this political equation.

Members rely on trusted colleagues to guide voting decisions because legislators cannot possibly inform themselves adequately about all the matters that require a vote. They depend instead on the expertise of others, most often members of committees (usually from their own party) with jurisdiction over the bills outside their own specialties. More generally, members have reason to listen to anyone who can supply them with essential information: political information about how constituents and other supporters will view their actions and technical information about what the legislation will do. They also have reason to weigh the views of anyone who can help or hinder them in winning reelection, advancing their careers in Washington, and having an impact on policy. Constituents' views count the most because they have the most direct control over members' careers, but the views of party leaders (as agents of their party colleagues), interest groups, and campaign contributors also shape decisions, especially on issues of little concern to constituents.

How influential is the president when the votes are finally cast? Occasionally presidents have been able to win against the odds by persuading wavering members of their party to stick with the team or by cutting special deals with pivotal members. A classic example occurred in 1993, when President Clinton's successful appeals to party loyalty were crucial to his razor-thin budget victories (218–216 in the House, 51–50 in the Senate, where Vice President Al Gore's vote broke a tie); no Republican in either chamber would support the budget because it included tax increases. Essential, too, were the bargains made to modify the bill to satisfy reluctant Democrats.[45] On most votes, however, the administration's wishes are by no means paramount. Thirty-four House Democrats voted against Obama's signature health care reform bill in 2010, for example; and 20 House Republicans voted against the repeal bill backed by Trump in 2017, as did the three Republican senators whose defection ended the effort that year.

Congressional Quarterly/Getty Images

House members use this electronic voting device to record their votes on matters coming to the floor. Electronic voting was first proposed as a time-saving device back in 1848 (using a system based on the telegraph) but was not adopted by the House until 1973. Despite the technology for instant voting, the process is sometimes delayed for hours as the majority's leaders work to bring party dissidents back into the fold to avoid defeat.

House and Senate party leaders also have limited influence at this stage of the process, at least if they are pushing for votes that might rile important constituents. Leaders exercise their greatest influence at earlier stages though control of the agenda and deal-making process, framing the ultimate choices that members face on the floor. But in doing so, their main task is to construct legislative packages that party members are comfortable supporting. If they are successful, no persuasion is necessary. If they fail, few members are likely to put party loyalty ahead of constituents' views except under the most intense pressure and on the party's most important bills. High levels of party loyalty on roll-call votes (see Figure 6.6) prevail in part because majority-party leaders keep party-splitting bills from reaching the floor.

In the House, unrecorded voice votes may be cast, but at the request of at least twenty members a recorded **roll-call vote** is taken. When voting by roll call, members insert a small plastic card into one of the more than forty stations scattered about the House floor and press a button for "yea," "nay," or "present" (indicating they were on the floor for the vote but did not take a side). Senators simply announce their votes when their names are called from the roll of members rather than record them by machine. Senators may also take unrecorded voice votes, but as a matter of senatorial courtesy a recorded roll-call vote is taken if any senator requests it.

## Reconciling Differences

Once passed, a bill is sent to the other chamber for consideration (if some version has not already been passed there). If the second chamber passes the bill unchanged, it is sent to the White House for the president's signature or veto. Routine legislation usually follows this route, but bills often pass the House and Senate in different versions, and the two bodies have to reconcile the differences before the bill can leave Congress. Sometimes a bill is shuttled back and forth between chambers, with adjustments made in each round until the two versions exactly agree. More commonly, one chamber simply drops its own and accepts the other chamber's version. If neither is willing to give in, reconciliation may become the job of a conference committee.

Party leaders in each house appoint a conference delegation that includes members of both parties, usually from among the standing committee members most actively involved for and against the legislation. The size of the delegation depends on the complexity of the legislation.

The House delegation to the conference handling the 1,300-page Clean Air Act amendments of 1990 consisted of 130 representatives from eight committees. The Senate got by with a delegation of nine from two committees. But the relative size of the delegations is not important, for each chamber votes as a separate unit in conference, and a bill is not reported out of conference to the House and Senate until it receives the approval of majorities of both delegations.

Conference committees are supposed to reconcile differences in the two versions of a bill without adding to or subtracting from the legislation. In practice, however, they occasionally do both. Conference committees generally exercise the widest discretion when the two versions are most discrepant. Once conferees reach agreement on a bill, they report the details to each chamber. A conference report is privileged—that is, it can be considered on the floor at any time without going through the usual scheduling process. The divisions of opinion in conference committees normally reflect the divisions in the chambers they represent, so majorities assembled in conference can usually be reproduced on the House and Senate floors. If both chambers approve the report, the bill is sent to the president.

Sometimes one or both chambers balk and send the conferees back to work, perhaps with instructions about what to change. If differences cannot be reconciled, the bill dies. This outcome is unusual, however; when a proposal has attracted enough support to make it this far and members face a choice to take it or leave it, they usually take it. This situation strengthens the hands of the committees that originally reported the legislation because the conference delegates are normally drawn from these committees and the conference gives them a chance to have the last word.

Once common, the use of conference committees has declined precipitously in recent years. From 1993 through 2004, an average of forty-two conference committees were appointed per Congress to reconcile House-Senate differences.[46] Since then, the number has fallen to single digits; only three were appointed during the 113th Congress, nine in the 114th, and five in the 115th. The conference committee process has become another victim of the polarized partisan warfare that has concentrated legislative deal-making in the hands of senior party leaders.

## To the President

Upon receiving a bill from Congress, the president has the choice of signing the bill into law; ignoring the bill, with the result that it becomes law in ten days (not counting Sundays); or vetoing the bill (see Chapter 7 for more information on the veto process). If Congress adjourns before the ten days are up, the bill fails because it was subject to a **pocket veto** (the president, metaphorically, stuck it in a pocket and forgot about it). When presidents veto a bill, they usually send a statement to Congress, and therefore to all Americans, that explains why they took such action.

Congressional override of a presidential veto requires a two-thirds vote in each chamber. If the override succeeds, the bill becomes law. Success is rare, however, because presidents usually can muster enough support from members of their own party in at least one chamber to sustain a veto. When a head count tells presidents that an override is possible, they hesitate to use the veto because the override would expose their political weakness. Of the 499 regular vetoes cast between 1945 and 2018, only 52 were overridden. Presidents also exercised 310 pocket vetoes, none of which could be overridden, over the same period.[47] Presidents often prevail without having to resort to a veto because members of Congress are reluctant to invest time and effort in legislation that will die on the president's desk. The exception is when congressional majorities want to stake out a position on a prominent issue to score political points. The veto, then, is a major weapon in the presidential arsenal; presidents can threaten to kill any legislative proposal they find unsatisfactory, usually leaving Congress with no choice but to cut presidents in on deals.

## A Bias against Action

Emerging from this review of the process and politics of ordinary congressional lawmaking is one central point: it is far easier to kill a bill than to pass one. Proponents of legislation have to win a sustained sequence of victories—in subcommittee, in committee, in Rules (in the House), in conference, on the floors of both chambers (repeatedly), and in the White House—to succeed. To do this supporters of a bill have to assemble not one but multiple majority coalitions. Opponents need win only once to keep a bill from going forward. The process imposes high transaction costs, conferring a strong bias in favor of the status quo.

### Unorthodox Lawmaking

The majority party can easily find its legislative agenda frustrated by the minority party when ordinary legislative procedures are followed. As party divisions in Congress have intensified and minority obstruction has become more common, majority-party leaders have improvised unorthodox procedures to enact legislation. In the House, these include designing complex special rules to structure debate and amendment to minimize the minority's influence, bypassing or overriding committees to draft bills directly, rewriting legislation in conference committee after it has passed the floor, combining separate bills into huge omnibus packages that leave members the choice of accepting all or getting nothing, and enacting continuing resolutions in lieu of passing formal budgets to fund the government. In the Senate, the minority party has probably contributed most to deviations from orthodoxy through the unbridled use of the filibuster, compelling leaders to negotiate supermajority coalitions of at least sixty votes to act on controversial issues. Majority Senate leaders have responded with procedural strategies designed to minimize the damage, such as filling the amendment tree. In dealing with important and controversial legislation, unorthodox procedures have in fact become the congressional norm.[48]

Unorthodox lawmaking requires a heavy investment of leaders' resources—time, energy, and favors—reflecting the high transaction costs incurred in getting Congress to act collectively on issues that provoke strong disagreement. Only a limited number of measures can receive such treatment, thus enhancing the **status quo bias** of legislative politics. Proposals that fall along the wayside can always be revived and reintroduced in the next Congress, however. Indeed, it is not at all unusual for many years to elapse between the initial introduction of a major piece of legislation and its final enactment. Proposals for national health insurance had been on the congressional agenda intermittently for more than sixty years before the ACA passed in 2010. Defeats are rarely final, but neither are most victories; the game is by no means over when a law is enacted. The real impact of legislation depends on how it is implemented by administrators and interpreted by the courts (see Chapters 8 and 9). And laws always are subject to revision or repeal by a later Congress; witness the ACA in the 115th. That victories or defeats almost always are partial, and conceivably temporary, contributes a great deal to making politics—cooperation in the face of disagreement—possible. Politicians recognize that taking half a loaf now does not mean they cannot go for a larger share in the future and that losses need not be irreversible.

## Evaluating Congress

Americans hold contradictory views about their national legislature. In the abstract, most people approve of the Constitution's institutional arrangements. Any proposals for change advanced by constitutional scholars and reformers are ignored by virtually everyone else. And Americans usually like their own representatives and senators, who always receive substantially higher approval ratings from constituents than does their institution. Most incumbents win reelection even when the public professes to be thoroughly fed up with national politics and the politicians of one or both parties. But Congress as it operates and its members as a class are rarely appreciated, and it is unusual for a majority of Americans to approve of its performance (see Figure 6.10).

The public's typical disdain for Congress reflects the low repute garnered by politicians as a class. Habitual contempt for politicians arises from the nature of politics itself. Americans use politics as a vehicle for social decisions even when they share no consensus about the best course of action. Politics, then, inevitably requires compromises and trades, the results of which leave no one fully satisfied. The alternative to compromise—stalemate—is often equally scorned by a public more inclined to view legislative gridlock as a product of partisan bickering than of intractable conflicts among legitimate values, interests, and beliefs. In reality, Congress's difficulty in deciding on a budget, reforming the health care system, or dealing with an array of social problems (poverty, inequality, education, job loss) reflects the absence of any public consensus on what should be done about these issues. The only consensus is that national leaders, when failing to act, have not done their job.

Congress's poor reputation also arises from the very nature of pluralism. In pluralist politics, adamant minorities frequently defeat apathetic majorities because the minorities invest more of their political resources—votes, money, persuasive efforts—in getting their way. Indeed, the ability of pluralist systems to weigh the intensity of preferences as well as to count heads is viewed as a major advantage because it means that groups tend to win when they care most and lose when they care least. But it also means that "special interests" often win out over general interests, leaving members of Congress perpetually open to the charge of violating the public trust.[49] Congress's reputation also suffers from recurrent if not widespread ethics scandals involving money, sex, and even drugs.

All of these sources of public disdain for members of Congress represent conditions to be coped with rather than problems that can be solved. Senators and representatives cannot avoid making political deals, representing conflicted publics, or paying special attention to intensely held views. And not all of them will resist the many opportunities for corrupt self-dealing that come with the job. Thus, members of Congress as a class are never likely to be revered by the public for any length of time.

Still, approval of Congress does vary in response to how it seems to be doing its job. The public prefers bipartisan agreement to partisan bickering; cooperation with the president

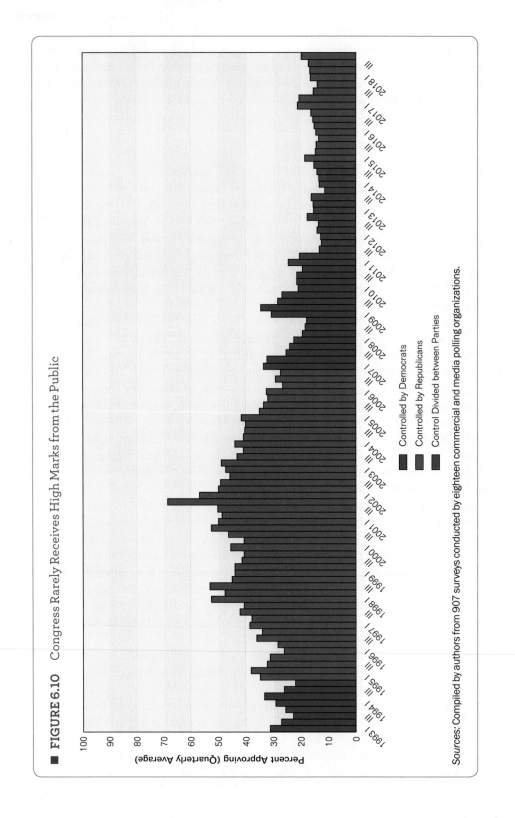

■ **FIGURE 6.10**  Congress Rarely Receives High Marks from the Public

■ Controlled by Democrats
■ Controlled by Republicans
■ Control Divided between Parties

*Sources:* Compiled by authors from 907 surveys conducted by eighteen commercial and media polling organizations.

over conflict between the branches; and, most of all, successful government policies. For example, in early 1998, on the heels of the 1997 balanced budget agreement between Clinton and the Republican Congress and against a background of a booming stock market and unemployment and inflation rates down to levels not seen since the 1960s, public approval of Congress in the Gallup poll reached 57 percent, up nearly 30 points from its low in 1992. But when Congress engaged in a highly partisan battle over impeaching Clinton for perjury and obstruction of justice in his attempt to cover up his sexual dalliance with a White House intern, its level of public approval fell sharply.

Evaluations of Congress became dramatically more positive in the wake of the al-Qaeda attacks on the United States in September 2001. The approval rating reached a record high of 84 percent a month after planes hit the World Trade Center and the Pentagon. With Congress itself under apparent biological attack from anthrax disseminated through the mail (its source was later found to be domestic and unrelated to the September 11 attacks) and displaying bipartisan resolve in supporting the Bush administration's initial proposals to combat terrorism, Congress-bashing went suddenly out of fashion. The distinction in the public mind between Congress as a revered constitutional invention and as a bunch of politicians doing the messy and often unsightly work of politics dissolved for a brief time, and Congress was included in the surge of patriotic affection for the symbols of American democracy the attacks had inspired (see Chapter 10). Soon, however, the public's view of Congress resumed its normal shape; within a year approval of Congress had fallen below 50 percent, and by the 2006 midterm election it was down to 25 percent. During the past decade, unrestrained partisan conflict has been far more common than bipartisan cooperation, so a large majority of the public has found fault with Congress most of the time. Since 2011, popular approval of its performance has rarely exceeded 20 percent.

Despite all its faults, perceived and real, the U.S. Congress remains the most powerful and independent legislature in the world. It has retained its power and independence for both constitutional and institutional reasons. The Constitution not only granted the House and Senate extensive legislative powers but also provided the basis for electoral independence from the executive. Congress's formal legislative powers and electoral independence would have been of little avail, however, had members not created effective institutional devices for acquiring information, coordinating action, managing conflict, and discouraging free riding. By developing the party and committee systems and securing the assistance of numerous staff and specialized research agencies, members of Congress have given themselves the organizational means to carry out, and thus to retain, their constitutional mandate. But their task is rarely easy nor the way smooth, for the Madisonian system that Congress epitomizes erects formidable barriers to collective action, and the range and complexity of contemporary political conflicts continually test Congress's fundamental ability to do politics successfully.

When Congress fails the test, as it often has in recent years, important policy decisions migrate to other institutions. As we shall see in the next chapter, presidents, facing stalemate on the Hill, are tempted to make policy by executive order. But without explicit legislative authorization, executive orders are subject to legal challenge, leaving it to the federal courts to determine their fate. Policy decisions thrashed out between the executive and the courts leave Congress, the "people's branch," on the sideline.

Since the 2016 election, Congress has also faced a fundamental challenge to its influence and integrity by an administration dedicated to disrupting the federal government across the board.

**for CQ Press**

**Want a better grade?**

Get the tools you need to sharpen your study skills. Access practice quizzes, eFlashcards, video, and multimedia at **edge.sagepub.com/kernell9e.**

President Donald Trump's demonstrated disdain for political customs, constitutional niceties, and demonstrable facts that might inhibit his pursuit of power and adulation has severely tested Congress's capacity to act as an independent force and check on the executive. During the 115th Congress, Republican majorities for the most part chose to ignore, downplay, or excuse Trump's transgressions of political norms as an acceptable price for furthering the party's conservative agenda. The Democrats controlling the House in the 116th Congress, with no such incentives, are certain to do the opposite.

## KEY TERMS

casework  248

closed rule  280

cloture  282

conditional party
   government  260

conference committees  268

discharge petition  282

earmarks  250

entitlements  272

filibuster  282

gerrymandering  238

joint committees  268

majority leader  260

majority whip  260

multiple referrals  271

open rule  280

pocket veto  289

"pork-barrel"
   legislation  250

president pro
   tempore  264

proportional representation  237

quorum  286

restricted rule  280

riders  283

roll-call vote  288

rules  256

select committees  268

seniority rule  256

Speaker of the House  258

special committees  268

standing committees  266

status quo bias  290

term limits  270

ticket-splitting  244

unanimous consent
   agreements  265

## SUGGESTED READINGS

Arnold, R. Douglas. *The Logic of Congressional Action.* New Haven, CT: Yale University Press, 1990. Explains how congressional leaders can manipulate the rules to overcome electorally induced free riding when they want to enact policies that impose short-term or concentrated costs to achieve longer-term or diffuse benefits.

Cox, Gary W., and Mathew D. McCubbins. *Legislative Leviathan: Party Government in the House.* Berkeley:

University of California Press, 1993. Lucid explanation of the logic that undergirds the House party organizations; makes a strong case that congressional parties are more powerful than most observers have assumed.

Davidson, Roger H., Walter J. Oleszek, Frances E. Lee, and Eric Schickler. *Congress and Its Members.* 15th ed. Thousand Oaks, CA: CQ Press, 2015. Thorough, authoritative text that is especially good at explaining rules and procedures.

Dodd, Lawrence D., and Bruce I. Oppenheimer. *Congress Reconsidered.* 11th ed. Thousand Oaks, CA: CQ Press, 2016. Offers historical and theoretical perspectives on congressional change and an up-to-date discussion of the contemporary Congress.

Fenno, Richard F., Jr. *Home Style: House Members in Their Districts.* Boston: Little, Brown, 1978. Fenno's close personal observation of House members' interactions with their constituents produces a wealth of insights about how representation actually works.

Jacobson, Gary C., and Jamie L. Carson. *The Politics of Congressional Elections.* 9th ed. New York: Rowman & Littlefield, 2016. A comprehensive look at congressional elections.

Kaiser, Robert G. *An Act of Congress: How America's Essential Institution Works, and How It Doesn't.* New York: Knopf, 2013. A fascinating and up-to-date case study of how a bill (the Dodd–Frank Wall Street Reform and Consumer Protection Act of 2012) became a law.

Lee, Francis. *Insecure Majorities: Congress and the Perpetual Campaign.* Chicago: University of Chicago Press, 2016. Explains how the battle for majority control leads to polarized conflict and legislative paralysis in Congress.

Mayhew, David R. *Congress: The Electoral Connection.* New Haven, CT: Yale University Press, 1974. Classic analysis of how electoral incentives shape almost every aspect of congressional organization and behavior.

Rohde, David W. *Parties and Leaders in the Postreform House.* Chicago: University of Chicago Press, 1991. Explains the decline and resurgence of party unity in the House over the past several decades, paying special attention to how the reforms of the 1970s fostered greater partisanship.

Sinclair, Barbara. *Unorthodox Lawmaking: New Legislative Processes in the U.S. Congress.* 5th ed. Thousand Oaks, CA: CQ Press, 2016. Explains how and why Congress has increasingly ignored its own standard legislative procedures to get its work accomplished.

Smith, Steven S. *The Senate Syndrome.* Norman: University of Oklahoma Press, 2014. An account of how increasingly polarized partisan conflict has fundamentally transformed the Senate in recent decades.

## REVIEW QUESTIONS

1. How do the differences between the House and the Senate reflect the competing interests of small and large states?

2. How does the electoral system established by the Constitution differ from that of other parliamentary democracies?

3. What constraints are placed on states when they draw districts for congressional elections? How can parties give their members an advantage through districting?

4. Why does the House have stricter rules and greater leadership control than does the Senate? How do these differences affect the day-to-day operation of the chambers?

5. If members are elected by majorities from their districts, why do interest groups sometimes prevail, even in conflicts with majority opinion?

6. Why have leaders adopted unorthodox procedures to enact legislation?

President Trump showing reporters his most recent executive order.

# The Presidency

"America does not stand still, and neither will I," declared President Obama in his State of the Union address at the beginning of the 2014 session of Congress. He added, "So wherever and whenever I can take steps without legislation to expand opportunity for more American families, that's what I'm going to do." Television viewers may have missed the significance of the president's promised "year of action." Some members of Congress attending the address may have mistakenly chalked up his comments to little more than grandstanding rhetoric. Yet they would have been wrong to do so. Stymied by a Republican-controlled Congress during much of his first term, President Obama had already begun unilaterally trying to achieve his policy goals. After Congress failed to enact the DREAM Act, in the summer of 2012 the president had instructed the Department of Homeland Security to defer deporting young illegal immigrants who had arrived in the United States before the age of five and had lived in the country for at least five years. By some estimates, over 1 million of these young immigrants could now register for temporary residency and work permits.

This action gave Republican leaders reason to believe that the president's State of the Union threat to go it alone portended more of the same. And they were correct. Over the next twelve months, President Obama continued to enlist executive actions that arguably dwarfed those issued earlier. During his last term with Republicans firmly controlling Congress, the president issued executive orders that extended overtime pay for millions of salaried workers, that prohibited federal contractors from discriminating against employees and job applicants based on their sexual orientation, and that extended deferred immigration enforcement of the parents of the children covered by this earlier unilateral action. These and other executive actions had Republicans (and Fox News) screaming for impeachment. They also went to court and succeeded in winning an injunction against the president's order extending DACA to family members.

Close observers of Washington politics attributed Obama's actions and the contretemps they fomented to the highly polarized Republican and Democratic parties' divided control of Congress and the presidency. Certainly, the partisan rhetoric had become toxic with efforts of both parties' moderates to foster compromise legislation failing on every important issue.

Donald Trump's victory in the 2016 election surprised virtually everyone who followed the campaigns and polls. Almost as shocking for Democrats, Trump's victory created a long coattail on which Republican majorities rode into both the House of Representatives and Senate. The 2016 Republican sweep appeared to rescue the new president from having to follow President Obama's go-it-alone, unilateral policymaking. Yet this is precisely how Trump proceeded. The president-elect instructed his staff to identify those campaign promises he could deliver immediately through executive order. He followed this up during his first weeks by issuing travel bans from a number of mostly Muslim countries, authorizing construction of the controversial XL gas pipeline, withholding federal grants to punish states and cities that refused to cooperate fully with immigration enforcement, unbridling the petroleum industry from Obama regulations, and loosening rules for employers in purchasing health insurance for employees. Add to these twenty-five more executive orders Trump issued during his first month in office. Altogether during his first two years in office, President Trump issued ninety executive orders and ninety-eight memoranda.

Even these numbers may understate Trump's disregard for separation of powers and his place within it. When caught by surprise during a news interview by the question if he had any plans to prevent children born in the United States from automatically becoming citizens, the president replied that his legal team had told him that he could reverse this policy through an executive order. (As we noted in Chapter 2, birthright citizenship is explicitly provided for in the Fourteenth Amendment.) "It was always told to me that you needed a constitutional amendment. Guess what? You don't," Trump said, declaring that he could do it by executive order. When the interviewer questioned the legality of this approach, Trump replied, "You can definitely do it with an act of Congress. But now they're saying I can do it just with an executive order. . . . It's in the process. It'll happen . . . with an executive order." A month later his target had switched from immigrants' children to the head of the Federal Reserve. He was looking for ways to remove the chair, whom he had appointed just months earlier. But once appointed, the head of this independent agency serves for a fixed term and is not subject to presidential removal. The next month he turned his sites back to building a border wall *without* congressional funding.

An Iranian-born science researcher holds out his boarding pass for a U.S.-bound flight just one week after President Donald Trump signed an executive order temporarily banning immigrants and refugees from seven Muslim-majority countries—including Iran—from traveling to the United States. Federal district courts quickly blocked the travel ban; eventually, the Supreme Court approved a revised ban and lifted the injunction preventing the ban's implementation.

Unquestionably, the modern presidency is a powerful office. Yet it lacks Congress's broad scope and detailed powers of Article I. With the exception of the section dealing with the president as commander in chief, Article II reads like an afterthought. From time to time presidents should report to Congress on the state of the nation; presidents may ask the bureaucracy for information, but there is no hint of centralized administration; presidents can appoint government officials, but one president (Andrew Johnson) was impeached when he removed a cabinet secretary. The veto sums up the president's legislative authority. It is not intended to confer any positive power on the executive. Rather, the presidency offered a convenient office with which to check Congress. How did we get from an office with modest authority to those modern presidents who seem to think that public policy is theirs to make with a stroke of the pen?

## The Historical Presidency

The trick in designing an energetic presidency lies in avoiding a Napoleon or Hitler, an ambitious individual who would use the temporary advantages conferred by a national crisis to permanently alter the constitutional order. By rejecting a plural office, the Framers accepted

Introduced by their member of Congress in return for past political support, nineteenth-century job seekers, hats in hand, approach the president for positions in his administration.

the proposition that, unlike the bicameral legislature, the executive would contain none of the internal checks provided by institutional design (described in *Federalist* No. 51) or factions (*Federalist* No. 10). The Constitutional Convention delegates finally solved the dilemma by giving the executive enough resources for coordinating national responses during emergencies but insufficient authority to usurp the Constitution. They achieved this objective—at least to the satisfaction of the majority that enacted Article II—by withholding certain executive powers, such as broad and easily invoked emergency powers that executives in other presidential systems have sometimes employed to get the upper hand over their political opponents. Power gravitates toward the office during moments of national urgency, but it does not involve suspension of other governmental actors' constitutional prerogatives. It remains confined to dealing with the emergency, and it dissipates as the crisis recedes or the government's response appears to fall short.

During the Republic's first century, presidents typically assumed a diminutive role as a governmental actor. Their accomplishments were mostly limited to their responses to wars, rebellions, and other national crises. In fact, early presidents played a larger role in conferring benefits to their political parties. Daily, filling vacancies in a growing federal bureaucracy consumed most of nineteenth-century presidents' time. Throughout the century, all federal employees—from the secretary of state to the postmaster in Cody, Wyoming—were appointed directly by the president or one of his agents. Large chunks of presidents' daily calendars were devoted to interviewing job seekers, listening to their party sponsors, and signing appointment letters. And because party colleagues in Congress and national party committees expected their nominees to be appointed, presidents could derive little political advantage from the appointment authority. Rather, it was a thankless task, befitting a clerk. "For every appointment," President Grover Cleveland observed ruefully, "I make one ingrate and ten enemies." Presidents took special care, however, in naming their cabinets. After all, these department heads represented important factions and interests within the president's party that had to be served if the president hoped to win renomination and election and enjoy his party's full support in Congress.

## The Era of Cabinet Government

Nineteenth-century Congress routed all matters related to administration and policy through the appropriate department secretary. When a president had a question about a policy, needed clarification on complaints or rumors about an agency head's performance, or sought advice on whether to sign or veto a bill, he consulted his cabinet. Indeed, the nineteenth-century department heads composing the cabinet routinely performed much of the work now carried out by the president's staff.

Clearly, a strong cabinet did not necessarily make for a strong president. Cabinet appointees, who were resourceful, independent, and frequently ambitious politicians, could not be expected to subordinate their own welfare and that of their department to the needs of their titular leader. An adviser to President Warren G. Harding may have only slightly exaggerated a basic truth in remarking, "The members of the cabinet are the president's natural enemies."[1] Thus a pattern of intersecting interests characterized president-cabinet relations: presidents selected their department heads for their political assets, such as their influence with a particular wing of their party in Congress or with the electorate (see Strategy and Choice box, "Lincoln and His Cabinet"). Those who joined the cabinet, however, were likely to pursue their own political and policy objectives and, perhaps incidentally, the president's (if indeed he harbored any). The result was a partnership based not on loyalty but on reciprocity: cabinet members helped the president achieve his limited political goals, and, by their cabinet appointment, he afforded them opportunities to pursue their agendas.

The Republican Congress passed the 1867 Tenure of Office Act to prevent President Andrew Johnson, elevated to office after President Lincoln's assassination, from ending Reconstruction by removing key administration officials without Senate confirmation. When Johnson ignored the law and dismissed his war secretary, the House of Representatives quickly impeached him, and the Senate came within a single vote of removing him from office.

The modern cabinet has lost much of its luster as an attractive office—that is, one with real political clout. Control over policy and even of department personnel has gravitated to the Oval Office—an important trend we track more fully shortly. Consequently, whereas ambitious politicians in the nineteenth century saw a cabinet post as a stepping-stone to the White House, modern politicians are more likely to view a stint in the cabinet as a suitable conclusion to a career in public service.

## Parties and Elections

A paramount concern for nineteenth-century politicians was winning control of the White House. After all, whichever party captured the presidency won control of several hundred thousand federal patronage jobs. Moreover, in this patronage era before election reforms guaranteed voters privacy and an easy opportunity to split their votes among the parties' slates of candidates, the party that won a state's presidential contest almost invariably gained control

**STRATEGY AND CHOICE**

# Lincoln and His Cabinet

Upon taking office in 1861, Republican president Abraham Lincoln confronted a nation threatening to dissolve. He also had to contend with a weak, young Republican Party composed of politicians who only recently had coalesced for the sole purpose of defeating the majority Democratic Party. To keep the party coalition together, Lincoln filled his cabinet with Republican leaders, even some of his rivals for the presidency.[a] Secretary of the Treasury Salmon Chase and Secretary of State William Seward, Lincoln's principal rivals for the presidential nomination, strongly disliked each other, but their support within the party and Congress kept both in Lincoln's cabinet.

Other cabinet officials of lesser stature but with impeccable political credentials were Pennsylvania's corrupt party boss and senator Simon Cameron, who was forced to resign the post of secretary of war, and Maryland Republican Party leader Montgomery Blair, who oversaw the patronage-rich Post Office Department. Blair's presence in the cabinet proved critical for he muscled the Maryland state legislature to defeat narrowly a motion calling for Maryland to secede from the Union.

Perhaps the most formidable cabinet member of all was the brusque Edwin Stanton, Cameron's replacement as secretary of war and a leader of the "war Republicans" in Congress. At times this gave him a veto over policy. "Stanton and I have an understanding," Lincoln wrote a friend. "If I send an order to him which cannot be consistently granted, he is to refuse it. This he sometimes does."[b] Thus, by surrendering control over large blocks of the executive branch to these self-interested, strong-willed politicians, President Lincoln succeeded in keeping the fragile Republican majority in Congress behind the unpopular Civil War.

---

[a]David Herbert Donald, "Lincoln, the Politician," in *Lincoln Reconsidered: Essays on the Civil War Era* (New York: Random House, 1956).

[b]David Herbert Donald, *Lincoln* (London: Jonathan Cape, 1995), 334.

Library of Congress

of all the other state and local offices on the ticket. As a result, the political party that carried the presidency almost always took control of Congress as well.

Presidential candidates were the engines that pulled the party trains. A look at the coverage of the president and Congress by daily newspapers in Cleveland, Ohio, from 1824 to 1876 reveals just how specialized the president's role was during this era (see Table 7.1). In total coverage (measured in column inches) presidents (or presidential candidates) moved to center stage in presidential election years and receded into the background during midterm election years, when they were not on the ballot. In 1840, 98 percent of all stories were centered on the president, and only 2 percent dealt with Congress. Ten years later, in a midterm election year, nearly the opposite was true. Unlike today, when presidents dominate the television network evening news, in the nineteenth century they received little media coverage outside of presidential election campaigns. Congress, not the government's chief clerk, held the spotlight.

At the national party nominating conventions, presidential candidates usually were valued a great deal more for their widespread popular appeal and willingness to distribute patronage according to party guidelines than for their policy pronouncements.* As a result, candidates with little experience in government frequently enjoyed an advantage over established politicians who might be associated with a particular faction of the party or who, as officeholders, had taken controversial positions on divisive national issues. National military heroes—Andrew Jackson, Zachary Taylor, and Ulysses S. Grant, and a number of generals who were nominated but lost—made fine presidential candidates. But for most of those who won, leadership ended on Election Day when their glorified "clerkship" began.

What, then, does the nineteenth-century presidency say about the role of the modern president? If the Constitution thrusts command authority on the office, its first century of occupants failed to notice. Yet the nineteenth-century experience is not wholly divorced from the circumstances in which modern presidents find themselves. Even then, the singular character of the office gave presidents a competitive advantage over other national politicians

**TABLE 7.1**  Nineteenth-Century Newspaper Coverage of Presidents: Heavy Only in Presidential Election Years

| ELECTION YEAR | PERCENTAGE OF POLITICAL NEWS DEVOTED TO | |
| --- | --- | --- |
| | PRESIDENT | CONGRESS |
| 1824 (presidential) | 43 | 57 |
| 1830 (midterm) | 40 | 60 |
| 1840 (presidential) | 98 | 2 |
| 1850 (midterm) | 16 | 84 |
| 1860 (presidential) | 76 | 24 |
| 1870 (midterm) | 19 | 81 |
| 1876 (presidential) | 70 | 30 |

*Source:* Samuel Kernell and Gary C. Jacobson, "Congress and the Presidency as News in the Nineteenth Century," *Journal of Politics* 49 (November 1987), 1016–1035.

*Note:* Percentages based on total column inches devoted to Congress (including members and committees) and the president (including cabinet and presidential candidates) by daily newspapers in Cleveland, Ohio, 1824–1876.

---

*There were, however, a few "litmus test" issues, such as the tariff, and during moments of national crisis the president's policy preferences would suddenly matter a great deal—consider Lincoln's position on slavery in the territories in 1860.

in attracting the public's attention. Their capacity to serve as a focal point—coordinating the efforts of state parties during national elections and occasionally in mobilizing the nation for war—offers a glimmer of national leadership that would shine far brighter in the next century.

## The Modern Presidency

By any measure the national government grew dramatically throughout the twentieth century. After World War I the United States somewhat reluctantly became a global power requiring presidents' increased attention to foreign relations. On the domestic front, the national government and presidential responsibilities grew at a similar pace. As noted in Chapter 3, large domains of services, once reserved exclusively for states and local communities—or set beyond the purview of all governments—came to be funded and regulated from Washington via an extensive network of grants-in-aid programs to the states.

Consider some of the myriad programs that make up modern agricultural policy. The U.S. Department of Agriculture (USDA) offers farmers a broad assortment of services from planting to marketing crops. The Occupational Safety and Health Administration (OSHA) regulates the working conditions of farmhands; the Environmental Protection Agency (EPA) regulates the use of pesticides; the Securities and Exchange Commission (SEC) regulates the farm commodities markets; and the USDA and Food and Drug Administration (FDA) inspect the sanitation of food processing and distribution facilities. Every other sector of the modern marketplace similarly involves a pervasive federal presence. (In the next chapter we systematically survey the growth of the federal bureaucracy and the problem this inevitably poses for elected officials in trying to translate constituents' demands into policy.) The point for us here is simply that the modern presidency reflects the tectonic shift of public policy from the state capitals to Washington. As a matter of course, legislation creating or revamping programs assigns presidents statutory authority to oversee and even make changes in policy and administration that serve the program's mission.

Even Congresses controlled by the opposition party routinely assign presidents broad discretion to administer policy. They have little choice because the Constitution's "take care" clause designates that the president "take Care that the Laws be faithfully executed." Moreover, the president appoints the executives who administer the departments, agencies, and courts. The president's executive responsibilities spill over to legislative initiative as Congress seeks guidance in creating annual budgets and periodically reauthorizing and revamping programs and bureaucracy.[*]

Of more recent origin, but just as important in defining the modern office, has been the emergence of **divided government** as the normal state of affairs in Washington. It pits a president against an opposition party that controls one or both chambers of Congress. For most of American history, party control was unified across the legislative and presidential branches. The winning presidential candidate customarily pulled his party's congressional candidates into office on his electoral coattails. Table 7.2 shows that from 1920 until the

---

[*]There is some evidence that they do so with strings attached. One study found opposition-controlled Congresses write longer laws on average as they try to anticipate efforts by unsympathetic administrations to suborn or redirect the policy. David Epstein and Sharon O'Halloran, *Delegating Powers* (New York: Cambridge University Press, 1999).

**TABLE 7.2**   The Growth of Divided Government, 1920–2018

| ELECTION YEAR | PRESIDENT | HOUSE OF REPRESENTATIVES | SENATE |
|---|---|:---:|:---:|
| 1920 | R (Harding) | R | R |
| 1922 | R (Coolidge) | R | R |
| 1924 | R (Coolidge) | R | R |
| 1926 | R (Coolidge) | R | R |
| 1928 | R (Hoover) | R | R |
| 1930 | R (Hoover) | D | R |
| 1932 | D (Roosevelt) | D | D |
| 1934 | D (Roosevelt) | D | D |
| 1936 | D (Roosevelt) | D | D |
| 1938 | D (Roosevelt) | D | D |
| 1940 | D (Roosevelt) | D | D |
| 1942 | D (Roosevelt) | D | D |
| 1944 | D (Roosevelt) | D | D |
| 1946 | D (Truman) | R | R |
| 1948 | D (Truman) | D | D |
| 1950 | D (Truman) | D | D |
| 1952 | R (Eisenhower) | R | R |
| 1954 | R (Eisenhower) | D | D |
| 1956 | R (Eisenhower) | D | D |
| 1958 | R (Eisenhower) | D | D |
| 1960 | D (Kennedy) | D | D |
| 1962 | D (Kennedy) | D | D |
| 1964 | D (Johnson) | D | D |
| 1966 | D (Johnson) | D | D |
| 1968 | R (Nixon) | D | D |
| 1970 | R (Nixon) | D | D |

*(Continued)*

**TABLE 7.2**   (Continued)

| ELECTION YEAR | PRESIDENT | HOUSE OF REPRESENTATIVES | SENATE |
|---|---|---|---|
| 1972 | R (Nixon) | D | D |
| 1974 | R (Ford) | D | D |
| 1976 | D (Carter) | D | D |
| 1978 | D (Carter) | D | D |
| 1980 | R (Reagan) | D | R |
| 1982 | R (Reagan) | D | R |
| 1984 | R (Reagan) | D | R |
| 1986 | R (Reagan) | D | D |
| 1988 | R (G. H. W. Bush) | D | D |
| 1990 | R (G. H. W. Bush) | D | D |
| 1992 | D (Clinton) | D | D |
| 1994 | D (Clinton) | R | R |
| 1996 | D (Clinton) | R | R |
| 1998 | D (Clinton) | R | R |
| 2000 | R (G. W. Bush) | R | D* |
| 2002 | R (G. W. Bush) | R | R |
| 2004 | R (G. W. Bush) | R | R |
| 2006 | R (G. W. Bush) | D | D† |
| 2008 | D (Obama) | D | D |
| 2010 | D (Obama) | R | D |
| 2012 | D (Obama) | R | D |
| 2014 | D (Obama) | R | R |
| 2016 | R (Trump) | R | R |
| 2018 | R (Trump) | D | R |

*Source:* Compiled by authors.

*Democrats gained control of the Senate after Vermont senator James Jeffords switched from Republican to independent (voting with the Democrats) in May 2001, breaking the 50–50 tie left by the 2000 elections.

†The Senate had forty-nine Democrats, forty-nine Republicans, and two independents.

first postwar election in 1946, divided government appeared only once (1931–1932), when Democrats won control of the House of Representatives, which ushered in a long-standing Democratic dominance of national politics beginning with the next election. Of the thirty-five Congresses since then, however, twenty-two have experienced divided party control in one or both chambers. (Chapter 12, "Political Parties," considers the various causes for this development.)

With the election of divided government, a kind of zero-sum game often ensues. Each side profits from the other side's failure. Mitch McConnell (R-Ky.), the leader of Senate Republicans, declared on the eve of the 2010 midterm elections: "The single most important thing we want to achieve is for President Obama to be a one-term president."[2] His comment attracted widespread criticism in the news media, but what distinguished McConnell's statement from the views of other party leaders when similarly situated was its candor rather than its sentiment.

And how do modern presidents deal with an opposition Congress? As relations with Congress become uncooperative, presidents rely more heavily on their authority to achieve necessarily more modest goals, which may amount mostly to preventing the congressional majority from enacting its preferred policies. Vetoes and threats to veto may become critical assets in forcing the legislature to pay attention to the president's preferences. Presidents have also responded to an opposition Congress by acting unilaterally and pulling decisions into the White House that were once made in the departments and agencies. This includes heavy reliance on executive orders, centralized administration, and broad assertions of executive privilege. Moreover, presidents carefully screen department and agency appointments to ensure that administrators will remain responsive to them and resist the pull of the opposition Congress.

The following sections assess modern presidential leadership against the backdrop of a more modest constitutional office. For purposes of discussion we assess presidential leadership across several spheres of government action: conduct of international affairs, administration of federal programs, and legislation. In the first sphere, the Constitution endows presidents with special advantages. The administrative presidency stands on less firm constitutional ground, but the sheer work of government has led to ever-increasing delegations of authority and responsibility for running the government. The president's legislative leadership depends heavily on the support from his copartisans in Congress.

## The President as Commander in Chief and Head of State

With several major European powers occupying territory bordering the United States, and frequently at war with one another, national security and foreign affairs were special concerns of delegates to the Constitutional Convention. The young nation's dismal record in international relations under the Articles of Confederation moved all but the most fearful delegates to shift this responsibility to the presidency. On the home front, the domestic uprising in 1786 by disgruntled Massachusetts farmers led by Daniel Shays, and the contagion of unrest that it spawned in the other colonies, exposed the Confederation's inability to provide national security.

### The Commander in Chief

The Constitution declares the president to be **commander in chief** of the nation's armed forces. The notion of putting the military under the control of a single individual was difficult for the Framers. One troubled convention delegate proposed limiting the military to no more than five thousand troops, provoking General George Washington to quip sarcastically that the Constitution also should limit invading armies to three thousand.[3] His point made, the Framers settled on a different kind of check on the president's powers as commander in chief: only Congress can declare war.

American history is replete with instances of presidents' ability to make the first move and thereby frame Congress's choice to either accept or reject their actions. In reality, the legislature may have little choice but to ratify the president's decisions. Within six months of the Confederate firing on Fort Sumter in 1861, President Abraham Lincoln suspended the writ of *habeas corpus* that prevented the Union Army from detaining civilians suspected of spying or even of just publicly opposing the war effort. He did not consult Congress before acting. Lincoln also approved a naval blockade of southern ports, extended voluntary military enlistment to a period of three years, increased the size of the army and navy, and authorized the purchase of materials, all without congressional sanction or even appropriation. Later, Lincoln justified his actions to Congress by relying exclusively on his authority as commander in chief: "The executive found the duty of employing the war

By giving the president full discretion to decide when to stop working through the UN and to invade Iraq, Congress assumed a measure of responsibility for the war's outcome.

power, in defense of the government, forced upon him. Whether strictly legal or not," he added, these measures "were ventured upon . . . trusting, then as now, that Congress would readily ratify them."[4]

History and recent experience alike demonstrate that Congress's war declaration authority does not resolve the problem of a president taking the nation into war. Presidents often commit troops and engage in hostilities and then go to Congress for authority to continue. We saw this dynamic at work in the aftermath of the September 11 terrorist attacks. For all practical purposes, the public and Congress gave the president a blank check to fight terrorism. Hardly anyone in Washington or the country second-guessed the president's decision to invade Afghanistan in search of Osama bin Laden. A year and a half later, Bush still retained the initiative in winning a Democratic Congress's grudging endorsement to invade Iraq. Presidents acting in this sequence can set Congress's agenda for a choice to continue the conflict or desist in such a way that places the legislature in a severe bind. Calls to pull back are branded as abandoning the troops in the field.

After the Democratic majority took control of Congress in 2007, it sought through a variety of measures to wind down the war in Iraq. After several false starts, Congress finally agreed to attach a rider to a supplemental funding bill for the Iraq War that tied funding to a timetable for withdrawal. President Bush promptly vetoed it and demanded a bill with no strings attached. As the date approached when existing funds for the war were projected to be depleted, the Democratic Congress and Republican president engaged in a game of chicken. To outsiders Congress appeared to hold the upper hand; if it did nothing, the American military would grind to a halt. Washington's political elite knew from experience that this prospect would, in fact, force Congress to back down in the face of withering criticism that its inaction would hamstring the ability of troops in the battlefield to defend themselves. Shortly after a failed attempt to override the veto, Congress capitulated and gave the president the funds he requested. That the president can take a military action and, with troops in the field, effectively oblige Congress to support it represents a conundrum that Congresses have struggled with throughout the nation's history.

Two numbers substantiate just how hollow is Congress's exclusive authority to declare war: 37,000 and 58,000. These are the numbers of American soldiers killed in the Korean and Vietnam Wars, respectively. In neither case did Congress declare war. In 1973 at the close of the Vietnam War, Congress sought to carve out new authority for itself by approving the **War Powers Act** over President Nixon's veto. The law requires the president to inform Congress within forty-eight hours of committing troops abroad in a military action. Moreover, the operation must end within sixty days unless Congress approves an extension. But neither the law's constitutionality nor its effectiveness in limiting the president's military authority has ever been tested. Over the decades Republican and Democratic presidents have continued to commit the military without seeking Congress's permission—witness Ronald Reagan's 1983 invasion of Grenada, George H. W. Bush's 1992 deployment of U.S. troops to Somalia as part of a United Nations (UN) peacekeeping force, Bill Clinton's commitment of American forces in the North Atlantic Treaty Organization's 1999 action against Yugoslavia, Barack Obama's 2011 participation in the UN's creation of a "no fly" zone over Libya, and Donald Trump's backing of Kurdish and other rebel forces in Syria. In fact, since 1989 U.S. armed forces have been almost continuously engaged somewhere in the world. Although members of Congress may question presidents' policies, Congress has not reined in presidents' ability to order an extended military engagement without a declaration of war.

## Head of State

The Confederation government, consisting of little more than a legislature, also found it difficult to transact foreign affairs. Even routine duties, such as responding to communications from foreign governments, proved to be an ordeal. To promote commerce, the states tried to fill this vacuum, but European merchants and governments were able to pit one state against another in a ruinous competition for markets and trade. The Framers discerned that a single executive would enjoy an inherent advantage over Congress in conducting foreign policy. With some misgivings, then, they provided the president with broader authority to transact diplomatic affairs than they were willing to allow on the domestic front.

From the outset, President George Washington interpreted the Constitution's provision "to receive Ambassadors and other public Ministers" to mean that he alone could decide whether the United States would recognize a new government and, accordingly, "receive" its ambassadors. The howls of protest in Congress that greeted this interpretation were echoed in the Capitol a century and a half later when President Harry Truman recognized the state of Israel. Seventy years later, the story continues with Trump recognizing Israel's relocation of its capital from Tel Aviv to Jerusalem.

The most important constitutional limitation on the president's leadership in foreign affairs is the requirement that a two-thirds majority of the Senate ratify treaties. At times, the Senate has rebuffed a president's leadership by rejecting a treaty negotiated by the White House. The most famous instance of this occurred at the close of World War I, when that chamber rejected the peace treaty that contained provisions for President Woodrow Wilson's brainchild, the League of Nations.* Overall, however, the Senate's ratification authority has proven less consequential than the Framers probably envisioned.

To sidestep difficulty in assembling a two-thirds majority of the Senate, especially when the chance of rejection is significant, presidents sometimes negotiate **executive agreements**, which are exempt from Senate ratification. Executive agreements, unlike treaties, take the form of joint declarations between the administration and a foreign government that they "agree" on how they will deal with each other on some issue. They are frequently used to implement a

SUSAN WALSH/AFP/Getty Images

During the summer of 2018, President Donald Trump and North Korea leader Kim Jong-un became the first leaders from these countries to meet and negotiate to end a decades-old nuclear standoff.

*It became the blueprint for the United Nations, created in the aftermath of World War II.

broader agreement contained in a treaty, or Congress has passed a law authorizing their negotiation. By one count nearly nine of ten executive agreements arise this way and are in step with the Senate majority's, if not its super-majority's, preferences.[5] But, certainly, presidents use them at times to end-run the Senate altogether. During the Vietnam War, Congress discovered that President Lyndon Johnson created several executive agreements tendering foreign aid funds to countries that kept token forces in Vietnam.[6]

If the chief attractiveness of executive agreements for presidents lies in avoiding an uncertain ratification process in the Senate, it is also their chief weakness. Where treaties have the same legal standing of federal law, a number of different officeholders can more easily undo or modify agreements. Treaties have escape clauses as well, but as a class, they are more secure from the kinds of encroachments that can afflict agreements. Congress can pass laws removing or amending these agreements; the courts can void them as violating current law; and presidents can rescind them. Our bargaining partners recognize this and, fearful of being played as "suckers" in a classic prisoner's dilemma game, may be less willing to make concessions to reach agreements that a new administration or Congress might renege on than to secure a more durable commitment of a treaty.

## The President as Chief Executive

The Framers' deep ambivalence about executive power is reflected in Article II's rambling provisions for the office. Compared with Article I's careful, detailed development of the structure and powers of Congress, Article II is long on generalities and short on details. It begins by stating, "The executive Power shall be vested in a President of the United States of America." Instead of proceeding to define that power, the article abruptly shifts to a lengthy description of the means of election, qualifications for office, succession procedure, and compensation.

Not until Section 2 does the Constitution confer meaningful administrative authority. It states that the president may appoint the officers of government "by and with the Advice and Consent of the Senate"—that is, by a majority confirmation vote. The Framers qualified this provision by allowing, "Congress may by Law vest the Appointment of such inferior Officers, as they think proper, in the President alone, in the Courts of Law, or in the Heads of Departments." For understanding the scope of presidents' appointment authority, it is useful to distinguish "principal" and "inferior" appointments. The former refers to those executive officers who directly exercise either constitutional or statutory responsibilities and therefore require Senate confirmation. These include, foremost, cabinet secretaries who oversee the departments, but also the next couple of tiers of executives, such as assistant secretaries and undersecretaries, who oversee programs and agencies within the departments.

Article II's Section 2 is more revealing in what it leaves unsaid about the president's administrative powers. At the outset, it declares simply that from time to time the president may "require the Opinion, in writing, of the principal Officer in each of the executive Departments." Then, as if the office's sketchy appointment and administrative authority fully equipped presidents, the Constitution, in Section 3, admonishes the president to "take Care that the Laws be faithfully executed."

But where does the Constitution enumerate the administrative tools presidents need to carry out this mandate? Conspicuously missing is any provision for executive departments or their administrative heads, who later would comprise the president's cabinet. Perhaps the Framers should be applauded for leaving the structure and work of administrative departments wholly to the discretion of future Congresses, to be determined in pace with the nationalization of public policy. This omission, however, precluded careful consideration of the administrative controls suitable to this new executive. The Framers could have foreseen the need for presidents to oversee budget proposals and subsequent spending, supervise personnel, and even countermand administrative decisions. These were, after all, familiar duties of eighteenth-century executives, just as they are today. Instead, in leaving the creation of the "several departments" to Congress, the Framers gave it the authority to define the president's role as chief executive.

### Authority via Delegation

The absence from the Constitution of any real administrative authority for the president left uncertain that the growth of the national government would elevate the president's control over public policy. Congress could have continued to keep presidents at bay, as it often did throughout the nineteenth century, by insisting that executive agencies report directly to congressional oversight committees. But as the obligations of government mounted, oversight began to tax Congress's time and resources and interfere with its ability to deliberate new policy. So instead of excluding the chief executive from administration, Congress found its interests best served by delegating to the White House a sizable share of administration and, with it necessarily, the discretion to adjust policy as the administration deems necessary. The fact that the same political party generally controlled both the legislative and executive branches during the first half of the twentieth century, a period of steady growth in the scope and number of federal programs, made it easier for Congress to transfer administrative responsibilities to the president. Given the scale of this, Congress really had no practical alternative.*

In writing public laws Congress can choose to delegate as much or as little rulemaking authority to the president as it thinks prudent. If it opts for too little, it freezes policy until the next act of Congress and may leave in place rigid programs that fail to respond to changing conditions. If, however, Congress delegates too much discretion to the executive, it may surrender control over important implementation decisions that could alter the intent of the legislation. In 1980 Congress erred in that direction when it passed the Paperwork Reduction Act, designed, as its name implies, to reduce the forms clogging the federal government and irritating citizens. When the U.S. Department of Health and Human Services proposed a survey of Americans' sexual practices to better understand and combat the AIDS epidemic, President Ronald Reagan, acting on his delegated power to implement the Paperwork Reduction Act, stopped the department from printing the surveys.

At times, politics more than programmatic necessity causes Congress to pass general policy after discovering that none of the more specific alternatives command a congressional majority. When legislators agree on a bill's goals but disagree on its specifics, they may deliberately swath its intent in vague language and leave it to the administration to deal with the details. At other times, members of Congress may find political advantage in delegating to

---

*As early as 1950, a survey found that over 1,100 public laws delegated discretionary authority to the White House. If such a survey were undertaken today, the number would, of course, be far larger.

the president broad responsibility for policies that might have politically unattractive outcomes. By "passing the buck," legislators hope to avoid blame. In the 1970s, for example, the principle that endangered species should be protected aroused far less controversy than any particular plan to achieve it. To avoid negative repercussions, Congress delegated to the U.S. Fish and Wildlife Service the discretion to establish criteria for classifying species as "endangered" and "threatened." Years later, when the service listed the northern spotted owl as a threatened species and limited the logging industry's access to Oregon's old-growth forests, the industry vented its anger at the agency and President George H. W. Bush—not at Congress. Not only did members of Congress escape retribution, but many subsequently won credit for softening the economic blow by passing a law that permitted timber companies to harvest fallen trees.

As indispensable as the executive office is for administering modern government's great variety of programs, the president is a tricky agent for Congress to delegate to. It is, after all, a separate

Contemplating the shock that his successor, General Dwight Eisenhower, would experience in the Oval Office, President Harry Truman remarked, "He'll sit here and he'll say, 'Do this! Do that!' And nothing will happen. Poor Ike—it won't be a bit like the Army. He'll find it very frustrating."

branch and thereby insulated from the kinds of control principals need to assure that their delegates comply with their preferences. Congress does not hire, nor can it easily fire, this agent. And because of the threat of a veto, Congress might find its hands tied when trying to rein in those presidents who are determined to take a program in a direction different from the one Congress intended. Moreover, with presidents separately elected, term limited, and (as shown in Table 7.2) frequently representing the other political party, presidents will rarely if ever view their role as Congress's dutiful agents. "Let anyone make the laws of the country, if I can construe them," quipped President William Howard Taft, this from an individual and in an era where presidents were not nearly so assertive as present-day White House occupants.[7]

A legislature that delegates too much discretion to a president may find that it surrendered control over the bureaucracy and the programs it administers. This is an important issue with a great deal at stake—environmental regulations, coverage of the Affordable Care Act, weapon systems, and trade agreements with other nations along with myriad other programs that constitute the work of modern government. Divided party control of these branches creates a dicey situation for politicians in both branches. This delegation dilemma renders the Constitution's seemingly simple and straightforward procedure of passing and sending presidents bills they either sign or veto so difficult and risky.

Although the Constitution confers on presidents little tangible authority to administer the executive branch, some presidents, judges, and law school professors regard Article II as offering presidents much greater authority than that specified in the Constitution. They read "The executive Power shall be vested in a President . . ." as conferring a broad mandate for presidents to undertake whatever actions they think necessary, so long as they do not explicitly run afoul of the law. Supreme Court justice Antonin Scalia expressed this view forcefully in a frequently cited passage he wrote in an opinion: "It is not for us to determine, and we have never presumed to determine, how much of the purely executive powers of government must be within the full control of the President. The Constitution prescribes that they *all* are."[8] Presidents Reagan and George W. Bush were vocal proponents of this expansive **unitary executive** theory of the presidency.* But all recent presidents who have found their policies frustrated by an opposition-controlled Congress have at one time or another acted as if the **unitary theory** were gospel as they sought to accomplish unilaterally those policies that Congress would not agree to.

## Unilateral Authority

Consider the administrative toolkit presidents have developed (or at least authority they claim to possess) to control government programs. At the outset of the chapter, we found Presidents Obama and Trump issuing numerous executive orders, some of which significantly altered government policy. Another, less conspicuous avenue involves informal instructions to their appointees. DACA originated with a letter to Homeland Security telling it to change its enforcement priorities. A large part of the work of the White House Office involves daily meetings and e-mails between the president's personal staff and their working contacts across the federal agencies. Of course, occasionally, administration executives will disagree with the president's policies or interpret their legal responsibilities differently. In such instances, presidents have a third source of control—replacing their department or agency executives.

News coverage of presidents' unilateral policymaking frequently refer to presidents' "executive actions." The last phrase has come in vogue over the past several administrations to refer to the increasing use of memoranda and informal letters to the departments.† Traditionally, presidents relied principally on **executive orders**. Since government officials began numbering and cataloguing them early in the twentieth century, presidents have issued nearly fourteen thousand executive orders. An early and one of the most famous of these was contained in the Pendleton Act of 1883, which inaugurated the civil service system. Initially, it converted only about 10 percent of the federal workforce from political patronage to merit appointments (see Chapter 8), but it also authorized the president to issue executive orders extending the civil service system to other classes of workers. Over the next half century, presidents issued a series of executive orders that shifted hundreds of thousands of employees into the civil service system.

---

*But one can find many other presidents expressing this sentiment at one time or another. "The most important factor in getting the right spirit in my administration," wrote Roosevelt, reflecting on his term, "was my insistence upon the theory that the executive power was limited only by specific restrictions and prohibitions appearing in the Constitution or imposed by Congress in its constitutional powers." Theodore Roosevelt, *The Works of Theodore Roosevelt* (New York: Scribner, 1926), 347.

†There is a third kind of unilateral presidential action called "proclamations." These are both more plentiful and less consequential, generally taking the form of commemoration—such as National Mentoring Month, National Stalking Awareness Month, and hundreds of others.

In recent years, presidents have increasingly enlisted an alternative administrative instruction called a **presidential memorandum**. These may at times read little differently than an executive order; they direct agencies to take specific actions as if the president were supervising its activities. When in late 2014 President Obama removed fear of deportation for nearly five million immigrants, he did so with a memorandum instructing the Department of Homeland Security to redirect its enforcement efforts. What is the difference, and why do presidents issue one instead of the other? Frankly, the differences are largely semantic. Both orders and memoranda enter the *Federal Register* as public notification of a new regulation or administrative action. Moreover, when issuing executive orders presidents cite specific provisions of the Constitution or public law as the basis for their action. Generally, so do memoranda, but not always.

Some critics suspect that the main reason why recent presidents have opted for the memorandum was to avoid attention and blame for acting unilaterally. President Obama and his allies in Congress sought to deflect criticism by observing that he had issued fewer executive orders than any president in over a century. Well, this is true, only because he had issued more memoranda than any of his predecessors. The opposite goal—to show that he is in charge—appears to motivate President Trump's numerous, highly public executive orders early in his administration.

Whether issued as executive orders or memoranda, executive actions are not laws in a couple of important respects. First, they are confined by the scope of the discretion delegated to the president. Note, for example, that President Obama repeatedly proposed immigration reform that would provide avenues for illegal immigrants currently in the United States to attain citizenship. But all that he could claim under current law was authority to concentrate scarce immigration control resources on some kinds of cases and not others.

Second, although executive actions *may* have the force of law, they lack its permanence. With certain exceptions, any president may revoke or alter an order with a new one. About a quarter of the nearly thousand executive orders issued from 1999 through 2018 dealt with a previous executive order. A few of these extended but the vast majority revoked a previous administration's order. And about half rescinded an order from the preceding administration. George W. Bush issued an order prohibiting funding for stem cell research. In one of his first official actions as president, Obama issued an order rescinding it. Congress can resist executive actions by withholding appropriations for those policies the executive order creates or by passing new law that explicitly revokes the order.

And federal courts have long shown a willingness to scrutinize executive orders more carefully than public laws. Judges ask such questions as whether the president's order is consistent with and allowed by current law or the Constitution. If not, the courts will likely void the order, as they did famously during the Korean War when President Truman issued an executive order seizing the nation's steel mills in order to avert a paralyzing national strike.

The most notable recent instance is a Texas federal district court's ruling that President Obama's order shielding millions of undocumented immigrants from immediate deportation (and giving them work permits) overreached his constitutional authority. In another case, a federal judge issued an injunction against the president's expansion of overtime wages for white-collar workers. President Trump's flurry of executive orders during his first month in office was met by a rush of lawsuits—sixty, by one count—challenging his unilateral actions.

When a federal district court suspended Trump's immigration ban within a week of its issuance, it became clear that the federal courts would not recede into the background with the arrival of the new administration. Because the Constitution does not specify in great detail the boundaries between administration and legislation, every generation has found politicians and judges trying to determine whether a president has the authority to take an action that some view as unconstitutional. They—including the judges—will frequently disagree on where to draw the line on presidential authority.

### Budgeting

Presidents carry out one of their most important "clerical" tasks when they formulate and send to Congress the annual budget for all federal programs. Yet budgeting also offers them an opportunity to set the spending priorities of the federal government. In fact, this authority exists because Congress long ago insisted that presidents assume responsibility for the government's bookkeeping. Until the 1920s, agencies sent their budget requests directly to the House Appropriations Committee, which held hearings, determined appropriations, and passed them on to the chamber for a vote and then over to the Senate for its consideration. During this process, no one formally solicited the president's views. But when the flow of department and agency budgets began to congest the legislative process, Congress in 1921 passed the Budget and Accounting Act, which gave the president responsibility for compiling budgets from the executive departments and submitting them to lawmakers as a single package. With this act Congress found itself strengthening the president's role in national policymaking.

The president's annual budget, submitted to Congress on the first Monday in February, culminates months of assembling and negotiating requests from the agencies to bring them into conformity with the White House's policy goals and proposed spending ceiling. The president's budget provides Congress with valuable technical and political information. Running into hundreds of pages, it supplies congressional committees with economic forecasts, projected tax revenues, baseline spending estimates for each department broken down by program, and other essential information for devising spending and taxation legislation. Politically the budget represents the president's "opening bid" in negotiations over how much the government should spend on particular programs and where the revenue will come from. Some years, the president's budget has sailed through Congress with minimal changes. Other years, Congress has ignored the president's proposals and written a wholly "congressional" budget, daring the chief executive to veto it. As we will see later in the chapter, presidential and congressional spending priorities can differ so much that compromise becomes a test of political will. And early in 2019, this test of will precipitated a government shutdown.

The growth in the president's administrative duties has ensured that Congress will generally give a chief executive's legislative proposals serious consideration. Beyond budgets, lawmakers expect presidents to advise them about problems with current policy and to recommend adjustments to improve performance. Presidents—and their appointees who administer federal agencies—enjoy an informational advantage, inherent in all delegation, that serves them well when proposing legislation. The administration will, at times, find that it can improve its chances of winning its favored bill by selectively withholding information from legislators. In a variety of ways, modern presidents' central role in administration ensures Congress's attention to their proposals. About 90 percent of presidents' initiatives are considered by some congressional committee or subcommittee.[9] Yet it does not assure their success. There are powerful electoral disincentives for opposition majorities to cooperate.

## The President as Legislator

In making new law the Constitution gives presidents only a modest role. They may call Congress into special session (little used, for the modern Congress is nearly always in session), and they are charged to report to Congress "from time to time" on the state of the nation. Singularly important is the veto. An opposition-controlled Congress may ignore presidents' speeches and declare their legislative initiatives DOA ("dead on arrival"), but they cannot ignore the veto. By requiring both chambers to assemble two-thirds majorities to override a veto, legislators must overcome serious transaction costs in order to legislate with disregard for the president's preferences. The veto is an authority well suited for presidents in this modern era when every White House occupant can expect to face an opposition-controlled House and/or Senate at some point during their tenure.

In assembling support for their legislation, presidents begin with their party allies in Congress. These men and women have a stake in their party leader's success, but this does not mean they will bow before the president's wishes. Members of Congress must, after all, attend to the interests of their constituents. Presidents cultivate the support of fellow partisans in Congress in many ways designed to strengthen members' standing back home. These include advocating spending on programs and public works (such as highways and water treatment plants) benefiting a district or state, appointing a member's congressional aide as an agency head, and visiting a lawmaker's district to generate local enthusiasm and financing for the next reelection campaign. Politicians in the White House and the two chambers of Congress follow the dictates of different electoral calendars. Consequently, presidents routinely confer with

their party's congressional leaders to determine which issues and stances attract support and to decide when to schedule presidential initiatives. The president's fellow partisans in Congress, conversely, do what they can to support their leader. Their shared party label might cause voters' assessments of the president's success to affect their own fortunes in the next election.

None of these incentives to cooperate is present in the president's relations with legislators from the opposition party. Indeed, opposition partisans in Congress correctly recognize that the president's legislative success might very well damage their vote count in the next election.

President Donald Trump arrives alongside Speaker of the House Paul Ryan (R) and Senate majority leader Mitch McConnell (C) as he prepares to speak to the press during a retreat with Republican lawmakers at Camp David in Thurmont, Maryland, January 6, 2018.

SAUL LOEB/AFP/Getty Images

Although no one wants to be perceived by voters as uncooperative or jockeying for narrow partisan advantage, both policy and politics generally give opposition-party legislators a stake in defeating the administration. As a consequence, opposition members' roll-call votes on average line up with the president's position less than half the time. Not a single Republican vote was cast in the House of Representatives for either the bailout legislation to deal with the financial crisis in 2009 or the Affordable Care Act (aka "Obamacare") in 2010. In 2017 Democrats returned the deed by uniformly voting against the Republican tax cut bill.

In appraising presidents as legislators, it is important to distinguish their leadership strategies and successes during unified and divided government. The former invites presidents to become legislative dynamos. All major spurts in congressional productivity have involved the presidents' early sponsorship and active promotion of their policies. Consider FDR's New Deal, Kennedy's New Frontier, Johnson's Great Society, and Obama's 2009 financial rescue plan—all famous bundles of legislation exceptional in the scope of their policies. It is no coincidence that they passed a Congress controlled by the president's party.

Conversely, during divided government, when the president confronts congressional majorities with different policy preferences and an opportunity to tarnish the president's standing with voters, several perverse political outcomes may occur. On issues where the

Jabin Botsford/The Washington Post via Getty Images

When the president and congressional leaders from the opposition party negotiate an agreement, each side may worry that the other side will renege on politically costly policy, leaving the other side being held responsible in the next election. At the close of 2018 with the government facing a shutdown over an appropriations bill that did not include funding for a border wall, the president invited incoming speaker Nancy Pelosi and Democratic Senate leader, Charles Schumer, to the White House for a negotiation. He did not tell them that the television crews would join them. The Democratic leaders viewed it as an ambush, but by most assessments, the media event turned out well for them after President Trump announced that he would take responsibility if the impasse shut down the government.

political parties differ sharply, neither side will be willing to compromise, and in the resulting gridlock the government accomplishes little and may even come to a virtual standstill.

## The Veto

The veto is the president's most formidable tool in dealing with a Congress controlled by the opposition political party. The Framers, ever alert to opportunities to introduce "checks and balances," were already familiar with the concept of an executive veto, exercised by most colonial and state governors. Unlike the president's administrative powers, the veto authority is defined quite precisely by the Constitution.* Over the past half century, presidents have averaged fewer than ten vetoes a year. The record belongs to Republican president Gerald Ford. Although he served less than one full term (from August 1974 until January 1977), Ford vetoed sixty-six bills. In the 1976 election he campaigned on his veto record, claiming that only a Republican in the White House would stand between hard-earned taxpayer dollars and the "spendthrift" Democratic Congress. Only twelve of Ford's vetoes were overridden, even though the Democrats commanded large majorities in both the House and Senate. Thus, Ford won many of the battles, but he lost the war—the election. President Obama issued the fewest—two—during his first six years. But throughout this period, his party controlled one or both chambers of Congress. After Republicans took over control of both the House and Senate in the 2014 elections, President Obama enlisted the veto ten times; none was overridden.

When dealing with an opposition Congress, presidents often use their veto authority to present a clear, self-enforcing means of asserting their policy preferences. Moreover, as Alexis de Tocqueville first observed in 1836, the public nature of the veto—frequently boosted by accompanying messages—enhances it as "a sort of appeal to the people," which modern presidents have not been shy about invoking whenever they discern public backing for their stands.[10] Earlier we noted that the Framers carefully tailored the president's veto authority to achieve seemingly contradictory goals: first, to check legislative abuses and second, to deny the executive the unilateral authority that in the hands of tyrants had proven so injurious to the welfare of ordinary citizens. The veto, with its strong but exclusively negative quality, seemed to meet both objectives.

Frequently, presidents may endorse a bill's purpose and its overall implementation but find some provisions highly objectionable. When the same party controls both branches, these disagreements are generally negotiated and resolved informally. Every party member facing another election has a stake in avoiding the appearance of internal conflict and disarray. It is during divided government that presidents will more often find themselves digging in and resisting legislation. Naturally, in these situations where they require significant changes before agreeing to a new policy, they would prefer to be able to remove those features they dislike and retain those they favor. The veto is not a very effective instrument for achieving this outcome. Congress will try to present them with a "take it or leave it" that they barely prefer to the status quo. The president signs a bill that gives Congress most of what it wants.

As divided party control has become the norm and partisan disagreements more contentious, presidents have sought in various ways to extricate themselves from the veto's take-it-or-leave-it choice. An early manifestation of this is impoundment (see Chapter 6,

---

*See section "Making Laws" in Chapter 6, p. 276, where the place of the veto in the legislative process is described in detail.

## LOGIC OF POLITICS
# The Veto Game

The veto game begins with the president and Congress at odds over a change in government policy (the status quo). If the two sides can agree on a change, a new policy will be created. If they continue to disagree and the president vetoes Congress's preferred policy, there is no change, and the status quo prevails. (It is assumed the congressional majority is too small to muster the two-thirds support needed for a veto override.) Within this context, three scenarios are possible:

### Scenario 1: The president and Congress have sharply different policy preferences.

This scenario depicts the simplest situation—and the only one that might actually end in a veto. Congress passes legislation changing the status quo. The president prefers the status quo, refuses to compromise, and simply vetoes the new legislation Congress has passed.

Anticipating this outcome, Congress may not even bother to create the legislation. When President Ronald Reagan (1981–1989) announced early in his first term that he would welcome legislation weakening certain provisions of the Clean Air Act, environmentalists in Congress knew that any attempt to strengthen the law during his tenure was doomed to failure. For the next eight years, then, the House Commerce subcommittee dealing with the environment occasionally held hearings but did not take action. The president's tacit veto trumped any real efforts to strengthen policy.

### Scenario 2: Congress favors a more drastic change in policy than does the president.

In Scenario 2 both Congress and the president want a change in the status quo, with Congress favoring a greater change than does the president. If Congress passes a law incorporating its preferences, the president will veto the bill because the administration favors the status quo more than the change Congress advocates. Nevertheless, Congress does not have to capitulate and precisely meet presidential demands. It only has to alter the original legislation enough to make the proposed policy marginally more attractive to the president than the status quo. Because the president's policy preferences are better served by signing than vetoing, the bill will become law.

When President George H. W. Bush (1989–1993) announced he would welcome a modest strengthening of the Clean Air Act, he shifted the game from Scenario 1 to Scenario 2. By stipulating early the provisions the bill would have to contain to win his signature, including a ceiling of $20 billion in new federal obligations, he was trying to signal precisely where the compromise should be. Democrats immediately went to work on new legislation, but they did not confine themselves to the changes the president had proposed. After all, they only had to provide him with a bill that he found marginally more attractive than current policy. In the end, the Democratic House and Senate passed a stronger bill than the president had wanted, and Bush reportedly spent almost the full ten days vacillating between a veto and a signature. Finally, Bush pronounced the legislation barely acceptable and signed into law the 1990 revision of the Clean Air Act. The president's temporizing and carping reflect how well congressional Democrats squeezed all they could from the president.

### Scenario 3: The president favors a more drastic policy change than does Congress.

In Scenario 3 the president and Congress swap places. The president favors a greater policy change than does Congress. Congress wants to change public policy as well, but by far less than does the president. Thus, Congress can confidently pass its preferred legislation and expect the president to sign it because the bill goes further in meeting the president's goal than does the status quo. In this situation the veto is worthless; Congress's preferences are enacted into policy.

In 1983 President Reagan sent Congress a budget calling for a 10 percent increase in defense spending. The Democratically controlled House agreed to only a 4 percent increase. When asked about the lower figure at a news conference, the president hinted that he might have to veto such

a bill. The Democrats, however, quickly turned the tables. On hearing of Reagan's comment, a Democratic leader retorted that the president had better be careful, for the next time the House might just lower the increase to 2 percent! President Reagan grudgingly signed the 4 percent increase.

These simple illustrations of veto policies reveal much about the role of the veto in presidential leadership. In the first instance, the veto allows the president to single-handedly preserve the status quo. In the second, it prescribes the kind of compromise that allows both sides to agree. In the third, the veto proves worthless in pushing Congress where it does not want to go.

p. 272) of appropriated funds. President Nixon signed the bills and then ignored their mandated spending, saying it would be inflationary. The Supreme Court ruled against the president,[11] but not before he signed a law allowing him to impound funds for forty-five days but no longer without a joint resolution passing Congress endorsing his action. This reform apparently passes muster constitutionally, for the courts have let it stand for a half century.

In contrast, a second reform, similarly intended to strengthen the president's hand in curtailing spending, was quickly struck down by the Supreme Court. Over the years some legal scholars and conservative politicians, looking for ways to control the growth of government, have flirted with the notion that the Constitution actually provides presidents with the opportunity to veto parts of enrolled bills. This **line-item veto** is enjoyed by forty-three states' governors. In 1996 the Republican majority in Congress anticipated winning the fall presidential election. They passed the Line Item Veto Act, providing that within five days of signing a bill into law, the president could formally reject its spending provisions and those tax breaks that affected fewer than a hundred persons or entities.* Before the Supreme Court declared it unconstitutional, ending its brief life, President Clinton actually invoked it to extract relatively minor policies from several bills.

The third approach presidents have enlisted to selectively enact parts of a bill is the **signing statement**. For decades presidents have issued statements representing their views about the bill they were signing. Most such statements are congratulatory, but during periods of divided government, presidents may include them with their signature to express their understanding of the legislation's purpose, perhaps to persuade some judge in the future to their point of view.

President George W. Bush issued so many signing statements that news reporters began counting them, and during the 2008 presidential campaign candidate Obama took

*Congress could repass the vetoed provisions with a simple majority vote, but the president could veto them as well.

Young Menachem and his dad at the Supreme Court. On this young man's case rests "separation of powers."

Bush to task for his numerous claims that he could ignore parts of dozens of new laws. Ironically, President Obama during his first term issued similarly issued signing statements—albeit significantly fewer. In signing the Defense Authorization Act of 2013 he singled out restrictions in the bill on transferring detainees out of military prisons in Afghanistan and Guantánamo Bay, Cuba. He signed the bill but then claimed his constitutional commander-in-chief responsibilities allowed him to override its limits, as he deemed necessary.

However, presidents usually do not follow through with their threat to sign but ignore a provision. For this reason, the courts have not definitively weighed in on the legal status of these signing statements. One Supreme Court case does suggest that presidents are on solid ground when they correctly size up the constitutional deficiency of a law. In 2002 Congress passed a bill allowing parents of children born in Jerusalem to list Israel as the child's place of birth. President George W. Bush signed the bill but stipulated that this provision infringed on "the president's constitutional authority to conduct the nation's foreign affairs," and that he would ignore it.* Menachem Zivotofsky, a U.S. citizen born in Jerusalem in 2002, wanted Israel listed as his birthplace on his passport. Menachem's parents insisted that the 2002 law be upheld and that their son's passport state that he is a citizen of Israel. In 2015, the Supreme Court disagreed. Future rulings may show whether Menachem's case influences decisions on the constitutionality of signing statements.

This brings us to the veto threat, the most pervasive effort presidents have taken to remove objectionable provisions from otherwise acceptable legislation. Presidents might be the last to vote, and then only to accept or reject a piece of legislation, but this does not mean that they will passively await the choice Congress presents them. Facing an opposition Congress, modern chief executives do all they can to break out of the Constitution's "take it or leave it" bind. Here presidents sometimes find threatening to veto proposed legislation useful. They commit in advance to veto a bill if it fails to include or omit certain provisions. More often than not threatened authorization bills fail to reach enrollment. Perhaps the president was insisting on too much change that legislators were unwilling to or could not accommodate. Those threatened bills that did pass and the president signed reflected a compromise constructed around

---

*Specifically, Bush said, the provision "could interfere with my ability as commander in chief to make time-sensitive determinations about the appropriate disposition of detainees in an active area of hostilities." If it operates "in a manner that violates constitutional separation of powers principles, my administration will implement it to avoid the constitutional conflict."

the veto threat. About half of the objectionable provisions were in the final bill dropped or substantially changed to accommodate the president.[12]

To be effective, a veto threat must be credible—that is, presidents must convince legislators that they are not bluffing. This strategy requires that the threat be explicit and leave the president little wiggle room. Moreover, it must be public—the more public the better—so that presidents will incur political embarrassment by backing down. Ronald Reagan is famous for his "make my day" and "line drawn in the sand" announcements in which he insisted that Congress give him legislation that reflected his preferences or suffer a veto. Of course, because such announcements may be politically costly, presidents do not issue them casually. Bravado stands against popular bills can backfire immediately in an adverse public response. In such instances Congress will be sure to pass the threatened bill in order to elicit the veto and remind voters just where the president stands. Heading into the 1992 presidential election the Democratic Congress passed the highly popular Family and Medical Leave Act despite President George H. W. Bush's veto threat. He promptly vetoed the bill. So what did Congress do? It changed the language slightly and passed it again and forced yet another veto.

■ **FIGURE 7.1**   Presidential Use of the Veto and Veto Threats

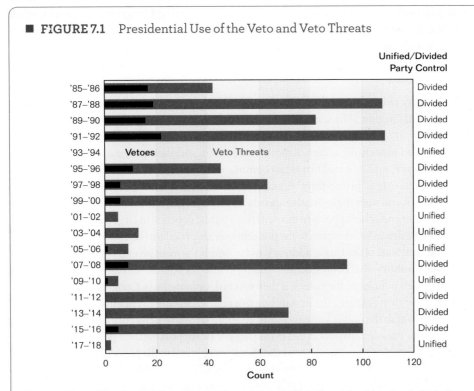

*Source:* Adapted from Scott M. Guenther and Samuel Kernell, "Veto Threat Bargaining on Authorization Legislation" (Ch. 6), in Samuel Kernell, *Veto Rhetoric* (Washington, DC: CQ Press), in preparation.

*Note:* The figures represent veto threats in presidents' Statements of Administration Policy targeting House bills pending floor consideration in the House of Representatives.

And tying one's own hands to gain credibility entails risks. Presidents cannot change their position without hurting themselves politically. As a result they rarely do. But whenever presidents ponder such a move, they invariably remember when George H. W. Bush accepted the Republican presidential nomination in 1988 by declaring, "Read my lips: no new taxes." Several years later, during a funding crisis that threatened to shut down the federal government, Bush relented and agreed to the Democratic Congress's demand for a tax increase. Immediately, politicians and the press howled that the president had lied to the American public. A major Republican consultant declared it to be "the most serious violation of any political pledge anybody has ever made."[13] During the 1992 campaign Bill Clinton ran ads showing the rousing convention pledge and questioning whether Bush could be trusted. Exit surveys found about a quarter of those who voted against Bush cited this broken promise as the chief reason for their vote.[14]

Even so, as we find in Figure 7.1, modern presidents threaten vetoes frequently. President Clinton averaged fifty-five threats per year during his six years (1995–2000) when Republicans controlled the House and Senate. President George W. Bush issued 214 explicit veto threats during his two terms. He even threatened legislation during the two Congresses when fellow Republicans controlled both chambers. President Obama issued 221 veto threats. President Trump formally threatened a veto only twice during his first Congress (the 115th), when Republicans controlled both chambers. With Democrats in firm control of the House of Representatives after the 2018 midterm elections, this will surely change.

## Going Public

Until the early twentieth century, presidents routinely satisfied their constitutional obligation (Article II, Section 3) by sending their state of the union messages to Congress by courier. There, an officer of Congress read the presidential communiqué, from all eyewitness reports, inaudibly to an inattentive audience more interested in socializing after a long adjournment. Today, however, sophisticated broadcast communications have transformed the **State of the Union address** into a "prime-time" event. It represents presidents' best opportunity to mold public opinion and steer the legislative agenda on Capitol Hill. The influence presidents derive from this event and other appeals to the American public depends in large part on the susceptibility of politicians in Washington to the political breezes presidents can stir up in the country.

The annual State of the Union address is today simply the most prominent instance of a strategy of **going public**—that is, presidents engaging in intensive public relations to promote themselves and their policies to the voters. If they succeed, opponents in Congress may fear voters' reprisals in the next election. Understanding this reality, popular presidents frequently exploit their ability to grab the public's attention and generate favorable news coverage for their legislative initiatives. Presidents who succeed in rallying public support for their policies may force the accommodation of a Congress otherwise indifferent or opposed to the president's ideas.

Evidence suggests that presidents view going public as a viable alternative to negotiating with the opposition on Capitol Hill. As a Clinton aide explained to reporters who were complaining about the heavy travel schedule, "Clinton has come to believe that if he keeps his approval ratings up and sells his message as he did during the campaign, there will be greater acceptability for his program. . . . The idea is that you have to sell it as if in a campaign."[15] Immediately after Senator Jeffords's defection in 2001 cost Republicans control of the Senate,

Having campaigned in 1988 on the slogan "Read my lips: no new taxes," President George H. W. Bush was hunted down by reporters in 1990 after he conceded a tax increase in negotiations with congressional Democrats. When reporters caught the president jogging one morning and baited him with his contradiction, he yelled, "Read my hips." In the national news story that followed, the president's response was reported as an expression of his disregard for his promises.

reporters asked President George W. Bush's chief of staff, Andrew Card, how the president would respond. Card replied that Bush might have to switch strategies and "use the bully pulpit a little more . . . to get [his legislation] moving." (Originating with President Theodore Roosevelt's characterization, "bully pulpit" refers to the advantageous position afforded the office for rallying public support.)

In the aftermath of reelection, President Bush used his 2005 State of the Union address to launch a "Sixty Stops in Sixty Days" blitzkrieg around the country to build a grassroots campaign for a massive overhaul of Social Security. His appearances were accompanied by extensive television advertising by the Republican National Committee and business groups supporting his privatization proposal, as well as by various groups opposed to his reforms. In pursuing this strategy Bush outdid Clinton by engaging Congress with unprecedented levels of travel to telegenic settings, speeches to appreciative audiences, and targeted television commercials.

If asked to name a president whose addresses drew a warm response from the American public, many would think first of Franklin Roosevelt, whose thirty nationally broadcast radio addresses, known as "fireside chats," rallied the American public during the Depression and World War II. Others might recall John Kennedy's speeches and live press conferences. Presidents Reagan and Clinton scored well in public relations. From this list of specialists in presidential rhetoric, we might conclude that nothing much has changed over the past half century. An examination of the number of times presidents have gone public, however, reveals a different picture. We can easily discern the steady growth in public relations undertaken by the White House in the rising number of presidential speeches and days devoted to political travel.

Today presidents devote a great deal of their time and energy, and the efforts of more than a quarter of their staff, to appealing directly to the American people for support for themselves and their policies. Though appearing on prime-time television is the most dramatic way of going public, presidents rely on this method sparingly, holding their major television addresses in check. They know they will lose the public's attention if they go to this well too often. During the energy crisis of the late 1970s, Jimmy Carter informed a consultant that he was about to deliver yet another nationally televised speech—the fifth!—on the need to conserve energy. Backed with polling data, the consultant talked him out of it, by arguing that the public had stopped paying attention to him.*

AP Photo/Mike Stewart, File

A familiar scene: a president meeting with representatives of a core constituency. In this instance, President Donald J. Trump speaks before members of the National Rifle Association.

---

*Several decades earlier, Franklin Roosevelt had made a similar point in private correspondence: "The public psychology . . . [cannot] be attuned for long periods of time to the highest note on the scale. . . . People tire of seeing the same name, day after day, in the important headlines of the papers and the same voice, night after night, over the radio." Douglass Cater, "How a President Helps Form Public Opinion," *New York Times Magazine*, February 26, 1961, 12.

Since the Carter years, the continued growth of cable and satellite subscription services has eroded presidents' capacity to enlist television to go public. In the 1960s, when viewers had few choices other than NBC, CBS, and ABC, these networks would agree to suspend commercial programming and broadcast the president's address.* They even used the same camera feeds; consequently, viewers had little recourse other than the apparently drastic alternative of turning off the television, which, as audience ratings indicate, very few did. Since 1970 the proportion of American households that subscribe to cable and satellite television has grown from 7 percent to over 90 percent, and the number of cable channels has multiplied dramatically. Viewers have more alternatives to watching a presidential speech than ever before. Consequently, presidents have increasingly focused their energies to tailoring appeals to targeted constituencies. Hence, domestic travel to annual meetings of trade associations and other groups (see Figure 7.3) to appeal for a group's support for a legislative initiative (minor addresses in Figure 7.2) represents the area of strongest growth in public relations from the White House.

Today, presidents occasionally deliver nationally televised addresses, but they are clearly on the wane. The bottom line for both presidents and television producers is the size of the audience. Aware that when viewers change channels, they often do not return for the rest of the evening, the big three television networks have increasingly balked at surrendering airtime to presidents for national addresses. A good indicator of presidents' shrinking national audiences can be found by comparing the number of households watching presidents' State of the Union addresses over time. President Obama's 2016 address drew barely 31 million viewers, setting a record for the smallest audience yet. This rating was a fifth smaller than his predecessor's last State of the Union address, and barely half that of Bill Clinton's. President Trump crowed that his 2018 audience share at 45 million households for his State of the Union address was the largest ever. Although it exceeded Obama's last two speeches, it fell short of other recent presidents' second-year addresses.

Mindful of the limitations of television, presidents communicate with voters in other ways. They take their messages to the public through appearances at graduation exercises, union conferences, and conventions held by trade and professional associations, where they can address the concerns of particular constituencies. Figure 7.2 reveals that these less visible, minor addresses have provided increasingly attractive vehicles for presidential communication.†

Presidential foreign and domestic travel, typically undertaken for different political purposes, has increased significantly in the past half century (see Figure 7.3). President Dwight Eisenhower's 1959 "goodwill tour" around the world is generally recognized as the first international presidential travel for which favorable publicity appeared to be the primary consideration. Subsequent presidents have favored the idea as well. By the end of his third year in office, George H. W. Bush was so conspicuously absent due to overseas travel that his

---

*The first instances of outright refusal occurred in the 1980s, when President Reagan encountered network resistance to his request for airtime on two separate occasions. In June 1992 the networks denied President George H. W. Bush a time slot for an evening press conference, and six of President Clinton's appearances (through January 1998) failed to attract full network coverage.

†At the end of 2019 we will count and post President Trump's speeches and travel on the book's website.

■ **FIGURE 7.2**   Presidential Addresses: Going Public More Often

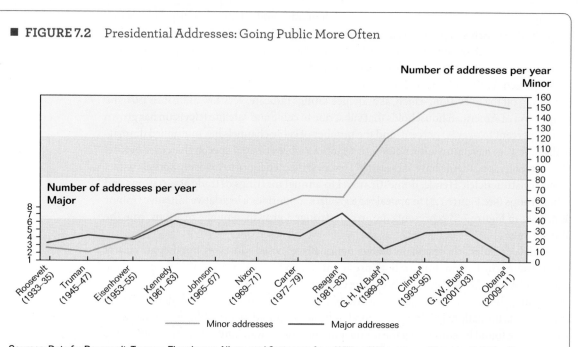

Sources: Data for Roosevelt, Truman, Eisenhower, Nixon, and Carter are from William W. Lammers, "Presidential Attention-Focusing Activities," in *The President and the American Public,* ed. Doris A. Graber (Philadelphia: Institute for the Study of Human Issues, 1982), Table 6-1, 152. Data for Kennedy, Johnson, Reagan, G. H. W. Bush, Clinton, and G. W. Bush are from the *Public Papers of the Presidents* series.

*Note:* Data reflect yearly averages. To eliminate public activities inspired by concerns of reelection rather than governing, only the first three years have been tabulated. For this reason, Gerald Ford's record of public activities during his two and one-half years of office has been ignored. Data on President Obama's first three years in office were calculated by Samuel Kernell and Josh Benjamin using www.whitehouse.gov/briefing-room/speeches-and-remarks.

[a]Includes television addresses only.

critics—especially his opponent in the next election, Bill Clinton—found a large segment of the public agreeing with him that the president was not paying enough attention to solving the economic recession at home.

Clinton had a special reason for his heavy domestic travel schedule: with third-party candidate Ross Perot in the race, Clinton had won the 1992 election with just 43 percent of the popular vote. By the 1996 election Clinton had averaged a visit to California, with its fifty-four electoral votes, every six weeks. Just as a precarious victory had motivated Clinton to travel, it also spurred his successor, George W. Bush, who eked out an Electoral College win. During his first three years in office, Bush logged nearly a third of his days in office traveling somewhere in the United States or abroad.

President Trump's extensive domestic travel during his first two years offered an opportunity to roast the Washington news media that he vilified during his presidential campaign. Although President Trump has also traveled extensively around the country, he has adopted

■ **FIGURE 7.3**    Going Public Involves More Presidential Travel

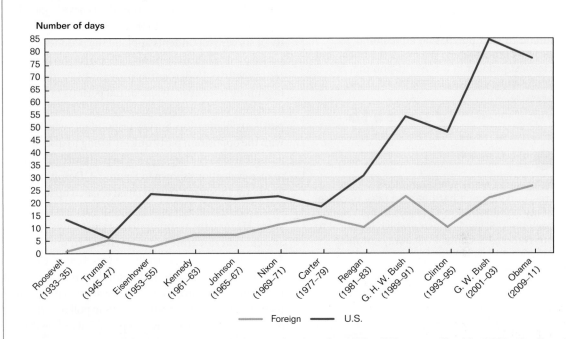

*Sources:* Data for Roosevelt, Truman, Eisenhower, Nixon, and Carter are from William W. Lammers, "Presidential Attention-Focusing Activities," in *The President and the American Public*, ed. Doris A. Graber (Philadelphia: Institute for the Study of Human Issues, 1982), Table 6-5, 160. Data for Kennedy, Johnson, Reagan, G. H. W. Bush, Clinton, and G. W. Bush are from the *Public Papers of the Presidents* series. See also Samuel Kernell, "The Presidency and the People: The Modern Paradox," in *The Presidency and the Political System*, ed. Michael Nelson (Washington, DC: CQ Press, 1984), 244.

*Note:* Data reflect yearly averages. To eliminate public activities inspired by concerns of reelection rather than governing, only the first three years have been tabulated. For this reason, Gerald Ford's record of public activities during his two and one-half years of office has been ignored. Data on President Obama's first three years in office were calculated by Samuel Kernell and Josh Benjamin using www.whitehouse.gov/schedule.

a different strategy than Clinton. Where Clinton sought to solidify support in states he had barely lost or barely won in 1992, Trump has concentrated instead on his raucous appeals to his most loyal supporters. Although they do little to broaden his support, they assured the president an enthusiastic, telegenic audience for news coverage. Where Trump has truly innovated in going public is in his use of social media. By the end of 2018 the president had averaged seven tweets a day to about 40 million followers. About 8 percent of the public report in surveys having directly read one of the president's Twitter messages, although three times that number have learned about one of his tweets via news coverage.[16]

The president's leadership of public opinion also rests on the public's appraisal of him as president. When an unpopular president issues public appeals, citizens will be inclined to ignore him and suspect base motives for his appeal. Long-term trends in presidents' approval

A sampling of President Trump's tweets during his first term.

ratings display a public that over the years has become increasingly critical of politicians who occupy the Oval Office. With one exception, presidents have begun their terms on *honeymoon* with the public, as a large majority of survey respondents applaud the president's early performance. The exception is Trump, who began his tenure with a 45 percent approval rating, the lowest beginning level ever. These initial periods of goodwill have become increasingly short-lived. One reason is partisan polarization. Survey respondents who identify with the opposition party quickly swing to disapproval, as indicated in the large spread in partisans' job performance evaluations shown in Figure 7.4. Despite a robust economy, President Trump failed to catch up to his predecessors in winning public support over the next two years. He remains as unpopular as any of his successors at a comparable time in their tenure. In one respect, Trump has fared significantly worse than the others. Never have Democrats and Republicans disagreed so much in their appraisal of the president's job performance as in November 2018. A Gallup poll reported that only 5 percent of Democrats approved of his job performance, but 91 percent of Republican respondents did so.

Polarized opinions pose both advantages and disadvantages. On the plus side, the nearly unanimous Republican voters' support will prevent other Republican candidates from straying far from Trump's fold. Those Republican senators who were Trump's most determined critics all left office in 2016. John McCain (AZ) died of cancer, and Jeff Flake (AZ) and Bob Corker (TN) both retired, as did a prominent Republican critic in the House, Trey Gowdy. If the president's support among Republican voters fades leading up to 2020, he will be left without any constituency. Another downside of polarized support is his limited ability to rally public support for his policies. The only people paying attention to his views are his ardent boosters.[17]

Presidents have many ways to communicate their views to the American public. But how do individual citizens communicate their views to the president? Well, certainly voting is vital and the kind of communication that elected officeholders covet. Many Americans do more; they write and call the president. So many do

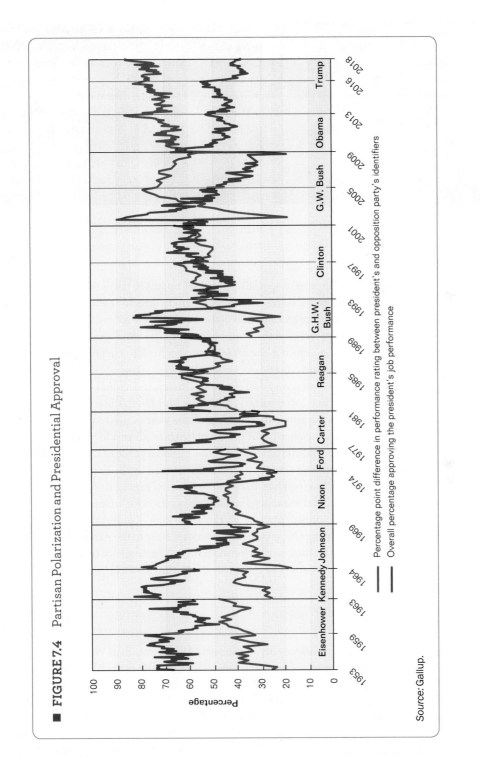

■ **FIGURE 7.4** Partisan Polarization and Presidential Approval

Percentage point difference in performance rating between president's and opposition party's identifiers

Overall percentage approving the president's job performance

*Source:* Gallup.

Pro-Trump rally in Tampa during summer 2018.

Anti-Trump rally in New York City during fall 2018.

so, the White House Office has a specialized staff set up just to tally and respond to opinions expressed in these communications. President Obama's director of presidential correspondence reported that his office received 100,000 e-mails, 10,000 letters, 3,000 phone calls, and 1,000 faxes. Oh yes, they received these numbers every day. And almost all of them ask the president for something—from a late social security check to curtailing nuclear proliferation.[18] Nearly a half million Americans went online to sign one of two petitions to Obama seeking a pardon for Steven Avery and Brendan Dassey, individuals convicted of murder and featured in the Netflix documentary, *Making a Murderer*. The president had to issue a statement explaining to the public that the defendants were convicted of a state crime in the Wisconsin courts, and consequently, the president had no authority to pardon them.[19]

Everything we have considered thus far about the emergence of the modern presidency implies vastly more work and activity than was envisioned by the Framers. As government programs have grown, Congress has delegated to the chief executive significant responsibility for managing the large bureaucracy and ample discretion for adapting policy to changing circumstances. Modern presidents aspire to be more than disinterested administrators, of course. Whether in lobbying Congress or in communicating to the public, they depend heavily on staff to help them do their work. Consequently, the emergence of modern presidential leadership has been accompanied by the steady development of a larger, more complex staffing system.

## The Institutional Presidency

As an organization the presidency began modestly. When President Washington summoned his secretary to help him with correspondence, Thomas Jefferson walked through the door with pen and paper. With such quality, who needs quantity? By the early 1800s the number of staff working in and around the White House was fewer than a dozen, of whom two or three were clerks who spent most of their time copying letters, receiving visitors, and running errands.[20] When Franklin Roosevelt entered the White House more than 130 years later, the president's staff had grown to about fifty, mostly "**detailed staff**" from another government agency sent over to lend the White House a hand. Agencies were happy to loan the president staff, for it ensured them inside information of what the president was up to. The Federal Bureau of Investigation and War Department were large contributors to the president's staff before the White House had its own.

Despite the growing workload associated with overseeing the executive branch departments, the presidency remained undeveloped as an organization. It depended largely on the president's daily assignments to unspecialized aides. By all assessments, Roosevelt was a master in managing his staff. Yet, coming into office in 1933 at the outset of the Great Depression, FDR's administration began with a frenzy of legislative and organizational activity. Congress appropriated nearly $5 billion with few strings attached. Fearful with some justification that many cabinet officials were holdovers of a succession of Republican administrations who were unsympathetic to the New Deal, the president persuaded Congress to give him the latitude to create more than a dozen new agencies outside the standing bureaucracy.* By the end of the second year, he complained repeatedly that personally managing the New Deal bureaucracy had turned the White House into a "five ring circus."

Moreover, FDR frequently bemoaned his inability to elicit advice from and give orders to the departments except through cabinet secretaries, many of whom had their own constituencies and incompatible ideas about their department's mission. Frustrated, he sometimes compared himself to "a power plant with no transmission lines." More than any of his predecessors, Roosevelt sought to take charge of the executive branch. Yet he was still yoked to a nineteenth-century office.

When in 1937 Louis Brownlow, one of a new breed of progressive public administration reformers, proposed that he form a committee to undertake a study of the president's staffing needs, Roosevelt jumped at the offer. A year later, the Brownlow Committee concluded its detailed analysis with the understated conclusion, "the president needs help." Likening the president to the chief executive officer of a large corporation, the report called for the creation of an organization dedicated to helping presidents be modern administrators. If the president was indeed the government's CEO, as Brownlow claimed, the office needed the same kinds of authority, expertise, and information modern corporate executives had at their fingertips. The recommendations in the **Brownlow report** failed to appreciate that the Constitution withholds from the presidency the kinds of command authority CEOs typically enjoy in running their businesses.

The chief executive's constitutional predicament was not lost on Congress, however. When a delighted President Roosevelt forwarded Brownlow's recommendations to Capitol Hill for enactment, he was rebuffed. Many in Congress, still angry over FDR's ill-fated attempt to pack the Supreme Court (described in Chapter 9), refused to act on the report's recommendations. Not until two years later, with the world edging toward the precipice of war, did Congress agree to a reduced form of Brownlow's staffing proposal. It created the Executive Office of the President as a collection of agencies designed to advise and otherwise assist

---

*The Works Progress Administration (WPA), for example, was not housed in the Department of the Interior, and over time it vied with that department's Public Works Administration (PWA) for funding and projects. Many of the other New Deal agencies remain familiar acronyms today: SEC (Security and Exchange Commission), NLRB (National Labor Relations Board), SSA (Social Security Administration), FHA (Federal Housing Administration), REA (Rural Electrification Administration), FCC (Federal Communications Administration), and TVA (Tennessee Valley Authority).

presidents. The staff would continue to grow in number and scope of activity. The responsibilities and resources available to modern presidents certainly set them apart from their nineteenth-century predecessors or any figure imagined at the Constitutional Convention.

Thus, the institutional presidency was born. Christened the **Executive Office of the President (EOP)**, it housed five "new" presidential agencies, two of which remain significant assets for present-day presidents: the Bureau of the Budget (reorganized and renamed the **Office of Management and Budget [OMB]** in 1970) and the **White House Office**, the president's personal staff system (see Figure 7.5).[21] This enlarged staff would allow presidents to keep tabs on the daily business of the departments and agencies. The Brownlow report called for the creation of the White House Office—comprising six loyal "Assistants to the President," who would serve the president with "a passion for anonymity." When President Roosevelt read this phrase, he reportedly chuckled and quipped that such an animal does not exist in Washington.*

■ **FIGURE 7.5**     Organization of the Executive Office of the President[a]

*Source:* Figure adapted from Bradley Patterson, "Key to the Organization Chart of the Obama White House Staff," Summer 2009, accessed at http://whitehousetransitionproject.org/resources/briefing/SixMonth/Patterson%20-%20BAMA%20WHITE%20HOUSE%20STAFF.pdf.

[a]Area proportionate to number of senior assistants. Offices concerned with residence, security, and administration of the White House are excluded.

[b]NSC includes the Homeland Security Council; does not include staff "detailed" from agencies.

***

*The rash of "kiss and tell" books from staff that has afflicted every presidency—and Trump's more than most—confirms FDR's suspicion.

Over the years the Executive Office of the President has housed those agencies the president or Congress would like to keep in the shadow of the White House. Typically, the dozen or so agencies that make up the acronym world of the modern EOP work much more closely with the president and the White House staff than they do with each other.* One can reasonably view the institutional presidency, as one political scientist aptly described it, as a "presidential branch of government separate and apart from the executive branch," which "sits across the table from the executive branch . . . and imperfectly attempts to coordinate both the executive and legislative branches in its own behalf."[22]

In performing classic staff functions, these agencies gather information from the departments and agencies (**National Security Council**, or **NSC**), Congress (OMB), or the broader policy environment (Council of Economic Advisers and Council on Environmental Quality), or they maintain the organization itself (Office of the Vice President and Office of Administration). With no programs to administer, the presidential bureaucracy does not require a field staff outside of Washington.

The largest and most important of the presidential agencies is the OMB. Staffed by accountants, economists, and tax lawyers, the OMB creates the president's annual budget request, monitors agency performance, solicits recommendations from the departments on **enrolled bills** (bills that have been passed in identical form by both houses of Congress and presented to the president for his signature), and performs **central clearance** over agencies' communications with Congress. Another important agency within the EOP is the NSC. Its statutory responsibility appears modest: to compile reports and advice from the State and Defense Departments and the Joint Chiefs of Staff and to keep the president well informed on international affairs. Yet the national security adviser, who heads this presidential agency, has at times assumed a role in conducting foreign policy that is close to that traditionally associated with the secretary of state.

The White House Office has grown in both number and complexity.

OMB staff read a proposed bill to decide which agencies' views should be solicited before sending recommendations to the White House.

Samuel Kernell

---

*Among locals, even the president sports an acronym, POTUS (the president of the United States).

What began as a small, informal group of half a dozen aides has evolved into a large, compartmentalized, multilayered bureaucracy. Richard Nixon assembled the largest staff, at almost 660. It probably would have continued to grow had the Watergate scandal that drove him from office not sent some Nixon aides to federal prison and turned the size of the White House staff into a campaign issue. Moreover, Congresses since then, most controlled by opposition parties, have reined in staff growth through budgets and legislative language limiting the president's ability to borrow staff from other agencies.

The present-day White House staff has leveled off at about 450 full-time positions. In large part the growth of staff follows the ever-expanding responsibilities of presidents, but it also springs from modern leadership strategies. Approximately a third of the staff attend to some aspect of public relations—travel, speeches, tending the press, and cultivating support among various constituencies. Similarly, as presidents have steadily centralized tasks that once were performed by their allies in the departments and agencies, they have added staff. Reputedly, no more than three or four of President Truman's aides ever dealt with vetting presidential appointments. Today, recruitment of appointees for the departments and federal judiciary is done almost exclusively from within the White House by a team of several dozen assistants.

In the early years small White House staffs were informally organized according to tasks and the working styles of the presidents. Franklin Roosevelt and Harry Truman favored a collegial organization in which they personally supervised their aides. Roosevelt resisted the notion of fixed staff assignments; throughout his term only his press secretary, appointments secretary, and legal counsel had well-defined duties and routines. FDR fostered competition by giving an aide projects that duplicated another aide's assignment. The staff was well aware of this practice, and therein lay its effectiveness. Aware that the president might already have been briefed on a subject, or soon would be, FDR's aides undertook their assignments with special diligence, not to be outdone. Not only were they thorough; they resisted the temptation to slant their reports to promote or nix a course of action according to their personal preferences. Through staff competition Roosevelt largely solved the "dependency" problem that afflicts all principals who rely on agents for information and advice.

Truman preferred more cooperative relations among his staff. He conducted a meeting each morning with ten to twelve of his "senior" staff to receive reports and give out assignments. Later presidents tried to emulate FDR's and Truman's collegial management styles, but as staffs grew, presidents found themselves devoting inordinate time to managing individuals whose positions were created to help the president get through the day. President Jimmy Carter was the last president to try to run the White House staff informally, but it proved so frustrating that he abandoned it in favor of an organization

AP Photo/File

H. R. Haldeman, chief of staff to President Richard Nixon, became entangled in the presidentially directed Watergate cover-up. After federal indictment in 1973, his boss asked him to resign his White House post, which he dutifully did. Haldeman subsequently served a brief prison term over this affair. In retirement he reflected on "the lessons of Watergate" in numerous public interviews and a memoir.

administered by a chief of staff. Perhaps reflecting his military background, President Eisenhower had introduced the more orderly and hierarchical organization headed by a chief of staff. His assistants had fixed routines, job titles, and middle-level supervisors. Whatever its advantages in clarifying day-to-day responsibilities and relieving the president from personally having to manage his agents, it rendered the president heavily reliant on and vulnerable to his chief's and other staff's assessment of what actions and policies he should embrace.*

The chief of staff has become a fixture in the White House. More broadly, specialists performing specific routine tasks have replaced yesterday's agents who depended on the president for assignments. Reflecting the more sophisticated division of labor, aides are recruited for specific offices and job titles according to their experience at different tasks. With several exceptions the **chief of staff system** has more to do with imposing a chain of command than with clarifying responsibilities and shielding the president from having to micromanage the staff's routine activities (see Figure 7.6).

At one time or another, all presidents have probably found the need to work through institutional channels irritating, even when they created these structures. None appears to have chafed at such confinement as much as President Trump. His first chief of staff lasted barely six months into his term. His second chief, John Kelly, was more successful, or at least was able to hold on to his job longer. By the end of the president's second year, he too was gone. Trump is the first president to be on his third chief within his first two years.

With its clear organizational lines, fixed assignments, and loyal and enthusiastic employees, one might think the White House staff system should run like a well-tuned engine. The facts, however, belie this naive expectation. Every recent president has experienced serious staffing problems that have erupted into public controversy, if not scandal. Many aides are motivated as much by interest in advancing a particular cause or policy agenda as by a desire to serve the president. This tendency is reinforced by outside pressures as key constituencies lobby for one of their own to be on the staff. "Everyone in the White House has a constituency," complained senior Reagan aide Michael Deaver.[23] In 1978 a Carter aide who sided with his Jewish constituency's opposition to the sale of reconnaissance jets to Saudi Arabia called a press conference and resigned in protest.[24] More often, staff will discreetly "leak" to the press information supporting their preferences. (The strategy of White House leaks is taken up more fully in Chapter 14.)

Most of the president's staff come to Washington lacking the experience suitable for their new position. Typically, many arrive at the White House fresh from the presidential campaign; others are sent over from the retinue of conservative and liberal think tanks of policy wonks who are attached politically to one of the political parties. Aides enter service committed to certain policies that may at times differ from the president's preferences. For example, rather than seek compromise on a controversial policy with members of Congress, campaign aides in the White House might wrongly advise their president to stand firm on constituency commitments and appeal for public support, even when reasonable accommodations are available.

Some staff members view their positions at the White House as way stations to lucrative careers. These aides may have a greater stake in the outcomes of decisions and making their mark

---

*On many issues Eisenhower's chief of staff instructed White House aides that if an issue could not be reduced to a single page, it was not ready for the president's consideration.

■ **FIGURE 7.6** Organization of the Trump White House, 2017

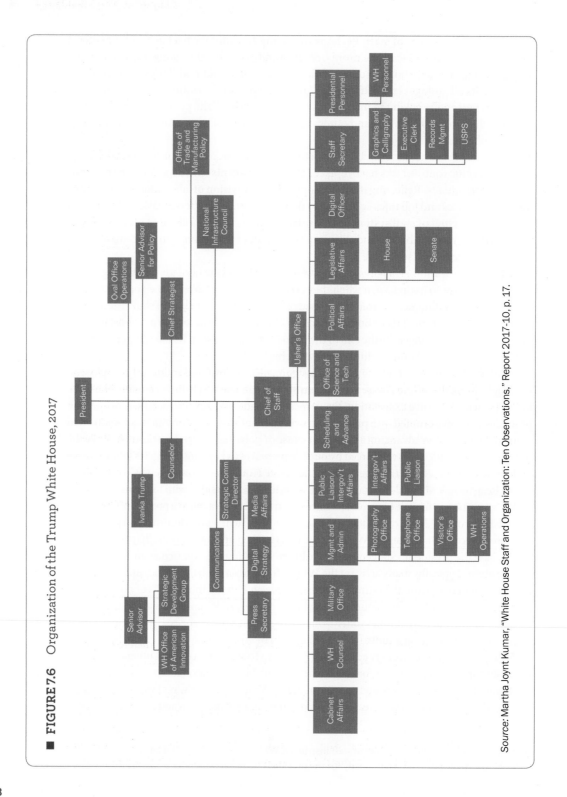

*Source:* Martha Joynt Kumar, "White House Staff and Organization: Ten Observations," Report 2017-10, p. 17.

President Trump speaks on the phone in the Oval Office, joined by Chief of Staff Reince Priebus, Vice President Pence, Senior Adviser Steve Bannon, Communications Director Sean Spicer, and National Security Adviser Michael Flynn. Only Pence, whose job is protected by the Constitution, remains.

on policy than in respecting the integrity of the organization's procedures—procedures designed to advance the presidential agenda. As staff members compete with others inside and outside the White House for influence, the tenets of orderly organization can crumble. Against these centrifugal forces stands the president, imploring aides to work tirelessly and anonymously on the president's behalf. Invariably, staff turnover is high, but none have come close to matching turnover in Trump's White House. Over the course of his first two years, sixty percent of Trump's senior White House aides departed. This compares to a quarter of Obama's and H. W. Bush's staff, a third of W. Bush's, and 40 percent of Clinton's.[25] Not surprisingly, this turnover has spawned a rash of former staff's "kiss and tell" books describing a White House in continuous turmoil.

## Conclusion

This chapter closely hews to the Constitution's plan for this new (really, novel) form of government. The introduction of Congress in the Constitution's Article I leaves no doubt that it is the singularly authoritative branch for deciding society's collective action commitments. The Framers envisioned a conservative biased process, and with coequal legislative chambers, they installed a substantial veto point well before an enrolled bill could be presented to the president. The subsequent internal development of these chambers only increased opportunities to block a majority's effort to pass a bill.

Students of Congress have long judged the Framers as largely having succeeded in designing Congress to frustrate small and brief majorities from imposing their preferences on public policy. Adding intense partisanship and regularly divided party control of one or both chambers to the mix introduces a scenario where gridlock is not just possible but likely. Yet issues continue to arrive in Washington, insisting on resolution. The flow of legislation through gridlocked Congresses may dwindle, but the need for governance continues unabated. Congress's inability to legislate creates a policy vacuum that presidents, whatever their political party or ideology, have willingly filled.

In the gridlock scenario the inherent advantage presidents enjoy is their ability to act. They can issue executive orders and other, less formal instructions to the agencies and departments. They may couch their actions as a temporary patch to a problem, awaiting passage of a more comprehensive policy. When Barack Obama created DACA in a letter to Homeland Security setting enforcement priorities and extending work permits and other benefits to a class of young undocumented immigrants, he justified his action as temporary, lasting only as long as necessary until Congress passed immigration reform. Temporary or not, Donald Trump has found that his predecessor's unilateral action cannot be so easily undone. Two years into his term, Trump has failed to deliver on his campaign promise to end DACA. Congress still has not passed reform, and, in the meantime, federal district judges have thrown up various procedural roadblocks to curtailing DACA.

Circumventing Congress with unilateral action does not mean the president controls policy. This alternative course simply transfers his dependence from Congress to the federal bureaucracy and the courts. Each of these sets of actors may hold policy preferences at odds with those of the president. Enamored with May Day military parades in France and Russia, President Trump ordered one for Memorial Day in Washington. The military resisted, citing expense and logistical problems and the likely damage the heavy armaments would pose for Pennsylvania Avenue. The president quietly dropped his plans for the parade. A more serious case of unresponsiveness for Trump can be found at the Justice Department. Despite continuously railing against the scope of special prosecutor Robert Mueller's investigation of Russia's social media interference with the 2016 election, the president has failed to alter the department's scrupulously maintained hands-off posture.

Unilateral policymaking lacks the durability of congressional policymaking. One glaring deficiency of the former is money. Presidents can announce a policy, but unless it is costless or the agency charged with action can transfer funds across programs, their aspirations for unilateral policy may be no more successful than were they to have submitted the policy to a gridlocked Congress. President Trump could send troops to reinforce the border in anticipation of the caravan of Central American asylum seekers without worrying about where the Pentagon would find the money. He could not, however, unilaterally build his fabled wall with its $25 billion price tag or even cover the first $5 billion installment without congressional funding.* But even if the bureaucracy backs the president and has the wherewithal to act, opponents have found sympathetic federal judges ready to block the president with national injunctions. So, it is fitting that the next two chapters shift the sights of our investigation to the bureaucracy and the judiciary to examine how these institutions respond to unilateral policymaking.

**Want a better grade?**

Get the tools you need to sharpen your study skills. Access practice quizzes, eFlashcards, video, and multimedia at **edge.sagepub.com/kernell9e.**

---

*In early 2019 President Trump threatened to invoke the National Emergencies Act to transfer construction funds from the military to border wall construction.

# KEY TERMS

Brownlow report   333

central clearance   335

chief of staff system   337

commander in chief   308

detailed staff   332

divided government   304

enrolled bill   335

executive agreement   310

Executive Office of the President (EOP)   334

executive orders   314

going public   324

line-item veto   321

National Security Council (NSC)   335

Office of Management and Budget (OMB)   334

presidential memorandum   315

signing statement   321

State of the Union address   324

"unitary executive"   314

unitary theory   314

War Powers Act   309

White House Office   334

# SUGGESTED READINGS

Howell, William G. *Thinking about the Presidency.* Princeton, NJ: Princeton University Press, 2013. This is an extended, thoughtful, pre-Trumpian essay on the paradox of presidential leadership. Continuing a theme introduced by Neustadt (see below) a half century earlier, Howell asks how presidents might parlay their formal authority into the power to satisfy public expectations.

Kernell, Samuel. *Going Public: New Strategies of Presidential Leadership.* 3rd ed. Washington, DC: CQ Press, 1997. The author develops more fully the argument summarized here that modern presidents are more inclined than were their predecessors to engage in public relations in seeking influence in Washington.

Neustadt, Richard E. *Presidential Power and the Modern Presidents: The Politics of Power from Roosevelt to Reagan.* 4th ed. New York: Free Press, 1990. This volume is *the* classic statement of the leadership predicament confronted by all presidents. Originally published in 1961 and in print ever since, the book is a touchstone for anyone aspiring to understand the American presidency.

Woodward, Bob. *Fear: Trump in the White House.* New York: Simon and Schuster, 2018. Legendary *Washington Post* reporter who reported Deep Throat's secrets about the nefarious goings on in the Nixon White House now turns his sights on the chaotic Trump administration.

# REVIEW QUESTIONS

1.  What are the powers granted to the president in the Constitution? What are the nonconstitutional sources of presidential power? When were these sources of power first tapped?

2.  What are executive orders? Executive agreements? What are the president's alternatives to using them?

3.  How did the presidency of the 1800s differ from that of today? In particular, how did the president's interactions with his party and his cabinet change over time?

4.  What are the trade-offs between the collegial and chief-of-staff models of presidential staff

organization? Which model seems to have predominated with recent presidents?

5. What is "going public"? What specific tools or resources are available to the president when he chooses to use this strategy?

6. How has the rise of cable and satellite television affected the president's ability to communicate with the public?

7. Why don't members of Congress go public as often as the president does? Why doesn't the president use this tactic on every issue?

The U.S. compound in Benghazi, Libya, went up in flames after an attack by Islamic militants killed four Americans, including the ambassador. Later reports by the State Department and by Congress pointed out the bureaucratic failures that slowed the American response.

# The Bureaucracy

## KEY QUESTIONS

- Who controls the bureaucracy? Is it the president? Congress? The courts? No one?

- How can the government grow while the bureaucracy shrinks?

- Why do efforts to make government agencies more accountable lead to the proliferation of red tape?

- How can elected officials design formal and informal mechanisms to oversee the implementation of laws by millions of unelected bureaucrats?

## CHAPTER OBJECTIVES

**8.1** Describe the development of the federal bureaucracy over time.

**8.2** Relate when the federal government grows most quickly, and why.

**8.3** Explain the bureaucracy's culture and the challenges it faces.

**8.4** Identify the tools that Congress and the president use to control bureaucracies.

**8.5** Discuss why red tape is often an important check on the operation of massive bureaucracies.

Just a year after a loose confederation of militias had overthrown longtime dictator Moammar Kadafi in Libya, the new American ambassador to the nation, J. Christopher Stevens, traveled from its capital of Tripoli to the city of Benghazi. Stevens was a widely respected diplomat who knew the country well. He was especially familiar with the coastal town—it was where he had arrived in Libya on a Greek cargo ship when the country was still in the throes of its civil war. As ambassador, he was returning to Benghazi to help create a new cultural center, modernize a hospital, and lay the groundwork to turn the temporary State Department facility there into a permanent outpost.

When Ambassador Stevens flew to Benghazi on September 10, 2012, he could bring only two diplomatic security agents along with him, leaving the other four serving in Libya at the time at the embassy in Tripoli. The reason these forces were spread so thin was that just a month earlier, the number of State Department security agents in the country had been reduced from thirty-four to six. But when the ambassador arrived in Benghazi, Central Intelligence Agency (CIA) agents on the ground briefed him about a "worsening security environment" due to rising activity by groups such as al-Qaeda, the Islamic Brethren, and Egyptian Islamic Jihad. Ambassador Stevens took these concerns seriously, with the final entry in his personal journal the next day noting the "Never ending security threats." Still, the ambassador continued with his work of meeting with members of the Local Council that helped run the city after the revolution deposed the Kadafi regime.

Beginning at 9:42 p.m., dozens of armed Islamic militants attacked the compound with explosives, rocket-propelled grenades, and heavy machine guns. As Ambassador Stevens and the six other Americans in the compound prepared to shelter in place and defend against the assault, the attackers started a massive diesel fire that sent toxic smoke into the compound. Stevens and State Department information officer Sean Smith died of smoke inhalation. Sounding the alarm up to other layers of the bureaucracy, one diplomatic security agent in the compound pleaded, "If you guys don't get here, we're all going to f——ing die."

The CIA agents posted nearby came to the aid of those in the compound, with the Americans fighting against continued attacks over more than eight hours. Though President Obama and top Pentagon officials quickly learned about the situation and authorized immediate military support, help did not reach the compound in time. By the end of the attacks, two former Navy SEALs and CIA operatives, Tyrone S. Woods and Glen Doherty, had also been killed.[*]

Did the Benghazi attacks take such a terrible toll—including the first ambassador killed in the line of duty since 1979—because of bureaucratic failures? The many reports released on the subject by Congress and the State Department do not agree on all aspects of exactly what created this vulnerability and how to strengthen security in the future but coalesce on a few central failings. An independent review by a former ambassador concluded that security at the compound was "grossly inadequate" and that State Department officials overseeing security displayed a "lack of proactive leadership." In the wake of the report's release in late 2012, four department officials were removed from their posts.[†]

The top leader of this bureaucracy, then–secretary of state Hillary Clinton, took responsibility for the attacks in Benghazi when she testified before Congress in 2013. The department's accountability

REUTERS/Jason Reed

Testifying before Congress, Hillary Clinton fights back tears as she describes watching the victims of the attack on the State Department's compound in Benghazi returned to the United States alongside President Obama.

---

[*]This material is drawn from Congress's 2016 "Report of the Select Committee on the Events Surrounding the 2012 Terrorist Attack in Benghazi," accessible at http://benghazi.house.gov/NewInfo, as well as the press reports noted.

[†]Michael R. Gordon and Eric Schmitt, "4 Are Out at State Department after Scathing Report on Benghazi Attack," *New York Times*, December 19, 2012.

■ **MAP 8.1**   Fighting Forces in Libya

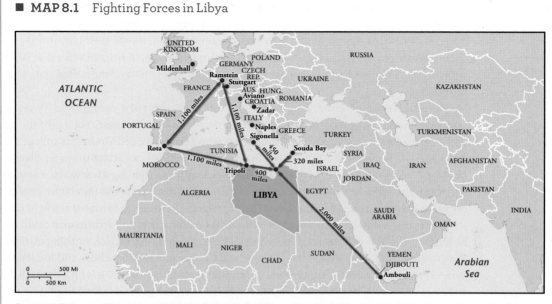

Source: U.S. House of Representatives, The Select Committee on Benghazi, "Report of the Select Committee on the Events Surrounding the 2012 Terrorist Attack in Benghazi as Ordered, Reported on July 8, 2016," p. vii, accessed at http://benghazi .house.gov/sites/republicans.benghazi.house.gov/files/documents/Cover.pdf.

Note: This map, included in Congress's 2016 "Report of the Select Committee on the Events Surrounding the 2012 Terrorist Attack in Benghazi," shows how far away all of the military's useful assets were from the State Department's facility in Benghazi, Libya, when four Americans were killed there.

review board provided twenty-nine recommendations to improve security at embassies and other offices around the world, and Secretary Clinton quickly accepted all of them. In her testimony, she admitted that "we do have to work harder and better to balance the risks and the opportunities. . . . For me, this is not just a matter of policy. It's personal."*

When Congress completed its final report, after a two-year, seven million dollar investigation, the U.S. military's bureaucracy also came under heavy criticism. The report concluded, "The assets ultimately deployed by the Defense Department in response to the Benghazi attacks were not positioned to arrive before the final, lethal attack." (See Map 8.1.) Marines stationed in Spain received conflicting orders about whether they would be sent in, but would not have arrived in time. According to the *New York Times*, "The 800-page report delivered a broad rebuke of the Defense Department, the Central Intelligence Agency and the State Department—and the officials who led them—for failing to grasp the acute security risks in Benghazi, and especially for maintaining outposts there that they could not protect."

The high-profile failure to protect Americans in Benghazi provides a dramatic illustration of the challenges faced every day by a federal bureaucracy charged with tasks as

*Transcript: Hillary Clinton Takes Responsibility for Benghazi Attack, Defends Actions in Emotional Testimony before Congress," *New York Daily News*, January 23, 2013.

mundane as delivering the mail and as critical as defending diplomats from a terrorist attack. Accomplishing either of those tasks requires the coordinated actions of thousands upon thousands of federal employees, each an expert in a specialized job but needing to work in concert with others. Coordinating their actions requires the ability to anticipate threats and challenges in an ever-changing world, and balancing the opportunities to serve that world with the risks inherent for public servants. This is the complexity—and the critical stakes—of **bureaucracy**.

Bureaucracy can seem deadly boring. No one ever inspired a young child by saying "Someday you could grow up to be a top bureaucrat of the United States!" Yet it is by the figurative and literal armies of federal bureaucrats who administer Pell Grants for college students, enforce the Clean Air Act, ensure that Medicare patients can access the most effective health care technologies, and organize the complex logistics of fighting a war that the work of American government is done. The energy of their individual efforts and the efficiency of the organizational structures that coordinate them determine whether government works or fails.

The example of Benghazi shows that the stakes of bureaucratic performance could not be higher. Without a system that puts policies effectively into practice, nothing else that Washington, D.C., does matters. Presidents and Congress may debate bills, and judges can issue orders, but none of these pronouncements implement themselves. It is only through the workings of a bureaucracy binding together millions of on-the-ground federal employees that the high-minded deliberations in our capitol translate into concrete change across the country and the world.

Clearly, government would cease to function at all without bureaucrats. But who occupies the diverse departments, agencies, bureaus, commissions, and other units of the executive branch that encompass the bureaucracy? What drives them or prevents their agencies from working perfectly? The many millions of individuals who carry out this work each have their own career goals, policy preferences, and human frailties that sometimes get in the way of government's working well.

The challenges faced by a bureaucratic system are multifaceted. Scholars Anthony Bertelli and Laurence Lynn phrase one of them simply: "While citizens and their representatives expect public managers to 'get the job done,' significant aspects of 'the job' that public managers are supposed to accomplish are often ambiguous. These unelected officials must decide what the law, circumstances, and common sense require of them in given situations. Once they have exercised their best judgment, it is all too common for these same citizens and their representatives . . . to say to an offending public manager, 'No, that's not the job we wanted you to do.'"[1] When bureaucrats go far beyond the bounds of what the public wants, they risk upsetting the balance that Alexander Hamilton laid out in *Federalist* No. 70, contrasting the need for "energy in the Executive" against the need for "safety." And when politicians seek to constrain bureaucrats, they run into the problem laid out by sociologist Max Weber in 1919. After observing the highly professionalized German bureaucracy, Weber noted how hard it was for generalist politicians to keep tabs on expert bureaucrats, who possessed information that lawmakers and the public did not.

All of these challenges are different facets of the basic dilemma of delegation, made more difficult by the fact that American bureaucracy forms the second of two layers of delegation. The American people delegate power to make their collective decisions to elected officials.

These lawmakers then hand over power to enforce and implement these decisions to the unelected bureaucrats whom they employ. Bureaucrats—ranging from cabinet secretaries to social workers to teachers to Drug Enforcement Administration agents—both serve and exert authority over the public. Enabling bureaucrats to understand what the public and lawmakers desire, and ensuring that they deliver it, is a constant and crucial challenge.

Though the Framers were largely silent on the design of American bureaucracy, the solution to this dilemma of delegation is built into our Constitution: our system of separated powers provides distinct checks on the bureaucracy. The executive branch employs all of these unelected officials, directing them through the thousands of top administrators who are appointed by the president. Congress attempts to control those who implement the laws it passes, both through the power of its purse strings and through oversight of administrative activities. The courts provide a vital check by upholding both administrative law and constitutional principles, forcing the bureaucracy to follow standardized processes and protecting against the tyranny of the majority. Highlighting how deeply connected the Federalists' system of separated powers is to the operation and legitimacy of the bureaucracy, the title of Bertelli and Lynn's book characterizes American administrators as *Madison's Managers*.

## The Development of the Federal Bureaucracy

The Framers viewed the executive as the necessary source of "energy" in government, but questions of administration received remarkably little attention at the Constitutional Convention, and the Constitution itself said little about how the executive branch was to be organized. As we saw in Chapter 7, it did authorize the president, with the advice and consent of the Senate, to appoint ambassadors, Supreme Court justices, heads of departments, and other senior executive branch officials. Congress was left with the task of establishing executive departments and determining how they would be staffed.

Throughout American history, Congress has created executive branch agencies with authority to implement the laws it passes, and presidents have necessarily delegated their executive chores to numerous subordinate agents. In the nation's earliest years these agents delivered the mail, collected customs duties (taxes on imported goods) and excise taxes (on alcohol and luxuries), prosecuted violations of federal laws, and managed relations with foreign nations. Surely the Framers did not envision anything like today's 184,000-member Department of Homeland Security (DHS) or the rest of the federal establishment, comprising some two thousand departments, bureaus, agencies, and commissions, which employ some 2.9 million nonmilitary personnel. But then they could not have anticipated the proliferation of demands for collective action that the next two centuries of social, economic, and technological change would provoke. A product of these demands, the modern bureaucracy also mirrors in a very direct way the pluralistic nature of American politics and society. Every new agency has been brought into being by a unique configuration of political demands and forces. Reflected in each agency's mandate and organization is the attempt of a successful policy coalition to preserve its victory through institutional design. The remarkable variety of arrangements adopted to administer government policies is largely a product of the endless search by Congress and the White House for ways to maximize the potential political benefits and minimize the potential political costs each time they decide to exercise and delegate their authority.

The end product is the extravagantly diverse collection of entities that now compose the federal bureaucracy.

## Modest Beginnings: The Dilemma of Delegation

From the beginning, Congress was wary of delegating too much power to the executive. The colonial experience with the king's governors and other royal officials was too fresh. But members of Congress also knew that delegation was unavoidable; the Continental Congress's attempt to make all administrative decisions through congressional committees had proved quite impractical. Delegate John Adams, for one, "found himself working eighteen-hour days just to keep up with the business of the 90 committees on which he served."[2]

With these experiences in mind, the First Congress began its work on the executive branch by reestablishing the departments that had existed under the Articles of Confederation: Treasury, Foreign Affairs (quickly renamed State after Congress decided to assign the department some domestic duties), and War. Congress also authorized the hiring of an attorney general to give the president and department heads legal advice. The larger departments were soon subdivided into more specialized offices, later called bureaus. For example, by 1801 the Treasury Department was dividing its work among units headed by a commissioner of revenue, who supervised tax collection; a purveyor in charge of buying military supplies; and an auditor who, among other duties, oversaw the operation of lighthouses. The Treasury Department also included a General Land Office to deal with the sale of public lands.[3] Congress readily agreed that each executive department should be headed by a single official responsible for its operations. There was far less consensus, however, about whether department heads were accountable to Congress or to the president. As noted earlier, presidents appointed senior officials, but appointments were subject to senatorial approval (see Chapter 7). Could presidents, then, dismiss officials without the consent of the Senate? The First Congress gave the president the sole right of removal, but only narrowly; Vice President John Adams cast the tie-breaking vote in the Senate.[4] The issue came up again during the Jackson administration (1829–1837) and later during Reconstruction (1865–1877) before it was finally settled in the president's favor: officials held their jobs at the pleasure of the chief executive. Nonetheless, many lower-level federal jobs such as local postmaster were, by the time of the Adams administration (1797–1801), effectively controlled by Congress. When the president turned to members of Congress for advice on appointments in their states and districts, they had quickly come to expect that it would be followed.

The dismissal controversy was one of many instances in which Congress faced the familiar dilemmas of delegation. The advantages of delegating authority to a unified executive that could energetically and efficiently implement laws were clear. But so was a potential drawback: executives might also pursue ends contrary to those desired by congressional majorities. Recognizing this drawback, Congress leveraged its authority to establish executive branch agencies and set their annual budgets as a way to balance the president's power.

The executive struggled with the same dilemma. Even the skimpy government of the Federalist period (1789–1801) was too large to be managed by the president and his cabinet secretaries without delegating authority to subordinate officials. Thus the executive also faced a standard principal–agent problem: how to ensure that agents acting ostensibly on its behalf would faithfully carry out official policies. As the nation has grown and the range of federal activities expanded, so has the challenge of keeping appointed officials responsive to elected officials, just as elected officials are, in their turn, supposed to be responsive to the citizenry. As we will see in this chapter, the various ways in which the government has tried to meet this challenge have had enduring consequences for the modern bureaucracy.

## The Federalist Years: A Reliance on Respectability

For many decades the federal government had few responsibilities, and so it was small. In fact, George Washington (1789–1797) had so few staff that he occasionally called on his cabinet chiefs to take dictation, making them secretaries in a less exalted sense.[5] Yet Washington and his successors still had to deal with the problem of delegation, heightened during the Republic's early days by long distances and primitive communications between the nation's capital and the states and cities where federal policies were administered.

During this period most federal government workers, laboring far from their bosses in the capital, were occupied with delivering the mail and collecting duties and taxes. The potential for corruption was considerable. President Washington believed that popular support for the young national government depended on honest and competent administration. Thus he sought to appoint civil servants of character and ability who were respected by their communities—in other words, men of superior education, means, family, and local reputation. The problem of delegation was to be met, in the first place, by choosing the right sort of people as agents. Other techniques also were used to ensure honest administration. Officials sometimes were required to post bonds of money or property that they would forfeit if they failed to perform their duties. Customs and alcohol tax collectors received a share of the proceeds from the sale of goods they seized from smugglers, giving them a financial incentive to detect and thwart smuggling. Heavy fines were imposed for giving or taking bribes.[6] President Washington's efforts to establish an honest, competent federal civil service largely succeeded. Although presidents remained free to dismiss officials at will, an informal custom of tenure during good behavior emerged and remained in place until the 1820s. Indeed, it was not uncommon for officials to pass positions on to their sons or nephews.[7] This practice, consistent with Federalist notions of government by respectable gentlemen, was contrary, however, to the democratic spirit that eclipsed Federalist views during the early decades of the nineteenth century.

## Democratization of the Civil Service: The Spoils System

The most prominent spokesman for this democratic spirit, President Andrew Jackson, argued that public offices held as, in effect, private property would "divert government from its legitimate ends and make it an engine for the support of the few at the expense of the many." Moreover, "the duties of all public officers are, or at least admit of being made, so plain and simple that men of intelligence may readily qualify themselves for their performance."[8] In other words, when it comes to governing, "no experience is necessary." Jackson thus advocated **rotation in office**; an official would serve in a position for a short, fixed period, then move on to something else, perhaps in government, but more often returning to private life. (The norm of rotation in office was also commonly practiced in Congress for much of the nineteenth century,

President Andrew Jackson's campaign to democratize public administration led to the distribution of government jobs to loyal party workers. This depiction of Jackson astride a gluttonous hog makes it clear that the "spoils system," as this practice came to be called, was by no means universally celebrated.

an informal forerunner of the modern term limits movement discussed in Chapter 15.) The Jacksonian idea was to democratize the civil service along with the rest of the political system.

The democratic ideal of rotation in office meshed with the practical need of party organizations to reward the activists they relied on to mobilize the expanding mass electorate (see Chapter 12). Who better deserved appointment to public office than the men who had proved their mettle by helping their political party to triumph? Debating this issue in 1835, Senator William Marcy, a New York Democrat, ensured himself a place in the history books by celebrating "the rule, that to the victor belong the spoils of the enemy,"[9] and giving the **spoils system**—the practice of the winning party's dispensing government jobs—its name. Once government jobs became a primary resource for maintaining party machines, members of Congress developed an even keener interest in influencing appointments to federal offices in their states and districts.

Ironically, rotation in office and the spoils system, meant to democratize administration, led instead to its bureaucratization. Bureaucratic organization arises when leaders try to solve the huge problems of coordination and delegation raised by many forms of large-scale collective action. Max Weber, the German sociologist, delineated more than a century ago the characteristic features of bureaucratic institutions:[10]

- a hierarchical structure of authority in which commands flow downward and information flows upward (for coordination and control);

- a division of labor (to reap the advantages of specialization in taking on complex tasks);

- a consistent set of abstract rules regarding what is to be done and who is to do it (for coordination among specialists, control over subordinates, and uniformity of action in each position regardless of who holds it);

- impersonality, treating everyone in the same category equally regardless of who they are as individuals (for consistency and impartiality);

- a career system, with appointment and advancement by demonstrated merit, and often considerable job security (to create incentives for loyal and effective performance); and

- specified goals toward which the collective action is aimed (unlike, for example, economic markets, in which individuals and firms have goals—making money— but the market as a whole does not).

The model bureaucracy is, in short, a purposive machine with interchangeable human parts designed to facilitate collective action (coordinating relevant actors, discouraging free riding, and enforcing cooperative agreements) while enabling principals to control agents. Centralized control is exercised over large numbers of people performing complex social tasks, greatly amplifying the power of whoever sits at the apex of the hierarchical pyramid. The classic example is an army, with its clear chain of command from the five-star general at the top down to the lowliest private at the bottom. Most modern corporations, government agencies, and even spiritual enterprises such as the Roman Catholic Church also have organized themselves bureaucratically for more effective central control over collective pursuits. But whatever its advantages, bureaucratic organization imposes heavy conformity costs on both bureaucrats and the people they deal with in return for reducing transaction costs and agency losses (see Chapter 1). The complex arrangements needed to ensure control quickly bred the kind of **red tape**—labyrinthine procedures, layers of paperwork (in quadruplicate!), demands for strict adherence to form—for which bureaucracies are legendary.

## Civil Service Reform

Under Jackson, the federal administration did not become fully bureaucratized in the Weberian sense; rotation in office precluded the development of government service as a career with job security and advancement based on merit. Only after the Civil War (1861–1865) were calls from citizens and reformers to adopt this additional component of bureaucracy finally heard. The emerging industrial economy raised administrative problems that a civil service composed of short-term amateurs was poorly suited to address. More important, financial scandals, particularly during Ulysses S. Grant's administration (1869–1877), fueled attacks on the spoils system and prompted political support for civil service reform.[11] Perhaps the most dramatic incident was the exposure of the Whiskey Ring, a massive conspiracy of revenue collectors and whiskey distillers to evade taxes, which, when exposed, led to 230 indictments and the resignation of one member of Grant's cabinet. Civil service reformers also exploited their pivotal positions as leaders of a swing constituency in an era of close two-party electoral competition.

Defenders of the old system did not give up easily, however, and reforms that protected officials from political firing and imposed merit criteria for hiring and advancement were extended gradually. The most compelling argument for reform was the assassination of President James Garfield in 1881 by a demented job seeker incensed at having lost a chance for a patronage appointment. The ensuing revulsion against the spoils system led in 1883 to

On July 2, 1881, Charles Guiteau, upset at being rejected for a patronage appointment, assassinated Republican president James A. Garfield in a Washington train station. Garfield died on September 19, 1881. The public uproar over the incident galvanized support in Congress for civil service reform.

passage of the Pendleton Act, the basis of the modern civil service. The act itself put only 10 percent of federal jobs under the merit system, but it authorized the president to extend coverage by executive order. Presidents from Grover Cleveland onward did exactly that, although, ironically, for the crassest of partisan motives. Each president about to relinquish office to the opposition party extended civil service protection to thousands of his own patronage appointees. By the time Franklin Roosevelt became president in 1933, 80 percent of federal workers were included in the merit system.[12] The merit system bred its own set of agency problems, however. Rotation in office may have left the government short on experience and efficiency, but it had kept officials in close touch with ordinary citizens and responsive to the elected politicians who appointed them. Some proponents of a professional civil service naively thought it would turn government agencies into efficient, politically neutral tools subject only to the will of policymakers in Congress and the White House. Career bureaucrats, however, inevitably develop their own personal and institutional interests, and the rules designed to protect them from political retaliation make it difficult to punish them for shirking or incompetence. They become the reigning experts in their bureau's procedures and policy domains, magnifying the problems of hidden action (principals unable to observe what agents are doing) and hidden information (agents knowing things that principals do not) inherent in principal–agent relationships (see the section "Delegation" in Chapter 1). Moreover, they can easily develop perspectives quite different from people outside government. Organized into unions, bureaucrats form a potent political force. These problems are compounded by a Constitution that compels Congress and the president to share, and compete for, control over administration; the agents can play their multiple principals against one another. The political attempts to come to terms with these problems are responsible for much of the complexity and diversity of the administrative units added to the federal government over the past century.

## An Expanding Government

Despite dramatic changes in *how* the government operated after Jackson, *what* it did changed very little. The number of federal officials grew along with the population, but they continued to perform the same limited set of tasks assigned during the Federalist period: collecting duties and taxes, delivering the mail, disposing of public lands in the West, granting patents, managing relations with foreign nations and Native Americans, and maintaining a small army and navy. The federal establishment began small and stayed that way for decades because most Americans wanted it that way. Cheap, limited government was part of the democratic creed professed by disciples of Thomas Jefferson and Jackson, and any attempts to expand the federal domain met firm resistance in Congress.

After the Civil War, however, the federal government began expanding its activities and personnel, and that trend, with a few exceptions, has continued to the present day. As Figure 8.1 reveals, federal employment grew steadily but not very steeply (except during World War I) from the 1870s until the New Deal period (1933–1941), when the rate of growth began to increase. World War II produced a dramatic surge in the size of the federal workforce that was only partially reversed afterward. The number of civil servants continued to trend upward until 1990, then underwent steady decline until the onset of the war on terrorism. As a proportion of the population, the federal workforce has actually been shrinking since the 1950s (see Figure 8.2). The federal government has not been shrinking in any other sense, however; politicians have found many ways to expand the government's activities without expanding its workforce.

Government could grow only if Congress and the president were willing to delegate authority to new agencies. Historically, the most common reasons for delegating authority have been to handle large-scale administrative tasks; to exploit expertise; to avoid blame for unpopular decisions; to make credible commitments to stable policy; or to deal with crises demanding swift, coordinated action. Varying goals have inspired varying degrees of delegation as well as different organizational strategies for limiting potential agency losses

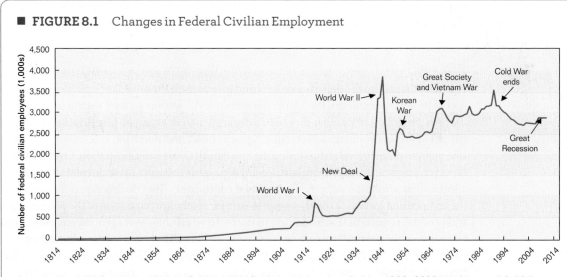

■ **FIGURE 8.1**   Changes in Federal Civilian Employment

*Sources:* Harold W. Stanley and Richard G. Niemi, *Vital Statistics on American Politics, 1999–2000* (Washington, DC: CQ Press, 2000), 259–256; data for 1999–2011 from U.S. Office of Personnel Management, *Federal Civilian Workforce Statistics, Employment and Trends,* bimonthly release.

■ **FIGURE 8.2**    Federal Civilian Employment Compared with the U.S. Population

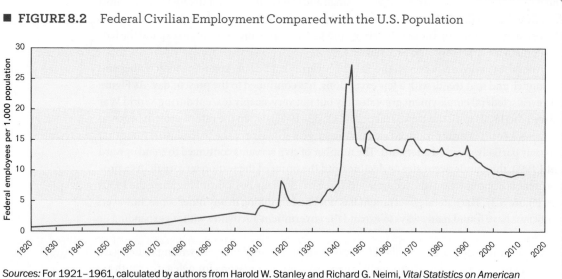

*Sources:* For 1921–1961, calculated by authors from Harold W. Stanley and Richard G. Neimi, *Vital Statistics on American Politics, 1999–2000* (Washington, DC: CQ Press, 2000), 259–260 and 355; U.S. Office of Personnel Management, *Federal Civilian Workforce Statistics, Employment and Trends*, bimonthly release; Bureau of the Census data accessed at www.census .gov/compendia/statab/cats/population.html.

(see Chapter 1). Political battles arising from conflicting goals within Congress and between Capitol Hill and the White House have also done much to shape and reshape bureaucratic institutions.

## The Cabinet

Agencies that rise to the department level and gain seats in the president's cabinet receive no special powers or privileges. Presidents can and do invite whomever they wish to serve in their cabinets, regardless of whether they head a department. For example, Lisa P. Jackson, administrator of the Environmental Protection Agency (EPA), and Ron Kirk, U.S. trade representative, enjoyed cabinet-level status during the first Barack Obama administration. Over the years, however, political entrepreneurs have fought vigorously to confer departmental status on the agencies that administer policies affecting their constituents. They do this in part for a leg up in the competition for scarce resources and in part for symbolic recognition of the political centrality of their concerns. Each addition to the roster of cabinet-level agencies represents and helps sustain the political triumph of a particular coalition. The history of the cabinet thus provides a concise, if incomplete, picture of the succession of social and economic interests that have become powerful enough to command this level of political recognition (see Table 8.1).

The symbolism of cabinet status was demonstrated by the creation of the Department of Education in 1979 and the Department of Veterans Affairs (VA) in 1988. By pushing through the legislation that established a cabinet-level Department of Education, President

**TABLE 8.1**   Origin of Cabinet-Level Departments

| | |
|---|---|
| 1789 | War, State, and Treasury (the attorney general, a part-time appointee, sat in on cabinet meetings as well) |
| 1798 | Navy (split off from War) |
| 1849 | Interior |
| 1870 | Justice (Office of the Attorney General was established in 1789 and elevated to department status in 1870) |
| 1889 | Agriculture (established in 1862 but not elevated to cabinet status until 1889) |
| 1903 | Labor (established as the Bureau of Labor in Interior in 1884; achieved cabinet status as the Department of Labor and Commerce in 1903; split from Commerce in 1913) |
| 1903 | Commerce (established as part of the Department of Labor and Commerce; split from Labor in 1913) |
| 1947 | Defense (combined War, Navy, and new Air Force Departments; initially called the National Military Establishment; renamed Defense in 1949) |
| 1965 | Housing and Urban Development |
| 1966 | Transportation |
| 1977 | Energy |
| 1979 | Health and Human Services (formerly Health, Education, and Welfare, 1953–1979) |
| 1979 | Education (established as a freestanding subcabinet department in 1867; placed in Interior a year later; eventually ended up in Health, Education, and Welfare, from which it split when it was raised to cabinet status) |
| 1988 | Veterans Affairs |
| 2002 | Homeland Security |

*Source:* Compiled by authors.

Jimmy Carter kept his promise to the teachers' groups whose support had been crucial to his bid for the White House. The elevation of the Veterans Administration to the Department of Veterans Affairs and to cabinet status was, among other things, a belated symbolic bow to veterans of the long, contentious Vietnam War as well as an effort by the Republican Reagan administration to woo the veteran vote. Neither department came with much in the way of new programs. Education took over programs and bureaus from the Department of Health, Education, and Welfare and other agencies; Veterans Affairs continued to do what it had done as an independent executive agency. Symbolism, then, played a major role in the creation of both departments. Proponents of the departments also hoped that cabinet status would strengthen each department's interests in the battle for government's limited resources, including the president's attention. But symbolism has its drawbacks. Until George W. Bush made education a centerpiece of his 2000 presidential campaign, Republican leaders had regularly sought to dismantle the Department of Education out of hostility to its largely Democratic clientele. And in 2014, the controversy over whether Veterans Affairs employees falsified records to obscure the long wait times for care at VA facilities led to the resignation of Veterans Affairs secretary Eric Shinseki.

Table 8.2 reports the size of each cabinet department, both in the number of employees and in the size of departmental budgets. The Department of Homeland Security, carved out of nearly two dozen agencies in the wake of the 9/11 attacks, is now behind only Defense and

**TABLE 8.2**   Projected Cabinet Department Staff and Budget Outlays: 2018 Budget

| DEPARTMENT | PERSONNEL (THOUSANDS) | BUDGET (BILLION DOLLARS) |
|---|---|---|
| Agriculture | 89 | 145.8 |
| Commerce | * | 9.9 |
| Defense | 741 | 612.5 |
| Education | 142 (along with HHS) | 63.9 |
| Energy | * | 28.2 |
| Health and Human Services | 142 (along with Education) | 1,167.9 |
| Homeland Security | 182 | 84.2 |
| Housing and Urban Development | * | 54.9 |
| Interior | 64 | 14.4 |
| Justice | 117 | 38.5 |
| Labor | * | 39.4 |
| State | * | 30.5 |
| Transportation | 55 | 79.7 |
| Treasury | 92 | 606.7 |
| Veterans Affairs | 359 | 176.8 |

Source: U.S. Office of Management and Budget, Historical Tables, Table 4.1, Table 16.1.

*Commerce, Energy, Housing and Urban Development, Labor, and State combine to form an "other" category with 246,000 employees.

Veterans Affairs in number of personnel, although other departments have much larger budgets, notably Treasury, which pays the interest on the public debt, and Health and Human Services (HHS), which administers the Medicare program. Altogether, the executive branch departments account for about 63 percent of the civilian government workforce and about 80 percent of the more than $3.7 trillion the federal government spends annually. The rest is accounted for by a host of agencies that, for a variety of calculated political reasons, have been placed outside the mainline departments.

One of the original four cabinet-level departments, the Treasury Department takes on tasks that range from advising the president on economic policy to the literal printing of money. Here Treasury Secretary Jack Lew is on Capitol Hill in April 2013, to testify before the House Ways and Means Committee to defend President Barack Obama's budget proposal for fiscal 2014.

## Noncabinet Agencies

The expansion of the federal government has not been confined to cabinet-level executive departments. Since the Civil War, Congress and the president have created an additional set of administrative bodies to make and carry out national policy. Most fall into one of three general categories: independent executive agencies, regulatory commissions, and government corporations.

### Independent Executive Agencies

Executive agencies are placed outside departments for one of several reasons, all political. Presidents promoting new initiatives that demand quick action may want to avoid placing bureaucratic layers between them and the responsible agency. For example, President Kennedy kept his cherished Peace Corps out of the stodgy and unsympathetic State Department. When the Soviet Union launched its space vehicle *Sputnik* in 1957, the National Aeronautics and Space Administration (NASA), established in 1958, was the administrative response. Its status as an independent executive agency reflected both the space program's urgency and the politicians' desire to keep it in civilian hands. NASA proved to be a brilliant organizational success, fulfilling President Kennedy's audacious dream of landing a man on the moon by 1969. Agencies also may report directly to the president to enhance the agency's prestige; the EPA, a candidate for cabinet status during the Clinton administration, is an example. In keeping with the president's role as commander in chief, the directors of national intelligence, the U.S. Arms Control and Disarmament Agency, and the Selective Service System all report directly to the president. Their independent status is intended, in part, to keep important defense-related activities—intelligence gathering, arms control negotiations, and the draft—under predominantly civilian control.

### Independent Regulatory Commissions

Unlike the independent executive agencies, independent regulatory commissions are designed to maintain their independence from the president and the executive departments. Congress adopted the commission form of administration to cope with new problems of delegation. The emergence after the Civil War of an industrial economy with a national market gave rise to economic dislocations and disputes on a scale too wide to be managed, as in the past, by local authorities. As a result, the railroads and the steel, oil, and banking industries became targets for national regulation. But Congress could not and did not want to do the regulating itself; the issues were too many, too technical, too dynamic, and too fraught with political conflict. The regulatory commission represents Congress's attempt to hedge against the potential political costs of delegation by restricting the influence of presidents and party politics on regulatory decisions. Table 8.3 lists the most important independent regulatory commissions.

A major reason for delegating authority to an independent agency is to avoid direct responsibility for unpopular decisions. In 1887 Congress set up the now-defunct Interstate Commerce Commission (ICC) to regulate the railroads in part because any decision made about shipping rates would likely anger some politically potent interest. The Postal Regulatory Commission takes the heat for increases in postage rates. The most striking case, however, is the Federal Reserve System, which makes decisions of enormous consequence for the entire economy (see the Logic of Politics box "Insulating the Fed" on p. 364). In this case and in others, the agency's independence helps insulate the president and Congress from the political fallout from unpopular decisions, explaining why both have been willing to accept this form of administration.

Over the years, the government's regulatory reach expanded in roughly three waves. The first, which swept in during the late nineteenth and early twentieth centuries as government sought to cope with a rapidly expanding national market economy, was regulation of the railroads (Interstate Commerce Commission), trusts (Federal Trade Commission), and monetary system (Federal Reserve System). The second, also economic in focus, occurred during the 1930s as part of the Roosevelt administration's response to the Great Depression. The government assumed responsibility for, among other things, the integrity of the banking system (Federal Deposit Insurance Corporation), the stock market (Securities and Exchange Commission), and labor relations (National Labor Relations Board). The third wave occurred during the 1960s and 1970s as a growing network of activist organizations lobbied successfully for federal protection of consumers (Consumer Product Safety Commission), motorists (National Transportation Safety Board), the environment (Environmental Protection Agency, Nuclear Regulatory Commission), and civil rights (Equal Employment Opportunity Commission).

The third wave did the most to expand the scope of regulation (see Figure 8.3). The dramatic growth in regulation during the 1970s, as measured by the number of pages in the **Federal Register** (which publishes all new administrative rules that have the force of law), was followed by a drop in the 1980s after the deregulation of the transportation and telecommunications sectors and the 1981 arrival of the Reagan administration, which was ideologically hostile to regulation. The Clinton administration clearly was not, and regulatory activity expanded once again during the 1990s before leveling off during the more antiregulatory

**TABLE 8.3**   Independent Regulatory Commissions

| AGENCY | YEAR ESTABLISHED | TERM OF SERVICE | SERVICE AT PRESIDENT'S DISCRETION? |
|---|---|---|---|
| Federal Reserve System (Fed) | 1913 | 14 | No |
| Federal Trade Commission (FTC) | 1914 | 7 | No |
| Federal Deposit Insurance Corporation (FDIC) | 1933 | 6 | No |
| Federal Communications Commission (FCC) | 1934 | 7 | No |
| Securities and Exchange Commission (SEC) | 1934 | 5 | Yes |
| National Labor Relations Board (NLRB) | 1935 | 5 | No |
| Federal Maritime Commission (FMC) | 1961 | 5 | No |
| Equal Employment Opportunity Commission (EEOC) | 1965 | 5 | Yes |
| National Transportation Safety Board (NTSB) | 1966 | 5 | Yes |
| Postal Regulatory Commission (PRC) | 1970 | 6 | No |
| Consumer Product Safety Commission (CPSC) | 1972 | 7 | No |
| Commodity Futures Trading Commission (CFTC) | 1975 | 5 | No |
| Federal Election Commission (FEC) | 1975 | 6 | No |
| Nuclear Regulatory Commission (NRC) | 1975 | 5 | No |

*Source:* Compiled by authors.

George W. Bush administration. The regulatory climate continues to shift in response to real-world events.

## Independent Government Corporations

When Congress puts the government in the business of delivering the kinds of services usually provided by private corporations, it sometimes imitates the corporate form of

■ **FIGURE 8.3**    The Growth of Federal Regulation

*Sources:* Harold W. Stanley and Richard G. Niemi, *Vital Statistics on American Politics, 2003–2004* (Washington, DC: CQ Press, 2003), 266; data for 2003–2015 compiled by author from the Office of the Federal Register, "Federal Register Pages Published 1936–2015."

administration as well. Like private corporations, government corporations are typically run by a chief executive officer, or CEO, under the supervision of a board of directors or commissioners and chosen in the same manner as members of regulatory commissions. Government corporations can buy and sell property, lend and borrow money, and sue or be sued like any other business. Congress, however, may put any constraints it chooses on their organization or activities.

Besides the U.S. Postal Service, the most important of the government corporations are the Tennessee Valley Authority (TVA) and the National Railroad Passenger Corporation, or Amtrak. The TVA was created in 1933, during the New Deal, to develop electric power, water transportation, and agriculture in the Tennessee Valley area, which at the time was poor and economically backward. Amtrak, launched in 1970, represents Congress's effort to maintain intercity rail passenger service, which had been dying out for want of investment and from competition from air, bus, and auto travel. The U.S. Postal Service actually predates the Constitution; it was established in 1777 by the Second Continental Congress. Known then as the Post Office Department, it was for much of its history the largest government agency delivering the most familiar government service. It also was a major source of congressional patronage during the heyday of patronage-based party politics in the latter decades of the nineteenth century (see Chapter 12). But politics did not promote efficiency or innovation in the postal service, and by the post–World War II economic expansion, the system's inadequacies had become quite evident. The agency was radically reorganized as a government corporation in 1970.

### Indirect Administration

Over the past sixty years federal spending in real (inflation-adjusted) dollars has increased by 670 percent, and federal programs and activities have mushroomed. Yet the federal workforce has scarcely grown at all (see Figure 8.1, page 355); in fact, as a proportion of the population (and total labor force) it has been falling for more than fifty years (see Figure 8.2, page 356). How can this be? The answer, as we saw in Chapter 3, is that many federal policies and programs are administered by someone else: state governments, private contractors, and grant recipients. State governments administer such major social welfare programs as Medicaid and Temporary Assistance for Needy Families. State and local agencies also carry out some of the federal government's regulatory work, such as enforcing air pollution rules and occupational health and safety standards. By delegating administrative duties to state and local government agencies, Congress can add programs, which voters like, without increasing the federal bureaucracy, which voters do not like.

The federal government also provides grants to private nonprofit organizations and to state and local governments to implement programs. For example, the Department of Education's programs for Indian education, special education, library construction, vocational education, and adult education are all carried out by nonfederal organizations funded by grants dispensed by the department. Nonfederal institutions, including universities, research laboratories, and think tanks, administer more than 80 percent of the federal government's scientific research funds.[13] The government also contracts with private companies for a countless variety of goods and services. The Department of Energy, for example, uses contractors to operate nuclear weapons plants; NASA uses contractors to load the space shuttle and to pick up its reusable engines after liftoff.[14] By one recent count, 1,931 private companies had contracts to work on counterterrorism programs in the United States. Contracts and grants thus provide another way for the federal government to take on more tasks without hiring more personnel. For politicians, the payoff can be significant. They can claim credit for reducing the size of the federal bureaucracy without reducing popular programs and services.

Because much of the government's work is performed by someone other than federal bureaucrats, a head count of federal personnel drastically understates the government's true size. According to one authoritative estimate, in 2005, in addition to the federal civilian workforce of 1.9 million, full-time equivalents of 7.6 million employees worked under federal contracts; 2.9 million held jobs created by federal grants; 767,000 worked for the Postal Service; and 1.4 million served in the armed forces, for a total federal workforce of 14.6 million.[15] Add the estimated 4.6 million in state and local positions created by federal mandates, and the total reaches 19 million.[16]

## Bureaucracy in Action

Who are the bureaucrats? The people who staff the myriad federal agencies by and large contradict the stereotypical image of "bureaucrat" prevalent in American popular culture. Accused variously of being inordinately "inflexible, rule-bound, cautious, impersonal, haughty, fearful, deceptive, alienated, or secretive," the reality disclosed by empirical research suggests, if anything, the contrary.[17] Moreover, the federal civil service mirrors the American population far more accurately than, say, Congress. Thirty percent are minorities, matching

# Insulating the Fed

Sometimes the task given an independent regulatory commission is such a hot potato that members of Congress, the president, and even lobbyists maintain a hands-off policy. When the task is the sensitive one of setting a nation's economic course, the logic of insulating the commission from political pressures makes imminent sense. The Federal Reserve System, popularly known as the Fed, is the most independent and powerful of the regulatory commissions. Its main responsibility is to make monetary policy.

Soon after President Trump appointed Jerome Powell as Fed Chair in 2018, the president began looking over his shoulder and criticizing the Fed's monetary policy.

The decisions handed down by the Fed influence the country's supply of credit and level of interest rates, which in turn affect the rates of inflation, unemployment, and economic growth. During periods of economic recession and high unemployment, the Fed buys securities from banks, increasing the banks' reserves so that they have more money to make loans. Interest rates then fall, stimulating investment that leads to faster economic growth and job formation. This makes everyone happy. When a booming economy and low unemployment bring (or sometimes even threaten) inflation, the Fed puts on the brakes by selling securities, which reduces the supply of money banks can lend, thereby raising interest rates. Profits fall, investment declines, the economy slows, and some people may lose their jobs. This does not make everyone happy.

Members of the Fed's board of governors are appointed by the president, with the Senate's approval, to a single fourteen-year term; they can be removed only for cause (evidence of wrongdoing). The board's chair, who dominates its deliberations and is appointed for a renewable four-year term, is one of the most influential people in government. During the long economic expansion and stock market boom of the 1990s,

the financial community scrutinized Chairman Alan Greenspan's every comment for omens about the future of interest rates, and every hint of an increase brought a sharp (but often temporary) drop in the price of stocks and bonds. When the economy later slowed after September 11, 2001, and stock prices tumbled, the Fed began reducing interest rates in an effort to stave off recession, cutting them eleven times in 2001 alone. In 2004, as signs of economic recovery set off inflation worries, the Fed began raising rates again. Rising interest rates contributed to a crisis in the housing market, forcing up mortgage costs while the price of houses was falling. Large financial institutions lost billions of dollars when many homeowners, especially those with variable-rate mortgages, could no longer meet their mortgage payments on houses now worth less than what they owed on them. It was left to Ben Bernanke, Greenspan's successor appointed in 2006, to deal with the financial fallout of the housing meltdown in 2008 by pumping $540 billion in loans into the money market funds in an attempt to unfreeze the credit market. Although this proved politically unpopular,

Bernanke was emboldened by the fact that he never had to run for reelection. Janet Yellen succeeded him in early 2014 and continued to inject billions of dollars into the U.S. economy in an attempt to drive down unemployment.

Presidents sometimes complain about the Fed's decisions, but they do not really desire greater control over the Fed because they do not want responsibility for its decisions. Neither does Congress, which even allows the Fed to finance itself through its own investments. Politically insulated, the Fed is left alone to take the heat for the painful steps sometimes needed to protect the nation's economy. Nonetheless, the Fed is usually careful to accommodate the fiscal policies of the president and Congress. Even when the president and Congress are genuinely unhappy with the Fed's actions, they dare not do much beyond grumbling about it because any real action to curb the Fed might spook the financial markets.

The election of Donald Trump brought a new dynamic to the long-standing relationship between the Fed and the president. During the 2016 campaign, candidate Trump called Federal Reserve chair Janet Yellen "highly political" and argued that "she's not raising rates for a very specific reason, because Obama told her not to." Trump appointed Jerome Powell, a former banker who had served on the Fed's board of governors, as Yellen's successor. Just months after Powell assumed command in February 2018, Trump criticized his approach to monetary policy, saying he was "not thrilled" about recent interest rate increases. Yet the Fed's insulation gives Powell the ability to brush off criticism, even from the leader of the free world.

*Sources:* Jeffrey E. Cohen, *Politics and Economic Policy in the United States* (Boston: Houghton Mifflin, 1997), 215–221 and Jeff Cox, "Trump Takes Another Shot at Fed Chairman Jerome Powell for Raising Rates," CNBC.com, August 20, 2018.

## LOGIC OF POLITICS
# The Deep State Writes an Op-Ed

During the first two years of his presidential administration, President Trump often aired his frustration over the fact that members of his bureaucracy did not always move policy in the direction he favored. Both his own appointees and civil servants who had long been in Washington came under fire when they appeared to be standing in the way of his agenda. The cardinal bureaucratic sin that aroused the most fury in the president was leaking information to the press, because leaks revealed both damaging details and embarrassing internal divisions.

Imagine the furor that arose, then, when an anonymous Trump administration official published an op-ed piece in the *New York Times* clearly stating that he (the pronoun used by the *Times*) and other top officials were actively working to undermine the president's agenda. Titled "I Am Part of the Resistance Inside the Trump Administration," the guest opinion essay revealed that Trump was facing a dilemma. "The dilemma—which he does not fully grasp—is that many of the senior officials in his own administration are working diligently from within to frustrate parts of his agenda and his worst inclinations." Calling the president's leadership style "impetuous, adversarial, petty and ineffective," the author vowed that he and other "unsung heroes" were

*(Continued)*

(Continued)

"trying to do what's right, even when Donald Trump won't."

President Trump, unsurprisingly, fumed. He tweeted that the piece was "gutless," then raised the question of whether it was "TREASON?" and finally tweeted that "If the GUTLESS anonymous person does indeed exist, the Times must, for National Security purposes, turn him/her over to government at once!" A series of officials, including Secretary of State Mike Pompeo, denied that they authored the essay. And allies of the president seized on this as one more piece of evidence that a "deep state" was actively trying to sabotage him.

What is the "deep state," and does this op-ed prove its existence? This term was imported into domestic politics from descriptions of a purported shadow government in Turkey that worked with organized crime groups to undermine the governing party during the 1990s. It gained currency among far-right groups allied with Trump (who has never used the term) as a description of something a bit less sinister: a group of career civil servants in government who collaborate with those in the private sector to move government in the direction they prefer, even though they have never been elected. Conservative news website Breitbart has published articles alleging that a deep state is aligning against Trump, and Republican Congressman Steve King reports that "we are talking about the emergence of a Deep State led by Barack Obama, and that is something that we should prevent."

Does the deep state really exist? The version of it that appears in far-right blogs—a hierarchical, coordinated shadow government that brings together private and public sector actors under the control of an ex-president, wielding unchecked power over the direction of policy—is clearly an unsupported conspiracy

While some conspiracy theorists posit that a many-tentacled "deep state" runs a shadow government undermining Donald Trump, the president does face the sort of internal divisions within his bureaucracy that frustrate the will of every president.

theory. Yet many observers of Washington, D.C., are describing something more mundane when they say "deep state." They mean that civil service and appointed officials alike often work, sometimes in loose collaboration, to prevent what they see as the unwise directives that come from the top of a presidential administration. They follow their own career incentives, professional norms, and sense of what is good policy, leaving presidents with the tremendous challenge of trying to compel their actions against their will. In a word, these members of the deep state are "bureaucrats," and quite typical bureaucrats at that. Although they rarely describe their resistance to presidential commands in *New York Times* op-eds, in every administration there are unelected officials deep inside, or even at the helms of, various agencies of the state, frustrating the presidents whose job it is to control them.

---

*Sources: Peter Baker and Maggie Haberman, "Trump Lashes Out after Reports of 'Quiet Resistance' by Staff," New York Times, September 5, 2018. Alana Abramson, "President Trump's Allies Keep Talking about the 'Deep State.' What's That?" Time.com, March 8, 2017.*

the overall population; 45 percent are women. Their range of skills matches that of workers in the private sector, as does their dedication to their jobs. Their views on most public or personal issues are indistinguishable from the views of other citizens—except that they place a higher value on civic participation and commitment to democratic values. Contrary to popular belief, civil servants generally perform their jobs as well as or better than people doing the same work in the private sector. Most, in fact, want to be good "agents," responsive to elected officials and supportive of the missions assigned to their agencies.[18] The federal bureaucracy displays numerous and sometimes severe shortcomings, to be sure, but these cannot be fairly blamed on the civil servants staffing the institutions. The vast majority spend their days managing programs and delivering services that most people would regard as essential to modern life: working to ensure the safety of food, drugs, consumer products, the workplace environment, and the transportation system; delivering the mail and keeping order in the nation's vast electronic communications systems; providing monthly retirement and unemployment checks to the millions of Americans who depend on them; attending to the needs of veterans; pursuing criminals and defending the nation from foreign enemies; and protecting the natural environment and responding to disasters, natural and man-made. The list could go on for pages. We tend to take such services for granted, paying attention only when something goes wrong, but we would certainly notice if they stopped.

## Bureaucratic Culture and Autonomy

In theory, bureaucratic agencies are subject to the authority of Congress, the president, and the courts, but bureaucrats are by no means always kept on a short leash; some agencies operate with substantial autonomy, whereas others are carefully monitored by their multiple principals. The ability of agencies to expand their autonomy—that is, to use their discretionary authority as they think best—depends on a variety of circumstances, not the least of which are the political skills of individual bureaucrats.

It is neither surprising nor necessarily a bad thing that government agencies strive for autonomy. During long service in agencies, people develop a strong sense of what their agency is supposed to do and how it is supposed to do it—that is, they absorb its **bureaucratic culture**. Political scientist James Q. Wilson defines an organization's culture as its "persistent, patterned way of thinking about the central tasks of and human relationships within [the] organization. Culture is to an organization what personality is to an individual. Like human culture generally, it is passed on from one generation to the next. It changes slowly, if at all."[19]

Bureaucrats imbued with their agency's culture come to dislike interference from outsiders ignorant of the problems, practices, and political environment the bureaucrats know so intimately. They also tend to value their agency's programs and services more highly than outsiders might and thus seek the resources and the freedom to carry out their missions in the way they believe is best. On the whole, then, there is nothing undesirable about having agencies staffed with people who have a strong sense of professionalism and confidence that their work is important and that they know best how to do it. A nation would not want its military officers, for example, to think any other way. The problem is that the very conditions that give an agency high morale and a strong sense of mission may encourage it to seek independence from political control.

**POLITICS TO POLICY**

# Can You Just Get Rid of Bureaucracy? The "Abolish ICE" Movement

As the Trump administration stepped up its "zero tolerance" approach to enforcing immigration laws in the summer of 2018, some of the groups resisting him stepped up their criticism of the bureaucracy charged with enforcing immigration laws within our borders, Immigration and Customs Enforcement (ICE). ICE, one of three agencies housed within the Department of Homeland Security since 2003, had long been a lightning rod for criticism from the left. But that summer, the #AbolishICE hashtag gained currency, "Occupy ICE" protesters shut down an ICE facility for a week, and Democratic congressman Mark Pocan of Wisconsin announced that he would introduce a bill to eliminate the agency. Leaders on the left from Senator Elizabeth Warren of Massachusetts to upstart candidate Alexandria Ocasio-Cortez in New York joined in the calls to abolish ICE.

What, exactly, would abolishing ICE mean? If Congress got rid of the agency, would immigration laws cease to be enforced within America's borders? Would the ICE agents who are tasked with taking on human trafficking or transnational criminal organizations lose their jobs? According to President Trump, this move would be a recipe for lawlessness. "Extremist Democrat politicians have called for the complete elimination of ICE," he tweeted. "These radical protesters want ANARCHY—but the only response they will find from our government is LAW AND ORDER!"

In fact, what Pocan, Warren, and Ocasio-Cortez were proposing was something a bit more boring than that. Calls for abolishing ICE are attempts not to end this agency's mission but to reshape its culture and constrain its actions through a

Erik Mcgregor/Pacific Press via ZUMA Wire

Immigrant rights advocates have focused their attention, somewhat surprisingly, on bureaucratic reorganization, calling for the abolition of Immigration and Customs Enforcement (ICE) in order to change how immigration laws are enforced.

bureaucratic reorganization. According to two former Homeland Security officials writing in the *Washington Post*, critics attack ICE for "being too aggressive and inadequately supervised; failing to distinguish among more and less urgent targets for removal; refusing to adopt criminal justice norms and protections for its targets; and at times interfering with state and local law enforcement." The agency's independence allowed this culture to develop and fueled the doubling in its number of deportation officers (from 3,127 to 6,400) and detention bids (from 18,000 to 40,520) since 2004. Abolishing the stand-alone agency and bringing it under the control of the Department of Justice, according to the arguments of its opponents, could focus its enforcement efforts on criminals and ensure that the typical constitutional norms of the criminal justice system are followed.

Even some leaders within ICE have called for a bureaucratic restructuring. In June 2018, nineteen special agents in charge of the Homeland Security Investigations (HSI) branch of ICE, which enforces crimes like human trafficking, proposed that they be split off from the Enforcement and Removal Operations (ERO) branch, which seeks out those who have immigrated illegally. In a letter to Homeland Security Secretary Kirstjen Nielsen, these special agents wrote that "the perception of HSI's investigative independence is unnecessarily impacted by the political nature of ERO's civil immigration enforcement." Though the acronyms may be hard for most people to keep track of, the basic message was that ERO's reputation was hampering the mission of HSI, spurring HSI's calls for autonomy.

What these proposals highlight is the real-world stakes of something as abstract as administrative reorganization. According to both the Democratic politicians and the HSI special agents, the structure of a bureaucratic agency can dramatically influence how it implements federal laws. Although abolishing ICE would not suspend any and all immigration laws, it could significantly impact how they are enforced.

*Sources:* Brittny Mejia, "ICE Faces Criticism from Public and Within," *Los Angeles Times*, July 1, 2018, and Margo Schlanger and Seth Grossman, "You've Heard the Calls to Abolish ICE. Here's What That Could Mean." Washington Post.com, July 9, 2018.

The development of distinctive bureaucratic cultures and missions also inhibits cooperation between agencies. The traditional mission of the Federal Bureau of Investigation, for example, has been to catch and punish lawbreakers, so it has come to value the kind of information that can be used to convict criminals in public court. The Central Intelligence Agency is charged with secretly monitoring potential foreign enemies and thwarting their plots, so it resists any release of information that might eventually expose its informers or methods. The two agencies also operate under very different sets of legal constraints imposed by Congress in response to actual or imaginable abuses of power. Hence even after September 11 the FBI and CIA have remained reluctant to share information, and getting them to cooperate in other ways has remained difficult.

For similar reasons, the integration of the DHS's disparate bureaucratic components, each imbued with its distinctive bureaucratic culture, into an institution capable of coping with the huge range of tasks needing coordinated attention if the United States were to be made secure from terrorist attack has proved a daunting task. The legislation creating DHS provided for a year of transition to get the department up and running, but the process has taken years to complete. Experts on mergers and acquisitions from the private sector—people who had overseen huge corporate acquisitions at General Electric, Hewlett-Packard, and Lockheed Martin—had to be solicited for advice, for no one else had experience with reorganization on such a grand scale.[20]

## Bureaucrats as Politicians

As partisans of their agencies and missions, bureaucrats are necessarily politicians. Indeed, the Weberian notion of civil servants who act as neutral instruments for implementing the policies chosen by their elected superiors has never taken hold in the United States. Agency officials operate in a world of competition for scarce resources, often intense conflicts among interests and values, and multiple bosses (principals). Scholars have proposed a variety of motives, in addition to the desire for autonomy, that might account for bureaucratic behavior. These motives include a quest for larger budgets, more subordinates, and greater authority; the chance to do some good; a preference for a stable, predictable environment; and the opportunity for career security and advancement. But whatever the goals, they can be achieved only through politics: mobilizing supporters, gathering allies, negotiating mutually beneficial deals with other politicians, keeping in touch with people whose cooperation is needed, and adapting to the realities of power.

The political environment of most government agencies is occupied by the House and Senate members of the subcommittees handling agencies' authorizing statutes and budgets, the committee and subcommittee staff, the political appointees who head agencies, the White House (especially its Office of Management and Budget), the interest groups affected by agency activities, and the federal courts. Occasionally, the news media and the broader public also show up on the radar screen. Bureaucrats' most important political relationship is usually the one with Congress, for it controls the organization, authority, budgets, and staffing—in fact, the very existence—of departments and bureaus. Although presidential appointees rarely stay in their agencies more than a few years, members of Congress and senior committee staff are in for the long haul, as are the interest groups that play an important role in Congress's political environment. Keeping Congress happy often means keeping interest groups happy.

Politically astute bureaucrats carefully cultivate members of Congress and their staffs. The principle is simple, though following it is sometimes far from simple: do things that help members achieve their goals and avoid doing things that have the opposite effect. Along the way, establish a reputation for competence and frugality. No one whose job relies on voters is going to defend bureaucratic ineptitude or malfeasance.* Keeping in touch, usually through congressional staff, also is crucial. Politicians and bureaucrats live in an uncertain, ever-changing world. Good information is a scarce and therefore valuable commodity (see Chapter 6). Information about their own activities is one political resource bureaucrats have in abundance. A regular exchange of intelligence helps both sides anticipate consequences and reduces the incidence of unpleasant surprises. Shrewd bureaucrats are responsive to informal suggestions as well as legislative mandates; they can take a hint. In short, bureaucrats prosper by convincing their congressional principals that they are good and faithful agents—never an easy task where hidden action and hidden information abound.

The survival of bureaucrats, like that of other politicians, also depends on having an appreciative constituency. Some agencies acquire organized constituencies at the moment of birth—the interests who lobbied them into existence. Others have to organize supporters themselves. An early secretary of commerce, for example, helped found the U.S. Chamber of Commerce. Many of the groups that now lobby on behalf of programs for the physically

---

*Just the opposite; for example, congressional outrage went into overdrive when, six months after the attacks of September 11, 2001, the Immigration and Naturalization Service (INS) sent word to the Florida flight school where two of the terrorists had been trained that the terrorists' student visas had been approved. The agency had granted approval the previous summer, before the attacks, but "backlogs and antiquated computers" had delayed delivery, and the INS had failed to recheck what was in the pipeline. Elizabeth A. Palmer and John Godfrey, "Sensenbrenner Leading the Charge for Immediate INS Overhaul," *CQ Weekly*, March 16, 2002, 705.

disabled, the mentally ill, and other disadvantaged people were brought into being through the efforts of government officials in social service agencies (for other examples, see Chapter 13).[21] Agencies that service politically feeble clienteles—such as the Bureau of Prisons (federal criminals) and the Agency for International Development (foreign countries)—inevitably suffer in the struggle for political attention and resources. Government agencies also try to cultivate broad public support, and most have public relations offices devoted to publicizing their activities.

Savvy bureaucrats design and manage their programs in ways that enhance political support in Congress. If feasible, programs

The National Aeronautics and Space Administration runs the U.S. space program, an expensive program ($19.3 billion in 2016) that has no direct impact on the lives of most Americans. To win support, NASA encourages the public to share in the excitement of space exploration by offering spectacular pictures and detailed information on websites devoted to each of its missions. This image is an artist's rendition of the view of the *Juno* spacecraft approaching Jupiter, where it arrived on July 4, 2016.

produce widely distributed local benefits even when their main purpose is to generate diffuse national benefits. For example, defense spending buys a diffuse national good—protection from potential enemy nations—but also helps the local economies where the money is spent. Aware of this aspect of military procurement, Pentagon officials protect weapons programs by making sure weapons components are produced in as many states and districts as possible.[22]

Bureaucrats also target benefits to key members of Congress. For example, from 1965 through 1974 a disproportionate share of grants for water and sewer facilities under a program administered by the Department of Housing and Urban Development went to the districts' subcommittee members who dealt with the program and to those conservatives who otherwise might have voted against it.[23] To sweeten such deals, bureaucrats make sure members of Congress take credit when local projects or grants are announced. They also try to stay in close touch with the organized interests active in their policy domains to anticipate and possibly head off political problems. The interest groups, for their part, naturally want to maintain cordial relations with "their" agencies as well.

## Bureaucratic Infighting

Agencies with different missions, clienteles, skills, and ideologies compete for influence, authority over policy, control of implementation, and resources. A striking example was the bitter infighting between the State and Defense Departments over guidance of policy toward the war in Iraq, when Defense secretary Donald Rumsfeld took a hawkish position early on while Secretary of State Colin Powell urged more caution. When President George W. Bush decided to wage a preemptive war in Iraq opposed by most of America's traditional allies, this represented an internal victory for Rumsfeld and the neoconservative intellectuals on his staff. Bureaucratic infighting also takes place within organizations. Many military professionals, for example, were unenthusiastic about the nation-building role they were assigned in Iraq. The armed forces are organized, equipped, and trained to fight wars, not to police cities, manage public works, or install democratic institutions. Thus they did not share their civilian bosses' ambition to control the process of rebuilding Iraq. Indeed, strong disagreements between civilian and military leaders are routine; in July 2010, General Stanley McChrystal, U.S. commander in Afghanistan, had to resign after comments from his staff highly critical of civilian administration officials, including Vice President Joe Biden and Obama's national security adviser, were reported in *Rolling Stone*.[24]

## Who Controls the Bureaucracy?

The more things elected representatives want the government to do, the more discretionary authority they must give to administrators. The proliferation of government agencies and programs during the New Deal and afterward has led critics to charge that Congress has abdicated its authority to the president, to an out-of-control bureaucracy, or to the clients the agencies serve.[25] The charges deserve to be taken seriously. Congress, in fact, has delegated a wide range of tasks, often with only the vaguest guidelines on how authority is to be exercised. In 1914, for example, Congress authorized the Federal Trade Commission to enforce laws against "unfair methods of competition . . . and unfair or deceptive acts or practices" without defining what these methods, acts, or practices were. At times, government agencies and programs have served private interests almost exclusively; the history of the Department of Agriculture is littered with examples. Regulatory commissions have sometimes served as the handmaidens of the interests they are supposed to regulate in the public interest. Until the mid-1970s, for example, the Civil Aeronautics Board (CAB) fought valiantly to protect the major airlines from competition. Congress often pays little attention to what its bureaucratic agents are doing, for administrative oversight is not a high priority (see Chapter 6). However, congressional majorities have found many ways in which to delegate authority without abdicating control. Legislators are fully aware of principal–agent dilemmas (though they do not think of them in those terms) and have strategies to cope with them.

These strategies can be placed into two general categories, named by political scientists Mathew McCubbins and Thomas Schwartz: "**police patrols**" and "**fire alarms**." In police patrol oversight, Congress works hard to directly monitor whether agencies are implementing laws faithfully and efficiently. When engaging in this type of work, members of Congress and their staffs investigate a sample of executive branch activities to detect and fix any deviations from legislative goals and, as bureaucrats notice that they are being watched, discourage future deviations. In fire alarm oversight, Congress designs procedures that allow interest groups and ordinary citizens to raise an alarm when something has gone wrong. Courts, agencies, and legislators can then solve problems that have been detected by interested parties. Although Congress itself may rush to the scene when a fire alarm is pulled, it leaves the monitoring of bureaucracies to those who have the highest stakes in their operation. This saves lawmakers a great amount of effort, while still allowing them to correct bureaucratic drift.

McCubbins and Schwartz argue that Congress conducts oversight primarily by setting up fire alarm mechanisms. Too much time can be wasted on police patrols where there is no crime, and the violations detected through patrols—which include investigative hearings, scientific studies, and field observation—may be so minor that no voters care about them. By contrast, when Congress enables fire alarm oversight by requiring agencies to make public reports and take comments on the rules that they would like to adopt, it exerts no effort on its own. When something goes wrong enough for the public to complain, Congress can come to the rescue and win the gratitude of voters. "Instead of sniffing for fires," McCubbins and Schwartz observe, "Congress places fire-alarm boxes on street corners, builds neighborhood fire houses, and sometimes dispatches its own hook-and-ladder in response to an alarm."[26] This section shows that legislators engage in both types of oversight, but fire alarms probably accomplish the most. Ironically, for rational reasons, Congress delegates to others much of the task of overseeing the agencies to which it has delegated power.

## Methods of Congressional Control

Congress operates from a position of overwhelming strength in its relationship to administrative agencies. It creates and empowers them by ordinary legislation, and it can eliminate or change them in the same way. Most agencies require new budget appropriations every year to continue functioning. Congress also has a say in who is appointed to head departments and bureaus. Indeed, some programs are set up with the explicit understanding that a particular individual will or, in some cases, will not be chosen to run it. Any president who wants an agency to thrive will choose appointees who can get on well with the agency's handlers in Congress. Bureaucratic agents recognize that, at some level, the very existence of their agency (and jobs) depends on at least the toleration of their congressional principals even when the principals seem to be paying no attention to what they are doing.

Congress uses a variety of methods to keep its bureaucratic agents in line. Among them are the sorts of costly activities that are most often part of police patrol oversight:

- **Hearings and investigations**, in which bureaucrats are called before subcommittees to explain and defend their decisions, and outsiders are sometimes invited to criticize them. Most agencies must testify annually about their activities before the House Appropriations subcommittee that has jurisdiction over their budgets.

- **Mandatory reports**, in which Congress requires executive agencies, even the president, to report on programs. For example, under an antidrug bill passed in 1986 the president is required to submit a report every March 1 on whether certain nations where illegal narcotics are produced or transshipped have "cooperated fully" with U.S. efforts to stem the drug traffic. Countries not certified as cooperating face a cutoff in U.S. aid.

- **Legislative vetoes**, which allow one or both houses of Congress (sometimes even individual House and Senate committees) to veto by majority vote an agency's policy proposals. Although the Supreme Court in 1983 declared the legislative veto unconstitutional because it violates the separation of powers, Congress continues to enact legislative vetoes, and agencies continue to send decisions to Congress for prior approval, knowing that Congress has other sanctions at its disposal if they do not.*

- **Committee and conference reports**, which often instruct agencies how Congress expects them to use their "discretion." Though not legally binding, bureaucrats ignore such instructions at their peril.

- **"Limitation riders,"** attached to appropriations bills, which forbid an agency to spend any of the money appropriated on activities specified by Congress in the riders (used to block agencies from issuing regulations opposed by Congress, among other things).[27]

- **Inspectors general**, with independent offices (outside the normal bureaucratic chain of command) in virtually every agency, who audit agency books and investigate activities on Congress's behalf.

- The **Government Accountability Office**, with a staff of more than five thousand, which audits programs and agencies and reports to Congress on their performance.

Congress can also guard against agency losses by putting a time limit on delegations of authority. For example, the expanded wiretap and surveillance authority included in the USA PATRIOT Act's broad grant of new powers to investigate and detain suspected terrorists enacted after September 11 was set to expire automatically by the end of 2005 unless Congress extended it. As former House majority leader Dick Armey explained, "We gave the Justice Department a huge increase in power" but with an expiration date "on the theory that would make them more responsive to oversight."[28] Congress extended the act's authority, slightly modified, in 2006.

A variety of procedural devices also are available to Congress for monitoring and controlling bureaucrats. Congress may not have the capacity to specify what bureaucrats are to do, but it can tell them how they have to do it. The broadest procedural requirements are found in the Administrative Procedure Act of 1946 (APA), which covers all rulemaking by government agencies unless an agency's legislative authorization specifies otherwise.

Congress normally regulates by delegating broad grants of authority to regulatory agencies and letting them fill in the details by making rules. These rules have the force of law, just as if Congress itself had enacted them. When an agency wants to make a rule, it first must give public notice in the *Federal Register*, outlining the proposed rule, disclosing the data and analysis on which it is based, and inviting written comments from the public. Public hearings may be held as well. The agency then responds to public comments, often in staggering depth,

---

*Nothing prevents Congress from passing legislation contrary to Supreme Court rulings, and Congress can have its way as long as it does not depend on the courts to enforce compliance. One scholar notes, "An agency might advise the committee: 'As you know, the requirement in this statute for committee prior-approval is unconstitutional under the Court's test.' Perhaps agency and committee staff will nod their heads in agreement—after which the agency will seek prior approval of the committee." Louis Fisher, in *Extensions*, a newsletter of the Carl Albert Congressional Research and Studies Center (Spring 1984): 2.

providing a comprehensive record of how and why the rule was promulgated and, on occasion, making modifications in the final rule. This process creates the rulemaking record that will be needed to justify the agency's decision if it is challenged in federal court.

These procedures serve several purposes. For one thing, they make rulemaking a public act, observable by members of Congress and anyone else—often, the interest groups who recognize how critical rulemaking is in their issue areas—who may be interested. They also give members of Congress and agency officials advance notice of the political fallout that any particular regulation would produce, allowing them to avoid political trouble. When the Federal Trade Commission proposed rules in 1982 requiring more complete disclosure of funeral costs and used car defects, undertakers and used car dealers protested loudly. Members of Congress, who were quickly reminded just how many undertakers and used car dealers they had in their districts and how influential they were, forced the agency to back down.[29]

In other words, the APA sets up a fire alarm mechanism that alerts members of Congress when delegated authority is being exercised in a way that might hurt them politically. In effect, it recruits interested outsiders to monitor the activities of bureaucratic agents on Congress's behalf.

When it chooses, Congress can fine-tune procedures to guarantee a desired balance of interests in regulatory policymaking. For example, the National Environmental Policy Act of 1969 requires federal agencies, as well as many other public and private entities, to consider what effects all major undertakings (construction projects, landfills, dredging schemes, and so forth) might have on the environment and to prepare environmental impact statements specifying the environmental effects of proposed projects and their alternatives. The act also gives private citizens legal **standing** to bring suit in federal court to challenge the adequacy of impact statements and, indirectly, the proposals they were intended to justify. Standing enables environmental groups and their lawyers to enforce compliance through the courts, ensuring that environmental interests will not be ignored. When Congress granted standing, it was setting up a fire alarm for environmental lawyers to pull.

How, then, do we reconcile this picture with news clips of members of Congress portraying themselves as enthusiastic bureaucracy bashers on the principle that "no politician ever lost votes by denouncing the bureaucracy"?[30] They are, in fact, the principal architects of the bureaucracy, and its design generally suits the political purposes of the congressional coalitions that create and sustain its various components. It is no accident that the division of responsibilities among agencies in the executive branch tends to mirror the division of legislative turf in the congressional committee and subcommittee systems. This is not to say, however, that Congress has exclusive control over the administration of agencies. The president and the federal courts also have a major say, and Congress itself is subject to pressure from interest groups, the media, and constituents on how it deals with administrative issues. Moreover, the fragmented political system can give agencies considerable room to maneuver in pursuit of their own ends.

## The President and the Bureaucracy

The president, who as the chief executive is charged by the Constitution with seeing that the laws are faithfully executed, sits officially atop the bureaucratic hierarchies of the executive branch. The heads of departments and other executive agencies and their immediate subordinates—the undersecretaries, assistant secretaries, and bureau chiefs—serve at the president's pleasure, as do members of some of the governing boards, commissions, foundations, institutes, and public corporations that make up the rest of the executive branch. With their duty to implement laws, power to appoint senior government officials, and other congressionally conferred grants of authority, presidents have enormous administrative responsibilities. The institutional realities, however, impose formidable barriers to presidential influence—let alone control—over the sprawling federal bureaucracy.

## The Power of Appointment

Presidents pursue their policy goals by appointing senior officials loyal to them and their ideas. American presidents enjoy much stronger appointment powers than other chief executives: the U.S. president appoints more than four thousand officials, whereas leaders in France, Britain, and Germany appoint one hundred to two hundred.[31] Yet appointments can come at a cost. The agencies within the U.S. government with the greatest percentage of presidential appointments tend to perform more poorly than agencies with a higher ratio of career civil servants.[32] What's more, when an agency run by presidential appointees fails, as the Federal Emergency Management Agency (FEMA) did during Hurricane Katrina, the public can hold the president personally accountable. FEMA was run by more appointees than other agencies, and headed by Michael Brown, whose prior experience consisted primarily of running the International Arabian Horse Association. After what was widely viewed as FEMA's incompetent management of Katrina's aftermath, Brown resigned, saying, "I think it's in the best interests of the agency and the best interest of the president."[33]

One limit on the power of appointment is that when the president appoints a top official to run a department or agency, it can become politically difficult to fire that official. Cabinet officials serve at the president's will. Thus, chief executives have the authority to fire their top bureaucrats but sometimes lack the political freedom to do so. Almost from the moment Donald Trump appointed Jeff Sessions to run the Department of Justice, the president and his attorney general found themselves at odds. The flashpoint of disagreement was Attorney General Sessions's decision to recuse himself from the investigation of the Trump campaign's possible links to Russia. Angered by this recusal, Trump clearly wanted Sessions out but

Kevin Dietsch/UPI

Soon after President Trump appointed Dr. Ronny L. Jackson, the White House physician under both Obama and Trump, to lead the Veteran Affairs Department, more than twenty of his current and former colleagues came forward with a series of accusations against him. These included charges that the White House medical office had a culture where "medications were freely distributed and lightly accounted for," as the *New York Times* reported, and that Dr. Jackson was frequently intoxicated. Though Trump stood by Dr. Jackson as "one of the finest people I have ever met," the president withdrew his nomination when it faced strong opposition in the Senate.[34]

feared the political backlash that would come from removing one of his top appointees from his position. The president attempted to pressure Sessions, even telling the newspaper the *Hill* that "I don't have an Attorney General. It's very sad," in September 2018. But the president clearly worried about the political backlash from firing him. In the end, the day after the 2018 midterm elections—timing that highlighted the political perils of such a move if it had been made even a few days earlier—Sessions submitted his resignation to President Trump "at your request."

### Senatorial Approval

Presidential appointments require Senate approval, and senators make the most of their authority. Rarely does the full Senate reject a nominee, but it is not unusual for an appointment to be withdrawn after an unfavorable committee vote or, earlier, after unfavorable publicity during a hearing on the appointment. In 2009 President Obama had to withdraw his first nomination for HHS secretary as it emerged that the nominee owed back taxes, and the president lost his first choice for commerce secretary when the nominee became the subject of a federal investigation (later dropped). Many nominations are not even made because presidents anticipate Senate opposition and decide the fight is not worth the political resources it would take to win. Senators also use the approval process to extract promises from appointees about what they will or will not do in office, further limiting administrative discretion. Seeking Senate approval in 2007, Michael Mukasey, George W. Bush's nominee to replace Attorney General Alberto Gonzales, who had resigned after months of harsh criticism for politicizing the Justice Department and for his role in setting the administration's policies on torture and surveillance, had to promise that he would resign if asked by the White House to violate the law or the Constitution. His confirmation was nearly derailed when he ducked the question of whether the technique of simulated drowning called "waterboarding" used to interrogate suspected terrorists constituted torture, but after declaring that he personally found the procedure "repugnant," he was confirmed on a 53–40 vote.[35]

Presidents have sometimes used "recess appointments" to appoint officials the Senate has refused to ratify. The Constitution allows the president to make temporary appointments of officials normally requiring Senate confirmation without Senate approval while the Senate is in recess (Article II, Section 2). Recess appointments expire at the end of the Senate's next session, and thus may last for as long as nearly two years. The Senate can block this ploy by remaining in pro forma session during break periods, such as the customary two-week Thanksgiving and five-week Christmas breaks. As long as a member officially gavels the Senate open and then gavels it closed at least once every four days—a process that takes only a few seconds—the Senate is formally in session and no recess appointments can be made. In December 2007 the Senate used this strategy to prevent George W. Bush, who had already made 171 such appointments during his presidency, from making any more.[36]

In addition to the Senate, the president may have to satisfy the clientele groups that care intensely about who heads "their" agency or risk alienating them and weakening the agency. Thus the secretary of labor requires the nod of the American Federation of Labor and Congress of Industrial Organizations (AFL-CIO), at least if the president is a Democrat; the chair of the Federal Reserve System must measure up on Wall Street; and the head of the National Institutes of Health needs the respect of the academic and research communities.

Clientele groups of the president also may benefit from the appointments process, because presidents often use appointments as symbolic payoffs to important factions in their party's electoral coalition. Recent presidents have taken pains to assemble administrations that recognize the racial, gender, and geographic diversity of the nation. For example, Obama's twenty-two cabinet-level appointees included six women, three Latinos, three Asian Americans, and two African Americans. Presidents also take care to ensure that their party's various ideological factions are acknowledged and represented. In making appointments for any reason, however, the president also must weigh competence; policy expertise may not be essential, but no president wants to be embarrassed by appointees too ignorant or unskilled to manage their agencies' business (such as FEMA head Michael Brown).

Once appointed, even initially loyal officials tend, as Richard Nixon's chief domestic aide famously put it, to "go off and marry the natives," becoming agents of their departments or bureaus instead of the president. Political appointees typically serve short terms—about two years—and often are unfamiliar with the rules, programs, and political relationships of the organizations they lead. To avoid disastrous mistakes, let alone to achieve anything positive, they need the candid advice and active cooperation of permanent civil servants. In return, they can offer effective advocacy of their agency's interests in the battles waged over programs and resources within both the administration and Congress.[37] In doing so, they may come to identify with the success of their agency rather than with that of the president, and thus pursue more programs and larger budgets—or defend programs and budgets from cuts—without regard for how their agency fits into the administration's overall program. Department and bureau heads also wield powers delegated directly to them by Congress, allowing them to bypass the president and further promote their independence from the president and their dependence on Congress.

### Mechanisms for Presidential Supervision

In an attempt to gain some control over the far-flung activities of the federal bureaucracy, presidents have built up their own supervisory bureaucracy in the Executive Office of the President (analyzed more fully in Chapter 7). The president's primary control instrument is the Office of Management and Budget, which oversees agency budgets and rulemaking and assembles the annual budget for all government agencies that the president is required to submit annually to Congress. The budget process allows presidents to emphasize their own priorities and policy goals. When Congress ignores presidents' recommendations—which it frequently does—presidents may use the veto to nudge that recalcitrant legislative body closer to their own budget preferences, as President Bush did with considerable success after the Democrats took control of Congress in 2007 (see Chapter 7).

For bureaucrats, favorable treatment in the president's budget is worth pursuing—so they have an incentive to keep the White House happy. But this inherently political relationship works two ways: the White House is much more likely to get its way if it can persuade political appointees and permanent civil servants that their best interests are served by doing what it wants. Because presidents do not hold undisputed authority over the executive branch, bargaining or indirect manipulation through mobilized interest groups or congressional allies is often more effective than issuing orders.[38]

By constitutional design, presidents enjoy special authority over agencies involved in diplomacy and national defense, and this authority is greatly magnified in times of national crisis. Moreover, public support for presidents is highest in such moments, so opposition to presidential demands carries unusually high political risks. President George W. Bush, like his predecessors, did not hesitate to use this institutional and popular wartime advantage to assert control over policy and institutions. Congress quickly complied with the president's request for legislation authorizing him "to use all necessary and appropriate force against the nations, organizations, or people that he determines planned, authorized, committed, or aided the terrorist attacks on the United States that occurred September 11, 2001."* He also won an extraordinary degree of authority to shape and run the DHS as he saw fit and a remarkably free hand on almost every aspect of the Iraq War. Pushing the limit, the administration had demanded total discretion in deciding how to spend $60 billion of the $78.5 billion sup-

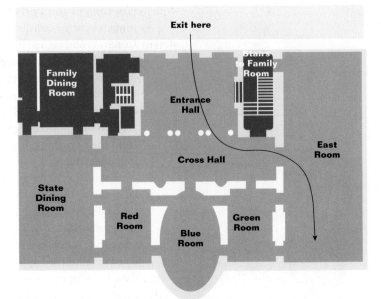

One guaranteed way to keep the White House unhappy is to leave it unprotected—in a literal, rather than political, sense. On September 19, 2014, a knife-wielding Iraq War veteran jumped over the White House fence, ran past several layers of security, made it into the building itself, and progressed as far as the East Room before being apprehended by the Secret Service. By October 1, under fire from members of Congress and apparently having lost the confidence of the White House, Secret Service director Julia Pierson resigned.

*Source:* KTLA, "White House Intruder: Secret Service Director Calls Incident 'Unacceptable,'" September 30, 2014; The White House, www.whitehouse.gov.

plemental appropriation for the war. Secretary of Defense Rumsfeld said flatly that "whatever is put forward by the Congress by way of money will be expended in a way that the president decides it should be expended."[39]

One of Donald Trump's first acts as president was designed to heighten his control of the bureaucracy and decrease what he saw as red tape: He signed an executive order stipulating that for any new regulation his administration added, two existing regulations needed to be repealed. His staff called it the "most significant administrative action in the world of regulatory reform since President Reagan."

## The Courts and the Bureaucracy

The third main branch of government, the judiciary, also shares authority over the bureaucracy. The United States inherited the English common law principle that the government, no less than individual citizens, is bound by law. Under this principle, a dispute between the

---

*This broad antiterrorism package (Public Law No. 107-56), enacted at the behest of the administration, passed 357–66 in the House and 98–1 in the Senate during the last week of October 2001.

iStock

Presidents seek to control bureaucrats in realms as seemingly innocuous as the regulation of movie theater popcorn. When White House deputy chief of staff Nancy-Ann DeParle got wind that the Food and Drug Administration (FDA) was considering a proposal forcing theaters to post nutritional information for buttered popcorn—which can contain more calories than two Big Macs!—as part of President Obama's national health care reform, she worried that it would be lampooned as an extreme example of nanny state intrusion into our daily lives. DeParle called the FDA Commission, which President Obama had appointed in 2010, and after a chilly conversation the FDA backed down.[40]

government and a private individual over whether the government is acting according to law—that is, a statute duly passed by Congress and signed by the president—comes before the courts as a normal lawsuit. The judge treats the government as any other party to a lawsuit, granting it no special status whatsoever. This tradition has strongly influenced the development of American administrative law. Judicial review of administrative decisions is taken for granted; regulatory commissions and agencies have, from the beginning, been constrained by the courts' defense of individual rights.

Expansion of the government's regulatory activities, particularly during the New Deal, put a host of bureaucratic agencies in the business of making rules and applying them—that is, agencies were authorized to make general rules, just like a legislature, and to adjudicate individual cases under them, just like a court. Federal courts maintained appellate jurisdiction over both sets of activities, hearing appeals on rules as well as their enforcement, and court decisions gradually imposed a set of procedural standards that Congress eventually codified in the Administrative Procedure Act of 1946.

Under the APA, any agency dealing with individual cases like a court must act like a court—that is, it must hold hearings conducted by neutral referees (now called administrative law judges). Parties may be represented by counsel, with written and oral testimony and opportunities for cross-examination. Decisions handed down by the agency must be issued in writing and justified on the evidence in the record. Those decisions that violate these procedures can be challenged and overturned in federal court. An agency that wants its judgments sustained must carefully follow the rules of administrative due process.

Over the years the federal courts have come to interpret the APA as requiring almost as much procedural care in making rules as in deciding cases. Courts have elaborated on and formalized the APA's notice and hearings requirements and now insist on a comprehensive, written justification backed by a complete record of all information and analysis that went into an agency's decision. The APA allows courts to invalidate rules only if they are "arbitrary and capricious," which would seem to give agencies wide latitude. Yet in the 1960s and 1970s the courts used judicial review "to create and impose on agencies a huge body of administrative law which was so complex and demanding that it allowed judges to strike down new agency rules whenever they pleased."[41] The courts were particularly interested in highly contentious, highly technical areas of regulation: the environment, health, and safety. Soon regulatory agencies adapted, however, by overwhelming the courts with reams of data and analysis, both to convince the judges they had made the most scientifically defensible choice and to make it more difficult for judges lacking technical expertise to say otherwise. The courts have since backed off a bit, but they still play a major role in shaping regulatory decisions.

Congress may, of course, rewrite the law if the courts invalidate rules that solid House and Senate majorities want to see implemented, and it may also alter the courts' jurisdiction over administrative matters. Yet any change must negotiate the usual congressional obstacle course, which, as we saw in Chapter 6, is by no means easy, particularly if the president prefers the courts' position. Congress does rectify both judicial and administrative decisions it does not like, but only under major provocation.

## Iron Triangles, Captured Agencies, and Issue Networks

The politics of program administration gives agency staff, members of Congress, and organized interest groups powerful incentives to form mutually beneficial alliances to manage policy in their areas of specialization. When successful, these alliances become **iron triangles**: narrowly focused subgovernments controlling policy in their domains, out of sight or oversight of the full Congress, the president, and the public at large. The classic examples operated in the areas of agriculture, water, and public works, where the active players enjoyed concentrated benefits—projects benefiting private interest groups, budgets and programs for administrators, and electoral support for congressional sponsors from grateful beneficiaries.[42] The broader public, excluded from the process, paid the diffuse costs.

Similarly, the politics of regulation allows the regulators to be "captured" by the very interests they are supposed to regulate. Once Congress establishes a regulatory agency in response to some threat to public welfare—whether it be railroad monopolies, dangerous or quack medicines, or impure processed food—the agency's dealings are with the very industries it should be regulating. Because industries have an enormous economic stake in how they are regulated, they become the primary source of political pressure on the regulators. Ironically, the regulated sectors also are the primary repository of the expertise—information and personnel—agencies need. Add to this the routine legislative mandate that the agency maintain the economic health of the industries it regulates, and the story is complete: regulators become the allies, if not agents, of the sector they regulate. At times, for example, the Food and Drug Administration catered to drug companies; the Interstate Commerce Commission ended up at the beck and call of established firms in the trucking industry; and the Civil Aeronautics Board, as noted earlier, protected the major airlines from competition.

In reality, though, iron triangles and captured agencies survive only as long as the costs they impose on everyone are small enough to avoid attracting serious attention from political entrepreneurs in Congress or the White House who may be scouting for popular issues to champion. For example, the CAB and the ICC no longer exist; the former was abolished in 1985, and ten years later the latter, by then more than one hundred years old, was finally put to rest. The marketplace now governs the sectors they once regulated. In the early 1960s one congressional coalition forced the FDA to impose much

### STRATEGY AND CHOICE
# A Fight with a Bureaucrat Goes Global

Presidents often disagree with the judgment calls made by top officials in their bureaucracies, on issues ranging from the right way to enact welfare reform to the proper response to a chemical weapons attack. It is much rarer that they disagree with the factual assessments that their advisors make on issues ranging from the impact of a welfare-to-work requirement or the identity of a chemical weapons attack's perpetrator. And it is unprecedented when they do so in public, while seated next to the leader of a rival world power.

Yet this is exactly what happened during President Donald Trump's Helsinki summit with Russian president Vladimir Putin in July 2018. Trump's director of national intelligence, Dan Coats, had clearly stated many times before the meeting that the U.S. intelligence community's assessment was that Russia interfered in the 2016 presidential election. Just before the Helsinki summit, his boss expressed doubts about this assessment, with Trump stating in a CBS Evening News interview on the summit's eve that "I don't know if I agree with that. I'd have to look." In Helsinki, when Trump and Putin were seated side-by-side, a reporter asked whether Trump believed Putin or his own intelligence officials. "My people came to me," Trump replied. "They said they think it's Russia. I have President Putin. He just said it's not Russia. I will say this, I don't see any reason why it would be." Putin was happy to add that "as for who to believe, who you can't believe, can you believe at all—you can't believe anyone."

This was a fight with the bureaucracy that went international, with many observers shocked at the spectacle of an American president seeming to side with Russia over the verdict reached by the U.S. intelligence community. Because the agreement came over an assessment of past fact rather than judgments about future actions, it was all the more surprising. For his part, Director Coats was unmoved in his view of what had happened in the 2016 elections and in his willingness to discuss it. After the summit, Coats was again asked about the issue. According to the former Republican senator, "We have been clear in our assessments of Russian meddling in

Presidents Trump and Putin found much to agree upon in their 2018 Helsinki Summit, leading to domestic criticism of Trump for appearing to side with Putin against his own intelligence agencies.

the 2016 election and their ongoing, pervasive efforts to undermine our democracy, and we will continue to provide unvarnished and objective intelligence in support of our national security."

Why did this bureaucrat continue to hold to his view, rather than getting in line behind the president? His individual incentives supported his bureaucratic independence. For Director Coat's reputation in the intelligence field and in government, following the norms of his profession to provide "unvarnished and objective" information was paramount. The many intelligence organizations under his leadership likely appreciated that he defended their assessment. Doing so likely damaged his working relationship with the president, but sometimes a bureaucrat's incentives are to protect a professional reputation more than to please a boss. For President Trump, apparently his calculation was that the risks in casting doubt upon the intelligence community's assessments were outweighed by the gains he made in pursuing other goals.

---

Sources: Eli Stokols and Sabra Ayres, "Trump Slams Russia Probe and Blames U.S. for Bad Relations with Putin as the Two Leaders Meet," *Los Angeles Times*, July 16, 2018; Eleanor Mueller, "Trump Second-Guessed DNI Coats on Cybersercurity before Sit-down with Putin," Politico.com, July 16, 2018.

*AP Photo/Pablo Martinez Monsivais*

tougher standards for proving the safety and efficacy of new drugs. The 1990s, however, saw another coalition compel it to ease up again on the ground that delays in approval of new drugs also hurt the public health.

Members of Congress learned from these experiences and designed new regulatory procedures to prevent the capture of agencies such as the EPA (see the discussion of standing, p. 375). The proliferation of self-proclaimed public interest groups in the 1960s also changed the political environments of many agencies, leaving them no option but to negotiate a far more complex, open, and conflict-ridden configuration of political forces (see Chapter 13). Thus scholars now talk of policy domains shaped by **issue networks**—amorphous, ever-changing sets of politicians, lobbyists, academic and think tank experts, and public interest entrepreneurs such as Ralph Nader—rather than iron triangles.[43]

Agencies adapted. The Department of Agriculture now pays attention to nutrition and other consumer concerns as well as to the needs of agribusiness. Today's EPA considers the economic as well as environmental effects of its decisions. But agencies do not always find it easy to adapt because new missions may go against the culture of an agency. For example, the U.S. Army Corps of Engineers, which for two centuries had been damming rivers, dredging harbors, and draining wetlands, was not eager to make cleaning up toxic wastes and protecting threatened ecosystems a high priority. But when the political environment changes, government agencies have little choice but to change as well.

## Bureaucratic Reform: A Hardy Perennial

Every modern president has viewed the federal bureaucracy as a problem that needs fixing. The Clinton administration's efforts focused on improving the delivery of bureaucratic services. Vice President Al Gore headed the administration's National Performance Review, which sought ways to "cast aside red tape"; encourage entrepreneurial administration that "put customers first"; decentralize authority to "empower those who work on the front lines"; and, in general, produce "better government for less" with a reduced workforce.[44] Not to be outdone, the Republican House freshmen elected in 1994 sought not merely to reinvent government but also to disinvent it. House Republicans proposed abolishing the Departments of Commerce, Energy, Education, and Housing and Urban Development, terminating many of their programs and bureaus and distributing the remainder to other departments. The George W. Bush administration tried another tack, proposing in 2001 to shrink government and increase efficiency by expanding "competitive sourcing" (letting firms in the private sector bid against government agencies for contracts to deliver government services) to include jobs currently performed by 425,000 civil servants, about one-fourth of the total federal workforce. Barack Obama took up the bureaucratic reform theme in his 2011 State of the Union address, promising to send Congress a proposal "to merge, consolidate, and reorganize the federal government in a way that best serves the goal of a more competitive America."[45]

Both the Republican and Democratic initiatives were imbued with political logic. Making government work like a business that depends on keeping customers happy has obvious appeal. So does getting rid of obsolete, wasteful programs and agencies and using competition to increase efficiency. Yet despite some success in improving the performance of several agencies and reducing the number of federal employees, the Clinton administration's goal of an efficient, customer-friendly bureaucracy remained largely unfilled. And House Republicans, though slashing some agency budgets and terminating a few programs, failed to eliminate any major agency, let alone whole cabinet departments. By 2003 the Bush administration's target for competitive sourcing had been reduced to 103,000 jobs in the face of congressional resistance and new, post-9/11 realities.[46] The fact is that the federal bureaucracy is hard to reform and still harder to prune because its actions and structure have a political logic of their own.

## The Logic of Red Tape

Red tape does not flourish by accident. It proliferates because it helps principals control and monitor their agents (the goal of the APA) and helps agents demonstrate to their principals that they are doing their jobs correctly. Many rules and procedures are adopted to ensure fair or at least equal treatment of each citizen by preventing unaccountable, arbitrary behavior. For example, federal agencies procuring goods and services from the private sector are bound by an elaborate set of requirements imposed on them by Congress.

Even after the Federal Acquisition Streamlining Act of 1994 simplified the rules, especially for relatively small purchases, the *Federal Acquisition Regulation*, which spells them out, still runs to more than five thousand pages. Bureaucrats have a strong incentive to follow the rules, for there is only one safe answer—"I followed the rules"—when a member of Congress asks pointedly why a favorite constituent did not get the contract.[47] By the same logic, bureaucrats like to have rules to follow. Detailed procedures protect as well as constrain bureaucrats, so red tape is frequently self-imposed.

Empowering bureaucrats on the front lines of service delivery may increase efficiency and even customer satisfaction, but it also may make it easier for bureaucrats to go astray. Each time an agency does so, Congress tends to write more elaborate procedures and add another layer of inspectors and auditors to keep it from happening again. Thus red tape often springs directly from Congress's desire to control administration. As a result, although Congress rails against red tape in general, it views with suspicion attempts to reduce the controls that generate it. Successful efforts at easing controls could reduce congressional ability to monitor and influence administration, a risk congressional majorities have been reluctant to accept, especially when the other party holds the White House.

Reformers seeking bureaucratic efficiency may also run into several other problems. Efficiency stems from using resources in a maximally productive way, so any assessment of efficiency must be based on measures of output. The output of many agencies defies measurement, however. Diplomats in the State Department are supposed to pursue the long-term security and economic interests of the nation. How do we measure their "productivity" in this endeavor? Complicating matters even more, agencies sometimes are assigned conflicting objectives. Is the Internal Revenue Service supposed to maximize tax compliance, requiring tough enforcement, or customer service, requiring flexible, sympathetic enforcement? Effective enforcement and effective customer service are not the same thing.

Because an agency's degree of success in accomplishing its vaguely defined ends is often impossible to measure, bureaucrats focus instead on outputs that can be measured: reports completed, cases processed, meetings held, regulations drafted, contracts properly concluded, forms filled out and filed. These means become the ends because they produce observable outputs for which bureaucrats can be held accountable. The result is yet more red tape. The notorious bureaucratic focus on process rather than product arises from the reality that, unlike private businesses, government agencies have no "bottom line" against which to measure the success or failure of their enterprise.

## The Bureaucratic Reward System

Conflicting goals and the lack of a bottom line hardly inspire the creative, "entrepreneurial" government envisioned by the Clinton-Gore National Performance Review. Entrepreneurs take risks proportionate to prospective rewards. Civil servants, by contrast, seldom profit personally from their attempts to make agencies more productive or customer-friendly. And if bold new approaches end in failure, they can count on being blasted in the media and in Congress. Bureaucrats are famously cautious for a good reason: a mistake is much more likely than a routine action to set off a fire alarm in Congress. If an alarm does sound and the routine was followed, the routine, rather than the bureaucrat, gets the blame.

The merit system rewards conscientious, long-term service; it does not encourage entrepreneurial risk taking. Congress could, of course, decide to give agency managers more authority to hire, promote, reward, redeploy, or fire personnel on the basis of their performance. But doing so would mean reducing the civil service protections put in place for well-considered political reasons: to avoid a partisan spoils system and to preserve congressional influence over administration.

The Clinton and Bush administrations' plans for reforming government inevitably included proposals to reduce bureaucratic waste and improve policy coordination by consolidating overlapping agencies and programs. Every president since Franklin Roosevelt has sought to do the same. And of course, it is easy to find examples of duplication, confused lines of authority, and conflict among the government's multifarious activities. Basic scientific research, for example, is funded by the National Science Foundation; the National Institutes of Health; the Departments of Energy, Agriculture, and Defense; and NASA. The National Park Service, the Forest Service, the Bureau of Land Management, and the U.S. Fish and Wildlife Service all manage public campgrounds. Responsibility for developing water resources is spread over five separate agencies. The government has programs to keep tobacco farming profitable and to discourage smoking. One agency subsidizes the lumber industry by building logging roads into national forests; another tries to curb it to protect endangered species. And the list could go on.

This duplication would all seem senseless if government pursued a coherent set of interrelated goals, but it does not. Government pursues overlapping, conflicting, or disconnected goals in response to the diverse demands Americans place on it. Each agency, and each program, reflects the coalition of forces that brought it into being and that now form its political environment. Different coalitions want different things and design different administrative institutions to get them.

In short, then, the problem of bureaucracy is not bureaucracy but politics. It is not impossible to reform, reinvent, streamline, or shrink the administrative leviathan, but it is impossible to do so without changing power relationships among interests and institutions. Deregulating the bureaucracy and empowering frontline bureaucrats would make agencies more efficient, but it also would make them less accountable to elected officials. Consolidating and rationalizing bureaucratic authority would reduce duplication, confusion, and expense, but it also would create losers whose interests or values would no longer enjoy undivided institutional attention. America's bureaucracy is disjointed because the political views of its people are fragmented. Bureaucrats face the challenging task of meeting the expectations of courts, Congress, and the president because our Constitution separates political power. Our nation's bureaucracy is characteristically American, reflecting the pluralistic politics and Madisonian institutions that shape all facets of our government.

**for CQ Press**

**Want a better grade?**

Get the tools you need to sharpen your study skills. Access practice quizzes, eFlashcards, video, and multimedia at **edge.sagepub.com/kernell9e.**

## KEY TERMS

bureaucracy 348
bureaucratic culture 367
committee and conference
    reports 374
*Federal Register* 360
fire alarms 372

Government Accountability
    Office 374
hearings and investigations 373
inspectors general 374
iron triangle 381
issue network 383
legislative veto 373

limitation riders 374
mandatory reports 373
police patrols 372
red tape 353
rotation in office 351
spoils system 352
standing 375

## SUGGESTED READINGS

Bertelli, Anthony M., and Laurence Lynn Jr. *Madison's Managers: Public Administration and the Constitution.* Baltimore: Johns Hopkins University Press, 2008. Combines political theory with political economy to show how American bureaucracy is both constrained and legitimized by the system of separated powers.

Gormley, William T., Jr., and Steven J. Balla. *Bureaucracy and Democracy: Accountability and Performance.* 2nd ed. Washington, DC: CQ Press, 2012. Discusses the factors that ultimately lead to bureaucratic successes and shortcomings, with a focus on accountability.

Lewis, David E. *The Politics of Presidential Appointments: Political Control and Bureaucratic Performance.* Princeton, NJ: Princeton University Press, 2008. Explains why some agencies have more appointees than others and how this affects bureaucratic performance.

Light, Paul C. *Thickening Government: Federal Hierarchy and the Diffusion of Accountability.* Washington, DC: Brookings, 1995. Considers how and why bureaucratic layers have multiplied and how this affects accountability and effectiveness.

Seidman, Harold. *Politics, Position, and Power: The Dynamics of Federal Organization.* 5th ed. New York: Oxford University Press, 1998. Discusses how politics shapes bureaucratic organizations and practices.

Shapiro, Martin. *Who Guards the Guardians? Judicial Control of Administration.* Athens: University of Georgia Press, 1988. A lucid and informative account of court–agency relations since the New Deal.

Skowronek, Stephen. *Building a New American State: The Expansion of National Administrative Capacities, 1877–1920.* Cambridge, UK: Cambridge University Press, 1982. Classic account of the development of the modern American bureaucracy, focusing on the civil service, the army, and agencies regulating the economy.

Waterman, Richard W. *Presidential Influence and the Administrative State.* Knoxville: University of Tennessee Press, 1989. Case studies from the Nixon, Carter, and Reagan administrations of presidential efforts to implement policies via the bureaucracy.

Wilson, James Q. *Bureaucracy: What Government Agencies Do and Why They Do It.* New York: Basic Books, 1989. If you read only one book on the bureaucracy, it should be this one.

# REVIEW QUESTIONS

1. Why is a bureaucracy necessary? What are the general characteristics of bureaucracies as set forth by Max Weber?

2. What powers does the president have over the bureaucracy? What powers does Congress have over the bureaucracy? Why would political actors ever choose to exercise less control over a bureaucratic actor?

3. How were members of the bureaucracy selected in George Washington's time? In Andrew Jackson's time? In Donald Trump's time? How do the ways in which bureaucrats get their jobs relate to their performance once in office?

4. How can the rules or procedures Congress establishes for bureaucratic agencies affect how those bureaucracies do their jobs?

5. If everybody hates "red tape," why does it still flourish? Why might bureaucrats themselves prefer to have detailed rules governing some of their actions?

The Supreme Court of the United States, Washington, D.C.

# The Federal Judiciary

**9**

By 1800 the leaders who had led the nation through the Revolution and adoption of the Constitution were divided into two warring camps. The ruling Federalist Party, led by John Adams and Alexander Hamilton, advocated for a vigorous national government, whereas the Democratic-Republican opposition, led by Thomas Jefferson and James Madison, favored less federal activity. Once allies, these two groups now despised and feared one another. Each believed that the future of the Republic rested on its party's victory in the presidential election of 1800. Consequently, that year's electoral campaign was one of the bitterest in American history.

Both sides indulged in negative campaigning, but the Federalists excelled at it; they attacked Jefferson as the devil incarnate. In political pamphlets and letters to the editor, the Federalists called Jefferson an "infidel" and "atheist," a darling of the French Revolution who favored the use of the guillotine, a proponent of majority rule (and thus apt to destroy the republican Constitution), a philanderer, and—perhaps the ultimate insult for a politician—a "philosopher." The author of one pamphlet added that Jefferson was not even a very good philosopher—barely adequate for a college professor but certainly not good enough for a president. The attack finally dredged the bottom in charging that Jefferson had written a "textbook" on American government that promoted abstract ideas and "hooted at experience."

Toward the end of the campaign both sides sensed that Jefferson could not be stopped, but neither anticipated the magnitude of the Democratic-Republican victory. Not only did the party walk away with the Electoral College vote, but it also took control of Congress. It was not clear who had been elected president, however, because of a quirk in the Constitution's rules that caused votes cast for a party's vice presidential candidate to be counted as if they were cast for the presidential candidate. As a result, when Jefferson and his running mate, Aaron Burr, ended up with the same number of electoral votes, they found themselves tied for the presidency. The apparent tie triggered a constitutional provision requiring the election to be decided by the House of Representatives, still controlled by the outgoing Federalists.*

During the weeks between the election and the House vote, rumors of conspiracies swirled across the nation. Would the Federalist Congress ignore the Constitution's technical glitch and ratify Jefferson's victory, or would it exploit the opportunity to deny the White House to this so-called freethinking radical? One scenario had the Federalists contriving a tie vote in the House, thus taking the presidential election beyond circumstances anticipated by the Constitution. Another had President Adams stepping down at the end of his term and Secretary of State John Marshall assuming caretaker control of the executive branch until a new presidential election could be called.† And yet another option, which clearly lay within the Constitution's provisions and was perhaps more seriously considered, had the Federalists electing Burr president as the lesser of two evils.‡ None of these options appeared feasible, however. Thus, after weeks of strategizing and perhaps a little soul searching, the Federalist Congress ratified the nation's choice, and Jefferson became the third president of the United States.

Had power not transferred peacefully in this first real test of the new Republic, the election of 1800 might have weakened the Constitution permanently. Failure here would have put the Constitution's integrity in doubt and left future politicians with a prisoner's dilemma of deciding whether to abide by the rules or to renege before the other side could. But the Federalists did not capitulate altogether. Their risky fallback strategy triggered a different kind of constitutional crisis with the unanticipated outcome of reconfiguring power among the branches of government, in particular the Supreme Court.

## Setting the Stage for Judicial Review

As they prepared to leave office, the Federalists passed the Judiciary Act of 1801. The law, designed to protect the Constitution against perceived Democratic-Republican schemes,

---

*The Twelfth Amendment corrected this problem in 1804.

†Evidently, Marshall seriously considered his elevation. He reportedly promoted it as "legal" among colleagues, and one biographer spotted Marshall's pen in anonymous newspaper endorsements of this option. On hearing of this plot, Virginia's Democratic-Republican governor and future president James Monroe warned vaguely that force would be enlisted to remove Marshall, Virginian or not. Donald O. Dewey, *Marshall versus Jefferson: The Political Background of* Marbury v. Madison (New York: Knopf, 1970), 42–43.

‡In the end, though, Burr proved to be Jefferson's ideal running mate; he scared many Federalists even more than did the radical from Monticello. Burr later took up dueling and assumed imperial aspirations—raising "soldier of fortune" armies to seize western territories from the French and create his own country.

sharply increased the number of district and appeals courts and conveniently created new judgeships, intending to pack these new judgeships with Federalists.* The partisan purpose of this last-minute reform was evident in the provision that shrank the size of the Supreme Court from six members to five members, but only after President Adams filled the current chief justice's vacancy. This provision would have denied the new Democratic-Republican administration the right to appoint a justice for a long time, if ever. With their scheme in place, President Adams nominated and the Senate quickly confirmed outgoing secretary of state John Marshall as the new chief justice.

At this point, the story turns from the grand drama of contending partisan armies to a soap opera about the personal foibles and ambitions of politicians. President Adams needed help processing the flurry of last-minute Federalist judicial appointments and so asked his new chief justice to stay on briefly as secretary of state. According to Jefferson, Adams was still signing appointment commissions at nine o'clock the evening before his departure from office. Apparently, in the rush, Marshall left on his desk a stack of signed and sealed justice of the peace commissions for the District of Columbia, five-year positions created to reward loyal Federalists. The next day Marshall, as chief justice of the United States, delivered the oath of office to the new president, his archrival, Thomas Jefferson.

Later, on discovering or being advised (the lore is inconsistent on this point) that some of the commissions had not been delivered but were lying around the office, Jefferson ordered that they be withdrawn. These commissions were the least of the Federalists' worries, however.

After the inauguration the Democratic-Republicans derided the judiciary as a "hospital of decayed politicians" and made clear their intention to repeal the Judiciary Act as soon as their Congress opened the following December. In a letter Jefferson expressed his party's sentiment: the Federalists "retired into the Judiciary as a strong hold . . . and from that battery all the works for republicanism are to be beaten down and erased by fraudulent use of the constitution."[1] In his message to the new Congress, Jefferson's intent was also clear: "The judiciary system of the United States, and especially that portion of it recently erected, will of course present itself to the contemplation of Congress." Indeed, in private, and apparently unbeknownst to Jefferson, some nervous Federalist politicians were urging their recently appointed judges to ignore the new Congress until the Marshall Court could come to their rescue. The convening of Congress promised an epic partisan battle in which the Democratic-Republicans controlled the presidency and (narrowly) both chambers of Congress, whereas the Federalists directed the federal judiciary.

But could Congress legally abolish courts and thereby remove life-tenured judges? More precisely, could Democratic-Republicans in Congress somehow be prevented from eliminating the Federalist-created judgeships? With repeal of the Judiciary Act imminent, Federalist politicians urged Marshall to defend the party's bulwark by voiding any such repeal legislation. This strategy presupposed, of course, that the Supreme Court possessed the authority, known as judicial review, to rule acts of Congress unconstitutional. Judicial review appears to have been implicitly provided in Article III of the Constitution, debated at the Constitutional Convention with some Framers assuming that the final wording of Article III included it but others—most notably James Madison—arguing that it did not, and brought up again, more hotly, at various states' ratifying conventions. Nearly everyone appeared to have accepted

---

*Article III of the Constitution gives Congress the power to establish lower federal courts.

that the Constitution's supremacy clause (Article VI) allowed the Supreme Court to exercise judicial review and veto *state* laws that trespassed on federal jurisdiction or violated the Constitution. But whether this unelected branch enjoyed authority comparable with the veto power of Congress and the president was altogether different—could the Supreme Court declare an act of Congress unconstitutional?

On February 3, 1802, by a 16–15 vote, the Senate repealed the Judiciary Act and eliminated the Federalist judgeships. All but one Democratic-Republican voted for repeal, and all Federalists voted against it. The House passed the repeal bill a month later, with only a single Democratic-Republican holdout, and Jefferson promptly signed it into law.[*] The Supreme Court had already decided that it would not or could not resist repeal, but Jefferson and his allies did not learn this until the Court's next session, in 1803.

On March 2, 1803, the long-anticipated showdown over the repeal of the Judiciary Act ended badly for the Federalists for the Court ruled in *Stuart v. Laird* that Congress had the authority under Article III to reorganize the judiciary.[2] The Federalist barricade had been dismantled; the Democratic-Republican victory was complete. The Federalist Party would never again win control of the presidency or either chamber of Congress.

Chief Justice Marshall had not caved in, however. The young Constitution had survived the election of 1800, the partisan confrontation surrounding the Judiciary Act, the Federalists' late-night machinations on the eve of Jefferson's inauguration, and the Democratic-Republicans' resolute resistance. As important as the peaceful, albeit difficult, transfer of government control was for the nation's future, it was followed by a comparably significant, and eventually better known, judicial event. Six days before the *Stuart* decision, the Marshall Court delivered another ruling that at the time was largely ignored as a toothless partisan maneuver. Subsequently, however, the *Marbury v. Madison* decision would come to be appreciated for establishing the Court's "coequal" status among the branches of the American government.

William Marbury and several other Federalists who had been denied their eleventh-hour justice of the peace commissions nearly two years earlier appealed to the Supreme Court for redress. They asked the Court to issue a **writ of mandamus**, a judicial instruction to a government officer—in this instance Secretary of State James Madison—to perform his duty and deliver the commissions. Based on the facts of the case, *Marbury v. Madison* did not seem the ideal vehicle for establishing "new" authority for the Court: the issue bordered on the trivial, and Chief Justice Marshall was himself deeply entangled in the dispute. His oversight as secretary of state, after all, had caused the problem in the first place. Moreover, a casual inspection of Marshall's options suggests that *Marbury* was a terrible case for a weak Court to face because it presented an apparent no-win situation. On the one hand, if the Court decided in favor of Marbury and ordered Madison to deliver the commissions, Marshall could reasonably assume that its decision would be ignored. (No administration official had even bothered to appear before the Court to defend Jefferson's decision to withdraw the commissions.) There was even talk in the Democratic-Republican press of impeaching the justices if they decided in Marbury's favor. Such a ruling, then, jeopardized the long-term health of the federal judiciary.

---

[*]To avoid colliding immediately with the Court, Congress then suspended the Court's schedule for the next thirteen months. This move not only eased the dismantling of the eliminated courts but also prevented the Court from continuing the partisan battle while Congress was out of session.

On the other hand, if Marshall ruled against Marbury, the Court would appear to be kowtowing to the Democratic-Republicans and confirming the judiciary's subordinate position. Faced with this dilemma, Marshall found an ideal solution that not only extricated the Court from its predicament but also established an important principle for the future.

In ruling on the case, Marshall asked three questions: First, does Marbury have a right to the commission? Second, do the laws of the United States afford him a remedy? Third, is the appropriate remedy a writ of mandamus issued by the Supreme Court? Marshall's affirmative answer to the first two questions boded well for Marbury. However, Marshall answered no to the third question, concluding that the Supreme Court did not have jurisdiction to hear the case.

Although dismissal by a court for lack of jurisdiction was nothing novel, Marshall's *reasoning* would have far-reaching consequences for the balance of power between the Court and Congress. Marshall's argument was as follows: Article III of the Constitution explicitly lists cases that are within the Supreme Court's original jurisdiction, and a writ of mandamus is not one of them.* Article III of the Constitution does not give Congress the power to *add* to the Court's original jurisdiction. Because the Judiciary Act of 1789 attempted to add a writ of mandamus to the Court's original jurisdiction, the act conflicts with the Constitution. In such a conflict, either the Constitution is superior to ordinary laws or it is on the same level as ordinary laws (and therefore may be altered when the legislature desires to change it). If the Constitution is not superior, then it would be a meaningless check on the powers of government. If, however, the Constitution is superior to ordinary laws, "then a legislative act contrary to the constitution is not law." Marshall then delivered the conclusion that solidified the Court's power of judicial review: because the Constitution is the supreme law of the land, acts of Congress that conflict with the Constitution are unconstitutional and, thus, void. In one of his most famous statements, Marshall wrote, "It is emphatically the province and duty of the judicial department *to say what the law is.*"[3] By refusing to hear the case, Marshall backed away from a confrontation he could not win and simultaneously asserted new judicial authority.

*Marbury v. Madison* did not immediately strengthen the Court's power in its relations with the president or Congress. After all, Marshall's ruling did not require that the other political actors do anything to affirm the Court's newfound authority. It required only that the Court refuse to act in Marbury's behalf. The *Marbury* decision is a testament to Marshall's strategic political skills, for Jefferson and the Democratic-Republicans remained confident that the Federalist bench had at last been tamed.†

However, the Court's ruling in *Marbury* proved to be one of the most important Supreme Court decisions in its history. It provided a precedent that the other branches' actors did not

---

*Cases of original jurisdiction are those that can be brought directly to the Supreme Court, without going to some lower court first.

†Although the Supreme Court left *Marbury* alone for much of the nineteenth century, there is evidence that early on it was accepted as legal dogma. *Marbury* was cited numerous times by lower courts and in lawyers' arguments. Whenever Jefferson encountered these citations, he objected. As late as 1823 he griped to one of his Supreme Court appointees, "This case of Marbury and Madison is continually cited by bench & bar, as if it were settled law, without any animadversion on its being *merely* an obiter dissertation by the Chief Justice." Letter from Jefferson to Justice William Johnson, June 12, 1823, cited in Dewey, *Marshall versus Jefferson*, 145 (emphasis added).

John Marshall (1755–1835) had never sat on the bench before his installation on the Supreme Court. Moreover, his legal education was limited to reading Blackstone's *Commentaries* with his father and three months of lectures by George Wythe at the College of William and Mary in 1780. Marshall's formidable powers of reasoning and leadership in unifying his colleagues behind unanimous decisions were complemented by an amiable disposition and "some little propensity for indolence."

repudiate (after all, the Court upheld Secretary of State Madison's action) and a rationale for the Court's broad authority to declare acts of Congress (and of the president) unconstitutional. This expansive vision of judicial review remained untested for nearly half a century, until the Court decided to enlist it in the infamous *Dred Scott* case. However, the Court's success in overturning key parts of the Missouri Compromise of 1820 had little to do with the other branches' acquiescence to its claimed authority and a lot to do with a sympathetic president in office and a Congress so riddled with internal disagreement that it could not nullify the ruling.

Over time, however, the other branches affirmed the Court's power of judicial review. When in 1895 the Supreme Court declared unconstitutional a federal law that taxed income derived from property, Congress implicitly conceded the Court's authority and turned to the laborious amendment process, eventually passing the Sixteenth Amendment.[4] Eighty years later another case testing and affirming judicial review arose. In *United States v. Nixon* the Supreme Court rejected President Richard M. Nixon's claim that the Watergate tapes were protected by executive privilege and ordered him to surrender the tapes to a special prosecutor. President Nixon largely complied, notwithstanding a mysterious eighteen-minute gap during a critical Oval Office conversation. Whether his compliance reflected heartfelt acceptance of the Court's power of review or recognition that balking would lead quickly to impeachment does not matter. The Supreme Court prevailed in asserting judicial review over actions of the executive.

Although the discussion of separation of powers later in the chapter makes clear that Congress and the president nevertheless sometimes refuse to abide by the Court's decisions, their general acknowledgment of the Court's power of judicial review has enhanced the Court's power vis-à-vis Congress and the president to a level that was not foreseen in 1803 when *Marbury v. Madison* was decided.

## Three Eras of the Court's Judicial Review

The Supreme Court's exercise of judicial review has varied substantially across different decades. Between 1790 and 1860, portions of only two federal laws were declared unconstitutional. The frequency with which the Court struck down acts of Congress and presidential executive orders remained low throughout the late nineteenth century, but as Table 9.1 shows, it surged during the 1920s and 1930s. The exercise of judicial review then receded to nineteenth-century levels over the next two decades, but in the 1960s an activist Court once again scrutinized federal and state laws alike. This ebb and flow of the Court's intrusion into the decisions of Congress and the president have marked the three eras in the modern Court's development.

In each of these three eras, the most important cases that came before the Court embodied particular unresolved questions about the interpretation of the Constitution. These questions first concerned nation versus state authority, then government regulation of the economy, and finally civil rights and liberties. As the controversy surrounding each issue developed, the federal judiciary confronted an upwelling of cases in which it asserted its preferences over those of other national, as well as state, officials.

## Nation versus State

During the first and least active of these issue eras (from the founding to the Civil War), the judiciary's most significant cases probed the unresolved jurisdictional boundaries between the national and state governments. Under Marshall's leadership, the Court generally favored national authority when it conflicted with states' rights. Reasoning that the national government had been approved directly by the citizenry in special ratification conventions, Marshall maintained that the national government's legitimacy was both independent of and superior to that of the individual states and concluded that the power of judicial review applied to the actions of state governments. As the rulings in the following historic cases illustrate, during the nineteenth century, the Court's major policy decisions frequently turned on the question of the federal government's authority vis-à-vis the authority of the states.

**TABLE 9.1**  The Supreme Court's Willingness to Declare State and Federal Laws Unconstitutional

| YEARS | FEDERAL | STATE AND LOCAL |
|---|---|---|
| 1790–1799 | 0 | 0 |
| 1800–1809 | 1 | 1 |
| 1810–1819 | 0 | 7 |
| 1820–1829 | 0 | 8 |
| 1830–1839 | 0 | 3 |
| 1840–1849 | 0 | 10 |
| 1850–1859 | 1 | 7 |
| 1860–1869 | 4 | 24 |
| 1870–1879 | 7 | 36 |
| 1880–1889 | 4 | 46 |
| 1890–1899 | 5 | 36 |
| 1900–1909 | 9 | 40 |
| 1910–1919 | 6 | 119 |
| 1920–1929 | 15 | 139 |
| 1930–1939 | 13 | 92 |
| 1940–1949 | 2 | 61 |
| 1950–1959 | 4 | 66 |
| 1960–1969 | 18 | 151 |
| 1970–1979 | 19 | 195 |
| 1980–1989 | 16 | 164 |
| 1990–1999 | 24 | 62 |
| 2000–2009 | 15 | 36 |
| 2010–2017 | 18 | 20 |
| Total | 182 | 1,335 |

*Sources:* Lawrence Baum, *The Supreme Court,* 13th ed. (Washington, DC: CQ Press, 2018), Table 5-2. Congressional Research Service, *The Constitution of the United States of America: Analysis and Interpretation* (Washington, DC: Government Printing Office, 2017), 2327–2619.

*Note:* Table shows the number of federal and state and local laws declared unconstitutional by the Supreme Court. The Court has always been more willing to exercise judicial review over the states than to apply the doctrine in striking down federal laws.

### McCulloch v. Maryland and National Supremacy

One of Marshall's historic decisions on national supremacy came in 1819 in *McCulloch v. Maryland*, a case that was, like *Marbury*, rooted in party conflict.[5] When in power, the Federalist Party created a nationally chartered bank and appointed party members to administer it. Showing their displeasure, several Democratic-Republican–controlled state governments, including Maryland's, sought to tax the national bank out of existence. In the *McCulloch* decision, Chief Justice Marshall, speaking for the Court, issued the famous declaration that "the power to tax involves the power to destroy." Thus, state taxation of federal property or its activities was unconstitutional. But first Marshall dealt with an even more fundamental issue. The state argued that in the absence of any provision in the Constitution explicitly authorizing Congress to charter a national bank, the national government had exceeded its authority. Marshall responded that the necessary and proper clause (Article I, Section 8) gave Congress a broad mandate to use "all means which are appropriate" to carry out any of its explicitly enumerated powers, as long as the means are plainly adapted to achieve such enumerated power(s) and not otherwise constitutionally prohibited. In *McCulloch*, the enumerated powers at issue included the power to levy and collect taxes, borrow money, and regulate commerce. Because the establishment of a national bank was an appropriate means plainly adapted to such enumerated powers, the Court rejected Maryland's argument that Congress had overstepped its constitutional bounds. The practical result in the case was that federal authority trumped state authority. In *Dred Scott*, decided thirty-eight years later, that result was reversed.

### Dred Scott v. Sandford and States' Rights

Despite its Federalist leanings, the Marshall Court could not permanently establish the explicit powers of the state and national governments. Marshall died in July 1835, and at the end of that year President Andrew Jackson selected Roger B. Taney to serve as the next chief justice. Jackson favored Taney largely because of his advocacy of states' rights, and, true to his reputation, Chief Justice Taney led the Court away from the national supremacy doctrine Marshall had crafted. Taney's effort culminated in *Dred Scott v. Sandford* (1857), which, as we found in Chapter 4, brought the nation to the brink of a civil war by claiming that African Americans were not citizens under the Constitution.[6] In addition to ruling that escaped slaves in the North had to be returned to their owners, Taney's majority opinion held that federal laws outlawing slavery north of the Mason–Dixon line (for example, as set in the Missouri Compromise) unconstitutionally infringed on settlers' territorial rights to self-government and private property.*

The overwhelming public outcry against Taney's reasoning left the Court—an unelected branch of government—seriously discredited. *Dred Scott v. Sandford* took on issues that were too important and divisive to be settled by judicial fiat. In the end, after politics failed, the enduring problems of states' rights and slavery could only be settled by war rather than by

---

*The opinion in *Dred Scott v. Sandford* was only the second time the Court had overruled an act of Congress. Considering that in the first instance, *Marbury*, the Court had merely asserted its authority but did so in such a way as to avoid reversing the president's action, the *Dred Scott* decision may represent the real, if inauspicious, beginning of judicial review of acts of Congress.

legislation or litigation. The defeat of the Confederacy in the Civil War signaled a decisive triumph for federal over state government.

After the Civil War, the Fourteenth and Fifteenth Amendments were ratified, and Congress passed laws that committed the Court to review state laws that ran counter to national statutes. The Court was not bound to support the federal government in every dispute, but it was obliged to devote more attention than ever before to policies emanating from the lower levels of government. Thus after 1860 the decisions striking down state and local laws increased markedly (see Table 9.1). Oliver Wendell Holmes Jr., one of the most distinguished Supreme Court justices of the early twentieth century, observed, "I do not think the United States would come to an end if we lost our power to declare an Act of Congress void. I do think the union would be imperiled if we could not make that declaration as to the laws of the several States."[7]

## Regulating the National Economy

The major issue during the second era of judicial review, from the end of the Civil War to the 1930s, was the government's regulation of the economy. Although the Civil War had settled the supremacy issue in favor of the national government, the actual scope of government powers at both levels remained uncertain. With the rapid industrial expansion after the war, Washington, D.C., and state capitals alike came under increasing pressure to regulate monopolies and to provide new services to the citizenry. Most such demands were brushed aside, but some, such as the call to regulate the railroads, proved politically irresistible. Invariably, whenever a state or, infrequently, the national government enacted a regulatory policy, it quickly found its way onto the docket of an unsympathetic Court.

### The Primacy of Property Rights

By the late nineteenth century, a constitutional tradition had developed that shielded business from economic regulation. The Framers considered the right to private property to be fundamental, and equated it with liberty. Indeed, it was the economic problems caused by the Articles of Confederation—namely, its failure to prevent state raids on property rights—that brought the

Congressional attempts to curb child labor by taxing the items produced were repeatedly rebuffed by the Supreme Court in the early twentieth century.

Library of Congress

delegates together in Philadelphia in the first place. Marshall shared the Framers' commitment to property, and during hard economic times the Court vigilantly protected the integrity of contracts against state efforts to annul them on behalf of debtors. Marshall wrote in one decision, "The people of the United States . . . have manifested a determination to shield themselves and their property from the effects of those sudden and strong passions to which men are exposed."[8]

After the Civil War the Court generally maintained its historical sympathy for property rights. The Fourteenth Amendment was adopted in 1868 to protect newly freed slaves from the repressive actions of the former Confederate states. The amendment said, in part, that no state shall "deprive any person of life, liberty, or property, without due process of law." As we saw in Chapter 4, the nineteenth-century Supreme Court discovered little basis in the due process clause to shield African Americans from disfranchisement and segregation. It did, however, find ample justification for protecting railroads and other businesses from regulation. To invoke the due process clause, the Court defined corporations as "persons."

The Supreme Court did not deliver a pro-business decision in every case, however. It consistently upheld state prohibitions against the sale of alcohol and occasionally affirmed state regulation of business when the public interest was at stake.[9] But this last criterion, "public interest," is ambiguous, and it prevented the Court from settling on a consistent doctrine. Consequently the states continued to test the boundaries of permissible regulation, and the early twentieth-century federal courts were inundated with these cases.

The Court's track record in work-hour regulation is one example. In *Lochner v. New York* (1905) the Court struck down a New York law restricting the work hours of bakers to a maximum of ten hours a day or sixty hours a week.[10] Laws "limiting the hours in which grown and intelligent men may labor to earn their living," the majority declared, "are mere meddlesome interferences with the rights of the individual." Three years later, however, the Court upheld an Oregon statute limiting the workday of female workers.*

During the 1920s the Supreme Court became decidedly more conservative on economic issues and with unprecedented vigor struck down laws regulating business in state after state. Figure 9.1 shows a steady rise in the number of economic measures overturned under the due process clause, reaching a peak of 133 from 1920 to 1929.[11] These decisions won the Court the enmity of many elected officials who found that the justices obstructed their efforts to respond to the demands and needs of their constituents.

After the great stock market crash of 1929, the nation plummeted into a deep economic depression. State and federal governments responded with numerous emergency economic reforms, many of which the Court narrowly affirmed. Yet as the Great Depression lingered on and the government intervened more substantially in the economy, the Court majority consistently ruled against regulation. From 1934 to 1937 the Court, still made up of justices who had been appointed before the Depression, struck down twelve statutes enacted during President Franklin D. Roosevelt's first term. These included laws creating emergency relief programs, controlling the production of coal and basic agricultural commodities, regulating child labor, and providing mortgage relief, especially to farmers.

---

*Muller v. Oregon*, 208 U.S. 412 (1908). Nine years later still, the Court disregarded *Lochner* altogether to uphold an Oregon law limiting to ten hours the workday of any person working in a "mill, factory, or manufacturing establishment." *Bunting v. Oregon*, 243 U.S. 426 (1917).

■ **FIGURE 9.1**   Changing Caseload of the Supreme Court by Decade

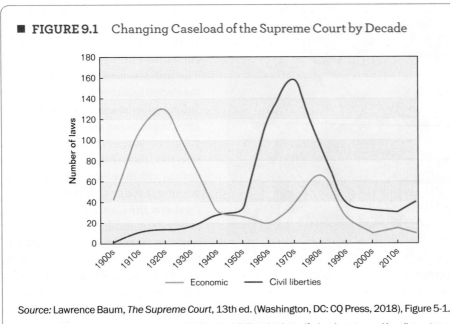

*Source:* Lawrence Baum, *The Supreme Court*, 13th ed. (Washington, DC: CQ Press, 2018), Figure 5-1.

*Note:* Figure shows the number of economic and civil liberties laws (federal, state, and local) overturned by the Supreme Court by decade. Civil liberties category does not include laws supportive of civil liberties.

### A National Consensus and the Court's About-Face

Earlier, the Civil War had ended slavery and rendered moot the *Dred Scott* decision. In this era of economic turmoil, resolution of the impasse between the Supreme Court and the elected branches of government required a direct confrontation. Shortly after his landslide reelection in 1936, President Roosevelt proposed a plan for revamping the judiciary. Its most consequential and controversial provision allowed the president to appoint an additional Supreme Court justice for every sitting justice over the age of seventy. Ostensibly the **Court-packing plan** would alleviate the backlog of cases on the Court's docket. With the opportunity to name as many as six new justices to the high bench, its real purpose was obvious—to give Roosevelt a Court majority sympathetic to his New Deal programs. Public reaction to the idea was generally negative, and the legislation failed in Congress, despite its lopsided Democratic majorities. Ultimately, however, victory went to Roosevelt. With a 5–4 decision in a case about regulating wage and working conditions in Washington State, the Court began to uphold the same type of economic regulations it had been rejecting for the past two years.[12]

The Court's about-face started when one justice began to favor federal economic assistance. Justice Owen Roberts's famed "switch in time that saved nine" allowed the Court to bend to the emerging national consensus that recovery required the government's active management of the economy. In the years after the Court-packing crisis, President Roosevelt sealed the Court's retreat from economic policy by filling vacant seats on the bench with appointees who were committed to the New Deal. He had many opportunities: from 1937

to 1941, seven members of the Court either died or retired. Only Roberts and Harlan Fiske Stone, whom Roosevelt raised to chief justice, remained. The justices, now more in tune with the elected branches' thinking about the federal government's role in the economy, began to pay attention to a different set of issues—civil rights and civil liberties. But whether the Court was dealing with the economy or civil rights, one thing became clear in the post–New Deal era: the Court's rulings shifted power dramatically to the federal government and away from the states. In the end, the dramatic conversion of the Supreme Court's agenda and its view of federal power came not through institutional reform, as might have been expected. Rather, it resulted from the replacement of retirees with a new generation of jurists in closer agreement with the president and Congress. We discuss shortly how the power to appoint like-minded judges is an important tool with which presidents influence the federal judiciary's policies and that, even for the *unelected* branch, politics matters.

## The Rise of Civil Rights and Civil Liberties

The third era of judicial review began in earnest in the 1940s. During this period the Court's concern was the relationship between the individual and government. We surveyed the broad scope of this new direction in Chapters 4 and 5; here we are interested in why the Supreme Court went in this particular direction.

A number of historical reasons for this development have been proposed, and all of them may be true. After abandoning a role to say what does and does not fall within Congress's authority to regulate interstate commerce, the federal judiciary found that much of its previous agenda of cases had been cleared. Some legal historians have suggested that the Supreme Court then strategically turned to a field where it could act unconstrained by the separation of powers system: the rights of individuals. The Court initially opened the door when it incorporated free speech rights through the Fourteenth Amendment, and other individual rights soon followed. In particular, incorporation benefited criminal defendants, who were then poised to make myriad claims that the Bill of Rights protected them from arbitrary actions by state and local law enforcement officials. Arising at the same time, as we found in Chapter 4, legal forces were assembling in the National Association for the Advancement of Colored People and elsewhere to challenge segregation and disenfranchisement in the federal courts. In sum, the confluence of historical forces sent new kinds of cases to the Supreme Court at a moment it was receptive to a fresh set of issues over which it could comfortably assert its authority.

## A Fourth Era? Reasserting Judicial Review and a Return to States' Rights

One common factor in the previous two eras was the Court's broad interpretation of Congress's power to regulate activity under the commerce clause. When the Supreme Court finally got pushed on board President Roosevelt's economic policies during the late 1930s and early 1940s, it did so by largely surrendering to Congress and the presidency responsibility for deciding what constituted "interstate commerce." In one of the most important laws of the civil rights era, Congress passed the Civil Rights Act of 1964 that barred segregation and discrimination in all forms of public accommodations. Citing its authority to regulate interstate commerce, Congress sought to prevent the "disruptive effect" of racial discrimination on interstate commerce. The Supreme Court agreed, thereby giving the federal government authority to regulate what might seem like purely local commerce—renting a hotel room, serving customers at restaurants, transportation services, and the like.[13] More generally, the broadly defined commerce clause gave the federal government authority to regulate virtually all commerce—much of it formerly under the exclusive jurisdiction of *state* governments. And with the exception of a few lone dissenting justices here and there, this expansive view of the commerce clause held for decades.

But things would start to change with the arrival of a more conservative Supreme Court led by Chief Justice William H. Rehnquist. Rehnquist—originally appointed by Richard Nixon—was elevated to chief justice by another Republican president, Ronald Reagan. In addition, Reagan was able to appoint three other justices who, as it turned out, were sympathetic to reining in the power of the federal government over the states. These four justices— Rehnquist, Sandra Day O'Connor, Antonin Scalia, and Anthony Kennedy—joined with Justice Clarence Thomas, a George H. W. Bush appointee, to decide a 1995 case that marked the arrival of the fourth era of assertive judicial review. In *United States v. Lopez*—for the first time in almost sixty years—the Court struck down legislation as exceeding Congress's powers under the commerce clause.[14] In a 5–4 decision written by Chief Justice Rehnquist, the Court held that gun possession in a school zone was not economic activity that could substantially affect interstate commerce. Five years later, with the same Republican-appointed justices in the majority, Chief Justice Rehnquist penned another 5–4 decision that made clear *Lopez* was not a fluke. In *United States v. Morrison,* the Court struck down part of the Violence Against Women Act as beyond the scope of Congress's commerce clause power on the ground that gender-motivated crimes of violence were not in any sense "economic activity."[15]

Underlying these decisions was the five-member majority's concern that the federal government had gone too far and encroached on areas that traditionally should be left to state governments. Thus, the Rehnquist Court was in effect rebalancing the power relationship between the federal and state governments. The current Supreme Court led by Chief Justice John Roberts has signaled that it will follow the groundwork laid by the Rehnquist Court. In its most high-profile decision to date, five members of the Court (in a majority opinion written by Chief Justice Roberts) held that Congress did not have the authority under the commerce clause to force individuals to purchase health insurance. Although the law was upheld by a different five-member majority under Congress's taxing power (see Politics to Policy box on page 404), the Roberts Court continued to scrutinize and limit new laws based on the assertion of the federal government's authority under the commerce clause.

In sum, this era's Supreme Court enlists its judicial review prerogative broadly. This can be easily seen in Table 9.1 by the comparatively large number of federal and state laws invalidated. The modern Court's assertiveness has placed it in position as the political system's chief referee keeping the political institutions in their proper orbits. In 1998 the Court struck down Congress's attempt to give the president a line-item veto (see Chapter 7). In 2001 it unanimously rejected an appeals court ruling that Congress delegated too much regulatory discretion to the Environmental Protection Agency (EPA) and, in effect, unconstitutionally abdicated its authority. And in 2008 the Court rejected President George W. Bush's executive order that Texas must retry a Mexican citizen convicted in a death penalty case because he had not been given the opportunity to consult with the Mexican consulate, as required by the World Court. Without explicit authorization by public law, the president's authority was insufficient to act alone. In these and other cases the Supreme Court acted as a disinterested third party applying the rule book—that is, the Constitution—to keep those officeholders who compete over public policy in their proper constitutional roles.

Another important aspect of the judiciary's referee role involves statutory interpretation. A significant share of the judiciary's modern caseload involves hearing challenges from plaintiffs both that a regulation or some other action causes them some financial injury and that the agency did not have the authority to take the action in the first place. Whenever the EPA issues a new pollution standard, there is a fair chance that an affected party will sue the agency, claiming that it exceeded its authority. The Court must determine whether the agency conformed substantively and procedurally to the law's guidelines.

In many other cases, the Court simply decides what the law says. Bankruptcy law protects retirement funds from liens by creditors. Does this include 401(k) savings accounts that can be withdrawn at any time but with a penalty before the individual reaches a certain age? Yes, the Court answered in 2005. Then, for the next session, it considered whether Social Security disability payments were similarly protected.[16] In many instances the modern federal judiciary acts as an extension of the bureaucracy. When the federal government believed that Apple Computer had violated antitrust laws in its deals with publishers over e-books, it could not, unlike governments in many other countries, directly penalize the company. Antitrust laws required that the government sue Apple and let a federal judge decide if the charges were true, and, if so, the penalty. By one count well over half the Court's decisions interpreting public laws from 2000 through 2011 took the form of statutory interpretation compared with just over a quarter that were decided on constitutional questions.[17] At times, the Court will even recommend changes in the law that will produce the intended results and resolve conflicting laws and ambiguous delegations of authority to the bureaucracy.[18]

## The Structure of the Federal Judiciary

The United States has several hundred federal courts, but only the Supreme Court is explicitly mentioned in the Constitution's Article III. The Framers knew more would be needed, but unable to agree whether to create a separate federal judiciary or have the state courts oversee the initial trials and lower-level appeals, they agreed to defer the decision and let Congress create "inferior" courts as necessary. Congress promptly did so in the Judiciary Act of 1789. Of the various types of courts Congress has created over the years, those of most interest here are **constitutional courts**, which are vested with the general judicial authority outlined in Article III.* (See Figure 9.2.) These lower-level courts, designed to handle litigation, exercise the same power of judicial review available to the Supreme Court. In this sense the entire federal judiciary serves as agents of the Supreme Court. The lower federal courts weigh the merits of a case against prescribed Supreme Court doctrine and presumably arrive at approximately the same decision the Supreme Court would have rendered had it heard the case.

As we have seen, Congress delegates work to specialized committees and sizable staffs to deal with the myriad issues and policies it handles. Similarly, the modern presidency includes a large retinue of highly specialized White House staff and the Office of Management and Budget (OMB) to monitor the hundreds of executive branch agencies. As with these other institutions, the Supreme Court's effectiveness also rests on delegation—in this case, on persuading the lower federal judiciary, by the strength of its opinions, to implement its policies.

■ **FIGURE 9.2**   The Structure of the Federal and State Court Systems

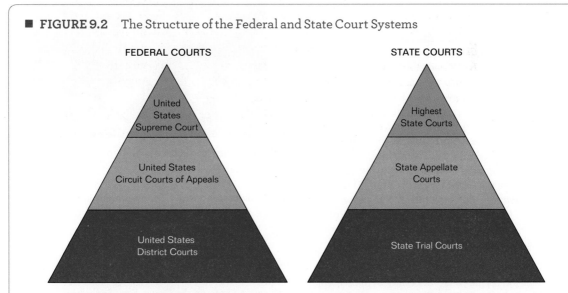

*Note:* In both the state system and the federal system, most cases begin at the bottom of the pyramid, in trial courts. Parties who lose at the trial level can usually appeal their case. In the federal system, a litigant appeals to the appropriate Circuit Court of Appeals, and in the state system, a litigant appeals to the appropriate state-level appellate court (although some states do not have courts at this level). At the top of the pyramid in the federal system is the U.S. Supreme Court, which has discretion over most appeals. At the top of each state's pyramid, there is also a court with ultimate authority to hear appeals; most are called the "Supreme Court" of that particular state.

---

*The nonconstitutional courts are classified as legislative courts. They are created by Congress under Article I and fulfill some special purpose; their judges are appointed by the president for fixed terms. Examples are the U.S. Court of Military Appeals, the U.S. Tax Court, and bankruptcy courts.

# Chief Justice Roberts Stands Alone and Puts His Stamp on the Roberts Court

Scholars often refer to different eras of the Court by the name of the chief justice who served during that time. As discussed in Chapter 5, the era in the 1960s in which the Court expanded the rights of criminal defendants is known as the Warren Court. The Rehnquist Court is known in part for rebalancing the relationship between the federal government and state governments.

In the spring of 2012, as the Supreme Court was preparing to decide the constitutionality of the Patient Protection and Affordable Care Act (also known as "Obamacare"), John Roberts had been chief justice for fewer than seven years. The highest-profile decision of the Roberts Court so far was *Citizens United,* discussed in Chapter 5. That decision was predictably 5–4, with the Court's conservative justices striking down sections of a bipartisan campaign finance reform law. In President Obama's State of the Union address in 2010 (just weeks after the Court's decision) he did something unusual for a sitting president: he openly and directly criticized the Court for its decision. This criticism was not just unusual but awkward: six of the justices (including Chief Justice Roberts) were sitting in the chamber, just steps away from the president.

This backdrop made the Court's pending decision on the constitutionality of the Patient Protection and Affordable Care Act all the more intriguing. Heightening the stakes was the fact that presidents since Teddy Roosevelt had tried to pass health care reform, and some, like Bill Clinton, had suffered political bruises in the process. And here stood Barack Obama, who could say he was the first to actually get it done. Would the Court's conservative justices undo President Obama's signature legislative achievement? Would this case provide further

U.S. Supreme Court

Chief Justice John Roberts

evidence—along with *Citizens United*—that the Roberts Court was nakedly partisan just like the elected branches?

Most assumed that the answer to those questions lay in the hands of one justice: Anthony Kennedy, the swing vote on the Court. Few—including the other eight justices—could have predicted that the real wild card would be Chief Justice Roberts. At the conference in which the justices voted, there were four votes to affirm, four votes to reverse.* Chief Justice Roberts spoke last and indicated that Congress had exceeded its powers under the commerce clause in creating the individual mandate. He then assigned himself the draft opinion.† The implication of course was that he would be drafting the majority opinion striking down the law.

In the end, Chief Justice Roberts did write the majority opinion. And he did side with the four conservative justices in holding that Congress did not have the power to pass the act under the commerce clause. But the shock was that the other part of his majority opinion *upheld* the Patient Protection and Affordable Care Act and its controversial individual mandate under Congress's power to tax. On that issue, he was the lone conservative who sided with the four "liberal" members of the Court.

What did this unique vote mean for the legacy of the Roberts Court? Much like Chief Justice John Marshall in *Marbury v. Madison,* Justice Roberts was able to avoid some unpalatable political consequences. If he had sided with Scalia, Thomas, Alito, and Kennedy in striking down the entire law, the Roberts Court's reputation would have been politicized beyond repair. The legacy of the Roberts Court might have been the institution's damaged legitimacy. And overturning the Court would have likely become an issue in the upcoming presidential campaign. On the other hand, had the Court upheld the law

under the commerce clause, Roberts would have been roundly criticized by fellow conservatives as undoing the work of his predecessors in redefining the commerce clause.

Perhaps the brilliance of Roberts's unique vote is that he made neither side completely happy, yet in the long term he enhanced the Court's credibility. As the chief justice stated the matter in his majority opinion, "Members of this Court are vested with the authority to interpret the law; we possess neither the expertise nor the prerogative to make policy judgments. Those decisions are entrusted to our Nation's elected leaders, who can be thrown out of office if the people disagree with them. It is not our job to protect the people from the consequences of their political choices." Justice Roberts sent a clear message, not to the president or Congress, but to the American people: if you don't like the Patient Protection and Affordable Care Act, take it up with the political branches, not the Court.

*Jeffrey Toobin, *The Oath: The Obama White House and the Supreme Court* (New York: Doubleday, 2012).

†When the chief justice is in the majority, he can assign the opinion to himself or to another justice.

## Jurisdiction of the Federal Courts

As almost every American law school student immediately learns, federal courts are courts of *limited* jurisdiction. The precise scope of federal court jurisdiction is not, in fact, so simple, which accounts for the semester-long law school courses devoted to this subject. Generally speaking, federal courts are authorized to hear two types of cases: those concerning "federal questions" and those involving citizens of different states. Among other things, **federal question** jurisdiction includes questions of U.S. constitutional law, such as the various civil liberties claims reviewed in Chapter 5. Or, more commonly, this jurisdiction involves the judiciary's interpreting and applying federal statutes in criminal and civil cases. For example, the Justice Department successfully sued Microsoft in federal court for engaging in monopolistic practices. The second major type of federal jurisdiction concerns cases where states or citizens of different states sue each other. The reasoning here is that a citizen of State A who is sued by a citizen of State B in State B might not be treated fairly by a court in State B.*

*Federal statutory law also imposes the requirement that the amount at issue between citizens of different states must be more than $75,000.

**TABLE 9.2**   The Federal Judiciary: Number of Judges

| COURT | CIRCUIT | DISTRICT |
|---|---|---|
| D.C. Circuit | 11 | 15 |
| 1st | 6 | 29 |
| 2nd | 13 | 62 |
| 3rd | 14 | 61 |
| 4th | 15 | 56 |
| 5th | 17 | 83 |
| 6th | 16 | 62 |
| 7th | 11 | 47 |
| 8th | 11 | 42 |
| 9th | 29 | 112 |
| 10th | 12 | 39 |
| 11th | 12 | 69 |
| Federal Circuit | 12 | — |

Source: Administrative Office of the U.S. Courts.

Note: Current as of December 2018, including vacancies.

Jurisdictional questions can be complicated by the fact that state courts also have jurisdiction over federal civil claims, unless Congress has given federal courts *exclusive* jurisdiction over certain kinds of federal cases, which it often does. Moreover, defendants can invoke "removal jurisdiction" to transfer a case filed from state court to federal court if the case could have originated there. As a practical matter, the vast majority of cases that can be heard in federal court usually will be heard in federal court instead of state court. In addition, a criminal defendant who has been convicted under a state criminal law in state court, but who feels that his federal constitutional rights have been violated, can appeal his case to the U.S. Supreme Court—although the defendant is generally required to first "exhaust" his appeals through the state court system. For example, the defendant in the seminal case of *Miranda v. Arizona,* after losing his appeal to the Supreme Court of Arizona, successfully appealed to the U.S. Supreme Court, which determined that the defendant's Fifth Amendment rights against self-incrimination had been violated.*

## The Supreme Court's Delegation

The federal judiciary is organized as a three-layered pyramid. At its base are ninety-four **district courts** staffed by approximately 667 authorized judgeships.[†] Every state has at least one district court, and the three largest states—California, New York, and Texas—have four. District courts are trial-level courts, and (with some exceptions) most cases in the federal system must start there. If one of the parties is not satisfied with the outcome of a case at the district court level, this party must appeal the case to one of the U.S. Courts of Appeals. There are currently thirteen **courts of appeals**, administered by approximately 179 authorized judgeships (see Table 9.2). Eleven separate geographic regions, or "circuits," cover the fifty states; a twelfth is assigned to the District of Columbia (see Map 9.1). The thirteenth, called the U.S. Court of Appeals for

*Finally, federal courts also have jurisdiction under federal law to hear habeas corpus petitions. Although a discussion of the complicated topic of habeas corpus is beyond the scope of this chapter, the basic idea is that a criminal defendant in state court may file an action in federal court, alleging that the state's incarceration violates the Constitution or other federal law.

[†]The most recent figure is for 2015. In addition, over 350 senior judges at the district court level preside over a reduced caseload.

■ **MAP 9.1** The Federal Judiciary

*Source:* United States Courts, Court Map, accessed at www.uscourts.gov/Home.aspx.

the Federal Circuit, has a nationwide jurisdiction and deals mostly with specialized federal law such as patent and trademark law. Usually sitting as three-judge panels, courts of appeals review district court decisions.

The Supreme Court is the court of final appeal. Under its appellate jurisdiction, the Court may hear cases appealed from the lower federal courts or directly from the highest state courts when an important constitutional question is in dispute. Through these channels, the Court receives the bulk of its work. Article III also gives the Court original trial court jurisdiction in all cases "affecting Ambassadors, other public Ministers and Consuls, and those in which a State shall be Party." This constitutional quirk required the Supreme Court in 1998 to hear a dispute between New York and New Jersey over which state "owned" Ellis Island, which is located at the mouth of the Hudson River. Original jurisdiction cases always have accounted for a small part of the Court's work—only about 160 cases in two hundred years.

The Supreme Court depends heavily on the lower courts behaving like loyal agents in deciding thousands of cases annually. The Court's lofty position at the apex of this pyramid of federal courts suggests a command over the subordinate courts' policies that in fact does not exist. Contrary to the clean lines of authority implied by the organizational structure, the judicial system is anything but a tightly supervised hierarchy. Rather, it is a decentralized organization, geographically dispersed across the nation's twelve circuits and administered at every level by independent, life-tenured judges. Moreover, there is some evidence that appeals court judges may, at times, seek cases and write decisions in ways that attract the attention of a president looking to fill a Supreme Court vacancy.[19] Unlike the presidency, which delegates oversight of the bureaucracy to the OMB, or the House and Senate, which delegate responsibility for drafting legislation to committees, the Supreme Court wields few administrative controls over the lower courts. Thus, successful implementation of the Supreme Court's policies is not guaranteed and depends greatly on the degree to which the justices concur in a course of action and on how clearly they communicate it to their colleagues throughout the judiciary.

## The Limits of Internal Control

If the Supreme Court truly sat atop a hierarchical organization, it would enjoy a far different relationship with the district and appeals courts. Like the CEO of a major corporation or a cabinet secretary, it would routinely supervise and give orders to its subordinate agents. Motivated by the knowledge that making the wrong choice might result in an unfavorable merit review, demotion, or even dismissal, subordinates would defer to their principal and seek guidance. None of these techniques to keep subordinates on the right track is available to the Supreme Court in steering decisions from the district and appellate courts. Instead, the life tenure of judges, which insulates the judiciary from the other branches, also insulates judges from one another.

Only Congress can remove a federal judge, and then only for serious offenses—not for incompetence or policy disagreement with the Supreme Court. Moreover, the Supreme Court cannot distribute the caseload to the lower courts; the distribution of cases depends on geographical jurisdictions created by Congress and, to some extent, litigants' choice of courts.

The Supreme Court also may have difficulty enforcing implementation of its decisions in the lower courts. Outright resistance to Supreme Court decisions by lower-court judges is unusual but does occur. Declaring that the Court "erred," an Alabama federal judge in 1983 upheld prayer in the public schools, in spite of the Court's prohibition of the practice.[20] In a capital punishment case in 1993 an appellate judge kept granting a stay of execution despite the Supreme Court's rejection of the defendant's appeal. When a lower court disregards a directive, the Court has several options available. It may hear the case a second time, rebuke the lower-court judge, issue a writ of mandamus ordering the lower-court judge to take a specified action, or assign the case to a different court. Because all such alternatives are costly in terms of the time and monitoring required, they illustrate the limits of Supreme Court control, though they also ensure that the Court will ultimately prevail if it feels sufficiently strongly on an issue.

More commonly, policy differences occur when lower-court judges take advantage of ambiguities arising from the particular facts of a case or in the language of Supreme Court doctrine to avoid complying with the higher court's preferences. This is precisely what happened in the aftermath of *Brown v. Board of Education*.[21] When the Court ordered public schools to desegregate with "all deliberate speed" instead of setting a deadline, it unwittingly invited segregationist federal judges throughout the South to move at a snail's pace.

Yet the Supreme Court is not helpless. It can reverse lower-court decisions when it disagrees; even the threat of reversal often deters deviations from Court doctrine. After all, a reversal represents a "defeat" for a judge, and those who suffer frequent reversals may damage their reputations. A poor reputation, in turn, alerts judges higher up to scrutinize their judgments carefully for incompetence or noncompliance with established precedents. Fearing reversal, most judges strategically temper their rulings to conform sufficiently with established doctrine, and thus to withstand litigants' efforts to persuade an appeals court or the Supreme Court to review the rulings.

Nonetheless, reversal remains an imperfect sanction. Some judges may be willing to risk a few reversals to defend strongly held views and to force other courts to reconsider current policy. In addition, given the Supreme Court's ability to control the number of cases it hears on appeal—a very small percentage of all cases are actually appealed—most circuit court judges realize that the probability of the Court reviewing their decisions is very low. However, a circuit court, like the liberal Ninth Circuit Court of Appeals in the West, can press its luck a bit too much. Over the past decade the Supreme Court has overturned the Ninth Circuit's judgments at more than twice the rate of the other appeals courts, and about half of these reversals brought a frequently divided Supreme Court into unanimous agreement.* As a result, the present Supreme Court monitors this wayward delegate closely. About one-third of all cases the Court reviews originate in this circuit, again about twice the share one would expect.

## Judicial Decision-Making

The pyramid shape of the court system accurately portrays the realities of the modern federal judiciary, at each level of which the caseload continues to mount. As alluded to earlier, the huge docket of the judicial branch means that the risk of reversal may not be so great. For the year ending in June 2016, nearly three hundred thousand new civil cases and eighty thousand criminal cases were filed in the federal district courts. During the same period over sixty thousand district decisions were appealed to the circuit courts.[22] The Supreme Court, in contrast, decided fewer than seventy-seven cases. By 2016 even this tiny number had shrunk to forty-eight. Several reasons possibly account for the Supreme Court's shrinking docket. In 1988 Congress passed a law that sharply curtailed the kinds of cases the Court *had* to consider.[23] Note in Figure 9.3 the docket began shrinking shortly after these previously mandated cases became discretionary. Moreover, in recent years the Court has been divided ideologically. Uncertain how a case will be decided, justices may be less comfortable taking up cases that could set important doctrine.[24]

---

*In one reversal in 2011, the unanimous Court, clearly exasperated, overruled a three-judge panel with a cryptic opinion: "The Court of Appeals offered a one-sentence conclusory explanation. That decision is as inexplicable as it is unexplained. It is reversed." David G. Savage, "High Court Restores Rape Conviction," *Los Angeles Times*, March 22, 2011.

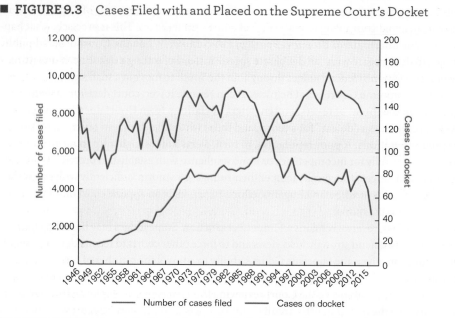

■ **FIGURE 9.3**   Cases Filed with and Placed on the Supreme Court's Docket

*Source:* Ken Moffett kindly supplied the total cases filed in the Supreme Court. The data include both paid and *informa pauperis* filings.

## Selecting Cases

In 1925, when the number of appeals began to grow at an alarming rate, the Supreme Court persuaded Congress to change the rules granting access to a hearing by the Court. Over the years these rules have been strengthened in favor of giving the Court greater discretion to choose the cases it reviews. Instead of having a right to "their day in court," litigants must file a **writ of certiorari** requesting that the Court order a lower court to send it the records of the trial in question. With this device, the Supreme Court gained control over its caseload, for the vast majority of cases arrive by this route. Indeed, the Court has managed to cut in half the number of cases it hears annually, despite a sixfold increase in the number of requests.

Discretionary control over its caseload solved only part of the Court's problem, however. From the eight thousand or so certiorari requests it receives each year, how does the Court decide which one hundred (or fewer) to review? In small, intimate work settings members need not delegate agenda control in order to coordinate their decisions. The Supreme Court's *rule of four* provides that when four justices support hearing a case the certiorari petition is granted.[25] Although this rule protects the prerogatives of individual justices, it does so at a cost to each member of having to cull through a mountain of petitions. Unlike congressional and presidential staffs numbering in the thousands, the Supreme Court is served not by a large bureaucracy to help it sort through that mountain and find cases that satisfy its criteria, but instead by a small retinue of law clerks. Each justice is permitted to hire up to four clerks, usually graduates of the country's most prestigious law schools, who spend a year or two at the Court. Most justices retain clerks who agree with them ideologically in the hope that they will read certiorari petitions the same way the justice would. Justice Clarence Thomas described his dependence on clerks as "mates in a foxhole."[26] Others have enlisted clerks who differ in their political views. This taxes the justice to some degree because he or she must view recommendations from these clerks with a measure of circumspection. On the other hand, this arrangement is well suited to give the justice a preview of the kinds of arguments other justices are likely to make.*

Because the opportunity to hear cases is limited, justices take a hard, strategic look at each petition before promoting it to their colleagues. Do the facts of the case allow the Court to arrive at a "clean" decision that will guide the lower courts? More important, will the justice's preference stand a chance of garnering the five votes necessary to win if the case is heard on its merits? If not, a justice who otherwise would want to hear a case may pass on it for fear of allowing the majority to establish even more firmly a policy he or she opposes.[27] Thus, deciding whether to hear a case is itself a major decision—and one fraught with political strategy. After all, as Chief Justice Rehnquist acknowledged, "There is an ideological division on the Court, and each of us has some cases we would like to see granted, and on the contrary some of the other members would not like to see them granted."[28] And because justices want to weigh in on cases in which they think the lower courts have made an error, cases granted certiorari have a good chance of being overturned. In a typical year almost two-thirds are.

### Resolving Lower-Court Disagreements

Recognizing that the Court has a strong stake in maintaining standards and coherence within this highly decentralized organization, justices look for cases they can use to resolve ambiguities and conflicting lower-court decisions. One example from the Court's 2013 session was *United States v. Woods,* where the Court resolved an appellate court split concerning a tax penalty provision in favor of the Internal Revenue Service. The issue in *Woods* had to do with whether the IRS could assess penalties at the partnership, as opposed to individual, level for certain misstatements. Another important circuit split emerged in November 2014, when the Sixth Circuit deviated from other courts in upholding state-level bans on same-sex marriage in Kentucky, Michigan, Ohio, and Tennessee. Because the Sixth Circuit ruling contradicted the other circuits, the Supreme Court weighed in with its historic decision that both the due process and equal protection clauses gave same-sex couples the right to marry.[29]

### Taking Cues from Others

In selecting cases for resolution, the justices economize by paying close attention to what others tell them. In addition to hearing from the plaintiff (or prosecutor in criminal cases) and

---

*It also offers the justice an opportunity to triangulate the opinions of his or her clerks in figuring out whether a case best suits the justice's interests. If one assumes that clerks are no different from anyone else in Washington in advancing some policies over others, judges are always exposed to the possibility that a clerk will promote a case that advances his or her point of view more than it does the justice's. If the justice can sample different points of view, he or she has a better prospect of determining whether it is a case the justice would like to hear.

defendant, the Court allows interested groups not party to the litigation—interest groups, businesses, and government agencies, among others—to submit **amicus curiae** (friend of the court) briefs arguing that a certiorari petition should be granted or denied. Just as interest groups testify before Congress in hearings, business, government, nonprofits, and other interest groups "testify" before the Supreme Court in these briefs. Of all the interested parties, the most important and prolific is the federal government itself. Through the office of the solicitor general, the administration lets the Court know which cases it thinks are important.

The anecdotal record has long acknowledged that the presence of *amicus curiae* briefs from prestigious sources increases a case's chances of being accepted by the Court. Liberal justices have long paid close attention to the cases championed by the NAACP and the American Civil Liberties Union—two groups introduced in Chapters 4 and 5, respectively, as institutions that perfected lawsuits to champion their views of civil rights and civil liberties. Conservative justices also appear to have *amicus* cue givers that have come on the scene over the past several decades. The National Rifle Association has sponsored key cases and provided courts with a rationale for reinterpreting the Second Amendment to include an individual's right to own firearms. The Heritage Foundation and Pacific Legal Foundation have supported a broader spectrum of cases they view as infringing on property rights and religious freedom.

The most active and important amicus of all is the U.S. government—specifically the **solicitor general**. This office is the chief attorney for the U.S. government. About half of the handful of cases the Supreme Court decides each year were accompanied by the solicitor general's brief urging the Court's consideration.[30] And in controversial cases—defined as those cases in which lower courts disagreed or various groups had filed *amicus curiae* briefs on both sides of the issue—the Court's decision to hear a case followed the solicitor general's recommendation more than 95 percent of the time.

At first glance, these figures suggest that the solicitor general acts as the Court's agenda setter. A subtler process is probably at work, however. The government and interest groups tend to promote those cases they think will attract the Court. In this way, they actually help the Court separate wheat from chaff and identify those decisions that most deserve the Court's attention. In lieu of an extensive bureaucracy to process nearly eight thousand cases, the Court has informally and effectively delegated some of this work to outside agents. When they sound an alarm, the Court pays attention.*

## Doctrine: Policymaking by the Court

Congress passes laws, courts make doctrine. Both are public policy, but they take very different forms. A public law typically assigns responsibility and appropriates money to a federal agency to achieve certain stated policy goals. A judicial policy decision, by contrast, typically states a rule or doctrine. In rendering decisions the Court prescribes guidelines for district and appeals judges to apply when trying similar cases. These guidelines are considered **judicial doctrine** that lower-court judges carefully weigh. Not only does judicial doctrine make

---

*And were they to abuse this influence by overtly calling attention to cases that they would like the Court to hear, but that do not really require its attention, they would find their legal briefs carrying less weight with the Court.

their jobs easier, it also provides valuable information for estimating how far lower courts can diverge from the Supreme Court's preferences before being reviewed and overturned.

Judicial doctrine assumes two forms: procedural and substantive. **Procedural doctrine** governs the specific ways in which the lower courts should do their work. **Substantive doctrine**, more akin to policymaking, guides judges on which party in a case should prevail. Sometimes the two doctrines clash, such as when the Court decides to change current policy—for example, a search and seizure doctrine—but in doing so, it repudiates existing methods or procedures that the lower courts have dutifully followed.

Former Chief Justice William Rehnquist, who served as a law clerk for Justice Robert Jackson (served 1941–1954), meets with his clerks to discuss pending cases.

Ken Heinen

## Procedural Doctrine

Like the managers of other decentralized organizations, the Supreme Court has sought to exercise control and to cope with its ever-growing caseload by establishing standard operating procedures prescribing how lower federal courts should decide cases. The most important such doctrine, **stare decisis** (Latin for "let the decision stand"), directs the lower courts, as well as the Supreme Court itself, to follow established precedent in deciding current cases. Generally precedents are earlier decisions that established a new substantive doctrine. Consider *Griswold v. Connecticut,* the case that established the implicit right of privacy (see Chapter 5). Especially at the appellate stages of a case, the plaintiff's and the defendant's lawyers invoke precedents that support their positions. To the extent that they follow *stare decisis,* the lower courts find it easier to extend the Supreme Court's preferences. This, in turn, frees the Court to monitor closely those decisions that fail to follow precedent or are otherwise unresolved.

Even when followed conscientiously, *stare decisis* cannot strictly determine the outcome of many cases; new and unusual circumstances arise for which existing doctrine offers little guidance. Or the doctrine may be ambiguous, perhaps reflecting uncertainty or disagreement among members of the Court over what the policy should be. Or, as happens frequently, the facts of a case may bring two doctrines into conflict. The ability to interpret doctrine and apply precedents to specific cases is an important skill. Among other things, a judge must decide whether a specific precedent applies to a particular case. Some judges develop strong reputations for writing convincing opinions that influence the way other judges think about comparable cases—that is, their opinions assume value as precedent.

Other procedural doctrines identify who may initiate cases in federal court and under what circumstances. Only litigants who are directly and adversely affected by the disputed action have the right, or standing—that is, sufficient personal stake in the outcome to bring the case to court (see also Chapter 8). In this era of divided party control of government in Washington and across the nation, a new class of actors has generally gained standing before federal courts: government officials. Members of Congress routinely sue the administration. November 2018 found Democratic members of the House and Senate litigating nearly a dozen active lawsuits against President Trump and his officials in the federal courts. Two hundred members of Congress won standing to sue the president for business dealings they claim violate the Constitution's emolument clause (Article I, Section 9) prohibiting government officials from profiting from a foreign government's gifts and other forms of compensation. Another lawsuit challenged the constitutionality of Trump's appointment of a nonconfirmed, "temporary" attorney general. During the Kavanaugh Supreme Court confirmation, Democrats on the judiciary committee sued for disclosure of additional documents on the judge's work in past Republican administrations.

The Court long ago established the principle that the judiciary would not rule on moot (otherwise resolved) or hypothetical issues. Do presidents have the authority to impound appropriated funds? The only way to find out is for a president to impound money and have someone file suit. Though at times highly inconvenient to other actors, this doctrine prevents the judiciary from becoming embroiled in hypothetical issues. Another important procedural doctrine establishes a boundary of federalism within the judiciary: only those cases in the state courts that raise a constitutional question at the outset—such as a civil liberty protected by the Bill of Rights—may be appealed to the federal judiciary and only after appeals through the state courts have been exhausted.

Bettmann/Getty Images

After inflaming white southerners with the Court's ruling in **Brown v. Board of Education** in 1954 and other groups throughout the country with liberal civil liberties rulings, Chief Justice Earl Warren became a target of a grassroots impeachment campaign. In this 1963 photo he accepts impeachment literature while passing picketers. No Supreme Court justice has ever been removed by impeachment.

### Substantive Doctrine

As the Supreme Court selects and decides cases, it is less interested in simply "seeing justice done" in a particular instance than in identifying standards and general characteristics of cases that will allow a decision to be applied to government policy as well as to future cases. In the *Miranda* decision discussed in Chapter 5, the

Court set out clear police procedures for protecting defendants against self-incrimination. Today thousands of local law enforcement jurisdictions follow the *Miranda* guidelines as a standard operating procedure when making an arrest.

Although the ideology of judges matters most at the higher levels where doctrine is made, current doctrine often leaves judges with abundant discretion in the lower courts. Aside from the conventional liberal-conservative distinction that applies to many cases, judgments also vary according to the way a judge views his or her role on the bench. A judge who in the absence of a clear violation of the Constitution or established doctrine will defer to the policies emanating from the elected branches is commonly described as exercising judicial **restraint**. Those who change doctrine to conform with their view of the Constitution in a changing society are exercising judicial **activism**. In modern political debate, the term *activist* has often been used pejoratively to describe a judge who seeks to substitute his or her policy views for the views of the legislature. The Warren Court during the 1960s was widely regarded as activist in that it reopened and changed doctrine in many areas of civil rights and civil liberties. During this era *activism* and *liberalism* were used more or less interchangeably in the news media to describe judges and their decisions. However, in the present era, with most of the activist views of the Warren Court solidified as established policy, activism is just as likely to be found among judges favoring a conservative policy agenda. Thus, as the Politics to Policy box "Judicial Activism" on the next page further explains, the term *activist* can apply to either a conservative or a liberal justice.

## Deciding Doctrine

Every Supreme Court decision contains two elements essential to creating doctrine. The first is the vote that decides the case in favor of one of the parties. The second is the opinion, a statement or set of statements in which the majority explains the rationale for its decision in a way that creates doctrine (that is, makes policy) and the minority, if there is one, articulates why it dissents.

A unanimous Court decision, simply because it is less likely to be reversed in the future, creates more compelling precedent than does a case decided by a 5–4 vote. After the justices express their views on a case and vote tentatively on the outcome in a private conference, the chief justice (if voting with the majority) assigns one of the majority the task of drafting an opinion.* The task is not insignificant; the author of an opinion voices the majority position and, in doing so, strongly influences the shape of that judicial policy.

Once the majority opinion is drafted, it often undergoes prolonged internal bargaining as the writer tries to persuade the other justices that its legal arguments are correct. The author of the opinion generally writes to maintain the decision's core support as well as appeal to dissenters who might be converted. In 1954 Chief Justice Warren used his considerable powers of persuasion to coax reluctant justices to abandon their disparate, and strongly held, positions on school desegregation and forge a unanimous opinion against segregation in *Brown v. Board of Education.*

Successful persuasion has its costs, however. Generally, to persuade colleagues to maintain or shift their positions, the drafter must change the opinion's language and perhaps blur

---

*If the chief justice is in the minority, the most senior associate justice in the majority is assigned the opinion.

## POLITICS TO POLICY
# Judicial Activism

*Judicial activism* is a term traditionally associated with "liberal" decisions by the courts. Commonly, it arises when a judge issues a ruling that broadens the conventional view of civil and criminal rights. In Chapter 5 we reviewed the activism of the Warren Supreme Court, which throughout the 1960s dramatically expanded the rights of criminal defendants. Activism also applies to instances in which a court intervenes beyond simply ruling whether legislation or, more commonly, implementation by a government agency violates the Constitution or some federal statute. Decisions described as activist are typically those in which a court actually prescribes how a policy needs to be changed or implemented to satisfy the judge's opinion of what is required for it to comply with the Constitution or some federal statute.

The term *activist*, objectively speaking, can be ascribed to judges who make decisions that can be categorized as either liberal or conservative. In other words, when judges are accused of being activists and substituting their policy views for those of elected officials or government agencies charged with implementing policy, the substantive outcome may be conservative. Here are two recent decisions—one conservative, one liberal—that have attracted the activist label.

*District of Columbia v. Heller* (decided in 2008) is a prime example of an activist decision that is also conservative. In *Heller,* the Supreme Court decided that the Second Amendment's right to bear arms was not a group right, but rather an individual right. This decision can be characterized as activist because it "both ignored precedent and invalidated a law adopted by a popularly elected government."[a] Furthermore, gun control advocates viewed the decision as conservative because the five members of

the Court in the majority were interpreting the Second Amendment in a way that made it harder for the elected branches of the federal government (and, as the Court held in a subsequent case, state governments) to regulate guns and, therefore, to address the consequences of violent crimes committed with guns.

By contrast, a recent decision that could be classified as liberal activism is one in which the Supreme Court upheld the decision by a three-judge district court ordering the state of California to reduce its prison population by approximately forty thousand inmates.[b] The lower court's order was the culmination of both a ten-year-old case and a nineteen-year-old case in which the plaintiffs alleged that California's overcrowded prisons failed to provide constitutionally adequate medical care and mental health care to prisoners. Although the district court noted that federal courts must proceed with caution when intervening in a state's affairs, the judges ultimately determined that the courts had no choice but to step in, and the Supreme Court agreed that the action was necessary to remedy the violation of prisoners' constitutional rights. The Supreme Court's decision can be seen as activist because the federal courts arguably are substituting their judgment for the judgment of the elected branches of the state of California. The decision also can be characterized as liberal because the court is protecting the constitutional rights of prisoners—a class of people not generally favored by conservatives, who are known for being "tough on crime."

---

[a]Erwin Chemerinsky, "The Supreme Court Gun Fight: A Case of Conservatism. A Case of Conservative Activism," *Los Angeles Times,* June 27, 2008.

[b]See *Brown v. Plata,* 131 S.Ct. 1910 (2011).

its message, allowing each member of the majority to find language in the opinion with which he or she can agree. Thus reluctant justices joined Warren's opinion in *Brown* on the condition that he not specify a time schedule for school desegregation. The consequences, we found in Chapter 4, were considerable. The failure to set a deadline allowed southern school boards to delay by first resisting and then engaging in token desegregation and tying up enforcement with litigation. The price of broad support among the justices may be vague, imperfectly enforced doctrine.

The prevalence of closely divided decisions—containing numerous opinions—is a modern development (see Figure 9.4). The rationale on which an opinion is based may be more consequential for future cases than for the decision itself. Because all justices wish to influence future decisions, each has an interest in opinion writing. A justice who disagrees with the majority of the Court may elect to explain why in a **dissenting opinion**. A justice who has unique reasons for supporting the majority may choose to write a **concurring opinion**. Concurring and dissenting opinions allow justices to provide their interpretations of what the majority opinion means. Although only the majority opinion counts as the Court's final decision in any given case, dissenting and concurring opinions may nonetheless influence reactions to the majority's position, by lower-court judges or by a future Supreme Court revisiting the policy.

Until passage of the Judiciary Act of 1925, which gave the Supreme Court greater control over its caseload, the Court decided far more cases than it considers today. Obligated to review many lower-court decisions with which it agreed, the Court before 1925 produced a large number of unanimous opinions. As the Supreme Court has freed itself to focus on cases that contain important, unresolved policy issues, the proportion of controversial cases has risen dramatically, and thus there are higher numbers of concurring and dissenting opinions.

Two other influences contributed to this rise in opinion writing. First, the Court stopped contesting the authority of Congress and the president to regulate economic activity and began applying the Bill of Rights to state—not just federal—actions. That the justices would not march in unison toward this new body of judicial doctrine is not surprising. The second influence has been the rise of divided party control of government—a pattern whose effects on the presidency were examined in Chapter 7. An important result of this political development has been an ideologically more heterogeneous Supreme Court.

## The Supreme Court's Place in the Separation of Powers

Judicial review seems to give the Court the last word on much of public policy. But we have found throughout our discussion, both here and in the earlier chapters on civil rights and civil liberties, that this is not necessarily so. Even when the Court's members agree on a decision and solve their internal compliance problem, the high court still faces formidable obstacles when its policy preferences differ sharply from those of Congress and the president. When the elected branches have decided on a course of action—even on controversial issues such as Roosevelt's New Deal or Obama's health care plan—they usually prevail.

■ **FIGURE 9.4**   Number of Dissenting and Concurring Opinions

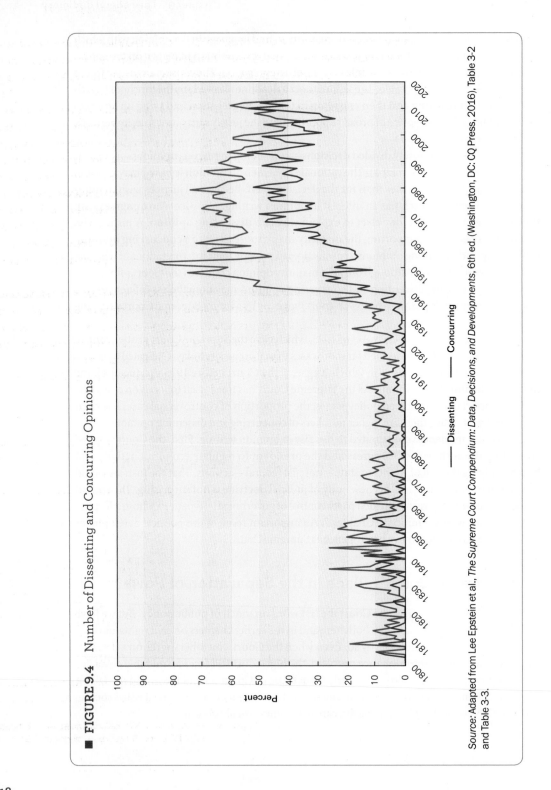

*Source:* Adapted from Lee Epstein et al., *The Supreme Court Compendium: Data, Decisions, and Developments,* 6th ed. (Washington, DC: CQ Press, 2016), Table 3-2 and Table 3-3.

The question that arose in Chapter 5 rears its perplexing head again here: how appropriate is it that unelected, life-tenured judges can decide on the constitutionality of acts of Congress? This arrangement does violate the democratic principle of majority rule, but it met the Framers' broader concerns that they create a balanced political system in which competing interests check one another. As we found in *Federalist* No. 10, the Framers were just as wary of popular majorities exploiting their control of government to pursue their own interests as were kings and other unelected rulers. Through the Constitution's separation of powers and checks and balances, the Framers appear to have planned for the judiciary to be part of the Constitution's balancing act.

But does not judicial review's seemingly absolute authority violate the republican principle of balance as much as it does the democratic principle of majority rule? Who is to guard this guardian? The constitutional amendment process offers one certain way to countermand the Court's ruling of unconstitutionality, but the process is difficult and rarely employed. The Constitution also empowers Congress to alter the size (and therefore the ideological complexion) of the Court as well as change its jurisdiction, but these ploys have been attempted even less frequently. Perhaps the rarity with which Congress has resorted to these difficult constitutional remedies reflects its ability to achieve adequate responsiveness through easier and less controversial means.

On close inspection, the federal judiciary appears to lack the kinds of internal resources that would allow it to be a powerful, autonomous policymaker. The limited veto authority offered by judicial review, the huge caseload, the lack of enforcement authority, and even the life tenure of its members at every level of organization limit the judiciary's capacity to be an assertive policymaker. Finally, the fact that presidents nominate federal judges and the Senate confirms them ensures that the judiciary will not long stray far from the mainstream of national opinion. The Court's decisions, just like those emanating from the other branches, come and often go; rarely are they final. In sum, the doctrine of judicial review has worked because it does not foreclose effective responses from the other branches. This is, of course, the principle we have found throughout our inquiry to lie at the core of America's republicanism.

## Absence of Judicial Enforcement

In 1974 President Richard Nixon refused to release Oval Office recordings of private conversations to the special prosecutor investigating the variety of misdeeds known as the Watergate scandal. When the two sides went to court, the Supreme Court, by an 8–0 vote, rejected Nixon's claim of executive privilege and instructed him to turn over the tapes to the special prosecutor, which he did.[31] The contents of the tapes led directly to his resignation. At this point the Court's role largely ended. Had Nixon defied the Court—and the press speculated that he might—Congress would have had to take the next step and decide whether his refusal constituted grounds for impeachment and removal from office.

The absence of enforcement authority has allowed Congress and the president at times to ignore Supreme Court rulings. As President Andrew Jackson famously remarked on learning that the Court had ruled his policies regarding removing Cherokee Indians from their land unconstitutional,[32] "They made their decision. Now, let them enforce it." Jackson ignored the decision and forced the Cherokee to give up their lands in return for land west of the Mississippi River. Many died on the trek later known as the Trail of Tears. In Chapter 4 we encountered another famous example of the Supreme Court's weak enforcement in *Brown v. the Topeka Board of Education*. In this case those state officials affected by this and follow-up decisions by other federal courts evaded enforcement by various subterfuges. Meaningful integration did not occur until implementation of the Civil Rights Act of 1964.

## Constitutional and Statutory Control

Several provisions of the Constitution equip Congress and the president with the power to rein in the Supreme Court when they disagree with its decisions. Article III allows Congress to set the jurisdiction of the Supreme Court and to create lower courts, which it did in 1787. Moreover, the Constitution is silent on the size of the Supreme Court, which means the Framers implicitly gave this authority to Congress. During the nineteenth century, Congress did, in fact, add to and subtract from the number of justices, but since 1869 the number has been set at nine. At times, when one of the political parties has captured control of the White House and Congress, it has expanded the size of the lower judiciary as a way of creating vacancies that can be filled with sympathetic judges.[33]

When all else fails, Congress may move to amend the Constitution (Article V). The Fourteenth Amendment's declaration that "all persons born or naturalized in the United States . . . are citizens of the United States" was designed to invalidate the Court's claim in *Dred Scott v. Sandford* that African Americans cannot be U.S. citizens. After repeated failures to persuade the Supreme Court that the Constitution does not forbid an income tax, Congress sent to the states the Sixteenth Amendment legalizing the personal income tax once and for all. The states ratified it in 1913.

The historical rarity of congressional attempts to amend the Constitution does not mean they are irrelevant to the relations between the elected branches and the judiciary. The recurrence of these attempts reminds justices that they cannot long impose a radically different interpretation of the Constitution without triggering a reaction from the elected branches. In 1937 President Roosevelt lost a Court-packing battle in which Congress rejected his proposal to expand the Court in order to win its approval of his New Deal programs to fight the Depression. His scheme failed in Congress, but FDR won the war in preventing the Supreme Court from overturning any more of his New Deal economic recovery policies. The conservatives on the Court confronted the stark reality of the superior authority of the elected branches, and so they nimbly began undoing precedents they had asserted only a few years before. Shortly thereafter, the Four Horsemen—the apocalyptic nickname given to the conservative justices who voted in unison against Roosevelt's policies—left the bench and were replaced by justices sympathetic to the New Deal.

Legislative responses to disagreeable Supreme Court interpretations to public laws are, by contrast, straightforward and routine. One study found that from 1967 through 1990 Congress averaged a dozen new laws a year explicitly designed to reverse or modify federal court rulings. And another study found that from 1954 through 1990 Congress passed new laws to reverse 41 of 569 Supreme Court decisions voiding state or federal laws in some way.[34] Moreover, Congress can effectively nullify an adverse judicial decision by writing a new public law that addresses the Court's concern or achieves the same goal in a somewhat different way.* The Supreme Court ruled that Congress cannot order local sheriffs to administer federal gun control procedures, but the ruling did not prevent Congress from tying such compliance to the eligibility for federal grants.

## Department of Justice

The Department of Justice assumes primary law enforcement responsibilities for the federal government and houses many well-known agencies, such as the Federal Bureau of Investigation (FBI), the Drug Enforcement Administration (DEA), and the Bureau of Alcohol, Tobacco, Firearms and Explosives (ATF). In addition, the Department of Justice is by far the most frequent and most important litigant in the federal court system, where it is the primary representative of the federal government. Indeed, the structure of the department parallels that of the federal courts, giving it the power (and efficiency) to press for legal action at all levels of the federal court system. The head of the department, the **attorney general** of the United States, can select cases and choose to file in courts where the Justice Department is most likely to win and create precedent for its legal position on an issue.

The department includes the U.S. attorneys, one for each of the ninety-four federal judicial districts. Presidential appointment and department supervision guarantee that U.S. attorneys serve as dutiful agents as they choose cases and enlist the court system to implement administration policy. In 1996, after a number of black churches had been firebombed, President Bill Clinton announced a special effort to find and prosecute the culprits. Over the next six months, several cases were prosecuted in federal court. Conversely, in the same year when California passed an initiative intended to legalize the use of marijuana for medicinal purposes, the U.S. attorneys stayed clear of prosecution, despite the Justice Department's warning that possession of marijuana remained a federal crime.

## Judicial Recruitment

The Constitution provides that all federal judges shall be nominated by the president with the "Advice and Consent" of the Senate (Article II, Section 2). Aside from voting judicial nominations up or down, senators have traditionally enjoyed a number of time-honored informal mechanisms for influencing judicial nominations. A long-standing practice, called **senatorial courtesy**, found presidents deferring to the preferences of copartisan (i.e., from the president's party) senators from the state where the district court was located. As late as the 1980s presidents would solicit names for nominations from their party's senators. They could reject them, but they generally accepted the senators' choices. This practice weakened during the civil rights era when Presidents Kennedy and Johnson rejected numerous southern Democratic senators' nominees who were unsympathetic to civil rights. Since then the tables have turned with presidents running their own searches for judges, although they continue to informally solicit names and vet nominees with senators from the relevant state.

---

*Moreover, about half of all Supreme Court decisions that involved interpretation of federal law became the specific subject of congressional hearings.

Appointments to the courts of appeals and Supreme Court have always tended to be more of a presidential prerogative. This makes sense in that these courts are more likely to take up constitutional questions. Nonetheless, even here senators have informally influenced the final choices. The practice of giving senators the prerogative of filing **blue slips** with the chairman of the Senate Judiciary Committee allowed those senators—even opposition party senators—who represented the state in which the nominee resided an opportunity to veto the administration's nominee. Unless both senators filed a blue slip endorsing the nominee, the chair would withhold hearings and the nomination would wither. The filibuster (see Chapter 6) offered a final avenue for resistance to nominations that again allowed opposition legislators to block objectionable nominees.

Over the decades the combined practices of senatorial courtesy, blue slips, and filibuster gave individual legislators and even the opposition party a significant measure of influence over recruitment. The net effect was moderation. Senators might propose district court judges to satisfy local political needs rather than someone wholly aligned with the party's ideological tendencies. And with holds and filibusters, even opposition legislators had a hand in nomination.

In recent years all these devices have eroded or been altogether discarded. The result has been the recruitment of judges who are more in tune with presidents' programmatic views and are generally more partisan. Although presidents, including President Trump, reportedly solicit names from their party's senators in identifying district court nominees, presidents no longer defer to their senators in their selections. The president's copartisans still have an important say in preventing an objectionable name from coming forward. The filibuster option has all but ended. Faced with a recalcitrant Republican opposition, Democratic majority leader Harry Reid in 2013 ruled that the filibuster would not be available to lower-court nominees. Once the Republican Party took over the Senate in 2017, its leaders extended this rule to the Supreme Court to prevent Democrats from blocking Trump's nominees. Finally, in the aftermath of the controversial, highly conflictual clearance on nominee Brett Kavanaugh in 2018, the Republican committee chair decided to ignore the blue slip objections of Democratic senator Dianne Feinstein directed at objectionable appeals court nominees from California. This appears to have created a precedent for future judiciary committee chairs to reject opposition senators' blue slips.

Senate confirmation of judicial nominations represents a modern veto game in reverse. The president

nominates, and the Senate accepts or rejects. In this game it is the Senate that confronts a "take it or leave it" decision that limits its opportunity to shape the result. When the White House and Senate are controlled by the same political party, the two sides cooperate informally to identify candidates both can support. As a consequence, nominees rarely encounter difficulty or delay in confirmation. Under divided government, however, the opposition party's rejection of the president's candidates—either outright or by inaction—has become increasingly common-place as the Senate has tried to insinuate its preferences into judicial nominations. How, then, can compromise occur when divided government threatens to stall the nomination process?

From the earliest days of the Republic, the president and Congress have appreciated the merits of appointing like-minded colleagues to the federal judiciary. As we saw in the open-ing of this chapter, the outgoing Federalists understood this as early as the 1790s, when they tried to stuff as many of their partisans as possible into this branch before vacating the pres-idency and Congress. But such strategies are unnecessary for administrations to leave their mark on the judiciary for the next decade or longer after they leave office. For six of his eight years in office President Obama would face an opposition Republican Senate with authority to confirm or deny office to his appointees. Yet he made 329 federal judgeship appointments or about a third of the federal judiciary!

A president's impact on the composition of the Court depends on the frequency with which vacancies arise—something over which the president typically has no influence. But vacancies do occur, and every recent president, except Jimmy Carter, has had via appoint-ments to Supreme Court vacancies an opportunity to shape the future direction of judicial policy. Largely through informal consultations among fellow party members, presidents develop a short list of potential nominees. Most modern nominees are already federal judges, making it easier for presidents to find candidates whose jurisprudence agrees with their own. Many future Supreme Court justices start their careers working in the White House or Justice Department for one of the party's past presidents. Increasingly, presi-dents rely on an ideologically kindred think tank to identify attractive can-didates. On the Republican side, 83 percent of President Trump's appeals court nominees are members of the Federalist Society. In fact, during the 2016 campaign Trump pledged to appoint "great judges," if he were elected—"all picked by Federalist Society." So far, he has honored that pledge.[35]

Presidents typically enlist sev-eral criteria in choosing a nominee. Understandably, presidents try to anticipate how a nominee will vote on currently controversial issues as well as those that may arise in the

THE PROCESS EXPLAINED...

HIM.

©2018 SEATTLE TIMES

RIGHT WING MEGA-DONORS | THE FEDERALIST SOCIETY | THE PRESIDENT | THE NOMINEE

David Horsey / The Seattle Times

A dozen or so conservative foundations heavily underwrite this nonprofit organization. These include the Koch family and its industries, Bradley Foundation, William and Flora Hewlett Foundation, John Templeton Foundation, Adolph Coors Foundation, and Texaco Chevron.

**TABLE 9.3**   Partisanship and Judicial Appointment: Percentage of District and Appellate Court Appointments from the President's Party*

|  | REAGAN | H. W. BUSH | CLINTON | W. BUSH | OBAMA | TRUMP (THROUGH '18) |
|---|---|---|---|---|---|---|
| **District** | 92% | 89% | 88% | 83% | 80% | 76% |
| **Appeals** | 96% | 69% | 85% | 92% | 88% | 93% |

*Sources:* Elliot Slotnick, Sara Schiavoni, and Sheldon Goldman, "Obama's Judicial Legacy: The Final Chapter," *Journal of Law and Courts*, Fall 2017, 363–422; Trump figures from Alliance for Justice: https://www.afj.org/; the Trump appointment percentages provided by Sheldon Goldman, personal correspondence.

*Percentage includes appointees who did not declare a party affiliation.

foreseeable future. One way of reducing uncertainty is to select nominees from the president's party—and, in fact, more than 90 percent of all nominees to the Supreme Court have shared the president's party affiliation. And as displayed in Table 9.3 the figure is not much lower for their appointments to the lower courts. Another involves examining prospective nominees' past decisions. In recent times, nearly all appointees served as appellate judges where they establish a record in overseeing and resolving disagreements arising from the district courts. Finally, presidents satisfy themselves that they are making the right choice in private interviews.

Of course, no infallible guide to choosing the "right" judge exists. Perhaps the most famous example of all of a justice surprising the appointing president occurred in President Dwight Eisenhower's nomination of Earl Warren, the governor of California, to serve as chief justice, reportedly as a reward for the crucial support the governor's delegation provided for Eisenhower's nomination at the 1952 Republican convention. Eisenhower later regretted his choice of Warren as well as that of another justice, William Brennan, who along with Warren

Eric Thayer/Getty Images

Chip Somodevilla/Getty Images

President Trump attends the swearing in ceremony of his two Supreme Court appointees: Neil Gorsuch (left) and Brett Kavanaugh (right).

proved too activist and liberal for Eisenhower's taste. Asked if he had made any mistakes as president, Eisenhower is widely reported as responding, "Yes, two, and they are both sitting on the Supreme Court."* His experience appears to be exceptional. Presidents, by and large, get the judges they put in office. In many respects, these life-tenure choices that successive administrations and congresses cannot undo represents their longest legacy to public policy. Figure 9.5 shows judges appointed three decades ago still deciding cases.

## Judicial Ideology

Judges enter office with established preferences about political issues of the day that differ little from those we expect to find with elected officeholders. Liberals tend to hold an expansive view of civil rights and the role of government in providing services to the citizens; conservatives, conversely, generally favor limited government and reliance instead on private transactions of the marketplace. Judges are not just robed politicians, however. By training, they strive to envelop their views into a consistent set of principles we have referred to as judicial doctrine. Yet the need to couch their decisions in broad principles does not greatly hamstring expression of their political beliefs and values.

■ **FIGURE 9.5**    Obama Appointed the Largest Share of Currently Active Federal Judges

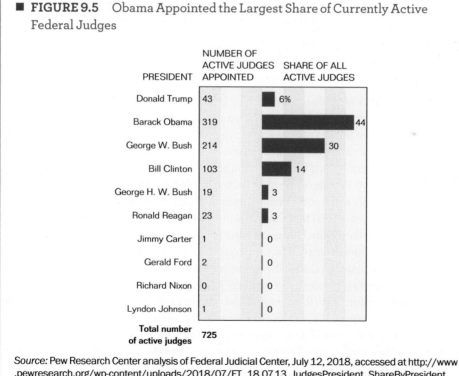

| PRESIDENT | NUMBER OF ACTIVE JUDGES APPOINTED | SHARE OF ALL ACTIVE JUDGES |
|---|---|---|
| Donald Trump | 43 | 6% |
| Barack Obama | 319 | 44 |
| George W. Bush | 214 | 30 |
| Bill Clinton | 103 | 14 |
| George H. W. Bush | 19 | 3 |
| Ronald Reagan | 23 | 3 |
| Jimmy Carter | 1 | 0 |
| Gerald Ford | 2 | 0 |
| Richard Nixon | 0 | 0 |
| Lyndon Johnson | 1 | 0 |
| **Total number of active judges** | 725 | |

*Source:* Pew Research Center analysis of Federal Judicial Center, July 12, 2018, accessed at http://www.pewresearch.org/wp-content/uploads/2018/07/FT_18.07.13_JudgesPresident_ShareByPresident.png. Chart reported in Adam Liptak and Alicia Parlapiano, *New York Times*, June 28, 2018.

---

*Eisenhower might not have used those exact words, but the story probably is an accurate reflection of his attitude toward these two justices.

■ **FIGURE 9.6**    The Distribution of Ideological Voting on the Supreme Court

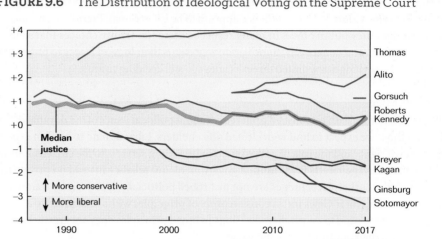

*Sources:* Ideology scores are based on voting patterns and developed from the Supreme Court Database by Lee Epstein, Washington University in St. Louis; and Andrew D. Martin and Kevin Quinn, University of Michigan. Chart reported in Adam Liptak and Alicia Parlapiano, *New York Times*, June 28, 2018.

*Note:* Red lines indicate justices appointed by a Republican, and blue lines by a Democrat.

With few exceptions, judges appointed by Democrats tend to be more liberal than their Republican counterparts. Consequently, when one party controls the presidency over time, the cumulative impact of new appointments can significantly shift judicial policy. As Republicans returned to the White House in 1953 for the first time in two decades, they encountered a Supreme Court wholly appointed by Democrats Roosevelt and Truman. But by the time President Eisenhower had left office in 1961, his five appointees constituted a "Republican" majority of the membership. Beginning with President Nixon, Republican presidents have appointed several times as many justices as have Democrats. With Republican success in winning the White House over the past four decades the federal judiciary has become distinctly more conservative. Consequently, all of the liberal minority in Figure 9.6 are Democratic appointees and all of the conservative majority, Republican.

Brett Kavanaugh's replacement of another "Republican" justice, Anthony Kennedy, may shift the Court even further to the right. Judicial watchers speculate that it may well create the most conservative Supreme Court since the New Deal. And with the two oldest current members (as of 2018), Ruth Bader Ginsburg (eighty-five) and Steven Breyer (eighty), among the Court's most liberal judges, the Trump administration may have additional opportunity to remake the Supreme Court.

Less evident is that presidential appointments of lower-level judges may similarly shift policy in a conservative or liberal direction, despite the fact that these judges are constrained by the appeals courts and Supreme Court who review and sometimes overturn their decisions. Research scoring the ideological stance of federal district judges' decisions finds that they tend to favor the ideological preferences of the president who appointed them. Figure 9.7 demonstrates that each set of judges appointed by a Democratic president on average scored more liberal than any set of judges appointed by a Republican president.

That justices do follow their ideological beliefs offers politicians who appoint and confirm them the advantage of predictability. This should be much appreciated by presidents who, in nominating these life-tenure officeholders, seek candidates who will continue the president's policies, as if they were dutiful delegates, long after the president leaves office. Far from undermining democratic responsibility, judicial **ideology** allows elected officeholders to tether the judiciary to majority opinion in the nation. But with judges appointed for life, at any given moment, the preferences of some of them may differ significantly from those of politicians who control Congress and the White House. This introduces the potential for conflict between the branches, with those wearing the robes asserting that they have the last word.

■ **FIGURE 9.7**   Percentage of Liberal Decisions by Federal District Judges according to the President Who Appointed Them

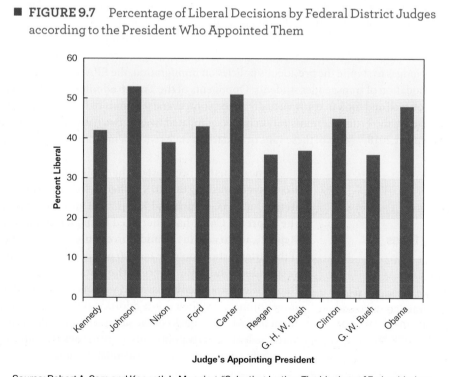

*Source:* Robert A. Carp and Kenneth L. Manning, "Selecting Justice: The Ideology of Federal Judges Appointed by President Barack Obama," in *Principles and Practice of American Politics*, 6th ed., ed. Samuel Kernell and Steven S. Smith (Washington, DC: CQ Press, 2015), 268.

## Does a Politicized Judiciary Alter Separation of Powers?

With judicial recruitment gravitating to the White House, the Senate is left with little more than a veto of objectionable nominees at the confirmation stage. As presidents have centralized recruitment of judges and bureaucrats, they have relied heavily on ideologically kindred think tanks and interest groups to find attractive candidates. Relying on these "outside" groups, presidents are more likely to select men and women who agree with their policies than if they depended on a state's senator to name a district judge or gave senators from the opposition political party an opportunity to block confirmation of the president's nominees. This helps explain why present-day federal judges closely reflect the party and ideology of the presidents who appointed them.

With Republican presidents consistently recruiting conservative judges, and Democrats just as dedicated to filling the judiciary with liberal judges, the selection process appears to be placing into life-tenure office judges willing to join the political fray to block the opposition party's policies. Those state attorneys general (see Chapter 3) and private organizations set up to challenge objectionable policies in court have nimbly sought decisions from those judges who agree with them and rule that a regulation or executive order or even a new law violates the Constitution. A recent appraisal of this trend concluded that "the justices now divide along party lines on major cases with greater frequency than at any time in decades."[36]

Moreover, increasingly these judges are willing to slap a national injunction against a policy's implementation. Obama was plagued by conservative litigants repeatedly finding sympathetic judges to stymie the president's policies on immigration, the EPA, regulations, and accommodation of transgender students. Opponents of the Trump administration learned this lesson well and took to court virtually all the controversial actions of President Trump. By one count, the Trump administration had accumulated twenty-two national injunctions by September 2018.[37] Most of these suits originated in states with Democratic state attorneys general.

### Want a better grade?

Get the tools you need to sharpen your study skills. Access practice quizzes, eFlashcards, video, and multimedia at **edge.sagepub.com/kernell9e.**

None of this has been lost on the public. Insider reports from experts tracking the 2018 midterm election campaigns noted that the Gorsuch and Kavanaugh appointments to the Supreme Court had energized both Democrats and Republicans to vote in the midterm elections. When asked if the latter justice could be fair, 90 percent of Democratic respondents said no, whereas the same percentage of Republican respondents answered yes.* As partisan judges issue injunctions, they invite additional litigants to seek them out. All this smacks of the same sentiment that motivated Federalist Party politicians to try to pack the judiciary after their defeat in the 1800 presidential election.

---

*The national poll of 3,980 respondents was conducted from October 14 through 20, 2018. David Lauter, "Trump Is Still a Drag on GOP," *Los Angeles Times* (October 22, 2018).

# KEY TERMS

activism  415

*amicus curiae*  412

attorney general  421

blue slip  422

concurring opinion  417

constitutional courts  403

court of appeals  406

Court-packing plan  399

dissenting opinion  417

district courts  406

federal question  405

ideology  427

judicial doctrine  412

procedural doctrine  413

restraint  415

rule of four  410

senatorial courtesy  421

solicitor general  412

*stare decisis*  413

substantive doctrine  413

writ of certiorari  410

writ of mandamus  392

# SUGGESTED READINGS

Baum, Lawrence. *The Supreme Court.* 13th ed. Thousand Oaks, CA: CQ Press, 2018. This text offers an excellent synthesis of research on the role of the judiciary in America's separated powers system.

Toobin, Jeffrey. *The Nine: Inside the Secret World of the Supreme Court.* New York: Random House, 2007. A highly readable account of recent politics on the Supreme Court, including "insider" stories on decision-making among the nine distinct personalities on the bench.

Woodward, Bob, and Scott Armstrong. *The Brethren: Inside the Supreme Court.* New York: Simon & Schuster, 1979. Not only highly readable, but generally regarded as an accurate fly-on-the-wall report of the inner workings of the Supreme Court.

# REVIEW QUESTIONS

1.  How does the Supreme Court's ability to delegate tasks compare with those of the other branches?

2.  Why is the judiciary regarded as the "least dangerous" branch of government?

3.  What features of the Court make it appear undemocratic?

4.  How does the Court enforce its decisions on lower courts? On the executive and legislative branches?

5.  How do executive branch attorneys influence the Court's agenda?

NFL quarterback Colin Kaepernick took a knee during the national anthem before a 2016 football game to protest the manner in which some police officers treat African Americans. Donald Trump weighed in on Twitter calling the action disrespectful to the flag and therefore to the country. Two years later, Nike revealed an ad featuring Kaepernick to celebrate the thirtieth anniversary of its "Just Do It" campaign—diving headfirst into the political battle between NFL players and the president of the United States.

# Public Opinion

# 10

Two years after he first knelt for the national anthem before an NFL game, former San Francisco 49ers quarterback Colin Kaepernick became the face of Nike's new "Just Do It" campaign. His initial action—and Nike's new ad—sparked a movement and back-lash among the public. Kaepernick's protest was meant to bring attention to the need for increased attention to the gaps in racial equality in America; particularly important at the time was the mistreatment of young black men by some police officers and the lack of accountability for the officers' actions.

The divisiveness over Kaepernick's refusal to stand for the anthem was amplified in 2017 when President Donald Trump weighed in on Kaepernick's action, asking Americans at one of his rallies if they'd like to see team owners fire "those sons of bitches" who refused to stand for the anthem, calling it "disrespectful" to the flag and military.

Three days after the president's statement, the Dallas Cowboys—known as "America's Team"—took the field in their pregame ceremony. Along with their owner and his family, they walked from the sideline, arms locked, and knelt for a moment to pray for equality and unity. They then returned to their sideline, arm in arm, and stood for the playing of the anthem. The next morning, the president took to social media to applaud the loud boos heard throughout the visiting stadium when the Cowboys took a knee, celebrating what he called the "great anger" it revealed at their actions.

The president's comments about football players and their owners helped to shape—and divide—public opinion, not only on issues of racial equality, but also on the NFL itself.* Before Trump weighed in on the matter, roughly 60 percent of Hillary Clinton's voters had a favorable view of the league, the same share as Trump voters. This was true even as Kaepernick protested in 2016. But in the fall of 2017, after the president's tweets, the share of his voters with favorable views of the NFL was cut in half. There was no shift among Clinton voters.

Voters changed their views on something as simple as a sports league based on what their political leaders were suggesting. They are even more likely to defer to political elites on matters more complicated such as foreign policy, taxes, and health care. Public opinion is an amalgam of people's beliefs, what they hear from leaders they like and respect, and what they have time to figure out.

Relying on party leaders to help form opinions may be an efficient cue for most voters. But if voters are simply relying on what politicians tell them to believe about important national issues, does this mean they don't have opinions on these issues themselves? How can people hold politicians accountable for their actions if voters simply believe the things party leaders tell them to believe?

If public opinion is merely the reflection of strategic politicians, what does this say about democracy and representation?

## What Is Public Opinion?

What is public opinion? The simplest definition, proposed more than fifty years ago by the eminent political scientist V. O. Key Jr., is that **public opinion** consists of "those opinions held by private persons which governments find it prudent to heed."[1] According to this definition, every government, democratic or otherwise, has to pay attention to public opinion in some fashion. Democracies differ from other forms of government in terms of which private persons governments find it prudent to heed (potential voters and those who can sway potential voters) and the main reason it is prudent to do so (an election is coming). In the United States basic constitutional guarantees—regular elections, broad suffrage, freedom of speech and press, freedom to form and join political organizations—allow citizens to express their views freely and compel government leaders to take the public's opinions into account if they want to keep their jobs. These guarantees also make it both possible and essential for political leaders and policy advocates to try to shape and mobilize public opinion on behalf of their causes.

The origins of these guarantees predate the Constitution, and American public opinion has from the beginning been treated as a political force to be alternatively shaped, mollified, or exploited. The object of the Federalists was to sway educated public opinion in favor of the Constitution, but national ratification was secured only when its proponents bowed to the

---

*See the evidence for this in a column about the Super Bowl at The Upshot in the *New York Times*, https://www.nytimes.com/interactive/2018/02/03/upshot/nfl-super-bowl-republicans.html.

widespread public demand that a bill of rights be added (see Chapter 2). In the first years of the Republic, leaders of the nascent parties quickly established newspapers to promote themselves and their policy proposals and to attack the ideas and character of their opponents.

The leaders of movements dedicated to the abolition of slavery, prohibition of alcoholic beverages, suffrage for women, and the end of the spoils system (see Chapters 8, 12, and 13) labored mightily to mold public opinion (through pamphlets, speeches, demonstrations, sermons, editorials, magazines, novels, and plays) and then to serve as agents for its political expression. Then, as now, interest group entrepreneurs sought to mobilize public opinion as a weapon in the policy wars, threatening electoral retaliation against leaders who refused to support their cause.

Modern efforts to measure, shape, and exploit public opinion have spawned two linked industries: scientific polling and public relations. The first is devoted to sounding out the public on an endless array of issues, and the other to marketing ideas, policies, and politicians. Before the advent of scientific polling, politicians gauged public opinion haphazardly, relying on information supplied by editorials, pamphleteers, local leaders, spokespersons for social causes, party activists, and sometimes even less conventional sources. According to one member of Congress who served in the 1930s, "This might sound odd, but myself and many other members of Congress that I knew, used to get a lot of ideas on how the general public felt by reading the walls in bathrooms in towns and cities that we were in."[2] Self-selected, perhaps angry, with axes to grind, such sources were of doubtful reliability. Even open expressions of public sentiments, such as marches, rallies, and riots, could not be taken at face value because they said nothing about the views of the majority who had stayed home. Not until well into the twentieth century was **scientific polling** developed as a tool for systematically investigating the opinions of ordinary people.

## Measuring Public Opinion

The basic techniques developed to measure public opinion accurately are simple in concept but often difficult to carry out in practice: select a random sample of the population of interest, ask the people in the sample some appropriate questions about their views, and count up their answers. The larger the sample, the more closely the sample's answers will approximate the answers the pollster would get if the entire population could be asked. As the sample gets larger, however, the rate of improvement in accuracy declines; it makes little sense to use a sample size larger than 1,200 to 1,500 people unless the outcomes of interest are divided by extremely small margins close to 50 percent. With numbers in the 1,200 to 1,500 range, researchers can be confident that, nineteen times out of twenty (95 percent of the time), the sample's division on a typical question will fall within 3 percentage points of the entire population's division. This is called the poll's margin of error, the maximum of which can be quickly approximated by dividing 1 by the square root of the total number of people in the sample. For example, if 45 percent of the respondents in a poll of 1,500 people say they approve of the president's job performance, chances are nineteen in twenty that the interval from 42 to 48 percent (45 percent plus or minus 3 points) covers the actual level of approval throughout the whole U.S. population. In order to reduce that interval to plus or minus 2 percentage points on either side of the sample estimate, a researcher would have to bear the cost of interviewing

1,000 more people—an increase of two-thirds the sample size to get a reduction of one-third in the margin of error. Strange as it may seem, a sample of 1,500 mirrors a population of 250 million just as accurately as it would a population of 10,000. Notice that the approximate formula for the margin of error does not require knowledge of the size of the entire population; it requires only the size of the sample.

A truly random sample of any large population is rarely feasible because there is no single directory where everyone is conveniently listed and so can be given an equal chance of being selected, which is what strict random sampling requires. Random sampling methods that don't give everyone in the population the same chance of being invited face potential biases if those who have low or zero chances of participating differ systematically from those who are invited.

Even for sampling methods that cover the entire population of interest, like when a list of registered voters is available, not everyone selected is willing to answer questions, and people who refuse differ systematically from the people who answer the pollster's questions (on average, refusers have less money, education, and political knowledge—also things that correlate with political attitudes). Methods have been developed to adjust for these problems—most often, weighting the responses of people in underrepresented demographic categories more heavily than the responses of those in overrepresented categories—but they work imperfectly, so no poll is completely free of the biases they introduce.

Another potential problem with interpreting polls lies in the questions, which respondents may not always understand or may answer incorrectly—by, for example, offering an instant opinion on an issue they have never thought about before. Even the most carefully designed question is subject to some measurement error because the fit between the words and concepts used in questions and how people actually think about issues is never perfect. Properly conducted polls with well-designed questions are nonetheless far less subject to distortion than any other method of measuring public opinion (see the "Straw Polls" box, which describes some pitfalls of alternative techniques for measuring public opinion).

From modest beginnings in the 1930s, opinion polling has grown into a vast industry producing an endless stream of information about the public's views on almost any conceivable matter. Presidents since Jimmy Carter (1977–1981) have had in-house pollsters take regular readings of the public's pulse. George W. Bush, who claimed to disdain polls, nonetheless maintained access to an estimated $1 million worth of public opinion research annually.[3] Barack Obama, described by his press secretary as "way too busy to sit around looking at polls," had access to more than $4 million in polling services via the Democratic National Committee during his first eighteen months in office.[4] In a rare move, recent Republican presidential candidate Donald Trump announced that he didn't have a pollster and wouldn't be hiring one. It wasn't until May 2016, after all the primary contests, that he eventually hired a notable Republican pollster to help him strategize for the general election.

Efforts to shape and channel public opinion have grown apace. As presidents have become more reliant on grassroots public support for winning policy battles, the line between campaigning and governing has blurred. Early in 1997, when campaign-weary news reporters asked Bill Clinton's press secretary why the president maintained such a heavy travel schedule even after winning reelection, he replied, "Campaigns are about framing a choice for the American people. . . . When you are responsible for governing you have to use the same tools of public persuasion to advance your program, to build public support for the direction you are attempting to lead."[5] George W. Bush followed suit, crisscrossing the country to, in his words, "gin up support" for his ten-year, $1.6 trillion tax cut in 2001 and repeating this tactic in 2005 in an unsuccessful attempt to rally a skeptical public behind his proposal to privatize part of Social Security. Obama did the same in an unsuccessful campaign to boost public support for his health care proposals. Trump may be the most interested in public opinion about his White House in general, notably tuning in to cable news to take the temperature of both the public and the Washington elite.

The president has no monopoly on the "tools of public persuasion." Virtually all large modern institutions—government agencies, political parties, corporations, universities, foundations, religious bodies, and so on—employ public relations specialists whose job it is to present the organization in the best possible light. Institutions also promote the *expression* of public opinion. Pollsters articulate public opinion by the very process of measuring it. A 1997 survey on issues raised by the threat of global warming discovered that 60 percent of Americans were apparently willing to pay an additional twenty-five cents per gallon for gasoline to reduce hydrocarbon emissions, a level of support that came as a surprise to people on both sides of the policy debate.[6]

Modern techniques for molding or measuring public opinion have contributed to the nationalization of American politics. Earlier strategies for gauging and shaping opinion depended on institutions such as newspapers and party organizations whose primary focus was local. The relevant publics were those of specific cities, towns, counties, and, to a lesser extent, states; national opinion emerged only as an aggregate of diversely measured local opinions. The advent of scientific polling has made it possible to measure and therefore to treat public opinion as a national phenomenon. National polls probe issues of national concern, raising their visibility in the minds of politicians, the news media, and the public alike. Organized efforts to shape public opinion have taken on national dimensions as well. To be sure, politicians who hold their jobs by the grace of local electorates maintain an abiding interest in local opinion (ask any member of Congress), but the institutional forces that shape local opinion have themselves become national in scope.

Finally, albeit unintentionally, the work to measure and shape public opinion has helped individual citizens to act collectively. Individual expressions of opinion to influence public policy are subject to the standard free-rider problem, because it is exceedingly unlikely that any single person's message will make a difference. But polls and mobilization campaigns can produce collective expressions of opinion that politicians ignore at their peril. And for most people, participation in a quick poll is relatively cost free, especially as survey research firms figure out how to let people take polls on their mobile phones and computers while preserving the scientific properties of the sample.

## The Origins of Public Opinion

Public opinion attracts all this attention because of its effect on political behavior, most notably voting, which is the main, sometimes only, political act of the great majority of ordinary citizens. Like the vote, public opinion has its political effect as an aggregate phenomenon, but also like the vote, it is no more than the sum of its individual parts. To make sense of public opinion, we need to understand the basis of individual opinions.

# Straw Polls

Newspapers and magazines had taken "straw polls" for a hundred years before the advent of scientific polling. The term refers to tossing straws in the air to see which way the wind is blowing. The *Harrisburg Pennsylvanian* sponsored the first known newspaper poll in 1824, correctly predicting that Andrew Jackson would win the popular vote in the presidential election. The polling techniques varied, but all allowed respondents to select themselves to be participants in the poll. Sometimes readers were invited to clip facsimile ballots from the paper, fill them out, and send them in, or they were mailed postcards that they were asked to complete and return.

The *Literary Digest*, a popular magazine, had used the postcard method successfully to forecast the presidential winner in every election from 1920 to 1932. In 1936 it again sent out ten million postcard ballots to names and addresses taken from telephone books, voter registration lists, club rosters, and lists of automobile owners and mail-order customers. The returned cards split 57 percent for Alf Landon, the Republican candidate, to 43 percent for Franklin Roosevelt, the Democratic president running for a second term. On Election Day Roosevelt defeated Landon, 62 percent to 38 percent, winning every state but Maine and Vermont.

How did the *Literary Digest* get it so wrong? First, its sample was badly biased for an election that, unlike the previous contests, divided the electorate strongly along economic lines. During the Great Depression, telephones and cars were luxuries that many Americans could not afford; those who could afford them were far more likely to favor Landon and the Republican Party. Second, the respondents selected themselves. Only 22 percent of those who were sent the postcard ballot responded. The kinds of people who respond to mail surveys are not typical; they tend to have more education, more money, and more ardent political views. Finally, the postcards were sent out too early (September) to pick up any late-breaking trends. Meanwhile, the fledgling Gallup poll, following more sophisticated sampling principles based on the science of probability (and drawing on a much smaller sample), accurately predicted Roosevelt's landslide victory.

Modern professional polls mainly avoid the pitfalls of straw polling, but this doesn't mean scientific polls always hit the mark. As we saw in the 2016 presidential election, polls will be off if the assumptions they make underlying their scientific approaches are also off. In 2016, particularly in states like Wisconsin, Michigan, and Pennsylvania, polls significantly underestimated Donald Trump's support. This could have had something to do with assumptions about the similarities of people who are the same age, race, gender, and party, for example, but who live in cities versus rural areas; or it could have had something to do with systematic differences in who responds to pollsters, differences related to candidate support. As response rates to traditional phone polls drop into single digits and the Internet and mobile platforms replace existing modes of communication, new methods of polling are developing that use the science of statistics to construct samples that *represent* the population without being *randomly drawn* from the population. Of course, pollsters still have to get the population right!

## Attitudes

Where do the individual opinions that collectively constitute public opinion originate? Most scholars who study public opinion believe that expressed opinions reflect underlying attitudes. An **attitude** is "an organized and consistent manner of thinking, feeling, and reacting with regard to people, groups, social issues, or, more generally, any event in one's environment."[7] An attitude thus combines feelings, beliefs, thoughts, and predispositions to react in a certain way. For example, a person's attitude toward the Republican Party might include feelings ("I trust the Republicans"), beliefs ("the Republican Party is against high taxes"), and an inclination to answer "Republican" to a pollster's question about which party handles the economy better. When invited to state opinions or cast votes, people respond in ways that express the underlying attitudes evoked by the choices they face.

Individuals differ widely in the attitudes they bring to bear on political choices. Some people have an elaborate set of informed, organized, internally consistent attitudes that allow them to understand, evaluate, and respond to almost any political phenomenon that catches their attention. Such people are unusual, however. Most people have more loosely structured sets of political attitudes, not necessarily consistent with one another or well informed by facts and concepts. And some people's attitudes are so rudimentary that they offer little guidance in making sense of or responding to political phenomena. People also differ in how strongly they hold attitudes. Some are intensely partisan—the "rock-ribbed Republicans" and "yellow-dog Democrats" (who would vote for a yellow dog if it were a Democrat) of political lore (for further discussions of partisan attitudes, see Chapters 11 and 12). Others maintain attitudes that are far more tentative and open to modification by new information or ideas. Individuals thus vary widely in how they form opinions and make political choices, and the forces that shape public opinion work in different ways on different people.

## Ideologies

Elaborately organized sets of political attitudes often take the form of political ideologies. In theory, ideologies promote consistency among political attitudes by connecting them to something greater, a more general principle or set of principles. In practice, ideologies often combine attitudes linked more by coalitional politics than by principle. The ideological labels commonly used in American politics are *liberal* and *conservative*. Over time, the meanings of these labels change, reflecting shifts in the clusters of issue positions adopted by rival sets of political leaders, who, like other people centrally involved in politics, routinely use ideological categories to simplify the complexities of political life.

In American politics today, **liberals** typically favor using government to reduce economic inequalities, champion the rights of disadvantaged groups such as racial minorities and women, and tolerate a more diverse range of social behaviors. They prefer a smaller defense establishment and usually are less willing to use military force in international politics. They believe that the rich should be taxed at higher rates to finance social welfare programs.

**Conservatives** distrust government and have greater faith in private enterprise and free markets, but they are more willing to use government to enforce traditional moral standards. They favor a larger military and more assertive pursuit of national self-interest. Conservatives advocate lower taxes, particularly on investment income, to stimulate growth and to restrict the government's capacity to finance social welfare programs. But these two sets of attitudes are by no means the only logical ways to combine political views. For example, some people are libertarians, who prefer to minimize government regulation of both social and economic behavior and oppose any military involvement except direct defense of U.S. territory. But these two standard combinations approximate current party alliances, with most liberals in the Democratic Party and most conservatives in the Republican Party. In YouGov surveys during the last presidential election, only 16 percent of Democrats described themselves as ideologically conservative, and only 3 percent of Republicans called themselves liberals.

Although *liberal* and *conservative* are used constantly in public discussions of politics and are familiar to everyone active in politics, these terms do not guide the political thinking of most citizens, nor do the opinions most people express fall neatly into one ideological category or the other. When asked to place themselves on a scale from very liberal to very conservative, a little less than half the people classify themselves as liberals or conservatives; the rest, about 24 percent, locate themselves in the middle, and another 29 percent do not place themselves at all.[8] Those who locate themselves on the scale tend to take positions on issues that are consistent with their chosen location, but a substantial minority take positions inconsistent with it. About half the adult population can apply the terms *liberal* and *conservative* correctly to political issues and figures, but only about one in five use these terms spontaneously to explain their own opinions on parties and candidates.[9] Ideological labels may be indispensable to politicians and pundits, but most citizens get by without them and feel no obligation to be consistently liberal or conservative.

Adopting a liberal or conservative pattern is not the only way people organize their political attitudes. Some studies suggest that a person's political attitudes reflect a small number of **core values**, such as individualism, support for equal opportunity, moral traditionalism, deservingness, or opposition to big government. A favorable attitude toward Republicans might reflect the values of individualism and opposition to big government. Attitudes that arise from the same core value will be in harmony, but because most people maintain more than one, attitudes also can conflict.[10] Psychologists have found that people are uncomfortable holding inconsistent attitudes and tend to modify one attitude or the other to reduce inconsistency when they become aware of it, mitigating, in the technical jargon, cognitive dissonance. Often, however, people remain blissfully unaware of inconsistencies among their attitudes, keeping them in separate mental compartments so they are not brought to mind at the same time by political figures and events. A citizen who dislikes "big government" but favors stricter regulation to protect consumers, workers, and the environment is by no means unusual.

## Partisanship

For most Americans, the political attitude that shapes opinions and organizes other political attitudes most consistently is their disposition toward the political parties. A large majority of Americans are willing to identify themselves as Republicans or Democrats and respond to political questions accordingly. Party identification is subject to varying interpretations, but they are complementary rather than mutually exclusive. The researchers who developed the concept in the 1950s viewed party identification as a psychological phenomenon—an identity. People who were willing to label themselves Democrats or Republicans identified with the party in the same way they might have identified with a region of the country or an ethnic or religious group: "I'm a New Yorker, an Irish Catholic, and a Democrat." The party preference was, literally, an element of an individual's personal identity, either rooted in powerful personal experiences (best exemplified by the millions who became Democrats during the Great Depression) or learned, along with similar identifications, from family and neighborhood. So interpreted, identification with a party was thought to establish an enduring orientation toward the political world. Voters might defect if they had strong enough reactions to particular candidates, issues, or events that ran counter to their party identification. But once these short-term forces were no longer present, the influence of party identification would reassert itself, and they would return to their partisan moorings. For most citizens, only quite powerful and unusual experiences would inspire permanent shifts of party allegiance.[11] The 2016 election is a good example of this notion. Even though many party leaders denounced Donald Trump as the party's nominee, they did not relinquish their party identification and become Democrats. The same is surely true for many voters.

Another interpretation emphasizes the practical rather than psychological aspects of party identification. People think of themselves as Democrats or Republicans because they have found, through past experience, that their party's politicians are more likely than the politicians of the other party to produce preferred results. Past experience is a more useful criterion than future promises or expectations because it is more certain. Party cues are recognized as imperfect, and people who are persuaded that a candidate of the other party would deal more effectively with their concerns vote for that candidate. If cumulative experience suggests that politicians of the preferred party are no longer predictably superior in this respect, the party preference naturally decays.[12] According to this interpretation, partisanship can change gradually in strength or direction without the psychological upheaval associated with revising one's personal identity.

But, again, these interpretations are not mutually exclusive. A party might be just a shorthand cue for some voters but a source of personal identity for others. Cumulative practical experience with leaders and policies might well strengthen or weaken an individual's sense of psychological identification with a party. Conversely, gut feelings about the parties may simply be the brain's efficient way of storing the results of cumulative experiences, providing a shortcut to action (deciding how to vote or to evaluate political actors and events) without further cognitive effort. However interpreted, party remains for a large majority of voters a default cue: unless there is a compelling reason to do otherwise, Americans interpret political phenomena in ways that favor the preferred party. For example, after George W. Bush was finally awarded Florida's electoral votes and thus the presidency in December 2000, 85 percent of self-identified Republicans thought that he had won fair and square, 11 percent that he had won on a technicality, and 3 percent that he had stolen the election. However, among self-identified Democrats, only 18 percent thought that he had won fair and square, 49 percent that he had won on a technicality, and 31 percent that he had stolen the election.[13] Reactions to Bill Clinton's impeachment in 1998 were sharply partisan: nearly two-thirds of self-identified

Republicans wanted him impeached and convicted, whereas about 85 percent of Democrats did not.[14] Even assessments of Donald Trump's intelligence break on party lines: after he was elected, a Quinnipiac College poll reported that 94 percent of Republicans think he is intelligent whereas only 51 percent of Democrats think so.

Such partisan discrepancies are not exceptional; indeed, responses to political actors and events have become increasingly polarized along party lines over the past thirty years. Reactions to George W. Bush and Barack Obama are illustrative. Bush entered the White House in 2001 with the widest partisan difference in job approval of any newly elected president since polling began more than fifty years ago (in no small part because of the partisan battles over the Florida vote count). Democrats rallied to his side in the upsurge of national solidarity inspired by the terrorist attacks of September 11, 2001 (see Figure 10.1), but the gap soon began to widen again. Among Republicans, Bush's approval rating stayed very high, whereas among Democrats it began a steady decline, briefly interrupted by reactions to the successful military phase of the Iraq War in April 2003 and the capture of Saddam Hussein in December 2003. By the fall of 2004, the gap between the parties' identifiers had widened to an average of more than 79 percentage points, an all-time high. Similar differences appeared in the distribution of responses to questions on almost anything having to do with the Bush administration and its policies. Partisan reactions to Obama were almost as polarized, but with the party positions switched. His signal policy initiative, health care reform, drew support from an average of 71 percent of Democrats but only 12 percent of Republicans.[15] In his first year in office, an average of 88 percent of Democrats and only 23 percent of Republicans approved of his performance. The 65-point spread is the largest of any president's first term—and evaluations of Obama only became more polarized as his term played out.[16] A Quinnipiac College poll from November 2016 estimated the difference between president-elect Trump's favorability ratings in the months before his inauguration as greater than 70 points.

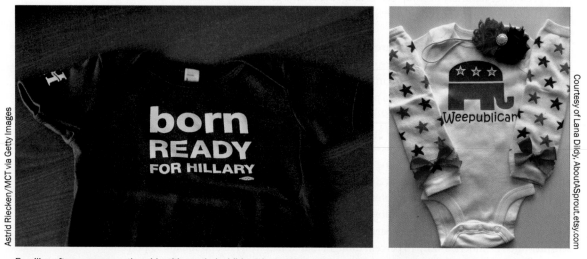

Astrid Riecken/MCT via Getty Images

Courtesy of Lana Dildy, AboutASprout.etsy.com

Families often pass on partisan identities to their children, just as they pass on religious and ethnic identities or a passion for the hometown sports teams. Usually the process is informal and unconscious, but such products as baby clothes are available to parents who don't want to leave anything to chance.

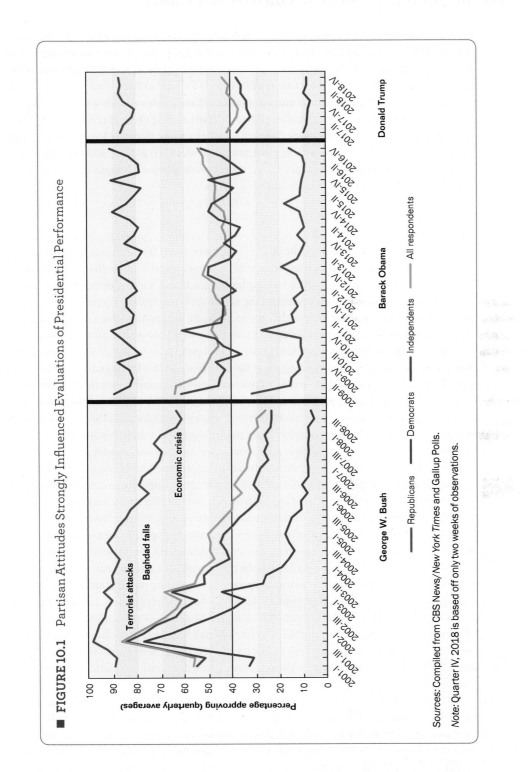

■ **FIGURE 10.1**  Partisan Attitudes Strongly Influenced Evaluations of Presidential Performance

*Sources:* Compiled from CBS News/*New York Times* and Gallup Polls.

*Note:* Quarter IV, 2018 is based off only two weeks of observations.

Party identification, like other attitudes, affects beliefs as well as opinions. Attitudes introduce bias into perceptions and interpretations of political information because people tend to
pay more attention and give more credence to sources and information that confirm rather
than challenge their beliefs. For example, a 2004 study found that Republicans outnumbered
Democrats in conservative radio commentator Rush Limbaugh's audience more than seven
to one, whereas Democrats outnumbered Republicans among viewers of Michael Moore's
anti–George W. Bush documentary *Fahrenheit 9/11* by more than five to one.[17] In general,
the more ambiguous the situation, the more prior attitudes such as party identification shape
beliefs; the 2000 Florida presidential election vote count is a classic example, for to this day no
one can conclusively say who really won.

## Acquiring Opinions

Where do the attitudes that underlie political opinions come from? In one way or another,
attitudes derive from the practical experience of growing up and living in the social and political world. The menu of possibilities is set by families, schools, friends, opinion leaders of all
kinds, and the mass media. People adopt the values and beliefs that pay off in some way—
for example, confirming identity with a group, pleasing others important to them, making
the world comprehensible, or validating material or psychological aspirations. Children
who grow up in families that talk about politics adopt political beliefs and values, just as they
adopt other beliefs and values imparted by the people who raise them and whose approval
they value. Schools reward the learning of political knowledge and values through the study
of the Declaration of Independence and the Constitution or the conduct of classroom elections; they also teach politics informally through the way teachers and other school officials
resolve conflicts and exercise authority. Later, peer groups—friends, fellow students, coworkers—become sources of political ideas and information and of incentives for paying attention
to them. The news media supply a steady stream of information and commentary designed
to shape people's thinking about politics. And even entertainment programming about politics (Showtime's *Homeland*, ABC's *Designated Survivor*, Netflix's *House of Cards*, or CBS's
*Madame Secretary*) can convey political ideas to unsuspecting viewers. Books, movies, and
television shows impart political values in ways that engage people's emotions as well as their
intellects. Movie offerings run the gamut from the classic and idealistic *Mr. Smith Goes to
Washington* and *All the President's Men* to the more cynical or satirical *BlacKkKlansman* or
*Wag the Dog*. **Political socialization**, as the process of acquiring political attitudes is known,
takes place during childhood and young adulthood, but new experiences can alter attitudes
at any stage of life. People who are out of work for the first time, or run the bureaucratic maze
of paperwork and regulations necessary to start a small business, or see how much the government takes out of their first paycheck, or try to keep a toxic waste incinerator out of their
neighborhood may well revise their attitudes toward government and politics in light of their
new experiences.

Although attitudes are certainly influenced by personal experiences, they are by no
means dominated by them. For example, most people base evaluations of the president's
economic performance on their beliefs about the national economy, not on their own family's economic fortunes (although even this may be influenced by a person's party identification). Large majorities may say the health care system is in crisis even though their

own medical arrangements are satisfactory. The perception that public schools are failing or crime is rampant creates a potent political issue even when most people are satisfied with their own local schools or feel safe in their neighborhoods. Indeed, when people rely solely on their own circumstances to make political judgments, it often is because they are unaware of what is happening more broadly and so have no other information to go on. Because politics is primarily about the provision of collective goods, and ordinary citizens can achieve political ends only through collective action, it is logical that political opinions would reflect attitudes

Sarah Shatz/CBS via Getty Images

In the CBS hit show *Madame Secretary*, Secretary of State Elizabeth McCord and her team balance foreign policy and diplomacy with the demands of domestic politics. In this episode, they are trying to hunt down a group that attacked the White House without starting a war.

arising more from collective than from personal experiences. For example, people can be unemployed for any number of reasons, but whatever the reason, their economic future is brighter when unemployment stands at 5 percent rather than 10 percent, and it therefore makes sense to use national rather than personal unemployment to judge the president's management of the economy.

Widely shared experiences give rise to the political ideas and opinions advanced by the various agents of political socialization. The experiences of slavery, segregation, and continuing racial prejudice have given many African Americans a view of politics that leads them to express greater support for government programs aimed at integrating schools, workplaces, and neighborhoods than is typical among whites. Millions of working people who were helped by Franklin Roosevelt's New Deal during the Great Depression developed an abiding loyalty to the Democratic Party. Some experiences fix political thinking for generations; it took a hundred years for white southerners to move beyond political attitudes forged in the Civil War and Reconstruction. Collective political attitudes and beliefs of this sort are grounded in experience, but not necessarily direct experience. Rather, they arise from how families, politicians, journalists, historians, storytellers, songwriters, moviemakers, and artists interpret events. Such interpretations offer socially based cues to "appropriate" attitudes for people who identify with a group but have not themselves shared its formative experiences. Conflicting attitudes arising from competing versions of experience underlie much of the diversity of political opinions both within and between social groups.

## Information

Generally, people tend to develop more complex, richly informed attitudes only when the payoff is greater than the cost of doing so. Individuals raised among politically active people, or who spend more years in school where they are exposed to political concepts and information, or whose jobs put them in touch with political affairs on a regular basis are more likely to develop elaborate and well-informed political views because they can do so without conscious effort. Most people, however, live in social settings where political ideas, events, and personalities are far down on the list of things their families and peers talk or care about, so they have neither the opportunity nor the incentive to develop informed, sophisticated political attitudes on their own. Because people are "cognitive misers," reluctant to pay the cost of acquiring information that has no practical payoff, they may rely more heavily on group cues—like from their political party—in order to express opinions. For people who lack a party affiliation, the opinions they express on issues often appear to be both uninformed and unstable.

Numerous polls have found the public to be surprisingly ignorant of basic political facts, concepts, and issues. A sampling of questions illustrating typical levels of public information on political matters is shown in the box "The Public's Political Knowledge." The percentages listed reveal that large majorities know some basic facts about the presidency and can identify major political figures such as the vice president and their state's governor. Smaller majorities know something about government institutions, such as the Supreme Court's authority to rule on the constitutionality of legislation or the president's power to appoint federal judges, and they understand basic political facts such as which party is more conservative. But more detailed policy questions and lower-level political figures go unnoticed by most of the public.

Chip Somodevilla/Getty Images

Hundreds of protesters occupy the center steps of the East Front of the U.S. Capitol after breaking through barricades to demonstrate against the confirmation of Supreme Court nominee Judge Brett Kavanaugh on October 6, 2018, in Washington, D.C.

# The Public's Political Knowledge

- 95 percent knew the length of the president's term (1989)

- 89 percent knew the meaning of *veto* (1989)

- 84 percent identified Dick Cheney as the vice president (2004)

- 82 percent knew the Democrats had a majority in the House of Representatives (2018)

- 75 percent knew it took a two-thirds vote to override a presidential veto (2006)

- 74 percent could identify Nancy Pelosi as Speaker of the House (2010)

- 73 percent identified the governor of their state (1989)

- 71 percent knew the Republicans are the more conservative party (2012)

- 62 percent knew Tony Blair was prime minister of Great Britain (2004)

- 57 percent (2012) and 83 percent (2018) knew which party had a majority in the Senate

- 52 percent knew each state has two U.S. senators (1978)

- 46 percent knew that the first ten amendments are called the Bill of Rights (1989)

- 41 percent knew it takes 60 votes to end a Senate filibuster (2018)

- 34 percent knew that John Roberts was chief justice of the Supreme Court (2012)

- 30 percent knew that the term of a U.S. representative is two years (1978)

- 25 percent could identify both senators from their state (1989)

- 25 percent knew that the term of U.S. senators is six years (1991)

- 20 percent could name two First Amendment rights (1989)

- 19 percent knew David Cameron was prime minister of Great Britain (2010)

- 2 percent could name two Fifth Amendment rights (1989)

*Sources:* The 2004 and 2008 entries are from the American National Election Studies; 2006 data are from the 2006 Congressional Election Survey of the Center on Congress of Indiana University; 2007, 2010, 2012, 2014, 2015, and 2018 data are from the Pew Research Center for the People and the Press; some 2012 data are from the Cooperative Campaign Analysis Project; other entries are from Michael X. Delli Carpini and Scott Keeter, *What Americans Know about Politics and Why It Matters* (New Haven, CT: Yale University Press, 1996).

In June 2014, the Pew Research Center asked people about the two major political parties. A survey of ten thousand Americans revealed that just months before the congressional elections, only 40 percent knew that Republicans had a majority in the House of Representatives and Democrats had a majority in the Senate. In 2015, just a few months after the death of Justice Antonin Scalia, only a third of Americans knew that there were three women on the Supreme Court.

The box also reveals that knowledge of political facts varies with the availability of free information about them. One source of free information on items in the list is the basic high school civics course. But people are most aware of leaders and events on the front page and the nightly television news. Less newsworthy figures and issues go largely unrecognized. The difference in recognition of Newt Gingrich (60 percent) and his successors Dennis Hastert (10 percent) and Nancy Pelosi (74 percent) during their respective terms as Speaker of the House is instructive. Although all three held the same formal position, Gingrich, as point man for the Republican "revolution" initiated in 1994, attracted far more attention from the news media than Hastert, so more people could identify him. Pelosi, celebrated as the first woman ever to serve as Speaker and a major figure (and Republican target) in health care reform politics, became even more prominent than Gingrich.

Ignorance does not necessarily prevent people from expressing opinions. Uninformed opinions are not very stable, however. The same person asked the same question at different times may well give different answers either because he or she didn't have a strong or real opinion in the first place or because of other contextual factors about how the question was asked.

Answers may be affected by even ostensibly minor changes in question wording. Public support for the Iraq War, for example, varied systematically according to how polls asked about it. People asked whether the United States "had made the right decision" in going to war were consistently the most supportive, whereas those asked whether "the result was worth the cost in American lives" were consistently the least supportive. The difference averaged about 10 percentage points (and more than 15 points during 2003 and 2004, when the war was still relatively popular).[18] Similarly, in surveys taken during 2009 and 2010, on average, 60 percent of Americans said no when asked whether the Afghanistan war had been a mistake, 53 percent said yes when asked if it had been the right decision, and 49 percent said it was "worth the cost," but only 45 percent said they "favored" the war.[19] Because wording can influence responses, poll questions are sometimes formulated to elicit maximum support for the views advocated by their sponsors. But even legitimate pollsters need to be careful about how their choice of words affects results—one reason why they asked so many different questions in probing public support for the wars in Iraq and Afghanistan. Sophisticated users of polling data recognize that polls always provide a *mediated* take on public opinion and pay close attention to the details of sampling and question wording when interpreting them.

## Framing

Social scientists have argued for years about whether unstable survey responses mean that many people's expressed opinions are not anchored in relevant attitudes or that survey questions are too crude to gauge attitudes accurately.[20] Although there are elements of truth in both views, the most important source of instability in a person's expressed opinions is probably **ambivalence**. Particular issues may evoke attitudes and beliefs that pull in opposite directions. When that happens, the response to a pollster's questions depends on which considerations come to mind first and seem most weighty. And that depends on the context: recent events, reference to particularly potent symbols or images (such as the mention of American lives or Saddam Hussein in questions about the Iraq War), or questions that have come earlier in the survey.

Some people might believe the poor deserve government help, but they also might detest welfare. Thus these people might well respond differently if asked about their views on "government programs to help the poor" rather than "welfare programs" (see Politics to Policy box "Public Opinion and Welfare Reform," page 462). They also might respond differently

### STRATEGY AND CHOICE
# Framing Hillary Clinton, Ted Cruz, and Marco Rubio

You might think that Donald Trump is good at giving people nicknames—he coined several of them for his opponents in the 2016 presidential election. His primary foes Ted Cruz and Marco Rubio became "Lyin' Ted" and "Little Marco." His general election opponent, Hillary Clinton, was dubbed "Crooked Hillary." But these are more than just nicknames; they are attempts to frame the choice before voters by casting—or framing—each candidate in a specific way. There's some evidence that this kind of linguistic move can work. Social scientists call it essentializing—it's the act of seeing a trait or characteristic of a person as an essential or undeniable feature of that person. Framing candidates in this way can drive people's attitudes and evaluations by both priming a trait and by associating it with the candidate in an explicit way. Sometimes, candidates make things worse by engaging the frame directly, like Rubio did by pointing out that Trump had "small hands" for his height.

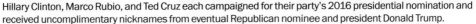

Hillary Clinton, Marco Rubio, and Ted Cruz each campaigned for their party's 2016 presidential nomination and received uncomplimentary nicknames from eventual Republican nominee and president Donald Trump.

depending on whether last night's TV documentary focused on the needs of homeless families or the costs of welfare programs. In other words, their responses are shaped by the considerations most recently brought to their attention because they think of them first.[21] The context frames the question, and the frame determines which attitudes govern the response.

**Framing** explains how both the mass media and political campaigns can affect people's expressed political opinions. The messages sent by the media and the candidates do not have to change underlying attitudes to change expressed opinions. All they have to do is frame the issue in a way that draws out one response rather than the other. For example, one experimental study found that tolerance for public rallies by the white supremacist Ku Klux Klan was significantly lower when framed by a television news story as a public order issue than when it was framed as a free speech issue.[22] Other studies have shown that the content of TV news programs affects the standards people use to evaluate presidents; people who have watched stories about a particular problem give greater weight to the president's performance on *that* problem when forming their overall evaluation of his performance.[23] Simply by covering some issues and ignoring others, the news media help define the political agenda (see Chapter 1), influencing which considerations are in the foreground when citizens make political judgments; in technical terms, they prime their audience to use particular frames in responding to political phenomena. Election campaigns, as we see in the next chapter, set out not to change people's political views but to bring to the forefront attitudes that favor their candidates. In the 2008 presidential campaign, John McCain tried to leverage his military experience and record as a war hero to make national security and foreign policy important considerations. In 2016, Donald Trump used that same war record to frame John McCain as a failure on the battlefield, remarking that he did not think the senator from Arizona was a war hero because he preferred to reserve the term *hero* for pilots who did not get shot down in combat. The same events—Senator McCain's record in combat—were framed in two different ways to sway public opinion in two presidential elections.

## Is Public Opinion Meaningful?

If large segments of the public are politically ignorant, hold inconsistent views, and can be manipulated by varying the words or context of questions, how can public opinion play its assigned role in democratic politics, which is to guide and constrain elected agents? The answer is that, despite the deficiencies uncovered by survey research, public opinion continues to play a crucial and effective part in American politics because a variety of formal and informal political institutions give it shape and force. And public opinion is meaningful because, although individual opinions may be badly informed and unstable, **aggregate public opinion**—the sum of all individual opinions—is both stable and coherent.

### Stability of Aggregate Public Opinion

The evidence for the stability of aggregate public opinion is impressive. When there is no obvious reason to expect significant change, the distribution of opinion tends to be highly stable. One study examined more than a thousand policy questions asked in identical form at least twice in surveys conducted between 1935 and 1990. In a majority of cases there was no appreciable change in the distribution of public responses between surveys, and nearly half of the changes that did occur were modest. On some questions, aggregate public opinion has followed a stable trend for several decades. Figure 10.2 illustrates the consistency of aggregate public opinion on whether the government is spending too little on health care. The figure shows a gentle upward trend with little year-to-year volatility from 1972 to 2008, and then, corresponding to public discourse about the Patient Protection and Affordable Care Act and its passage in 2010, the percentage of people saying we are spending "too little" on protecting

■ **FIGURE 10.2**    Public Opinion on Health Care Spending: Too Little

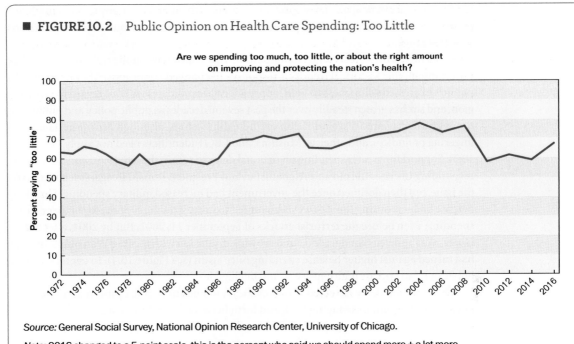

**Are we spending too much, too little, or about the right amount
on improving and protecting the nation's health?**

*Source:* General Social Survey, National Opinion Research Center, University of Chicago.

*Note:* 2016 changed to a 5-point scale, this is the percent who said we should spend more + a lot more.

■ **FIGURE 10.3**    Growing Acceptance of Women and Minorities as Presidential Candidates

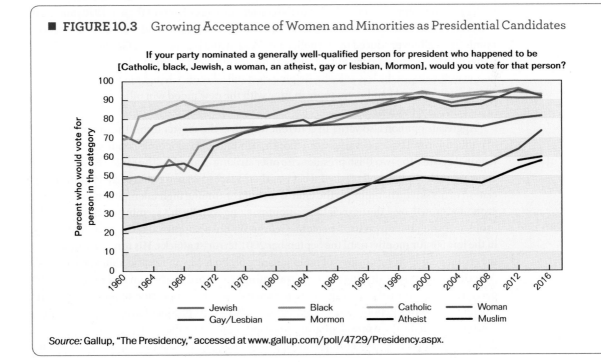

**If your party nominated a generally well-qualified person for president who happened to be
[Catholic, black, Jewish, a woman, an atheist, gay or lesbian, Mormon], would you vote for that person?**

*Source:* Gallup, "The Presidency," accessed at www.gallup.com/poll/4729/Presidency.aspx.

the nation's health drops to levels previously seen in the mid-1980s. Even this remarkable piece of legislation did not shift opinion on spending for health care outside of its previously observed range.

Typically, when substantial changes in the distribution of public opinion occur, they reflect intelligible historical trends or responses to changed conditions.[24] For example, the public's expressed willingness to vote for presidential candidates without regard to race, religion, and sex has grown steadily over the past several decades as public policy and public sentiment turned against discrimination on these dimensions, although Mormons face some lingering prejudices, and atheists, Muslims, and LBGT identifiers need not apply (see Figure 10.3). Support for greater spending on national defense rose in the late 1970s and early 1980s, responding to crises in Iran and Afghanistan and President Ronald Reagan's leadership on the issue, but then declined once the government had increased military spending. Shrinking defense budgets during the 1990s eventually led to greater public support for higher defense spending, even before the terrorist attacks of September 11, 2001. But by 2004, after a large increase in the defense budget and amid growing disillusion with the Iraq War, public opinion had turned against higher defense spending once again (see Figure 10.4). In aggregate, then, public opinion appears both consistent and intelligible.[25]

Other studies have detected broad cyclical changes in public opinion across a range of issues, with opinion swinging back and forth between liberal and conservative "moods." The inevitable shortcomings of both the liberal and conservative approaches to government eventually make the opposition's ideas more attractive. Experience with conservative policies moves public opinion in a liberal direction, whereas experience with liberal policies makes the public more conservative.[26] For example, the liberal expansion of the welfare state in the 1960s under Lyndon Johnson eventually led to the conservative tax revolts of the late 1970s and early 1980s and the election of Reagan, a conservative Republican, as president. The growing economic inequalities produced by the policies of Reagan and his successor, George H. W. Bush, revived, at least temporarily, public support for government programs to improve the economic well-being of the less affluent, helping elect Bill Clinton. Changes in mood bring about changes in policy, as candidates more in tune with the new mood win office and many of the holdovers adapt to survive.

Aggregate opinion also varies in coherent ways over the shorter term. The president's level of public approval typically varies from month to month with economic conditions and international events. The two Bush presidencies offer striking examples. The senior Bush's level of approval in the Gallup poll reached what was then a record 83 percent in early 1991 in appreciation of his skillful handling of the Gulf War, but continuing high unemployment and slow economic growth over the next eighteen months, along with Bush's seeming inattention to the problem, brought it down to 32 percent. George W. Bush's approval ratings had been stuck in the low 50s for months until the September 2001 terrorist attacks. His forceful response to the crisis and the strong upsurge of national unity provoked by the attacks rallied virtually all Americans to his side, driving his approval ratings to record levels—up to a remarkable 92 percent in one national poll. **Aggregate partisanship**—the proportion of poll respondents labeling themselves Republicans or Democrats—also affects presidential approval. There is a greater partisan divide in presidential approval today (and over the last two presidencies) than there has ever been. Donald Trump's low approval rating is a product of extremely low ratings

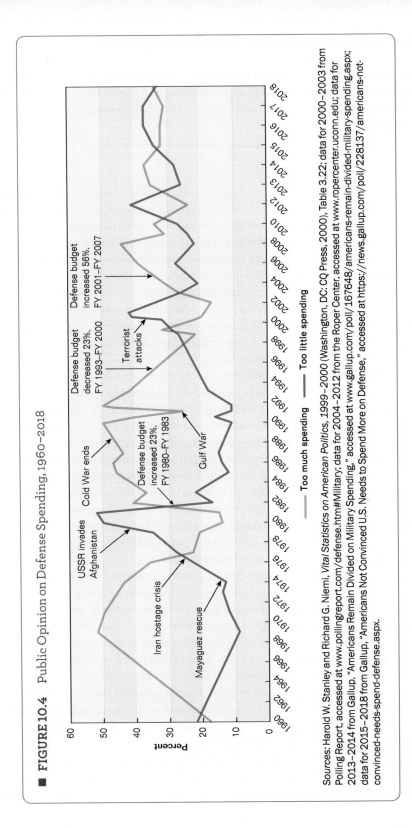

**■ FIGURE 10.4** Public Opinion on Defense Spending, 1960–2018

*Sources:* Harold W. Stanley and Richard G. Niemi, *Vital Statistics on American Politics, 1999–2000* (Washington, DC: CQ Press, 2000), Table 3.22; data for 2000–2003 from Polling Report, accessed at www.pollingreport.com/defense.htm#Military; data for 2004–2012 from the Roper Center, accessed at www.ropercenter.uconn.edu; data for 2013–2014 from Gallup, "Americans Remain Divided on Military Spending," accessed at www.gallup.com/poll/167648/americans-remain-divided-military-spending.aspx; data for 2015–2018 from Gallup, "Americans Not Convinced U.S. Needs to Spend More on Defense," accessed at https://news.gallup.com/poll/228137/americans-not-convinced-needs-spend-defense.aspx.

among Democrats and extremely high ratings among Republicans. This partisan separation provides stability to the president's approval rating, as it does to other public opinion results. Attitudes that have a strong partisan cue are likely to have more stability than those that are not partisan.

## Opinion Leadership

How can stable and coherent public opinion arise from unstable and incoherent individual opinions? Part of the answer lies in the aggregation process itself. When survey responses are added together, **measurement errors** (from the mismatch of survey questions with the attitudes they are supposed to measure) and random individual changes tend to cancel one another out; therefore, the average remains the same if circumstances remain the same. The more important part of the answer lies in the division of labor between the minority of the public that is attentive and informed and the much larger majority that is neither. A small segment of the public forms opinions by paying close attention to political events and issues. The uninformed and inattentive majority routinely free rides when forming opinions by taking cues from members of this attentive segment. In aggregate, public opinion is given rationality and coherence by these **opinion leaders**.[27]

Opinion leadership arises naturally as people respond to different incentives. The widespread ignorance of political facts and issues does not mean that most Americans are dunces. Indeed, in an important sense political ignorance is rational. It takes time and energy to become informed. Political issues and processes often are exceedingly complicated, and even the most devoted student of politics cannot hope to master them all. Most citizens, on most political questions, receive no tangible payoff from becoming better informed. People are unlikely to improve either U.S. policy or their own lives by developing a better understanding of the Israeli-Palestinian conflict. The same goes for health care policy. Better information holds no promise of a better outcome because the views of any single individual are so unlikely to be decisive. It makes sense to gather information about options when we get to make the decision (e.g., what kind of car to buy), but not when our influence on the choice is effectively nil (e.g., what kind of helicopters the Marines should buy).

Suppose we do want to participate in politics, if only in a small way, by voting or by responding to a public opinion poll. Or suppose friends are discussing politics. To join in, we need to adopt some positions on the issues. But how do we know which side of an issue to favor, and why, without investing the time and effort to learn about it? If we are like most people, we rationally free ride on the efforts of others, following the cues given by people we consider informed and whose biases we know. They may be people we know personally—friends, relatives, or coworkers who pay special attention to politics; community activists; or leaders in our places of worship. They may be public figures—political leaders, TV or radio personalities, and newspaper columnists. Organizations such as the Sierra Club, the Roman Catholic Church, and the U.S. Chamber of Commerce may be sources of cues. Thus instead of learning about an endless variety of complicated political issues, all we have to learn is whose attitudes reliably match or contradict our own and then follow their cues. Their biases need not match ours for the cues to be useful; sometimes we can determine what we are for by noting who is against it, and vice versa. In effect, we avoid incurring information costs by delegating opinion formation to (we hope) reliable agents chosen for that purpose.

**Cognitive shortcuts** of this sort are available because interested people and groups have a stake in gathering and disseminating political information. Some people find politics as fascinating as others do baseball and enjoy being recognized by friends as political mavens. But most people who traffic in political information do so to pursue their power and policy goals more effectively. The activities and biases of information specialists usually reflect their institutional roles. Tobacco company officials need to know everything that is said about the dangers of secondhand smoke to counter these claims and defend corporate profits. The American Cancer Society's staff seeks out and publicizes information emphasizing the damage

The popularity among young-adult viewers of shows like Comedy Central's *The Daily Show* and HBO's *Last Week Tonight* has made the comedian a genuine if reluctant opinion leader. The ironic finding by a poll taken during the 2004 presidential campaign that people who watch these shows were better informed than people who watched only regular network or cable news programs or read newspapers is no doubt more the result of self-selection than of pure information—in other words, people who watch satirical news programs are already very interested and informed about current events.

tobacco does to the nation's health and health care budgets. Think tanks such as the American Enterprise Institute (conservative) and the Center for American Progress (liberal) sponsor research and issue reports designed to further their ideological agendas. Newspaper columnists and radio talk show hosts are paid to express opinions on political issues. Professional politicians and those with political ambitions also need to master issues and be prepared to discuss them. A pluralist political system breeds—and depends on—opinion leaders of many kinds.

The sources of opinion leadership differ from issue to issue, as does the audience for policy. Many political issues go unnoticed except by distinct **issue publics**—subsets of the population who are better informed than everyone else about an issue because it touches them more directly and personally. Farmers pay attention to farm programs; retired people (and their doctors) keep tabs on Medicare policy; research scientists monitor National Science Foundation budgets and rules. Citizens committed to a moral cause, such as protecting animal rights, banning abortion, or protecting civil liberties, form issue publics for policies affecting their cause. Most policy domains are of concern only to issue publics, so it is usually their opinions, not mass opinion, that matter to politicians. Together, opinion leaders and issue publics are the main conduits of public opinion in a pluralist political system. They apply most of the routine pressures felt by government officials engaged in the day-to-day making of public policy on the countless matters dealt with by the federal government. By the same token, their interest makes them the targets of most organized attempts to sway and mobilize public opinion for political ends.

*Fred Lee/ABC via Getty Images*

Aggregate public opinion, then, is, given its coherence and focus by opinion leaders, typically based in institutions, whose knowledge, ideas, proposals, and debates define the positions and options from which ordinary citizens, acting logically as cognitive misers, adopt their expressed views. This conclusion does not mean that public opinion is routinely manipulated by self-serving elites (although there is no shortage of attempts to do so); pluralist competition usually denies any particular opinion leader a monopoly. Opinion leaders maintain their leadership status only if people choose to follow them.

The aggregate stability of popular views reveals that, in an often confused and poorly articulated way, people do have a real basis for the opinions they express. They respond to opinion leaders not randomly but in ways that are consistent with the values and notions about politics they have accumulated during their lives. Cognitive shortcuts would be of no value if they did not bring people somewhere near the destination they would have reached by taking the longer path.[28] Agents can be fired; opinion leaders, therefore, lead by expressing the political sentiments of those who follow them. This is why politicians, who are fully aware of how fickle and poorly informed people's expressed opinions may be, still think twice about going against the polls. Aggregate opinion is meaningful, and aggregates are what count when a politician is running for reelection or trying to get a bill passed.

For this reason, public opinion, at least as measured by polls, is regularly if not invariably found to influence public policy. One summary study concluded that public opinion significantly affected public policy in three-quarters of the fifty-two possible instances examined in thirty separate research studies; the more prominent the issue, the more likely public opinion was to be influential.[29]

## The Content of Public Opinion

Political opinions reflect people's underlying values and beliefs about how the world works. This fact is no less true of second- or thirdhand opinions—those derived, respectively, from one other person or from an opinion leader through another person—than of original opinions, which are formed through personal experience. This is because core values and beliefs influence people's choice of cue-givers (recall who listens to Rush Limbaugh and who to Michael Moore). Americans share a broad consensus on basic political

"Mr. President, the people have spoken ... and they're not making any sense."

values that puts real limits on what is politically possible. Yet within these bounds, Americans find plenty on which to disagree. Consensus on the basics makes politics—defined here as reaching agreement on a course of common, or collective, action despite disagreement on the purposes of the action—***possible***; disagreement within this general consensus makes politics ***necessary***.

## Consensus on the System

Opinion polls find that almost every American supports the institutional underpinnings of modern democracy: the right of every citizen to vote; the freedom to speak, write, and work with others for political goals; the right to due process and equal treatment by courts and other government agencies. Although each of these principles was once controversial (see Chapters 4 and 11), opposition to them has now virtually disappeared from public life.

When it comes to the practical application of these abstract values, however, consensus breaks down. When a poll taken in 1940 asked a sample of Americans, "Do you believe in freedom of speech?" 97 percent said yes. When those who answered yes were asked, "Do you believe in it to the extent of allowing fascists and communists to hold meetings and express their views in the community?" 76 percent said no. In 1940, the year these questions were posed, war was raging in Europe, and both fascism and communism loomed as serious threats. But even in calmer times, many people who say they favor First Amendment rights would deny them to people with unpopular views. Polls taken in the mid-1970s found 82 percent agreeing that "nobody has the right to tell another person what he should or should not read," but also 50 percent agreeing that "books that preach the overthrow of the government should be banned from the library."[30] A 2007 survey found Americans were divided on the question of whether "freedom of speech should . . . extend to groups that are sympathetic to terrorists," with 50 percent saying it should, and 45 percent saying it should not.[31] When the abstract value of free expression comes up against the more tangible matters of national security or social order, free expression does not always come out on top. It is therefore important to note that free speech and other democratic values find stronger support among the minority of Americans who specialize in politics; those who play the political game are more supportive of its rules.[32]

Other basic political values are also hedged. Large majorities say they favor free enterprise and dislike government meddling in the economy, but majorities just as large back laws regulating businesses in order to protect the environment or the health and safety of workers and consumers. Again, people who pay more attention to politics are more likely to recognize the implications of one position or another and to offer more consistent sets of opinions. But almost everyone holds political values and beliefs that clash. Forced to choose, people have to consider trade-offs; sometimes political conflict and compromise even occur in our own heads.

At one level, the values of democracy and capitalism are not compatible. Democracy treats people as equals and permits majorities to rule. Capitalism extols liberty, not equality. It distributes its rewards unequally and leaves crucial economic decisions (what products to produce, what jobs to offer, where to build factories) in the hands of individuals and private corporations, whose goals are profits. The fear that democracy would bring economic ruin by allowing popular majorities to despoil the wealthy minority was a central motive behind the

Steven Kazlowski/Barcroft Medi via Getty Images

Majorities of Americans value free enterprise, job opportunities, cheap and abundant energy, and an unobtrusive government, but majorities also value clean air and water, the continued survival of wild creatures in their natural environments, and some measure of protection from market risks. The tension among such competing values—symbolized here by endangered polar bears on the Arctic National Wildlife Refuge, a fragile environment holding substantial oil deposits—creates personal as well as political dilemmas, especially when the price of gasoline skyrockets.

Constitution's elaborate avoidance of direct popular rule. But the fear proved to be groundless because Americans have come to make sharp distinctions about the kinds of equality they consider appropriate. Just about everyone favors political equality. Support for equal opportunity is at least as strong: statements such as "everyone in America should have an equal right to get ahead" and "children should have equal education opportunities" are accepted almost without dissent when posed in opinion polls.[33] Americans have also come to support equal pay for equal work and generally to oppose workplace discrimination against any person based on age, race, ethnicity, gender, or sexual orientation.

Very little popular support exists, however, for mandating equal outcomes. Asked whether, under a fair economic system, all people would earn about the same or people with more ability would earn higher salaries, 7 percent chose the first option, 78 percent the second.[34] Nor is there much support for affirmative action programs intended to remedy past discrimination against women or racial minorities by putting them first in line for jobs and school admissions. When CNN asked in a 2013 poll whether people approved of programs that give admissions preference to college and law school students from racial minority groups, only 29 percent approved of the programs (although vaguer forms of affirmative action are generally supported—question wording is highly consequential in this area). The result is that Americans, renowned since Alexis de Tocqueville's day for their egalitarian social and political values, tolerate huge—and growing—differences in wealth and well-being among individuals and groups.

## Politicians: A Suspect Class

Americans approve overwhelmingly of the U.S. political system and its symbols; pride in the Constitution and the flag are nearly universal. They are normally far less pleased, however, with the people they elect to run the system. Criticizing the government is a national pastime with a pedigree longer than baseball's, but the public's distrust of government and its practitioners deepened markedly over the last half of the twentieth century. Figure 10.5 traces the public's varying cynicism about government through a set of questions that have been asked repeatedly in the biennial American National Election Studies and occasionally in other surveys. More than in the 1950s and 1960s, Americans in recent years have been inclined to believe that public officials are "crooked" and that the government wastes tax money, cannot be trusted to do what is right, is run by a few big interests for their own benefit, and does not care about ordinary people.

■ **FIGURE 10.5**    Americans' Varying Cynicism about Government

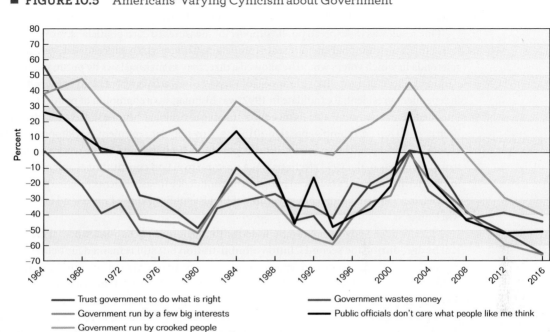

Percent

Legend:
— Trust government to do what is right
— Government run by a few big interests
— Government run by crooked people
— Government wastes money
— Public officials don't care what people like me think

*Sources:* Compiled from American National Election Studies, CBS News/*New York Times*, PEW, and Gallup Polls.

*Note:* The entries are the percentage of respondents expressing confidence in government minus the percentage expressing a lack of confidence in government on each question. The questions are:

1.  How much of the time do you think you can trust the government in Washington to do what is right—just about always, most of the time, or only some of the time? ("Always" or "most of the time" minus "some" or "none of the time.")

2.  Do you think that people in government waste a lot of money we pay in taxes, waste some of it, or don't waste very much of it? ("Some" or "not much" minus "a lot.")

3.  Would you say that the government is pretty much run by a few big interests looking out for themselves or that it is run for the benefit of all? ("Benefit of all" minus "a few big interests.")

4.  Please tell me if you agree or disagree with this statement: Public officials don't care what people like me think. ("Disagree" minus "agree.")

5.  Do you think that quite a few of the people running the government are crooked, not very many are crooked, or hardly any of them are crooked? ("Hardly any" or "not many" minus "quite a few.")

2016 "crooked" changed scales to "How many people running government are corrupt? All, most, about half, a few, or none?" (Value is "None" or "A Few" minus "About half," "Most," or "All").

The most common explanation for these trends is that the conflicts over civil rights and the Vietnam War in the 1960s, followed closely by the Watergate scandal that drove a president from office (note the sharp drops in 1974), led to a more critical press and a disillusioned public. Confidence revived somewhat with the economy in 1984, but later problems, including a stagnant economy during the George H. W. Bush administration (1989–1993), large federal budget deficits, assorted political scandals in the late 1990s, the need for the Supreme Court to intervene in the 2000 presidential election, and a pervasive sense that the United States was moving in the wrong direction, kept public distrust of government high.

One result was widespread public support for measures to curb politicians: term limits for legislators, constitutional amendments compelling Congress to balance the budget, national referenda in which voters would be allowed a direct say in making laws by putting them on a national ballot. A large part of the appeal of Ross Perot, who won 19 percent of the vote as an independent presidential candidate in 1992, was his image as a champion of political reforms intended to make elected officials more accountable to ordinary people; indeed, this may have been part of Donald Trump's appeal in 2016, too. Any popular sentiment as widespread as this is bound to find political sponsors. Indeed, part of the Republicans' strategy for taking control of Congress in the 1994 elections was a promise to act on constitutional amendments to impose term limits and a balanced budget. The confidence measurements reached a low point in 1994, evidence of the anger at government that Republicans both fanned and exploited to win Congress.

Confidence in government rebounded with the booming economy and balanced federal budget during the second Clinton administration but still remained far below what it was in the 1950s. This trend continued through the first year of George W. Bush's presidency until the al-Qaeda attacks on the United States effectively reframed the issue. The events of September 11, 2001, and their aftermath had an immediate and dramatic effect on how Americans responded to polling questions about their government and its leaders. Not only did Bush's approval rating shoot to record highs, but so did approval of Congress (84 percent in one poll, topping the previous high of 57 percent) and congressional leaders. The proportion of respondents who said they trusted the government in Washington to do what is right "almost always" or "most of the time," which had been below 45 percent in every poll since the Watergate scandal in 1974 and had fallen as low as 18 percent in the early 1990s, jumped to 56 percent. The sharp rise in expressed support for government and its leaders reflected a radical change in the context in which people thought about these questions. Under deadly attack from shadowy foreign enemies, Americans rallied behind their government as the defender and institutional embodiment of American democracy. For a brief time, politicians and other government officials enjoyed the kind of broad public support normally reserved for such national symbols as the flag and the Constitution. Moreover, the attacks were a forceful reminder of the need for a government capable of organizing and sustaining collective action in pursuit of that most fundamental of public goods, security from foreign attack. In this context, the ordinary annoyances and frustrations people associate with government and politics became decidedly secondary.

This mood did not, however, survive the reemergence of politics as usual and the increasingly bitter partisan differences provoked by the Iraq War and other Bush administration decisions. By 2008, amid deep public discontent with the war, the economy, and the overall direction of the country, cynicism again dominated Americans' views of their elected leaders. And the first four years of the Obama administration, beset by stubbornly high unemployment, rising budget deficits, and increasing U.S. casualties in Afghanistan, did little to stop the trend. Further, in late 2011, ratings agencies downgraded the nation's credit score for the first time in history. One agency, Standard & Poor's, accompanied its downgrade with a strong critique of the political brinksmanship in Congress that prevented the government from increasing its debt ceiling, saying that this style of politics renders the U.S. government "less stable, less effective, and less predictable" in managing its finances. The widespread belief that the government couldn't be trusted to do anything right was growing—a Pew Research Center poll in December 2017 revealed that a vast majority of Americans thought the government could only be trusted some or none of the time. Only 18 percent said it could be trusted most of the time or just about always.

## Public Opinion on Issues

Popular agreement on the fundamentals of representative democracy does not translate into agreement on every important policy area. In each of three broad domains—the economy, social and cultural issues, and foreign policy—the central issues have consistently generated wide divisions of opinion. It is crucial to understand how these differences split the public because these factions form the raw material from which political leaders try to construct majority coalitions. When the public is divided in different ways on different issues and lacks consensus on which are most important, strategies for assembling and maintaining party coalitions become more difficult to conceive and execute.

### Economic Issues

Although Americans mainly believe in capitalism, almost no one believes that private businesses should be completely unregulated or that the things people value should be allocated exclusively by an unfettered free market. Political conflict occurs over how far the government should go in regulating business and redressing market-driven economic and social inequalities. Historically, the trend has been toward an ever-larger government role in managing economic affairs, with notable expansions in the 1930s under Franklin Roosevelt's New Deal policies, in the 1960s with Lyndon Johnson's Great Society programs, and in the 1970s with new laws to protect consumers and the environment (see Chapter 8). After the 2016 presidential election, Donald Trump and his administration began to dismantle many of these regulations.

More specifically, large majorities typically support stable or increased government spending for programs that serve (or will eventually serve) nearly everyone: Social Security (pensions for the disabled or retired), Medicare (medical care for retirees), and unemployment insurance (cash for people laid off from jobs). Social Security is so popular that politicians call it "the third rail of American politics—touch it and you are dead" (referring to the high-voltage rail from which subway trains draw their power). George W. Bush's 2005 campaign to whip up support for reforming the program implicitly acknowledged the danger; the president spent months traveling the country telling audiences that Social Security needed a major overhaul to remain fiscally sound without mentioning that, absent major tax increases that Bush had ruled out, the overhaul would have to include substantial cuts in promised future benefits. Other individual government programs designed to improve health and welfare also command broad support—with a few revealing exceptions (see the Politics to Policy box "Public Opinion and Welfare Reform," page 462, which lists some typical poll results and illustrates how such opinions can affect major policy decisions).

By and large, Americans seem to support a wide range of economic and social welfare policies that commonly are classified as liberal. But when it comes to principles, as opposed to programs, Americans are much more likely to think of themselves as conservatives. Majorities also agree with conservative politicians who say that taxes are too high, that the government wastes a lot of money, that bureaucrats are too meddlesome, and that people ought to take care of themselves rather than depend on government handouts.

### Social, Cultural, and Moral Issues

Politics is about the distribution of goods, which can be moral as well as material. The great struggles to abolish slavery, achieve votes for women, prohibit alcohol, and end racial segregation were driven largely by moral rather than economic considerations. Today social and moral issues produce some of the most heated political controversies. Questions about abortion; religion in public life; and the rights of women, ethnic and racial minorities, immigrants, and the LBGT population make up an important part of the political agenda. These issues raise conflicting considerations that are difficult to reconcile, not only between opposed groups but also for individuals in their own minds.

In modern times abortion is the best-known example. Since the Supreme Court handed down its *Roe v. Wade* ruling in 1973, thereby overturning state laws making abortions illegal, the abortion issue has become a defining one for multiple political generations. Groups with starkly opposing positions have dominated the public debate. According to a Quinnipiac poll completed in July 2018 neither extreme position holds a majority—although more people now believe abortion should be legal in all or most circumstances. At one extreme, however, are those who want the law to forbid abortion as murder making it always illegal (roughly 20 percent); at the other are those who object to any restriction on a woman's right to have an abortion, meaning it should always be legal, regardless of the circumstance (roughly a quarter).

AP Photo/Jason DeCrow

The abstract ideal of equal rights is widely shared by Americans, but its application is often vigorously disputed. On June 26, 2013, the U.S. Supreme Court decided to invalidate parts of the Defense of Marriage Act and to uphold a lower-court ruling that struck down California's controversial Proposition 8—that banned same-sex marriage. Edie Windsor, plaintiff in *United States v. Windsor*, is shown here on the right.

Aggregate public opinion on abortion has been highly stable over the years but is acutely sensitive to how the issue is framed. Figure 10.6 shows the trends in responses to one set of questions posed regularly in polls since 1965. After an initial increase in support for legalized abortion (coinciding with *Roe v. Wade*), aggregate opinion has changed little. Large majorities in both parties think abortion should be legal if the pregnancy resulted from rape or would endanger the woman's health. The public is much more evenly split on whether abortion for financial reasons should be legal. Other variations in the question wording produce a similar spread.

Abortion is the kind of issue that has defied political resolution

■ **FIGURE 10.6**  Public Support for Abortion Rights: Dependent on the Reason for the Abortion

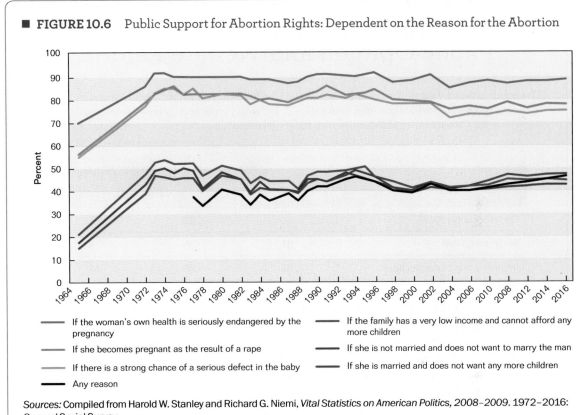

——— If the woman's own health is seriously endangered by the pregnancy

——— If she becomes pregnant as the result of a rape

——— If there is a strong chance of a serious defect in the baby

——— Any reason

——— If the family has a very low income and cannot afford any more children

——— If she is not married and does not want to marry the man

——— If she is married and does not want any more children

*Sources:* Compiled from Harold W. Stanley and Richard G. Niemi, *Vital Statistics on American Politics, 2008–2009. 1972–2016:* General Social Survey.

because the wide disagreement on values leaves little space for agreement on action. Generally, however, opinion and policy on abortion has followed the nation's overall trend toward liberalization on social issues. The last two Supreme Court decisions related to abortion (*Planned Parenthood v. Casey* in 1992 and *Whole Woman's Health v. Hellerstedt* in 2016) have soundly reaffirmed women's rights to have abortions. Thus exploitation of the issue politically is becoming a delicate undertaking. In running for president in 2008, John McCain had to maintain a firm pro-life position to attract support from conservative Christians, many of whom were Republicans primarily because the party was committed to banning abortion, without leading uncommitted moderates to worry that "choice" would immediately be threatened if he were to win. In 2012, Mitt Romney balanced these demands by changing his once pro-choice position to a pro-life stance. In 2016, Donald Trump, who also used to be pro-choice but then switched, went further, saying that if abortion were illegal he thought women who got illegal abortions should be punished with possible jail time. After outcries from both parties, he immediately recanted the statement.

**POLITICS TO POLICY**
# Public Opinion and Welfare Reform

The public is broadly supportive of major social spending programs—except those that evoke the wrong frames. Consider the public's responses to the following question: "Should spending on the following programs increase, stay the same, or decrease?"

| | INCREASE (%) | STAY THE SAME (%) | DECREASE (%) |
|---|---|---|---|
| Social Security (2018) | 50 | 43 | 5 |
| Medicare (2018) | 57 | 35 | 6 |
| Improving and protecting health (2014) | 57 | 28 | 13 |
| Health care (2018) | 38 | 47 | 12 |
| Education (2018) | 70 | 23 | 7 |
| Welfare (2018) | 24 | 42 | 32 |
| Aid to poor people (2014) | 62 | 24 | 12 |
| Food stamps (2000) | 16 | 51 | 33 |
| Supplemental Nutritional Assistance Program, formerly food stamps (2018) | 37 | 39 | 19 |
| Solving problem of the homeless (1996) | 58 | 31 | 11 |
| Veterans' medical benefits (2017) | 77 | 19 | 2 |

*Source:* Compiled from multiple sources.

*Note:* Percentages may not add to one hundred due to rounding.

Only a tiny minority wants the government to spend less on Social Security, health, the public schools, and the homeless than it is already spending. Programs whose names evoke the wrong symbols, however, enjoy much less support. Here, for example, 32 percent would reduce spending on "welfare," and only 24 percent would increase it, although 62 percent would increase spending on "aid to poor people"—overlooking the fact that welfare *is* aid to poor people. This is a clear example of framing. Most Americans think government should help the poor, but the word *welfare* conjures up images, however unfair, of people living off the hard work of the taxpayers. Charity is seen as a virtue, but so is self-reliance, and poverty issues can be framed in terms of either one.

Images and frames matter. In 1996 the Republican Congress sent Bill Clinton a welfare reform bill that cut back on federal assistance to poor people. Among other things, the bill imposed a time limit on welfare eligibility for the first time since the adoption of the original assistance program in the 1930s. It also slashed the food stamp program, which apparently shares welfare's negative connotations (see the entry for food stamps in the table). Most congressional Democrats opposed the bill, but, facing reelection, Clinton signed it anyway because it was widely supported by a public that had applauded his previous campaign promise to "end welfare as we know it."

*Sources:* The 1996 data are from the American National Election Studies; 2013 data are from the Pew Research Center for the People and the Press; 2014 data are from the General Social Survey; 2017 and 2018 data are from a Kaiser Family Foundation poll (April and January, respectively) and a Politico/ Harvard School of Public Health poll (June).

Despite long-standing differences in the extreme positions on abortion, Americans are increasingly taking moderate to liberal positions on other social issues. According to the Pew Research Center, formal prayer in public schools, banned by Supreme Court decisions in the early 1960s, once received overwhelming support but now receives only a slight majority of public support (57 percent). Likewise, support for legalizing marijuana has now overtaken opposition with 52 percent favoring its legal use. In 2001, 57 percent of Americans opposed same-sex marriage, but in 2016, 55 percent supported it. According to an NBC/*Wall Street Journal* poll in July 2015, 64 percent of Americans support giving undocumented immigrants a pathway to citizenship or grant of citizenship relative to 32 percent who want to find, arrest, and deport them immediately. Similarly, a majority of Americans believe that the U.S.-born children of undocumented immigrants should continue to be deemed U.S. citizens, as the law of birthright citizenship demands, even though President Trump disagrees.

One area in which opinion leans the other way is on the question of whether public schools should be required to allow transgender students to use bathrooms and locker rooms that are consistent with the gender they identify with instead of the gender they were born. In a May 2016 Quinnipiac College poll, 56 percent of Americans thought public schools should not be required to allow this. The topic drew national attention after the state of North Carolina passed a law barring transgender people from using the bathroom of the sex they identify with and again after the Obama administration responded by writing a letter to every public school in the country warning them that as a condition of receiving federal funds they must allow students to use facilities matching their gender identity.

### Foreign Policy

In 2016, Hillary Clinton's experience as secretary of state, coupled with Donald Trump's priming of the threat from terrorists like ISIS, made foreign policy and national defense a focus of the campaign. During the 2004 and 2008 election campaigns, issues of foreign policy, particularly regarding the war in Iraq, shared a bit of the spotlight with the national economy. In light of the war's controversial justification and growing cost in American life and treasure, this was not at

Fifteen years after the attacks of September 11, 2001, and the start of wars in Iraq and Afghanistan, a unique study by the Program for Public Consultation asked Americans to consider arguments for and against cutting military spending.[35] Most people (76 percent) thought the national defense budget should be cut—with an average reduction of about 20 percent. Interestingly, one of the areas people slated for small cuts was funding for special forces. These highly trained special operations forces (Green Berets, Army Rangers, Delta Force operators, and Navy SEALs, as well as elite aviators, Marines, and even special canine units) undertake covert missions against terrorist groups and elite or irregular forces. It was a team of special forces operators (a Navy SEAL team) that killed Osama bin Laden in the spring of 2011. Survey respondents recommended a 10 percent cut to special forces, while recommending support for conventional ground forces be cut by 23 percent. Across all areas, Democrats cut more than Republicans, but in terms of support for special forces, independents recommended an increase in funding for these operators.

all surprising. But these recent elections are unusual. Except when Americans are dying overseas, foreign policy issues tend to be remote from everyday experience, and few people pay sustained attention to foreign affairs. Recent terrorist attacks may be changing this, making foreign policy seem more relevant to everyone's lives. Despite Americans' increasing interaction with terrorism, public opinion on foreign policy remains particularly responsive to opinion leadership. The president is the most important opinion leader on foreign policy, but presidential influence varies according to whether other opinion leaders—rival politicians, foreign policy experts, and news commentators—agree or disagree with the White House.[36] Since World War II large majorities have supported an active international role for the United States, but backing for particular policies has been much more variable. In the summer of 2016, the Pew Research Center reported that 57 percent of Americans agreed that the United States should deal with its own problems and let other countries deal with their problems. This "nation-first" mentality has routinely been a feature of European public opinion, but it is a change in the United States. For example, in 2010, the share of people who believed in such nationalism was 10 points lower—at roughly 47 percent. Whether this marked change is due to the opinion leadership of Donald Trump or Americans' increasing fears of terrorism is difficult to isolate, but public opinion on America's role in the world is changing.

Until the breakup of the Soviet Union at the end of 1991, the Cold War conflict between the United States and the Soviet Union framed both public and elite thinking on foreign affairs. The avowed U.S. objective of "containing" the Soviet Union to prevent the expansion of communism enjoyed broad public acceptance, but the public did not agree on all of the actions taken in the name of containment. Both the Korean and Vietnam wars lost popular support as casualties mounted.[37] Later, majorities opposed proposals by the Reagan and Bush administrations to give military assistance to the Nicaraguan contras in their civil war against the avowedly socialist Sandinista government. In all these cases, public divisions reflected in a direct way the divisions among opinion leaders. In general, opinion on whether to take a tougher or more conciliatory approach to dealing with the Soviets varied with U.S. perceptions of Soviet behavior; events such as the Soviet invasion of Afghanistan in 1979 to prop up a threatened communist regime made a tougher line more popular, whereas arms control agreements and summit meetings between the United States and the Soviet Union during the Cold War years made conciliation more popular.[38]

National leaders reached no new consensus on a guiding framework for U.S. foreign policy during the post–Cold War era of the 1990s, so neither did the public. The war against Iraq to liberate Kuwait in 1991 attracted widespread public support even before its stunning success because Iraq's invasion threatened the U.S. economy (by putting the Persian Gulf oil supply at risk) and the closest U.S. ally in the region, Israel. But the Clinton administration had great difficulty building popular support for policies aimed at resolving conflicts in Somalia, Bosnia, Haiti, and Kosovo, partly because the administration itself was vague about what was at stake for the nation in these conflicts and partly because other opinion leaders opposed the administration's policies.

Drift and division on foreign policy issues ended almost instantly with the assaults on the World Trade Center and the Pentagon in 2001. Foreign policy issues became, tragically, anything but remote. The Bush administration moved immediately to direct virtually all of its foreign policy resources to mounting a multifaceted war on terrorism. Leaders in both parties overwhelmingly supported the administration's initial actions, and so did the public; in October 2001 polls, nine of ten Americans said they backed the ongoing military action against the terrorist organizations and the Taliban government in Afghanistan. A large majority was even willing to accept several thousand U.S. casualties if that was what it took to succeed.[39] With the United States itself in harm's way, little opinion leadership was at first necessary; indeed, any leader who did not support a vigorous, conspicuous response would have been badly out of step with mass opinion. But after the initial rout of the Taliban in Afghanistan with the fall of Kandahar and the Battle of Tora Bora in December 2001, the administration's shift of focus to Iraq was not so uniformly applauded. That war became less popular over time as citizens and leaders divided increasingly along party lines over the wisdom of the invasion, especially after a major premise of the war, that Iraq possessed WMDs, was discredited. The war in Afghanistan consistently attracted greater popular support and was less divisive than the war in Iraq, although both eventually provoked unusually wide partisan divisions. Majorities in every partisan category backed the Obama administration's decision to expand U.S. troop levels in Afghanistan to combat the resurgent Taliban in 2009, but as American casualties mounted and the war dragged on with few signs of progress, support continued to slide. Rather than sharing a consensus on foreign policy, the public is increasingly divided along party lines, not only over the ongoing wars but also over the legitimacy of preemptive wars and the value of working with allies or the United Nations. In May 2014, President Obama announced that the American military would return to Afghanistan in an advisory capacity to help Afghan forces combat the "remnants of al-Qaeda." By September 2014, after months of violence in the region, including the execution of a U.S. journalist, the announcement of U.S.-led airstrikes in Syria against an insurgent group called the Islamic State met with support by a wide majority of the American population—roughly 70 percent.[40] By 2015, only a third of the country agreed with President Obama's decision to leave troops in Afghanistan. In 2017, Donald Trump announced he, too, was leaving troops in Afghanistan. Because partisanship plays a role in opinions on the topic (both parties' presidents made the same choice), support for the policy went up by about 10 points under Trump's leadership.

Few contest the necessity of combating terrorism to protect the U.S. homeland, but there has been little agreement on how best to accomplish this goal. In some sense, living with the threat of terrorism has become the "new normal" for most people. Ten years after the attacks in 2001, most Americans thought the United States was "neither winning nor losing" the war on terror—a pattern that does not differ by party identification. In December 2015, a CNN/ORC poll conducted after terrorist attacks in a Paris nightclub and at a San Bernardino, California, holiday party found that 75 percent of Americans were not satisfied with the way the war on terror was proceeding—up from 61 percent in 2007. These opinions also cross party lines, with 59 percent of Democrats, 79 percent of independents, and 86 percent of Republicans expressing dissatisfaction with the current course of action.

## Effects of Background on Public Opinion

People's opinions on specific issues reflect the knowledge, beliefs, and values they have acquired over their lifetimes. The public's diverse points of view often represent differences in background, education, and life experiences. When polling data are analyzed, these differences show up in the way opinions vary with demographic characteristics such as race, ethnicity, gender, income, education, region, religion, and age. Politicians pay close attention to group differences because they determine feasible coalition-building strategies.

### Race and Ethnicity

Unlike in the past, a large majority of white Americans now reject segregation and support equal opportunity for all races, but they disagree on what, if anything, should be done about the lingering effects of racial discrimination and persisting areas of inequality. A 2016 Gallup survey asked respondents if colleges and universities should admit students based solely on merit or whether they should consider other factors like a student's race or ethnicity in order to increase the diversity of the student population. A quarter of white Americans, 29 percent of Latinos, and 44 percent of black Americans thought colleges should consider race and ethnicity. In other words, most people—regardless of race—preferred admissions decisions be made based solely on merit.

Americans of different races also have decidedly different views on law enforcement. A July 2016 CBS/*New York Times* poll asked whether people thought police in most communities were more likely to use deadly force against a black person or a white person or whether race had nothing to do with the use of deadly force. Seventy-five percent of African Americans but only 36 percent of whites thought police were more likely to use deadly force against blacks. Similarly, nearly half of white respondents thought the police in their communities were doing an excellent job, whereas only 13 percent of black respondents felt this way.

These contrasting views reflect the profoundly different perceptions and life experiences of African Americans, Hispanics, and whites in American society. African Americans, Hispanics, Native Americans, and

AP Photo/Mike Groll

In November 2014, President Obama issued an executive action to shield as many as 5 million undocumented immigrants from deportation and extend protections under the DREAM Act. Like so many other polarizing issues, public opinion was sharply divided by party identification and by race. In this rally at the New York State Capitol, supporters of the DREAM Act hold up portraits of undocumented students who were not eligible for college tuition assistance in the state because of their legal status.

Asian Americans—along with other groups of diverse national origins—share a history of discrimination based on race; many have experienced it firsthand. Whites tend to think that legal equality has now been achieved and that any special effort to overcome the effects of past discrimination is unfair. In 2017, a National Public Radio commissioned survey revealed that more than half of white Americans believe discrimination against whites exists in America.

On all these issues, the views of African Americans are closer to the positions taken by the Democratic Party, and African Americans vote overwhelmingly Democratic. As a result, they are a crucial part of the Democratic coalition. Only twice since World War II has the Democratic presidential candidate won more of the white vote than the Republican candidate (Lyndon Johnson in 1964 and Bill Clinton in 1996); every other Democratic victory (Harry Truman in 1948, John Kennedy in 1960, Jimmy Carter in 1976, Bill Clinton in 1992, and Barack Obama in 2008 and 2012) has depended on huge majorities among African Americans to offset narrower Republican majorities among whites. African Americans also gave Al Gore his popular plurality in 2000, awarding him more than 90 percent of their votes.[41] Not surprisingly, they voted for Barack Obama, the first African American to run for president on a major-party ticket, almost unanimously.[42]

More generally, other minority groups show distinctive patterns of issue opinion and voting behavior, but in most instances these patterns reflect the group's economic status rather than particularly ethnic views. Hispanics tend to have lower incomes and so favor more extensive government services and the Democratic Party; Asian Americans tend to have higher incomes and so are economically more conservative and more Republican than Hispanics. But there are enormous differences within these broad categories in the ethnic backgrounds and economic status of subgroups. Hispanics include Cuban Americans, Puerto Ricans, Mexican Americans, immigrants from the nations of Central America, and people whose roots in the Southwest go back centuries. Asian Americans include people of Korean, Japanese, Chinese, Vietnamese, Philippine, and Laotian extraction, some further divided into different eras of immigration and regions of origin.

Generalizing about group opinions is risky, although one pattern seems to hold: ethnic minorities express strong and distinctive political views on issues directly affecting their groups. Cuban Americans are deeply concerned about U.S. policy toward Cuba, a focus that brought them closer to Republicans. Mexican Americans are far more likely than other groups to oppose the denial of public education and health care to undocumented immigrants, a view that brings them closer to Democrats.

## Gender

On many issues, the sexes think alike, but on some things they do not. Women are consistently less inclined than men to support the use of violence in foreign and domestic policy and to favor diplomacy over conflict. Women also have more favorable attitudes toward social welfare spending and regulations designed to protect the environment, consumers, and children.[43] The reasons for these differences are still a matter of debate. What is known is that they have created a "gender gap" in recent electoral politics, with women more supportive than men of the Democratic Party and its candidates, and men more supportive of Republicans. In 2008 Barack Obama's vote ran about 7 percentage points higher among women than among men; unmarried women are especially likely to favor Democrats and account for most of the difference between the sexes.[44] In 2016, a wider gender gap emerged when 52 percent of men compared with 41 percent of women cast ballots for Donald Trump according to exit polls on Election Day. Hillary Clinton's support among women came largely from nonwhite women and white women with college educations. White women with only high school educations voted for Trump 61 percent to 34 percent.

It is interesting to note that women and men do not differ much on sex-related issues. Both show high levels of support for women and men having an equal role in society and politics; the sexes do not differ in distribution of opinions on abortion.

## Income and Education

The politicians who designed the Constitution thought the most enduring political conflicts would pit the poor against the rich. Surveys find abundant evidence that opinions differ among income classes, but the differences are modest compared with those found in most other modern industrial nations. People with lower incomes are more inclined to support spending on government services helpful to people like them: Social Security, student loans, food stamps, child care, and help for the homeless. People with higher incomes are notably less enthusiastic about government spending on social programs or taxing higher incomes at higher rates. Economic self-interest easily explains these differences: people getting more of the benefits tend to see greater merit in social programs than do those paying more of the costs.

On noneconomic issues, however, higher-income groups tend to be more liberal than lower-income groups. This difference has less to do with income than it does with education. People in higher-income groups tend to have more years of formal education, and the more education people have, the more likely they are to take the liberal side on issues such as abortion, LBGT and gender equality, freedom of speech, and rights generally.

## Religion

Religion has played an important role in American political life since the founding of the first colonies. A large majority of Americans profess a religious affiliation, and more people belong to religious groups than to any other kind of organization. Religious beliefs shape values, including many of the values people pursue through political action. The movements to abolish slavery, prohibit alcohol, extend civil rights to African Americans, end the war in Vietnam, and ban abortion have all been strongly imbued with religious ideals.

Differences in religious beliefs often underlie differences in political opinions. Not surprisingly, religious beliefs influence opinions on more social issues than economic issues. People who are secular (no religious preference), Jewish, or members of one of what scholars call the mainline Protestant denominations, such as Episcopalians, Presbyterians, and Congregationalists, tend to be more liberal on social issues. Evangelical Protestants, such as Southern Baptists and Pentecostals, tend to be very conservative. Roman Catholics, who form the largest single denomination, fall in between, but only on average; a wide variety of social views are supported by various organizations within the Catholic Church.

*Noah Rabinowitz, Denver Post*

Despite the fact that the Constitution mandates a separation of church and state, religion and politics come together more often than people realize. When states give employees days off for religious observances or when government scholarships are given to students at colleges affiliated with specific churches, people have argued the separation of church and state is violated. In January 2012, the Freedom From Religion Foundation erected this billboard off Route 295 in Warwick, Rhode Island. The foundation placed its first billboard in Madison, Wisconsin, in 2007 and since then has placed 695 billboards in sixty-one American cities.

Regardless of religious affiliation, the more active people are in religious life, the more socially conservative they are likely to be.

Beginning with the Reagan administration, the Republican Party has made a concerted effort to win the support of evangelical Protestants and other religious conservatives, with a good deal of success. Although the country as a whole was split down the middle between Bush and Gore in 2000, white voters of the religious right went for Bush, 80 percent to 18 percent.[45] Aware of this fact, Bush's 2004 reelection campaign made a special effort to organize get-out-the-vote drives through churches. Even in 2008, when economic issues were far more salient than social issues, white, born-again Christians gave McCain 74 percent of their votes.[46] Christian conservatives have become so large and active an element in the Republican coalition that they now dominate the party organization in many states. In 2012, white, born-again Christians made up slightly more than a third of the Republican primary electorate. These voters supported Rick Santorum and other candidates who dropped out early in the timeline, like Michele Bachmann and Rick Perry, over Mitt Romney (only 20 percent favored Romney) for the party nomination. In 2016, these divisions within the Republican primary electorate were rendered irrelevant as Donald Trump leveraged a different set of attitudes on his path to victory.

### Other Demographic Divisions

Other demographic divisions of opinion are worth noting. Younger voters tend to be more liberal than their elders on social and economic issues; they are, for example, much more supportive of same-sex marriage. City dwellers are more liberal than residents of suburbs, small towns, or rural areas. People living near the coasts or in the upper Midwest tend to be more liberal than people living in the South, the plains, or the mountain states, particularly on cultural issues. The red state–blue state division made so much of in recent presidential elections reflects this culturally based regional divide. White southerners once stood out starkly from the rest of the population in their opposition to racial integration, but the gap has almost entirely disappeared.

Differences of opinion among major social groups constitute the raw material of electoral politics. Candidates and parties trying to win elections have no choice but to piece together coalitions out of the material at hand. The more affluent voters tend to be economic conservatives but social liberals; voters with more modest incomes combine economic liberalism with social conservatism. Social issues have recently given Republicans a wedge to split the Democratic coalition by appealing to the social conservatism of voters who, on economic issues, think like Democrats, but as the nation is liberalizing on average, the payoff from this appeal is shrinking. Similarly, Democrats have countered by using issues such as abortion rights and gun control to woo highly educated voters (particularly women) whose economic interests place them closer to Republicans.

## Public Opinion: A Vital Component of American Politics

The vast network of organizations engaged in measuring or trying to influence public opinion attests to its crucial influence in American politics. But the complexity of the network also underlines the reality that public opinion's influence is rarely simple or unmediated. Individual opinions become public opinion only when aggregated, and organizations and leaders do the aggregating. Polling organizations reveal and express public opinion even as they measure it. Politicians and other policy advocates give it shape, focus, and force through their efforts to persuade and activate citizens to support their causes. The mass media report and interpret the collective political experiences that become the material basis for individual opinions. Opinion leaders provide the cues that the rationally ignorant majority uses as shortcuts to forming its opinion. Individual opinions, although rooted in personal values and experiences, are both shaped by and expressed through leaders and institutions.

Leaders and institutions do not, however, control public opinion. People choose which leaders to follow and which messages to heed according to the values and beliefs they accumulate over a lifetime. Their assessments of parties, issues, candidates, and other political phenomena, derived from personal observations and life experiences as well as from families and friends, retain a strong practical component, reflecting real interests and needs. For most people, basic political orientations, whether reflections of ideologies, a few core values, or simple party preferences, are quite resistant to change. The raw individual material that goes into the construction of public opinion is not particularly malleable, and neither, therefore, is aggregate opinion. Candidates, policy advocates, and anyone else whose political goals require public support (or at least acquiescence) have little choice but to work within the formidable if often hazy constraints imposed by public attitudes. They succeed, if at all, by framing the choice favorably rather than by changing minds. This is clearest in the electoral context, which is the subject of the next chapter.

**⑤SAGE edge™**
**for CQ Press**

**Want a better grade?**

Get the tools you need to sharpen your study skills. Access practice quizzes, eFlashcards, video, and multimedia at **edge.sagepub.com/kernell9e.**

# KEY TERMS

aggregate partisanship    450
aggregate public opinion    448
ambivalence    446
attitude    437
cognitive shortcut    453

conservative    438
core values    438
framing    447
issue publics    453
liberal    437

measurement error    452
opinion leader    452
political socialization    442
public opinion    432
scientific polling    433

# SUGGESTED READINGS

Asher, Herbert. *Polling and the Public: What Every Citizen Should Know.* 9th ed. Washington, DC: CQ Press, 2016. A nontechnical primer for citizens who wish to become smarter, more critical consumers of polls and the media stories that report them.

Page, Benjamin I., and Robert Y. Shapiro. *The Rational Public.* Chicago: University of Chicago Press, 1992. Mass public opinion responds in reasonable ways to national political events and experiences.

Stimson, James A. *Tides of Consent: How Public Opinion Shapes American Politics*. 2nd ed. New York: Cambridge University Press, 2015. Broad trends in public opinion on a wide range of policy issues, or public "moods," both shape and reflect broad trends in national policy. At the most general level, government policies do respond to public preferences.

Zaller, John. *Nature and Origins of Mass Opinion*. New York: Cambridge University Press, 1992. Four simple axioms about how people respond to political information generate a rich variety of models of how public opinion shifts in response to events and to elite persuasion.

## REVIEW QUESTIONS

1. How have modern techniques for molding and measuring public opinion contributed to the nationalization of American politics?

2. Do voters think in terms of ideologies? Are voters' attitudes generally consistent? If not, what explains the inconsistency?

3. Because aggregate opinion is simply the combination of all individual opinions, how can it be more stable and coherent than individual opinion?

4. Who are opinion leaders? Why might typical individuals rely on the statements or positions of these opinion leaders in forming their own opinions? What are the limits on how much these opinion leaders can control public opinion?

5. In which areas does the American public agree or disagree on basic political values and policies? How does this agreement or disagreement make politics possible or necessary?

Bill Clark/CQ Roll Call

AP Photo/John Raoux

Erik McGregor/Pacific Press/LightRocket via Getty Images

*Top:* Kyrsten Sinema defeated her Republican opponent to take the seat previously held by John McCain in Arizona. She is the first woman the state has sent to the Senate and is the first openly bisexual U.S. senator. *Middle:* After a statewide recount, Republican governor Rick Scott was named the next senator from Florida, defeating the Democratic incumbent in an election many called a "blue wave." *Bottom:* Alexandria Ocasio-Cortez, a 28-year-old, Bronx-born Latina and member of the Democratic Socialists of America, defeated a ten-term Democratic congressman in a primary and became the youngest woman ever elected to the U.S. Congress.

# Voting, Campaigns, and Elements

# 11

## KEY QUESTIONS

- If Americans cherish the right to vote, why do so many neglect to exercise it?

- Why is political party identification, which many Americans discount, still the best single predictor of how people will vote?

- If attentive and informed voters are likely to be turned off by negative advertisements, why do campaigns pour so much money into running them?

- Does the American system of campaign finance facilitate or undermine democratic accountability?

## CHAPTER OBJECTIVES

**11.1** Explain the logic of elections in a democracy.

**11.2** Describe how different segments of American society obtained the right to vote.

**11.3** Discuss the factors that affect how people vote.

**11.4** Summarize the role of campaigns in elections.

**11.5** Relate the principal–agent theory as it applies to elections.

Elections invite citizens to choose leaders and register their opinions on how they have performed. In 2018, Donald Trump asked voters to cast their ballot as if he were on it—and many did—turning the House over to his opponents for the first time in eight years. The Senate remained in Republican hands, for Democrats lost some seats in states Trump won in 2016 (like Ben Nelson's loss to Rick Scott in Florida*) but also picked up seats previously held by Republicans (like Kyrsten Sinema's taking the seat held by Arizona's John McCain*). The aftermath of the 2016 and 2018 elections is a divided government—Democrats hold a clear majority in the House, Republicans added two seats to their majority in the Senate, and a Republican sits in the Oval Office.

The change in party makeup was not the only shift to come from the 2018 elections. Washington is significantly more diverse in 2019, continuing the increasingly important role of identity in American politics and better reflecting the nation's population. There are 127 women serving in Congress in 2019, the most ever. Midterm voters also sent the first Native Americans, the first Muslim women, and the youngest woman ever elected to Congress (Alexandria Ocasio-Cortez*). The election also added to the diversity of Congress by increasing the number of LGBT, black, Hispanic, and Asian members.

The parties continue to fight to define how best to serve Americans—and what it means to *be* an American. Alongside traditional topics like

*Photos of Sinema, Scott, and Ocasio-Cortez are on the previous page.

prosperity and peace, changing U.S. demographics are making issues related to racial, ethnic, and religious identities increasingly important to voters at the polls in both presidential and midterm elections. Understanding people's reaction to the nation's changing context is key to understanding how the parties and candidates compete for votes in 2020 and beyond.

Elections are best thought of as the link between the governed and those who govern them. They enable ordinary citizens, in aggregate, to reward or punish elected officials for their performance in office and to influence national policy by selecting or replacing leaders according to their actions or proposals. Elections not only prompt elected officials to take voters' views into account when they make policy choices but also provide a reason for citizens to think about and form opinions on issues and candidates. For candidates and their parties, these opinions serve as the raw material of electoral politics. As we saw in Chapter 10, Americans are divided on a broad range of political issues. Often, the divisions do not form consistent patterns; different groups come together on different issues. The challenge for each candidate or party is to find ways to persuade voters of disparate and often conflicting views to agree on a common action or candidate and to vote for their side. Building coalitions—getting people to agree on an action in the absence of agreement on the purposes of the action—is what pluralist politics is all about, and it is as fundamental to electoral politics as it is to governing. The challenge for voters is to figure out which candidate or party will best serve their interests and represent their values. The way voters, candidates, and parties attempt to meet these challenges is the subject of this chapter. To begin, we need to examine the logic of elections and their historical development in the United States.

## The Logic of Elections

Democracy in America is representative democracy. James Madison, in defending the Constitution in *Federalist* No. 10, adopted the term *republic* to emphasize the distinction between democracy as eighteenth-century Americans saw it and the proposed new system:

> The two great points of difference between a democracy and a republic are: first, the delegation of the government, in the latter, to a small number of citizens elected by the rest; secondly, the greater number of citizens, and greater sphere of country, over which the latter may be extended.

The sheer size of the new nation made self-government by direct democracy impossible (imagine the transaction costs). If the American people were to govern themselves at all, they would have to do it indirectly through the delegation of their authority to a small number of representative agents. But delegation raised the unavoidable danger, immediately acknowledged by Madison, that these agents might use their authority to serve themselves rather than the people they are supposed to represent: "Men of fractious tempers, of local prejudices, or of sinister designs, may, by intrigue, by corruption, or by other means, first obtain the suffrages [votes], and then betray the interests of the people."

As noted in Chapter 1, any delegation of authority raises the possibility of agency loss. Whenever we engage people to act on our behalf, we face the risk that they will put their interests ahead of ours. Worse, it is often difficult to tell whether they are faithful agents because we cannot see what they do or know why they are doing it. The problem of delegation has no perfect solution. One effective, if *imperfect,* solution adopted by representative democracies is to hold regular, free, competitive elections. Elections ameliorate the delegation problem in several ways. First, they give ordinary citizens a say in who represents them. Second, the prospect of future elections gives officeholders who want to keep (or improve) their jobs a motive to be responsive agents. And third, elections provide powerful incentives for the small set of citizens who want to replace the current officeholders to keep a close eye on representatives and to tell everyone else about any misconduct they detect.

Elections do not guarantee faithful representation; indeed, many Americans today do not feel faithfully represented (see Figure 10.5, page 457), even though the United States holds more elections for more public offices than any other nation in the world. But the absence of regular, free, competitive elections does make it unlikely that ordinary citizens will be represented at all. Competitive elections in which virtually all adult citizens are eligible to vote are the defining feature of modern democratic governments.

# The Right to Vote

The practice of selecting leaders by ballot arrived in North America with the first settlers from England. So, too, did the practice of limiting suffrage. Every colony imposed a property qualification for voting, and many denied the franchise to Catholics, Jews, Native Americans, and freed black slaves. Women were rarely allowed to vote.

Many of these restrictions survived the Revolution intact; only about half of the free adult male population was eligible to vote at the time the Constitution was adopted. The story since that time has been the progressive, if sometimes frustratingly slow, extension of the franchise to virtually all adult citizens (defined as people who have celebrated their eighteenth birthdays) not in prisons or mental institutions. Every expansion of suffrage had to overcome both philosophical objections and resistance rooted in the mundane calculations of political advantage. The triumph of (nearly) universal adult suffrage reflects the powerful appeal of democratic ideas, combined with profound social changes, the struggles of dedicated activists, and the perpetual scramble of politicians for votes.

## Wider Suffrage for Men

The property qualifications and voting restrictions brought over from England in colonial times reflected the basic social realities there. Most adults were poor, illiterate, and dependent; they were servants, tenants, hired hands, or paupers. Members of the upper-class minority—a well-born, prosperous, and educated elite—took for granted their right to govern. They were not about to risk the existing social order, which served them so well, by extending voting rights to people whose interests might be better served by changing it. The trip across the Atlantic took some of the bite out of the property qualifications. Land was easier to acquire and far more evenly distributed in the colonies than in England, so a larger proportion of adult men qualified to vote. In the more fluid colonial communities, property restrictions often were enforced laxly if at all. By the revolutionary period any "respectable" man—meaning white, Protestant, and gainfully employed—was, in practice, allowed to vote in many places.[1]

The Revolutionary War exerted a powerful influence on the demands to enlarge the franchise. The rallying cry against England of "no taxation without representation," initially a demand for home rule, also implied that anyone who paid taxes should have the right to vote. Men who risked their lives in the fight for independence felt entitled to full political citizenship regardless of wealth. More important and longer lasting, the ringing pronouncements in the Declaration of Independence that "all men are created equal" and enjoy unalienable rights to "Life, Liberty, and the pursuit of Happiness" and that governments derive "their just powers from the consent of the governed" left little ground for denying voting rights to any citizen.

Still, universal suffrage for (white) men was not fully achieved until the 1840s in the wake of the triumph of Jacksonian democracy. The rear-guard defense of suffrage restrictions rested on traditional arguments: people without a stake in the social order should not have a voice in governing it. If every man were allowed to vote, the votes of those dependent on the wealthy for their livelihoods—employees, tenant farmers, servants, and apprentices—would be controlled by their patrons, enhancing the power of the rich. If, to avoid such untoward influence, a secret ballot were used, the more numerous poor might support unscrupulous demagogues promoting schemes to redistribute wealth. The argument for limiting suffrage boiled down to this: only the independent and virtuous were fit to govern, and the best evidence of independence and virtue was being a property-holding, white, Protestant man.

Gradually, however, this view lost ground to the argument for political equality implicit in the Declaration of Independence, and opposition to universal male suffrage became a political liability. The more democratic the electorate, the more politically suicidal it was to oppose more democracy. French observer Alexis de Tocqueville noted the following with his usual clarity:

> There is no more invariable rule in the history of society: the further electoral rights are extended, the greater is the need of extending them; for after each concession the strength of the democracy increases, and its demands increase with its strength. . . . Concession follows concession, and no stop can be made short of universal suffrage.[2]

## Suffrage for Women

As Tocqueville correctly observed, the democratic logic that justified giving the vote to all white men did not stop there; it also nurtured demands that all adult citizens, regardless of race or sex, be eligible to vote. For more than a century, race, sex, and the institution of slavery interacted to complicate suffrage politics. The women's suffrage movement grew directly out of the antislavery movement, sharing its underlying ideals and some of its activists. Suffragists felt betrayed when the Civil War amendments (formally, if not in practice) enfranchised the newly freed black men but not white or black women. The largely successful effort by white southerners to purge blacks from the electorate after the end of Reconstruction (see Chapter 4) raised a major barrier to giving women the vote. Southern whites opposed any action that might focus national attention on repressive local electoral practices. As one Mississippi senator candidly put it in the 1880s, "We are not afraid to maul a black man over the head if he dares to vote but we can't treat women, even black women, that way. No, we'll allow no woman suffrage. It may be right, but we won't have it."[3]

The resistance to women's suffrage was gradually overcome by a combination of social change—the expansion of education for both sexes, the entry of women into the workforce outside the home—and political need. Western territories (later states) were the first to grant women the right to vote, not because places like Wyoming and Utah were hotbeds of radical democracy but because women were expected to vote for "family values" in raw frontier communities. The campaign for suffrage sometimes took on nativist overtones, proposing to use women's votes to uphold Anglo-Saxon civilization; indeed, many suffragists did not object to the literacy tests, poll taxes,

The campaign to give women the right to vote was fueled by the hope that their presence in the electorate would improve the moral tone of political life. This 1909 cartoon, captioned "Shall women vote? No, they might disturb the existing order of things," suggests that the existing order was thoroughly corrupt and thus ought to be disturbed.

and other devices designed to keep the "wrong" sorts of people out of the electorate. As women's suffrage grew at the state and local levels, politicians competing for women's votes naturally supported further expansion. Once party politicians sensed an irresistible trend, they scrambled to make sure their side was not stigmatized for standing in the way. Only southern Democrats held out to the bitter end; the defense of white supremacy trumped everything else.[4] The Nineteenth Amendment to the Constitution, adopted in 1920, finally guaranteed women everywhere the right to vote.

## Suffrage for African Americans and Young Americans

Despite ratification of the Civil War amendments, the effective extension of the vote to blacks and other minorities came much later as a result of social changes and the political incentives they produced. The story, crowned by the landmark Voting Rights Act of 1965, is told in Chapter 4.

The most recent expansion of voting rights—the Twenty-Sixth Amendment (1971), which lowered the voting age of citizens to eighteen years—also was a political move, one provoked by the Vietnam War. The idea appealed to antiwar activists because young people were so prominent in their movement. Politicians who supported the war also endorsed the amendment because it enfranchised the troops fighting in Vietnam, most of whom were under the age of twenty-one. The movement echoed the logic advanced after the Revolutionary War that those who risk their lives on the battlefield ought to have a voice in governing the nation they are defending.

Consider, though, what consequences did *not* ensue from the formal expansions of suffrage. The propertyless did not despoil the propertied; hence the conformity cost most dreaded by defenders of limited suffrage never materialized. Votes for women did not immediately transform electoral politics in any measurable way: no distinctive pattern of women's voting was evident until the 1980s, following a steep increase in the proportion of single working women in the electorate. The only discernible consequence of granting eighteen-year-olds the right to vote was a decline in the percentage of those eligible who turn out to vote. The Fourteenth and Fifteenth Amendments did not prevent a century of racial discrimination at the polls. Only the Voting Rights Act quickly and effectively achieved its goals of increasing African American voting in states practicing discrimination.

## Who Uses the Right to Vote?

Most Americans agree that the right to vote is the very essence of democracy. On Memorial Day and other holidays the nation honors the soldiers who have fought and died for that privilege. If the right to vote is so valuable, then, why do millions of Americans choose not to exercise it?

It might seem paradoxical that many people who think that the right to vote is worth dying for do not bother to go to the polls. But this reality is not paradoxical at all: it is inherent in the logic of elections. The benefits of elections—in both the broad sense of maintaining democratic accountability and in the narrower sense of electing a preferred candidate—are collective benefits. People enjoy these payoffs even if they have not helped produce them by voting. It makes perfect sense for citizens to insist on the right to vote, for it gives leaders a reason to care about people's interests, opinions, and values. But it makes equal sense not to bother voting if the only purpose in voting is to influence leaders. After all, the likelihood that any single vote will influence anyone or anything is minute. Totaled up, votes are decisive; individually, they count for next to nothing. Why, then, spend the time and energy required to go to the polls if individual participation, or its absence, makes no difference in the outcome of the election? The real question is not so much why millions of Americans do not vote, but why millions of Americans forgo free riding and do vote in elections where they are unlikely to be pivotal (in small elections where the chances of swaying the outcome are not negligible, it may not be rational to free ride!).

The same logic applies to gathering information about the competing candidates and parties if a person chooses to vote. There is no point in investing time, energy, or money in becoming better informed about electoral options because the payoff for casting the "right" vote—for the candidate who would, in the voter's view, do the best job—is for all practical purposes nil. If there is no real chance that a vote will be decisive, it is of no consequence whether the vote is right or wrong. Ignorance, like abstention from voting, is rational.

Followed to its logical conclusion, this line of reasoning would lead to the collapse of electoral politics and thus to the collapse of democracy: no voters, no accountability, no consent of the governed. In practice, however, these free-rider problems are overcome, but they are overcome quite imperfectly and in ways that have important consequences for how American democracy actually works.

The share of eligible voters who go to the polls has varied widely over American history (turnout patterns are traced in Chapter 12). The most important change in the past half century was the sharp decline in voter turnout between 1968 and 1972. Since then, an average of only about 58 percent of the eligible electorate has bothered to register and vote in presidential elections; even the hotly contested 2016 presidential race inspired a turnout of only 60 percent of those eligible to register. The 2018 midterm elections set a century-long record for midterm turnout—nearly half of eligible voters went to the polls. By comparison, in 2014, midterm turnout was 37 percent. Variations in turnout pose the questions we address in this section: who votes, why, and to what effect? Why do turnout rates vary, and does it matter?

## Individual Factors Affecting Turnout

A great deal of research has gone into figuring out who votes, who does not, and how to get people who don't usually vote to do so. Age and education have the strongest influence on voting, but many other things affect turnout as well. African Americans and Hispanics are less likely to vote (taking all other factors into account), as are people who live in southern states or states bordering the South. People with deeper roots in their communities (longtime residents, homeowners, church members, and people with jobs) are more likely to go to the polls, as are individuals with greater confidence in their own ability to understand and engage in politics (internal efficacy, as it is known in political science) and in their ability to influence the decisions of government (external efficacy). Turnout also is higher among people with stronger partisan views and electoral preferences and those who live in areas with active parties and competitive campaigns. Finally, turnout is higher where legal barriers to registration are lower.

Why is sex missing from this list of influences on voting? Other things being equal, the voting rates for men and women were roughly the same for a long time, but recently this has started to change—and change steadily year after year. Today, it is estimated that given comparable incomes, educations, and ages, a woman is 5 percentage points more likely to turn out than a man in presidential elections. Also absent are measures of trust in government and beliefs about government responsiveness; the cynical and distrusting are as likely to vote as everyone else. This point contradicts a popular explanation for the decline in participation between the 1960s and 1990s—that it resulted from the dramatic increase in public cynicism and mistrust since 1960.[5]

The explanation for these general patterns is straightforward. Voting and other forms of political participation, such as contributing money or time to campaigns, writing letters to elected officials, and attending political meetings, incur costs but produce benefits. People participate when they can meet the costs and appreciate the benefits. Those with money, education, experience, free time, and self-confidence find it easier to meet the costs; those with a greater psychological stake in politics—from a concern with issues, a sense of obligation to carry out their duties as citizens, or a strong interest in parties or candidates—receive greater benefits (also mainly psychological) from participation. Voting, therefore, is rational for the millions of individuals who derive personal satisfaction from going to the polls. Expressing themselves through voting outweighs the typically modest cost of casting a ballot.

## Institutional Factors Affecting Turnout

Differences in participation cannot be explained completely by individual differences in resources and psychological involvement, however. The institutional context—for example, variations in registration laws—affects turnout. The more onerous the registration requirement, the higher the cost of voting. In the decades after the Civil War, southern states adopted devices such as poll taxes, literacy tests, and the requirement that voters reregister periodically to discourage African Americans from voting. In many cases, these practices discouraged poor whites from participating as well. But after the Voting Rights Act of 1965 banned literacy tests and authorized the Justice Department to oversee voter registration in states with a history of flagrant racial discrimination, voting among African Americans (and whites) increased sharply. Still, the effects of old practices linger. Even with the end of formal and informal restrictions on voting and the advent of two-party competition in their region, southerners are notably less likely to vote than are Americans who reside elsewhere. Schemes to skew the electorate for political advantage are by no means a thing of the past. Prior to the 2012 election, more than a dozen states adopted a requirement that voters show a picture ID at the polls, raising the cost of participation for poor and minority voters, who are less likely to possess driver's licenses or passports. Such groups are also more likely to vote for Democrats, and all but one of the state governments that adopted this requirement were controlled by Republicans.

Social circumstances also play a crucial part in stimulating turnout. Social connections create personal incentives to participate when, for example, coworkers take note of who is performing their citizen's duty to vote (and who is wearing the "I voted" sticker). These connections also provide plenty of free information through casual conversation touching on politics. Even more significant, however, are the deliberate efforts of political activists of all kinds to get people to vote. Often, people participate because they are asked, a fact that has never been a secret to politicians. The desire to win elections has inspired extensive efforts

REUTERS/Trish Badger

Despite efforts by groups like Rock the Vote to register and mobilize young people, this group votes in disproportionately low numbers relative to other groups in the nation. Because they don't turn out in elections, politicians tend to ignore the needs and demands of young people, opting instead to address the concerns of those who actually vote on Election Day.

## STRATEGY AND CHOICE
# Personal Politics: Mobilization

Beginning in 1998, two political scientists at Yale University conducted a series of experiments on voter turnout on nearly thirty thousand registered voters in New Haven, Connecticut. The experiments were done "in the field" during actual elections and involved canvassing, phone calls, and direct mail—all aimed at encouraging people to get out and vote in the upcoming election. The League of Women Voters was a partner in the project and helped in the development of the scripts and the implementation of the experiment.[6]

Hyoung Chang, *The Denver Post*

Through a series of random assignments, a sample of registered voters was divided into treatment and control groups. Roughly 11,000 people received no treatments; 7,369 were sent at least one mailing but nothing else; 2,686 got only personal contact; and 958 were contacted only on the phone. The remaining 7,567 people received a mix of the mail and phone call efforts. Of these three types of voter contact, one emerged as massively more effective than the others: personal contact. A personal visit increased turnout by almost 9 percentage points. The other methods didn't even come close.

To encourage people to turn out and vote, the researchers used three different appeals in their messaging. The first was a plea to civic duty that reminded people that "democracy depends on the participation of our country's citizens." The second focused on the closeness of the election outcome, underscoring for voters that their ballot

could be pivotal. The final message highlighted neighborhood solidarity and said, "Politicians sometimes ignore a neighborhood's problems if the people in that neighborhood don't vote." Which one worked the best? As you might have guessed, the largest effect seemed to have come from the message stressing the closeness of the election—and therefore increasing people's chances of being pivotal to the outcome. The differences between the messages were large (5 percent for neighborhood solidarity and 12 percent for closeness), but even so, the differences were not big enough to be sure that the effects of the messages weren't all the same on average.

The work of these Yale professors and their students gave rise to a renewed interest in canvassing by both political parties—but with a twist. Randomized experiments were built in to campaign operations to assess the effectiveness of different tactics.

by candidates, parties, interest groups, and other campaigners to get their potentially free-riding supporters to show up at the polls. The massive and effective turnout efforts mounted by the Obama campaigns in 2008 and 2012 are cases in point. Not surprisingly, research has shown that one of the most effective ways to turn a nonvoter into a voter is through a personal appeal—often done at the doorstep—asking the nonvoter to make a plan for how, when, and where he or she will vote on Election Day. Personal appeals, and social pressure from others, work well in stimulating turnout. A study by two political scientists in 2008 showed that mailing postcards to registered voters with the names of people who lived on their blocks and who stayed home on the last Election Day increased turnout by double digits! No one wants to be the person on their block who shirked his or her civic duty.[7] The mailing was by far the best way to increase turnout in elections.

The assorted demographic and institutional influences on voting produce an electorate in which wealthy, well-educated, older white people are overrepresented and the poor, uneducated, young, and nonwhite are underrepresented. Unequal resources are only part of the reason. The other is that people with social advantages are more likely to be mobilized by parties, interest groups, and campaign organizations. Political leaders deploy their scarce resources efficiently, targeting the people who are cheapest to reach and likeliest to respond. In other words, they go after people like themselves (educated and relatively affluent), people already organized and identified by membership in voluntary associations, and people whose social characteristics already incline them to participate. It takes an extraordinary effort backed by abundant organizational resources to counteract this tendency.

In general, the smaller the electorate, the greater its upper-class bias. Logically, a biased electorate should produce biased policy because politicians naturally cater to the people whose votes control their futures. In times of tight budgets, for example, Congress has been more willing to cut social welfare programs benefiting poor people (food stamps, job training programs, and Aid to Families with Dependent Children) than to cut social welfare programs benefiting the politically active middle class (Social Security and Medicare).

## How Do Voters Decide?

Casting a vote is making a prediction about the future—that electing one candidate will produce a better outcome in some relevant sense than electing another candidate. To make such a prediction, a voter has to choose the standards for "better" and "relevant" and then determine which candidate best meets the standards. These choices are made under conditions of considerable uncertainty, and because the likelihood of casting a decisive vote is so tiny, people find it makes little sense to put much effort into acquiring information that might reduce uncertainty. Thus they economize by using simple cues as cognitive shortcuts and by relying heavily, if selectively, on the free information delivered by the news media, campaign advertising, opinion leaders, and their own experience to inform their predictions.

## Past Performance and Incumbency

One way to predict the future is to look at the past. Voters may treat an election as a referendum on the incumbent's or majority party's performance in office. Has the current agent done an adequate job of serving the voters' values and interests? One simple rule is to vote for incumbents who have performed well. The question then becomes, performance on what? The answer depends on the office, the circumstances, and what the voter considers important. Presidents seeking reelection often are held accountable for the national economy—the rates of inflation, unemployment, and economic growth. Economic problems probably cost Jimmy Carter and George H. W. Bush their jobs, whereas a strong economy contributed to Ronald Reagan's reelection in 1984 and to Bill Clinton's in 1996. The question famously posed by Reagan captures this standard: "Are you better off now than you were four years ago?" Since the New Deal, for example, the change in the nation's growth rate (the gross domestic product) in the first six months of the election year serves as a strong predictor of whether the incumbent president's party will win reelection. When the economy is growing the incumbent party is typically returned to office—75 percent of the time to be exact. This robust relationship provides evidence on the stability of presidential election outcomes and how closely they are tied to the government's performance in office. In 2016, for example, this prediction yielded an incredibly close election outcome, one essentially on the 50–50 mark.

Although one party may benefit from the state of the nation's economy, the other looks to focus the election on something else; thus, some presidents also may be reviewed for their conduct of foreign policy. Dwight Eisenhower's success in ending the war in Korea helped ensure his reelection in 1956; Carter's inability to obtain the release of the U.S. diplomats held hostage by Iran damaged his reelection chances in 1980. The performance of representatives and senators, by contrast, is often measured by their success in providing services and projects for their states and districts or in casting acceptable votes in Congress (see Chapter 6). But some voters hold the president's party as a whole responsible, casting their congressional votes according to how well they think the administration has governed. Voters unhappy with President Bush and the Iraq War took it out on congressional Republicans in 2006; similarly, voters objecting to President Obama, his policies, and the sorry state of the economy punished Democratic candidates for Congress in the 2010 and 2014 midterm elections. In 2006, 2010, and 2018 the president's party lost majority control of the House and, in 2006 and 2014, the Senate as well.

## Assessing the Issues and Policy Options

How can voters assess performance efficiently? Personal experience supplies a good deal of politically relevant information. Looking for a job, shopping at the supermarket, or trying to get a mortgage to buy a house teaches people about unemployment, inflation, and interest rates. Taking out a student loan or applying for veterans' benefits teaches something about government programs. Millions of retired Americans are keenly aware of the size of their monthly Social Security checks. The threat of a military draft certainly raised the political consciousness of college-age Americans during the Vietnam War. Those without direct experience with certain issues learn about them through the news media. For example, crime became a bigger public issue in the 1990s than it had been a decade earlier—even though the crime rate had actually declined—because of the greater emphasis the news media put on it. And, of course, Americans needed no direct personal experience of terrorist attacks and the Iraq War for these events to shape their judgments of George W. Bush's fitness for reelection in 2004.

Another strategy for predicting which candidate will be the more satisfactory agent is to compare the future policy options each represents. By the positions they take on issues, by their overall ideological stances, or by their party affiliations, candidates offer choices among alternative national policies. Which policy positions matter? The answer depends on the voters and current circumstances. For voters with strong views on abortion, any difference between candidates on this issue may be enough to settle their choice. **Single-issue voters** also coalesce around causes such as gun control (its most adamant opponents) and environmental protection (its most adamant proponents). Instead of a single issue, other voters may consider bundles of issues, choosing between, say, the expectations of lower taxes and more generous social spending. The times also may determine which issues become important to voters. Civil rights became critical in the 1964 election when the Republican candidate, Senator Barry Goldwater of Arizona, voted against the Civil Rights Act of 1964. What to do about Vietnam dominated voter opinion while American soldiers were fighting there. Similarly, the wisdom of invading Iraq was central to voters' deliberations in 2004. Iraq was expected to be the central issue again in 2008, but with the collapse of housing prices, frozen credit markets, a plummeting stock market, and a looming recession, the economy overwhelmed all other issues. In 2016 issues like immigration and terrorism played a central role as Donald Trump highlighted a series of terrorist attacks in the year prior to the election and stoked people's fears of undocumented people through his campaign rhetoric.

## Voter Cues and Shortcuts

The news media and the campaigns supply plenty of free information about candidates' positions on issues and policy promises. But voters cannot take the information at face value, for candidates have an incentive to misrepresent themselves (and their opponents) to win votes. Voters can deal with this problem by taking cues from opinion leaders (see Chapter 10). In electoral politics, opinion leadership is often formalized through endorsements from organizations and individuals. A candidate supported by NARAL Pro-Choice America, Reverend Jesse Jackson, or the Sierra Club is certain to have different policy objectives from one endorsed by the Christian Coalition, the NRA, the National Taxpayers Union, or the Tea Party Express.

Voters also make predictions based on the candidates' personal characteristics. One set of personal considerations includes qualities such as competence, experience, honesty, knowledge, and leadership skills. Another set includes characteristics such as sex, race, ethnicity, age, and place of residence. The rationale for such criteria is straightforward. Voters cannot anticipate all the problems and issues that will come up after the election, nor can they easily monitor the behavior of their elected officials. Much of what these agents do is out of public sight, and much of the information they act on is unknown to their constituents. Under these

Mark Cornelison/Lexington Herald-Leader/TNS via Getty Images

Affiliations or endorsements from well-known interest groups give voters cheap and reliable cues about the policy inclinations of candidates. Here, Republican presidential candidate Donald Trump speaks at the National Rifle Association (NRA) convention in May 2016, an unmistakable signal to voters on either side of the gun control issue that Trump stood with the NRA against greater regulation of firearms.

circumstances, using personal criteria makes a great deal of sense. A candidate's demographic features give voters clues about his or her personal values. Voters feel that people who are like them in some tangible way are more likely to think and act as they would in the same circumstances. As an African American, Barack Obama faced the challenge of convincing a majority of voters that, although he may not look like them, he nonetheless understood their needs and values and would thus be an effective agent for them. His rival in 2012, Mitt Romney, with a fortune estimated to be worth $230 million, struggled to persuade voters of modest means that he could nonetheless feel their economic pain. In 2016, Hillary Clinton banked on the fact that a candidate's competence, background, and character could give voters clues about how far he or she can be trusted to do the right thing even when no one is watching. She never missed an opportunity to point out that her opponent, Donald Trump, was unfit for office. Of course, Trump did the same and had the help of the director of the Federal Bureau of Investigation (FBI), James Comey, who in the middle of the campaign released a report saying Secretary Clinton was "careless" in her handling of classified documents while she was at the State Department.

The most important information shortcut voters use to make predictions is the **party label**. A large majority of voters continue to take their cues from party affiliations, even though popular attitudes toward parties as institutions tend to range from indifference to outright hostility.[8] The party label provides useful information for both **performance voting** (voting for the party in control, or "in-party," when one thinks the government is performing well; voting for the "outs" when one thinks the party in charge is performing poorly) and **issue voting** (the typical positions of Republicans and Democrats differ in predictable ways on many issues). Most voters drastically simplify their electoral evaluations and decisions by developing a consistent bias in favor of the candidates of one of the major parties, making the party label the most influential "endorsement" of all.

## The Power of Party Identification

As the best single predictor of the vote in federal elections, **party identification** is a central focus of modern electoral research (see Chapter 10). Since the 1950s a nationally sponsored survey, the American National Election Study, has asked scientifically selected samples of the American public a set of questions probing the strength and direction of their partisanship. In recent years, a new set of projects, the Cooperative Election Studies, has also started asking people the same questions. Respondents are first asked, "Generally speaking, do you usually think of yourself as a Republican, a Democrat, an independent, or what?" Those who answer "Democrat" or "Republican" are then asked, "Would you call yourself a strong Democrat (Republican) or a not very strong Democrat (Republican)?" Those who answer "independent" or something else are then asked, "Do you think of yourself as closer to the Republican Party or the Democratic Party?" Answers to these questions locate respondents on a seven-point scale: strong Democrats, weak Democrats, independents leaning Democratic, pure independents, independents leaning Republican, weak Republicans, and strong Republicans. This scale serves as the standard measure of party identification.

Party identification has proved to be a strong predictor of the vote in any election in which candidates run under party labels. In 2016, for example, about 90 percent of partisans voted for their own party's presidential candidate, whereas independents split their votes 48–42 for

■ **FIGURE 11.1**  Partisan Voting in Presidential Elections

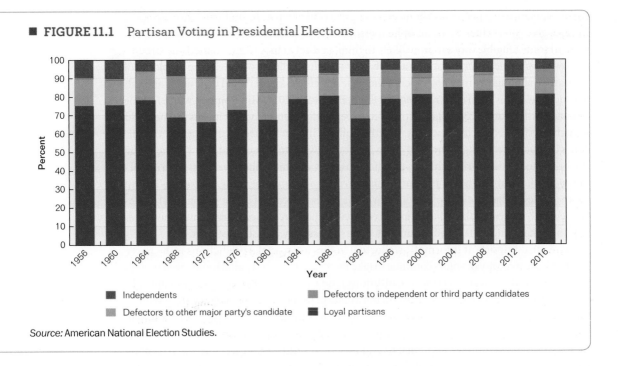

Source: American National Election Studies.

Trump. In general, the weaker a survey respondent's partisanship, the more likely he or she is to vote for a minor-party candidate.

The connection between party identification and vote choice varies over time but is always powerful. Figure 11.1 shows that in elections from 1956 through 2016, typically about 80 percent of presidential voters were self-identified partisans supporting their party's candidate. Their portion of the electorate has been growing since the 1970s. The proportion defecting to the opposing party's candidate ranged from 7.6 percent to 24.1 percent, and the proportion voting for independent or third-party candidates varied from less than 1 percent to 15.3 percent. Usually, fewer than 10 percent are pure independents who claim to favor neither party. Still, there are enough independents and partisan defectors to keep party identification alone from determining who wins or loses elections.

## Election Campaigns

If voters are short of information and uncertain about their choices, the candidates and their allies are only too happy to help them out. Experienced campaigners are fully aware of voters' reliance on free information and cognitive shortcuts, and they concoct strategies for winning votes accordingly. Each campaign emphasizes selected facts and cues aimed at getting at least a plurality of voters to the polls. The choice among strategic options depends on what the candidate and campaign staff believe will work in this contest in this year with this electorate. Campaigns are intensely pragmatic, opportunistic affairs, highly variable because they must adapt to circumstances that are highly variable—the office in question, whether the contest is a primary or general election, and current political events and issues. Nonetheless, all competitive campaigns have features in common because they face many of the same challenges.

## The Basic Necessities: Candidates and Messages

The basic necessities of any campaign are a candidate, a message, and a way to inform voters about both. A **candidate** is a person who can be portrayed as sufficiently qualified and trustworthy for the job. Achieving this status is not as simple as it sounds. Members of the House of Representatives often run unopposed because no one is willing to take them on in the primary or general election. Even more often, members run against candidates so lacking in political experience, talent, temperament, or background that voters do not consider them seriously as viable choices. Sometimes, although less frequently, senators are equally lucky: Senator Jim DeMint of South Carolina, for example, was opposed in 2010 by a candidate who raised no money, did almost no campaigning, and was under federal indictment on an obscenity charge.[9] Who do you think won?

Because potential candidates think strategically, the quality of House and Senate candidates varies with their prospects for success. The smaller the chances of winning, the less likely the talented and ambitious are to run (see Strategy and Choice box, "To Run or Not to Run"). Presidential contests usually attract plenty of political talent, but even the pool of presidential candidates may be affected by expectations: when President George H. W. Bush seemed unbeatable in 1991 after the Gulf War triumph, some prominent Democratic presidential prospects decided not to run, leaving room for Arkansas governor Bill Clinton, a relative unknown, to move to the front of the pack.

The 2016 presidential race cast doubt on many of the long-standing beliefs about what candidates needed to do to win elections—and what they could do and still remain viable options. Donald Trump won the endorsement of only nine newspapers in the nation; few copartisans endorsed him; he raised far less money than his opponent and ran many fewer ads on television—and he won the presidency. Future candidates should take note, however, of an important element of Trump's candidacy that likely made him the exception rather than the rule: his preexisting fame. As one of the world's richest billionaires, with his name on everything from grand hotels to neckties, Donald Trump was a household name before he even declared his candidacy. Add to this his long run as the host of one of television's most popular reality shows, *The Apprentice,* and you begin to understand how people may have believed they knew everything they needed to know about Donald Trump before he even started campaigning, something that is unlikely to be true for future candidates who want to follow his campaign tactics but don't have his preexisting level of fame.

### Getting out the Message
The **message** is the answer to the voter's question: why should I vote for this candidate rather than another? It tells voters why, in their terms, this particular candidate is their best choice. Messages are shaped by candidates' theories about the political beliefs, perceptions, values, and responses of different segments of the electorate. Uncertainty is so pervasive and good information about voters so valuable that campaigns invest heavily in research—if they can afford it.

## STRATEGY AND CHOICE
# To Run or Not to Run

Variations in the quality of House and Senate candidates reflect the rational strategies of people interested in successful political careers. Politically ambitious people with the skills, resources, and experience to be effective candidates hesitate to try to move up the political ladder unless they are likely to succeed, for defeat will stall, and may effectively end, a career in politics. Unless conditions are promising—say, the incumbent is in political trouble or the seat is open—the strongest potential candidates will stay out of the race and leave the field to weaker candidates for whom defeat will be less costly to their already unpromising careers.

As politicians decide to run or not to run, they also gauge the national partisan breezes. A strong economy, the absence of party scandal, or a president who enjoys the public's support might tilt the election toward the president's fellow party members, whereas the opposite conditions will shift the political winds toward the out-party's candidates. Because quality candidates have career investments to protect, more will come forward when national conditions are favorable to their side. Moreover, because the presence of quality candidates greatly affects the election outcome, their anticipated responses will tend to reinforce and magnify the effect of national conditions on congressional elections. Think of it this way: high-quality candidates wait to run until the national context suggests they have the best chance of winning.

In fall of 2001 Democratic and Republican Party officials were busy trying to entice quality candidates to run in the 2002 midterm elections. With economic indicators pointing mostly toward recession, Democrats were optimistic that they might take back control of the House and strengthen their grip on the Senate. Then

on September 11 the terrorist attacks on the World Trade Center and the Pentagon totally changed the national agenda. Suddenly potential challengers in both parties found it unseemly to tout their partisan aspirations for political office. At the same time, many of the mostly Republican incumbents who had been leaning toward retirement announced that they would do their patriotic duty and serve another term. Context matters. Knowledgeable observers from both political parties concluded that the terrorist attacks and subsequent events deterred many quality Democratic candidates and limited the party's prospects in the 2002 elections.

The political climate in 2006 was far different. The unpopularity of the Bush administration and the Iraq War was apparent well before the election (see Chapter 10), encouraging vigorous Democratic challenges and discouraging potentially strong Republican candidates from taking on Democratic incumbents. Anticipating a favorable national tide, Democratic operatives, candidates, and contributors positioned themselves to exploit it. As a result, the Democrats picked up thirty Republican seats while losing none of their own.[a] Effectively exploiting similarly favorable national conditions in 2008, the Democrats picked up another twenty-one House seats. The tide turned decisively in 2010, when popular unhappiness with the economy and the general direction of the country promised a banner year for Republicans. In 2018, the tide turned once again as Democratic voters—stinging from a narrow loss in 2016—returned the House to the Democrats and ushered in the most diverse set of House members in history, a direct reaction to the focus on identity issues in 2016.

---

[a]Gary C. Jacobson, "Referendum: The 2006 Midterm Congressional Elections," *Political Science Quarterly* 122 (Spring 2007): 1–24.

Presidential campaigns can afford it, and they use the full range of research techniques. They run hundreds of opinion surveys and conduct numerous **focus group** sessions in which a small number of ordinary citizens are observed as they talk with one another about political candidates, issues, and events. Presidential campaigns use focus groups to test their general themes as well as the specific advertisements promoting those themes. They monitor the effects of campaign ads and events with daily tracking polls that sample citizens' views on a continuing basis to measure changes in responses. In 1988 there was nothing accidental about the Bush campaign's relentless attacks on the Democratic opponent, Michael Dukakis, for being "soft on crime." Nor was it simple intuition in 1992 that made Clinton's campaign manager, James Carville, put up the now-famous sign reminding himself and the rest of the staff of their campaign's most powerful theme: "the economy, stupid." Nor was there anything mysterious about Clinton in 1996 endlessly repeating the vow to protect "Medicare, Medicaid, education, and the environment," or about George W. Bush choosing to define himself as a "compassionate conservative" in 2000 and as the nation's shield against terrorism in 2004, or in Barack Obama's effort to tie John McCain to Bush's unpopular legacy in 2008, or in the 2012 Obama campaign's depiction of Mitt Romney as a cold-hearted capitalist with retrograde social views. In each case the campaign's research told it that these messages were winners.

In 2016, both the Trump and Clinton campaigns settled on the same idea for their messages but from opposite points of view. Understanding that the changing demographic composition of the country was making people's attitudes about race and ethnicity more important in their political decision-making, both candidates leveraged this in their campaigns. The Trump campaign focused on "making America great again" by identifying groups of people as being like "us" or being like "them." The "us" group included people like Trump whereas the "them" group often included the media, protestors, and people who did not exhibit "American values." During the campaign, Trump said he wanted to keep undocumented citizens out of the country, deport those who were currently in the country, and ban the entry of Muslims to the country until the government could figure out "what the hell is going on." He proposed a divided nation of "us" versus "them." The Clinton campaign message took exactly the opposite approach to the same idea. Her message, "stronger together," was routinely coupled with images of people from all walks of life—different ethnicities, different kinds of couples, children and adults—everyone together in Clinton's notion of a strong country celebrating its differences. She proposed a unified nation of "togetherness."

These examples illustrate something else about campaign messages: they are chosen opportunistically. Slow economic growth during the administration of George H. W. Bush handed the Clinton campaign in 1992 a powerful, ready-made theme, and the campaign really would have been stupid not to make the most of it. This holds for the Obama campaign in 2008 as well; its strongest argument for replacing the Republicans was an economic collapse larger than any seen in recent memory. Clinton's questionable candor about his draft record, experimentation with marijuana, and alleged extramarital affairs handed the Bush campaign its central message in 1992: Bill Clinton was too untrustworthy to be president. By embracing "compassionate conservatism," the younger Bush sought to attract moderate swing voters weary of the Democratic administration but repelled by the hardline conservatism displayed by congressional Republicans. Bush also vowed repeatedly to "uphold the honor and dignity of the office" of president, a not-so-subtle appeal to voters disgusted by Bill Clinton's behavior. Imagine how different the 2004 campaigns would have been had the terrorist attacks of September 2001 never occurred, or how different the 2008 campaigns would have been had the economy been booming and had Bush been popular. The messages candidates use in their campaigns depend very much on two things: the national context and who is running against them. In 2016, the economy was so mixed that coupled with the Democrats seeking a third term in office, the election was predicted to be a very close one from the outset. This is perhaps one of the reasons why neither candidate spent much time discussing the nation's economy—it didn't help either one of them very much.

The same opportunistic strategy is applied to congressional races. The House bank scandal (see Chapter 6) gave House challengers a powerful message for their 1992 campaigns: vote the self-serving deadbeats out of office. The controversial hearings in 1991 over the nomination of Clarence Thomas to the Supreme Court provided another stick. Anita Hill's accusations that Thomas sexually harassed her were handled clumsily by a committee of middle-aged men, who, many thought, "just didn't get it." The result was that a candidate's sex became an important shorthand cue for many congressional voters in 1992, who thus elected nineteen additional women to the House (raising the total at the time to forty-seven) and four to the Senate (for a total of six). In 2018, Donald Trump's exclusionary rhetoric and the nomination of Brett Kavanaugh and subsequent hearings led to the most women ever elected to Congress—127.

Candidates work hard to convey the message that they do "get it," that they understand and care about the concerns of their fellow citizens. Like other job seekers, candidates prepare glowing résumés highlighting their credentials, experience, and accomplishments. But they also try to show that, regardless of their backgrounds, they share some common ground with voters of all sorts. Patrician Yale graduate George H. W. Bush advertised his fondness for pork rinds and bass fishing to connect with ordinary folks during his campaign in 1988. Bill Clinton's impromptu saxophone jams showed that he could be just one of the gang. It is a robust appetite for votes, not food, that leads candidates to eat bagels and lox at a corner deli in a Jewish neighborhood in the morning, black-eyed peas at an African American church at lunch, and green chili enchiladas at a Mexican American fiesta in the evening. The implicit message is empathy: "Though I may not be one of you, I appreciate your culture and understand your needs and concerns, so I can serve effectively as your agent."

Actions intended to symbolize a candidate's concerns do not always work as planned, however. In 1972 the Democratic candidate, Senator George McGovern of South Dakota, displayed his ignorance rather than appreciation of Jewish culture when he ordered milk to go with his kosher hot dog while campaigning in a Jewish neighborhood in Queens, New York. Handed a tamale while campaigning among Mexican American voters in San Antonio in 1976, Gerald Ford took a vigorous bite out of the inedible cornhusk wrapper, a gaffe that made all the network news broadcasts. During the 1988 presidential campaign, Michael Dukakis reaped widespread ridicule, not enhanced credentials on defense issues, when news broadcasts showed him peering out dolefully from under an ill-fitting helmet while riding on an Army tank.[10] In 2012, Mitt Romney expressed his enthusiasm for the U.S. auto industry by telling a Detroit audience, "I drive a Mustang and a Chevy pickup truck. Ann [his wife] drives a couple of Cadillacs," inadvertently reinforcing the Democrats' depiction of him as an out-of-touch millionaire. In each instance, the action conveyed a message subverting the one intended. Campaign advisers may want to display their candidates as all things to all people, but the human material often proves recalcitrant.

Acquiring and maintaining a public image appropriate to the office sought is a particular challenge for presidential candidates, who are subject to intense scrutiny by both their opponents and the news media over many months of campaigning. Most presidential primaries now take place so early in the election year—roughly two-thirds of the states select convention delegates for one or both parties by the end of March—that campaigns begin shortly after the midterm election, if not earlier. In years with crowded primary fields (at one time six Democrats and seventeen Republicans were officially in the race for the 2016 nominations) aspirants have to fight for attention and to make sure that they, rather than their opponents or skeptical reporters, shape their public images. Candidates blessed with famous names (in 2000 George W. Bush, governor of Texas and son of a former president, and Elizabeth Dole, holder of cabinet positions in the Reagan and George H. W. Bush administrations, president of the Red Cross, and wife of the 1996 Republican candidate, Bob Dole; in 2008 and 2016 Hillary Clinton; and perhaps the most famous of all, Donald Trump in 2016) and ample money enjoy a distinct advantage in these endeavors, but front-runners also become all the other candidates' favorite targets, and the candidate with the most money doesn't always win the nomination, as Howard Dean learned in 2004, Romney learned in 2008, and Jeb Bush learned in 2016.

Televised debates are another special challenge for presidential candidates trying to convey the message that they are right for the job. For clear front-runners, especially those not fully comfortable in front of television cameras, the risks of damaging missteps during a debate outweigh the potential gains from winning it. But the media and public now expect debates, so there is no graceful way to avoid them. For challengers and candidates behind in the polls, the nationally televised debates offer a chance to share equal billing with the leader and to make up lost ground before the largest audiences of the campaign. Independent candidate Ross Perot, for example, made the most of his opportunity in 1992, stealing the first debate from Bush and Clinton with his folksy style, populist rhetoric, and handmade charts, thereby giving his candidacy a boost.[11] Usually, however, independent and minor-party candidates are excluded; Ralph Nader and Pat Buchanan protested vigorously but fruitlessly when they were kept out of the debates in 2000 on the ground that their support in preelection polls was too low to make them viable candidates and thus eligible to participate. Only Obama and McCain shared the debate stage in 2008; Obama, looking younger and calmer than his better-known opponent, was the consensus winner of all three of their debates, giving his candidacy an important boost. Ironically, Obama's first debate with Mitt Romney in 2012 nearly derailed his reelection bid; Romney's forceful performance and Obama's lackluster responses turned an Obama lead into a tie in the preelection horse-race polls. In 2016, the candidacy of a reality TV star transformed the debates into major television events. In 2012, 67 million people watched the first Obama-Romney debate, but 83 million tuned in for the first Clinton-Trump debate in 2016—the largest audience for a presidential debate since the first debate more than sixty years ago. The second closest was the single 1980 debate between Jimmy Carter and Ronald Reagan, to which 80 million people tuned in.

Debates rarely cover new campaign ground, but they remain popular among the media and public because they show the presidential candidates up close under sustained pressure. They may also help frame the choice in clear terms for voters, but the effects of debates in general elections are largely ignorable.

### Political Advertising and Attacks

The effects of ads, whether promotional or attack, are likely small and fleeting. This is why candidates advertise so much—they have to maintain a sustained advertising effort to keep the effects from disappearing. It is also why they advertise so much near Election Day—they have to keep their message fresh in voters' minds. Advertisements are special forms of communication because they combine visual and aural elements in unique ways. Viewers see images and words on the screen. They hear background sounds, music, and voice-overs too. Critically, they can be seeing and hearing all of these things at the same time. In this way, ads are a special medium. Although no single element of the ad may be misleading or untrue, the combination of the elements may lead viewers to draw a misleading inference. It's the way the parts of the ad make up the whole that makes political advertising powerful. For example, an ad that shows an image of children and a voice-over that says, "The lack of health care in America is a big problem" invites viewers to draw the inference that the lack of health care is a big problem for kids. But when the ad-maker supplies one more element—an on-screen piece of text that reads "14 percent uninsured"—the ad takes on a new meaning. Now, the viewer is led to conclude that 14 percent of kids in America are uninsured. It's actually 14 percent of adults. Only 5 percent of kids are uninsured. You can watch collections of campaign ads from presidential races going back to 1952 at the online exhibit called the Living Room Candidate (www.livingroomcandidate.org). As you watch the ads, pay attention to how the ad-makers use these elements to persuade viewers.

Campaign messages emphasizing one candidate's personal suitability for the job invite rebuttals from the other side. **Negative or attack campaigning**, pointed personal criticism of the other candidate, is thus a normal if sometimes ugly component of the electoral process—and an effective one. Negative ads exploit voters' uncertainty inherent in the delegation of authority to powerful agents. Research suggests that negative ads inform people about both candidates and may also increase interest in elections. There is little evidence that people stay home on Election Day because they dislike attack ads.[12]

As negative campaigns have proved effective, candidates have sought to erect defenses against them. In 1988 Bush campaign adviser Lee Atwater created a series of attack ads that succeeded in branding Dukakis, who began the campaign unfamiliar to most voters, as a far-out liberal, soft on crime and weak on defense. Four years later, Clinton's strategists, determined to prevent a similar fate for their candidate, organized a rapid response team that blanketed the news media with forceful rebuttals of every charge made by Bush or his supporters, often on the same day charges were made. They also replied swiftly to negative television ads. For example, within forty-eight hours of the broadcast of a spot criticizing Clinton for his tax record while governor of Arkansas, the Clinton campaign produced, tested with a focus group, revised, and aired its own spot that included some text from the Bush ad with "UNTRUE" stamped across it.[13] The idea was to counter negative messages before they could sink in. The wisdom of this strategy was apparent in 2004, when John Kerry was evidently hurt by his slow reaction to charges from a group calling itself the Swift Boat Vets and POWs for Truth that had mounted an independent campaign harshly assailing his Vietnam service. In 2008 the McCain campaign's attempt to portray Obama as someone who, as Sarah Palin put it in her stump speech, "pals around with terrorists" was forcefully countered by the Obama campaign (and by Obama himself during the third debate), and most Americans came to regard the charge as unfair.[14]

One common explanation among commentators for Romney's loss in 2012 was his campaign's ineffective response to ads broadcast in swing states during the spring and summer, when many voters were just getting to know him, attacking him as a greedy venture capitalist, indifferent to the fates of people working for the companies he made a fortune buying, restructuring, and selling. Uncovering the effects of campaign ads on final vote choice, however, is challenging, because campaigns are cumulative, contemporaneous, and competitive enterprises. In other words, one side's gains may be immediately negated by the other side's response to those initial gains, making the observed effect of all this campaign effort small to nonexistent. The media like to report on elections as if they are boxing matches, with one side about to deliver a knock-out blow, but in reality, campaigns are more like a tug-of-war, with both sides pulling equally hard on the rope and the flag in the middle barely moving.[15]

This was not the case in 2016, which provides a unique chance to sort out whether campaign ads move people. In 2012, the candidates and groups advertising on their behalf ran nearly the same number of ads in the general election. In 2016, however, Hillary Clinton outadvertised Donald Trump by a factor of about three to one. All told, there were nearly 390,000 ads aired on behalf of Clinton and 123,000 on behalf of Trump. Interestingly, most of Clinton's advertisements were about the candidates' fitness for office—namely Trump's failings on that score. Nearly 76 percent of the appeals in Clinton's advertisements between June 1 and Election Day were about candidate traits. Almost half of Trump's appeals were about this, too. It seems in 2016 both candidates thought their best approach was to frame the other person as unfit to serve the highest office in the land (see Figure 11.2).

Between June and October, Clinton outadvertised Trump by at least 80 percent to 20 percent in eighteen states: Alabama, Arizona, California, Colorado, Florida, Iowa, Massachusetts, Nebraska, Nevada, New Hampshire, North Carolina, Ohio, Pennsylvania, South Carolina, Tennessee, Vermont, Virginia, and West Virginia. Trump outadvertised Clinton by at least 80 percent to 20 percent in only four states: Maine, Michigan, Texas, and Wisconsin.

Using these imbalances and the candidate vote share on each day in each state (as forecasted by the Upshot at the *New York Times*), you can see how the change in each candidate's share of the advertising in each state over this period affected the change in their vote share over the same time. As a candidate's vote share goes up, so do his or her poll numbers. In places like Arizona and Tennessee, where Clinton was on the air nearly alone between June and October, she gained nearly 5 points in vote share over the same time. Because candidates control only their own advertising efforts and not their opponent's, they don't have control

Negative campaign ads are a staple, if often disdained, component of presidential campaigns. The most effective ones take advantage of a candidate's constraints. Here, a super PAC reminds voters of the phrases Donald Trump has used to describe women, words like *bimbo* and *fat pig*. The ad reminds viewers that Trump has routinely disrespected women and is meant to suggest he is unfit to lead.

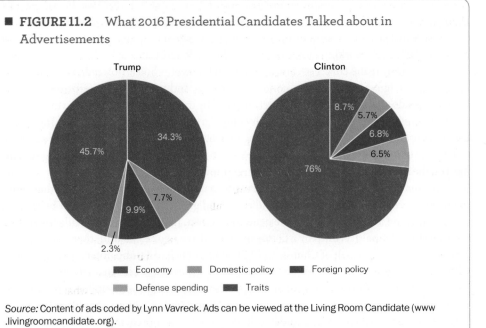

■ **FIGURE 11.2**  What 2016 Presidential Candidates Talked about in Advertisements

*Source:* Content of ads coded by Lynn Vavreck. Ads can be viewed at the Living Room Candidate (www .livingroomcandidate.org).

over where on the horizontal axis a state ends up. This makes it unlikely that they are just particularly good at guessing where there are easy votes to pick up by advertising there and more likely that the dominance of the advertising space is driving the increasing vote shares. On average, Clinton probably picked up about 2.6 points in the places she outadvertised Trump between June and October 2016.

Negative or not, campaign ads are rarely subtle, for their targets are the rationally ignorant, marginally involved voters who have not already made up their minds—not the informed political sophisticates or the confirmed partisans for whom the information provided by campaigns is superfluous. As one campaign consultant put it,

> The voters have a lot more important things on their minds than political campaigns. . . . Most of the people we are trying to reach with our message don't think about [campaigns] at all until late October. They don't read all the news magazines, the *Wall Street Journal,* and two local dailies. They don't watch CNN and C-SPAN. They watch "Wheel of Fortune," and they think about politics and campaigns less than five minutes a week.[16]

Simplicity, repetition, exaggeration, and symbolism (images of home, family, neighborhood, and flag) are therefore the staples of campaign advertising. Accuracy is not a priority; as Romney's chief pollster put it, "We're not going to let our campaign be dictated by fact checkers."[17] Flat-out lies are typically avoided in campaign ads, although 2016 saw a surge in the number of false claims made during the campaign. Campaigns "source" the facts they use in their campaign ads with citations at the bottom of the screen to think tanks or government agencies that support their view or information. Of course, a supporting source can be found for almost any piece of information, and the same voters who watch *Wheel of Fortune* are also unlikely to know the difference between the Government Accountability Office in the U.S. government and the U.S. Office of the Comptroller General, which may—or may not—be as objective an arbiter of information.

In the end, a successful campaign comes down to several basics. Its goal is to win a majority of votes, not every vote. Planners begin by using past voting records, polling, and telephone or door-to-door canvassing to figure out who is certain to support the candidate, who is up for grabs, and who is certain to support the opponent. The central clue here, at least for general elections, is the voter's party identification. The campaign is designed to appeal to the first two groups but especially to the second—particularly if, as is usually the case, the first does not amount to a majority. Campaign staffs find out where the swing voters live, what they care about, and what their mood and concerns are this year. The most sophisticated operations also now use the reams of commercially available data on individuals' characteristics, values, and tastes in "**microtargeting**" specific campaign messages to those they think are the most susceptible. Campaign strategists work to frame the choice—establish what the election is about—in a way that underlines their candidate's strengths and plays down his or her weaknesses. In doing so, they develop a simple, coherent campaign theme that explains both why the candidate should be elected and why the opponent should not. Finally, they repeat the theme ad nauseam to reach the crucial late-deciding voters who pay almost no attention to politics. None of these things, however, can be accomplished without money.

## The Other Necessity: Campaign Money

No matter how qualified candidates are or how powerful their message, neither will count for much if voters never hear about them. Thus the third requirement of a competitive campaign is an effective way to communicate with voters. For most of America's history, party organizations and newspapers were the chief conduits for political propaganda. Parties organized marches, rallies, and picnics; supplied the speakers; did the door-to-door canvassing of potential voters; and distributed pamphlets, broadsides, and posters bearing the campaign message. The campaign itself was a team affair, agitating for the election of all the party's candidates, although the spotlight usually was on the top of the ticket.

After World War II, however, patronage-based party organizations declined, and television gained popularity as a campaign medium (see Chapter 12). As a result, parties gradually lost their central role in campaigns, to the point that by the 1960s campaigns had largely become the province of individual candidates and their personal organizations. Candidates had to assemble their own campaign teams, raise the funds, hire the consultants and technical specialists, and design and execute their own individual campaign strategies, sometimes with the help of their national or local party organizations but often without it.

We may now be entering the post-television era—a time when on-demand viewing and personally cultivated media environments are beginning to dominate the way people interact with content. In 2016, for example, Donald Trump ran very few television ads relative to

Hillary Clinton. Instead, Trump dominated the media environment by tweeting his often provocative thoughts regularly. These tweets generated coverage by mainstream media as well as new media. More important, this strategy didn't cost him anything. Tweeting or sharing on other social media platforms is free. On the one hand, these platforms may help equalize the playing field for candidates, allowing those who cannot or do not want to raise money the opportunity to reach some of the same audiences as those candidates who can afford to advertise and do. On the other hand, we don't want to generalize too much from the campaign of a multibillionaire, reality TV star—Donald Trump may be the exception, not the new rule.

Most of the activities of typical campaigns cost money. Modern campaigns for federal office are expensive. There is simply no way for most candidates to organize and plan a campaign, do research, develop and package a message, and get that message out to potential voters on the cheap. Genuine electoral competition that gives voters a choice of agents and gives the winners an incentive to remain faithful (lest they be replaced) requires that candidates raise and spend money. According to the Center for Responsive Politics, the 2000 presidential election cost roughly $1.4 billion. In 2004, that number jumped to $1.9 billion, and in 2008 it catapulted up to $2.8 billion, the most ever. The 2012 contest was slightly less expensive at $2.6 billion, and the 2016 cycle came in at just over $1 billion.

The lack of spending by presidential candidates in 2016, however, should not be taken as a sign that the importance of money in politics is waning. The non–presidential year spending is equally impressive. In 2014, for example, total spending by all interested parties was $3.6 billion. Candidates and parties accounted for $2.7 billion of that and outside groups $700 million. Individual races were as pricey as ever, but 2016 and 2018 exceeded these numbers, making the last congressional races the priciest in history with more than $5 billion spent by all interested parties. Senate candidates in competitive races can spend upward of $25 million on their campaigns. Even House campaigns can be expensive, with many candidates spending multiple millions of dollars on their efforts.

### Regulating Campaign Money

Currently, all of the money spent on major campaigns for federal offices comes from private sources.* Privately financed elections inevitably raise two related problems for American democracy. First, democracy demands political equality: one person, one vote. But because money is distributed unequally, its role in electoral politics threatens democratic equality. Second, privately financed elections raise the suspicion that elected officials will serve as agents of their contributors rather than of their constituents. The dilemma, then, is that meaningful elections require money, but the pursuit of money may subvert the very purpose of elections.

---

*Federal matching funds are available for presidential candidates in both the nominating phase of the campaign and the general election campaign, separately. Serious (read *all*) candidates now refuse these funds from the government to avoid the spending limits they must adhere to if they accept the money. The first presidential candidate to do this in a general election was Barack Obama in 2008. It is unlikely any presidential candidates will ever return to using public funds to mount their campaigns for this limits what they can spend. In 2016, the limit was $96 million. If they refuse public financing, they can spend as much as they can raise. Clinton spent roughly $500 million and Trump about $250 million.

Efforts to resolve this dilemma through regulation have generally failed. Prior to the 1970s, campaign money was effectively unregulated. Congress had, from time to time, passed limits on contributions and spending, but the limits were easily circumvented and never enforced. This casual attitude toward campaign money faded with the spread of candidate-centered campaigns and the rise of broadcast campaigning, both of which quickly drove up costs. Higher costs accelerated not only the demand for campaign money but also the fear that the winners would favor contributors over constituents.

Congress's response was the Federal Election Campaign Act of 1971 (FECA), extensively amended in 1974. FECA provided partial public funding for presidential campaigns and required full public reporting of and strict limits on all contributions and expenditures in federal elections. It also established the Federal Election Commission to enforce the law and to collect and publish detailed information on campaign contributions and expenditures. The Supreme Court, in *Buckley v. Valeo* (1976), upheld the reporting requirements and contribution limits (to prevent "corruption or the appearance of corruption") but rejected spending limits on the ground that they interfered with political speech protected by the First Amendment.[18] Presidential candidates, however, could be required to abide by spending limits as a condition of receiving public funds for their campaigns. Also in *Buckley* the Court overturned, again on First Amendment grounds, ceilings on how much of their own money candidates could spend on their campaigns and on how much anyone could spend to agitate for or against candidates independently of candidates' campaigns.

Concerned that spending limits were choking off traditional local party activity in federal elections, Congress liberalized FECA in 1979, amending the act to allow unrestricted contributions and spending for state and local party-building and get-out-the-vote activities. A 1996 Court decision gave party organizations the right to unfettered independent spending as well.[19] Funds for these activities were commonly called **soft money**, as contrasted with the "hard money" raised and spent under FECA's limitations. When the unregulated soft money contributions to party committees ballooned, soft money became the favorite target of campaign finance reformers, and in March 2002 Congress passed the Bipartisan Campaign Reform Act (BCRA), which among other reforms prohibited parties from raising or spending soft party money for federal candidates. Aided by the high emotions generated by the presidential race, the parties countered by raising vastly increased sums of hard money, and many former soft money donors redirected their contributions to so-called 527 committees (named after the section of the tax code dealing with them) and to 501(c) committees ("charitable" groups under the tax code that can finance campaigns if they maintain the notion that they are merely informing voters, not advocating the election or defeat of particular candidates). Such committees together spent about $500 million on independent campaigns for—or, more often, against—the presidential candidates in 2004 and another $400 million in 2008. BCRA's attempt to limit independent campaigning by such groups was struck down by the Supreme Court in 2007. The Court went further in 2010, overturning precedent (in *Citizens United v. Federal Election Commission*) to invalidate any restriction on independent campaign spending by any organization, including corporations and labor unions, on the ground that groups enjoyed the same First Amendment protections as individuals.[20] The effect of these decisions is evident in the growth of nonparty independent and electioneering efforts by groups, which grew from $300 million in 2004 to about $1 billion in 2012 and nearly $1.5 billion in 2016.

**POLITICS TO POLICY**

# Soft Money Finds a New Home

The story of how campaign finance reform led to the flood of "soft money" in presidential election campaigns, and how reforms aimed at stemming the flood merely rechanneled it, exemplify the partisan conflicts, dilemmas, and unanticipated consequences that vex campaign finance policy. With their party in debt after the 1968 election, congressional Democrats embraced reform proposals that would limit campaign spending and finance presidential campaigns with public funds. Republican opposition to these reforms collapsed in the wake of the Watergate scandal, in which campaign finance abuses had figured prominently. After Richard Nixon resigned in August 1974 to avoid impeachment, his successor, Gerald Ford, who like Nixon opposed public financing of campaigns, reluctantly agreed to sign the Federal Election Campaign Act amendments, conceding that "the times demand this legislation."

Use of the new system in the 1976 elections exposed an unanticipated problem. To meet spending limits, the presidential campaigns focused on mass media advertising to take advantage of its efficiencies and maintained tight central control of all other campaign activity to avoid violating the law. State and local parties had little chance to participate, and the absence of the familiar paraphernalia of grassroots campaigns—bumper stickers, lapel buttons, yard signs—was widely noted and lamented. To preserve a role for local parties and grassroots activists in presidential campaigns, Congress in 1979 amended FECA to permit state and local parties to raise and spend money on party building, voter registration, and get-out-the-vote activities. No limits were placed on contributions or expenditures for these purposes, and, until the law was amended again in 1988, the sums involved did not even have to

be reported to the Federal Election Commission. These funds were nicknamed "soft money" to distinguish them from the tightly regulated "hard money" governed by the public funding system.

Permissive interpretations by the Federal Election Commission and the federal courts of what constituted "party building" allowed presidential candidates to raise and spend unlimited sums under the legal fiction that they were merely helping fertilize the grass roots. Consequently, presidential campaign finance became almost as wide open as it had been before the reforms of the 1970s. For years, partisan disagreements kept Congress from reforming the system, but finally in 2002, scandals surrounding the collapse of energy giant Enron, a generous donor of both hard and soft campaign money to both parties, induced majorities in both houses to pass the Bipartisan Campaign Reform Act despite strong opposition from Republican leaders. Among other things, BCRA banned soft money contributions to the parties, completely depriving them of this source of funds.

But soft money did not disappear. Tax-exempt groups organized under regulations in section 527 of the revenue code can raise unlimited money to spend on voter **mobilization**, issue advocacy, and almost any other campaign activity as long as they refrain from expressly advocating the election or defeat of a federal candidate and do not coordinate their activities with parties or candidates. In response to BCRA, most large soft money donors shifted to supporting 527 committees, whose financial participation in federal elections jumped from $151 million in 2002 to $405 million in 2004. With the Supreme Court's 2010 decision in

*Citizens United v. Federal Election Commission* tossing out all limits on independent spending, including campaigns paid for out of corporate and union treasuries, the total spent independently on federal campaigns by parties and political action committees reached nearly $1.5 billion in 2016. In April 2014, in *McCutcheon v. Federal Election Commission,* the Supreme Court removed the aggregate limit that individuals could give to candidates and parties,

too, although individuals must still adhere to the limits per candidate or party.

*Sources: Dollar Politics,* 3rd ed. (Washington, DC: Congressional Quarterly, 1982), 8–24; Frank J. Sorauf, *Inside Campaign Finance* (New Haven, CT: Yale University Press, 1992), 147–150; Steve Weissman and Ruth Hassan, "BCRA and the 527 Groups," in *The Election after Reform: Money, Politics, and the Bipartisan Campaign Reform Act,* ed. Michael Malbin (Lanham, MD: Rowman and Littlefield, 2006); http://reporting.sunlightfoundation.com/2012/return_on_investment; and Center for Responsive Politics.

### The Flow of Campaign Money

Although proponents of the original FECA had hoped to rein in the costs of campaigns, the flow of campaign money has continued to outpace inflation. Total funding from all sources for the general election campaigns for president rose from $453 million in 1996 to $676 million in 2000, $1.3 billion in 2004, and more than $2 billion in 2008, 2012, and 2016. Spending in House and Senate campaigns also has continued to grow since FECA took effect, rising by averages of about 9 percent in House elections and 12 percent in Senate elections (in inflation-adjusted dollars) from one election year to the next. Both supply and demand have driven campaign spending up. The supply of contributions continues to grow because the stakes represented by elections are so great, and the Internet has made it easier to connect with like-minded citizens and donors.

Although presidential candidates typically raise and spend about the same amount of money, House and Senate spending averages mask the huge variation in the amounts available to individual congressional candidates or spent on their behalf. Some candidates raise and spend millions, whereas others have to make do with almost nothing. A select minority of races attract heavy independent spending; the rest are largely ignored.

All types of contributors and independent spenders, with the possible exception of the candidates themselves, distribute their funds strategically. They avoid wasting resources on hopeless candidacies, preferring instead to put their money behind their favorites in races they expect to be close, where campaigning and therefore campaign spending might make a difference. Contributors also favor likely winners whose help they might need after the election. In practice, then, congressional incumbents, usually safe—or, at worst, in tight races for reelection—have the least trouble raising campaign funds. How much they actually acquire depends in good part on how much they think they need; the safer they feel, the less they raise and spend.

Does it matter how much candidates for down-ballot races are able to raise and spend? It matters only to the degree that a lack of money prevents candidates from getting their messages out and reaching voters. Campaign money has little to do with the results of general elections for president. The presidential candidates' campaigns always are at least adequately

Broadly speaking, campaign finance now operates through two parallel systems. Money going directly to candidates or parties is subject to limits on the size of contributions and full public disclosure of sources. Presidential candidates who accept public funds also must observe spending limits, though McCain was the last candidate who did so (and for the general election only). But in the other system, money raised and spent outside of the parties' and candidates' campaigns is not subject to limits or, in some forms, disclosure of contributors. In practice, this means that any citizen who wants to invest any amount of money in campaign activities can find a legal way to do so, and anonymously at that. These anonymous sources of funds have become known as dark money.

financed, and huge sums of additional money are now spent by party organizations and independent committees on the candidates' behalf. Add to this the abundant free information the media transmit about presidential candidates, and the resources are nearly always balanced—of course the content of these things may not be balanced!

Campaign money does matter in presidential primaries, in which rationally ignorant voters cannot rely on party labels as default cues and so need to know something about the candidates. Well-known candidates have a leg up, but lesser-known contenders, to have any chance at all, need to get the attention of voters, which almost always requires spending substantial sums of money. Held in January or February at the beginning of the primary season, the Iowa caucuses and New Hampshire primary once gave unknowns such as Jimmy Carter (1976) and Bill Clinton (1992) an opportunity to parlay relatively inexpensive early successes into fund-raising bonanzas for later primaries (see Chapter 12). But with so many states now holding primaries in February and March, candidates have little time to exploit unexpected success and cannot compete effectively without raising a great deal of money before the election year begins. In fact, the year before the election is now called the "invisible primary" because of the importance of fund-raising leading up to those first contests in the election year. In 2016, despite raising more money than any other contender, Jeb Bush was unable to turn his fund-raising success into votes. Donald Trump, who had raised virtually no money in the year before the election, went on to come in close in Iowa and win New Hampshire—setting the trajectory for his subsequent nomination. Money is not the key to winning—strategy, messaging, and a candidate's comparative advantage are all important elements of success.

In House and Senate races, money—specifically, the lack of it—is frequently decisive. Typically, half of Senate incumbents and 70 percent to 80 percent of House incumbents win by default because their opponents spend too little money to make a race of it (see Figure 11.3).

■ **FIGURE 11.3**   Incumbent versus Challenger: Campaign Spending in Contested House Elections

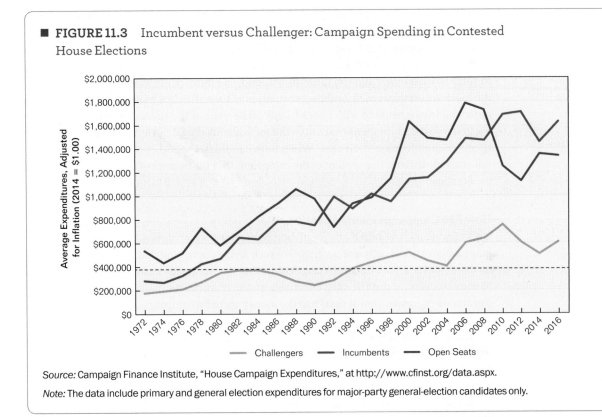

Source: Campaign Finance Institute, "House Campaign Expenditures," at http://www.cfinst.org/data.aspx.

Note: The data include primary and general election expenditures for major-party general-election candidates only.

Voters tend to reject candidates they know nothing about in favor of those they recognize. In the elections held from 1980 through 2008, an average of 92 percent of House voters and 96 percent of Senate voters recognized the incumbent's name. Awareness of the challengers was much less common; over the same period only 54 percent recognized the House challenger's name and 77 percent the Senate challenger's name. Challengers who do not improve substantially on these averages have no chance of winning, and few can do so without heavy campaign spending. But campaign spending has little effect on awareness of incumbents because voters already are familiar with them before the campaign begins.[21]

Campaign money, then, is much more important to challengers (and obscure candidates of any kind) than it is to incumbents or other well-known candidates. In House elections the more challengers spend, the more likely they are to win, but few spend enough to be competitive. Most House challengers spend less than $200,000. As challenger spending increases, so does the likelihood of winning. Curiously, though, the opposite appears true for incumbents. They are much more likely to spend at high levels, yet the higher their spending, the more likely they are to lose.

This surprising fact is a by-product of the strategies pursued by contributors and candidates. The more threatened incumbents feel, the more they raise and spend, but the additional effort does not fully offset the threat that provokes it. For incumbents, then, spending lavishly is a sign of electoral weakness that is ultimately registered at the polls. For challengers, higher spending is a sign, as well as a source, of electoral strength. Challengers with better prospects (attractive candidates with potentially effective messages) are able to raise more money; and the more they spend, the more professional their campaigns, the more voters they reach, and the more support they attract. Challengers do not have to outspend incumbents to win. Indeed, only 20 percent of the successful House challengers in the past decade spent more than the incumbents they defeated. They simply have to spend enough to make their case. When both candidates spend enough money to mount full-scale campaigns, the content of the campaigns, not the balance of resources, determines the outcome.

### How Are Campaign Funds Spent?

Once candidates have raised campaign money, they have to decide how to spend it, unless, like many congressional incumbents, they face such feeble opposition that they are free to pass it on to other candidates, donate to party committees, or stash it away for some future contest. No one is certain about the most effective way to use scarce campaign resources. The most commonly expressed view is that "half the money spent on campaigns is wasted. The trouble is, we don't know which half."

Because a fundamental goal of every campaign is to reach voters with the candidate's message, the largest expense is advertising, with television and radio ads leading the way. Presidential and Senate campaigns make heavier use of television advertising, whereas House campaigns use more "persuasion mail." The reason is efficiency. Media markets in large metropolitan areas may include as many as thirty House districts (e.g., greater New York). Thus House candidates opting for broadcast advertising have to pay for a station's entire audience, not just that fraction living in the target district. Mailings, by contrast, can be targeted precisely to district residents. Still, House campaigners with enough money often use television even where it is inefficient because it is the only way to reach many potential voters and avoids the risk of campaign brochures being tossed out as "junk mail."

Only a small proportion of spending goes for traditional campaigning—speeches, rallies, soliciting votes door to door, and shaking hands at the factory gate. Yet these activities remain a major part of every campaign because candidates hope to extend their impact far beyond the immediate audience by attracting news coverage. Campaigns display considerable imagination in coming up with gimmicks that will gain free media exposure; indeed, campaign professionals work so hard for it that they prefer to call it "earned" media. One particularly brave House challenger even traveled with a large pig to underline his opposition to the incumbent's "pork barrel politics." What local TV station could resist the visuals? Another tactic is running paid ads designed to provoke controversy. The ensuing news coverage then spreads the message to an audience much larger than the one originally exposed to the ad. Of course in 2016, Donald Trump pioneered the use of Twitter as a way to garner free media coverage. It is hard to believe that when Barack Obama became president in 2008, no prior officeholder had ever had a mobile device. There was considerable discussion before Obama's inauguration about whether the president would be allowed to carry a Blackberry! (The reason was security concerns about presidential communications.)

In pursuing favorable news coverage, presidential campaigns were already in a class by themselves, but Trump took things to a new level. Modern presidential campaigns are basically made-for-TV productions. Candidates tolerate grueling travel schedules, participate in countless carefully staged events, and compose pithy "sound bites" and tweets—short comments designed to be excerpted—to get their messages on the news and out to the voters. Although the media have changed, there are a lot of similarities between the goal of George H. W. Bush's "Read my lips. No new taxes" in 1988 and Donald Trump's "I refuse to call Megyn Kelly a bimbo. That would not be politically correct" in 2016. Large rallies are another successful example of staged events aimed at generating media coverage. Whether Bill Clinton and Al Gore's bus tour, Barack Obama's stadium speeches, or Donald Trump's overnight sold-out crowds, candidates view these events as ways to demonstrate popularity and enthusiasm—all for a TV audience far beyond the location of the event itself. Presidential candidates also exploit soft news and entertainment shows. In recent elections, both parties' candidates have made multiple appearances on television's talk and comedy shows. In 2008, Sarah Palin and Hillary Clinton went on *Saturday Night Live* to joke with Tina Fey and Amy Poehler, who had been parodying them in the comedy show's sketches, and John McCain went on David Letterman's show to stop the needling Letterman had been giving him for having canceled an appearance a few weeks earlier. In 2015, Donald Trump made multiple appearances with Jimmy Fallon on the *Tonight Show* and also hosted *Saturday Night Live*. The campaigns take these events seriously, for these shows likely reach audiences who do not otherwise pay much attention to political news.

When it comes to media coverage, the rich get richer, and the poor get ignored. The best-funded campaigns (for president or hotly contested Senate seats) get the most attention from the news media. Poorly funded candidates may be desperate for news coverage because they cannot afford to buy airtime, yet the very fact of their poverty makes them look like sure losers and therefore not worth covering. Campaigns that must depend on the news media to get their messages out invariably fail. Trump, of course, was different because he was already famous as a reality TV star and billionaire.

A large share of congressional campaign funds pays for expenses not directly connected to reaching voters. One study found that nearly a quarter of the money spent went into overhead—staff salaries, office and furniture rental, computers and other equipment, telephone calls, travel, legal and accounting services, and the like. Every serious campaign now also has a digital presence and branding designed to attract volunteers and contributors as well as to get out the campaign's message. Fund-raising is another major expense, particularly for Senate candidates, who spend 20 percent of their money on just raising more money. Because of their larger constituencies, Senate candidates usually have to raise bigger sums than House candidates do.

## Where Are Presidential Campaign Funds Spent?

Presidential candidates invest heavily in television advertising, the most effective way to reach an electorate of more than 100 million people. In recent elections the campaigns have together spent hundreds of millions of dollars on television time. Decisions about where to spend the money are dominated by the design of the Electoral College (see box "The Electoral College"), which encourages a strategy of focusing on states with large numbers of electoral votes that are not securely in one party's camp rather than on the national electorate. Whoever wins the

# The Electoral College

## Where the Big States Hold the Cards

The Constitution's formula for allocating electoral votes to each state is simple: number of senators plus the number of representatives equals the number of votes in the Electoral College. This formula heavily favors the populous states, which not only have a lot of electoral votes but, following a rule adopted by all states except Nebraska and Maine, award all their electoral votes to the candidate receiving the most votes. This winner-take-all rule means that California with its 55 electoral votes, Texas with 38, and New York and Florida with 29 each carry the most electoral weight. Based on the 2010 census, the ten most populous states in the nation control 256 of the 270 electoral votes needed to elect a president. By contrast, the thirteen least populous states have only 46 electoral votes—fewer than those held by the largest state, California.

The largest states do not necessarily see the most action, however, because some of them are reliably in one party's column. In recent elections, California and New York have been safely Democratic, while Republicans have had a lock on Texas. White House hopefuls plan their campaign stops accordingly, heavily crisscrossing those vote-rich states that are not firmly in one party's hands—such as Florida, Ohio, North Carolina, and Virginia in 2012—at the expense of the vote-poor states and those not considered in play.

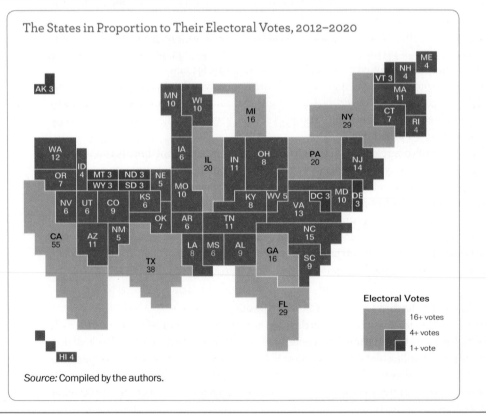

The States in Proportion to Their Electoral Votes, 2012–2020

Electoral Votes
16+ votes
4+ votes
1+ vote

*Source:* Compiled by the authors.

An ongoing criticism of the Electoral College system is that a candidate can win a plurality of the popular vote nationally but still not be elected because of failure to gain a majority in the Electoral College. This happened to presidential candidates Andrew Jackson in 1824, Samuel J. Tilden in 1876, Grover Cleveland in 1888, Al Gore in 2000, and Hillary Clinton in 2016. Jackson and Cleveland succeeded, however, in their next runs for the office. More typically, the electoral vote merely exaggerates the margin of victory of the winner of the popular vote. In 1992, for example, Bill Clinton won 43.3 percent of the popular vote but 68.7 percent of the electoral vote; Barack Obama won 52.6 percent of the popular vote but 67.7 percent of the electoral vote in 2008, and 51.1 percent of the popular vote but 61.2 percent of the electoral vote in 2012. The 2000 and 2004 elections, however, proved exceptions to the rule. In 2000, George W. Bush's share of the popular vote (47.8 percent) nearly equaled his slice of the electoral vote (50.4 percent); the two figures were equally close in 2004, when Bush won 50.7 percent of the popular vote and 53.2 percent of the electoral vote. Despite the lack of fidelity between the margins in the popular vote and the Electoral College vote, bounding contests by geography has some advantages. One of them is the ability to contain the effects of fraud. If someone managed to manipulate the vote in two large metropolitan areas, like New York and Los Angeles, for example, the Electoral College makes it difficult for this manipulation to determine the outcome of the election, more so than under a method that relied solely on popular vote margins.

most popular votes in a state, except for Maine and Nebraska, gets all of its electoral votes no matter how narrow the margin of victory.* The object of a presidential campaign, then, is to piece together enough state victories to win at least 270 electoral votes.

When the election is expected to be close, the obvious strategy is to concentrate on states that polls indicate could go either way and to ignore entirely states that seem locked up by either side. For example, in 2012, the campaigns focused on a narrow set of so-called battleground states that preelection surveys suggested were seriously in play. Both candidates invested heavily in the largest of these states in 2012—Florida (29 electoral votes), Pennsylvania (20), Ohio (18), and initially Michigan (16; the Romney campaign ceded Michigan early in the fall). But in 2016, only Hillary Clinton was on the air for much of the summer. She focused on some of the same states as the candidates did in 2012—Florida, Pennsylvania, and Ohio—and outadvertised Donald Trump in those states by nearly two to one. But she set aside places like Michigan and Wisconsin, where Trump was outadvertising her over the summer. The vast majority of the TV campaign ads were broadcast in battleground-state media markets, with Florida and Ohio seeing the majority. Most are also shown on broadcast television networks during and around the local and morning news programs.

Even a large imbalance in advertising, however, may not be able to overcome controversial events that get reported in the news. As Election Day drew near in 2016, lingering doubts about Clinton's use of a private e-mail server reemerged as the FBI director sent a letter to Congress regarding e-mails between Clinton and her aides that were discovered on a laptop

*In Maine and Nebraska the electoral vote can be divided if one congressional district votes for a candidate who loses statewide.

Justin Sullivan/Getty Images

Democratic presidential candidate Hillary Clinton speaks at a campaign rally in Michigan just one day before the election in 2016. Despite her campaigning in several key states in the days leading up to the election and a barrage of advertising, Clinton lost Michigan along with Wisconsin and Pennsylvania. Winning just 77,000 more votes in these three states would have given her the advantage in the Electoral College and the White House.

the bureau had just seized as part of the Anthony Wiener sexting investigation. After the news broke, the Clinton campaign went on the air with ads in Michigan and Wisconsin, but even after the FBI director exonerated Clinton a few days later of any additional wrongdoing in the matter of the server, she lost both Michigan and Wisconsin, along with Ohio, Florida, and Pennsylvania. These losses gave Trump more than enough Electoral College votes, and he became the president-elect of the United States on November 8, 2016.

The story of the 2016 election is more complicated than Trump's Electoral College victory implies. Despite handily winning the Electoral College, Trump lost the popular vote by nearly 3 million. This is largely a function of the fact that Clinton did better than Obama in 2012 in places like California, Arizona, and Texas (places with large populations of Latino voters), but she did worse almost everywhere else, particularly in places like West Virginia, Ohio, and Iowa.

The 2016 election provides two examples of money not being the key to winning—Jeb Bush in the primaries and Clinton in the general election—but these unexpected outcomes both have one thing in common: Donald Trump. Because of this, it is premature to generalize about future elections and the role of campaigns and money.

## The Logic of Elections Revisited

Despite all the problems with U.S. elections, they work remarkably well to preserve American democracy. Regular, free, competitive elections guard the nation against the dangers that inevitably arise when citizens delegate authority to governments. Elections allow citizens, as principals, to pick their agents and to fire and replace those whose performance falls short. The threat of replacement provides elected officials with a powerful incentive to listen to their constituents. Elections also create incentives for entrepreneurs and organizations to solve the free-rider and coordination problems that beset citizens acting as collective principals. Aspiring leaders and their political allies compete for votes by keeping an eye on officials and informing citizens about their shortcomings, paying the information costs that individual citizens would not rationally pay. Similarly, by getting out the vote on Election Day they turn citizens who might otherwise rationally abstain from casting a ballot into voters. They also bear much of the cost, through polling and focus groups, of keeping track of what citizens want from their agents in government, again making up for the lack of rational incentives for individual political expression. But all of these activities cost money, and the campaign finance system presents its own set of agency problems that are not easily solved.

Elections also induce candidates and campaigns to help solve the massive coordination problem faced by millions of voters trying to act collectively to control or replace their agents. By offering competing frames for a voting decision, they clarify and focus the electoral choice to the point where rationally ignorant voters can manage it. Candidates' opportunistic choice of issues puts voters' concerns on the agenda and helps make election results intelligible: in 2012, for example, a crucial issue really *was* the appropriate strategy for invigorating the economy and bringing down the deficit. When candidates form relatively stable coalitions with other would-be leaders—that is, combine into political parties—they narrow the choices to a manageable number, often as few as two. Indeed, party labels simplify voters' choices across offices and over a series of elections. They also allow voters to hold elected officials collectively responsible for their performance in office. In other words, elections create strong links between public opinion and government action. *But they do so only because politically ambitious people have found that it serves their own purposes to engage in the activities that forge the links.* One durable institutional by-product of political ambition pursued under American electoral rules, the party system, is the subject of the next chapter.

**⑨SAGE edge™**
for CQ Press

**Want a better grade?**

Get the tools you need to sharpen your study skills. Access practice quizzes, eFlashcards, video, and multimedia at **edge.sagepub.com/kernell9e.**

# KEY TERMS

candidate  489
focus group  491
issue voting  487
message  489
microtargeting  497

mobilization  500
negative or attack
  campaigning  494
party identification  487
party label  487

performance voting  487
single-issue voters  485
soft money  499

## SUGGESTED READINGS

Campbell, Angus, Philip E. Converse, Warren E. Miller, and Donald E. Stokes. *The American Voter.* Chicago: University of Chicago Press, 1976. First published in 1960, this seminal survey-based study of American voting behavior presents the classic psychological theory of party identification. It is still essential reading for every student of American politics.

Downs, Anthony. *An Economic Theory of Democracy.* New York: Harper and Row, 1957. The seminal theoretical work explaining how electoral and party politics reflect rational strategies of candidates and voters.

Fiorina, Morris P. *Retrospective Voting in American National Elections.* New Haven, CT: Yale University Press, 1981. Survey-based study supporting the Downsian theory of party identification as a running tally of positive and negative experiences with the parties' performance in government.

Lupia, Arthur, and Mathew D. McCubbins. *The Democratic Dilemma: Can Citizens Learn What They Need to Know?* New York: Cambridge University Press, 1998. The answer, according to the theory and experimental evidence reported in this book, is a clear yes; despite "rational ignorance," people use freely available cues to make reasoned choices among candidates.

Popkin, Samuel L. *The Reasoning Voter: Communication and Persuasion in Presidential Campaigns.* 2nd ed. Chicago: University of Chicago Press, 1994. How voters use "gut reasoning" and information shortcuts to decide how to vote in primary and general elections for president.

Popkin, Samuel L. *The Candidate: What It Takes to Win—and Hold—the White House.* New York: Oxford University Press, 2012. The three things presidential campaigns have to accomplish to win, and why what got you there won't keep you there when you run for reelection.

Rosenstone, Steven J., and John Mark Hansen. *Mobilization, Participation, and Democracy in America.* New York: Macmillan, 1993. The most prominent and intractable question in American politics is why voter turnout has declined over the past thirty years. Rosenstone and Hansen offer the closest thing we have to an answer that is actually supported by evidence.

Sides, John, and Lynn Vavreck. *The Gamble: Choice and Chance in the 2012 Presidential Election.* Princeton, NJ: Princeton University Press, 2013. The effects of campaigns are hard to uncover because elections are like a tug-of-war, not a boxing match. Both sides fight hard with roughly equal resources to win votes.

Vavreck, Lynn. *The Message Matters: The Economy and Presidential Campaigns.* Princeton, NJ: Princeton University Press, 2009. What matters in campaigns and thus election outcomes is not just the state of the economy but how candidates and campaigns react to it.

## REVIEW QUESTIONS

1.  What are the potential problems with delegating authority to representatives in government? How do elections help reduce these risks?

2.  What benefits do people get from voting? Which of these benefits do they still receive if they personally do not vote?

3. Voting, in effect, makes voters choose between a future governed by candidate A and one governed by candidate B. Most voters can't predict the future. What tools allow voters to make these predictions of future performance?

4. What is the most important personal characteristic for predicting a person's vote in a federal election for president or Congress?

5. What is the most important aggregate statistic in predicting which party is likely to win a presidential election?

6. What do candidates spend most of their money on? Is money enough to win? Does it help all candidates equally? What type of candidate benefits the most from increased spending?

National conventions display party politics in its most colorful and distilled form. Here, Donald Trump and his running mate, Mike Pence, are greeted with unrestrained enthusiasm by delegates to the 2016 Republican National Convention.

Win McNamee/Getty Images

# Political Parties

# 12

## KEY QUESTIONS

- Why does a nation as diverse as the United States sustain only two major parties?

- If the first generation of leaders elected under the Constitution rejected political parties on principle, why did they create them anyway?

- Today national party conventions merely certify the winners of primary elections instead of choosing the presidential nominees, as they did in the past. So why do the parties continue to hold these gatherings?

- Ninety percent of Americans claim they always vote for the person best suited for the job, regardless of party. Why, then, is party-line voting so prevalent, and why are partisans so polarized?

## CHAPTER OBJECTIVES

**12.1** Describe the origins of political parties and their basic features.

**12.2** Summarize the development and evolution of the party systems.

**12.3** Discuss the revival of partisanship over the past two decades and how modern parties are structured.

**12.4** Assess modern parties' influence and effectiveness as a vehicle for politicians and voters to act collectively within the established institutional framework.

In 2016, billionaire real estate investor Donald Trump executed a hostile takeover of the Republican Party. Nearly the entire Republican establishment—elected leaders, elder statesmen, most major campaign contributors, and many prominent conservative pundits—opposed his nomination. They objected variously to his personality, character, inexperience, temperament, and unorthodox positions on economic and foreign policy issues. They considered Trump's divisive rhetoric targeting immigrants and minorities a threat to the party's short- and long-term prospects by alienating, perhaps permanently, growing segments of the electorate.[1] Trump swept the primaries anyway by tapping into the rich vein of right-wing populist disdain for cultural, corporate, media, and political elites found in a large faction of Republican voters. Failing to derail Trump's candidacy, many prominent Republican leaders stayed away from the nominating convention and declined to endorse him afterward. Most House and Senate candidates running on the Republican ticket initially backed Trump rather than risk offending his supporters, but some deserted after a 2005 videotape showed Trump bragging about his sexual exploits, including groping assaults on women.

A lot of ordinary Republican voters also had serious reservations about their party's nominee; during the month before the election, an average of 30 percent expressed unfavorable opinions of Trump, compared with the more typical 8 percent expressing unfavorable opinions of Republican nominee Mitt Romney in 2012.[2] On average, only 70 percent said Trump was qualified to be president; only 62 percent said he has the right temperament for the office; and only 57 percent said he respects women.[3] Most Democratic leaders supported Trump's opponent, Hillary Clinton, but ordinary Democrats, especially those who had supported her main opponent in the primaries, Bernie Sanders, were less enthusiastic; 18 percent held an unfavorable opinion of her, compared with 8 percent for Barack Obama in 2012.

As these numbers show, in 2016 both presidential candidates, but Trump in particular, went into the general election with divided parties and historically low levels of popularity within their parties and among the general public. Most voters, as usual, also took a dim view of the parties themselves. Large majorities of Americans claim they vote for the candidate they think is best suited for the office, regardless of party. Typically, more than half tell pollsters that the two major parties "do such a poor job that a third major party is needed."[4] Most Americans also usually say they prefer that control of government be divided between the parties rather than monopolized by one party.[5] The situation in 2016 thus seemed ripe for voters to desert their party (crossing party lines or voting for third-party candidates) or split their tickets (voting for different parties' candidates for president and Congress) in large numbers. They did not. Nearly 95 percent voted for a major-party presidential candidate.

For partisans, antipathy toward the other party and its presidential candidate swamped any reservations voters may have had about their own,[6] and self-identified Republicans and Democrats voted nearly as loyally for their presidential and congressional candidates as they had in 2012, which featured the highest incidence of party-line voting in at least seven decades.[7] Election results set a new record for consistency across states and districts. For the first time in history, every Senate contest was won by the party that won the state's electoral votes. The coincidence of party victories at the House district level was nearly as high, approaching 92 percent. Despite Trump's highly unorthodox and disruptive candidacy and the internal divisions within both parties exposed by the primary contests, differences between the parties remained far more important to voters, and the election of 2016 was as partisan, polarized, and nationalized as it had been in 2012.[8]

Clearly, reports of the parties' demise, common a couple of decades ago, no longer match reality.[9] Indeed, anyone who looks at how people vote and evaluate politicians, which candidates win elections, and how the nation is governed will have to conclude that the two major parties rarely have been healthier. A large majority of voters are willing to identify themselves as Republicans or Democrats, and, of these partisans, a very large majority routinely vote loyally for their party's candidates. Rarely does anyone win state or federal office without a major-party nomination; as of 2019, all fifty state governors and all but two of the 535 members of Congress were either Democrats or Republicans.* Moreover, party remains the central organizing instrument in government (see Chapter 6).

---

*Two independents serve in the 116th Congress (2019–2020): Senator Bernie Sanders of Vermont and Senator Angus King of Maine. Of the 7,383 citizens serving in state legislatures in 2019, only thirty-two (0.43 percent) were neither Democrats nor Republicans.

The wide gap between people's opinions about and behavior toward political parties has deep roots in American history. None of the politicians who designed the Constitution or initially sought to govern under it thought parties were a good idea—including the very people who unwittingly created them. Even in their heyday in the latter part of the nineteenth century, parties never lacked articulate critics or public scorn. Still, parties began to develop soon after the founding of the nation and, in one guise or another, have formed an integral part of the institutional machinery of American politics ever since. The chief reason for their longevity is that the institutions created by the Constitution make the payoffs for using parties—to candidates, voters, and elected officeholders—too attractive to forgo. American political parties represent the continuing triumph of pure political expedience.

Although expedience explains the existence of the parties, the activities that maintain them contribute to successful democratic politics in unforeseen ways. Indeed, the unintended consequences of party work are so important that most political scientists agree with E. E. Schattschneider, who said that "political parties created democracy and [that] modern democracy is unthinkable save in terms of parties."[10] Parties recruit and train leaders, foster political participation, and teach new citizens democratic habits and practices. Beyond that, they knit citizens and leaders together in electoral and policy coalitions and allow citizens to hold their elected agents collectively responsible for what the government does. They also help channel and constrain political conflicts, promoting their peaceful resolution. Finally, parties organize the activities of government, facilitating the collective action necessary to translate public preferences into public policy (see Chapters 6 and 7). In short, political parties make mass democracy possible.

This chapter examines the origin and development of national parties in the United States and explains what parties are, why and how they were invented, and how they have evolved.

Scholars have proposed a variety of formal definitions of **political party**. Two of the most prominent stand in clear contrast to each other (except in their conventional sexism). Edmund Burke, an eighteenth-century British politician and political philosopher, defined a party as "a body of men united for promoting by their joint endeavors the national interest, upon some particular principle in which they are all agreed."[11] Anthony Downs, in his modern classic *An Economic Theory of Democracy,* defined a party as "a team of men seeking to control the governing apparatus by gaining office in a duly constituted election."[12] Although rhetorical references to principle are a staple of party politics, the American parties have displayed a shared appetite for public office a good deal more consistently than they have for the pursuit of shared principles.

## The Constitution's Unwanted Offspring

The Constitution contains no mention of political parties. During the nation's founding, parties were widely considered to be dangerous to good government and public order, especially in republics (see box "No One Wanted to Party"). In such an intellectual climate, no self-respecting leader would openly set out to organize a political party.

The pervasive fear of parties reflected both historical experience and widely held eighteenth-century social beliefs. Factional conflict brought to mind the bloody religious and political wars of England's past and the internal strife that destroyed the republics in ancient

## No One Wanted to Party

In the early years of the United States, conventional wisdom inveighed against political parties. Benjamin Franklin spoke out against the "infinite mutual abuse of parties, tearing to pieces the best of characters."[a] In *Federalist* No. 10 James Madison called them a species of "faction," which, by definition, holds intentions "adverse to the rights of other citizens, or to the permanent and aggregate interests of the community." George Washington used his farewell address to "warn . . . in the most solemn manner against the baneful effects of the Spirit of Party, generally,"[b] and his successor, John Adams, averred that "a division of the republic into two great parties . . . is to be dreaded as the greatest political evil under our Constitution."[c] Even Thomas Jefferson once declared, "If I could not get to heaven but with a party, I would not go there at all."[d]

[a]Richard Hofstadter, "The Idea of a Party System," in *After the Constitution: Party Conflict in the New Republic*, ed. Lance Banning (Belmont, CA: Wadsworth, 1989), 20.

[b]Nobel E. Cunningham, ed., *The Making of the American Party System: 1789 to 1809* (Englewood Cliffs, NJ: Prentice Hall, 1965), 16.

[c]Hofstadter, "The Idea of a Party System," 20.

[d]Richard Hofstadter, *The Idea of a Party System: The Rise of Legitimate Opposition in the United States, 1780–1840* (Berkeley: University of California Press, 1970), 123.

Greece and Rome and, later, the city-states of Renaissance Italy. Society was viewed ideally as a harmonious whole, its different parts sharing common interests that all wise and honest authorities would dutifully promote. People in authority saw themselves as agents acting on behalf of the whole community; any organized opposition was therefore misguided at best, treasonous at worst. Accepting the same perspective, rivals justified their opposition by imagining that those in power were betrayers of the community's trust. When the leaders of the new government took the steps that led to the creation of the first political parties, they did not expect or want party competition to become a permanent feature of American politics. Rather, their aim was to have the common good—their version, naturally—prevail and their opponents consigned to oblivion. The first parties were created as temporary expedients.

Expedient they were, but temporary they were not. The First Amendment's guarantees of freedom to speak, write, and assemble ensured that party activities would be legal. Beyond that, the framework of institutions established by the Constitution created powerful incentives for undertaking the activities that created and sustained parties. The design of the Constitution also had a profound effect on the kind of parties that developed. The party system has changed in important ways over the years as political entrepreneurs have adapted parties to new purposes and opportunities, but the basic features that reflect the constitutional system have reappeared in every period.

### Incentives for Party Building

The political incentives that spawned parties are transparent. In any system where collective choices are made by voting, organization pays. When action requires winning majorities on a continuing basis in multiple settings, organization is absolutely essential. The Constitution's

provisions for enacting laws and electing leaders therefore put a huge premium on building majority alliances across institutions and electoral units. Parties grew out of the efforts of political entrepreneurs to build such alliances and to coordinate the collective activity necessary to gain control of and use the machinery of government.

### To Build Stable Legislative and Electoral Alliances

The first American parties appeared in Congress when leaders with opposing visions of the nation's future began competing for legislative votes. Passing legislation requires majority support in the House and Senate. Any leader wanting to get Congress to act has to identify enough supporters to make up a majority, arrange a common course of action, and then get supporters to show up and vote. To control policy consistently, then, legislative leaders found it advantageous to cultivate a stable group of supporters, forming durable alliances that sharply reduced the transaction costs of negotiating a winning coalition on each new proposal. Because lawmaking powers are shared by three institutions—the presidency, the House, and the Senate—the value of alliances that cross institutional boundaries was also obvious.

Given the diversity of American society, it is impossible for stable alliances of any appreciable size to be built solely on shared interests or values. Rather, alliances are, by necessity, coalitions: participants have to agree to cooperate on action even though they have different,

Both major parties are coalitions with internal divisions over policy and ideology that often threaten to pull them apart. Desire for majority status, however, provides a powerful incentive for party factions to hang together despite their disagreements.

even conflicting reasons for doing so. Holding diverse coalitions together takes continuing political effort, for participants cooperate only as long as it serves their purposes. The sustained organizational effort needed to keep legislative coalitions working in harmony produces legislative parties.

Organized competition for votes in Congress leads directly to organized competition for votes in congressional elections. Coalitions vying for majority status need to recruit like-minded candidates and work to elect them; successful legislative alliances in Washington depend on successful electoral alliances in the states and districts. The organizational work required to negotiate and maintain electoral alliances expands legislative parties into electoral parties.

The presidential selection rules also offer compelling reasons for building electoral alliances across districts and states. The Constitution assigns selection of the president to the Electoral College or, if no candidate wins a majority of electors, to the House of Representatives. Many early observers expected the House to make the choice most of the time, believing that sectional jealousies would keep a majority of electors from uniting behind a single candidate. In fact, sectional rivalries and the competing ambitions of the larger states were constant sources of political friction. The incentives embodied in the rules for selecting the president provide a powerful counterweight to sectionalism, however. If an alliance can recruit and elect people pledged to one candidate in enough states, it can win the presidency. The alternative is to stack the House of Representatives with enough supporters to make the alliance's choice prevail should no candidate win a majority in the Electoral College. In either case, the problem is to sustain cooperation among numerous politicians, often with divergent purposes and interests, across great distances. To the degree that the effort succeeds, the result is a national party organization.

### To Mobilize Voters

No matter how well organized, electoral alliances fail if they cannot get enough people to vote for their candidates. The competition for votes motivates alliance leaders to attract voters and get them to the polls. In the early days of the Republic, electioneering followed traditional forms. The natural agents of a harmonious society were thought to be its most prominent and successful members, and a community's interests were assumed to be safest in the hands of those with superior breeding, education, and experience in public affairs. Restrictions on suffrage were common (see Chapter 11). Those who could vote made their preferences known orally and in public, a practice that encouraged deference to the local gentry. The elections themselves were decided largely on a personal basis; contests, if they arose, were between individuals backed by their personal followers. In such circumstances, open pursuit of political office was thought to be unseemly, and campaigns had to be conducted on the sly, through friends and allies. This is not to say that election campaigns were unknown; after all, the techniques of soliciting support and rounding up votes had been known for centuries because elections had been held for centuries. But they were techniques designed for small communities with even smaller electorates that, for the most part, took their cues from local worthies.

After the adoption of the Constitution, property and other qualifications for (white male) voting were progressively reduced or eliminated, and the egalitarian spirit of the frontier gradually eclipsed the habits of deference, even in the older states. As the size of the electorate increased, so did the task of identifying and attracting supporters and getting them to show up at the polls. Whoever could win over these new voters would enjoy a distinct political advantage. The networks of leaders and activists assembled to mobilize electoral support became the first party organizations.

### To Develop New Electoral Techniques

Once organized, electoral parties initiated new relationships between voters and elected leaders. The personal appeals and services that candidates had used to win the support of their neighbors since colonial times did not disappear, but they were, by themselves, inadequate for reaching a much larger, dispersed, and anonymous electorate. Party organizers turned to mass communications—newspapers, pamphlets, public letters, and printed speeches—designed to excite voters with emotional appeals on issues. The temptation to press hot buttons was irresistible when campaigns sought to persuade politically unsophisticated and uninvolved people that they had a stake in the election and a compelling reason to vote. Anyone trying to mobilize citizens to vote also has to overcome the electorate's tendency to free ride, for a party's victory is a collective good that its supporters get to enjoy whether or not they vote (see Chapter 11). Since the beginning, then, much of the work of campaigns has been aimed at overcoming, by one means or another, the free-rider problem.

### To Use Party Labels and Enforce Collective Responsibility

Voters need a way to distinguish among candidates, and party labels offer a serviceable shorthand cue that keeps voting decisions cheap and simple—as long as the labels are informative. The more accurately a candidate's party label predicts what he or she will do in office, the more useful it is to voters and the more voters will rely on party cues in making their choices. In addition, the more voters rely on party cues, the more valuable party labels

KAMIL KRZACZYNSKI/AFP/Getty Images

Getting voters to the polls is among the oldest and most important party activities, and the Democrats' successful mobilization efforts were crucial to their takeover of the House in 2018. Exploiting the antipathy toward the Trump presidency common among ordinary Democrats, activists and their allies raised the total vote for their House candidates by more than 25.1 million over their 2014 midterm total. Counterefforts by Republican Party activists offset these gains only partially, adding 10.9 million voters to their 2014 totals. In combination, the parties' efforts produced the highest midterm turnout in a century, 50.3 percent (see Figure 12.3), up from 36.7 percent in 2014.

are to candidates. Would-be leaders adopt one of the existing political identities to benefit from the electorate's cue-taking habits. Local candidates join national party alliances even though local political divisions may have no logical relation to the issues that national parties fight about.

Once they have adopted the party label, however, politicians have a personal stake in maintaining the value of their party's "brand name," which may impose conformity costs by requiring the subordination of their own views and ambitions to the party's welfare and reputation. Party labels allow voters to reward or punish elected officials as a group for their performance in office. If voters do not like what the government is doing and want to "throw the rascals out," they have an easy way to identify the rascals: they are members of the majority party. The threat of collective punishment gives the majority party a strong incentive to govern in ways that please voters. Parties, then, developed into three-part systems connecting (1) the party in government, an alliance of current officeholders cooperating to shape public policy; (2) the party organization, dedicated to electing the party's candidates; and (3) the party in the electorate, composed of those voters who identify with the party and regularly vote for its nominees.[13]

## Basic Features of the Party System

Parties emerged, then, not because anyone thought they were a good idea but because the institutional structures and processes established by the Constitution made them too useful to forgo. Their obvious value to elected leaders competing for political goods, to candidates competing for office and groups competing for political power, and to voters in search of cognitive shortcuts to voting decisions guaranteed that parties' practical virtues would be rediscovered by every political generation. Parties have not always taken the same form, to be sure. But certain features reappear in every historical party system because they reflect the basic constitutional structure of American government. These features include competition between two major parties made up of decentralized, fragmented party coalitions maintained by professional politicians.

### Two-Party Competition

During the first few Congresses, national leaders gradually divided into two major camps, initiating a pattern of two-party competition that has continued, with a few brief interruptions, to this day. Americans tend to think of a **two-party system** as normal, but other modern democracies have more than two parties (see Figure 12.1). It is, in fact, remarkable that a people continually divided by region, religion, race, and ethnicity, not to mention social beliefs and economic interests, could fit into as few as two major political camps. But this pattern has continued for a compelling reason. In any election where a single winner is chosen by plurality vote (whoever gets the most votes wins), there is a strong tendency for serious competitors to be reduced to two because people tend to vote strategically. If their favorite party's candidate has no chance to win, they turn to the less objectionable of the major-party candidates who does have a chance to win (see Logic of Politics box, "Third-Party Blues"). This tendency is so strong that scholars have given it the status of a law, known as Duverger's law, named after the

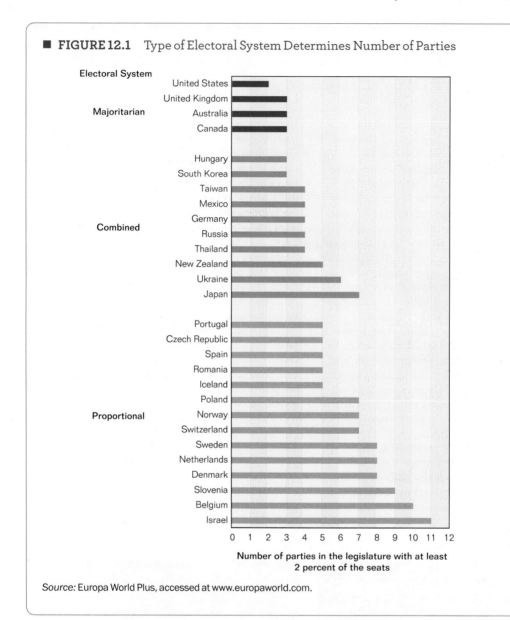

**■ FIGURE 12.1** Type of Electoral System Determines Number of Parties

*Source:* Europa World Plus, accessed at www.europaworld.com.

French political scientist who articulated it.[14] Office seekers, aware of this pattern, usually join one of the two competitive parties rather than pursuing office as independents or third-party nominees.

This logic is sufficiently compelling that, at most, only an election or two is required after the disruption of old party alliances and the appearance of new party coalitions for voters to

## LOGIC OF POLITICS
# Third-Party Blues

Third-party and independent candidates have a hard time with the winner-take-all electoral system. Even in 2016, when both parties nominated unpopular presidential candidates disliked by an unusual number of voters in their own parties, support for the minor-party alternatives—Gary Johnson (Libertarian) and Jill Stein (Green)—faded over the election season, dropping from an average of 12 percent in August to below 7 percent late in the election year, and ending up at 4.3 percent (3.3 and 1.0 percent, respectively) in November. Voters who preferred one of them but believed—correctly—that they could not win voted for Hillary Clinton or Donald Trump in an effort to keep their least favorite candidate from winning. By arguing that "a vote for Johnson or Stein is a vote for Trump," the Clinton campaign sought to win back disaffected Democrats whose top priority was keeping Trump out of the White House. The Republicans made a variation of this pitch—"a vote for Johnson is a vote for Clinton"—to voters who preferred Johnson to Trump but Trump to Clinton. Only voters whose disdain for both major-party candidates exceeded their desire to elect the lesser of two evils cast ballots for minor-party or independent candidates.

In the end, then, only those third parties (or independent candidates) that manage to supplant one of the two reigning parties as a viable option in voters' minds gain rather than lose support from strategic voters. The last time this occurred on a national scale was 1856, when the Republicans surged ahead of the Whigs, who were fatally split over the slavery issue.

Third-party and independent candidates can be influential despite their electoral futility, however. Ralph Nader, candidate of the Green Party in 2000, gave George W. Bush the presidency. Had he not been on the ballot in Florida, any plausible redistribution of the ninety-seven thousand votes he received would have given the state to Al Gore (most of Nader's support came from liberals who preferred Gore to Bush). Nader immediately became the exemplar of the dangers of "wasting" a vote, and when he ran again in 2004 his national vote total dropped from 2,882,995 (2.74 percent) to 443,830 (0.37 percent), and he was not a factor.

Even when independent and third-party candidates do not affect the outcome, the policies and ideas they promote may survive them through adoption by one, sometimes

Helen H. Richardson/The Denver Post via Getty Images

Gary Johnson

© Wally McNamee/CORBIS/ Corbis via Getty Images

(From left) George H. W. Bush, Ross Perot, and Bill Clinton

both, of the major parties. For example, many of the regulatory innovations sought by the Populist Party in the 1890s became part of the Democrats' New Deal after 1932. George Wallace's 1968 campaign theme of law and order soon found its way into many Republican campaigns. And the legislative term limits advocated by Ross Perot in his surprisingly successful independent candidacy in 1992 (Perot won no states but 19 percent of the popular vote) ended up in the Republicans' 1994 "Contract with America." Third-party movements thus contribute to the policy agendas of the major-party coalitions even as the winner-take-all electoral system continues to deny third-party candidates public office.

narrow the viable choices down to two. Competition for survival, not to mention victory, puts strong pressure on party leaders to assemble broad coalitions, extending the party's hand to the voters ready to give up on their first choice. Any idea promoted by a third party that proves to be popular with voters is subject to poaching by one, or sometimes both, of the established parties maneuvering to coopt the disaffected. Thus, incentives to expand electoral coalitions also help reduce the number of parties to two.

This 1884 Republican poster explains to voters why they should vote Republican. High tariffs supported working families because they kept products made by cheap foreign labor out of the country. With protection, the factories hum (compare smokestacks), food is on the table, and Mom does not yell at the kids. Note also the prominence given party labels during the nineteenth century.

Elections in the United States have almost always been winner-take-all affairs, so the rules have continually worked to reduce the viable options to two. An alternative kind of electoral system—proportional representation, under which a party receives legislative seats in proportion to its share of votes—is used in many democracies. This system helps preserve smaller parties because votes for their candidates are not wasted (hence the proportional systems listed in Figure 12.1 produce an average of 7.1 legislative parties), but it has never been tried in the United States on any significant scale. Once two-party competition was in place, both parties had a stake in preserving electoral rules that discriminate against third parties.

Strictly speaking, the winner-take-all logic applies only within a given electoral unit (a single congressional district or state, for example); it does not require that the same two parties face each other in every electoral unit. But for purposes of electing a president, the entire United States works as a single electoral unit. The contest for the presidency became so central to electoral politics that it shaped party competition for lesser offices as well.

From the 1940s to the 1970s the Democratic Party balanced northern presidential nominees with southern vice presidential nominees to appeal to the divergent political views of Democratic voters in these regions, especially on the race issue. Despite the sometimes bitter relations between the candidates and their staffs, in 1960 Massachusetts-born John Kennedy was compelled to team up with Texan Lyndon Johnson to strengthen his bid for the South. An August 1960 campaign stop in Amarillo, Texas, was one of their few joint appearances. In fact, most of the time these candidates ran separate campaigns in different parts of the country, with little coordination between them. At the bottom of the photo is Lyndon Johnson's wife, Lady Bird Johnson.

Digital Image © The Museum of Modern Art/Licensed by SCALA/Art Resource, NY

### Decentralized, Fragmented Party Coalitions

Another reason the two-party pattern endures is that federalism fragments the political system. Historically, national parties have been assembled from diverse state and local political factions concerned chiefly with the vibrant politics of their states, counties, or cities. The decentralized policymaking system allowed these local parties to work together to elect national leaders while going their own way on matters closer to home. National leaders could maintain diverse, unwieldy coalitions because many of the factions within them had little contact with one another except when choosing the party's presidential candidate. Indeed, since the beginning the major parties have been diverse, unwieldy coalitions, ready to fly apart unless carefully maintained. Skillful management and the compelling need to hold these factions together for any chance at office have usually, but by no means always, kept the parties from self-destructing.

### Professional Politicians

At the time the Constitution was adopted, political leadership was the prerogative of success-ful and prominent men who viewed service in public office as a temporary duty that fell to members of their class. As organization became essential to winning public office, political power flowed into the hands of people with the skills to build networks of party workers, man-age alliances of local leaders, and mobilize voters on Election Day. Personal wealth, education, and status were still advantages, but they no longer were essential. Of those attracted to party politics, many were ambitious people who latched onto the party as a vehicle for personal advancement; opportunism made no small contribution to the emergence of political parties.

Eventually the variety and frequency of elections generated by the multilayered federal system made party management a full-time job in many places. To maintain the electoral machinery, party managers had to attract resources and reward the efforts of party workers. Thus **patronage**—jobs, offices, government contracts, business licenses, and so forth—grew in importance. By the 1840s, when they were fully developed, parties had become ends in themselves to the thousands of local politicos who depended on them, one way or another, for their livelihood. That dependence ended in the late nineteenth and early twentieth centuries, however, when reforms largely destroyed the patronage-based party organizations. Today, full-time professionals manage the parties, and party activists are mainly amateurs who volun-teer their time.

## Development and Evolution of the Party Systems

The historical development of parties (see Figure 12.2) reveals how they were shaped by pol-iticians' strategic reactions to the opportunities and challenges posed by the Constitution. Scholars of a generation ago identified a sequence of five (possibly now six) distinct historical party systems. Although more recent research suggests that party evolution has been more continuous and less periodic than implied by this schema, it remains useful for identifying important innovations that have shaped and reshaped the parties.[15]

The first party system (1790–1824) illustrates the logic that led to the creation of national parties. Institutional innovation in the second party system (1824–1860) set parties on their basic organizational course. The full flowering and then decline of party machines under Progressive assault characterized the third (1860–1894) and fourth (1894–1932) party sys-tems. Each of these systems also was defined by its distinctive pair of rival coalitions, but the coalitional nature of American parties is clearest in the creation and erosion of the party coa-litions of the fifth party system (1932–?). The party coalitions have changed enough since the 1950s to suggest that a sixth party system is now in place, although there is no consensus on its date of origin.

### The First Party System: The Origin of American Parties

The American party system was born in the first few Congresses as leaders with opposing views on national political issues sought to have their views prevail. Alexander Hamilton, sec-retary of the Treasury in George Washington's administration, proposed an ambitious and

■ **FIGURE 12.2**  American Political Parties

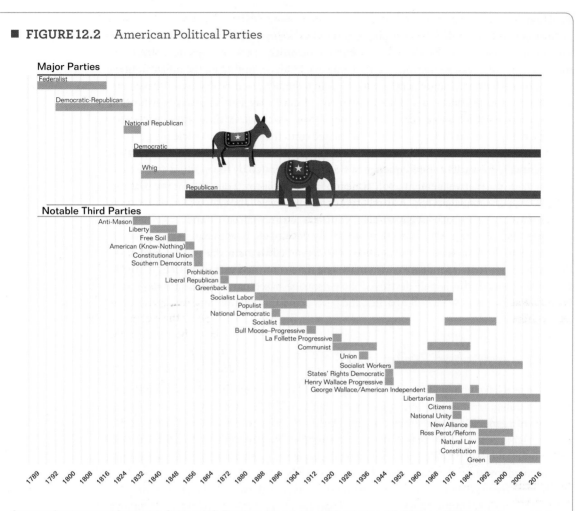

Sources: *Congressional Quarterly's Guide to U.S. Elections,* 5th ed., Vol. 1 (Washington, DC: CQ Press, 2006). Updates provided by Rhodes Cook and the authors.

Note: Throughout U.S. history there have been more than 1,500 political parties. For this chart *Congressional Quarterly* editors have selected those parties that achieved national significance during presidential election years. The spaces between the rules on this chart indicate the election year only. For example, the Constitutional Union Party and the Southern Democrats were in existence for the 1860 election only and were gone by 1864.

controversial set of measures designed to foster economic development. Other prominent leaders, notably James Madison and Thomas Jefferson, who saw no constitutional basis for the federal government doing any such thing, opposed Hamilton's program. The two sides also disagreed on foreign policy: Hamilton and his allies wanted strong ties with England, whereas Jefferson's group leaned toward France.

Hamilton's pursuit of votes in Congress led him to create what was, in effect, a legislative party. He cultivated a stable group of allies soon labeled "Federalists" because of their endorsement of a strong national government. Members of Congress who opposed Hamilton's policies gradually coalesced under the leadership of Jefferson and Madison. Protesting the alleged aristocratic inclinations of Hamilton's group, they styled themselves as Republicans. Members of this party also were called Democratic-Republicans until the 1820s, when they became known simply as Democrats. Today, the Democratic Party is the oldest political party in the world.

As the Federalists continued to roll up legislative victories, the Democratic-Republicans realized they needed more votes in Congress if they were to prevail. That meant getting more like-minded people into Congress, which meant recruiting and electing candidates. Because senators were chosen by state legislatures, the Democratic-Republican national leaders began to pay attention to state elections as well. The Federalists recognized the same realities and reached the same conclusions. The two groups began to compete in elections.

The presidential election required the parties' attention as well, for the Federalists had demonstrated the importance of controlling the presidency as well as Congress. The Constitution had left it up to the states to decide how to select their presidential electors. A number of selection procedures were tried—most commonly popular election, selection by the state legislature, or some combination of the two. The Framers expected the electors to be prominent local men who would deliberate with others from their states before deciding how to cast their votes.[16] Challenging Adams for the presidency in 1800, Jefferson and his Democratic-Republican allies realized that these deliberations could be circumvented if they recruited and elected a majority of electors pledged to support Jefferson. By reaching out to local political leaders who were potential electors and to the growing mass of voters who chose the electors and state legislators, Jefferson successfully patched together an alliance of state and local factions, which led to a historic victory for his Democratic-Republicans and the ousting of the Federalists (see Chapter 9).*

It is no accident that the Democratic-Republicans did the innovating: the history of party building is largely a story of the "outs" finding new ways to become the "ins." The losers then imitate successful innovations. The Federalists tried with uneven success to duplicate the Democratic-Republicans' organizational efforts. They were hampered, however, by their nostalgia for deferential politics—the feeling that "better" people like them were by right the natural leaders—which left them uncomfortable making popular appeals to an increasingly egalitarian electorate.

With the designation of competing slates of electors pledged to support specific presidential candidates, the candidates replaced individual electors as the objects of the voters' decisions. The practice of pledging therefore went a long way toward democratizing the choice of president. In doing so, it strengthened the president's hand within the constitutional system as an executive chosen by the people and beholden to them, not other politicians.

---

*Jefferson's victory was complicated by the fact that he and his running mate, Aaron Burr, won the same number of electoral votes; the tie had to be broken by the outgoing House of Representatives, where Federalist votes put Jefferson over the top. The Twelfth Amendment, adopted in 1804, altered the counting procedure to assure this could not happen again.

The first parties were by no means the elaborate national organizations that emerged a generation later. Both parties' coalitions were unstable, lacking even uniform names. Any loyalty felt by politicians or voters did not extend much beyond the immediate issue or election. When their pro-British leanings put them on the wrong side in the War of 1812, the Federalists faded as a national force. In the aftermath of the party's collapse, politicians and informed observers hoped that party competition—and therefore parties—would disappear. The idea that organized opposition would or should be a permanent part of American national politics was still unorthodox.

## The Second Party System: Organizational Innovation

By the second decade of the nineteenth century the Democratic-Republicans had eclipsed the Federalists nearly everywhere. James Monroe crushed the Federalists' last presidential nominee in 1816 and was reelected without significant opposition in 1820. The Monroe years were so lacking in party conflict that the period was dubbed the Era of Good Feelings. But the end of party conflict did not mean the end of political conflict; it only meant that political battles were fought within the remaining party. Without the need for unity to win national elections, party networks fell apart. Personal and factional squabbles reemerged to replace party conflict in most states. One immediate consequence was a dramatic falloff in voter participation in presidential elections: turnout among eligible voters dropped from more than 40 percent in 1812 to less than 10 percent in 1820—eloquent testimony to the parties' crucial role in mobilizing voters (see Figure 12.3).

Party competition revived with a fight for the presidency. Under the first party system, the parties' congressional **caucuses** (members assembled with their allies to make party decisions) nominated presidential candidates—a natural development because electoral competition began as an extension of party competition in Congress. This method became a problem, however, when the Federalists dissolved, leaving almost everyone in Congress a nominal Democratic-Republican. With one party so dominant, whoever picked its nominee effectively picked the president. The caucus, then, could have its way as long as there was a general consensus among its members on the nominee, as in the case of Monroe. Without a consensus, the caucus lost influence and legitimacy.

In 1824, after Monroe, no fewer than five serious candidates—all of them Democratic-Republicans—sought the presidency. The congressional caucus nominated William Crawford, who came in third in the electoral vote and dead last in the popular vote. Andrew Jackson, hero of the Battle of New Orleans in the War of 1812, won the most popular and electoral votes but a majority of neither. John Quincy Adams came in second, and House Speaker Henry Clay came in third in popular votes but fourth in the Electoral College. (The remaining candidate, John C. Calhoun, withdrew early and was elected vice president instead.) Because no candidate received a majority of electors, the election was thrown into the House of Representatives. There, Clay gave his support to Adams, who, upon taking office, made Clay his secretary of state—and, hence, the heir apparent to the White House, for Adams was the fourth president in a row who had previously served as secretary of state.

Jackson's supporters were outraged that a "corrupt bargain" had denied "Old Hickory" his rightful place in the White House. In the midst of that outrage a shrewd New York politician,

■ **FIGURE 12.3**    Voter Turnout in Presidential and Midterm Elections, 1789–2018

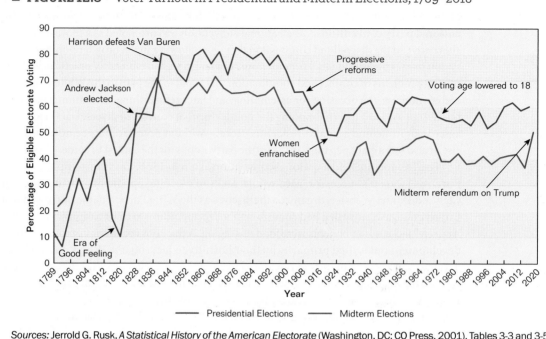

*Sources:* Jerrold G. Rusk, *A Statistical History of the American Electorate* (Washington, DC: CQ Press, 2001), Tables 3-3 and 3-5. Data for 1998–2018 are from Michael P. McDonald, "Voter Turnout," accessed at www.electproject.org/home/voter-turnout/voter-turnout-data.

Martin Van Buren, recognized the opportunity to build a new political coalition. Believing that a national party along the lines of the old Jeffersonian alliance of "the planters of the South and the plain Republicans of the north"[17] would have the best chance of containing the most explosive issues of the day, particularly slavery, Van Buren reconstructed the Democratic Party using Jackson as the rallying point. Central committees set up in Washington and Nashville, Jackson's hometown, promoted the formation of state organizations, which in turn promoted Jackson clubs or committees in towns and counties. Aided by a nationwide chain of newspapers established to support the cause, Van Buren and Jackson used this network to spread propaganda that kept Jackson and the "wrong" done him in the public consciousness. Local politicians, recognizing Jackson's popularity as a vehicle for their own ambitions, rallied voters with meetings, marches, barbecues, and hickory pole raisings.[18]

Supporters of President Adams had no choice but to put together a network of their own. Adams detested parties and had sought during his administration to build a coalition that incorporated all factions of the old Democratic-Republican and Federalist Parties. He did nothing himself to cultivate electoral allies. Yet his backers, in the process of nominating electors and candidates for other offices and working to get people to vote for them, created what amounted to an Adams party. As one historian has put it, "Just by standing for reelection Adams brought a national party into being."[19]

### National Conventions

Jackson's smashing victory in 1828 was, among other things, a powerful lesson in the value of political organization. The 1832 election, which he also won handily, featured the first **national party conventions**.* The national convention was promoted as a more democratic alternative to the discredited congressional caucus, allowing much broader popular participation in making presidential nominations. But it also was an eminently practical device for solving problems of conflict and coordination that stand in the path to the White House. The convention was the occasion for assembling, and later refurbishing, the national party coalition. It provided a forum for doing the politicking that convinced diverse party factions to agree to unite behind a single presidential ticket—without necessarily agreeing on anything else. It also was a giant pep rally, firing up the party troops for the contest to come.

The Democrats held a national convention again in 1836, this time to nominate Van Buren as Jackson's successor. Meanwhile, Jackson's leading opponents, including Henry Clay and Daniel Webster, organized themselves as the Whig Party, a name borrowed from British political history that had come to symbolize opposition to royal tyranny, which "King Andrew" Jackson's opponents were fond of alleging. A fractious coalition promoting national development but united primarily by their hostility to Jackson, the Whigs did not hold a national convention but instead attempted to divide and conquer by running three regional candidates. Their plan was to combine their strength behind the strongest candidate in the Electoral College or, failing that, to throw the election into the House.

When that strategy flopped in 1836, the Whigs turned to a ploy that won the party its only two presidential victories: nominating a popular military hero without known political coloration and obscuring party divisions by not writing a platform. The Whig nominee in 1840 was William Henry Harrison, hero of the Battle of Tippecanoe (fought against a confederation of Native American tribes in 1811) and extolled as a rough-hewn man of the people. He defeated Van Buren in a contest that moved party competition to an entirely new level.

The 1840 campaign extended organized two-party competition to every state in the nation, framing not only the contest for president but also competition for offices at all levels of government. Competition inspired unprecedented efforts to involve and mobilize ordinary voters, turning political campaigns into the most exciting spectacles the era offered. As one historian of the period observed,

> Those tens of thousands of men and women who attended the mammoth Whig festival at Nashville in 1840; those untold millions who carried torches, donned uniforms, chanted slogans, or cheered themselves hoarse at innumerable parades and rallies; those puffed-up canvassers of wards, servers of rum, and distributors of largess; and all those simple folk who whipped themselves into a fury of excitement and anxiety as each election day approached, were thrilling to a grand dramatic experience, even a cathartic experience. There was no spectacle, no contest, in America that could match an election campaign.[20]

---

*Actually, the Anti-Masonic Party had held a convention in 1831, and Jackson's loosely organized opponents, calling themselves National Republicans, had convened a small national gathering that year as well. But the Democratic convention that met in Baltimore to renominate Jackson in 1832 is considered the original full-scale national party convention.

In effect, the parties solved the problem of free riding endemic to mass electorates by making participation exciting, emotionally compelling, and fun. One sign of their success was a dramatic increase in turnout (see Figure 12.3). In 1824 only 27 percent of the eligible electorate (adult white men) bothered to vote in the presidential election. When Jackson was elected in 1828, turnout rose to 55 percent, and it stayed at about that level for the next two presidential contests. In 1840 fully 78 percent of the eligible voters took part. More striking evidence of the crucial role of parties—and party competition—in making mass democracy a reality could scarcely be imagined.

### The Spoils System

Parties on the rise always attract opportunists. The politicians who flocked to Jackson's banner or joined his Whig opponents were not, for the most part, altruists; rather, they carried on the party work because they were ambitious for an office or other favors. These motives are neither surprising nor appalling. Parties pursue a collective good: victory for their candidates and policies. All who prefer the winner benefit from the party's victory whether or not they contribute to it. Thus, without some prospect of private reward for party activists as well, the free-rider problem would have left parties stillborn. The men who worked to elect Jackson or Harrison took as their right the spoils of victory—mainly government jobs but also contracts to supply goods and services to the government or special projects from which they might profit.

The pursuit of political spoils, which came to be known as the spoils system (see Chapter 8), intensified party competition and put a heavy premium on winning. On the positive side, putting victory ahead of principle made parties open and inclusive. For a time, broad national coalitions helped manage the dangerous intersectional conflict over slavery and other divisive issues. The high stakes also inspired imaginative efforts to mobilize the first mass electorate in history. On the negative side, the desire to win contributed to corruption, moral myopia regarding slavery, and public cynicism about the honesty and motives of politicians. In either case, the Democrats and Whigs of the second party system set the pattern for the future: every successful American party has cared more about winning elections than about furthering a consistent set of principles.

Indeed, principled conflict is often a threat to party coalitions. Established party politicians put unity first because their careers depend on it, but voters and activists have no such stake and may care very deeply about the positions a party takes on controversial issues. The Whigs and the Democrats built coalitions around differences on tariffs, banking, and other economic policies. But both parties had northern and southern wings and so were badly split by the slavery issue. Leaders tried to keep slavery off the political agenda, but this proved impossible. When the extension of slavery became the dominant national issue, the coalitions that formed the second party system fell apart. For the first and only time in U.S. history, a third party emerged to supplant one of the two dominant parties.

### The Third Party System: Entrepreneurial Politics

The Republican Party, organized in 1854 as a coalition of antislavery forces, is unusual only in the success of its challenge to the two-party establishment. Third parties have arisen time and again, but most have failed to attract enough of a following to become more than obscure

refuges for the disaffected. On a few occasions, however, third parties have managed to shake up the system, leaving notable traces in party politics long after they have disappeared. The Anti-Masonic Party and the American (Know-Nothing) Party are examples from the pre–Civil War era (see Figure 12.2). Both sprouted in periods of economic distress and social crisis, originating as antiparties—movements of "the people" against corrupt and compromising party regulars. As soon as they showed a capacity to win elections, however, they attracted opportunists seeking to jump-start political careers. For some ambitious men, the protest party was a way station to a position of leadership in a major party. Anti-Masons joined the Whigs; Know-Nothings joined the Republicans.

The Republican Party was formed in opposition to the Kansas-Nebraska Act (1854), which overturned limits on the extension of slavery to the territories enacted earlier in the Missouri Compromise of 1820 and the Compromise of 1850. It drew leaders and followers from two earlier antislavery parties as well as the Know-Nothings, antislavery Whigs, and dissident Democrats. Its adopted name laid claim to the mantles of both the Jeffersonian Republicans and the National Republicans who had backed Adams against Jackson.

Although founded on the slavery issue, the Republican Party was by no means a single-issue party. It also appealed to business and commercial interests by promising a protective tariff and a transcontinental railway and to farmers by promising free land for homesteading. On only its second try the party elected a president, Abraham Lincoln. His victory over divided opposition in 1860 triggered the South's secession from the Union and then the Civil War, from which the Republicans emerged as the party of victory and union. For the next generation the party sought to retain its ascendancy by appealing variously to patriotism, national expansion, and laissez-faire capitalism and by distributing pensions to Civil War veterans and protective tariffs to manufacturers. The end of Reconstruction in 1876 restored local control to white southern politicians (see Chapter 4) and left the newly revived Democratic Party, dominant in the South and with pockets of strength in the West, border states, and northern urban areas, a nearly equal competitor for national power.

### Party Machines

Party organizations reached their peak of development during the third party system. Patronage—jobs, contracts, development rights, zoning favors—generated by the rapid growth of industrial cities provided the capital; party entrepreneurs provided the management. The classic **party machines** were built on simple principles of exchange: party politicians provided favors and services to people throughout the year in return for their votes on Election Day. They found an eager market for their offerings among the growing population of poor immigrants whose basic needs—shelter, food, fuel, jobs, and help in adapting to a new and bewildering country—were far more pressing than any concern for party programs or ideologies.

The late-nineteenth-century party machines represented the culmination of trends reaching back to the Jacksonian era. Politics had become a full-time profession for thousands of individuals. Those who took it up were mostly "men of slender social distinction, whose training came not from the countinghouse or the university, but from the street gang, the saloon, the fire department, the political club."[21] Winning local elections to keep the patronage flowing was the paramount goal of party professionals; issues, programs, and candidates (national

as well as local) mattered only insofar as they could help or hinder that goal. National parties were contentious alliances of local party organizations competing for patronage.

## The Progressive Attack

Party machines were regularly attacked as corrupt and inefficient, run by party hacks incapable of dealing with problems created by the growth of large industry and national markets. Reformers, working almost entirely from within the two-party system, sought to destroy the party machines by depriving party leaders of the capacity to reward followers. Eventually, they succeeded. The most important changes were introduced during what is now called the **Progressive Era**—the decades just before and after the turn of the twentieth century, overlapping the end of the third party system and the beginning of the fourth. The most important reforms were the civil service, the Australian ballot, and primary elections.

After passage of the Pendleton Act in 1883, reformers began to replace the spoils system with a civil service system in most jurisdictions. Under the spoils system, the winning party filled appointive government jobs with its faithful workers; the civil service system turned government jobs into professional careers. Appointment and advancement depended on merit, not political pull, and civil servants could not be fired except "for cause"—failing to do their jobs or committing crimes (see Chapter 8). As more government jobs were brought under civil service, the rewards for party work shrank, reducing the number of party workers.

Another reform associated with the Progressive Era was the secret ballot. Prior to the 1890s each party produced its own ballots (listing only its candidates), which were handed to voters outside the polling place. Because party ballots were readily distinguishable, voters could not keep their choices to themselves or easily vote a **split ticket**—that is, vote for candidates of different parties for different offices—for this required manipulating several ballots. The system invited corruption and intimidation; party workers could monitor voters and reward or punish them accordingly. Thus between 1888 and 1896, 90 percent of the states adopted the **Australian ballot**, named for its country of origin. The new type of ballot, still in use today, was prepared by the government, listed candidates from all parties, and was marked in the privacy of a voting booth. This change made it much more difficult for parties

The advent of the Australian ballot allowed voters to pick candidates across parties. With whole-party tickets at an end, candidate-centered campaigns began their ascendancy.

to exchange favors for votes because it left no (legal) way for the party to know if voters had kept their side of the bargain.

With adoption of the Australian ballot, the government became involved in party nominations, for someone had to determine officially which parties and names would be listed on the government-produced ballot. Laws were passed to regulate party nominating conventions and, later, to allow a party's voters to nominate candidates through **primary elections**. Strong party machines were still able to dominate primaries, but as party organizations were weakened by other changes, primaries deprived them of a crucial political resource: the ability to control access to elective public office by controlling nominations.

Progressives advocated, and in many places achieved, other reforms intended to detach local politics from national politics on the ground that "there is no Republican or Democratic way to pave a street" (forgetting that Democrats and Republicans may have different priorities in deciding whose streets to pave, who gets the paving contract, and who pays for it). At the local level, elections were made officially "nonpartisan" and held separately from federal elections. States also adopted laws requiring would-be voters to register before Election Day (to reduce the possibilities of fraud) and to pass literacy tests (unlike the old party-produced ballots, the Australian ballot could be used only by literate voters). At the national level a constitutional amendment, ratified in 1913, took the choice of U.S. senators from the state legislatures and gave it to the voters, eliminating the party politics that had governed the selection of senators.

Although ostensibly aimed at rooting out corruption and cleaning up electoral politics, progressive reforms also were designed to enhance the political clout of the "right" kind of people—educated middle- and upper-middle-class folks like the reformers themselves—at the expense of poor urban immigrants and their leaders "of slender social distinction." Stricter voter registration laws discriminated against the poor and uneducated. Literacy tests had the same effect and were used widely in the South to disenfranchise African Americans and sometimes poor whites.

Progressive reforms were adopted to varying degrees in almost every state. And on the whole they worked, weakening or destroying party machines and preventing their resurrection. Vigorous party organizations did survive, though, in some places, often for many years. For example, a tightly controlled Democratic machine ran Chicago until the 1970s. Over the long run, however, progressive reforms deprived state and local party organizations—the basic building blocks of national parties—of much of their political power.

## Consequences of Progressive Reforms

These changes had several important consequences for electoral politics. First, turnout declined. Tighter registration laws, the Australian ballot, and literacy tests discouraged voting. With fewer jobs and favors to reward the party workers, fewer people were willing to do the work that wedded voters to the party and brought them to the polls. According to Figure 12.3, from the Civil War to the 1890s about 80 percent of the eligible electorate voted in presidential elections. By the 1910s turnout had fallen to around 60 percent. It fell further when women were enfranchised in 1920; many women initially ignored politics as "men's business," and women's turnout levels—which today surpass men's—took a half century to pull even. Turnout declined most among poor and uneducated people, the very citizens most

dependent on parties for incentives to vote. (For more on turnout, see Chapter 11.)

The reforms also began to shift the focus of electoral politics from parties to candidates. When party organizations controlled nominations and voters chose between whole-party tickets, political careers were bound tightly to parties. With the advent of the Australian ballot and primary elections, these bonds weakened. Candidates could win nominations with or without the party's blessing by appealing directly to voters; they could campaign separately from the party's team because voters could now split their tickets more easily. The full flowering of candidate-centered electoral politics

President Franklin Roosevelt and his allies assembled the Democrats' New Deal coalition from remarkably diverse segments of American society. In this 1936 photo Roosevelt chats with members of one group served by New Deal policies, North Dakota farmers who have received drought relief grants.

had to await the development of modern communication technologies, but the seeds were planted by the progressive reforms.

By altering the incentives to perform party work, reforms also contributed to changes in the demographics and goals of party organizations. Traditional party organizations were built on material incentives attractive to working-class people; consequently, parties concentrated on winning elections to keep the material benefits flowing. As their resource base shrank, patronage-based parties were supplanted by party organizations made up of middle-class people inspired by nonmaterial incentives—devotion to a particular candidate, issue, or ideology—people for whom a party victory was often less important than the success of their preferred candidate or cause.

Paradoxically, the Progressive Era left the Republicans and Democrats organizationally weaker but more entrenched than ever in the political system. Once considered private groups, parties were now treated by the law in many states as essentially public entities charged with managing elections. Regulations tended to privilege the two major parties and discriminate against new parties and independent candidates. Moreover, the advent of primary elections encouraged dissidents to work within the established parties because outsiders could now compete for control of the party's machinery and name. Why should malcontents buck the long odds against winning under a new party label when they could convert an established party to their cause? For insurgent outsider Donald Trump, seizing control of the existing Republican Party through the primary system offered a much more promising road to the White House than an independent candidacy would have offered. Other examples include conservative Christian activists, inspired by their opposition to *Roe v. Wade* (see Chapter 5), who took over the Republican Party apparatus in many states and soon made their positions

on social issues such as abortion and gay rights the party's official positions, and the antigovernment Tea Party activists who mounted their insurgency within the Republican Party rather than setting up a party of their own. No new party has come close to challenging either of the major parties since the nineteenth century, but those parties have suffered some convulsive changes as the result of challenges from within.

## The Fourth Party System: Republican Ascendancy

From the end of Reconstruction in 1876 until 1894, the third American party system settled into place, and the Republicans and Democrats competed on nearly even terms. In 1896 the Democrats reacted to a severe economic downturn by adopting the platform of the People's Party, or Populists, a party of agrarian protest against high railroad rates and the gold standard, and nominating William Jennings Bryan, a candidate with strong Populist sympathies. The Republican campaign persuaded many urban workers that the Democrats' proposal to make silver as well as gold a monetary standard threatened their livelihoods (arguing that "sound" money backed by gold was the backbone of the financial system that sustained the industrial economy) and so converted them into Republicans. The reaction to the agrarian takeover of the Democrats left the Republicans with a clear national majority for the next generation; the new alignment is commonly designated the fourth party system.

The Republican Party ultimately lost its ascendancy to the Great Depression. Having taken credit for the prosperity of the 1920s with policies highly favorable to financial institutions and industrial corporations, the Republicans and their president, Herbert Hoover, were saddled with the blame for the economic devastation and high unemployment that followed the 1929 stock market crash. Franklin Roosevelt, the Democratic candidate, defeated Hoover in the 1932 election. Roosevelt's New Deal solidified a new coalition of interests that gave the Democrats a popular majority. Despite the coalition's slow demise since the 1960s, the Democratic Party has retained that majority—sometimes barely—to this day.

## The Fifth Party System: The New Deal Coalition

Nothing illustrates the diversity of American party coalitions more strikingly than does the **New Deal coalition**, which brought together Democrats of every conceivable background. It united white southern segregationists with northern African Americans (few southern African Americans could vote), progressive intellectuals with machine politicians, union members and their families with the poorest farmers, Roman Catholics with Southern Baptists. These diverse groups agreed on only one thing—electing Democrats—while having very different reasons for wanting to do so.

Some were attracted by Roosevelt's New Deal policies, which, in tackling the Depression's devastation, radically expanded the federal government's responsibility for, and authority over, the economic and social welfare of all Americans. The Wagner Act of 1935, known as organized labor's "bill of rights," cemented union support. Public works programs pulled in poor and unemployed citizens, including northern African Americans (who until then favored the party of Lincoln), and provided patronage for urban machines. Farm programs appealed to distressed rural voters. Progressive intellectuals applauded the federal government's expanded role in attending to the economic welfare of citizens. The adoption of the Social Security and unemployment insurance systems earned the gratitude of working people whose economic insecurity had been so painfully exposed by the Depression.

Other groups were part of the Democratic coalition by tradition. Southern whites were still expressing political identities forged in the Civil War. Roman Catholics, already disproportionately Democratic, had become overwhelmingly so in 1928, when the party chose Al Smith, the first of their faith to be nominated for president by a major party. Jews in the cities of the East and Midwest also had supported Smith, in reaction to the rural and small-town Protestant bigotry his candidacy had provoked, and stayed with the Democrats under Roosevelt, an early and staunch enemy of Nazi Germany.

The opposing Republican coalition was a smaller, inverted image of the Democratic coalition: business and professional people, upper-income white Protestants, residents of smaller towns and cities in the Northeast and Midwest, and ideological conservatives. It was united by what it opposed: Roosevelt's New Deal programs and the greatly enlarged federal bureaucracy they engendered (see Chapter 8), which Republicans excoriated as unconstitutional, unwise, and un-American.

### Erosion of the New Deal Coalition

The complexities of coalition politics aside, national electoral competition during the New Deal period was organized around a single question: are you for or against the New Deal? As long as that was the question, the New Deal alignment held. But when new issues became the focus of electoral politics, the Democratic coalition began to unravel. The Republicans opened the way for new issues to shape electoral politics by finally recognizing that the major New Deal programs were there to stay; a party in search of a national majority cannot cling forever to losing positions. When they finally regained the White House in 1952 (using the old Whig ploy of nominating a military hero, General Dwight Eisenhower), it was on a promise not to repeal the New Deal but to administer its programs more frugally. Once that question was settled, other issues could come to the fore.

The first and most important of these issues was civil rights for African Americans (discussed in detail in Chapter 4). As the Democrats became the party of civil rights, white southerners began to depart. At about the same time, the war in Vietnam also split the Democrats, largely along the fault lines of class. The party machine politicians and labor leaders whose blue-collar constituents supplied most of the soldiers generally supported the war, as did most southern Democrats. Opposition was led by liberal intellectuals and was most conspicuous on elite university campuses. New controversies over the bounds of acceptable social behavior deepened the split as sexual freedom, pornography, abortion, women's rights, and gay rights became the stuff of politics.

Traditional Democratic constituencies also were divided over new economic initiatives. The Great Society programs enacted during Lyndon Johnson's presidency (1963–1969) lacked the broad appeal of the New Deal. The major New Deal programs—Social Security, unemployment insurance, and Medicare (a New Deal–type program, although not enacted until 1965)—serve politically active majorities. Great Society programs—housing subsidies, school nutrition programs, Head Start, food stamps, and Medicaid—serve a politically apathetic minority: the poor. For many working-class and middle-class Democrats, the New Deal was for "us," but the Great Society's War on Poverty was for "them."

The Republicans, although less diverse than their rivals, could not avoid some serious divisions of their own. The conservative and moderate wings struggled for dominance from the New Deal period until the 1980s. Conservatives took over the national party in 1964, nominating one of their own, Senator Barry Goldwater of Arizona, for president. Goldwater's vote against the Civil Rights Act of 1964 endeared him to southern segregationists but alienated moderates in his own party, as did his hostility to the core New Deal programs. His overwhelming defeat left the party temporarily in tatters. It quickly recovered, however, by taking advantage of the deep divisions within the old Democratic coalition to win five of the next six presidential elections.

Republican candidates since Richard Nixon have sought to build winning coalitions by combining affluent economic conservatives (and, since 2010, antigovernment Tea Party enthusiasts) with white middle-class and working-class nationalists and social conservatives, particularly from what is called the Christian Right. To attract economic conservatives, the Republicans declared war on taxation, regulation, welfare, and deficit spending; to win over social conservatives, they offered law and order, patriotism (opposition to the Vietnam War left Democrats vulnerable here), and "traditional family values," defined to mean a ban on

abortion, promotion of prayer in public schools, and opposition to same-sex marriage. But this coalition was not much more united than its Democratic counterpart. Many affluent economic conservatives were not attracted to the Christian Right's social agenda, and many social conservatives of modest means remained reluctant to expose themselves to the mercies of an unfettered free market. Trump's candidacy in 2016 split the party along a different though related dimension, pitting an enthusiastic constituency of blue-collar whites, particularly men, who applauded his verbal assaults on undocumented immigrants; Muslims; free trade; "political correctness"; and political, economic, and media elites against the more educated, affluent, cosmopolitan, and economically orthodox Republicans who were put off by both the style and content of Trump's campaign. These divisions remained during his first two years in office, but mainly at the elite level; most ordinary Republicans continued to offer Trump overwhelming support, and the Republican Party of today is unquestionably Trump's party.

### Changing the Rules

Divisions within the parties' electoral coalitions during the 1960s were played out in intraparty battles that reshaped the parties as organizations. One major result was the progressive-style reform of presidential nominations. The Democrats' nominating practices had fallen into disrepute because many southern delegations were discriminating against black voters just recently activated by the civil rights movement. It was the Vietnam War, however, that triggered wholesale reform. When those Democrats opposed to American involvement in Vietnam sought to nominate an antiwar candidate in 1968, they found the diverse, arcane state procedures for selecting delegates to the national nominating convention a formidable barrier. Only fifteen states held primary elections, and in some of them support in primaries did not translate into convention delegates. In Pennsylvania, for example, the antiwar candidate, Senator Eugene McCarthy, won 72 percent of the primary votes, but Vice President Hubert Humphrey got 80 percent of Pennsylvania's convention delegates. Party leaders chose the delegates in most states, so leaders from the larger states dominated the convention.

In 1968 the convention was still the quadrennial coming together of diverse and fractious state party organizations that it had been since the 1830s. Most party regulars were, by habit, loyal to their president, Lyndon Johnson, and his anointed successor, Vice President Humphrey. Meeting in Chicago, the Democrats nominated Humphrey while antiwar protests filled the streets outside the convention hall. When the demonstrations got out of hand, they were violently suppressed by the Chicago police on the orders of Mayor Richard J. Daley, boss of the strongest surviving party machine and a major Humphrey backer. The party's internal divisions, dramatized by the riots and exposed to the world on national television, doomed the Democratic ticket and led to the election of Richard Nixon as president.

### Primary Elections and Caucuses

To repair the Democratic coalition and restore the convention's legitimacy, a party commission (the McGovern-Fraser Commission) drew up a new set of criteria specifying that convention delegations had to be chosen in a process that was "open, timely, and representative." The state parties could comply in one of two ways. They could hold a primary election, the outcome of which would determine at least 90 percent of the state's delegation. Or they could hold local party caucuses open to all Democrats, who would select delegates to a meeting at the

county, congressional district, or state level. These delegates would in turn elect delegates to the national convention. The easiest option was the primary, and most state parties have adopted it.

In another change, the winner-take-all method of allocating delegates went out the window. Instead of awarding all of a state's delegates to the top vote getter, the new rules allocated delegates proportionately to candidates according to the share of votes they received in the primary or the caucus.* To meet the "representativeness" standard, delegations had to include more minorities, women, and young adults. Because most elected officeholders were white men over thirty, these rules meant that many of them could no longer attend the convention.

The Democrats' delegate selection rules created a whole new ball game. Previously the party's supreme plum, its presidential nomination, had been conferred by party leaders, who sought to pick a winner who would be obligated to them and therefore send presidential favors their way. Moreover, they wanted a candidate who would help the whole party ticket on Election Day. Now the nomination goes to the candidate who can best mobilize support in primary elections. If party leaders are to exercise any influence in this process, they must do it by delivering endorsements, money, and other electoral resources to their favorite before and during the primary season.

The new process may be "fairer," as intended, but it has threatened other party goals, namely winning and governing. In some years, the candidate who most excites the activist minority who show up for primary elections (turnout is typically 20 percent to 30 percent of eligible voters) is not even the best vote getter among Democrats generally, let alone the broader electorate. For example, Senator George McGovern, the 1972 nominee, was the choice of antiwar Democrats but no one else; he won only 38 percent of the general election vote, the worst showing for a Democrat since the New Deal realignment.

Battles between Vietnam War demonstrators and the Chicago police outside the 1968 Democratic National Convention caused a revolt in the convention, culminating in the removal of the Chicago mayor, Richard J. Daley (pictured left, with fist raised), as a delegate. Not only did the last of the party machine mayors depart, but the turmoil also stimulated the party to install reforms that have dramatically altered the way the political parties nominate their presidential candidates.

*The Republican Party also adopted primary elections as the basic method of choosing delegates but allows states to maintain a winner-take-all process.

The system also allows outsiders with tenuous links to other party leaders to compete. Jimmy Carter, an obscure one-term governor of Georgia, won the nomination and then the White House in 1976 but, inexperienced in the ways of Washington, found it nearly impossible to work effectively with his party in Congress (see Chapter 7).[22] Responding to such problems, the Democrats altered their rules several more times to give party regulars more influence in the selection process. Prominent elected officials—governors, senators, and representatives—are now automatically among the convention delegates. These so-called **superdelegates** accounted for 712, or 15 percent, of the 4,763 votes at the Democrats' 2016 convention. They favored Hillary Clinton over Bernie Sanders by a wide margin, but she also won a clear majority (54.4 percent) of the elected delegates, so, as in previous years, superdelegate votes did not change the outcome. If they ever did so, supporters of the candidate with the most elected delegates would no doubt be outraged, splitting the party badly, a potential downside overlooked when the party added superdelegates to the mix. Recognizing this problem, Democrats altered the rules again. In 2020, two-thirds of the superdelegates will be bound to state primary and caucus results; the other third, made up of senators, governors, and representatives, will still have a free vote.

The nomination process enables the parties to solve the coordination problem posed by competing presidential aspirants. Sometimes party elites do the coordinating; if they can reach broad agreement on which candidate to support, they can be decisive, as the nomination of George W. Bush in 2000 illustrated. Bush initially faced a crowded field of twelve candidates, but by the beginning of the delegate selection process (the Iowa caucuses on January 24), six had dropped out, and by early February only Senator John McCain remained a serious rival. Acceptable to all factions, Bush swept away the competition by persuading the Republican Party establishment, elected officials and campaign donors alike, that his candidacy offered the best chance of returning the White House to Republican control. In 2016, in contrast, it took much longer for the field of seventeen Republican aspirants to shrink. A large majority of party leaders and donors opposed the eventual winner, Donald Trump, but they failed to rally behind a single alternative and their efforts to head off Trump's nomination proved ineffective. Coordination was accomplished instead by Trump, who made himself a vehicle for expressing the anti-elite, anti-establishment sentiments common among a large segment of the Republican base. Trump assumed a lead over the crowded Republican field shortly after announcing his candidacy in June 2015 and never relinquished it (see Figure 12.4a). His strongest rivals—initially surgeon Ben Carson, then Texas senator Ted Cruz—were also outsiders opposed to and by the Republican establishment. Trump eventually won 46.6 percent of Republican primary votes and 62.4 percent of the convention delegates.

Early in 2016, Hillary Clinton appeared to be the consensus solution to the Democrats' coordination problem, but Bernie Sanders's challenge from the left turned her anticipated coronation march into a long slog (see Figure 12.4b). Sanders's appeal to the party's young white liberals cut Clinton's lead in national polls from an average of 25 points in December to single digits in April. Clinton barely eked out a win in Iowa and lost badly to Sanders in New Hampshire, states where liberal whites populate the Democratic coalition. She ran much stronger than Sanders among older and minority voters, and their numbers in subsequent primaries allowed her to survive these and later setbacks. But the divisions within the party

■ **FIGURE 12.4A**   Republican Nomination Preferences, 2015–2016

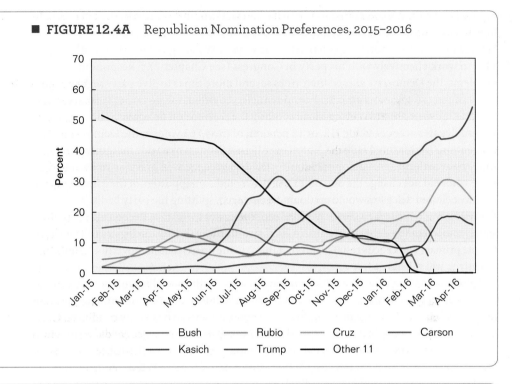

■ **FIGURE 12.4B**   Democratic Nomination Preferences, 2015–2016

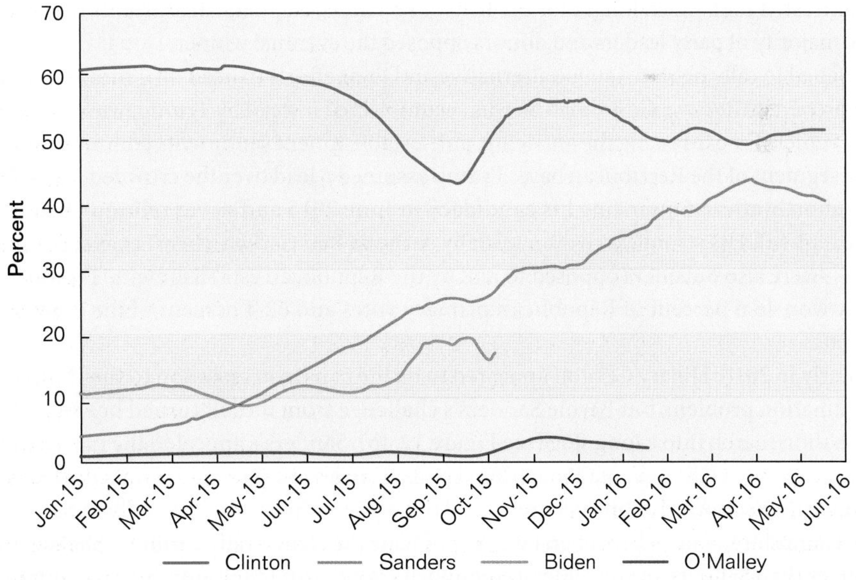

*Sources:* Compiled by authors from data at www.pollingreport.com/2016.htm, http://elections
.huffingtonpost.com/pollster/2016-national-democratic-primary, and http://elections.huffingtonpost.com/
pollster/2016-national-gop-primary.

exposed in the primary were never fully healed, and Clinton's effort to reconstruct the coalition that had twice elected Barack Obama fell short.

## The Conventions Evolve

Now that primaries and caucuses effectively determine the parties' nominees, the purpose and meaning of national conventions have changed. Conventions were once venues for state and local party leaders to renegotiate their complex coalitions and to choose a torchbearer around whom the troops could rally. Now, delegates belong to candidates, not party officials. Conventions no longer choose the party's candidate; caucus activists and voters in primaries do. Renewing the party coalition and rallying the faithful remain crucial, especially after divisive primary contests. But conveying an attractive image and message to citizens watching the action back home on television is an even more important goal.

In 2016, both parties' conventions became venues for efforts to patch up party divisions arising from a bruising primary season as well as for trumpeting the candidates' central campaign themes for the fall (see Chapter 11). Unity proved elusive at the Republican convention in Cleveland. Many senior Republican leaders, including former presidents and presidential candidates, senators, and governors—traditionally prominent convention participants—elected to stay away. Some delegates not reconciled to Trump's nomination sought unsuccessfully to pass a resolution freeing delegates to vote for any candidate. Cruz, given the prime-time speaking spot customarily granted the second place candidate in return for endorsing the winner, pointedly refused to endorse Trump, telling Republicans instead to "vote their consciences." Nonetheless, the convention sealed Trump's takeover of the party, as speaker after speaker reiterated the populist themes of his campaign while excoriating Clinton and Obama. His vice presidential choice, Indiana governor Mike Pence, was an orthodox economic and social conservative and thus attractive to important Republican factions beyond Trump's populist core. Pence helped bring the party together during the general election campaign, a classic instance of balancing the party ticket to broaden its appeal.

The 2016 Democratic convention was also contentious. To bring Sanders's supporters on board, Clinton gave his appointees a major influence on the party platform, making it the most liberal ever adopted (for examples, see the box on pp. 554–555). Although Sanders offered Clinton strong support in his prime-time speech and pleaded with his delegates to join him, not all complied. The exposure of Democratic National Committee (DNC) e-mails (determined by U.S. intelligence agencies to be the work of Russian hackers) revealing that its leaders tilted toward Clinton outraged Sanders supporters, some of whom walked out and joined street demonstrations against her nomination. The DNC's chair, Debbie Wasserman Schultz, had to resign, giving up her role as convention chair.

Both parties, then, found it difficult to overcome internal divisions in 2016. Both came together sufficiently to make the general election a highly partisan affair, with the vast majority of voters remaining loyal to their party's candidate. But for both, the divisions exposed during the primaries and conventions remain in place, and the internal struggles over who and what the parties stand for will continue.

Both 2016 conventions featured long rosters of speakers—politicians from all levels of government, leaders of various organizations, celebrities, former military officers, exemplary citizens, and the candidates' children. An emphasis on diversity in age, race and ethnicity, gender, and background is typical, sometimes belying the much more homogenous composition

Chip Somodevilla/Getty Images

Joe Raedle/Getty Images

Each party's 2016 convention featured an eloquent speech by the candidate's spouse designed to soften and humanize the candidate's image. Melania Trump's speech was one of the few appearances she made during the campaign. Bill Clinton's participation was unique, both as the potential first husband and first former president to perform this role. He has delivered a prime-time address at every Democratic convention since 1988.

of the delegations, particularly on the Republican side; the message is that all are welcome. These efforts serve as a reminder that conventions, in addition to refurbishing the party coalitions for the fall campaign, aim to show voters what sorts of people make up the party and what groups and causes they champion. A party's self-display at its national convention is not without risk, as both parties have had more than one occasion to discover. Party activists often hold more extreme views on the issues of the day than do ordinary party voters, who may question whether the party actually represents their values and interests. The problem is illustrated in the box "Voters versus Party Activists in 2008: Differences of Opinion," which compares the views of voters who identify themselves as Republicans or Democrats with the views of the respective party's convention delegates in 2008. On almost every question the opinions of convention delegates are more sharply divided than those of their parties' voters; on average, the respective delegations' responses differ by about 60 percentage points. On a few issues, delegates' views are also quite distinct from the views of party supporters (Democrats on abortion; Republicans on health care policy). It is easy to understand why many voters would see the Republicans as too conservative and the Democrats as too liberal to represent their views reliably. However, the responses show that ordinary Democratic and Republican voters differ on many issues as well. The average difference in responses among the parties' voters is about 38 percentage points. No comparable studies exist for 2012 or 2016, but the party platforms, excerpted on pages 554–555, frequently express positions clearly more appealing to the party's ideological activists than to its more moderate voters.

### Consequences of Fractured Alignments

When issues arise that split the existing party coalitions, partisan identities weaken, and the party label may not provide the information voters want. The fracturing of the New Deal alignments in the 1960s and 1970s and the difficulty party politicians faced in reconstructing stable coalitions around new issues reduced the importance of party cues to voters, who became less certain about which political camp they belonged in. The consequences of this breakdown were abundantly evident in election and polling results. Party-line voting declined, and ticket splitting increased (see Figure 12.5, p. 547). With voters substituting personal cues for party cues, the electoral advantage enjoyed by congressional incumbents grew (for details, see section "Candidate-Centered versus Party-Centered Electoral Politics" in Chapter 6, pp. 244–247). The electorate became more volatile, with wider swings of party fortunes between elections. Independent and third-party candidates increased their take. Between 1932 and 1964, no minor party or independent candidate received more than 3 percent of the vote. Between 1968 and 1996, three candidates in four races exceeded that margin: George Wallace (14 percent in 1968), John Anderson (7 percent in 1980), and Ross Perot (19 percent in 1992, 8 percent in 1996).

These electoral changes made divided partisan control of governments more common. American voters now regularly if not invariably divide control of the White House and Congress between the parties (see Table 7.2, p. 305). Do they do it on purpose? Certainly, moderate voters might prefer divided government because it allows each party to block the other's more extreme proposals and forces both parties to compromise when making policy.[23] People who simply distrust politicians also might prefer to have the parties in a position to check each other. Despite this logic, there is little evidence that many people deliberately split their votes to achieve moderate policies or to make "ambition counteract ambition." Divided government is partly a by-product of voters applying different criteria for different offices, responding to the specific options in each contest, or making trade-offs among their incompatible preferences (for low taxes but generous middle-class entitlements, for less regulation but more protection from environmental and market risks).[24] It is also partly a consequence of the Republicans' structural advantage from a more efficient distribution of their regular voters, which, for example, allowed them to win a majority of House seats in 2012 with a minority of votes cast nationwide for U.S. representatives while their candidate was losing the presidency by five million votes (see box "The Republican Gerrymander in 2012" in Chapter 6, p. 240). And it occurs when voters deliver a negative midterm referendum on the president, as in 1994, 2010, and 2018. But even if few people deliberately vote for divided government, most are usually happy when they get it. For example, in 2016, a year when 90 percent of voters in the American National Election Studies voted for the same party's candidate for president and U.S. representative, 54 percent said they preferred to have the presidency and Congress split between the parties, whereas only 20 percent preferred to have one party control both branches (the rest said it did not matter).

### Media and Money

The weakening of party influence on voters in the 1960s and 1970s was hastened by technological changes and the growing availability of campaign resources—money, skill, activists—from sources other than political parties. The most important technological innovation was

Voters versus Party Activists in 2008

| DIFFERENCES OF OPINION | DEMOCRATIC DELEGATES | DEMOCRATIC VOTERS | REPUBLICAN VOTERS | REPUBLICAN DELEGATES |
|---|---|---|---|---|
| 1. Ideology: Liberal | 43% | 48% | 5% | 0% |
| Moderate | 50 | 34 | 30 | 26 |
| Conservative | 3 | 16 | 63 | 72 |
| 2. The United States did the right thing in taking military action in Iraq. | 2 | 14 | 71 | 80 |
| 3. Prefer health coverage for all and higher taxes to lower taxes leaving some without health coverage. | 94 | 90 | 40 | 7 |
| 4. Protecting the environment is more important than developing new sources of energy. | 25 | 30 | 9 | 3 |
| 5. Gun control laws should be made more strict. | 62 | 71 | 32 | 8 |
| 6. Illegal immigration is a very serious issue. | 15 | 36 | 63 | 58 |
| 7. Same-sex couples should be allowed to marry legally. | 55 | 49 | 11 | 6 |
| 8. Abortion should be generally available to those who want it rather than under stricter limits or not permitted. | 70 | 43 | 19 | 0 |
| 9. The condition of the economy is good. | 2 | 7 | 40 | 57 |
| 10. The 2001 Bush tax cuts should be made permanent. | 7 | 34 | 62 | 91 |

Source: CBS News/New York Times polls, July–August 2008, accessed at www.cbsnews.com/htdocs/pdf/RNCDelegates_issues.pdf and www.cbsnews.com/htdocs/pdf/RNCDelegates_who_are_they.pdf.

Note: Percentage indicates the proportion of each group that agreed with each numbered statement.

■ **FIGURE 12.5** Split-Ticket Voting

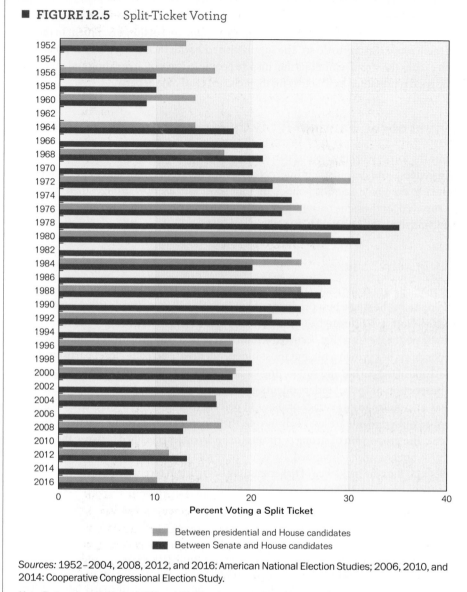

*Percent Voting a Split Ticket*

Between presidential and House candidates
Between Senate and House candidates

*Sources:* 1952–2004, 2008, 2012, and 2016: American National Election Studies; 2006, 2010, and 2014: Cooperative Congressional Election Study.

*Note:* Data not available for 1954 and 1962 and not yet in for 2018.

the advent of television as a campaign medium, but newer technologies, such as computerized direct mail, mass-produced campaign videos, and later Twitter and the Internet, contributed as well. These media enabled candidates with sufficient resources to reach voters directly without the help of parties; Ross Perot was able to conduct a surprisingly successful campaign in 1992 with no party at all behind him.

The technology of modern campaigns is expensive, driving up the demand for campaign funds. The supply rose to meet the demand because a growing economy provided more money for people to invest in politics, and the expanding role of the government in their lives gave them more reasons to do so. The supply also rose with increasing partisan polarization, which excites the strong emotions that inspire people to leave off free riding and invest in the public good represented by a victory for their chosen candidate or party.

## Revival of the Parties: A Sixth Party System?

Despite the forces working against parties, despite the public's doubts about the value of parties in general, and despite their internal divisions, the Democratic and Republican Parties continue to dominate electoral politics. In some ways, they are now stronger than ever. Parties have survived for the same reasons they came into being: elected officials, candidates, and voters still find them indispensable.

### Partisanship Endures

Large majorities of Americans still call themselves Democrats or Republicans, and party affiliation remains the single best predictor of how people will vote. The distribution of partisan identities from 1952 through 2016, shown in Figure 12.6, is surprisingly stable despite the dramatic political events that occurred within that period. The proportion calling themselves independents has grown a bit, but most independents are actually closet partisans leaning toward one of the parties and supporting its candidates as consistently as do weak partisans.[25] The proportion of "pure" independents grew from 6 percent in 1952 to 15 percent in 1976 but has since fallen to an average of about 11 percent over the past two decades. Because self-described independents are less likely to vote, their share of the electorate is actually closer to 5 percent. The proportion of strong partisans (of both parties) declined between the 1950s and the 1970s but has since rebounded. Partisans have also grown more loyal to their party's candidates, and thus the incidence of ticket splitting has fallen in recent elections to levels last seen in the 1960s (see Figure 12.5).

### Party Differences

Voters may not think much of parties, but most still admit to a party preference and use parties to guide their voting decisions. They do so because, despite the divisions within the party coalitions and regardless of how they feel about parties in general, the party labels still carry valuable information about candidates (see box "2016 Party Platforms"), continuing to provide the cheap, shorthand cue so useful to rationally ignorant voters. Indeed, more people think party labels offer clearer guidance now than at any time since 1952; over the past thirty years, the proportion of Americans seeing important differences in what the parties stand for has grown from about half to nearly 80 percent (see Figure 12.7).

Party differences are in fact clear-cut. Republicans typically favor a smaller, cheaper federal government; they advocate lower taxes, less regulation of business, and lower spending on social welfare. They would be more generous only to the Defense Department.

**■ FIGURE 12.6**  Americans' Continuing Identification with a Major Party

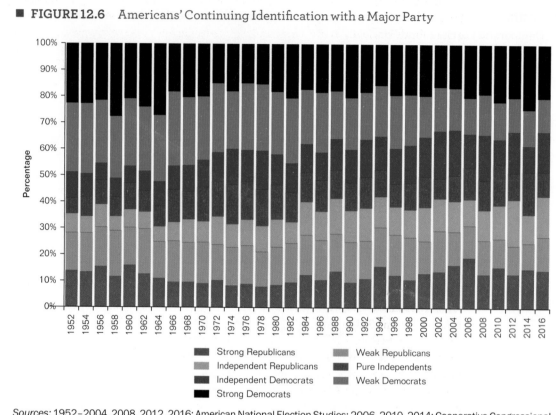

Strong Republicans  Weak Republicans
Independent Republicans  Pure Independents
Independent Democrats  Weak Democrats
Strong Democrats

*Sources:* 1952–2004, 2008, 2012, 2016: American National Election Studies; 2006, 2010, 2014: Cooperative Congressional Election Study.

Republicans oppose stricter gun control, restrictions on campaign spending, and a pathway to citizenship for undocumented immigrants, whereas Democrats favor all three. Democrats are more inclined to regulate business on behalf of consumers and the environment and are more supportive of government programs designed to improve domestic welfare; they would spend less on national defense. Democrats are more concerned with "fairness" and equality, Republicans with letting free enterprise flourish. Republicans would ban abortion and gay marriage and allow official prayer in public schools; Democrats would not. Republicans want to reduce immigration and build a wall on the Mexican border; Democrats do not. Democrats accept the overwhelming scientific consensus that human activity is warming the planet, with potentially disastrous consequences, and advocate government action to cut greenhouse gas emissions; Republicans either deny human responsibility for global warming or consider it insufficiently menacing to justify government intervention. Not all candidates adhere to their party's modal positions; some Republicans support freedom of choice on abortion, and some Democrats advocate large defense budgets; Donald Trump's rejection of free trade is a clear departure from Republican orthodoxy. But the party label continues to distinguish

■ **FIGURE 12.7**    Americans Increasingly See Important Differences in What the Republican and Democratic Parties Stand For

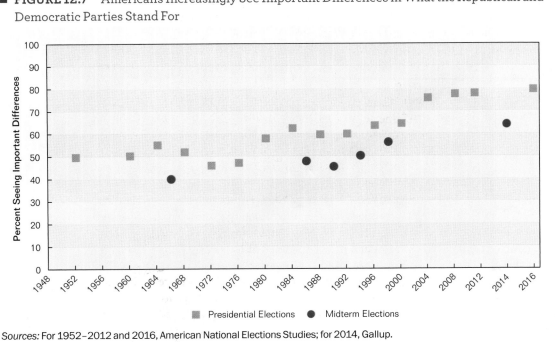

Sources: For 1952–2012 and 2016, American National Elections Studies; for 2014, Gallup.

candidates from one another on many issues with considerable accuracy. As the predictive accuracy of party labels has grown in recent decades, so has the usefulness—and therefore use—of party cues.

## Changes in the Party Coalitions

The party coalitions of the 2000s still retain traces of the New Deal alignment (for example, lower-income voters are still more likely to be Democrats and higher-income voters Republicans), but they have undergone several crucial changes since the 1960s. In the 1950s white southerners were overwhelmingly Democratic, but they responded to the civil rights revolution—and the Republicans' "southern strategy" to exploit the discontent civil rights aroused—by moving gradually but steadily into the Republican camp. A solid majority of white southerners now identify themselves as Republicans. African Americans favored Democrats even before the 1960s, but the magnitude of the Democratic advantage more than doubled in the 1960s, has remained huge ever since, and was reinforced by Obama's two candidacies. Latino voters, representing a growing share of the electorate, have also become an important component of the Democratic coalition, in part as a reaction to the hard-line stance against undocumented immigrants taken by many Republican politicians, exemplified by President Trump.

Men have become more Republican, whereas women have not, creating the famous "gender gap" between the parties.* The Democratic advantage among Catholics has shrunk, and religiously active voters in all Christian denominations have become relatively more Republican, whereas secular voters have become more Democratic.

Changes in the party coalitions have been extensive enough to suggest that a sixth party system is now in place. Because the changes occurred gradually and at different times, the new system's starting date is unclear: some analysts propose 1968, whereas others say 1980 or 1984. Whatever the timing, the most salient difference between the current and New Deal party systems is the Republican Party's increased strength, exemplified by its winning majorities in the House and Senate in six straight elections (1994–2004), unprecedented since the fourth party system, its retaking of the House in 2010 and the Senate in 2014, erasing the Democratic gains of 2006 and 2008, and its sweeping national victory in 2016 (now partially erased by the Democrats' 2018 takeover of the House).

The Republicans' competitive status is threatened, however, by demographic trends. The Republican coalition includes a disproportionate share of white (86 percent), male, older, less educated, religiously active, and socially conservative Americans, all shrinking segments of the electorate. The Democratic coalition is younger, more female, better educated, and more secular and includes a much larger share of minority voters (43 percent), including Latinos, the fastest growing segment of the electorate.[26] Younger voters tend to be more secular and socially liberal and are likely to remain so as they age. Mitt Romney's inability to attract more young, nonwhite, secular, and female voters in 2012 was widely viewed by Republican analysts as a sign that their party faced long-term decline if it did not expand its appeal beyond its current, diminishing base. Trump challenged that perspective in 2016 when he won the electoral if not the popular vote by outperforming Romney among whites, especially white men without college degrees, who were key to his victories in several swing states. More generally, as America has become more diverse racially and ethnically, whites have responded by becoming more conservative and Republican, while racial and ethnic minorities have remained predominantly liberal and Democratic. Thus, although the parties have grown increasingly divergent demographically—a trend contributing to partisan polarization—the electorate's changing demographic profile has yet to shift the partisan balance in the Democrats' favor.[27]

A second distinctive feature of the current party system is that partisan differences on issues and policy are wider and deeper than they were during the New Deal party system. The widening ideological divide between the parties in Congress over the past several decades (see Figure 6.7 on p. 262) has been echoed, to varying degrees, at all levels of the party system. In general, the more actively engaged Americans are in politics, the more polarized along party

---

*The American National Election Studies from 1964 through 1978 found women to be, on average, only about 2 percentage points more Democratic in their partisanship than men. In studies conducted from 1980 through 1990, however, women averaged 6 percentage points more Democratic; since then, the gender gap in party identification has grown to about 10 percentage points. These differences show up in presidential voting, with the Democratic candidate running better among women than among men by about 10 percentage points in 2000, 7 points in 2004, 5 points in 2008 and 2012, and 7 points in 2016. In 2018, the gender gap in the House vote was more than 11 points. For a general discussion of the gender gap in party identification, see Warren E. Miller and J. Merrill Shanks, *The New American Voter* (Cambridge, MA: Harvard University Press, 1996), 141–145.

lines they have become. Partisan differences in ideology and policy have widened the most among political professionals; campaign contributors; and the amateur activists who walk precincts and staff phone banks for candidates, put up yard signs, and encourage their friends and neighbors to vote for their side. To a lesser extent, partisan polarization has also increased among people whose participation is limited to voting; it has not increased only among the politically inactive and uninvolved.[28] Scholars still debate whether Americans as a whole have become more polarized in their opinions on political issues, but there is abundant evidence that they have responded to the clearer cues issuing from the more polarized political class by sorting themselves more consistently into the party that best fits their own political beliefs and preferences.[29] People who call themselves conservatives and express conservative opinions on policy issues are much more likely to identify as Republicans, and self-identified liberals and people holding liberal policy views are more likely to identify as Democrats, than was the case a few decades ago.

The sorting process has been gradual; it has been most noticeable among conservative southern whites, but it is by no means confined to them. Figure 12.8 illustrates some consequences. The Republican coalition, predominantly conservative from the start, has grown substantially more so. The proportion of Republicans placing themselves to the right of center on a 7-point scale that ranged from very conservative to very liberal grew from 54 percent in 1972 to 72 percent in 2016, while the proportion left of center fell from 13 percent to 4 percent. Meanwhile Democrats grew more liberal, with the proportion placing themselves left of center rising from 36 percent to 60 percent and the proportion right of center falling from 25 percent to 13 percent. Over the same period, the share of Republicans placing themselves

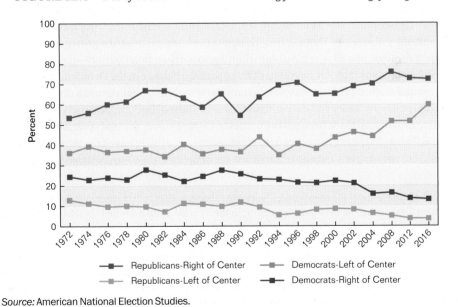

■ **FIGURE 12.8**  Party Identification and Ideology Are Increasingly Aligned

Republicans-Right of Center
Republicans-Left of Center
Democrats-Left of Center
Democrats-Right of Center

Source: American National Election Studies.

in the middle of the scale dropped 10 points (down to 24 percent in 2016), and the share of Democrats by 13 points (down to 27 percent). The emergence of polarized, nearly evenly balanced party coalitions has ratcheted up electoral competition for federal offices, spurring the invigoration of national party organizations and the formation of lavishly funded auxiliary organizations devoted to electing the party's candidates.

## Modern Party Organizations

On paper the modern Democratic and Republican Parties might be depicted as pyramidal organizations. Each party's sovereign body is its national nominating convention, which officially elects the national party chair and ratifies the states' selections to the party's national committee (the Republican National Committee or the Democratic National Committee). The national committee, with at least two members from each state, is charged with conducting the party's affairs between national conventions and hiring and directing a large professional staff. Below the national committees are the state committees and chairs, which oversee the committees representing congressional and state legislative districts and counties. Further subdivisions include diverse township, city, ward, and precinct committees, also with formal leaders, some chosen by caucuses, some in primary elections.*

### Control

In reality, however, the national parties are far from orderly hierarchies, and at most levels they are controlled by elected politicians, not party officials. The national party's chair is always the choice of the party's presidential nominee, and the national committee's primary task is to win or retain the presidency, although it engages in other forms of party building between presidential contests. House and Senate candidates have their own separate national campaign organizations—all under the control of their respective party's congressional leaders (see Chapter 6).

Elected officials also usually control state parties, which are in no way subordinate to the national parties; governors are frequently the most powerful figures in their state parties, for example. State parties often have little influence over local organizations, and both state and local parties are sometimes split into personal, ideological, or regional factions. Local party offices sometimes go begging, and on occasion insurgent groups have been able to take over party committee and leadership posts just by getting their people to show up at the usually lightly attended caucuses or precinct conventions where such choices are made. That is how, for example, Christian conservatives came to control local Republican Party organizations in some places in the 1990s, including Texas, South Carolina, and Minnesota.[30]

Although they continue to display the organizational fragmentation that has always characterized them, the American parties of today are in some ways more closely linked than ever. Both national parties and many state organizations have become modern,

---

*Party organization at the state and local levels is highly varied, reflecting differences in historical development, local custom, and state law. Moreover, in many places the formal party units are joined by a diverse set of party clubs, caucuses, factional organizations, and allied interest groups that also participate in party politics.

# 2016 Party Platforms

These excerpts from the 2016 Democratic and Republican platforms reveal some of the differences between positions typically held by the parties. But few voters learn of these differences by reading the platforms. Rather, they learn about the parties' positions through political news and campaign advertising.

| | REPUBLICANS | DEMOCRATS |
|---|---|---|
| **Abortion** | We assert the sanctity of human life and affirm that the unborn child has a fundamental right to life which cannot be infringed. We support a human life amendment to the Constitution. | We believe unequivocally . . . that every woman should have access to quality reproductive health care services, including safe and legal abortion—regardless of where she lives, how much money she makes, or how she is insured. |
| **Taxes** | We oppose tax policies that deliberately divide Americans or promote class warfare. . . . Any value added tax or national sales tax must be tied to the simultaneous repeal of the Sixteenth Amendment, which established the federal income tax. . . . We . . . support making the federal tax code so simple and easy to understand that the IRS becomes obsolete and can be abolished. | At a time of massive income and wealth inequality, we believe the wealthiest Americans and largest corporations must pay their fair share of taxes. . . . We will end deferrals so that American corporations pay United States taxes immediately on foreign profits and can no longer escape paying their fair share of U.S. taxes by stashing profits abroad. |
| **Guns** | We support firearm reciprocity legislation to recognize the right of law-abiding Americans to carry firearms . . . in all 50 states. We support constitutional carry statutes. . . . We oppose . . . laws that would restrict magazine capacity or ban the sale of the most popular and common modern rifle. . . . We oppose federal licensing or registration of law-abiding gun owners, registration of ammunition, and restoration of the ill-fated Clinton gun ban. | We will expand and strengthen background checks and close . . . loopholes in our current laws; repeal the Protection of Lawful Commerce in Arms Act (PLCAA) to revoke the . . . legal immunity protections gun makers and sellers now enjoy; and keep weapons of war—such as assault weapons and large capacity ammunition magazines—off our streets. . . . The U.S. Centers for Disease Control and Prevention must have the resources it needs to study gun violence as a public health issue. |
| **Same-sex marriage** | We condemn the Supreme Court's ruling in *United States v. Windsor*, which . . . removed the ability of Congress to define marriage policy in federal law. We also condemn the Supreme Court's . . . ruling in *Obergefell v. Hodges* . . . [which] robbed 320 million Americans of their legitimate constitutional authority to define marriage as the union of one man and one woman. | Democrats applaud last year's decision by the Supreme Court that recognized that LGBT people—like other Americans—have the right to marry the person they love. |
| **Climate change** | Climate change is far from this nation's most pressing national security issue. . . . We oppose any carbon tax. . . . We will . . . forbid the EPA to regulate carbon dioxide. . . . We reject the agendas of both the Kyoto Protocol and the Paris Agreement. | Climate change is an urgent threat and a defining challenge of our time. . . . Carbon dioxide, methane, and other greenhouse gases should be priced to reflect their negative externalities. . . . Climate change is too important to wait for climate deniers and defeatists in Congress to start listening to science, and [we] support using every tool available to reduce emissions now. |
| **Health care** | Improving healthcare must start with repeal of . . . the Affordable Care Act. . . . We will reduce mandates and enable insurers and providers of care to increase healthcare options and contain costs. . . . We will return to the states their . . . role of regulating local insurance markets, limit federal requirements on both private insurance and Medicaid . . . we propose to block grant Medicaid and other payments. | Health care is a right, not a privilege. . . . We took a . . . step toward the goal of universal health care by passing the Affordable Care Act. . . . Democrats will never falter in our . . . fight to guarantee health care as a fundamental right for every American. . . . Americans should be able to access public coverage through a public option, and those over 55 should be able to opt in to Medicare. |

| | REPUBLICANS | DEMOCRATS |
|---|---|---|
| **Immigration** | We oppose any form of amnesty. . . . The executive amnesties of 2012 and 2014 . . . [are] unlawful . . . [and] must be immediately rescinded by a Republican president. [We] support building a wall along our southern border and protecting all ports of entry. . . . Asylum should be limited to cases of political, ethnic or religious persecution. . . . Refugees who cannot be carefully vetted cannot be admitted to the country, especially those whose homelands have been the breeding grounds for terrorism. | We need to . . . fix our broken immigration system . . . and create a path to citizenship for law-abiding families who are here. . . . We must fix family backlogs and defend against those who would exclude or eliminate legal immigration avenues and denigrate immigrants. We will defend and implement President Obama's Deferred Action for Childhood Arrivals and Deferred Action for Parents of Americans executive actions to help DREAMers, parents of citizens, and lawful permanent residents avoid deportation. |
| **Social Security** | Its current course will lead to a financial and social disaster. . . . Current retirees and those close to retirement can be assured of their benefits. . . . All options should be considered to preserve Social Security. . . . We oppose tax increases and believe in the power of markets to create wealth and to help secure the future of our Social Security system. | We will fight every effort to cut, privatize, or weaken Social Security, including attempts to raise the retirement age, diminish benefits by cutting cost-of-living adjustments, or reducing earned benefits. |
| **Death penalty** | The constitutionality of the death penalty is firmly settled by its explicit mention in the Fifth Amendment. . . . We condemn the Supreme Court's erosion of the right of the people to enact capital punishment in their states. | We will abolish the death penalty, which has proven to be a cruel and unusual form of punishment. . . . The application of the death penalty is arbitrary and unjust. The cost to taxpayers far exceeds those of life imprisonment. It does not deter crime. |
| **Minimum wage** | Minimum wage is an issue that should be handled at the state and local level. | Americans should earn at least $15 an hour. . . . We should raise the federal minimum wage to $15 an hour over time and index it. |
| **Voter identification** | We are concerned . . . that some voting procedures may be open to abuse. . . . We support legislation to require proof of citizenship when registering to vote and secure photo ID when voting. We strongly oppose litigation against states exercising their sovereign authority to enact such laws. | We will continue to fight against discriminatory voter identification laws, which disproportionately burden young voters, diverse communities, people of color, low-income families, people with disabilities, the elderly, and women. |
| **Campaign finance** | Freedom of speech includes the right to devote resources to whatever cause or candidate one supports. . . . We support repeal of federal restrictions on political parties in McCain-Feingold [and] raising or repealing contribution limits. | Big money is drowning out the voices of everyday Americans . . . Democrats support a constitutional amendment to overturn the Supreme Court's decisions in *Citizens United* and *Buckley v. Valeo* [allowing unlimited campaign spending]. |
| **Financial regulation** | We must overturn the regulatory nightmare, created by the Dodd-Frank law. | We will . . . vigorously implement, enforce, and build on President Obama's landmark Dodd-Frank financial reform law. |
| **Cuba** | The current Administration's "opening to Cuba" was a shameful accommodation to the demands of its tyrants. . . . We call on the Congress to uphold current U.S. law which sets conditions for the lifting of sanctions on the island: Legalization of political parties, an independent media, and free and fair internationally-supervised elections. | In Cuba, we will build on President Obama's historic opening and end the travel ban and embargo. We will also stand by the Cuban people and support their ability to decide their own future and to enjoy the same human rights and freedoms that people everywhere deserve. |

*Sources:* Adapted from 2016 Republican and Democratic platforms, accessed at https://prod-cdn-static.gop.com/static/home/data/platform.pdf and www.demconvention.com/wp-content/uploads/2016/07/Democratic-Party-Platform-7.21.16-no-lines.pdf.

businesslike enterprises with permanent offices, professional staffs, and relatively stable budgets, producing a stronger institutional basis for ongoing coordination and cooperation in pursuit of power.

### Organizational Innovations

Although both major parties have had permanent national committees since before the Civil War, only since the 1970s have national organizations played a significant role in party politics. Democrats began to nationalize their party structure when the various post-1968 reform commissions operating out of national headquarters imposed rules on state and local parties. But Republicans led the way after that as they sought to undo the damage inflicted by the Watergate scandal and other troubles that cost their president, Gerald Ford, the 1976 election. The first step was to raise money—lots of it. Republican operatives perfected the new technique of computerized direct-mail fund-raising, developing lists of people willing to send modest checks in response to regular solicitations to create a steady source of income for the party. Their growing success during the early 1980s, when they were raising 80 percent of their money through mail-in checks averaging less than thirty dollars, is documented in Figure 12.9.

With the money coming in, Republicans enlarged their organization staff and began to provide a host of services to their candidates. Today they help candidates for federal office raise money, comply with campaign finance regulations, design polls, set up websites, research opponents' records, put together lists of voters to contact, and design campaign strategy. They also contribute some money directly to candidates' campaign war chests. Republican candidates are helped indirectly as well by the money and training the national party has contributed to state and local Republican organizations across the nation to strengthen the party at the grass roots. In addition, the campaign committees stepped up efforts to identify, recruit, and train effective candidates for Congress and, in some instances, for state offices as well.[31]

Democrats were shocked into a similar effort to expand the services offered by their national party committees when in 1980 they lost both the White House (to Ronald Reagan) and their Senate majority. They played catch-up in fund-raising until 2008, when they outspent the Republicans for the first time (see Figure 12.9). Contrary to expectations, the ban on soft party money enacted in 2002 (see Chapter 11) did not put them at further disadvantage, for they were able to make up much of the difference by raising more hard dollars. Republicans, too, vastly increased their take of hard money, and between them, the parties raised $1.59 billion for the 2004 federal election campaigns, $1.75 billion for the 2008 campaigns, $2.09 billion for 2012, and more than $2.11 billion for 2016. Instead of transferring soft money to state parties to help federal candidates as they had in the past, the Hill committees simply switched to spending hard money on independent campaigns (separate from the candidates' campaigns) in the most competitive congressional races. Spending of this sort exceeded $232 million in 2018, up from a mere $2.9 million in 2002.[32]

Both parties have now also adopted the most up-to-date technology to perform the oldest of party tasks, getting potentially free-riding supporters to the polls. They have compiled massive databases, with detailed information about tens of millions of individual voters, which are used to support sophisticated local efforts to get out the vote. This traditional party

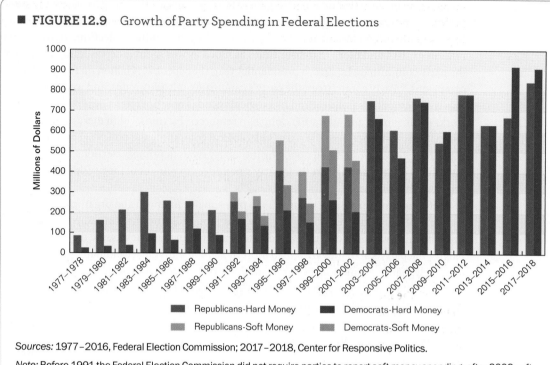

**■ FIGURE 12.9**   Growth of Party Spending in Federal Elections

Republicans-Hard Money        Democrats-Hard Money
Republicans-Soft Money        Democrats-Soft Money

*Sources:* 1977–2016, Federal Election Commission; 2017–2018, Center for Responsive Politics.

*Note:* Before 1991 the Federal Election Commission did not require parties to report soft money spending; after 2002 soft money was banned.

activity has grown more important because, with fewer voters willing to cross party lines, winning depends increasingly on mobilizing core supporters. Both parties recognized this reality in 2018 and made extraordinary efforts to get their people to the polls. Both succeeded, but Democrats to a much greater extent than Republicans, and this was crucial to their takeover of the House. Their efforts produced the highest midterm voting participation rates in a century, with an estimated 50.3 percent of eligible citizens casting ballots, 13 points higher than in 2014 and 10 points higher than the midterm average for the last four decades (see Figure 12.3).[33] The total vote for Republican candidates in House elections nationally was about 10.9 million higher than in the previous midterm in 2014, but the total vote for Democratic candidates was 25.1 million higher. In the twenty-eight districts Democrats took from Republicans where comparisons with 2014 are possible, the average Republican vote total was up 21 percent over 2014, but the average Democratic vote total was up more than 200 percent. Voter participation in Senate elections was also up sharply over 2014, by averages of 46 percent in the ten most competitive states and 29 percent in the rest. Big turnout increases in the Republican-leaning states of Indiana (61 percent) and Missouri (58 percent) were instrumental in defeating the Democratic incumbents and enlarging the Republican Senate majority. The remarkable jump in participation reflected Donald Trump's unique capacity to incite partisan passions among activists and voters on both sides.[34]

Outside groups also now participate extensively in campaigning for (or more often against) candidates, mainly but not exclusively as auxiliaries of the parties; such groups spent $1.1 billion on independent campaigns in the 2018 midterm election, up from $560 million in 2014 and more than four times as much as was spent independently in 2018 by the party committees. In 2016, a presidential year, they spent $1.4 billion on federal election campaigns.[35] Party committees, the party's candidates, outside groups, and wealthy individuals with compatible political and ideological agendas now operate as flexible partisan networks for acquiring and allocating campaign resources. Factions within these networks often compete for influence over the party's ideological coloration and policy agenda, mainly by supporting their favorites and opposing intraparty rivals in primary elections, but they unite after the primaries to support their party's nominees in pursuit of the presidency and congressional majorities.

Although modern parties continue to play a major financial and organizational role in electoral politics, they have clearly lost the near monopoly they had on campaign resources until the mid-twentieth century. Candidates, rather than party tickets, are the focus of campaigns; the party's activities are aimed more at helping individual candidates compete more effectively than at promoting the party brand. According to political scientist John Aldrich, "A new form of party has emerged, one that is 'in service' to its ambitious politicians but not 'in control' of them as the mass party [of the past] sought to be."[36] Whatever influence the party organizations do exercise over politicians is shared by the wealthy interests and individuals who now invest so heavily in their campaigns.

## Expediency Persists

American parties developed and continue to endure because they have proved so useful to politicians and voters attempting to act collectively within the institutional framework established by the Constitution. The federal system offers powerful incentives for organizing and expanding both legislative and electoral coalitions—that is, political parties—to win and exercise political power. For one thing, it rewards political entrepreneurs who can organize collective action across government institutions and electoral arenas. For another, it prompts voters to use party labels to simplify their decisions, giving politicians a reason to cooperate with party leaders to maintain the value of the party's "brand name."

Although the party coalitions have shifted periodically in response to new national issues and conflicts, producing five—perhaps now six—more or less distinct party systems, the basic pattern of competition between two broad, usually fractious coalitions persists. The two-party system arises from strategic voting in the winner-take-all competition for the presidency (and for all other federal offices as well) and has been strengthened by laws (mandating, for example, primary elections) that treat the parties as official components of the electoral machinery. Party coalitions remain fractious because party entrepreneurs pursuing majorities must combine diverse groups that are neither natural allies nor disposed to pay high conformity costs for the party's sake. But these coalitions persist because the payoffs for cooperation (and the costs of splitting) are so obvious. Progressive Era reforms, followed by the development of new technologies of communication after the Second World War, weakened traditional party organizations and ended their monopoly control

of campaigns, but parties continue to play a central role in electoral politics. Despite their expressed disdain for parties, voters still rely heavily on party cues in making their decisions because party labels continue to provide useful, cheap information about candidates. Party entrepreneurs, for their part, have simply redesigned party organizations to operate more effectively in today's media-based electoral arena. They are walking down the trail blazed by Jefferson and Van Buren, and for the same reason: to elect those who share their views so that they may shape public policy to their liking.

**⑤SAGE edge™**
**for CQ Press**

**Want a better grade?**

Get the tools you need to sharpen your study skills. Access practice quizzes, eFlashcards, video, and multimedia at **edge.sagepub.com/kernell9e.**

## KEY TERMS

Australian ballot   533
caucus   528
national party convention   530
New Deal coalition   537

party machines   532
patronage   525
political party   515
primary election   534

Progressive Era   533
split ticket   533
superdelegates   541
two-party system   520

## SUGGESTED READINGS

Aldrich, John H. *Why Parties? The Origin and Transformation of Party Politics in America.* Chicago: University of Chicago Press, 1995. An astute theoretical and historical analysis of American parties that deepens and extends the approach taken in this text.

Chambers, William Nesbit, and Walter Dean Burnham, eds. *The American Party Systems: Stages of Political Development.* 2nd ed. New York: Oxford University Press, 1975. Fascinating historical essays on American party development. The essay by Eric L. McKitrick explaining how partisan politics helped Abraham Lincoln and how its absence hurt Jefferson Davis during the Civil War is especially instructive.

Cohen, Jeffrey E., Richard Fleisher, and Paul Kantor, eds. *American Political Parties: Decline or Resurgence?* Washington, DC: CQ Press, 2001. Historical and contemporary materials explore changes in American parties and analyze party weaknesses, the reasons for

revitalization, and the responsibilities of parties in a democracy.

DiSalvo, Daniel. *Engines of Change: Party Factions in American Politics 1868–2010.* New York: Oxford University Press, 2012. The Tea Party is only the latest instance of a party faction strongly influencing a party's policy agenda, nominations, and governing strategies.

Levandusky, Matthew. *The Partisan Sort: How Liberals Became Democrats and Conservatives Became Republicans.* Chicago: University of Chicago Press, 2009. Details how Americans have increasingly sorted themselves into the political party that best fits their ideological and policy preferences, contributing to the growth in party polarization over the past several decades.

Mayhew, David R. *Electoral Realignments: A Critique of an American Genre.* New Haven, CT: Yale University Press, 2002. As its title suggests, the idea of

periodic party realignments of the kind discussed in this chapter is examined and questioned in this book.

Mayhew, David R. *Placing Parties in American Politics.* Princeton, NJ: Princeton University Press, 1986. To understand why some states developed strong party organizations and others did not, read this book.

Noel, Hans. *Political Ideologies and Political Parties in America.* New York: Cambridge University Press, 2013. Examines how the development of coherent liberal and conservative ideologies has shaped the development of the contemporary parties.

Riordan, William L., ed. *Plunkitt of Tammany Hall.* New York: Dutton, 1963. According to the subtitle, "a series of very plain talks on very practical politics, delivered by George Washington Plunkitt, the Tammany Philosopher, from his rostrum—the New York County Court House bootblack stand." Includes a good introductory essay on nineteenth-century party machine politics.

Sundquist, James L. *The Dynamics of the Party System.* Rev. ed. Washington, DC: Brookings, 1983. Highly detailed study of historical party realignments; for those who prefer complex stories to simple ones.

## REVIEW QUESTIONS

1. Where did U.S. parties first arise? Why did they prove necessary in this setting? Why did parties spread from there to other areas of politics?

2. Why do third parties tend to do so poorly in U.S. elections? Why do such parties do so much better in other democracies?

3. How has the nomination process for party candidates changed over time? If national conventions no longer decide on the party's presidential nominee, why are they still held?

4. How do party activists differ from rank-and-file voters of their party? What consequences does this difference have for American politics?

5. How and why have the parties become more polarized on ideology and issues over the past several decades?

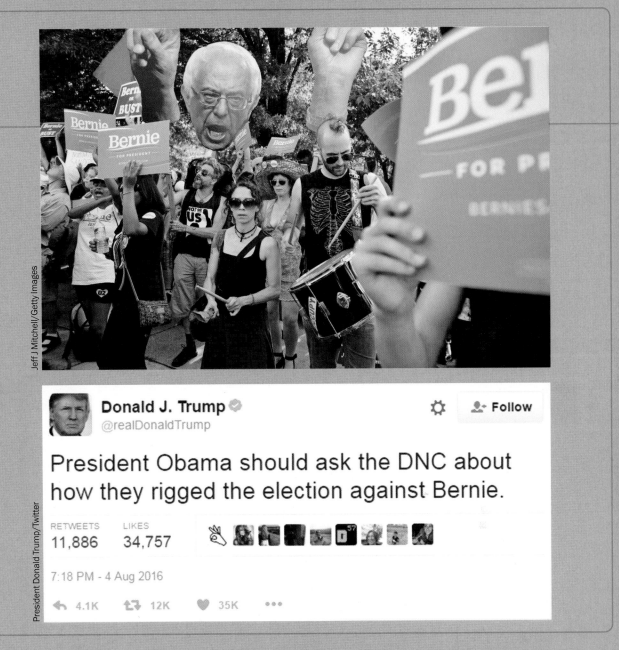

Throughout his campaign, Bernie Sanders drew legions of supporters with his full-throated attack on what he saw as a rigged system controlled by the biggest political donors and the most powerful private interest groups. Donald Trump, railing first against the rules of the primary election and later against a political system that he saw as biased against the average American, often leveled the same charge.

# Interest Groups

# 13

Is our system rigged? Over and again throughout their insurgent campaigns for the presidency in 2016, both Republican Donald J. Trump and Democrat Bernie Sanders charged that the fix was in for American politics, with big-money groups getting their way in policy battles while the rest of us have no voice in the halls of power. "I have joined the political arena so that the powerful can no longer beat up on people that cannot defend themselves," Trump said when he accepted the Republican Party's nomination for president. "Nobody knows the system better than me," he allowed, "which is why I alone can fix it." And in a debate with Hillary Clinton, Sanders laid out his explanation of why the United States does not have a single-payer health care system: "Do you know why we can't do what every other country—major country on Earth is doing? It's because we have a campaign finance system that is corrupt, we have super PACs, we have the pharmaceutical industry pouring hundreds of millions of dollars into campaign contributions and lobbying, and the private insurance companies as well." In a striking moment of comity between the real estate mogul and the former socialist, Trump tweeted his congratulations to @BernieSanders for winning the Indiana primary even while "the dysfunctional system is totally rigged against him!"

Although Sanders and Trump stated their critique of the system in bolder terms than before and harnessed the viral power of Twitter and other social media to spread their message, their complaint is nothing new. From the Founders' concerns about the might of factions to political scientists' warnings about bias in the interest group system, observers of American politics—and, indeed, of every modern democracy—have always worried that organized groups with narrow, self-interested goals will wield outsized power. Surveying the history of this debate and testing claims about the unequal distribution of political power, three leading scholars, Kay Lehman Schlozman, Sidney Verba, and Henry Brady, write that "American politicians have long claimed to speak for those who have no voice." But, they conclude after examining a comprehensive body of evidence, "the disparities in political voice across various segments of society are so substantial and so persistent as to preclude equal consideration. Public officials cannot consider voices they do not hear, and it is more difficult to pay attention to voices that speak softly."

In many political debates, then, well-heeled **interest groups** and individuals have a louder voice than the less affluent. Does this mean that money rules politics, all the time and in every venue? The biggest stage in American politics—the presidential election—offered in 2016 an instructive case in what America's super PACs (political action committees) and richest donors can and cannot buy in politics. The very success of the Trump and Sanders campaigns—which attracted far more votes than the campaigns of many super PAC–funded adversaries—demonstrates that big money from rich donors is neither necessary nor sufficient to do well in an election. Trump's campaign was especially effective, trouncing opponents aided by massive "independent expenditure" campaigns that could raise money in unlimited chunks. Super PACs and other donors spent $121 million to help Jeb Bush in this way, $109 million went to Marco Rubio, and $67 million of outside expenditures supported Ted Cruz, according to the Center for Responsive Politics. Less than $10 million in big outside contributions went to help Donald Trump, yet he convincingly defeated all of these opponents in a system he claimed was rigged against him.

If their massive campaign contributions do not always carry the day, then, what do rich interests think they are getting from their political investments? The internal e-mails hacked from the servers of the Democratic National Committee (DNC) in July 2016 offered an instructive and often entertaining look into the exchange of political dollars for favors deep inside the corridors of power. What big-dollar donors mostly wanted, the e-mail chains made clear, were invitations to social events. One donor who had raised $679,650 for the party and for President Obama asked for an extra ticket to Joe Biden's holiday party and inquired about whether she would be included in an exclusive November gathering in the White House: "Not assuming I am invited . . . just mentioning/asking, if in case, I am invited :)." DNC staffers went back and forth with each other over who should be seated next to the president at a dinner party or invited to play golf with him, comparing the amounts given by competing donors over recent years. Of course, social access could easily translate into political influence. But when a contributor brazenly asked for a contact who had "clout" because "I have a very importance client/ friend needed access with someone within the administration. So I promise him I would investigate," his ungrammatical and impolitic e-mail was brushed off and later disavowed.*

---

*The leaked e-mails and their links to political access were reported on by Nicholas Confessore and Steve Eder, "In Hacked DNC Emails, a Glimpse of How Big Money Works," *New York Times*, July 25, 2016.

In Congress as in a party organization, big money can often help an interest group but does not always carry the day. For instance, when they crafted the financial reform legislation that followed the stock market crash of 2008–2009, members of Congress largely rebuffed the lobbying efforts of the big banks—the villains of the crash, in the minds of most Americans— even though they spent $600 million in an attempt to influence Washington, D.C., with their 1,500 lobbyists. Politicians ignored most demands of the unpopular Wall Street interests. But in the legislation, they carved out exemptions for a Main Street interest, the local car dealers located in nearly every legislator's district. This interest group spent a mere $10 million on lobbying the financial reform bill, but with populist rhetoric, an unblemished image, and strategically located members working to their advantage, auto dealers were the rare financial interest that emerged from financial reform unscathed.

Looking at who lost and who won in this policy fight with billion-dollar stakes teaches valuable lessons about the role of interest groups in our nation. Interest groups are omnipresent in American politics, but not omnipotent. Lobbyists may show up everywhere in Washington, D.C., but they by no means dictate what goes on there. Part of why we see interest groups being so active is that they need to work so hard for the opportunity to make their pitch to elected officials and to be heard over the cacophony of competing voices. Large, well-heeled lobbies have suffered shocking defeats, and smaller groups have won surprising victories. The enduring power of the electoral connection that ties lawmakers to voters can explain why they may sometimes ignore powerful lobbyists, and the logic of collective action shows why there is often lobbying strength in small numbers.

Although the dynamics of interest group power vary from time to time and group to group, their presence on the political scene remains a constant. Interest groups and lobbying are inevitable and, indeed, essential components of modern democratic politics. They also are a continual source of problems for democracy. The American political system could not function without the endlessly busy work of organized interests and their representatives trying to sway policy in their favor. Yet there has never been a time in American history when they have not been under attack from one quarter or another as threats to democracy itself. This chapter looks at why interest groups are both essential and problematic.

## The Logic of Lobbying

The logic of lobbying is transparent. People who want to influence government decisions that affect their lives and welfare quickly recognize the advantages of banding together with others of like mind and asking astute and powerful friends to help out. Governments, for their part, have good reason to welcome **lobbying**, defined as appeals from citizens and groups for favorable policies and decisions. Even officials in blatantly nondemocratic governments find life considerably easier if they have the support, or at least the acquiescence, of the governed (as any parent knows). Such officials cannot estimate the costs and benefits of alternative actions without having some idea of how people will react to their initiatives. All governments also need the information, political as well as technical, that people and organizations outside the government are in the best position to provide—for a price. Elected officials, looking to keep their jobs, try to accommodate the people who command valuable electoral

resources—votes, money, organizational structures, and skills. And always and everywhere, at least a few government officials have been willing to trade favors for personal "gifts" of every imaginable sort.

Modern politics also breeds professional **lobbyists**. For the same reason they hire lawyers to represent them in court, people hire agents who are specialists to represent them before legislatures and executive agencies. Like courts, modern legislatures and bureaucracies are complex institutions bound by arcane rules, procedures, and customs. People wanting these institutions to act on their behalf are more likely to succeed if they are represented by agents who understand how the institutions work and enjoy warm personal friendships with the key institutional players.

Lobbying as a profession thus emerged with modern representative government and has flourished with the growing scope and complexity of government activities. Figure 13.1 shows that lobbying is now the costliest route through which interest groups attempt to influence government. This figure reports the total amount that all groups—whether they were political action committees or simply collections from individuals—spent on campaign contributions to congressional candidates in recent election cycles, compared with lobbying expenditures. As you can see, even though campaign contributions are the most frequent source of citizen concern about government being "bought and sold," they are merely the tip of the influence

■ **FIGURE 13.1**   Lobbying Expenditures Dwarf Campaign Contributions to Congress

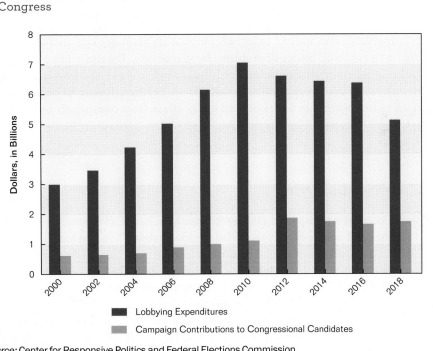

*Source:* Center for Responsive Politics and Federal Elections Commission.

*Note:* Figures are shown for a two-year campaign or lobbying cycle.

iceberg. Interest groups spend billions more every cycle on lobbying than they do on campaign contributions. This shows that interest groups value their representation on K Street (the street in Washington where top lobbyists traditionally located their offices) as much as they worry about who represents voters on Capitol Hill.

This comparison, along with the billions of dollars devoted to both lobbying and campaign contributions, also raises concerns about the legitimacy of interest groups and lobbyists. Their very presence, not to mention any political success they may achieve, raises the suspicion that "special interests" win at the expense of the "public interest." Even people who deny that the public interest can be defined objectively—as do many modern political scientists— often argue that successful lobbying subverts the basic principles of democratic equality and majority rule. Groups vary widely in wealth and in how readily they can be organized for collective action, creating marked imbalances in the representation of social interests. Moreover, policy gridlock and political paralysis in the face of pressing national problems are commonly blamed on the cacophony of competing interests. For these reasons, organized political interests have been attacked and criticized as long as they have existed.

## The Origins of Interest Group Politics in the United States

James Madison, with his usual cogency, captured the dilemma posed by politically active groups in his famous discussion of factions in *Federalist* No. 10. For Madison, factions were by definition pernicious, pursuing selfish aims contrary to the rights of others or to the public interest. As such, factions were, in Madison's view, a major threat to popular government: "The instability, injustice, and confusion introduced into the public councils" by the "dangerous vice" of faction "have, in truth, been the mortal diseases under which popular governments have everywhere perished." (The full text of *Federalist* No. 10 appears in the appendix.)

Why, then, not just get rid of factions? Madison's answer was that factions could be eliminated only by "destroying the liberty which is essential to [their] existence . . . [or by] giving every citizen the same opinions, the same passions, and the same interests." He found the first cure "worse than the disease" because popular government is supposed to protect liberty; he found the second impossible: "As long as the reason of man continues to be fallible, and he is at liberty to exercise it, different opinions will be formed."

Practically speaking, then, to maintain the freedoms specified in the First Amendment— to speak, publish, assemble, and "petition the Government for a redress of grievances"—a political system must tolerate factions even though they may be, as by Madison's definition, opposed to the public good. Political parties, interest groups, lobbyists, and peaceful political organizations of all kinds are, in effect, licensed by the Constitution and can be suppressed only by violating its principles.

Should we therefore think of interest groups only as a necessary evil in a free political system, as a threat to the polity that needs to be contained through institutional design? Madison seemed to take this view, and as we saw in Chapter 2, his solution was to divide authority among federal institutions. This fragmentation of authority would prevent any single faction from dominating the others. The wide variety of competing interests could then use this institutional machinery to thwart each other's selfish designs. Later observers of American politics

have seen positive value in the groups that work energetically to further the varied interests of so many segments of our diverse society, celebrating the pluralism both of our citizens and of the groups representing them. Both approaches focus on institutional and social pluralism, a key characteristic of America's political history and current realities.

Madison's discussion of factions, though abstract, was anything but academic. Organized attempts to influence government decisions have been an integral part of American politics since the nation's earliest days. During the colonial era, merchants, manufacturers, and ethnic and religious minorities actively sought favorable policies from the authorities in London as well as from colonial governors and assemblies. By the middle of the eighteenth century, such groups had developed most of the techniques of persuasion still used today. Colonial interests submitted petitions to the government, hired agents to "handle the delicate work involved in extracting concessions from ministers and lesser bureaucrats," examined the voting records of legislators to identify prospective supporters, organized letter-writing campaigns, reminded legislators that a group's supporters were among their constituents, and formed logrolling coalitions with other interests.[1] The eighteenth century also witnessed the invention of the **public interest lobby** and the tactic of appealing to the general public for support of an outsider group's goals. The chief innovator was the English radical John Wilkes, whose Bill of Rights Society promoted a general cause—the expansion of suffrage—rather than defending any particular interest. Disdaining the customary methods of friendly persuasion, the Wilkesites attacked government officials.[2] Similar organizations appeared in the colonies, the best known of which was the Sons of Liberty. Among other subversive activities, this group threw the Boston Tea Party.

After the Revolutionary War, the American political system allowed "factions" to flourish. French visitor Alexis de Tocqueville noted with astonishment the abundance and variety of organized groups in the United States: "In no country in the world has the principle of association been more successfully used, or applied to a greater multitude of objects, than in America. . . . There is no end which the human will despairs of attaining through the combined power of individuals united into a society."[3] Such associations included the American Anti-Slavery Society (founded in 1833); the National Trades' Union (1834), which lobbied for a ten-hour workday;* and the American Temperance Union (1836), which lobbied for a halt to the sale of alcoholic beverages. Like Madison, Tocqueville thought that such associations could be dangerous to public order and good government, but his observations convinced him that voluntary groups were essential to an egalitarian social and political system.[4] When large-scale industrial corporations began to flex their political muscles after the Civil War, citizens outraged by political corruption formed new associations to agitate for reform. Over time, these groups succeeded in reorganizing government at all levels and rewriting the rules of electoral and party politics (see Chapters 8 and 12). As with the Sanders and Trump campaigns, they formed movements and groups aimed at overturning a rigged system dominated by other interest groups.

---

*Employers of this era could demand as much work time as their employees would tolerate. People desperate for employment put up with workdays of twelve to fourteen hours, sometimes even more during the lengthy days of summer.

PUCK.

THE BOSSES OF THE SENATE.

Joseph Keppler, one of the most popular political cartoonists of his day, pays tribute to the "Bosses of the Senate." By 1889 the Senate was known as the millionaires' club. The presiding officer was a Wall Street banker, and its principal members represented the oil, lumber, railroad, insurance, silver, gold, utility, and manufacturing interests. Note that the "People's Entrance" is "closed." This cartoon could run in a newspaper today, for a 2009 analysis published in *Roll Call* found that fifty senators each had a net worth of more than $1 million.

The groups that had so impressed Tocqueville in the 1830s had been largely local and short-lived. By the twentieth century, however, large-scale organizations like the national labor and business groups just mentioned began to proliferate. They turned into constant fixtures in campaigns, and their representatives began to take up permanent residence in Washington, D.C., and in state capitols. Interest group activity became an industry unto itself, which is now centered on K Street in Washington but reaches everywhere that key policy decisions are made. Americans now have a permanent organizational base to attend to their political interests, whether these interests happen to be protecting the right to bear arms, the right to make reproductive choices, or even the right to surf (through the lobbying of the Surfrider Foundation). Interest groups are now an institution in American politics, potent and enduring.

## The Pluralist Defense of Interest Groups

With the emergence of stable political associations as major players in national politics, scholars began to study interest groups. One result was the first systematic defense of their

## POLITICS TO POLICY
# High School Students Turned Gun Control Lobbyists

### An Interest Group Born from a Mass Shooting Vows #NeverAgain

After the horrific mass shooting at a high school in Parkland, Florida, on February 14, 2018, left seventeen dead, it seemed likely that the familiar script of a gun violence tragedy would play out yet again. In the shooting's immediate wake, politicians in the press and the broad public through social media pledged that their thoughts and prayers were with the victims, families, and survivors. Very soon, a fractious political debate broke out, with gun control advocates arguing that stricter laws could have prevented the shooting while gun rights defenders disputed those claims and railed against the politicization of a tragedy. It looked like each side would become further entrenched, gridlock on the issue would stall any legislative action, and survivors would be left alone with their thoughts and prayers once the news cycle moved on. What had happened after mass shootings in Orlando; Las Vegas; and Sutherland Springs, Texas, looked destined to occur again.

But, remarkably, this pattern was broken by the high school students who had witnessed the shooting and refused to allow the nation to forget it. Their call to action began with viral videos they took at Marjory Stoneman Douglas High during the Valentine's Day massacre and with the raw, emotional interviews they gave to the national media in the days that followed. What turned it from an impassioned response into an impactful movement was the more mundane yet highly effective organizing they did in the following weeks. The students became unapologetic lobbyists for gun control, creating a grassroots interest group that put together, in five

Nicholas Kamm/AFP/Getty Images

short weeks, one of the most successful marches on Washington in decades. An estimated two million protesters participated in the March 24 March for Our Lives, flooding the National Mall or taking part in one of the 850 sibling marches held around the world.

The Parkland students pulled off this unprecedented feat—no group of teenagers had organized a protest movement approaching this scale before—by employing the traditional tools and tactics of interest groups outlined in this chapter. First, they harnessed the crush of media attention that followed the shooting to clarion calls for change. "We can't ignore the issues of gun control that this tragedy raises," vowed junior Cameron Kasky. "And so, I'm asking—no, demanding—we take action now." They used social media, a realm in which any teenager surpasses the skills of nearly all adults, to spread their message and call out the interest group they saw as their primary protagonist, the Nation Rifle Association (NRA). Emma Gonzalez, the buzzcut student who soon emerged as a leading voice of the movement, did not have a Twitter account before the shooting but within two weeks had garnered more followers than the NRA. The Parkland students-turned-organizers

even adopted the #NeverAgain hashtag as their group's name. Just like any interest group, the Parkland students fund-raised, creating a GoFundMe page that attracted $4 million in donations in addition to the $2 million they received from celebrities like George Clooney, Steven Spielberg, and Oprah.

Instead of feeling alienated from the political process, they dove straight into it. Junior class president Jaclyn Corin led a group of 100 Stoneman Douglas students to Tallahassee to lobby the state legislature, demanding gun control legislation that banned the sort of AR-15 assault rifles and high-capacity magazines used by the shooter. Although they fell short of that lofty goal, they succeeded in pushing the Florida legislature to pass, and Republican governor Rick

Scott to sign, a bill that banned the bump stocks that make rifles fire faster, raised the minimum age for a gun purchase to 21, and created a waiting period for gun buyers. This was the first major gun control bill passed in the state in two decades. Even though the NRA opposed the legislation, sixty-seven Republicans who had been endorsed by the NRA voted for it. Within weeks of a tragedy, high school students from Parkland, Florida, created, funded, and put into action an interest group that defeated one of the nation's most powerful lobbying organizations and promised more action in the years to come.

---

*Sources:* Charlotte Alter, "The School Shooting Generation Has Had Enough," Time.com, March 22, 2018; Emanuella Grinberg and Nadeem Muaddi, "How the Parkland Students Pulled Off a Massive National Protest in Only 5 Weeks," March 26, 2018.

---

legitimate role in a modern democracy. The case was made most fully by political scientist David Truman in his influential book *The Governmental Process*, published in 1951.[5] Truman viewed the proliferation of political interest groups as a natural and largely benign consequence of economic development. These groups formed spontaneously whenever shared interests were threatened or could be enhanced by political action. Modern industrial society, characterized by an ever more elaborate division of labor, became awash in interests and therefore in interest groups. As society became progressively more fragmented and variegated, so did the universe of associations.

Because groups were free to organize and participate in an open political system, the political process balanced competing interests, just as James Madison had promised. If established groups advocated policies that threatened the interests of other citizens, the threatened would organize to defend themselves. Demands provoked counterdemands, and so policies embodied the numerous compromises and trade-offs necessary for building winning coalitions within and between political institutions. Aware that overreaching would stir opposition, established groups prudently moderated their demands. Thus unorganized interests constrained active groups even when they were not represented by lobbies of their own.

Clearly, then, this view of American pluralism did not embrace the customary disdain of "special interests." Rather, interest groups were regarded as essential and valuable participants in the democratic politics of a modern industrial society. Without their participation, policy would be made in far greater ignorance of what citizens actually wanted from their government.

As a description of reality, this sunny conception of pluralism was open to some obvious criticisms. No one doubted that organized groups often were important political players; this was not at issue. But it was also undeniable that the groups most visibly active in

politics did not, by any stretch of the imagination, form a balanced cross section of economic or social interests. Some interests, such as those of large industrial corporations, seemed to be vastly overrepresented; other interests, such as those of migrant laborers and the unemployed, were not represented at all. "The flaw in the pluralist heaven," as political scientist E. E. Schattschneider put it, "is that the heavenly chorus sings with a strong upper-class accent."[6] The power and resources possessed by lobbyists tend to reflect the power that the groups they represent have in society. This compounds the inequalities present in the nation. Observers who are not swayed by Truman's defense of interest group pluralism worry that the close connections between K Street and Capitol Hill allow the affluent and informed to use the machinery of government for their narrow benefit while unorganized groups go unheard.

## The Problem of Collective Action

A subtler but equally important explanation for the observed bias in group representation lies in the way the incentives for collective action and the barriers to organization vary across different types of groups. The explanation, developed by economist Mancur Olson in *The Logic of Collective Action* (1965), begins by pointing out that classical pluralists such as Truman were mistaken in assuming that people would form interest groups spontaneously to promote or defend shared interests.[7] Someone has to take on the work of organizing the group and finding the resources to keep it going. And to succeed, organizers have to overcome a standard collective action problem: most political interest groups pursue collective goods that, by definition, all group members will enjoy whether or not they help provide them. Rational self-interest could lead to universal free riding, dooming the organization and the effort unless some way is found around this difficulty.

This collective action problem poses more of a challenge to some interests than others, Olson pointed out, with the scale of the group and the stakes of its involvement in public policy determining whether its members are likely to work together toward their common goal. These factors help us understand why, for instance, there is no powerful lobby working on behalf of airline passengers, whereas airlines themselves are well organized and influential. First, small groups are easier to organize than large groups. Most of us fly at one time or another, and everyone who flies is annoyed at having to pay an extra fee to check a bag or eat lunch. But it would be very difficult to sign every passenger up as a dues-paying member of a group dedicated to passing a law prohibiting these fees. The transaction costs involved in bringing together a handful of airlines to oppose such a law are much lower than the costs of building an association of millions of passengers. For the small community of airlines, free-rider problems are less severe, because free riders—in this case, airlines that do not contribute to an industry-wide lobbying effort—are more readily detected and subject to pressure to cooperate in defending the industry. Second, interests with a great deal at stake in a policy domain are more readily organized for political action than are people with little at stake. (Airline fees are a minor annoyance to all of us, but they are a source of billions of dollars in much-needed revenue for airlines.) When prospective costs or benefits of a policy are large, so are incentives to invest in political action. When the support for a group is a mile wide but only an inch deep, as it is for airline passenger rights, coordination becomes difficult, and the potential for political power often goes unfulfilled.

Group size and stakes often are inversely related, compounding the bias. For a few fortunate groups, a single member might have enough at stake to justify paying the entire cost of pursuing the group's collective interests. ExxonMobil, for example, might find it profitable to invest in lobbying for repeal of price controls on gasoline even if it has to pay the entire cost of producing a benefit that would have to be shared with all gasoline producers (a small group—just ten companies control 79 percent of U.S. domestic refining capacity). By contrast, many widely shared, diffuse collective interests will be poorly represented if those who share them behave rationally and remain free riders.

This analysis may explain why lobbies representing narrow economic interests predominate in Washington, but it raises a new question: why are there nonetheless so many vigorous lobbies claiming to speak for widespread, diffuse interests? Indeed, one of the most striking changes in the interest group universe over the past three decades has been the proliferation of organizations claiming to represent millions of citizens devoted to some version of the "public interest." How have the leaders of public interest groups, which have broad public support but are seemingly too large and focused on issues with stakes that are too low in order to organize effectively, solved the collective action problem that should have doomed them?

One reason behind the proliferation of public interest groups is that some people who care passionately about an issue do not act like coldly rational calculators. They are willing to contribute to groups espousing causes they care about without worrying about whether their contributions will make any appreciable difference. *Moral incentives*, the personal satisfactions of active self-expression, trump the economist's concept of rationality for the countless concerned citizens who send checks to groups pursuing environmental protection, a ban on abortion, political reform, same-sex marriage or its abolition, animal rights, and a host of other social causes. These groups did not arise spontaneously through the action of concerned citizens; most were put together by enterprising activists supported by charitable foundations, wealthy individuals, or the government itself. Yet many are sustained by dues and small contributions from a large number of private citizens.

But another important route to organizing public interest groups recognizes that many of us do act rationally, and provides concrete benefits to those who join. Many of the most successful organizations circumvent the collective action problem by offering *selective incentives*—benefits that can be denied to individuals who do not join and contribute. The American Automobile Association (AAA), an interest group founded in 1902 to push for the construction of more roads, actively lobbies Congress on issues such as vehicle safety, car theft, and gasoline prices. But for the vast majority of members, joining AAA is a way to get roadside assistance, maps, and discounts at motels. By offering these selective benefits, the group solved a collective action problem similar to the one faced by airline passengers. Other massive lobbies have followed the same path. Attorneys become members of state bar associations in order to practice law, physicians join the American Medical Association to qualify for malpractice insurance and to receive the association's journal, and farmers seek membership in the American Farm Bureau Federation to receive the assistance of county farm agents. Groups that initially attract members by providing them with individual benefits may invest some of their resources in pursuing collective benefits through political action. The largest interest group in the United States by far, AARP, was formed to market insurance to senior citizens and thrives by providing members with a variety of selective benefits. Indeed, to a

### LOGIC OF POLITICS
# The Political Power of Small Numbers

Mancur Olson's 1965 book *The Logic of Collective Action* may have been the first academic work to lay out the organizational advantage conferred on a small group with intense interests, but he was not the first to recognize it. Representative Clem Miller, a young congressman from California's north coast, saw exactly this logic at play when he compared the lobbying efforts of two agricultural groups in 1959. Both groups, the walnut growers and the poultrymen, faced economic collapse as record production levels drove prices so low that small farmers were taking a loss on every nut or egg they sold. Lawmakers were sympathetic to the plight of each type of farmer. Both groups lobbied Congress for relief. Only one, though, won political action, and the secret to its success lay in its size and concentration of interests.

inga spence/Alamy

Because walnut growers had bumper crops in both 1958 and 1959, their nuts and foreign imports flooded the market to drive down prices. All walnut farmers faced an economic problem. Organizing the industry to ask for a solution, though, was relatively easy. Walnut farming was concentrated in California, and the independent growers had already organized themselves into associations that effectively reduced their numbers. "The walnut industry is well organized," Congressman Miller observed. "This is easy to understand. One marketing cooperative controls seventy per cent of the state's productive." Instead of asking for help with disparate voices, the small network of marketing associations worked together in unison. They laid the groundwork for a successful lobbying effort by coordinating grassroots efforts in much the same way that the "Main Street" car dealers did, detailed in this chapter's opening vignette. "Each California congressman received a personal, carefully reasoned, five-page letter," Congressman Miller recounted. "Quite properly, the group worked through the congressman in whose district the association offices and many growers are located." The growers then hired a lobbyist who identified a solution—the government could buy surplus walnuts for school lunches, using the tariffs collected on imported nuts—and traveled to Washington to press their case. After making allies of their representatives, the farmers stood with members of Congress to demand that the secretary of agriculture take action. Under withering political pressure, he eventually complied.

Though no less needy or sympathetic, the poultrymen won no such governmental assistance. At first glance, this seems surprising because so many chicken farmers spread across the nation petitioned Congress for help. Independent poultrymen, who did not work through marketing associations, were being driven to bankruptcy by an oversupply of eggs and meat produced by new, bank-financed industrial farms. The sector was thus split internally. It did not help the cause that poultrymen came from many different states whose legislators were not as used to working together as the California congressional delegation. After a loose confederation agitated for a committee hearing, more than two hundred chicken farmers descended on Washington, D.C., and testified for two days about their plight.

Yet despite numbers that dwarfed the walnut growers, they never hired a lobbyist to help press their case in a strategic fashion. They came and left Congress without proposing a concrete solution. "All of the men were active poultrymen who had to get back to their flocks," Miller pointed out. "Who was going to coordinate policy between New Jersey, California, Alabama, Wisconsin, Georgia, and Kansas? The answer from them was, 'No one.'" Without a single voice to carry the ball, even the impassioned testimony of so many farmers led nowhere. Congress passed a weak resolution, and the many poultrymen suffered.

*Source:* Clem Miller, "The Walnut Growers and Poultrymen," in *Member of the House: Letters of a Congressman*, edited by John W. Baker (New York: Charles Scribner's Sons, 1962).

remarkable extent the interest groups that now throng the nation's capital are offshoots of organizations that fulfill many goals of their members extending far beyond political action but are politically powerful nonetheless.

## Contemporary Interest Groups

The exact dimensions of the present-day interest group universe are unknown, but it is expanding. According to one estimate, the number of lobbying organizations more than tripled between the 1960s and the 1990s; a subsequent analysis indicated a further doubling between 2000 and 2005.[8] The website Lobbyists.info, an authoritative directory of interest groups and lobbyists, lists approximately twenty-two thousand lobbyists serving a host of corporations, labor unions, trade and professional associations, political action committees, and advocacy groups, including lawyers registered as lobbyists, public relations consultants, and think tank staff. In addition to the active lobbying organizations sponsored by private sector organizations, government entities—states, cities, counties, and their agencies—are behind much lobbying activity. No fewer than 168 California government bodies employ Washington, D.C., representatives. So do more than three hundred colleges and universities, 148 Native American tribes, sixteen ethnic groups, and more than one hundred religious organizations.[9] More than twenty-seven thousand individuals are registered as lobbyists with Congress, and more than one hundred thousand Washingtonians are employed somewhere in the lobbying industry.[10] Like other industries, lobbying has its ups and downs. When congressional Republicans and President Obama frequently deadlocked over policy after the 2010 elections, lobbying firms took a financial hit because of the policy slowdown. "Historically, when you look at the third and fourth quarter of election years, we've been down," explained an executive with Patton Boggs, D.C.'s largest lobbying firm. In election years, he added, "you have a reduced number of legislative fights that occur in the third and fourth quarter."[11]

Most advocacy groups also are the creatures of preexisting institutions. From abolition to temperance to civil rights to nuclear disarmament to the "right to life," churches and synagogues have provided a stable institutional base for organizing movements pursuing social and political change. Most of the self-designated public interest groups that have proliferated in recent decades initially were financed by patrons—philanthropic foundations, corporations, wealthy individuals, or the government itself—and many depend on continuing subsidies for significant parts of their budgets. The interests of welfare recipients, the mentally ill, children, and the homeless do not lack advocates, even though such groups themselves are not organized for collective action. Their causes have been taken up by lobbies representing the social service professionals (mostly government employees) who run the programs that serve these groups. Political campaigns can spawn lobbying groups. After the 2012 presidential election, a group of President Obama's key advisers formed a tax-exempt advocacy group, Organizing for Action, that aimed to turn the president's electoral coalition into a grassroots advocacy network (and to do so more successfully than its 2009 incarnation, Organizing for America). The group leased the sophisticated voter data sets and outreach software that the Obama campaign had developed, essentially becoming an extension of the campaign itself. In the vast realm of organized interests in the United States, there are even groups that claim to speak for the whales and mount civil disobedience campaigns to stop them from being hunted (see box "The Cetacean Lobby").

Not every group depends on outside assistance for its resources. Prominent public interest groups such as Common Cause, Public Citizen, and the Public Interest Research Group are financed principally by membership dues and small donations, as are many of the large environmental lobbies, such as the Sierra Club, the National Audubon Society, and the Wilderness Society. These and other organizations have taken advantage of modern computer technology to solicit and maintain a mass membership and donor base through Internet and direct-mail appeals to current and prospective supporters. Because they depend mostly on moral incentives—persuading people to invest in collective goods despite the temptation to free ride on the efforts of others—their memberships and budgets fluctuate with circumstances. They tend to grow when opponents run the government and shrink when sympathetic politicians are in power.

## Why Have Interest Groups Proliferated?

Several interacting factors have contributed to the rapid proliferation of interest groups since the 1960s. For one thing, the *social ferment* initiated by the civil rights movement and continued by the Reagan-era conservative and right-to-life movements has inspired and instructed the stream of organizations that agitated for social change. Some led the opposition to the war in Vietnam; others asserted the rights of women, gays, Native Americans, Hispanics, Asians, and people with disabilities. Environmental and consumer groups emerged, along with the antiabortion and conservative Christian movements and animal rights organizations. In 2010, both the Occupy movement and the Tea Party galvanized millions of Americans on the left and right. Today, mass movements on both sides of the immigration issue and on gun control and gun rights have mobilized sizable segments of society. The list could (and no doubt will) go on. Organizers of **social movements**—amorphous aggregates of people sharing general values and a desire for social change—quickly imitate successful innovations, and each new group has been able to draw on the experience of its predecessors.

The clientele for such groups has come from a growing and increasingly well-educated and affluent middle class, people with a surplus of money or time to invest in causes that excite their moral imaginations strongly enough to discourage free riding. Technological innovations—e-mail appeals, campaigns run via Facebook or Twitter, and "microtargeted" mail that

# The Cetacean Lobby

Although its goals and tactics are certainly unique, the Sea Shepherd Conservation Society has much in common with other public interest groups. It is led by a charismatic, if controversial, political entrepreneur. To fund its activities, it relies on large donations from wealthy individuals as well as dues from a small but passionate base of members. And it has taken advantage of the new media masterfully to raise its profile and expand its mass support, through the television show *Whale Wars*.

After his radical tactics got him kicked out of Greenpeace, the environmental group he helped found, Paul Watson organized Sea Shepherd to stop the hunting of minke whales and endangered fin whales carried out by the Institute of Cetacean Research. The institute, which despite its subsidy from the Japanese government produces little actual research and instead sells the meat of the whales it catches, complains that Sea Shepherd's tactics of confronting whaling ships violate international law and endanger its crews. This notoriety has attracted the support of many rich and famous animal rights activists, including

GERARD JULIEN/AFP/Getty Images

Las Vegas magnate Steve Wynn (who helped Sea Shepherd buy a submarine) and *The Price Is Right* host Bob Barker (who donated funds to purchase the ship that bears his name). Most effectively, this interest group has capitalized on the primary "advance" in television—reality shows—by starring in the Animal Planet show *Whale Wars*. Every week, interested viewers can watch Sea Shepherd confront the Japanese whaling fleet with its unique form of radical civil disobedience, practiced by a crew that makes up for its maritime inexperience with an immense reservoir of outrage.

uses consumer databases to identify those who would likely support a movement and tailor a message to their concerns—have made it easier and cheaper than ever before for entrepreneurial leaders to establish and maintain organizations that have a large number of geographically scattered and socially unconnected members.

Successful groups inspire opponents as well as imitators. Corporate and business leaders whose interests were threatened by the political gains of environmental and consumer groups organized to defend themselves. Legislation that added to their regulatory burden and threatened the bottom line was a powerful stimulus to political action by industries and firms. Business leaders also sought to beef up the intellectual case for their side by financing think tanks* dedicated to promoting conservative ideas and policies—among them the

---

*Think tank* is the common term for an organization that employs or sponsors professional intellectuals to study issues of public policy and to prepare books, reports, newspaper essays and opinion pieces, magazine articles, and speeches promoting their conclusions. Most, though not all, adhere to some identifiable ideology that reflects the values and interests of their sponsors.

Hoover Institution, the American Enterprise Institute, the Heritage Foundation, and the Cato Institute.[12] The most important part of the dynamic behind the expanding interest group universe, however, has been the *encouragement of the federal government itself*. In addition to stimulating the organization of business interests, the growing scope of government activity has encouraged the proliferation of organizations in the nonprofit and public sectors:

> The growth, during the twentieth century, of public schools, parks and forest pre-serves, agricultural research stations, public hospitals, and social welfare agencies of all kinds stimulated the creation of numerous professional associations made up of the providers of these new public services. *These groups often were created at the suggestion of public officials who realized the political value of organized constituents working to promote their programs from outside of government.*[13] [emphasis added]

Prominent examples include private business groups such as the U.S. Chamber of Commerce and the Business Roundtable, which were created under the leadership of sec-retaries of commerce in, respectively, the Taft and Nixon administrations; the American Farm Bureau Federation, which developed from a network of official advisory committees to the U.S. Department of Agriculture's county agents; and the National Organization for Women (NOW), a leading feminist organization. Indeed, the women's movement itself was jump-started by the government. In the early 1960s the Kennedy administration spon-sored legislation that encouraged the creation of a commission on the status of women in every state. Later, the state and federal governments funded a series of conferences on women's issues. In 1966 some delegates to the annual meeting of state commissioners on the status of women, frustrated by how their position as government officials limited their ability to take political action, sought a voice by founding NOW, which could work outside government.[14]

The federal government also has contributed to the proliferation of interest groups through the tax code. Many groups qualify as nonprofit organizations, which are exempt from most taxes, and donors may deduct contributions to some kinds of nonprofit groups from their taxable income. The government also subsidizes the mass mailings of nonprofit groups through special postal rates. These organizations do face some restrictions on their political activity, however; they may educate, but they are not supposed to lobby openly or to engage in partisan electoral politics. The philanthropic foundations that fund many advocacy groups are themselves creatures of tax policy; rich people and families put their assets into foundations as a legal way to avoid income and inheritance taxes. Administrations also subsidize some polit-ically favored organizations by hiring them to conduct studies or carry out specific projects. Groups thrive in good part because public policy has encouraged them to do so.

Finally, although discussions of pluralist politics commonly assume that government programs emerge in response to interest group demands, in reality it often is the other way around: interests (and interest groups) arise *in defense of government programs*. Typically, groups benefiting from government programs get organized and active only after the pro-grams are in place. For example, most of the potent groups defending the interests of elderly people emerged after the enactment of Social Security (1935), Medicare (1965), and the Older

SAUL LOEB/AFP/Getty Images

Organized in 2009 as a reaction to President Obama's economic stimulus, bank bailout, and health care policies, the Tea Party is a set of loosely confederated interest groups that have given voice to populist anger across the nation. Various state and local Tea Party groups mobilized their members at town hall meetings, at marches on Washington (like the 2012 march shown here), and in Republican primaries to nominate Tea Party loyalists in the 2010, 2012, and 2014 elections. Many Tea Party adherents embraced Donald Trump's campaign in 2016 and supported the candidates he backed in 2018.

Americans Act of 1965; AARP did not become the eight-hundred-pound gorilla of American politics until these programs were already in place to defend.

With or without the deliberate instigation of government officials, new policies create constituencies ripe for organization. People who adapt their plans to existing policies (on tax credits for capital investments, for example) develop a stake in continuation of the policies. And it is easier to mobilize people to defend what they already have than to pursue the more doubtful prospective benefits they do not yet enjoy—that is, the threat of loss is a more power- ful spur to action than the hope of gain.[15] In general, the more the government does, the more incentives it creates for organized political action.

## Fragmentation and Specialization

The expanding interest group universe also reflects the fragmentation of old interests and the growing division of labor among groups sharing the same broad goals. New organizations form when new issues pull old groups apart; increasingly complex issues and fragmented pol- icy processes force groups to specialize to be effective. Meanwhile, as links between diverse problems have become more transparent, a wider range of organized interests has pushed into formerly isolated issue domains.

Farm policy, for example, was for many years the exclusive domain of the farm bloc, an alliance composed of a handful of interest groups (most notably the American Farm Bureau Federation), Department of Agriculture officials, and members of Congress from the farm states who sat on the agriculture and appropriations committees and subcommittees. Together, they formed a classic iron triangle that dominated federal agriculture policy (see Chapter 8). Today, more than two hundred organizations attempt to shape agricultural policy in a far more diffuse policy environment. Commodity groups (representing, for example, growers of wheat, cotton, corn, soybeans, rice, sugar beets, and peanuts, as well as producers of milk, honey, beef, chicken, and wool) have been joined by groups concerned with nutrition, sustainability, food safety, international trade, "locavore" eating habits, farm credit, food processing and distribution, environmental quality, and the welfare of rural residents. A study of 130 of these groups found that only one in six pursued a broad agenda; the rest addressed only a narrow range of policy issues in their chosen niches.[16] The participants are far too many and diverse to form anything resembling the stable, exclusive iron triangle of old.

The growth of federally sponsored medical research has also spawned a variety of specialized lobbying organizations. Various bodily organs (heart, lungs, brain, kidneys, eyes) as well as diseases (HIV/AIDS, diabetes, epilepsy, cystic fibrosis, arthritis, lupus) have their own advocacy groups. Cancer research is promoted not only by the American Cancer Society but by groups specializing in its various forms (breast, prostate, ovarian, leukemia, lymphoma). Associations lobby for more investment in curing birth and developmental diseases (spina bifida, cystic fibrosis), maladies of youth (sudden infant death syndrome) and age (osteoporosis), and mental as well as physical illnesses (bipolar disorder, autism, alcoholism). All want the health research budget to grow, but each also works to expand the share devoted to its particular specialty.

Specialization responds not only to changes in the external environment but also to organizational imperatives. To survive, an interest group must convince its individual or institutional backers that their continued investment is worthwhile. To do so, it must distinguish itself from similar outfits competing for the same constituency by showing that its contribution is unique. Some have done so spectacularly, with either high-profile events (such as the Susan G. Komen Race for the Cure

AP Photo/Haraz Ghanbari

Michael J. Fox, actor, Parkinson's disease patient, and founder of the Michael J. Fox Foundation for Parkinson's Research, confers with Senator Orrin Hatch on Capitol Hill as they jointly advocate for passage of a bill that would fund stem cell research into this and other diseases. Groups successfully pressuring Congress to devote more resources to combating "their" disease have inspired imitators, making this strategy increasingly common.

walk to fight breast cancer) or famous spokespeople (such as the Michael J. Fox Foundation for Parkinson's Research). Most groups survive by staking an exclusive claim to leadership and expertise on a particular subset of issues. To avoid mutually destructive poaching, potential competitors for the same constituency reach informal accommodations, deferring to each other's issue turf. Opponents do not threaten an interest group's health; indeed, as we saw earlier in this chapter, powerful opponents often invigorate a group. A group is in the greatest danger from similar groups appealing to the same supporters. This problem makes the formation of coalitions tricky. Groups often have to form alliances to succeed politically, but to be submerged in a coalition threatens the loss of a group's special identity. Thus many groups are reluctant to participate in coalitions and join them only temporarily for specific purposes.[17] Nonetheless, groups with common interests—and no fear of losing their separate identities—do sometimes form new groups that are, in effect, standing coalitions. More than a few of the organizations listed in *Washington Representatives* are coalitions of other groups that are themselves representatives of institutions. There is even a National Association of Business Political Action Committees (NABPAC), representing 132 business **political action committees (PACs)** that themselves represent corporations and trade associations. NABPAC advises its members on PAC management, fund-raising, and candidates and testifies in defense of PACs in congressional hearings on campaign finance legislation.

## What Do Interest Groups Do?

What do all these interest groups spend their time doing? For most, the first objective is not political influence but simple survival. Interest group leaders keep their organizations in business by cultivating and retaining patrons willing to pay the bills or supply other essential resources. This activity not only absorbs a great deal of time and energy but also strongly shapes a group's political activity. Organizations that survive on small contributions from a mass membership, for example, have no choice but to focus on the issues that continue to generate contributions. Common Cause, which initially advocated a broad range of civic reforms, has spent much of its time in recent decades agitating for campaign finance reform because the issue always tops the list when members are surveyed at membership renewal time.

Lobbying groups that represent corporations and trade associations have to pass muster with executives or boards of directors who may have only a shaky understanding of political realities. As a result, group leaders may spend as much time explaining government to their patrons as they do explaining their patrons' interests to government officials. They also may spend more time engineering a consensus among patrons on what the group's policy goals should be than pursuing the goals themselves. For example, "representatives of the Peanut Growers Group . . . spent considerably more time agreeing on what they would contest in the 1985 farm bill than they did working to get it."[18] In short, interest group leaders and their constituents are involved in a principal–agent relationship, with all the familiar problems and challenges such relationships pose (described in Chapter 1). On a more mundane level, group officials must manage their offices—hiring and firing, assigning work, and keeping staff productive and content. All of this activity adds up; interest group officials spend a good deal of their time just keeping the organization going.

## Insider Tactics: Trafficking in Information and Cultivating Access

Interest groups have proliferated in Washington, D.C., in part because the federal government's expanded activities affect almost everything that people care about deeply, giving them plenty of reasons to defend or extend their interests. But to do so they first must know when and how their interests are at stake, not always a simple matter in a world of complex issues and processes. Meanwhile, political decision makers, facing the same complex and uncertain world, are always hungry for information about the potential consequences of different courses of action. The informational needs of politicians and interest groups create a basis for mutually beneficial exchanges. The importance of these exchanges was confirmed when officials from a representative sample of 175 organizations with Washington offices were asked to specify their most important activities: exchanging and presenting information topped the list, shown in Table 13.1.[19]

The information provided by interest groups is inherently suspect, of course, for, as government officials realize, it is intended not merely to inform but also to persuade. Thus much of what goes on between lobbyists and government officials is aimed at establishing sufficient trust to permit mutually beneficial exchanges of information. For example, lobbyists spend a lot of their time just keeping in touch with the government officials—members of Congress, congressional staff, bureaucrats—who deal with their issues so they can know when their interests are at stake. Much of their work lies in responding to proposals or actions, and early warning of a proposed action often is essential to an effective response. Lobbyists also gather intelligence by regularly reading newspapers, blogs, and more specialized publications and talking to other lobbyists as well as to government officials. Keeping in touch facilitates cordial relations with the officials they might do business with someday. People are more inclined to listen to friends than to strangers, but even mere acquaintance makes it easier to interpret, and therefore take into account, a lobbyist's pitch. Indeed, just being visible is important: "*You have to be seen. Even if the legislators don't know who you are, if they see you often enough, they'll start to feel you belong.*"[20] When an issue of concern to an interest group does arise, information is central to persuading government officials to act. Decision makers need two related types of information: technical and political. The Environmental Protection Agency cannot carry out its mandate, and Congress cannot legislate clean air or water, without a great deal of technical information on the dangers of, say, greenhouse gases. Many important policy questions are fiendishly complex; government officials, wishing to avoid disastrous, costly mistakes, welcome any information that reduces uncertainty and the likelihood of nasty surprises. Knowing this, interest groups provide volumes of technical information designed to show that their preferred course of action will produce superior results and that policies they oppose will fail, cost too much, or produce new disasters.

Political information tells politicians how voters are likely to react to alternative policies. Lobbyists, not surprisingly, take pains to point out that the actions they favor will please a politician's supporters and the actions they oppose will have the opposite effect. Whenever possible, they carefully frame proposals in terms consistent with prevailing currents of public opinion. They may conduct scientific public opinion polls to demonstrate support for their side or artfully craft a communications strategy to put the best possible spin on their client's position. Following the attacks of September 11, 2001, many lobbyists repackaged their

**TABLE 13.1**    What Lobbying Groups Say They Do

| | ACTIVITY | PERCENTAGE ENGAGING IN ACTIVITY |
|---|---|---|
| 1. | Testifying at hearings | 99 |
| 2. | Contacting government officials directly to present the group's point of view | 98 |
| 3. | Engaging in informal contacts with officials—at conventions, over lunch, and so forth | 95 |
| 4. | Presenting research results or technical information | 92 |
| 5. | Sending letters to members of the group to inform them about its activities | 92 |
| 6. | Entering into coalitions with other groups | 92 |
| 7. | Attempting to shape the implementation of policies | 90 |
| 8. | Talking with people from the media | 89 |
| 9. | Consulting with government officials to plan legislative strategy | 86 |
| 10. | Helping draft legislation | 85 |
| 11. | Inspiring letter-writing or telegram campaigns | 84 |
| 12. | Shaping the government's agenda by raising new issues and calling attention to ignored problems | 84 |
| 13. | Mounting grassroots lobbying efforts | 80 |
| 14. | Having influential constituents contact their members of Congress | 80 |
| 15. | Helping draft regulations, rules, or guidelines | 78 |
| 16. | Serving on advisory commissions and boards | 76 |
| 17. | Alerting members of Congress about the effects of a bill on their districts | 75 |
| 18. | Filing suit or otherwise engaging in litigation | 72 |
| 19. | Making financial contributions to electoral campaigns | 58 |
| 20. | Doing favors for officials who need assistance | 56 |
| 21. | Attempting to influence appointments to public office | 53 |
| 22. | Publicizing candidates' voting records | 44 |
| 23. | Engaging in direct-mail fund-raising for the group | 44 |
| 24. | Running advertisements in the media about the group's position on issues | 31 |
| 25. | Contributing work or personnel to electoral campaigns | 24 |
| 26. | Making public endorsements of candidates for office | 22 |
| 27. | Engaging in protest demonstrations | 20 |

*Source:* From a survey of interest groups reported in Kay Lehman Schlozman and John T. Tierney, *Organized Interests and American Democracy,* copyright © 1985. Reprinted by permission of Pearson Education, Inc., Upper Saddle River, New Jersey.

policy pitches as ways for Congress to fight terrorism by doing everything from drilling for oil in Alaska to reestablishing telecommunications monopolies to including California-grown dates in the food packages air-dropped into Afghanistan during the holy month of Ramadan.

Because politicians know that lobbyists are advocates, when can they trust a lobbyist's information? Only when both sides expect to have a continuing relationship. Rational choice analyses of many games show that when they are repeated over and over, the players have far greater incentives to cooperate with one another and to be truthful and straightforward in their dealings. Lobbying is, in this way, like a repeated game. A lobbyist who needs to stay in a politician's good graces on a continuing basis must maintain credibility or go out of business. If information turns out to be misleading or inflicts political damage, its source will never be heeded again.

Lobbyists do have ways of increasing the credibility of their messages. One reason they arrange for scientists or scholars to testify at congressional committee hearings is to back technical claims with evidence from more neutral sources. Testimony also allows groups to put their cases into the public record that will later guide the interpretation of laws by courts and administrative agencies. Because arranging testimony is costly for a lobbyist, it demonstrates to members of Congress that the group represented really does care about the issue under discussion. Testimony also is a way for lobbyists to show the people who pay their bills that they are doing their jobs. Often the same representatives of a group show up at the same subcommittee hearings and give the same testimony year after year, not because they expect to be effective but because the activity fits their job description. They are sustaining the organization, if not the cause.

The credibility of political information is enhanced when a group mobilizes its constituency as a part of the lobbying effort. Supportive letters, e-mails, and phone calls from the districts of key members of Congress reinforce the impression that a favorable vote is in their best interests. A representative or senator who is skeptical of messages coming from some hired gun in Washington may be convinced by evidence that some constituents care enough to put time and effort into sending the same message. This is why the automobile dealers who fought for an exemption from the financial reform bill of 2010 were so successful, as we saw in this chapter's introduction. They were able to mount a significant grassroots campaign for the exemption in every congressional district, relying on dealership owners and their employees, rather than slick K Street lobbyists, to carry the message directly to their representatives. The dealers won because they could call on a political resource that Goldman Sachs and other Wall Street banks fighting the bill did not possess. Lobbying by informing requires *access*, the professional lobbyist's indispensable stock in trade. Persuasive information does no good if it does not reach decision makers. Politicians grant access to people who can help them achieve their own goals. These people are the representatives of politically important interests in their constituencies, the supporters who help finance their campaigns, the men and women who have provided valuable information or assistance in the past—in other words, the people who can help them do what they want to do more effectively. Indeed, successful lobbying is political persuasion in its purest form: a lobbyist must get people to do what he or she wants them to do by convincing them that the action serves their goals.

Legislators and other government officials always have more things to do than they have time to do them. An interest group can encourage a sympathetic politician to spend time on

**STRATEGY AND CHOICE**

# Why Spend Millions on Lobbying?

## Because It Is Worth Billions

To everyday Americans, the dollar figures in the disclosures that lobbying groups are required to make detailing how much they spend to have a voice in American politics can be mind-boggling. Every three months, group after group after group spends hundreds of thousands or even millions of dollars to make its case for or against legislation. A single health insurance association, Blue Cross/Blue Shield, spent over $24 million on lobbying in 2017, followed closely by telecom giant AT&T ($20 million), Google's parent company Alphabet Inc. ($18 million), and aerospace giant Boeing ($17 million). What could possibly justify these massive expenditures?

The even more massive stakes of national politics make all of these lobbying fees a good investment, and then some. Take, for instance, the battle that brewed on K Street in late 2017 when Congress considered, and eventually passed, a massive overhaul of the tax system. The process of moving from a nine-page outline of the bill at the beginning of fall to the 600-page legislation that passed shortly before Christmas presented an opportunity for quickly mobilizing groups to shape its details. The Trump administration proposed to cut corporate and individual tax rates but to balance some of those cuts with increases that would affect specific types of individuals or sectors of the economy. Just as Mancur Olson's logic would predict, the narrow groups with the most to win or lose mobilized quickly, and expensively.

It was a good time to be a lobbyist. During the tax reform debate, 2,065 groups hired more than 6,000 lobbyists in their attempts to advocate for or against the bill or to push for particular provisions that would help their members or the companies they represented. Large trade groups that brought together broad coalitions of businesses in support of the corporate tax cut spent the most. The Business Roundtable spent $17.35 million and the U.S. Chamber of Commerce $16.8 million on lobbying in just three months, and their members ended up on the winning side. Fighting hard to preserve the tax deductions that homeowners receive for their state and local taxes, the National Association of Realtors spent $22 million on lobbying that fall and won only a partial victory by protecting the first $10,000 of these tax deductions. One of their allies in this fight, the American Federation of Teachers, set its lobbying record for a quarter by spending $500,000.

Just as active in the debate were individual corporations looking to protect their narrower interests. The cable giant Comcast filed sixty reports of hiring lobbyists on the tax bill that year, in which the company successfully fought off attempts to get rid of the advertising tax deduction for businesses, which would have hurt the cable television advertising market. Microsoft came to the table to preserve the research and development tax credit, which gives them a tax break on the money they spend to pay scientists and engineers to lead their product innovations. Both Anheuser-Busch and Altria, the world's largest cigarette company and owner of several wine brands, worked hard to lower excise taxes on their products. They lost on cigarettes but won on alcohol, with the excise tax on beer, wine, and liquor dropping by 16%.

Few of these details of the tax bill made it into the headlines that covered it. Yet their vital importance to the companies they affected were attested to by the millions that these companies invested in lobbying. And low-profile issues are often the realm in which lobbyists can operate most efficiently, because they do not have to

*(Continued)*

(Continued)

swim against the tides of public opinion. In the words of Benjamin Waterhouse, author of the book *Lobbying America: The Politics of Business from Nixon to NAFTA*, "Where lobbyists are especially effective is in the weeds, where no one can see them."

*Sources:* Center for Responsive Politics, "Top Spenders," accessed at https://www.opensecrets.org/lobby/top.php?showYear=2017&indexType=s; Alexia Fernandez Campbell, "The 4 Companies That Lobbied Most on Tax Overhaul—and What They Got for It," Vox.com, December 7, 2017; and Ben Brody, "Business Groups Spent Big on Lobbying during the Tax Overhaul," Bloomberg.com, January 23, 2018.

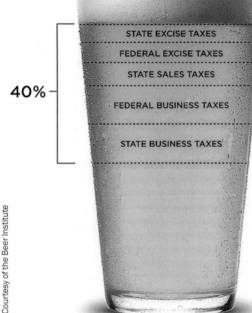

STATE EXCISE TAXES

FEDERAL EXCISE TAXES

STATE SALES TAXES

**40%**

FEDERAL BUSINESS TAXES

STATE BUSINESS TAXES

**Federal and state excise taxes.** When you combine the federal excise tax of $18 per barrel with state duties, it amounts to four cents of every dollar spent on beer.[2]

**Sales, wholesale, hotel, over-the-bar and local excise taxes.** State and county taxes account for four cents of every dollar spent on beer.[2]

**Federal and state business taxes.** Brewers, distributers and retailers are subject to the same taxes every other business pays. This accounts for 32 cents for every dollar spent on beer.[2]

Courtesy of the Beer Institute

BEER INSTITUTE

BeerInstitute.org

As an industry, we're proud to do our part in keeping America great. But the truth is, we're doing more than our fair share, shouldering a higher tax burden than just about every other consumer product.

As part of the 2017 tax cut legislation, excise taxes on beer, wine, and liquor dropped by sixteen percent after a lobbying campaign led by groups such as Anheuser-Busch and the Beer Institute.

its issue by making it cheaper (in time and staff resources) for the politician to do so. (See Table 13.1, page 583, for some of the things lobbying groups can do to help politicians.) By helping officials plan legislative strategy, assemble legislative coalitions, draft legislation, organize hearings, and write rules and regulations, lobbyists will not so much change minds as activate politicians already on their side by reducing the politicians' cost of getting involved.

Interest groups also can make the jobs of regulators and other bureaucrats easier. Congress usually writes general legislation, leaving decisions on the detailed rules and regulations up to the administrative agencies. The Administrative Procedure Act of 1946 requires that all such proposed rules and regulations be published in the *Federal Register* before they are promulgated and that public hearings be held on them if anyone objects (see Chapter 8). An important task of many group officials is to monitor the *Federal Register* for proposed rules that might affect their group's interests and to provide research and testimony in opposition or support.

For their part, regulators, hoping to avoid writing rules that get shot down by appeals to the courts or Congress, keep in touch with politically potent groups in the sectors they regulate. Often the relationship is formalized through the creation of advisory groups representing the relevant private interests, which can be consulted on a continuing basis. About one thousand such groups exist, including the Interagency Committee on Smoking and Health of the U.S. Department of Health and Human Services and the Department of Agriculture's Burley Tobacco Advisory Committee.[21] Again, the benefits are mutual. On one hand, the interests represented on the advisory group have permanent access to decision makers, so their views are guaranteed a hearing. On the other hand, the regulators can get an early reading on the likely reaction to their proposals and maintain a conduit to the groups whose interests they affect. Interest group officials, sitting on the inside, develop a greater appreciation for technical, legal, and political grounds for regulatory decisions and may end up lobbying their own members to accept them.

Interest groups also can be valuable to bureaucrats as allies in dealing with the elected officials who control their budgets. During the Cold War, for example, all three branches of the military mobilized civilian support groups to help fight the battles in Congress and, more important, with one another for a larger share of the defense pie. The Navy League, Air Force Association, and Association of the U.S. Army lobbied vigorously for the programs and weapons systems sought by their respective services and against those of rival services. Each organization enjoyed the financial support of the defense contractors who proposed to build the weapons systems it advocated.

## Outsider Tactics: Altering the Political Forces

The **insider tactics** just described depend on personal access to government officials and work through mutually beneficial exchanges between lobbyists and politicians. The ***outsider tactics*** used by interest groups do not require any personal contact with politicians and may take the form of implicit or explicit threats—real pressure—rather than offers of reciprocally helpful exchanges. The strategy is to persuade politicians to act as the group desires by altering the political forces they feel obliged to heed.

One common tactic is use of the mass media to shape public opinion. The Center for Responsive Politics tries to generate support for its campaign finance reform proposals by assembling and publicizing reports on campaign contributions and spending. Think tanks regularly hold press conferences to bring attention to research reports on public issues. The Children's Defense Fund assembles and publicizes reports on childhood poverty to encourage public pressure on Congress to spend more on programs for poor children. Other groups try to get the media to buy their version of the public interest on, for example, the danger from pesticides or the incidence of breast cancer so that the threat of bad publicity will hang over the heads of politicians who oppose their demands.

Demonstrations—picketing, marches, sit-ins—are another time-honored outsider device. The principal techniques, around for centuries, were used by antislavery groups, suffragists, and prohibitionists, but they were perfected in their contemporary form by civil rights groups in the 1950s and 1960s and have since been widely imitated by a host of social movements. Demonstrations are intended to focus public attention on the cause. Freedom marches in the South brought the issue of segregation—and the brutality of its defenders— into the homes of Americans everywhere through the then-fresh medium of television (see Chapter 4). Demonstrations also may show the breadth of support for a cause. In the early 1970s opponents of the Vietnam War amassed hundreds of thousands of demonstrators in Washington, D.C., for this purpose. Beginning in the late 1990s, protesters at World Trade Organization meetings and other top economic summits have engaged in vigorous, anarchic, and puppet-filled activities. Civil disobedience—sit-ins and other demonstrations that openly violate the law—dramatizes the intensity of commitment; it is difficult to ignore a cause for which large numbers of people are willing to go to jail. Finally, demonstrations foster group solidarity—shared work and risk are powerful bonding agents—and thus may strengthen the organization. Demonstrations are used most often by groups that do not enjoy insiders' access. They have become so familiar in Washington, D.C., that, unless they are extraordinary in some way, the news media pay little attention to them.

Carolyn Cole/Los Angeles Times via Getty Images

Mass demonstrations are a staple tactic of groups trying to get government leaders to pay attention to their issue. Throughout 2011, the Occupy movement staged some of the most energetic, sustained demonstrations in a generation, taking over public parks first near Wall Street and then across the nation to protest against economic inequality and corporate power. Along with the Tea Party movement, which came from the diametrically opposite pole of the political spectrum, Occupy heralded a new era of movement politics in the United States. Yet because Occupy avoided traditional lobbying techniques and hierarchical organization—indeed, because most of those camping out were fundamentally opposed to such traditional routes to influence—the group's ultimate impact was ephemeral.

Reports, news conferences, and demonstrations aimed at putting issues on the agenda and compelling government officials to do something about them depend on media attention. If the news media ignore them, they fail. Private interests that wish to publicize their views without the uncertainties of relying on free coverage may, if they can afford the cost, buy advertising. After its disastrous oil spill in the Gulf of Mexico, BP spent more than $93 million on the television, newspaper, and radio "Making It Right" public relations campaign designed to demonstrate all that the company was doing to help the Gulf Coast recover. Of course, this campaign itself backfired when members of Congress from affected areas attacked BP for spending money cleaning up its image instead of their beaches and fisheries.

Insider and outsider strategies are not mutually exclusive, and groups may use either or both, depending on circumstances and opportunities. The health insurance industry employs top Washington professionals for its day-to-day insider lobbying, but in 2009 and 2010 it adopted outsider tactics to fight Barack Obama's health care reform package. Most organizations, however, tend to specialize in one strategy or the other. Groups with money and expertise whose issues are narrow or nonconflictual usually take the insider route. Large groups whose issues are conspicuous and contentious are more likely to operate from the outside, relying on **grassroots lobbying**, mobilizing members to send messages that reiterate the group's demands to their senators and representatives. For example, when the National Rifle Association wants to prevent new restrictions on firearms, its members shower Congress with letters, e-mails, faxes, and phone calls supporting its position. The intended message is that people who care enough to write on an issue care enough to vote for members of Congress according to their stance on the issue. A rough rule of thumb is that the amount of attention that elected officials pay to these sorts of communication is directly proportional to the amount of thought and effort that real voters put into them. Members of Congress discount patently stimulated mail—that is, hundreds of identically worded letters—that may count for less than a handful of spontaneous, original messages. Indeed, some supposedly grassroots efforts, particularly those run by firms specializing in the business, are so patently artificial that they are dismissed as "Astroturf campaigns."

This is not news to the organizations that use this tactic, so some contrive to make the process seem more personal and less mechanical. Some groups provide appropriate letters that vary in wording, typeface, and styles of stationery; others ask members to use their own words but to emphasize suggested themes. Members may be urged to write in longhand, even to use colloquial grammar, to make messages appear more authentic.

Outsider tactics differ from insider tactics because they impose real pressure, even threats—sometimes veiled, sometimes not—pushing politicians to act in ways they otherwise would prefer not to. Politicians, then, are far more resentful of outsider lobbying tactics than of insider ones. Any student who has interned in a Capitol Hill office has seen the reaction when an interest group mounts a campaign to jam the legislator's phone lines for the day with calls from irate constituents, many of whom may not be well versed in the pros and cons of a policy. Indeed, such tactics can backfire when overdone; the pose of "standing up to pressure" has its political attractions, after all.

## Litigation

One tactic equally available to insiders and outsiders is litigation. Interest groups snubbed by lawmakers or regulators may seek redress in court, challenging hostile laws or regulations.

### STRATEGY AND CHOICE
# Lobbying with a Social Network

Lobbyists who work in Washington, D.C., or state capitols know that their influence over legislators depends, to a great extent, on how well they can organize grassroots supporters. When the pleas they make in the halls of power are echoed by thousands of e-mails or phone calls from real voters, legislators' ears perk up. The trick for lobbyists is to find the voters who support their general cause, provide them with timely information about a bill that is up for a key vote, and give them an easy way to reach lawmakers. This is, of course, easier written than done, but digital social networks hold out the promise to reweight the calculus of political activism and deliver policy victories to those who can access them.

Whereas Uber was able to take advantage of its social media presence to direct thirty-seven thousand tweets toward the Washington, D.C., City Council, its old-school opponents, taxi drivers, used the more traditional method of parking and honking on Pennsylvania Avenue when the council was considering a crackdown on ride-sharing services.

PAUL J. RICHARDS/AFP/Getty Images

The car ride-sharing company Uber has provided clear proof of the concept that electronic advocacy can be incredibly effective when a company is in constant digital touch with its consumers. After the Washington, D.C., City Council floated a proposal in 2013 that would have dramatically driven up ride-sharing rates, Uber used its connected consumer base to protest, virtually. Uber riders flooded the D.C. City Council with fifty thousand e-mails and thirty-seven thousand tweets, forcing lawmakers to back down. Crediting this electronic grassroots movement for the victory, then Uber CEO Travis Kalanick explained his company's chief lobbying tactic: "What we do in those situations is we go big on social media. We say, 'Be active, speak up, send an email to an elected official or a regulator.'"[a] The next year, Uber beat back legislation in California's state legislature that it claimed would have driven Uber out of the state. The company set up a hashtag, #CAlovesUber, and provided its customers with both the phone numbers and the Twitter handles of legislators on the committee that was hearing the bill. In the end, Uber's lobbyist was able to deliver seventeen thousand signatures opposing the bill to its author, who dramatically amended it.

These victories demonstrate a huge advantage that Uber and other companies in the sharing economy have in the lobbying game: they can reach their customer base instantly and cheaply. Taxi drivers can't do this, and neither can Coca-Cola or Ford Motor Co. And if using social networks confers a political advantage, what about the social networks themselves? A collaboration between academics and Facebook during the 2010 elections showed that huge numbers of voters could be mobilized to turn out through social media messages.[b] If you were a legislator, would you author a bill that threatened Facebook, Twitter, or Instagram?

Uber's lobbying success shows that one of the most valuable pieces of lobbying real estate is a home base within your supporters' social networks. And it helps if those supporters are in the generation who live most of their lives online and think nothing of shooting off a quick e-mail. If political activism can be done on a smartphone while riding across a city in a cool black car, it

becomes nearly costless. This can help lobbyists get around collective action problems, activate their base with the touch of a few buttons, and win critical political battles.

---

[a]Jennifer Martinez and Brendan Sasso, "Uber Used Social Media to Beat Local Regs," *The Hill*, January 23, 2013.

[b]Robert M. Bond, Christopher J. Fariss, Jason J. Jones, Adam D. I. Kramer, Cameron Marlow, Jaime Settle, and James H. Fowler, "A 61-Million-Person Experiment in Social Influence and Political Mobilization," *Nature* 489 (2012): 295–298.

This strategy is especially attractive to groups that can rest claims on constitutional rights and that do not have the political clout to influence elected politicians. During the 1940s and 1950s, when many black citizens were effectively denied the right to vote and there was only limited public sympathy for their cause, civil rights groups used the courts extensively (see Chapter 4). People in jail or accused of crimes, unpopular religious minorities, and groups on the political fringe—none of whom are likely to be championed by officials who depend directly on voters for their jobs—have all found redress in court. But then so have General Motors, Philip Morris, and Microsoft. Despite the notable court victories of some groups on the margins of society, large corporations with deep pockets make the most frequent and effective political use of litigation.

Although about one-third of the Washington representatives of interest groups are lawyers, only a small proportion of interest groups list litigation as their predominant activity. Using the courts to good purpose often requires winning legislative battles in the first place. For example, environmental groups, notably the Environmental Defense Fund, have been able to use the courts effectively because the National Environmental Policy Act (1969) was deliberately designed to make it easy for private citizens to go to court to enforce environmental regulations.

In court cases in which they do not participate directly, interest groups may attempt to influence judicial decisions by submitting amicus curiae or "friend of the court" briefs. Such briefs present evidence and arguments intended to strengthen one side under the guise of supplying judges with information on social facts relevant to the decision. Today, amicus briefs are filed in more than 90 percent of the cases heard by the Supreme Court.[22] Controversial cases generate the most amicus filings; *Webster v. Reproductive Health Services*, an important abortion rights case decided in 1989, attracted seventy-five amicus briefs signed by hundreds of organizations.[23] Court decisions seem to be affected by neither the numerical balance of amicus briefs nor the status of their sponsors, but the more briefs submitted with a case, the more likely the Court is to hear the case (see Chapter 9).

Organized interests also seek to shape court decisions indirectly by lobbying on judicial appointments. Nearly three hundred groups joined the battles over Senate approval of Supreme Court nominees Robert Bork (1987) and Clarence Thomas (1991), liberals winning

Kevin Roose for New York Magazine.

From the "politics makes strange bedfellows" department comes the appearance of Grover Norquist, president of Americans for Tax Reform and one of the conservative movement's most prolific fund-raisers, at 2014's Burning Man festival. Why? Norquist has long believed that Silicon Valley entrepreneurs should join rather than oppose his small-government movement and wanted to make it clear to them that he and his allies are not social sticks-in-the-mud. So he turned up at Burning Man, which has drawn tech leaders like Sergey Brin, Mark Zuckerberg, and Elon Musk, to hang out with event organizers and ride in a car decorated to look like a spider on July 28, 2014. Or, as a *Vanity Fair* writer dubbed it, "The Day Burning Man Died."

the first by derailing Bork, conservatives the second by elevating Thomas.[24] Less extensive but still vigorous lobbying campaigns faced off over the nominations of Chief Justice John G. Roberts Jr. in 2005 and Justice Samuel A. Alito Jr. in 2006. Lower-court appointments also attract the attention of interest groups, with liberal groups calling on Senate Democrats to stall many of George W. Bush's appeals and circuit court appointees throughout his two terms and conservative groups working with Republican senators to filibuster many judges appointed by Barack Obama at the beginning of his administration.

## Electoral Politics and Political Action Committees

Both outsiders and insiders use electoral politics to influence elected officials, but insiders offer electoral help, whereas outsiders more commonly threaten electoral harm. Groups unhappy with current policy always can try to replace the current decision makers with friendlier ones by recruiting and financing challengers, but this tactic is used mainly by partisan or ideological organizations. For example, GOPAC, chaired by Georgia Republican Newt Gingrich from 1986 to 1995, when he became House Speaker, nurtured the political careers of many of the Republican freshmen elected to the House in 1994. EMILY's List, a group dedicated to recruiting and training pro-choice women to run for office, has played an important role in many campaigns since the early 1990s. More typically, though, groups monitor and publicize the voting records of elected officials on their key issues. The idea is to identify friends and enemies so that campaign contributors and voters sympathetic to the group know which politicians to reward and which to punish. Interest groups act most conspicuously in electoral politics, however, through PACs.

As noted in Chapter 11, modern election campaigns are unavoidably expensive. Candidates who are not independently wealthy have to rely primarily on private individuals and PACs to pay the bills. In their modern form, PACs are a creation of the Federal Election Campaign Act of 1971 (FECA; as amended in 1974). FECA encouraged groups to form PACs by clarifying their legal status and specifying rules under which they could legitimately participate in financing campaigns; it also put the financial activities of PACs on the public record. To qualify as a *multicandidate committee* (the legal term for a political action committee), a PAC must raise money from at least fifty people and contribute to at least five candidates. The maximum contribution is $5,000 per candidate per campaign, which means, in effect, $10,000 (because a candidate can raise $5,000 each for the primary and general election campaigns). By contrast, individuals may contribute only $2,400 per candidate per campaign.

### Growth of PACs

The number of PACs grew dramatically in the first decade after FECA was enacted but then leveled out at about four thousand in the mid-1980s and has remained near that level since then (see Figure 13.2). PAC contributions to candidates grew similarly, increasing by 375 percent between 1974 and 1986 (see Figure 13.3). Thereafter PAC contributions grew only modestly until 2000, when the bitter legacy of impeachment politics and the closely fought battle for control of both houses of Congress inspired a new surge of PAC spending, which continued to grow through 2018. The sharp increase in PAC activity during FECA's first decade and the continuing financial importance of PACs since then are at the center of a lively controversy, for PAC generosity raises an obvious question: what do PACs get in return for their contributions? Indeed, assaults on the legitimacy of interest groups now focus commonly on PACs.

The term *PAC* is applied to a diverse set of organizations. The categories of PACs used by the Federal Election Commission (FEC) in reporting financial activities—labor, corporate, corporation without stock, cooperative, trade/membership/health, and nonconnected— merely hint at the variety.* Some amount to little more than an entrepreneur with a mailing list; others are adjuncts of huge corporations or labor unions. Some pass out millions of dollars in every election cycle; others exist only on paper. Donations may be made at the sole discretion of the PAC director or only after extensive input from the PAC's contributors. The goals of some are immediate, narrow, and self-interested; others pursue long-term objectives based on broad ideological visions. Most PACs just give money, but a few also provide campaign

---

*The first two PAC categories, labor and corporate, are self-explanatory, as is the minor category of corporations without stock. Cooperatives, another minor category, are special economic entities owned by their members, such as the dairy cooperatives run by groups of dairy farmers. The trade/ membership/health category includes PACs representing trade, business, and professional associations. Nonconnected PACs have no separate organizational sponsor; the category includes a wide variety of ideological and single-issue groups.

■ **FIGURE 13.2**    The Growth of PACs

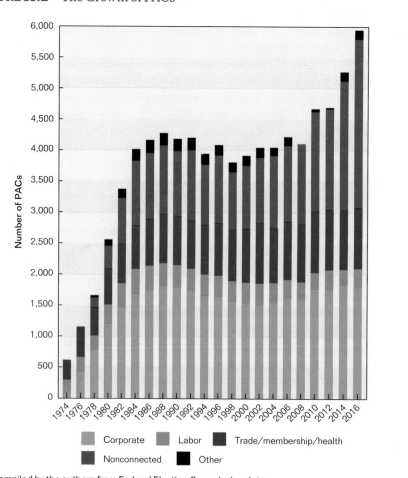

*Source:* Compiled by the authors from Federal Election Commission data.

workers, offer endorsements (who would not want to be regarded as a "friend of small business"?), produce advertising, advise on campaign strategies, get out the vote, and recruit and
train candidates.

Upon which candidates do PACs choose to bestow these gifts? When they pursue the
short-term goal of access to those in control of Washington's policy machinery, PACs
will shift their contribution patterns as control of Congress shifts. In the years before 1994,
when the Democrats controlled Congress, many business-oriented PACs supported incumbent Democrats who seemed certain to be reelected, switching to Republican challengers only when their prospects looked extraordinarily promising. Although most business
groups are closer to Republicans ideologically, they were reluctant to risk loss of access by
offending Democratic incumbents when they ran for Congress. The short-term pursuit of

**■ FIGURE 13.3**   The Increase in PAC Contributions to Congressional Candidates

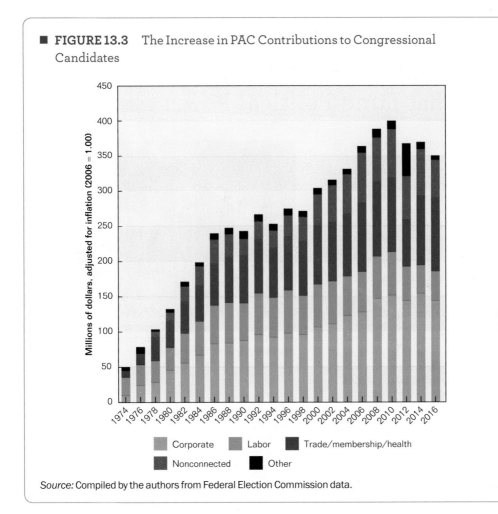

*Source:* Compiled by the authors from Federal Election Commission data.

access to Democrats was at odds with the long-term goal that these business groups had of aiding Republicans who were more sympathetic to their requests. When Republicans took control after 1994, the short- and long-term goals of business PACs were more easily reconciled. Republican leaders threatened retaliation against PACs that continued to support Democrats.[25] As New York representative Bill Paxon, chair of the National Republican Congressional Committee, put it,

> Our members have felt they were carrying the legislative water for many of these groups who then gave their money to the other side. It's very difficult for me to argue that people should open their arms to those who are embracing their opponents. I certainly am not going to embrace someone who's constantly stabbing me in the back. We're making sure that the members know who's wielding the knife.[26]

LOGIC OF POLITICS
# Labor Unions, Free Riding, and the Fees that Fund Political Power

Often countering the role business groups play in electoral politics and lobbying, labor organizations have an important, and well-funded, voice in public policy debates. A landmark 2018 U.S. Supreme Court decision, though, threatens that voice by overturning forty years of precedent in the law governing how unions collect their dues. In the language we introduce in Chapter 1, the *Janus v. American Federation of State, County, and Municipal Employees* (AFSCME) decision overrode the solution that unions had found to their free-rider problem.

At issue was whether workers who did not want to join a union could be compelled to pay a union's "agency fees," which cover the exercise of collective bargaining rights, against their will. Workers have long been able to opt out of paying the portion of union dues that go to political purposes—the basis of the PAC contributions that appear in Figure 13.3—but were forced to pay the collective bargaining fees. The 5–4 majority decision in this case, written by Justice Alito, held that compelling nonunion workers to do so violated their First Amendment rights. AFCME, the union that represents state, county, and municipal employees, collectively bargains with these governments, and so the result of those bargains by its nature affects public policy. Forcing nonunion workers to pay these fees, then, involved them in advocating public policy changes that they might disagree with, and so the Court decision freed them from this "compelled subsidization of private speech."

From the point of view of unions, however, this removed from their toolkit a key solution to the collective action problem that they very often face. When unions bargain collectively with an employee, they seek benefits that every employee will share in. Whether they win raises, improved benefits, or specific changes such as a smaller student-teacher ratio for an education union or the lower nurse-to-patient ratios that public health care unions frequently fight for, every employee shares in the victory. But not everyone would like

AP Photo/Jacquelyn Martin

Union leaders and grassroots labor activists worry that the Supreme Court's 2018 *Janus* decision will dramatic reduce the power of unions to bargain collectively by constraining their ability to charge the "agency fees" that fund this bargaining.

to pay their union agency fees. Even if someone did not object on free speech grounds to what their union advocated, they could be tempted to simply free ride on the efforts of others, refusing to pay their agency fees but gladly taking advantage of the benefits. The solution by unions in many states was to work with lawmakers to force everyone to pay these fees, whether they wanted to join the union or not. Analogous to the individual mandate to purchase health insurance under Obamacare, this solution to the free-riding problem has been enshrined in many states' laws and approved by a prior Supreme Court decision.

After the *Janus v. AFCME* case, though, union dues and thus union power may take a hit. The nation's largest teachers union expected to lose 200,000 members and $28 million from its budget. Stanford professor Terry Moe observed after the decision that "members and money are power in politics. This will weaken the teachers unions nationwide as a political force."

*Sources:* Dana Goldstein and Erica L. Green, "What the Supreme Court's Janus Decision Means for Teacher Unions," *New York Times*, June 27, 2018; Brian Miller, "Unpacking the Janus Decision," Forbes.com, June 27, 2018.

Thus, whereas in the four elections from 1988 to 1994 Democrats received an average of 54 percent of corporate PAC contributions to House candidates, in the four subsequent elections Democrats received an average of only 34 percent. In 2007, the first year after the Democrats resumed control of the House, their share went back up to 49 percent.[27]

Some PACs also conduct independent campaigns for or against specific candidates, a practice that has become increasingly common in recent elections. For a campaign to be independent, it must not coordinate its activities with the candidate's campaign. The law does not limit independent expenditures, but they must be reported to the FEC. In the 2008 campaign cycle, for example, 146 PACs spent a total of $135 million on independent campaigns for or against particular House, Senate, and presidential candidates. Although the size of independent PAC expenditures is unlimited, PACs are still required to raise the funds for these expenditures in small chunks, putting a functional limit on what they can raise and spend. The landmark *Citizens United v. Federal Election Commission* decision, handed down by the Supreme Court in 2010, removed even this constraint. By a 5–4 margin, the Court held that independent spending by corporations and by unions was speech protected by the First Amendment and thus could not be prohibited or limited. Instead of having to work hard to raise money for its PAC and then spend PAC money on an independent campaign, a corporation or union can now use money directly from its treasury to fund political advertisements on behalf of or in opposition to a candidate. With the funding floodgates opened, independent expenditures rose to $220 million with a month still to go in the 2010 campaigns, nearly doubling the 2008 figure even though the White House was not at stake.[28] So-called super PACs emerged, such as one named American Crossroads that raised more than $24 million from corporations and individuals to spend on behalf of conservative candidates in the midterm elections. Although it also empowers labor groups on the left, the *Citizens United* decision again raises the specter that the unequal distribution of wealth in society will directly translate into a distribution of interest group power that favors the most affluent voters on each side of the ideological spectrum.

### PAC Influence

How does PAC activity affect public policy? According to one view, PACs corrupt the entire legislative process, giving citizens "the best Congress money can buy" because members vote with an eye more to the interests of their PAC donors than to those of their constituents or the nation. Proponents of this view say that PAC contributions buy votes and policy, period.[29] The evidence usually offered for this charge, however, is largely circumstantial or anecdotal. An investigative reporter or a campaign reform lobby such as the Center for Responsive Politics reveals that members supporting legislation desired by some interest groups—milk producers, used car dealers, physicians, the banking industry, and the National Rifle Association are examples—got more campaign money from PACs representing the group than did members who opposed the legislation.

Such evidence is inconclusive, however. PAC officials counter that they are merely helping elect legislators who share their own conception of the public interest. It would be bizarre indeed if PACs distributed money randomly to friend and foe alike; no one should expect them to be that careless. The fact is, no simple matching of contributions to roll-call votes (recorded votes cast on the floor of the House or Senate) or other activities can prove that PACs buy

# What, Exactly, Do PAC Contributions Buy?

Numbers never lie, but it is always tricky to interpret what the numbers like those in this figure mean when it comes to interpreting patterns in PAC contributions. These data come from a report issued by the Center for Responsive Politics, a leading government think tank, titled *Big Labor Gave Big Support to Health Reform Supporters, Health Interests Lent More Support to Opponents.* It shows how much members of Congress who supported or opposed 2010's landmark health care reform bill received in contributions from labor PACs and from health care industry groups.

The figure shows a clear correlation between the source of a representative's campaign cash and how he or she voted on this bill, a correlation that shows up on bill after bill in Congress. Does this mean that campaign contributions "buy" the votes of members of Congress? Did the supporters of Obama's plan—all of whom were Democrats—back it simply because they relied so heavily on the support of the labor groups who advocated its passage? Did the opponents of health care reform, nearly all Republicans, oppose it in order to court contributions from the health care industry?

One interpretation of the link between money and votes answers both these questions in the affirmative, contending that PAC contributions influence the votes of legislators who are bought and sold to the highest bidder. In this view, PAC contributions buy votes in Congress. Another view, though, holds that lawmakers are unlikely to shift their positions on such a high-profile, hotly contested issue as health care reform, and instead posits that representatives are able to raise large sums of money from a PAC because they have already taken clear positions on the side of that interest. In this view, PAC contributions are aimed at helping friendly candidates win office.

The PACs that work for the interests of labor or business groups have broad ideological agendas. Their goal is to maximize the number of seats held by people sympathetic to their views, changing policies by changing representatives

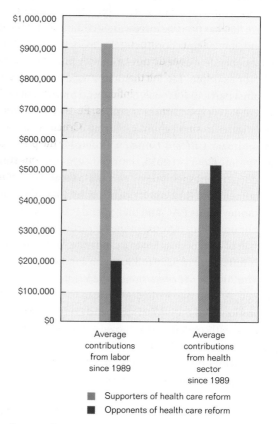

*Sources:* Compiled by authors from various sources.

rather than by persuading representatives to change policies. Thus they support both incumbents and promising challengers, often concentrating their resources on the closest races in which their contributions will do the most good. The PACs of groups that want to buy as much access as possible—or even attempt to buy votes—will focus their money only on incumbents, especially those in the safest seats. Exploring the complex patterns that link levels of competition to PAC contributions can tell us what interest groups think they are buying. Simply observing a correlation between money and voting behavior, on the other hand, is insufficient evidence to indict lobbyists or lawmakers.

influence. More careful scholarly studies have found that PAC contributions are driven almost entirely by party, ideology, and state or district interests and exert, at most, only a modest effect on a legislator's decisions. On issues that attract little public attention and do not divide members along party or ideological lines, votes appear to reflect, in a modest way, prior PAC contributions. But these are rare issues indeed. Despite the many tales of members who vote to please financial backers or who demand money from lobbyists in return for help, there is little reliable evidence that policy is being bought wholesale by special interests.[30] This is not to say, however, that PAC contributions do not have other effects on some members of Congress. Both members and PAC officials admit that, at minimum, contributions ensure access—a necessary if not sufficient condition for insider influence. Doors are open to lobbyists representing groups who have supported members' campaigns. Furthermore, roll-call votes are by no means the only important decisions shaping legislation. Crucial choices are made before bills reach the floor, but little is known about how PACs influence the preliminary stages of the legislative process. One study did find, however, that PAC contributions stimulated committee activity on behalf of the PAC's legislative goals.[31] Interest groups are not likely to put much time, energy, and money into PAC activities without some perceived legislative payoff.

Still, there are some formidable barriers to PAC influence. Many important issues generate conflicts among well-organized interests, giving members access to PAC money no matter which side they take and thus freeing them to take whatever side is consistent with their personal or district preferences. Given the variety of sources of campaign money available to incumbents—private individuals and parties as well as the thousands of PACs—most should have little difficulty financing campaigns without putting their principles on the block. Again, the representation of such a vast array of interests through PACs buttresses David Truman's pluralist defense of interest groups. Furthermore, the point of campaigns is to win elections, not raise money. Campaign contributions are a means to an end—winning votes and elections—not the end in themselves. For incumbents, the marginal return on campaign spending is small; the prospective value, in votes, of even the maximum PAC contribution ($10,000) is tiny. Thus it makes no sense for a member, to please a PAC, to take a stand that produces even a small net loss of voter support. The sentiments of a member's constituents, when they can be estimated, far outweigh campaign contributions in determining roll-call votes.

Finally, one fact, often overlooked, is that members of Congress are in a much stronger position to influence PACs than PACs are to influence them. Like other forms of lobbying, the activities undertaken by PACs are largely defensive. They ignore invitations to fund-raisers held by legislators at their peril because they risk losing access and putting the interests they represent at a competitive disadvantage. Yet for politicians, granting access is relatively cheap; it does not promise action—it promises merely the opportunity to be heard. Groups are thus "awash in access but often subordinate in influence."[32] PACs that cannot afford to say no or to offend members by funding their challengers are scarcely the powerhouses of legend.

It is important to remember that PACs are not themselves lobbying organizations, though lobbyists sometimes organize PACs to try to bolster the political clout of the interest groups they represent. In fact, PACs form a relatively small, quite specialized part of the interest group universe, and only a small portion of the money spent to influence politics passes through them. Most politically active interest groups do not form PACs at all. Rather, they use one or more of the other methods described in this chapter to influence politics. If PACs were to be abolished tomorrow, interest group politics would continue unabated.

## Interest Group Politics: Controversial and Thriving

Former member of Congress Mick Mulvaney, when he was serving as head of the Consumer Financial Protection Bureau during the Trump administration, made an unusually candid admission of how lobbyists employ both insider tactics and PAC contributions to influence politics. In an April 2018 speech to the American Bankers Association, he urged them to lobby lawmakers energetically, and to back up this lobbying with campaign contributions, to pursue the association's policy agenda. "We had a hierarchy in my office in Congress," Mulvaney recounted. "If you're a lobbyist who never gave us money, I didn't talk to you. If you're a lobbyist who gave us money, I might talk to you." His comments drew harsh criticism from his former colleagues, such as Democratic senator Bob Casey of Pennsylvania, who said, "This is supposed to be a government by the people, for the people. Not a government of the thieves and the money changers. Mick Mulvaney is a disgrace." In the same speech that he talked about meeting with lobbyists, though, Mulvaney also insisted that his doors remained even more open to everyday constituents. "If you came from back home and sat in my lobby, I talked to you without exception, regardless of the financial contributions."[33]

The debates about potential "pay-to-play" politics in Washington, D.C., are only the most recent variation on the enduring theme that special interest lobbies subvert democracy and trample the public interest. Scholarly critics of mid-twentieth-century interest group politics emphasized two faults. The first was captured by Schattschneider's oft-quoted observation, noted earlier, that in the pluralist paradise, "the heavenly chorus sings with a strong upper-class accent"—that is, group representation is biased in favor of wealthy corporations and affluent individuals. The second was that rampant pluralism had let private interests hijack public authority. The mutually advantageous iron triangles formed by interest groups, agencies, and congressional subcommittees allowed special interests to dominate their policy domains. Agencies established to protect the public were soon captured by the very interests they were supposed to be regulating.

As we saw in Chapter 8, few observers today fret about iron triangles or captured agencies. The rise of public interest groups and the fragmentation of the interest group universe, as well as the ability of legislators to learn from past mistakes, broke up the iron triangles and liberated (or eliminated) the captured regulatory agencies. Public interest groups kept the spotlight on agencies and changed the political equation by promising political benefits (good publicity, a reputation as the defender of citizens) to elected officials who pursued the groups' versions of the public interest and by threatening political damage to those who did not. Organizational fragmentation undermined old accommodations: the more than two hundred organizations active in agricultural policy, for example, cannot form stable, autonomous alliances with agencies and legislators.[34] Changes in the way Congress operates also contributed to the breakup of iron triangles. During the 1970s, the legislative process became more open and permeable, committee and subcommittee autonomy declined, and influence over policy became more widely distributed. There were simply too many potential players for stable subgovernments to persist. Since then, the growing legislative dominance of party leaders has proven equally inhospitable to them.

The demise of iron triangles, however, has not ended the criticism of pluralist politics. The charge of class bias remains plausible. Business organizations and other groups representing well-heeled interests still account for the largest share of lobbying expenditures by far (see Figure 13.4). Even public interest groups represent largely upper-middle-class clientele—well-educated people with enough discretionary income to indulge in expressive contributions to causes they deem worthy. The interests of poor people, welfare mothers, and the homeless may be represented, but only through the financial contributions of the more affluent people and organizations presuming to speak for them.[35]

Although iron triangles no longer reign, the proliferation of groups that contributed to their demise has created problems of its own. The clamor of competing groups is blamed for **policy gridlock**. With more active players, policy advocates find it harder to assemble winning coalitions. And with so many groups capable of vigorously defending themselves, some observers argue that it is impossible to initiate any change that imposes concentrated costs to achieve general benefits even if the benefits greatly outweigh the costs.[36]

Examples of policy gridlock are plentiful. The long battle to reduce the budget deficits during the 1980s and 1990s (and resumed with vigor in the 111th Congress, 2009–2010) is one. Although nearly everyone pays lip service to the ideal of a balanced budget, every spending program and every tax break is defended by organized beneficiaries, whereas deficit reduction, a diffuse collective good, inspires far less active organized support.

■ **FIGURE 13.4**   Business Dominates Lobbying Expenditures

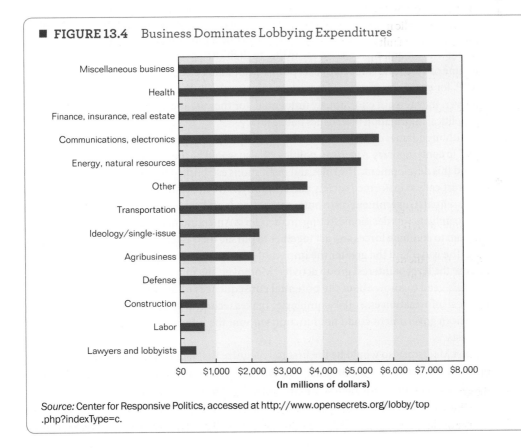

*Source:* Center for Responsive Politics, accessed at http://www.opensecrets.org/lobby/top .php?indexType=c.

Yet if interest group politics produced only gridlock and maintenance of the status quo, then we would not have seen the passage of landmark health care and financial reform legislation in 2010. Both were stridently opposed by a multitude of interest groups, but the public spotlight shining on the issues and the active arm-twisting done by President Barack Obama and then–House Speaker Nancy Pelosi made siding with constituents or party leaders a better payoff for legislators than siding with potential contributors. And, of course, there were influential interest groups on both sides of these bills, ready to back in the next election the lawmakers who stood with them. If our rich ecosystem of interest group politics did not allow major policy shifts, then the airline, telecommunications, and trucking industries would never have been deregulated; tax reform would have failed in 1986 and in 2017; major deficit reduction packages would not have been enacted in the 1990s and in the 2010s; and Medicare would not have been overhauled in 2003. Interest groups may shape but rarely stifle progress on the biggest issues facing lawmakers.

The health care bill demonstrated that a president claiming a policy mandate and legislative leaders using every trick up their sleeves are still the primary forces in the policy process. Specialized, fragmented groups are dependent on members of Congress or White House officials to build and lead legislative coalitions. Legislators control access, an essential commodity in ever greater demand because of the growing number of interest groups. As the real insiders, members of Congress are in the best position to know when particular interests are likely to be at stake—crucial information for lobbyists facing a political world fraught with uncertainty. Moreover, opposing groups often simply cancel one another out, leaving politicians free to pick and choose among interests according to their own personal or partisan beliefs. There are some obvious and important exceptions—not many elected officials are willing to cross AARP, for example—but most interest groups exercise little clout individually. Collectively, however, they remain enormously influential, for they are the main source of the technical and political information that shapes public policy.

Although James Madison would be astonished at the proliferation of organized "factions" in contemporary American politics, he also would be the first to acknowledge the logic behind this development. The rules and institutions established by the Constitution, adapted to a drastically transformed society and economy, have made interest groups both inevitable and essential. Government distributes scarce goods and values, creating incentives for citizens to influence its decisions. Acting on their First Amendment rights, citizens exercise their freedom to combine forces and act together to pursue their interests and values through politics. The wider and the greater the impact of government decisions, the more diverse and intense the level of interest group activity. Moreover, the more government does, the more officials need to know about the potential consequences of their choices. Elections make political information essential; complexity makes technical information essential. Modern American government could not function without the information supplied by organized interests.

Yet Madison also would be the first to recognize that factions continue to raise serious problems for American democracy. The interest group universe, though remarkably large and diverse, favors some interests at the expense of others. The resources needed to gain influence—money, access, and expertise—are distributed very unevenly. And some groups are able to overcome the barriers to collective action more easily than others. Narrow private interests thus often enjoy an advantage over broader ones. If the system is not rigged, it is assuredly tilted.

These problems are somewhat mitigated by electoral incentives; candidates for public office rationally champion widely shared values and interests whether or not these have wealthy or well-organized advocates. The advent of many lobbying groups dedicated to some moral vision of the public good also has mitigated the problems just described. The institutional and social pluralism Madison thought would cope adequately with the "mischiefs of faction" has grown ever more luxuriant, embracing more groups that are more highly specialized and linked in increasingly complex ways. This change has raised the specter of hyperpluralism and policy gridlock, but interest groups can only stop action on the biggest problems when there is no popular consensus behind a single solution. Congress and the president find it difficult to balance the budget not simply because special interests defend every spending program and every tax break but also because there is no popular consensus on what combination of spending cuts and tax increases should be made to balance it (or, indeed, that balancing the budget is the most important goal of government). The conflicts among organized interests mirror, and sometimes crystallize, divisions and uncertainties prevalent among Americans. To paraphrase the comic strip character Pogo, we have met the special interests, and they are us.

**$SAGE edge**™
for CQ Press

**Want a better grade?**

Get the tools you need to sharpen your study skills. Access practice quizzes, eFlashcards, video, and multimedia at **edge.sagepub.com/kernell9e.**

## KEY TERMS

| | | |
|---|---|---|
| grassroots lobbying   589 | moral incentives   573 | public interest lobby   568 |
| insider tactics   587 | outsider tactics   587 | selective incentives   573 |
| interest groups   564 | policy gridlock   601 | social movements   576 |
| lobbying   565 | political action committee | |
| lobbyists   566 | (PAC)   581 | |

## SUGGESTED READINGS

Cigler, Allan J., Burdett A. Loomis, and Anthony J. Nownes. *Interest Group Politics.* 9th ed. Washington, DC: CQ Press, 2016. A collection of contemporary essays that examine the development of organized interests and recent changes in interest group politics. The book covers such topics as the Internet as an organizational tool, the political role of corporate lobbyists, and interest groups and gridlock.

Derthick, Martha A. *Up in Smoke: From Legislation to Litigation in Tobacco Politics.* Washington, DC: CQ Press, 2012. A thorough case study of how an interest group has sought to influence the policymaking process and—in recent decades—consistently lost despite its tight organization and deep corporate pockets.

Drutman, Lee. *The Business of America Is Lobbying: How Corporations Became Politicized and Politics Became More Corporate.* New York: Oxford University Press, 2015. A thorough account of Washington-based interest group activity today. It shows how much money is spent on lobbying—especially compared with campaign spending—and how lobbying activity has grown as government relations professionals become entrenched within corporations and push to expand their budgets.

Lowi, Theodore J. *The End of Liberalism: The Second Republic of the United States.* 2nd ed. New York: Norton, 1979. A vigorous scholarly polemic arguing that private interest groups have taken control of bureaucratic agencies, allowing special interests to dominate policymaking and thereby subvert democracy.

Moe, Terry M. *The Organization of Interests: Incentives and the Internal Dynamics of Interest Groups.* Chicago: University of Chicago Press, 1988. A critique and revision of Mancur Olson's seminal argument in *The Logic of Collective Action*, which asserts that political entrepreneurs and nonmaterial incentives often are able to solve the free-rider problem.

Nownes, Anthony J. *Total Lobbying: What Lobbyists Want (and How They Try to Get It).* Cambridge, UK: Cambridge University Press, 2006. An analysis of the activities lobbyists engage in, combined with in-depth interviews with lobbyists that reveal their goals and strategies.

Olson, Mancur. *The Logic of Collective Action: Public Goods and the Theory of Groups.* Cambridge, MA: Harvard University Press, 1965. A classic analysis of how the free-rider problem hampers organization for voluntary collective action and how the problem can be overcome.

Schlozman, Kay Lehman, Sidney Verba, and Henry E. Brady. *The Unheavenly Chorus: Unequal Political Voice and the Broken Promise of American Democracy.* Princeton, NJ: Princeton University Press, 2012. An authoritative look at how a voter's level of affluence and education affects political participation, and how these inequalities in participation affect political representation.

# REVIEW QUESTIONS

1. What sorts of benefits do politicians receive from lobbyists? If these groups are so beneficial, why do citizens view them with such suspicion?

2. What actions has the government taken to foster interest groups? How do governmental policies themselves create potential interest groups?

3. How do "insider" and "outsider" lobbying tactics differ? What situations favor the use of each? When might an interest group choose to enlist litigation as it tries to influence policy?

4. What do political action committees (PACs) get in return for their donations to candidates? What evidence exists that such contributions are corrupting our political system?

5. How will the Supreme Court's *Citizens United v. Federal Election Commission* decision shape the role of interest groups in federal elections? Are there ways to reconcile the protection of First Amendment rights of interest groups with concerns about their influence over elections and policy?

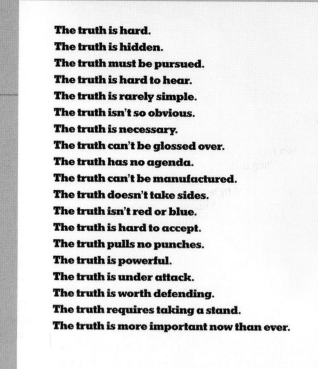

In the wake of Donald Trump's election as president, he declared the media were "the enemy of the people." Media organizations responded to his election by branding themselves as protectors of the truth. Among others, the *New York Times* and the *Washington Post* explicitly reminded citizens that "democracy dies in darkness" and that "the truth is hard."

# Media

# 14

## KEY QUESTIONS

- What role do the news media play in a democracy? Are current news organizations fulfilling this role?

- Is traditional news as collected by legacy organizations an objective "mirror reflection" of what happens in the world, or is it a subjective collection of stories? What about news as represented on social media?

- How does media affect different people in different ways?

## CHAPTER OBJECTIVES

**14.1** Summarize the development of media as a business and the role technology has played over time.

**14.2** Discuss the ways in which the news is a consumer product and how that influences legacy news organizations, digital-only sites, and social media outlets.

**14.3** Explain the demand for news and how news affects people.

**14.4** Describe the relationship between politicians and reporters.

"Democracy Dies in Darkness," reads the new masthead on the *Washington Post*. CNN is reminding Americans that they stand for "Facts First" in a series of advertisements about apples not being called bananas. The *New York Times* is branding itself through an ad campaign proclaiming, "The Truth is hard." Donald Trump has accused the media of reporting "fake news" and of being "the enemy of the people," and legacy media outlets are hitting back, reminding Americans that they are aligned with the foundations of a free society: truth, facts, and helping voters hold elected leaders accountable.

News media and the way we consume news has changed over the last decade. More news is being produced, delivered, and shared on digital platforms than at any point in our nation's history, but the role of the media as an independent check on government has not changed—nor has its influence on citizens. As we think about what drives media coverage and what effects it has on politicians and voters, it will be helpful to keep in mind the different platforms on which news can be encountered in our current context. We'll focus on three: traditional, legacy news outlets (like the *New York Times*, CBS News, or CNN); digital-only platforms that may contain content provided by people who aren't reporters (think of blogs like the *Huffington Post*, *Daily Kos*, *Red State*, or sites like Vox.com and 538.com); and social media platforms where legacy articles can be shared or original content can be posted (think of Facebook, Instagram, WhatsApp, or Snapchat). Each platform is important in understanding the role of news in American politics—and each may play different roles in helping citizens coordinate with one another to solve collective action problems.

# Development of the News Business

Traditional, legacy **news outlets** are organizations that gather, package, and transmit the news through some proprietary communications technology. When we talk about legacy outlets we are talking about organizations that base the majority of their content on the work of trained reporters. This distinction separates legacy outlets from two other types of news-providing media we talk about in the chapter—digital-only platforms like blogs and natively online news, and social media sites like Facebook and Twitter. To characterize legacy news media as businesses does not discredit their integrity as suppliers of vital civic information. Since the introduction of mass circulation and advertising, the news media have been in continual competition to increase the audiences for their product.

## The Economics of Early Newspapers

In colonial times almost no one earned a living solely by publishing the news. Instead, most early newspapers were run by people in related businesses, such as print shop owners and postmasters, who ventured into the news business because their marginal printing and delivery costs made newspaper publishing a viable sideline.[1] Still, producing newspapers in the colonial era was an extremely expensive undertaking. It was not unusual for newspapers to feature "breaking news" that had occurred two months earlier.

The news in colonial days took vast amounts of time and effort. Every page had to be composed (in reverse) from individual pieces of metal type. And the act of printing a single impression on paper with a wooden, hand-cranked press required thirteen separate steps. The best printers of the day could manage to print only 240 impressions an hour. By the mid-1770s approximately twenty-five weekly newspapers were serving the colonies. With the emergence of the Federalist and Democratic-Republican parties in the 1790s, commercial concerns redirected newspapers toward politics. Almost immediately the parties launched newspapers wherever they competed in order to advance their particular vision for the Republic. Objective reporting had little place in these partisan organs. Instead, their pages advocated party platforms, promoted candidates, and attacked the opposition.[2] These party-sponsored newspapers did not attract large audiences. According to one estimate, during the first few decades of the Republic the number of subscribers held steady at approximately four thousand, most of whom were likely voters, already committed to a party.[3] The laws of supply and demand could not be defied for the long term, however; the papers had to be subsidized by the parties.

Thus, during the early days of the Republic, newspaper publishers came to serve as the agents of the party politicians who hired and fired them. Readers were more or less incidental to this relationship, except that publishers needed sufficient numbers of subscribers to justify the party's financial support. These publishers' real principals were the politicians who recruited and financed them. Publishers knew that if their papers lacked sufficient partisan fervor, their sponsor might withdraw its subsidy. Moreover, the government subsidy also might disappear if the party lost the election. Consequently, the newspapers championed their party as if their survival depended on it—because it did. In sum, within a couple of decades of ratification of the First Amendment, the notion that the "free press" would guard the citizenry's liberties against the designs of ambitious politicians had been replaced by dedicated partisan boosterism.

The changeable fortunes of political parties in election years provided a poor foundation for building a business. Many editors probably wanted to extricate themselves from the grip of their partisan principals, not so much to justify the Framers' faith in the press as to place their small businesses on a more secure financial footing. Somehow they would have to break their financial dependence on political parties.

## Rise of the Penny Press

Liberation from party subsidies began in the 1830s with the adaptation of steam power to printing and the development of faster, more reliable cylinder presses. These two technologies introduced dramatic economies of scale, allowing publishers to sell papers more cheaply, increase their audiences, and, in the process, split away from party sponsorship. The *New York Sun* was the first paper to enlist this new technology, but not until several years later, when the *Sun*'s competitor, the *New York Herald,* hit the newsstands, was the full potential for cultivating a mass readership realized.

The *Herald* sold for a penny, whereas most of the competition was still wedded to six-cent limited editions. Soon the *Herald*'s readership was twice that of its nearest competitor, and advertising revenues soared. The success of the "penny press" depended on more than price, however.* To attract new readers, the *Herald* and the dozen imitators that soon surfaced in the nation's largest markets expanded the realm of the news to include human-interest stories and coverage of crime, business, and social events. Not only did these topics squeeze out space devoted to party politics, but editors muted their partisan affiliations to appeal to a broader audience.† To supply copy for newspapers' expanded coverage—particularly coverage of the war with Mexico—the *Sun* joined with several dozen other papers to create the Associated Press (AP). It remains the dominant wire service today and is increasingly enlisted as newspapers cut back their overseas and Washington news bureaus.

Competition for a mass readership became even more intense at the end of the nineteenth century. Screaming headlines and sensational stories tempted newsstand browsers. Critics of these devices, many of whom worked for competing papers, derided these papers as **"yellow journalism"**—a reference to the yellow ink in which the comic strips, especially the nightshirt-clad Yellow Kid in Joseph Pulitzer's *New York World,* were printed.[4] These criticisms impressed publishers around the country less than did the huge circulations and profits

---

*Several contemporaneous social changes also aided the rise of the penny press. Sidney Kobre identifies these factors as the growth of cities, the modernization of transportation, the rise of a larger working class, the onset of mass production of consumer items, and increases in literacy, among others. Sidney Kobre, *The Development of American Journalism* (Dubuque, IA: William C. Brown, 1969), 208.

†In the first edition of the *Herald*, its publisher, John Gordon Bennett, a longtime Democratic Party functionary who had clashed with others in the party, denounced allegiances to all political parties and political principles. He claimed that the *Herald* would support no party or faction. Instead, he said, it would concentrate on reporting the news "stripped of verbiage and coloring." Michael Schudson, *Discovering the News: A Social History of American Newspapers* (New York: Basic Books, 1978), 22.

megapublishers like Pulitzer and Hearst were accumulating (see box "The Megapublishers"). From 1870 to 1900 the circulation of the nation's daily newspapers grew from roughly two and a half million to more than fifteen million. By 1904 there were twelve million readers of Sunday papers.

Publishers of established successful newspapers in one city often tried to repeat their success elsewhere. The result was the emergence of the great modern newspaper chain. By 1935, William Randolph Hearst owned twenty-four dailies and sixteen Sunday newspapers from New York to Los Angeles. Indeed, at one point he could boast that nearly one in four Americans read one of his papers.[5]

Newspapers were the beginning of what we now think of as "the news," but over the past half century the extensive power of newspapers has eroded substantially. First radio, then television, and more recently the Internet have all provided competition for newspapers.

## Emergence of Radio and Television

In 1920 Westinghouse launched the nation's first commercial radio station, KDKA, in Pittsburgh. Within a few years five hundred stations were broadcasting to an audience of two million. By 1930 just over 40 percent of all households owned radios.[6] Despite its advantages, radio initially had little to do with civic affairs. During its first decade, most radio news consisted of brief on-the-hour announcements, which the newspapers welcomed because they believed readers would then turn to them for the "whole story."

For several decades radio threatened to eclipse newspapers as the primary news medium. As early as 1940 *Fortune* magazine reported that most respondents to its reader survey claimed to get their news mainly from the radio. President Franklin D. Roosevelt noted the rapid growth of radios as a common household appliance and strategically used radio communication during his presidency. Altogether he delivered thirty "fireside chats" on the radio.

Throughout World War II Roosevelt's fireside chats and regular news broadcasts kept the American public informed about the war's progress—documents in Roosevelt's files indicate that 79 percent of all households heard the president discuss Japan's attack on Pearl Harbor on the radio. Today, radio remains a significant but distinctly secondary source of news. Rather, the medium has found a special niche in the talk radio format—particularly in syndicated and call-in programs with a conservative slant on public affairs. One 2004 study found national and local conservative talk programs totaled forty thousand broadcast hours a week throughout the country, compared with only three thousand for liberal talk shows.[7] Although television technology was developed by the 1930s, the television broadcast industry did not take root until the close of the war in 1945 as national production turned from weapons to consumer goods. The 1950s witnessed astonishing growth as the public embraced television as an essential home appliance. From 1950 to 1960 the television audience exploded from six million to sixty million viewers, more than 88 percent of U.S. households.[8] By the end of the 1960s the penetration of television into America's homes was nearly complete. Households with televisions outnumbered those with indoor plumbing. Just as newspapers had to adapt to radio, so too did radio with the rise of television.

# The Megapublishers

### Joseph Pulitzer and William Randolph Hearst

Via different routes, publishers Joseph Pulitzer and William Randolph Hearst came to New York and competed fiercely for readers. From the innovations their rivalry fostered, the modern mass-circulation newspaper was created. Pulitzer arrived first. He had begun as a reporter for a German-language newspaper in St. Louis. After a brief stint in the state legislature, he decided his calling was that of crusading publisher. He bought a couple of ailing dailies, merged them into the present-day *St. Louis Post-Dispatch*, and demonstrated that by expanding the market to the "common man," large dailies could be profitable. With the purchase of the *World* in 1883, Pulitzer took his strategy to the most important testing ground in the nation, New York City, with its millions of recent immigrants who were not being targeted for marketing by the mainstream dailies.

George Rinhart/Corbis via Getty Images

Hearst was named managing editor of the *San Francisco Examiner* in 1887 when he was only twenty-four years old. His father, George Hearst, a wealthy California investor and U.S. senator, had owned the newspaper for seven years. Eight years later, in 1895, the younger Hearst bought the *New York Journal* and challenged the *World*.

For a while, Hearst (like Pulitzer) became infatuated with holding public office. He served in the House of Representatives for two terms but gave it up to dedicate himself to "yellow journalism." Hearst's insatiable political ambition and megalomania were captured by actor, writer, and producer Orson Welles in his 1941 classic film *Citizen Kane* (see photo).

Both men used their newspapers to promote causes. Hearst's paper, like the man, was more flamboyant and erratic in its commitments. His political views vacillated from the radical left to the radical right. When he boosted Franklin Roosevelt for the Democratic Party nomination in 1932, he did so vigorously and with hyperbolic praise; his ardor was repeated a few years later when he turned against Roosevelt. Pulitzer, by contrast, used his editorial pages (as well as the news articles themselves) to promote consistently liberal causes. Freedom of speech, personal liberty, and the excesses of "money power" were the staples of his commentaries.

In 1912 Pulitzer, in a bequest to Columbia University, established annual awards for achievements in journalism and letters. The coveted Pulitzer Prize is awarded annually on the recommendations of an advisory board at the Columbia School of Journalism.

CBS Photo Archive/Getty Images

On location in Vietnam in the aftermath of the Tet Offensive in 1968, CBS anchor Walter Cronkite broke from the standard of objective journalism when he concluded his report with the judgment that the war would end in a stalemate. At the same time, U.S. military leaders were privately concluding that the severe casualties inflicted on the Vietcong and North Vietnamese forces constituted a decisive victory for the United States. Nonetheless, Cronkite's assessment confirmed the numerous news images, and one month later President Lyndon B. Johnson announced he would not seek reelection.

Nationally, the three major networks (ABC, CBS, and NBC) dominated audience shares and news programming. This was the era of network anchors as national celebrities. With nightly audience shares in the tens of millions, Walter Cronkite, Chet Huntley, David Brinkley, John Chancellor, and Howard K. Smith projected objectivity and authority as guides to current events. For many Americans the nightly evening network news became their chief source of news.

But as with every other news technology reviewed here, market dominance is never permanent. Even at the peak of network television in the early 1980s, when 42 percent of the television audience regularly tuned into one of the three evening network news programs, cable was on the horizon. Over the next two decades cable and satellite, which initially served a largely rural niche market that lay beyond clear over-the-air broadcast signals, would take away a large chunk of the networks' market share in all programming areas, including news. In 1970 fewer than 10 percent of viewers received cable. Over time, as cable providers began to invest heavily in laying lines into urban and suburban markets, they began offering substantially more channels to lure new subscribers. Where in 1970 the average subscriber had seven channels available, today this subscriber enjoys hundreds of options. Cable providers' strategy of innovation and marketing succeeded. By 2000, the share of television households subscribing to cable or comparable satellite services was just short of 90 percent—but today, that number has fallen to about 78 percent as streaming digital media is displacing wired cable or satellite in people's homes.

## The Digital Revolution: Internet and Mobile

As televisions were taking hold in American households in the 1950s, the electronic computer was emerging on the scientific scene in labs and universities around the world. In 1969, the first point-to-point message between remote computers was sent from University of California, Los Angeles, computer science professor Leonard Kleinrock's lab in Boelter Hall to Douglas Engelbart's lab at the Stanford Research Institute in Menlo Park, California. With the transmission of the word *login* (successful on the second try!) what we think of as today's Internet was born. A decade or so later, the protocols to link multiple networks together were standardized, and the concept of a worldwide web of computers was introduced. By the early 1990s commercial Internet service providers began to emerge, and by 1995 the Internet, which began as an idea funded by government and research entities, was fully commercialized. A private good became a public good, but not one people could use by free riding—they would have to pay. Just how the public would get to access this collective good would take coordination among government agencies, research scientists, and the business community. This web of networks was uncharted territory, and without some mutually agreed-on paths its use and development would be wildly inefficient.

In the early days, most people accessed the World Wide Web from computers connected to the Internet through analog telephone lines. The transmission of data was accomplished using a device called a modem—a "*mo*dulator-*dem*odulator" that translated between analog and digital signals. Connectivity was slow, but progress was fast. In 1985, the FCC opened up unused portions of the digital broadcast spectrum for commercial use, and soon, a group of engineers and businesspeople came together to solve a basic collective action problem facing the industry: if commercial enterprises were going to leverage the connectivity of the World Wide Web, they had to make devices that could connect to the Internet and even connect to one another from anywhere; in other words, they all agreed on the goal, but they needed to agree on the path to that goal. The fruits of this work (see Strategy and Choice box, "Wi-Fi Brings Sectors Together to Solve Coordination Problems") are what we today call Wi-Fi technology, and in 1999 Apple put a Wi-Fi adapter in each of its new laptops, ushering in a new era of Internet connectivity. Continued cooperation between government entities and technology researchers and companies has resulted in subsequent advances in connectivity, particularly among mobile networks. The first commercially available mobile phones to connect to the Internet were launched in the late 1990s in Europe and Asia.

By 2001, Americans were able to read their e-mail and surf the web on their mobile phones. As with the other transitions to newly emerging technologies, digital news has changed the industry for newspapers, radio (through podcasts), and television (through streaming). Podcasts are a great example of the way digital streaming has changed news provision and consumption. There are now more than a half a million active podcasts with nearly 20 million episodes.

The *New York Times*' breakout podcast hit *The Daily* is an example of how digital has transformed the role of legacy outlets—and opened up space for the second type of media: digital only. *The Daily* is routinely

The first e-mail was sent from this computer on the UCLA campus to a computer at Stanford. The growth of such rapid-fire communication over the World Wide Web significantly changed the ways in which information is shared.

© Dan Murphy

## STRATEGY AND CHOICE
# Wi-Fi Brings Sectors Together to Solve Coordination Problems

Wi-Fi, the short-range wireless broadband technology that so many of us rely on, is the result of surprising cooperation among telecommunication regulators, business entrepreneurs, and engineers—three groups who may not have realized their interests were aligned but who solved coordination problems to make progress. It started in 1985 when the Federal Communications Commission opened up several bands of the wireless spectrum (900 MHz, 2.4 GHz, and 5.8 GHz) for use without a government license. Initially, wireless equipment makers developed their own proprietary methods of operating on the newly opened bands. This meant that equipment from one vendor could not talk to equipment from another—limiting the potential uses of wireless technology and decreasing each company's potential sales. Competitors soon realized that through cooperating with one another to set a standard method of wireless connection, they could all potentially benefit. The market was essentially suffering because of the chaos surrounding wireless connectivity.

Researchers from NCR Corporation and Bell Labs worked with the Institute of Electrical and Electronics Engineers (IEEE) to define the wireless connectivity standards. The IEEE committee, called 802.11, worked for many years to minimize conformity costs across the various vendors with interests in the market. The final set of standards was not in keeping with every company's preferences but was acceptable to 75 percent of the committee members. Transaction costs may have been high, but the committee managed to keep conformity costs relatively low.

Engineers started building wireless connectors to meet the standards, and companies started making compatible devices. By 2000, the technology was standardized and named "Wi-Fi," and Apple began offering Wi-Fi adapters on all of its iBooks. Today, Americans own countless devices that connect to the Internet using Wi-Fi technology, including televisions, cameras, phones, computers, and even cars. The "Internet of Things" is growing.

The story of Wi-Fi demonstrates clearly that cooperation among government agencies and competing businesses can create a market—and a highly profitable one at that. All the market needed to flourish was someone to help the various actors coordinate their behavior.

one of the top ten podcasts listened to each month nationwide—averaging somewhere around a million downloads each week. The show interviews *Times* reporters about their stories running in the paper that day and has recently been syndicated for terrestrial radio by American Public Media.

At the same time digital and online technology has enabled legacy outlets to embrace new ways to connect citizens to the news, it has also provided a platform for politicians and those who are not reporters to insert themselves directly into the news cycle. Blogs, Facebook posts, and tweets are now mechanisms through which anyone with an Internet connection can make or cover news. These efforts often blur the line between reporting and people's opinions and make it possible for people to be confused about whether they are consuming fact-based reporting.

## A Tragedy of the Commons: Broadcast Technology Introduces Regulation

The advent of radio not only introduced a major new player to a news industry; it exploited a commons—the airwaves—that drew government into the regulation of the news for the first time. During the early 1920s hundreds of stations came on the air, creating massive congestion problems across the broadcasting spectrum. Stations overcrowded desirable spots on the radio dial, causing signal interference and threatening to reduce this new medium to an unintelligible Tower of Babel. Broadcasters acting individually could not solve this classic tragedy of the commons. Soon, they accepted that the airwaves were a public good instead of their private property. The solution was to establish a government commission that could license stations to occupy a particular spot on the bandwidth. Because the airwaves belonged to the public, the Communications Act of 1934 reasoned that in return for their exclusive licenses, broadcasters must "serve the public interest, convenience and necessity." Although the law explicitly prohibited government censorship, it did not precisely define what the mandate to serve the public interest entailed. Responsibility for interpreting and implementing Congress's legislative intent was given to a new independent agency (see Chapter 8), the Federal Communications Commission.

The 1934 law also instituted the **equal time** provision, which required stations to provide equal access to candidates for office. And by lodging this authority in an independent agency, they removed it as a resource for some future political party. The FCC also has the responsibility to regulate cable and Internet providers, but the regulations have not addressed the same tragedy of the commons issues as they have for free-to-air broadcast networks. In these cases, the FCC has mandated that cable providers also provide local network channels to subscribers at no cost; it has also weighed in on whether Internet providers can discriminate about what content they serve to users and at what speeds (often called net neutrality).

## An Ever-Changing News Media

As a business, the news industry has been continuously transformed by technological advances as competing producers have sought a greater share of their potential market. The trend clearly points toward ever-expanding access to greater amounts of information. In this respect, market competition has provided a collective good in offering more people easier access to a greater variety of news. From the early days of the Republic, when several dozen weekly and a few daily newspapers delivered the national news, to today, when streaming sites receive millions of downloads, the history of the news media is essentially market responses to changing communications technology. New communications technology does not drive an old technology out of business but instead forces these suppliers to be creative and leverage the technology in productive ways. On the whole, innovation in mass communications has resulted in a dramatic expansion of news as a consumer product in a highly competitive marketplace.

## Legacy News as a Consumer Product: How the News Gets "Made"

News—the kind produced by legacy outlets—is expensive to produce. Reporters, editors, producers, fact checkers, and a host of supporting professionals are required for every story every day. This makes news a consumer product that must pay attention to the bottom line. The news is a business, and like all businesses, without profits it will cease to exist.

Complicating the quest for consumers by legacy news outlets is the rise of the Internet as a mode of information transmission. Not only have digital-only outlets sprung up, but social media sites like Facebook, Snapchat, Instagram, and WhatsApp have given people a platform and voice to both forward news they think is relevant to their followers and to express their own views on topics they think are important. Of course social media is not news media, but when people use the social platforms to share or imitate news, the lines can be blurred.

In addition to these blurry lines, the proliferation of alternative media gives viewers the opportunity to opt out of consuming political information altogether—why watch news when there are baking competitions to watch? Even for those attentive to legacy news, the profusion of programming choices may allow consumers to select sources they find most congenial to their political views, thus reinforcing preexisting beliefs instead of providing new information. To grab people's attention in this crowded space, media respond with more sensationalized headlines, photos, and video. The fast production of the news makes both production and consumption of news challenging.

Despite these challenges, things seem to be heading in the right direction. A report by the Pew Research Center's Project for Excellence in Journalism (PEJ) shows that among people interested in news, the ease of accessing media means more time spent reading, watching, and listening to trusted legacy media sources. In a crowded marketplace, consumers are looking for trusted brands, not just brands they like or information masquerading as news produced by citizens wanting to be heard.

### Legacy News Producers: Reporters and Their News Organizations

Both the legacy broadcast and print news outlets rely heavily on the talents of their reporters and correspondents, who work directly with politicians and other sources in uncovering stories and following leads. Sometimes a close relationship with a source will allow the reporter to scoop a story for his or her news organization or gain an exclusive interview. In their own words, reporters often say their job is about relationships with people who will give them the information they need.

The role of reporter is so pivotal to making news that a professional creed has grown up around the job, setting its members apart from others who work in the news business. Reporters make the initial decisions about the newsworthiness of a story and may play the chief role in defining the context or framework within which the story will be eventually reported. Within their organizations, reporters may act as a story's sponsor; "selling" a story to the editor is a venerable challenge and a source of journalistic pride.

## The Beat

Both legacy newspapers and broadcast media cover the regular sources of important stories systematically by permanently assigning reporters to certain venues, traditionally called **beats**. At the national level, regular news beats include the White House, Congress, the Supreme Court, the State Department, and the Pentagon. Moreover, during political campaigns reporters are assigned to cover each of the major candidates. At the White House, reporters receive much of their information at the daily briefings conducted by the president's press secretary. In fact, nearly all government agencies and senior officials have press staffs responsible for providing the media with information. More often than not, these are the agents who initiate "news" by issuing a statement or talking with a reporter. Beginning with the Afghanistan war, the military began taking reporters beyond briefings and **embedding** them in military units, in part to avoid a credibility gap and engender sympathetic coverage (see Strategy and Choice box, "The Military's Media Strategy"). Donald Trump has challenged these norms—often forgoing the daily briefings and revoking reporters' credentials to enter the White House.

The beat system has several important implications for news. Because news organizations rely on a continuous flow of stories, beat reporters routinely file stories or updates throughout the day; they remain close to their assigned beat in case something happens. In a 24-hour world of news, being ready when news breaks is important. Beats allow news organizations to work efficiently because their agents in the field can specialize in particular sectors of the government.

Another implication of the beat system is that reporters for rival publications and networks tend to write about the same events. Moreover, while on the beat they are in daily contact with other correspondents from other news organizations whom they tend to regard more as colleagues than competitors. The White House press corps consists of members of an organized club that has been in continuous operation for over a half century. Given the proximity in which reporters on the same beat work, news reports emanating from a particular beat tend to be similar across newspapers and even across the news media. Twitter, a favorite way for national journalists to communicate, has only exacerbated this tendency. Occasionally these social dynamics create a conspicuously narrow or skewed representation of an event. On such occasions, critics charge reporters with practicing **pack journalism**, in which journalists follow the same story in the same way because they talk to one another while reporting and read one another's copy for validation of their own reporting or interpretations.

## Reporting

Increased media competition has given rise to many forms of news programming and presentation. The Pew Research Center's Project for Excellence in Journalism convened a nationwide conversation among journalists that resulted in a statement of nine principles of journalism. Two of those principles are worth noting: (1) that journalism is in essence a discipline of verification and (2) that its practitioners must maintain an independence from those they cover. About the principle of verification:

> Journalists rely on a professional discipline for verifying information . . . a consistent method of testing information—a transparent approach to evidence—precisely so that personal and cultural biases would not undermine the accuracy of

## STRATEGY AND CHOICE
# The Military's Media Strategy

During the Civil War, a newspaper correspondent tried to acquit himself with Union general William Tecumseh Sherman by saying that he simply sought to report the truth. Sherman instructed him to take the next train out of town: "The truth, eh? No sir!... We don't want the enemy any better informed than he is. Make no mistake about that train." Until recently military authorities could aspire to control news from the front. As long as the military could manage the news effectively, it could prevent useful information from falling into enemy hands, and it could bury failures and promote sympathetic coverage. The first Persian Gulf War, in 1991, was probably the last conflict in which the military could hope to "contain" news reports from the front.

An embedded journalist, left, communicates with his newsroom during an attack near Baghdad as U.S. Marines take up positions around the capital.

Scott Peterson/Getty Images

Relations between the military and the news media during the Afghanistan and Iraq wars displayed features similar to the relations between politicians and the news media. Advancing communications technology liberated journalists from transmission centers, removing them from military oversight and censorship. Hundreds of journalists roamed Afghanistan, unescorted and unconfined. At times, American soldiers found themselves approaching not the enemy but swarms of network and freelance reporters representing news media from all over

the world. As one officer remembered ruefully, soon after a firefight with the Taliban forces in a remote village, reporters from Al Jazeera, the Arab television news network, showed up to conduct live interviews and transmit graphic images of civilian casualties while the American soldiers looked on. As war approached in March 2003, a small army of print and broadcast journalists descended on Iraq equipped with satellite phones and video transmission backpacks. General Sherman's policy of banishing the news media from the front was simply no longer viable.

their work. The method is objective, not the journalist. Seeking out multiple witnesses, disclosing as much as possible about sources, and asking various sides for comment all signal such standards. This discipline of verification is what separates journalism from other modes of communication, such as propaganda, fiction or entertainment.

And about independence:

Independence is an underlying requirement of journalism, a cornerstone of its reliability. Independence of spirit and mind, rather than neutrality, is the principle journalists must keep in focus. While editorialists and commentators are not neutral, the source of their credibility is still their accuracy, intellectual fairness, and ability to inform—not their devotion to a certain group or outcome.

Verification and independence are cornerstones of journalistic integrity and ethics. As news organizations produce more programming and fill more web space, the levels of verification, independence, and reporting may vary.

## Selecting the News

To accommodate various limitations, the news media must exercise discretion in allocating time and sometimes space to news stories. Even with the Internet, being on the front or landing page of a news site is still coveted. The media employ various criteria in deciding which stories to cover. The first criterion is often the authority and status of the source alongside the importance of the story—even if the source will be unnamed. Of course, presidents command front pages and lead stories. Behind the president are members of the Senate, who edge out their counterparts in the House of Representatives.[9] Even staff with important knowledge about timely stories can command attention from reporters.

A second criterion for running a story is its level of controversy: conflict, drama, and disagreement are preferable to consensus. As journalists attempt to sell stories to editors and news organizations compete with one another, the news media often create controversy where it does not exist. A third criterion, closely related to the second, is negativity—bad news is often preferred to good news because it is dramatic. In 1993, when asked pointedly in a press conference why he thought his popularity had dropped 15 percentage points in only two months, President Clinton quickly shot back, "I bet not five percent of the American people know that we passed a budget . . . and it passed by the most rapid point of any budget in 17 years. I bet not one in 20 American voters knows that because . . . success and the lack of discord are not as noteworthy as failure."[10]

To the extent that reporters and their editors actively filter and interpret messages in a way that favors conflict over consensus and bad news over good, the news media do not serve as a strictly neutral conduit for the flow of civic information to their intended audience. Beyond a bias in the tone and type of coverage, many people accuse legacy media outlets of having an ideological slant. The *New York Times* and MSNBC are thought to lean left, and the *Washington Times* and Fox News the opposite. Recent work by media scholars Matt Gentzkow and Jesse Shapiro suggests that this variation may be driven by consumer demand—people like media that comports with their view of the world. They find little effect of media ownership, politicians' demand for stories, or reporters' ideologies on the slant of news coverage.[11]

## News as the Product of Politics

From 1962 until his retirement in 1981, Walter Cronkite anchored the *CBS Evening News*. During his tenure, public opinion surveys repeatedly found him to be one of the most trusted persons in the country. When Cronkite matter-of-factly closed each broadcast with his signature statement, "And that's the way it is," the American public believed him. But news reporting is never a simple, objective "mirror image" of reality.

Most political news does not actually claim to report only events. Unless covering a crisis, most news stories about politics come from interviews, press conferences, and news releases—activities done with the purposive goal of making news. This "political talk" assumes many forms—from official declarations to "off the record" conversations with a reporter over lunch. Politicians undertake these activities because they are important to political success. As naturally garrulous as elected officeholders may appear on camera, political purpose lies behind all their efforts to make news. They may be simply trying to garner favorable publicity or to build public support for their position on some issue. Frequently, the ultimate target of their efforts is not the public but other politicians in Washington. But whatever the strategy underlying their public utterances, they must in every instance persuade a reporter that what they have to say is worth transmitting to an audience. This is not as easy as it may seem.

Earlier chapters noted some of the many news-making activities undertaken with specific purposes in mind—activities such as the publication of the *Federalist,* interest groups' creation of websites and newsletters for their members, the selection of Birmingham and Selma as sites for major civil rights demonstrations, campaign advertising, and the staging by presidents of bill-signing ceremonies in the White House Rose Garden. In each of these instances, someone—James Madison in one instance, Reverend Martin Luther King Jr. in another—made news in order to influence the preferences of the public and, ultimately, the positions of other leaders.

Most political news derives more from what people are *saying* than from what they are *doing,* but this does not necessarily diminish its status as news or its value to the audience. Much of what specialists and officials have to say is invaluable to a public trying to make sense of a particular set of facts or group of actions. For example, a scientist publishes a paper offering a new explanation for climate change; the chair of the Federal Reserve Board interprets the latest economic indicators at a congressional briefing; the head of a local housing agency announces a critical shortage of shelters for the homeless. In deciding to portray the gravity of a problem and in selecting the information to disclose—including whether to disclose it at all and when—these experts and officials are using the news media to achieve some political purpose.

Unlike television commercials produced by inspired Madison Avenue copywriters or academic journal articles hammered into submission by solitary professors, political news does not spring forth as the product of a single actor or set of collaborators. Rather, it is the joint product of two sets of independent actors—politicians and the news media—frequently competing with one another to define the story. As they engage each other in an enterprise of news making, they do so to achieve different and frequently incompatible goals. Politicians seek to influence the course of political events. Not surprisingly, they want news stories to cast them and their positions on the issues in the most favorable light. Those in the business of reporting and producing the news must keep a keen eye on their audience's interest in the proposed story and the willingness of their readers or viewers to rely on their coverage over that of a competitor. Reporters find it pays to demonstrate independence from their political sources and not simply pass along what politicians would like the public to know. The relationship between politicians and reporters, then, reflects a tension between reciprocity and competition. Occasionally, unhappiness over the other side's performance erupts publicly in charges and countercharges. Politicians typically complain that the news media are biased and uninformed; reporters may charge that they, or the news, are being manipulated. This tension was actively on display during the 2016 presidential election as Donald Trump vacillated between

# Twenty-First-Century Media: Mediums Change, but the Craft Endures

There's no doubt technology is changing the way news is made, produced, and consumed, but how different is the actual act of reporting in the Internet age? To find out, we went to three of the nation's top political reporters and interviewed them about the changing nature of their job.

### Dan Balz: A Cut above the Norm

Dan Balz has covered nine presidential elections for the *Washington Post* and is one of America's great political journalists. In 2011 the White House Correspondents' Association awarded him the Merriman Smith award for excellence in his coverage of the president under the pressure of imminent deadline. Balz has had many front-page stories, despite the tremendous amount of competition for the paper's most coveted spot. Speaking about the real estate under the paper's masthead, Balz says, "Those stories that make it do so because the news is compelling and exclusive."

A front-page story at the *Post* gets scrutinized at the highest levels—going all the way to the paper's executive and managing editors. "Some front-page stories sail onto the page," Balz reports. "Others get surgery because they don't quite measure up in some way but are of enough import to justify the extra work." Qualities that increase a story's chance of making it to the top spot include having a fresh or original angle and writing that is a "cut or two above the norm," he says.

Front-page stories have always gotten more attention than stories inside the paper, but the pressure to be fast and first online is changing these editorial standards. The Internet operates as a fast-paced environment and brings a palpable competition to stay abreast of breaking

*Washington Post* reporter Dan Balz always looks for a compelling story.

Alex Wong/Getty Images for Meet the Press

news, "even," Balz adds, "if it is not all that compelling."

Balz's impression of the Internet is an "insatiable beast" that results in stories sometimes being written in great haste. The demand for speed, he says, "can sometimes mean mistakes that would be caught under normal circumstances slip by." But, he cautions, "if there are people who take the attitude that mistakes on the web can be cleaned up and therefore aren't as bothersome as mistakes in the print edition, they are a distinct minority."

### Mark Barabak: The Craft of Journalism

Mark Z. Barabak is one of America's top political reporters. He wrote his first political story in the

*(Continued)*

(Continued)

late 1970s, when he was just sixteen years old, and he's been practicing the craft of journalism, in one way or another, ever since. Barabak has reported from forty-eight states, covering nine presidential elections, Capitol Hill, the White House, and one of only two successful gubernatorial recall elections in our nation's history. In his thirty-five years as a reporter, he has seen a lot of technological changes but none greater than the development of the Internet and its impact on the production and consumption of news.

Barabak acknowledges that digital technology has made some aspects of reporting easier, citing the ability to research, view, and read primary sources from any connected device or to watch video sources on websites such as YouTube. But he also stresses that the things that made reporters great in the 1960s and 1970s are the same things that make reporters stand out today. "The craft," he says, "is still the craft."

What Barabak is getting at is that in the era of Internet and cable news a scoop has been redefined to mean beating another reporter online or on the air by a matter of seconds. But reporters' careers, Barabak warns, are not elevated by getting a breaking news story out thirty seconds before another reporter. The kind of reporting that propels careers to greatness, he says, is the kind that results in having something no one else has—an angle no one else has seen or an analysis no one else has thought of. How does a reporter get this kind of exclusive content? The answer may surprise you. "It takes relationships to break stories," Barabak says. "Trust and relationships. These are the things a reporter's career is built on." Despite the ubiquity of information available online, the news business is still very much a people business.

Barabak admits, though, that there are important ways technology is changing the news. In a world of unlimited information, trusted sources of news are becoming more valuable in his view, not less.

Jeff Zeleny is one of CNN's White House reporters and lives in Washington, D.C.

AP Photo/Lauren Victoria Burke

"What I do, what journalists do—take a huge amount of information, synthesize, and present it in a cogent and clear fashion—is more important than ever." Perhaps because of this, Barabak is not worried about the future of newspapers in the digital age. "People have been saying that newspapers are dying my whole career," he recalls. He worries a bit about the economics of it but not enough to give him great pause. "If you're a newspaperman, you live with the uncertainty," he concludes.

### Jeff Zeleny: Big Fish, Big Pond

Jeff Zeleny graduated from the University of Nebraska in 1996 with degrees in journalism and political science. Since then he has traveled to all fifty states, six continents, and more than three dozen countries. Only five years after graduating from college, Zeleny won a Pulitzer Prize for his work with colleagues at the *Chicago Tribune*. As national political correspondent for the *New York Times*, he traveled around the world with President Obama. In the spring of 2013, Zeleny made the move to TV news when hired by ABC News as senior Washington correspondent. He is now one of CNN's White House reporters. In very little time, he has proven himself to be one of the nation's top political reporters.

What advice does Zeleny have for college students who want to become journalists or for young reporters starting out? "There's no substitute for good reporting," he says. "The digital age and the fast-paced world of Twitter have not eliminated the need to knock on doors and talk to voters." In fact, Zeleny thinks today's chaotic media environment actually elevates the need to connect with real people in real communities—and to listen to them. "I am always amazed at what I learn from just listening," he says.

Zeleny's advice to young reporters is simple: be a big fish in a small pond. Starting out at the *Des Moines Register* and covering the Iowa caucuses made Zeleny a young, go-to "big fish" during the Iowa caucuses in 2000. When the national media arrived in Des Moines, Zeleny was there to help them connect with Iowa insiders and political elites. He might have started out as a big fish in a small pond, but today he's a big fish in any pond. With dozens of bylines on the front page of the *New York Times* during his time at the paper, Zeleny is writing American politics into history. Does he worry that new forms of media are diminishing the demand for high-quality reporting? Not too much. "The media may have changed," he says, "but the craft of journalism remains just that, a craft."

making himself readily available to reporters (even calling in unexpectedly to some news programs) and making himself available only to Sean Hannity on Fox News.

When politicians participate in news making, they usually have two audiences in mind: the public and fellow politicians. Although elected officeholders are always on the lookout for ways to improve the public's estimate of their service, much of their news-making activity is really an attempt to communicate with other politicians. The reason is simple: public statements often capture their colleagues' attention and force a response when a private communication will not. For example, when a president threatens publicly to veto legislation nearing a floor vote in Congress, the threat gains credibility by having been publicized. If Congress were to pass the legislation anyway and a veto were not forthcoming, the president would damage his reputation both on Capitol Hill and with the public. Recognizing this, legislators regard public threats more seriously than threats conveyed privately.

Every elected politician in Washington has a press secretary on staff to generate favorable news about the boss. The president's press secretary probably has the biggest job of them all, befitting the importance of public opinion to modern presidential leadership. The institutions within which these politicians serve offer them numerous occasions to generate favorable news. Members of Congress can, among other things, conduct public hearings, publicly state their issue positions on the floor of their chamber in front of C-SPAN's cameras, and insert speeches and press releases into the *Congressional Record*. Every time a president steps outside the White House, he is trailed by the White House press corps, which looks for a story in a presidential speech, an appearance in an elementary school classroom, or even a foray into a department store to shop. In late 2009 President Obama and his advisers knew that presidential travel and media appearances on long-form talk shows ensured the network television coverage required to keep health care reform in the news and on the minds of a reluctant Congress. In one week's time the president was on *60 Minutes, The Late Show with David Letterman,* and five Sunday talk shows. Members of the White House press corps, who literally go everywhere with the president unless the "lid is on" (and assurances are made to them that no news will be made in their absence), could conclude little other than health care reform was the most important topic in the nation at that time.

One venerable news strategy used by politicians to transact politics with one another is the **trial balloon**. A politician "floats" a policy or some other idea with a reporter on the condition that the source of the story remain anonymous. If the story containing the proposal elicits a favorable response from others in Washington, the politician then publicly announces the proposal. Presidents often float trial balloons by persuading a member of Congress to propose a policy, allowing the president to gauge the political breezes before committing to a course of action.

Another discreet news-making strategy equally available to presidents, members of Congress, and lesser government officials is the news **leak**. This political term, first listed in Noah Webster's American dictionary in 1832, refers to giving strategically consequential information to the news media on the condition that its source not be identified by name. The "leaker" may be seeking to influence the public, other politicians, or both. The most common leaks involve a source revealing something good about itself or bad about someone else.[12] More than simply scoring points, the most important leaks force an action or a response from others in Washington. Arguably, the most famous leaker in American history was "Deep Throat," who continuously provided news reporters at the *Washington Post* leads for investigating the June 1972 break-in at Democratic headquarters at the Watergate Hotel. Later, as revelations mounted, a special Senate committee began conducting a formal, nationally televised investigation. Deep Throat continued his news leaks, leading Senate investigators to new and productive avenues of inquiry into the Watergate scandal, ultimately ending in Richard Nixon's resignation from the presidency and the sentencing of numerous White House aides to federal prison.

AP Photo/Schwarz

When Mark Felt revealed (and *Washington Post* reporter Bob Woodward confirmed) that he was Deep Throat in May 2005, it ended over three decades of continuous speculation. Felt was the second in command at the Federal Bureau of Investigation (FBI) and headed its day-to-day operations, which gave him direct access to hundreds of FBI interviews investigating the Watergate burglary. Suspecting complicity in the break-in and subsequent cover-up in the leadership of the Justice Department and White House, Felt claimed he had no alternative to spurring investigation through news leaks. Shortly before his tenure as Deep Throat, Felt had become embittered with the Nixon administration after being passed over as J. Edgar Hoover's successor at the Bureau.

Today, the costs associated with figuring out how to anonymously leak sensitive documents have been reduced by Julian Assange, the founder in 2006 of WikiLeaks. The website describes itself as a multinational media organization and library. WikiLeaks anonymously publishes large quantities (usually databases) of confidential materials involving war, spying, and corruption. During the 2016 presidential campaign, WikiLeaks released over 33,000 pages of private e-mails from the account of John Podesta, Hillary Clinton's campaign chairman. Stories using this leaked information were numerous. Despite the fact that the e-mails were stolen, there was little the Clinton campaign could do to stop their publication as the tests for prior restraint (a limit on the media, see below) are so demanding and the thief was unknown.

An interesting variant that appeared more than once during the massive leaking that accompanied the Clinton White House affair and scandal was the "inoculating" leak. Independent counsel Kenneth Starr, who was investigating the affair between President Clinton and a White House intern, denied serving as the source of leaks and then blamed Clinton's staff. He chided White House aides for peremptorily releasing unfavorable information in order to minimize any future damage when the news became public. The president's lawyer, David Kendall, vigorously challenged Starr's assertions, arguing that the independent counsel's office had waged an ongoing campaign of leaks and then placed blame on the president.* Virtually every administration in recent decades has at one time or another become entangled in a major scandal or conflict that was begun or fueled by leaks. In its eight years, President George W. Bush's administration had to deal with several major controversies based on leaked information. In the Valerie Plame scandal (see box "The Dicey Game of Leaks"), White House aides were finally exposed as leaking information that revealed the identity of a CIA operative in a vendetta directed at her husband, a diplomat who had recently criticized the administration in a newspaper op-ed essay.

With the rise of WikiLeaks, leaks have become even more daunting as outside parties try to hack into Internet servers where sensitive information is hosted to steal documents like e-mails in order to leak them to sites like WikiLeaks, where reporters then read and cover the stories the leaks generate.

### Strategic Relations between Politicians and Reporters

Politicians have long enlisted the cutting-edge communications technology of their age. The **franking privilege** gave nineteenth-century members of Congress free access to the postal system, and it is still embraced by their present-day counterparts. Today politicians take to social media to communicate directly with voters—but also to get the attention of reporters. There are other ways to generate purely positive coverage: foreign travel and visits to disaster sites almost always engender favorable news reports (although Donald Trump has had

---

*Howard Kurtz said, "The White House decided the way that it could inoculate itself was to do the leaking itself, to do what they called document dumps, to get this stuff out, take their hits early . . . [and when] Fred Thompson and other investigating senators came along, the White House could say, 'Well this is old news. This has all been in the papers. We already know all this stuff.'" Interview on *Nightline*, ABC News, March 11, 1998.

# The Dicey Game of Leaks

Protecting the anonymity of sources has long been a cherished right of the news industry. Some argue that extending such a guarantee to a source—say, a government official, such as Mark Felt (also known as Deep Throat), who is leaking information revealing the participation of other government officials in a lie—represents the highest service this "fourth branch of government" can perform for the public. Generally, leaks also make for great stories that attract large consumer interest. But leaks do not necessarily speak truth to politics. What happens when government officials anonymously leak information, including false information, to gain some political advantage over other politicians? Are news reporters being manipulated by government officials who benefit by remaining anonymous while spinning stories to their advantage or attacking those who disagree with them? Or are reporters—men and women proud of their savvy pursuit of a scoop—in cahoots with the politicians to break a stunning story?

All of these questions were raised by the Valerie Plame scandal, which showed that the use of "leaking" sources can be a very dangerous political game. In February 2002, the Central Intelligence Agency (CIA) sent former diplomat Joe Wilson to Africa to investigate whether Iraq had purchased uranium from Niger. Wilson's subsequent report back to the CIA concluded that the sources documenting such a purchase were not credible. Almost a year and a half later, Wilson wrote an op-ed piece in the *New York Times* in which he criticized President George W. Bush's continuing reference to the African uranium purchase to make his case for the invasion of Iraq. Eight days later Wilson's wife, Valerie Plame—a career CIA operative—was "outed" in the *Washington Post* by veteran syndicated columnist Robert Novak, who

referred to his sources merely as "two senior administration officials."

The firestorm that followed centered on two questions: who were these anonymous officials who leaked Plame's identity to the press—effectively ending her career, endangering field operatives, and possibly violating a criminal law in the process—and was the purpose of the leak to retaliate against her husband for criticizing the Bush administration?

It would take three years and the appointment of a special prosecutor, Patrick Fitzgerald, to answer the first question. Novak's sources included Karl Rove, President Bush's close friend and senior adviser, and Richard Armitage, then assistant secretary of state. But the biggest controversy centered on special prosecutor Fitzgerald's questioning of Judith Miller, a reporter for the *New York Times* who researched but never actually wrote a story about Joe Wilson and the administration's response to his claims. In the end, Miller spent twelve weeks in jail for refusing to reveal her source—who turned out to be Vice President Dick Cheney's chief of staff, I. Lewis "Scooter" Libby, who was later convicted of perjury for his role in the Plame affair. Miller and her paper claimed that the "freedom of the press" allowed her to shield sources from revelation, even when crimes were involved. Federal courts recognize a vague, weak shield right by insisting the investigators first pursue other avenues to the information. But unlike many states that have passed strong **shield laws** that protect journalists from having to testify about their sources in court, the Supreme Court has never agreed that the "freedom of the press" implies this professional freedom. Eventually, the Miller case turned from a professional cause célèbre to a sordid instance of a journalist abetting a vengeful government official's effort to ruin someone's career.

missteps here; similarly President George W. Bush's delayed response to Hurricane Katrina engendered the public's enmity). In 2012 when Hurricane Sandy hit the New Jersey and New York shoreline, few were surprised to find the president on the scene immediately, even though the election was only about a week away.

Television viewers crave visual images, and savvy politicians have learned how to create irresistible ones. In the 1950s anticommunist witch-hunter Senator Joseph McCarthy always appeared with loose sheets of paper that he could wave at any live camera and claim contained his list of 205 or 81 or 57 (the number changed daily) known communists in the State Department.[13] Civil rights leaders in the 1960s realized that by confronting southern segregation through often violent television images of segregationists in action, they could validate their claims of racism to the rest of the nation. The movement's success with highly telegenic passive resistance continues to inspire the media strategies of those who protest to advance a cause.

In many respects, relations between politicians and reporters have not changed much since the early days of the Republic, when a newspaperwoman spotted President John Quincy Adams skinny-dipping in the Potomac and threatened to scream if he came out of the water before giving her an interview on his policy toward the state banks.[14] (Adams had been hiding in the White House, hoping to avoid public statements on the issue.) This amusing scene is a reminder of the tension inherent in the relationship between politicians and reporters. If they could, each side would exploit the other for each possesses (and would prefer not to surrender) something the other needs. The politician needs sympathetic access to voters, and the reporter requires information that makes for a good story. Both are, in some sense, costly to obtain. No working journalist wants to appear to be a publicist for some politician. And the conveyed information that best serves the politician's purposes will rarely coincide with that good story coveted by the reporter. President Adams clearly thought no story at all would best suit his purposes, but the intrepid reporter caught him in an unguarded moment. This obstacle to cooperation is precisely what the Framers had in mind when they placed protection for the press immediately after freedom of speech in the First Amendment. Anyone suspicious of the concentration of government authority should applaud the wariness with which the press and politicians deal with each other.

## How Legacy News Is Produced: Content and Form

Walter Lippmann, a newspaper columnist and cofounder of *The New Republic,* worried about democracy and its future. Writing in the 1920s, he saw a particular role for journalism in fostering democracy, and he had concerns about whether he and his colleagues were up to the task. He wrote, in *Liberty and the News,* that "the news of the day as it reaches the newspaper office is an incredible medley of fact, propaganda, rumor, suspicion, clues, hopes, and fears. And the task of selecting and ordering that news is one of the truly sacred and priestly offices in a democracy. For the newspaper is in all literalness the bible of democracy, the book out of which a people determines its conduct." Lippmann's vision of the press was one of sifting through the propaganda, rumor, fact, and fear to emerge with "the news"—the information that a good citizen needed to know to function in democracy.

# Blogs and Digital Media

Blogs and other forms of digital media have come a long way since they hit the digital scene in 1997. No longer just a collection of personal diaries and musings, blogs and online news today span all topics and points of view—from personal thoughts to high-quality reporting from journalists at legacy newspapers. This has changed the publishing industry, aspects of public relations, politics, the entertainment industry, and journalism.

One of the most popular news destinations on the web started as a blog: the *Huffington Post* (www .huffingtonpost.com). It has over one thousand authors and covers topics from the Academy Awards to presidential elections. Founded in 2005, in 2012 it became the first digital media outlet in the United States to win a Pulitzer Prize for its original coverage about wounded veterans. Some who write for this outlet are reporters, others are actors, professors, lawyers, or other people with domain expertise. This makes the product interesting but further blurs the line between *reporting* and editorializing.

Digital-only media have influenced and continue to influence politics and journalism in important ways. In 1998, Matt Drudge's news aggregator, the Drudge Report (www.drudgereport.com), scooped *Newsweek*'s Michael Isikoff by suggesting an inappropriate relationship existed between President Bill Clinton and a White House intern. The story led to the impeachment of President Clinton. Similarly, various blogs claim credit for bringing to light (and to the mainstream media) the questionable provenance of the documents on which Dan Rather, the *CBS Evening News* anchor, based his reporting during the 2004 presidential election when he questioned the service of President George W. Bush in the Texas Air National Guard. The documents were later determined to have come from people who lied about their origins and several CBS News employees lost their jobs.

In 2014, several digital-only news sites debuted, including the Upshot (at the *New York Times*), Vox.com, and FiveThirtyEight.com. All focus on policy, politics, sports, and culture using a data-analytic approach—a recent trend in journalism called data journalism. Twitter has also proven itself to be an important space for journalism. Reporters promoting their stories, and therefore their brand, often take to Twitter to engage with other reporters, potential sources, experts, and even readers. Sometimes these public connections help solve coordination problems by serving as a focal point for people with the same interests who previously had a hard time finding one another.

This vision of the press requires a sophisticated cadre of both journalists and citizens that is perhaps unrealistic, but it is surely the aspiration of high-quality news operations to fulfill this role, or perhaps an even greater role in the connected twenty-first century—to enable people to be citizens of the world in which they live. But whereas Lippmann saw the challenges to journalism center on honing the craft of reporting, today's challenges are more complicated. Competition for news audiences, the twenty-four-hour news cycle, the Internet, and social media have brought about structural changes to the news business that would surely make Lippmann shudder.

It is worth repeating: news organizations are businesses. And businesses have to make money, or they cease to exist. It is important to a functioning democracy to have a fully operational, high-quality press in place (recall the *Washington Post* addition to the masthead, "Democracy Dies in Darkness"), but news organizations exist independently from government in America and are, for the most part, profit-seeking operations. Most of the profits come from advertisers who want to expose audiences to their products. Because of this, although central to a healthy democracy, news outlets do everything they can to attract and keep an audience.

### Sensationalization

One of the easiest ways to do this is to give citizens what they want, which may be very different from what they need. This includes the slant of news, which we talked about earlier, and also drama, controversy, and intrigue—all of which help grab people's attention.

### Speed

Another way modern news outlets try to attract audiences is by being the place to go for breaking news. In other words, they want to be first. But they also want to be right. It does an outlet no good to be quick to publish or broadcast stories that are always incomplete or wrong. Many outlets rush the news so as not to be left behind but end up running headlines and stories that need to be corrected or are just flat-out wrong. The tension reporters, editors, and producers feel while reporting illustrates an often inherent incompatibility of trying to be both first and right.

Another way news programming has adjusted to gain audiences has been to try to entertain people while delivering some news. This is often referred to as "infotainment"—a combination of information and entertainment. These shows or websites are typically low on reporting—that is, they have very little verification, and the host or writer is rarely independent from the topic or guests on the program. Some people refer to **infotainment** news platforms as "soft" news programming, as opposed to news produced through the craft of reporting, which is often called "hard" news. Although soft news contains less reporting, it may be more engaging and entertaining. In fact, work by political scientists Matt Baum and Sam Kernell shows that for people not that interested in public affairs or current events, soft news programming—and even programs like *The Daily Show* and *Saturday Night Live,* which are almost pure entertainment programs—can prove highly informative.[15] The downside, however, is that it also provides more opportunities to mix argument and assertion in with fact and verification, leading to more shouting matches—and more blurred lines.

## How News on Social Media Is Generated

There are of course no beats or editors making decisions about what to cover on most social media sites (although some have reporters, editors, and producers generating news segments). In fact, on sites like Facebook, Twitter, WhatsApp, Snapchat, or Instagram most of the time users decide "what to cover" or, in these cases, "what to share" with people who follow them or to whom they are writing directly. Some of what users share may be based on independent, verifiable reporting by legacy outlet reporters, but some is not. Social media sites provide users with the opportunity not just to share news but to create content that looks like news—blurring the lines between what is actual news coverage and what is not. One of the ways that social media and legacy media have become similar (and thus a way that makes it harder to tell the difference) is in the style of their presentations—sensationalized, speedy, and controversial.

The effects of competition, sensationalization, speed, and the proliferation of infotainment programming have taken their toll on the press. This is part of the reason why Donald Trump's accusations about "fake news" seem plausible to some people. In fact, some things that seem like news are not based on independent reporting (the soft news shows and sites). And some stories promoted on social media literally are faked stories. Changes in the way news is produced and consumed sets the context for the appeal of Trump's accusation.

In 2018, the Pew Research Center asked Americans to rate the fairness and believability of news sources. Most Americans say that news outlets tend to favor one side of the political debate over the other. Still, 71 percent of people say they go into a national news story expecting it to be accurate. And even more reassuring for legacy media organizations is the fact that people trust the information they get from the national and local news vastly more than information they get from social media. Overall, 71 percent trust the information they get from national news outlets. Only 33 percent trust the information they get from social media. Both numbers have gone down over the last couple of years (see Figure 14.1).

The trends in news fairness and trustworthiness have a partisan split to them—much like everything else in American politics at the moment. Among Republicans, more than 80 percent believe the news is biased; the number is smaller (52 percent) but still large among Democrats. There is also a 23-point gap between partisans on the question of whether the news media are trustworthy, with 35 percent of Democrats saying "very trustworthy" and only 12 percent of Republicans sharing this view. Similar gaps emerge on questions relating to whether the news keeps people informed and whether it keeps elites from doing things they shouldn't by playing a watchdog role (see Figure 14.2).

■ **FIGURE 14.1**  Few Americans Think Information They Get on Social Media Is Trustworthy

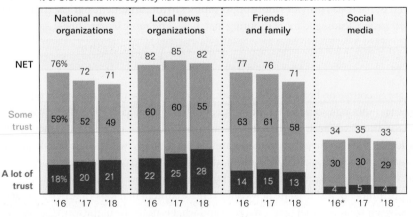

*% of U.S. adults who say they have **a lot or some** trust in information from . . .*

*Source:* Pew Research Center.

*In 2016, trust of information from social media was only asked of and based on web-using U.S. adults.

■ **FIGURE 14.2** Stark Partisan Divides Remain in the American Public's Views of the News Media

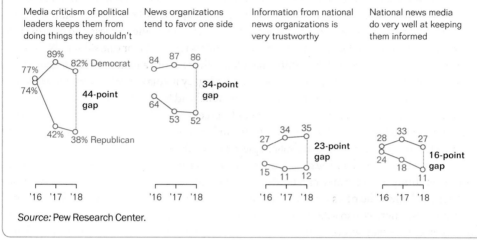

*% of U.S. adults who say . . .*

Media criticism of political leaders keeps them from doing things they shouldn't

News organizations tend to favor one side

Information from national news organizations is very trustworthy

National news media do very well at keeping them informed

*Source:* Pew Research Center.

## Limits on the Media

In the modern era public policy has buttressed the news media's independence. The idea that the press should be fair is left to the marketplace to address—and it has balanced viewpoints in a specific way—across programming, not always within it. Lawsuits by disgruntled candidates, for example, charging unfair treatment from the local press have always fallen on deaf ears in the courts. Hypothetically, anyone can start a news outlet, and certainly, anyone can set up a website or a blog. During the modern era the courts have extended the First Amendment's categorical language in two important areas of journalism that have served to insulate news producers from government censorship and intimidation, despite Donald Trump's attempts to limit reporters' access to the White House. These concern government efforts at prior restraint and the press's exposure to libel and slander laws.

### Prior Restraint

When a government seeks to *prevent* the publication and dissemination of written and recorded speech, it is exercising **prior restraint**. Beginning with a 1931 decision, the Supreme Court has consistently taken a dim view of this form of censorship.* Perhaps the most famous application of this doctrine occurred in 1971 when the *New York Times* and other newspapers

---

*The case establishing this doctrine is *Near v. Minnesota*, 283 U.S. 697 (1931). Jay Near was the editor of a small Minnesota newspaper who used his paper as a forum for vilifying Jews and politicians. After a state judge ordered him to stop publication, Near challenged the state law that allowed local courts and law enforcement to shut down a "malicious, scandalous, and defamatory newspaper, magazine, or other periodical." In enunciating new doctrine, the Court did acknowledge that national security might sometimes require government censorship.

announced their intent to publish the Pentagon Papers, an immense, top-secret compilation of U.S. government decisions and information about the Vietnam War.[16] The Nixon administration won an injunction against publication in a district court with the argument that publication would undermine national security at a moment when the war was still raging. In striking down the lower court's decision to suspend publication, the Supreme Court emphasized its four-decades-old precedent: "Any system of prior restraints of expression comes to this Court bearing a heavy presumption against its constitutional validity." In other words, the government had to demonstrate—and in this case had failed to do so—that publication of the documents would damage national security. Today this presumption lives on, and prior restraint is rarely permitted, except in "troopship" circumstances, when a news report threatens to endanger the lives of American soldiers by publicly disclosing their position.

### Slander and Libel

A similar strain of judicial reasoning crops up in libel doctrine. (This covers both written—**libel**—and spoken—**slander**—forms of false and malicious information that damages another person's reputation.) Civil litigation involving private citizens follows well-established standards of what constitutes libel and appropriate monetary damages, but when one party is a newspaper and the other a public figure—such as a politician, televangelist, or movie star—an altogether different doctrine kicks in. Simply stated, public figures largely forfeit legal recourse to protect their reputation. Not only must injured individuals prove that the story was false; they must also prove that the news producer acted with "malice" by publishing the damaging story it knew to be false. This test raises the bar of proof so high that politicians and other public figures stand little chance of winning in court.[17]

The idea behind these institutions is to make the press relatively free from any real threat of being sued, so that it will feel less constrained in seeking and speaking truth to politics—a desirable goal and perhaps a necessity of a healthy democracy. Critics, on the other hand, charge that such a high threshold of proof gives news media free rein to distort public figures' actions and motives.

## Demand for and Effects of News

### Where People Get Their News

Overall, Americans prefer watching the news to reading it, surfing the web for it, or listening to it, according to Pew Research. Most of the watching happens on television (and most of that is local news), although more watching of news takes place on the Internet year by year. The web is popular among the 34 percent of the population who prefer to read the news, with 63 percent of those people saying they read the news online (across all kinds of sources, legacy news and others). There are differences across ages. Young people are more likely to use the Internet to consume news than older people (see Figure 14.3).

There are endless ways for Americans to get news. Today, nearly every household in America has a radio, a television, and at least one mobile-connected device. About 90 percent of households have an Internet connection. Still, many people do not know or understand the basic operations of government or topical matters of the day. Put simply, many people are just not interested in politics or what is happening in Washington, their state capitol, or town hall.

But even among those who consume news and are interested in these things, the effect of news consumption is quite small.

## How the Media Influence Citizens

The plethora of news products raises complex questions about how and how well the American public learns about politics. Years ago, news choices were much more limited. For most individuals, the news consisted of the morning newspaper and one of the network nightly news programs. Everyone received similar doses of information at the same time. Now that news is ubiquitous, Americans enjoy far greater latitude in deciding what news to consume and when. What does the increasing abundance of news imply for the average citizen trying to make sense of politics in Washington?

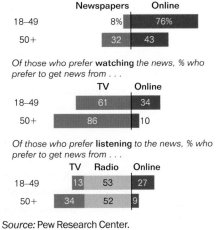

■ **FIGURE 14.3**   Digital Preferences Driven by the Young

*Source:* Pew Research Center.

### Agenda Setting and Priming

What effects does watching the news really have? A landmark set of experiments done in the 1980s found that readers and watchers of news were influenced by what the press covered in a very specific way: it shaped what they thought *about,* not what they *thought.* The latter we often refer to as *persuasion*—and it is quite hard to accomplish. Media researchers call the former effects **agenda setting** when they relate to issues or topics and **priming** when they relate to the criteria with which we evaluate candidates or elected leaders.

The press have the power to shape people's priorities, but not to persuade them or change their attitudes about issues or politicians. For example, when people see stories about the environment, they tend to think the environment is a more important issue than they would have in the absence of those stories—but their opinions about whether to spend more money on clean air or water are left unchanged. This is what we mean when we say the media can tell us what to think about but not what to think.

Agenda setting and priming may not seem as powerful as persuasion, but if an issue or topic benefits one party or candidate more than the other, making that issue more important to people's considerations can be an important effect. You don't have to change people's minds to change the decisions they make.

### Going Newsless

Choices about how to consume news and how much to consume will reflect differences in lifestyles and interests, and citizens today may consume more news content than ever. Or, paradoxically, they may consume less. The same communications technologies broadening the availability of news are even more actively expanding the range of entertainment options. With so many choices, fewer citizens may be tuning into news and current affairs programming than in the past.

### Political Polarization

One might think that the profusion of news across the spectrum of political ideology would result in a better-informed citizenry. Moreover, as consumers sample a variety of viewpoints, they might become more tolerant—or at least more sophisticated—in appreciating alternative points of view on controversial issues. Neither result is necessarily true. The main effect appears to lie in giving consumers the latitude to select news producers according to their assessment of their reliability. Moreover, the multitude of news choices allows consumers to avoid information that contradicts their prior beliefs. Hence, the profusion of news via cable television and the Internet might contribute to the trend toward partisan and ideological polarization (see Chapter 12) among those interested in politics.

Perhaps surprisingly, there is little evidence that the increase in polarization is being shaped by social media—a popular accusation after the 2016 presidential election. In a 2018 paper published in the *Proceedings of the National Academy of Science*, economists Levi Boxell, Matthew Gentzkow, and Jesse Shapiro examine the role of the Internet and social media in driving polarization. They find that polarization has increased the most among the demographic groups least likely to use the Internet and social media—those older than sixty-five. When they compare this group to people aged eighteen to thirty-nine, they find increased polarization among older Americans who are much less likely to consume news online or use social media generally. They conclude that the Internet explains a very small share of the increase in polarization overall.

### Fake News

It is one thing to suggest that social media may not be driving increased polarization, but what about concerns over stories that are fake? After the 2016 election, two things made concerns about "fake news" rise to the top of people's minds. The first was a series of stories shared via social media that were literally made up—things like the pope endorsing Donald Trump or Hillary Clinton running a human trafficking ring out of a pizza parlor in Washington, D.C. This first type of fake news is made up of stories that are intentionally and verifiably false. The second thing in the aftermath of the 2016 election is Trump's accusations that mainstream media are "fake news" and "the enemy of the people." We have already discussed the fact that persuasion via news reporting is difficult (in fact, largely nonexistent) and that most Americans largely expect news reports to be accurate. Trump's efforts to paint the news as useless or even malicious seem to be falling largely on deaf ears. But what effects—if any—do sensationalized, intentionally, and legitimately fake news stories shared on social media have on people's attitudes and behaviors? It is unlikely that they persuade people any more than other news stories, and there is some evidence to back that up.

In 2017, Hunt Allcott and Matthew Gentzkow set out to discover what role fake news played in the 2016 presidential election. Their definition of fake news rules out unintentional reporting mistakes, rumors that do not originate from a particular news article, conspiracy theories, satire that is unlikely to be misconstrued as factual, false statements by politicians, and reports that are slanted or misleading but not outright false. If these are the things fake news is *not*, what exactly is it? Allcott and Gentzkow wrote that fake news articles originate on several types of websites with legitimate sounding names, like "NationalReport.net." Some are established entirely to print intentionally fabricated and misleading articles. Others contain articles that might be interpreted as factual when seen out of context but are meant to be satirical. The websites are often short-lived and disappear after elections.

Allcott and Gentzkow discuss the origins of fake news, saying that separate investigations by BuzzFeed and the *Guardian* after the 2016 election revealed that more than one hundred fake news sites were run by teenagers in the small town of Veles, Macedonia. Another site responsible for four of the ten most popular fake news stories on Facebook was run by a twenty-four-year-old Romanian man. A U.S. company called Disinfomedia owns many fake news sites, and its owner claims to employ twenty to twenty-five writers. Why are these people doing this? One reason is money. News articles that go viral draw significant advertising revenue. According to Allcott and Gentzkow, the teenagers in Veles produced stories favoring both Trump and Clinton that earned them tens of thousands of dollars. But another reason people do this is political. Some fake news providers seek to advance candidates they favor.

After showing that most people get to fake news sites from social medial (as opposed to a web search, for example) and that only a small share of campaign news is delivered via social media, Allcott and Gentzkow assess the role of fake news through a survey done after the election. In the survey they presented fifteen headlines. For each headline, the survey asked whether respondents recalled seeing it ("Do you recall seeing this reported or discussed before the election?") and whether they believed it ("At the time of the election, would your best guess have been that this statement was true?"). They did this for headlines that were legitimate and big—what they call "big true" headlines—and for "small true" stories that were real but not major stories. Then, they asked about fake news headlines that appeared during the campaign. Finally, they asked about headlines they made up (this was the placebo group; no one could have possibly seen these headlines). The results are shown in Figure 14.4 and should be examined carefully. The left bars present the share of respondents who recall seeing the headlines in each category, and the right bars present the share of respondents who recall seeing and believing the headlines.

What jumps out about these results? First, notice the difference between the share of adults who recall seeing (and believing) major true headlines and any other category. More than 60 percent say they saw the big and true headlines during the campaign, compared to just over 20 percent who say they saw the minor, true headlines. Second, notice that the share of people seeing fake news stories is nearly the same as the share of people who say they have seen headlines that were impossible for them to have seen—the placebo headlines. This is important because just as many people said they saw something they literally could not have seen as said they saw a fake news headline in 2016. Because of this similarity, it is impossible to know whether those reporting seeing fake news stories really saw them at all. Think of it this way: the placebo results suggest that about 15 percent of people will say they have seen things they have not (we know this because it is impossible for them to have seen the placebo headlines). If 15 percent of people then say they saw fake news headlines in 2016, what are we to make of that result? For the major headlines, we can subtract 15 percent from the 60 percent who say they recall seeing them and conclude somewhere around 45 percent may have actually seen the big and true headlines. But for the fake news headlines we are left with no one after we take away the 15 percent.

Allcott and Gentzkow's findings are consistent with what we would expect given the volume of fake news stories relative to real news stories and the difficulties of persuasion detailed

■ **FIGURE 14.4**    Percentage of U.S. Adult Population That Recalls Seeing or Believing Election News

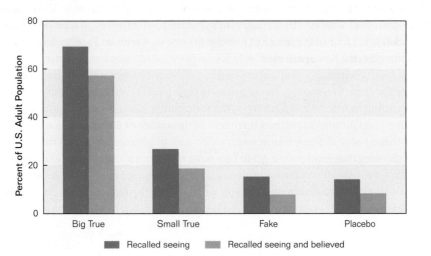

*Source: Journal of Economic Perspectives* 31(2) (Spring 2017): 211–236.

*Notes:* In the postelection survey, authors Allcott and Gentzkow presented fifteen headlines. For each headline, the survey asked whether respondents recalled seeing the headline ("Do you recall seeing this reported or discussed before the election?") and whether they believed it ("At the time of the elections, would your best guess have been that this statement was true?"). The left bars present the share of respondents who recall seeing the headlines in each category, and the right bars present the share of respondents who recall seeing and believed the headlines. "Big True" headlines are major headlines leading up to the election; "Small True" headlines are the minor fact-checked headlines the authors gathered from Snopes and PolitiFact. The placebo fake news headlines were made up for the research and never actually circulated. Observations are weighted for national representativeness.

earlier. This doesn't mean that social media platforms—where most fake news stories are seen— shouldn't try to curb the sharing of intentionally false news links. And after 2016, some did.

In 2018, Hunt Allcott, Matthew Gentzkow, and Chuan Yu measured the spread of content from 570 fake news websites and 10,240 fake news stories on Facebook and Twitter between January 2015 and July 2018. They found that user interactions with false content rose steadily on both Facebook and Twitter through the end of 2016, but since then, interactions with false content have fallen sharply on Facebook while continuing to rise on Twitter. In comparison, interactions with other content (news, business, or culture) have followed similar trends on both platforms. The results suggest that Facebook's efforts to limit the diffusion of misinformation after the 2016 election may have had a meaningful impact.

If Lippmann were here today looking at the modern news environment, what would he say? That there is more news would likely please him, but that its quality as the gatekeeper of important information varies would no doubt displease him. Famous American news anchor and reporter Edward R. Murrow worried in the 1960s that truth was always at a disadvantage in the broadcast environment because it took time. Paraphrasing Winston Churchill, Murrow said, "A lie can go around the world while the truth is still getting his pants on"—an observation more apt today than it was decades ago when Murrow anchored the news.[18]

News producers, from journalism professionals to corporate owners, fondly refer to themselves as occupying the "fourth branch" of government, perhaps envisioning their role as the gatekeepers Lippmann conjured up. We turn now to an evaluation of how this oversight branch is faring in the new age of media.

## News Media as the "Fourth Branch"

The collective action problems citizens face in monitoring their elected leaders require some type of coordinating mechanism to solve. When citizens succeed in finding this mechanism, their politicians will be motivated to serve their constituency faithfully, or they will run the risk of defeat in the next election. In other contexts (most notably in political control of the bureaucracy), gaining access to information is no small task. Agents inherently enjoy an informational advantage over the principals they serve. They are quick to disclose information that places their performance in a favorable light and to conceal that which damages their reputations. We have already examined one solution the Framers devised to counteract the information deficit—frequent elections. Presumably, the Framers expected that ambitious challengers coveting the incumbent's office would ferret out incompetence and malfeasance in office.\* But when challengers fail to perform due diligence on this score, or when there are no challengers, the press fills the void.

The early appearance of a free press in the First Amendment, which occupied—then as now—a special status within the Bill of Rights, is not happenstance. Both proponents and opponents of the Constitution's ratification agreed that the press had been crucial in mobilizing public protests and boycotts and coordinating the colonies' efforts during the early days of the independence movement. Recognized as a bulwark against tyranny, no one objected to including freedom of the press alongside freedom of speech and religion. Thomas Jefferson explained to a friend his rationale for listing it at the beginning of his proposed Bill of Rights: "The basis of our government being the opinion of the people, the very first object should be to keep that right."† In sweeping language, the First Amendment constructs a wall between the government and the press: "Congress shall make no law . . . abridging the freedom of speech,

---

\*Even opponents of the Constitution's ratification endorsed frequent elections but charged that the Framers did only a half-hearted job in installing the safeguards of elections. With the campaign slogan "Tyranny begins where annual elections end," Patrick Henry hammered ratification advocates on the grounds that elections were too infrequent.

†In a favorite often-quoted passage of journalists, Jefferson added with customary rhetorical flare, "Were it left to me to decide whether we should have a government without newspapers or newspapers without a government, I should not hesitate a moment to prefer the latter." But with the accumulated bruises that accompany public life, Jefferson came to despise the partisan press. During his long retirement at Monticello, Jefferson prided himself on never picking up a "putrid" newspaper and turning to poetry instead. Meanwhile, down the road at Montpelier, his longtime political partner James Madison spent his retirement (he outlived all of the Constitution's other Framers) poring over news from Washington and firing off letters to the editor to correct wrongheaded news and opinions.

or of the press." Journalists are understandably inclined to see this provision as establishing a "fourth branch" of government charged with monitoring and reporting the self-interested actions of politicians in the other branches.

Despite the apparent consensus behind the principle of freedom of the press, the practices of the new government initially went in the opposite direction. The First Congress sent the Bill of Rights amendments to the states for ratification; the Fifth Congress passed the Sedition Act in 1798. It expressly forbade any criticism of the president and Congress, both controlled by the Federalist Party, that contained "any false, scandalous and malicious writing . . . to bring [government officials] . . . into contempt or disrepute or to excite against them . . . the hatred of the good people of the United States." After passage, the John Adams administration promptly arrested twenty-five people and convicted eleven, mostly newspaper editors aligned with the emerging Democratic-Republican opposition. The resulting political uproar contributed to the Federalist debacle in the 1800 election from which it never recovered. Newly installed president Jefferson pardoned all convicted under this act, and the new Democratic-Republican–controlled Congress passed resolutions of apology and compensation. The real lesson of this early test came with the disastrous political consequences of blatantly breaching press freedom.*

## Politician–Press Relations Then and Now

Veteran newspaper reporters sometimes wax nostalgically about the "good old days" when print journalists ruled the news and worked closely with politicians based on mutual trust and profit. The good old days probably never were as rosy as hindsight allows, and despite the downsides of social media one upside is the ease with which reporters and politicians can communicate directly with citizens—and with one another. Information is no longer scarce. Then as now, the president is at the center of the news media's attention. During his years in the White House, Franklin D. Roosevelt (1933–1945) didn't have Twitter, so he conducted 998 biweekly press conferences with a regular group of White House correspondents. The president used these "family gatherings," as he called them, as occasions to make significant announcements. Today, the president just repeatedly tweets his reactions to major events and the media cover them as official statements.

In Roosevelt's day, reporters favored press conferences because they created a level playing field and limited competition for stories. They came to the Oval Office expecting hard news that would secure them a byline on the front page of the next day's paper. "[Roosevelt] never sent reporters away empty-handed," reminisced one veteran, adding that correspondents "are all for a man who can give them several laughs and a couple of top-head dispatches in a twenty-minute visit."[19] In return, the correspondents gave Roosevelt and his New Deal full and generally sympathetic coverage. Today, there is mass competition to cover the president's tweets by everyone from White House correspondents to an accountant in Idaho—anyone with an Internet connection and a social media platform can not only read the president's

---

*The most famous of those arrested was Vermont newspaper editor Matthew Lyon, who won election to Congress while in jail awaiting trial. In the deadlocked election of 1800 decided in the House of Representatives, Lyon cast the decisive vote for Thomas Jefferson.

official statements but write about them, too. The openness of the process has contributed to the blurred lines between what is reporting and what is not.

Throughout our inquiry into the logic of American politics, we see that collective action generally involves two or more actors successfully solving a prisoner's dilemma. Each participant has to agree to forgo some short-term advantage, pay some cost, or accept risk that the other side will break an agreement in order to secure a more attractive outcome through cooperation. Institutions create settings that bring these actors together and ensure that any agreements will be honored. Thus far, we have examined how governmental institutions allow politicians to engage in mutually profitable exchange by solving this dilemma. Here, a more informal institution, Roosevelt's biweekly open press conferences, regulated by the ground rules of hard news and no favoritism, allowed the president and the press to cooperate to achieve their separate goals. Both sides, then, got what they needed from their long-standing relationship. Two key elements of the setting that allowed this relationship between the president and the press corps to succeed in overcoming each side's temptation to exploit the other was the community's stability and small size. The president served as an authoritative and routinely available source for more than a dozen years, a long enough time for trust to develop, where each party knew the other intimately.

The Washington, D.C., of today contains a far larger, more diverse population of news producers. They compete as much with one another as with politicians in ferreting out stories. One could sense this emerging reconfiguration as early as 1961, when President John F. Kennedy conducted his first press conference on live prime-time television. Network news bureaus relished their newfound access to the press conference and quickly turned Roosevelt's "family gathering" into a media event. Veteran news reporters understandably despised the intrusion of network cameras, likening it to "making love in Carnegie Hall."[20] Derision toward modern television-based journalism remains commonplace (to learn why, see Strategy and Choice box, "The Shrinking Presidential Sound Bite"). The problem print correspondents had with television journalism ran deeper, though. The television cameras reported stories instantly. With television, print coverage became nearly obsolete. Substitute Internet for television and we are experiencing this shift again. The medium of Internet communication is ill-suited for the cultivation of cozy politician–press relations. Rather, it is conducive to the flourishing of a prisoner's dilemma between reporters and government officials, one that arises from competition and manipulation.

Some students of the news media attribute the modern era's strained relations between politicians and the press to the widespread suspicion among reporters that presidents will lie to them whenever it serves their interest and they think they can get away with it. Veteran journalists point to two specific events—Vietnam and Watergate—as critical in fostering a pervasive and enduring **credibility gap**. Charges of presidential manipulation became daily occurrences during the Vietnam War, which took place largely on Lyndon Johnson's watch. Before the credibility gap had much chance to dissipate, the Watergate scandal broke, and eventually, through the persistent efforts of reporters, President Nixon was forced to resign in 1974. The most recent rendition of Washington correspondents protesting that they were duped was the Bush administration's campaign of false claims about the imminent threat of Saddam Hussein's chemical, biological, and nuclear weapons of mass destruction in order to justify an invasion of Iraq. In the aftermath of September 11, 2001, and with the United States at war in

**STRATEGY AND CHOICE**

# The Shrinking Presidential Sound Bite

## A Tweet!

Politicians' survival depends on successful adaptation. Whereas in 1968 presidential candidates could speak on camera during news segments for an average of about forty seconds without interruption, by the 1980s they were lucky to achieve an average allotment of nine seconds.[a] How did they adapt to this change? For one thing, they stopped trying to present an argument (most of their sentences were too long). Instead, they developed **sound bites**, catchy phrases and slogans that encapsulated their appeal to viewers. Another adaptation is happening now—the reduction of these sound bites to 280 characters to enable broadcast on Twitter.

No single candidate or president has exemplified this adaptation better than Donald Trump. According to *Politico*, between 2009 (when Trump started using Twitter) and 2017, Trump increased his volume of tweets from fewer than twenty-five a week in 2009 to occasionally more than two hundred a week in 2015 and 2016. On June 16, 2015, after making a public announcement, he tweeted, "I am officially running for President of the United States. #MakeAmericaGreatAgain." At the end of 2016, Trump had roughly 17 million Twitter followers, and his most popular tweet during the campaign was shared 25,580 times and liked by 20,022 people.

To get a sense for how Trump has made Twitter his megaphone for announcements on politics and policy, consider this December 6, 2016, tweet (six weeks before his inauguration): "Boeing is building a brand new 747 Air Force One for future presidents, but costs are out of control, more than $4 billion. Cancel Order!" This tweet sparked a flurry of news stories about a variety of topics, including the public targeting of a single

In October 2016, with polls showing Democratic candidate Hillary Clinton in the lead, Trump tweeted that the election was rigged by the media and pollsters. A month after his November win, the CIA reported Russian interference in the election. President-elect Trump called it a "conspiracy theory" and tweeted a rebuke of the report and calls for an investigation.

company by the future president. How effective are Trump's tweets at garnering attention? Boeing's stock dropped two dollars a share (1.5 percent) just after the comment and took the remainder of the day to recover to the previous day's closing value. A few weeks after his victory, Trump's campaign manager called Trump's use of Twitter "a great way" to "cut through the noise or silence." Lots of politicians tweet, but Trump's knack for saying things in this medium that are sharp and controversial is unique. He has figured out a way to coordinate coverage onto the topics he wants in the news exactly when he wants them there, virtually rendering the strategic work of coming up with the day's traditional sound bite irrelevant.

*Source:* Daniel C. Hallin, *The Presidency, the Press, and the People* (La Jolla: University of California Extension, 1993).

[a]Daniel C. Hallin, "Sound Bite News: Television Coverage of Elections, 1968–1988," in *Do the Media Govern? Politicians, Voters, and Reporters in America*, ed. Shanto Iyengar and Richard Reeves (Thousand Oaks, CA: Sage, 1997), 57–65.

Afghanistan, the national press adopted a largely uncritical stance toward these claims. Vietnam, Watergate, and the Iraq War—all falling within the professional careers of many of today's news editors and senior reporters—have conditioned reporters to greet all White House claims with a suspicion of duplicity. Yet even without these major press failings, a credibility gap would probably still color the politician–press relationship. It is embedded in the tension between the preferred news story of reporters and that of politicians. In the absence of institutions designed for their mutual benefit, such as Roosevelt's "family gatherings," the news media's relationship with politicians is likely to remain one of mutual suspicion.

**for CQ Press**

**Want a better grade?**

Get the tools you need to sharpen your study skills. Access practice quizzes, eFlashcards, video, and multimedia at **edge.sagepub.com/kernell9e.**

## KEY TERMS

agenda setting   633

beat   617

credibility gap   639

embedding   617

equal time   615

franking privilege   625

infotainment   629

leak   624

libel   632

news outlets   608

pack journalism   617

priming   633

prior restraint   631

shield laws   626

slander   632

sound bite   640

trial balloon   624

"yellow journalism"   609

## SUGGESTED READINGS

Allcott, Hunt, and Matthew Gentzkow. *Social Media and Fake News in the 2016 Election.* National Bureau of Economic Research (2017). Available at https://www.nber.org/papers/w23089.pdf.

Allcott, Hunt, Matthew Gentzkow, and Chuan Yu. *Trends in the Diffusion of Misinformation on Social Media.* Stanford University (2018). Available at https://web.stanford.edu/~gentzkow/research/fake-news-trends.pdf.

Baum, Matthew A. *Soft News Goes to War.* Princeton, NJ: Princeton University Press, 2003. This book successfully resolves two inconsistent findings in public opinion research: a public expressing less interest in foreign affairs than in previous times but scoring as well informed as in the past. Baum presents persuasive evidence that many who shun formal news do, nonetheless, become informed via "soft" news entertainment programs.

Boxell, Levi, Matthew Gentzkow, and Jesse M. Shapiro. "Greater Internet Use Is Not Associated with Faster Growth in Political Polarization among U.S. Demographic Groups." *PNAS* 114 (40) (2017): 10612–10617.

Hamilton, James T. *All the News That Is Fit to Sell.* Princeton, NJ: Princeton University Press, 2004. An economist examines modern television programming practices as a product of business strategies. A well-written book in which the author explains the decline of traditional news and the rise of infotainment.

Kovach, Bill, and Tom Rosenstiel. *Blur: How to Know What's True in the Age of Information Overload.* New York: Bloomsbury Press, 2011.

## REVIEW QUESTIONS

1. How do market forces shape the frequency, tone, and reliability of news in the digital age?

2. How has the Internet changed the production of news? What is the difference between legacy media, digital-only media, and social media?

3. How did the rise of newspaper chains affect the political influence of the press? What ultimately eroded the political power of these chains? How and why has the influence of newspapers continued to decline today?

4. How and why do politicians seek to manipulate the news? What strategies do they use to generate beneficial coverage?

5. What resources do politicians have that might allow them to "go around" the press and communicate with the public directly? In general, how successful are these attempts?

The passage of policy always requires political deal making. The logic that creates policy problems can often also stand in the way of political solutions, or it can bring leaders with diametrically opposed ideologies together to reap shared political rewards. Here, Republican president Donald Trump and Democratic congressional leader Nancy Pelosi, often the fiercest of political foes, shake hands.

# Is There a Logic to American Policy?

# 15

## KEY QUESTIONS

- How does the logic of collective action dictate that narrow interests will often organize to stop the passage of a policy that threatens them, while the general public fails to rally behind it even if it would yield broad benefits? Under what conditions can this logic be overcome?

- If both parties might gain in the long run from reaching a compromise deal on a controversial policy, why would neither side have the courage to step forward with a proposal?

- What policies fit into the tragedy of the commons framework in which every player has an individual incentive to degrade a common resource? What solutions to this problem are offered by the Framers' tool kit, and what forces stand in the way of reaching a resolution?

- Considering that politicians and everyday Americans disagree so strongly about so many issues, how can there be any logic to policy at all?

## CHAPTER OBJECTIVES

**15.1** Describe how free riding influences U.S. health care reform efforts.

**15.2** Explain how the tragedy of the commons complicates nations' attempts to address climate change.

**15.3** Identify the political costs and benefits of teetering on a fiscal cliff.

**15.4** Relate the ways that entitlement programs such as Medicare and Social Security are subject to the prisoner's dilemma.

**15.5** Discuss the collective action challenges to achieving meaningful tax reform.

A discernible logic—intuited by the Founders when they designed our institutions, formally described by academics in the twentieth century, and practiced today by political strategists and everyday voters alike—guides American politics. It can help explain why the House delegates power to a Speaker and to its committees, or why some types of interest groups are better organized than others. Logic clarifies the incentives to build parties with strong brand names, lets us understand why some people vote whereas others abstain, and even explains why we elect politicians rather than relying on a monarch or governing ourselves through direct democracy.

But does the same logic at work in our politics also drive American policy? At first glance, the legislation that comes out of Washington, D.C., and state capitols may seem illogical, a piecemeal reaction to societal problems and foreign policy dilemmas that rarely appears to resolve policy challenges permanently. Except in rare cases of national consensus brought by a war or an economic crisis, major policies are bitterly contested at the time that they pass and often lead to a political backlash against their authors. If there is logic to policy, why do we disagree about it so much of the time, and what prevents it from being perfectly successful?

A policy challenge is not logical in the same way that a math problem is logical. There is rarely a single solution that dominates all others and about which leaders need only to think long and hard enough to reach. But understanding the concepts covered by this book can yield insights into the sources of policy problems, point to possible solutions, and at the same time explain why agreement on those solutions is often difficult to reach. First, the logic of collective action that we introduce in Chapter 1 and use throughout this text is often what creates the policy challenges that leaders must face. Logic explains why these problems are so vexing, but it also holds out hope for answers: the same tool kit used by the Framers to address these problems and create our institutions can be used to help resolve even the most complex policy puzzles.

The Framers, reacting against the arbitrary authority exercised by a king, dispersed political power widely across the different institutions of American government. As a result, no one can dictate a solution on his or her own. Policymakers must work through deeply political processes, which bring a new set of challenges in reaching agreement. And collective action suggests why consensus is so hard to come by. When societal goals are at odds with individually rational actions—as we have illustrated so many times throughout this book—any legislation will have policy winners and losers. Logic can help us understand who loses and why they will often fight so hard to preserve the policy status quo.

Finally, understanding logic can help us to identify when a policy problem is ripe for a solution or when a proposal seems doomed to failure. Multiple logics can be at play in a complex political environment, sometimes setting a force like electoral pressure from voters against organized opposition from well-funded interest groups. The most successful policymakers and politicians are those who can diagnose the dynamics of such situations, find a window of policy opportunity, and act quickly to capitalize on them, thus bringing lasting change in the ideological direction they favor.

In this concluding chapter, we apply the same collective action logic that we applied to America's political institutions to the policymaking process. Through five vignettes, we show how health reform advocates needed to stop "Young Invincibles" from free riding, why the tragedy of the commons dynamic makes it so difficult for any single nation to address global climate change, and why Washington, D.C., often edges right up to a "fiscal cliff" but never quite tumbles over. We explain why those who would reform Social Security and Medicare face the same dilemma that prisoners locked in separate interrogation rooms face, then compare two efforts to overhaul the tax system. These stories examine in-depth instances of policy progress but also of policy failure. In all of them, we probe below the surface of political events to explain why elected officials made the policy choices they did. There may not be perfect rationality in every deal that Congress and the president reach, but a clear logic determines the nature of the challenges they jointly face, the mechanisms at their disposal to address these problems, and the political processes through which they bargain. In the end, understanding these concepts helps predict what choices are made and what issues remain unresolved through America's deceptively logical way of making policy.

## Free Riding and Health Care

With so much discussion in the health policy debates of recent decades focused on fixing the problem of the uninsured, it is puzzling at first glance that anyone who might be able to afford it would decide not to buy medical insurance. Who wouldn't want to be covered in case they got sick or hurt? Buying insurance might seem rational, yet a closer look at the incentives (and disincentives) Americans faced before the adoption of the Affordable Care Act (ACA) shows why it might make perfect sense to remain uninsured—as long as you also remain healthy.

Picture yourself as a perfectly healthy twenty-five-year-old, without a whole lot of extra money to spend. Like most twenty-five-year-olds, you might think you will stay healthy forever, regardless of how many rocks you climb or germs you encounter. Sure, you think, you might need to see a doctor every so often, but paying for a few visits will not cost as much as a monthly health insurance premium. As long as you stay healthy, this is looking like a pretty good deal. But what if something terrible happens and you find yourself in an emergency room? You might know that a federal law guarantees that an emergency room must provide you with services and care regardless of your ability to pay. (This 1986 law, the Emergency Medical Treatment and Active Labor Act, applies to all emergency rooms that accept Medicare, the health insurance program for senior citizens. Functionally, this means nearly every emergency room in the country, because all of them want to be able to treat Medicare patients. The health insurance program seniors have paid into their whole lives is thus what keeps the doors of emergency rooms open to you.) Of course, you'll still be legally responsible for paying for that care eventually, but the hospital can't turn you away simply because you are uninsured. If it turns out that you do have a serious condition that will cost thousands of dollars to treat, that's going to create a major financial strain for you and perhaps lead to a disastrous bankruptcy. But as long as you do not get hurt or sick, you think, you will be fine.*

This mentality creates what the insurance industry calls the "**Young Invincibles**," the group of healthy patients who forgo insurance, knowing that the health care and emergency systems set up to cover those who do buy insurance will be there for them if something catastrophic occurs. In the language of collective action we introduced in Chapter 1, they are free riding. The Young Invincibles can take advantage of many of the benefits of the health care safety net that everyone else's insurance premiums provide, without paying the costs themselves. Of course, they have always been a minority of the uninsured. Most of those who lack insurance simply have no way to afford it. But millions of healthy people have made the choice to free ride in this way. "Though not all young invincibles are playing the odds by choice," explained one 2009 study, "about 9 percent of uninsured people between the ages 18 and 24 have received affordable offers of insurance through their employers. . . . Another 14 percent could afford to buy coverage on the private market."[1]

---

*Lest you think that forgoing insurance and relying solely on the emergency room is a wonderful idea, consider these facts: "In 2013, nearly 40% of uninsured adults said they had outstanding medical bills, and a fifth said they had medical bills that caused serious financial strain. These bills can quickly translate into medical debt since most of the uninsured have low or moderate incomes and have little, if any, savings." See Kaiser Family Foundation, "Key Facts about the Uninsured Population," October 29, 2014, accessed at http://kff.org/uninsured/fact-sheet/key-facts-about-the-uninsured-population/, December 2014.

The free-riding incentives that keep so many Young Invincibles out of the insurance market are exacerbated by the high costs so many of them face. If you do not have a steady job with a company that offers health care benefits, you will pay much higher insurance premiums. That's because not only do big companies pay all or a large share of their employees' premiums, but the federal government also provides a tax subsidy for these benefits that covers nearly a third of their costs. Without a job that provides health care, you pay a larger insurance bill, all on your own.

This creates the cruel calculus that has kept so many Americans uninsured for so long. If you are young and healthy but do not work for an employer who provides health benefits, you could face a steep monthly insurance bill. Because health care is so expensive, it will definitely be worth paying if you get sick or hurt. But you could gamble, free riding on the emergency room system subsidized by those who do have insurance. Who takes that gamble? People who have not been sick and have been generally free of injuries in the past. This part of the population—who of course would rack up smaller medical bills, making them cheaper for an insurance company to cover—decides not to buy coverage. To use an insurance industry term, they pull out of the "risk pool."

Who is left in that pool? The part of the population who likely knew that they would need more health care and who then incur higher medical bills. The healthy (and cheap!) patients get out of the risk pool, leaving the sicker (and more expensive) Americans in it. Now what does that do to next year's insurance premiums? Because insurance companies need to pay more to cover an increasingly expensive risk pool, and because technological advances drive the costs of health care up so steeply, premiums rise. Of course, this creates a vicious cycle, with rising costs pushing even more Americans off of insurance. Healthy young people face an even greater incentive to forgo it, with this sorting of the risk pool compounding the free-rider problem.

The policy challenge, then, is to get everyone into the same risk pool. One way to do that is to offer a carrot, by making taxpayer-subsidized premiums available to everyone, not just to those with good jobs. That is one of the key provisions of President Obama's Affordable Care Act: it funds tax credits for low-income and middle-income Americans that cover a significant portion of their insurance premiums. This makes the health coverage plans—still run by private insurance companies but usually selected through the federal government's HealthCare.gov website or through state exchanges—dramatically cheaper. But it does *not* make insurance free. Even with the subsidy, there remain individual incentives for people who are healthy and expect to stay that way to free ride.

The policy solution to that problem brought the most critical, but perhaps the most controversial, aspect of Obamacare: its individual mandate to purchase insurance. The ACA required all Americans to buy health insurance by January 1, 2014, or pay a penalty. The size of that fee, which is paid to the Internal Revenue Service on your tax returns, depends on your income, and some Americans are exempt. The basic idea is that the individual mandate stops free riding by making it illegal. It is thus a classic example of the "command" approach to a policy problem, drawing on the first and most powerful of the items in the Framers' tool kit that we introduced in Chapter 2. The mandate has the additional benefit—as long as the penalty is enough of a deterrent to free riding and the tax credits are sufficiently large to make insurance affordable—of placing everyone into the same risk pool, which will keep premiums down in the future.

Though it is central to the health care law that bears his name, President Obama did not invent the individual mandate. As many Americans were surprised to learn during the debate about Obamacare during the 2012 election, the mandate's most prominent forerunner was the Mitt Romney–backed health care reform in Massachusetts. The idea itself had come from conservative groups, including think tanks like the Heritage Foundation and the American Enterprise Institute, in the late 1980s. It was even championed as part of a Republican alternative to the universal health coverage plan put forth by Bill and Hillary Clinton in 1993.

Part of its appeal to those on the right was that the individual mandate was based on economic logic. In a television commercial aired by Governor Romney in 2006, he advocated for his comprehensive health reform package by arguing that the individual mandate would prevent free riding.* In a January 2008 presidential primary debate, then-candidate Romney explained the rationale behind the mandate: "Yes, we said, look, if people can afford to buy it, either buy the insurance or pay your own way," he said. "Don't be free-riders."[2] And on the day he signed his landmark bill into law in Massachusetts, Governor Romney talked about how it would stop the uninsured from relying on emergency rooms for all of their care but avoid paying their bills. "It's a Republican way of reforming the market," Romney said of the mandate. "Because, let me tell you, having thirty million people in this country without health insurance and having those people show up when they get sick, and expect someone else to pay, that's a Democratic approach. That's the wrong way. The Republican approach is to say, 'You know what? Everybody should have insurance. They should pay what they can afford to pay. If they need help, we will be there to help them, but no more free ride.'"[3]

Yet with the level of party polarization that we have in modern American politics, it should not be surprising that the bipartisan intellectual consensus around the mandate as a solution to free riding collapsed into a partisan political battle royal over "socialized medicine" during the passage of Obamacare in 2010 and thereafter. Certainly, the ACA contains so many provisions that it is hard to say what aspect is most controversial. Throughout the legislative debate and through the act's implementation, however, the individual mandate has been its tallest political lightning rod. Command approaches to policy problems are rarely popular, especially when everyone is forced to obey a government command that may bring collective benefits but works against the individual incentives of some people. An adviser both to the White House and to Governor Romney stirred up a furor in 2014, when his indelicate comments describing the political liability created by the individual mandate went viral. (See the Logic of Politics box "#Grubergate and the Perils of Making Free Riders Pay Up.") The mandate has remained unpopular, with a 2015 Rasmussen poll showing that only 37 percent of Americans support it.

The individual mandate was also the basis of the ACA's most threatening legal challenge. At the heart of the judicial controversy was the age-old battle between the federal government and the states, waged through the reinterpretation of a venerable constitutional provision. Does the Constitution give Congress the authority to command Americans across the states to buy insurance? As we describe in Chapter 3's discussion of federalism, the Supreme Court's 1824 *Gibbons v. Ogden* decision invoked the Constitution's commerce clause to give the federal government the power to prevent states from engaging in mutually

---

*You can watch that commercial on the *Logic* website at http://edge.sagepub.com/kernell8e.

Joe Raedle/Getty Images

Mitt Romney fully grasped and clearly articulated the problem of free riding in the health care system when he created a universal health care system as governor of Massachusetts. He is shown here, with the late senator Ted Kennedy and others, signing the bill in 2006.

destructive competition and to open the door to federal involvement in many aspects of Americans' daily lives. Nearly two centuries later, opponents of the ACA and proponents of states' rights argued that the individual mandate went far beyond the regulation of interstate commerce. Anticipating the passage of Obamacare, Virginia's state legislature passed a law making it illegal to require mandatory health insurance for Virginians. The day after Obama signed his federal bill, Virginia's attorney general, Ken Cuccinelli II, filed suit against it. On his blog Cuccinelli argued, "It is unconstitutional because the federal government is claiming that the source of its power for imposing the mandate is the Constitution's Commerce Clause, which gives the federal government the power to 'regulate commerce among the several states. . . .' We argue that if someone isn't buying insurance, then—by definition—he is not participating in commerce."[4]

The first federal judge to hear the case, U.S. District Judge Henry E. Hudson, agreed. Judge Hudson's December 2010 ruling threw out the mandate, saying that the commerce clause did not grant Obama and Congress the authority to require all Americans to buy health insurance. The same constitutional clause that has empowered the federal government for so long was thus used as a check on national power. This set in motion the Supreme Court battle over the mandate and other aspects of the law in *National Federation of Independent Business (NFIB) v. Sebelius*. Although the Supreme Court upheld the health care law's constitutionality in 2012, it did not reverse Hudson's reasoning: the Court ruled that although an insurance mandate could not be justified by the commerce clause, it constituted a "tax" and thus fell under Congress's powers of taxation (see Chapter 7). In that 5–4 decision, the Court saved a central plank of Obamacare. Perhaps it also saved Obama's reelection campaign. What it likely did not do, though, is preserve the ability of Congress to stop free riding in other realms. If the commerce clause can only be used to force people to stop doing something, but not to compel them to take affirmative action, it will be trickier for Congress to use the command tool from the Framers' tool kit. To prevent free riding, lawmakers must force free riders to pay up and, thus, to engage in commerce. Depending on how future Courts interpret it, the *NFIB v. Sebelius* case could make that more difficult in the future.

Yet another challenge to ending free riding in the health care realm is to implement new health insurance marketplaces so smoothly that even the Young Invincibles will use them to find the best plans, pay the lowest possible premiums, and stay in the risk pool. The agency charged with designing HealthCare.gov turned the rollout of the website into an initial policy and public relations disaster. The site was so hard to use that it seemed, early on, that many would end up free riding and paying their penalty to the Internal Revenue Service simply because of the logistical hurdles to signing up. But after intense efforts at a technological fix and a publicity overhaul, the website was in working order by the March 31, 2014, deadline, allowing 7.1 million Americans to sign up.

The long-term challenge for the proponents of universal coverage will be to keep Americans enrolled, because so many of these new registrants are the young and healthy Americans who had forgone coverage in the past. Although President Trump and congressional Republicans failed to repeal Obamacare or the individual mandate itself in early 2017, Trump was successful in eliminating the tax penalty for failing to follow the mandate later that year. Without a penalty, the mandate may become a policy with no consequence. As Obamacare is implemented by the Trump administration, it will be a huge challenge to keep healthy people in the risk pool. This will always remain a concern, because in health care—as in so many policy areas—there are often incentives for individuals to free ride.

## The Obstacles to Taking Domestic Action to Stop Global Climate Change

It is difficult for policymakers of any ideological stripe to argue that global climate change is something to be ignored. Faced with a scientific consensus that average temperatures are slowly but steadily rising, and that the culprit is the greenhouse gases emitted in the course of providing energy, heat, food, and transportation for humans, politicians are confronted with an unavoidable policy problem.[5] The comprehensive report released by the Intergovernmental Panel on Climate Change in November 2014 warned that unless the unrestricted use of fossil fuels is phased out by 2100, the world faces "severe, pervasive and irreversible damage." With the release of the report, United Nations secretary general Ban Ki-moon declared, "Science has spoken. There is no ambiguity in their message. Leaders must act. Time is not on our side."[6]

Why, then, have leaders taken so long to act? Why, decades after scientists began to chart the link between carbon dioxide emissions and rising temperatures, have policymakers—especially in Washington, D.C.—taken so few steps to slow climate change? The simple and unfortunate answer is that greenhouse gas emissions represent a classic case of the tragedy of the commons. This collective action problem is introduced in Chapter 1 and used to explain the decline of the cod fishing industry. It also explains the far more frightening damage that all nations have some incentive to inflict upon the environment, yet no single nation can act alone to prevent.

Our atmosphere, like a cod fishery, is a common resource that every nation has access to and no nation can be blocked from degrading. In a cod fishery, every boat's crew faces an incentive to catch as many fish as it can as quickly as possible because it knows that other crews will do the same thing. Because no one exerts control over the full common resource, no crew can compel the others to fish at a sustainable rate, leaving everyone to catch as much as they can at a frenzied pace that could lead to the collapse of the fishery's ecosystem. The same tragedy is occurring in the commons of the global environment. No nation exerts exclusive control over the atmosphere above it. Greenhouse gasses from coal-burning power plants in the United States mix with those from plants in China and India, methane emissions from Brazil's massive cattle farms, and diesel emissions from trucks in Europe and container ships all around the world.

Facing certain worldwide environmental damage, why doesn't each nation simply reduce its emissions? Because of the uncertainty that others will follow suit. If one country acts unilaterally while the others continue to produce greenhouse gases unabated, it will only gain a marginal reduction in worldwide emissions (the benefits of which will be shared equally by every nation) in exchange for paying all of the costs for retooling its energy infrastructure. The calculus of acting alone rarely adds up. As a result, most nations have found it in their individual interests to continue to deplete the common resource of the environment, burning the least expensive fuels rather than shifting to cleaner technologies in a comprehensive fashion. Inaction is, in a cynical sense, rational. Even though everyone might be better off if all nations acted together to restrict greenhouse gas emissions, no country has an incentive to pay all of the costs of reducing emissions by itself.

Recognizing that climate change represents an epic tragedy of the **global commons** raises another question: why has there been no fully ratified international treaty to bind all nations together to cut greenhouse gases? After all, this sort of regulatory solution is the mechanism that has saved many fisheries. Part of the explanation is that a debate over equity between developed and still-developing nations further vexes this environmental policy problem. Developing countries such as China, India, and Brazil argue that they need to burn fuel from the cheapest possible sources, even if these are the dirtiest, until they catch up with other nations' prosperity. After all, they charge, the United States and Western European countries relied on cheap coal to bring them from the Industrial Revolution into their postwar affluence, starting the trend toward climate change in the first place. Developing nations want the right to take the same route and point out that their per capita emissions still lag far behind other big countries. (For a comparison of both per capita and total emissions by different nations, see the carbon footprint maps in Figure 15.1.) Addressing climate change, some argue, is a luxury only rich nations can afford.

This dynamic has stood as a barrier to reaching effective international accords on climate change. Developing nations do not want to commit to emission reductions that would slow their economic growth, whereas rich nations such as the United States do not want to act alone as others continue to pollute. For a generation, that standoff has curtailed the impact of international bargains, most prominently the **Kyoto Protocol**. Long before that agreement was reached in Japan, a deal reached in Berlin mandated that rich nations would do all of the greenhouse gas reductions in the near term, and a set of developing nations that included China would face no limits. American officials bristled at the notion that the United States would be asked to clean up the commons while others got a free ride. In 1997, just as the Kyoto negotiations were about to get under way, West Virginia senator Robert Byrd raged, "It is the Berlin mandate—and the fact that it lets the developing world off the hook scot-free—that will seriously harm the global environment in future years." The Senate then voted 95–0 to demand that developing nations cut

# ■ FIGURE 15.1   Carbon Emissions by Nation

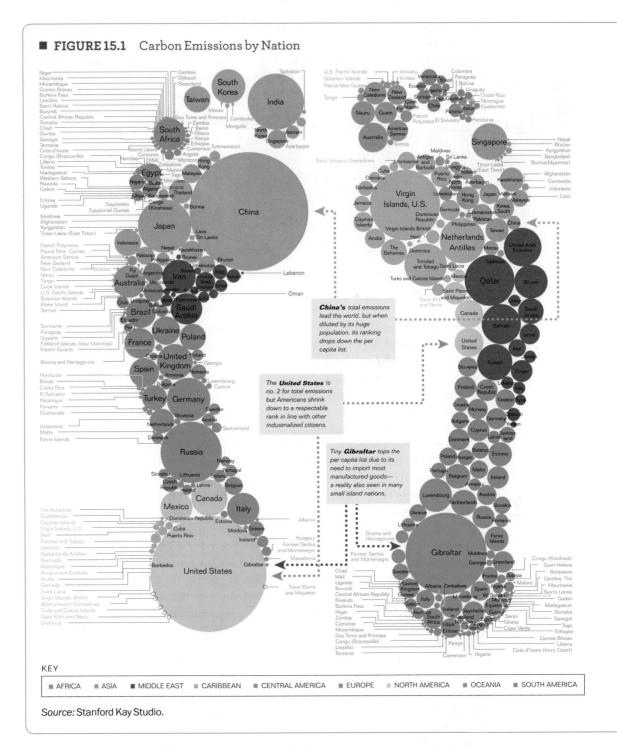

China's total emissions lead the world, but when diluted by its huge population, its ranking drops down the per capita list.

The United States is no. 2 for total emissions but Americans shrink down to a respectable rank in line with other industrialized citizens.

Tiny Gibraltar tops the per capita list due to its need to import most manufactured goods—a reality also seen in many small island nations.

KEY

■ AFRICA   ■ ASIA   ■ MIDDLE EAST   ■ CARIBBEAN   ■ CENTRAL AMERICA   ■ EUROPE   ■ NORTH AMERICA   ■ OCEANIA   ■ SOUTH AMERICA

Source: Stanford Kay Studio.

Chinese schoolchildren cheer President Obama and President Xi Jinping during the November 2014 meeting at which the world's two top climate polluters vowed to reduce their carbon emissions.

their greenhouse gas emissions as part of an international agreement.[7]

Because the Senate must ratify treaties, this did not bode well for the prospects of the Kyoto deal. Following the Berlin directive, the new agreement did not apply to the Chinas of the world. The thirty-seven nations that eventually pledged to abide by it agreed to cut their emissions by an average of 4.2 percent from their 1990 levels, with the cuts taking place from 2008 to 2012. President Bill Clinton signed it but warned that the United States—then and still the world's largest greenhouse gas polluter—would not ratify the protocol unless China and other developing nations joined it. They did not, so the United States did not, and it eventually withdrew altogether. The nations that did sign generally met their obligations, in part because of the worldwide economic recession that reduced demand for energy just as the Kyoto deadlines approached. Yet as it expired in 2012, an article in the authoritative journal *Science* summarized it as "The Kyoto Protocol: Hot Air," noting that "the reductions made under the treaty were dwarfed by the rise in emissions not covered by the accord, especially in Asia. Since 2000, $CO_2$ emissions in China have nearly tripled ..., and those in India have doubled."

Despite the best efforts of the European Union, whose members have pledged to reduce emissions by 40 percent by 2030, the world seemed caught in the stalemate between the United States and China, each polluting the commons at an alarming rate. Then, late in 2014, came a glimmer of hope. That November Presidents Barack Obama and Xi Jinping issued a joint announcement from Beijing that both of their countries intended to reach an "ambitious 2015 agreement that reflects the principle of common but differentiated responsibilities and respective capabilities" at the UN climate conference in Paris. The United States committed to cutting emissions by 26 to 28 percent by 2025, and China announced its intention to begin reductions by 2030.[8] Nine months in the making, this deal by the world's two biggest climate polluters renewed hope that a new international framework can succeed. "For once, the US is not being seen as the Great Satan of $CO_2$," wrote one journalist at the beginning of the meetings. "Thanks to their joint initiative with China, the two countries are taking a bow as leaders of the fight against rising temperatures."[9]

Turning the new sense of optimism into a concrete framework, 195 nations came together in Paris in December 2015 to settle on a plan to save the environmental commons. The **Paris Agreement** reached by these nations, including the United States, China, and nearly every major producer of greenhouse gases, proposed to bind the world together in an aggressive plan to limit global warming to less than two degrees Celsius over preindustrial levels. The logic of the tragedy of the commons dictates that this sort of comprehensive approach, with all polluters vowing to release less carbon into the atmosphere, is the only way to push individual nations toward a collective solution. The Paris Agreement was explicitly structured to avoid the tragedy of the commons. The plan could not go into effect until it was adopted by at least fifty-five countries that produce 55 percent of the world's greenhouse gases, a mechanism designed to discourage free riding. With the United States, China, the European Union, and nearly 200 nations on board, the Paris Agreement entered into effect on November 4, 2016.

World leaders celebrate the completion of the Paris Agreement in December 2015, a promising solution to the tragedy of the climate change commons that was soon thrown into doubt when the United States defected from this global accord soon after the election of President Trump.

Four days later, Donald Trump was elected president. Trump campaigned against the agreement, and in June 2017, he officially withdrew the United States from it. "The Paris accord will undermine our economy," President Trump argued, while claiming that it "puts us at a permanent disadvantage."[10] Because of the way the agreement was structured, the effect date of American withdrawal will not come until November 2020, but the political reaction at home and abroad has been swift. Leaders around the world worried that the United States was attempting to free ride on the efforts of other nations. In America, on the same day the president withdrew from the accord, a group of thirty mayors, three governors, eighty university presidents, and the leaders of over one hundred businesses pledged to abide by the Paris Agreement and even attempted to work with the UN to join it formally. The most consequential decision to determine the future of climate policy, though, will not be made by governors, mayors, presidents, or UN negotiators. In November 2020, when American voters choose the next president at the same time President Trump's withdrawal from the agreement goes into effect, these voters will likely determine the approach the world's biggest economy will take to the planet's most threatening policy challenge.[11]

## High-Stakes Maneuvering: Why We Tiptoe up to, but Have Not Fallen off, the Fiscal Cliff

Though it has gained new currency in the past few years, the term *fiscal cliff* has a lexicographic history that goes back over a century. It draws on a quaint predecessor, the "fiscal precipice," used in the debate over free silver in 1893. The term **fiscal cliff** was coined in the *New York Times* in 1957. During the 1970s and 1980s, it was often used to describe the teetering finances of federal, state, and local governments.*

---

*You can watch that commercial on the *Logic* website at http://edge.sagepub.com/kernell9e.

But the mother of all fiscal cliffs came in late 2012, as President Obama tried to translate the political buoyancy that came along with an overwhelming reelection victory into newfound policy influence over taxation rates and government spending, the two spheres that jointly define fiscal policy. He ran into stiff opposition from the Republican-controlled Congress, which contained many Tea Party members elected with fiscal goals in diametric opposition to the president's positions. Both sides faced a looming deadline of December 31, 2012. When the clock struck midnight on New Year's Eve, the tax cuts passed under George W. Bush and debated throughout the 2012 campaign were due to expire. That was also the day that delayed spending cuts, passed just the year before, would go into effect if no deal could be reached. These cuts, dubbed "budget sequestration," affected a full range of programs supported by both parties and nearly every type of voter—Social Security, Medicaid, government workers, military pay, and veterans' benefits. If the tax increases and spending cuts went into effect together, so the logic went, financial pandemonium would ensue for everyone. Although the federal deficit would drop dramatically, which would bring long-term benefits, it would do so at the cost of jacking up rates for many taxpayers and trimming the federal spending that stimulates growth. The U.S. economy could, in a politically juicy term, fall off the fiscal cliff.

Media coverage of the fiscal cliff was feverish, filled with warnings of the dire consequences of inaction. Both parties were motivated to make a deal. Democrats knew that some of their core constituencies would be hit hard by sequestration cuts and that their president would take the blame if a plunge off the cliff sent the economy spiraling back down. But Republican voting blocs were not immune from the cuts either, for they applied to active-duty military and to veterans. And many in the GOP wanted desperately to retain the tax cuts that represented part of Bush's legacy. Because both sides faced multiple policy losses in the absence of a deal, both had numerous reasons to give something up and come to the table.

As the "fiscal cliff" loomed on December 31, 2012, members of both parties had an incentive to hold on to their policy demands until just before they sent the nation's budget over the cliff, in order to extract the best possible deal from the other side.

Technically, when the ball dropped on Times Square at midnight that year, the nation went over the fiscal cliff. But not for long, because a deal already in the works was consummated even before Americans on the West Coast toasted the New Year. The compromise bill passed the Senate at 2:00 a.m. on January 1, 2013, cleared the House the following evening, and was signed by President Obama the next day. (On vacation in Honolulu, he had to sign it using his "autopen," a mechanical device that can replicate his signature from afar.) The deal, called the American

## LOGIC OF POLITICS

# #Grubergate and the Perils of Making Free Riders Pay Up

One of the challenges to designing a policy that prevents free riding is that it will, by definition, impose costs on one segment of the electorate by forcing the free riders to begin to pay their way. In 2014, the Obama administration took the heat for doing this through the Affordable Care Act, which forced even healthy Americans to purchase health insurance. Many of them reacted angrily. Of course, it didn't help that an economics professor who had helped design Obamacare—and before that, Mitt Romney's health care plan in Massachusetts—called American voters "stupid."

MIT professor Jonathan Gruber is a leading authority on the economics of health care reform and has created complex statistical models to simulate the impact of policy changes on how much different types of people would have to pay for their medical care. Because his expertise is obviously relevant to designing efficient policy mechanisms, he was brought in as a consultant to help Governor Romney and the Massachusetts legislature create their landmark health care reform bill in 2006. Then he was hired as a consultant to the White House during the debate leading up to the passage of the ACA. Although he was not a principal architect of that bill, he was paid $400,000 for his work and once advised President Obama on it in the Oval Office.

Gruber's close connection to Obama created a major political problem for the president and the public perception of the legislation when a video of Gruber discussing its passage surfaced in 2014. The point he was trying to make was that one political challenge the bill faced was that healthy Americans who chose not to purchase health insurance in the past, or who bought bare-bones coverage, would be forced to pay more when they were placed into the same risk pool as Americans with more health challenges (ending their free ride). The video of his comments to fellow economists left the impression that this aspect of Obamacare—which was widely debated at the time—was hidden from the public. "If it made it explicit the healthy people pay in and sick people get money," Gruber said about the law, "it

Chip Somodevilla/Getty Images

MIT economics professor Jonathan Gruber, whose mathematical simulations were important to the design of both Mitt Romney's Massachusetts universal health care law and the Affordable Care Act, was forced to answer tough questions—"Are you stupid?" asked Representative Darrell Issa—in Congress after implying that the "stupidity of the American voter" was what prompted free riders to support the passage of Obamacare.

would not have passed." Digging his hole a bit deeper, Professor Gruber, with all the charm and political acumen characteristic of an economist, explained, "Lack of transparency is a huge political advantage. And basically, you know, call it stupidity of the American voter or whatever."

Predictably, this led to outrage, spread by the hashtag #grubergate. The social media campaign and attendant furor over Gruber's comments have, according to the *Washington Post*, "recast (somewhat) the debate over Obamacare." Gruber was forced to testify before Congress in December 2014 and apologize for his "glib, thoughtless, and sometimes downright insulting comments." Yet although they were embarrassing and perhaps politically damaging to the law he helped pass, Professor Gruber's remarks did accurately point out that when a policy clamps down on free riding, some people will have to pay more.

*Sources:* Aaron Blake, "Jonathan Gruber's Big Apology, Translated," *Washington Post: The Fix*, December 9, 2014; Jason Millman, "Meet Jonathan Gruber, the Man Who's Willing to Say What Everyone Else Is Only Thinking about Obamacare," *Washington Post: Wonkblog*, November 12, 2014.

Taxpayer Relief Act of 2012, brought much smaller tax increases than the ones due to go into effect, with only the richest few Americans seeing their taxes rise at all, in return for delaying the sequestration cuts. But the cuts were delayed by only two months, with the promise that a more permanent deficit reduction deal could be crafted by then.

In the eyes of many, President Obama emerged from the year-end drama with more gains than losses. The very richest Americans saw their Bush-era tax cuts disappear, and the middle class hung onto their breaks. But congressional Republicans won some concessions as well, most prominently the promise of spending cuts in the coming months. After the Senate acted, Obama concluded, "While neither Democrats nor Republicans got everything they wanted, this agreement is the right thing to do for our country and the House should pass it without delay." The House did, just before the financial markets opened, and the crisis was averted.[12]

The same logic—accompanied by even more hyperventilation—drove the countdown to a possible default on the nation's sovereign debt at the end of the fiscal year on August 1, 2011. That crisis really would have brought an immediate and irreparable reputational cost to the United States and possibly its first-ever credit downgrading by bond rating agencies. A true cliff, that episode was resolved with a deal that both increased the nation's ability to borrow and led to the creation of a bipartisan deficit reduction committee charged with identifying the sorts of painful spending cuts and tax increases that could reduce borrowing in the future.[13] Of course, that deal only increased the debt ceiling temporarily. When national borrowing approached the limit again on October 17, 2013, another round of furious negotiations began. Republicans in Congress demanded that, in exchange for postponing a government default by another year, all President Obama had to do was agree to a delay in the implementation of the Affordable Care Act, a vote on comprehensive tax reform, and fast-tracking the construction of the Keystone XL Pipeline. With the president refusing to cut an early deal, the federal government went into a partial shutdown on October 1 as the deadline later that month still loomed. The day before the ceiling was reached, Democrats and Republicans reached a deal to pass a continuing resolution to reopen government and continue borrowing until the next deadline was reached.[14]

Though it appeared that the election of President Donald Trump along with a Republican Congress in 2016 would dramatically change the bargaining dynamic, brinksmanship returned early in his administration. Looking toward a series of deadlines in the fall of 2017 that could have brought a default on the national debt and a government shutdown, Trump tweeted that the country "needs a good 'shutdown' in September." Why do leaders, over and over again, pass policies creating deadlines like the fiscal cliff? And why do negotiations so regularly run right up to the final moments, then just as reliably end up in a midnight deal? First, laying out a definite schedule that leads to dire policy consequences creates the pressure of a deadline. It is human nature to respond to deadlines, which have motivated students and professors alike into increased productivity. But the most important logic of a fiscal cliff or a debt ceiling is that it motivates both sides to reach a compromise. Even in our polarized political times, lawmakers can force one another into making concessions when disaster looms after a deadline. It makes the unpalatable palatable, at least compared with an alternative that is even more grim.

Of course, deals are hard to reach until just before the deadline, because both sides face strategic incentives and popular pressure to hold out for the best deal possible. The dynamic is like a staring match, with neither side wanting to be the first to blink and offer its opponent a good deal. If one party caved a week early, the interest groups and voters who support it would wonder, with good cause, if they could have gotten more by negotiating longer and harder. So no one reaches agreement until they are staring just over the cliff.

Consider how different this is from the normal policymaking process. In everyday negotiations over bills in Washington, D.C., nothing too terrible happens if the bill fails. Policy stays at the status quo, and usually at least one side can live with that. That means you rarely see both sides at the negotiating table. But a cliffhanging deadline fundamentally changes the dynamic; when neither side can stomach the consequences of going over the deadline without a deal, both will come to the table in good faith. A deadline does not always bring major progress. The 2012 fiscal cliff led to a much more consequential compromise than the debt ceiling debates of 2011 and 2013. But we have seen these crises regularly resolved, not a day before the pending apocalypse.

## The Prisoner's Dilemma of Entitlement Reform

Sometimes the logic of a policy challenge can create a set of political costs and payoffs that stand in the way of reaching a compromise; thus the eternal issue of **entitlement reform**. Entitlements are the federal programs that Americans are entitled to benefit from once they reach a certain age or condition, with Medicare and Social Security being the two most prominent. The fact that these two programs—which provide health care and pensions for senior citizens—represent a guarantee of coverage creates both the policy challenge of keeping the programs solvent and the political barrier to making any cuts that would maintain their solvency.

Here, in simplified form, is how Social Security and Medicare operate. When you work, you pay into both programs through earmarked taxes that are withdrawn from every paycheck. (These are the FICA, or Federal Insurance Contributions Act, taxes that so mysteriously reduce your take-home pay.) As long as you make more than $4,880 a year, you earn full credits toward receiving Social Security when you retire. When you turn sixty-five, you receive health insurance through Medicare and a monthly Social Security check. (You can retire as early as sixty-two or as late as seventy, but your Social Security check will be smaller if you retire early or larger if you start collecting your benefits later.)[15]

Everyone who has paid into this system receives these benefits, no matter how rich or poor they are. That gives Medicare and Social Security a tremendously broad base of political support. It also, of course, makes them tremendously expensive. The retirement benefits for all are funded by money paid in by people who are still working. When there are lots of people working and relatively few retirees, both programs take in far more money than they pay out and put the surplus into "trust funds." That was the case for many decades after World War II, when the baby boom generation made good salaries in an expanding economy. Now, as those baby boomers are retiring, as they are expected to live longer into retirement, as the costs of providing their medical care rise, as lower birthrates have reduced the number of workers, and as wages have stagnated, the equation has reversed. In the coming decades, Medicare and Social Security will pay out more money to retirees than they take in from workers, drying up their trust funds by 2030 (for Medicare) and 2033 (for Social Security). Simple economic and demographic logic sets both programs on a path toward fiscal insolvency. In 2014, the boards of trustees for the two funds issued a report that began by clearly stating, "Neither Medicare

BUDGET SHADOWS

Solving America's
Entitlement Dilemma

To install:  1) Insert this disk in drive A:
            2) Select "Run" from the File menu.
            3) Type a:\Install and press [ENTER]

Prepared by the Staff of the
Bipartisan Commission on
Entitlement and Tax Reform        Disk 1 of 2

Wikimedia Commons

To make entitlement reform as exciting as stealing automobiles or crushing candy, in 1994 the Bipartisan Commission on Entitlement and Tax Reform took the innovative step of designing the Budget Shadows video game, letting players solve the looming Medicare and Social Security shortfalls. The committee distributed the game through the nascent World Wide Web and on floppy disks like this one.

nor Social Security can sustain projected long-run program costs in full under currently scheduled financing, and legislative changes are necessary to avoid disruptive consequences for beneficiaries and taxpayers."[16] There is a clear consensus that we face a policy problem. With both funds teetering financially, all of the constituencies that rely on them—senior citizens, the doctors and nursing homes who care for seniors, today's workers who want a secure retirement—know that they would benefit themselves if the programs' finances were shored up. Doing so will certainly involve some pain, but in the long term it will bring gains to the health of the programs overall. Why, then, haven't politicians reached a deal that guarantees the solvency of entitlements far into the future?

The simple reason why this policy challenge has persisted for so long is that there is so much to lose, politically, from offering a painful solution, and so much for each party to gain by letting the other party go first in proposing it. As we noted in Chapter 1, this puts Republicans and Democrats in a prisoner's dilemma. Like two people accused of a crime and interrogated in separate rooms, both parties know that they could benefit from reaching a landmark entitlement reform deal, if they could just trust the other side to come to the table. With both sides cooperating on meaningful reform, they could move these critical programs toward solvency and at the same time demonstrate that Washington, D.C., can deliver bipartisan compromise. This would give them policy as well as political gains. But of course any such deal will have some unpopular aspects: shoring up the funds means reducing benefit levels, raising the retirement age, increasing FICA payments, or diverting tax dollars from other programs.

What if one party moves first in making such a proposal? The other party could sit back and criticize it, playing politics rather than coming to the negotiating table. If that happens, there is no landmark deal. For the side that made the bold political move, the payoffs are all bad. The trust funds remain at risk over the long run, and the bold party takes a big, short-term hit for having the temerity to suggest that seniors or workers should have to give something up to secure their entitlement. All of the political benefits will accrue to the party that does nothing but criticize and win points with senior citizens—a reliable voting bloc—for defending their programs. Looking at this logic, making a strong move toward entitlement reform does not look very wise. If both parties play it safe and criticize any reform proposals, neither side puts itself at much political risk. Washington is still seen as dysfunctional, so both parties take a slight hit to their reputations, but no one gains a big electoral advantage. Anticipating that this is what the other party will do, neither party will risk taking a bold step, and we are stuck with the policy status quo.

The table that follows, which parallels the description of Betty Grable and Victor Mature's dilemma laid out in our introduction, lists the payoffs both parties face. If they could only trust the other side to go along with them in reforming entitlements—just as two prisoners would like to trust each other to remain silent—everyone would be better off. They would like to end up with the landmark policy payoff in the top left corner. But because the electoral incentives to let the other side propose reform while your party merely criticizes it are so strong, reaching this cooperative equilibrium is unlikely. Instead, both sides will likely defect—the equivalent of two prisoners ratting each other out—by criticizing reform and attempting to win on the issue in the next election. With each side playing the same strategy of criticizing reform, both parties lose a little bit of their reputation for effectiveness, and everyone misses the opportunity to gain through a cooperative reform deal.

Diagnosing the strategic incentives created by the prisoner's dilemma logic at work here helps explain why policy progress has been so difficult, while at the same time offering a glimmer of hope for a solution. The way to get to cooperation is to set up some institution that allows the two players to communicate and make a credible commitment to following through on reform. With two prisoners, that would mean talking and then issuing a joint plea of not guilty. The Washington, D.C., version of this institution is a bipartisan commission. In fact, this is the approach that has previously yielded temporary success in the realm of entitlement reform. In 1981 President Ronald Reagan and Congress appointed a commission, headed by future Federal Reserve chair Alan Greenspan, to deal with a looming short-term funding crisis—Social Security was due to run out of money in a mere two years. With the momentum created by this pending debacle, and with members that included powerful Senate and House leaders from both parties, the Greenspan Commission produced a consensus set of recommendations by January 1983 that were enacted into law later that year. There remains debate over whether the commission as a whole put together the deal or whether commission members like Democratic senator Pat Moynihan and Republican senator Bob Dole were the prime movers, but the definite lesson is that it was successful because members of both parties locked arms around a single plan to increase payroll taxes and raise the retirement age to 67 by 2026.

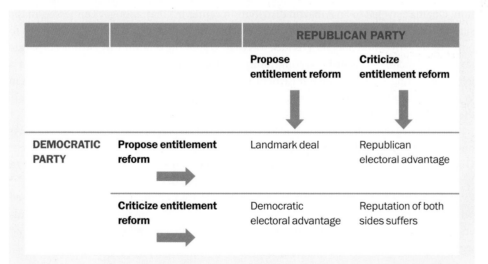

| | | REPUBLICAN PARTY | |
|---|---|---|---|
| | | Propose entitlement reform | Criticize entitlement reform |
| **DEMOCRATIC PARTY** | **Propose entitlement reform** | Landmark deal | Republican electoral advantage |
| | **Criticize entitlement reform** | Democratic electoral advantage | Reputation of both sides suffers |

Unfortunately, that deal simply delayed Social Security's insolvency, while doing nothing to fix Medicare. So a decade later, President Bill Clinton and Congress returned to the same playbook by appointing the Bipartisan Commission on Entitlement and Tax Reform, cochaired by Democratic senator Bob Kerrey and Republican senator John Danforth. The commission was able to reach agreement only on the scope of the problem but not on a set of solutions. Without a looming crisis in the next few years, they took creative approaches to giving the public a full sense of the threat. The commission even created a computer game that gave the public the opportunity to try their own hand at entitlement reforms.[17] Yet the gaming community did not embrace the chance to make grand theft automatic payroll deduction increases, and the commission folded without making any policy recommendations. Reform efforts have sputtered since then, with both parties quick to pounce on any reform proposals that their opponents make unilaterally. Until we get closer to the cliffs of the Social Security and Medicare fund insolvency, it appears that the prisoner's dilemma logic will stand in the way of landmark entitlement reform.

## The Success and Failure of Collective Action: A Tale of Two Tax Reforms

Tax reform—admittedly not a glamorous issue but one with enormous consequences for the state of the economy and the lives of millions every April 15—is a perennial issue in American politics that heated up once again during the 2012 presidential campaign. Tea Party activist Herman Cain's campaign centered around his "9–9-9" proposal, in which all taxpayers would pay the same flat rate (any guesses as to what that rate would be?). Texas governor Rick Perry prominently featured his plan, and former Massachusetts governor Mitt Romney vowed, "We'll replace the Obama job-killing tax policies with sweeping tax reform to jumpstart job creation."[18] The eventual winner of the campaign, Barack Obama, also pledged to pass major reforms.

Yet like all recent attempts at sweeping changes to the nation's tax code, the president's plan ran into steep opposition created by the eternal logic of politics. After winning reelection, Obama traveled to an Amazon distribution center in Chattanooga, Tennessee, in the summer of 2013 to propose a compromise on tax reform that would deliver policy wins to both conservatives and liberals. His idea was to help spur the economy by cutting corporate tax rates, something the business community had long wanted, while creating middle-class jobs by spending $50 billion on infrastructure projects (a priority of labor groups). "If folks in Washington really want a 'grand bargain,' how about a grand bargain for middle-class jobs?" the president asked the crowd of two thousand.[19]

As it turned out, folks in the nation's capital wanted no part of the president's bargain. As one reporter covering the announcement and the reaction it garnered explained, "President Obama wisely chose to unveil his new corporate tax reform in Tennessee—because in Washington his so-called 'grand bargain' instantly flopped. Congress was unimpressed."[20] Even though it was delivered from Obama's bully pulpit as part of a nationwide tour focused on policies that would stimulate the economy, the plan went nowhere. Republican leaders immediately attacked it, the business community failed to embrace it, and it led to no legislation.

Perhaps that was because, with the House firmly under Republican control at the time, only the deliberate efforts of a leading GOP lawmaker could lead to a major tax overhaul. That explanation was soon put to a test. After three years of hearings and consultation, powerful House Ways and Means Committee chair Dave Camp, a Republican from Michigan, released his voluminous plan to revise the tax code the next February. Yet this did not set the stage for 2014 to become the year of tax reform either. The ambitious plan would have flattened the progressive income tax out into just two rates, reducing the marginal rate paid by the highest earners from 39.6 percent to 25 percent. It would have paid for this by eliminating many tax deductions and loopholes, while at the same time imposing surtaxes on the biggest banks and the wealthiest individuals. The "loopholes" it proposed to close included deductions for health insurance, mortgage interest, student loans, retirement savings, and a type of interest paid to private equity managers. The plan appeared, in some ways, to seek to please the majority of Americans but make legislative enemies of some of the wealthiest and most powerful forces in Washington. Every group that benefited from the loopholes, in addition to the biggest banks, quickly rallied against it.

Almost immediately after Chairman Camp unveiled his 979-page plan, Washington insiders began to profess it "dead on arrival." Just a few days later, fellow Republican and House Speaker John Boehner, when asked whether Chairman Camp's bill would come up for a vote in 2014, literally laughed. Then, when asked for his thoughts about the specifics of Camp's plan, the Speaker "began by replying, 'Blah, blah, blah' and spoke in generalities."[21] This was not a warm welcome from the most powerful member of Camp's party or an auspicious omen for his bill's chances of success. But it was accurate, for Camp's plan went nowhere, and its author retired from Congress at the end of the year.

How can tax reform proposals that promise to help so many be blocked by the few? The answer lies in the logic of collective action that economist Mancur Olson illuminated in 1965 (see the Logic of Politics box, "The Political Power of Small Numbers," in Chapter 13). To organize effectively, people need to be motivated to join and lead groups. When a policy like tax reform promises to bring small benefits to a large group, paradoxically, it is a challenge to get this group mobilized. Support for the policy may be a mile wide, but because it is only an inch deep—and because people can reap its rewards no matter whether they work for its passage or not—few will be motivated to press for it. By contrast, when a small group would pay high costs if a policy bill passes, all of its members face an incentive to work hard to stop it because each has a strong individual

**LOGIC OF POLITICS**

# The Structure of Government and Anti-Tobacco Laws

Sometimes the very structure of American government itself shapes the way in which policy is made. As we demonstrated in Chapters 2 and 3, the Framers separated powers between branches of the federal government and spread authority across the federal system so that no king would rule the United States. This puts in place steep obstacles for anyone aiming to make sweeping policy changes throughout the nation. But it also creates many points through which crusaders can access our policymaking apparatus, giving them other options to turn toward when they are stymied in one branch.

This complex structure has shaped the path of the fifty-year crusade to put tight shackles on the advertisement and sale of that most American of products—tobacco. This battle was first fought in the ordinary arenas of politics, with health advocates lobbying Congress and winning incremental successes during their decades of sustained work. Yet the innovation that led to a policy breakthrough was the move away from Washington, D.C., and into the offices of state attorneys general, a transition from leadership by public officials to the entrepreneurship of private tort lawyers, and a shift in venue from legislatures to the courts. The anti-smoking movement achieved many of its policy goals, but only after transforming its policymaking strategy. The book *Up In Smoke*, by political scientist Martha Derthick, tells the story of the protracted, contentious, and surprising journey toward today's strict regulation of the tobacco industry.

The anti-smoking movement began in earnest in 1964 when a panel of experts convened by the U.S. surgeon general released a comprehensive report showing that men who smoked died of lung cancer ten times as often as nonsmokers and that "cigarette smoking is a health hazard of sufficient importance in the United States to warrant appropriate remedial action." This was an open invitation for Congress to regulate a product that was so ubiquitous that 4,345 cigarettes were sold a year per every American adult. Yet Congress, where policy was literally made in smoke-filled rooms quite often at that time, was slow to act. The watered-down bill it passed the next year required labels on cigarette packs warning that smoking "may be hazardous to your health" but allowed tobacco companies to continue to advertise their products with no warnings. The federal law also occupied the field of policy, thus preempting all of the states from enacting stricter regulations (see Chapter 3's discussion of federal preemption). Finally, because smokers had been warned, tobacco companies were in many ways shielded from liability. The legislation was condemned by the *New York Times* as "a shocking piece of special interest legislation . . . a bill to protect the economic health of the tobacco industry by freeing it of proper regulation."

Through a series of cautious compromises, tobacco policy began to change incrementally. Congress banned television and radio advertising in 1970 but still allowed newspaper and magazine ads like the popular "Joe Camel" cartoons that appealed to adults and children alike. Executive agencies created separate smoking sections on airplanes and interstate buses in the early 1970s before Congress banned smoking in planes by 1990. In a series of laws, Congress raised cigarette taxes from eight cents per pack to twenty-four cents, and made some grants-in-aid to states contingent upon enforcing their bans on selling tobacco to those under eighteen.

Part of the reason why the progress of anti-smoking legislation through the normal Washington legislative process was so incremental and modest was that many leading politicians of the era were smokers themselves. Long before he was president, Ronald Reagan appeared in this advertisement for Chesterfields, and Joe Camel gave cool appeal to Camel cigarettes.

What had changed that allowed this legislative process? In the early years, the industry flexed its political muscle through its chief lobbyist, Earle Clements, a former U.S. senator from Kentucky and Senate whip under Majority Leader Lyndon Johnson. He coordinated their D.C. activities through the Tobacco Institute, facing loosely organized opposition. By the 1980s, just as Clements was retiring, the American Cancer Society, the American Lung Association, and the American Heart Association banded together to create their own formalized lobbying group to counter the Tobacco Institute. And they advocated in a more sympathetic Congress in which the aftermath of Watergate brought in liberal lawmakers to replace many committee chairs from tobacco-producing southern states. This was a bipartisan effort, with California Democrats like Representative Henry Waxman joined in the anti-tobacco fight by Republican senators such as Orrin Hatch of Utah and Robert Packwood of Oregon. By 1998, an R. J. Reynolds executive was astounded by Congress's transformed attitude toward tobacco companies, remarking that committees that used to be welcoming were "treating us like we were war criminals in the Nuremberg trials."

States and cities also began to act on their own. San Francisco banned workplace smoking in 1983, and by 1990, 213 California cities and counties had such bans in place. States began passing heavy excise taxes to discourage smoking, while at the same time generating funds to pay for its societal costs, with Michigan's seventy-five-cent-per-pack tax leading the way. Utah banned ads on billboards, and the city of Cincinnati banned advertisements near schools, playgrounds, and parks. Still, this created only a patchwork of anti-smoking laws. Advocates looked at even their successes as half measures, a series of important yet modest reforms that reduced smoking rates but were not strict enough to bring their hoped-for elimination of a health threat that costs so many lives.

The major breakthrough did come from the states, but not from their legislatures or governors. In the 1990s, state attorneys general began to sue tobacco companies that had been "unjustly enriched" and had cost the states billions in medical expenses to care for their addicted and afflicted residents. The states were advised by Harvard law professors and worked with private attorneys who agreed to invest in the massive amounts of legal research required to

*(Continued)*

(Continued)

take on Big Tobacco, in exchange for a financial share of any judgment they would help win.

As state after state joined the flagship case led by Mississippi, the industry—spending hundreds of millions a year in legal fees and pressured by nervous shareholders—agreed to a "Master Settlement Agreement" with all of the states filing suit in November 1998. In addition to paying billions to each state in order to reduce their future liability, the tobacco companies agreed to an extraordinary set of regulations. Tobacco companies would cease advertising on billboards everywhere, stop sponsoring most concerts and sports teams, and no longer give away merchandise and clothing emblazoned with their brands. They could not go bankrupt. The companies even agreed to give up a fundamental role that interest groups play in American politics: they disbanded their lobbying arm, the

Tobacco Institute, and pledged not to lobby against state and local legislative proposals aimed at stopping youth smoking. By shifting political power dynamics, this legal deal aimed to shape future legislative actions on tobacco policy. Importantly, this deal was simply negotiated between attorneys representing the states and those working for tobacco companies. Judges and juries did not weigh in directly, and Congress and the president were also kept out of the room of the most profound shift in the history of U.S. tobacco policy. The normal checks and balances were absent from this process, illustrating that the many avenues of influence present in American democracy can create an extraordinary variety of policymaking processes.

*Source:* Martha A. Derthick, *Up in Smoke: From Legislation to Litigation in Tobacco Politics*, 3rd ed. (Washington, DC: CQ Press, 2012).

stake in the outcome. This is exactly the dynamic at work in the failed tax reform efforts of 2012 through 2014. Most Americans would have benefitted a bit by seeing their tax rates fall. But if a few small groups were stripped of their loopholes, each would face massive losses.

Consequently, the narrow interests who feared losing their loopholes mobilized like never before. These groups spent so much to lobby on the bill that one observer dubbed it the "Build a Vacation Home for a Tax Lobbyist Act." The majority of Americans who would have each gained a bit through the passage of tax reform stayed silent. The mobilized few defeated the unorganized many, just as Olson would have predicted, and neither President Obama nor Ways and Means Chairman Camp's proposal went anywhere.

Yet in 2017, President Trump and congressional leaders were able to deliver on a tax bill, the landmark legislative achievement of the Trump administration to that point. How were they able to succeed where their predecessors had failed? Certainly, the fact that the 2016 election delivered control of the White House, Senate, and House of Representatives to the Republicans put in place the necessary conditions for the passage of this bill. But party control alone was not sufficient to ensure its passage, and many congressional observers doubted that the GOP would be able to hold together the coalition necessary to deliver the votes.

One key reason the tax bill of 2017 passed was that it followed Olsonian logic, flipping the script that doomed earlier efforts at tax reform. It delivered huge benefits to a narrow group of interests ready to mobilize in favor of the bill in Congress. These interests—the corporations that would benefit directly from the tax cut—sent their lobbyists from K Street to Capitol Hill to advocate for its passage. In a Strategy and Choice box in Chapter 13 titled "Why Spend

Millions on Lobbying? Because It Is Worth Billions," we chronicle the vast amounts spent by the organized interest groups who lobbied on the 2017 tax bill. A total of 2,065 interest groups hired more than 6,000 lobbyists and spent tens of millions of dollars lobbying on the tax bill, with the vast majority of this activity supporting its passage.

How were President Trump, House Speaker Paul Ryan, and Senate Majority Leader Mitch McConnell able to get these groups on their side of the tax bill? By reshaping the policy substance of the bill in a way that dramatically changed its politics. Calling it "tax reform" might be a stretch, because the bill was, fundamentally, a

President Trump was able to deliver on a tax reform bill after President Obama and Republican congressional leaders had failed by harnessing the logic of collective action: his bill provided both broad and narrow benefits in the short term, while pushing its costs off into the future.

Reuters/Carlos Barria

tax cut. Whereas prior bills had paid for the broad cuts they delivered by getting rid of loopholes that thus increased tax revenues, the 2017 bill reduced taxes on (nearly) everyone, for a total of $1.5 trillion in cuts over ten years. This was, according to Treasury Department reports, the fourth largest tax cut passed since 1968, and it delivered a tax cut to 80 percent of Americans.[22] The bill was particularly good for corporations: the corporate rate was cut from 35 percent to 21 percent, and these cuts were made permanent, whereas the individual tax cuts are due to expire in 2025. This ensured that corporations, who had much to gain, would lobby heavily for the bill. They did.

Corporations and most taxpayers were the short-term winners in this bill. Who were the losers? One group that lost, a minority of taxpayers, turned out to have little political clout. Most of the 20 percent of individuals who will pay higher taxes reside in states that charge steep state and local taxes, which used to be fully deductible from federal taxes. Now only the first $10,000 of these taxes can be deducted. Yet most of these high-tax states are blue states with many Democratic representatives in Congress, who were not planning to vote for the bill anyway. Thus the financial hit they took cost President Trump's plan very little support, another example of political ingenuity played out through a policy detail. The other group that lost is amorphous: the future. Because the tax cuts were not balanced by tax increases, the bill will add its $1.5 trillion cost to the federal deficits and debt. How will that be paid for? Mostly likely by cuts in government services at some point down the road, but because those costs did not have to be made explicit, they did not generate concrete political opposition. And because the debt is something that affects everyone, but only by a small amount, adding to it did not galvanize any narrow constituency. The 2017 tax bill was, from Mancur Olson's perspective, the perfect bill to make many friends and few enemies.

Even so, with its clear benefits for corporations, but bill was not popular. At the time of its passage, a CNN poll found that 55 percent of Americans opposed the plan, with only 33 percent

## STRATEGY AND CHOICE
# Saying No to Getting to Yes: Why an Immigration Deal Has Proven Elusive

For decades, reaching a comprehensive deal on immigration policy has eluded America's policymakers. The issue has stayed on top of the minds of voters in election after election, but negotiations in Washington, D.C., have collapsed year after year. The hope for reaching a deal though bipartisan groups like the "Gang of Eight" senators who proposed a bill in 2013 and the "Gang of Six" who announced a proposal in early 2018 have all been dashed when centrists have failed to garner the support of enough members of either party. President Obama could not move major immigration legislation through Congress—though he did create the popular Deferred Action for Childhood Arrivals (DACA) program through unilateral action—and so far President Trump has been unable to pass a bill, though he unilaterally moved to phase out DACA.

Why has getting to yes on immigration reform been so difficult? At first glance, many of the ingredients for a potential bipartisan deal seem to be in place. Both sides want to see major changes in immigration policy. Immigrant rights advocates and liberal lawmakers have a policy wish list: a path toward citizenship for those who immigrated without documents, protections especially for those brought to America as children, and more opportunities for people from all countries to immigrate legally. Those concerned with illegal immigration and conservative politicians also want to see changes to the policy status quo: increased security at the border, restrictions on the number of family members who can follow an immigrant into America legally, and a consideration of the job skills legal immigrants would bring. Voters on both sides care strongly about the issue and want to see something done about the problem. Although they do not agree on the solutions,

John Moore/Getty Images

Images like this of immigrant families being separated at the border galvanized public opinion against the Trump administration's "zero tolerance" immigration policy in summer 2018, but a comprehensive immigration solution has proved elusive.

there is nothing inherently contradictory about each side's policy proposals: stronger borders, a path to citizenship, a permanent DACA program, and a reduction in family immigration rights are not logically incompatible.

Yet they have proved to be politically incompatible. This was demonstrated again in the summer of 2018, when a popular consensus about a crisis on the southwest border with Mexico seemed to make conditions ripe for a compromise. But, in another episode of the long-running saga on immigration policy, Congress followed the same old script and failed to reach a deal. The crisis was the separation of families that took place at the border in ever increasing numbers after then–attorney general Jeff Sessions ordered, in April 2018, the immediate adoption of a "zero tolerance" policy that led to the criminal prosecution of any adult caught crossing the border. When adults were prosecuted, it resulted in the separation of 2,342 children from their parents from early May to mid-June, when

President Trump signed an executive order reversing the practice of separating families. People of every ideological stripe were horrified by images of frightened children being detained without their parents. With a popular consensus on one aspect of immigration policy, the conditions seemed to be ripe for a deal.

Moderate Republicans pushed for a vote that May on a bipartisan deal they had negotiated with many Democrats. GOP congressional leaders, though, did not want to lose control of the process and could not support some of the policy compromises necessary to get Democratic votes. They used their control over the agenda to keep the bipartisan bill off the floor of the House of Representatives. Although Republican moderates attempted to use a "discharge petition" signed by 218 members of the House to force a vote on their bipartisan deal, they fell two votes short. Instead, House leaders allowed a vote on their version of a deal. The bill that reached the floor on June 27 would have ended family separation at the border and included a path to citizenship for some young immigrants, provisions favored by the left. But it would have also provided $25 billion to build President Trump's border wall and restricted family-based immigration, ideas key to the right. The president,

though he had sent mixed messages a few days earlier, sent a last-minute tweet supporting the deal. To show that he really meant it, he used all caps: "HOUSE REPUBLICANS SHOULD PASS THE STRONG BUT FAIR IMMIGRATION BILL, KNOWN AS GOODLATTE II, IN THEIR AFTERNOON VOTE TODAY."

Not enough Republicans were swayed, and no Democrats budged. The bill was killed, 301–121, just as so many deals before it had died. Each side's convictions have proved to be too strong to reach an immigration compromise. Although both would gain some policies from their wish list in any deal, they would also lose by backing their opponent's proposals. Looking at this calculus, neither side yet sees this as, on balance, a good policy deal. And the political cost of making any compromise has risen as the topic becomes ever more controversial. Electoral shifts and policy realities can always change the dynamics, but so far the conditions are not in place for a grand bargain on immigration.

---

*Sources:* Mike Debonis and John Wagner, "House Rejects Immigration Bill Pushed by Trump in Last-Minute Tweet," *Washington Post*, June 27, 2018; Camila Domonoske, "What We Know: Family Separation and 'Zero Tolerance' at the Border," npr.org, June 19, 2018.

favoring it. This did not discourage President Trump. "The Tax Cuts are so large and so meaningful," he tweeted, "and yet the Fake News is working overtime to follow the lead of their friends, the defeated Dems, and only demean. This is truly a case where the results will speak for themselves, and very soon. Jobs, Jobs, Jobs!"[23] With the president's strong support, the bill passed narrowly in the House and by a party line vote in the Senate. President Trump was able to claim the biggest victory of his first year in office because the policy approach of his tax bill created, in a way that perfectly followed the logic laid out by Mancur Olson, good politics.

## Conclusion

All of these stories point out the complexities of the policy challenges that America's elected officials face, showing how difficult they are to resolve through a government system that spreads power across branches and levels that possess the incentives and authority to thwart one another's policy moves. The same underlying logic that drives these examples may also be applied to the myriad other policy challenges that the nation faces today and is certain to face in the future. Although the specific details of every policy realm are always important, common themes abound. Immigration politics is a bit like entitlement reform, in which each part faces electoral costs if it moves too aggressively on its own, preventing a comprehensive deal that might benefit both sides. The same tragedy of the commons logic that makes solving global climate change so hard also applies to the more mundane issue of "pork" projects in every congressional district because it is individually rational for each representative to over-graze the commons of the federal budget by spending too much in his or her district. In foreign policy, when the United States issues an ultimatum to another country, that friend or foe has every incentive to push right up to the deadline or territorial boundary in order to extract the best possible deal for itself, just as both parties walk to the edge of the fiscal cliff.

The vignettes in this concluding chapter—which draw on both the logical dilemmas posed in Chapter 1 and the solutions used by the Founders and throughout American history—are designed to give readers a new way to think about the policies they read about in today's news. Of course, they do not promise easy policy solutions. The stories illustrate both policy success and policy failure. One lesson of this chapter is that policymaking in a decentralized, combative political system is never easy.

Yet neither is it impossible. One reason is that talented leaders who understand the policy dynamics at play, as well as the mechanisms of the nation's policymaking institutions, can uncover ways to move government in their desired direction. They do not do so by discovering one undisputed solution, as in an elementary math problem. In none of these vignettes does the logic of collective action yield a simple policy solution or a single political strategy. Instead, it reveals the nature of policy challenges, points those who would solve them toward a tool kit of responses, and outlines the obstacles that any new idea will face in Washington, D.C. The policymakers who have succeeded have done so because they think strategically about all of these dynamics. By mastering policy and political logic, they have changed a nation.

**SAGE edge**™
for CQ Press

**Want a better grade?**

Get the tools you need to sharpen your study skills. Access practice quizzes, eFlashcards, video, and multimedia at **edge.sagepub.com/kernell9e.**

# KEY TERMS

## SUGGESTED READINGS

Birnbaum, Jeffrey H., and Alan S. Murray. *Showdown at Gucci Gulch: Lawmakers, Lobbyists, and the Unlikely Triumph of Tax Reform.* New York: Vintage Books, 1987. Two journalists tell the inside story of the surprising passage of the Tax Reform Act of 1986, which brought Democratic legislators together with President Reagan to overhaul the tax code.

Cohen, Richard E. *Washington at Work: Back Rooms and Clean Air.* New York: Macmillan, 1992. Written by a longtime Capitol Hill journalist, this inside account of the passage of the Clean Air Act Amendments of 1990 both describes the difficulty in resolving pollution issues—which are driven by a tragedy of the commons logic—and shows how major deals often emerge from behind Washington's closed doors.

Intergovernmental Panel on Climate Change. *Climate Change 2014: Synthesis Report.* Available at http://www.ipcc.ch. This authoritative report created by hundreds of scientists synthesizes the scientific literature on the causes and consequences of climate change, and contains a summary for policymakers.

Staff of the *Washington Post. Landmark: The Inside Story of America's New Health-Care Law.* Washington, DC: Washington Post, 2010. Covering both the passage of the Affordable Care Act and the policy history and dynamics of the quest to move toward universal health insurance, this volume provides a detailed look at a major policymaking episode.

## REVIEW QUESTIONS

1. What collective action problem makes a solution to global climate change so difficult? What possible solutions can be found in the Framers' tool kit, and what political debates stand in the way of these solutions?

2. Why did tax reform fail so miserably in 2014 and then pass so triumphantly in 2017? What factors shifted to reshape the interest group activity that either opposed or advocated tax changes?

3. If you were a party leader addressing entitlement reform, and faced the potential payoffs laid out in our prisoner's dilemma table, what strategy would you choose? What would be the opposing party's best response to this strategy, and what payoffs would this lead to for you? Could you make your party better off if you chose a different strategy?

4. How do deadlines such as the fiscal cliff change the politics of the policymaking process? Comparing this dynamic with normal negotiations over a proposed bill, how does a deadline change the game? Does it do so for the better or for worse?

5. What do you think about the morality of the logic of policy? That is, do individuals have a responsibility to behave in ways that make policies work best for society as a whole, or can they simply act in a manner that is individually rational?

# Reference Material

## Appendixes

# Appendix 1

## Articles of Confederation

To all to whom these Presents shall come, we the undersigned Delegates of the States affixed to our Names send greeting.

Articles of Confederation and perpetual Union between the states of New Hampshire, Massachusetts-bay Rhode Island and Providence Plantations, Connecticut, New York, New Jersey, Pennsylvania, Delaware, Maryland, Virginia, North Carolina, South Carolina and Georgia.

### Article I

The Stile of this Confederacy shall be **"The United States of America."**

### Article II

Each state retains its sovereignty, freedom, and independence, and every power, jurisdiction, and right, which is not by this Confederation expressly delegated to the United States, in Congress assembled.

### Article III

The said States hereby severally enter into a firm league of friendship with each other, for their common defense, the security of their liberties, and their mutual and general welfare, binding themselves to assist each other, against all force offered to, or attacks made upon them, or any of them, on account of religion, sovereignty, trade, or any other pretense whatever.

### Article IV

The better to secure and perpetuate mutual friendship and intercourse among the people of the different States in this Union, the free inhabitants of each of these States, paupers, vagabonds, and fugitives from justice excepted, shall be entitled to all privileges and immunities of free citizens in the several States; and the people of each State shall free ingress and regress to and from any other State, and shall enjoy therein all the privileges of trade and commerce, subject to the same duties, impositions, and restrictions as the inhabitants thereof respectively, provided that such restrictions shall not extend so far as to prevent the removal of property imported into any State, to any other State, of which the owner is an inhabitant; provided also that no imposition, duties or restriction shall be laid by any State, on the property of the United States, or either of them.

If any person guilty of, or charged with, treason, felony, or other high misdemeanor in any State, shall flee from justice, and be found in any of the United States, he shall, upon demand of the Governor or executive power of the State from which he fled, be delivered up and removed to the State having jurisdiction of his offense.

Full faith and credit shall be given in each of these States to the records, acts, and judicial proceedings of the courts and magistrates of every other State.

### Article V

For the most convenient management of the general interests of the United States, delegates shall be annually appointed in such manner as the legislatures of each State shall direct, to meet in Congress on the first Monday in November, in every year, with a power reserved to each State to recall its delegates, or any of them, at any time within the year, and to send others in their stead for the remainder of the year.

No State shall be represented in Congress by less than two, nor more than seven members; and no person shall be capable of being a delegate for more than three years in any term of six years; nor shall any person, being a delegate, be capable of holding any office under the United States, for which he, or another for his benefit, receives any salary, fees or emolument of any kind.

Each State shall maintain its own delegates in a meeting of the States, and while they act as members of the committee of the States.

In determining questions in the United States in Congress assembled, each State shall have one vote.

Freedom of speech and debate in Congress shall not be impeached or questioned in any court or place out of Congress, and the members of Congress shall be protected in their persons from arrests or imprisonments, during the time of their going to and from, and attendance on Congress, except for treason, felony, or breach of the peace.

## Article VI

No State, without the consent of the United States in Congress assembled, shall send any embassy to, or receive any embassy from, or enter into any conference, agreement, alliance or treaty with any King, Prince or State; nor shall any person holding any office of profit or trust under the United States, or any of them, accept any present, emolument, office or title of any kind whatever from any King, Prince or foreign State; nor shall the United States in Congress assembled, or any of them, grant any title of nobility.

No two or more States shall enter into any treaty, confederation or alliance whatever between them, without the consent of the United States in Congress assembled, specifying accurately the purposes for which the same is to be entered into, and how long it shall continue.

No State shall lay any imposts or duties, which may interfere with any stipulations in treaties, entered into by the United States in Congress assembled, with any King, Prince or State, in pursuance of any treaties already proposed by Congress, to the courts of France and Spain.

No vessel of war shall be kept up in time of peace by any State, except such number only, as shall be deemed necessary by the United States in Congress assembled, for the defense of such State, or its trade; nor shall any body of forces be kept up by any State in time of peace, except such number only, as in the judgement of the United States in Congress assembled, shall be deemed requisite to garrison the forts necessary for the defense of such State; but every State shall always keep up a well-regulated and disciplined militia, sufficiently armed and accoutered, and shall provide and constantly have ready for use, in public stores, a due number of filed pieces and tents, and a proper quantity of arms, ammunition and camp equipage.

No State shall engage in any war without the consent of the United States in Congress assembled, unless such State be actually invaded by enemies, or shall have received certain advice of a resolution being formed by some nation of Indians to invade such State, and the danger is so imminent as not to admit of a delay till the United States in Congress assembled can be consulted; nor shall any State grant commissions to any ships or vessels of war, nor letters of marque or reprisal, except it be after a declaration of war by the United States in Congress assembled, and then only against the Kingdom or State and the subjects thereof, against which war has been so declared, and under such regulations as shall be established by the United States in Congress assembled, unless such State be infested by pirates, in which case vessels of war may be fitted out for that occasion, and kept so long as the danger shall continue, or until the United States in Congress assembled shall determine otherwise.

## Article VII

When land forces are raised by any State for the common defense, all officers of or under the rank of colonel, shall be appointed by the legislature of each State respectively, by whom such forces shall be raised, or in such manner as such State shall direct, and all vacancies shall be filled up by the State which first made the appointment.

## Article VIII

All charges of war, and all other expenses that shall be incurred for the common defense or general welfare, and allowed by the United States in Congress assembled, shall be defrayed out of a common treasury, which shall be supplied by the several States in proportion to the value of all land within each State, granted or surveyed for any person, as such land and the buildings and improvements thereon shall be estimated according to such mode as the United States in Congress assembled, shall from time to time direct and appoint.

The taxes for paying that proportion shall be laid and levied by the authority and direction of the legislatures of the several States within the time agreed upon by the United States in Congress assembled.

## Article IX

The United States in Congress assembled, shall have the sole and exclusive right and power of determining on peace and war, except in the cases mentioned in the sixth article—of sending and receiving ambassadors—entering into treaties and alliances, provided that no treaty of commerce shall be made whereby the legislative power of the respective States shall be restrained from imposing such imposts and duties on foreigners, as their own people are subjected to, or from prohibiting the exportation or importation of any species of goods or commodities whatsoever—of establishing rules for deciding in all cases, what captures on land or water shall be legal, and in what manner prizes taken by land or naval forces in the service of the United States shall be divided or appropriated—of granting letters of marque and reprisal in times of peace—appointing courts for the trial of piracies and felonies commited on the high seas and establishing courts for receiving and determining finally appeals in all cases of captures, provided that no member of Congress shall be appointed a judge of any of the said courts.

The United States in Congress assembled shall also be the last resort on appeal in all disputes and differences now subsisting or that hereafter may arise between two or more States concerning boundary, jurisdiction or any other causes whatever; which authority shall always be exercised in the manner following. Whenever the legislative or executive authority or lawful agent of any State in controversy with another shall present a petition to Congress stating the matter in question and praying for a hearing, notice thereof shall be given by order of Congress to the legislative or executive authority of the other State in controversy, and a day assigned for the appearance of the parties by their lawful agents, who shall then be directed to appoint by joint consent, commissioners or judges to constitute a court for hearing and determining the matter in question: but if they cannot agree, Congress shall name three persons out of each of the United States, and from the list of such persons each party shall alternately strike out one, the petitioners beginning, until the number shall be reduced to thirteen; and from that number not less than seven, nor more than nine names as Congress shall direct, shall in the presence of Congress be drawn out by lot, and the persons whose names shall be so drawn or any five of them, shall be commissioners or judges, to hear and finally determine the controversy, so always as a major part of the judges who shall hear the cause shall agree in the determination: and if either party shall neglect to attend at the day appointed, without showing reasons, which Congress shall judge sufficient, or being present shall refuse to strike, the Congress shall proceed to nominate three persons out of each State, and the secretary of Congress shall strike in behalf of such party absent or refusing; and the judgement and sentence of the court to be appointed, in the manner before prescribed, shall be final and conclusive; and if any of the parties shall refuse to submit to the authority of such court, or to appear or defend their claim or cause, the court shall nevertheless proceed to pronounce sentence, or judgement, which shall in like manner be final and decisive, the judgement or sentence and other proceedings being in either case transmitted to Congress, and lodged among the acts of Congress for the security of the parties concerned: provided that every commissioner, before he sits in judgement, shall take an oath to be administered by one of the judges of the supreme or superior court of the State, where the cause shall be tried, 'well and truly to hear and determine the matter in question, according to the best of his judgement, without favor, affection or hope of reward': provided also, that no State shall be deprived of territory for the benefit of the United States.

All controversies concerning the private right of soil claimed under different grants of two or more States, whose jurisdictions as they may respect such lands, and the States which passed such grants are adjusted, the said grants or either of them being at the same time claimed to have originated antecedent to such settlement of jurisdiction, shall on the petition of either party to the Congress of the United States, be finally determined as near as may be in the same manner as is before prescribed for deciding disputes respecting territorial jurisdiction between different States.

The United States in Congress assembled shall also have the sole and exclusive right and power of regulating the alloy and value of coin struck by their own authority, or by that of the respective States—fixing the standards of weights and measures throughout the United States—regulating the trade and managing all affairs with the Indians, not members of any of the States, provided that the legislative right of any State within its own limits be not infringed or violated—establishing or regulating post offices from one State to another, throughout all the United States, and exacting such postage on the papers passing through the same as may be requisite to defray the expenses of the said office—appointing all officers of the land forces, in the service of the United States, excepting regimental officers—appointing all the officers of the naval forces, and commissioning all officers whatever in the service of the United States—making rules for the government and regulation of the said land and naval forces, and directing their operations.

The United States in Congress assembled shall have authority to appoint a committee, to sit in the recess of Congress, to be denominated 'A Committee of the States', and to consist of one delegate from each State; and to appoint such other committees and civil officers as may be necessary for managing the general

affairs of the United States under their direction—to appoint one of their members to preside, provided that no person be allowed to serve in the office of president more than one year in any term of three years; to ascertain the necessary sums of money to be raised for the service of the United States, and to appropriate and apply the same for defraying the public expenses—to borrow money, or emit bills on the credit of the United States, transmitting every half-year to the respective States an account of the sums of money so borrowed or emitted—to build and equip a navy—to agree upon the number of land forces, and to make requisitions from each State for its quota, in proportion to the number of white inhabitants in such State; which requisition shall be binding, and thereupon the legislature of each State shall appoint the regimental officers, raise the men and cloath, arm and equip them in a solid-like manner, at the expense of the United States; and the officers and men so cloathed, armed and equipped shall march to the place appointed, and within the time agreed on by the United States in Congress assembled. But if the United States in Congress assembled shall, on consideration of circumstances judge proper that any State should not raise men, or should raise a smaller number of men than the quota thereof, such extra number shall be raised, officered, cloathed, armed and equipped in the same manner as the quota of each State, unless the legislature of such State shall judge that such extra number cannot be safely spread out in the same, in which case they shall raise, officer, cloath, arm and equip as many of such extra number as they judge can be safely spared. And the officers and men so cloathed, armed, and equipped, shall march to the place appointed, and within the time agreed on by the United States in Congress assembled.

The United States in Congress assembled shall never engage in a war, nor grant letters of marque or reprisal in time of peace, nor enter into any treaties or alliances, nor coin money, nor regulate the value thereof, nor ascertain the sums and expenses necessary for the defense and welfare of the United States, or any of them, nor emit bills, nor borrow money on the credit of the United States, nor appropriate money, nor agree upon the number of vessels of war, to be built or purchased, or the number of land or sea forces to be raised, nor appoint a commander in chief of the army or navy, unless nine States assent to the same: nor shall a question on any other point, except for adjourning from day to day be determined, unless by the votes of the majority of the United States in Congress assembled.

The Congress of the United States shall have power to adjourn to any time within the year, and to any place within the United States, so that no period of adjournment be for a longer duration than the space of six months, and shall publish the journal of their proceedings monthly, except such parts thereof relating to treaties, alliances or military operations, as in their judgement require secrecy; and the yeas and nays of the delegates of each State on any question shall be entered on the journal, when it is desired by any delegates of a State, or any of them, at his or their request shall be furnished with a transcript of the said journal, except such parts as are above excepted, to lay before the legislatures of the several States.

## Article X

The Committee of the States, or any nine of them, shall be authorized to execute, in the recess of Congress, such of the powers of Congress as the United States in Congress assembled, by the consent of the nine States, shall from time to time think expedient to vest them with; provided that no power be delegated to the said Committee, for the exercise of which, by the Articles of Confederation, the voice of nine States in the Congress of the United States assembled be requisite.

## Article XI

Canada acceding to this confederation, and adjoining in the measures of the United States, shall be admitted into, and entitled to all the advantages of this Union; but no other colony shall be admitted into the same, unless such admission be agreed to by nine States.

## Article XII

All bills of credit emitted, monies borrowed, and debts contracted by, or under the authority of Congress, before the assembling of the United States, in pursuance of the present confederation, shall be deemed and considered as a charge against the United States, for payment and satisfaction whereof the said United States, and the public faith are hereby solemnly pledged.

## Article XIII

Every State shall abide by the determination of the United States in Congress assembled, on all questions which by this confederation are submitted to them. And the Articles of this Confederation shall be inviolably observed by every State, and the Union shall be perpetual; nor shall any alteration at any time hereafter be made in any of them; unless such alteration be agreed to in a Congress of the United States, and be afterwards confirmed by the legislatures of every State.

And Whereas it hath pleased the Great Governor of the World to incline the hearts of the legislatures we respectively represent in Congress, to approve of, and to authorize us to ratify the said Articles of Confederation and perpetual Union. Know Ye that we the undersigned delegates, by virtue of the power and authority to us given for that purpose, do by these presents, in the name and in behalf of our respective constituents, fully and entirely ratify and confirm each and every of the said Articles of Confederation and perpetual Union, and all and singular the matters and things therein contained: And we do further solemnly plight and engage the faith of our respective constituents, that they shall abide by the determinations of the United States in Congress assembled, on all questions, which by the said Confederation are submitted to them. And that the Articles thereof shall be inviolably observed by the States we respectively represent, and that the Union shall be perpetual.

In Witness whereof we have hereunto set our hands in Congress. Done at Philadelphia in the State of Pennsylvania the ninth day of July in the Year of our Lord One Thousand Seven Hundred and Seventy-Eight, and in the Third Year of the independence of America.

Agreed to by Congress 15 November 1777

In force after ratification by Maryland, 1 March 1781

# Appendix 2

## Declaration of Independence

*On June 11, 1776, the responsibility to "prepare a declaration" of independence was assigned by the Continental Congress, meeting in Philadelphia, to five members: John Adams, Benjamin Franklin, Thomas Jefferson, Robert Livingston, and Roger Sherman. Impressed by his talents as a writer, the committee asked Jefferson to compose a draft. After modifying Jefferson's draft the committee turned it over to Congress on June 28. On July 2 Congress voted to declare independence; on the evening of July 4, it approved the Declaration of Independence.*

In Congress, July 4, 1776,
The unanimous Declaration of the thirteen united States of America,

When in the Course of human events, it becomes necessary for one people to dissolve the political bands which have connected them with another, and to assume among the Powers of the earth, the separate and equal station to which the Laws of Nature and of Nature's God entitle them, a decent respect to the opinions of mankind requires that they should declare the causes which impel them to the separation.

We hold these truths to be self-evident, that all men are created equal, that they are endowed by their Creator with certain unalienable Rights, that among these are Life, Liberty and the pursuit of Happiness. That to secure these rights, Governments are instituted among Men, deriving their just powers from the consent of the governed. That whenever any form of Government becomes destructive of these ends, it is the Right of the People to alter or to abolish it, and to institute new Government, laying its foundation on such principles and organizing its powers in such form, as to them shall seem most likely to effect their Safety and Happiness. Prudence, indeed, will dictate that Government long established should not be changed for light and transient causes; and accordingly all experience hath shown, that mankind are more disposed to suffer, while evils are sufferable, than to right themselves by abolishing the forms to which they are accustomed. But when a long train of abuses and usurpations, pursuing invariably the same Object evinces a design to reduce them under absolute Despotism, it is their right, it is their duty, to throw off such Government, and to provide new Guards for their future security. Such has been the patient sufferance of these Colonies; and such is now the necessity which constrains them to alter their former Systems of Government. The history of the present King of Great Britain is a history of repeated injuries and usurpations, all having in direct object the establishment of an absolute Tyranny over these States. To prove this, let Facts be submitted to a candid world.

He has refused his Assent to Laws, the most wholesome and necessary for the public good.

He has forbidden his Governors to pass Laws of immediate and pressing importance, unless suspended in their operation till his Assent should be obtained; and when so suspended, he has utterly neglected to attend to them.

He has refused to pass other Laws for the accommodation of large districts of people, unless those people would relinquish the right of Representation in the

Legislature, a right inestimable to them and formidable to tyrants only.

He has called together legislative bodies at places unusual, uncomfortable, and distant from the depository of their Public Records, for the sole purpose of fatiguing them into compliance with his measures.

He has dissolved Representative Houses repeatedly, for opposing with manly firmness his invasions on the rights of the people.

He has refused for a long time, after such dissolutions, to cause others to be elected; whereby the Legislative Powers, incapable of Annihilation, have returned to the People at large for their exercise; the State remaining in the mean time exposed to all the dangers of invasion from without, and convulsions within.

He has endeavored to prevent the population of these States; for that purpose obstructing the Laws of Naturalization of Foreigners; refusing to pass others to encourage their migration hither, and raising the conditions of new Appropriations of Lands.

He has obstructed the Administration of Justice, by refusing his Assent to Laws for establishing Judiciary Powers.

He has made Judges dependent on his Will alone, for the tenure of their offices, and the amount and payment of their salaries.

He has erected a multitude of New Offices, and sent hither swarms of Officers to harass our People, and eat out their substance.

He has kept among us, in times of peace, Standing Armies without the Consent of our legislature.

He has affected to render the Military independent of and superior to the Civil Power.

He has combined with others to subject us to a jurisdiction foreign to our constitution, and unacknowledged by our laws; giving his Assent to their acts of pretended legislation:

For quartering large bodies of armed troops among us:

For protecting them, by a mock Trial, from Punishment for any Murders which they should commit on the Inhabitants of these States:

For cutting off our Trade with all parts of the world:

For imposing taxes on us without our Consent:

For depriving us in many cases, of the benefits of Trial by Jury:

For transporting us beyond Seas to be tried for pretended offences:

For abolishing the free System of English Laws in a neighbouring Province, establishing therein an Arbitrary government, and enlarging its Boundaries so as to render it at once an example and fit instrument for introducing the same absolute rule into these Colonies:

For taking away our Charters, abolishing our most valuable Laws, and altering fundamentally the Forms of our Governments:

For suspending our own Legislature, and declaring themselves invested with Power to legislate for us in all cases whatsoever.

He has abdicated Government here, by declaring us out of his Protection and waging War against us.

He has plundered our seas, ravaged our Coasts, burnt our towns, and destroyed the lives of our people.

He is at this time transporting large armies of foreign mercenaries to compleat the works of death, desolation and tyranny, already begun with circumstances of Cruelty & perfidy scarcely parallel in the most barbarous ages, and totally unworthy the Head of a civilized nation.

He has constrained our fellow Citizens taken Captive on the high Seas to bear Arms against their Country, to become the executioners of their friends and Brethren, or to fall themselves by their Hands.

He has excited domestic insurrections amongst us, and has endeavoured to bring on the inhabitants of our frontiers, the merciless Indian Savages, whose known rule of warfare, is an undistinguished destruction of all ages, sexes and conditions.

In every stage of these Oppressions We have Petitioned for Redress in the most humble terms: Our repeated Petitions have been answered only by repeated injury. A Prince, whose character is thus marked by every act which may define a Tyrant, is unfit to be the ruler of a free People.

Nor have We been wanting in attention to our British brethren. We have warned them from time to time of attempts by their legislature to extend an unwarrantable jurisdiction over us. We have reminded them of the circumstances of our emigration and settlement here. We have appealed to their native justice and magnanimity, and we have conjured them by the ties of our common kindred to disavow these usurpations, which would inevitably interrupt our connections and correspondence. They too have been deaf to the voice of justice and of consanguinity. We must, therefore, acquiesce in the necessity, which denounces our Separation, and hold them, as we hold the rest of mankind, Enemies in War, in Peace Friends.

We, therefore, the Representatives of the United States of America, in General Congress, Assembled, appealing to the Supreme Judge of the world for the rectitude of our intentions, do, in the Name, and by Authority of the good People of these Colonies, solemnly publish and declare, That these United Colonies are, and of Right ought to be Free and Independent States; that they are Absolved from all Allegiance to the British Crown, and that all political connection between them and the State of Great Britain, is and ought to be totally dissolved; and that as Free and Independent States, they have full Power to levy War, conclude Peace, contract Alliances, establish Commerce, and to do all other Acts and Things which Independent States may of right do. And for the support of this Declaration, with a firm reliance on the Protection of Divine Providence, we mutually pledge to each other our Lives, our Fortunes and our sacred Honor.

John Hancock

**New Hampshire:**
Josiah Bartlett
William Whipple
Matthew Thornton

**Massachusetts Bay:**
John Hancock
Samuel Adams
John Adams
Robert Treat Paine
Elbridge Gerry

**Rhode Island:**
Stephen Hopkins
William Ellery

**Connecticut:**
Roger Sherman
Samuel Huntington
William Williams
Oliver Wolcott

**New York:**
William Floyd
Philip Livingston
Francis Lewis
Lewis Morris

**Pennsylvania:**
Robert Morris
Benjamin Rush
Benjamin Franklin
John Morton
George Clymer
James Smith
George Taylor
James Wilson
George Ross

**Delaware:**
Caesar Rodney
George Read
Thomas McKean

**Georgia:**
Button Gwinnett
Lyman Hall
George Walton

**Maryland:**
Samuel Chase
William Paca
Thomas Stone
Charles Carroll of Carrollton

**Virginia:**
George Wythe
Richard Henry Lee
Thomas Jefferson
Benjamin Harrison
Thomas Nelson Jr.
Francis Lightfoot Lee
Carter Braxton

**North Carolina:**
William Hooper
Joseph Hewes
John Penn

**South Carolina:**
Edward Rutledge
Thomas Heyward Jr.
Thomas Lynch Jr.
Arthur Middleton

**New Jersey:**
Richard Stockton
John Witherspoon
Francis Hopkinson
John Hart
Abraham Clark

# Appendix 3

## Constitution of the United States

*The United States Constitution was written at a convention that Congress called on February 21, 1787, for the purpose of recommending amendments to the Articles of Confederation. Every state but Rhode Island sent delegates to Philadelphia, where the convention met that summer. The delegates decided to write an entirely new constitution, completing their labors on September 17. Nine states (the number the Constitution itself stipulated as sufficient) ratified by June 21, 1788.*

*The Framers of the Constitution included only six paragraphs on the Supreme Court. Article III, Section 1, created the Supreme Court and the federal system of courts. It provided that "[t]he judicial power of the United States, shall be vested in one supreme Court," and whatever inferior courts Congress "from time to time" saw fit to establish. Article III, Section 2, delineated the types of cases and controversies that should be considered by a federal—rather than a state—court. But beyond this, the Constitution left many of the particulars of the Supreme Court and the federal court system for Congress to decide in later years in judiciary acts.*

We the People of the United States, in Order to form a more perfect Union, establish Justice, insure domestic Tranquility, provide for the common defence, promote the general Welfare, and secure the Blessings of Liberty to ourselves and our Posterity, do ordain and establish this Constitution for the United States of America.

## Article I

**Section 1.** All legislative Powers herein granted shall be vested in a Congress of the United States, which shall consist of a Senate and House of Representatives.

**Section 2.** The House of Representatives shall be composed of Members chosen every second Year by the People of the several States, and the Electors in each State shall have the Qualifications requisite for Electors of the most numerous Branch of the State Legislature.

No Person shall be a Representative who shall not have attained to the age of twenty five Years, and been seven Years a Citizen of the United States, and who shall not, when elected, be an Inhabitant of that State in which he shall be chosen.

[Representatives and direct Taxes shall be apportioned among the several States which may be included within this Union, according to their respective Numbers, which shall be determined by adding to the whole Number of free Persons, including those bound to Service for a Term of Years, and excluding Indians not taxed, three fifths of all other Persons.][1] The actual Enumeration shall be made within three Years after the first Meeting of the Congress of the United States, and within every subsequent Term of ten Years, in such Manner as they shall by Law direct. The Number of Representatives shall not exceed one for every thirty Thousand, but each State shall have at Least one Representative; and until such enumeration shall be made, the State of New Hampshire shall be entitled to chuse three, Massachusetts eight, Rhode-Island and Providence Plantations one, Connecticut five, New-York six, New Jersey four, Pennsylvania eight, Delaware one, Maryland six, Virginia ten, North Carolina five, South Carolina five, and Georgia three.

When vacancies happen in the Representation from any State, the Executive Authority thereof shall issue Writs of Election to fill such Vacancies.

The House of Representatives shall chuse their Speaker and other Officers; and shall have the sole Power of Impeachment.

**Section 3.** The Senate of the United States shall be composed of two Senators from each State, [chosen by the Legislature thereof,]² for six Years; and each Senator shall have one Vote.

Immediately after they shall be assembled in Consequence of the first Election, they shall be divided as equally as may be into three Classes. The Seats of the Senators of the first Class shall be vacated at the Expiration of the second Year, of the second Class at the Expiration of the fourth Year, and of the third Class at the Expiration of the sixth Year, so that one third may be chosen every second Year; [and if Vacancies happen by Resignation, or otherwise, during the Recess of the Legislature of any State, the Executive thereof may make temporary Appointments until the next Meeting of the Legislature, which shall then fill such Vacancies.]³

No Person shall be a Senator who shall not have attained to the Age of thirty Years, and been nine Years a Citizen of the United States, and who shall not, when elected, be an Inhabitant of that State for which he shall be chosen.

The Vice President of the United States shall be President of the Senate, but shall have no Vote, unless they be equally divided.

The Senate shall chuse their other Officers, and also a President pro tempore, in the Absence of the Vice President, or when he shall exercise the Office of President of the United States.

The Senate shall have the sole Power to try all Impeachments. When sitting for that Purpose, they shall be on Oath or Affirmation. When the President of the United States is tried, the Chief Justice shall preside: And no Person shall be convicted without the Concurrence of two thirds of the Members present.

Judgment in Cases of Impeachment shall not extend further than to removal from Office, and disqualification to hold and enjoy any Office of honor, Trust or Profit under the United States: but the Party convicted shall nevertheless be liable and subject to Indictment, Trial, Judgment and Punishment, according to Law.

**Section 4.** The Times, Places and Manner of holding Elections for Senators and Representatives, shall be prescribed in each State by the Legislature thereof; but the Congress may at any time by Law make or alter such Regulations, except as to the Places of chusing Senators.

The Congress shall assemble at least once in every Year, and such Meeting shall [be on the first Monday in December],⁴ unless they shall by Law appoint a different Day.

**Section 5.** Each House shall be the Judge of the Elections, Returns and Qualifications of its own Members, and a Majority of each shall constitute a Quorum to do Business; but a smaller Number may adjourn from day to day, and may be authorized to compel the Attendance of absent Members, in such Manner, and under such Penalties as each House may provide.

Each House may determine the Rules of its Proceedings, punish its Members for disorderly Behaviour, and, with the Concurrence of two thirds, expel a Member.

Each House shall keep a Journal of its Proceedings, and from time to time publish the same, excepting such Parts as may in their Judgment require Secrecy; and the Yeas and Nays of the Members of either House on any question shall, at the Desire of one fifth of those Present, be entered on the Journal.

Neither House, during the Session of Congress, shall, without the Consent of the other, adjourn for more than three days, nor to any other Place than that in which the two Houses shall be sitting.

**Section 6.** The Senators and Representatives shall receive a Compensation for their Services, to be ascertained by Law, and paid out of the Treasury of the United States. They shall in all Cases, except Treason, Felony and Breach of the Peace, be privileged from

Arrest during their Attendance at the Session of their respective Houses, and in going to and returning from the same; and for any Speech or Debate in either House, they shall not be questioned in any other Place.

No Senator or Representative shall, during the Time for which he was elected, be appointed to any civil Office under the Authority of the United States, which shall have been created, or the Emoluments whereof shall have been encreased during such time; and no Person holding any Office under the United States, shall be a Member of either House during his Continuance in Office.

***Section 7.*** All Bills for raising Revenue shall originate in the House of Representatives; but the Senate may propose or concur with Amendments as on other Bills.

Every Bill which shall have passed the House of Representatives and the Senate, shall, before it become a Law, be presented to the President of the United States; If he approve he shall sign it, but if not he shall return it, with his Objections to that House in which it shall have originated, who shall enter the Objections at large on their Journal, and proceed to reconsider it. If after such Reconsideration two thirds of that House shall agree to pass the Bill, it shall be sent, together with the Objections, to the other House, by which it shall likewise be reconsidered, and if approved by two thirds of that House, it shall become a Law. But in all such Cases the Votes of both Houses shall be determined by yeas and Nays, and the Names of the Persons voting for and against the Bill shall be entered on the Journal of each House respectively. If any Bill shall not be returned by the President within ten Days (Sundays excepted) after it shall have been presented to him, the Same shall be a Law, in like Manner as if he had signed it, unless the Congress by their Adjournment prevent its Return, in which Case it shall not be a Law.

Every Order, Resolution, or Vote to which the Concurrence of the Senate and House of Representatives may be necessary (except on a question of Adjournment) shall be presented to the President of the United States; and before the Same shall take Effect, shall be approved by him, or being disapproved by him, shall be repassed by two thirds of the Senate and House of Representatives, according to the Rules and Limitations prescribed in the Case of a Bill.

***Section 8.*** The Congress shall have Power To lay and collect Taxes, Duties, Imposts and Excises, to pay the Debts and provide for the common Defence and general Welfare of the United States; but all Duties, Imposts and Excises shall be uniform throughout the United States;

To borrow Money on the credit of the United States;

To regulate Commerce with foreign Nations, and among the several States, and with the Indian Tribes;

To establish an uniform Rule of Naturalization, and uniform Laws on the subject of Bankruptcies throughout the United States;

To coin Money, regulate the Value thereof, and of foreign Coin, and fix the Standard of Weights and Measures;

To provide for the Punishment of counterfeiting the Securities and current Coin of the United States;

To establish Post Offices and post Roads;

To promote the Progress of Science and useful Arts, by securing for limited Times to Authors and Inventors the exclusive Right to their respective Writings and Discoveries;

To constitute Tribunals inferior to the supreme Court;

To define and punish Piracies and Felonies committed on the high Seas, and Offences against the Law of Nations;

To declare War, grant Letters of Marque and Reprisal, and make Rules concerning Captures on Land and Water;

To raise and support Armies, but no Appropriation of Money to that Use shall be for a longer Term than two Years;

To provide and maintain a Navy;

To make Rules for the Government and Regulation of the land and naval Forces;

To provide for calling forth the Militia to execute the Laws of the Union, suppress Insurrections and repel Invasions;

To provide for organizing, arming, and disciplining, the Militia, and for governing such Part of them as may be employed in the Service of the United States, reserving to the States respectively, the Appointment of the Officers, and the Authority of training the Militia according to the discipline prescribed by Congress;

To exercise exclusive Legislation in all Cases whatsoever, over such District (not exceeding ten Miles square) as may, by Cession of particular States, and the Acceptance of Congress, become the Seat of the Government of the United States, and to exercise like Authority over all Places purchased by the Consent of the Legislature of the State in which the Same shall be, for the Erection of Forts, Magazines, Arsenals, dock-Yards, and other needful Buildings;—And

To make all Laws which shall be necessary and proper for carrying into Execution the foregoing Powers, and all other Powers vested by this Constitution in the Government of the United States, or in any Department or Officer thereof.

**Section 9.** The Migration or Importation of such Persons as any of the States now existing shall think proper to admit, shall not be prohibited by the Congress prior to the Year one thousand eight hundred and eight, but a Tax or duty may be imposed on such Importation, not exceeding ten dollars for each Person.

The Privilege of the Writ of Habeas Corpus shall not be suspended, unless when in Cases of Rebellion or Invasion the public Safety may require it.

No Bill of Attainder or ex post facto Law shall be passed.

No Capitation, or other direct, Tax shall be laid, unless in Proportion to the Census or Enumeration herein before directed to be taken.[5]

No Tax or Duty shall be laid on Articles exported from any State.

No Preference shall be given by any Regulation of Commerce or Revenue to the Ports of one State over those of another; nor shall Vessels bound to, or from, one State, be obliged to enter, clear, or pay Duties in another.

No Money shall be drawn from the Treasury, but in Consequence of Appropriations made by Law; and a regular Statement and Account of the Receipts and Expenditures of all public Money shall be published from time to time.

No Title of Nobility shall be granted by the United States: And no Person holding any Office of Profit or Trust under them, shall, without the Consent of the Congress, accept of any present, Emolument, Office, or Title, of any kind whatever, from any King, Prince, or foreign State.

**Section 10.** No State shall enter into any Treaty, Alliance, or Confederation; grant Letters of Marque and Reprisal; coin Money; emit Bills of Credit; make any Thing but gold and silver Coin a Tender in Payment of Debts; pass any Bill of Attainder, ex post facto Law, or Law impairing the Obligation of Contracts, or grant any Title of Nobility.

No State shall, without the Consent of the Congress, lay any Imposts or Duties on Imports or Exports, except what may be absolutely necessary for executing its inspection Laws: and the net Produce of all Duties and Imposts, laid by any State on Imports or Exports, shall be for the Use of the Treasury of the United States; and all such Laws shall be subject to the Revision and Controul of the Congress.

No State shall, without the Consent of Congress, lay any Duty of Tonnage, keep Troops, or Ships of War in time of Peace, enter into any Agreement or Compact with another State, or with a foreign Power, or engage in War, unless actually invaded, or in such imminent Danger as will not admit of delay.

## Article II

**Section 1.** The executive Power shall be vested in a President of the United States of America. He shall hold his Office during the Term of four Years, and, together with the Vice President, chosen for the same Term, be elected, as follows:

Each State shall appoint, in such Manner as the Legislature thereof may direct, a Number of Electors, equal to the whole Number of Senators and Representatives to which the State may be entitled in the Congress: but no Senator or Representative, or Person holding an Office of Trust or Profit under the United States, shall be appointed an Elector.

[The Electors shall meet in their respective States, and vote by Ballot for two Persons, of whom one at least shall not be an Inhabitant of the same State with themselves. And they shall make a List of all the Persons voted for, and of the Number of Votes for each; which List they shall sign and certify, and transmit sealed to the Seat of the Government of the United States, directed to the President of the Senate. The President of the Senate shall, in the Presence of the Senate and House of Representatives, open all the Certificates, and the Votes shall then be counted. The Person having the greatest Number of Votes shall be the President, if such Number be a Majority of the whole Number of Electors appointed; and if there be more than one who have such Majority, and have an equal Number of Votes, then the House of Representatives shall immediately chuse by Ballot one of them for President; and if no Person have a Majority, then from the five highest on the list the said House shall in like Manner chuse the President. But in chusing the President, the Votes shall be taken by States, the Representation from each State having one Vote; A quorum for this Purpose shall consist of a Member or Members from two thirds of the States, and a Majority of all the States shall be necessary to a Choice. In every Case, after the Choice of the President, the Person having the greatest Number of Votes of the Electors shall be the Vice President. But if there should remain two or more who have equal Votes, the Senate shall chuse from them by Ballot the Vice President.][6]

The Congress may determine the Time of chusing the Electors, and the Day on which they shall give their Votes; which Day shall be the same throughout the United States.

No Person except a natural born Citizen, or a Citizen of the United States, at the time of the Adoption of this Constitution, shall be eligible to the Office of President; neither shall any Person be eligible to that Office who shall not have attained to the Age of thirty five Years, and been fourteen Years a Resident within the United States.

In Case of the Removal of the President from Office, or of his Death, Resignation, or Inability to discharge the Powers and Duties of the said Office,[7] the Same shall devolve on the Vice President, and the Congress may by Law provide for the Case of Removal, Death, Resignation or Inability, both of the President and Vice President, declaring what Officer shall then act as President, and such Officer shall act accordingly, until the Disability be removed, or a President shall be elected.

The President shall, at stated Times, receive for his Services, a Compensation, which shall neither be encreased nor diminished during the Period for which he shall have been elected, and he shall not receive within that Period any other Emolument from the United States, or any of them.

Before he enter on the Execution of his Office, he shall take the following Oath or Affirmation:—"I do solemnly swear (or affirm) that I will faithfully execute the Office of President of the United States, and will to the best of my Ability, preserve, protect and defend the Constitution of the United States."

*Section 2.* The President shall be Commander in Chief of the Army and Navy of the United States, and of the Militia of the several States, when called into the actual Service of the United States; he may require the Opinion, in writing, of the principal Officer in each of the executive Departments, upon any Subject relating to the Duties of their respective Offices, and he shall have Power to grant Reprieves and Pardons for Offences against the United States, except in Cases of Impeachment.

He shall have Power, by and with the Advice and Consent of the Senate, to make Treaties, provided two thirds of the Senators present concur; and he shall nominate, and by and with the Advice and Consent of the Senate, shall appoint Ambassadors, other public Ministers and Consuls, Judges of the supreme Court, and all other Officers of the United States, whose Appointments are not herein otherwise provided for, and which shall be established by Law: but the Congress may by Law vest the Appointment of such inferior Officers, as they think proper, in the President alone, in the Courts of Law, or in the Heads of Departments.

The President shall have Power to fill up all Vacancies that may happen during the Recess of the Senate, by granting Commissions which shall expire at the End of their next Session.

**Section 3.** He shall from time to time give to the Congress Information of the State of the Union, and recommend to their Consideration such Measures as he shall judge necessary and expedient; he may, on extraordinary Occasions, convene both Houses, or either of them, and in Case of Disagreement between them, with Respect to the Time of Adjournment, he may adjourn them to such Time as he shall think proper; he shall receive Ambassadors and other public Ministers; he shall take Care that the Laws be faithfully executed, and shall Commission all the Officers of the United States.

**Section 4.** The President, Vice President and all civil Officers of the United States, shall be removed from Office on Impeachment for, and Conviction of, Treason, Bribery, or other high Crimes and Misdemeanors.

## Article III

**Section 1.** The judicial Power of the United States, shall be vested in one supreme Court, and in such inferior Courts as the Congress may from time to time ordain and establish. The Judges, both of the supreme and inferior Courts, shall hold their Offices during good Behaviour, and shall, at stated Times, receive for their Services, a Compensation, which shall not be diminished during their Continuance in Office.

**Section 2.** The judicial Power shall extend to all Cases, in Law and Equity, arising under this Constitution, the Laws of the United States, and Treaties made, or which shall be made, under their Authority; —to all Cases affecting Ambassadors, other public Ministers and Consuls; —to all Cases of admiralty and maritime Jurisdiction; —to Controversies to which the United States shall be a Party; —to Controversies between two or more States; —between a State and Citizens of another State;[8] —between Citizens of different States; —between Citizens of the same State claiming Lands under Grants of different States, and between a State, or the Citizens thereof, and foreign States, Citizens or Subjects.[8]

In all Cases affecting Ambassadors, other public Ministers and Consuls, and those in which a State shall be Party, the supreme Court shall have original Jurisdiction. In all the other Cases before mentioned, the supreme Court shall have appellate Jurisdiction, both as to Law and Fact, with such Exceptions, and under such Regulations as the Congress shall make.

The Trial of all Crimes, except in Cases of Impeachment, shall be by Jury; and such Trial shall be held in the State where the said Crimes shall have been committed; but when not committed within any State, the Trial shall be at such Place or Places as the Congress may by Law have directed.

**Section 3.** Treason against the United States, shall consist only in levying War against them, or in adhering to their Enemies, giving them Aid and Comfort. No Person shall be convicted of Treason unless on the Testimony of two Witnesses to the same overt Act, or on Confession in open Court.

The Congress shall have Power to declare the Punishment of Treason, but no Attainder of Treason shall work Corruption of Blood, or Forfeiture except during the Life of the Person attainted.

## Article IV

**Section 1.** Full Faith and Credit shall be given in each State to the public Acts, Records, and judicial Proceedings of every other State. And the Congress may by general Laws prescribe the Manner in which such Acts, Records and Proceedings shall be proved, and the Effect thereof.

**Section 2.** The Citizens of each State shall be entitled to all Privileges and Immunities of Citizens in the several States.

A Person charged in any State with Treason, Felony, or other Crime, who shall flee from Justice, and be found in another State, shall on Demand of the executive Authority of the State from which he fled, be delivered up, to be removed to the State having Jurisdiction of the Crime.

[No Person held to Service or Labour in one State, under the Laws thereof, escaping into another, shall, in Consequence of any Law or Regulation therein, be discharged from such Service or Labour, but shall be delivered up on Claim of the Party to whom such Service or Labour may be due.][9]

**Section 3.** New States may be admitted by the Congress into this Union; but no new State shall be formed or erected within the Jurisdiction of any other State; nor any State be formed by the Junction of two or more States, or Parts of States, without the Consent of the Legislatures of the States concerned as well as of the Congress.

The Congress shall have Power to dispose of and make all needful Rules and Regulations respecting the Territory or other Property belonging to the United States; and nothing in this Constitution shall be so construed as to Prejudice any Claims of the United States, or of any particular State.

**Section 4.** The United States shall guarantee to every State in this Union a Republican Form of Government, and shall protect each of them against Invasion; and on Application of the Legislature, or of the Executive (when the Legislature cannot be convened) against domestic Violence.

## Article V

The Congress, whenever two thirds of both Houses shall deem it necessary, shall propose Amendments to this Constitution, or, on the Application of the Legislatures of two thirds of the several States, shall call a Convention for proposing Amendments, which, in either Case, shall be valid to all Intents and Purposes, as Part of this Constitution, when ratified by the Legislatures of three fourths of the several States, or by Conventions in three fourths thereof, as the one or the other Mode of Ratification may be proposed by the Congress; Provided [that no Amendment which may be made prior to the Year One thousand eight hundred and eight shall in any Manner affect the first and fourth Clauses in the Ninth Section of the first Article; and][10] that no State, without its Consent, shall be deprived of its equal Suffrage in the Senate.

## Article VI

All Debts contracted and Engagements entered into, before the Adoption of this Constitution, shall be as valid against the United States under this Constitution, as under the Confederation.

This Constitution, and the Laws of the United States which shall be made in Pursuance thereof; and all Treaties made, or which shall be made, under the Authority of the United States, shall be the supreme Law of the Land; and the Judges in every State shall be bound thereby, any Thing in the Constitution or Laws of any State to the Contrary notwithstanding.

The Senators and Representatives before mentioned, and the Members of the several State Legislatures, and all executive and judicial Officers, both of the United States and of the several States, shall be bound by Oath or Affirmation, to support this Constitution; but no religious Test shall ever be required as a Qualification to any Office or public Trust under the United States.

## Article VII

The Ratification of the Conventions of nine States, shall be sufficient for the Establishment of this Constitution between the States so ratifying the Same.

Done in Convention by the Unanimous Consent of the States present the Seventeenth Day of September in the Year of our Lord one thousand seven hundred and Eighty seven and of the Independence of the United States of America the Twelfth. IN WITNESS whereof We have hereunto subscribed our Names,

George Washington, President and deputy from Virginia, and thirty-eight other delegates.

[The language of the original Constitution, not including the Amendments, was adopted by a convention of the states on September 17, 1787, and was subsequently ratified by the states on the following dates: Delaware, December 7, 1787; Pennsylvania, December 12, 1787; New Jersey, December 18, 1787; Georgia, January 2, 1788; Connecticut, January 9, 1788; Massachusetts, February 6, 1788; Maryland, April 28, 1788; South Carolina, May 23, 1788; New Hampshire, June 21, 1788.

Ratification was completed on June 21, 1788.

The Constitution subsequently was ratified by Virginia, June 25, 1788; New York, July 26, 1788; North Carolina, November 21, 1789; Rhode Island, May 29, 1790; and Vermont, January 10, 1791.]

# Amendments

## Amendment I

(First ten amendments ratified December 15, 1791.)

Congress shall make no law respecting an establishment of religion, or prohibiting the free exercise thereof; or abridging the freedom of speech, or of the press; or the right of the people peaceably to assemble, and to petition the Government for a redress of grievances.

## Amendment II

A well regulated Militia, being necessary to the security of a free State, the right of the people to keep and bear Arms, shall not be infringed.

## Amendment III

No Soldier shall, in time of peace be quartered in any house, without the consent of the Owner, nor in time of war, but in a manner to be prescribed by law.

## Amendment IV

The right of the people to be secure in their persons, houses, papers, and effects, against unreasonable searches and seizures, shall not be violated, and no Warrants shall issue, but upon probable cause, supported by Oath or affirmation, and particularly describing the place to be searched, and the persons or things to be seized.

## Amendment V

No person shall be held to answer for a capital, or otherwise infamous crime, unless on a presentment or indictment of a Grand Jury, except in cases arising in the land or naval forces, or in the Militia, when in actual service in time of War or public danger; nor shall any person be subject for the same offence to be twice put in jeopardy of life or limb; nor shall be compelled in any criminal case to be a witness against himself, nor be deprived of life, liberty, or property, without due process of law; nor shall private property be taken for public use, without just compensation.

## Amendment VI

In all criminal prosecutions, the accused shall enjoy the right to a speedy and public trial, by an impartial jury of the State and district wherein the crime shall have been committed, which district shall have been previously ascertained by law, and to be informed of the nature and cause of the accusation; to be confronted with the witnesses against him; to have compulsory process for obtaining witnesses in his favor, and to have the Assistance of Counsel for his defence.

## Amendment VII

In Suits at common law, where the value in controversy shall exceed twenty dollars, the right of trial by jury shall be preserved, and no fact tried by a jury, shall be otherwise re-examined in any Court of the United States, than according to the rules of the common law.

## Amendment VIII

Excessive bail shall not be required, nor excessive fines imposed, nor cruel and unusual punishments inflicted.

## Amendment IX

The enumeration in the Constitution, of certain rights, shall not be construed to deny or disparage others retained by the people.

## Amendment X

The powers not delegated to the United States by the Constitution, nor prohibited by it to the States, are reserved to the States respectively, or to the people.

## Amendment XI
### (Ratified February 7, 1795)

The Judicial power of the United States shall not be construed to extend to any suit in law or equity, commenced or prosecuted against one of the United States by Citizens of another State, or by Citizens or Subjects of any Foreign State.

## Amendment XII
### (Ratified June 15, 1804)

The Electors shall meet in their respective states and vote by ballot for President and Vice-President, one of whom, at least, shall not be an inhabitant of the same state with themselves; they shall name in their ballots the person voted for as President, and in distinct ballots the person voted for as Vice-President, and they shall make distinct lists of all persons voted for as President, and of all persons voted for as Vice-President, and of the number of votes for each, which lists they shall sign and certify, and transmit sealed to the seat of the government of the United States, directed to the President of the Senate; — The President of the Senate shall, in the presence of the Senate and House of Representatives, open all the certificates and the votes shall then be counted; — The person having the greatest number of votes for President, shall be the President, if such number be a majority of the whole number of Electors appointed; and if no person have such majority, then from the persons having the highest numbers not exceeding three on the list of those voted for as President, the House of Representatives shall choose immediately, by ballot, the President. But in choosing the President, the votes shall be taken by states, the representation from each state having one vote; a quorum for this purpose shall consist of a member or members from two-thirds of the states, and a majority of all the states shall be necessary to a choice. [And if the House of Representatives shall not choose a President whenever the right of choice shall devolve upon them, before the fourth day of March next following, then the Vice-President shall act as President, as in the case of the death or other constitutional disability of the President. —][11] The person having the greatest number of votes as Vice-President, shall be the Vice-President, if such number be a majority of the whole number of Electors appointed, and if no person have a majority, then from the two highest numbers on the list, the Senate shall choose the Vice-President; a quorum for the purpose shall consist of two-thirds of the whole number of Senators, and a majority of the whole number shall be necessary to a choice. But no person constitutionally ineligible to the office of President shall be eligible to that of Vice-President of the United States.

## Amendment XIII
### (Ratified December 6, 1865)

**Section 1.** Neither slavery nor involuntary servitude, except as a punishment for crime whereof the party shall have been duly convicted, shall exist within the United States, or any place subject to their jurisdiction.

**Section 2.** Congress shall have power to enforce this article by appropriate legislation.

## Amendment XIV
### (Ratified July 9, 1868)

**Section 1.** All persons born or naturalized in the United States, and subject to the jurisdiction thereof, are citizens of the United States and of the State wherein they reside. No State shall make or enforce any law which shall abridge the privileges or immunities of citizens of the United States; nor shall any State deprive any person of life, liberty, or property, without due process of law; nor deny to any person within its jurisdiction the equal protection of the laws.

**Section 2.** Representatives shall be apportioned among the several States according to their respective numbers, counting the whole number of persons in each State, excluding Indians not taxed. But when the right to vote at any election for the choice of electors for President and Vice President of the United States, Representatives in Congress, the Executive and Judicial officers of a State, or the members of the Legislature thereof, is denied to any of the male inhabitants of such State, being twenty-one years of age,[12] and citizens of the United States, or in any way abridged, except for participation in rebellion, or other crime, the basis of representation therein shall be reduced in the proportion which the number of such male citizens shall bear to the whole number of male citizens twenty-one years of age in such State.

**Section 3.** No person shall be a Senator or Representative in Congress, or elector of President and Vice President, or hold any Office, civil or military, under the United States, or under any State, who, having previously taken an oath, as a member of

Congress, or as an officer of the United States, or as a member of any State legislature, or as an executive or judicial officer of any State, to support the Constitution of the United States, shall have engaged in insurrection or rebellion against the same, or given aid or comfort to the enemies thereof. But Congress may by a vote of two-thirds of each House, remove such disability.

**Section 4.** The validity of the public debt of the United States, authorized by law, including debts incurred for payment of pensions and bounties for services in suppressing insurrection or rebellion, shall not be questioned. But neither the United States nor any State shall assume or pay any debt or obligation incurred in aid of insurrection or rebellion against the United States, or any claim for the loss or emancipation of any slave; but all such debts, obligations and claims shall be held illegal and void.

**Section 5.** The Congress shall have power to enforce, by appropriate legislation, the provisions of this article.

## Amendment XV
### (Ratified February 3, 1870)

**Section 1.** The right of citizens of the United States to vote shall not be denied or abridged by the United States or by any State on account of race, color, or previous condition of servitude.

**Section 2.** The Congress shall have power to enforce this article by appropriate legislation.

## Amendment XVI
### (Ratified February 3, 1913)

The Congress shall have power to lay and collect taxes on incomes, from whatever source derived, without apportionment among the several States, and without regard to any census or enumeration.

## Amendment XVII
### (Ratified April 8, 1913)

The Senate of the United States shall be composed of two Senators from each State, elected by the people thereof, for six years; and each Senator shall have one vote. The electors in each State shall have the qualifications requisite for electors of the most numerous branch of the State legislatures.

When vacancies happen in the representation of any State in the Senate, the executive authority of such State shall issue writs of election to fill such vacancies: *Provided,* That the legislature of any State may empower the executive thereof to make temporary appointments until the people fill the vacancies by election as the legislature may direct.

This amendment shall not be so construed as to affect the election or term of any Senator chosen before it becomes valid as part of the Constitution.

## Amendment XVIII
### (Ratified January 16, 1919)

**Section 1.** After one year from the ratification of this article the manufacture, sale, or transportation of intoxicating liquors within, the importation thereof into, or the exportation thereof from the United States and all territory subject to the jurisdiction thereof for beverage purposes is hereby prohibited.

**Section 2.** The Congress and the several States shall have concurrent power to enforce this article by appropriate legislation.

**Section 3.** This article shall be inoperative unless it shall have been ratified as an amendment to the Constitution by the legislatures of the several States, as provided in the Constitution, within seven years from the date of the submission hereof to the States by the Congress.[13]

## Amendment XIX
### (Ratified August 18, 1920)

The right of citizens of the United States to vote shall not be denied or abridged by the United States or by any State on account of sex.

Congress shall have power to enforce this article by appropriate legislation.

## Amendment XX
### (Ratified January 23, 1933)

**Section 1.** The terms of the President and Vice President shall end at noon on the 20th day of January, and the terms of Senators and Representatives at noon on the 3d day of January, of the years in which such terms would have ended if this article had not been ratified; and the terms of their successors shall then begin.

**Section 2.** The Congress shall assemble at least once in every year, and such meeting shall begin at noon on the 3d day of January, unless they shall by law appoint a different day.

**Section 3.**[14] If, at the time fixed for the beginning of the term of the President, the President elect shall have died, the Vice President elect shall become President. If a President shall not have been chosen before the time fixed for the beginning of his term, or if the President elect shall have failed to qualify, then the Vice President elect shall act as President until a President shall have qualified; and the Congress may by law provide for the case wherein neither a President elect nor a Vice President elect shall have qualified, declaring who shall then act as President, or the manner in which one who is to act shall be selected, and such person shall act accordingly until a President or Vice President shall have qualified.

**Section 4.** The Congress may by law provide for the case of the death of any of the persons from whom the House of Representatives may choose a President whenever the right of choice shall have devolved upon them, and for the case of the death of any of the persons from whom the Senate may choose a Vice President whenever the right of choice shall have devolved upon them.

**Section 5.** Sections 1 and 2 shall take effect on the 15th day of October following the ratification of this article.

**Section 6.** This article shall be inoperative unless it shall have been ratified as an amendment to the Constitution by the legislatures of three-fourths of the several States within seven years from the date of its submission.

## Amendment XXI
### (Ratified December 5, 1933)

**Section 1.** The eighteenth article of amendment to the Constitution of the United States is hereby repealed.

**Section 2.** The transportation or importation into any State, Territory, or possession of the United States for delivery or use therein of intoxicating liquors, in violation of the laws thereof, is hereby prohibited.

**Section 3.** This article shall be inoperative unless it shall have been ratified as an amendment to the Constitution by conventions in the several States, as provided in the Constitution, within seven years from the date of the submission hereof to the States by the Congress.

## Amendment XXII
### (Ratified February 27, 1951)

**Section 1.** No person shall be elected to the office of the President more than twice, and no person who has held the office of President, or acted as President, for more than two years of a term to which some other person was elected President shall be elected to the office of the President more than once. But this Article shall not apply to any person holding the office of President when this Article was proposed by the Congress, and shall not prevent any person who may be holding the office of President, or acting as President, during the term within which this Article becomes operative from holding the office of President or acting as President during the remainder of such term.

**Section 2.** This article shall be inoperative unless it shall have been ratified as an amendment to the Constitution by the legislatures of three-fourths of the several States within seven years from the date of its submission to the States by the Congress.

## Amendment XXIII
### (Ratified March 29, 1961)

**Section 1.** The District constituting the seat of Government of the United States shall appoint in such manner as the Congress may direct:

A number of electors of President and Vice President equal to the whole number of Senators and Representatives in Congress to which the District would be entitled if it were a State, but in no event more than the least populous State; they shall be in addition to those appointed by the States, but they shall be considered, for the purposes of the election of President and Vice President, to be electors appointed by a State; and they shall meet in the District and perform such duties as provided by the twelfth article of amendment.

**Section 2.** The Congress shall have power to enforce this article by appropriate legislation.

## Amendment XXIV
## (Ratified January 23, 1964)

**Section 1.** The right of citizens of the United States to vote in any primary or other election for President or Vice President, for electors for President or Vice President, or for Senator or Representative in Congress, shall not be denied or abridged by the United States or any State by reason of failure to pay any poll tax or other tax.

**Section 2.** The Congress shall have power to enforce this article by appropriate legislation.

## Amendment XXV
## (Ratified February 10, 1967)

**Section 1.** In case of the removal of the President from office or of his death or resignation, the Vice President shall become President.

**Section 2.** Whenever there is a vacancy in the office of the Vice President, the President shall nominate a Vice President who shall take office upon confirmation by a majority vote of both Houses of Congress.

**Section 3.** Whenever the President transmits to the President pro tempore of the Senate and the Speaker of the House of Representatives his written declaration that he is unable to discharge the powers and duties of his office, and until he transmits to them a written declaration to the contrary, such powers and duties shall be discharged by the Vice President as Acting President.

**Section 4.** Whenever the Vice President and a majority of either the principal officers of the executive departments or of such other body as Congress may by law provide, transmit to the President pro tempore of the Senate and the Speaker of the House of Representatives their written declaration that the President is unable to discharge the powers and duties of his office, the Vice President shall immediately assume the powers and duties of the office as Acting President.

Thereafter, when the President transmits to the President pro tempore of the Senate and the Speaker of the House of Representatives his written declaration that no inability exists, he shall resume the powers and duties of his office unless the Vice President and a majority of either the principal officers of the executive departments or of such other body as Congress may by law provide, transmit within four days to the President pro tempore of the Senate and the Speaker of the House of Representatives their written declaration that the President is unable to discharge the powers and duties of his office. Thereupon Congress shall decide the issue, assembling within forty-eight hours for that purpose if not in session. If the Congress, within twenty-one days after receipt of the latter written declaration, or, if Congress is not in session, within twenty-one days after Congress is required to assemble, determines by two-thirds vote of both Houses that the President is unable to discharge the powers and duties of his office, the Vice President shall continue to discharge the same as Acting President; otherwise, the President shall resume the powers and duties of his office.

## Amendment XXVI
## (Ratified July 1, 1971)

**Section 1.** The right of citizens of the United States, who are eighteen years of age or older, to vote shall not be denied or abridged by the United States or by any State on account of age.

**Section 2.** The Congress shall have power to enforce this article by appropriate legislation.

## Amendment XXVII
## (Ratified May 7, 1992)

No law varying the compensation for the services of the Senators and Representatives shall take effect, until an election of Representatives shall have intervened.

*Source:* U.S. Congress, House, Committee on the Judiciary, *The Constitution of the United States of America, as Amended*, 100th Cong., 1st sess., 1987, H Doc 100–94.

## Notes:

1. The part in brackets was changed by section 2 of the Fourteenth Amendment.
2. The part in brackets was changed by the first paragraph of the Seventeenth Amendment.
3. The part in brackets was changed by the second paragraph of the Seventeenth Amendment.
4. The part in brackets was changed by section 2 of the Twentieth Amendment.
5. The Sixteenth Amendment gave Congress the power to tax incomes.
6. The material in brackets was superseded by the Twelfth Amendment.
7. This provision was affected by the Twenty-fifth Amendment.
8. These clauses were affected by the Eleventh Amendment.
9. This paragraph was superseded by the Thirteenth Amendment.
10. Obsolete.
11. The part in brackets was superseded by section 3 of the Twentieth Amendment.
12. See the Nineteenth and Twenty-sixth Amendments.
13. This amendment was repealed by section 1 of the Twenty-first Amendment.
14. See the Twenty-fifth Amendment.

# Appendix 4

## Federalist No. 10

The Same Subject Continued: The Union as a Safeguard Against Domestic Faction and Insurrection.

From the New York Packet
Friday, November 23, 1787.

Author: James Madison

To the People of the State of New York:

AMONG the numerous advantages promised by a wellconstructed Union, none deserves to be more accurately developed than its tendency to break and control the violence of faction. The friend of popular governments never finds himself so much alarmed for their character and fate, as when he contemplates their propensity to this dangerous vice. He will not fail, therefore, to set a due value on any plan which, without violating the principles to which he is attached, provides a proper cure for it. The instability, injustice, and confusion introduced into the public councils, have, in truth, been the mortal diseases under which popular governments have everywhere perished; as they continue to be the favorite and fruitful topics from which the adversaries to liberty derive their most specious declamations. The valuable improvements made by the American constitutions on the popular models, both ancient and modern, cannot certainly be too much admired; but it would be an unwarrantable partiality, to contend that they have as effectually obviated the danger on this side, as was wished and expected. Complaints are everywhere heard from our most considerate and virtuous citizens, equally the friends of public and private faith, and of public and personal liberty, that our governments are too unstable, that the public good is disregarded in the conflicts of rival parties, and that measures are too often decided, not according to the rules of justice and the rights of the minor party, but by the superior force of an interested and overbearing majority. However anxiously we may wish that these complaints had no foundation, the evidence, of known facts will not permit us to deny that they are in some degree true. It will be found, indeed, on a candid review of our situation, that some of the distresses under which we labor have been erroneously charged on the operation of our governments; but it will be found, at the same time, that other causes will not alone account for many of our heaviest misfortunes; and, particularly, for that prevailing and increasing distrust of public engagements, and alarm for private rights, which are echoed from one end of the continent to the other. These must be chiefly, if not wholly, effects of the unsteadiness and injustice with which a factious spirit has tainted our public administrations.

By a faction, I understand a number of citizens, whether amounting to a majority or a minority of the whole, who are united and actuated by some common impulse of passion, or of interest, adversed to the rights of other citizens, or to the permanent and aggregate interests of the community.

There are two methods of curing the mischiefs of faction: the one, by removing its causes; the other, by controlling its effects.

There are again two methods of removing the causes of faction: the one, by destroying the liberty which is essential to its existence; the other, by giving to every citizen the same opinions, the same passions, and the same interests.

It could never be more truly said than of the first remedy, that it was worse than the disease. Liberty is to faction what air is to fire, an aliment without which it instantly expires. But it could not be less folly to abolish liberty, which is essential to political life, because it nourishes faction, than it would be to wish the annihilation of air, which is essential to animal life, because it imparts to fire its destructive agency.

The second expedient is as impracticable as the first would be unwise. As long as the reason of man continues fallible, and he is at liberty to exercise it, different opinions will be formed. As long as the connection subsists between his reason and his self-love, his opinions and his passions will have a reciprocal influence on each other; and the former will be objects to which the latter will attach themselves. The diversity in the faculties of men, from which the rights of property originate, is not less an insuperable obstacle to a uniformity of interests. The protection of these faculties is the first object of government. From the protection of different and unequal faculties of acquiring property, the possession of different degrees and kinds of property immediately results; and from the influence of these on the sentiments and views of the respective proprietors, ensues a division of the society into different interests and parties.

The latent causes of faction are thus sown in the nature of man; and we see them everywhere brought into different degrees of activity, according to the different circumstances of civil society. A zeal for different opinions concerning religion, concerning government, and many other points, as well of speculation as of practice; an attachment to different leaders ambitiously contending for pre-eminence and power; or to persons of other descriptions whose fortunes have been interesting to the human passions, have, in turn, divided mankind into parties, inflamed them with mutual animosity, and rendered them much more disposed to vex and oppress each other than to co-operate for their common good. So strong is this propensity of mankind to fall into mutual animosities, that where no substantial occasion presents itself, the most frivolous and fanciful distinctions have been sufficient to kindle their unfriendly passions and excite their most violent conflicts. But the most common and durable source of factions has been the various and unequal distribution of property. Those who hold and those who are without property have ever formed distinct interests in society. Those who are creditors, and those who are debtors, fall under a like discrimination. A landed interest, a manufacturing interest, a mercantile interest, a moneyed interest, with many lesser interests, grow up of necessity in civilized nations, and divide them into different classes, actuated by different sentiments and views. The regulation of these various and interfering interests forms the principal task of modern legislation, and involves the spirit of party and faction in the necessary and ordinary operations of the government.

No man is allowed to be a judge in his own cause, because his interest would certainly bias his judgment, and, not improbably, corrupt his integrity. With equal, nay with greater reason, a body of men are unfit to be both judges and parties at the same time; yet what are many of the most important acts of legislation, but so many judicial determinations, not indeed concerning the rights of single persons, but concerning the rights of large bodies of citizens? And what are the different classes of legislators but advocates and parties to the causes which they determine? Is a law proposed concerning private debts? It is a question to which the creditors are parties on one side and the debtors on the other. Justice ought to hold the balance between them. Yet the parties are, and must be, themselves the judges; and the most numerous party, or, in other words, the most powerful faction must be expected to prevail. Shall domestic manufactures be encouraged, and in what degree, by restrictions on foreign manufactures? are questions which would be differently decided by the landed and the manufacturing classes, and probably by neither with a sole regard to justice and the public good. The apportionment of taxes on the various descriptions of property is an act which seems to require the most exact impartiality; yet there is, perhaps, no legislative act in which greater opportunity and temptation are given to a predominant party to trample on the rules of justice. Every shilling with which they overburden the inferior number, is a shilling saved to their own pockets.

It is in vain to say that enlightened statesmen will be able to adjust these clashing interests, and render them all subservient to the public good. Enlightened statesmen will not always be at the helm. Nor, in many cases, can such an adjustment be made at all without taking into view indirect and remote considerations, which will rarely prevail over the immediate interest which one party may find in disregarding the rights of another or the good of the whole.

The inference to which we are brought is, that the CAUSES of faction cannot be removed, and that relief is only to be sought in the means of controlling its EFFECTS.

If a faction consists of less than a majority, relief is supplied by the republican principle, which enables the majority to defeat its sinister views by regular vote. It may clog the administration, it may convulse the society; but it will be unable to execute and mask its violence under the forms of the Constitution. When a majority is included in a faction, the form of popular government, on the other hand, enables it to sacrifice to its ruling passion or interest both the public good and the rights of other citizens. To secure the public good and private rights against the danger of such a faction, and at the same time to preserve the spirit and the form of popular government, is then the great object to which our inquiries are directed. Let me add that it is the great desideratum by which this form of government can be rescued from the opprobrium under which it has so long labored, and be recommended to the esteem and adoption of mankind.

By what means is this object attainable? Evidently by one of two only. Either the existence of the same passion or interest in a majority at the same time must be prevented, or the majority, having such coexistent passion or interest, must be rendered, by their number and local situation, unable to concert and carry into effect schemes of oppression. If the impulse and the opportunity be suffered to coincide, we well know that neither moral nor religious motives can be relied on as an adequate control. They are not found to be such on the injustice and violence of individuals, and lose their efficacy in proportion to the number combined together, that is, in proportion as their efficacy becomes needful.

From this view of the subject it may be concluded that a pure democracy, by which I mean a society consisting of a small number of citizens, who assemble and administer the government in person, can admit of no cure for the mischiefs of faction. A common passion or interest will, in almost every case, be felt by a majority of the whole; a communication and concert result from the form of government itself; and there is nothing to check the inducements to sacrifice the weaker party or an obnoxious individual. Hence it is that such democracies have ever been spectacles of turbulence and contention; have ever been found incompatible with personal security or the rights of property; and have in general been as short in their lives as they have been violent in their deaths. Theoretic politicians, who have patronized this species of government, have erroneously supposed that by reducing mankind to a perfect equality in their political rights, they would, at the same time, be perfectly equalized and assimilated in their possessions, their opinions, and their passions.

A republic, by which I mean a government in which the scheme of representation takes place, opens a different prospect, and promises the cure for which we are seeking. Let us examine the points in which it varies from pure democracy, and we shall comprehend both the nature of the cure and the efficacy which it must derive from the Union.

The two great points of difference between a democracy and a republic are: first, the delegation of the government, in the latter, to a small number of citizens elected by the rest; secondly, the greater number of citizens, and greater sphere of country, over which the latter may be extended.

The effect of the first difference is, on the one hand, to refine and enlarge the public views, by passing them through the medium of a chosen body of citizens, whose wisdom may best discern the true interest of their country, and whose patriotism and love of justice will be least likely to sacrifice it to temporary or partial considerations. Under such a regulation, it may well happen that the public voice, pronounced by the representatives of the people, will be more consonant to the public good than if pronounced by the people themselves, convened for the purpose. On the other hand, the effect may be inverted. Men of factious tempers, of local prejudices, or of sinister designs, may, by intrigue, by corruption, or by other means, first obtain the suffrages, and then betray the interests, of the people. The question resulting is, whether small or extensive republics are more favorable to the election of proper guardians of the public weal; and it is clearly decided in favor of the latter by two obvious considerations:

In the first place, it is to be remarked that, however small the republic may be, the representatives must be raised to a certain number, in order to guard against the cabals of a few; and that, however large it may be, they must be limited to a certain number, in order to guard against the confusion of a multitude. Hence, the number of representatives in the two cases not being in proportion to that of the two constituents, and being proportionally greater in the small republic, it follows that, if the proportion of fit characters be not less in the large than in the small republic, the former will present a greater option, and consequently a greater probability of a fit choice.

In the next place, as each representative will be chosen by a greater number of citizens in the large than in the small republic, it will be more difficult for unworthy candidates to practice with success the vicious arts by which elections are too often carried; and the suffrages of the people being more free, will be more likely to centre in men who possess the most attractive merit and the most diffusive and established characters.

It must be confessed that in this, as in most other cases, there is a mean, on both sides of which inconveniences will be found to lie. By enlarging too much the number of electors, you render the representatives too little acquainted with all their local circumstances and lesser interests; as by reducing it too much, you render him unduly attached to these, and too little fit to comprehend and pursue great and national objects. The federal Constitution forms a happy combination in this respect; the great and aggregate interests being referred to the national, the local and particular to the State legislatures.

The other point of difference is, the greater number of citizens and extent of territory which may be brought within the compass of republican than of democratic government; and it is this circumstance principally which renders factious combinations less to be dreaded in the former than in the latter. The smaller the society, the fewer probably will be the distinct parties and interests composing it; the fewer the distinct parties and interests, the more frequently will a majority be found of the same party; and the smaller the number of individuals composing a majority, and the smaller the compass within which they are placed, the more easily will they concert and execute their plans of oppression. Extend the sphere, and you take in a greater variety of parties and interests; you make it less probable that a majority of the whole will have a common motive to invade the rights of other citizens; or if such a common motive exists, it will be more difficult for all who feel it to discover their own strength, and to act in unison with each other. Besides other impediments, it may be remarked that, where there is a consciousness of unjust or dishonorable purposes, communication is always checked by distrust in proportion to the number whose concurrence is necessary.

Hence, it clearly appears, that the same advantage which a republic has over a democracy, in controlling the effects of faction, is enjoyed by a large over a small republic,—is enjoyed by the Union over the States composing it. Does the advantage consist in the substitution of representatives whose enlightened views and virtuous sentiments render them superior to local prejudices and schemes of injustice? It will not be denied that the representation of the Union will be most likely to possess these requisite endowments. Does it consist in the greater security afforded by a greater variety of parties, against the event of any one party being able to outnumber and oppress the rest? In an equal degree does the increased variety of parties comprised within the Union, increase this security. Does it, in fine, consist in the greater obstacles opposed to the concert and accomplishment of the secret wishes of an unjust and interested majority?

Here, again, the extent of the Union gives it the most palpable advantage.

The influence of factious leaders may kindle a flame within their particular States, but will be unable to spread a general conflagration through the other States. A religious sect may degenerate into a political faction in a part of the Confederacy; but the variety of sects dispersed over the entire face of it must secure the national councils against any danger from that source. A rage for paper money, for an abolition of debts, for an equal division of property, or for any other improper or wicked project, will be less apt to pervade the whole body of the Union than a particular member of it; in the same proportion as such a malady is more likely to taint a particular county or district, than an entire State.

In the extent and proper structure of the Union, therefore, we behold a republican remedy for the diseases most incident to republican government. And according to the degree of pleasure and pride we feel in being republicans, ought to be our zeal in cherishing the spirit and supporting the character of Federalists.

PUBLIUS.

# Appendix 5

## Federalist No. 51

The Structure of the Government Must Furnish the Proper Checks and Balances Between the Different Departments

From the New York Packet.
Friday, February 8, 1788.

Author: James Madison

To the People of the State of New York:

TO WHAT expedient, then, shall we finally resort, for maintaining in practice the necessary partition of power among the several departments, as laid down in the Constitution? The only answer that can be given is, that as all these exterior provisions are found to be inadequate, the defect must be supplied, by so contriving the interior structure of the government as that its several constituent parts may, by their mutual relations, be the means of keeping each other in their proper places. Without presuming to undertake a full development of this important idea, I will hazard a few general observations, which may perhaps place it in a clearer light, and enable us to form a more correct judgment of the principles and structure of the government planned by the convention.

In order to lay a due foundation for that separate and distinct exercise of the different powers of government, which to a certain extent is admitted on all hands to be essential to the preservation of liberty, it is evident that each department should have a will of its own; and consequently should be so constituted that the members of each should have as little agency as possible in the appointment of the members of the others. Were this principle rigorously adhered to, it would require that all the appointments for the supreme executive, legislative, and judiciary magistracies should be drawn from the same fountain of authority, the people, through channels having no communication whatever with one another. Perhaps such a plan of constructing the several departments would be less difficult in practice than it may in contemplation appear. Some difficulties, however, and some additional expense would attend the execution of it. Some deviations, therefore, from the principle must be admitted. In the constitution of the judiciary department in particular, it might be inexpedient to insist rigorously on the principle: first, because peculiar qualifications being essential in the members, the primary consideration ought to be to select that mode of choice which best secures these qualifications; secondly, because the permanent tenure by which the appointments are held in that department, must soon destroy all sense of dependence on the authority conferring them.

It is equally evident, that the members of each department should be as little dependent as possible on those of the others, for the emoluments annexed to their offices. Were the executive magistrate, or the judges, not independent of the legislature in this particular, their independence in every other would be merely nominal. But the great security against a gradual concentration of the several powers in the same department, consists in giving to those who administer each department the necessary constitutional means and personal motives to resist encroachments of the others. The provision for defense must in this, as in all other cases, be made commensurate to the danger of attack. Ambition must be made to counteract ambition. The interest of the man must be connected with the constitutional rights of the place. It may be a reflection on human nature, that such devices should be necessary to control the abuses of government. But what is government itself, but the greatest of all reflections on human nature? If men were angels, no government would be necessary. If angels were to govern men, neither external nor internal controls on government would be necessary. In framing a government which is to be administered by men over men, the great difficulty lies in this: you must first enable the government to control the governed; and in the next place oblige it to control itself.

A dependence on the people is, no doubt, the primary control on the government; but experience has taught mankind the necessity of auxiliary precautions. This policy of supplying, by opposite and rival interests, the defect of better motives, might be traced through the whole system of human affairs, private as well as public. We see it particularly displayed in all the subordinate distributions of power, where the constant aim is to divide and arrange the several offices in such a manner as that each may be a check on the other that the private interest of every individual may be a sentinel over the public rights. These inventions of prudence cannot be less requisite in the distribution of the supreme powers of the State. But it is not possible to give to each department an equal power of self-defense. In republican government, the legislative authority necessarily predominates. The remedy for this inconveniency is to divide the legislature into different branches; and to render them, by different modes of election and different principles of action, as little connected with each other as the nature of their common functions and their common dependence on the society will admit. It may even be necessary to guard against dangerous encroachments by still further precautions. As the weight of the legislative authority requires that it should be thus divided, the weakness of the executive may require, on the other hand, that it should be fortified.

An absolute negative on the legislature appears, at first view, to be the natural defense with which the executive magistrate should be armed. But perhaps it would be neither altogether safe nor alone sufficient. On ordinary occasions it might not be exerted with the requisite firmness, and on extraordinary occasions it might be perfidiously abused. May not this defect of an absolute negative be supplied by some qualified connection between this weaker department and the weaker branch of the stronger department, by which the latter may be led to support the constitutional rights of the former, without being too much detached from the rights of its own department? If the principles on which these observations are founded be just, as I persuade myself they are, and they be applied as a criterion to the several State constitutions, and to the federal Constitution it will be found that if the latter does not perfectly correspond with them, the former are infinitely less able to bear such a test.

There are, moreover, two considerations particularly applicable to the federal system of America, which place that system in a very interesting point of view. First. In a single republic, all the power surrendered by the people is submitted to the administration of a single government; and the usurpations are guarded against by a division of the government into distinct and separate departments. In the compound republic of America, the power surrendered by the people is first divided between two distinct governments, and then the portion allotted to each subdivided among distinct and separate departments. Hence a double security arises to the rights of the people. The different governments will control each other, at the same time that each will be controlled by itself. Second. It is of great importance in a republic not only to guard the society against the oppression of its rulers, but to guard one part of the society against the injustice of the other part. Different interests necessarily exist in different classes of citizens. If a majority be united by a common interest, the rights of the minority will be insecure.

There are but two methods of providing against this evil: the one by creating a will in the community independent of the majority that is, of the society itself; the other, by comprehending in the society so many separate descriptions of citizens as will render an unjust combination of a majority of the whole very improbable, if not impracticable. The first method prevails in all governments possessing an hereditary or self-appointed authority. This, at best, is but a precarious security; because a power independent of the society may as well espouse the unjust views of the major, as the rightful interests of the minor party, and may possibly be turned against both parties. The second method will be exemplified in the federal republic of the United States. Whilst all authority in it will be derived from and dependent on the society, the society itself will be broken into so many parts, interests, and classes of citizens, that the rights of individuals, or of the minority, will be in little danger from interested combinations of the majority.

In a free government the security for civil rights must be the same as that for religious rights. It consists in the one case in the multiplicity of interests, and in the other in the multiplicity of sects. The degree of security in both cases will depend on the number of interests and sects; and this may be presumed to depend on the extent of country and number of people comprehended under the same government. This view of the subject must particularly recommend a proper federal system to all the sincere and considerate friends of republican government, since it shows that in exact proportion as the territory of the Union may be formed into more circumscribed Confederacies, or States oppressive combinations of a majority will be facilitated: the best security, under the republican forms, for the rights of every class of citizens, will be diminished: and consequently the stability and independence of some member of the government, the only other security, must be proportionately increased. Justice is the end of government. It is the end of civil society. It ever has been and ever will be pursued until it be obtained, or until liberty be lost in the pursuit. In a society under the forms of which the stronger faction can readily unite and oppress the weaker, anarchy may as truly be said to reign as in a state of nature, where the weaker individual is not secured against the violence of the stronger; and as, in the latter state, even the stronger individuals are prompted, by the uncertainty of their condition, to submit to a government which may protect the weak as well as themselves; so, in the former state, will the more powerful factions or parties be gradually induced, by a like motive, to wish for a government which will protect all parties, the weaker as well as the more powerful.

It can be little doubted that if the State of Rhode Island was separated from the Confederacy and left to itself, the insecurity of rights under the popular form of government within such narrow limits would be displayed by such reiterated oppressions of factious majorities that some power altogether independent of the people would soon be called for by the voice of the very factions whose misrule had proved the necessity of it. In the extended republic of the United States, and among the great variety of interests, parties, and sects which it embraces, a coalition of a majority of the whole society could seldom take place on any other principles than those of justice and the general good; whilst there being thus less danger to a minor from the will of a major party, there must be less pretext, also, to provide for the security of the former, by introducing into the government a will not dependent on the latter, or, in other words, a will independent of the society itself. It is no less certain than it is important, notwithstanding the contrary opinions which have been entertained, that the larger the society, provided it lie within a practical sphere, the more duly capable it will be of self-government. And happily for the REPUBLICAN CAUSE, the practicable sphere may be carried to a very great extent, by a judicious modification and mixture of the FEDERAL PRINCIPLE.

PUBLIUS.

# Appendix 6

## Political Party Affiliations in Congress and the Presidency, 1789–2015[*]

| YEAR | CONGRESS | HOUSE | | SENATE | | PRESIDENT |
|------|----------|-------|---|--------|---|-----------|
| | | MAJORITY PARTY | PRINCIPAL MINORITY PARTY | MAJORITY PARTY | PRINCIPAL MINORITY PARTY | |
| 1789–1791 | 1st | AD-38 | Op-26 | AD-17 | Op-9 | F (Washington) |
| 1791–1793 | 2nd | F-37 | DR-33 | F-16 | DR-13 | F (Washington) |
| 1793–1795 | 3rd | DR-57 | F-48 | F-17 | DR-13 | F (Washington) |
| 1795–1797 | 4th | F-54 | DR-52 | F-19 | DR-13 | F (Washington) |
| 1797–1799 | 5th | F-58 | DR-48 | F-20 | DR-12 | F (John Adams) |
| 1799–1801 | 6th | F-64 | DR-42 | F-19 | DR-13 | F (John Adams) |
| 1801–1803 | 7th | DR-69 | F-36 | DR-18 | F-13 | DR (Jefferson) |
| 1803–1805 | 8th | DR-102 | F-39 | DR-25 | F-9 | DR (Jefferson) |
| 1805–1807 | 9th | DR-116 | F-25 | DR-27 | F-7 | DR (Jefferson) |
| 1807–1809 | 10th | DR-118 | F-24 | DR-28 | F-6 | DR (Jefferson) |
| 1809–1811 | 11th | DR-94 | F-48 | DR-28 | F-6 | DR (Madison) |
| 1811–1813 | 12th | DR-108 | F-36 | DR-30 | F-6 | DR (Madison) |
| 1813–1815 | 13th | DR-112 | F-68 | DR-27 | F-9 | DR (Madison) |
| 1815–1817 | 14th | DR-117 | F-65 | DR-25 | F-11 | DR (Madison) |
| 1817–1819 | 15th | DR-141 | F-42 | DR-34 | F-10 | DR (Monroe) |
| 1819–1821 | 16th | DR-156 | F-27 | DR-35 | F-7 | DR (Monroe) |
| 1821–1823 | 17th | DR-158 | F-25 | DR-44 | F-4 | DR (Monroe) |
| 1823–1825 | 18th | DR-187 | F-26 | DR-44 | F-4 | DR (Monroe) |
| 1825–1827 | 19th | AD-105 | J-97 | AD-26 | J-20 | DR (John Q. Adams) |
| 1827–1829 | 20th | J-119 | AD-94 | J-28 | AD-20 | DR (John Q. Adams) |
| 1829–1831 | 21st | D-139 | NR-74 | D-26 | NR-22 | DR (Jackson) |
| 1831–1833 | 22nd | D-141 | NR-58 | D-25 | NR-21 | D (Jackson) |
| 1833–1835 | 23rd | D-147 | AM-53 | D-20 | NR-20 | D (Jackson) |
| 1835–1837 | 24th | D-145 | W-98 | D-27 | W-25 | D (Jackson) |
| 1837–1839 | 25th | D-108 | W-107 | D-30 | W-18 | D (Van Buren) |
| 1839–1841 | 26th | D-124 | W-118 | D-28 | W-22 | D (Van Buren) |
| 1841–1843 | 27th | W-133 | D-102 | W-28 | D-22 | W (W. Harrison) W (Tyler) |

| YEAR | CONGRESS | HOUSE | | SENATE | | PRESIDENT |
| | | MAJORITY PARTY | PRINCIPAL MINORITY PARTY | MAJORITY PARTY | PRINCIPAL MINORITY PARTY | |
|---|---|---|---|---|---|---|
| 1843–1845 | 28th | D-142 | W-79 | W-28 | D-25 | W (Tyler) |
| 1845–1847 | 29th | D-143 | W-77 | D-31 | W-25 | D (Polk) |
| 1847–1849 | 30th | W-115 | D-108 | D-36 | W-21 | D (Polk) |
| 1849–1851 | 31st | D-112 | W-109 | D-35 | W-25 | W (Taylor) |
| | | | | | | W (Fillmore) |
| 1851–1853 | 32nd | D-140 | W-88 | D-35 | W-24 | W (Fillmore) |
| 1853–1855 | 33rd | D-159 | W-71 | D-38 | W-22 | D (Pierce) |
| 1855–1857 | 34th | R-108 | D-83 | D-42 | R-15 | D (Pierce) |
| 1857–1859 | 35th | D-131 | R-92 | D-35 | R-20 | D (Buchanan) |
| 1859–1861 | 36th | R-113 | D-101 | D-38 | R-26 | D (Buchanan) |
| 1861–1863 | 37th | R-106 | D-42 | R-31 | D-11 | R (Lincoln) |
| 1863–1865 | 38th | R-103 | D-80 | R-39 | D-12 | R (Lincoln) |
| 1865–1867[1] | 39th | U-145 | D-46 | U-42 | D-10 | U (Lincoln) |
| | | | | | | U (A. Johnson) |
| 1867–1869 | 40th | R-143 | D-49 | R-42 | D-11 | R (A. Johnson) |
| 1869–1871 | 41st | R-170 | D-73 | R-61 | D-11 | R (Grant) |
| 1871–1873 | 42nd | R-139 | D-104 | R-57 | D-17 | R (Grant) |
| 1873–1875 | 43rd | R-203 | D-88 | R-54 | D-19 | R (Grant) |
| 1875–1877 | 44th | D-181 | R-107 | R-46 | D-29 | R (Grant) |
| 1877–1879 | 45th | D-156 | R-137 | R-39 | D-36 | R (Hayes) |
| 1879–1881 | 46th | D-150 | R-128 | D-43 | R-33 | R (Hayes) |
| 1881–1883 | 47th | R-152 | D-130 | R-37 | D-37 | R (Garfield) |
| | | | | | | R (Arthur) |
| 1883–1885 | 48th | D-200 | R-119 | R-40 | D-36 | R (Arthur) |
| 1885–1887 | 49th | D-182 | R-140 | R-41 | D-34 | D (Cleveland) |
| 1887–1889 | 50th | D-170 | R-151 | R-39 | D-37 | D (Cleveland) |
| 1889–1891 | 51st | R-173 | D-159 | R-37 | D-37 | R (B. Harrison) |
| 1891–1893 | 52nd | D-231 | R-88 | R-47 | D-39 | R (B. Harrison) |
| 1893–1895 | 53rd | D-220 | R-126 | D-44 | R-38 | D (Cleveland) |
| 1895–1897 | 54th | R-246 | D-104 | R-43 | D-39 | D (Cleveland) |
| 1897–1899 | 55th | R-206 | D-134 | R-46 | D-34 | R (McKinley) |
| 1899–1901 | 56th | R-185 | D-163 | R-53 | D-26 | R (McKinley) |
| 1901–1903 | 57th | R-198 | D-153 | R-56 | D-29 | R (McKinley) |
| | | | | | | R (T. Roosevelt) |
| 1903–1905 | 58th | R-207 | D-178 | R-58 | D-32 | R (T. Roosevelt) |
| 1905–1907 | 59th | R-250 | D-136 | R-58 | D-32 | R (T. Roosevelt) |
| 1907–1909 | 60th | R-222 | D-164 | R-61 | D-29 | R (T. Roosevelt) |
| 1909–1911 | 61st | R-219 | D-172 | R-59 | D-32 | R (Taft) |
| 1911–1913 | 62nd | D-228 | R-162 | R-49 | D-42 | R (Taft) |
| 1913–1915 | 63rd | D-290 | R-127 | D-51 | R-44 | D (Wilson) |
| 1915–1917 | 64th | D-231 | R-193 | D-56 | R-39 | D (Wilson) |
| 1917–1919 | 65th | D-216 | R-210 | D-53 | R-42 | D (Wilson) |

*(Continued)*

(Continued)

| YEAR | CONGRESS | HOUSE | | SENATE | | PRESIDENT |
| | | MAJORITY PARTY | PRINCIPAL MINORITY PARTY | MAJORITY PARTY | PRINCIPAL MINORITY PARTY | |
|---|---|---|---|---|---|---|
| 1919–1921 | 66th | R-237 | D-191 | R-48 | D-47 | D (Wilson) |
| 1921–1923 | 67th | R-300 | D-132 | R-59 | D-37 | R (Harding) |
| 1923–1925 | 68th | R-225 | D-207 | R-51 | D-43 | R (Coolidge) |
| 1925–1927 | 69th | R-247 | D-183 | R-54 | D-40 | R (Coolidge) |
| 1927–1929 | 70th | R-237 | D-195 | R-48 | D-47 | R (Coolidge) |
| 1929–1931 | 71st | R-267 | D-163 | R-56 | D-39 | R (Hoover) |
| 1931–1933 | 72nd | D-216 | R-218 | R-48 | D-47 | R (Hoover) |
| 1933–1935 | 73rd | D-313 | R-117 | D-59 | R-36 | D (F. Roosevelt) |
| 1935–1937 | 74th | D-322 | R-103 | D-69 | R-25 | D (F. Roosevelt) |
| 1937–1939 | 75th | D-333 | R-89 | D-75 | R-17 | D (F. Roosevelt) |
| 1939–1941 | 76th | D-262 | R-169 | D-69 | R-23 | D (F. Roosevelt) |
| 1941–1943 | 77th | D-267 | R-162 | D-66 | R-28 | D (F. Roosevelt) |
| 1943–1945 | 78th | D-222 | R-209 | D-57 | R-38 | D (F. Roosevelt) |
| 1945–1947 | 79th | D-243 | R-190 | D-56 | R-38 | D (F. Roosevelt) D (Truman) |
| 1947–1949 | 80th | R-246 | D-188 | R-51 | D-45 | D (Truman) |
| 1949–1951 | 81st | D-263 | R-171 | D-54 | R-42 | D (Truman) |
| 1951–1953 | 82nd | D-234 | R-199 | D-48 | R-47 | D (Truman) |
| 1953–1955 | 83rd | R-221 | D-213 | R-48 | D-46 | R (Eisenhower) |
| 1955–1957 | 84th | D-234 | R-201 | D-48 | R-47 | R (Eisenhower) |
| 1957–1959 | 85th | D-233 | R-200 | D-49 | R-47 | R (Eisenhower) |
| 1959–1961 | 86th | D-283 | R-153 | D-64 | R-34 | R (Eisenhower) |
| 1961–1963 | 87th | D-262 | R-175 | D-64 | R-36 | D (Kennedy) |
| 1963–1965 | 88th | D-258 | R-176 | D-67 | R-33 | D (Kennedy) D (L. Johnson) |
| 1965–1967 | 89th | D-295 | R-140 | D-68 | R-32 | D (L. Johnson) |
| 1967–1969 | 90th | D-248 | R-187 | D-64 | R-36 | D (L. Johnson) |
| 1969–1971 | 91st | D-243 | R-192 | D-58 | R-42 | R (Nixon) |
| 1971–1973 | 92nd | D-255 | R-180 | D-54 | R-44 | R (Nixon) |
| 1973–1975 | 93rd | D-242 | R-192 | D-56 | R-42 | R (Nixon) R (Ford) |
| 1975–1977 | 94th | D-291 | R-144 | D-60 | R-37 | R (Ford) |
| 1977–1979 | 95th | D-292 | R-143 | D-61 | R-38 | D (Carter) |
| 1979–1981 | 96th | D-277 | R-158 | D-58 | R-41 | D (Carter) |
| 1981–1983 | 97th | D-242 | R-192 | R-53 | D-46 | R (Reagan) |
| 1983–1985 | 98th | D-269 | R-166 | R-54 | D-46 | R (Reagan) |
| 1985–1987 | 99th | D-253 | R-182 | R-53 | D-47 | R (Reagan) |
| 1987–1989 | 100th | D-258 | R-177 | D-55 | R-45 | R (Reagan) |
| 1989–1991 | 101st | D-260 | R-175 | D-55 | R-45 | R (G. H. W. Bush) |
| 1991–1993 | 102nd | D-267 | R-167 | D-56 | R-44 | R (G. H. W. Bush) |
| 1993–1995 | 103rd | D-258 | R-176 | D-57 | R-43 | D (Clinton) |
| 1995–1997 | 104th | R-230 | D-204 | R-52 | D-48 | D (Clinton) |
| 1997–1999 | 105th | R-226 | D-207 | R-55 | D-45 | D (Clinton) |
| 1999–2001 | 106th | R-223 | D-211 | R-55 | D-45 | D (Clinton) |
| 2001–2003 | 107th | R-221 | D-212 | D-50 | R-50 | R (G. W. Bush) |

| YEAR | CONGRESS | HOUSE | | SENATE | | PRESIDENT |
| | | MAJORITY PARTY | PRINCIPAL MINORITY PARTY | MAJORITY PARTY | PRINCIPAL MINORITY PARTY | |
|---|---|---|---|---|---|---|
| 2003–2005 | 108th | R-229 | D-204 | R-51 | D-48 | R (G. W. Bush) |
| 2005–2007 | 109th | R-232 | D-202 | R-55 | D-44 | R (G. W. Bush) |
| 2007–2009 | 110th | D-233 | R-202 | D-49 | R-49 | R (G. W. Bush) |
| 2009–2011 | 111th | D-254 | R-175 | D-57 | R-40 | D (Obama) |
| 2011–2013 | 112th | R-242 | D-193 | D-53 | R-47 | D (Obama) |
| 2013–2015 | 113th | R-232 | D-200 | D-53 | R-45 | D (Obama) |
| 2015–2017 | 114th | R-246 | D-188 | R-54 | D-44 | D (Obama) |
| 2017–2019 | 115th | R-240 | D-193 | R-52 | D-46 | R (Trump) |
| *2019– | 116th | D-235 | R-199 | R-53 | D-47 | R (Trump) |

*Sources:* For data through the 33rd Congress, see U.S. Bureau of the Census, *Historical Statistics of the United States, Colonial Times to 1970* (Washington, D.C.: Government Printing Office, 1975), 1083–1084; for data after the 33rd Congress, see U.S. Congress, Joint Committee on Printing, *Official Congressional Directory* (Washington, D.C.: Government Printing Office, 2008), 553–554; for 2008 election data see *CQ Politics Election 2008*, www.cqpolitics.com/wmspage.cfn?parm1=2. See also http://innovation.cq.com/election_night08?tab2=f; for 2010 election data, see http://www.rollcall.com/politics/. For 2012 election data, see the Office of the Clerk of the U.S. House of Representatives, http://clerk.house.gov/member_info/cong.aspx.

*Notes:* Figures are for the beginning of the first session of each Congress. Key to abbreviations: AD—Administration; AM—Anti-Masonic;

D—Democratic; DR—Democratic-Republican; F—Federalist; J—Jacksonian; NR—National Republican; Op—Opposition; R—Republican;

U—Unionist; W—Whig.

1. The Republican Party ran under the Union Party banner in 1864.

*Numbers current as of time of publication.

# Appendix 7

## Summary of Presidential Elections, 1789–2016

| YEAR | NO. OF STATES | CANDIDATES | | ELECTORAL VOTE | | POPULAR VOTE | |
|------|---------------|------------|---|----------------|---|--------------|---|
| 1789[a] | 10 | Fed.<br>George Washington | | Fed.<br>69 | | —[b] | |
| 1792[a] | 15 | Fed.<br>George Washington | | Fed.<br>132 | | —[b] | |
| 1796[a] | 16 | Dem.-Rep.<br>Thomas Jefferson | Fed.<br>John Adams | Dem.-Rep.<br>68 | Fed.<br>71 | —[b] | |
| 1800[a] | 16 | Dem.-Rep.<br>Thomas Jefferson<br>Aaron Burr | Fed.<br>John Adams<br>Charles Cotesworth<br>Pinckney | Dem.-Rep<br>73 | Fed.<br>65 | —[b] | |
| 1804 | 17 | Dem.-Rep.<br>Thomas Jefferson<br><br>George Clinton | Fed.<br>Charles Cotesworth<br>Pinckney<br>Rufus King | Dem.-Rep<br>162 | Fed.<br>14 | —[b] | |
| 1808 | 17 | Dem.-Rep.<br>James Madison<br><br>George Clinton | Fed.<br>Charles Cotesworth<br>Pinckney<br>Rufus King | Dem.-Rep<br>122 | Fed.<br>47 | —[b] | |
| 1812 | 18 | Dem.-Rep.<br>James Madison<br>Elbridge Gerry | Fed.<br>George Clinton<br>Jared Ingersoll | Dem.-Rep<br>128 | Fed.<br>89 | —[b] | |
| 1816 | 19 | Dem.-Rep.<br>James Monroe<br>Daniel D. Tompkins | Fed.<br>Rufus King<br>John Howard | Dem.-Rep<br>183 | Fed.<br>34 | —[b] | |
| 1820 | 24 | Dem.-Rep<br>James Monroe<br>Daniel D. Tompkins | —[c] | Dem.-Rep<br>231 | —[c] | —[b] | |
| 1824[d] | 24 | Dem.-Rep<br>Andrew Jackson<br>John C. Calhoun | Dem.-Rep<br>John Q. Adams<br>Nathan Sanford | Dem.-Rep<br>99 | Dem.-Rep.<br>84 | Dem.-Rep<br>151,271<br>41.3% | Dem.-Rep<br>113,122<br>30.9% |

| YEAR | NO. OF STATES | CANDIDATES | | ELECTORAL VOTE | | POPULAR VOTE | |
|---|---|---|---|---|---|---|---|
| 1828 | 24 | Dem.-Rep.<br>Andrew Jackson<br>John C. Calhoun | Nat.-Rep.<br>John Q. Adams<br>Richard Rush | Dem.-Rep.<br>178 | Nat.-Rep.<br>83 | Dem.-Rep.<br>642,553<br>56.0% | Nat.-Rep.<br>500,897<br>43.6% |
| 1832[e] | 24 | Dem.<br>Andrew Jackson<br>Martin Van Buren | Nat.-Rep.<br>Henry Clay<br>John Sergeant | Dem.<br>219 | Nat.-Rep.<br>49 | Dem.<br>701,780<br>54.2% | Nat.-Rep.<br>484,205<br>37.4% |
| 1836[f] | 26 | Dem.<br>Martin Van Buren<br>Richard M. Johnson | Whig<br>William H. Harrison<br>Francis Granger | Dem.<br>170 | Whig<br>73 | Dem.<br>764,176<br>50.8% | Whig<br>550,816<br>36.6% |
| 1840 | 26 | Dem.<br>Martin Van Buren<br>Richard M. Johnson | Whig<br>William H. Harrison<br>John Tyler | Dem.<br>60 | Whig<br>234 | Dem.<br>1,128,854<br>46.8% | Whig<br>1,275,390<br>52.9% |
| 1844 | 26 | Dem.<br>James Polk<br>George M. Dallas | Whig<br>Henry Clay<br>Theodore Frelinghuysen | Dem.<br>170 | Whig<br>105 | Dem.<br>1,339,494<br>49.5% | Whig<br>1,300,004<br>48.1% |
| 1848 | 30 | Dem.<br>Lewis Cass<br>William O. Butler | Whig<br>Zachary Taylor<br>Millard Fillmore | Dem.<br>127 | Whig<br>163 | Dem.<br>1,233,460<br>42.5% | Whig<br>1,361,393<br>47.3% |
| 1852 | 31 | Dem.<br>Franklin Pierce<br>William R. King | Whig<br>Winfield Scott<br>William A. Graham | Dem.<br>254 | Whig<br>42 | Dem.<br>1,607,510<br>50.8% | Whig<br>1,386,942<br>43.9% |

| YEAR | NO. OF STATES | CANDIDATES | | ELECTORAL VOTE | | POPULAR VOTE | |
|---|---|---|---|---|---|---|---|
| | | DEM. | REP. | DEM. | REP. | DEM. | REP. |
| 1856[g] | 31 | James Buchanan<br>John C. Breckinridge | John C. Fremont<br>William L. Dayton | 174 | 114 | 1,836,072<br>45.3% | 1,342,345<br>33.1% |
| 1860[h] | 33 | Stephen A. Douglas<br>Herschel V. Johnson | Abraham Lincoln<br>Hannibal Hamlin | 12 | 180 | 1,380,202<br>29.5% | 1,865,908<br>39.8% |
| 1864[i] | 36 | George B. McClellan<br>George H. Pendleton | Abraham Lincoln<br>Andrew Johnson | 21 | 212 | 1,812,807<br>45.0% | 2,218,388<br>55.0% |
| 1868[j] | 37 | Horatio Seymour<br>Francis P. Blair Jr. | Ulysses S. Grant<br>Schuyler Colfax | 80 | 214 | 2,708,744<br>47.3% | 3,013,650<br>52.7% |
| 1872[k] | 37 | Horace Greeley<br>Benjamin Gratz Brown | Ulysses S. Grant<br>Henry Wilson | | 286 | 2,834,761<br>43.8% | 3,598,235<br>55.6% |
| 1876 | 38 | Samuel J. Tilden<br>Thomas A. Hendricks | Rutherford B. Hayes<br>William A. Wheeler | 184 | 185 | 4,288,546<br>51.0% | 4,034,311<br>47.9% |
| 1880 | 38 | Winfield S. Hancock<br>William H. English | James A. Garfield<br>Chester A. Arthur | 155 | 214 | 4,444,260<br>48.2% | 4,446,158<br>48.3% |
| 1884 | 38 | Grover Cleveland<br>Thomas A. Hendricks | James G. Blaine<br>John A. Logan | 219 | 182 | 4,874,621<br>48.5% | 4,848,936<br>48.2% |

(Continued)

(Continued)

| YEAR | NO. OF STATES | CANDIDATES | | ELECTORAL VOTE | | POPULAR VOTE | |
|------|------|------|------|------|------|------|------|
| | | DEM. | REP. | DEM. | REP. | DEM. | REP. |
| 1888 | 38 | Grover Cleveland / Allen G. Thurman | Benjamin Harrison / Levi P. Morton | 168 | 233 | 5,534,488 / 48.6% | 5,443,892 / 47.8% |
| 1892[l] | 44 | Grover Cleveland / Adlai E. Stevenson | Benjamin Harrison / Whitelaw Reid | 277 | 145 | 5,551,883 / 46.1% | 5,179,244 / 43.0% |
| 1896 | 45 | William J. Bryan / Arthur Sewall | William McKinley / Garret A. Hobart | 176 | 271 | 6,511,495 / 46.7% | 7,108,480 / 51.0% |
| 1900 | 45 | William J. Bryan / Adlai E. Stevenson | William McKinley / Theodore Roosevelt | 155 | 292 | 6,358,345 / 45.5% | 7,218,039 / 51.7% |
| 1904 | 45 | Alton B. Parker / Henry G. Davis | Theodore Roosevelt / Charles W. Fairbanks | 140 | 336 | 5,028,898 / 37.6% | 7,626,593 / 56.4% |
| 1908 | 46 | William J. Bryan / John W. Kern | William H. Taft / James S. Sherman | 162 | 321 | 6,406,801 / 43.0% | 7,676,258 / 51.6% |
| 1912[m] | 48 | Woodrow Wilson / Thomas R. Marshall | William H. Taft / James S. Sherman | 435 | 8 | 6,293,152 / 41.8% | 3,486,333 / 23.2% |
| 1916 | 48 | Woodrow Wilson / Thomas R. Marshall | Charles E. Hughes / Charles W. Fairbanks | 277 | 254 | 9,126,300 / 49.2% | 8,546,789 / 46.1% |
| 1920 | 48 | James M. Cox / Franklin D. Roosevelt | Warren G. Harding / Calvin Coolidge | 127 | 404 | 9,140,884 / 34.2% | 16,133,314 / 60.3% |
| 1924[n] | 48 | John W. Davis / Charles W. Bryant | Calvin Coolidge / Charles G. Dawes | 136 | 382 | 8,386,169 / 28.8% | 15,717,553 / 54.1% |
| 1928 | 48 | Alfred E. Smith / Joseph T. Robinson | Herbert C. Hoover / Charles Curtis | 87 | 444 | 15,000,185 / 40.8% | 21,411,991 / 58.2% |
| 1932 | 48 | Franklin D. Roosevelt / John N. Garner | Herbert C. Hoover / Charles Curtis | 472 | 59 | 22,825,016 / 57.4% | 15,758,397 / 39.6% |
| 1936 | 48 | Franklin D. Roosevelt / John N. Garner | Alfred M. Landon / Frank Knox | 523 | 8 | 27,747,636 / 60.8% | 16,679,543 / 36.5% |
| 1940 | 48 | Franklin D. Roosevelt / Henry A. Wallace | Wendell L. Willkie / Charles L. McNary | 449 | 82 | 27,263,448 / 54.7% | 22,336,260 / 44.8% |
| 1944 | 48 | Franklin D. Roosevelt / Harry S. Truman | Thomas E. Dewey / John W. Bricker | 432 | 99 | 25,611,936 / 53.4% | 22,013,372 / 45.9% |
| 1948[o] | 48 | Harry S. Truman / Alben W. Barkley | Thomas E. Dewey / Earl Warren | 303 | 189 | 24,105,587 / 49.5% | 21,970,017 / 45.1% |
| 1952 | 48 | Adlai E. Stevenson II / John J. Sparkman | Dwight D. Eisenhower / Richard M. Nixon | 89 | 442 | 27,314,649 / 44.4% | 33,936,137 / 55.1% |
| 1956[p] | 48 | Adlai E. Stevenson II / Estes Kefauver | Dwight D. Eisenhower / Richard M. Nixon | 73 | 457 | 26,030,172 / 42.0% | 35,585,245 / 57.4% |
| 1960[q] | 50 | John F. Kennedy / Lyndon B. Johnson | Richard M. Nixon / Henry Cabot Lodge | 303 | 219 | 34,221,344 / 49.7% | 34,106,671 / 49.5% |
| 1964 | 50* | Lyndon B. Johnson / Hubert H. Humphrey | Barry Goldwater / William E. Miller | 486 | 52 | 43,126,584 / 61.1% | 27,177,838 / 38.5% |

| YEAR | NO. OF STATES | CANDIDATES | | ELECTORAL VOTE | | POPULAR VOTE | |
|---|---|---|---|---|---|---|---|
| | | DEM. | REP. | DEM. | REP. | DEM. | REP. |
| 1968[f] | 50* | Hubert H. Humphrey Edmund S. Muskie | Richard M. Nixon Spiro T. Agnew | 191 | 301 | 31,274,503 42.7% | 31,785,148 43.4% |
| 1972[s] | 50* | George McGovern Sargent Shriver | Richard M. Nixon Spiro T. Agnew | 17 | 520 | 29,171,791 37.5% | 47,170,179 60.7% |
| 1976[t] | 50* | Jimmy Carter Walter F. Mondale | Gerald R. Ford Robert Dole | 297 | 240 | 40,830,763 50.1% | 39,147,793 48.0% |
| 1980 | 50* | Jimmy Carter Walter F. Mondale | Ronald Reagan George H. W. Bush | 49 | 489 | 35,483,883 41.0% | 43,904,153 50.7% |
| 1984 | 50* | Walter F. Mondale Geraldine Ferraro | Ronald Reagan George H. W. Bush | 13 | 525 | 37,577,185 40.6% | 54,455,075 58.8% |
| 1988[u] | 50* | Michael S. Dukakis Lloyd Bentsen | George H. W. Bush Dan Quayle | 111 | 426 | 41,809,074 45.6% | 48,886,097 53.4% |
| 1992 | 50* | William J. Clinton Albert Gore | George H. W. Bush Dan Quayle | 370 | 168 | 44,909,326 43.0% | 39,103,882 37.4% |
| 1996 | 50* | William J. Clinton Albert Gore | Robert J. Dole Jack F. Kemp | 379 | 159 | 47,402,357 49.2% | 39,198,755 40.7% |
| 2000 | 50* | Albert Gore Joseph I. Lieberman | George W. Bush Richard B. Cheney | 266 | 271 | 50,992,335 48.4% | 50,455,156 47.9% |
| 2004 | 50* | John Kerry John Edwards | George W. Bush Richard B. Cheney | 252 | 286 | 59,026,013 47.3% | 62,025,554 50.7% |
| 2008 | 50* | Barack Obama Joe Biden | John McCain Sarah Palin | 365 | 173 | 69,498,459 52.9% | 59,948,283 45.6% |
| 2012 | 50* | Barack Obama Joe Biden | Mitt Romney Paul Ryan | 332 | 206 | 62,611,250 51.5% | 59,134,475 48.5% |
| 2016 | 50* | Hillary Clinton Tim Kaine | Donald J. Trump Michael Pence | 227** | 304** | 65,844,610 48.1% | 62,979,636 46% |

*Sources:* Harold W. Stanley and Richard G. Niemi, *Vital Statistics on American Politics, 2007–2008* (Washington, D.C.: CQ Press, 2008), 26–30; *CQ Press Guide to U.S. Elections*, 5th ed. (Washington, D.C.: CQ Press, 2006), 715–719; for the 2008 election: for presidential race electoral vote data, see *CQ Politics Election 2008*, http://innovation.cq.com/election_night08?tab2=f. For presidential race popular vote data, see the *New York Times*' Presidential Big Board, http://elections.nytimes.com/2008/results/president/votes.html. 2012 election data calculated from Politico, 2012 Presidential Election, http://www.politico.com/2012-election/map/#/President/2012/; 2016 election data from *The New York Times* at www.nytimes.com/elections/results/president.

*Note:* Dem.-Rep.—Democratic-Republican; Fed.—Federalist; Nat.-Rep.—National-Republican; Dem.—Democratic; Rep.—Republican.

a. Elections from 1789 through 1800 were held under rules that did not allow separate voting for president and vice president.

b. Popular vote returns are not shown before 1824 because consistent, reliable data are not available.

c. 1820: One electoral vote was cast for John Adams and Richard Stockton, who were not candidates.

d. 1824: All four candidates represented Democratic-Republican factions. William H. Crawford received 41 electoral votes and Henry Clay received 37 votes. Because no candidate received a majority, the election was decided (in Adams's favor) by the House of Representatives.

e. 1832: Two electoral votes were not cast.

f. 1836: Other Whig candidates receiving electoral votes were Hugh L. White, who received 26 votes, and Daniel Webster, who received 14 votes.

g. 1856: Millard Fillmore, Whig-American, received 8 electoral votes.

h. 1860: John C. Breckinridge, southern Democrat, received 72 electoral votes. John Bell, Constitutional Union, received 39 electoral votes.

i. 1864: Eighty-one electoral votes were not cast.

j. 1868: Twenty-three electoral votes were not cast.

k. 1872: Horace Greeley, Democrat, died after the election. In the Electoral College, Democratic electoral votes went to Thomas Hendricks, 42 votes; Benjamin Gratz Brown, 18 votes; Charles J. Jenkins, 2 votes; and David Davis, 1 vote. Seventeen electoral votes were not cast.

l. 1892: James B. Weaver, People's Party, received 22 electoral votes.

m. 1912: Theodore Roosevelt, Progressive Party, received 88 electoral votes.

n. 1924: Robert M. La Follette, Progressive Party, received 13 electoral votes.

o. 1948: J. Strom Thurmond, States' Rights Party, received 39 electoral votes.

p. 1956: Walter B. Jones, Democrat, received 1 electoral vote.

q. 1960: Harry Flood Byrd, Democrat, received 15 electoral votes.

r. 1968: George C. Wallace, American Independent Party, received 46 electoral votes.

s. 1972: John Hospers, Libertarian Party, received 1 electoral vote.

t. 1976: Ronald Reagan, Republican, received 1 electoral vote.

u. 1988: Lloyd Bentsen, the Democratic vice-presidential nominee, received 1 electoral vote for president.

* Fifty states plus the District of Columbia.

** Clinton received 227 electoral votes, of the 232 electors pledged to vote for her; Trump received 304 votes of the 306 electors pledged to vote for him.

# Glossary

**activism:** When judges deliberately shape judicial doctrine to conform to their personal view of the Constitution and social policy.

**affirmative action:** Policies or programs designed to expand opportunities for minorities and women and usually requiring that an organization take measures to increase the number or proportion of minorities and women in its membership or employment.

**agency loss:** The discrepancy between what citizens ideally would like their agents to do and how the agents actually behave.

**agenda control:** The capacity to set the choices available to others.

**agenda setting:** Occurs when readers and watchers of news that relates to issues or topics are influenced by what the press covers in a very specific way—it influences what they think *about*, not what they *think*.

**agent:** Someone who makes and implements decisions on behalf of someone else.

**aggregate partisanship:** The distribution, or percentage, of the electorate that identifies with each of the political parties.

**aggregate public opinion:** In a democracy, the sum of all individual opinions.

**ambivalence:** A state of mind produced when particular issues evoke attitudes and beliefs that pull in opposite directions.

**amicus curiae:** "Friend of the court." A brief filed in a lawsuit by an individual or group that is not party to the lawsuit but that has an interest in the outcome.

**Antifederalists:** A loosely organized group (never a formal political party) that opposed ratification of the Constitution, which the group believed would jeopardize individual freedom and states' rights. After ratification, the efforts of the Antifederalists led to adoption of the first ten amendments, the Bill of Rights.

**Articles of Confederation:** The compact among the thirteen original states that formed the basis of the first national government of the United States from 1777 to 1789, when it was supplanted by the Constitution.

**attitude:** An organized and consistent manner of thinking and feeling about people, groups, social issues, or, more generally, any event in one's environment.

**attorney general:** The head of the Justice Department. As the nation's chief legal officer, the attorney general of the United States represents the federal government's interests in law courts throughout the nation. The attorney general is also the chief law enforcement officer.

**Australian ballot:** A ballot prepared and distributed by government officials that places the names of all candidates on a single list and is filled out by voters in private. First adopted in the United States in 1888, the Australian ballot replaced oral voting and party-supplied ballots.

**authority:** The right to make and implement a decision.

**bargaining:** A form of negotiation in which two or more parties who disagree propose exchanges and concessions to find a course of acceptable collective action.

**beat:** A regularly assigned venue that a news reporter covers on an ongoing basis.

**bicameral legislature:** A legislature composed of two houses or chambers. The U.S. Congress (House and Senate) and every U.S. state legislature (with the exception of Nebraska's, which is unicameral) are bicameral legislatures.

**bicameralism:** The practice of having two legislative or parliamentary chambers that share power.

**Bill of Rights:** The first ten amendments to the U.S. Constitution.

**black codes:** Laws enacted by southern legislatures after the Civil War that prevented former slaves from voting and holding certain jobs, among other prohibitions.

**block grant:** A broad grant of money given by the federal government to a state government. The grant specifies the general area (such as education or health services) in which the funds may be spent but leaves it to the state to determine the specific allocations.

**blue slip:** In the Senate, a form in which a home state senator can write their views of a federal judicial nominee before a confirmation hearing can be scheduled. The process is a tradition that has been followed by both parties in the spirit of bipartisanship.

***Brandenburg* test:** A legal framework used to determine whether free speech can be limited in cases where it stands to incite violence or a crime.

**Brownlow report:** Report issued in 1937 by the President's Committee on Administrative Management that likened the president to the CEO of a large corporation and concluded that the president needed a professional staff.

**bureaucracy:** A complex structure of offices, tasks, and rules in which employees have specific responsibilities and work within a hierarchy of authority. Government bureaucracies are charged with implementing policies.

**bureaucratic culture:** The norms and regular patterns of behavior found within a bureaucratic organization. Different agencies often develop their own norms, which shape the behavior of those who work in the agency.

**cabinet:** The formal group of presidential advisers who head the major departments and agencies of the federal government. Cabinet members are chosen by the president and approved by the Senate.

**candidate:** A person who is running for elected office.

**casework:** The activity undertaken by members of Congress and their staffs to solve constituents' problems with government agencies.

**caucus:** A closed meeting of a political or legislative group to choose candidates for office or to decide issues of policy.

**central clearance:** A presidential directive requiring that all executive agency proposals, reports, and recommendations to Congress—mostly in the form of annual reports and testimony at authorization and appropriations hearings—be certified by the Office of Management and Budget as consistent with the president's policy.

**checks and balances:** A constitutional mechanism giving each branch some oversight and control of the other branches. Examples are the presidential veto, Senate approval of presidential appointments, and judicial review of presidential and congressional actions.

**chief of staff system:** The means by which a chain of command is imposed on the president's staff. The system clarifies responsibilities and shields the president from having to micromanage the staff's routine activities.

**civil liberties:** Constitutional and legal protections from government interference with personal rights and freedoms such as freedom of assembly, speech, and religion.

**civil rights:** The powers or privileges conferred on citizens by the Constitution and the courts that entitle them to make claims upon the government. Civil rights protect individuals from arbitrary or discriminatory treatment at the hands of the government.

**clear and present danger test:** A rule used by the Supreme Court to distinguish between speech protected and not protected by the First Amendment. Under this rule, the First Amendment does not protect speech aimed at inciting an illegal action.

**clear and probable danger test:** A rule introduced by Chief Justice Fred Vinson for the courts to enlist in free expression cases: "In each case [the courts] must ask whether the gravity of the 'evil,' discounted by its probability, justifies such invasion of free speech as is necessary to avoid the danger."

**closed rule:** An order from the House Rules Committee limiting floor debate on a particular bill and disallowing or limiting amendment.

**cloture:** A parliamentary procedure used to close debate. Cloture is used in the Senate to cut off filibusters. Under the current Senate rules, three-fifths of senators, or sixty, must vote for cloture to halt a filibuster except on presidential nominations to offices other than Supreme Court justice.

**coalition:** An alliance of unlike-minded individuals or groups to achieve some common purpose such as lobbying, legislating, or campaigning for the election of public officials.

**cognitive shortcut:** A mental device allowing citizens to make complex decisions based on a small amount of information. For example, a candidate's party label serves as a shortcut by telling voters much about his or her positions on issues.

**collective action:** An action taken by a group of like-minded individuals to achieve a common goal.

**collective goods:** Goods that are collectively produced and freely available for anyone's consumption.

**command:** The authority of one actor to dictate the actions of another.

**commander in chief:** The title given to the president by the Constitution that denotes the president's authority as the head of the national military.

**commerce clause:** The clause in Article I, Section 8, of the Constitution that gives Congress the authority to regulate commerce with other nations and among the states.

**committee and conference reports:** Documents submitted by committees that often instruct agencies on how Congress expects them to use their "discretion." Though not legally binding, bureaucrats ignore such instructions at their peril.

**Common Core:** A national set of education standards in mathematics and English language arts/literacy that outline what students should know and be able to do at the end of each grade (K–12).

**community standards:** The Supreme Court's 1973 ruling that a work is obscene if it is "utterly without redeeming social importance" and "to the average person, applying contemporary 'community standards,' the dominant theme of the material, taken as a whole, appeals to prurient interests."

**compromise:** Settlement in which each side concedes some of its preferences in order to secure others.

**concurring opinion:** A written opinion by a Supreme Court justice who agrees with the decision of the Court but disagrees with the rationale for reaching that decision.

**conditional party government:** The degree of authority delegated to and exercised by congressional leaders; varies with and is conditioned by the extent of election-driven ideological consensus among members.

**confederation:** A political system in which states or regional governments retain ultimate authority except for those powers they expressly delegate to a central government.

**conference committee:** A temporary joint committee of the House and Senate appointed to reconcile the differences between the two chambers on a particular piece of legislation.

**conformity costs:** The difference between what a person ideally would prefer and what the group with which that person makes collective decisions actually does. Individuals pay conformity costs whenever collective decisions produce policy outcomes that do not best serve their interests.

**conservative:** In the United States, a proponent of a political ideology that favors small or limited government, an unfettered free market, self-reliance, and traditional social norms.

**constitution:** A document outlining the formal rules and institutions of government and the limits placed on its powers.

**constitutional courts:** Category of federal courts vested with the general judicial authority outlined in Article III of the Constitution. The most important are the Supreme Court, the courts of appeals, and the ninety-four district courts. Their authority derives from that of the Supreme Court, and they are supposed to conform to its decisions.

**coordination:** The act of organizing a group to achieve a common goal. Coordination remains a prerequisite for effective collective action even after the disincentives to individual participation (that is, prisoner's dilemma problems) have been solved.

**core values:** Moral beliefs held by citizens that underlie their attitudes toward political and other issues. As integral parts of an individual's identity, these beliefs are stable and resistant to change.

**court of appeals:** The second tier of courts in the federal judicial system (between the Supreme Court and the district courts). One court of appeals serves each of eleven regions, or circuits, plus one for the District of Columbia.

**Court-packing plan:** An attempt by President Franklin Roosevelt, in 1937, to remodel the federal judiciary. Its purpose ostensibly was to alleviate the overcrowding of federal court dockets by allowing the president to appoint an additional Supreme Court justice for every sitting justice over the age of seventy. The legislation passed the House of Representatives but failed in the Senate by a single vote. If it had passed, Roosevelt could have added six new justices to the high bench, thereby installing a new Court majority sympathetic to his New Deal programs.

**credibility gap:** The widespread suspicion among reporters that presidents will lie to the media when doing so serves their interest and they think they can get away with it.

**cruel and unusual punishments:** Criminal penalties not considered appropriate by a society that involve torture or can result in death when the death penalty has not been ordered.

**cutthroat competition:** Competition among states that involves adopting policies that each state would prefer to avoid. For example, states engage in cutthroat competition when they underbid one another on tax breaks to attract businesses relocating their facilities.

**Declaration of Independence:** The document drafted by Thomas Jefferson and adopted by the Second Continental Congress on July 4, 1776, declaring the independence of the thirteen colonies from Great Britain.

**de facto segregation:** Segregation that results from practice rather than from law.

**de jure segregation:** Segregation enacted into law and imposed by the government.

**delegation:** The act of one person or body authorizing another person or body to perform an action on its behalf. For example, Congress often delegates authority to the president or administrative agencies to decide the details of policy.

**detailed staff:** Staff from another government agency sent to assist the White House.

**direct democracy:** A system of government in which citizens make policy decisions by voting on legislation themselves rather than by delegating that authority to their representatives.

**discharge petition:** A petition that removes a measure from a committee to which it has been referred in order to make it available for floor consideration. In the House a discharge petition must be signed by a majority of House members (218).

**dissenting opinion:** The written opinion of one or more Supreme Court justices who disagree with the ruling of the Court's majority. The opinion outlines the rationale for their disagreement.

**district courts:** The trial courts of original jurisdiction in the federal judicial system. The ninety-four district courts are the third tier of the federal judicial system, below the Supreme Court and the courts of appeals.

**divided government:** A term used to describe government when one political party controls the

executive branch and the other political party controls one or both houses of the legislature.

**dual federalism:** A system of government in which the federal government and state governments each have mutually exclusive spheres of action.

**due process clause:** A clause found in both the Fifth and Fourteenth Amendments to the Constitution protecting citizens from arbitrary action by the national and state governments.

**earmarks:** Money set aside by Congress in the federal budget to pay for projects in the home district of a member of Congress.

**elastic clause:** Allows Congress to "make all Laws which shall be necessary and proper for carrying into Execution the foregoing Powers."

**Electoral College:** A body of electors in each state, chosen by voters, who formally elect the president and vice president of the United States. Each state's number of electoral votes equals its representation in Congress; the District of Columbia has three votes. An absolute majority of the total electoral vote is required to elect a president and vice president.

**embedding:** Military media strategy of putting journalists among military units in the field.

**enrolled bill:** A bill that has been passed by both the Senate and the House and has been sent to the president for approval.

**entitlement:** A benefit every eligible person has a legal right to receive that cannot be taken away without a change in legislation or due process in court.

**entitlement reform:** The "reform" of entitlements is a political code word for cuts to maintain the long-term solvency of the Social Security and Medicare system, to which senior citizens are entitled upon reaching a certain age.

**enumerated powers:** The explicit powers given to Congress by the Constitution in Article I, Section 8. These include the powers of taxation, coinage of money, regulation of commerce, and provision for the national defense.

**equal protection clause:** A Fourteenth Amendment clause guaranteeing all citizens equal protection of the laws. The courts have interpreted the clause to bar discrimination against minorities and women.

**equal time:** A "fairness" rule established by the Federal Communications Commission to ensure that broadcasters offer balanced coverage of controversial issues. If a radio or television station sells or gives airtime to one candidate for political office, it must provide other candidates with equal time.

**establishment of religion clause:** The first clause of the First Amendment. The establishment clause prohibits the national government from establishing a national religion.

**exclusionary rule:** A judicial rule prohibiting the police from using at trial evidence obtained through illegal search and seizure.

**executive agreement:** An agreement between the president and one or more other countries. An executive agreement is similar to a treaty, but unlike a treaty, it does not require the approval of the Senate.

**Executive Office of the President (EOP):** A collection of agencies that help the president oversee department and agency activities, formulate budgets and monitor spending, craft legislation, and lobby Congress. The major components of the EOP, established in 1939 by President Franklin Roosevelt, include the White House Office, Office of Management and Budget, National Security Council, and Council of Economic Advisers, among other agencies.

**executive order:** A presidential directive to an executive agency establishing new policies or indicating how an existing policy is to be carried out.

**externality:** Public goods or bads generated as by-products of private activity. For example, air pollution is an externality (public bad) because it is, in part, the by-product of the private activity of driving a car.

**faction:** A group of people sharing common interests who are opposed to other groups with competing interests. James Madison defined a faction as any group with objectives contrary to the general interests of society.

**fast-track authority:** Impermanent power granted by Congress to the president to negotiate international trade agreements.

**federal question:** A case directly involving the U.S. Constitution, federal laws, or treaties.

*Federal Register:* A government publication listing all proposed federal regulations.

**federalism:** A system of government in which power is divided between a central government and several regional governments. In the United States the division is between the national government and the states.

**Federalists:** Name given to two related, but not identical, groups in late-eighteenth-century American politics. The first group, led by Alexander Hamilton and James Madison, supported ratification of the Constitution in 1787 and 1788. Subsequently, Hamilton and John Adams led the second group, the Federalist Party, which dominated national politics during the administrations of George Washington (1789–1797) and Adams (1797–1801).

**filibuster:** A tactic used in the Senate to halt action on a bill. It involves making long speeches until the majority retreats. Senators, once holding the floor, have unlimited time to speak unless a cloture vote is passed by three-fifths (sixty) of the members.

**fire alarms:** The type of oversight in which Congress does not act directly but instead sets up processes that allow organized groups and private individuals to detect failures in the implementation of laws and to alert Congress.

**fiscal cliff:** A term that describes the teetering finances of federal, state, and local governments.

**focal point:** Focus identified by participants when coordinating their energies to achieve a common purpose.

**focus group:** A method of gauging public opinion by observing a small number of people brought together to discuss specific issues, usually under the guidance of a moderator.

**framing:** Providing a context that affects the criteria citizens use to evaluate candidates, campaigns, and political issues.

**franking privilege:** The legal right of each member of Congress to send official mail postage-free under his or her signature.

**free exercise clause:** The second clause of the First Amendment. The free exercise clause forbids the national government from interfering with the exercise of religion.

**free-rider problem:** A situation in which individuals can receive the benefits from a collective activity whether or not they helped to pay for it, leaving them with no incentive to contribute.

**Fugitive Slave Law:** The 1850 law compelling northerners to honor southerners' property claims to slaves, passed in return for the South's agreeing to admit California as a free state (and hence lose its ability to block legislation in the Senate).

**gerrymandering:** Drawing legislative districts in such a way as to give one political party a disproportionately large share of seats for the share of votes its candidates win.

**global commons:** A common resource used by the international community, such as the environment.

**going public:** Presidents "go public" when they engage in intensive public relations to promote their policies to the voters and thereby induce cooperation from other elected officeholders in Washington.

**government:** The institutions and procedures through which people are ruled.

**Government Accountability Office:** Office with a staff of more than five thousand that audits programs and agencies and reports to Congress on their performance.

**grandfather clauses:** Statutes stating that only those people whose grandfather had voted before Reconstruction could vote, unless they passed a literacy or wealth test. After the Civil War this mechanism was used to disenfranchise African Americans.

**grants-in-aid:** Funds given by Congress to state or local governments for a specific purpose.

**grassroots lobbying:** Lobbying conducted by rank-and-file members of an interest group.

**Great Compromise:** The agreement between large and small states at the Constitutional Convention (1787) that decided the selection and composition of Congress. The compromise stipulated that the lower chamber (House of Representatives) be chosen by direct popular vote and that the upper chamber (Senate) be selected by the state legislatures. Representation in the House would be proportional to a state's population; in the Senate each state would have two members.

**gridlock:** A legislative "traffic jam" often precipitated by divided government. Gridlock occurs when presidents confront opposition-controlled Congresses with policy preferences and political stakes that are in direct competition with their own and those of their party. Neither side is willing to compromise, the government accomplishes little, and federal operations may even come to a halt.

**hate crime:** A violent crime directed against individuals, property, or organizations solely because of the victims' race, gender, national origin, or sexual orientation.

**hearings and investigations:** Meetings in which bureaucrats are called before subcommittees to explain and defend their decisions, and outsiders are sometimes invited to criticize them. Most agencies must testify annually about their activities before the House Appropriations subcommittee that has jurisdiction over their budgets.

**home rule:** Power given by a state to a locality to enact legislation and manage its own affairs locally. Home rule also applies to Britain's administration of the American colonies.

**ideology:** A comprehensive, integrated set of views about government and politics.

**incitement:** The government cannot forbid "advocacy of the use of force or of law violation" unless the advocacy is "directed to inciting or producing imminent lawless action and is likely to incite or produce such action."

**incorporation:** The Supreme Court's extension of the guarantees of the Bill of Rights to state and local governments through its various interpretations of the Fourteenth Amendment.

**infotainment:** Increasingly popular, nontraditional source of political information that combines news and entertainment. Examples include talk shows and political comedy programs.

**initiative:** An approach to direct democracy in which a proposal is placed on an election ballot when the requisite number of registered voters have signed petitions.

**insider tactics:** Interest group activity that includes normal lobbying on Capitol Hill, working closely with members of Congress, and contributing money to incumbents' campaigns. Contrasts with *outsider tactics*.

**inspectors general:** Positions with independent offices (outside the normal bureaucratic chain of command) in virtually every government agency that audit agency books and investigate activities on Congress's behalf.

**institution:** In a democracy, an organization that manages potential conflicts between political rivals, helps them to find mutually acceptable solutions, and makes and enforces the society's collective agreements. Among the prominent federal political institutions in the United States are Congress, the presidency, and the Supreme Court.

**institutional design:** The construction of political institutions and processes for managing conflicts and reaching collective agreements between competing interests.

**interest groups:** Organized groups of people seeking to influence public policy.

**iron triangle:** A stable, mutually beneficial political relationship among a congressional committee (or subcommittee), an administrative agency, and organized interests concerned with a particular policy domain.

**issue network:** A loose, informal, and highly variable web of relationships among representatives of various interests involved in a particular area of public policy.

**issue publics:** Groups of citizens who are more attentive to particular areas of public policy than average citizens because such groups have some special stake in the issues.

**issue voting:** Voting for candidates based on their positions on specific issues, as opposed to their party or personal characteristics.

**Jim Crow laws:** A series of laws enacted in the late nineteenth century by southern states to institute segregation. These laws created "whites only" public accommodations such as schools, hotels, and restaurants.

**joint committees:** Permanent congressional committees made up of members of both the House and the Senate. Joint committees do not have any legislative authority; they monitor specific activities and compile reports.

**judicial doctrine:** The practice of prescribing in a decision a set of rules that are to guide future decisions on similar cases. Used by the Supreme Court to guide the lower courts in making decisions.

**judicial review:** The authority of a court to declare legislative and executive acts unconstitutional and therefore invalid.

**Kyoto Protocol:** An international agreement on climate change that commits its signatories to setting internationally binding emission reduction targets.

**leak:** Strategically consequential information given to reporters on the condition that its source not be identified by name.

**legislative veto:** A procedure that allows one or both houses of Congress to reject an action taken by the president or an executive agency. In 1983 the Supreme Court declared legislative vetoes unconstitutional, but Congress continues to enact legislation incorporating the veto.

***Lemon* test:** The most far-reaching of the controversial cases in which the Supreme Court specified three conditions every state law must satisfy to avoid running afoul of the establishment of religion prohibition: the statute in question "must have a secular legislative purpose," such as remedial education; the statute's "primary effect must be one that neither advances nor inhibits religion"; and the statute must not foster "an excessive government entanglement with religion."

**libel:** A published falsehood or statement resulting in the defamation of someone's character. The First Amendment does not protect libelous statements.

**liberal:** In the United States, a proponent of a political ideology that favors extensive government action to redress social and economic inequalities and tolerates social behaviors that conservatives view as deviant. Present-day liberals advocate policies benefiting the poor, minority groups, labor unions, women, and the environment and oppose government imposition of traditional social norms.

**limitation riders:** Amendments, attached to appropriations bills, that forbid an agency to spend any of the money appropriated on activities specified by Congress.

**line-item veto:** A procedure, available in 1997 for the first time, permitting a president to cancel amounts of new discretionary appropriations (budget authority), as well as new items of direct spending (entitlements) and certain limited tax benefits, unless Congress disapproves by law within a specified period of time. It was declared unconstitutional in 1998.

**literacy test:** A legal barrier used to exclude African Americans from voting. Local white registrars would require prospective black voters to read and interpret arcane passages of the state's constitution. Because few satisfied these registrars' rigorous demands, by 1910 fewer than 10 percent of black men were voting in the South.

**lobbying:** Activities through which individuals, interest groups, and other institutions seek to influence public policy by persuading government officials to support their groups' position.

**lobbyists:** Professionals who work to influence public policy in favor of their clients' interests.

**logroll:** The result of legislative vote trading. For example, legislators representing urban districts may vote for an agricultural bill provided that legislators from rural districts vote for a mass transit bill.

**majority leader:** The formal leader of the party controlling a majority of the seats in the House or the Senate. In the Senate the majority leader is the head of the majority party. In the House the majority leader ranks second in the party hierarchy behind the Speaker.

**majority (minority) whip:** Majority (minority) party official in Congress charged with managing communications between party leaders and members.

**majority rule:** The principle that decisions should reflect the preferences of more than half of those voting. Decision-making by majority rule is one of the fundamental procedures of democracy.

**mandatory reports:** Method by which Congress keeps its bureaucratic agents in line, in this case requiring executive agencies—even the president—to report on programs.

**matching grant:** A grant of money given by the federal government to a state government for which the federal government provides matching funds, usually between one and two dollars, for every dollar the state spends in some area.

**measurement error:** Uncertainties in public opinion, as revealed by responses to polls, that arise from the imperfect connection between the wording of survey questions and the terms in which people understand and think about political objects.

**message:** In a political campaign, the central thematic statement of why voters ought to prefer one candidate over others.

**microtargeting:** The process of targeting very specific groups of potential voters. For example, using databases that combine voter rolls with credit card purchase information or grocery store savings club records to identify potential supporters.

*Miranda* **rule:** Requirement that police inform suspects that they have a right to remain silent and a right to have counsel while being interrogated. Failure to inform suspects of their rights will result in any confession or evidence thus obtained being inadmissible against them at trial.

**mobilization:** Also known as "getting out the vote." Mobilization occurs when activists working for parties, candidates, or interest groups ask members of the electorate to vote.

**moral incentives:** The personal satisfactions of active self-expression through contribution or other involvement to social causes.

**multiple referral:** The act of sending a proposed piece of legislation to more than one committee in the same chamber.

**national party convention:** A gathering of delegates to select a party's presidential and vice presidential ticket and to adopt its national platform.

**National Security Council (NSC):** The highest advisory body to the president on military and diplomatic issues. Established in 1947, this agency in the Executive Office of the President helps the president coordinate the actions of government agencies, including the State and Defense Departments and the Joint Chiefs of Staff, into a single cohesive policy for dealing with other nations.

**nationalists:** Constitutional reformers led by James Madison and Alexander Hamilton who sought to replace the Articles of Confederation. Opposed at the Constitutional Convention (1787) by states' rights proponents, the nationalists favored a strong national legislature elected directly by the citizenry rather than the states and a national government that could veto any state laws it deemed unfit.

**nationalization:** Shifting to the national government responsibilities traditionally exercised by the states.

**necessary and proper clause:** The last clause of Article I, Section 8, of the Constitution. This clause grants Congress the authority to make all laws that are "necessary and proper" and to execute those laws.

**negative or attack campaigning:** Campaign content that attacks an opponent's position on an issue, performance in office, or personal traits.

**neutrality test:** Policy favored by justices in establishment of religion decisions. The justices used the neutrality test not so much to prevent favoritism among religious groups as to root out policies that preferred religious groups generally over nonreligious groups engaged in a similar activity.

**New Deal coalition:** An electoral alliance that was the basis of Democratic dominance from the 1930s to the early 1970s. The alliance consisted of Catholics, Jews, racial minorities, urban residents, organized labor, and white southerners.

**New Jersey Plan:** New Jersey delegate William Paterson's proposal for reforming the Articles of Confederation. Introduced at the Constitutional Convention (1787), the New Jersey Plan was favored by delegates who supported states' rights.

**news outlets:** The organizations that gather, package, and transmit the news through some proprietary communications technology.

**nominating convention:** A political convention used to select a candidate to run in an upcoming election.

**nullification:** A legal doctrine that allows a state to void any federal law that could be deemed unconstitutional.

**obscenity:** Defined as publicly offensive acts or language, usually of a sexual nature, with no redeeming social value. The Supreme Court has offered varying definitions in its rulings over the years.

**office:** Subdivision of some government departments that confers on its occupants specific authority and responsibilities.

**Office of Management and Budget (OMB):** Previously known as the Bureau of the Budget, OMB is the most important agency in the Executive Office of the President. The budget bureau, created in 1921 to act as a central clearinghouse for all budget requests, was renamed and given increased responsibilities in 1970. OMB advises the president on fiscal and economic policies, creates the annual federal budget, and monitors agency performance, among other duties.

**open rule:** A provision governing debate of a pending bill and permitting any germane amendment to be offered on the floor of the House.

**opinion leader:** A citizen who is highly attentive to and involved in politics or some related area and to whom other citizens turn for political information and cues.

**outsider tactics:** Interest group activities designed to influence elected officials by threatening to impose political costs on them if they do not respond. Tactics

include marches, demonstrations, campaign contributions to opponents, and electoral mobilization.

**pack journalism:** A method of news gathering in which news reporters all follow the same story in the same way because they read one another's copy for validation of their own.

**Paris Agreement:** The international agreement reached in December 2015 by developed and developing nations alike to reduce their greenhouse gas emissions, beginning in 2020, through the United Nations Framework Convention on Climate Change.

**parliamentary government:** A form of government in which the chief executive is chosen by the majority party or by a coalition of parties in the legislature.

**party identification:** An individual's enduring affective or instrumental attachment to one of the political parties; the most accurate single predictor of voting behavior.

**party label:** A label carrying the party's "brand name," incorporating the policy positions and past performance voters attribute to it.

**party machines:** State or local party organizations based on patronage. They work to elect candidates to public offices that control government jobs and contracts, which, in turn, are used by party leaders (often denigrated as "bosses") to reward the subleaders and activists who mobilize voters for the party on Election Day.

**patronage:** The practice of awarding jobs, grants, licenses, or other special favors in exchange for political support.

**penumbras:** Judicially created rights based on various guarantees of the Bill of Rights. The right to privacy is not explicitly stated in the Constitution, but the Supreme Court has argued that this right is implicit in various clauses found throughout the Bill of Rights.

**performance voting:** Basing votes for a candidate or party on how successfully the candidate or party performed while in office.

**pluralism:** A theory describing a political system in which all significant social interests freely compete with one another for influence over the government's policy decisions.

**plurality:** Rule in electing members of Congress by which the candidate who receives the most votes wins, regardless of whether the plurality reaches a majority.

**pocket veto:** A method by which the president vetoes a bill passed by both houses of Congress by failing to act on it within ten days of Congress's adjournment.

**police patrols:** The type of oversight in which Congress directly monitors agencies to ensure they are implementing laws faithfully, doing this visibly so bureaucrats will notice that they are being watched and stay in line.

**policy gridlock:** Political paralysis in the face of pressing national problems.

**political action committee (PAC):** A federally registered fund-raising group that pools money from individuals to give to political candidates and parties.

**political party:** A coalition of people who seek to control the machinery of government by winning elections. Not specifically mentioned in the Constitution, political parties make mass democracy possible by, among other functions, coordinating the group activities necessary to translate public preferences into public policy.

**political socialization:** The process by which citizens acquire their political beliefs and values.

**politicians:** A small group of professionals tasked by society with discovering and coordinating mutually attractive collective decisions.

**politics:** The process through which individuals and groups reach agreement on a course of common, or collective, action—even as they disagree on the intended goals of that action.

**poll tax:** A tax imposed on people when they register to vote. In the decades after the Civil War this tax was used primarily to disenfranchise black voters. With passage of the Twenty-Fourth Amendment, in 1964, it became unconstitutional.

**popular sovereignty:** Citizens' delegation of authority to their agents in government, with the ability to rescind that authority.

**"pork barrel" legislation:** Legislation that provides members of Congress with federal projects and programs for their individual districts.

**power:** An officeholder's actual influence with other officeholders and, as a consequence, over the government's actions.

**preemption legislation:** Laws passed by Congress that override or preempt state or local policies. The power of preemption derives from the supremacy clause (Article VI) of the Constitution. (See also *supremacy clause*.)

**preferences:** Individuals' choices, reflecting economic situation, religious values, ethnic identity, or other valued interests.

**president pro tempore:** In the absence of the vice president, the formal presiding officer of the Senate. The honor is usually conferred on the senior member of the majority party, but the post is sometimes rotated among senators of the majority party.

**presidential memorandum:** A presidential directive to an agency directing it to alter its administration of policies along lines prescribed in the memorandum. When a presidential memorandum is published in the *Federal Register*, it assumes the same legal standing of an executive order.

**primary election:** An election held before the general election in which voters decide which of a party's candidates will be the party's nominee for the general election.

**priming:** Occurs when readers and watchers of news that relates to the criteria with which we evaluate candidates or elected leaders are influenced by what the press covers in a very specific way—it influences what they think *about*, not what they *think*.

**principal:** Someone who possesses decision-making authority; may delegate their authority to *agents*, who then exercise it on behalf of the principals.

**prior restraint:** A government agency's act to prohibit the publication of material or speech before the fact. The courts forbid prior restraint except under extraordinary conditions.

**prisoner's dilemma:** A situation in which two (or more) actors cannot agree to cooperate for fear that the other will find its interest best served by reneging on an agreement.

**private goods:** Benefits and services over which the owner has full control of their use.

**privatize:** To prevent a common resource from being overexploited by tying the benefit of its consumption to its cost.

**privileges and immunities clause:** The clause in Section I of the Fourteenth Amendment stipulating that "no State shall make or enforce any law which shall abridge the privileges or immunities of citizens of the United States."

**procedural doctrine:** Principle of law that governs how the lower courts do their work.

**Progressive Era:** A period of American history extending roughly from 1880 to 1920 and associated with the reform of government and electoral institutions in an attempt to reduce corruption and weaken parties.

**proportional representation:** An electoral system in which legislative seats are awarded to candidates or parties in proportion to the percentage of votes received.

**public goods:** Goods collectively produced and freely available for anyone's consumption.

**public interest lobby:** A group that promotes some conception of the public interest rather than the narrowly defined economic

or other special interests of its members.

**public opinion:** "Those opinions held by private persons which governments find it prudent to heed."

**quorum:** The minimum number of congressional members who must be present for the transaction of business. Under the Constitution, a quorum in each house is a majority of its members: 218 in the House and 51 in the Senate when there are no vacancies.

**quotas:** Specific shares of college admissions, government contracts, and jobs set aside for population groups that have suffered from past discrimination. The Supreme Court has rejected the use of quotas wherever it has encountered them.

**race to the bottom:** When states "race," or compete, to provide a minimum level of services (such as welfare spending) or regulation (such as tax incentives for corporations). There remains much debate over whether states do indeed race toward the bottom.

**racial profiling:** Identifying the suspects of a crime solely on the basis of their race or ethnicity.

**red tape:** Excessive paperwork leading to bureaucratic delay. The term originated in the seventeenth century, when English legal and governmental documents were bound with red-colored tape.

**referendum:** An approach to direct democracy in which a state legislature proposes a change to the state's laws or constitution that all the voters subsequently vote on.

**regulation:** Setting up rules limiting access to a common resource and monitoring and penalizing those who violate them.

**representative government:** A political system in which citizens select government officials who, acting as their agents, deliberate and commit the citizenry to a course of collective action.

**republic:** A form of democracy in which power is vested in elected representatives.

**restraint:** The judicial action of deferring to the policies emanating from the elected branches in the absence of a clear violation of the Constitution or established doctrine.

**restricted rule:** A provision that governs consideration of a bill and specifies and limits the kinds of amendments that may be made on the floor of the House of Representatives.

**rider:** An amendment to a bill that is not germane to the legislation.

**roll-call vote:** Vote taken by a call of the roll to determine whether a quorum is present, to establish a quorum, or to vote on a question. Usually the House uses its electronic voting system for a roll call, but when the system is malfunctioning the Speaker directs the clerk to read the names. The Senate does not have an electronic voting system; its roll is always called by a clerk.

**rotation in office:** The practice of citizens serving in public office for a limited term and then returning to private life.

**rule:** A provision that governs consideration of a bill by the House of Representatives by specifying how the bill is to be debated and amended.

**rule of four:** A rule used by the Supreme Court stating that when four justices support hearing a case the certiorari petition is granted.

**scientific polling:** Tool developed in the twentieth century for systematically investigating the opinions of ordinary people, based on random samples.

**segregation:** The political and social practice of separating whites and blacks into dual and highly unequal schools, hospitals, prisons, public parks, housing, and public transportation.

**select committee:** A temporary legislative committee created for a specific purpose and dissolved after its tasks are completed.

**selective incentives:** Private goods or benefits that induce rational actors to participate in a collective effort to provide a collective good.

**selective incorporation:** The Supreme Court's gradual process of assuming guardianship of civil liberties by applying piecemeal the various provisions of the Bill of Rights to state laws and practices.

**senatorial courtesy:** An informal practice in which senators are given veto power over federal judicial appointments in their home states.

**seniority rule:** The congressional practice of appointing as committee or subcommittee chairs the members of the majority with the most years of committee service.

**separate but equal doctrine:** The Supreme Court–initiated doctrine that separate but equivalent facilities for African Americans and whites are constitutional under the equal protection clause of the Fourteenth Amendment.

**separation of powers:** The distribution of government powers among several political institutions. In the United States, at the national level power is divided between the three branches: Congress, the president, and the Supreme Court.

**shared federalism:** A system in which the national and state governments share in providing citizens with a set of goods.

**Shays's Rebellion:** Uprising of 1786 led by Daniel Shays, a former captain in the Continental Army and a bankrupt Massachusetts farmer, to protest the state's high taxes and aggressive debt collection policies. The rebellion demonstrated a fundamental weakness of the Articles of Confederation—its inability to keep the peace—and stimulated interest in strengthening the national government, leading to the Philadelphia convention that framed the Constitution.

**shield laws:** Laws that protect journalists from having to testify about their sources in court.

**signing statement:** A statement issued by the president that is intended to modify implementation or ignore altogether provisions of a new law.

**simple majority:** A majority of 50 percent plus one.

**single-issue voters:** People who base their votes on candidates' or parties' positions on one particular issue of public policy, regardless of the candidates' or parties' positions on other issues.

**slander:** Forms of false and malicious information that damage another person's reputation.

**social movements:** Amorphous aggregates of people sharing general values and a desire for social change.

**soft money:** Money used by political parties for voter registration, public education, and voter mobilization. Until 2002, when Congress passed legislation outlawing soft money, the government had imposed no limits on contributions or expenditures for such purposes.

**solicitor general:** The official responsible for representing the U.S. government before the Supreme Court. The solicitor general is a ranking member of the U.S. Department of Justice.

**sound bite:** A catchy phrase or slogan that encapsulates a politician's message, broadcast especially on television news programs.

**Speaker of the House:** The presiding officer of the House of Representatives. The Speaker is elected at the beginning of each congressional session on a party-line vote. As head of the majority party, the Speaker has substantial control over the legislative agenda of the House.

**special committee:** A temporary legislative committee, usually lacking legislative authority.

**split ticket:** The act of voting for candidates from different political parties for different offices—for example, voting for a Republican for president and a Democrat for senator.

**spoils system:** A system in which newly elected officeholders award government jobs to political supporters and members of the same political party. The term originated in the saying "to the victor go the spoils."

**standing:** The right to bring legal action.

**standing committee:** A permanent legislative committee specializing in a particular legislative area. Standing committees have stable memberships and stable jurisdictions.

*stare decisis:* "Let the decision stand." In court rulings, a reliance on precedents, or previous rulings, in formulating decisions in new cases.

**State of the Union address:** A message to Congress under the constitutional directive that the president shall "from time to time give to the Congress Information of the State of the Union, and recommend to their Consideration such Measures as he shall judge necessary and expedient."

**states' rights:** Safeguards against a too-powerful national government that were favored by one group of delegates to the Constitutional Convention (1787). States' rights advocates supported retaining those features of the Articles of Confederation that guarded state prerogatives, such as state participation in the selection of national officeholders and equal representation for each state regardless of population.

**status quo bias:** Institutional bias that fundamentally favors continuation of current public policy.

**substantive doctrine:** Principle that guides judges on which party in a case should prevail—akin to policymaking.

**suffragists:** Women who campaigned in the early twentieth century for the right of women to vote.

**superdelegate:** A delegate to the Democratic National Convention who is eligible to attend because he or she is an elected party official. The Democrats reserve a specific set of delegate slots for party officials.

**supermajority:** A majority larger than a simple 51 percent majority, which is required for extraordinary legislative actions such as amending the Constitution or certain congressional procedures. For example, in the Senate sixty votes are required to stop a filibuster.

**supremacy clause:** A clause in Article VI of the Constitution declaring that national laws are the "supreme" law of the land and therefore take precedence over any laws adopted by states or localities.

**"take care" clause:** The provision in Article II, Section 3, of the Constitution instructing the president to "take Care that the Laws be faithfully executed."

**Tenth Amendment:** The amendment that offers the most explicit endorsement of federalism to be found in the Constitution: "The powers not delegated to the United States by the Constitution, nor prohibited by it to the States, are reserved to the States respectively, or to the people."

**term limits:** A movement begun during the 1980s to limit the number of terms both state legislators and members of Congress can serve.

**ticket-splitting:** (See *split ticket.*)

**Title IX:** A provision added to a federal aid to higher education law in 1972 that implements antidiscrimination policies based on gender. The Civil Rights Act of 1964 prohibits gender-based discrimination in principal. Title IX spells out federal oversight of colleges' and universities' practices initially with regard to support of intercollegiate sports but increasingly with regard to sexual harassment.

**tragedy of the commons:** A situation in which group members overexploit a common resource, causing its destruction.

**transaction costs:** The costs of doing political business reflected in the time and effort required to compare preferences and negotiate compromises in making collective decisions.

**trial balloon:** Policy announced by the president in order to test public opinion and floated either by members of Congress or the media.

**two-party system:** A political system in which only two major parties compete for all of the elective offices. Third-party candidates usually have few, if any, chances of winning elective office.

**tyranny:** A form of government in which the ruling power exploits its authority and permits little popular control.

**unanimous consent agreement:** A unanimous resolution in the Senate restricting debate and limiting amendments to bills on the floor.

**unitary executive:** When a president claims prerogative to attach signing statements to bills and asserts his or her right to modify implementation or ignore altogether provisions of a new law that encroaches on his or her constitutional prerogatives as the chief executive or as commander in chief.

**unitary government:** A system of government in which a single government unit holds the power to govern the nation (in contrast to a federal system, in which power is shared among many governing units). (See also *federalism*.)

**unitary theory:** A theory of American constitutional law holding that the president has the power to control the entire executive branch. The doctrine is rooted in Article II of the Constitution.

**veto:** The formal power of the president to reject bills passed by both houses of Congress. A veto can be overridden by a two-thirds vote in each house.

**Virginia Plan:** Constitutional blueprint drafted by James Madison that sought to reform the Articles of Confederation. Introduced at the Constitutional Convention (1787), the plan proposed a tripartite national government, but unlike the subsequent Constitution, it provided for a popularly elected legislature that would dominate national policymaking.

**voting rules:** Rules prescribing who votes and the minimum number of votes required to accept a proposal or elect a candidate.

**War Powers Act:** Law that requires the president to inform Congress within forty-eight hours of committing troops abroad in a military action.

**whistle-blower laws:** Whistle blower laws encourage employees to disclose information about government actions that are illegal, wasteful, or corrupt by protecting their job status from reprisals. In some cases, these laws provide whistle-blowers with generous rewards for recovering resources. This device helps principals keep tabs on their agents.

**White House Office:** Agency in the Executive Office of the President (EOP) that serves as the president's personal staff system. Although the entire EOP does the president's business, the White House staff consists of the president's personal advisers, who oversee the political and policy interests of the administration.

**white primary:** A practice that permitted political parties to exclude African Americans from voting in primary elections. Because historically in the South winning the Democratic primary was tantamount to winning the general election, this law in effect disenfranchised black voters in southern states.

**writ of certiorari:** An order given by a superior court to an appellate court that directs the lower court to send up a case the superior court has chosen to review. This is the central means by which the Supreme Court determines what cases it will hear.

**writ of mandamus:** "We command." A court-issued writ commanding a public official to carry out a specific act or duty.

**"yellow journalism":** Style of journalism born of intense competition and characterized by screaming headlines and sensational stories. Coined at the end of the nineteenth century, the term referred to the yellow ink in which the *New York World*'s comic strips were printed.

**Young Invincibles:** Young adults who typically have not had major health crises and who thus feel "invincible" and are unlikely to purchase health insurance.

# Notes

## Chapter 1

1. James Harrington, *The Commonwealth of Oceana and a System of Politics* (1656; reprinted, ed. J. G. Pocock, New York: Cambridge University Press, 1992).
2. C. R. Hallpike, "Functionalist Interpretations of Primitive Warfare," *Man* (September 1973). Cited in Russell Hardin, "Hobbesian Political Order," *Political Theory* (May 1991): 168.
3. Thomas Hobbes, *Leviathan, or the Matter, Forme, & Power of a Commonwealth Ecclesiasticall and Civill* (1651; reprint, Oxford: Clarendon Press, 1958).
4. Russell Gold and Erin Ailworth, "Oil Firms' Predicament: Who Should Cut Output?" *Wall Street Journal,* December 23, 2014.
5. Ryan Lizza, "The Final Push," *The New Yorker,* October 29, 2012, 67.
6. Moriah Balingit and Danielle Douglas-Gabriel, "'Preparing for the Worst': Unions Brace for Loss of Members and Fees in Wake of Supreme Court Ruling," *Washington Post,* June 27, 2018.
7. Mark Kurlansky, *Cod: A Biography of the Fish That Changed the World* (New York: Walker, 1997).
8. Nathaniel Philbrick, *Mayflower* (New York: Viking, 2006), 165.
9. Eric M. Anicich, Roderick I. Swaab, and Adam D. Galinsky, "Hierarchical Cultural Values Predict Success and Mortality in High-Stakes Teams," *Proceedings of the National Academy of Sciences,* 112 (2015).
10. They were, among others, the French philosopher Baron de Montesquieu (1689–1755) and the English philosopher John Locke (1632–1704).

## Chapter 2

1. Wayne Carp, *To Starve the Army at Pleasure: Continental Army Administration and American Political Culture, 1775–1783* (Chapel Hill: University of North Carolina Press, 1984), 197. During 1780 Washington frequently repeated this warning in correspondence with political leaders.
2. Letter from John Adams to Timothy Pickering, August 22, 1822, in *John Adams, Life and Works,* Vol. 2, ed. Charles Francis Adams (Boston: Little, Brown, 1850–1856).
3. This expression comes from Revolutionary War general Nathanael Greene—see Carp, *To Starve the Army at Pleasure,* 196. Remarkably, although the field commanders showered Congress with contempt, none ever suggested that the military could do a better job of running the government.
4. Gordon S. Wood, *The Creation of the American Republic: 1776–1787* (New York: Norton, 1969), 405–410.
5. Letter to Thomas Jefferson, October 17, 1788, in William T. Hutchinson et al., eds., *The Papers of James Madison,* Vol. 9 (Chicago: University of Chicago Press, 1962).
6. This discussion follows David P. Szatmary's treatment in *Shays's Rebellion: The Making of an Agrarian Insurrection* (Amherst: University of Massachusetts Press, 1980), 120–134.
7. John Locke, *Essay Concerning the True Original Extent and End of Civil Government. Second Treatise of Government,* ed. C. B. Macpherson (Indianapolis, IN: Hackett, 1980).
8. William Lee Miller, *The Business of May Next: James Madison and the Founding* (Charlottesville: University Press of Virginia, 1992), 87.
9. *Marbury v. Madison,* 1 Cr. 137 (1803).
10. Quoted in James MacGregor Burns, *The Vineyard of Liberty* (New York: Vintage, 1983), 28.
11. Catherine Drinker Bowen, *Miracle at Philadelphia: The*

*Story of the Constitutional Convention, May to September 1787* (Boston: Atlantic–Little, Brown, 1966), 278.

12. See Locke, *Essay Concerning the True Original Extent and End of Civil Government;* and David Hume, "The Perfect Commonwealth," in *Essays, Moral, Political, and Literary,* ed. Eugene F. Miller (Indianapolis, IN: Liberty Fund, 1987). In 1776 Madison had urged fellow members of the Virginia House of Burgesses to embrace a multitude of religious sects in promoting religious reform, proposing that "all men are equally entitled to enjoy the free exercise of religion, according to the dictates of conscience." Ralph Ketcham, *James Madison: A Biography* (Charlottesville: University Press of Virginia, 1990), 72. In an essay on the "vices" of republican governments, Madison fleshed out the argument more fully and applied it to political factions. Also see Douglas Adair, "'That Politics May Be Reduced to a Science,' David Hume, James Madison and the Tenth *Federalist,*" *Huntington Library Quarterly* (1957), reprinted in Douglas Adair, *Fame and the Founding Fathers* (New York: Norton, 1974), 93–106.

13. This argument is developed more fully in Samuel Kernell, "'The True Principles of Republican Government': Reassessing James Madison's Political Science," in *James Madison: The Theory and Practice of Republican Government,* ed. Samuel Kernell (Stanford, CA: Stanford University Press, 2003).

14. Eric Schmitt, "Testing of a President: The Votes; Impeachment Doubts Erode Slim Republican Majority," *New York Times,* November 19, 1998.

15. William G. Howell and Terry M. Moe, *Relic: How Our Constitution Undermines Effective Government* (New York: Basic Books, 2016).

## Chapter 3

1. Jazmine Ulloa and Liam Dillon, "Sessions, State Officials at 'War' over Immigration," *Los Angeles Times,* March 8, 2018, p. A1.

2. Joseph Tafani, "Continuing a Fierce Assault on 'Sanctuary' Policies, Sessions Attacks a California Bill," *Los Angeles Times,* September 19, 2017, accessed at http://www.latimes.com/politics/la-na-pol-sessions-sanctuary-20170919-story.html in September 2018.

3. Kristine Phillips, "In Message of Defiance to Trump, Lawmakers Vote to Make California a Sanctuary State," *Washington Post,* September 16, 2017, accessed at https://www.washingtonpost.com/news/politics/wp/2017/09/16/in-message-of-defiance-to-trump-lawmakers-vote-to-make-california-a-sanctuary-state/?utm_term=.f822a2d66d97 in September 2018.

4. This definition comes directly from Parris N. Glendening and Mavis Mann Reeves, *Pragmatic Federalism,* 2nd ed. (Pacific Palisades, CA: Pacific Palisades, 1984), 11.

5. This quotation is from Howard L. McBain, *The Law and the Practice of Municipal Home Rule* (New York: Columbia University Press, 1916), 15. Dillon was an Iowa Supreme Court justice who set forth the doctrine that local governments were fully subordinate to states in an 1868 decision (*Clinton v. Cedar Rapids and Missouri River R. R.,* 24 Iowa 455) and an 1872 book. It was the U.S. Supreme Court's 1907 decision in *Hunter v. Pittsburgh* (207 U.S. 161) that applied Dillon's rule to local governments across the nation.

6. For a review of contemporary state-local relations, see Russell L. Hanson, *Governing Partners: State-Local Relations in the United States* (Boulder, CO: Westview, 1998).

7. William H. Riker, "The Senate and American Federalism," *American Political Science Review* 49 (1955): 452–469.

8. For a discussion of the Senate's special role in spawning presidential candidates, see Nelson W. Polsby, *Political Innovation in America* (New Haven, CT: Yale University Press, 1984).

9. See Article I, Section 9.

10. The elastic clause also is known as the necessary and proper clause.

11. *McCulloch v. Maryland,* 4 Wheat. 316 (1819).

12. *Gibbons v. Ogden,* 22 U.S. 1 (1824).

13. This history is well told by Robert H. Wiebe in *The Search for Order, 1877–1920* (New York: Hill & Wang, 1967).

14. The case was *United States v. F. W. Darby Lumber Co.,* 312 U.S. 100 (1941). Passage cited in Lee Epstein and Thomas G. Walker, *Constitutional Law for a Changing America: A Short Course,* 3rd ed. (Washington, DC: CQ Press, 2005), 192–193.

15. The "welfare magnets" idea and the initial evidence that states raced to the bottom in welfare payments were introduced in Paul E. Peterson and Mark C. Rom, *Welfare Magnets: The Case for a National Welfare Standard* (Washington, DC: Brookings, 1990). The findings of the literature that this book inspired have been critiqued by Craig Volden in "The Politics of Competitive Federalism: A Race to the Bottom in Welfare Benefits?" *American Journal of Political Science* 46 (2002): 352–363.

16. Louis Uchitelle, "States Pay for Jobs, but It Doesn't Always Pay Off," *New York Times,* November 10, 2003.

17. *South Dakota v. Dole,* 483 U.S. 203 (1987).

18. *Garcia v. San Antonio Metropolitan Transit Authority,* 469 U.S. 528 (1985).

19. Kenneth T. Palmer and Edward B. Laverty, "The Impact of *United States v. Lopez* on Intergovernmental Relations: A Preliminary Assessment," *Publius* 26 (Summer 1996): 109–126. This revisionism continued in a 1997 case in which the Court invalidated a provision of the 1993 Brady handgun law that required local law enforcement officials to run background checks on purchasers of handguns. Dan Carney, "Brady Decision Reflects Effort to Curb Congress' Authority," *Congressional Quarterly Weekly Report,* June 28, 1997, 1524–1525.

20. John Kincaid, "Constitutional Federalism: Labor's Role in Displacing Places to Benefit Persons," *PS* (June 1993): 172.

21. Quoted on page 1127 of Wallace Oates, "An Essay on Fiscal Federalism," *Journal of Economic Literature* 37 (September 1999): 1120–1149.

22. L. Nye Stevens, *Unfunded Mandates—Reform Act Has Had Little Effect on Agencies' Rulemaking Actions,* Report to the Committee on Governmental Affairs, U.S. Senate (Washington, DC: General Accounting Office, 1998).

23. Quoted from David Brian Robertson, *Federalism and the Making of America* (New York and London: Routledge, 2012), 8.

## Chapter 4

1. Sam Howe Verhovek, "Americans Give in to Race Profiling," *New York Times,* September 23, 2001.

2. "Guidance for Screeners and Other Security Personnel," U.S. Department of Transportation, Federal Aviation Administration, accessed at www.dot.gov/airconsumer.

3. Henry Weinstein et al., "After the Attack; Law Enforcement," *Los Angeles Times,* September 24, 2001.

4. Harold Sullivan proposes this distinction in *Civil Rights and Liberties: Provocative Questions and Evolving Answers* (New York: Prentice Hall, 2001), 1–2.

5. John M. Broder, "Clinton, Softening Slap at Senate, Names 'Acting' Civil Rights Chief," *New York Times,* December 16, 1997.

6. Mary B. Norton et al., *People and a Nation: A History of the United States,* Vol. 1, 5th ed. (Boston: Houghton Mifflin, 1987), 238.

7. Chaplain W. Morrison, *Democratic Politics and Sectionalism: The Wilmot Proviso Controversy* (Chapel Hill: University of North Carolina Press, 1967).

8. *Dred Scott v. Sandford,* 19 How. 393 (1857).

9. Quoted in C. Vann Woodward, *The Burden of Southern History* (Baton Rouge: Louisiana State University Press, 1968), 95.

10. Ibid.

11. C. Vann Woodward, *Reunion and Reaction: The Compromise of 1877 and the End of Reconstruction* (Boston: Little, Brown, 1966).

12. *Plessy v. Ferguson,* 163 U.S. 737 (1896).

13. Edward G. Carmines and James A. Stimson, *Issue Evolution: Race and the Transformation of American Politics* (Princeton, NJ: Princeton University Press, 1989).

14. *Brown v. Board of Education of Topeka,* 347 U.S. 483 (1954).

15. *Smith v. Allwright,* 321 U.S. 649 (1944).

16. *Sweatt v. Painter,* 339 U.S. 629 (1950).

17. *Brown v. Board of Education,* 349 U.S. 294 (1955).

18. David J. Garrow, *Bearing the Cross: Martin Luther King, Jr., and the Southern Christian Leadership Conference* (New York: Morrow, 1986), 91.

19. Dennis Chong elaborates on these issues in his *Collective Action and the Civil Rights Movement* (Chicago: University of Chicago Press, 1991).

20. Paul Burstein, "Public Opinion, Demonstrations, and the Passage of Anti-discrimination Legislation," *Public Opinion Quarterly* 43 (1979): 157–172.

21. Taylor Branch, *Parting the Waters: America in the King Years, 1954–1963* (New York: Simon & Schuster, 1988).

22. Ibid.

23. Robert M. Axelrod, "Where the Votes Come From: An Analysis of Electoral Coalitions, 1952–1958," *American Political Science Review* (March 1972).

24. From Gary Orfield, *Congressional Power: Congress and Social Change* (New York: Harcourt Brace Jovanovich, 1975), 102.

25. Eilperin, Juliet. "What's changed for African Americans since 1963, by the numbers," *Washington Post,* August 22, 2013.

26. *Shelby County, Alabama v. Holder,* 570 U.S. ___ (2013).

27. *Crawford v. Marion County Election Board,* 553 U.S. 181 (2008).

28. Wendy R. Weiser and Lawrence Norden, "Voting Law Changes in 2012," Brennan Center for Justice at New York University School of Law.

29. *Regents of the University of California v. Bakke,* 438 U.S. 265 (1978).

30. The 1987 case is *Johnson v. Transportation Agency of Santa Clara County*; the 1995 case, *Adarand Constructors, Inc. v. Peña,* 515 U.S. 200 (1995).

31. *Gratz v. Bollinger,* 539 U.S. 244 (2003), involved the undergraduate point system, whereas *Grutter v. Bollinger,* 539 U.S. 306 (2003), concerned the law school's consideration of race as a variable.

32. *Fisher v. University of Texas,* No. 14-981.

33. Alexander Keyssar, *The Right to Vote* (New York: Basic Books, 2000); Judith Apter Klinghoffer and Lois Elkis, "The Petticoat Electors: Women's Suffrage in New Jersey, 1776–1807," *Journal of the Early Republic* 12 (1992): 159–193.

34. Ibid., 177.

35. The rise of the abortion issue after the Supreme Court legalized abortions in its 1973 *Roe v. Wade* decision stalled the ERA. Jane Mansbridge, *Why We Lost the ERA* (Chicago: University of Chicago Press, 1986).

36. The case that triggered Congress's response was *Grove City College v. Bell,* 465 U.S. 555 (1984).

37. This estimate is based on "Charge Statistics," compiled by the EEOC and reported on its website, accessed at www.eeoc.gov/eeoc/statistics/enforcement/charges.cfm.

38. *Romer v. Evans,* 517 U.S. 620 (1996).

39. The list, updated in 2004, is contained in the General Accounting Office report located at www.gao.gov/new.items/d04353r.pdf.

40. *United States v. Windsor.*

41. *Obergefell et al. v. Hodges, Director, Ohio Department of Health,* No. 14-556.

# Chapter 5

1. Pew Research Center, "Perceptions of How Blacks Are Treated in the U.S. Vary Widely by Race," June 2016, accessed at http://www.pewsocialtrends.org/2016/06/27/on-views-of-race-and-inequality-blacks-and-whites-are-worlds-apart/st_2016-06-27_race-inequality-overview-02/.

2. *Tennessee v. Garner,* 471 U.S. 1 (1985).

3. *Plumhoff v. Rickard,* 12–1117 (2014).

4. From a speech to Congress, June 8, 1789. Quoted in *The Papers of James Madison,* ed. William T. Hutchinson et al. (Chicago: University of Chicago Press, 1962), 197–206.

5. *Employment Division, Department of Human Resources of Oregon v. Smith,* 494 U.S. 872 (1990).

6. *City of Boerne v. Flores,* 136 L. Ed. 2d 709 (1997).

7. Donald S. Lutz, "The State Constitutional Pedigree of the U.S. Bill of Rights," *Publius* 22 (Spring 1992): 19–45.

8. Quoted in Alpheus Thomas Mason, *The States' Rights Debate* (New York: Oxford University Press, 1972), 174. Madison informed the House of Representatives, "I will not propose a single alteration which I do not wish to see take place, as proper in itself, or proper because it is wished by

a respectable number of my fellow citizens."

9. *Barron v. Baltimore,* 7 Pet. 243 (1833).

10. This discussion of incorporation follows the presentation in Lee Epstein and Thomas G. Walker, *Constitutional Law for a Changing America: Rights, Liberties, and Justice,* 5th ed. (Washington, DC: CQ Press, 2004), 75–97. Indeed, this text provides a thorough review and treatment of all issues described in this chapter.

11. *The Butchers' Benevolent Association of New Orleans v. The Crescent City Livestock Landing and Slaughterhouse Co.; Esteban v. Louisiana* (the *Slaughterhouse Cases*), 16 Wall. 36 (1873).

12. *Hurtado v. California,* 110 U.S. 516 (1884).

13. *Gitlow v. New York,* 268 U.S. 652 (1925).

14. *Dennis v. United States,* 341 U.S. 494 (1951).

15. *Brandenburg v. Ohio,* 395 U.S. 444 (1969).

16. *Rice v. Paladin Press* (1997), Fourth Circuit, and *Planned Parenthood v. American Coalition of Life Activists* (2002), Ninth Circuit.

17. https://www.thefire.org/speech-code-of-the-month-lafayette-college/

18. https://medium.com/informed-and-engaged/8-ways-college-student-views-on-free-speech-are-evolving-963334babe40

19. *Jacobellis v. Ohio,* 378 U.S. 184 (1964).

20. Craig R. Ducat, *Constitutional Interpretation: Rights of the Individual* (Boston: Cengage Learning, 2008).

21. *Roth v. United States,* 354 U.S. 476 (1957).

22. *Miller v. California,* 413 U.S. 15 (1973).

23. Epstein and Walker, *Constitutional Law,* 371–372.

24. *Sheppard v. Maxwell,* 384 U.S. 333 (1966).

25. *Globe Newspaper Co. v. Superior Court,* 457 U.S. 596 (1982).

26. Ralph Ketcham, *James Madison* (Charlottesville: University Press of Virginia, 1971), 166.

27. *Bradfield v. Roberts,* 175 U.S. 291 (1899).

28. *Everson v. Board of Education,* 330 U.S. 1 (1947).

29. Frank J. Sorauf, *The Wall of Separation* (Princeton, NJ: Princeton University Press, 1976), 257.

30. *Lemon v. Kurtzman; Earley v. DiCenso,* 403 U.S. 602 (1971).

31. *Lynch v. Donnelly,* 465 U.S. 668 (1984); *County of Allegheny v. ACLU, Greater Pittsburgh Chapter,* 492 U.S. 573 (1989).

32. Leonard W. Levy, *The Establishment Clause* (New York: Macmillan, 1986), 128.

33. *Board of Education of Kiryas Joel Village School District v. Grumet,* 512 U.S. 687 (1994).

34. *Agostini v. Felton,* 521 U.S. 203 (1997); *Mitchell v. Helms,* 530 U.S. 793 (2000); *Zelman v. Simmons-Harris,* 536 U.S. 639 (2002).

35. The case is *Locke v. Davey,* 540 U.S. 712 (2004). Linda Greenhouse, "States Allowed to Avoid Subsidy of Divinity Study," *New York Times,* February 26, 2004.

36. *Engel v. Vitale,* 370 U.S. 421 (1962).

37. *School District of Abington Township v. Schempp,* 374 U.S. 203 (1963).

38. Dan Carney, "With Barely a Prayer of Ratification, Religious Freedom Amendment Opens Perennial Election-Year Debate," *CQ Weekly,* June 6, 1998, 1530.

39. *Wallace v. Jaffree,* 472 U.S. 38 (1985).

40. *Lee v. Weisman,* 505 U.S. 577 (1992).

41. Robert Birkby, "The Supreme Court in the Bible Belt: Tennessee Reaction to the *Schempp* Decision," *American Journal of Political Science* 10 (1966): 304.

42. Kevin Sack, "In South, Prayer Is a Form of Protest: A Ruling Is Opposed in Classrooms, Courtroom and Statehouse," *New York Times,* November 8, 1997, A7.

43. *Employment Division, Department of Human Resources of Oregon v. Smith.*

44. *Church of the Lukumi Babalu Aye, Inc., et al. v. City of Hialeah,* 508 U.S. 502, 533 (1993).

45. *District of Columbia v. Heller,* 554 U.S. 570 (2008).

46. *McDonald v. Chicago,* 561 U.S. 3025 (2010).

47. *United States v. Masciandaro,* 638 F.3d 458, 475 (4th Cir. 2011).

48. Cited in Kenneth Janda, Jeffrey M. Berry, and Jerry Goldman, *The Challenge of Democracy,* 4th ed. (Boston: Houghton Mifflin, 1995), 537.

49. *Brown v. Mississippi,* 297 U.S. 278 (1936).

50. Harold W. Stanley and Richard G. Niemi, *Vital Statistics on American Politics, 2007–2008* (Washington, DC: CQ Press, 2007), 155.

51. *Katz v. United States,* 389 U.S. 347 (1967).

52. *Kyllo v. United States,* 533 U.S. 27 (2001).

53. *Riley v. California,* 13–132 (2014)

54. For a full discussion of each of these conditions, see Epstein and Walker, *Constitutional Law,* 509–541.

55. *Mapp v. Ohio,* 367 U.S. 643 (1961).

56. *United States v. Leon,* 468 U.S. 897 (1984); *Massachusetts v. Sheppard,* 468 U.S. 981 (1984).

57. *Hudson v. Michigan,* 547 U.S. 586 (2006).

58. *United States v. Jones,* 132 S.Ct. 945 (2012).

59. See Robert Barnes, "Supreme Court: Warrants Needed in GPS Tracking," *Washington Post,* January 23, 2012.

60. *Malloy v. Hogan,* 378 U.S. 1 (1964).

61. *Miranda v. Arizona,* 384 U.S. 436 (1966).

62. *Dickerson v. United States,* 530 U.S. 428 (2000).

63. *Gideon v. Wainwright,* 372 U.S. 335 (1963).

64. *Argersinger v. Hamlin,* 407 U.S. 25 (1972).

65. *Missouri v. Frye,* 132 S.Ct. 1399 (2012).

66. *Strickland v. Washington,* 466 U.S. 668 (1984).

67. Charles Lane, "Death Penalty of Md. Man Is Overturned," *Washington Post,* June 23, 2003.

68. *Gregg v. Georgia,* 428 U.S. 153 (1976).

69. The discriminatory jury selection case is *Foster v. Chatman,* No. 14-8349. *Hurst v. Florida,* No. 14-7505, further tightened past Court rulings that only the jury can decide whether conditions were present that permitted a death penalty sentence.

70. *Griswold v. Connecticut,* 381 U.S. 479 (1965).

71. *Eisenstadt v. Baird,* 410 U.S. 113 (1972), extended access to contraceptives to unmarried women.

72. *Planned Parenthood of Southeastern Pennsylvania v. Casey,* 505 U.S. 833 (1992).

73. Linda Greenhouse, "In New York Visit, O'Connor Foresees Limits on Freedom," *New York Times,* September 29, 2001.

## Chapter 6

1. Based on 216 surveys from twelve survey organizations and reported at www .pollingreport.com/health.htm.

2. Rachel Roubein, "Timeline: The GOP's Failed Effort to Repeal ObamaCare," *The Hill,* September 27, 2017, at https:// thehill.com/policy/healthcare/ other/352587-timeline-the-gop-effort-to-repeal-and-replace-obamacare.

3. Henry C. Jackson, "6 Promises Trump Has Made about Health Care," *Politico,* March 13, 2017, at www.politico .com/story/2017/03/trump-obamacare-promises-236021.

4. Thomas Kaplan, Jennifer Steinhauer, and Robert Pear, "Trump, in Zigzag, Calls House Republicans' Health Bill 'Mean,'" *New York Times,* June 13, 2017, at www .nytimes.com/2017/06/13/us/ politics/trump-in-zigzag-calls-house-republicans-health-bill-mean.html.

5. On average in 2017 and 2018, 54 percent of people expressing an opinion favored the ACA and 46 percent opposed it. See the survey data

reported at www.pollingreport .com/health.htm.

6. *Wesberry v. Sanders,* 376 U.S. 1 (1964).

7. *Thornburg v. Gingles,* 478 U.S. 30 (1986).

8. *Davis v. Bandemer,* 478 U.S. 109 (1986).

9. *Thornburg v. Gingles.*

10. *Shaw v. Reno,* 590 U.S. 630 (1993).

11. *Miller v. Johnson,* 515 U.S. 900 (1995).

12. Alan I. Abramowitz and Jeffrey A. Segal, *Senate Elections* (Ann Arbor: University of Michigan Press, 1992), 18.

13. The Progressive Era and its effects on U.S. politics are described more fully in Chapter 12, "Political Parties."

14. Jerrold G. Rusk, "The Effects of the Australian Ballot Reform on Split Ticket Voting, 1876–1908," in *Controversies in Voting Behavior,* ed. Richard G. Niemi and Herbert F. Weisberg (San Francisco: W. H. Freeman, 1976), 485–486.

15. Gary C. Jacobson, *The Politics of Congressional Elections,* 7th ed. (New York: Longman, 2009), 27–45.

16. Norman J. Ornstein, Thomas E. Mann, Andrew Rugg, and Michael J. Malbin, *Vital Statistics on Congress,* Tables 5-11 and 5-12, at www.aei.org/publication/ vital-statistics-on-congress.

17. Figure 6.1 averages three common measures of the incumbency advantage. One is the "slurge," which is the average of the "sophomore surge" (the average gain in vote share won by candidates running as incumbents for the first time compared

to their vote share in their initial election, adjusted for the national partisan swing) and the "retirement slump" (the average drop in the party's vote from the previous election when the incumbent departs, again adjusted for the swing); the other two are variants of the Gelman-King index. For details on their sources and construction, see Gary C. Jacobson, "Barack Obama and Nationalized Electoral Politics in the 2014 Midterm," *Political Science Quarterly* 130 (Spring 2015).

18. A similar if more erratic trend is evident for Senate incumbents as well; see Gary C. Jacobson, "It's Nothing Personal: The Decline of the Incumbency Advantage in Congressional Elections," delivered at the Annual Meeting of the Midwest Political Science Association, Chicago, April 3–6, 2014.

19. Gary C. Jacobson, "The Triumph of Polarized Partisanship: Donald Trump's Improbable Victory and the Nationalization of Electoral Politics in 2016," *Political Science Quarterly* 132 (Spring 2017), 9–41; Gary C. Jacobson, "Extreme Referendum: Donald Trump and the 2018 Midterm Elections," *Political Science Quarterly*, forthcoming.

20. John Kingdon, *Congressmen's Voting Decisions,* 2nd ed. (New York: Harper and Row, 1981), 47–50.

21. Kerry Young, "An Earmark by Any Other Name," *CQ Weekly,* November 22, 2010, 2700.

22. Citizens against Government Waste, *2018 Congressional Pig Book,* at www.cagw.org/ reporting/pig-book; see also www.cagw.org/reporting/ pig-book#historical_trends.

23. Roger H. Davidson, Walter J. Oleszek, and Frances E. Lee, *Congress and Its Members,* 11th ed. (Washington, DC: CQ Press, 2008), 124.

24. David R. Mayhew, *Congress: The Electoral Connection* (New Haven, CT: Yale University Press, 1974), 87–97.

25. Tom Murse, "All 21 Government Shutdowns in U.S. History," at www .thoughtco.com/government-shutdown-history-3368274.

26. Sarah A. Binder, *Minority Rights, Majority Rule: Partisanship and the Development of Congress* (Cambridge, UK: Cambridge University Press, 1997).

27. Gary W. Cox and Mathew D. McCubbins, *Legislative Leviathan: Party Government in the House* (Berkeley: University of California Press, 1993), part 2.

28. David W. Rohde, *Parties and Leaders in the Postreform House* (Chicago: University of Chicago Press, 1991), chap. 3.

29. Ibid., 31–49.

30. Jennifer Stenihauer, "Republicans Who Have Opposed Leadership See Committee Assignments Stripped," *New York Times,* December 3, 2012.

31. Diana Evans, *Greasing the Wheels: Using Pork Barrel Projects to Build Majority Coalitions in Congress* (Cambridge, UK: Cambridge University Press, 2004).

32. George B. Galloway, *The History of the House of Representatives* (New York: Crowell, 1961), 12.

33. Barbara Hinckley, *Stability and Change in Congress,* 4th ed. (New York: Harper and Row, 1988), 155.

34. Richard E. Cohen, Siobhan Gorman, and Sydney J. Freedberg Jr., "National Security: The Ultimate Turf War," *National Journal,* January 4, 2003.

35. Ibid.

36. Ibid.

37. Barbara Sinclair, *Unorthodox Lawmaking: New Legislative Processes in the U.S. Congress,* 5th ed. (Washington, DC: CQ Press, 2017), 147.

38. Joseph White and Aaron Wildavsky, *The Deficit and the Public Interest: The Search for Responsible Budgeting in the 1980s* (Berkeley: University of California Press, 1989), chaps. 16–17.

39. Don Wolfensberger, "The New Congressional Staff: Politics at the Expense of Policy," *Brookings Report,* March 21, 2014, at www.brookings .edu/blog/fixgov/2014/03/21/ the-new-congressional-staff-politics-at-the-expense-of-policy.

40. Sinclair, *Unorthodox Lawmaking,* chaps. 2–3.

41. Mathew D. McCubbins and Thomas Schwartz, "Congressional Oversight Overlooked: Police Patrols vs. Fire Alarms," *American Journal of Political Science* 28 (February 1984): 165–179.

42. Sinclair, *Unorthodox Lawmaking,* 126.

43. Sean M. Theriault, *The Gingrich Senators: The Roots of Partisan Warfare in Congress* (New York: Oxford University Press, 2013).

44. Kingdon, *Congressmen's Voting Decisions,* 47–54.

45.  George Hager and David S. Cloud, "Democrats Tie Their Fate to Clinton's Budget Bill," *Congressional Quarterly Weekly Report,* August 7, 1993, 2212–2219.

46.  Walter J. Oleszek, *Congressional Procedures and the Policy Process* (Thousand Oaks, CA: Sage, 2014), 336.

47.  Harold W. Stanley and Richard G. Niemi, *Vital Statistics on American Politics,* 6th ed. (Washington, DC: Congressional Quarterly, 1998), 252; http://en .wikipedia.org/wiki/List_of_ United_States_presidential_ vetoes.

48.  Sinclair, *Unorthodox Lawmaking,* 5; Steven S. Smith, *The Senate Syndrome* (Norman: University of Oklahoma Press, 2014), 231–250.

49.  John R. Hibbing and Elizabeth Theiss-Morse, *Congress as Public Enemy: Public Attitudes toward American Political Institutions* (New York: Cambridge University Press, 1995), 46–61.

# Chapter 7

1.  Richard E. Neustadt, *Presidential Power and the Modern Presidents: The Politics of Power from Roosevelt to Reagan* (New York: Free Press, 1990), 34.

2.  Michael O'Brien, "McConnell: GOP's 'only' option is to defeat Obama in 2012," *The Hill,* November 4, 2010.

3.  Marcus Cunliffe, *The Presidency* (Boston: Houghton Mifflin, 1968).

4.  Quotation from David Herbert Donald, "Lincoln, the Politician," in *Lincoln Reconsidered: Essays on the Civil War Era* (New York: Random House, 1956).

5.  Loch K. Johnson, *The Making of International Agreements: Congress Confronts the Executive* (New York: New York University Press), 1994.

6.  Louis Fisher, *The Politics of Shared Power,* 3rd ed. (Washington, DC: CQ Press, 1993), 156–157.

7.  Louis Fisher, *Constitutional Conflicts between Congress and the President,* 3rd ed. (Lawrence: University Press of Kansas, 1991), 103.

8.  *Morrison v. Olson,* 487 U.S. 654, 705 (1988).

9.  This figure covers presidential initiatives from 1935 through 1996. Jon R. Bond and Richard Fleisher, *Polarized Politics* (Washington, DC: CQ Press, 2000), 120.

10.  Alexis de Tocqueville, *Democracy in America,* ed. J. P. Mayer (Garden City, NY: Doubleday, 1969), 122.

11.  *Train v. City of New York*, 420 U.S. 35 (1975).

12.  Hans H. G. Hassell and Samuel Kernell, "Veto Rhetoric and Legislative Riders," *American Journal of Political Science* 60(4) (2016): 845–859.

13.  Jack Germond, *Mad as Hell: Revolt at the Ballot Box, 1992* (New York: Warner Books, 1993).

14.  Glenn Kessler, "Grover Norquist's History Lesson: George H. W. Bush, 'No New Taxes,' and the 1992 Election," *Washington Post,* November 26, 2012.

15.  Alison Mitchell, "Clinton Seems to Keep Running though the Race Is Run and Won," *New York Times,* February 12, 1997, A1, A12.

16.  Brandon Cole, "Trump Has 15 Million Fake Twitter Followers," *Newsweek,* March 22, 2018.

17.  Samuel Kernell and Laurie L. Rice, "Cable and Partisan Polarization of the President's Audience," *Presidential Studies Quarterly* 41 (2011): 693–711.

18.  William G. Howell, *Thinking about the Presidency* (Princeton, NJ: Princeton University Press, 2013).

19.  Daniel Victor, "No 'Making a Murderer' Pardon from Obama, White House Says," *New York Times*, January 8, 2016.

20.  Noble E. Cunningham Jr., *In Pursuit of Reason: The Life of Thomas Jefferson* (Baton Rouge: Louisiana State University Press, 1987).

21.  John Hart, *The Presidential Branch: From Washington to Clinton,* 2nd ed. (Chatham, NJ: Chatham House, 1995), 31.

22.  Nelson W. Polsby, "Some Landmarks in Presidential-Congressional Relations," in *Both Ends of the Avenue: The President, the Executive Branch, and the Congress,* ed. Anthony King (Washington, DC: American Enterprise, 1983), cited in Charles O. Jones, *The Presidency in a Separated System,* 2nd ed. (Washington, DC: Brookings, 2005).

23.  Quoted in Samuel Kernell, "New and Old Lessons on White House Management," in *Executive Leadership in Anglo-American Systems,* ed. Colin Campbell and Margaret

Jane Wyszomirski (Pittsburgh: University of Pittsburgh Press, 1991), 350.

24. Terence Smith, "Carter Liaison Aide with Jews to Quit White House," *New York Times,* March 9, 1978.

25. Kathryn Dunn Tenpas, Elaine Kamarck, and Nicholas W. Zeppos, "Tracking Turnover in the Trump Administration," Brookings Institution, November 7, 2018, www.brookings.edu/research/tracking-turnover-in-the-trump-administration.

## Chapter 8

1. Anthony M. Bertelli and Laurence Lynn Jr., *Madison's Managers: Public Administration and the Constitution* (Baltimore: Johns Hopkins University Press, 2006), 2.

2. Michael Nelson, "A Short, Ironic History of Bureaucracy," *Journal of Politics* 44 (1982): 750.

3. Leonard D. White, *The Jeffersonians: A Study in Administrative History, 1801–1829* (New York: Macmillan, 1961), 139–140.

4. James Q. Wilson, "The Rise of the Bureaucratic State," in *The American Commonwealth, 1976,* ed. Nathan Glazer and Irving Kristol (New York: Basic Books, 1976), 78.

5. Nelson, "A Short, Ironic History of Bureaucracy," 756.

6. Leonard D. White, *The Federalists: A Study in Administrative History* (New York: Macmillan, 1961), 427–431.

7. White, *The Jeffersonians,* 357.

8. Quoted in Leonard D. White, *The Jacksonians: A Study in Administrative History, 1829–1861* (New York: Macmillan, 1963), 318.

9. Ibid., 320.

10. Max Weber, "Bureaucracy," in *Essays in Sociology,* translated by H. H. Gerth and C. Wright Mills (New York: Oxford University Press, 1962), 196–244.

11. Paul P. Van Riper, *History of the United States Civil Service* (Evanston, IL: Row, Peterson, 1958), 74–75.

12. Nelson, "A Short, Ironic History of Bureaucracy," 767.

13. Harold Seidman and Robert Gilmour, *Politics, Position, and Power: From the Positive to the Regulatory State* (New York: Oxford University Press, 1986), 316–319.

14. Paul C. Light, *The True Size of Government* (Washington, DC: Brookings, 1999), 24.

15. Paul C. Light, "The New True Size of Government," Research Brief No. 2, Robert F. Wagner Graduate School of Public Service, New York University, August 2006, 11.

16. Paul C. Light, "Fact Sheet on the New True Size of Government," Center for Public Service, Brookings Institution (September 5, 2003), accessed at http://www.brookings.edu/research/articles/2003/09/05politics-light.

17. Charles T. Goodsell, *The Case for Bureaucracy: A Public Administration Polemic,* 4th ed. (Washington, DC: CQ Press, 2004), 141.

18. Ibid., 84–111.

19. James Q. Wilson, Bureaucracy: *What Government Agencies Do and Why They Do It* (New York: Basic Books, 1989), 91.

20. Martin Kady II, "Security's Swelling Price Tag," *CQ Weekly,* January 11, 2003, 75.

21. Jack L. Walker, *Mobilizing Interest Groups in America: Patrons, Professions, and Social Movements* (Ann Arbor: University of Michigan Press, 1991), 30–33.

22. Kenneth R. Mayer, *The Political Economy of Defense Contracting* (New Haven, CT: Yale University Press, 1991), 158–174.

23. R. Douglas Arnold, *Congress and the Bureaucracy: A Theory of Influence* (New Haven, CT: Yale University Press, 1979), 136–137.

24. Michael Hastings, "The Runaway General," *Rolling Stone,* July 8–22, 2010.

25. Theodore J. Lowi, *The End of Liberalism*: *The Second Republic of the United States,* 2nd ed. (New York: Norton, 1979).

26. Mathew D. McCubbins and Thomas Schwarz, "Congressional Oversight Overlooked: Police Patrols versus Fire Alarms," *American Journal of Political Science* 28(1): 165–179, p. 166.

27. Jason A. McDonald, "Limitation Riders and Congressional Influence over Bureaucratic Decisions," *American Political Science Review* 104 (November 2010): 766–782.

28. David Nather, "Congress as Watchdog: Asleep on the Job," *CQ Weekly,* May 22, 2004, 1193.

29. Wilson, *Bureaucracy,* 82–83.

30. Ibid., 235.

31. National Commission on the Public Service, *Leadership for*

*America: Rebuilding the Public Service* (Washington, DC: Brookings, 1989).

32. David E. Lewis, *The Politics of Presidential Appointments: Political Control and Bureaucratic Performance* (Princeton, NJ: Princeton University Press, 2008).

33. Ron Fournier, "FEMA Director Mike Brown Resigns," Associated Press, September 12, 2005.

34. Nicholas Fandos and Peter Baker, "White House Withdraws Jackson Nomination for V.A. Chief Amid Criticism," *New York Times*, April 26, 2018.

35. Carl Hulse, "Mukasey Wins Vote in Senate, Despite Doubts," *New York Times*, November 9, 2007, A1.

36. Henry B. Hogue, "Recess Appointments: Frequently Asked Questions," Congressional Research Service, January 9, 2012, accessed at http://www.senate.gov/CRSReports/crs-publish.cfm?pid=%270DP%2BP\W%3B%20P%20%20%0A; Paul Kane, "The Fastest Gavel in the Senate," *New York Times*, December 31, 2007, A13.

37. Hugh Heclo, *Government of Strangers: Executive Politics in Washington* (Washington, DC: Brookings, 1977), 195–198.

38. Richard W. Waterman, *Presidential Influence and the Administrative State* (Knoxville: University of Tennessee Press, 1989), chap. 7.

39. Joseph J. Schatz, "Has Congress Given Bush Too Free a Spending Hand?" *CQ Weekly*, April 12, 2003, 858.

40. Gardiner Harris, "White House and the FDA Often at Odds," *New York Times*, April 2, 2012.

41. Martin Shapiro, *Who Guards the Guardians? Judicial Control of Administration* (Athens: University of Georgia Press, 1988), 57.

42. Douglas Cater, *Power in Washington* (New York: Vintage, 1964).

43. Hugh Heclo, "Issue Networks and the Executive Establishment," in *The New American Political System*, ed. Anthony King (Washington, DC: American Enterprise Institute, 1978), 87–124.

44. Joel D. Aberbach, "The Federal Executive under Clinton," in *The Clinton Presidency: First Appraisals*, ed. Colin Campbell and Bert A. Rockman (Chatham, NJ: Chatham House, 1996), 179.

45. Transcript of Obama's State of the Union address, accessed at http://www.npr.org/2011/01/26/133224933/transcript-obamas-state-of-union-address, January 25, 2011.

46. Goodsell, *The Case for Bureaucracy*, 146.

47. Ibid.

## Chapter 9

1. Letter from Jefferson to John Dickinson, December 19, 1801, cited in Donald O. Dewey, *Marshall versus Jefferson: The Political Background of* Marbury v. Madison (New York: Knopf, 1970), 63.

2. *Stuart v. Laird,* 1 Cr. 299 (1803).

3. *Marbury v. Madison,* 1 Cr. (5 U.S.) 137 at 177–180 (1803); emphasis added.

4. *Pollock v. Farmers' Loan & Trust Co.,* 157 U.S. 429 (1895).

5. *McCulloch v. Maryland,* 4 Wheat. 316 (1819).

6. *Dred Scott v. Sandford,* 19 How. (60 U.S.) 393 (1857).

7. Quoted by Paul Brest and Sanford Levinson in *Processes of Constitutional Decisionmaking,* 3rd ed. (Boston: Little, Brown, 1992), 75.

8. *Fletcher v. Peck,* 6 Cr. 87 (1810).

9. *Munn v. Illinois,* 94 U.S. 113 (1877); *Mugler v. Kansas,* 123 U.S. 623 (1887).

10. *Lochner v. New York,* 198 U.S. 45 (1905).

11. Robert McCloskey and Sanford Levinson, eds., *The American Supreme Court,* 2nd ed. (Chicago: University of Chicago Press, 1994); Lawrence Baum, *The Supreme Court,* 6th ed. (Washington, DC: CQ Press, 1998), 208.

12. *West Coast Hotel Co. v. Parrish,* 300 U.S. 379 (1937).

13. *Heart of Atlanta Motel, Inc. v. United States,* 379 U.S. 241 (1964).

14. *United States v. Lopez,* 514 U.S. 549 (1995).

15. *United States v. Morrison,* 529 U.S. 598 (2000).

16. David G. Savage, "IRAs Shielded in Bankruptcy, Justices Rule," *Los Angeles Times,* April 5, 2005; "Justices to Decide if Social Security Can Be Seized," *Los Angeles Times,* April 26, 2005.

17. Supreme Court Database, accessed at http://scdb.wustl.edu.

18. Lori Hausegger and Lawrence Baum, "Inviting Congressional Action: A Study of Supreme Court Motivations in Statutory

Interpretation," *American Journal of Political Science* 43 (January 1999): 162–185.

19. R. C. Black and R. J. Owens, "Courting the President: How Circuit Court Judges Alter Their Behavior for Promotion to the Supreme Court," *American Journal of Political Science* 60 (2016): 30–43.

20. *Jaffree v. Board of School Commissioners,* 554 F. Supp. 1104, 1128 (S.D. Ala. 1983).

21. *Brown v. Board of Education,* 347 U.S. 483 (1954).

22. Figures accessed at http://www.uscourts.gov/statistics-reports.

23. "Supreme Court Case Selections Act of 1988," Pub. L. No. 100-352.

24. Ryan J. Owens and David A. Simon, "Explaining the Supreme Court's Shrinking Docket," *William and Mary Law Review* 53 (2012): 1219–1285.

25. Jeffrey R. Lax, "Certiorari and Compliance in the Judicial Hierarchy: Discretion, Reputation, and the Rule of Four," *Journal of Theoretical Politics* 15 (2003): 61–86.

26. Adam Liptak, "Polarization of Supreme Court Is Reflected in Justices' Clerks," *New York Times,* September 6, 2010.

27. Peter Linzer, "The Meaning of Certiorari Denials," *Columbia Law Review* 79 (1979): 1227–1305.

28. David O'Brien, *Storm Center: The Supreme Court in American Politics,* 4th ed. (New York: Norton, 1996).

29. *Obergefell v. Hodges,* 576 U.S. ___ (2015).

30. Gregory A. Caldeira and John R. Wright, "Organized Interests and Agenda Setting in the U.S. Supreme Court," *American Political Science Review* 82 (1988): 1109–1127.

31. *United States v. Nixon,* 418 U.S. 683 (1974).

32. *Worcester v. Georgia,* 31 U.S. (6 Pet.) 515 (1832).

33. Mathew McCubbins, Roger G. Knoll, and Barry R. Weingast, "Political Control of the Judiciary: A Positive Theory of Judicial Doctrine and the Rule of Law," *University of Southern California Law Review* (September 1995): 1631–1683.

34. See William N. Eskridge Jr., "Overriding Supreme Court Statutory Interpretation Decisions," *Yale Law Journal* 101 (1991): 331–455; and James Meernik and Joseph Ignagni, "Judicial Review and Coordinate Construction of the Constitution," *American Journal of Political Science* 41 (April 1997): 446–467.

35. Jason Zengerle, "How the Trump Administration Is Remaking the Courts," *New York Times,* August 22, 2018.

36. Alan I. Abramowitz, *The Great Alignment: Race, Party Transformation, and the Rise of Donald Trump* (New Haven: Yale University Press, 2018).

37. Byron Tau and Andrew Duehren, "Republicans Take Aim at Judges Issuing Nationwide Rulings," *Wall Street Journal,* September 13, 2018.

## Chapter 10

1. V. O. Key Jr., *Public Opinion and American Democracy* (New York: Knopf, 1967), 14.

2. Quoted in Susan Herbst, *Numbered Voices: How Opinion Polling Has Shaped American Politics* (Chicago: University of Chicago Press, 1993), 108.

3. Joshua Green, "The Other War Room," *Washington Monthly,* April 2002, accessed at http://washingtonmonthly.com/features/2001/0204.green.html.

4. Sam Stein, "Obama Mocks Polls but Spends More on Them ($4.4M) Than Bush Did," July 29, 2010, accessed at www.huffingtonpost.com/2010/07/29/obama-mocks-polls-but-spe_n_663553.html.

5. Alison Mitchell, "Clinton Seems to Keep Running though the Race Is Run and Won," *New York Times,* February 2, 1997, A1.

6. "Survey Bolsters Global Warming Fight," *Los Angeles Times,* November 21, 1997, A4.

7. William W. Lambert and Wallace E. Lambert, *Social Psychology* (Englewood Cliffs, NJ: Prentice Hall, 1964), 50.

8. Estimates from the American National Election Studies Cumulative Data File for 2000 through 2016 using only in-person interviews.

9. Robert S. Erikson and Kent L. Tedin, *American Public Opinion,* 5th ed. (Boston: Allyn & Bacon, 1995), 65–78.

10. Stanley Feldman and John Zaller, "The Political Culture of Ambivalence: Ideological Responses to the Welfare State," *American Journal of Political Science* 36 (1992): 268–307.

11. Angus Campbell et al., *The American Voter* (New York: Wiley, 1960), chaps. 6 and 7.

12. Morris P. Fiorina, *Retrospective Voting in American National Elections* (New Haven, CT: Yale University Press, 1981), chap. 5.

13. Gallup/*USA Today* poll, December 15–17, 2000, available from the Roper Center, University of Connecticut.

14. Gary C. Jacobson, "Public Opinion and the Impeachment of Bill Clinton," in *British Elections and Parties Review*, vol. 10, ed. Philip Cowley, David Denver, Andrew Russell, and Lisa Harrison (London: Frank Cass, 2000), 1–31.

15. Gary C. Jacobson, "Barack Obama and the American Public: The First 18 Months" (paper presented at the Annual Meeting of the American Political Science Association, Washington, DC, September 2–5, 2010), 17.

16. John Sides and Lynn Vavreck, *The Gamble: The Hand You're Dealt* (Princeton, NJ: Princeton University Press, 2012), 22.

17. Annenberg Public Policy Center, "Fahrenheit 9/11 Viewers and Limbaugh Listeners about Equal in Size Even though They Perceive Two Different Nations," Press Release, August 3, 2004.

18. Support was about 9 points higher if "removing Saddam Hussein" replaced "the result of the war" in the question that mentioned the loss of American lives. See Gary C. Jacobson, *A Divider, Not a Uniter: George W. Bush and the American People* (New York: Pearson, 2006), 129.

19. From data reported at www.pollingreport.com/afghan

.htm. The number of surveys averaged to produce these four percentages was six, fourteen, eight, and sixteen, respectively.

20. Philip E. Converse, "The Nature of Belief Systems in Mass Publics," in *Ideology and Discontent*, ed. David Apter (New York: Free Press, 1964); Christopher Achen, "Mass Political Attitudes and Survey Response," *American Political Science Review* 69 (1995): 1218–1231.

21. Zaller and Feldman, "A Simple Theory of Survey Response," 585–586.

22. Thomas E. Nelson, Rosalee A. Clawson, and Zoe M. Oxley, "Media Framing of a Civil Liberties Conflict and Its Effect on Tolerance," *American Political Science Review* 91 (September 1977): 567–583.

23. Shanto Iyengar and Donald R. Kinder, *News That Matters* (Chicago: University of Chicago Press, 1987), 63–72.

24. Benjamin I. Page and Robert Y. Shapiro, *The Rational Public* (Chicago: University of Chicago Press, 1992), 63.

25. Ibid., 130.

26. James A. Stimson, *Public Opinion in America: Moods, Cycles, and Swings* (Boulder, CO: Westview Press, 1991), 29–31.

27. Stimson, *Public Opinion*, 125.

28. Arthur Lupia and Mathew D. McCubbins, *The Democratic Dilemma: Can Citizens Learn What They Really Need to Know?* (New York: Cambridge University Press, 1998).

29. Paul Burstein, "The Impact of Public Opinion on Public Policy: A Review and an Agenda," *Political Research Quarterly* 56 (March 2003): 29–40.

30. Herbert McClosky and John Zaller, *The American Ethos* (Cambridge, MA: Harvard University Press, 1984), 38.

31. Pew Research Center for the People and the Press survey, December 12, 2006, to January 9, 2007, accessed at www.pollingreport.com/terror.htm.

32. Herbert McClosky and Ada Brill, *Dimensions of Tolerance* (New York: Basic Books, 1983).

33. McClosky and Zaller, *The American Ethos*, 83.

34. Ibid., 84.

35. The study can be found here: http://www.worldpublicopinion.org/pipa/pdf/may12/DefenseBudget_May12_rpt.pdf.

36. Richard A. Brody, *Assessing the President* (Stanford, CA: Stanford University Press, 1991).

37. John E. Mueller, *War, Presidents, and Public Opinion* (New York: Wiley, 1973), 58–63.

38. Mark Peffley and Jon Hurwitz, "International Events and Foreign Policy Beliefs: Public Responses to Changing U.S.-Soviet Relations," *American Journal of Political Science* 36 (May 1992): 431–461.

39. See http://pollingreport.com/terror.htm.

40. ABC News/*Washington Post* poll, September 24, 2014.

41. According to American National Election Study, 2000, Gore won 91 percent of the black vote; the Election Day exit polls put the figure at 90 percent.

42. Ninety-nine percent of black voters in the 2008 American National Election Studies and in Gallup's surveys said they

had voted for Obama; in the National Exit Poll, it was 95 percent.

43. The Pew Research Center, March 29, 2012, "The Gender Gap: Three Decades Old, as Wide as Ever."

44. "Election Polls—Presidential Vote by Groups," Gallup Report, accessed at www .gallup.com/poll/139880/ Election-Polls-Presidential-Vote-Groups.aspx#1.

45. Voter News Service exit poll, November 7, 2000, available from the Roper Center, University of Connecticut.

46. National Exit Poll, accessed at www.cnn.com/ ELECTION/2008/results/ polls/#val=US P00p2.

## Chapter 11

1. Chilton Williamson, *American Suffrage: From Property to Democracy 1760–1860* (Princeton, NJ: Princeton University Press, 1960), 49.

2. Alexis de Tocqueville, *Democracy in America,* Vol. 1 (New York: Vintage, 1990), 57.

3. Quoted by David Morgan in *Suffragists and Democrats: The Politics of Women's Suffrage in America* (East Lansing: Michigan State University Press, 1972), 84.

4. Ibid., 124.

5. Steven J. Rosenstone and John Mark Hansen, *Mobilization, Participation, and Democracy in America* (New York: Macmillan, 1993), 150.

6. Alan S. Gerber, Donald P. Green, and Christopher W. Larimer, "Social Pressure and Voter Turnout: Evidence from a Large-Scale Field Experiment," *American Political Science Review* 102, no. 1 (2008): 33–48.

7. Gerber, Green, and Larimer, "Social Pressure and Voter Turnout."

8. Martin P. Wattenberg, *The Decline of American Political Parties, 1952–1992* (Cambridge, MA: Harvard University Press, 1994), 155–157, 171–180.

9. Jordan Fabian, "DeMint Challenger Greene Pulls in 28 Percent in Loss," *The Hill,* November 3, 2010, accessed at http://thehill.com/blogs/blog-briefing-room/news/127421-demint-challenger-greene-pulls-in-28-percent-in-loss.

10. Samuel L. Popkin, *The Reasoning Voter: Communication and Persuasion in Presidential Campaigns,* 2nd ed. (Chicago: University of Chicago Press, 1994), 1.

11. Paul R. Abramson, John H. Aldrich, and David W. Rohde, *Change and Continuity in the 1992 Elections* (Washington, DC: CQ Press, 1994), 56–57.

12. John G. Geer and Lynn Vavreck, "Negativity, Information, and Candidate Position-Taking," *Political Communication* 31 (2014): 218–236; Richard R. Lau, Lee Sigelman, and Ivy Brown Rovner, "The Effects of Negative Political Campaigns: A Meta-Analytic Reassessment," *Journal of Politics* 69, no. 4 (2007): 1176–1209.

13. Nelson W. Polsby and Aaron Wildavsky, *Presidential Elections,* 9th ed. (Chatham, NJ: Chatham House, 1996), 215–216.

14. ABC News/*Washington Post* poll of likely voters taken October 17–19, 2008, accessed at www.pollingreport.com/ wh08.htm.

15. John Sides and Lynn Vavreck, *The Gamble: Choice and Chance in the 2012 Presidential Election* (Princeton, NJ: Princeton University Press, 2013).

16. Joel Bradshaw, "Strategy, Theme, and Message" (paper presented at the Conference on Campaign Management, American University, Washington, DC, December 10–11, 1992), 114.

17. Michael Cooper, "Campaigns Play Loose with Truth in Fact-Check Age," *New York Times,* August 31, 2012, accessed at http://www.nytimes.com/ 2012/09/01/us/politics/fact-checkers-howl-but-both-sides-cling-to-false-ads.html.

18. *Buckley v. Valeo,* 424 U.S. 1 (1976).

19. *Colorado Republican Federal Campaign Committee v. Federal Election Commission,* 518 U.S. 604 (1996).

20. *Citizens United v. Federal Election Commission,* 130 S. Ct. 876 (2010).

21. Gary C. Jacobson, *The Politics of Congressional Elections,* 7th ed. (New York: Longman, 2009), 124–134.

## Chapter 12

1. Gary C. Jacobson, "Polarization, Gridlock, and Presidential Campaign Politics in 2016," *Annals of the American Academy of Political and Social Sciences* 667 (September 2016): 223–237.

2. The 2012 data are from Gallup, CBS News/*New York Times,* CNN, and Pew surveys; the

2016 data are from Gallup, *Economist*/YouGov, CBS News/*New York Times*, ABC News/*Washington Post*, and Fox News surveys.

3. Averages from six *Economist*/YouGov surveys taken in October and November 2016.

4. In the Gallup poll taken September 4–12, 2018, 57 percent of respondents said they were of that opinion, and 35 percent said they were not (accessed at https://news.gallup.com/poll/244106/third-party-25102018-trending.aspx?); a Suffolk University/*USA Today* survey conducted February 11–15, 2016, found similar sentiments: 53 percent want more parties, whereas 34 percent said the major parties were enough (accessed at www.suffolk.edu/academics/10741.php).

5. American National Election Studies, 2004–2016.

6. In the preelection polls cited in endnote 2, not only did an average of 91 percent of partisans typically express unfavorable opinion of the other party's candidate, but for both candidates about 80 percent chose the "very unfavorable" option; the comparable figures for Obama and Romney had been 54 percent and 48 percent, respectively.

7. The National Exit Poll found that Democrats were a bit less loyal to Clinton than they had been to Obama (the split for him was 92–7 compared with 89–9 for her) and Republicans were also a bit less loyal to Trump (90–7 compared with 93–6 for Romney), but by

historic standards, these were still high levels of party loyalty. Party-line voting was even more prevalent in the House races (93–6 when both parties are combined), and the level of ticket splitting that can be estimated from the National Exit Poll remained very low, about 6.8 percent compared with 6.5 percent estimated from the 2012 edition of the poll.

8. Gary C. Jacobson, "Congress: Nationalized, Polarized, and Partisan," *The Elections of 2016*, ed. Michael Nelson (Washington, DC: CQ Press, 2017).

9. Martin P. Wattenberg, *The Decline of American Political Parties, 1952–1994* (Cambridge, MA: Harvard University Press, 1996); Everett Carll Ladd, "1996 Vote: The 'No Majority' Realignment Continues," *Political Science Quarterly* 112 (Spring 1997): 1–23.

10. E. E. Schattschneider, *Party Government* (New York: Holt, Rinehart, & Winston, 1942), 1.

11. Edmund Burke, *Thoughts on the Causes of the Present Discontents*, ed. W. Murison (Cambridge, UK: Cambridge University Press, 1930).

12. Anthony Downs, *An Economic Theory of Democracy* (New York: Harper & Row, 1957), 25.

13. This conceptual trinity, originally proposed by V. O. Key Jr., is used routinely by political scientists who study parties. See *Politics, Parties, and Pressure Groups* (New York: Thomas Crowell, 1964), 163–165.

14. Maurice Duverger, *Political Parties* (New York: Wiley, 1954), 217.

15. David R. Mayhew, *Electoral Realignments: A Critique of an American Genre* (New Haven, CT: Yale University Press, 2002).

16. See Alexander Hamilton's discussion of the Electoral College in *Federalist* No. 68. This device is described in Chapter 7, "The Presidency."

17. Quoted in Richard H. Brown, "The Missouri Crisis, Slavery, and the Politics of Jacksonianism," in *After the Constitution: Party Conflict in the New Republic*, ed. Lance Banning (Cambridge, MA: Harvard University Press, 1964), 446.

18. Michael F. Holt, *Political Parties and American Political Development from the Age of Jackson to the Age of Lincoln* (Baton Rouge: Louisiana State University Press, 1992), 41.

19. James S. Chase, *Emergence of the Presidential Nominating Convention, 1798–1832* (Urbana: University of Illinois Press, 1973), 85.

20. Richard P. McCormick, "Political Development and the Second Party System," in *The American Party Systems: Stages of Political Development*, 2nd ed., ed. William Nesbit Chambers and Walter Dean Burnham (New York: Oxford University Press, 1975), 108.

21. Ibid., 8.

22. Nelson W. Polsby, *Consequences of Party Reform* (New York: Oxford University Press, 1983), chaps. 2 and 3.

23. Morris P. Fiorina, *Divided Government*, 2nd ed. (Boston: Allyn & Bacon, 1996), 72–81.

24. Gary C. Jacobson, *The Electoral Origins of Divided Government* (Boulder, CO:

Westview Press, 1990), 105–120.

25. Bruce E. Keith et al., *The Myth of the Independent Voter* (Berkeley: University of California Press, 1992), chap. 4.

26. Pew Research Center, "The Parties on the Eve of the 2016 Election: Two Coalitions, Moving Further Apart," accessed at www.people-press.org/2016/09/13/the-parties-on-the-eve-of-the-2016-election-two-coalitions-moving-further-apart/.

27. Ibid.; Marissa Abrajano and Zoltan L. Hajnal, *White Backlash: Immigration, Race, and American Politics* (Princeton, NJ: Princeton University Press, 2015).

28. Alan I. Abramowitz, *The Disappearing Center: Engaged Citizens, Polarization, and American Democracy* (New Haven, CT: Yale University Press, 2010), chap. 3.

29. Morris P. Fiorina, *Culture War? The Myth of a Polarized America* (New York: Pearson, 2005); Marc J. Hetherington and Jonathan D. Weiler, *Authoritarianism and Polarization in American Politics* (New York: Cambridge University Press, 2009); Matthew Levendusky, *The Partisan Sort: How Liberals Became Democrats and Conservatives Became Republicans* (Chicago: University of Chicago Press, 2009).

30. Mark Rozell and Clyde Wilcox, eds., *God at the Grass Roots: The Christian Right in the 1994 Elections* (Lanham, MD: Rowman & Littlefield, 1995).

31. Paul S. Herrnson, *Party Campaigning in the 1980s*

32. Center for Responsive Politics, at www.opensecrets.org/outsidespending/index.php.

33. Michael P. McDonald, 2018 November General Election Turnout Rates, United States Election Project, at www.electproject.org/2018gm.

34. Gary C. Jacobson, "Donald Trump and the 2018 Midterm Elections," *Political Science Quarterly* 134 (Spring 2019), forthcoming

35. Center for Responsive Politics, at www.opensecrets.org/outsidespending/index.php.

36. John H. Aldrich, *Why Parties? The Origin and Transformation of Party Politics in America* (Chicago: University of Chicago Press, 1995), 273.

## Chapter 13

1. Alison Gilbert Olson, *Making the Empire Work: London and American Interest Groups, 1690–1790* (Cambridge, MA: Harvard University Press, 1992), 56.

2. Ibid., 146.

3. Alexis de Tocqueville, *Democracy in America*, ed. Andrew Hacker (New York: Washington Square, 1964), 71.

4. Ibid., 182.

5. David B. Truman, *The Governmental Process* (New York: Knopf, 1951).

6. E. E. Schattschneider, *The Semisovereign People: A Realist's View of Democracy in America* (Hinsdale, IL: Dryden, 1960), 34–35.

7. Mancur Olson, *The Logic of Collective Action: Public Goods

and the Theory of Groups* (Cambridge, MA: Harvard University Press, 1965).

8. Jack L. Walker Jr., *Mobilizing Interest Groups in America: Patrons, Professions, and Social Movements* (Ann Arbor: University of Michigan Press, 1991), 1; Jeffrey Birnbaum, "The Road to Riches Is Called K Street," *Washington Post*, June 22, 2005, A01.

9. *Washington Representatives*, 31st ed. (Bethesda, MD: Columbia Books, 2007).

10. James A. Thurber, "Lobbying Reform: The Importance of Enforcement and Transparency," testimony before the Senate Committee on Rules and Administration, February 8, 2006, accessed at https://www.american.edu/spa/ccps/upload/Rules-committee-2006.pdf.

11. Byron Tau and Tarini Parti, "K Street Sings the Blues," *Politico*, January 23, 1013.

12. David Vogel, *Fluctuating Fortunes: The Political Power of Business in America* (New York: Basic Books, 1988), 220–227.

13. Walker, *Mobilizing Interest Groups*, 29.

14. Ibid., 31.

15. Daniel Kahneman and Amos Tversky, "Prospect Theory: An Analysis of Decision under Risk," *Econometrica* 47 (1979): 263–291.

16. William P. Browne, "Issue Niches and the Limits of Interest Group Influence," in *Interest Group Politics*, 3rd ed., eds. Allan J. Cigler and Burdett A. Loomis (Washington, DC: CQ Press, 1991), 348.

17. James Q. Wilson, *Political Organizations* (New York: Basic Books, 1973), chap. 13.

18. Browne, "Issue Niches and the Limits of Interest Group Influence," 356.

19. Kay Lehman Schlozman and John T. Tierney, *Organized Interests and American Democracy* (New York: Harper & Row, 1986), 150.

20. Unidentified lobbyist quoted in Jeffrey M. Berry, *The Interest Group Society* (Boston: Little, Brown, 1984), 117; emphasis in the original.

21. Schlozman and Tierney, *Organized Interests*, 333.

22. Kevin T. McGuire, *Understanding the U.S. Supreme Court* (Boston: McGraw-Hill, 2001), 151.

23. Karen O'Connor, "Lobbying the Justices or Lobbying for Justice?" in *The Interest Group Connection: Electioneering, Lobbying, and Policymaking in Washington*, 2nd ed., eds. Paul S. Herrnson, Ronald G. Shaiko, and Clyde Wilcox (Washington, DC: CQ Press, 2005), 319–340.

24. Gregory A. Caldeira and John R. Wright, "Lobbying for Justice: Organized Interests, Supreme Court Nominations, and the United States Senate," *American Journal of Political Science* 42 (April 1998): 510.

25. Andrew J. Polsky, "Giving Business the Business," *Dissent* (Winter 1996): 33–36.

26. Jonathan D. Salant and David S. Cloud, "To the '94 Election Victors Go the Fundraising Spoils," *Congressional Quarterly Weekly Report*, April 15, 1995, 1056.

27. Campaign Finance Institute, "PAC Fundraising Swings Democratic over the First Nine Months of 2007," November 8, 2007, accessed at www.cfinst.org/pr/prRelease .aspx?ReleaseID=167.

28. See Fredreka Schouten, "Campaign Spending by Outside Groups Skyrockets," *USA Today*, October 15, 2010.

29. See, for example, Philip Stern, *The Best Congress Money Can Buy* (New York: Pantheon, 1988); Brooks Jackson, *Honest Graft: Big Money and the American Political Process* (New York: Knopf, 1988); and Elizabeth Drew, *Politics and Money: The New Road to Corruption* (New York: Macmillan, 1983).

30. John R. Wright, *Interest Groups and Congress* (Boston: Allyn and Bacon, 1996), 136–145; Frank J. Sorauf, *Inside Campaign Finance: Myths and Realities* (New Haven, CT: Yale University Press, 1992), 163–174; Stephen Ansolabehere, John de Figueiredo, and James Snyder Jr., "Why Is There So Little Money in U.S. Politics?" *Journal of Economic Perspectives* 17 (2003): 105–130.

31. Richard L. Hall and Frank W. Wayman, "Buying Time: Monied Interests and the Mobilization of Bias in Congressional Committees," *American Political Science Review* 84 (1990): 797–820.

32. Robert S. Salisbury, *Institutions and Interests: Substance and Structure in American Politics* (Pittsburgh, PA: University of Pittsburgh Press, 1992), 348.

33. Both quotes are from James Hohmann, "The Daily 202: Mick Mulvaney's Confession Highlights the Corrosive Influence of Money in Politics," April 25, 2018, *Washington Post*, accessed at washingtonpost.com.

34. William P. Browne, *Private Interests, Public Policy, and American Agriculture* (Lawrence: University Press of Kansas, 1988), 248–252.

35. Schlozman and Tierney, *Organized Interests*, 399–403.

36. Lester C. Thurow, *The Zero-Sum Society* (New York: Basic Books, 1980); Mancur Olson, *The Rise and Decline of Nations* (New Haven, CT: Yale University Press, 1982).

## Chapter 14

1. Timothy Cook, *Governing with the News: The News Media as a Political Institution* (Chicago: University of Chicago Press, 1998), 22.

2. Richard Hofstadter, *The Idea of the Party System* (Berkeley: University of California Press, 1969), 8.

3. Thomas C. Leonard, *The Power of the Press: The Birth of American Political Reporting* (New York: Oxford University Press, 1986), 57.

4. Willard Grosvenor Bleyer, *Main Currents of the History of American Journalism* (Boston: Houghton Mifflin, 1927), 377.

5. Alfred M. Lee, *The Daily Newspaper in America* (New York: Macmillan, 1937), 214–217.

6. *Historical Statistics of the United States: Colonial Times to 1970*, Vols. 1 and 2 (Washington, DC: Government Printing Office, 1975), series R104–5.

7. Julia Angwin and Sarah McBride, "Radio's

Bush-Bashing Air America Is Back in Fighting Form," *Wall Street Journal,* January 28, 2005.

8. Edwin Emery, *The Press and America,* 2nd ed. (Englewood Cliffs, NJ: Prentice Hall, 1962), 107–124.

9. Stephen Hess, *Live from Capitol Hill* (Washington, DC: Brookings, 1991).

10. Transcript, presidential press conference, May 7, 1993, Washington, DC.

11. Matthew Gentzkow and Jess M. Shapiro, "What Drives Media Slant? Evidence from U.S. Daily Newspapers," *Econometrica* 78, no. 1 (2010): 35.

12. Howard Kurtz of the *Washington Post,* interview on *Nightline,* ABC News, January 30, 1998.

13. Richard H. Rovere, *Senator Joe McCarthy* (Cleveland, OH: Meridian, 1966), 124.

14. Paul F. Boller Jr., *Presidential Anecdotes* (New York: Penguin, 1982), 63–64.

15. Matthew A. Baum and Samuel Kernell, "Has Cable Ended the Golden Age of Presidential Television?" *American Political Science Review* 93, no. 1 (1999): 99–114.

16. *New York Times Co. v. United States,* 403 U.S. 713 (1971).

17. The Court first employed this doctrine in 1964 in *New York Times Co. v. Sullivan,* 376 U.S. 254 (1964).

18. Murrow is quoted in Bill Kovach and Tom Rosenstiel, *Blur: How to Know What's True in the Age of Information Overload* (New York: Bloomsbury Press, 2011).

19. James E. Pollard, *The Presidents and the Press* (New York: Macmillan, 1947), 775.

20. Cited in Worth Bingham and Ward S. Just, "The President and the Press," *Reporter* 26 (April 12, 1962): 20.

## Chapter 15

1. See Christopher Weaver, "People Who Choose Not to Have Health Insurance," Kaiser Health News, October 3, 2009, accessed at http:// kaiserhealthnews.org/news/ npr-voluntarily-uninsured-explainer/, December 2014.

2. Quoted in Elspeth Reeve, "Four Things Romney Wishes He Hadn't Said about Romneycare," *The Wire,* June 29, 2012.

3. Quoted in Ryan Lizza, "Romney's Dilemma: How His Greatest Achievement Has Become His Biggest Liability," *The New Yorker,* June 6, 2011.

4. See Rosalind S. Helderman and Amy Goldstein, "Federal Judge in Va. Strikes Down Part of Health-Care Law," *Washington Post,* December 14, 2010; "Health Mandate Fight Hinges on Commerce Clause," National Public Radio, December 14, 2010; Ken Cuccinelli, "Why Virginia Is Suing the Federal Government over the New Health Care Law," accessed at http://www.oag .state.va.us/FAQs/FAQ_Why_ VA_Suing.html, February 2011.

5. See National Research Council, *Advancing the Science of Climate Change* (Washington, DC: National Academies Press, 2010).

6. Matt McGrath, "Fossil Fuels Should Be Phased Out by 2100 Says IPCC," BBC News, November 2, 2014.

7. See Quirin Schiermeier, "The Kyoto Protocol: Hot Air," *Science,* November 28, 2012.

8. See "U.S.-China Joint Announcement on Climate Change," White House Press Release, November 12, 2014, accessed at http:// www.whitehouse.gov/the-press-office/2014/11/11/ us-china-joint-announcement-climate-change, December 2014.

9. Matt McGrath, "Will Kerry Strike Gold at Lima Climate Talks?" BBC News, December 11, 2014.

10. Barnini Chakraborty, "Paris Agreement on Climate Change: US Withdraws as Trump Calls It 'Unfair,'" Foxnews.com, June 1, 2017.

11. Hiroko Tabuchi and Henry Fountain, "Bucking Trump, These Cities, States, and Companies Commit to Paris Accord," *New York Times,* June 1, 2017.

12. Jonathan Weisman, "Senate Passes Legislation to Allow Taxes on Affluent to Rise," *New York Times,* January 1, 2013.

13. Jeanne Sahadi, "Debt Ceiling: What the Deal Will Do," CNN Money, August 2, 2011.

14. Lori Montgomery and Rosalind S. Helderman, "Obama Signs Bill to Raise Debt Limit, Reopen Government," *Washington Post,* October 16, 2013.

15. See Social Security Administration, "Frequently

Asked Questions," accessed at https://faq.ssa.gov/link/portal/34011/34019/ArticleFolder/418/Retirement, December 2014.

16. Social Security and Medicare Boards of Trustees, "A Summary of the 2014 Annual Reports," accessed at http://www.ssa.gov/oact/trsum/, December 2014.

17. For a full history of the commission and its legacy, see Social Security Administration, "Report of the Bipartisan Commission on Entitlement and Tax Reform," accessed at http://www.ssa

.gov/history/reports/Kerrey Danforth/KerreyDanforth.htm, December 2014; and U.S. Chamber of Commerce, "Sin of Commission: 20 Years of Neglect on Entitlement Reform," accessed at https://www.uschamber.com/blog/sin-commission-20-years-neglect-entitlement-reform, December 2014.

18. Jeanne Sahadi, "Obama vs. Romney on Taxes," CNN Money, July 5, 2012.

19. Mark Landler and Jackie Calmes, "Obama Proposes Deal over Taxes and Jobs," New York Times, July 30, 2013.

20. Eric Pianin, "Tax Reform: No Takers for Obama's 'Grand Bargain,'" The Fiscal Times, July 31, 2013.

21. Russell Berman and Bernie Becker, "Boehner Scoffs at Tax Reform Vote," The Hill, February 26, 2014.

22. Sam Petulla and Tal Yellin, "The Biggest Tax Cut in History? Not Quite," CNN.com, January 30, 2018.

23. Deirdre Walsh, Phil Mattingly, Ashley Killough, Lauren Fox, and Kevin Liptak, "White House, GOP Celebrate Passing Sweeping Tax Bill," CNN.com, December 20, 2017.

# Index

Figures/images, boxes, tables, maps, and notes are indicated by f, b, t, m, and n following the page number.

# About the Authors

**Samuel Kernell** is distinguished emeritus professor of political science at the University of California, San Diego, where he has taught since 1977. Kernell's research interests focus on the presidency, political communication, and American political history. His books include *Going Public: New Strategies of Presidential Leadership*, 4th edition; *Strategy and Choice in Congressional Elections*, 2nd edition (with Gary C. Jacobson); and *Party Ballots, Reform, and the Transformation of America's Electoral System* (with Erik J. Engstrom). He has also edited *Parallel Politics: Economic Policymaking in Japan and the United States*; *The Politics of Divided Government* (with Gary W. Cox); and *James Madison: The Theory and Practice of Republican Government*. He is presently writing *Veto Rhetoric: Presidential Leadership in Divided Government*, which CQ Press will publish in 2020.

**Gary C. Jacobson** is distinguished emeritus professor of political science at the University of California, San Diego, where he taught from 1979 to 2016. He previously taught at Trinity College; the University of California, Riverside; Yale University; and Stanford University. Jacobson specializes in the study of U.S. elections, parties, interest groups, public opinion, and Congress. He is the author of *Money in Congressional Elections*; *The Politics of Congressional Elections*, 9th edition; *The Electoral Origins of Divided Government*; *A Divider, Not a Uniter: George W. Bush and the American People*, 2nd edition; and *Presidents and Parties in the Public Mind*; he is the coauthor of *Strategy and Choice in Congressional Elections*, 2nd edition. Jacobson is a fellow of the American Academy of Arts and Sciences.

**Thad Kousser** is professor of political science and department chair at the University of California, San Diego (UCSD). He has served as a legislative aide in the California, New Mexico, and U.S. Senates. He is the author of *Term Limits and the Dismantling of State Legislative Professionalism*, coauthor of *The Power of American Governors*, and coeditor of *The New Political Geography of California* and of *Politics in the American States*, 11th edition. Kousser has been awarded the UCSD Academic Senate's Distinguished Teaching Award and serves as coeditor of the journal *Legislative Studies Quarterly*.

**Lynn Vavreck** is the Marvin Hoffenberg Professor of American Politics and Public Policy at the University of California, Los Angeles (UCLA), and a contributor to The Upshot at the *New York Times*. She is the author of *Identity Crisis: The 2016 Presidential Campaign and the Battle for the Meaning of America* and the award-winning book *The Gamble: Choice and Chance in the 2012 Presidential Campaign*. In 2014, she hosted and interviewed Hillary Clinton at UCLA's Luskin Lecture on Thought Leadership, and in 2015 she was awarded an Andrew F. Carnegie Fellowship to investigate the influence of political advertising. Her research has been supported by the National Science Foundation, and she has served on the advisory boards of both the British and American National Election Studies. At UCLA she teaches courses on campaigns, elections, and public opinion.